W9-DGW-797

For Reference

Not to be taken from this room

NORTH
AMERICAN
INDUSTRY
CLASSIFICATION
SYSTEM

United States, 2002
EXPANDED EDITION
WITH ADDED "BRIDGES"

Appendix C. NAICS 2002 TO SIC 1987

Appendix D. SIC 1987 TO NAICS 2002

EXECUTIVE OFFICE OF THE PRESIDENT
OFFICE OF MANAGEMENT AND BUDGET

Published and for sale by:
CLAITOR'S PUBLISHING DIVISION
P.O. Box 261333, Baton Rouge, LA 70826-1333
800-274-1403 (In LA 225-344-0476)
Fax: 225-344-0480
Internet address:
e mail: claitors@claitors.com
World Wide Web: http://www.claitors.com

*We acknowlege the input and assistance of the U. S. Census Bureau, since much of the following is extracted from their web site at http://www.census.gov

Dedication

The Office of Management and Budget (OMB) is indebted to the many individuals and organizations whose vision, insights, and energies have made NAICS United States a reality.

This NAICS United States manual is dedicated to the memory of **Linda M. Dill,** *of the Social Security Administration, who worked on the Administrative and Maintenance Subcommittees until her death.*

Foreword

The Instituto Nacional de Estadística, Geografía e Informática (INEGI) of Mexico, Statistics Canada, and the United States Office of Management and Budget, through its Economic Classification Policy Committee, have jointly updated the system of classification of economic activities that makes the industrial statistics produced in the three countries comparable. The North American Industry Classification System (NAICS) revision for 2002 is scheduled to go into effect for reference year 2002 in Canada and the United States, and 2003 in Mexico. NAICS was originally developed to provide a consistent framework for the collection, analysis and dissemination of industrial statistics used by government policy analysts, by academics and researchers, by the business community, and by the public. Revisions for 2002 were made to account for our rapidly changing economies.

Classifications serve as a lens through which to view the data they classify. NAICS is the first industry classification system that was developed in accordance with a single principle of aggregation, the principle that producing units that use similar production processes should be grouped together. NAICS also reflects, in a much more explicit way, the enormous changes in technology and in the growth and diversification of services that have marked recent decades. Though NAICS differs from other industry classification systems, statistics compiled on NAICS are comparable with statistics compiled according to the latest revision of the United Nations' International Standard Industrial Classification (ISIC, Revision 3) for some 60 high level groupings.

The actual classification reveals only the tip of the work carried out by dedicated staff from INEGI, Statistics Canada, and U.S. statistical agencies. It is through their efforts, painstaking analysis, and spirit of accommodation that NAICS has emerged as a harmonized international classification of economic activities.

Preface

Statistics Canada, Mexico's Instituto Nacional de Estadística, Geografía e Informática (INEGI), and the Economic Classification Policy Committee (ECPC) of the United States, acting on behalf of the Office of Management and Budget, created a common classification system that replaced the existing classification of each country, the Standard Industrial Classification (1980) of Canada, the Mexican Classification of Activities and Products (1994), and the Standard Industrial Classification (1987) of the United States.

The North American Industry Classification System (NAICS) is unique among industry classifications in that it is constructed within a single conceptual framework. Economic units that have similar production processes are classified in the same industry, and the lines drawn between industries demarcate, to the extent practicable, differences in production processes. This supply-based, or production-oriented, economic concept was adopted for NAICS because an industry classification system is a framework for collecting and publishing information on both inputs and outputs, for statistical uses that require that inputs and outputs be used together and be classified consistently. Examples of such uses include measuring productivity, unit labor costs, and the capital intensity of production, estimating employment-output relationships, constructing input-output tables, and other uses that imply the analysis of production relationships in the economy. The classification concept for NAICS will produce data that facilitate such analyses.

In the design of NAICS, attention was given to developing production-oriented classifications for (a) new and emerging industries, (b) service industries in general, and (c) industries engaged in the production of advanced technologies. These special emphases are embodied in the particular features of NAICS, discussed below. These same areas of special emphasis account for many of the differences between the structure of NAICS and the structures of industry classification systems in use elsewhere. NAICS provides enhanced industry comparability among the three North American Free Trade Agreement (NAFTA) trading partners, while also increasing compatibility with the two-digit level of the International Standard Industrial Classification (ISIC, Rev. 3) of the United Nations.

NAICS divides the economy into 20 sectors. Industries within these sectors are grouped according to the production criterion. Though the goods/services distinction is not explicitly reflected in the structure of NAICS, four sectors are largely goods-producing and 16 are entirely services-producing industries.

A key feature of NAICS is the Information sector that groups industries that primarily create and disseminate a product subject to copyright. The NAICS Information sector brings together those activities that transform information into a commodity that is produced and distributed, and activities that provide the means for distributing those products, other than through traditional wholesale-retail distribution channels. A few of the new and important industries created in this sector for the 2002 revision include: Internet service providers and Web search portals, and Internet publishing and broadcasting. Also included in the Information sector are telecommunications; newspaper, book, and periodical publishing; motion picture and sound recording industries; libraries; and other information services.

Another feature of NAICS is a sector for Professional, Scientific, and Technical Services, that comprises establishments engaged in activities where human capital is the major input. The industries within this sector are each defined by the expertise and training of the service provider. The sector includes such industries as offices of lawyers, engineering services, architectural services, advertising agencies, and interior design services.

A sector for Arts, Entertainment, and Recreation greatly expands the number of industries providing services in these three areas.

Another key sector, Health Care and Social Assistance, recognizes the merging of the boundaries of health care and social assistance. The industries in this sector are arranged in an order that reflects the range and extent of health care and social assistance provided. Some important industries are family planning centers, outpatient mental health and substance abuse centers, and community care facilities for the elderly.

In the Manufacturing sector, an important subsector, Computer and Electronic Product Manufacturing, brings together industries producing electronic products and their components. Establishments that manufacture computers, communications equipment, and semiconductors, for example, are grouped into the same subsector because of the inherent technological similarities of their production processes, and the likelihood that these technologies will continue to converge in the future. The reproduction of packaged software is placed in this sector, rather than in the services sector, because the reproduction of packaged software is a manufacturing process, and the product moves through the wholesale and retail distribution systems like any other manufactured product. NAICS acknowledges the importance of these electronic industries, their rapid growth over the past several years and the likelihood that these industries will, in the future, become even more important in the economies of the three North American countries.

This NAICS structure reflects the levels at which data comparability was agreed upon by the three statistical agencies. The boundaries of all the sectors of NAICS have been delineated. In most sectors, NAICS provides for compatibility at the industry (five-digit) level. During the 2002 revision, five-digit comparability was obtained in the construction sector for all areas except one industry group. This was a major achievement and goal of the 2002 revision. However, for real estate, utilities, finance and insurance, and for three of the four subsectors in other services (except public administration), three-country compatibility will occur either at the industry group (four-digit) or subsector (three-digit) levels. For these sectors, differences in the economies of the three countries prevent full compatibility at the NAICS industry level. For wholesale trade, retail trade, and public administration, the three countries' statistical agencies have agreed, at this time, only on the boundaries of the sector (two-digit level). Below the agreed upon level of compatibility, each country may add additional detailed industries, as necessary to meet national needs, provided that this additional detail aggregates to the NAICS level.

The United States has adopted the revised classification in its statistical programs for reference years beginning on or after 2002. Agencies may adopt the 2002 NAICS earlier at their discretion.

Acknowledgments

The first revision of the North American Industry Classification System (NAICS) was an immense undertaking requiring the time, energy, creativity, and cooperation of numerous people and organizations throughout the three countries. The work that has been accomplished is a testament to the individual and collective willingness of many persons and organizations both inside and outside government to contribute to the development of NAICS. Within the United States, NAICS was revised under the guidance of the Office of Management and Budget by the Economic Classification Policy Committee (ECPC). Members of the ECPC were **John R. Kort** and **Kenneth Johnson,** Bureau of Economic Analysis, U.S. Department of Commerce; **Thomas L. Mesenbourg, Carole A. Ambler** (retired Chair), and **John B. Murphy** (current Chair), Bureau of the Census, U.S. Department of Commerce; and **George S. Werking,** Bureau of Labor Statistics, U.S. Department of Labor; and ex officio, **Paul Bugg,** Office of Management and Budget.

The ECPC established two U.S. interagency subcommittees to work with their counterparts in Canada and Mexico to revise specific portions of the structure of NAICS. Eight U.S. government agencies provided staff for these subcommittees. Their contributions were invaluable. The agencies that generously made their staff available to support this process were as follows: Bureau of the Census; Bureau of Economic Analysis; Bureau of Labor Statistics; International Trade Administration; International Trade Commission; Internal Revenue Service; National Agricultural Statistics Service; and the Social Security Administration.

NAICS Revision Subcommittees:

Construction—**Michael J. Zampogna** (retired), Chair, Bureau of the Census; **Barry Rappaport**, Chair, Bureau of the Census
Wholesale Trade—**John R. Trimble**, Chair, Bureau of the Census
The ECPC established an additional subcommittee to coordinate the maintenance and upkeep of the system within the U.S. and with Canada and Mexico. Membership in this U.S. Maintenance Subcommittee included the Bureau of the Census, the Bureau of Economic Analysis, the Bureau of Labor Statistics, and the Social Security Administration.

Maintenance Subcommittee:

Michael J. Zampogna (retired), Co-Chair; **Wanda K. Dougherty**, Chair, Bureau of the Census
John B. Murphy, former Co-Chair; **David Talan**, Bureau of Labor Statistics
Paula C. Young (retired); **Jeffrey H. Lowe**, Bureau of Economic Analysis
Linda M. Dill (deceased), Social Security Administration

In addition to the parties listed above, the ECPC would like to acknowledge the dedicated staff of the **Economic Product and Industry Classification Branch** at the Bureau of the Census. Their hard work and dedication was invaluable in the preparation of the NAICS United States, 2002 manuscript for publication.

Contents

EXPLANATION OF SYMBOLS

In NAICS United States Structure

Symbol	Explanation
US	United States industry only.
CAN	United States and Canadian industries are comparable.
MEX	United States and Mexican industries are comparable.
[Blank]	[No superscript symbol] Canadian, Mexican, and United States industries are comparable.

In Part I, Titles and Descriptions

Symbol	Explanation
US	United States industry only.
CAN	United States and Canadian industries are comparable.
MEX	United States and Mexican industries are comparable.
[Blank]	[No superscript symbol] Canadian, Mexican, and United States industries are comparable.

In Appendix A

Symbol	Explanation
US	United States industry only.
CAN	United States and Canadian industries are comparable.
MEX	United States and Mexican industries are comparable.
[Blank]	[No superscript symbol] Canadian, Mexican, and United States industries are comparable.
*	Part of

In Appendix B

Symbol	Explanation
pt	Part of

Introduction

Background

In 1937, the Central Statistical Board established an Interdepartmental Committee on Industrial Classification "to develop a plan of classification of various types of statistical data by industries and to promote the general adoption of such classification as the standard classification of the Federal Government.[1]" The List of Industries for manufacturing was first available in 1938, with the List of Industries for nonmanufacturing following in 1939. These Lists of Industries became the first Standard Industrial Classification (SIC) for the United States.

The SIC was developed for use in the classification of establishments by type of activity in which they are primarily engaged; for purposes of facilitating the collection, tabulation, presentation, and analysis of data relating to establishments; and for promoting uniformity and comparability in the presentation of statistical data collected by various agencies of the United States Government, State agencies, trade associations, and private research organizations. The SIC covered the entire field of economic activities by defining industries in accordance with the composition and structure of the economy.

Since the inception of the SIC in the 1930s, the system has been periodically revised to reflect the economy's changing industrial composition and organization. The last revision of the SIC was in 1987.

Rapid changes in both the U.S. and world economies brought the SIC under increasing criticism. In 1991, an International Conference on the Classification of Economic Activities was convened in Williamsburg, Virginia, to provide a forum for responding to such criticism and to explore new approaches to classifying economic activity. In July 1992, the Office of Management and Budget (OMB) established the Economic Classification Policy Committee (ECPC) and charged it with a "fresh slate" examination of economic classifications for statistical purposes. The ECPC prepared a number of issue papers regarding classification, consulted with outside users, and ultimately joined with Mexico's Instituto Nacional de Estadística, Geografía e Informática (INEGI) and Statistics Canada to develop the North American Industry Classification System (NAICS), that replaced the 1987 U.S. SIC and the classification systems of Canada (1980 SIC) and Mexico (1994 Mexican Classification of Activities and Products (CMAP)).

The dynamic nature of world economies continues to impact classification systems. NAICS was revised in 2002 to achieve two main goals. The first goal was increased comparability among the three countries for selected areas. To that end, the construction sector has been revised and comparability has been achieved, for the most part, at the NAICS industry (five-digit) level. The second goal was to identify additional industries for new and emerging activities. In the United States,

---

[1] Pearce, Esther, History of the Standard Industrial Classification, Executive Office of the President, Office of Statistical Standards, U.S. Bureau of the Budget, Washington, DC, July 1957 (mimeograph).

industries were created for electronic shopping, electronic auctions, Web search portals, Internet service providers, and Internet publishing and broadcasting.

The impact of NAICS on various countries has brought about a renewed effort for additional convergence with the many industry classifications used throughout the world. Future revisions of NAICS will continue to strive for greater global comparability.

Purpose of NAICS

NAICS is an industry classification system that groups establishments into industries based on the activities in which they are primarily engaged. It is a comprehensive system covering the entire field of economic activities, producing and nonproducing. There are 20 sectors in NAICS and 1,179 industries in NAICS United States.

NAICS was initially developed and subsequently revised by Mexico's INEGI, Statistics Canada, and the U.S. ECPC (the latter acting on behalf of OMB) to provide common industry definitions for Canada, Mexico, and the United States that will facilitate economic analyses of the economies of the three North American countries. The statistical agencies in the three countries produce information on inputs and outputs, industrial performance, productivity, unit labor costs, and employment. NAICS, which is based on a production-oriented concept, ensures maximum usefulness of industrial statistics for these and similar purposes.

NAICS United States is used by U.S. statistical agencies to facilitate the collection, tabulation, presentation, and analysis of data relating to establishments; and to provide uniformity and comparability in the presentation of statistical data describing the U.S. economy. NAICS United States is designed for statistical purposes. Although the classification also may be used for various administrative, regulatory and taxation purposes, the requirements of government agencies that use it for nonstatistical purposes played no role in its development or subsequent revision.

Development of NAICS

The U.S. ECPC established by OMB in 1992 was chaired by the Bureau of Economic Analysis, U.S. Department of Commerce, with representatives from the Bureau of the Census, U.S. Department of Commerce, and the Bureau of Labor Statistics, U.S. Department of Labor. The ECPC was asked to examine economic classifications for statistical purposes and to determine the desirability of developing a new industry classification system for the United States based on a single economic concept. On March 31, 1993, OMB published a **Federal Register** notice (58FR16990–17004) announcing the intention to revise the SIC for 1997, the establishment of the ECPC, and the process for revising the SIC.

In July 1994, the OMB announced plans to develop a new industry classification system in cooperation with Mexico's INEGI and Statistics Canada. The new system—NAICS—replaces the current U.S. SIC. The concepts of the new system and the principles upon which NAICS was to be developed were announced in a July 26, 1994 **Federal Register** notice (59FR38092–38096) and were as follows:

1. NAICS will be erected on a production-oriented or supply-based conceptual framework. This means that producing units that use identical or similar production processes will be grouped together in NAICS.

2. The system will give special attention to developing production-oriented classifications for (a) new and emerging industries, (b) service industries in general, and (c) industries engaged in the production of advanced technologies.

3. Time series continuity will be maintained to the extent possible. However, changes in the economy and proposals from data users must be considered. In addition, adjustments will be required for sectors where the United States, Canada, and Mexico have incompatible industry classification definitions in order to produce a common industry system for all three North American countries.

4. The system will strive for compatibility with the two-digit level of the International Standard Industrial Classification of All Economic Activities (ISIC, Rev. 3) of the United Nations.

The structure of NAICS was developed in a series of meetings among the three countries. Public proposals for individual industries from all three countries were considered for acceptance if the proposed industry was based on the production-oriented concept of the system. In the United States, public comments also were solicited as groups of subsectors of NAICS were completed and agreed upon by the three countries. The ECPC published the proposed industries for those subsectors in a series of five successive **Federal Register** notices, in 1995 and 1996, asking for comments from interested data users.

Revision of NAICS for 2002

OMB published a notification of intention to complete portions of NAICS in a February 25, 1999, **Federal Register** notice (FR 64 9416–9419). This notice solicited comments on the advisability of revising the NAICS 1997 Structure for 2002 and solicited proposals for the creation of new industries in the Construction and Wholesale Trade Sectors, modifications to the national industries for department stores and non-store retailers, and changes necessary to NAICS 1997 identified during the implementation of NAICS 1997.

After considering all proposals from the public, consulting with a large number of U.S. data users and industry groups, and undertaking extensive discussions with Statistics Canada and Mexico's Instituto Nacional de Estadística, Geografía e Informática (INEGI), a revised industrial structure for NAICS was developed that would apply to all three North American countries. This includes a revised structure for both the Construction and Information sectors and additional U.S. industry detail in the Retail Trade sector. Statistics Canada and INEGI sought comments on the proposed revisions. Further discussions were held among the three countries to consider public comments received from all three countries. The United States has chosen to restructure the Wholesale Trade sector to more accurately reflect production function differences between those wholesalers that take title to goods and those that do not, and to better capture the rapidly-growing business-to-business electronic markets developing in the United States. These changes for the United States did not impact comparability among the three partners in NAICS. In an April 20, 2000 **Federal Register** notice (FR 65 21242–21282) OMB published the proposed structure of NAICS United States, 2002, and formalized adoption in a **Federal Register** notice (FR 66 3826–3827) on January 16, 2001.

Conceptual Framework

NAICS is erected on a production-oriented or supply-based conceptual framework that groups establishments into industries according to similarity in the processes used to produce goods or services. A production-oriented industry classification system ensures that statistical agencies in the three countries can produce information on inputs and outputs, industrial performance, productivity, unit labor costs, employment, and other statistics and structural changes occurring in each of the three economies.

When an industry is defined on a production-oriented concept, producing units within the industry's boundaries share a basic production process; they use closely similar technology. In the language of economics, producing units within an industry share the same production functions; producing units in different industries have different production functions. The boundaries between industries thus demarcate, in principle, differences in production processes and production technologies.

The reasoning behind the three countries' decision to base NAICS on a production-oriented concept is summarized as follows: An industry is a grouping of economic activities. Though it inevitably groups the products of the economic activities that are included in the industry definition, it is not solely a grouping of products; put another way, an industry groups producing units. Accordingly, an industry classification system provides a framework for collecting data on inputs and outputs together.

The uses of economic data that require that data on inputs and outputs be used together and be collected on the same basis, include production analyses, productivity measurement, and studying input usage and input intensities. The North American statistical agencies developed NAICS using a production-oriented concept as the framework for two reasons: (1) an industry classification system groups producing units, not products or services; and (2) groupings of producing units permit the collection of data on inputs and outputs on a comparable basis, which is required for production-oriented analysis, but do not facilitate a comprehensive collection of data on the total output of any particular good or service, which is required for market-oriented analysis. Thus, the efficient organizing concept of an industry classification system is production-oriented rather than market-oriented.

Structure of NAICS

The structure of NAICS is hierarchical. The first two digits of the structure designate the NAICS sectors that represent general categories of economic activities.

NAICS classifies all economic activities into 20 sectors. The NAICS sectors, their two-digit codes, and the distinguishing activities of each are:

11 Agriculture, Forestry, Fishing and Hunting—Activities of this sector are growing crops, raising animals, harvesting timber, and harvesting fish and other animals from farms, ranches, or the animals' natural habitats.

21 Mining—Activities of this sector are extracting naturally occurring mineral solids, such as coal and ore; liquid minerals, such as crude petroleum; and gases, such as natural gas; and beneficiating (e.g., crushing, screening, washing, and flotation) and other preparation at the mine site, or as part of mining activity.

22 Utilities—Activities of this sector are generating, transmitting, and/or distributing electricity, gas, steam, and water and removing sewage through a permanent infrastructure of lines, mains, and pipe.

23 Construction—Activities of this sector are erecting buildings and other structures (including additions); heavy construction other than buildings; and alterations, reconstruction, installation, and maintenance and repairs.

31-33 Manufacturing—Activities of this sector are the mechanical, physical, or chemical transformation of material, substances, or components into new products.

42 Wholesale Trade—Activities of this sector are selling or arranging for the purchase or sale of goods for resale; capital or durable nonconsumer goods; and raw and intermediate materials and supplies used in production, and providing services incidental to the sale of the merchandise.

44-45 Retail Trade—Activities of this sector are retailing merchandise generally in small quantities to the general public and providing services incidental to the sale of the merchandise.

48-49 Transportation and Warehousing—Activities of this sector are providing transportation of passengers and cargo, warehousing and storing goods, scenic and sightseeing transportation, and supporting these activities.

51 Information—Activities of this sector are distributing information and cultural products, providing the means to transmit or distribute these products as data or communications, and processing data.

52 Finance and Insurance—Activities of this sector involve the creation, liquidation, or change in ownership of financial assets (financial transactions) and/ or facilitating financial transactions.

53 Real Estate and Rental and Leasing—Activities of this sector are renting, leasing, or otherwise allowing the use of tangible or intangible assets (except copyrighted works), and providing related services.

54 Professional, Scientific, and Technical Services—Activities of this sector are performing professional, scientific, and technical services for the operations of other organizations.

55 Management of Companies and Enterprises—Activities of this sector are the holding of securities of companies and enterprises, for the purpose of owning controlling interest or influencing their management decision, or administering, overseeing, and managing other establishments of the same company or enterprise and normally undertaking the strategic or organizational planning and decision making of the company or enterprise.

56 Administrative and Support and Waste Management and Remediation Services—Activities of this sector are performing routine support activities for the day-to-day operations of other organizations.

61 Educational Services—Activities of this sector are providing instruction and training in a wide variety of subjects.

62 Health Care and Social Assistance—Activities of this sector are providing health care and social assistance for individuals.

71 Arts, Entertainment, and Recreation—Activities of this sector are operating or providing services to meet varied cultural, entertainment, and recreational interests of their patrons.

72 Accommodation and Food Services—Activities of this sector are providing customers with lodging and/or preparing meals, snacks, and beverages for immediate consumption.

81 Other Services (except Public Administration)—Activities of this sector are providing services not elsewhere specified, including repairs, religious activities, grantmaking, advocacy, laundry, personal care, death care, and other personal services.

92 Public Administration—Activities of this sector are administration, management, and oversight of public programs by Federal, State, and local governments.

NAICS uses a six-digit coding system to identify particular industries and their placement in this hierarchical structure of the classification system. The first two digits of the code designate the sector, the third designates the subsector, the fourth digit designates the industry group, the fifth digit designates the NAICS industry, and the sixth digit designates the national industry. A zero as the sixth digit generally indicates that the NAICS industry and the U.S. industry are the same.

The subsectors, industry groups, and NAICS industries, in accord with the conceptual principle of NAICS, are production-oriented combinations of establishments. However, the production distinctions become more narrowly defined as one moves down the hierarchy.

NAICS agreements permit each country to designate detailed industries, below the level of a NAICS industry, to meet national needs. The United States has such industry detail in many places in the classification system to recognize large, important U.S. industries that cannot be recognized in the other countries because of size, specialization, or organization of the industry.

Typically the level at which comparable data will be available for Canada, Mexico, and the United States is the five-digit NAICS industry; for some sectors (or subsectors or industry groups) however, the three countries agreed upon the boundaries at a higher level of detail rather than the detailed industry structure (five-digit). Agreement was reached at the sector level for utilities; wholesale trade; retail trade; and public administration and at the subsector level for finance; personal and laundry services; religious, grantmaking, civic, and professional and similar organizations; and waste management and remediation services. For insurance and real estate, the three countries agreed on comparability at the industry group level. The 2002 revision effort obtained comparability at the five-digit level for most areas of the construction sector.

Differences in the economies of the three countries or time constraints necessitated these modifications. For each of these sectors, except wholesale trade and public administration, Canada and the United States have agreed upon an industry structure and hierarchy to ensure comparability of statistics between those two countries. Canada and the United States also have established the same national detail (six-digit) industries where possible, adopting the same codes to describe comparable industries. For this reason, the numbers of the U.S. industries may not be consecutive. In a few cases, it was necessary for the United States to use all of the numbers available to establish its six-digit detail so that the same six-digit codes do not represent comparable industries in the U.S. and Canada.

NAICS with U.S. detail will be known as NAICS United States (denoted by "US" in Appendix A and a superscript "US" at the end of the title in Part I) while Canada and Mexico will produce six-digit detail and will publish that detail as NAICS Canada and NAICS (SCIAN in Spanish) Mexico.

Definition of an Establishment

NAICS is a classification system for establishments. The establishment as a statistical unit is defined as the smallest operating entity for which records provide information on the cost of resources materials, labor, and capital employed to produce the units of output. The output may be sold to other establishments and receipts or sales recorded, or the output may be provided without explicit charge, that is, the good or service may be "sold" within the company itself.

The establishment, in NAICS United States, is generally a single physical location, where business is conducted or where services or industrial operations are performed (for example, a factory, mill, store, hotel, movie theater, mine, farm, airline terminal, sales office, warehouse, or central administrative office). There are cases where records identify distinct and separate economic activities performed at a single physical location (e.g., shops in a hotel). These retailing activities, operated out of the same physical location as the hotel, are identified as separate establishments and classified in retail trade while the hotel is classified in accommodations. In such cases, each activity is treated as a separate establishment provided:

(1) no one industry description in the classification includes such combined activities; (2) separate reports can be prepared on the number of employees, their wages and salaries, sales or receipts, and expenses; and (3) employment and output are significant for both activities.

Exceptions to the single location exist for physically dispersed operations, such as construction, transportation, and communication. For these activities the individual sites, projects, fields, networks, lines, or systems of such dispersed activities are not normally considered to be establishments. The establishment is represented by those relatively permanent main or branch offices, terminals, stations, and so forth, that are either (1) directly responsible for supervising such activities, or (2) the base from which personnel operate to carry out these activities.

Although an establishment may be identical with the enterprise (company), the two terms should not be confused. An enterprise (company) may consist of more than one establishment. Such multiunit enterprises may have establishments in more than one industry in NAICS. If such enterprises have a separate establishment primarily engaged in providing headquarters services, these establishments are classified in NAICS Sector 55, Management of Companies and Enterprises.

Although all establishments have output, they may or may not have receipts. In large enterprises it is not unusual for establishments to exist that solely serve other establishments of the same enterprise (auxiliary establishments). In such cases, these units often do not collect receipts from the establishments they serve. This type of support (captive) activity is found throughout the economy and involves goods producing activities as well as services. Units that carry out support activities for the enterprise to which they belong are classified, to the extent feasible, according to the NAICS code related to their own activity. This means that warehouses providing storage facilities for their own enterprise will be classified as warehouses.

Determining an Establishment's Industry Classification

An establishment is classified to an industry when its primary activity meets the definition for that industry. Because establishments may perform more than one activity, it is necessary to determine procedures for identifying the primary activity of the establishment.

In most cases, if an establishment is engaged in more than one activity, the industry code is assigned based on the establishment's principal product or group of products produced or distributed, or services rendered. Ideally, the principal good or service should be determined by its relative share of current production costs and capital investment at the establishment. In practice, however, it is often necessary to use other variables such as revenue, shipments, or employment as proxies for measuring significance.

There are two types of combined activities that are given special attention in NAICS. They are vertical integration and joint production. These combined activities have an economic basis and occur in both goods-producing and services-producing sectors. In some cases, there are efficiencies to be gained from combining certain activities in the same establishment. Some of these combinations occur so commonly or frequently that their combination can be treated as a third activity in its own right and explicitly classified in a specific industry.

One approach to classifying these activities would be to use the primary activity rule, that is, whichever activity is largest. However, the fundamental principle of NAICS is that establishments that employ the same production process should be classified in the same industry. If the premise that the combined activities correspond to a distinct third activity is accepted, then using the primary activity rule would place establishments performing the same combination of activities in different industries, thereby violating the production principle of NAICS. A second reason for NAICS recognizing combined activities is to improve the stability of establishment classification, both over time and among the various agencies that implement the classification. An establishment should remain classified in the same industry unless its production process changes, and different agencies should code the same establishment or type of establishment in the same way. A consistent treatment of establishments with combined activities is more likely if they are classified to a single industry.

Vertical integration involves consecutive stages of fabrication or production processes in which the output of one step is the input of the next. In general, establishments will be classified based on the final process in a vertically integrated production environment, unless specifically identified as classified in another industry. For example, paper may be produced either by establishments that first produce pulp and then consume that pulp to produce paper or by those establishments producing paper from purchased pulp. NAICS specifically specifies that both of these types of paper-producing processes should be classified in NAICS 32212, Paper Mills, the industry, or the final step in paper manufacturing, rather than in NAICS 32211, Pulp Mills. In other cases, NAICS specifies that vertically integrated establishments be classified in the industry representing the first stage of the manufacturing process. For example, steel mills that make steel and also perform other activities such as producing steel castings are classified in NAICS 33111, Iron and Steel Mills and Ferroalloy Manufacturing, the first stage of the manufacturing process.

The joint production of goods or services represents the second type of combined activities. For example, automobile dealers both sell and repair autos; automotive parts dealers may both sell parts and repair automobiles; and musical instrument stores may both sell and rent instruments. In the manufacturing sector, establishments may make two different products such as women's dresses and women's suits, activities that are classified in two different NAICS United States detailed industries. In general, receipts/sales and revenue data are used as a proxy to determine primary activity for these establishments. The assumption is that the activity generating the most receipts is also the activity using the most resources and most indicative of the production process.

In some cases, however, these combined activities have been assigned to a specific NAICS industry. Most of these activities involve either the sale and repair of goods or the sale and rental of goods in the same establishment. For example, establishments that both sell automobile parts and repair automobiles are classified in NAICS 44131, Automotive Parts and Accessories Stores, and those music stores that both sell and rent musical instruments are classified in NAICS 45114, Musical Instrument and Supplies Stores. In other cases, specific industries have been identified for these combined activities, such as NAICS 44711, Gasoline Stations with Convenience Stores.

Classification rules related to the agreement to permit individual country detail at the six-digit level for NAICS sometimes results in less comparable NAICS industries at the five-digit level and above. For example in NAICS, the assignment of the industry code is at the most detailed level of the classification (the six-digit U.S. detail code), except for agriculture. That is, if the value of an establishment's production consists of 30 percent from computers, 30 percent from computer storage devices, and 40 percent from semiconductors and related devices, it will be classified in U.S. detail industry 334413, Semiconductor and Related Device Manufacturing, that will be aggregated to NAICS 33441, Semiconductor and Other Electronic Component Manufacturing, the level that comparable information is shown for all three countries. If the classification for the above example were at the five-digit NAICS level, that establishment would be classified in NAICS 33411, Computer and Peripheral Equipment Manufacturing. There would then be more comparable information at the NAICS level, but it would be impossible to classify this establishment to a U.S. detail six-digit industry.

In agriculture, however, NAICS coding begins at the top of the structure and continues down to the most detailed level (the six-digit U.S. detail code). The existence of a 50 percent rule in agriculture, rather than the plurality rule used elsewhere, and the presence of combination industries based on families of related agricultural products with none accounting for 50 percent or more of production require a top down coding procedure rather than coding at the most detailed level first as is done in the balance of the classification.

Use of Reporting Units Other than Establishments

NAICS is based on the economic principle that establishments should be grouped together based on their production processes. The NAICS definition of the establishment ensures that, at some level, "establishments": (1) identify the most refined (generally smallest) individual entity possible; (2) can provide the information needed when surveying economic activity; and (3) when aggregated, approximate the statistical universe of economic activity. Each economic survey program, in practice, will need to determine whether the establishment is the most appropriate reporting unit to meet the three criteria listed above with respect to the program's objectives. If not, an alternative reporting unit may have to be identified.

For example, an economic survey of employment or wage data may choose the establishment—generally a physical location—as the reporting unit. Physical locations generally have records for the number of employees and their wages readily available. Therefore, it is reasonable to expect that separate wage and employment data would be available for each switching station in a multiunit telecommunications carrier enterprise and the physical location is a logical choice for the reporting unit.

If the economic survey collects output data, the individual switching stations would not have the total number of telephone calls or a complete accounting of inputs and outputs of the multiunit telecommunications carrier. If a telephone call is routed through three different switching stations and the price is determined at a fourth location, all of the related locations would need to be merged into an alternative reporting unit to measure the volume and value of the output. In this case, the physical location would not be an appropriate reporting unit. The level of aggregation of physical units required to create reporting units will vary greatly depending on the business activity being studied. To efficiently define reporting units, statistical surveys need to evaluate the characteristics of the activities being studied and the organizational structure of the entities producing goods or services. In some cases, the physical location is appropriate, sometimes units will need to be grouped based on homogeneous production characteristics or geographical groupings, and in other cases, the enterprise (company) may form the most appropriate reporting unit.

The practical variation in reporting unit definitions affects comparability of data. A count of units defined as physical locations will be different from a count of units defined based on the need for complete input and output records in the telecommunications industries. It is critical that each data provider clearly identifies the reporting unit definition used when presenting summary statistics. The analysis of statistical data from a variety of sources requires the transparency of clearly defined reporting units.

While the reporting unit definition can vary, NAICS is a classification system for establishments, and is based on grouping establishments with similar production function characteristics.

Comparison of NAICS to the International Standard Industrial Classification (ISIC)

Recognizing the need for international comparability of economic statistics, the United Nations (UN) first adopted an International Standard Industrial Classification (ISIC) system in 1948. Revisions to the ISIC structure and codes were adopted by the UN's Statistical Commission in 1958, 1968, and 1989.[2]

Similar to NAICS, ISIC was designed primarily to provide classifications for grouping activities (rather than enterprises or firms), and the primary focus for the ISIC classification system is the kind of activity in which establishments or other

---

[2] International Standard Industrial Classification of all Economic Activities, Statistical Papers, Series M., No. 4, Department of International Economic and Social Affairs, Statistical Office, United Nations, New York, 1958, International Standard Industrial Classification of All Economic Activities, Statistical Papers, Series M., No. 4, Rev. 2, Department of International Economic and Social Affairs, Statistical Office, United Nations, New York, 1968. International Standard Industrial Classification of All Economic Activities, Statistical Papers, Series M., No. 4., Rev. 3, Department of International Economic and Social Affairs, Statistical Office, United Nations, New York, 1990.

statistical entities are engaged. The main criteria employed in delineating divisions and groups (the two- and three-digit categories, respectively) of ISIC are: (a) the character of the goods and services produced; (b) the uses to which the goods and services are put; and (c) the inputs, the process, and the technology of production.

The third classification criterion of the ISIC is the conceptual foundation of NAICS, and thus, NAICS is aligned more closely with ISIC than was the 1987 SIC system. However, there are differences between the NAICS and ISIC classification schemes. Most important, perhaps, is the single (production process) conceptual framework of NAICS. As noted elsewhere, this is unique among industry classifications. Distinctions also were made during ISIC's development with regard to (1) select characteristics of goods and services produced; (2) the range of kinds of activity frequently carried out under the same ownership or control; (3) differences between enterprises in scale, organization of activities, capital requirements, and finance; and (4) the pattern of categories at various levels of classification in national classifications.

The ISIC, Rev. 3 groups economic activity into 17 broad Sections, 60 Divisions, 159 Groups, and 292 Classes. In the coding system, Sections are distinguished by the letters A through Q and the Divisions, Groups, and Classes are identified as the two-digit, three-digit, and four-digit groupings, respectively. NAICS United States groups economic activity into 20 sectors (two-digit), 100 subsectors (three-digit), 317 industry groups (four-digit), 725 NAICS industries (five-digit, of which 484 are comparable among all three countries), and 1,179 six-digit industries. Of the 1,179 six-digit industry codes, 669 identify an economic type unique to the United States (a U.S. industry), but within the general NAICS structure.

In the development and subsequent revision of NAICS industries, the statistical agencies of the three countries strove to create industries that did not cross ISIC two-digit boundaries. While this general goal was met in the initial development of NAICS, continuing efforts are underway to identify and evaluate the differences between NAICS and ISIC.

NAICS United States Structure

The following page contains a summary table of the NAICS United States structure. This table shows the counts of subsectors, industry groups, industries, and United States detail industries for each of the NAICS sectors.

Following the summary table is a complete numerical list of the NAICS United States structure. This list displays the codes and official full titles for the sectors, subsectors, industry groups, industries, and United States detail industries. It also indicates the comparability of the codes with NAICS Canada and NAICS Mexico.

Part II of this manual contains a numerical list of short titles that are recommended for use when space limitations preclude the use of the full titles for the dissemination of data classified to NAICS.

NAICS United States Structure

Sector	Name	Sub-sectors (3-digit)	Industry Groups (4-digit)	NAICS Industries (5-digit)	6-digit Industries U.S. Detail	6-digit Industries Same as 5-digit	6-digit Industries Total
11	Agriculture, Forestry, Fishing and Hunting	5	19	42	32	32	64
21	Mining	3	5	10	28	1	29
22	Utilities	1	3	6	6	4	10
23	Construction	3	10	28	4	27	31
31-33	Manufacturing	21	86	184	408	65	473
42	Wholesale Trade	3	19	71	0	71	71
44-45	Retail Trade	12	27	61	24	51	75
48-49	Transportation and Warehousing	11	29	42	25	32	57
51	Information	7	16	30	12	24	36
52	Finance and Insurance	5	11	32	15	27	42
53	Real Estate and Rental and Leasing	3	8	19	9	15	24
54	Professional, Scientific, and Technical Services	1	9	35	17	30	47
55	Management of Companies and Enterprises	1	1	1	3	0	3
56	Administrative and Support and Waste Management and Remediation Services	2	11	29	23	20	43
61	Educational Services	1	7	12	7	10	17
62	Health Care and Social Assistance	4	18	30	16	23	39
71	Arts, Entertainment, and Recreation	3	9	23	3	22	25
72	Accommodation and Food Services	2	7	11	7	8	15
81	Other Services (except Public Administration)	4	14	30	30	19	49
92	Public Administration	8	8	29	0	29	29
	Total	100	317	725	669	510	1179

11 Agriculture, Forestry, Fishing and Hunting

111 Crop Production

1111 Oilseed and Grain Farming

11111	Soybean Farming
111110	Soybean Farming
11112	Oilseed (except Soybean) Farming
111120	Oilseed (except Soybean) Farming[CAN]
11113	Dry Pea and Bean Farming
111130	Dry Pea and Bean Farming[CAN]
11114	Wheat Farming
111140	Wheat Farming
11115	Corn Farming
111150	Corn Farming[CAN]
11116	Rice Farming
111160	Rice Farming
11119	Other Grain Farming
111191	Oilseed and Grain Combination Farming[US]
111199	All Other Grain Farming[US]

1112 Vegetable and Melon Farming

11121	Vegetable and Melon Farming
111211	Potato Farming[CAN]
111219	Other Vegetable (except Potato) and Melon Farming[CAN]

1113 Fruit and Tree Nut Farming

11131	Orange Groves
111310	Orange Groves
11132	Citrus (except Orange) Groves
111320	Citrus (except Orange) Groves[CAN]
11133	Noncitrus Fruit and Tree Nut Farming
111331	Apple Orchards[US]
111332	Grape Vineyards[US]
111333	Strawberry Farming[US]
111334	Berry (except Strawberry) Farming[US]
111335	Tree Nut Farming[US]
111336	Fruit and Tree Nut Combination Farming[US]
111339	Other Noncitrus Fruit Farming[US]

1114 Greenhouse, Nursery, and Floriculture Production

11141	Food Crops Grown Under Cover
111411	Mushroom Production[CAN]
111419	Other Food Crops Grown Under Cover[CAN]
11142	Nursery and Floriculture Production

111421   Nursery and Tree Production[CAN]
111422   Floriculture Production[CAN]

1119   Other Crop Farming

11191   Tobacco Farming
111910   Tobacco Farming
11192   Cotton Farming
111920   Cotton Farming
11193   Sugarcane Farming
111930   Sugarcane Farming
11194   Hay Farming
111940   Hay Farming[CAN]
11199   All Other Crop Farming
111991   Sugar Beet Farming[US]
111992   Peanut Farming[MEX]
111998   All Other Miscellaneous Crop Farming[US]

112 Animal Production

1121   Cattle Ranching and Farming

11211   Beef Cattle Ranching and Farming, including Feedlots
112111   Beef Cattle Ranching and Farming[US]
112112   Cattle Feedlots[US]
11212   Dairy Cattle and Milk Production
112120   Dairy Cattle and Milk Production
11213   Dual-Purpose Cattle Ranching and Farming[MEX]
112130   Dual-Purpose Cattle Ranching and Farming[MEX]

1122   Hog and Pig Farming

11221   Hog and Pig Farming
112210   Hog and Pig Farming[CAN]

1123   Poultry and Egg Production

11231   Chicken Egg Production
112310   Chicken Egg Production[CAN]
11232   Broilers and Other Meat Type Chicken Production
112320   Broilers and Other Meat Type Chicken Production
11233   Turkey Production
112330   Turkey Production
11234   Poultry Hatcheries
112340   Poultry Hatcheries
11239   Other Poultry Production
112390   Other Poultry Production[MEX]

1124 Sheep and Goat Farming

11241	Sheep Farming
112410	Sheep Farming^{CAN}
11242	Goat Farming
112420	Goat Farming

1125 Animal Aquaculture

11251	Animal Aquaculture
112511	Finfish Farming and Fish Hatcheries^{US}
112512	Shellfish Farming^{US}
112519	Other Animal Aquaculture^{US}

1129 Other Animal Production

11291	Apiculture
112910	Apiculture
11292	Horses and Other Equine Production
112920	Horses and Other Equine Production
11293	Fur-Bearing Animal and Rabbit Production
112930	Fur-Bearing Animal and Rabbit Production
11299	All Other Animal Production
112990	All Other Animal Production^{MEX}

113 Forestry and Logging

1131 Timber Tract Operations

11311	Timber Tract Operations
113110	Timber Tract Operations

1132 Forest Nurseries and Gathering of Forest Products

11321	Forest Nurseries and Gathering of Forest Products
113210	Forest Nurseries and Gathering of Forest Products^{CAN}

1133 Logging

11331	Logging
113310	Logging^{MEX}

114 Fishing, Hunting and Trapping

1141 Fishing

11411	Fishing
114111	Finfish Fishing^{US}
114112	Shellfish Fishing^{US}
114119	Other Marine Fishing^{US}

1142 Hunting and Trapping

11421	Hunting and Trapping
114210	Hunting and Trapping

115 Support Activities for Agriculture and Forestry

1151 Support Activities for Crop Production

11511	Support Activities for Crop Production
115111	Cotton Ginning[US]
115112	Soil Preparation, Planting, and Cultivating[US]
115113	Crop Harvesting, Primarily by Machine[US]
115114	Postharvest Crop Activities (except Cotton Ginning)[US]
115115	Farm Labor Contractors and Crew Leaders[US]
115116	Farm Management Services[US]

1152 Support Activities for Animal Production

11521	Support Activities for Animal Production
115210	Support Activities for Animal Production

1153 Support Activities for Forestry

11531	Support Activities for Forestry
115310	Support Activities for Forestry

21 Mining

211 Oil and Gas Extraction

2111 Oil and Gas Extraction

21111	Oil and Gas Extraction
211111	Crude Petroleum and Natural Gas Extraction[US]
211112	Natural Gas Liquid Extraction[US]

212 Mining (except Oil and Gas)

2121 Coal Mining

21211	Coal Mining
212111	Bituminous Coal and Lignite Surface Mining[US]
212112	Bituminous Coal Underground Mining[US]
212113	Anthracite Mining[US]

2122 Metal Ore Mining

21221	Iron Ore Mining
212210	Iron Ore Mining
21222	Gold Ore and Silver Ore Mining
212221	Gold Ore Mining[MEX]
212222	Silver Ore Mining[MEX]
21223	Copper, Nickel, Lead, and Zinc Mining
212231	Lead Ore and Zinc Ore Mining[CAN]
212234	Copper Ore and Nickel Ore Mining[US]
21229	Other Metal Ore Mining

212291	Uranium-Radium-Vanadium Ore Mining[CAN]
212299	All Other Metal Ore Mining[CAN]

2123   Nonmetallic Mineral Mining and Quarrying

21231	Stone Mining and Quarrying
212311	Dimension Stone Mining and Quarrying[US]
212312	Crushed and Broken Limestone Mining and Quarrying[US]
212313	Crushed and Broken Granite Mining and Quarrying[US]
212319	Other Crushed and Broken Stone Mining and Quarrying[US]
21232	Sand, Gravel, Clay, and Ceramic and Refractory Minerals Mining and Quarrying
212321	Construction Sand and Gravel Mining[MEX]
212322	Industrial Sand Mining[US]
212324	Kaolin and Ball Clay Mining[US]
212325	Clay and Ceramic and Refractory Minerals Mining[US]
21239	Other Nonmetallic Mineral Mining and Quarrying
212391	Potash, Soda, and Borate Mineral Mining[US]
212392	Phosphate Rock Mining[US]
212393	Other Chemical and Fertilizer Mineral Mining[US]
212399	All Other Nonmetallic Mineral Mining[US]

213 Support Activities for Mining

2131   Support Activities for Mining

21311	Support Activities for Mining
213111	Drilling Oil and Gas Wells
213112	Support Activities for Oil and Gas Operations[US]
213113	Support Activities for Coal Mining[US]
213114	Support Activities for Metal Mining[US]
213115	Support Activities for Nonmetallic Minerals (except Fuels) Mining[US]

22   Utilities

221 Utilities[CAN]

2211   Electric Power Generation, Transmission and Distribution

22111	Electric Power Generation[CAN]
221111	Hydroelectric Power Generation[CAN]
221112	Fossil Fuel Electric Power Generation[CAN]
221113	Nuclear Electric Power Generation[CAN]
221119	Other Electric Power Generation[CAN]

22112	Electric Power Transmission, Control, and Distribution[CAN]
221121	Electric Bulk Power Transmission and Control[CAN]
221122	Electric Power Distribution[CAN]

2212 Natural Gas Distribution[CAN]

22121	Natural Gas Distribution[CAN]
221210	Natural Gas Distribution[CAN]

2213 Water, Sewage and Other Systems[CAN]

22131	Water Supply and Irrigation Systems[CAN]
221310	Water Supply and Irrigation Systems[CAN]
22132	Sewage Treatment Facilities[CAN]
221320	Sewage Treatment Facilities[CAN]
22133	Steam and Air-Conditioning Supply[CAN]
221330	Steam and Air-Conditioning Supply[CAN]

23 Construction

236 Construction of Buildings

2361 Residential Building Construction

23611	Residential Building Construction
236115	New Single-Family Housing Construction (except Operative Builders)[US]
236116	New Multifamily Housing Construction (except Operative Builders)[US]
236117	New Housing Operative Builders [US]
236118	Residential Remodelers [US]

2362 Nonresidential Building Construction

23621	Industrial Building Construction
236210	Industrial Building Construction[CAN]
23622	Commercial and Institutional Building Construction
236220	Commercial and Institutional Building Construction[CAN]

237 Heavy and Civil Engineering Construction

2371 Utility System Construction

23711	Water and Sewer Line and Related Structures Construction
237110	Water and Sewer Line and Related Structures Construction[CAN]
23712	Oil and Gas Pipeline and Related Structures Construction

237120   Oil and Gas Pipeline and Related Structures Construction[CAN]

23713   Power and Communication Line and Related Structures Construction

237130   Power and Communication Line and Related Structures Construction[CAN]

2372 Land Subdivision

23721   Land Subdivision
237210   Land Subdivision[CAN]

2373 Highway, Street, and Bridge Construction

23731   Highway, Street, and Bridge Construction
237310   Highway, Street, and Bridge Construction[CAN]

2379 Other Heavy and Civil Engineering Construction

23799   Other Heavy and Civil Engineering Construction
237990   Other Heavy and Civil Engineering Construction[CAN]

238 Specialty Trade Contractors

2381 Foundation, Structure, and Building Exterior Contractors

23811   Poured Concrete Foundation and Structure Contractors[CAN]

238110   Poured Concrete Foundation and Structure Contractors[CAN]

23812   Structural Steel and Precast Concrete Contractors
238120   Structural Steel and Precast Concrete Contractors[CAN]
23813   Framing Contractors[CAN]
238130   Framing Contractors[CAN]
23814   Masonry Contractors[CAN]
238140   Masonry Contractors[CAN]
23815   Glass and Glazing Contractors[CAN]
238150   Glass and Glazing Contractors[CAN]
23816   Roofing Contractors[CAN]
238160   Roofing Contractors[CAN]
23817   Siding Contractors[CAN]
238170   Siding Contractors[CAN]
23819   Other Foundation, Structure, and Building Exterior Contractors[CAN]

238190   Other Foundation, Structure, and Building Exterior Contractors[CAN]

2382 Building Equipment Contractors

23821   Electrical Contractors
238210   Electrical Contractors

23822   Plumbing, Heating, and Air-Conditioning Contractors

238220   Plumbing, Heating, and Air-Conditioning Contractors[CAN]

23829   Other Building Equipment Contractors

238290   Other Building Equipment Contractors[MEX]

2383 Building Finishing Contractors

23831   Drywall and Insulation Contractors

238310   Drywall and Insulation Contractors[CAN]

23832   Painting and Wall Covering Contractors

238320   Painting and Wall Covering Contractors

23833   Flooring Contractors

238330   Flooring Contractors

23834   Tile and Terrazzo Contractors

238340   Tile and Terrazzo Contractors

23835   Finish Carpentry Contractors

238350   Finish Carpentry Contractors

23839   Other Building Finishing Contractors

238390   Other Building Finishing Contractors

2389 Other Specialty Trade Contractors

23891   Site Preparation Contractors

238910   Site Preparation Contractors

23899   All Other Specialty Trade Contractors

238990   All Other Specialty Trade Contractors[CAN]

31-33 Manufacturing

311 Food Manufacturing

3111 Animal Food Manufacturing

31111   Animal Food Manufacturing

311111   Dog and Cat Food Manufacturing[CAN]

311119   Other Animal Food Manufacturing[CAN]

3112 Grain and Oilseed Milling

31121   Flour Milling and Malt Manufacturing

311211   Flour Milling[CAN]

311212   Rice Milling[US]

311213   Malt Manufacturing[US]

31122   Starch and Vegetable Fats and Oils Manufacturing

311221   Wet Corn Milling[CAN]

311222   Soybean Processing[US]

311223   Other Oilseed Processing[US]

311225   Fats and Oils Refining and Blending[CAN]

| 31123 | Breakfast Cereal Manufacturing |
| 311230 | Breakfast Cereal Manufacturing |

3113   Sugar and Confectionery Product Manufacturing

31131	Sugar Manufacturing
311311	Sugarcane Mills^{US}
311312	Cane Sugar Refining^{US}
311313	Beet Sugar Manufacturing^{US}
31132	Chocolate and Confectionery Manufacturing from Cacao Beans
311320	Chocolate and Confectionery Manufacturing from Cacao Beans
31133	Confectionery Manufacturing from Purchased Chocolate
311330	Confectionery Manufacturing from Purchased Chocolate
31134	Nonchocolate Confectionery Manufacturing
311340	Nonchocolate Confectionery Manufacturing

3114   Fruit and Vegetable Preserving and Specialty Food Manufacturing

31141	Frozen Food Manufacturing
311411	Frozen Fruit, Juice, and Vegetable Manufacturing^{MEX}
311412	Frozen Specialty Food Manufacturing^{MEX}
31142	Fruit and Vegetable Canning, Pickling, and Drying
311421	Fruit and Vegetable Canning^{US}
311422	Specialty Canning^{US}
311423	Dried and Dehydrated Food Manufacturing^{US}

3115   Dairy Product Manufacturing

31151	Dairy Product (except Frozen) Manufacturing
311511	Fluid Milk Manufacturing^{CAN}
311512	Creamery Butter Manufacturing^{US}
311513	Cheese Manufacturing^{US}
311514	Dry, Condensed, and Evaporated Dairy Product Manufacturing^{US}
31152	Ice Cream and Frozen Dessert Manufacturing
311520	Ice Cream and Frozen Dessert Manufacturing

3116   Animal Slaughtering and Processing

31161	Animal Slaughtering and Processing
311611	Animal (except Poultry) Slaughtering^{CAN}
311612	Meat Processed from Carcasses^{US}
311613	Rendering and Meat Byproduct Processing^{US}
311615	Poultry Processing^{CAN}

3117   Seafood Product Preparation and Packaging

31171   Seafood Product Preparation and Packaging
311711   Seafood Canning^US
311712   Fresh and Frozen Seafood Processing^US

3118   Bakeries and Tortilla Manufacturing

31181   Bread and Bakery Product Manufacturing
311811   Retail Bakeries^CAN
311812   Commercial Bakeries^US
311813   Frozen Cakes, Pies, and Other Pastries
           Manufacturing^US
31182   Cookie, Cracker, and Pasta Manufacturing
311821   Cookie and Cracker Manufacturing^CAN
311822   Flour Mixes and Dough Manufacturing from
           Purchased Flour ^CAN
311823   Dry Pasta Manufacturing^CAN
31183   Tortilla Manufacturing
311830   Tortilla Manufacturing

3119   Other Food Manufacturing

31191   Snack Food Manufacturing
311911   Roasted Nuts and Peanut Butter Manufacturing^CAN
311919   Other Snack Food Manufacturing^CAN
31192   Coffee and Tea Manufacturing
311920   Coffee and Tea Manufacturing^CAN
31193   Flavoring Syrup and Concentrate Manufacturing
311930   Flavoring Syrup and Concentrate Manufacturing
31194   Seasoning and Dressing Manufacturing
311941   Mayonnaise, Dressing, and Other Prepared Sauce
           Manufacturing^US
311942   Spice and Extract Manufacturing^US
31199   All Other Food Manufacturing
311991   Perishable Prepared Food Manufacturing^US
311999   All Other Miscellaneous Food Manufacturing^US

312 Beverage and Tobacco Product Manufacturing

3121   Beverage Manufacturing

31211   Soft Drink and Ice Manufacturing
312111   Soft Drink Manufacturing^MEX
312112   Bottled Water Manufacturing^MEX
312113   Ice Manufacturing^MEX
31212   Breweries
312120   Breweries
31213   Wineries
312130   Wineries^CAN

31214   Distilleries
312140   Distilleries^{CAN}

3122   Tobacco Manufacturing

31221   Tobacco Stemming and Redrying
312210   Tobacco Stemming and Redrying
31222   Tobacco Product Manufacturing
312221   Cigarette Manufacturing^{MEX}
312229   Other Tobacco Product Manufacturing^{US}

313 Textile Mills

3131   Fiber, Yarn, and Thread Mills

31311   Fiber, Yarn, and Thread Mills
313111   Yarn Spinning Mills^{US}
313112   Yarn Texturizing, Throwing, and Twisting Mills^{US}
313113   Thread Mills^{MEX}

3132   Fabric Mills

31321   Broadwoven Fabric Mills
313210   Broadwoven Fabric Mills
31322   Narrow Fabric Mills and Schiffli Machine
          Embroidery
313221   Narrow Fabric Mills^{US}
313222   Schiffli Machine Embroidery^{US}
31323   Nonwoven Fabric Mills
313230   Nonwoven Fabric Mills
31324   Knit Fabric Mills
313241   Weft Knit Fabric Mills^{US}
313249   Other Knit Fabric and Lace Mills^{US}

3133   Textile and Fabric Finishing and Fabric Coating Mills

31331   Textile and Fabric Finishing Mills
313311   Broadwoven Fabric Finishing Mills^{US}
313312   Textile and Fabric Finishing (except Broadwoven
          Fabric) Mills^{US}
31332   Fabric Coating Mills
313320   Fabric Coating Mills

314 Textile Product Mills

3141   Textile Furnishings Mills

31411   Carpet and Rug Mills
314110   Carpet and Rug Mills
31412   Curtain and Linen Mills
314121   Curtain and Drapery Mills^{US}
314129   Other Household Textile Product Mills^{US}

3149 Other Textile Product Mills

31491	Textile Bag and Canvas Mills
314911	Textile Bag Mills[US]
314912	Canvas and Related Product Mills[US]
31499	All Other Textile Product Mills
314991	Rope, Cordage, and Twine Mills[US]
314992	Tire Cord and Tire Fabric Mills[US]
314999	All Other Miscellaneous Textile Product Mills[US]

315 Apparel Manufacturing

3151 Apparel Knitting Mills

31511	Hosiery and Sock Mills
315111	Sheer Hosiery Mills[US]
315119	Other Hosiery and Sock Mills[US]
31519	Other Apparel Knitting Mills
315191	Outerwear Knitting Mills[US]
315192	Underwear and Nightwear Knitting Mills[US]

3152 Cut and Sew Apparel Manufacturing

31521	Cut and Sew Apparel Contractors[CAN]
315211	Men's and Boys' Cut and Sew Apparel Contractors[US]
315212	Women's, Girls', and Infants' Cut and Sew Apparel Contractors[US]
31522	Men's and Boys' Cut and Sew Apparel Manufacturing[CAN]
315221	Men's and Boys' Cut and Sew Underwear and Nightwear Manufacturing[CAN]
315222	Men's and Boys' Cut and Sew Suit, Coat, and Overcoat Manufacturing[CAN]
315223	Men's and Boys' Cut and Sew Shirt (except Work Shirt) Manufacturing[US]
315224	Men's and Boys' Cut and Sew Trouser, Slack, and Jean Manufacturing[US]
315225	Men's and Boys' Cut and Sew Work Clothing Manufacturing[US]
315228	Men's and Boys' Cut and Sew Other Outerwear Manufacturing[US]
31523	Women's and Girls' Cut and Sew Apparel Manufacturing[CAN]
315231	Women's and Girls' Cut and Sew Lingerie, Loungewear, and Nightwear Manufacturing[CAN]
315232	Women's and Girls' Cut and Sew Blouse and Shirt Manufacturing[CAN]

315233	Women's and Girls' Cut and Sew Dress Manufacturing[CAN]
315234	Women's and Girls' Cut and Sew Suit, Coat, Tailored Jacket, and Skirt Manufacturing[CAN]
315239	Women's and Girls' Cut and Sew Other Outerwear Manufacturing[CAN]
31529	Other Cut and Sew Apparel Manufacturing[CAN]
315291	Infants' Cut and Sew Apparel Manufacturing[CAN]
315292	Fur and Leather Apparel Manufacturing[CAN]
315299	All Other Cut and Sew Apparel Manufacturing[CAN]

3159   Apparel Accessories and Other Apparel Manufacturing

31599	Apparel Accessories and Other Apparel Manufacturing
315991	Hat, Cap, and Millinery Manufacturing[MEX]
315992	Glove and Mitten Manufacturing[US]
315993	Men's and Boys' Neckwear Manufacturing[US]
315999	Other Apparel Accessories and Other Apparel Manufacturing[US]

316 Leather and Allied Product Manufacturing

3161   Leather and Hide Tanning and Finishing

31611	Leather and Hide Tanning and Finishing
316110	Leather and Hide Tanning and Finishing

3162   Footwear Manufacturing

31621	Footwear Manufacturing
316211	Rubber and Plastics Footwear Manufacturing[US]
316212	House Slipper Manufacturing[US]
316213	Men's Footwear (except Athletic) Manufacturing[US]
316214	Women's Footwear (except Athletic) Manufacturing[US]
316219	Other Footwear Manufacturing[US]

3169   Other Leather and Allied Product Manufacturing

31699	Other Leather and Allied Product Manufacturing
316991	Luggage Manufacturing[US]
316992	Women's Handbag and Purse Manufacturing[US]
316993	Personal Leather Good (except Women's Handbag and Purse) Manufacturing[US]
316999	All Other Leather Good Manufacturing[US]

321 Wood Product Manufacturing

3211   Sawmills and Wood Preservation

32111	Sawmills and Wood Preservation

321113   Sawmills^{US}
321114   Wood Preservation^{CAN}

3212   Veneer, Plywood, and Engineered Wood Product Manufacturing

32121   Veneer, Plywood, and Engineered Wood Product Manufacturing
321211   Hardwood Veneer and Plywood Manufacturing^{CAN}
321212   Softwood Veneer and Plywood Manufacturing^{CAN}
321213   Engineered Wood Member (except Truss) Manufacturing^{US}
321214   Truss Manufacturing^{US}
321219   Reconstituted Wood Product Manufacturing^{US}

3219   Other Wood Product Manufacturing

32191   Millwork
321911   Wood Window and Door Manufacturing^{CAN}
321912   Cut Stock, Resawing Lumber, and Planing^{US}
321918   Other Millwork (including Flooring)^{US}
32192   Wood Container and Pallet Manufacturing
321920   Wood Container and Pallet Manufacturing
32199   All Other Wood Product Manufacturing
321991   Manufactured Home (Mobile Home) Manufacturing^{CAN}
321992   Prefabricated Wood Building Manufacturing^{CAN}
321999   All Other Miscellaneous Wood Product Manufacturing^{CAN}

322 Paper Manufacturing

3221   Pulp, Paper, and Paperboard Mills

32211   Pulp Mills
322110   Pulp Mills^{MEX}
32212   Paper Mills
322121   Paper (except Newsprint) Mills^{CAN}
322122   Newsprint Mills^{CAN}
32213   Paperboard Mills
322130   Paperboard Mills^{CAN}

3222   Converted Paper Product Manufacturing

32221   Paperboard Container Manufacturing
322211   Corrugated and Solid Fiber Box Manufacturing^{CAN}
322212   Folding Paperboard Box Manufacturing^{CAN}
322213   Setup Paperboard Box Manufacturing^{US}
322214   Fiber Can, Tube, Drum, and Similar Products Manufacturing^{US}
322215   Nonfolding Sanitary Food Container Manufacturing^{US}

32222	Paper Bag and Coated and Treated Paper Manufacturing
322221	Coated and Laminated Packaging Paper and Plastics Film Manufacturing[US]
322222	Coated and Laminated Paper Manufacturing[US]
322223	Plastics, Foil, and Coated Paper Bag Manufacturing[US]
322224	Uncoated Paper and Multiwall Bag Manufacturing[US]
322225	Laminated Aluminum Foil Manufacturing for Flexible Packaging Uses[US]
322226	Surface-Coated Paperboard Manufacturing[US]
32223	Stationery Product Manufacturing
322231	Die-Cut Paper and Paperboard Office Supplies Manufacturing[US]
322232	Envelope Manufacturing[US]
322233	Stationery, Tablet, and Related Product Manufacturing[US]
32229	Other Converted Paper Product Manufacturing
322291	Sanitary Paper Product Manufacturing[CAN]
322299	All Other Converted Paper Product Manufacturing[CAN]

323 Printing and Related Support Activities

3231 Printing and Related Support Activities

32311	Printing
323110	Commercial Lithographic Printing[US]
323111	Commercial Gravure Printing[US]
323112	Commercial Flexographic Printing[US]
323113	Commercial Screen Printing[CAN]
323114	Quick Printing[CAN]
323115	Digital Printing[CAN]
323116	Manifold Business Forms Printing[CAN]
323117	Books Printing[US]
323118	Blankbook, Looseleaf Binders, and Devices Manufacturing[US]
323119	Other Commercial Printing[US]
32312	Support Activities for Printing
323121	Tradebinding and Related Work[US]
323122	Prepress Services[US]

324 Petroleum and Coal Products Manufacturing

3241 Petroleum and Coal Products Manufacturing

32411	Petroleum Refineries
324110	Petroleum Refineries

32412	Asphalt Paving, Roofing, and Saturated Materials Manufacturing
324121	Asphalt Paving Mixture and Block Manufacturing[CAN]
324122	Asphalt Shingle and Coating Materials Manufacturing[CAN]
32419	Other Petroleum and Coal Products Manufacturing
324191	Petroleum Lubricating Oil and Grease Manufacturing[MEX]
324199	All Other Petroleum and Coal Products Manufacturing[US]

325 Chemical Manufacturing

3251 Basic Chemical Manufacturing

32511	Petrochemical Manufacturing
325110	Petrochemical Manufacturing
32512	Industrial Gas Manufacturing
325120	Industrial Gas Manufacturing
32513	Synthetic Dye and Pigment Manufacturing
325131	Inorganic Dye and Pigment Manufacturing[US]
325132	Synthetic Organic Dye and Pigment Manufacturing[US]
32518	Other Basic Inorganic Chemical Manufacturing
325181	Alkalies and Chlorine Manufacturing[CAN]
325182	Carbon Black Manufacturing[US]
325188	All Other Basic Inorganic Chemical Manufacturing[US]
32519	Other Basic Organic Chemical Manufacturing
325191	Gum and Wood Chemical Manufacturing[US]
325192	Cyclic Crude and Intermediate Manufacturing[US]
325193	Ethyl Alcohol Manufacturing[US]
325199	All Other Basic Organic Chemical Manufacturing[US]

3252 Resin, Synthetic Rubber, and Artificial Synthetic Fibers and Filaments Manufacturing

32521	Resin and Synthetic Rubber Manufacturing
325211	Plastics Material and Resin Manufacturing[US]
325212	Synthetic Rubber Manufacturing[MEX]
32522	Artificial and Synthetic Fibers and Filaments Manufacturing
325221	Cellulosic Organic Fiber Manufacturing[US]
325222	Noncellulosic Organic Fiber Manufacturing[US]

3253 Pesticide, Fertilizer, and Other Agricultural Chemical Manufacturing

32531	Fertilizer Manufacturing
325311	Nitrogenous Fertilizer Manufacturing[US]
325312	Phosphatic Fertilizer Manufacturing[US]
325314	Fertilizer (Mixing Only) Manufacturing[CAN]
32532	Pesticide and Other Agricultural Chemical Manufacturing
325320	Pesticide and Other Agricultural Chemical Manufacturing

3254 Pharmaceutical and Medicine Manufacturing

32541	Pharmaceutical and Medicine Manufacturing
325411	Medicinal and Botanical Manufacturing[US]
325412	Pharmaceutical Preparation Manufacturing[US]
325413	In-Vitro Diagnostic Substance Manufacturing[US]
325414	Biological Product (except Diagnostic) Manufacturing[US]

3255 Paint, Coating, and Adhesive Manufacturing

32551	Paint and Coating Manufacturing
325510	Paint and Coating Manufacturing
32552	Adhesive Manufacturing
325520	Adhesive Manufacturing

3256 Soap, Cleaning Compound, and Toilet Preparation Manufacturing

32561	Soap and Cleaning Compound Manufacturing
325611	Soap and Other Detergent Manufacturing[US]
325612	Polish and Other Sanitation Good Manufacturing[US]
325613	Surface Active Agent Manufacturing[US]
32562	Toilet Preparation Manufacturing
325620	Toilet Preparation Manufacturing

3259 Other Chemical Product and Preparation Manufacturing

32591	Printing Ink Manufacturing
325910	Printing Ink Manufacturing
32592	Explosives Manufacturing
325920	Explosives Manufacturing
32599	All Other Chemical Product and Preparation Manufacturing
325991	Custom Compounding of Purchased Resins[CAN]
325992	Photographic Film, Paper, Plate, and Chemical Manufacturing[MEX]
325998	All Other Miscellaneous Chemical Product and Preparation Manufacturing[US]

326 Plastics and Rubber Products Manufacturing

3261 Plastics Product Manufacturing

32611	Plastics Packaging Materials and Unlaminated Film and Sheet Manufacturing
326111	Plastics Bag Manufacturing[CAN]
326112	Plastics Packaging Film and Sheet (including Laminated) Manufacturing[US]
326113	Unlaminated Plastics Film and Sheet (except Packaging) Manufacturing[US]
32612	Plastics Pipe, Pipe Fitting, and Unlaminated Profile Shape Manufacturing
326121	Unlaminated Plastics Profile Shape Manufacturing[CAN]
326122	Plastics Pipe and Pipe Fitting Manufacturing[CAN]
32613	Laminated Plastics Plate, Sheet (except Packaging), and Shape Manufacturing
326130	Laminated Plastics Plate, Sheet (except Packaging), and Shape Manufacturing
32614	Polystyrene Foam Product Manufacturing
326140	Polystyrene Foam Product Manufacturing
32615	Urethane and Other Foam Product (except Polystyrene) Manufacturing
326150	Urethane and Other Foam Product (except Polystyrene) Manufacturing
32616	Plastics Bottle Manufacturing
326160	Plastics Bottle Manufacturing
32619	Other Plastics Product Manufacturing
326191	Plastics Plumbing Fixture Manufacturing[CAN]
326192	Resilient Floor Covering Manufacturing[US]
326199	All Other Plastics Product Manufacturing[US]

3262 Rubber Product Manufacturing

32621	Tire Manufacturing
326211	Tire Manufacturing (except Retreading)[MEX]
326212	Tire Retreading[MEX]
32622	Rubber and Plastics Hoses and Belting Manufacturing
326220	Rubber and Plastics Hoses and Belting Manufacturing
32629	Other Rubber Product Manufacturing
326291	Rubber Product Manufacturing for Mechanical Use[US]
326299	All Other Rubber Product Manufacturing[US]

327 Nonmetallic Mineral Product Manufacturing

3271 Clay Product and Refractory Manufacturing

32711   Pottery, Ceramics, and Plumbing Fixture
Manufacturing

327111   Vitreous China Plumbing Fixture and China and
Earthenware Bathroom Accessories
Manufacturing[US]

327112   Vitreous China, Fine Earthenware, and Other
Pottery Product Manufacturing[US]

327113   Porcelain Electrical Supply Manufacturing[US]

32712   Clay Building Material and Refractories
Manufacturing

327121   Brick and Structural Clay Tile Manufacturing[US]

327122   Ceramic Wall and Floor Tile Manufacturing[US]

327123   Other Structural Clay Product Manufacturing[US]

327124   Clay Refractory Manufacturing[US]

327125   Nonclay Refractory Manufacturing[US]

3272   Glass and Glass Product Manufacturing

32721   Glass and Glass Product Manufacturing

327211   Flat Glass Manufacturing[MEX]

327212   Other Pressed and Blown Glass and Glassware
Manufacturing[US]

327213   Glass Container Manufacturing[US]

327215   Glass Product Manufacturing Made of Purchased
Glass[CAN]

3273   Cement and Concrete Product Manufacturing

32731   Cement Manufacturing

327310   Cement Manufacturing

32732   Ready-Mix Concrete Manufacturing

327320   Ready-Mix Concrete Manufacturing

32733   Concrete Pipe, Brick, and Block Manufacturing

327331   Concrete Block and Brick Manufacturing[US]

327332   Concrete Pipe Manufacturing[US]

32739   Other Concrete Product Manufacturing

327390   Other Concrete Product Manufacturing[CAN]

3274   Lime and Gypsum Product Manufacturing

32741   Lime Manufacturing

327410   Lime Manufacturing

32742   Gypsum Product Manufacturing

327420   Gypsum Product Manufacturing

3279   Other Nonmetallic Mineral Product Manufacturing

32791   Abrasive Product Manufacturing

327910   Abrasive Product Manufacturing

32799   All Other Nonmetallic Mineral Product
Manufacturing

327991   Cut Stone and Stone Product Manufacturing[US]
327992   Ground or Treated Mineral and Earth Manufacturing[US]
327993   Mineral Wool Manufacturing[US]
327999   All Other Miscellaneous Nonmetallic Mineral Product Manufacturing[US]

331 Primary Metal Manufacturing

3311 Iron and Steel Mills and Ferroalloy Manufacturing

33111   Iron and Steel Mills and Ferroalloy Manufacturing
331111   Iron and Steel Mills[US]
331112   Electrometallurgical Ferroalloy Product Manufacturing[US]

3312 Steel Product Manufacturing from Purchased Steel

33121   Iron and Steel Pipe and Tube Manufacturing from Purchased Steel
331210   Iron and Steel Pipe and Tube Manufacturing from Purchased Steel
33122   Rolling and Drawing of Purchased Steel
331221   Rolled Steel Shape Manufacturing[CAN]
331222   Steel Wire Drawing[CAN]

3313 Alumina and Aluminum Production and Processing

33131   Alumina and Aluminum Production and Processing
331311   Alumina Refining[US]
331312   Primary Aluminum Production[US]
331314   Secondary Smelting and Alloying of Aluminum[US]
331315   Aluminum Sheet, Plate, and Foil Manufacturing[US]
331316   Aluminum Extruded Product Manufacturing[US]
331319   Other Aluminum Rolling and Drawing[US]

3314 Nonferrous Metal (except Aluminum) Production and Processing

33141   Nonferrous Metal (except Aluminum) Smelting and Refining
331411   Primary Smelting and Refining of Copper[MEX]
331419   Primary Smelting and Refining of Nonferrous Metal (except Copper and Aluminum)[MEX]
33142   Copper Rolling, Drawing, Extruding, and Alloying
331421   Copper Rolling, Drawing, and Extruding[US]
331422   Copper Wire (except Mechanical) Drawing[US]
331423   Secondary Smelting, Refining, and Alloying of Copper[US]

33149   Nonferrous Metal (except Copper and Aluminum) Rolling, Drawing, Extruding, and Alloying
331491   Nonferrous Metal (except Copper and Aluminum) Rolling, Drawing, and Extruding[US]
331492   Secondary Smelting, Refining, and Alloying of Nonferrous Metal (except Copper and Aluminum)[US]

3315 Foundries

33151   Ferrous Metal Foundries
331511   Iron Foundries[CAN]
331512   Steel Investment Foundries[US]
331513   Steel Foundries (except Investment)[US]
33152   Nonferrous Metal Foundries
331521   Aluminum Die-Casting Foundries[US]
331522   Nonferrous (except Aluminum) Die-Casting Foundries[US]
331524   Aluminum Foundries (except Die-Casting)[US]
331525   Copper Foundries (except Die-Casting)[US]
331528   Other Nonferrous Foundries (except Die-Casting)[US]

332 Fabricated Metal Product Manufacturing

3321 Forging and Stamping

33211   Forging and Stamping
332111   Iron and Steel Forging[US]
332112   Nonferrous Forging[US]
332114   Custom Roll Forming[US]
332115   Crown and Closure Manufacturing[US]
332116   Metal Stamping[US]
332117   Powder Metallurgy Part Manufacturing[US]

3322 Cutlery and Handtool Manufacturing

33221   Cutlery and Handtool Manufacturing
332211   Cutlery and Flatware (except Precious) Manufacturing[US]
332212   Hand and Edge Tool Manufacturing[US]
332213   Saw Blade and Handsaw Manufacturing[US]
332214   Kitchen Utensil, Pot, and Pan Manufacturing[US]

3323 Architectural and Structural Metals Manufacturing

33231   Plate Work and Fabricated Structural Product Manufacturing
332311   Prefabricated Metal Building and Component Manufacturing[CAN]
332312   Fabricated Structural Metal Manufacturing[US]

332313   Plate Work Manufacturing[US]
33232   Ornamental and Architectural Metal Products
         Manufacturing
332321   Metal Window and Door Manufacturing[CAN]
332322   Sheet Metal Work Manufacturing[US]
332323   Ornamental and Architectural Metal Work
         Manufacturing[US]

3324   Boiler, Tank, and Shipping Container Manufacturing

33241   Power Boiler and Heat Exchanger Manufacturing
332410   Power Boiler and Heat Exchanger Manufacturing
33242   Metal Tank (Heavy Gauge) Manufacturing
332420   Metal Tank (Heavy Gauge) Manufacturing
33243   Metal Can, Box, and Other Metal Container
         (Light Gauge) Manufacturing
332431   Metal Can Manufacturing[CAN]
332439   Other Metal Container Manufacturing[CAN]

3325   Hardware Manufacturing

33251   Hardware Manufacturing
332510   Hardware Manufacturing

3326   Spring and Wire Product Manufacturing

33261   Spring and Wire Product Manufacturing
332611   Spring (Heavy Gauge) Manufacturing[CAN]
332612   Spring (Light Gauge) Manufacturing[US]
332618   Other Fabricated Wire Product Manufacturing[US]

**3327   Machine Shops; Turned Product; and Screw, Nut, and
Bolt Manufacturing**

33271   Machine Shops
332710   Machine Shops
33272   Turned Product and Screw, Nut, and Bolt
         Manufacturing
332721   Precision Turned Product Manufacturing[US]
332722   Bolt, Nut, Screw, Rivet, and Washer
         Manufacturing[US]

3328   Coating, Engraving, Heat Treating, and Allied Activities

33281   Coating, Engraving, Heat Treating, and Allied
         Activities
332811   Metal Heat Treating[US]
332812   Metal Coating, Engraving (except Jewelry and
         Silverware), and Allied Services to
         Manufacturers[US]
332813   Electroplating, Plating, Polishing, Anodizing, and
         Coloring[US]

3329   Other Fabricated Metal Product Manufacturing

33291   Metal Valve Manufacturing

332911   Industrial Valve Manufacturing[US]

332912   Fluid Power Valve and Hose Fitting
         Manufacturing[US]

332913   Plumbing Fixture Fitting and Trim
         Manufacturing[US]

332919   Other Metal Valve and Pipe Fitting
         Manufacturing[US]

33299   All Other Fabricated Metal Product
         Manufacturing

332991   Ball and Roller Bearing Manufacturing

332992   Small Arms Ammunition Manufacturing[US]

332993   Ammunition (except Small Arms)
         Manufacturing[US]

332994   Small Arms Manufacturing[US]

332995   Other Ordnance and Accessories Manufacturing[US]

332996   Fabricated Pipe and Pipe Fitting Manufacturing[US]

332997   Industrial Pattern Manufacturing[US]

332998   Enameled Iron and Metal Sanitary Ware
         Manufacturing[US]

332999   All Other Miscellaneous Fabricated Metal
         Product Manufacturing[US]

333 Machinery Manufacturing

**3331   Agriculture, Construction, and Mining Machinery
         Manufacturing**

33311   Agricultural Implement Manufacturing

333111   Farm Machinery and Equipment Manufacturing[US]

333112   Lawn and Garden Tractor and Home Lawn and
         Garden Equipment Manufacturing[US]

33312   Construction Machinery Manufacturing

333120   Construction Machinery Manufacturing

33313   Mining and Oil and Gas Field Machinery
         Manufacturing

333131   Mining Machinery and Equipment
         Manufacturing[US]

333132   Oil and Gas Field Machinery and Equipment
         Manufacturing[US]

3332   Industrial Machinery Manufacturing

33321   Sawmill and Woodworking Machinery
         Manufacturing

333210   Sawmill and Woodworking Machinery
         Manufacturing

33322	Plastics and Rubber Industry Machinery Manufacturing
333220	Plastics and Rubber Industry Machinery Manufacturing
33329	Other Industrial Machinery Manufacturing
333291	Paper Industry Machinery Manufacturing[CAN]
333292	Textile Machinery Manufacturing[MEX]
333293	Printing Machinery and Equipment Manufacturing[MEX]
333294	Food Product Machinery Manufacturing[US]
333295	Semiconductor Machinery Manufacturing[US]
333298	All Other Industrial Machinery Manufacturing[US]

3333   Commercial and Service Industry Machinery Manufacturing

33331	Commercial and Service Industry Machinery Manufacturing
333311	Automatic Vending Machine Manufacturing[US]
333312	Commercial Laundry, Drycleaning, and Pressing Machine Manufacturing[US]
333313	Office Machinery Manufacturing[US]
333314	Optical Instrument and Lens Manufacturing[US]
333315	Photographic and Photocopying Equipment Manufacturing[US]
333319	Other Commercial and Service Industry Machinery Manufacturing[US]

3334   Ventilation, Heating, Air-Conditioning, and Commercial Refrigeration Equipment Manufacturing

33341	Ventilation, Heating, Air-Conditioning, and Commercial Refrigeration Equipment Manufacturing
333411	Air Purification Equipment Manufacturing[US]
333412	Industrial and Commercial Fan and Blower Manufacturing[US]
333414	Heating Equipment (except Warm Air Furnaces) Manufacturing[US]
333415	Air-Conditioning and Warm Air Heating Equipment and Commercial and Industrial Refrigeration Equipment Manufacturing[US]

3335   Metalworking Machinery Manufacturing

33351	Metalworking Machinery Manufacturing
333511	Industrial Mold Manufacturing[CAN]
333512	Machine Tool (Metal Cutting Types) Manufacturing[US]

333513	Machine Tool (Metal Forming Types) Manufacturing[US]
333514	Special Die and Tool, Die Set, Jig, and Fixture Manufacturing[US]
333515	Cutting Tool and Machine Tool Accessory Manufacturing[US]
333516	Rolling Mill Machinery and Equipment Manufacturing[US]
333518	Other Metalworking Machinery Manufacturing[US]

3336 Engine, Turbine, and Power Transmission Equipment Manufacturing

33361	Engine, Turbine, and Power Transmission Equipment Manufacturing
333611	Turbine and Turbine Generator Set Units Manufacturing[CAN]
333612	Speed Changer, Industrial High-Speed Drive, and Gear Manufacturing[US]
333613	Mechanical Power Transmission Equipment Manufacturing[US]
333618	Other Engine Equipment Manufacturing[US]

3339 Other General Purpose Machinery Manufacturing

33391	Pump and Compressor Manufacturing
333911	Pump and Pumping Equipment Manufacturing[US]
333912	Air and Gas Compressor Manufacturing[US]
333913	Measuring and Dispensing Pump Manufacturing[US]
33392	Material Handling Equipment Manufacturing
333921	Elevator and Moving Stairway Manufacturing[US]
333922	Conveyor and Conveying Equipment Manufacturing[US]
333923	Overhead Traveling Crane, Hoist, and Monorail System Manufacturing[US]
333924	Industrial Truck, Tractor, Trailer, and Stacker Machinery Manufacturing[US]
33399	All Other General Purpose Machinery Manufacturing
333991	Power-Driven Handtool Manufacturing[US]
333992	Welding and Soldering Equipment Manufacturing[US]
333993	Packaging Machinery Manufacturing[US]
333994	Industrial Process Furnace and Oven Manufacturing[US]
333995	Fluid Power Cylinder and Actuator Manufacturing[US]
333996	Fluid Power Pump and Motor Manufacturing[US]

333997   Scale and Balance (except Laboratory) Manufacturing[US]

333999   All Other Miscellaneous General Purpose Machinery Manufacturing[US]

334 Computer and Electronic Product Manufacturing

3341 Computer and Peripheral Equipment Manufacturing

33411   Computer and Peripheral Equipment Manufacturing

334111   Electronic Computer Manufacturing[US]

334112   Computer Storage Device Manufacturing[US]

334113   Computer Terminal Manufacturing[US]

334119   Other Computer Peripheral Equipment Manufacturing[US]

3342 Communications Equipment Manufacturing

33421   Telephone Apparatus Manufacturing

334210   Telephone Apparatus Manufacturing

33422   Radio and Television Broadcasting and Wireless Communications Equipment Manufacturing

334220   Radio and Television Broadcasting and Wireless Communications Equipment Manufacturing

33429   Other Communications Equipment Manufacturing

334290   Other Communications Equipment Manufacturing

3343 Audio and Video Equipment Manufacturing

334310   Audio and Video Equipment Manufacturing

334310   Audio and Video Equipment Manufacturing

3344 Semiconductor and Other Electronic Component Manufacturing

33441   Semiconductor and Other Electronic Component Manufacturing

334411   Electron Tube Manufacturing[US]

334412   Bare Printed Circuit Board Manufacturing[US]

334413   Semiconductor and Related Device Manufacturing[US]

334414   Electronic Capacitor Manufacturing[US]

334415   Electronic Resistor Manufacturing[US]

334416   Electronic Coil, Transformer, and Other Inductor Manufacturing[US]

334417   Electronic Connector Manufacturing[US]

334418   Printed Circuit Assembly (Electronic Assembly) Manufacturing[US]

334419   Other Electronic Component Manufacturing[US]

3345   Navigational, Measuring, Electromedical, and Control Instruments Manufacturing

33451   Navigational, Measuring, Electromedical, and Control Instruments Manufacturing

334510   Electromedical and Electrotherapeutic Apparatus Manufacturing[US]

334511   Search, Detection, Navigation, Guidance, Aeronautical, and Nautical System and Instrument Manufacturing[CAN]

334512   Automatic Environmental Control Manufacturing for Residential, Commercial, and Appliance Use[US]

334513   Instruments and Related Products Manufacturing for Measuring, Displaying, and Controlling Industrial Process Variables[US]

334514   Totalizing Fluid Meter and Counting Device Manufacturing[US]

334515   Instrument Manufacturing for Measuring and Testing Electricity and Electrical Signals[US]

334516   Analytical Laboratory Instrument Manufacturing[US]

334517   Irradiation Apparatus Manufacturing[US]

334518   Watch, Clock, and Part Manufacturing[US]

334519   Other Measuring and Controlling Device Manufacturing[US]

3346   Manufacturing and Reproducing Magnetic and Optical Media

33461   Manufacturing and Reproducing Magnetic and Optical Media

334611   Software Reproducing[US]

334612   Prerecorded Compact Disc (except Software), Tape, and Record Reproducing[US]

334613   Magnetic and Optical Recording Media Manufacturing[US]

335 Electrical Equipment, Appliance, and Component Manufacturing

3351   Electric Lighting Equipment Manufacturing

33511   Electric Lamp Bulb and Part Manufacturing

335110   Electric Lamp Bulb and Part Manufacturing

33512   Lighting Fixture Manufacturing

335121   Residential Electric Lighting Fixture Manufacturing[US]

335122   Commercial, Industrial, and Institutional Electric Lighting Fixture Manufacturing[US]

335129   Other Lighting Equipment Manufacturing[US]

3352 Household Appliance Manufacturing

33521 Small Electrical Appliance Manufacturing

335211 Electric Housewares and Household Fan Manufacturing[US]

335212 Household Vacuum Cleaner Manufacturing[US]

33522 Major Appliance Manufacturing

335221 Household Cooking Appliance Manufacturing[US]

335222 Household Refrigerator and Home Freezer Manufacturing[US]

335224 Household Laundry Equipment Manufacturing[US]

335228 Other Major Household Appliance Manufacturing[US]

3353 Electrical Equipment Manufacturing

33531 Electrical Equipment Manufacturing

335311 Power, Distribution, and Specialty Transformer Manufacturing[CAN]

335312 Motor and Generator Manufacturing[CAN]

335313 Switchgear and Switchboard Apparatus Manufacturing[US]

335314 Relay and Industrial Control Manufacturing[US]

3359 Other Electrical Equipment and Component Manufacturing

33591 Battery Manufacturing

335911 Storage Battery Manufacturing[US]

335912 Primary Battery Manufacturing[US]

33592 Communication and Energy Wire and Cable Manufacturing

335921 Fiber Optic Cable Manufacturing[US]

335929 Other Communication and Energy Wire Manufacturing[US]

33593 Wiring Device Manufacturing

335931 Current-Carrying Wiring Device Manufacturing[US]

335932 Noncurrent-Carrying Wiring Device Manufacturing[US]

33599 All Other Electrical Equipment and Component Manufacturing

335991 Carbon and Graphite Product Manufacturing[MEX]

335999 All Other Miscellaneous Electrical Equipment and Component Manufacturing[MEX]

336 Transportation Equipment Manufacturing

3361 Motor Vehicle Manufacturing

33611 Automobile and Light Duty Motor Vehicle Manufacturing

336111   Automobile Manufacturing[US]
336112   Light Truck and Utility Vehicle Manufacturing[US]
33612   Heavy Duty Truck Manufacturing
336120   Heavy Duty Truck Manufacturing

3362 Motor Vehicle Body and Trailer Manufacturing

33621   Motor Vehicle Body and Trailer Manufacturing
336211   Motor Vehicle Body Manufacturing[CAN]
336212   Truck Trailer Manufacturing[CAN]
336213   Motor Home Manufacturing[US]
336214   Travel Trailer and Camper Manufacturing[US]

3363 Motor Vehicle Parts Manufacturing

33631   Motor Vehicle Gasoline Engine and Engine Parts Manufacturing
336311   Carburetor, Piston, Piston Ring, and Valve Manufacturing[US]
336312   Gasoline Engine and Engine Parts Manufacturing[US]
33632   Motor Vehicle Electrical and Electronic Equipment Manufacturing
336321   Vehicular Lighting Equipment Manufacturing[US]
336322   Other Motor Vehicle Electrical and Electronic Equipment Manufacturing[US]
33633   Motor Vehicle Steering and Suspension Components (except Spring) Manufacturing
336330   Motor Vehicle Steering and Suspension Components (except Spring) Manufacturing
33634   Motor Vehicle Brake System Manufacturing
336340   Motor Vehicle Brake System Manufacturing
33635   Motor Vehicle Transmission and Power Train Parts Manufacturing
336350   Motor Vehicle Transmission and Power Train Parts Manufacturing
33636   Motor Vehicle Seating and Interior Trim Manufacturing
336360   Motor Vehicle Seating and Interior Trim Manufacturing
33637   Motor Vehicle Metal Stamping
336370   Motor Vehicle Metal Stamping
33639   Other Motor Vehicle Parts Manufacturing
336391   Motor Vehicle Air-Conditioning Manufacturing[US]
336399   All Other Motor Vehicle Parts Manufacturing[US]

3364 Aerospace Product and Parts Manufacturing

33641   Aerospace Product and Parts Manufacturing

336411	Aircraft Manufacturing[US]
336412	Aircraft Engine and Engine Parts Manufacturing[US]
336413	Other Aircraft Parts and Auxiliary Equipment Manufacturing[US]
336414	Guided Missile and Space Vehicle Manufacturing[US]
336415	Guided Missile and Space Vehicle Propulsion Unit and Propulsion Unit Parts Manufacturing[US]
336419	Other Guided Missile and Space Vehicle Parts and Auxiliary Equipment Manufacturing[US]

3365 Railroad Rolling Stock Manufacturing

| 33651 | Railroad Rolling Stock Manufacturing |
| 336510 | Railroad Rolling Stock Manufacturing |

3366 Ship and Boat Building

33661	Ship and Boat Building
336611	Ship Building and Repairing[CAN]
336612	Boat Building[CAN]

3369 Other Transportation Equipment Manufacturing

33699	Other Transportation Equipment Manufacturing
336991	Motorcycle, Bicycle, and Parts Manufacturing[US]
336992	Military Armored Vehicle, Tank, and Tank Component Manufacturing[US]
336999	All Other Transportation Equipment Manufacturing[US]

337 Furniture and Related Product Manufacturing

3371 Household and Institutional Furniture and Kitchen Cabinet Manufacturing

33711	Wood Kitchen Cabinet and Countertop Manufacturing
337110	Wood Kitchen Cabinet and Countertop Manufacturing
33712	Household and Institutional Furniture Manufacturing
337121	Upholstered Household Furniture Manufacturing[CAN]
337122	Nonupholstered Wood Household Furniture Manufacturing[US]
337124	Metal Household Furniture Manufacturing[US]
337125	Household Furniture (except Wood and Metal) Manufacturing[US]
337127	Institutional Furniture Manufacturing[CAN]

337129 Wood Television, Radio, and Sewing Machine Cabinet Manufacturing[US]

3372 Office Furniture (including Fixtures) Manufacturing

33721 Office Furniture (including Fixtures) Manufacturing
337211 Wood Office Furniture Manufacturing[US]
337212 Custom Architectural Woodwork and Millwork Manufacturing[US]
337214 Office Furniture (except Wood) Manufacturing[CAN]
337215 Showcase, Partition, Shelving, and Locker Manufacturing[CAN]

3379 Other Furniture Related Product Manufacturing

33791 Mattress Manufacturing
337910 Mattress Manufacturing
33792 Blind and Shade Manufacturing
337920 Blind and Shade Manufacturing

339 Miscellaneous Manufacturing

3391 Medical Equipment and Supplies Manufacturing

33911 Medical Equipment and Supplies Manufacturing
339111 Laboratory Apparatus and Furniture Manufacturing[US]
339112 Surgical and Medical Instrument Manufacturing[US]
339113 Surgical Appliance and Supplies Manufacturing[US]
339114 Dental Equipment and Supplies Manufacturing[US]
339115 Ophthalmic Goods Manufacturing[US]
339116 Dental Laboratories[US]

3399 Other Miscellaneous Manufacturing

33991 Jewelry and Silverware Manufacturing
339911 Jewelry (except Costume) Manufacturing[US]
339912 Silverware and Hollowware Manufacturing[US]
339913 Jewelers' Material and Lapidary Work Manufacturing[US]
339914 Costume Jewelry and Novelty Manufacturing[US]
33992 Sporting and Athletic Goods Manufacturing
339920 Sporting and Athletic Goods Manufacturing
33993 Doll, Toy, and Game Manufacturing
339931 Doll and Stuffed Toy Manufacturing[US]
339932 Game, Toy, and Children's Vehicle Manufacturing[US]
33994 Office Supplies (except Paper) Manufacturing
339941 Pen and Mechanical Pencil Manufacturing[US]
339942 Lead Pencil and Art Good Manufacturing[US]

339943	Marking Device Manufacturing[US]
339944	Carbon Paper and Inked Ribbon Manufacturing[US]
33995	Sign Manufacturing
339950	Sign Manufacturing
33999	All Other Miscellaneous Manufacturing
339991	Gasket, Packing, and Sealing Device Manufacturing[US]
339992	Musical Instrument Manufacturing[US]
339993	Fastener, Button, Needle, and Pin Manufacturing[US]
339994	Broom, Brush, and Mop Manufacturing[US]
339995	Burial Casket Manufacturing[MEX]
339999	All Other Miscellaneous Manufacturing[US]

42   Wholesale Trade

423 Merchant Wholesalers, Durable Goods[US]

4231   Motor Vehicle and Motor Vehicle Parts and Supplies Merchant Wholesalers[US]

42311	Automobile and Other Motor Vehicle Merchant Wholesalers[US]
423110	Automobile and Other Motor Vehicle Merchant Wholesalers[US]
42312	Motor Vehicle Supplies and New Parts Merchant Wholesalers[US]
423120	Motor Vehicle Supplies and New Parts Merchant Wholesalers[US]
42313	Tire and Tube Merchant Wholesalers[US]
423130	Tire and Tube Merchant Wholesalers[US]
42314	Motor Vehicle Parts (Used) Merchant Wholesalers[US]
423140	Motor Vehicle Parts (Used) Merchant Wholesalers[US]

4232   Furniture and Home Furnishing Merchant Wholesalers[US]

42321	Furniture Merchant Wholesalers[US]
423210	Furniture Merchant Wholesalers[US]
42322	Home Furnishing Merchant Wholesalers[US]
423220	Home Furnishing Merchant Wholesalers[US]

4233   Lumber and Other Construction Materials Merchant Wholesalers[US]

42331	Lumber, Plywood, Millwork, and Wood Panel Merchant Wholesalers[US]

423310	Lumber, Plywood, Millwork, and Wood Panel Merchant Wholesalers[US]
42332	Brick, Stone, and Related Construction Material Merchant Wholesalers[US]
423320	Brick, Stone, and Related Construction Material Merchant Wholesalers[US]
42333	Roofing, Siding, and Insulation Material Merchant Wholesalers[US]
423330	Roofing, Siding, and Insulation Material Merchant Wholesalers[US]
42339	Other Construction Material Merchant Wholesalers[US]
423390	Other Construction Material Merchant Wholesalers[US]

4234 Professional and Commercial Equipment and Supplies Merchant Wholesalers[US]

42341	Photographic Equipment and Supplies Merchant Wholesalers[US]
423410	Photographic Equipment and Supplies Merchant Wholesalers[US]
42342	Office Equipment Merchant Wholesalers[US]
423420	Office Equipment Merchant Wholesalers[US]
42343	Computer and Computer Peripheral Equipment and Software Merchant Wholesalers[US]
423430	Computer and Computer Peripheral Equipment and Software Merchant Wholesalers[US]
42344	Other Commercial Equipment Merchant Wholesalers[US]
423440	Other Commercial Equipment Merchant Wholesalers[US]
42345	Medical, Dental, and Hospital Equipment and Supplies Merchant Wholesalers[US]
423450	Medical, Dental, and Hospital Equipment and Supplies Merchant Wholesalers[US]
42346	Ophthalmic Goods Merchant Wholesalers[US]
423460	Ophthalmic Goods Merchant Wholesalers[US]
42349	Other Professional Equipment and Supplies Merchant Wholesalers[US]
423490	Other Professional Equipment and Supplies Merchant Wholesalers[US]

4235 Metal and Mineral (except Petroleum) Merchant Wholesalers[US]

| 42351 | Metal Service Centers and Other Metal Merchant Wholesalers[US] |

423510   Metal Service Centers and Other Metal Merchant Wholesalers[US]

42352   Coal and Other Mineral and Ore Merchant Wholesalers[US]

423520   Coal and Other Mineral and Ore Merchant Wholesalers[US]

4236   Electrical and Electronic Goods Merchant Wholesalers[US]

42361   Electrical Apparatus and Equipment, Wiring Supplies, and Related Equipment Merchant Wholesalers[US]

423610   Electrical Apparatus and Equipment, Wiring Supplies, and Related Equipment Merchant Wholesalers[US]

42362   Electrical and Electronic Appliance, Television, and Radio Set Merchant Wholesalers[US]

423620   Electrical and Electronic Appliance, Television, and Radio Set Merchant Wholesalers[US]

42369   Other Electronic Parts and Equipment Merchant Wholesalers[US]

423690   Other Electronic Parts and Equipment Merchant Wholesalers[US]

4237   Hardware, and Plumbing and Heating Equipment and Supplies Merchant Wholesalers[US]

42371   Hardware Merchant Wholesalers[US]

423710   Hardware Merchant Wholesalers[US]

42372   Plumbing and Heating Equipment and Supplies (Hydronics) Merchant Wholesalers[US]

423720   Plumbing and Heating Equipment and Supplies (Hydronics) Merchant Wholesalers[US]

42373   Warm Air Heating and Air-Conditioning Equipment and Supplies Merchant Wholesalers[US]

423730   Warm Air Heating and Air-Conditioning Equipment and Supplies Merchant Wholesalers[US]

42374   Refrigeration Equipment and Supplies Merchant Wholesalers[US]

423740   Refrigeration Equipment and Supplies Merchant Wholesalers[US]

4238   Machinery, Equipment, and Supplies Merchant Wholesalers[US]

42381   Construction and Mining (except Oil Well) Machinery and Equipment Merchant Wholesalers[US]

423810	Construction and Mining (except Oil Well) Machinery and Equipment Merchant Wholesalers[US]
42382	Farm and Garden Machinery and Equipment Merchant Wholesalers[US]
423820	Farm and Garden Machinery and Equipment Merchant Wholesalers[US]
42383	Industrial Machinery and Equipment Merchant Wholesalers[US]
423830	Industrial Machinery and Equipment Merchant Wholesalers[US]
42384	Industrial Supplies Merchant Wholesalers[US]
423840	Industrial Supplies Merchant Wholesalers[US]
42385	Service Establishment Equipment and Supplies Merchant Wholesalers[US]
423850	Service Establishment Equipment and Supplies Merchant Wholesalers[US]
42386	Transportation Equipment and Supplies (except Motor Vehicle) Merchant Wholesalers[US]
423860	Transportation Equipment and Supplies (except Motor Vehicle) Merchant Wholesalers[US]

4239 Miscellaneous Durable Goods Merchant Wholesalers[US]

42391	Sporting and Recreational Goods and Supplies Merchant Wholesalers[US]
423910	Sporting and Recreational Goods and Supplies Merchant Wholesalers[US]
42392	Toy and Hobby Goods and Supplies Merchant Wholesalers[US]
423920	Toy and Hobby Goods and Supplies Merchant Wholesalers[US]
42393	Recyclable Material Merchant Wholesalers[US]
423930	Recyclable Material Merchant Wholesalers[US]
42394	Jewelry, Watch, Precious Stone, and Precious Metal Merchant Wholesalers[US]
423940	Jewelry, Watch, Precious Stone, and Precious Metal Merchant Wholesalers[US]
42399	Other Miscellaneous Durable Goods Merchant Wholesalers[US]
423990	Other Miscellaneous Durable Goods Merchant Wholesalers[US]

424 Merchant Wholesalers, Nondurable Goods[US]

4241 Paper and Paper Product Merchant Wholesalers[US]

| 42411 | Printing and Writing Paper Merchant Wholesalers[US] |

424110   Printing and Writing Paper Merchant
Wholesalers^{US}

42412   Stationery and Office Supplies Merchant
Wholesalers^{US}

424120   Stationery and Office Supplies Merchant
Wholesalers^{US}

42413   Industrial and Personal Service Paper Merchant
Wholesalers^{US}

424130   Industrial and Personal Service Paper Merchant
Wholesalers^{US}

4242   Drugs and Druggists' Sundries Merchant Wholesalers^{US}

42421   Drugs and Druggists' Sundries Merchant
Wholesalers^{US}

424210   Drugs and Druggists' Sundries Merchant
Wholesalers^{US}

**4243   Apparel, Piece Goods, and Notions Merchant
Wholesalers^{US}**

42431   Piece Goods, Notions, and Other Dry Goods
Merchant Wholesalers^{US}

424310   Piece Goods, Notions, and Other Dry Goods
Merchant Wholesalers^{US}

42432   Men's and Boys' Clothing and Furnishings
Merchant Wholesalers^{US}

424320   Men's and Boys' Clothing and Furnishings
Merchant Wholesalers^{US}

42433   Women's, Children's, and Infants' Clothing and
Accessories Merchant Wholesalers^{US}

424330   Women's, Children's, and Infants' Clothing and
Accessories Merchant Wholesalers^{US}

42434   Footwear Merchant Wholesalers^{US}

424340   Footwear Merchant Wholesalers^{US}

4244   Grocery and Related Product Merchant Wholesalers^{US}

42441   General Line Grocery Merchant Wholesalers^{US}

424410   General Line Grocery Merchant Wholesalers^{US}

42442   Packaged Frozen Food Merchant Wholesalers^{US}

424420   Packaged Frozen Food Merchant Wholesalers^{US}

42443   Dairy Product (except Dried or Canned)
Merchant Wholesalers^{US}

424430   Dairy Product (except Dried or Canned)
Merchant Wholesalers^{US}

42444   Poultry and Poultry Product Merchant
Wholesalers^{US}

424440   Poultry and Poultry Product Merchant
Wholesalers^{US}

42445	Confectionery Merchant Wholesalers[US]
424450	Confectionery Merchant Wholesalers[US]
42446	Fish and Seafood Merchant Wholesalers[US]
424460	Fish and Seafood Merchant Wholesalers[US]
42447	Meat and Meat Product Merchant Wholesalers[US]
424470	Meat and Meat Product Merchant Wholesalers[US]
42448	Fresh Fruit and Vegetable Merchant Wholesalers[US]
424480	Fresh Fruit and Vegetable Merchant Wholesalers[US]
42449	Other Grocery and Related Products Merchant Wholesalers[US]
424490	Other Grocery and Related Products Merchant Wholesalers[US]

4245 Farm Product Raw Material Merchant Wholesalers[US]

42451	Grain and Field Bean Merchant Wholesalers[US]
424510	Grain and Field Bean Merchant Wholesalers[US]
42452	Livestock Merchant Wholesalers[US]
424520	Livestock Merchant Wholesalers[US]
42459	Other Farm Product Raw Material Merchant Wholesalers[US]
424590	Other Farm Product Raw Material Merchant Wholesalers[US]

4246 Chemical and Allied Products Merchant Wholesalers[US]

42461	Plastics Materials and Basic Forms and Shapes Merchant Wholesalers[US]
424610	Plastics Materials and Basic Forms and Shapes Merchant Wholesalers[US]
42469	Other Chemical and Allied Products Merchant Wholesalers[US]
424690	Other Chemical and Allied Products Merchant Wholesalers[US]

4247 Petroleum and Petroleum Products Merchant Wholesalers[US]

42471	Petroleum Bulk Stations and Terminals[US]
424710	Petroleum Bulk Stations and Terminals[US]
42472	Petroleum and Petroleum Products Merchant Wholesalers (except Bulk Stations and Terminals)[US]
424720	Petroleum and Petroleum Products Merchant Wholesalers (except Bulk Stations and Terminals)[US]

4248   Beer, Wine, and Distilled Alcoholic Beverage Merchant Wholesalers[US]

42481	Beer and Ale Merchant Wholesalers[US]
424810	Beer and Ale Merchant Wholesalers[US]
42482	Wine and Distilled Alcoholic Beverage Merchant Wholesalers[US]
424820	Wine and Distilled Alcoholic Beverage Merchant Wholesalers[US]

4249   Miscellaneous Nondurable Goods Merchant Wholesalers[US]

42491	Farm Supplies Merchant Wholesalers[US]
424910	Farm Supplies Merchant Wholesalers[US]
42492	Book, Periodical, and Newspaper Merchant Wholesalers[US]
424920	Book, Periodical, and Newspaper Merchant Wholesalers[US]
42493	Flower, Nursery Stock, and Florists' Supplies Merchant Wholesalers[US]
424930	Flower, Nursery Stock, and Florists' Supplies Merchant Wholesalers[US]
42494	Tobacco and Tobacco Product Merchant Wholesalers[US]
424940	Tobacco and Tobacco Product Merchant Wholesalers[US]
42495	Paint, Varnish, and Supplies Merchant Wholesalers[US]
424950	Paint, Varnish, and Supplies Merchant Wholesalers[US]
42499	Other Miscellaneous Nondurable Goods Merchant Wholesalers[US]
424990	Other Miscellaneous Nondurable Goods Merchant Wholesalers[US]

425 Wholesale Electronic Markets and Agents and Brokers[US]

4251   Wholesale Electronic Markets and Agents and Brokers[US]

42511	Business to Business Electronic Markets[US]
425110	Business to Business Electronic Markets[US]
42512	Wholesale Trade Agents and Brokers[US]
425120	Wholesale Trade Agents and Brokers[US]

44-45 Retail Trade

441 Motor Vehicle and Parts Dealers[CAN]

4411   Automobile Dealers[CAN]

44111	New Car Dealers[CAN]
441110	New Car Dealers[CAN]

44112   Used Car Dealers^{CAN}
441120   Used Car Dealers^{CAN}

4412   Other Motor Vehicle Dealers^{CAN}

44121   Recreational Vehicle Dealers^{CAN}
441210   Recreational Vehicle Dealers^{CAN}
44122   Motorcycle, Boat, and Other Motor Vehicle
          Dealers^{CAN}
441221   Motorcycle Dealers^{US}
441222   Boat Dealers^{US}
441229   All Other Motor Vehicle Dealers^{US}

4413   Automotive Parts, Accessories, and Tire Stores^{CAN}

44131   Automotive Parts and Accessories Stores^{CAN}
441310   Automotive Parts and Accessories Stores^{CAN}
44132   Tire Dealers^{CAN}
441320   Tire Dealers^{CAN}

442 Furniture and Home Furnishings Stores^{CAN}

4421   Furniture Stores^{CAN}

44211   Furniture Stores^{CAN}
442110   Furniture Stores^{CAN}

4422   Home Furnishings Stores^{CAN}

44221   Floor Covering Stores^{CAN}
442210   Floor Covering Stores^{CAN}
44229   Other Home Furnishings Stores^{CAN}
442291   Window Treatment Stores^{CAN}
442299   All Other Home Furnishings Stores^{US}

443 Electronics and Appliance Stores^{CAN}

4431   Electronics and Appliance Stores^{CAN}

44311   Appliance, Television, and Other Electronics
          Stores ^{CAN}
443111   Household Appliance Stores^{US}
443112   Radio, Television, and Other Electronics Stores^{US}
44312   Computer and Software Stores^{CAN}
443120   Computer and Software Stores^{CAN}
44313   Camera and Photographic Supplies Stores^{CAN}
443130   Camera and Photographic Supplies Stores^{CAN}

444 Building Material and Garden Equipment and Supplies Dealers^{CAN}

4441   Building Material and Supplies Dealers^{CAN}

44411   Home Centers^{CAN}

444110   Home Centers[CAN]
44412   Paint and Wallpaper Stores[CAN]
444120   Paint and Wallpaper Stores[CAN]
44413   Hardware Stores[CAN]
444130   Hardware Stores[CAN]
44419   Other Building Material Dealers[CAN]
444190   Other Building Material Dealers[CAN]

4442   Lawn and Garden Equipment and Supplies Stores[CAN]

44421   Outdoor Power Equipment Stores[CAN]
444210   Outdoor Power Equipment Stores[CAN]
44422   Nursery, Garden Center, and Farm Supply Stores[CAN]
444220   Nursery, Garden Center, and Farm Supply Stores[CAN]

445 Food and Beverage Stores[CAN]

4451 Grocery Stores[CAN]

44511   Supermarkets and Other Grocery (except Convenience) Stores[CAN]
445110   Supermarkets and Other Grocery (except Convenience) Stores[CAN]
44512   Convenience Stores[CAN]
445120   Convenience Stores[CAN]

4452 Specialty Food Stores[CAN]

44521   Meat Markets[CAN]
445210   Meat Markets[CAN]
44522   Fish and Seafood Markets[CAN]
445220   Fish and Seafood Markets[CAN]
44523   Fruit and Vegetable Markets[CAN]
445230   Fruit and Vegetable Markets[CAN]
44529   Other Specialty Food Stores[CAN]
445291   Baked Goods Stores[CAN]
445292   Confectionery and Nut Stores[CAN]
445299   All Other Specialty Food Stores[CAN]

4453 Beer, Wine, and Liquor Stores[CAN]

44531   Beer, Wine, and Liquor Stores[CAN]
445310   Beer, Wine, and Liquor Stores[CAN]

446 Health and Personal Care Stores[CAN]

4461 Health and Personal Care Stores[CAN]

44611   Pharmacies and Drug Stores[CAN]
446110   Pharmacies and Drug Stores[CAN]

44612	Cosmetics, Beauty Supplies, and Perfume Stores^{CAN}
446120	Cosmetics, Beauty Supplies, and Perfume Stores^{CAN}
44613	Optical Goods Stores^{CAN}
446130	Optical Goods Stores^{CAN}
44619	Other Health and Personal Care Stores^{CAN}
446191	Food (Health) Supplement Stores^{CAN}
446199	All Other Health and Personal Care Stores^{CAN}

447 Gasoline Stations^{CAN}

4471 Gasoline Stations^{CAN}

44711	Gasoline Stations with Convenience Stores^{CAN}
447110	Gasoline Stations with Convenience Stores^{CAN}
44719	Other Gasoline Stations^{CAN}
447190	Other Gasoline Stations^{CAN}

448 Clothing and Clothing Accessories Stores^{CAN}

4481 Clothing Stores^{CAN}

44811	Men's Clothing Stores^{CAN}
448110	Men's Clothing Stores^{CAN}
44812	Women's Clothing Stores^{CAN}
448120	Women's Clothing Stores^{CAN}
44813	Children's and Infants' Clothing Stores^{CAN}
448130	Children's and Infants' Clothing Stores^{CAN}
44814	Family Clothing Stores^{CAN}
448140	Family Clothing Stores^{CAN}
44815	Clothing Accessories Stores^{CAN}
448150	Clothing Accessories Stores^{CAN}
44819	Other Clothing Stores^{CAN}
448190	Other Clothing Stores^{US}

4482 Shoe Stores^{CAN}

44821	Shoe Stores^{CAN}
448210	Shoe Stores^{CAN}

4483 Jewelry, Luggage, and Leather Goods Stores^{CAN}

44831	Jewelry Stores^{CAN}
448310	Jewelry Stores^{CAN}
44832	Luggage and Leather Goods Stores^{CAN}
448320	Luggage and Leather Goods Stores^{CAN}

451 Sporting Goods, Hobby, Book, and Music Stores^{CAN}

4511 Sporting Goods, Hobby, and Musical Instrument Stores^{CAN}

45111   Sporting Goods Stores^{CAN}
451110   Sporting Goods Stores^{CAN}
45112   Hobby, Toy, and Game Stores^{CAN}
451120   Hobby, Toy, and Game Stores^{CAN}
45113   Sewing, Needlework, and Piece Goods Stores^{CAN}
451130   Sewing, Needlework, and Piece Goods Stores^{CAN}
45114   Musical Instrument and Supplies Stores^{CAN}
451140   Musical Instrument and Supplies Stores^{CAN}

4512   Book, Periodical, and Music Stores^{CAN}

45121   Book Stores and News Dealers^{CAN}
451211   Book Stores^{US}
451212   News Dealers and Newsstands^{US}
45122   Prerecorded Tape, Compact Disc, and Record Stores^{CAN}
451220   Prerecorded Tape, Compact Disc, and Record Stores^{CAN}

452 General Merchandise Stores^{CAN}

4521   Department Stores^{CAN}

45211   Department Stores^{CAN}
452111   Department Stores (except Discount Department Stores)^{US}
452112   Discount Department Stores^{US}

4529   Other General Merchandise Stores^{CAN}

45291   Warehouse Clubs and Supercenters^{CAN}
452910   Warehouse Clubs and Supercenters^{CAN}
45299   All Other General Merchandise Stores^{CAN}
452990   All Other General Merchandise Stores^{US}

453 Miscellaneous Store Retailers^{CAN}

4531   Florists^{CAN}

45311   Florists^{CAN}
453110   Florists^{CAN}

4532   Office Supplies, Stationery, and Gift Stores^{CAN}

45321   Office Supplies and Stationery Stores^{CAN}
453210   Office Supplies and Stationery Stores^{CAN}
45322   Gift, Novelty, and Souvenir Stores^{CAN}
453220   Gift, Novelty, and Souvenir Stores^{CAN}

4533   Used Merchandise Stores^{CAN}

45331   Used Merchandise Stores^{CAN}
453310   Used Merchandise Stores^{CAN}

4539   Other Miscellaneous Store Retailers^{CAN}

45391	Pet and Pet Supplies Stores^{CAN}
453910	Pet and Pet Supplies Stores^{CAN}
45392	Art Dealers^{CAN}
453920	Art Dealers^{CAN}
45393	Manufactured (Mobile) Home Dealers^{CAN}
453930	Manufactured (Mobile) Home Dealers^{CAN}
45399	All Other Miscellaneous Store Retailers^{CAN}
453991	Tobacco Stores^{US}
453998	All Other Miscellaneous Store Retailers (except Tobacco Stores)^{US}

454 Nonstore Retailers^{CAN}

4541   Electronic Shopping and Mail-Order Houses^{CAN}

45411	Electronic Shopping and Mail-Order Houses^{CAN}
454111	Electronic Shopping^{US}
454112	Electronic Auctions^{US}
454113	Mail-Order Houses^{US}

4542   Vending Machine Operators^{CAN}

45421	Vending Machine Operators^{CAN}
454210	Vending Machine Operators^{CAN}

4543   Direct Selling Establishments^{CAN}

45431	Fuel Dealers^{CAN}
454311	Heating Oil Dealers^{US}
454312	Liquefied Petroleum Gas (Bottled Gas) Dealers^{US}
454319	Other Fuel Dealers^{US}
45439	Other Direct Selling Establishments^{CAN}
454390	Other Direct Selling Establishments^{CAN}

48-49   Transportation and Warehousing

481 Air Transportation

4811   Scheduled Air Transportation

48111	Scheduled Air Transportation
481111	Scheduled Passenger Air Transportation^{US}
481112	Scheduled Freight Air Transportation^{US}

4812   Nonscheduled Air Transportation

48121	Nonscheduled Air Transportation
481211	Nonscheduled Chartered Passenger Air Transportation^{US}

481212   Nonscheduled Chartered Freight Air Transportation[US]

481219   Other Nonscheduled Air Transportation[US]

482 Rail Transportation

4821 Rail Transportation

48211   Rail Transportation
482111   Line-Haul Railroads[US]
482112   Short Line Railroads[CAN]

483 Water Transportation

4831 Deep Sea, Coastal, and Great Lakes Water Transportation

48311   Deep Sea, Coastal, and Great Lakes Water Transportation
483111   Deep Sea Freight Transportation[US]
483112   Deep Sea Passenger Transportation[US]
483113   Coastal and Great Lakes Freight Transportation[US]
483114   Coastal and Great Lakes Passenger Transportation[US]

4832 Inland Water Transportation

48321   Inland Water Transportation
483211   Inland Water Freight Transportation[US]
483212   Inland Water Passenger Transportation[US]

484 Truck Transportation

4841 General Freight Trucking

48411   General Freight Trucking, Local
484110   General Freight Trucking, Local[CAN]
48412   General Freight Trucking, Long-Distance
484121   General Freight Trucking, Long-Distance, Truckload[CAN]
484122   General Freight Trucking, Long-Distance, Less Than Truckload[CAN]

4842 Specialized Freight Trucking

48421   Used Household and Office Goods Moving
484210   Used Household and Office Goods Moving
48422   Specialized Freight (except Used Goods) Trucking, Local
484220   Specialized Freight (except Used Goods) Trucking, Local[US]
48423   Specialized Freight (except Used Goods) Trucking, Long-Distance

| | 484230 | Specialized Freight (except Used Goods) Trucking, Long-Distance[US] |

485 Transit and Ground Passenger Transportation

4851 Urban Transit Systems

48511   Urban Transit Systems
485111   Mixed Mode Transit Systems[US]
485112   Commuter Rail Systems[US]
485113   Bus and Other Motor Vehicle Transit Systems[US]
485119   Other Urban Transit Systems[US]

4852 Interurban and Rural Bus Transportation

48521   Interurban and Rural Bus Transportation
485210   Interurban and Rural Bus Transportation

4853 Taxi and Limousine Service

48531   Taxi Service
485310   Taxi Service[CAN]
48532   Limousine Service
485320   Limousine Service

4854 School and Employee Bus Transportation

48541   School and Employee Bus Transportation
485410   School and Employee Bus Transportation

4855 Charter Bus Industry

48551   Charter Bus Industry
485510   Charter Bus Industry

4859 Other Transit and Ground Passenger Transportation

48599   Other Transit and Ground Passenger Transportation
485991   Special Needs Transportation[US]
485999   All Other Transit and Ground Passenger Transportation[US]

486 Pipeline Transportation

4861 Pipeline Transportation of Crude Oil

48611   Pipeline Transportation of Crude Oil
486110   Pipeline Transportation of Crude Oil

4862 Pipeline Transportation of Natural Gas

48621   Pipeline Transportation of Natural Gas
486210   Pipeline Transportation of Natural Gas

4869 Other Pipeline Transportation

48691	Pipeline Transportation of Refined Petroleum Products
486910	Pipeline Transportation of Refined Petroleum Products
48699	All Other Pipeline Transportation
486990	All Other Pipeline Transportation

487 Scenic and Sightseeing Transportation

4871 Scenic and Sightseeing Transportation, Land

48711	Scenic and Sightseeing Transportation, Land
487110	Scenic and Sightseeing Transportation, Land

4872 Scenic and Sightseeing Transportation, Water

48721	Scenic and Sightseeing Transportation, Water
487210	Scenic and Sightseeing Transportation, Water

4879 Scenic and Sightseeing Transportation, Other

48799	Scenic and Sightseeing Transportation, Other
487990	Scenic and Sightseeing Transportation, Other

488 Support Activities for Transportation

4881 Support Activities for Air Transportation

48811	Airport Operations
488111	Air Traffic Control
488119	Other Airport Operations[CAN]
48819	Other Support Activities for Air Transportation
488190	Other Support Activities for Air Transportation

4882 Support Activities for Rail Transportation

48821	Support Activities for Rail Transportation
488210	Support Activities for Rail Transportation

4883 Support Activities for Water Transportation

48831	Port and Harbor Operations
488310	Port and Harbor Operations
48832	Marine Cargo Handling
488320	Marine Cargo Handling
48833	Navigational Services to Shipping
488330	Navigational Services to Shipping[MEX]
48839	Other Support Activities for Water Transportation
488390	Other Support Activities for Water Transportation

4884 Support Activities for Road Transportation

48841	Motor Vehicle Towing
488410	Motor Vehicle Towing
48849	Other Support Activities for Road Transportation

        488490   Other Support Activities for Road
                 Transportation^{CAN}

4885   Freight Transportation Arrangement

        48851   Freight Transportation Arrangement
        488510   Freight Transportation Arrangement^{US}

4889   Other Support Activities for Transportation

        48899   Other Support Activities for Transportation
        488991   Packing and Crating^{US}
        488999   All Other Support Activities for Transportation^{US}

491 Postal Service

4911   Postal Service

        49111   Postal Service
        491110   Postal Service

492 Couriers and Messengers

4921   Couriers

        49211   Couriers
        492110   Couriers

4922   Local Messengers and Local Delivery

        49221   Local Messengers and Local Delivery
        492210   Local Messengers and Local Delivery

493 Warehousing and Storage

4931   Warehousing and Storage

        49311   General Warehousing and Storage
        493110   General Warehousing and Storage^{CAN}
        49312   Refrigerated Warehousing and Storage
        493120   Refrigerated Warehousing and Storage
        49313   Farm Product Warehousing and Storage
        493130   Farm Product Warehousing and Storage
        49319   Other Warehousing and Storage
        493190   Other Warehousing and Storage

51 Information

511 Publishing Industries (except Internet)

5111   Newspaper, Periodical, Book, and Directory Publishers

        51111   Newspaper Publishers
        511110   Newspaper Publishers^{CAN}
        51112   Periodical Publishers
        511120   Periodical Publishers^{CAN}

51113	Book Publishers
511130	Book Publishers^{CAN}
51114	Directory and Mailing List Publishers
511140	Directory and Mailing List Publishers^{CAN}
51119	Other Publishers
511191	Greeting Card Publishers^{US}
511199	All Other Publishers^{US}

5112 Software Publishers

51121	Software Publishers
511210	Software Publishers

512 Motion Picture and Sound Recording Industries

5121 Motion Picture and Video Industries

51211	Motion Picture and Video Production
512110	Motion Picture and Video Production^{CAN}
51212	Motion Picture and Video Distribution
512120	Motion Picture and Video Distribution
51213	Motion Picture and Video Exhibition
512131	Motion Picture Theaters (except Drive-Ins)^{US}
512132	Drive-In Motion Picture Theaters^{US}
51219	Postproduction Services and Other Motion Picture and Video Industries
512191	Teleproduction and Other Postproduction Services^{US}
512199	Other Motion Picture and Video Industries^{US}

5122 Sound Recording Industries

51221	Record Production
512210	Record Production
51222	Integrated Record Production/Distribution
512220	Integrated Record Production/Distribution
51223	Music Publishers
512230	Music Publishers
51224	Sound Recording Studios
512240	Sound Recording Studios
51229	Other Sound Recording Industries
512290	Other Sound Recording Industries

515 Broadcasting (except Internet)

5151 Radio and Television Broadcasting

51511	Radio Broadcasting
515111	Radio Networks^{US}
515112	Radio Stations^{US}
51512	Television Broadcasting
515120	Television Broadcasting

5152 **Cable and Other Subscription Programming**

    51521   Cable and Other Subscription Programming

    515210   Cable and Other Subscription Programming

516 Internet Publishing and Broadcasting

5161 **Internet Publishing and Broadcasting**

    51611   Internet Publishing and Broadcasting

    516110   Internet Publishing and Broadcasting

517 Telecommunications

5171 **Wired Telecommunications Carriers**

    51711   Wired Telecommunications Carriers

    517110   Wired Telecommunications Carriers

5172 **Wireless Telecommunications Carriers (except Satellite)**

    51721   Wireless Telecommunications Carriers (except Satellite)

    517211   Paging[US]

    517212   Cellular and Other Wireless Telecommunications[US]

5173 **Telecommunications Resellers**

    51731   Telecommunications Resellers

    517310   Telecommunications Resellers

5174 **Satellite Telecommunications**

    51741   Satellite Telecommunications

    517410   Satellite Telecommunications

5175 **Cable and Other Program Distribution**

    51751   Cable and Other Program Distribution

    517510   Cable and Other Program Distribution

5179 **Other Telecommunications**

    51791   Other Telecommunications

    517910   Other Telecommunications

518 Internet Service Providers, Web Search Portals, and Data Processing Services

5181 **Internet Service Providers and Web Search Portals**

    51811   Internet Service Providers and Web Search Portals

    518111   Internet Service Providers[US]

    518112   Web Search Portals[US]

5182 **Data Processing, Hosting, and Related Services**

51821   Data Processing, Hosting, and Related Services
518210   Data Processing, Hosting, and Related Services

519 Other Information Services

5191 Other Information Services

51911   News Syndicates
519110   News Syndicates
51912   Libraries and Archives
519120   Libraries and Archives^{US}
51919   All Other Information Services
519190   All Other Information Services

52 Finance and Insurance

521 Monetary Authorities—Central Bank

5211 Monetary Authorities—Central Bank

52111   Monetary Authorities—Central Bank
521110   Monetary Authorities—Central Bank

522 Credit Intermediation and Related Activities

5221 Depository Credit Intermediation^{CAN}

52211   Commercial Banking^{US}
522110   Commercial Banking^{US}
52212   Savings Institutions^{US}
522120   Savings Institutions^{US}
52213   Credit Unions^{CAN}
522130   Credit Unions^{CAN}
52219   Other Depository Credit Intermediation^{CAN}
522190   Other Depository Credit Intermediation^{CAN}

5222 Nondepository Credit Intermediation^{CAN}

52221   Credit Card Issuing^{CAN}
522210   Credit Card Issuing^{CAN}
52222   Sales Financing^{CAN}
522220   Sales Financing^{CAN}
52229   Other Nondepository Credit Intermediation^{CAN}
522291   Consumer Lending^{CAN}
522292   Real Estate Credit^{US}
522293   International Trade Financing^{US}
522294   Secondary Market Financing^{US}
522298   All Other Nondepository Credit Intermediation^{US}

5223 Activities Related to Credit Intermediation^{CAN}

52231   Mortgage and Nonmortgage Loan Brokers^{CAN}
522310   Mortgage and Nonmortgage Loan Brokers^{CAN}

52232	Financial Transactions Processing, Reserve, and Clearinghouse Activities[CAN]
522320	Financial Transactions Processing, Reserve, and Clearinghouse Activities[US]
52239	Other Activities Related to Credit Intermediation[CAN]
522390	Other Activities Related to Credit Intermediation[CAN]

523 Securities, Commodity Contracts, and Other Financial Investments and Related Activities

5231 Securities and Commodity Contracts Intermediation and Brokerage

52311	Investment Banking and Securities Dealing[CAN]
523110	Investment Banking and Securities Dealing[CAN]
52312	Securities Brokerage[CAN]
523120	Securities Brokerage[CAN]
52313	Commodity Contracts Dealing[CAN]
523130	Commodity Contracts Dealing[CAN]
52314	Commodity Contracts Brokerage[CAN]
523140	Commodity Contracts Brokerage[CAN]

5232 Securities and Commodity Exchanges

52321	Securities and Commodity Exchanges
523210	Securities and Commodity Exchanges

5239 Other Financial Investment Activities

52391	Miscellaneous Intermediation[CAN]
523910	Miscellaneous Intermediation[CAN]
52392	Portfolio Management[CAN]
523920	Portfolio Management[CAN]
52393	Investment Advice[CAN]
523930	Investment Advice[CAN]
52399	All Other Financial Investment Activities[CAN]
523991	Trust, Fiduciary, and Custody Activities[US]
523999	Miscellaneous Financial Investment Activities[US]

524 Insurance Carriers and Related Activities

5241 Insurance Carriers

52411	Direct Life, Health, and Medical Insurance Carriers[CAN]
524113	Direct Life Insurance Carriers[US]
524114	Direct Health and Medical Insurance Carriers[US]
52412	Direct Insurance (except Life, Health, and Medical) Carriers[CAN]

   524126   Direct Property and Casualty Insurance Carriers[US]

   524127   Direct Title Insurance Carriers[US]

   524128   Other Direct Insurance (except Life, Health, and Medical) Carriers[US]

   52413   Reinsurance Carriers[CAN]

   524130   Reinsurance Carriers[US]

5242   Agencies, Brokerages, and Other Insurance Related Activities

   52421   Insurance Agencies and Brokerages[CAN]

   524210   Insurance Agencies and Brokerages[CAN]

   52429   Other Insurance Related Activities[CAN]

   524291   Claims Adjusting[CAN]

   524292   Third Party Administration of Insurance and Pension Funds[US]

   524298   All Other Insurance Related Activities[US]

525 Funds, Trusts, and Other Financial Vehicles[US]

5251   Insurance and Employee Benefit Funds[US]

   52511   Pension Funds[US]

   525110   Pension Funds[US]

   52512   Health and Welfare Funds[US]

   525120   Health and Welfare Funds[US]

   52519   Other Insurance Funds[US]

   525190   Other Insurance Funds[US]

5259   Other Investment Pools and Funds[US]

   52591   Open-End Investment Funds[US]

   525910   Open-End Investment Funds[US]

   52592   Trusts, Estates, and Agency Accounts[US]

   525920   Trusts, Estates, and Agency Accounts[US]

   52593   Real Estate Investment Trusts[US]

   525930   Real Estate Investment Trusts[US]

   52599   Other Financial Vehicles[US]

   525990   Other Financial Vehicles[US]

53   Real Estate and Rental and Leasing

531 Real Estate

5311   Lessors of Real Estate

   53111   Lessors of Residential Buildings and Dwellings[CAN]

   531110   Lessors of Residential Buildings and Dwellings[US]

   53112   Lessors of Nonresidential Buildings (except Miniwarehouses)[CAN]

531120   Lessors of Nonresidential Buildings (except Miniwarehouses)^{CAN}

53113   Lessors of Miniwarehouses and Self-Storage Units^{CAN}

531130   Lessors of Miniwarehouses and Self-Storage Units^{CAN}

53119   Lessors of Other Real Estate Property^{CAN}

531190   Lessors of Other Real Estate Property^{CAN}

5312 Offices of Real Estate Agents and Brokers

53121   Offices of Real Estate Agents and Brokers

531210   Offices of Real Estate Agents and Brokers

5313 Activities Related to Real Estate

53131   Real Estate Property Managers^{CAN}

531311   Residential Property Managers^{US}

531312   Nonresidential Property Managers^{US}

53132   Offices of Real Estate Appraisers^{CAN}

531320   Offices of Real Estate Appraisers^{CAN}

53139   Other Activities Related to Real Estate^{CAN}

531390   Other Activities Related to Real Estate^{CAN}

532 Rental and Leasing Services

5321 Automotive Equipment Rental and Leasing

53211   Passenger Car Rental and Leasing

532111   Passenger Car Rental^{CAN}

532112   Passenger Car Leasing^{CAN}

53212   Truck, Utility Trailer, and RV (Recreational Vehicle) Rental and Leasing

532120   Truck, Utility Trailer, and RV (Recreational Vehicle) Rental and Leasing^{CAN}

5322 Consumer Goods Rental

53221   Consumer Electronics and Appliances Rental

532210   Consumer Electronics and Appliances Rental

53222   Formal Wear and Costume Rental

532220   Formal Wear and Costume Rental

53223   Video Tape and Disc Rental

532230   Video Tape and Disc Rental

53229   Other Consumer Goods Rental

532291   Home Health Equipment Rental^{US}

532292   Recreational Goods Rental^{US}

532299   All Other Consumer Goods Rental^{US}

5323 General Rental Centers

53231   General Rental Centers

532310   General Rental Centers

5324   Commercial and Industrial Machinery and Equipment Rental and Leasing

53241   Construction, Transportation, Mining, and Forestry Machinery and Equipment Rental and Leasing

532411   Commercial Air, Rail, and Water Transportation Equipment Rental and Leasing[US]

532412   Construction, Mining, and Forestry Machinery and Equipment Rental and Leasing[US]

53242   Office Machinery and Equipment Rental and Leasing

532420   Office Machinery and Equipment Rental and Leasing

53249   Other Commercial and Industrial Machinery and Equipment Rental and Leasing

532490   Other Commercial and Industrial Machinery and Equipment Rental and Leasing[CAN]

533 Lessors of Nonfinancial Intangible Assets (except Copyrighted Works)

5331   Lessors of Nonfinancial Intangible Assets (except Copyrighted Works)

53311   Lessors of Nonfinancial Intangible Assets (except Copyrighted Works)

533110   Lessors of Nonfinancial Intangible Assets (except Copyrighted Works)

54   Professional, Scientific, and Technical Services

541 Professional, Scientific, and Technical Services

5411   Legal Services

54111   Offices of Lawyers

541110   Offices of Lawyers

54112   Offices of Notaries

541120   Offices of Notaries

54119   Other Legal Services

541191   Title Abstract and Settlement Offices[US]

541199   All Other Legal Services[US]

5412   Accounting, Tax Preparation, Bookkeeping, and Payroll Services

54121   Accounting, Tax Preparation, Bookkeeping, and Payroll Services

541211   Offices of Certified Public Accountants[US]

541213   Tax Preparation Services[CAN]

541214   Payroll Services[US]
541219   Other Accounting Services[US]

5413 Architectural, Engineering, and Related Services

54131   Architectural Services
541310   Architectural Services
54132   Landscape Architectural Services
541320   Landscape Architectural Services
54133   Engineering Services
541330   Engineering Services
54134   Drafting Services
541340   Drafting Services
54135   Building Inspection Services
541350   Building Inspection Services
54136   Geophysical Surveying and Mapping Services
541360   Geophysical Surveying and Mapping Services
54137   Surveying and Mapping (except Geophysical) Services
541370   Surveying and Mapping (except Geophysical) Services
54138   Testing Laboratories
541380   Testing Laboratories

5414 Specialized Design Services

54141   Interior Design Services
541410   Interior Design Services
54142   Industrial Design Services
541420   Industrial Design Services
54143   Graphic Design Services
541430   Graphic Design Services
54149   Other Specialized Design Services
541490   Other Specialized Design Services

5415 Computer Systems Design and Related Services

54151   Computer Systems Design and Related Services
541511   Custom Computer Programming Services[US]
541512   Computer Systems Design Services[US]
541513   Computer Facilities Management Services[US]
541519   Other Computer Related Services[US]

5416 Management, Scientific, and Technical Consulting Services

54161   Management Consulting Services
541611   Administrative Management and General Management Consulting Services[CAN]
541612   Human Resources and Executive Search Consulting Services[CAN]

541613	Marketing Consulting Services[US]
541614	Process, Physical Distribution, and Logistics Consulting Services[US]
541618	Other Management Consulting Services[US]
54162	Environmental Consulting Services
541620	Environmental Consulting Services
54169	Other Scientific and Technical Consulting Services
541690	Other Scientific and Technical Consulting Services

5417 Scientific Research and Development Services

54171	Research and Development in the Physical, Engineering, and Life Sciences
541710	Research and Development in the Physical, Engineering, and Life Sciences[CAN]
54172	Research and Development in the Social Sciences and Humanities
541720	Research and Development in the Social Sciences and Humanities[CAN]

5418 Advertising and Related Services

54181	Advertising Agencies
541810	Advertising Agencies
54182	Public Relations Agencies
541820	Public Relations Agencies
54183	Media Buying Agencies
541830	Media Buying Agencies
54184	Media Representatives
541840	Media Representatives
54185	Display Advertising
541850	Display Advertising
54186	Direct Mail Advertising
541860	Direct Mail Advertising
54187	Advertising Material Distribution Services
541870	Advertising Material Distribution Services
54189	Other Services Related to Advertising
541890	Other Services Related to Advertising[MEX]

5419 Other Professional, Scientific, and Technical Services

54191	Marketing Research and Public Opinion Polling
541910	Marketing Research and Public Opinion Polling
54192	Photographic Services
541921	Photography Studios, Portrait[US]
541922	Commercial Photography[US]
54193	Translation and Interpretation Services

541930	Translation and Interpretation Services
54194	Veterinary Services
541940	Veterinary Services[CAN]
54199	All Other Professional, Scientific, and Technical Services
541990	All Other Professional, Scientific, and Technical Services

55 Management of Companies and Enterprises

551 Management of Companies and Enterprises

5511 Management of Companies and Enterprises

55111	Management of Companies and Enterprises
551111	Offices of Bank Holding Companies[US]
551112	Offices of Other Holding Companies[US]
551114	Corporate, Subsidiary, and Regional Managing Offices[CAN]

56 Administrative and Support and Waste Management and Remediation Services

561 Administrative and Support Services

5611 Office Administrative Services

| 56111 | Office Administrative Services |
| 561110 | Office Administrative Services |

5612 Facilities Support Services

| 56121 | Facilities Support Services |
| 561210 | Facilities Support Services |

5613 Employment Services

56131	Employment Placement Agencies
561310	Employment Placement Agencies
56132	Temporary Help Services
561320	Temporary Help Services
56133	Professional Employer Organizations
561330	Professional Employer Organizations

5614 Business Support Services

56141	Document Preparation Services
561410	Document Preparation Services
56142	Telephone Call Centers
561421	Telephone Answering Services[US]
561422	Telemarketing Bureaus[MEX]
56143	Business Service Centers
561431	Private Mail Centers[US]

561439   Other Business Service Centers (including Copy Shops)[US]
56144   Collection Agencies
561440   Collection Agencies
56145   Credit Bureaus
561450   Credit Bureaus
56149   Other Business Support Services
561491   Repossession Services[US]
561492   Court Reporting and Stenotype Services[US]
561499   All Other Business Support Services[US]

5615   Travel Arrangement and Reservation Services

56151   Travel Agencies
561510   Travel Agencies
56152   Tour Operators
561520   Tour Operators
56159   Other Travel Arrangement and Reservation Services
561591   Convention and Visitors Bureaus[US]
561599   All Other Travel Arrangement and Reservation Services[US]

5616   Investigation and Security Services

56161   Investigation, Guard, and Armored Car Services
561611   Investigation Services[CAN]
561612   Security Guards and Patrol Services[CAN]
561613   Armored Car Services[CAN]
56162   Security Systems Services
561621   Security Systems Services (except Locksmiths)[CAN]
561622   Locksmiths[CAN]

5617   Services to Buildings and Dwellings

56171   Exterminating and Pest Control Services
561710   Exterminating and Pest Control Services
56172   Janitorial Services
561720   Janitorial Services[MEX]
56173   Landscaping Services
561730   Landscaping Services
56174   Carpet and Upholstery Cleaning Services
561740   Carpet and Upholstery Cleaning Services
56179   Other Services to Buildings and Dwellings
561790   Other Services to Buildings and Dwellings[MEX]

5619   Other Support Services

56191   Packaging and Labeling Services
561910   Packaging and Labeling Services
56192   Convention and Trade Show Organizers

561920 Convention and Trade Show Organizers
56199 All Other Support Services
561990 All Other Support Services

562 Waste Management and Remediation Services

5621 Waste Collection^{CAN}

56211 Waste Collection^{CAN}
562111 Solid Waste Collection^{US}
562112 Hazardous Waste Collection^{US}
562119 Other Waste Collection^{US}

5622 Waste Treatment and Disposal^{CAN}

56221 Waste Treatment and Disposal^{CAN}
562211 Hazardous Waste Treatment and Disposal^{US}
562212 Solid Waste Landfill^{US}
562213 Solid Waste Combustors and Incinerators^{US}
562219 Other Nonhazardous Waste Treatment and Disposal^{US}

5629 Remediation and Other Waste Management Services^{CAN}

56291 Remediation Services^{CAN}
562910 Remediation Services^{CAN}
56292 Materials Recovery Facilities^{CAN}
562920 Materials Recovery Facilities^{CAN}
56299 All Other Waste Management Services^{CAN}
562991 Septic Tank and Related Services^{US}
562998 All Other Miscellaneous Waste Management Services^{US}

61 Educational Services

611 Educational Services

6111 Elementary and Secondary Schools

61111 Elementary and Secondary Schools^{CAN}
611110 Elementary and Secondary Schools^{CAN}

6112 Junior Colleges

61121 Junior Colleges
611210 Junior Colleges^{CAN}

6113 Colleges, Universities, and Professional Schools

61131 Colleges, Universities, and Professional Schools
611310 Colleges, Universities, and Professional Schools^{CAN}

6114 Business Schools and Computer and Management Training

61141	Business and Secretarial Schools
611410	Business and Secretarial Schools[CAN]
61142	Computer Training
611420	Computer Training[CAN]
61143	Professional and Management Development Training
611430	Professional and Management Development Training[CAN]

6115   Technical and Trade Schools

61151	Technical and Trade Schools
611511	Cosmetology and Barber Schools[US]
611512	Flight Training[US]
611513	Apprenticeship Training[US]
611519	Other Technical and Trade Schools[US]

6116   Other Schools and Instruction

61161	Fine Arts Schools
611610	Fine Arts Schools[CAN]
61162	Sports and Recreation Instruction
611620	Sports and Recreation Instruction[CAN]
61163	Language Schools
611630	Language Schools[CAN]
61169	All Other Schools and Instruction
611691	Exam Preparation and Tutoring[US]
611692	Automobile Driving Schools[US]
611699	All Other Miscellaneous Schools and Instruction[US]

6117   Educational Support Services

61171	Educational Support Services
611710	Educational Support Services

62   Health Care and Social Assistance

621 Ambulatory Health Care Services

6211   Offices of Physicians

62111	Offices of Physicians
621111	Offices of Physicians (except Mental Health Specialists)[US]
621112	Offices of Physicians, Mental Health Specialists[US]

6212   Offices of Dentists

62121	Offices of Dentists
621210	Offices of Dentists[CAN]

6213   Offices of Other Health Practitioners

62131	Offices of Chiropractors
621310	Offices of Chiropractors[CAN]
62132	Offices of Optometrists
621320	Offices of Optometrists
62133	Offices of Mental Health Practitioners (except Physicians)
621330	Offices of Mental Health Practitioners (except Physicians)[CAN]
62134	Offices of Physical, Occupational and Speech Therapists, and Audiologists
621340	Offices of Physical, Occupational and Speech Therapists, and Audiologists[CAN]
62139	Offices of All Other Health Practitioners
621391	Offices of Podiatrists[US]
621399	Offices of All Other Miscellaneous Health Practitioners[US]

6214 Outpatient Care Centers

62141	Family Planning Centers
621410	Family Planning Centers[CAN]
62142	Outpatient Mental Health and Substance Abuse Centers
621420	Outpatient Mental Health and Substance Abuse Centers[CAN]
62149	Other Outpatient Care Centers
621491	HMO Medical Centers[US]
621492	Kidney Dialysis Centers[US]
621493	Freestanding Ambulatory Surgical and Emergency Centers[US]
621498	All Other Outpatient Care Centers[US]

6215 Medical and Diagnostic Laboratories

62151	Medical and Diagnostic Laboratories
621511	Medical Laboratories[US]
621512	Diagnostic Imaging Centers[US]

6216 Home Health Care Services

| 62161 | Home Health Care Services |
| 621610 | Home Health Care Services |

6219 Other Ambulatory Health Care Services

62191	Ambulance Services
621910	Ambulance Services[MEX]
62199	All Other Ambulatory Health Care Services
621991	Blood and Organ Banks[US]
621999	All Other Miscellaneous Ambulatory Health Care Services[US]

622 Hospitals

6221 General Medical and Surgical Hospitals

62211   General Medical and Surgical Hospitals
622110   General Medical and Surgical Hospitals[US]

6222 Psychiatric and Substance Abuse Hospitals

62221   Psychiatric and Substance Abuse Hospitals
622210   Psychiatric and Substance Abuse Hospitals[CAN]

6223 Specialty (except Psychiatric and Substance Abuse) Hospitals

62231   Specialty (except Psychiatric and Substance Abuse) Hospitals
622310   Specialty (except Psychiatric and Substance Abuse) Hospitals[CAN]

623 Nursing and Residential Care Facilities

6231 Nursing Care Facilities

62311   Nursing Care Facilities
623110   Nursing Care Facilities[CAN]

6232 Residential Mental Retardation, Mental Health and Substance Abuse Facilities

62321   Residential Mental Retardation Facilities
623210   Residential Mental Retardation Facilities[CAN]
62322   Residential Mental Health and Substance Abuse Facilities
623220   Residential Mental Health and Substance Abuse Facilities[US]

6233 Community Care Facilities for the Elderly

62331   Community Care Facilities for the Elderly
623311   Continuing Care Retirement Communities[US]
623312   Homes for the Elderly[US]

6239 Other Residential Care Facilities

62399   Other Residential Care Facilities
623990   Other Residential Care Facilities[US]

624 Social Assistance

6241 Individual and Family Services

62411   Child and Youth Services
624110   Child and Youth Services[CAN]
62412   Services for the Elderly and Persons with Disabilities

624120   Services for the Elderly and Persons with Disabilities^{CAN}

62419   Other Individual and Family Services

624190   Other Individual and Family Services^{CAN}

6242   Community Food and Housing, and Emergency and Other Relief Services

62421   Community Food Services

624210   Community Food Services^{CAN}

62422   Community Housing Services

624221   Temporary Shelters^{US}

624229   Other Community Housing Services^{US}

62423   Emergency and Other Relief Services

624230   Emergency and Other Relief Services^{CAN}

6243   Vocational Rehabilitation Services

62431   Vocational Rehabilitation Services

624310   Vocational Rehabilitation Services^{CAN}

6244   Child Day Care Services

62441   Child Day Care Services

624410   Child Day Care Services^{CAN}

71   Arts, Entertainment, and Recreation

711   Performing Arts, Spectator Sports, and Related Industries

7111   Performing Arts Companies

71111   Theater Companies and Dinner Theaters

711110   Theater Companies and Dinner Theaters^{US}

71112   Dance Companies

711120   Dance Companies^{CAN}

71113   Musical Groups and Artists

711130   Musical Groups and Artists^{CAN}

71119   Other Performing Arts Companies

711190   Other Performing Arts Companies^{CAN}

7112   Spectator Sports

71121   Spectator Sports

711211   Sports Teams and Clubs^{CAN}

711212   Racetracks^{US}

711219   Other Spectator Sports^{US}

7113   Promoters of Performing Arts, Sports, and Similar Events

71131   Promoters of Performing Arts, Sports, and Similar Events with Facilities

711310   Promoters of Performing Arts, Sports, and Similar Events with Facilities[US]

71132   Promoters of Performing Arts, Sports, and Similar Events without Facilities

711320   Promoters of Performing Arts, Sports, and Similar Events without Facilities[MEX]

7114   Agents and Managers for Artists, Athletes, Entertainers, and Other Public Figures

71141   Agents and Managers for Artists, Athletes, Entertainers, and Other Public Figures

711410   Agents and Managers for Artists, Athletes, Entertainers, and Other Public Figures

7115   Independent Artists, Writers, and Performers

71151   Independent Artists, Writers, and Performers

711510   Independent Artists, Writers, and Performers

712 Museums, Historical Sites, and Similar Institutions

7121   Museums, Historical Sites, and Similar Institutions

71211   Museums

712110   Museums[US]

71212   Historical Sites

712120   Historical Sites

71213   Zoos and Botanical Gardens

712130   Zoos and Botanical Gardens[CAN]

71219   Nature Parks and Other Similar Institutions

712190   Nature Parks and Other Similar Institutions

713 Amusement, Gambling, and Recreation Industries

7131   Amusement Parks and Arcades

71311   Amusement and Theme Parks

713110   Amusement and Theme Parks[CAN]

71312   Amusement Arcades

713120   Amusement Arcades

7132   Gambling Industries

71321   Casinos (except Casino Hotels)

713210   Casinos (except Casino Hotels)

71329   Other Gambling Industries

713290   Other Gambling Industries[US]

7139   Other Amusement and Recreation Industries

71391   Golf Courses and Country Clubs

713910   Golf Courses and Country Clubs

71392   Skiing Facilities

713920	Skiing Facilities
71393	Marinas
713930	Marinas
71394	Fitness and Recreational Sports Centers
713940	Fitness and Recreational Sports Centers[CAN]
71395	Bowling Centers
713950	Bowling Centers
71399	All Other Amusement and Recreation Industries
713990	All Other Amusement and Recreation Industries[CAN]

72 Accommodation and Food Services

721 Accommodation

7211 Traveler Accommodation

72111	Hotels (except Casino Hotels) and Motels
721110	Hotels (except Casino Hotels) and Motels[US]
72112	Casino Hotels
721120	Casino Hotels
72119	Other Traveler Accommodation
721191	Bed-and-Breakfast Inns[CAN]
721199	All Other Traveler Accommodation[US]

7212 RV (Recreational Vehicle) Parks and Recreational Camps

72121	RV (Recreational Vehicle) Parks and Recreational Camps
721211	RV (Recreational Vehicle) Parks and Campgrounds[CAN]
721214	Recreational and Vacation Camps (except Campgrounds)[US]

7213 Rooming and Boarding Houses

| 72131 | Rooming and Boarding Houses |
| 721310 | Rooming and Boarding Houses[CAN] |

722 Food Services and Drinking Places

7221 Full-Service Restaurants

| 72211 | Full-Service Restaurants |
| 722110 | Full-Service Restaurants[CAN] |

7222 Limited-Service Eating Places

72221	Limited-Service Eating Places
722211	Limited-Service Restaurants[US]
722212	Cafeterias[US]
722213	Snack and Nonalcoholic Beverage Bars[US]

7223   Special Food Services

72231	Food Service Contractors
722310	Food Service Contractors
72232	Caterers
722320	Caterers
72233	Mobile Food Services
722330	Mobile Food Services

7224   Drinking Places (Alcoholic Beverages)

72241	Drinking Places (Alcoholic Beverages)
722410	Drinking Places (Alcoholic Beverages)[CAN]

81   Other Services (except Public Administration)

811   Repair and Maintenance

8111   Automotive Repair and Maintenance

81111	Automotive Mechanical and Electrical Repair and Maintenance
811111	General Automotive Repair[CAN]
811112	Automotive Exhaust System Repair[CAN]
811113	Automotive Transmission Repair[US]
811118	Other Automotive Mechanical and Electrical Repair and Maintenance[US]
81112	Automotive Body, Paint, Interior, and Glass Repair
811121	Automotive Body, Paint, and Interior Repair and Maintenance[CAN]
811122	Automotive Glass Replacement Shops[CAN]
81119	Other Automotive Repair and Maintenance
811191	Automotive Oil Change and Lubrication Shops[US]
811192	Car Washes[CAN]
811198	All Other Automotive Repair and Maintenance[US]

8112   Electronic and Precision Equipment Repair and Maintenance

81121	Electronic and Precision Equipment Repair and Maintenance
811211	Consumer Electronics Repair and Maintenance[MEX]
811212	Computer and Office Machine Repair and Maintenance[US]
811213	Communication Equipment Repair and Maintenance[US]
811219	Other Electronic and Precision Equipment Repair and Maintenance[US]

8113 Commercial and Industrial Machinery and Equipment (except Automotive and Electronic) Repair and Maintenance

> 81131 Commercial and Industrial Machinery and Equipment (except Automotive and Electronic) Repair and Maintenance
>
> 811310 Commercial and Industrial Machinery and Equipment (except Automotive and Electronic) Repair and Maintenance[CAN]

8114 Personal and Household Goods Repair and Maintenance

> 81141 Home and Garden Equipment and Appliance Repair and Maintenance
>
> 811411 Home and Garden Equipment Repair and Maintenance[CAN]
>
> 811412 Appliance Repair and Maintenance[CAN]
>
> 81142 Reupholstery and Furniture Repair
>
> 811420 Reupholstery and Furniture Repair
>
> 81143 Footwear and Leather Goods Repair
>
> 811430 Footwear and Leather Goods Repair
>
> 81149 Other Personal and Household Goods Repair and Maintenance
>
> 811490 Other Personal and Household Goods Repair and Maintenance[CAN]

812 Personal and Laundry Services

8121 Personal Care Services[CAN]

> 81211 Hair, Nail, and Skin Care Services[CAN]
>
> 812111 Barber Shops[US]
>
> 812112 Beauty Salons[US]
>
> 812113 Nail Salons[US]
>
> 81219 Other Personal Care Services[CAN]
>
> 812191 Diet and Weight Reducing Centers[US]
>
> 812199 Other Personal Care Services[US]

8122 Death Care Services[CAN]

> 81221 Funeral Homes and Funeral Services[CAN]
>
> 812210 Funeral Homes and Funeral Services[CAN]
>
> 81222 Cemeteries and Crematories[CAN]
>
> 812220 Cemeteries and Crematories[CAN]

8123 Drycleaning and Laundry Services[CAN]

> 81231 Coin-Operated Laundries and Drycleaners[CAN]
>
> 812310 Coin-Operated Laundries and Drycleaners[CAN]
>
> 81232 Drycleaning and Laundry Services (except Coin-Operated)[CAN]

812320   Drycleaning and Laundry Services (except Coin-Operated)[CAN]
81233   Linen and Uniform Supply[CAN]
812331   Linen Supply[US]
812332   Industrial Launderers[US]

8129 Other Personal Services[CAN]

81291   Pet Care (except Veterinary) Services[CAN]
812910   Pet Care (except Veterinary) Services[CAN]
81292   Photofinishing[CAN]
812921   Photofinishing Laboratories (except One-Hour)[CAN]
812922   One-Hour Photofinishing[CAN]
81293   Parking Lots and Garages[CAN]
812930   Parking Lots and Garages[CAN]
81299   All Other Personal Services[CAN]
812990   All Other Personal Services[CAN]

813 Religious, Grantmaking, Civic, Professional, and Similar Organizations

8131 Religious Organizations[CAN]

81311   Religious Organizations[CAN]
813110   Religious Organizations[CAN]

8132 Grantmaking and Giving Services[CAN]

81321   Grantmaking and Giving Services[CAN]
813211   Grantmaking Foundations[US]
813212   Voluntary Health Organizations[US]
813219   Other Grantmaking and Giving Services[US]

8133 Social Advocacy Organizations[CAN]

81331   Social Advocacy Organizations[CAN]
813311   Human Rights Organizations[US]
813312   Environment, Conservation and Wildlife Organizations[US]
813319   Other Social Advocacy Organizations[US]

8134 Civic and Social Organizations[CAN]

81341   Civic and Social Organizations[CAN]
813410   Civic and Social Organizations[CAN]

8139 Business, Professional, Labor, Political, and Similar Organizations[CAN]

81391   Business Associations[CAN]
813910   Business Associations[CAN]
81392   Professional Organizations[CAN]
813920   Professional Organizations[CAN]

81393	Labor Unions and Similar Labor Organizations[CAN]
813930	Labor Unions and Similar Labor Organizations[CAN]
81394	Political Organizations[CAN]
813940	Political Organizations[CAN]
81399	Other Similar Organizations (except Business, Professional, Labor, and Political Organizations)[CAN]
813990	Other Similar Organizations (except Business, Professional, Labor, and Political Organizations)[CAN]

814 Private Households

8141 Private Households

| 81411 | Private Households |
| 814110 | Private Households |

92 Public Administration

921 Executive, Legislative, and Other General Government Support[US]

9211 Executive, Legislative, and Other General Government Support[US]

92111	Executive Offices[US]
921110	Executive Offices[US]
92112	Legislative Bodies[US]
921120	Legislative Bodies[US]
92113	Public Finance Activities[US]
921130	Public Finance Activities[US]
92114	Executive and Legislative Offices, Combined[US]
921140	Executive and Legislative Offices, Combined[US]
92115	American Indian and Alaska Native Tribal Governments[US]
921150	American Indian and Alaska Native Tribal Governments[US]
92119	Other General Government Support[US]
921190	Other General Government Support[US]

922 Justice, Public Order, and Safety Activities[US]

9221 Justice, Public Order, and Safety Activities[US]

92211	Courts[US]
922110	Courts[US]
92212	Police Protection[US]
922120	Police Protection[US]
92213	Legal Counsel and Prosecution[US]

922130	Legal Counsel and Prosecution[US]
92214	Correctional Institutions[US]
922140	Correctional Institutions[US]
92215	Parole Offices and Probation Offices[US]
922150	Parole Offices and Probation Offices[US]
92216	Fire Protection[US]
922160	Fire Protection[US]
92219	Other Justice, Public Order, and Safety Activities[US]
922190	Other Justice, Public Order, and Safety Activities[US]

923 Administration of Human Resource Programs[US]

9231 Administration of Human Resource Programs[US]

92311	Administration of Education Programs[US]
923110	Administration of Education Programs[US]
92312	Administration of Public Health Programs[US]
923120	Administration of Public Health Programs[US]
92313	Administration of Human Resource Programs (except Education, Public Health, and Veterans' Affairs Programs)[US]
923130	Administration of Human Resource Programs (except Education, Public Health, and Veterans' Affairs Programs)[US]
92314	Administration of Veterans' Affairs[US]
923140	Administration of Veterans' Affairs[US]

924 Administration of Environmental Quality Programs[US]

9241 Administration of Environmental Quality Programs[US]

92411	Administration of Air and Water Resource and Solid Waste Management Programs[US]
924110	Administration of Air and Water Resource and Solid Waste Management Programs[US]
92412	Administration of Conservation Programs[US]
924120	Administration of Conservation Programs[US]

925 Administration of Housing Programs, Urban Planning, and Community Development[US]

9251 Administration of Housing Programs, Urban Planning, and Community Development[US]

| 92511 | Administration of Housing Programs[US] |
| 925110 | Administration of Housing Programs[US] |

92512	Administration of Urban Planning and Community and Rural Development[US]
925120	Administration of Urban Planning and Community and Rural Development[US]

926 Administration of Economic Programs[US]

9261 Administration of Economic Programs[US]

92611	Administration of General Economic Programs[US]
926110	Administration of General Economic Programs[US]
92612	Regulation and Administration of Transportation Programs[US]
926120	Regulation and Administration of Transportation Programs[US]
92613	Regulation and Administration of Communications, Electric, Gas, and Other Utilities[US]
926130	Regulation and Administration of Communications, Electric, Gas, and Other Utilities[US]
92614	Regulation of Agricultural Marketing and Commodities[US]
926140	Regulation of Agricultural Marketing and Commodities[US]
92615	Regulation, Licensing, and Inspection of Miscellaneous Commercial Sectors[US]
926150	Regulation, Licensing, and Inspection of Misccellaneous Commercial Sectors[US]

927 Space Research and Technology[US]

9271 Space Research and Technology[US]

92711	Space Research and Technology[US]
927110	Space Research and Technology[US]

928 National Security and International Affairs[US]

9281 National Security and International Affairs[US]

92811	National Security[US]
928110	National Security[US]
92812	International Affairs[US]
928120	International Affairs[US]

Frequently Asked Questions About Economic Classifications

1. What is the purpose of an industry classification system?
   - An industry classification system facilitates the collection, tabulation, presentation, and analysis of data relating to establishments and ensures that data about the U.S. economy published by U.S. statistical agencies are uniform and comparable. NAICS ensures that such data are uniform and comparable among the North American countries.

2. What is an establishment?
   - An establishment is generally a single, physical location at which economic activity occurs (e.g., store, factory, farm, etc.). An enterprise, on the other hand, may consist of more than one location performing the same or different types of economic activities. Each establishment of that enterprise is assigned a NAICS code.

3. In which industry is my company classified?
   - NAICS is an establishment classification system, not a company classification system. To determine in which industry each establishment of your company is classified, you should first identify the primary activity of each establishment and then go to the alphabetic list of activities in the NAICS United States Manual. Find that activity in the alphabetic index, turn to the industry description of the specified code, read the definition of the industry as printed in the description, and determine if that description fits the activities of your establishment. Electronic references are available at http://www.census.gov/naics.

4. How are NAICS codes assigned?
   - NAICS codes are assigned to each establishment of an enterprise based on the primary activity of that establishment. When a company applies for an Employer Identification Number (EIN), information about the type of activity in which that business is engaged is requested in order to assign a NAICS code. In addition, statistical programs such as those conducted by the Census Bureau and the Bureau of Labor Statistics assign NAICS codes based on information reported to them.

5. How do I apply for a NAICS code?
   - As explained above, NAICS codes are assigned based on the primary activity of the business establishment. You may contact the appropriate agency assigning codes for your particular need (see 4. Above).

6. Have the Small Business Administration's size standards been updated to reflect the NAICS 2002 codes?
   - You should contact the Office of Size Standards of the Small Business Administration, 409 Third Street SW, Washington, DC 20416 for this information. They can be reached at 202-205-6618.

7. How do the NAICS codes affect the Environmental Protection Agency's regulations?
   - You should contact the Environmental Protection Agency at 202-260-3071 for answers to those questions.

8. When will NAICS codes be used in Federal Procurement regulations?
   • You should contact the U.S. General Services Administration at 202-205-6618.

Select U.S. Government Agencies Involved in Trade and Industry

Department of Agriculture

James L. Whitten Building
Independent Ave and 14th St SW
Washington, DC 20250

Phone: (202) 720-3631
http://www.usda.gov

Economic Research Service

1301 New York Ave
Washington, DC 20005-4788

Phone: (202) 219-0300
Fax: (202) 219-0146

National Agricultural Statistics Service

South Agriculture Building
Room 4117-S
Washington, DC 20250

Phone: (202) 720-2707
Fax: (202) 720-9013

Department of Commerce

Herbert C. Hoover Building
14th St and Pennsylvania Ave NW
Washington, DC 20230

Phone: (202) 482-2000
http://www.doc.gov

Bureau of Economic Analysis
1441 L St NW
Washington, DC 20230

Phone: (202) 606-9600
Fax: (202) 606-5311

Bureau of Census
Services Division
FOB #3, Room 2633
Suitland, MD 20746

Phone: (301) 457-2668
Fax: (301) 457-1343

Bureau of Export Administration
Herbert C. Hoover Building
Room 3989
17th St and Pennsylvania Ave NW
Washington, DC 20230

Phone: (202) 482-1455
Fax: (202) 482-2387

Economic Development Administration
Herbert C. Hoover Building
Room 7800
17th St and Pennsylvania Ave NW
Washington, DC 20230

Phone: (202) 482-5081
Fax: (202) 482-0995

International Trade Administration
Assistant Secretary for Trade Development
Office of Trade and Economic Analysis
14th St and Constitution Ave NW
Room 2825
Washington, DC 20230

Phone: (202) 482-5145
Fax: (202) 482-4614
http://www.ita.doc.gov

Minority Business Development Agency
Herbert C. Hoover Building
Room 5053
17th and Pennsylvania Ave NW
Washington, DC 20230

Phone: (202) 482-5061
Fax: (202) 501-4698

National Institute of Standards and Technology
Gaithersburg, MD 20899

Phone: (301) 975-2300

Patent and Trademark Office
2021 Jefferson Davis Highway
Arlington, VA 22202

Phone: (703) 305-8600
Fax: (703) 305-8664

Department of Energy

Administrator for Energy Information Administration
James Forrestal Building
1000 Independence Ave NW
Washington, DC 20585

Phone: (202) 586-4361
http://www.eia.doe.gov

Department of Labor

Francis Perkins Building
3rd St and Constitution Ave NW
Washington, DC 20210

Phone: (202) 219-5000
http://www.dol.gov

Bureau of Labor Statistics
Postal Square Building, Suite 4040
2 Massachusetts Ave NE
Washington, DC 20212

Phone: (202) 606-6623
Fax: (202) 606-6619
http:/www.bls.gov

Occupational Safety and Health Administration
Frances Perkins Building, Room S2315
3rd St and Constitution Ave NW
Washington, DC 20210

Phone: (202) 219-6091

Department of State

2201 C St NW
Washington, DC 20520

Phone: (202) 647-4000

Department of Transportation

400 7th St SW
Washington, DC 20590

Phone (202) 366-4000
http://www.dot.gov

Bureau of Transportation Statistics
400 7th St SW
Washington, DC 20590

Phone: (202) 366-3282
http://www.bts.gov

Department of Treasury

15th St and Pennsylvania Ave NW
Washington, DC 20220

Phone: (202) 622-2000
http://www.ustreas.gov

Internal Revenue Service
Internal Revenue Building
1111 Constitution Ave NW
Washington, DC 20224

Phone: (202) 566-5000
http://www.irs.ustreas.gov

Executive Office of the President

Office of Management and Budget
Old Executive Office Building (OEOB)
Washington, DC 20503

Phone: (202) 395-4840
http://www.whitehouse.gov/WH/EOP/OMB/html/ombhome.html

Independent Agencies

**Board of Governors of the Federal Reserve System
(Federal Reserve Board)**
20th and C Sts NW
Washington, DC 20551

Phone   (202) 452-3000
http://www.bog.frb.fed.us/

Environmental Protection Agency
401 M St SW
Washington, DC 20460

Phone: (202) 260-4700
http://www.epa.gov

General Services Administration
1800 F St NW
Washington, DC 20405

Phone   (202) 501-0800
http://www.gsa.gov

International Trade Commission
500 E. St SW
Washington, DC 20436

Phone: (202) 205-1819
http://www.usitc.gov

Small Business Administration

409 3rd St SW
Washington, DC 20416

Phone: (202) 205-6600
Fax: 205-7064
http://www.sba.gov

Part I

Titles and Descriptions of Industries

Sector 11—Agriculture, Forestry, Fishing and Hunting

The Sector as a Whole

The Agriculture, Forestry, Fishing and Hunting sector comprises establishments primarily engaged in growing crops, raising animals, harvesting timber, and harvesting fish and other animals from a farm, ranch, or their natural habitats.

The establishments in this sector are often described as farms, ranches, dairies, greenhouses, nurseries, orchards, or hatcheries. A farm may consist of a single tract of land or a number of separate tracts which may be held under different tenures. For example, one tract may be owned by the farm operator and another rented. It may be operated by the operator alone or with the assistance of members of the household or hired employees, or it may be operated by a partnership, corporation, or other type of organization. When a landowner has one or more tenants, renters, croppers, or managers, the land operated by each is considered a farm.

The sector distinguishes two basic activities: agricultural production and agricultural support activities. Agricultural production includes establishments performing the complete farm or ranch operation, such as farm owner-operators, tenant farm operators, and sharecroppers. Agricultural support activities include establishments that perform one or more activities associated with farm operation, such as soil preparation, planting, harvesting, and management, on a contract or fee basis.

Excluded from the Agriculture, Forestry, Hunting and Fishing sector are establishments primarily engaged in agricultural research and establishments primarily engaged in administering programs for regulating and conserving land, mineral, wildlife, and forest use. These establishments are classified in Industry 54171, Research and Development in the Physical, Engineering, and Life Sciences; and Industry 92412, Administration of Conservation Programs, respectively.

111 Crop Production

Industries in the Crop Production subsector grow crops mainly for food and fiber. The subsector comprises establishments, such as farms, orchards, groves, greenhouses, and nurseries, primarily engaged in growing crops, plants, vines, or trees and their seeds.

The industries in this subsector are grouped by similarity of production activity, including biological and physiological characteristics and economic requirements, the length of growing season, degree of crop rotation, extent of input specialization, labor requirements, and capital demands. The production process is typically completed when the raw product or commodity grown reaches the "farm gate" for market, that is, at the point of first sale or price determination.

US—United States industry only. CAN—United States and Canadian industries are comparable. MEX—United States and Mexican industries are comparable. Blank—Canadian, Mexican, and United States industries are comparable.

Establishments are classified to the crop production subsector when crop production (i.e., value of crops for market) accounts for one-half or more of the establishment's total agricultural production. Within the subsector, establishments are classified to a specific industry when a product or industry family of products (i.e., oilseed and grain farming, vegetable and melon farming, fruit and tree nut farming) account for one-half or more of the establishment's agricultural production. Establishments with one-half or more crop production with no one product or family of products of an industry accounting for one-half of the establishment's agricultural production are treated as general combination crop farming and are classified in Industry 11199, All Other Crop Farming.

Industries in the Crop Production subsector include establishments that own, operate, and manage and those that operate and manage. Those that manage only are classified in Subsector 115, Support Activities for Agriculture and Forestry.

1111 Oilseed and Grain Farming

This industry group comprises establishments primarily engaged in (1) growing oilseed and/or grain crops and/or (2) producing oilseed and grain seeds. These crops have an annual life cycle and are typically grown in open fields.

11111 Soybean Farming
See industry description for 111110 below.

111110 Soybean Farming

This industry comprises establishments primarily engaged in growing soybeans and/or producing soybean seeds.

Cross-References.

Establishments engaged in growing soybeans in combination with grain(s) with the soybeans or grain(s) not accounting for one-half of the establishment's agricultural production (value of crops for market) are classified in U.S. Industry 111191, Oilseed and Grain Combination Farming.

11112 Oilseed (except Soybean) Farming
See industry description for 111120 below.

111120 Oilseed (except Soybean) Farming^{CAN}

This industry comprises establishments primarily engaged in growing fibrous oilseed producing plants and/or producing oilseed seeds, such as sunflower, safflower, flax, rape, canola, and sesame.

US—United States industry only. CAN—United States and Canadian industries are comparable. MEX—United States and Mexican industries are comparable. Blank—Canadian, Mexican, and United States industries are comparable.

Cross-References. Establishments primarily engaged in—

- Growing soybeans—are classified in Industry 111110, Soybean Farming; and
- Growing oilseed(s) in combination with grain(s) with no one oilseed (or family of oilseeds) or grain(s) (or family of grains) accounting for one-half of the establishment's agricultural production (value of crops for market)— are classified in U.S. Industry 111191, Oilseed and Grain Combination Farming.

11113 Dry Pea and Bean Farming
See industry description for 111130 below.

111130 Dry Pea and Bean Farming[CAN]

This industry comprises establishments primarily engaged in growing dry peas, beans, and/or lentils.

Cross-References.

Establishments primarily engaged in growing fresh green beans and peas are classified in U.S. Industry 111219, Other Vegetable (except Potato) and Melon Farming.

11114 Wheat Farming
See industry description for 111140 below.

111140 Wheat Farming

This industry comprises establishments primarily engaged in growing wheat and/or producing wheat seeds.

Cross-References.

Establishments growing wheat in combination with oilseed(s) with the wheat or oilseed(s) not accounting for one-half of the establishment's agricultural production (value of crops for market) are classified in U.S. Industry 111191, Oilseed and Grain Combination Farming.

11115 Corn Farming
See industry description for 111150 below.

111150 Corn Farming[CAN]

This industry comprises establishments primarily engaged in growing corn (except sweet corn) and/or producing corn seeds.

Cross-References. Establishments primarily engaged in—

- Growing sweet corn—are classified in U.S. Industry 111219, Other Vegetable (except Potato) and Melon Farming; and

- Growing corn in combination with oilseed(s) with the corn or oilseed(s) not accounting for one-half of the establishment's production (value of crops for market)—are classified in U.S. Industry 111191, Oilseed and Grain Combination Farming.

11116 Rice Farming
See industry description for 111160 below.

111160 Rice Farming

This industry comprises establishments primarily engaged in growing rice (except wild rice) and/or producing rice seeds.

Cross-References. Establishments primarily engaged in—

- Growing wild rice—are classified in U.S. Industry 111199, All Other Grain Farming; and

- Engaged in growing rice in combination with oilseed(s) with the rice or oilseed(s) not accounting for one-half of the establishment's agricultural production (value of crops for market)—are classified in U.S. Industry 111191, Oilseed and Grain Combination Farming.

11119 Other Grain Farming

This industry comprises establishments primarily engaged in (1) growing grain(s) and/or producing grain seeds (except wheat, corn, and rice) or (2) growing a combination of grain(s) and oilseed(s) with no one grain (or family of grains) or oilseed (or family of oilseeds) accounting for one-half of the establishment's agriculture production (value of crops for market). Combination grain(s) and oilseed(s) establishments may produce oilseed(s) and grain(s) seeds and/or grow oilseed(s) and grain(s).

Illustrative Examples:

Barley farming	Rye farming
Milo farming	Sorghum farming
Oat farming	Wild rice farming
Oilseed and grain combination farming	

Cross-References. Establishments primarily engaged in—

- Growing wheat—are classified in U.S. Industry 11114, Wheat Farming;

- Growing corn (except sweet corn)—are classified in U.S. Industry 11115, Corn Farming;

- Growing sweet corn—are classified in U.S. Industry 11121, Vegetable and Melon Farming; and

- Growing rice (except wild rice)—are classified in U.S. Industry 11116, Rice Farming.

111191 Oilseed and Grain Combination Farming[US]

This U.S. industry comprises establishments engaged in growing a combination of oilseed(s) and grain(s) with no one oilseed (or family of oilseeds) or grain (or family of grains) accounting for one-half of the establishment's agricultural production (value of crops for market). These establishments may produce oilseed(s) and grain(s) seeds and/or grow oilseed(s) and grain(s).

Cross-References.

Establishments engaged in growing one grain (or family of grains) or oilseed (or family of oilseeds) accounting for one-half of the establishment's agriculture production (value of crops for market) are classified in Industry Group 1111, Oilseed and Grain Farming accordingly by the prominent grain(s) or oilseed(s) grown.

111199 All Other Grain Farming[US]

This U.S. industry comprises establishments primarily engaged in growing grains and/or producing grain(s) seeds (except wheat, corn, rice, and oilseed(s) and grain(s) combinations).

Illustrative Examples:

Barley farming	Sorghum farming
Oat farming	Wild Rice farming
Rye farming	

US—United States industry only. CAN—United States and Canadian industries are comparable. MEX—United States and Mexican industries are comparable. Blank—Canadian, Mexican, and United States industries are comparable.

Cross-References. Establishments primarily engaged in—

- Growing wheat—are classified in Industry 111140, Wheat Farming;
- Growing corn—are classified in Industry 111150, Corn Farming;
- Growing rice (except wild rice)—are classified in Industry 111160, Rice Farming;
- Growing sweet corn—are classified in U.S. Industry 111219, Other Vegetable (except Potato) and Melon Farming; and
- Growing a combination of grain(s) and oilseed(s) with no one grain (or family of grains) or oilseed (or family of oilseeds) accounting for one-half of the establishment's agricultural production (value of crops for market)—are classified in U.S. Industry 111191, Oilseed and Grain Combination Farming.

1112 Vegetable and Melon Farming

This industry group comprises establishments primarily engaged in growing root and tuber crops (except sugar beets and peanuts) or edible plants and/or producing root and tuber or edible plant seeds. The crops included in this group have an annual growth cycle and are grown in open fields. Climate and cultural practices limit producing areas but often permit the growing of a combination of crops in a year.

11121 Vegetable and Melon Farming

This industry comprises establishments primarily engaged in one or more of the following: (1) growing vegetable and/or melon crops; (2) producing vegetable and melon seeds; and (3) growing vegetable and/or melon bedding plants.

Cross-References. Establishments primarily engaged in—

- Growing sugar beets—are classified in Industry 11199, All Other Crop Farming;
- Growing vegetables and melons under glass or protective cover—are classified in Industry 11141, Food Crops Grown Under Cover;
- Growing dry peas and beans—are classified in Industry 11113, Dry Pea and Bean Farming;
- Growing corn (except sweet corn)—are classified in Industry 11115, Corn Farming;
- Canning, pickling, and/or drying (artificially) vegetables—are classified in Industry 31142, Fruit and Vegetable Canning, Pickling and Drying; and

- Growing fruit on trees and other fruit-bearing plants (except melons)—are classified in Industry Group 1113, Fruit and Tree Nut Farming.

111211 Potato Farming^{CAN}

This U.S. industry comprises establishments primarily engaged in growing potatoes and/or producing seed potatoes (except sweet potatoes).

Cross-References. Establishments primarily engaged in—

- Growing sweet potatoes, cassava, and yams—are classified in U.S. Industry 111219, Other Vegetable (except Potato) and Melon Farming; and

- Canning or drying potatoes—are classified in Industry 31142, Fruit and Vegetable Canning, Pickling and Drying.

111219 Other Vegetable (except Potato) and Melon Farming^{CAN}

This U.S. industry comprises establishments primarily engaged in one or more of the following: (1) growing melons and/or vegetables (except potatoes; dry peas; dry beans; field, silage, or seed corn; and sugar beets); (2) producing vegetable and/or melon seeds; and (3) growing vegetable and/or melon bedding plants.

Illustrative Examples:

Carrot farming	Squash farming
Green bean farming	Sweet potato farming
Melon farming (e.g., cantaloupe, casaba, honeydew, watermelon)	Tomato farming
	Vegetable (except potato) and melon farming
Pepper farming (e.g., bell, chili, green, red, sweet peppers)	Watermelon farming

Cross-References. Establishments primarily engaged in—

- Growing potatoes—are classified in U.S. Industry 111211, Potato Farming;

- Growing sugar beets—are classified in U.S. Industry 111991, Sugar Beet Farming;

- Growing vegetables and melons under glass or protective cover—are classified in U.S. Industry 111419, Other Food Crops Grown Under Cover;

- Growing dry peas and beans—are classified in Industry 111130, Dry Pea and Bean Farming;

- Growing corn (except sweet corn)—are classified in Industry 111150, Corn Farming;

- Canning, pickling, and/or drying (artificially) vegetables—are classified in Industry 31142, Fruit and Vegetable Canning, Pickling and Drying; and

- Growing fruit on trees and other fruit-bearing plants (except melons)—are classified in Industry Group 1113, Fruit and Tree Nut Farming.

1113 Fruit and Tree Nut Farming

This industry group comprises establishments primarily engaged in growing fruit and/or tree nut crops. The crops included in this industry group are generally not grown from seeds and have a perennial life cycle.

11131 Orange Groves
See industry description for 111310 below.

111310 Orange Groves

This industry comprises establishments primarily engaged in growing oranges.

11132 Citrus (except Orange) Groves
See industry description for 111320 below.

111320 Citrus (except Orange) Groves[CAN]

This industry comprises establishments primarily engaged in growing citrus fruits (except oranges).

Illustrative Examples:

Citrus groves (except oranges)	Mandarin groves
Grapefruit groves	Tangelo groves
Lemon groves	Tangerine groves

Cross-References.

Establishments primarily engaged in growing oranges are classified in Industry 111310, Orange Groves.

11133 Noncitrus Fruit and Tree Nut Farming

This industry comprises establishments primarily engaged in one or more of the following: (1) growing noncitrus fruits (e.g., apples, grapes, berries, peaches);

(2) growing tree nuts (e.g., pecans, almonds, pistachios); or (3) growing a combination of fruit(s) and tree nut(s) with no one fruit (or family of fruit) or family of tree nuts accounting for one-half of the establishment's agriculture production (value of crops for market).

Cross-References. Establishments primarily engaged in—

- Harvesting berries or nuts from native and noncultivated plants—are classified in Industry 11321, Forest Nurseries and Gathering of Forest Products; and
- Canning and/or drying (artificially) fruit—are classified in Industry 31142, Fruit and Vegetable Canning, Pickling and Drying.

111331 Apple Orchards^{US}

This U.S. industry comprises establishments primarily engaged in growing apples.

Cross-References.

Establishments engaged in growing apples in combination with tree nut(s) with the apples or family of tree nuts not accounting for one-half of the establishment's agriculture production (i.e., value of crops for market) are classified in U.S. Industry 111336, Fruit and Tree Nut Combination Farming.

111332 Grape Vineyards^{US}

This U.S. industry comprises establishments primarily engaged in growing grapes and/or growing grapes to sun dry into raisins.

Cross-References. Establishments primarily engaged in—

- Drying grapes artificially—are classified in U.S. Industry 311423, Dried and Dehydrated Food Manufacturing; and
- Growing grapes in combination with tree nut(s) with the grapes or family of tree nuts not accounting for one-half of the establishment's agriculture production (i.e., value of crops for market)—are classified in U.S. Industry 111336, Fruit and Tree Nut Combination Farming.

111333 Strawberry Farming^{US}

This U.S. industry comprises establishments primarily engaged in growing strawberries.

Cross-References.

Establishments engaged in growing strawberries in combination with tree nut(s) with the strawberries or family of tree nuts not accounting for one-half of the establishment's agriculture production (i.e., value of crops for market) are classified in U.S. Industry 111336, Fruit and Tree Nut Combination Farming.

111334 Berry (except Strawberry) Farming[US]

This U.S. industry comprises establishments primarily engaged in growing berries.

Illustrative Examples:

Berry (except strawberries) farming	Cranberry farming
Blackberry farming	Currant farming
Blueberry farming	Raspberry farming

Cross-References. Establishments primarily engaged in—

- Growing strawberries—are classified in U.S. Industry 111333, Strawberry Farming;

- Harvesting berries from native and noncultivated bushes or vines—are classified in Industry 113210, Forest Nurseries and Gathering of Forest Products; and

- Growing berries in combination with tree nut(s) with the berries or family of tree nuts not accounting for one-half of the establishment's agriculture production (i.e., value of crops for market)—are classified in U.S. Industry 111336, Fruit and Tree Nut Combination Farming.

111335 Tree Nut Farming[US]

This U.S. industry comprises establishments primarily engaged in growing tree nuts.

Illustrative Examples:

Almond farming	Pistachio farming
Filbert farming	Tree nut farming
Macadamia farming	Walnut farming
Pecan farming	

Cross-References. Establishments primarily engaged in—

- Growing coconut and coffee—are classified in U.S. Industry 111339, Other Noncitrus Fruit Farming; and

---

US—United States industry only. CAN—United States and Canadian industries are comparable. MEX—United States and Mexican industries are comparable. Blank—Canadian, Mexican, and United States industries are comparable.

- Growing tree nut(s) in combination with fruit(s) with no one fruit (or family of fruit or of tree nuts) accounting for one-half of the establishment's agriculture production (i.e., value of crops for market)—are classified in U.S. Industry 111336, Fruit and Tree Nut Combination Farming.

111336 Fruit and Tree Nut Combination Farming[US]

This U.S. industry comprises establishments primarily engaged in growing a combination of fruit(s) and tree nut(s) with no one fruit (or family of fruit) or family of tree nuts accounting for one-half of the establishment's agriculture production (i.e., value of crops for market).

Cross-References.

Establishments engaged in growing fruit(s) or the family of tree nut(s) accounting for one-half of the establishment's agriculture production (i.e., value of crops for market) are classified in Industry Group 1113, Fruit and Tree Nut Farming accordingly by the prominent fruit(s) or tree nut(s) grown.

111339 Other Noncitrus Fruit Farming[US]

This U.S. industry comprises establishments primarily engaged in growing noncitrus fruits (except apples, grapes, berries, and fruit(s) and tree nut(s) combinations).

Illustrative Examples:

Apricot farming	Fig farming
Banana farming	Noncitrus fruit farming
Cherry farming	Peach farming
Coffee farming	Pineapple farming
Date farming	Prune farming

Cross-References. Establishments primarily engaged in—

- Growing apples—are classified in U.S. Industry 111331, Apple Orchards;

- Growing grapes including sun drying of grapes into raisins—are classified in U.S. Industry 111332, Grape Vineyards;

- Growing strawberries—are classified in U.S. Industry 111333, Strawberry Farming;

- Growing berries (except strawberries)—are classified in U.S. Industry 111334, Berry (except Strawberry) Farming;

US—United States industry only. CAN—United States and Canadian industries are comparable. MEX—United States and Mexican industries are comparable. Blank—Canadian, Mexican, and United States industries are comparable.

- Drying fruit artificially—are classified in U.S. Industry 311423, Dried and Dehydrated Food Manufacturing; and

- Growing noncitrus fruit(s) in combination with tree nut(s) with no one fruit (or family of fruits) or family of tree nuts accounting for one-half of the establishment's agriculture production (i.e., value of crops for market)—are classified in U.S. Industry 111336, Fruit and Tree Nut Combination Farming.

1114 Greenhouse, Nursery, and Floriculture Production

This industry group comprises establishments primarily engaged in growing crops of any kind under cover and/or growing nursery stock and flowers. "Under cover" is generally defined as greenhouses, cold frames, cloth houses, and lath houses. The crops grown are removed at various stages of maturity and have annual and perennial life cycles. The nursery stock includes short rotation woody crops that have growth cycles of 10 years or less.

11141 Food Crops Grown Under Cover

This industry comprises establishments primarily engaged in growing food crops (e.g., fruits, melons, tomatoes) under glass or protective cover.

Cross-References.

Establishments primarily engaged in growing vegetable and melon bedding plants are classified in Industry 11121, Vegetable and Melon Farming.

111411 Mushroom Production[CAN]

This U.S. industry comprises establishments primarily engaged in growing mushrooms under cover in mines underground, or in other controlled environments.

111419 Other Food Crops Grown Under Cover[CAN]

This U.S. industry comprises establishments primarily engaged in growing food crops (except mushrooms) under glass or protective cover.

Illustrative Examples:

Alfalfa sprout farming, grown under cover	Hydroponic crop farming
	Melon farming, grown under cover
Fruit farming, grown under cover	Vegetable farming, grown under cover

---

US—United States industry only. CAN—United States and Canadian industries are comparable. MEX—United States and Mexican industries are comparable. Blank—Canadian, Mexican, and United States industries are comparable.

Cross-References.

Establishments primarily engaged in growing mushrooms under cover are classified in U.S. Industry 111411, Mushroom Production.

11142 Nursery and Floriculture Production

This industry comprises establishments primarily engaged in (1) growing nursery and floriculture products (e.g., nursery stock, shrubbery, cut flowers, flower seeds, foliage plants) under cover or in open fields and/or (2) growing short rotation woody trees with a growing and harvesting cycle of 10 years or less for pulp or tree stock (e.g., cut Christmas trees, cottonwoods).

Cross-References. Establishments primarily engaged in—

- Growing vegetable and melon bedding plants—are classified in Industry 11121, Vegetable and Melon Farming;
- Operating timber tracts (i.e., growing cycle greater than 10 years)—are classified in Industry 11311, Timber Tract Operations; and
- Retailing nursery, tree stock, and floriculture products primarily purchased from others—are classified in Industry 44422, Nursery, Garden Center, and Farm Supply Stores.

111421 Nursery and Tree Production^{CAN}

This U.S. industry comprises establishments primarily engaged in (1) growing nursery products, nursery stock, shrubbery, bulbs, fruit stock, sod, and so forth, under cover or in open fields and/or (2) growing short rotation woody trees with a growth and harvest cycle of 10 years or less for pulp or tree stock.

Cross-References. Establishments primarily engaged in—

- Growing vegetable and melon bedding plants—are classified in Industry 11121, Vegetable and Melon Farming;
- Operating timber tracts (i.e., growing cycle greater than 10 years)—are classified in Industry 113110, Timber Tract Operations; and
- Retailing nursery, tree stock, and floriculture products primarily purchased from others—are classified in Industry 444220, Nursery, Garden Center, and Farm Supply Stores.

111422 Floriculture Production^{CAN}

This U.S. industry comprises establishments primarily engaged in growing and/or producing floriculture products (e.g., cut flowers and roses, cut cultivated

US—United States industry only. CAN—United States and Canadian industries are comparable. MEX—United States and Mexican industries are comparable. Blank—Canadian, Mexican, and United States industries are comparable.

greens, potted flowering and foliage plants, and flower seeds) under cover and in open fields.

Cross-References.

Establishments primarily engaged in retailing floriculture products primarily purchased from others are classified in Industry 444220, Nursery, Garden Center, and Farm Supply Stores.

1119 Other Crop Farming

This industry group comprises establishments primarily engaged in (1) growing crops (except oilseed and/or grain; vegetable and/or melon; fruit and tree nut; and greenhouse, nursery, and/or floriculture products). These establishments grow crops, such as tobacco, cotton, sugarcane, hay, sugar beets, peanuts, agave, herbs and spices, and hay and grass seeds; or (2) growing a combination of crops (except a combination of oilseed(s) and grain(s) and a combination of fruit(s) and tree nut(s)).

11191 Tobacco Farming
See industry description for 111910 below.

111910 Tobacco Farming

This industry comprises establishments primarily engaged in growing tobacco.

11192 Cotton Farming
See industry description for 111920 below.

111920 Cotton Farming

This industry comprises establishments primarily engaged in growing cotton.

Cross-References.

Establishments primarily engaged in ginning cotton are classified in U.S. Industry 115111, Cotton Ginning.

11193 Sugarcane Farming
See industry description for 111930 below.

US—United States industry only. CAN—United States and Canadian industries are comparable. MEX—United States and Mexican industries are comparable. Blank—Canadian, Mexican, and United States industries are comparable.

111930 Sugarcane Farming

This industry comprises establishments primarily engaged in growing sugarcane.

11194 Hay Farming
See industry description for 111940 below.

111940 Hay Farming^{CAN}

This industry comprises establishments primarily engaged in growing hay, alfalfa, clover, and/or mixed hay.

Cross-References. Establishments primarily engaged in—

- Growing grain hay—are classified in Industry Group 1111, Oilseed and Grain Farming; and
- Growing grass and hay seeds—are classified in U.S. Industry 111998, All Other Miscellaneous Crop Farming.

11199 All Other Crop Farming

This industry comprises establishments primarily engaged in (1) growing crops (except oilseeds and/or grains; vegetables and/or melons; fruits and/or tree nuts; greenhouse, nursery and/or floriculture products; tobacco; cotton; sugarcane; or hay) or (2) growing a combination of crops (except a combination of oilseed(s) and grain(s); and a combination of fruit(s) and tree nut(s)) with no one crop or family of crops accounting for one-half of the establishment's agricultural production (i.e., value of crops for market).

Illustrative Examples:

Agave farming	Hay seed farming
Algae farming	Maple sap gathering
General combination crop farming	Peanut farming
(except oilseed and grain; vegetables	Spice farming
and melons; fruit and nut combinations)	Sugar beet farming
Grass seed farming	Tea farming

Cross-References. Establishments primarily engaged in—

- Growing oilseeds and/or wheat, corn, rice, or other grains—are classified in Industry Group 1111, Oilseed and Grain Farming;
- Growing vegetables and/or melons—are classified in Industry Group 1112, Vegetable and Melon Farming;

US—United States industry only. CAN—United States and Canadian industries are comparable. MEX—United States and Mexican industries are comparable. Blank—Canadian, Mexican, and United States industries are comparable.

- Growing fruits and/or tree nuts—are classified in Industry Group 1113, Fruit and Tree Nut Farming;
- Growing greenhouse, nursery, and/or floriculture products—are classified in Industry Group 1114, Greenhouse, Nursery, and Floriculture Production;
- Growing tobacco—are classified in Industry 11191, Tobacco Farming;
- Growing cotton—are classified in Industry 11192, Cotton Farming;
- Growing sugarcane—are classified in Industry 11193, Sugarcane Farming; and
- Growing hay—are classified in Industry 11194, Hay Farming.

111991 Sugar Beet Farming[US]

This U.S. industry comprises establishments primarily engaged in growing sugar beets.

Cross-References.

Establishments primarily engaged in growing beets (except sugar beets) are classified in U.S. Industry 111219, Other Vegetable (except Potato) and Melon Farming.

111992 Peanut Farming[MEX]

This U.S. industry comprises establishments primarily engaged in growing peanuts.

111998 All Other Miscellaneous Crop Farming[US]

This U.S. industry comprises establishments primarily engaged in one of the following: (1) growing crops (except oilseeds and/or grains; vegetables and/or melons; fruits and/or tree nuts; greenhouse, nursery and/or floriculture products; tobacco; cotton; sugarcane; hay; sugar beets; or peanuts); (2) growing a combination of crops (except a combination of oilseed(s) and grain(s); and a combination of fruit(s) and tree nut(s)) with no one crop or family of crop(s) accounting for one-half of the establishment's agricultural production (i.e., value of crops for market); or (3) gathering tea or maple sap.

Illustrative Examples:

Agave farming	Grass seed farming
Algae farming	Hay seed farming

US—United States industry only. CAN—United States and Canadian industries are comparable. MEX—United States and Mexican industries are comparable. Blank—Canadian, Mexican, and United States industries are comparable.

General combination crop farming
(except oilseed and grain; vegetables
and melons; fruit and tree nut
combinations)

Hop farming
Mint farming
Spice farming

Cross-References. Establishment primarily engaged in—

- Growing oilseeds and/or wheat, corn, rice, or other grains—are classified in Industry Group 1111, Oilseed and Grain Farming;
- Growing vegetables and/or melons—are classified in Industry Group 1112, Vegetable and Melon Farming;
- Growing fruits and/or tree nuts—are classified in Industry Group 1113, Fruit and Tree Nut Farming;
- Growing greenhouse, nursery and/or floriculture products—are classified in Industry Group 1114, Greenhouse, Nursery, and Floriculture Production;
- Growing tobacco—are classified in Industry 111910, Tobacco Farming;
- Growing cotton—are classified in Industry 111920, Cotton Farming;
- Growing sugarcane—are classified in Industry 111930, Sugarcane Farming;
- Growing hay—are classified in Industry 111940, Hay Farming;
- Growing sugar beets—-are classified in U.S. Industry 111991, Sugar Beet Farming; and
- Growing peanuts—are classified in U.S. Industry 111992, Peanut Farming.

112 Animal Production

Industries in the Animal Production subsector raise or fatten animals for the sale of animals or animal products. The subsector comprises establishments, such as ranches, farms, and feedlots primarily engaged in keeping, grazing, breeding, or feeding animals. These animals are kept for the products they produce or for eventual sale. The animals are generally raised in various environments, from total confinement or captivity to feeding on an open range pasture.

The industries in this subsector are grouped by important factors, such as suitable grazing or pasture land, specialized buildings, type of equipment, and the amount and types of labor required. Establishments are classified to the Animal Production subsector when animal production (i.e., value of animals for market) accounts for one-half or more of the establishment's total agricultural production. Establishments with one-half or more animal production with no one animal product or family of animal products of an industry accounting for one-half of the establishment's agricultural production are treated as combination animal farming classified to Industry 11299, All Other Animal Production.

1121 Cattle Ranching and Farming

This industry group comprises establishments primarily engaged in raising cattle, milking dairy cattle, or feeding cattle for fattening.

11211 Beef Cattle Ranching and Farming, including Feedlots

This industry comprises establishments primarily engaged in raising cattle (including cattle for dairy herd replacements), or feeding cattle for fattening.

Cross-References. Establishments primarily engaged in—

- Milking dairy cattle—are classified in Industry 11212, Dairy Cattle and Milk Production; and
- Operating stockyards for transportation and not buying, selling, or auctioning livestock—are classified in Industry 48899, Other Support Activities for Transportation.

112111 Beef Cattle Ranching and Farming[US]

This U.S. industry comprises establishments primarily engaged in raising cattle (including cattle for dairy herd replacements).

Cross-References.

Establishments primarily engaged in milking dairy cattle are classified in Industry 112120, Dairy Cattle and Milk Production.

112112 Cattle Feedlots[US]

This U.S. industry comprises establishments primarily engaged in feeding cattle for fattening.

Cross-References.

Establishments primarily engaged in operating stockyards for transportation and not buying, selling, or auctioning livestock are classified in U.S. Industry 488999, All Other Support Activities for Transportation.

11212 Dairy Cattle and Milk Production
See industry description for 112120 below.

112120 Dairy Cattle and Milk Production

This industry comprises establishments primarily engaged in milking dairy cattle.

Cross-References. Establishment primarily engaged in—
- Raising dairy herd replacements—are classified in U.S. Industry 112111, Beef Cattle Ranching and Farming; and
- Milking goats—are classified in Industry 112420, Goat Farming.

11213 Dual-Purpose Cattle Ranching and Farming^{MEX}
See industry description for 112130 below.

112130 Dual-Purpose Cattle Ranching and Farming^{MEX}

This industry comprises establishments primarily engaged in raising cattle for both milking and meat production.

Cross-References. Establishments primarily engaged in—
- Milking dairy cattle—are classified in Industry 11212, Dairy Cattle and Milk Production;
- Raising cattle or feeding cattle for fattening—are classified in Industry 11211, Beef Cattle Ranching and Farming, including Feedlots; and
- Operating stockyards for transportation and not buying, selling, or auctioning livestock—are classified in U.S. Industry 488999, All Other Support Activities for Transportation.

1122 Hog and Pig Farming

11221 Hog and Pig Farming
See industry description for 112210 below.

112210 Hog and Pig Farming^{CAN}

This industry comprises establishments primarily engaged in raising hogs and pigs. These establishments may include farming activities, such as breeding, farrowing, and the raising of weanling pigs, feeder pigs, or market size hogs.

Cross-References.

Establishments primarily engaged in operating stockyards for transportation and not buying, selling, or auctioning livestock are classified in U.S. Industry 488999, All Other Support Activities for Transportation.

US—United States industry only. CAN—United States and Canadian industries are comparable. MEX—United States and Mexican industries are comparable. Blank—Canadian, Mexican, and United States industries are comparable.

1123 Poultry and Egg Production

This industry group comprises establishments primarily engaged in breeding, hatching, and raising poultry for meat or egg production.

11231 Chicken Egg Production
See industry description for 112310 below.

112310 Chicken Egg Production^{CAN}

This industry comprises establishments primarily engaged in raising chickens for egg production. The eggs produced may be for use as table eggs or hatching eggs.

Cross-References.

Establishments primarily engaged in raising chickens for the production of meat are classified in Industry 112320, Broilers and Other Meat Type Chicken Production.

11232 Broilers and Other Meat Type Chicken Production
See industry description for 112320 below.

112320 Broilers and Other Meat Type Chicken Production

This industry comprises establishments primarily engaged in raising broilers, fryers, roasters, and other meat type chickens.

Cross-References.

Establishments primarily engaged in raising chickens for egg production are classified in Industry 112310, Chicken Egg Production.

11233 Turkey Production
See industry description for 112330 below.

112330 Turkey Production

This industry comprises establishments primarily engaged in raising turkeys for meat or egg production.

US—United States industry only. CAN—United States and Canadian industries are comparable. MEX—United States and Mexican industries are comparable. Blank—Canadian, Mexican, and United States industries are comparable.

11234 Poultry Hatcheries
See industry description for 112340 below.

112340 Poultry Hatcheries

This industry comprises establishments primarily engaged in hatching poultry of any kind.

11239 Other Poultry Production
See industry description for 112390 below.

112390 Other Poultry Production[MEX]

This industry comprises establishments primarily engaged in raising poultry (except chickens for meat or egg production and turkeys).

Illustrative Examples:

Duck production
Emu production
Geese production

Ostrich production
Pheasant production
Quail production

Cross-References. Establishments primarily engaged in—

- Raising aviary birds, such as parakeets, canaries, and love birds,—are classified in Industry 112990, All Other Animal Production;
- Raising chickens for egg production—are classified in Industry 112310, Chicken Egg Production;
- Raising broilers and other meat type chickens—are classified in Industry 112320, Broilers and Other Meat Type Chicken Production;
- Raising turkeys—are classified in Industry 112330, Turkey Production; and
- Raising swans, peacocks, flamingos or other "adornment birds"—are classified in Industry 112990, All Other Animal Production.

1124 Sheep and Goat Farming

This industry group comprises establishments primarily engaged in raising sheep, lambs, and goats, or feeding lambs for fattening.

11241 Sheep Farming
See industry description for 112410 below.

112410 Sheep Farming^{CAN}

This industry comprises establishments primarily engaged in raising sheep and lambs, or feeding lambs for fattening. The sheep or lambs may be raised for sale or wool production.

Cross-References.

Establishments primarily engaged in operating stockyards for transportation and not buying, selling, or auctioning livestock are classified in U.S. Industry 488999, All Other Support Activities for Transportation.

11242 Goat Farming
See industry description for 112420 below.

112420 Goat Farming

This industry comprises establishments primarily engaged in raising goats.

1125 Animal Aquaculture

11251 Animal Aquaculture

This industry comprises establishments primarily engaged in the farm raising of finfish, shellfish, or any other kind of animal aquaculture. These establishments use some form of intervention in the rearing process to enhance production, such as holding in captivity, regular stocking, feeding, and protecting from predators.

Cross-References.

Establishments primarily engaged in the catching or taking of fish and other aquatic animals from their natural habitat are classified in Industry 11411, Fishing.

112511 Finfish Farming and Fish Hatcheries^{US}

This U.S. industry comprises establishments primarily engaged in (1) farm raising finfish (e.g., catfish, trout, goldfish, tropical fish, minnows) and/or (2) hatching fish of any kind.

Cross-References.

Establishments primarily engaged in the catching or taking of finfish from their natural habitat are classified in U.S. Industry 114111, Finfish Fishing.

US—United States industry only. CAN—United States and Canadian industries are comparable. MEX—United States and Mexican industries are comparable. Blank—Canadian, Mexican, and United States industries are comparable.

112512 Shellfish Farming[US]

This U.S. industry comprises establishments primarily engaged in farm raising shellfish (e.g., crayfish, shrimp, oysters, clams, mollusks).

Cross-References.

Establishments primarily engaged in the catching or taking of shellfish from their natural habitat are classified in U.S. Industry 114112, Shellfish Fishing.

112519 Other Animal Aquaculture[US]

This U.S. industry comprises establishments primarily engaged in farm raising animal aquaculture (except finfish and shellfish). Alligator, frog, or turtle production is included in this industry.

Cross-References. Establishments primarily engaged in—

- Miscellaneous fishing activities, such as catching or taking of terrapins, turtles, and frogs in their natural habitat,—are classified in U.S. Industry 114119, Other Marine Fishing;
- Farm raising finfish—are classified in U.S. Industry 112511, Finfish Farming and Fish Hatcheries; and
- Farm raising shellfish—are classified in U.S. Industry 112512, Shellfish Farming.

1129 Other Animal Production

This industry group comprises establishments primarily engaged in raising animals and insects (except cattle, hogs and pigs, poultry, sheep and goats, animal aquaculture) for sale or product production. These establishments are primarily engaged in raising one of the following: bees, horses and other equines, rabbits and other fur-bearing animals, and so forth, and producing products, such as honey and other bee products. Establishments primarily engaged in raising a combination of animals with no one animal or family of animals accounting for one-half of the establishment's agricultural production (i.e., value of animals for market) are included in this industry group.

11291 Apiculture

See industry description for 112910 below.

112910   Apiculture

This industry comprises establishments primarily engaged in raising bees. These establishments may collect and gather honey; and/or sell queen bees, packages of bees, royal jelly, bees' wax, propolis, venom, and/or other bee products.

11292   Horses and Other Equine Production
See industry description for 112920 below.

112920   Horses and Other Equine Production

This industry comprises establishments primarily engaged in raising horses, mules, donkeys, and other equines.

Cross-References.

- Establishments primarily engaged in equine boarding are classified in Industry 115210, Support Activities for Animal Production; and
- Equine owners entering horses in racing or other spectator sporting events are classified in U.S. Industry 711219, Other Spectator Sports.

11293   Fur-Bearing Animal and Rabbit Production
See industry description for 112930 below.

112930   Fur-Bearing Animal and Rabbit Production

This industry comprises establishments primarily engaged in raising fur-bearing animals including rabbits. These animals may be raised for sale or for their pelt production.

Cross-References.

Establishments primarily engaged in the trapping or hunting of wild fur-bearing animals are classified in Industry 114210, Hunting and Trapping.

11299   All Other Animal Production
See industry description for 112990 below.

112990   All Other Animal Production[MEX]

This industry comprises establishments primarily engaged in: (1) raising animals (except cattle, hogs and pigs, poultry, sheep and goats, animal aquaculture, apiculture, horses and other equines; and fur-bearing animals including rabbits); or (2) raising a combination of animals, with no one animal or family of animals accounting for one-half of the establishment's agricultural production (i.e., value of animals for market) are included in this industry.

Illustrative Examples:

Bird production (e.g., canaries, parakeets, parrots)
Combination animal farming (except dairy, poultry)
Companion animals production (e.g., cats, dogs)
Deer production
Laboratory animal production (e.g., rats, mice, guinea pigs)
Llama production
Worm production

Cross-References. Establishments primarily engaged in—

- Raising cattle, dairy cattle or feeding cattle for fattening—are classified in Industry Group 1121, Cattle Ranching and Farming;

- Raising hogs and pigs—are classified in Industry Group 1122, Hog and Pig Farming;

- Raising poultry and raising poultry for egg production—are classified in Industry Group 1123, Poultry and Egg Production;

- Raising sheep and goats—are classified in Industry Group 1124, Sheep and Goat Farming;

- Raising animal aquaculture—are classified in Industry Group 1125, Animal Aquaculture;

- Raising bees—are classified in Industry 112910, Apiculture;

- Raising horses and other equines—are classified in Industry 112920, Horses and Other Equine Production; and

- Raising fur-bearing animals including rabbits—are classified in Industry 112930, Fur-Bearing Animal and Rabbit Production.

113 Forestry and Logging

Industries in the Forestry and Logging subsector grow and harvest timber on a long production cycle (i.e., of 10 years or more). Long production cycles use different production processes than short production cycles, which require more horticultural interventions prior to harvest, resulting in processes more similar to those found in the Crop Production subsector. Consequently, Christmas tree production and other production involving production cycles of less than 10 years, are classified in the Crop Production subsector.

US—United States industry only. CAN—United States and Canadian industries are comparable. MEX—United States and Mexican industries are comparable. Blank—Canadian, Mexican, and United States industries are comparable.

Industries in this subsector specialize in different stages of the production cycle. Reforestation requires production of seedlings in specialized nurseries. Timber production requires natural forest or suitable areas of land that are available for a long duration. The maturation time for timber depends upon the species of tree, the climatic conditions of the region, and the intended purpose of the timber. The harvesting of timber (except when done on an extremely small scale) requires specialized machinery unique to the industry. Establishments gathering forest products, such as gums, barks, balsam needles, rhizomes, fibers, Spanish moss, and ginseng and truffles, are also included in this subsector.

1131 Timber Tract Operations

11311 Timber Tract Operations
See industry description for 113110 below.

113110 Timber Tract Operations

This industry comprises establishments primarily engaged in the operation of timber tracts for the purpose of selling standing timber.

Cross-References. Establishments primarily engaged in—

- Acting as lessors of land with trees as real estate property—are classified in Industry 53119, Lessors of Other Real Estate Property;

- Growing short rotation woody trees (i.e., growing and harvesting cycle is 10 years or less)—are classified in U.S. Industry 111421, Nursery and Tree Production; and

- Cutting timber—are classified in Industry 113310, Logging.

1132 Forest Nurseries and Gathering of Forest Products

11321 Forest Nurseries and Gathering of Forest Products
See industry description for 113210 below.

113210 Forest Nurseries and Gathering of Forest Products[CAN]

This industry comprises establishments primarily engaged in (1) growing trees for reforestation and/or (2) gathering forest products, such as gums, barks, balsam needles, rhizomes, fibers, Spanish moss, ginseng, and truffles.

US—United States industry only. CAN—United States and Canadian industries are comparable. MEX—United States and Mexican industries are comparable. Blank—Canadian, Mexican, and United States industries are comparable.

Cross-References. Establishments primarily engaged in—

- Gathering tea and maple sap—are classified in U.S. Industry 111998, All Other Miscellaneous Crop Farming; and
- Processing maple syrup into other products—are classified in Industry 31199, All Other Food Manufacturing.

1133 Logging

11331 Logging
See industry description for 113310 below.

113310 Logging[MEX]

This industry comprises establishments primarily engaged in one or more of the following: (1) cutting timber; (2) cutting and transporting timber; and (3) producing wood chips in the field.

Cross-References.

Establishments primarily engaged in trucking timber are classified in Industry 484220, Specialized Freight (except Used Goods) Trucking, Local.

114 Fishing, Hunting and Trapping

Industries in the Fishing, Hunting, and Trapping subsector harvest fish and other wild animals from their natural habitats and are dependent upon a continued supply of the natural resource. The harvesting of fish is the predominant economic activity of this subsector and it usually requires specialized vessels that, by the nature of their size, configuration and equipment, are not suitable for any other type of production, such as transportation.

Hunting and trapping activities utilize a wide variety of production processes and are classified in the same subsector as fishing because the availability of resources and the constraints imposed, such as conservation requirements and proper habitat maintenance, are similar.

1141 Fishing

11411 Fishing

This industry comprises establishments primarily engaged in the commercial catching or taking of finfish, shellfish, or miscellaneous marine products from a natural habitat, such as the catching of bluefish, eels, salmon, tuna, clams, crabs, lobsters, mussels, oysters, shrimp, frogs, sea urchins, and turtles.

Cross-References. Establishments primarily engaged in—

- Farm raising finfish, shellfish or other marine animals—are classified in Industry 11251, Animal Aquaculture; and
- Gathering and processing (known as "floating factory ships") seafood into canned seafood products—are classified in Industry 31171, Seafood Product Preparation and Packaging.

114111 Finfish Fishing[US]

This U.S. industry comprises establishments primarily engaged in the commercial catching or taking of finfish (e.g., bluefish, salmon, trout, tuna) from their natural habitat.

Cross-References. Establishments primarily engaged in—

- Farm raising finfish—are classified in U.S. Industry 112511, Finfish Farming and Fish Hatcheries; and
- Gathering and processing (known as "floating factory ships") seafood into canned seafood products—are classified in U.S. Industry 311711, Seafood Canning.

114112 Shellfish Fishing[US]

This U.S. industry comprises establishments primarily engaged in the commercial catching or taking of shellfish (e.g., clams, crabs, lobsters, mussels, oysters, sea urchins, shrimp) from their natural habitat.

Cross-References.

Establishments primarily engaged in farm raising shellfish are classified in U.S. Industry 112512, Shellfish Farming.

114119 Other Marine Fishing[US]

This U.S. industry comprises establishments primarily engaged in the commercial catching or taking of marine animals (except finfish and shellfish).

Cross-References. Establishments primarily engaged in—

- Raising animal aquaculture (except finfish and shellfish)—are classified in U.S. Industry 112519, Other Animal Aquaculture;

US—United States industry only. CAN—United States and Canadian industries are comparable. MEX—United States and Mexican industries are comparable. Blank—Canadian, Mexican, and United States industries are comparable.

- The commercial catching or taking of finfish from their natural habitat—are classified in U.S. Industry 114111, Finfish Fishing; and

- The commercial catching or taking of shellfish from their natural habitat—are classified in U.S. Industry 114112, Shellfish Fishing.

1142 Hunting and Trapping

11421 Hunting and Trapping

See industry description for 114210 below.

114210 Hunting and Trapping

This industry comprises establishments primarily engaged in one or more of the following: (1) commercial hunting and trapping; (2) operating commercial game preserves, such as game retreats; and (3) operating hunting preserves.

Cross-References. Establishments primarily engaged in—

- Operating nature preserves—are classified in Industry 712190, Nature Parks and Other Similar Institutions; and

- Farm raising rabbits and other fur-bearing animals—are classified in Industry 112930, Fur-Bearing Animal and Rabbit Production.

115 Support Activities for Agriculture and Forestry

Industries in the Support Activities for Agriculture and Forestry subsector provide support services that are an essential part of agricultural and forestry production. These support activities may be performed by the agriculture or forestry producing establishment or conducted independently as an alternative source of inputs required for the production process for a given crop, animal, or forestry industry. Establishments that primarily perform these activities independent of the agriculture or forestry producing establishment are in this subsector.

1151 Support Activities for Crop Production

11511 Support Activities for Crop Production

This industry comprises establishments primarily engaged in providing support activities for growing crops.

US—United States industry only. CAN—United States and Canadian industries are comparable. MEX—United States and Mexican industries are comparable. Blank—Canadian, Mexican, and United States industries are comparable.

Illustrative Examples:

Aerial dusting or spraying (i.e., using
 specialized or dedicated aircraft)
Cotton ginning
Cultivating services

Farm management services
Planting crops
Vineyard cultivation services

Cross-References. Establishments primarily engaged in—

- Performing crop production that are generally known as farms, orchards, groves, or vineyards (including sharecroppers and tenant farms)—are classified in the appropriate crop industry within Subsector 111, Crop Production;
- Providing support activities for forestry—are classified in Industry 11531, Support Activities for Forestry;
- Landscaping and horticultural services, such as lawn and maintenance care and ornamental shrub and tree services,—are classified in Industry 56173, Landscaping Services;
- Land clearing, land leveling, and earth moving for terracing, ponds, and irrigation—are classified in Industry 23891, Site Preparation Contractors;
- Artificially drying and dehydrating fruits and vegetables—are classified in Industry 31142, Fruit and Vegetable Canning, Pickling and Drying;
- Stemming and redrying tobacco—are classified in Industry 31221, Tobacco Stemming and Redrying;
- Providing water for irrigation—are classified in Industry 22131, Water Supply and Irrigation Systems; and
- Buying farm products, such as fruits or vegetables, for resale to other wholesalers or retailers, and preparing them for market or further processing—are classified in Industry 42448, Fresh Fruit and Vegetable Merchant Wholesalers.

115111 Cotton Ginning[US]

This U.S. industry comprises establishments primarily engaged in ginning cotton.

115112 Soil Preparation, Planting, and Cultivating[US]

This U.S. industry comprises establishments primarily engaged in performing a soil preparation activity or crop production service, such as plowing, fertilizing, seed bed preparation, planting, cultivating, and crop protecting services.

US—United States industry only. CAN—United States and Canadian industries are comparable. MEX—United States and Mexican industries are comparable. Blank—Canadian, Mexican, and United States industries are comparable.

Cross-References. Establishments primarily engaged in—

- Land clearing, land leveling, and earth moving for terracing, ponds, and irrigation—are classified in Industry 238910, Site Preparation Contractors; and

- Providing water for irrigation—are classified in Industry 221310, Water Supply and Irrigation Systems.

115113 Crop Harvesting, Primarily by Machine[US]

This U.S. industry comprises establishments primarily engaged in mechanical harvesting, picking, and combining of crops, and related activities. The machinery used is provided by the servicing establishment.

Cross-References. Establishments primarily engaged in—

- Providing personnel for manual harvesting—are classified in U.S. Industry 115115, Farm Labor Contractors and Crew Leaders; and

- Providing farm management services (i.e., a contract or fee basis) and arranging or contracting crop mechanical or manual harvesting operations for the farm(s) it manages—are classified in U.S. Industry 115116, Farm Management Services.

115114 Postharvest Crop Activities (except Cotton Ginning)[US]

This U.S. industry comprises establishments primarily engaged in performing services on crops, subsequent to their harvest, with the intent of preparing them for market or further processing. These establishments provide postharvest activities, such as crop cleaning, sun drying, shelling, fumigating, curing, sorting, grading, packing, and cooling.

Cross-References. Establishments primarily engaged in—

- Ginning cotton—are classified in U.S. Industry 115111, Cotton Ginning;

- Artificially drying and dehydrating fruits and vegetables—are classified in U.S. Industry 311423, Dried and Dehydrated Food Manufacturing;

- Stemming and redrying tobacco—are classified in Industry 312210, Tobacco Stemming and Redrying;

- Buying farm products for resale to other wholesalers or retailers and preparing them for market or further processing—are classified in Industry 424480, Fresh Fruit and Vegetable Merchant Wholesalers; and

---

US—United States industry only. CAN—United States and Canadian industries are comparable. MEX—United States and Mexican industries are comparable. Blank—Canadian, Mexican, and United States industries are comparable.

- Providing farm management services (i.e., a contract or fee basis) and arranging or contracting postharvesting crop activities for the farm(s) it manages—are classified in U.S. Industry 115116, Farm Management Services.

115115 Farm Labor Contractors and Crew Leaders^{US}

This U.S. industry comprises establishments primarily engaged in supplying labor for agricultural production or harvesting.

Cross-References. Establishments primarily engaged in—

- Providing machine harvesting—are classified in U.S. Industry 115113, Crop Harvesting, Primarily by Machine; and
- Providing farm management services (i.e., a contract or fee basis) and arranging or contracting farm labor for the farm(s) it manages—are classified in U.S. Industry 115116, Farm Management Services.

115116 Farm Management Services^{US}

This U.S. industry comprises establishments primarily engaged in providing farm management services on a contract or fee basis usually to citrus groves, orchards, or vineyards. These establishments always provide management and may arrange or contract for the partial or the complete operations of the farm establishment(s) it manages. Operational activities may include cultivating, harvesting, and/or other specialized agricultural support activities.

Cross-References.

Establishments primarily engaged in crop production that are generally known as farms, orchards, groves, or vineyards (including share croppers and tenant farms), are classified in the appropriate crop industry within Subsector 111, Crop Production.

1152 Support Activities for Animal Production

11521 Support Activities for Animal Production
See industry description for 115210 below.

115210 Support Activities for Animal Production

This industry comprises establishments primarily engaged in performing support activities related to raising livestock (e.g., cattle, goats, hogs, horses, poultry, sheep). These establishments may perform one or more of the following: (1) breeding services for animals, including companion animals (e.g., cats, dogs, pet birds); (2) pedigree record services; (3) boarding horses; (4) dairy herd improvement activities; (5) livestock spraying; and (6) sheep dipping and shearing.

1153 Support Activities for Forestry

11531 Support Activities for Forestry
See industry description for 115310 below.

115310 Support Activities for Forestry

This industry comprises establishments primarily engaged in performing particular support activities related to timber production, wood technology, forestry economics and marketing, and forest protection. These establishments may provide support activities for forestry, such as estimating timber, forest firefighting, forest pest control, and consulting on wood attributes and reforestation.

Cross-References.

Establishments primarily engaged in the public administration and conservation of forest lands are classified in Industry 924120, Administration of Conservation Programs.

Sector 21—Mining

The Sector as a Whole

The Mining sector comprises establishments that extract naturally occurring mineral solids, such as coal and ores; liquid minerals, such as crude petroleum; and gases, such as natural gas. The term mining is used in the broad sense to include quarrying, well operations, beneficiating (e.g., crushing, screening, washing, and flotation), and other preparation customarily performed at the mine site, or as a part of mining activity.

The Mining sector distinguishes two basic activities: mine operation and mining support activities. Mine operation includes establishments operating mines, quarries, or oil and gas wells on their own account or for others on a contract or fee basis. Mining support activities include establishments that perform exploration (except geophysical surveying) and/or other mining services on a contract or fee basis (except mine site preparation and construction of oil/gas pipelines).

Establishments in the Mining sector are grouped and classified according to the natural resource mined or to be mined. Industries include establishments that develop the mine site, extract the natural resources, and/or those that beneficiate (i.e., prepare) the mineral mined. Beneficiation is the process whereby the extracted material is reduced to particles that can be separated into mineral and waste, the former suitable for further processing or direct use. The operations that take place in beneficiation are primarily mechanical, such as grinding, washing, magnetic separation, and centrifugal separation. In contrast, manufacturing operations primarily use chemical and electrochemical processes, such as electrolysis and distillation. However, some treatments, such as heat treatments, take place in both the beneficiation and the manufacturing (i.e., smelting/refining) stages. The range of preparation activities varies by mineral and the purity of any given ore deposit. While some minerals, such as petroleum and natural gas, require little or no preparation, others are washed and screened, while yet others, such as gold and silver, can be transformed into bullion before leaving the mine site.

Mining, beneficiating, and manufacturing activities often occur in a single location. Separate receipts will be collected for these activities whenever possible. When receipts cannot be broken out between mining and manufacturing, establishments that mine or quarry nonmetallic minerals, beneficiate the nonmetallic minerals into more finished manufactured products are classified based on the primary activity of the establishment. A mine that manufactures a small amount of finished products will be classified in Sector 21, Mining. An establishment that mines whose primary output is a more finished manufactured product will be classified in Sector 31-33, Manufacturing.

US—United States industry only. CAN—United States and Canadian industries are comparable. MEX—United States and Mexican industries are comparable. Blank—Canadian, Mexican, and United States industries are comparable.

211 Oil and Gas Extraction

Industries in the Oil and Gas Extraction subsector operate and/or develop oil and gas field properties. Such activities may include exploration for crude petroleum and natural gas; drilling, completing, and equipping wells; operating separators, emulsion breakers, desilting equipment, and field gathering lines for crude petroleum and natural gas; and all other activities in the preparation of oil and gas up to the point of shipment from the producing property. This subsector includes the production of crude petroleum, the mining and extraction of oil from oil shale and oil sands, and the production of natural gas, sulfur recovery from natural gas, and recovery of hydrocarbon liquids.

Establishments in this subsector include those that operate oil and gas wells on their own account or for others on a contract or fee basis. Establishments primarily engaged in providing support services, on a fee or contract basis, required for the drilling or operation of oil and gas wells (except geophysical surveying and mapping, mine site preparation, and construction of oil/gas pipelines) are classified in Subsector 213, Support Activities for Mining.

2111 Oil and Gas Extraction

21111 Oil and Gas Extraction

This industry comprises establishments primarily engaged in operating and/or developing oil and gas field properties and establishments primarily engaged in recovering liquid hydrocarbons from oil and gas field gases. Such activities may include exploration for crude petroleum and natural gas; drilling, completing, and equipping wells; operation of separators, emulsion breakers, desilting equipment, and field gathering lines for crude petroleum and natural gas; and all other activities in the preparation of oil and gas up to the point of shipment from the producing property. This industry includes the production of crude petroleum, the mining and extraction of oil from oil shale and oil sands, the production of natural gas, sulfur recovery from natural gas, and the recovery of hydrocarbon liquids from oil and gas field gases. Establishments in this industry operate oil and gas wells on their own account or for others on a contract or fee basis.

Cross-References. Establishments primarily engaged in—

- Performing oil field services for operators on a contract or fee basis—are classified in Industry 21311, Support Activities for Mining;
- Manufacturing acyclic and cyclic aromatic hydrocarbons from refined petroleum or liquid hydrocarbons—are classified in Industry 32511, Petrochemical Manufacturing;

- Refining crude petroleum into refined petroleum and liquid hydrocarbons—are classified in Industry 32411, Petroleum Refineries; and

- Recovering helium from natural gas—are classified in Industry 32512, Industrial Gas Manufacturing.

211111 Crude Petroleum and Natural Gas Extraction[US]

This U.S. industry comprises establishments primarily engaged in (1) the exploration, development and/or the production of petroleum or natural gas from wells in which the hydrocarbons will initially flow or can be produced using normal pumping techniques or (2) the production of crude petroleum from surface shales or tar sands or from reservoirs in which the hydrocarbons are semisolids. Establishments in this industry operate oil and gas wells on their own account or for others on a contract or fee basis.

Cross-References. Establishments primarily engaged in—

- Performing oil field services for operators on a contract or fee basis—are classified in Industry 21311, Support Activities for Mining;

- Refining crude petroleum into refined petroleum and liquid hydrocarbons—are classified in Industry 324110, Petroleum Refineries; and

- Recovering helium from natural gas—are classified in Industry 325120, Industrial Gas Manufacturing.

211112 Natural Gas Liquid Extraction[US]

This U.S. industry comprises establishments primarily engaged in the recovery of liquid hydrocarbons from oil and gas field gases. Establishments primarily engaged in sulfur recovery from natural gas are included in this industry.

Cross-References. Establishments primarily engaged in—

- Manufacturing acyclic and cyclic aromatic hydrocarbons from refined petroleum or converting refined petroleum into liquid hydrocarbons (petrochemicals) and/or recovering liquid hydrocarbons—are classified in Industry 325110, Petrochemical Manufacturing;

- Refining crude petroleum into refined petroleum and liquid hydrocarbons—are classified in Industry 324110, Petroleum Refineries; and

- Recovering helium from natural gas—are classified in Industry 325120, Industrial Gas Manufacturing.

US—United States industry only. CAN—United States and Canadian industries are comparable. MEX—United States and Mexican industries are comparable. Blank—Canadian, Mexican, and United States industries are comparable.

212 Mining (except Oil and Gas)

Industries in the Mining (except Oil and Gas) subsector primarily engage in mining, mine site development, and beneficiating (i.e., preparing) metallic minerals and nonmetallic minerals, including coal. The term "mining" is used in the broad sense to include ore extraction, quarrying, and beneficiating (e.g., crushing, screening, washing, sizing, concentrating, and flotation), customarily done at the mine site.

Beneficiation is the process whereby the extracted material is reduced to particles which can be separated into mineral and waste, the former suitable for further processing or direct use. The operations that take place in beneficiation are primarily mechanical, such as grinding, washing, magnetic separation, centrifugal separation, and so on. In contrast, manufacturing operations primarily use chemical and electrochemical processes, such as electrolysis, distillation, and so on. However some treatments, such as heat treatments, take place in both stages: the beneficiation and the manufacturing (i.e., smelting/refining) stages. The range of preparation activities varies by mineral and the purity of any given ore deposit. While some minerals, such as petroleum and natural gas, require little or no preparation, others are washed and screened, while yet others, such as gold and silver, can be transformed into bullion before leaving the mine site.

Establishments in the Mining (except Oil and Gas) subsector include those that have complete responsibility for operating mines and quarries (except oil and gas wells) and those that operate mines and quarries (except oil and gas wells) for others on a contract or fee basis. Establishments primarily engaged in providing support services, on a contract or fee basis, required for the mining and quarrying of minerals are classified in Subsector 213, Support Activities for Mining.

2121 Coal Mining

21211 Coal Mining

This industry comprises establishments primarily engaged in one or more of the following: (1) mining bituminous coal, anthracite, and lignite by underground mining, auger mining, strip mining, culm bank mining, and other surface mining; (2) developing coal mine sites; and (3) beneficiating (i.e., preparing) coal (e.g., cleaning, washing, screening, and sizing coal).

Cross-References. Establishments primarily engaged in—

   • Manufacturing code oven products in coke oven establishments—are classified in Industry 32419, Other Petroleum and Coal Products Manufacturing; and

---

- Manufacturing coal products in steel mills—are classified in Industry 33111, Iron and Steel Mills and Ferroalloy Manufacturing.

212111 Bituminous Coal and Lignite Surface Mining[US]

This U.S. industry comprises establishments primarily engaged in one or more of the following: (1) surface mining of bituminous coal and lignite; (2) developing bituminous coal and lignite surface mine sites; (3) surface mining and beneficiating (e.g., cleaning. washing, screening, and sizing coal) of bituminous coal; or (4) beneficiating (e.g., cleaning, washing, screening, and sizing coal), but not mining, bituminous coal.

Cross-References. Establishments primarily engaged in—

- Manufacturing coke oven products in coke oven establishments—are classified in U.S. Industry 324199, All Other Petroleum and Coal Products Manufacturing;
- Underground mining of bituminous coal—are classified in U.S. Industry 212112, Bituminous Coal Underground Mining; and
- Mining and/or beneficiating anthracite coal—are classified in U.S. Industry 212113, Anthracite Mining.

212112 Bituminous Coal Underground Mining[US]

This U.S. industry comprises establishments primarily engaged in one or more of the following: (1) underground mining of bituminous coal; (2) developing bituminous coal underground mine sites; and (3) underground mining and beneficiating of bituminous coal (e.g., cleaning, washing, screening, and sizing coal).

Cross-References. Establishments primarily engaged in—

- Manufacturing coke oven products in coke oven establishments—are classified in U.S. Industry 324199, All Other Petroleum and Coal Products Manufacturing;
- Surface mining and/or beneficiating of bituminous coal or lignite—are classified in U.S. Industry 212111, Bituminous Coal and Lignite Surface Mining; and
- Mining and/or beneficiating anthracite coal—are classified in U.S. Industry 212113, Anthracite Mining.

212113 Anthracite Mining[US]

This U.S. industry comprises establishments primarily engaged in one or more of the following: (1) mining anthracite coal; (2) developing anthracite coal mine

---

sites; and (3) beneficiating anthracite coal (e.g., cleaning, washing, screening, and sizing coal).

Cross-References. Establishments primarily engaged in—

- Manufacturing coke oven products in coke oven establishments—are classified in U.S. Industry 324199, All Other Petroleum and Coal Products Manufacturing;
- Surface mining and/or beneficiating bituminous coal or lignite—are classified in U.S. Industry 212111, Bituminous Coal and Lignite Surface Mining; and
- Underground mining of bituminous coal—are classified in U.S. Industry 212112, Bituminous Coal Underground Mining.

2122 Metal Ore Mining

This industry group comprises establishments primarily engaged in developing mine sites or mining metallic minerals, and establishments primarily engaged in ore dressing and beneficiating (i.e., preparing) operations, such as crushing, grinding, washing, drying, sintering, concentrating, calcining, and leaching. Beneficiating may be performed at mills operated in conjunction with the mines served or at mills, such as custom mills, operated separately.

21221 Iron Ore Mining
See industry description for 212210 below.

212210 Iron Ore Mining

This industry comprises establishments primarily engaged in (1) developing mine sites, mining, and/or beneficiating (i.e., preparing) iron ores and manganiferous ores valued chiefly for their iron content and/or (2) producing sinter iron ore (except iron ore produced in iron and steel mills) and other iron ore agglomerates.

Cross-References.

Establishments primarily engaged in manufacturing pig iron ore are classified in U.S. Industry 331111, Iron and Steel Mills.

21222 Gold Ore and Silver Ore Mining

This industry comprises establishments primarily engaged in developing the mine site, mining, and/or beneficiating (i.e., preparing) ores valued chiefly for their gold and or silver content. Establishments primarily engaged in the transformation of the gold and silver into bullion or dore bar in combination with mining activities are included in this industry.

Cross-References.

Establishments primarily engaged in manufacturing gold or silver bullion or dore bar without mining are classified in Industry 33141, Nonferrous Metal (except Aluminum) Smelting and Refining.

212221 Gold Ore Mining[MEX]

This U.S. industry comprises establishments primarily engaged in developing the mine site, mining, and/or beneficiating (i.e., preparing) ores valued chiefly for their gold content. Establishments primarily engaged in transformation of the gold into bullion or dore bar in combination with mining activities are included in this industry.

Cross-References.

Establishments primarily engaged in manufacturing gold bullion or dore bar without mining are classified in U.S. Industry 331419, Primary Smelting and Refining of Nonferrous Metal (except Copper and Aluminum).

212222 Silver Ore Mining[MEX]

This U.S. industry comprises establishments primarily engaged in developing the mine site, mining, and/or beneficiating (i.e., preparing) ores valued chiefly for their silver content. Establishments primarily engaged in transformation of the silver into bullion or dore bar in combination with mining activities are included in this industry.

Cross-References.

Establishments primarily engaged in manufacturing silver bullion or dore bar without mining are classified in U.S. Industry 331419, Primary Smelting and Refining of Nonferrous Metal (except Copper and Aluminum).

21223 Copper, Nickel, Lead, and Zinc Mining

This industry comprises establishments primarily engaged in developing the mine site, mining, and/or beneficiating (i.e., preparing) ores valued chiefly for their copper, nickel, lead, or zinc content. Beneficiating includes the transformation of ores into concentrates.

US—United States industry only. CAN—United States and Canadian industries are comparable. MEX—United States and Mexican industries are comparable. Blank—Canadian, Mexican, and United States industries are comparable.

Cross-References. Establishments primarily engaged in—

- Refining copper concentrates—are classified in Industry 33141, Nonferrous Metal (except Aluminum) Smelting and Refining; and

- Developing the mine site, mining, and/or beneficiating iron and manganiferous ores valued for their iron content—are classified in Industry 21221, Iron Ore Mining.

212231 Lead Ore and Zinc Ore Mining^CAN

This U.S. industry comprises establishments primarily engaged in developing the mine site, mining, and/or beneficiating (i.e., preparing) lead ores, zinc ores, or lead-zinc ores.

212234 Copper Ore and Nickel Ore Mining^US

This U.S. industry comprises establishments primarily engaged in: (1) developing the mine site, mining, and/or beneficiating (i.e, preparing) copper and/or nickel ores; and (2) recovering copper concentrates by the precipitation, leaching, or electrowinning of copper ore.

Cross-References.

Establishments primarily engaged in refining copper concentrates are classified in U.S. Industry 331411, Primary Smelting and Refining of Copper.

21229 Other Metal Ore Mining

This industry comprises establishments primarily engaged in developing the mine site, mining, and/or beneficiating (i.e., preparing) metal ores (except iron and manganiferous ores valued for their iron content, gold ore, silver ore, copper, nickel, lead, and zinc ore).

Illustrative Examples:

Antimony ores mining and/or beneficiating	Tantalum ores mining and/or beneficiating
Columbite ores mining and/or beneficiating	Tungsten ores mining and/or beneficiating
Ilmenite ores mining and/or beneficiating	Uranium-radium-vanadium ores mining and/or beneficiating
Molybdenum ores mining and/or beneficiating	

Cross-References. Establishments primarily engaged in—

- Developing the mine site, mining, and/or beneficiating iron and manganiferous ores valued chiefly for their iron content—are classified in Industry 21221, Iron Ore Mining;

- Developing the mine site, mining, and/or beneficiating ores valued chiefly for their gold or silver content—are classified in Industry 21222, Gold Ore and Silver Ore Mining;

- Developing the mine site, mining, and/or beneficiating ores valued chiefly for their copper, nickel, lead, or zinc content—are classified in Industry 21223, Copper, Nickel, Lead, and Zinc Mining; and

- Enriching uranium—are classified in Industry 32518, Other Basic Inorganic Chemical Manufacturing.

212291 Uranium-Radium-Vanadium Ore Mining[CAN]

This U.S. industry comprises establishments primarily engaged in developing the mine site, mining, and/or beneficiating (i.e., preparing) uranium-radium-vanadium ores.

Cross-References.

Establishments primarily engaged in enriching uranium are classified in U.S. Industry 325188, All Other Basic Inorganic Chemical Manufacturing.

212299 All Other Metal Ore Mining[CAN]

This U.S. industry comprises establishments primarily engaged in developing the mine site, mining, and/or beneficiating (i.e., preparing) metal ores (except iron and manganiferous ores valued for their iron content, gold ore, silver ore, copper, nickel, lead, zinc, and uranium-radium-vanadium ore).

Illustrative Examples:

Antimony ores mining and/or
  beneficiating
Columbite ores mining and/or
  beneficiating
Ilmenite ores mining and/or beneficiating
Molybdenum ores mining and/or
  beneficiating

Rare-earth metal ores mining and/or
  beneficiating
Tantalum ores mining and/or
  beneficiating
Tungsten ores mining and/or
  beneficiating

Cross-References. Establishments primarily engaged in—

- Developing the mine site, mining, and/or beneficiating iron and manganiferous ores valued for their iron content—are classified in Industry 212210, Iron Ore Mining;

US—United States industry only. CAN—United States and Canadian industries are comparable. MEX—United States and Mexican industries are comparable. Blank—Canadian, Mexican, and United States industries are comparable.

- Developing the mine site, mining, and/or beneficiating ores valued chiefly for their gold or silver content—are classified in Industry 21222, Gold Ore and Silver Ore Mining;

- Developing the mine site, mining, and/or beneficiating ores valued chiefly for their copper, nickel, lead, or zinc content—are classified in Industry 21223, Copper, Nickel, Lead, and Zinc Mining; and

- Developing the mine site, mining, and/or beneficiating uranium-radium-vanadium ores—are classified in U.S. Industry 212291, Uranium-Radium-Vanadium Ore Mining.

2123 Nonmetallic Mineral Mining and Quarrying

This industry group comprises establishments primarily engaged in developing mine sites, or in mining or quarrying nonmetallic minerals (except fuels). Also included are certain well and brine operations, and preparation plants primarily engaged in beneficiating (e.g., crushing, grinding, washing, and concentrating) nonmetallic minerals.

Beneficiation is the process whereby the extracted material is reduced to particles which can be separated into mineral and waste, the former suitable for further processing or direct use. The operations that take place in beneficiation are primarily mechanical, such as grinding, washing, magnetic separation, and centrifugal separation. In contrast, manufacturing operations primarily use chemical and electrochemical processes, such as electrolysis and distillation. However, some treatments, such as heat treatments, take place in both the beneficiation and the manufacturing (i.e., smelting/refining) stages. The range of preparation activities varies by mineral and the purity of any given ore deposit. While some minerals, such as petroleum and natural gas, require little or no preparation, others are washed and screened, while yet others, such as gold and silver, can be transformed into bullion before leaving the mine site.

21231 Stone Mining and Quarrying

This industry comprises (1) establishments primarily engaged in developing the mine site, mining or quarrying dimension stone (i.e., rough blocks and/or slabs of stone), or mining and quarrying crushed and broken stone and/or (2) preparation plants primarily engaged in beneficiating stone (e.g., crushing, grinding, washing, screening, pulverizing, and sizing).

Cross-References. Establishments primarily engaged in—

- Producing lime—are classified in Industry 32741, Lime Manufacturing; and

---

- Quarrying and dressing dimension stone—are classified Industry 32799, All Other Nonmetallic Mineral Product Manufacturing.

212311 Dimension Stone Mining and Quarrying[US]

This U.S. industry comprises establishments primarily engaged in developing the mine site and/or mining or quarrying dimension stone (i.e., rough blocks and/ or slabs of stone).

Cross-References.

Establishments primarily engaged in dressing dimension stone and manufacturing stone products are classified in U.S. Industry 327991, Cut Stone and Stone Product Manufacturing.

212312 Crushed and Broken Limestone Mining and Quarrying[US]

This U.S. industry comprises (1) establishments primarily engaged in developing the mine site, mining or quarrying crushed and broken limestone (including related rocks, such as dolomite, cement rock, marl, travertine, and calcareous tufa); and (2) preparation plants primarily engaged in beneficiating limestone (e.g., grinding or pulverizing).

Cross-References. Establishments primarily engaged in—

- Producing lime—are classified in Industry 327410, Lime Manufacturing; and
- Mining or quarrying bituminous limestone—are classified U.S. Industry 212319, Other Crushed and Broken Stone Mining and Quarrying.

212313 Crushed and Broken Granite Mining and Quarrying[US]

This U.S. industry comprises: (1) establishments primarily engaged in developing the mine site, and/or mining or quarrying crushed and broken granite (including related rocks, such as gneiss, syenite, and diorite); and (2) preparation plants primarily engaged in beneficiating granite (e.g., grinding or pulverizing).

212319 Other Crushed and Broken Stone Mining and Quarrying[US]

This U.S. industry comprises: (1) establishments primarily engaged in developing the mine site and/or mining or quarrying crushed and broken stone (except limestone and granite); (2) preparation plants primarily engaged in beneficiating

---

US—United States industry only. CAN—United States and Canadian industries are comparable. MEX—United States and Mexican industries are comparable. Blank—Canadian, Mexican, and United States industries are comparable.

(e.g., grinding and pulverizing) stone (except limestone and granite); and (3) establishments primarily engaged in mining or quarrying bituminous limestone and bituminous sandstone.

Illustrative Examples:

Bituminous limestone mining and/or
  beneficiating
Bituminous sandstone mining and/or
  beneficiating

Marble crushed and broken stone mining
  and/or beneficiating
Sandstone crushed and broken stone
  mining and/or beneficiating

Cross-References. Establishments primarily engaged in—

- Mining or quarrying crushed and broken limestone—are classified in U.S. Industry 212312, Crushed and Broken Limestone Mining and Quarrying; and

- Mining or quarrying crushed and broken granite—are classified in U.S. Industry 212313, Crushed and Broken Granite Mining and Quarrying.

21232 Sand, Gravel, Clay, and Ceramic and Refractory Minerals Mining and Quarrying

This industry comprises (1) establishments primarily engaged in developing the mine site and/or mining, quarrying, dredging for sand and gravel, or mining clay, (e.g., china clay, paper clay and slip clay) and (2) preparation plants primarily engaged in beneficiating (e.g., washing, screening, and grinding) sand and gravel, clay, and ceramic and refractory minerals.

Cross-References. Establishments primarily engaged in—

- Calcining, dead burning, or otherwise processing (i.e., beyond basic preparation) clay or refractory minerals—are classified in Industry 32799, All Other Nonmetallic Mineral Product Manufacturing;

- Shaping, molding, baking, burning, or hardening nonclay ceramics, clay and nonclay refractories, and structural clay products—are classified in Industry 32712, Clay Building Material and Refractories Manufacturing; and

- Shaping, molding, glazing, and firing pottery, ceramics, and plumbing fixtures—are classified in Industry 32711, Pottery, Ceramics and Plumbing Fixture Manufacturing.

212321 Construction Sand and Gravel Mining[MEX]

This U.S. industry comprises establishments primarily engaged in one or more of the following: (1) operating commercial grade (i.e., construction) sand and

---

US—United States industry only. CAN—United States and Canadian industries are comparable. MEX—United States and Mexican industries are comparable. Blank—Canadian, Mexican, and United States industries are comparable.

gravel pits; (2) dredging for commercial grade sand and gravel; and (3) washing, screening, or otherwise preparing commercial grade sand and gravel.

Cross-References.

Establishments primarily engaged in mining industrial grade sand are classified in U.S. Industry 212322, Industrial Sand Mining.

212322 Industrial Sand Mining[US]

This U.S. industry comprises establishments primarily engaged in one or more of the following: (1) operating industrial grade sand pits; (2) dredging for industrial grade sand; and (3) washing, screening, or otherwise preparing industrial grade sand.

Cross-References.

Establishments primarily engaged in mining commercial (i.e., construction) grade gravel are classified in U.S. Industry 212321, Construction Sand and Gravel Mining.

212324 Kaolin and Ball Clay Mining[US]

This U.S. industry comprises (1) establishments primarily engaged in developing the mine site and/or mining kaolin or ball clay (e.g., china clay, paper clay, and slip clay) and (2) establishments primarily engaged in beneficiating (i.e., preparing) kaolin or ball clay.

Cross-References.

Establishments primarily engaged in calcining, dead burning, or otherwise processing (i.e., beyond basic preparation) kaolin and ball clay are classified in U.S. Industry 327992, Ground or Treated Mineral and Earth Manufacturing.

212325 Clay and Ceramic and Refractory Minerals Mining[US]

This U.S. industry comprises establishments primarily engaged in one or more of the following: (1) mining clay (except kaolin and ball), ceramic, or refractory minerals; (2) developing the mine site for clay, ceramic, or refractory minerals; and (3) beneficiating (i.e., preparing) clay (except kaolin and ball), ceramic, or refractory minerals.

Illustrative Examples:

Bentonite mining and/or beneficiating   Magnesite mining and/or beneficiating

---

US—United States industry only. CAN—United States and Canadian industries are comparable. MEX—United States and Mexican industries are comparable. Blank—Canadian, Mexican, and United States industries are comparable.

Common clay mining and/or beneficiating
Feldspar mining and/or beneficiating
Fire clay mining and/or beneficiating
Fuller's earth mining and/or beneficiating

Nepheline syenite mining and/or
  beneficiating
Shale (except oil shale) mining and/or
  beneficiating

Cross-References. Establishments primarily engaged in—

- Shaping, molding, baking, burning, or hardening clay and nonclay refractories, and structural clay products—are classified in Industry 32712, Clay Building Material and Refractories Manufacturing;

- Developing the mine site, mining, and/or beneficiating kaolin or ball clay—are classified in U.S. Industry 212324, Kaolin and Ball Clay Mining; and

- Shaping, molding, glazing, and firing pottery, ceramics, and plumbing fixtures—are classified in Industry 32711, Pottery, Ceramics and Plumbing Fixture Manufacturing.

21239 Other Nonmetallic Mineral Mining and Quarrying

This industry comprises establishments primarily engaged in developing the mine site, mining, and/or milling or otherwise beneficiating (i.e., preparing) nonmetallic minerals (except coal, stone, sand, gravel, clay, ceramic, and refractory minerals).

Illustrative Examples:

Barite mining and/or beneficiating
Borate, natural, mining and/or
  beneficiating
Peat mining and/or beneficiating

Phosphate rock mining and/or
  beneficiating
Potash mining and/or beneficiating
Rock salt mining and/or beneficiating

Cross-References. Establishments primarily engaged in—

- Mining or quarrying dimension stone—are classified in Industry 21231, Stone Mining and Quarrying;

- Mining or quarrying sand, gravel, clay and ceramic and refractory minerals—are classified in Industry 21232, Sand, Gravel, Clay, and Ceramic and Refractory Minerals Mining and Quarrying;

- Calcining, dead burning, or otherwise processing (i.e., beyond basic preparation) minerals, such as talc, mica, feldspar, barite, and soapstone—are classified in Industry 32799, All Other Nonmetallic Mineral Product Manufacturing;

- Manufacturing boron compounds and potassium salts—are classified in Industry 32518, Other Basic Inorganic Chemical Manufacturing;

- Manufacturing table salt—are classified in Industry 31194, Seasoning and Dressing Manufacturing;

- Manufacturing salt (except table salt)—are classified in Industry 32599, All Other Chemical Product and Preparation Manufacturing; and

- Manufacturing phosphoric acid, superphosphates, or other phosphatic fertilizer materials—are classified in Industry 32531, Fertilizer Manufacturing.

212391 Potash, Soda, and Borate Mineral Mining[US]

This U.S. industry comprises establishments primarily engaged in developing the mine site, mining and/or milling, or otherwise beneficiating (i.e., preparing) natural potassium, sodium, or boron compounds. Drylake brine operations are included in this industry, as well as establishments engaged in producing the specified minerals from underground and open pit mines.

Cross-References. Establishments primarily engaged in—

- Manufacturing boron compounds and potassium salts—are classified in U.S. Industry 325188, All Other Basic Inorganic Chemical Manufacturing;

- Manufacturing sodium carbonate—are classified in U.S. Industry 325181, Alkalies and Chlorine Manufacturing; and

- Manufacturing table salt—are classified in U.S. Industry 311942, Spice and Extract Manufacturing.

212392 Phosphate Rock Mining[US]

This U.S. industry comprises establishments primarily engaged in developing the mine site, mining, milling, and/or drying or otherwise beneficiating (i.e., preparing) phosphate rock.

Cross-References.

Establishments primarily engaged in manufacturing phosphoric acid, superphosphates, or other phosphatic fertilizer materials are classified in U.S. Industry 325312, Phosphatic Fertilizer Manufacturing.

212393 Other Chemical and Fertilizer Mineral Mining[US]

This U.S. industry comprises establishments primarily engaged in developing the mine site, mining, milling, and/or drying or otherwise beneficiating (i.e., preparing) chemical or fertilizer mineral raw materials (except potash, soda, boron, and phosphate rock).

US—United States industry only. CAN—United States and Canadian industries are comparable. MEX—United States and Mexican industries are comparable. Blank—Canadian, Mexican, and United States industries are comparable.

Illustrative Examples:

Barite mining and/or beneficiating

Celestite mining and/or beneficiating

Fluorspar mining and/or beneficiating

Rock salt mining and/or beneficiating

Sulfur mining and/or beneficiating

Cross-References. Establishment primarily engaged in—

- Mining and/or milling or otherwise beneficiating natural potassium, sodium, or boron compounds—are classified in U.S. Industry 212391, Potash, Soda, and Borate Mineral Mining;

- Manufacturing industrial salt—are classified in U.S. Industry 325998, All Other Miscellaneous Chemical Product and Preparation Manufacturing;

- Mining, milling, drying, and/or sintering or otherwise beneficiating phosphate rock—are classified in U.S. Industry 212392, Phosphate Rock Mining; and

- Manufacturing table salt—are classified in U.S. Industry 311942, Spice and Extract Manufacturing.

212399 All Other Nonmetallic Mineral Mining[US]

This U.S. industry comprises establishments primarily engaged in developing the mine site, mining and/or milling or otherwise beneficiating (i.e., preparing) nonmetallic minerals (except stone, sand, gravel, clay, ceramic, refractory minerals, chemical and fertilizer minerals).

Illustrative Examples:

Gypsum mining and/or beneficiating

Mica mining and/or beneficiating

Pyrophyllite mining and/or beneficiating

Soapstone mining and/or beneficiating

Talc mining and/or beneficiating

Cross-References. Establishments primarily engaged in—

- Mining or quarrying dimension stone—are classified in Industry 21231, Stone Mining and Quarrying;

- Mining, quarrying, or beneficiating sand, gravel, clay, and ceramic and refractory minerals—are classified in Industry 21232, Sand, Gravel, Clay, and Ceramic and Refractory Minerals Mining and Quarrying;

- Mining, quarrying or beneficiating natural potash, soda, and borate—are classified in U.S. Industry 212391, Potash, Soda, and Borate Mineral Mining; and

- Mining and/or milling or otherwise beneficiating phosphate rock—are classified in U.S. Industry 212392, Phosphate Rock Mining.

---

213 Support Activities for Mining

Industries in the Support Activities for Mining subsector group establishments primarily providing support services, on a contract or fee basis, required for the mining and quarrying of minerals and for the extraction of oil and gas. Establishments performing exploration (except geophysical surveying and mapping) for minerals, on a contract or fee basis, are included in this subsector. Exploration includes traditional prospecting methods, such as taking core samples and making geological observations at prospective sites.

The activities performed on a contract or fee basis by establishments in the Support Activities for Mining subsector are also often performed in-house by mining operators. These activities include: taking core samples, making geological observations at prospective sites, excavating slush pits and cellars, and such oil and gas operations as spudding in, drilling in, redrilling, directional drilling, well surveying; running, cutting, and pulling casings, tubes and rods; cementing wells, shooting wells; perforating well casings; acidizing and chemically treating wells; and cleaning out, bailing, and swabbing wells.

2131 Support Activities for Mining

21311 Support Activities for Mining

This industry comprises establishments primarily engaged in providing support services, on a contract or fee basis, required for the mining and quarrying of minerals and for the extraction of oil and gas. Drilling, taking core samples, and making geological observations at prospective sites (except geophysical surveying and mapping) for minerals, on a contract or fee basis, is included in this industry.

Cross-References. Establishments primarily engaged in—

- Performing geophysical surveying and mapping services for minerals (i.e., coal, metal ores, oil and gas, and nonmetallic minerals) on a contract or fee basis—are classified in Industry 54136, Geophysical Surveying and Mapping Services;
- Mining, quarrying, and/or beneficiating on a contract or fee basis—are classified in Subsector 212, Mining (except Oil and Gas) based on the mineral mined; and
- Operating oil and gas field properties on a contract or fee basis—are classified in Subsector 211, Oil and Gas Extraction based on the activity.

213111 Drilling Oil and Gas Wells

This U.S. industry comprises establishments primarily engaged in drilling oil and gas wells for others on a contract or fee basis. This industry includes contractors that specialize in spudding in, drilling in, redrilling, and directional drilling.

Cross-References. Establishments primarily engaged in—

- Performing exploration (except geophysical surveying and mapping) services for oil and gas on a contract or fee basis—are classified in U.S. Industry 213112, Support Activities for Oil and Gas Operations; and

- Performing geophysical surveying and mapping services for oil and gas on a contract or fee basis—are classified in Industry 541360, Geophysical Surveying and Mapping Services.

213112 Support Activities for Oil and Gas Operations[US]

This U.S. industry comprises establishments primarily engaged in performing support activities on a contract or fee basis for oil and gas operations (except site preparation and related construction activities). Services included are exploration (except geophysical surveying and mapping); excavating slush pits and cellars, well surveying; running, cutting, and pulling casings, tubes, and rods; cementing wells, shooting wells; perforating well casings; acidizing and chemically treating wells; and cleaning out, bailing, and swabbing wells.

Cross-References. Establishments primarily engaged in—

- Contract drilling for oil and gas—are classified in U.S. Industry 213111, Drilling Oil and Gas Wells;

- Operating oil and gas field properties on a contract or fee basis—are classified in Subsector 211, Oil and Gas Extraction, based on the activity;

- Performing geophysical surveying and mapping services for oil and gas on a contract or fee basis—are classified in Industry 541360, Geophysical Surveying and Mapping Services;

- Oil and gas pipeline and related structures construction—are classified in Industry 237120, Oil and Gas Pipeline and Related Structures Construction; and

- Site preparation and related construction activities on a contract or fee basis—are classified in Industry 238910, Site Preparation Contractors.

213113 Support Activities for Coal Mining[US]

This U.S. industry comprises establishments primarily engaged in providing support activities for coal mining (except site preparation and related construction activities) on a contract or fee basis. Exploration for coal is included in this industry. Exploration includes traditional prospecting methods, such as taking core samples and making geological observations at prospective sites.

Cross-References. Establishments primarily engaged in—

- Performing geophysical surveying and mapping services for coal on a contract or fee basis—are classified in Industry 541360, Geophysical Surveying and Mapping Services;
- Operating coal mines or quarries on a contract or fee basis—are classified in Industry Group 2121, Coal Mining, based on the type of coal mined; and
- Site preparation and related construction activities on a contract or fee basis—are classified in Industry 238910, Site Preparation Contractors.

213114 Support Activities for Metal Mining[US]

This U.S. industry comprises establishments primarily engaged in providing support activities (except site preparation and related construction activities) on a contract or fee basis for the mining and quarrying of metallic minerals and for the extraction of metal ores. Exploration for minerals is included in this industry. Exploration (except geophysical surveying and mapping services) includes traditional prospecting methods, such as taking core samples and making geological observations at prospective sites.

Cross-References. Establishments primarily engaged in—

- Performing geophysical surveying and mapping services for metallic minerals on a contract or fee basis—are classified in Industry 541360, Geophysical Surveying and Mapping Services;
- Operating metallic mineral mines or quarries on a contract or fee basis—are classified in Industry Group 2122, Metal Ore Mining, based on the type of ore mined; and
- Site preparation and related construction activities on a contract or fee basis—are classified in Industry 238910, Site Preparation Contractors.

213115 Support Activities for Nonmetallic Minerals (except Fuels) Mining[US]

This U.S. industry comprises establishments primarily engaged in providing support activities, on a fee or contract basis, for the mining and quarrying of nonmetallic minerals (except fuel) and for the extraction of nonmetallic minerals (except site preparation and related construction activities). Exploration for minerals is included in this industry. Exploration (except geophysical surveying and mapping services) includes traditional prospecting methods, such as taking core samples and making geological observations at prospective sites.

Cross-References. Establishments primarily engaged in—

- Performing geophysical surveying and mapping services for nonmetallic minerals on a contract or fee basis—are classified in Industry 541360, Geophysical Surveying and Mapping Services;

- Operating nonmetallic mineral mines or quarries on a contract or fee basis— are classified in Industry Group 2123, Nonmetallic Mineral Mining and Quarrying, based on the type of mineral mined or quarried; and

- Site preparation and related construction activities—are classified in Industry 238910, Site Preparation Contractors.

Sector 22—Utilities

The Sector as a Whole

The Utilities sector comprises establishments engaged in the provision of the following utility services: electric power, natural gas, steam supply, water supply, and sewage removal. Within this sector, the specific activities associated with the utility services provided vary by utility: electric power includes generation, transmission, and distribution; natural gas includes distribution; steam supply includes provision and/or distribution; water supply includes treatment and distribution; and sewage removal includes collection, treatment, and disposal of waste through sewer systems and sewage treatment facilities.

Excluded from this sector are establishments primarily engaged in waste management services classified in Subsector 562, Waste Management and Remediation Services. These establishments also collect, treat, and dispose of waste materials; however, they do not use sewer systems or sewage treatment facilities.

221 Utilities^{CAN}

Industries in the Utilities subsector provide electric power, natural gas, steam supply, water supply, and sewage removal through a permanent infrastructure of lines, mains, and pipes. Establishments are grouped together based on the utility service provided and the particular system or facilities required to perform the service.

2211 Electric Power Generation, Transmission and Distribution

This industry group comprises establishments primarily engaged in generating, transmitting, and/or distributing electric power. Establishments in this industry group may perform one or more of the following activities: (1) operate generation facilities that produce electric energy; (2) operate transmission systems that convey the electricity from the generation facility to the distribution system; and (3) operate distribution systems that convey electric power received from the generation facility or the transmission system to the final consumer.

22111 Electric Power Generation^{CAN}

This industry comprises establishments primarily engaged in operating electric power generation facilities. These facilities convert other forms of energy, such as water power (i.e., hydroelectric), fossil fuels, nuclear power, and solar power,

---

into electrical energy. The establishments in this industry produce electric energy and provide electricity to transmission systems or to electric power distribution systems.

Cross-References.

Establishments primarily engaged in operating trash incinerators that also generate electricity are classified in Industry 56221, Waste Treatment and Disposal.

221111 Hydroelectric Power Generation^{CAN}

This U.S. industry comprises establishments primarily engaged in operating hydroelectric power generation facilities. These facilities use water power to drive a turbine and produce electric energy. The electric energy produced in these establishment is provided to electric power transmission systems or to electric power distribution systems.

221112 Fossil Fuel Electric Power Generation^{CAN}

This U.S. industry comprises establishments primarily engaged in operating fossil fuel powered electric power generation facilities. These facilities use fossil fuels, such as coal, oil, or gas, in internal combustion or combustion turbine conventional steam process to produce electric energy. The electric energy produced in these establishments are provided to electric power transmission systems or to electric power distribution systems.

221113 Nuclear Electric Power Generation^{CAN}

This U.S. industry comprises establishments primarily engaged in operating nuclear electric power generation facilities. These facilities use nuclear power to produce electric energy. The electric energy produced in these establishments are provided to electric power transmission systems or to electric power distribution systems.

221119 Other Electric Power Generation^{CAN}

This U.S. industry comprises establishments primarily engaged in operating electric power generation facilities (except hydroelectric, fossil fuel, nuclear). These facilities convert other forms of energy, such as solar, wind, or tidal power, into electrical energy. The electric energy produced in these establishment is provided to electric power transmission systems or to electric power distribution systems.

US—United States industry only. CAN—United States and Canadian industries are comparable. MEX—United States and Mexican industries are comparable. Blank—Canadian, Mexican, and United States industries are comparable.

Cross-References. Establishments primarily engaged in—

- Operating trash disposal incinerators that also generate electricity—are classified in U.S. Industry 562213, Solid Waste Combustors and Incinerators;

- Operating hydroelectric power generation facilities—are classified in U.S. Industry 221111, Hydroelectric Power Generation;

- Operating fossil fuel powered electric power generation facilities—are classified in U.S. Industry 221112, Fossil Fuel Electric Power Generation; and

- Operating nuclear electric power generation facilities—are classified in U.S. Industry 221113, Nuclear Electric Power Generation.

22112 Electric Power Transmission, Control, and Distribution[CAN]

This industry comprises establishments primarily engaged in operating electric power transmission systems, controlling (i.e., regulating voltages) the transmission of electricity, and/or distributing electricity. The transmission system includes lines and transformer stations. These establishments arrange, facilitate, or coordinate the transmission of electricity from the generating source to the distribution centers, other electric utilities, or final consumers. The distribution system consists of lines, poles, meters, and wiring that deliver the electricity to final consumers.

Cross-References.

Establishments primarily engaged in generating electric energy are classified in Industry 22111, Electric Power Generation.

221121 Electric Bulk Power Transmission and Control[CAN]

This U.S. industry comprises establishments primarily engaged in operating electric power transmission systems and/or controlling (i.e., regulatory voltage) the transmission of electricity from the generating source to distribution centers or other electric utilities. The transmission system includes lines and transformer stations.

Cross-References. Establishments primarily engaged in—

- Generating electric energy—are classified in Industry 22111, Electric Power Generation; and

- Distributing electricity to final consumers—are classified in U.S. Industry 221122, Electric Power Distribution.

221122 Electric Power Distribution^{CAN}

This U.S. industry comprises electric power establishments primarily engaged in either (1) operating electric power distribution systems (i.e., consisting of lines, poles, meters, and wiring) or (2) operating as electric power brokers or agents that arrange the sale of electricity via power distribution systems operated by others.

Cross-References. Establishments primarily engaged in—

- Generating electric energy—are classified in Industry 22111, Electric Power Generation; and

- Transmitting electricity between generating sources or distribution centers— are classified in U.S. Industry 221121, Electric Bulk Power Transmission and Control.

2212 Natural Gas Distribution^{CAN}

22121 Natural Gas Distribution^{CAN}
See industry description for 221210 below.

221210 Natural Gas Distribution^{CAN}

This industry comprises: (1) establishments primarily engaged in operating gas distribution systems (e.g., mains, meters); (2) establishments known as gas marketers that buy gas from the well and sell it to a distribution system; (3) establishments known as gas brokers or agents that arrange the sale of gas over gas distribution systems operated by others; and (4) establishments primarily engaged in transmitting and distributing gas to final consumers.

Cross-References. Establishments primarily engaged in—

- Pipeline transportation of natural gas from process plants to local distribution systems—are classified in Industry 486210, Pipeline Transportation of Natural Gas; and

- Retailing liquified petroleum (LP) gas via direct selling—are classified in U.S. Industry 454312, Liquefied Petroleum Gas (Bottled Gas) Dealers.

2213 Water, Sewage and Other Systems^{CAN}

22131 Water Supply and Irrigation Systems^{CAN}
See industry description for 221310 below.

US—United States industry only. CAN—United States and Canadian industries are comparable. MEX—United States and Mexican industries are comparable. Blank—Canadian, Mexican, and United States industries are comparable.

221310 Water Supply and Irrigation Systems^{CAN}

This industry comprises establishments primarily engaged in operating water treatment plants and/or operating water supply systems. The water supply system may include pumping stations, aqueducts, and/or distribution mains. The water may be used for drinking, irrigation, or other uses.

22132 Sewage Treatment Facilities^{CAN}
See industry description for 221320 below.

221320 Sewage Treatment Facilities^{CAN}

This industry comprises establishments primarily engaged in operating sewer systems or sewage treatment facilities that collect, treat, and dispose of waste.

Cross-References. Establishments primarily engaged in—

- Operating waste treatment or disposal facilities (except sewer systems or sewage treatment facilities)—are classified in Industry 56221, Waste Treatment and Disposal;

- Pumping (i.e., cleaning) septic tanks and cesspools—are classified in U.S. Industry 562991, Septic Tank and Related Services; and

- Cleaning and rodding sewers and catch basins—are classified in U.S. Industry 562998, All Other Miscellaneous Waste Management Services.

22133 Steam and Air-Conditioning Supply^{CAN}
See industry description for 221330 below.

221330 Steam and Air-Conditioning Supply^{CAN}

This industry comprises establishments primarily engaged in providing steam, heated air, or cooled air. The steam distribution may be through mains.

US—United States industry only. CAN—United States and Canadian industries are comparable. MEX—United States and Mexican industries are comparable. Blank—Canadian, Mexican, and United States industries are comparable.

Sector 23—Construction

The Sector as a Whole

The construction sector comprises establishments primarily engaged in the construction of buildings or engineering projects (e.g., highways and utility systems). Establishments primarily engaged in the preparation of sites for new construction and establishments primarily engaged in subdividing land for sale as building sites also are included in this sector.

Construction work done may include new work, additions, alterations, or maintenance and repairs. Activities of these establishments generally are managed at a fixed place of business, but they usually perform construction activities at multiple project sites. Production responsibilities for establishments in this sector are usually specified in (1) contracts with the owners of construction projects (prime contracts) or (2) contracts with other construction establishments (subcontracts).

Establishments primarily engaged in contracts that include responsibility for all aspects of individual construction projects are commonly known as general contractors, but also may be known as design-builders, construction managers, turnkey contractors, or (in cases where two or more establishments jointly secure a general contract) joint-venture contractors. Construction managers that provide oversight and scheduling only (i.e., agency) as well as construction managers that are responsible for the entire project (i.e., at risk) are included as general contractor type establishments. Establishments of the "general contractor type" frequently arrange construction of separate parts of their projects through subcontracts with other construction establishments.

Establishments primarily engaged in activities to produce a specific component (e.g., masonry, painting, and electrical work) of a construction project are commonly known as specialty trade contractors. Activities of specialty trade contractors are usually subcontracted from other construction establishments but, especially in remodeling and repair construction, the work may be done directly for the owner of the property.

Establishments primarily engaged in activities to construct buildings to be sold on sites that they own are known as operative builders, but also may be known as speculative builders or merchant builders. Operative builders produce buildings in a manner similar to general contractors, but their production processes also include site acquisition and securing of financial backing. Operative builders are most often associated with the construction of residential buildings. Like general contractors, they may subcontract all or part of the actual construction work on their buildings.

There are substantial differences in the types of equipment, work force skills, and other inputs required by establishments in this sector. To highlight these differences and variations in the underlying production functions, this sector is divided into three subsectors.

US—United States industry only. CAN—United States and Canadian industries are comparable. MEX—United States and Mexican industries are comparable. Blank—Canadian, Mexican, and United States industries are comparable.

Subsector 236, Construction of Buildings, comprises establishments of the general contractor type and operative builders involved in the construction of buildings. Subsector 237, Heavy and Civil Engineering Construction, comprises establishments involved in the construction of engineering projects. Subsector 238, Specialty Trade Contractors, comprises establishments engaged in specialty trade activities generally needed in the construction of all types of buildings.

Force account construction is construction work performed by an enterprise primarily engaged in some business other than construction for its own account and use, using employees of the enterprise. This activity is not included in the construction sector unless the construction work performed is the primary activity of a separate establishment of the enterprise. The installation and the ongoing repair and maintenance of telecommunications and utility networks is excluded from construction when the establishments performing the work are not independent contractors. Although a growing proportion of this work is subcontracted to independent contractors in the Construction Sector, the operating units of telecommunications and utility companies performing this work are included with the telecommunications or utility activities.

236 Construction of Buildings

The Construction of Buildings subsector comprises establishments primarily responsible for the construction of buildings. The work performed may include new work, additions, alterations, or maintenance and repairs. The on-site assembly of precut, panelized, and prefabricated buildings and construction of temporary buildings are included in this subsector. Part or all of the production work for which the establishments in this sector have responsibility may be subcontracted to other construction establishments—usually specialty trade contractors.

Establishments in this subsector are classified based on the types of buildings they construct. This classification reflects variations in the requirements of the underlying production processes.

2361 Residential Building Construction

23611 Residential Building Construction

This Industry comprises establishments primarily responsible for the construction or remodeling and renovation of single-family and multifamily residential buildings. Included in this industry are residential housing general contractors (i.e., new construction, remodeling or renovating existing residential structures), operative builders and remodelers of residential structures, residential project construction management firms, and residential design-build firms.

US—United States industry only. CAN—United States and Canadian industries are comparable. MEX—United States and Mexican industries are comparable. Blank—Canadian, Mexican, and United States industries are comparable.

Cross-References. Establishments primarily engaged in—

- Performing specialized construction work on houses and other residential buildings, generally on a subcontract basis—are classified in Subsector 238, Specialty Trade Contractors;
- Performing manufactured (mobile) home setup and tie-down work—are classified in Industry 23899, All Other Specialty Trade Contractors; and
- Constructing and leasing residential buildings on their own account—are classified in Industry 53111, Lessors of Residential Buildings and Dwellings.

236115 New Single-Family Housing Construction (except Operative Builders)[US]

This U.S. industry comprises general contractor establishments primarily responsible for the entire construction of new single-family housing, such as single-family detached houses and town houses or row houses where each housing unit (1) is separated from its neighbors by a ground-to-roof wall and (2) has no housing units constructed above or below. This industry includes general contractors responsible for the on-site assembly of modular and prefabricated houses. Single-family housing design-build firms and single-family construction management firms acting as general contractors are included in this industry.

Cross-References. Establishments primarily engaged in—

- Building single-family houses on their own account for sale as operative or speculative builders—are classified in U.S. Industry 236117, New Housing Operative Builders;
- Remodeling or repairing existing houses and other residential buildings— are classified in U.S. Industry 236118, Residential Remodelers;
- Performing manufactured (mobile) home setup and tie-down work—are classified in Industry 238990, All Other Specialty Trade Contractors;
- Performing specialized construction work on houses and other residential buildings, generally on a subcontract basis—are classified in Subsector 238, Specialty Trade Contractors; and
- Constructing and leasing residential buildings on their own account—are classified in Industry 531110, Lessors of Residential Buildings and Dwellings.

236116 New Multifamily Housing Construction (except Operative Builders)[US]

This U.S. industry comprises general contractor establishments responsible for the construction of new multifamily residential housing units (e.g., high-rise, garden, and town house apartments and condominiums where each unit is not separated from its neighbors by a ground-to-roof wall). Multifamily design-build firms and multifamily housing construction management firms acting as general contractors are included in this industry.

Cross-References. Establishments primarily engaged in—

- Building multifamily buildings on their own account for sale as operative or speculative builders—are classified in U.S. Industry 236117, New Housing Operative Builders;

- Remodeling or repairing existing multifamily housing and other residential buildings—are classified in U.S. Industry 236118, Residential Remodelers;

- Performing specialized construction work on multifamily housing and other residential buildings, generally on a subcontract basis—are classified in Subsector 238, Specialty Trade Contractors; and

- Constructing and leasing residential buildings on their own account—are classified in Industry 531110, Lessors of Residential Buildings and Dwellings.

236117 New Housing Operative Builders^{US}

This U.S. industry comprises operative builders primarily responsible for the entire construction of new houses and other residential buildings, single-family and multifamily, on their own account for sale. Operative builders are also known as speculative or merchant builders.

Cross-References. Establishments primarily engaged in—

- Building single-family houses for others as general contractors—are classified in U.S. Industry 236115, New Single-Family Housing Construction (except Operative Builders);

- Building multifamily residential buildings for others as general contractors—are classified in U.S. Industry 236116, New Multifamily Housing Construction (except Operative Builders);

- Remodeling or repairing existing houses and other residential buildings, either for others or on own account for sale—are classified in U.S. Industry 236118, Residential Remodelers;

- Performing specialized construction work on houses or other residential buildings, generally on a subcontract basis—are classified in Subsector 238, Specialty Trade Contractors; and

---

- Constructing and leasing residential buildings on their own account—are classified in Industry 531110, Lessors of Residential Buildings and Dwellings.

236118 Residential Remodelers[US]

This U.S. industry comprises establishments primarily responsible for the remodeling construction (including additions, alterations, reconstruction, maintenance and repair work) of houses and other residential buildings, single-family and multifamily. Included in this industry are remodeling general contractors, operative remodelers, remodeling design-build firms, and remodeling project construction management firms.

Cross-References. Establishments primarily engaged in—

- Building single-family houses for others as general contractors—are classified in U.S. Industry 236115, New Single-Family Housing Construction (except Operative Builders);
- Building multifamily buildings for others as general contractors—are classified in U.S. Industry 236116, New Multifamily Housing Construction (except Operative Builders);
- Building houses or other residential buildings, on their own account for sale as operative or speculative builders—are classified in U.S. Industry 236117, New Housing Operative Builders;
- Remodeling nonresidential buildings—are classified in Industry Group 2362, Nonresidential Building Construction, based on the type of structure being remodeled;
- Performing specialized construction work on houses or other residential buildings generally on a subcontract basis—are classified in Subsector 238, Specialty Trade Contractors; and
- Constructing and leasing residential buildings on their own account—are classified in Industry 531110, Lessors of Residential Buildings and Dwellings.

2362 Nonresidential Building Construction

This industry group comprises establishments primarily responsible for the construction (including new work, additions, alterations, maintenance, and repairs) of nonresidential buildings. This industry group includes nonresidential general contractors, nonresidential operative builders, nonresidential design-build firms, and nonresidential project construction management firms.

US—United States industry only. CAN—United States and Canadian industries are comparable. MEX—United States and Mexican industries are comparable. Blank—Canadian, Mexican, and United States industries are comparable.

23621 Industrial Building Construction
See industry description for 236210 below.

236210 Industrial Building Construction^{CAN}

This industry comprises establishments primarily responsible for the construction (including new work, additions, alterations, maintenance, and repairs) of industrial buildings (except warehouses). The construction of selected additional structures, whose production processes are similar to those for industrial buildings (e.g., incinerators, cement plants, blast furnaces, and similar nonbuilding structures), is included in this industry. Included in this industry are industrial building general contractors, industrial building operative builders, industrial building design-build firms, and industrial building construction management firms.

Illustrative Examples:

Assembly plant construction
Cannery construction
Cement plant construction
Chemical plant (except petrochemical) construction
Factory construction
Food processing plant construction
Furnace, industrial plant, construction

Mine loading and discharging station construction
Paper or pulp mill construction
Pharmaceutical manufacturing plant construction
Steel mill construction
Waste disposal plant (except sewage treatment) construction

Cross-References. Establishments primarily engaged in—

- Constructing oil refineries and petrochemical plant—are classified in Industry 237120, Oil and Gas Pipeline and Related Structures Construction;

- Constructing water treatment plants, sewage treatment plants, and pumping stations for water and sewer systems—are classified in Industry 237110, Water and Sewer Line and Related Structures Construction;

- Constructing power generation plants (except hydroelectric)—are classified in Industry 237130, Power and Communication Line and Related Structures Construction;

- Constructing industrial warehouses—are classified in Industry 236220, Commercial and Institutional Building Construction; and

- Performing specialized construction work on industrial buildings, generally on a subcontract basis—are classified in Subsector 238, Specialty Trade Contractors.

23622 Commercial and Institutional Building Construction
See industry description for 236220 below.

236220 Commercial and Institutional Building Construction^{CAN}

This industry comprises establishments primarily responsible for the construction (including new work, additions, alterations, maintenance, and repairs) of commercial and institutional buildings and related structures, such as stadiums, grain elevators, and indoor swimming pools. This industry includes establishments responsible for the on-site assembly of modular or prefabricated commercial and institutional buildings. Included in this industry are commercial and institutional building general contractors, commercial and institutional building operative builders, commercial and institutional building design-build firms, and commercial and institutional building project construction management firms.

Illustrative Examples:

Airport building construction
Arena construction
Barrack construction
Farm building construction
Fire station construction
Grain elevator construction
Hospital construction
Hotel construction
Indoor swimming pool construction
Office building construction
Parking garage construction
Prison construction

Radio and television broadcast studio
 construction
Religious building (e.g., church,
 synagogue, mosque, temple)
 construction
Restaurant construction
School building construction
Shopping mall construction
Warehouse construction (e.g.,
 commercial, industrial, manufacturing,
 private)

Cross-References. Establishments primarily engaged in—

- Constructing structures that are integral parts of utility systems (e.g., storage tanks, pumping stations) or are used to produce products for these systems (e.g., power plants, refineries)—are classified in Industry Group 2371, Utility System Construction, based on type of construction project;

- Performing specialized construction work on commercial and institutional buildings generally on a subcontract basis—are classified in Subsector 238, Specialty Trade Contractors; and

- Constructing buildings on their own account for rent or lease—are classified in Industry Group 5311, Lessors of Real Estate.

237 Heavy and Civil Engineering Construction

The Heavy and Civil Engineering Construction subsector comprises establishments whose primary activity is the construction of entire engineering projects (e.g., highways and dams), and specialty trade contractors, whose primary activity is the production of a specific component for such projects. Specialty trade contractors in Heavy and Civil Engineering Construction generally are performing activities that are specific to heavy and civil engineering construction projects and are not normally performed on buildings. The work performed may include new work, additions, alterations, or maintenance and repairs.

Specialty trade activities are classified in this subsector if the skills and equipment present are specific to heavy or civil engineering construction projects. For example, specialized equipment is needed to paint lines on highways. This equipment is not normally used in building applications so the activity is classified in this subsector. Traffic signal installation, while specific to highways, uses much of the same skills and equipment that are needed for electrical work in building projects and is therefore classified in Subsector 238, Specialty Trade Contractors.

Construction projects involving water resources (e.g., dredging and land drainage) and projects involving open space improvement (e.g., parks and trails) are included in this subsector. Establishments whose primary activity is the subdivision of land into individual building lots usually perform various additional site-improvement activities (e.g., road building and utility line installation) and are included in this subsector.

Establishments in this subsector are classified based on the types of structures that they construct. This classification reflects variations in the requirements of the underlying production processes.

2371 Utility System Construction

This industry group comprises establishments primarily engaged in the construction of distribution lines and related buildings and structures for utilities (i.e., water, sewer, petroleum, gas, power, and communication). All structures (including buildings) that are integral parts of utility systems (e.g., storage tanks, pumping stations, power plants, and refineries) are included in this industry group.

23711 Water and Sewer Line and Related Structures Construction
See industry description for 237110 below.

237110 Water and Sewer Line and Related Structures Construction^{CAN}

This industry comprises establishments primarily engaged in the construction of water and sewer lines, mains, pumping stations, treatment plants and storage tanks. The work performed may include new work, reconstruction, rehabilitation, and repairs. Specialty trade contractors are included in this group if they are engaged in activities primarily related to water and sewer line and related structures construction. All structures (including buildings) that are integral parts of water

---

and sewer networks (e.g., storage tanks, pumping stations, water treatment plants, and sewage treatment plants) are included in this industry.

Illustrative Examples:

Distribution line, sewer and water, construction
Fire hydrant installation
Irrigation systems construction
Pumping station, water and sewage system, construction
Reservoir construction
Sewage disposal plant construction
Sewer main, pipe, and connection, construction

Storm sewer construction
Water main and line construction
Water system storage tank and tower construction
Water treatment plant construction
Water well drilling, digging, boring, or sinking (except water intake wells in oil and gas fields)

Cross-References.

Establishments primarily engaged in constructing marine facilities (e.g., ports), flood control structures, dams, or hydroelectric power generation facilities are classified in Industry 237990, Other Heavy and Civil Engineering Construction.

23712 Oil and Gas Pipeline and Related Structures Construction
See industry description for 237120 below.

237120 Oil and Gas Pipeline and Related Structures Construction[CAN]

This industry comprises establishments primarily engaged in the construction of oil and gas lines, mains, refineries, and storage tanks. The work performed may include new work, reconstruction, rehabilitation, and repairs. Specialty trade contractors are included in this group if they are engaged in activities primarily related to oil and gas pipeline and related structures construction. All structures (including buildings) that are integral parts of oil and gas networks (e.g., storage tanks, pumping stations, and refineries) are included in this industry.

Illustrative Examples:

Distribution line, gas and oil, construction
Gas main construction
Gathering line, gas and oil field, construction
Natural gas pipeline construction
Natural gas processing plant construction

Oil refinery construction
Petrochemical plant construction
Pumping station, gas and oil transmission, construction
Storage tank, natural gas or oil, tank farm or field, construction

Cross-References.

Establishments primarily engaged in building chemical plants (except petrochemical) and similar process or batch facilities are classified in Industry 236210, Industrial Building Construction.

23713 Power and Communication Line and Related Structures Construction
See industry description for 237130 below.

237130 Power and Communication Line and Related Structures Construction[CAN]

This industry comprises establishments primarily engaged in the construction of power lines and towers, power plants, and radio, television, and telecommunications transmitting/receiving towers. The work performed may include new work, reconstruction, rehabilitation, and repairs. Specialty trade contractors are included in this group if they are engaged in activities primarily related to power and communication line and related structures construction. All structures (including buildings) that are integral parts of power and communication networks (e.g., transmitting towers, substations, and power plants) are included.

Illustrative Examples:

Alternative energy (e.g., geothermal, ocean wave, solar, wind) structure construction
Cellular phone tower construction
Co-generation plant construction
Communication tower construction
Electric light and power plant (except hydroelectric) construction
Electric power transmission line and tower construction

Nuclear power plant construction
Power line stringing
Radio transmitting tower construction
Satellite receiving station construction
Telephone line stringing
Transformer station and substation, electric power, construction
Underground cable (e.g., cable television, electricity, telephone) laying

Cross-References. Establishments primarily engaged in—

- Constructing hydroelectric generating facilities—are classified in Industry 237990, Other Heavy and Civil Engineering Construction;

- Constructing broadcast studios and similar nonresidential buildings—are classified in Industry 236220, Commercial and Institutional Building Construction;

- Performing electrical work within buildings—are classified in Industry 238210, Electrical Contractors;

US—United States industry only. CAN—United States and Canadian industries are comparable. MEX—United States and Mexican industries are comparable. Blank—Canadian, Mexican, and United States industries are comparable.

- Line slashing or cutting (except maintenance)—are classified in Industry 238910, Site Preparation Contractors;

- Installing and maintaining communication transmission lines performed by telecommunications companies—are classified in Subsector 517, Telecommunications;

- Locating underground utility lines prior to digging—are classified in Industry 561990, All Other Support Services; and

- Tree and brush trimming for overhead utility lines—are classified in Industry 561730, Landscaping Services.

2372 Land Subdivision

23721 Land Subdivision
See industry description for 237210 below.

237210 Land Subdivision[CAN]

This industry comprises establishments primarily engaged in servicing land and subdividing real property into lots, for subsequent sale to builders. Servicing of land may include excavation work for the installation of roads and utility lines. The extent of work may vary from project to project. Land subdivision precedes building activity and the subsequent building is often residential, but may also be commercial tracts and industrial parks. These establishments may do all the work themselves or subcontract the work to others. Establishments that perform only the legal subdivision of land are not included in this industry.

Cross-References. Establishments primarily engaged in—

- Constructing buildings, for sale, on lots they subdivide—are classified in Industry Group 2361, Residential Building Construction, or Industry Group 2362, Nonresidential Building Construction, based on the type of construction project;

- Installing roads on a subcontract basis for land subdividers—are classified in Industry 237310, Highway, Street, and Bridge Construction;

- Installing utilities on a subcontract basis for land subdividers—are classified in Industry Group 2371, Utility System Construction;

- Preparing land owned by others for building construction—are classified in Industry 238910, Site Preparation Contractors;

- Constructing buildings, for rent or own use, on lots they subdivide—are classified in Industry Group 5311, Lessors of Real Estate; and

---

US—United States industry only. CAN—United States and Canadian industries are comparable. MEX—United States and Mexican industries are comparable. Blank—Canadian, Mexican, and United States industries are comparable.

- Legal subdivision of land without land preparation—are classified elsewhere in the classification system based on the primary activity of the establishment.

2373 Highway, Street, and Bridge Construction

23731 Highway, Street, and Bridge Construction
See industry description for 237310 below.

237310 Highway, Street, and Bridge Construction[CAN]

This industry comprises establishments primarily engaged in the construction of highways (including elevated), streets, roads, airport runways, public sidewalks, or bridges. The work performed may include new work, reconstruction, rehabilitation, and repairs. Specialty trade contractors are included in this group if they are engaged in activities primarily related to highway, street, and bridge construction (e.g., installing guardrails on highways).

Illustrative Examples:

Airport runway construction	Painting traffic lanes or parking lot
Causeway construction	Pothole filling, highway, road, street, or
Culverts, highway, road, and street,	bridge
construction	Resurfacing, highway, road, street, or
Elevated highway construction	bridge
Guardrail construction	Sign erection, highway, road, street, or
Highway line painting	bridge

Cross-References. Establishments primarily engaged in—

- Constructing tunnels—are classified in Industry 237990, Other Heavy and Civil Engineering Construction;

- Highway lighting and signal installation—are classified in Industry 238210, Electrical Contractors;

- Painting bridges—are classified in Industry 238320, Painting and Wall Covering Contractors; and

- Constructing parking lots and private driveways and sidewalks, or erecting billboards—are classified in Industry 238990, All Other Specialty Trade Contractors.

2379 Other Heavy and Civil Engineering Construction

23799 Other Heavy and Civil Engineering Construction
See industry description for 237990 below.

US—United States industry only. CAN—United States and Canadian industries are comparable. MEX—United States and Mexican industries are comparable. Blank—Canadian, Mexican, and United States industries are comparable.

237990 Other Heavy and Civil Engineering Construction^{CAN}

This industry comprises establishments primarily engaged in heavy and engineering construction projects (excluding highway, street, bridge, and distribution line construction). The work performed may include new work, reconstruction, rehabilitation, and repairs. Specialty trade contractors are included in this group if they are engaged in activities primarily related to engineering construction projects (excluding highway, street, bridge, distribution line, oil and gas structure, and utilities building and structure construction). Construction projects involving water resources (e.g., dredging and land drainage), development of marine facilities, and projects involving open space improvement (e.g., parks and trails) are included in this industry.

Illustrative Examples:

Channel construction
Dam construction
Dock construction
Dredging (e.g., canal, channel, ditch, waterway)
Earth retention system construction
Flood control project construction
Golf course construction
Horizontal drilling (e.g., cable, pipeline, sewer installation)
Hydroelectric generating station construction

Land drainage contractors
Marine construction
Microtunneling contractors
Nuclear waste disposal site construction
Park ground and recreational open space improvement construction
Railroad construction
Subway construction
Trenching, underwater
Tunnel construction

Cross-References. Establishments primarily engaged in—

- Constructing water mains, sewers, and related structures—are classified in Industry 237110, Water and Sewer Line and Related Structures Construction;

- Constructing oil and gas pipelines and related structures—are classified in Industry 237120, Oil and Gas Pipeline and Related Structures Construction;

- Constructing power and communication transmission lines and related structures—are classified in Industry 237130, Power and Communication Line and Related Structures Construction;

- Constructing highways, streets, and bridges—are classified in Industry 237310, Highway, Street, and Bridge Construction; and

- Trenching (except underwater)—are classified in U.S. Industry 238910, Site Preparation Contractors.

238 Specialty Trade Contractors

The Specialty Trade Contractors subsector comprises establishments whose primary activity is performing specific activities (e.g., pouring concrete, site preparation, plumbing, painting, and electrical work) involved in building construction or other activities that are similar for all types of construction but that are not responsible for the entire project. The work performed may include new work, additions, alterations, maintenance, and repairs. The production work performed by establishments in this subsector is usually subcontracted from establishments of the general contractor type or operative builders but, especially in remodeling and repair construction, work also may be done directly for the owner of the property. Specialty trade contractors usually perform most of their work at the construction site, although they may have shops where they perform prefabrication and other work. Establishments primarily engaged in preparing sites for new construction are also included in this subsector.

There are substantial differences in types of equipment, work force skills, and other inputs required by specialty trade contractors. Establishments in this subsector are classified based on the underlying production function for the specialty trade in which they specialize. Throughout the Specialty Trade Contractors subsector, establishments commonly provide both the parts and labor required to complete work. For example, electrical contractors supply the current-carrying and noncurrent-carrying wiring devices that are required to install a circuit. Plumbing, Heating and Air-Conditioning contractors also supply the parts required to complete a contract.

Establishments that specialize in activities primarily related to heavy and civil engineering construction that are not normally performed on buildings, such as the painting of lines on highways are classified in Subsector 237, Heavy and Civil Engineering Construction.

Establishments that are primarily engaged in selling construction materials are classified in Sector 42, Wholesale Trade, or Sector 44-45, Retail Trade, based on the characteristics of the selling unit.

2381 Foundation, Structure, and Building Exterior Contractors

This industry group comprises establishments primarily engaged in the specialty trades needed to complete the basic structure (i.e., foundation, frame, and shell) of buildings. The work performed may include new work, additions, alterations, maintenance, and repairs.

23811 Poured Concrete Foundation and Structure Contractors^{CAN}

See industry description for 238110 below.

US—United States industry only. CAN—United States and Canadian industries are comparable. MEX—United States and Mexican industries are comparable. Blank—Canadian, Mexican, and United States industries are comparable.

238110 Poured Concrete Foundation and Structure Contractors[CAN]

This industry comprises establishments primarily engaged in pouring and finishing concrete foundations and structural elements. This industry also includes establishments performing grout and shotcrete work. The work performed may include new work, additions, alterations, maintenance, and repairs.

Illustrative Examples:

Concrete work (except paving)
Concrete pouring and finishing
Concrete pumping (i.e., placement)
Footing and foundation concrete
  contractors

Gunite contractors
Mud-jacking contractors
Shotcrete contractors

Cross-References. Establishments primarily engaged in—

- Constructing or paving streets, highways, and public sidewalks—are classified in Industry 237310, Highway, Street, and Bridge Construction;
- Concrete sealing, coating, waterproofing, or dampproofing—are classified in Industry 238390, Other Building Finishing Contractors; and
- Paving residential driveways, commercial parking lots, and other private parking areas—are classified in Industry 238990, All Other Specialty Trade Contractors.

23812 Structural Steel and Precast Concrete Contractors
See industry description for 238120 below.

238120 Structural Steel and Precast Concrete Contractors[CAN]

This industry comprises establishments primarily engaged in: (1) erecting and assembling structural parts made from steel or precast concrete (e.g., steel beams, structural steel components, and similar products of precast concrete); and/or (2) assembling and installing other steel construction products (e.g., steel rods, bars, rebar, mesh, and cages) to reinforce poured-in-place concrete. The work performed may include new work, additions, alterations, maintenance, and repairs.

Illustrative Examples:

Concrete product (e.g., structural precast,
  structural prestressed) installation
Erecting structural steel

Precast concrete panel, slab, or form
  installation
Rebar contractors
Reinforcing steel contractors

| Placing and tying reinforcing rod at a construction site | Structural steel contractors |

Cross-References.

Establishments primarily engaged in pouring concrete at the construction site for building foundations or structural elements are classified in Industry 238110, Poured Concrete Foundation and Structure Contractors.

23813 Framing Contractors^CAN

See industry description for 238130 below.

238130 Framing Contractors^CAN

This industry comprises establishments primarily engaged in structural framing and sheathing using materials other than structural steel or concrete. The work performed may include new work, additions, alterations, maintenance, and repairs.

Illustrative Examples:

Building framing (except structural steel)	Steel framing contractors
Foundation, building, wood, contractors	Wood frame component (e.g., truss)
Framing contractors	fabrication on site
Post frame contractors	

Cross-References. Establishments primarily engaged in—

- Finish carpentry—are classified in Industry 238350, Finish Carpentry Contractors; and

- Installing structural steel or precast concrete framing or structural elements—are classified in Industry 238120, Structural Steel and Precast Concrete Contractors.

23814 Masonry Contractors^CAN

See industry description for 238140 below.

238140 Masonry Contractors^CAN

This industry comprises establishments primarily engaged in masonry work, stone setting, brick laying, and other stone work. The work performed may include new work, additions, alterations, maintenance, and repairs.

US—United States industry only. CAN—United States and Canadian industries are comparable. MEX—United States and Mexican industries are comparable. Blank—Canadian, Mexican, and United States industries are comparable.

Illustrative Examples:

Block laying
Brick laying
Concrete block laying
Foundation (e.g., brick, block, stone),
  building, contractors

Marble, granite, and slate, exterior,
  contractors
Masonry pointing, cleaning, or caulking
Stucco contractors

Cross-References. Establishments primarily engaged in—

- Erecting the basic structure of buildings by pouring concrete—are classified in Industry 238110, Poured Concrete Foundation and Structure Contractors;

- Interior marble, granite and slate work—are classified in Industry 238340, Tile and Terrazzo Contractors; and

- Laying precast stones or bricks for patios, sidewalks, and driveways; or paving residential driveways, commercial parking lots and other private parking areas—are classified in Industry 238990, All Other Specialty Trade Contractors.

23815 Glass and Glazing Contractors[CAN]

See industry description for 238150 below.

238150 Glass and Glazing Contractors[CAN]

This industry comprises establishments primarily engaged in installing glass panes in prepared openings (i.e., glazing work) and other glass work for buildings. The work performed may include new work, additions, alterations, maintenance, and repairs.

Illustrative Examples:

Decorative glass and mirror installation
Glass cladding installation
Glass coating and tinting (except
  automotive) contractors
Glass installation (except automotive)
  contractors

Glazing contractors
Stained glass installation
Window pane or sheet installation

Cross-References. Establishments primarily engaged in—

- Installing prefabricated window units—are classified in Industry 238350, Finish Carpentry Contractors; and

- The replacement, repair, and/or tinting of automotive glass—are classified in U.S. Industry 811122, Automotive Glass Replacement Shops.

US—United States industry only. CAN—United States and Canadian industries are comparable. MEX—United States and Mexican industries are comparable. Blank—Canadian, Mexican, and United States industries are comparable.

23816 Roofing Contractors[CAN]

See industry description for 238160 below.

238160 Roofing Contractors[CAN]

This industry comprises establishments primarily engaged in roofing. This industry also includes establishments treating roofs (i.e., spraying, painting, or coating) and installing skylights. The work performed may include new work, additions, alterations, maintenance, and repairs.

Illustrative Examples:

Painting, spraying, or coating, roof   Sheet metal roofing installation
Shake and shingle, roof, installation   Skylight installation

Cross-References. Establishments primarily engaged in—

- Installing roof trusses and sheathing attached to trusses—are classified in Industry 238130, Framing Contractors; and

- Installing downspouts, gutters, fascia, and soffits—are classified in Industry 238170, Siding Contractors.

23817 Siding Contractors[CAN]

See industry description for 238170 below.

238170 Siding Contractors[CAN]

This industry comprises establishments primarily engaged in installing siding of wood, aluminum, vinyl or other exterior finish material (except brick, stone, stucco, or curtain wall). This industry also includes establishments installing gutters and downspouts. The work performed may include new work, additions, alterations, maintenance, and repairs.

Illustrative Examples:

Downspout, gutter, and gutter guard   Fascia and soffit installation
installation   Siding (e.g., vinyl, wood, aluminum)

Cross-References. Establishments primarily engaged in—

- Installing brick, stone, or stucco building exterior finish materials—are classified in Industry 238140, Masonry Contractors;

- Installing curtain wall—are classified in Industry 238190, Other Foundation, Structure, and Building Exterior Contractors; and

---

- Installing sheet metal duct work—are classified in Industry 238220, Plumbing, Heating, and Air-Conditioning Contractors.

23819 Other Foundation, Structure, and Building Exterior Contractors[CAN]

See industry description for 238190 below.

238190 Other Foundation, Structure, and Building Exterior Contractors[CAN]

This industry comprises establishments primarily engaged in building foundation and structure trades work (except poured concrete, structural steel, precast concrete, framing, masonry, glass and glazing, roofing, and siding). The work performed may include new work, additions, alterations, maintenance, and repairs.

Illustrative Examples:

Curtain wall, metal, installation
Decorative steel and wrought iron work installation
Fire escape installation
Forms for poured concrete, erecting and dismantling
Ornamental metal work installation
Welding, on site, contractors

Cross-References: Establishments primarily engaged in—

- Poured concrete foundation and structure work—are classified in Industry 238110, Poured Concrete Foundation and Structure Contractors;

- Installation of structural steel or precast concrete building components—are classified in Industry 238120, Structural Steel and Precast Concrete Contractors;

- Framing buildings—are classified in Industry 238130, Framing Contractors;

- Masonry work—are classified in Industry 238140, Masonry Contractors;

- Glass and glazing work—are classified in Industry 238150, Glass and Glazing Contractors;

- Installing or repairing roofs—are classified in Industry 238160, Roofing Contractors; and

- Installing siding—are classified in Industry 238170, Siding Contractors.

2382 Building Equipment Contractors

This industry group comprises establishments primarily engaged in installing or servicing equipment that forms part of a building mechanical system (e.g., electricity, water, heating, and cooling). The work performed may include new work, additions, alterations, or maintenance and repairs. Contractors installing specialized building equipment, such as elevators, escalators, service station equipment, and central vacuum cleaning systems are also included.

23821 Electrical Contractors

See industry description for 238210 below.

238210 Electrical Contractors^{CAN}

This industry comprises establishments primarily engaged in installing and servicing electrical wiring and equipment. Electrical contractors included in this industry may include both the parts and labor when performing work. Electrical contractors may perform new work, additions, alterations, maintenance, and repairs.

Illustrative Examples:

Airport runway lighting contractors
Alarm system (e.g., fire, burglar),
  electric, installation only
Audio equipment (except automotive)
  installation contractors
Cable television hookup contractors
Cable splicing, electrical or fiber optic
Computer and network cable installation
Environmental control system installation
Fiber optic cable (except transmission
  line) contractors

Highway, street, and bridge lighting and
  electrical signal installation
Home automation system installation
Lighting system installation
Telecommunication equipment and
  wiring (except transmission line)
  installation contractors
Traffic signal installation

Cross-References. Establishments primarily engaged in—

- Installing and maintaining telecommunications lines by telecommunications companies—are classified in Subsector 517, Telecommunications;

- Constructing power and communication transmission lines—are classified in Industry 237130, Power and Communication Line and Related Structures Construction; and

- Burglar and fire alarm installation combined with sales, maintenance, or monitoring services—are classified in U.S. Industry 561021, Security Systems Services (except Locksmiths).

23822 Plumbing, Heating, and Air-Conditioning Contractors

See industry description for 238220 below.

US—United States industry only. CAN—United States and Canadian industries are comparable. MEX—United States and Mexican industries are comparable. Blank—Canadian, Mexican, and United States industries are comparable.

238220 Plumbing, Heating, and Air-Conditioning Contractors^{CAN}

This industry comprises establishments primarily engaged in installing and servicing plumbing, heating, and air-conditioning equipment. Contractors in this industry may provide both parts and labor when performing work. The work performed may include new work, additions, alterations, maintenance, and repairs.

Illustrative Examples:

Cooling tower installation
Duct work (e.g., cooling, dust collection, exhaust, heating, ventilation) installation
Fire sprinkler system installation
Fireplace, natural gas, installation
Furnace installation
Heating, ventilation, and air-conditioning (HVAC) contractors
Lawn sprinkler system installation
Mechanical contractors
Refrigeration system (e.g., commercial, industrial, scientific) installation
Sewer hook-up and connection, building

Cross-References. Establishments primarily engaged in—

- Installing electrical controls for HVAC systems—are classified in Industry 238210, Electrical Contractors; and

- Duct cleaning—are classified in Industry 561790, Other Services to Buildings and Dwellings.

23829 Other Building Equipment Contractors
See industry description for 238290 below.

238290 Other Building Equipment Contractors^{US}

This industry comprises establishments primarily engaged in installing or servicing building equipment (except electrical; plumbing; heating, cooling, or ventilation equipment). The repair and maintenance of miscellaneous building equipment is included in this industry. The work performed may include new work, additions, alterations, maintenance, and repairs.

Illustrative Examples:

Automated and revolving door installation
Boiler and pipe insulation installation
Commercial-type door installation
Conveyor system installation
Dismantling large-scale machinery and equipment
Lightning protection equipment (e.g., lightning rod) installation
Machine rigging
Millwrights
Overhead door, commercial- or industrial-type, installation
Revolving door installation

Elevator installation
Escalator installation
Gasoline pump, service station,
 installation

Satellite dish, household-type,
 installation
Vacuum cleaning system, built-in,
 installation

Cross-References. Establishments primarily engaged in—

- Manufacturing of industrial equipment with incidental installation—are classified in Sectors 31-33, Manufacturing; and

- Repair and maintenance of commercial refrigeration equipment or production equipment—are classified in Industry 811310, Commercial and Industrial Machinery and Equipment (except Automotive and Electronic) Repair and Maintenance.

2383 Building Finishing Contractors

This industry group comprises establishments primarily engaged in the specialty trades needed to finish buildings. The work performed may include new work, additions, alterations, or maintenance and repairs.

23831 Drywall and Insulation Contractors
See industry description for 238310 below.

238310 Drywall and Insulation Contractors^{CAN}

This industry comprises establishments primarily engaged in drywall, plaster work, and building insulation work. Plaster work includes applying plain or ornamental plaster, and installation of lath to receive plaster. The work performed may include new work, additions, alterations, maintenance, and repairs.

Illustrative Examples:

Acoustical ceiling tile and panel
 installation
Drop ceiling installation
Drywall contractors
Fresco (i.e., decorative plaster finishing)
 contractors
Gypsum board installation

Lathing contractors
Plastering (i.e., ornamental, plain)
 contractors
Soundproofing contractors
Taping and finishing drywall
Wall cavity and attic space insulation
 installation

Cross-References. Establishments primarily engaged in—

- Applying stucco—are classified in Industry 238140, Masonry Contractors; and

---

- Insulating pipes and boilers—are classified in Industry 238290, Other Building Equipment Contractors.

23832 Painting and Wall Covering Contractors
See industry description for 238320 below.

238320 Painting and Wall Covering Contractors[CAN]

This industry comprises establishments primarily engaged in interior or exterior painting or interior wall covering. The work performed may include new work, additions, alterations, maintenance, and repairs.

Illustrative Examples:

Bridge painting	Ship painting contractors
House painting	Wallpaper hanging and removal
Paint and wallpaper stripping	contractors
Paperhanging or removal contractors	

Cross-References. Establishments primarily engaged in—

- Painting lines on highways, streets, and parking lots—are classified in Industry 237310, Highway, Street, and Bridge Construction;
- Roof painting—are classified in Industry 238160, Roofing Contractors; and
- Installing wood paneling—are classified in Industry 238350, Finish Carpentry Contractors.

23833 Flooring Contractors
See industry description for 238330 below.

238330 Flooring Contractors[CAN]

This industry comprises establishments primarily engaged in the installation of resilient floor tile, carpeting, linoleum, and hard wood flooring. The work performed may include new work, additions, alterations, maintenance, and repairs.

Illustrative Examples:

Carpet, installation only	Resilient floor tile or sheet (e.g.,
Floor laying, scraping, finishing, and	linoleum, rubber, vinyl), installation only
refinishing	Resurfacing hardwood flooring
Hardwood flooring, installation only	Vinyl flooring contractors

Cross-References. Establishments primarily engaged in—

- Laying concrete flooring—are classified in Industry 238110, Poured Concrete Foundation and Structure Contractors;
- Installing stone or ceramic floor tile—are classified in Industry 238340, Tile and Terrazzo Contractors; and
- Selling and installing carpet and other flooring products as retail establishments—are classified in Sector 44-45, Retail Trade.

23834 Tile and Terrazzo Contractors
See industry description for 238340 below.

238340 Tile and Terrazzo Contractors[CAN]

This industry comprises establishments primarily engaged in setting and installing ceramic tile, stone (interior only), and mosaic and/or mixing marble particles and cement to make terrazzo at the job site. The work performed may include new work, additions, alterations, maintenance, and repairs.

Illustrative Examples:

Ceramic tile installation	Mosaic work
Mantel, marble or stone, installation	Stone flooring installation
Marble, granite, and slate, interior installation contractors	Tile (except resilient) laying and setting

Cross-References. Establishments primarily engaged in—

- Exterior marble, granite, and slate work—are classified in Industry 238140, Masonry Contractors;
- Manufacturing precast terrazzo products—are classified in Industry 327390, Other Concrete Product Manufacturing; and
- Installing, without selling resilient floor tile—are classified in Industry 238330, Flooring Contractors.

23835 Finish Carpentry Contractors
See industry description for 238350 below.

238350 Finish Carpentry Contractors[CAN]

This industry comprises establishments primarily engaged in finish carpentry work. The work performed may include new work, additions, alterations, maintenance, and repairs.

Illustrative Examples:

Built-in wood cabinets constructed on
  site
Counter top, residential-type, installation
Door and window frame construction
Garage door, residential-type, installation
Millwork installation
Molding or trim, wood or plastic,
  installation

Paneling installation
Prefabricated kitchen and bath cabinet,
  residential-type, installation
Ship joinery contractors
Window and door, residential type, of
  any material, prefabricated, installation

Cross-References. Establishments primarily engaged in—

- Installing skylights—are classified in Industry 238160, Roofing Contractors;

- Framing—are classified in Industry 238130, Framing Contractors; and

- Building custom kitchen and bath cabinets (except free standing) in a shop are—classified in Industry 337110, Wood Kitchen Cabinet and Countertop Manufacturing.

23839 Other Building Finishing Contractors
See industry description for 238390 below.

238390 Other Building Finishing Contractors[CAN]

This industry comprises establishments primarily engaged in building finishing trade work (except drywall, plaster and insulation work; painting and wall covering work; flooring work; tile and terrazzo work; and finish carpentry work). The work performed may include new work, additions, alterations, or maintenance and repairs.

Illustrative Examples:

Bath tub refinishing on site
Closet organizer system installation
Concrete coating, glazing, or sealing
Countertop and cabinet, metal (except
  residential-type), installation
Drapery fixture (e.g., hardware, rods,
  tracks) installation
Fabricating metal cabinets or countertops
  on site

Modular furniture system attachment and
  installation
Trade show exhibit installation and
  dismantling
Waterproofing contractors
Window shade and blind installation

Cross-References. Establishments primarily engaged in—

- Installing drywall, plaster or insulation—are classified in Industry 238310, Drywall and Insulation Contractors;

- Installing or removing paint or wall coverings—are classified in Industry 238320, Painting and Wall Covering Contractors;

- Installing or repairing wood floors, resilient flooring, and carpet—are classified in Industry 238330, Flooring Contractors;

- Setting tile or performing terrazzo work—are classified in Industry 238340, Tile and Terrazzo Contractors; and

- Finish carpentry—are classified in Industry 238350, Finish Carpentry Contractors.

2389 Other Specialty Trade Contractors

23891 Site Preparation Contractors
See industry description for 238910 below.

238910 Site Preparation Contractors^{CAN}

This industry comprises establishments primarily engaged in site preparation activities, such as excavating and grading, demolition of buildings and other structures, septic system installation, and house moving. Earth moving and land clearing for all types of sites (e.g., building, nonbuilding, mining) is included in this industry. Establishments primarily engaged in construction equipment rental with operator (except cranes) are also included.

Illustrative Examples:

Blasting, building demolition
Concrete breaking and cutting for
  demolition
Cutting new rights of way
Demolition, building and structure
Dewatering contractors
Dirt moving for construction
Equipment rental (except crane),
  construction, with operator
Excavating, earthmoving, or land
  clearing contractors

Foundation digging (i.e., excavation)
Foundation drilling contractors
Grading construction sites
Line slashing or cutting (except
  maintenance)
Septic system contractors
Trenching (except underwater)
Underground tank (except hazardous)
  removal
Wrecking, building or other structure

Cross-References. Establishments primarily engaged in—

- Earth retention or underwater trenching—are classified in Industry 237990, Other Heavy and Civil Engineering Construction;

- Crane rental with operator—are classified in Industry 238990, All Other Specialty Trade Contractors;

US—United States industry only. CAN—United States and Canadian industries are comparable. MEX—United States and Mexican industries are comparable. Blank—Canadian, Mexican, and United States industries are comparable.

- Overburden removal as an activity prior to mineral removal from quarries or open pit mines—are classified in Sector 21, Mining;

- Drilling oil and gas field water intake wells—are classified in U.S. Industry 213111, Support Activities for Mining;

- Dismantling tanks in oil fields—are classified in U.S. Industry 213112, Drilling Oil and Gas Wells;

- Construction equipment rental without an operator—are classified in U.S. Industry 532412, Construction, Mining, and Forestry Machinery and Equipment Rental and Leasing;

- Tree and brush trimming for overhead utility lines—are classified in Industry 561730, Landscaping Services; and

- Nuclear power plant decommissioning and environmental remediation work, such as the removal of underground steel tanks for hazardous materials—are classified in Industry 562910, Remediation Services.

23899 All Other Specialty Trade Contractors
See industry description for 238990 below.

238990 All Other Specialty Trade Contractors[CAN]

This industry comprises establishments primarily engaged in specialized trades (except foundation, structure, and building exterior contractors; building equipment contractors; building finishing contractors; and site preparation contractors). The specialty trade work performed includes new work, additions, alterations, maintenance, and repairs.

Illustrative Examples:

Billboard erection	Outdoor swimming pool construction
Crane rental with operator	Paver, brick (e.g., driveway, patio,
Cleaning building interiors during and	sidewalk), installation
immediately after construction	Paving, residential and commercial
Driveway paving or sealing	driveway and parking lot
Fence installation	Sandblasting building exteriors
Interlocking brick and block installation	Scaffold erecting and dismantling
Manufactured (mobile) home, set up and	Steeplejack work
tie-down	

Cross-References. Establishments primarily engaged in—

- Foundation, structure, and building exterior work—are classified in Industry Group 2381, Foundation, Structure, and Building Exterior Contractors;

US—United States industry only. CAN—United States and Canadian industries are comparable. MEX—United States and Mexican industries are comparable. Blank—Canadian, Mexican, and United States industries are comparable.

- Installing, repairing, or maintaining building mechanical systems—are classified in Industry Group 2382, Building Equipment Contractors;

- Finishing buildings—are classified in Industry Group 2383, Building Finishing Contractors;

- Paving public highways, streets, and roads—are classified in Industry 237310, Highway, Street, and Bridge Construction;

- Construction equipment rental with an operator (except cranes) or preparing land for building construction—are classified in Industry 238910, Site Preparation Contractors;

- Construction equipment rental without an operator—are classified in U.S. Industry 532412, Construction, Mining, and Forestry Machinery and Equipment Rental and Leasing;

- Radon testing—are classified in Industry 541380, Testing Laboratories;

- Power washing and other building exterior cleaning (except sandblasting)— are classified in Industry 561790, Other Services to Buildings and Dwellings; and

- Environmental remediation work, such as asbestos abatement—are classified in Industry 562910, Remediation Services.

Sector 31-33—Manufacturing

The Sector as a Whole

The Manufacturing sector comprises establishments engaged in the mechanical, physical, or chemical transformation of materials, substances, or components into new products. The assembling of component parts of manufactured products is considered manufacturing, except in cases where the activity is appropriately classified in Sector 23, Construction.

Establishments in the Manufacturing sector are often described as plants, factories, or mills and characteristically use power-driven machines and materials-handling equipment. However, establishments that transform materials or substances into new products by hand or in the worker's home and those engaged in selling to the general public products made on the same premises from which they are sold, such as bakeries, candy stores, and custom tailors, may also be included in this sector. Manufacturing establishments may process materials or may contract with other establishments to process their materials for them. Both types of establishments are included in manufacturing.

The materials, substances, or components transformed by manufacturing establishments are raw materials that are products of agriculture, forestry, fishing, mining, or quarrying as well as products of other manufacturing establishments. The materials used may be purchased directly from producers, obtained through customary trade channels, or secured without recourse to the market by transferring the product from one establishment to another, under the same ownership.

The new product of a manufacturing establishment may be finished in the sense that it is ready for utilization or consumption, or it may be semifinished to become an input for an establishment engaged in further manufacturing. For example, the product of the alumina refinery is the input used in the primary production of aluminum; primary aluminum is the input to an aluminum wire drawing plant; and aluminum wire is the input for a fabricated wire product manufacturing establishment.

The subsectors in the Manufacturing sector generally reflect distinct production processes related to material inputs, production equipment, and employee skills. In the machinery area, where assembling is a key activity, parts and accessories for manufactured products are classified in the industry of the finished manufactured item when they are made for separate sale. For example, a replacement refrigerator door would be classified with refrigerators and an attachment for a piece of metal working machinery would be classified with metal working machinery. However, components, input from other manufacturing establishments, are classified based on the production function of the component manufacturer. For example, electronic components are classified in Subsector 334, Computer and Electronic Product Manufacturing and stampings are classified in Subsector 332, Fabricated Metal Product Manufacturing.

Manufacturing establishments often perform one or more activities that are classified outside the Manufacturing sector of NAICS. For instance, almost all manufacturing has some captive research and development or administrative operations, such as accounting, payroll, or management. These captive services are treated the same as captive manufacturing activities. When the services are provided by separate establishments, they are classified to the NAICS sector where such services are primary, not in manufacturing.

The boundaries of manufacturing and the other sectors of the classification system can be somewhat blurry. The establishments in the manufacturing sector are engaged in the transformation of materials into new products. Their output is a new product. However, the definition of what constitutes a new product can be somewhat subjective. As clarification, the following activities are considered manufacturing in NAICS:

Milk bottling and pasteurizing;
Water bottling and processing;
Fresh fish packaging (oyster shucking, fish filleting);
Apparel jobbing (assigning of materials to contract factories or shops for fabrication or other contract operations) as well as contracting on materials owned by others;
Printing and related activities;
Ready-mixed concrete production;
Leather converting;
Grinding of lenses to prescription;
Wood preserving;
Electroplating, plating, metal heat treating, and polishing for the trade;
Lapidary work for the trade;
Fabricating signs and advertising displays;
Rebuilding or remanufacturing machinery (i.e., automotive parts)
Ship repair and renovation;
Machine shops; and
Tire retreading.

Conversely, there are activities that are sometimes considered manufacturing, but which for NAICS are classified in another sector (i.e., not classified as manufacturing). They include:

1. Logging, classified in Sector 11, Agriculture, Forestry, Fishing and Hunting is considered a harvesting operation;

2. The beneficiating of ores and other minerals, classified in Sector 21, Mining, is considered part of the activity of mining;

3. The construction of structures and fabricating operations performed at the site of construction by contractors, is classified in Sector 23, Construction;

4. Establishments engaged in breaking of bulk and redistribution in smaller lots, including packaging, repackaging, or bottling products, such as liquors or chemicals; the customized assembly of computers; sorting of scrap; mixing paints to customer order; and cutting metals to customer order, classified in Sector 42, Wholesale Trade or Sector 44-45, Retail Trade, produce a modified version of the same product, not a new product; and

5. Publishing and the combined activity of publishing and printing, classified in Sector 51, Information, perform the transformation of information into a

product where as the value of the product to the consumer lies in the information content, not in the format in which it is distributed (i.e., the book or software diskette).

311 Food Manufacturing

Industries in the Food Manufacturing subsector transform livestock and agricultural products into products for intermediate or final consumption. The industry groups are distinguished by the raw materials (generally of animal or vegetable origin) processed into food products.

The food products manufactured in these establishments are typically sold to wholesalers or retailers for distribution to consumers, but establishments primarily engaged in retailing bakery and candy products made on the premises not for immediate consumption are included.

Establishments primarily engaged in manufacturing beverages are classified in Subsector 312, Beverage and Tobacco Product Manufacturing.

3111 Animal Food Manufacturing

31111 Animal Food Manufacturing

This industry comprises establishments primarily engaged in manufacturing food and feed for animals from ingredients, such as grains, oilseed mill products, and meat products.

Cross-References. Establishments primarily engaged in—

- Slaughtering animals for feed—are classified in Industry 31161, Animal Slaughtering and Processing; and

- Manufacturing vitamins and minerals for animals—are classified in Industry 32541, Pharmaceutical and Medicine Manufacturing.

311111 Dog and Cat Food Manufacturing[CAN]

This U.S. industry comprises establishments primarily engaged in manufacturing dog and cat food from ingredients, such as grains, oilseed mill products, and meat products.

Cross-References. Establishments primarily engaged in—

- Manufacturing food for animals (except dog and cat)—are classified in U.S. Industry 311119, Other Animal Food Manufacturing;

- Slaughtering animals for feed—are classified in Industry 31161, Animal Slaughtering and Processing; and

- Manufacturing vitamins and minerals for dogs and cats—are classified in Industry 32541, Pharmaceutical and Medicine Manufacturing.

311119 Other Animal Food Manufacturing[CAN]

This U.S. industry comprises establishments primarily engaged in manufacturing animal food (except dog and cat) from ingredients, such as grains, oilseed mill products, and meat products.

Cross-References. Establishments primarily engaged in—

- Manufacturing dog and cat foods—are classified in U.S. Industry 311111, Dog and Cat Food Manufacturing;

- Slaughtering animals for feed—are classified in Industry 31161, Animal Slaughtering and Processing; and

- Manufacturing vitamins and minerals for animals—are classified in Industry 32541, Pharmaceutical and Medicine Manufacturing.

3112 Grain and Oilseed Milling

31121 Flour Milling and Malt Manufacturing

This industry comprises establishments primarily engaged in one or more of the following: (1) milling flour or meal from grains or vegetables; (2) preparing flour mixes or doughs from flour milled in the same establishment; (3) milling, cleaning, and polishing rice; and (4) manufacturing malt from barley, rye, or other grains.

Cross-References. Establishments primarily engaged in—

- Preparing breakfast cereals from flour milled in the same establishment— are classified in Industry 31123, Breakfast Cereal Manufacturing;

- Crushing soybeans or wet milling corn and vegetables—are classified in Industry 31122, Starch and Vegetable Fats and Oils Manufacturing;

- Manufacturing prepared flour mixes or doughs from flour ground else- where—are classified in Industry 31182, Cookie, Cracker, and Pasta Manu- facturing;

- Brewing malt beverages—are classified in Industry 31212, Breweries;

- Mixing purchased dried and dehydrated ingredients with purchased rice—are classified in Industry 31199, All Other Food Manufacturing;

- Drying and/or dehydrating ingredients and packaging them with purchased rice—are classified in Industry 31142, Fruit and Vegetable Canning, Pickling, and Drying; and

- Manufacturing malt extract and syrups—are classified in Industry 31194, Seasoning and Dressing Manufacturing.

311211 Flour Milling^{CAN}

This U.S. industry comprises establishments primarily engaged in (1) milling flour or meal from grains (except rice) or vegetables and/or (2) milling flour and preparing flour mixes or doughs.

Cross-References. Establishments primarily engaged in—

- Preparing breakfast cereals from flour milled in the same establishment—are classified in Industry 311230, Breakfast Cereal Manufacturing;

- Manufacturing prepared flour mixes or doughs from flour ground elsewhere—are classified in U.S. Industry 311822, Flour Mixes and Dough Manufacturing from Purchased Flour;

- Milling rice or cleaning and polishing rice—are classified in U.S. Industry 311212, Rice Milling;

- Wet milling corn and vegetables—are classified in U.S. Industry, 311221, Wet Corn Milling; and

- Crushing soybean and extracting soybean oil—are classified in U.S. Industry 311222, Soybean Processing.

311212 Rice Milling^{US}

This U.S. industry comprises establishments primarily engaged in one of the following: (1) milling rice; (2) cleaning and polishing rice; or (3) milling, cleaning, and polishing rice. The establishments in this industry may package the rice they mill with other ingredients.

Cross-References. Establishments primarily engaged in—

- Drying and/or dehydrating ingredients and packaging them with purchased rice—are classified in U.S. Industry 311423, Dried and Dehydrated Food Manufacturing; and

- Mixing purchased dried and/or dehydrated ingredients with purchased rice—are classified in U.S. Industry 311999, All Other Miscellaneous Food Manufacturing.

311213 Malt Manufacturing[US]

This U.S. industry comprises establishments primarily engaged in manufacturing malt from barley, rye, or other grains.

Cross-References. Establishments primarily engaged in—

- Brewing malt beverages—are classified in Industry 312120, Breweries; and
- Manufacturing malt extract and syrups—are classified in U.S. Industry 311942, Spice and Extract Manufacturing.

31122 Starch and Vegetable Fats and Oils Manufacturing

This industry comprises establishments primarily engaged in one or more of the following: (1) wet milling corn and vegetables; (2) crushing oilseeds and tree nuts; (3) refining and/or blending vegetable oils; (4) manufacturing shortening and margarine; and (5) blending purchased animal fats with vegetable fats.

Cross-References. Establishments primarily engaged in—

- Manufacturing table syrups from corn syrup and starch base dessert powders—are classified in Industry 31199, All Other Food Manufacturing;
- Reducing maple sap to maple syrup—are classified in Industry 11199, All Other Crop Farming;
- Milling flour or meal from grains and vegetables—are classified in Industry 31121, Flour Milling and Malt Manufacturing;
- Wet milling corn to produce nonpotable ethyl alcohol—are classified in Industry 32519, Other Basic Organic Chemical Manufacturing;
- Rendering or refining animal fats and oils—are classified in Industry 31161, Animal Slaughtering and Processing; and
- Manufacturing laundry starches—are classified in Industry 32561, Soap and Cleaning Compound Manufacturing.

311221 Wet Corn Milling[CAN]

This U.S. industry comprises establishments primarily engaged in wet milling corn and other vegetables (except to make ethyl alcohol). Examples of products

---

US—United States industry only. CAN—United States and Canadian industries are comparable. MEX—United States and Mexican industries are comparable. Blank—Canadian, Mexican, and United States industries are comparable.

made in these establishments are corn sweeteners, such as glucose, dextrose, and fructose; corn oil; and starches (except laundry).

Cross-References. Establishments primarily engaged in—

- Refining and/or blending corn oil from purchased oils—are classified in U.S. Industry 311225, Fats and Oils Refining and Blending;
- Manufacturing sweetening syrups from corn syrup and starch base dessert powders—are classified in U.S. Industry 311999, All Other Miscellaneous Food Manufacturing;
- Reducing maple sap to maple syrup—are classified in U.S. Industry 111998, All Other Miscellaneous Crop Farming;
- Milling (except wet milling) corn—are classified in U.S. Industry 311211, Flour Milling;
- Wet milling corn to produce nonpotable ethyl alcohol—are classified in U.S. Industry 325193, Ethyl Alcohol Manufacturing; and
- Manufacturing laundry starches—are classified in U.S. Industry 325612, Polish and Other Sanitation Good Manufacturing.

311222 Soybean Processing[US]

This U.S. industry comprises establishments engaged in crushing soybeans. Examples of products produced in these establishments are soybean oil, soybean cake and meal, and soybean protein isolates and concentrates.

Cross-References. Establishments primarily engaged in—

- Refining and/or blending soybean oil from purchased oil—are classified in U.S. Industry 311225, Fats and Oils Refining and Blending;
- Wet milling corn and other vegetables—are classified in U.S. Industry 311221, Wet Corn Milling; and
- Crushing oilseeds (except soybeans) and tree nuts—are classified in U.S. Industry 311223, Other Oilseed Processing.

311223 Other Oilseed Processing[US]

This U.S. industry comprises establishments engaged in crushing oilseeds (except soybeans) and tree nuts, such as cottonseeds, linseeds, peanuts, and sunflower seeds.

Cross-References. Establishments primarily engaged in—

- Wet milling corn and other vegetables—are classified in U.S. Industry 311221, Wet Corn Milling;

US—United States industry only. CAN—United States and Canadian industries are comparable. MEX—United States and Mexican industries are comparable. Blank—Canadian, Mexican, and United States industries are comparable.

- Crushing soybeans—are classified in U.S. Industry 311222, Soybean Processing; and

- Refining and/or blending vegetable, oilseed, and tree nut oils from purchased oils—are classified in U.S. Industry 311225, Fats and Oils Refining and Blending.

311225 Fats and Oils Refining and Blending[CAN]

This U.S. industry comprises establishments primarily engaged in one or more of the following: (1) manufacturing shortening and margarine from purchased fats and oils; (2) refining and/or blending vegetable, oilseed, and tree nut oils from purchased oils; and (3) blending purchased animal fats with purchased vegetable fats.

Cross-References. Establishments primarily engaged in—

- Refining and/or blending soybean oil in soybean crushing mills—are classified in U.S. Industry 311222, Soybean Processing;

- Refining and/or blending corn oil made by wet corn milling—are classified in U.S. Industry 311221, Wet Corn Milling;

- Refining and/or blending oilseeds (except soybeans) and tree nuts in crushing mills—are classified in U.S. Industry 311223, Other Oilseed Processing; and

- Rendering or refining animal fats and oils—are classified in Industry 31161, Animal Slaughtering and Processing.

31123 Breakfast Cereal Manufacturing
See industry description for 311230 below.

311230 Breakfast Cereal Manufacturing

This industry comprises establishments primarily engaged in manufacturing breakfast cereal foods.

Cross-References. Establishments primarily engaged in—

- Manufacturing nonchocolate-coated granola bars and other types of breakfast bars—are classified in Industry 311340, Nonchocolate Confectionery Manufacturing;

- Manufacturing chocolate-coated granola bars from purchased chocolate— are classified in Industry 311330, Confectionery Manufacturing from Purchased Chocolate;

- Manufacturing chocolate-coated granola bars from cacao beans—are classified in Industry 311320, Chocolate and Confectionery Manufacturing from Cacao Beans; and

- Manufacturing coffee substitutes from grain—are classified in Industry 311920, Coffee and Tea Manufacturing.

3113 Sugar and Confectionery Product Manufacturing

This industry group comprises (1) establishments that process agricultural inputs, such as sugarcane, beet, and cacao, to give rise to a new product (sugar or chocolate), and (2) those that begin with sugar and chocolate and process these further.

31131 Sugar Manufacturing

This industry comprises establishments primarily engaged in manufacturing raw sugar, liquid sugar, and refined sugar from sugarcane, raw cane sugar and sugarbeets.

Cross-References. Establishments primarily engaged in—

- Manufacturing corn sweeteners by wet milling corn—are classified in Industry 31122, Starch and Vegetable Fats and Oils Manufacturing;

- Manufacturing table syrups from corn syrup and starch base dessert powders—are classified in Industry 31199, All Other Food Manufacturing;

- Reducing maple sap to maple syrup—are classified in Industry 11199, All Other Crop Farming; and

- Manufacturing synthetic sweeteners (i.e., sweetening agents), such as saccharin and sugar substitutes (i.e., synthetic sweetener blended with other ingredients),—are classified in Subsector 325, Chemical Manufacturing.

311311 Sugarcane Mills[US]

This U.S. industry comprises establishments primarily engaged in processing sugarcane.

Cross-References. Establishments primarily engaged in—

- Manufacturing refined cane sugar from raw cane sugar—are classified in U.S. Industry 311312, Cane Sugar Refining;

- Manufacturing beet sugar—are classified in U.S. Industry 311313, Beet Sugar Manufacturing;

- Manufacturing corn sweeteners by wet milling corn—are classified in U.S. Industry 311221, Wet Corn Milling;
- Manufacturing table syrups from corn syrup—are classified in U.S. Industry 311999, All Other Miscellaneous Food Manufacturing; and
- Manufacturing synthetic sweeteners (i.e., sweetening agents), such as saccharin and sugar substitutes (i.e., synthetic sweetener blended with other ingredients),—are classified in Subsector 325, Chemical Manufacturing.

311312 Cane Sugar Refining[US]

This U.S. industry comprises establishments primarily engaged in refining cane sugar from raw cane sugar.

Cross-References. Establishments primarily engaged in—

- Processing and refining sugarcane—are classified in U.S. Industry 311311, Sugarcane Mills;
- Manufacturing beet sugar—are classified in U.S. Industry 311313, Beet Sugar Manufacturing;
- Manufacturing corn sweeteners by wet milling corn—are classified in U.S. Industry 311221, Wet Corn Milling;
- Reducing maple sap to maple syrup—are classified in U.S. Industry 111998, All Other Miscellaneous Crop Farming;
- Manufacturing table syrups from corn syrup—are classified in U.S. Industry 311999, All Other Miscellaneous Food Manufacturing; and
- Manufacturing synthetic sweeteners (i.e., sweetening agents), such as saccharin and sugar substitutes (i.e., synthetic sweetener blended with other ingredients),—are classified in Subsector 325, Chemical Manufacturing.

311313 Beet Sugar Manufacturing[US]

This U.S. industry comprises establishments primarily engaged in manufacturing refined beet sugar from sugarbeets.

Cross-References. Establishments primarily engaged in—

- Manufacturing raw cane sugar and/or refined cane sugar from sugarcane—are classified in U.S. Industry 311311, Sugarcane Mills;
- Manufacturing refined cane sugar from raw cane sugar—are classified in U.S. Industry 311312, Cane Sugar Refining;

- Manufacturing corn sweeteners by wet milling corn—are classified in U.S. Industry 311221, Wet Corn Milling;
- Manufacturing table syrups from corn syrup—are classified in U.S. Industry 311999, All Other Miscellaneous Food Manufacturing;
- Reducing maple sap to maple syrup—are classified in U.S. Industry 111998, All Other Miscellaneous Crop Farming; and
- Manufacturing synthetic sweeteners (i.e., sweetening agents), such as saccharin and sugar substitutes (i.e., synthetic sweetener blended with other ingredients),—are classified in Subsector 325, Chemical Manufacturing.

31132 Chocolate and Confectionery Manufacturing from Cacao Beans
See industry description for 311320 below.

311320 Chocolate and Confectionery Manufacturing from Cacao Beans

This industry comprises establishments primarily engaged in shelling, roasting, and grinding cacao beans and making chocolate cacao products and chocolate confectioneries.

Cross-References. Establishments primarily engaged in—

- Manufacturing, not for immediate consumption, chocolate confectioneries from chocolate made elsewhere—are classified in Industry 311330, Confectionery Manufacturing from Purchased Chocolate;
- Manufacturing, not for immediate consumption, nonchocolate candies—are classified in Industry 311340, Nonchocolate Confectionery Manufacturing;
- Preparing and selling confectioneries for immediate consumption—are classified in U.S. Industry 722213, Snack and Nonalcoholic Beverage Bars; and
- Retailing confectioneries not for immediate consumption made elsewhere— are classified in U.S. Industry 445292, Confectionery and Nut Stores.

31133 Confectionery Manufacturing from Purchased Chocolate
See industry description for 311330 below.

311330 Confectionery Manufacturing from Purchased Chocolate

This industry comprises establishments primarily engaged in manufacturing chocolate confectioneries from chocolate produced elsewhere. Included in this

US—United States industry only. CAN—United States and Canadian industries are comparable. MEX—United States and Mexican industries are comparable. Blank—Canadian, Mexican, and United States industries are comparable.

industry are establishments primarily engaged in retailing chocolate confectionery products not for immediate consumption made on the premises from chocolate made elsewhere.

Cross-References. Establishments primarily engaged in—

- Manufacturing chocolate confectioneries from cacao beans—are classified in Industry 311320, Chocolate and Confectionery Manufacturing from Cacao Beans;
- Manufacturing nonchocolate confectioneries—are classified in Industry 311340, Nonchocolate Confectionery Manufacturing;
- Retailing confectioneries not for immediate consumption made elsewhere—are classified in U.S. Industry 445292, Confectionery and Nut Stores; and
- Preparing and selling confectioneries for immediate consumption—are classified in U.S. Industry 722213, Snack and Nonalcoholic Beverage Bars.

31134 Nonchocolate Confectionery Manufacturing
See industry description for 311340 below.

311340 Nonchocolate Confectionery Manufacturing

This industry comprises establishments primarily engaged in manufacturing nonchocolate confectioneries. Included in this industry are establishments primary engaged in retailing nonchocolate confectionery products not for immediate consumption made on the premises.

Cross-References. Establishments primarily engaged in—

- Manufacturing chocolate confectioneries from cacao beans—are classified in Industry 311320, Chocolate and Confectionery Manufacturing from Cacao Beans;
- Manufacturing chocolate confectioneries from chocolate made elsewhere—are classified in Industry 311330, Confectionery Manufacturing from Purchased Chocolate;
- Retailing confectioneries not for immediate consumption made elsewhere—are classified in U.S. Industry 445292, Confectionery and Nut Stores;
- Preparing and selling confectioneries for immediate consumption—are classified in U.S. Industry 722213, Snack and Nonalcoholic Beverage Bars; and
- Roasting, salting, drying, cooking, or canning nuts and seeds—are classified in U.S. Industry 311911, Roasted Nuts and Peanut Butter Manufacturing.

3114 Fruit and Vegetable Preserving and Specialty Food Manufacturing

This industry group includes (1) establishments that freeze food and (2) those that use preservation processes, such as pickling, canning, and dehydrating. Both types begin their production process with inputs of vegetable or animal origin.

31141 Frozen Food Manufacturing

This industry comprises establishments primarily engaged in manufacturing frozen fruit, frozen juices, frozen vegetables, and frozen specialty foods (except seafood), such as frozen dinners, entrees, and side dishes; frozen pizza; frozen whipped toppings; and frozen waffles, pancakes, and french toast.

Cross-References. Establishments primarily engaged in—

- Manufacturing frozen dairy specialties—are classified in Industry 31152, Ice Cream and Frozen Dessert Manufacturing;

- Manufacturing frozen bakery products—are classified in Industry 31181, Bread and Bakery Product Manufacturing;

- Manufacturing frozen seafood products—are classified in Industry 31171, Seafood Product Preparation and Packaging; and

- Manufacturing frozen meat products—are classified in Industry 31161, Animal Slaughtering and Processing.

311411 Frozen Fruit, Juice, and Vegetable Manufacturing[MEX]

This U.S. industry comprises establishments primarily engaged in manufacturing frozen fruits; frozen vegetables; and frozen fruit juices, ades, drinks, cocktail mixes and concentrates.

Cross-References.

Establishments primarily engaged in manufacturing frozen specialty foods are classified in U.S. Industry 311412, Frozen Specialty Food Manufacturing.

311412 Frozen Specialty Food Manufacturing[MEX]

This U.S. industry comprises establishments primarily engaged in manufacturing frozen specialty foods (except seafood), such as frozen dinners, entrees, and side dishes; frozen pizza; frozen whipped topping; and frozen waffles, pancakes, and french toast.

US—United States industry only. CAN—United States and Canadian industries are comparable. MEX—United States and Mexican industries are comparable. Blank—Canadian, Mexican, and United States industries are comparable.

Cross-References. Establishments primarily engaged in—

- Manufacturing frozen dairy specialties—are classified in Industry 311520, Ice Cream and Frozen Dessert Manufacturing;

- Manufacturing frozen bakery products—are classified in U.S. Industry 311813, Frozen Cakes, Pies, and Other Pastries Manufacturing;

- Manufacturing frozen fruits, frozen fruit juices, and frozen vegetables— are classified in U.S. Industry 311411, Frozen Fruit, Juice, and Vegetable Manufacturing;

- Manufacturing frozen meat products—are classified in Industry 31161, Animal Slaughtering and Processing; and

- Manufacturing frozen seafood products—are classified in U.S. Industry 311712, Fresh and Frozen Seafood Processing.

31142 Fruit and Vegetable Canning, Pickling, and Drying

This industry comprises establishments primarily engaged in manufacturing canned, pickled, and dried fruits, vegetables, and specialty foods. Establishments in this industry may package the dried or dehydrated ingredients they make with other purchased ingredients. Examples of products made by these establishments are canned juices; canned baby foods; canned soups (except seafood); canned dry beans; canned tomato-based sauces, such as catsup, salsa, chili, spaghetti, barbeque, and tomato paste, pickles, relishes, jams and jellies, dried soup mixes and bullions, and sauerkraut.

Cross-References. Establishments primarily engaged in—

- Manufacturing canned dairy products—are classified in Industry 31151, Dairy Product (except Frozen) Manufacturing;

- Manufacturing canned seafood soups and seafood products—are classified in Industry 31171, Seafood Product Preparation and Packaging;

- Manufacturing canned meat products—are classified in Industry 31161, Animal Slaughtering and Processing;

- Milling rice and packaging it with other ingredients or manufacturing vegetable flours and meals—are classified in Industry 31121, Flour Milling and Malt Manufacturing;

- Manufacturing dry pasta and packaging it with other ingredients—are classified in Industry 31182, Cookie, Cracker, and Pasta Manufacturing;

- Mixing purchased dried and/or dehydrated potatoes, rice, and pasta and packaging them with other purchased ingredients; mixing purchased dried and/or dehydrated ingredients for soup mixes and bouillon; and manufacturing canned puddings—are classified in Industry 31199, All Other Food Manufacturing;

- Manufacturing dry salad dressing and dry sauce mixes—are classified in Industry 31194, Seasoning and Dressing Manufacturing; and

- Manufacturing canned fruit and vegetable drinks, cocktails, and ades—are classified in Industry 31211, Soft Drink and Ice Manufacturing.

311421 Fruit and Vegetable Canning[US]

This U.S. industry comprises establishments primarily engaged in manufacturing canned, pickled, and brined fruits and vegetables. Examples of products made in these establishments are canned juices; canned jams and jellies; canned tomato-based sauces, such as catsup, salsa, chili, spaghetti, barbeque, and tomato paste; pickles, relishes, and sauerkraut.

Cross-References. Establishments primarily engaged in—

- Manufacturing canned baby foods, canned soups (except seafood), and canned specialty foods (except seafood)—are classified in U.S. Industry 311422, Specialty Canning;

- Manufacturing canned seafood soups and canned seafood products—are classified in U.S. Industry 311711, Seafood Canning;

- Manufacturing canned meat products—are classified in Industry 31161, Animal Slaughtering and Processing; and

- Manufacturing canned fruit and vegetable drinks, cocktails, and ades—are classified in U.S. Industry 312111, Soft Drink Manufacturing.

311422 Specialty Canning[US]

This U.S. industry comprises establishments primarily engaged in manufacturing canned specialty foods. Examples of products made in these establishments are canned baby food, canned baked beans, canned soups (except seafood), canned spaghetti, and other canned nationality foods.

Cross-References. Establishments primarily engaged in—

- Manufacturing canned dairy products—are classified in U.S. Industry 311514, Dry, Condensed, and Evaporated Dairy Product Manufacturing;

- Manufacturing canned fruits, canned vegetables, and canned juices—are classified in U.S. Industry 311421, Fruit and Vegetable Canning;

US—United States industry only. CAN—United States and Canadian industries are comparable. MEX—United States and Mexican industries are comparable. Blank—Canadian, Mexican, and United States industries are comparable.

- Manufacturing canned seafood soups and canned seafood products—are classified in U.S. Industry 311711, Seafood Canning;
- Manufacturing canned meat products—are classified in Industry 31161, Animal Slaughtering and Processing; and
- Manufacturing canned puddings—are classified in U.S. Industry 311999, All Other Miscellaneous Food Manufacturing.

311423 Dried and Dehydrated Food Manufacturing[US]

This U.S. industry comprises establishments primarily engaged in (1) drying (including freeze-dried) and/or dehydrating fruits, vegetables, and soup mixes and bouillon and/or (2) drying and/or dehydrating ingredients and packaging them with other purchased ingredients, such as rice and dry pasta.

Cross-References. Establishments primarily engaged in—

- Milling rice and packaging it with other ingredients—are classified in U.S. Industry 311212, Rice Milling;
- Manufacturing dry pasta and packaging it with other ingredients—are classified in U.S. Industry 311823, Dry Pasta Manufacturing;
- Manufacturing vegetable flours and meals—are classified in U.S. Industry 311211, Flour Milling;
- Mixing purchased dried and/or dehydrated potatoes, rice, and dry pasta, and packaging them with other purchased ingredients, and mixing purchased dried and/or dehydrated ingredients for soup mixes and bouillon—are classified in U.S. Industry 311999, All Other Miscellaneous Food Manufacturing; and
- Manufacturing dry salad dressing and dry sauce mixes—are classified in U.S. Industry 311942, Spice and Extract Manufacturing.

3115 Dairy Product Manufacturing

This industry group comprises establishments that manufacture dairy products from raw milk, processed milk, and dairy substitutes.

31151 Dairy Product (except Frozen) Manufacturing

This industry comprises establishments primarily engaged in one or more of the following: (1) manufacturing dairy products (except frozen) from raw milk and/or processed milk products; (2) manufacturing dairy substitutes (except frozen)

---

from soybeans and other nondairy substances; and (3) manufacturing dry, condensed, concentrated, and evaporated dairy and dairy substitute products.

Cross-References. Establishments primarily engaged in—

- Manufacturing cheese-based salad dressings—are classified in Industry 31194, Seasoning and Dressing Manufacturing;

- Manufacturing margarine or margarine-butter blends—are classified in Industry 31122, Starch and Vegetable Fats and Oils Manufacturing;

- Manufacturing frozen whipped toppings—are classified in Industry 31141, Frozen Food Manufacturing; and

- Manufacturing ice cream, frozen yogurt, and other frozen dairy desserts—are classified in Industry 31152, Ice Cream and Frozen Dessert Manufacturing.

311511 Fluid Milk Manufacturing^{CAN}

This U.S. industry comprises establishments primarily engaged in (1) manufacturing processed milk products, such as pasteurized milk or cream and sour cream and/or (2) manufacturing fluid milk dairy substitutes from soybeans and other nondairy substances.

Cross-References. Establishments primarily engaged in—

- Manufacturing dry mix whipped toppings, canned milk, and ultra high temperature milk— are classified in U.S. Industry 311514, Dry, Condensed, and Evaporated Dairy Product Manufacturing;

- Manufacturing frozen whipped toppings—are classified in U.S. Industry 311412, Frozen Specialty Food Manufacturing; and

- Manufacturing ice cream and frozen yogurt and other frozen desserts—are classified in Industry 311520, Ice Cream and Frozen Dessert Manufacturing.

311512 Creamery Butter Manufacturing^{US}

This U.S. industry comprises establishments primarily engaged in manufacturing creamery butter from milk and/or processed milk products.

Cross-References.

Establishments primarily engaged in manufacturing margarine or margarine-butter blends are classified in U.S. Industry 311225, Fats and Oils Refining and Blending.

US—United States industry only. CAN—United States and Canadian industries are comparable. MEX—United States and Mexican industries are comparable. Blank—Canadian, Mexican, and United States industries are comparable.

311513 Cheese Manufacturing[US]

This U.S. industry comprises establishments primarily engaged in (1) manufacturing cheese products (except cottage cheese) from raw milk and/or processed milk products and/or (2) manufacturing cheese substitutes from soybean and other nondairy substances.

Cross-References. Establishments primarily engaged in—

- Manufacturing cheese-based salad dressings—are classified in U.S. Industry 311941, Mayonnaise, Dressing, and Other Prepared Sauce Manufacturing; and

- Manufacturing cottage cheese—are classified in U.S. Industry 311511, Fluid Milk Manufacturing.

311514 Dry, Condensed, and Evaporated Dairy Product Manufacturing[US]

This U.S. industry comprises establishments primarily engaged in manufacturing dry, condensed, and evaporated milk and dairy substitute products.

Cross-References. Establishments primarily engaged in—

- Manufacturing fluid milk products—are classified in U.S. Industry 311511, Fluid Milk Manufacturing;

- Manufacturing creamery butter—are classified in U.S. Industry 311512, Creamery Butter Manufacturing; and

- Manufacturing cheese products—are classified in U.S. Industry 311513, Cheese Manufacturing.

31152 Ice Cream and Frozen Dessert Manufacturing
See industry description for 311520 below.

311520 Ice Cream and Frozen Dessert Manufacturing

This industry comprises establishments primarily engaged in manufacturing ice cream, frozen yogurts, frozen ices, sherbets, frozen tofu, and other frozen desserts (except bakery products).

Cross-References. Establishments primarily engaged in—

- Manufacturing frozen bakery products—are classified in U.S. Industry 311813, Frozen Cakes, Pies, and Other Pastries Manufacturing; and

---

US—United States industry only. CAN—United States and Canadian industries are comparable. MEX—United States and Mexican industries are comparable. Blank—Canadian, Mexican, and United States industries are comparable.

- Manufacturing ice cream and ice milk mixes—are classified in U.S. Industry 311514, Dry, Condensed, and Evaporated Dairy Product Manufacturing.

3116 Animal Slaughtering and Processing

31161 Animal Slaughtering and Processing

This industry comprises establishments primarily engaged in one or more of the following: (1) slaughtering animals; (2) preparing processed meats and meat byproducts; and (3) rendering and/or refining animal fat, bones, and meat scraps. This industry includes establishments primarily engaged in assembly cutting and packing of meats (i.e., boxed meats) from purchased carcasses.

Cross-References. Establishments primarily engaged in—

- Manufacturing canned meat for baby food—are classified in Industry 31142, Fruit and Vegetable Canning, Pickling, and Drying;
- Manufacturing meat-based animal feeds from carcasses—are classified in Industry 31111, Animal Food Manufacturing;
- Blending purchased animal fats with vegetable fats—are classified in Industry 31122, Starch and Vegetable Fats and Oils Manufacturing;
- Manufacturing canned and frozen specialty foods containing meat, such as nationality foods (e.g., enchiladas, pizza, egg rolls) and frozen dinners,—are classified in Industry Group 3114, Fruit and Vegetable Preserving and Specialty Food Manufacturing;
- Drying, freezing, or breaking eggs—are classified in Industry 31199, All Other Food Manufacturing; and
- Cutting meat (except box meat)—are classified in Industry 42447, Meat and Meat Product Merchant Wholesalers.

311611 Animal (except Poultry) Slaughtering[CAN]

This U.S. industry comprises establishments primarily engaged in slaughtering animals (except poultry and small game). Establishments that slaughter and prepare meats are included in this industry.

Cross-References. Establishments primarily engaged in—

- Processing meat and meat byproducts (except poultry and small game) from purchased meats—are classified in U.S. Industry 311612, Meat Processed from Carcasses;

US—United States industry only. CAN—United States and Canadian industries are comparable. MEX—United States and Mexican industries are comparable. Blank—Canadian, Mexican, and United States industries are comparable.

- Slaughtering and/or processing poultry and small game—are classified in U.S. Industry 311615, Poultry Processing;
- Rendering lard and other animal fats and oils, animal fat, bones, and meat scraps—are classified in U.S. Industry 311613, Rendering and Meat Byproduct Processing; and
- Manufacturing canned and frozen specialty foods containing meat, such as nationality foods (e.g., enchiladas, egg rolls, pizza) and frozen dinners,— are classified in Industry Group 3114, Fruit and Vegetable Preserving and Specialty Food Manufacturing.

311612 Meat Processed from Carcasses[US]

This U.S. industry comprises establishments primarily engaged in processing or preserving meat and meat byproducts (except poultry and small game) from purchased meats. This industry includes establishments primarily engaged in assembly cutting and packing of meats (i.e., boxed meats) from purchased meats.

Cross-References. Establishments primarily engaged in—

- Slaughtering animals (except poultry and small game)—are classified in U.S. Industry 311611, Animal (except Poultry) Slaughtering;
- Slaughtering poultry and small game—are classified in U.S. Industry 311615, Poultry Processing;
- Rendering animal fat, bones, and meat scraps—are classified in U.S. Industry 311613, Rendering and Meat Byproduct Processing;
- Manufacturing canned meats for baby food—are classified in U.S. Industry 311422, Specialty Canning;
- Manufacturing meat-based animal feeds from carcasses—are classified in Industry 31111, Animal Food Manufacturing;
- Manufacturing canned and frozen specialty foods containing meat, such as nationality foods (e.g., enchiladas, egg rolls, pizza) and frozen dinners,— are classified in Industry Group 3114, Fruit and Vegetable Preserving and Specialty Food Manufacturing; and
- Cutting meat (except boxed meat)—are classified in U.S. Industry 424470, Meat and Meat Product Merchant Wholesalers.

311613 Rendering and Meat Byproduct Processing[US]

This U.S. industry comprises establishments primarily engaged in rendering animal fat, bones, and meat scraps.

US—United States industry only. CAN—United States and Canadian industries are comparable. MEX—United States and Mexican industries are comparable. Blank—Canadian, Mexican, and United States industries are comparable.

Cross-References.

Establishments primarily engaged in blending purchased animal fats with vegetable fats are classified in U.S. Industry 311225, Fats and Oils Refining and Blending.

311615 Poultry Processing[CAN]

This U.S. industry comprises establishments primarily engaged in (1) slaughtering poultry and small game and/or (2) preparing processed poultry and small game meat and meat byproducts.

Cross-References. Establishments primarily engaged in—

- Slaughtering animals (except poultry and small game) and/or preparing meats—are classified in U.S. Industry 311611, Animal (except Poultry) Slaughtering;

- Preparing meat and meat byproducts (except poultry and small game) from purchased meats—are classified in U.S. Industry 311612, Meat Processed from Carcasses;

- Rendering animal fat, bones, and meat scraps—are classified in U.S. Industry 311613, Rendering and Meat Byproduct Processing;

- Canning poultry and small game for baby food—are classified in U.S. Industry 311422, Specialty Canning;

- Producing meat-based animal feeds from carcasses—are classified in Industry 31111, Animal Food Manufacturing;

- Manufacturing canned and frozen meat products, such as nationality foods (e.g., enchiladas, egg rolls, pizza) and frozen dinners,—are classified in Industry Group 3114, Fruit and Vegetable Preserving and Specialty Food Manufacturing; and

- Drying, freezing, and breaking eggs—are classified in U.S. Industry 311999, All Other Miscellaneous Food Manufacturing.

3117 Seafood Product Preparation and Packaging

31171 Seafood Product Preparation and Packaging

This industry comprises establishments primarily engaged in one or more of the following: (1) canning seafood (including soup); (2) smoking, salting, and drying seafood; (3) eviscerating fresh fish by removing heads, fins, scales, bones, and entrails; (4) shucking and packing fresh shellfish; (5) processing marine fats and oils; and (6) freezing seafood. Establishments known as "floating factory ships'' that are engaged in the gathering and processing of seafood into canned seafood products are included in this industry.

311711 Seafood Canning^{US}

This U.S. industry comprises establishments primarily engaged in (1) canning seafood (including soup) and marine fats and oils and/or (2) smoking, salting, and drying seafood. Establishments known as ''floating factory ships'' that are engaged in the gathering and processing of seafood into canned seafood products are included in this industry.

Cross-References.

Establishments primarily engaged in preparing fresh and frozen seafood and marine fats and oils are classified in U.S. Industry 311712, Fresh and Frozen Seafood Processing.

311712 Fresh and Frozen Seafood Processing^{US}

This U.S. industry comprises establishments primarily engaged in one or more of the following: (1) eviscerating fresh fish by removing heads, fins, scales, bones, and entrails; (2) shucking and packing fresh shellfish; (3) manufacturing frozen seafood; and (4) processing fresh and frozen marine fats and oils.

Cross-References.

Establishments primarily engaged in canning and curing seafood are classified in U.S. Industry 311711, Seafood Canning.

3118 Bakeries and Tortilla Manufacturing

31181 Bread and Bakery Product Manufacturing

This industry comprises establishments primarily engaged in manufacturing fresh and frozen bread and other bakery products.

Cross-References. Establishments primarily engaged in—

- Manufacturing cookies and crackers—are classified in Industry 31182, Cookie, Cracker, and Pasta Manufacturing;

- Preparing and selling bakery products (e.g., cookies, pretzels) for immediate consumption—are classified in Industry 72221, Limited-Service Eating Places;

US—United States industry only. CAN—United States and Canadian industries are comparable. MEX—United States and Mexican industries are comparable. Blank—Canadian, Mexican, and United States industries are comparable.

- Retailing bakery products not for immediate consumption made elsewhere—are classified in Industry 44529, Other Specialty Food Stores; and

- Manufacturing pretzels (except soft)—are classified in Industry 31191, Snack Food Manufacturing.

311811 Retail Bakeries^{CAN}

This U.S. industry comprises establishments primarily engaged in retailing bread and other bakery products not for immediate consumption made on the premises from flour, not from prepared dough.

Cross-References. Establishments primarily engaged in—

- Retailing bakery products not for immediate consumption made elsewhere—are classified in U.S. Industry 445291, Baked Goods Stores;

- Preparing and selling bakery products (e.g., cookies, pretzels) for immediate consumption—are classified in U.S. Industry 722213, Snack and Nonalcoholic Beverage Bars;

- Manufacturing fresh or frozen breads and other fresh bakery (except cookies and crackers) products—are classified in U.S. Industry 311812, Commercial Bakeries; and

- Manufacturing cookies and crackers—are classified in U.S. Industry 311821, Cookie and Cracker Manufacturing.

311812 Commercial Bakeries^{US}

This U.S. industry comprises establishments primarily engaged in manufacturing fresh and frozen bread and bread-type rolls and other fresh bakery (except cookies and crackers) products.

Cross-References. Establishments primarily engaged in—

- Retailing bread and other bakery products not for immediate consumption made on the premises from flour, not from prepared dough—are classified in U.S. Industry 311811, Retail Bakeries;

- Manufacturing frozen bakery products (except bread)—are classified in U.S. Industry 311813, Frozen Cakes, Pies, and Other Pastries Manufacturing;

- Preparing and selling bakery products (e.g., cookies, pretzels) for immediate consumption—are classified in U.S. Industry 722213, Snack and Nonalcoholic Beverage Bars;

- Retailing bakery products not for immediate consumption made elsewhere—are classified in U.S. Industry 445291, Baked Goods Stores;
- Manufacturing cookies and crackers—are classified in U.S. Industry 311821, Cookie and Cracker Manufacturing; and
- Manufacturing pretzels (except soft)—are classified in U.S. Industry 311919, Other Snack Food Manufacturing.

311813 Frozen Cakes, Pies, and Other Pastries Manufacturing[US]

This U.S. industry comprises establishments primarily engaged in manufacturing frozen bakery products (except bread), such as cakes, pies, and doughnuts.

Cross-References. Establishments primarily engaged in—

- Manufacturing frozen breads—are classified in U.S. Industry 311812, Commercial Bakeries;
- Retailing bakery products not for immediate consumption made on the premises from flour, not from prepared dough—are classified in U.S. Industry 311811, Retail Bakeries;
- Preparing and selling bakery products (e.g., cookies, pretzels) for immediate consumption—are classified in U.S. Industry 722213, Snack and Nonalcoholic Beverage Bars;
- Manufacturing cookies and crackers—are classified in U.S. Industry 311821, Cookie and Cracker Manufacturing; and
- Retailing bakery products not for immediate consumption made elsewhere—are classified in U.S. Industry 445291, Baked Goods Stores.

31182 Cookie, Cracker, and Pasta Manufacturing

This industry comprises establishments primarily engaged in one of the following: (1) manufacturing cookies and crackers; (2) preparing flour and dough mixes and dough from flour ground elsewhere; and (3) manufacturing dry pasta. The establishments in this industry may package the dry pasta they manufacture with other ingredients.

Cross-References. Establishments primarily engaged in—

- Preparing and selling bakery products (e.g., cookies, pretzels) for immediate consumption—are classified in Industry 72221, Limited-Service Eating Places;

- Retailing bakery products not for immediate consumption made elsewhere—are classified in Industry 44529, Other Specialty Food Stores;
- Manufacturing bakery products (e.g., bread, cookies, pies)—are classified in Industry 31181, Bread and Bakery Product Manufacturing;
- Milling flour and preparing flour mixes or doughs—are classified in Industry 31121, Flour Milling and Malt Manufacturing;
- Manufacturing canned pasta specialties—are classified in Industry 31142, Fruit and Vegetable Canning, Pickling, and Drying;
- Manufacturing fresh pasta—are classified in Industry 31199, All Other Food Manufacturing;
- Manufacturing pretzels (except soft)—are classified in Industry 31191, Snack Food Manufacturing;
- Mixing purchased dried and/or dehydrated ingredients with purchased dry pasta—are classified in Industry 31199, All Other Food Manufacturing; and
- Drying and/or dehydrating ingredients and packaging them with purchased dry pasta—are classified in Industry 31142, Fruit and Vegetable Canning, Pickling, and Drying.

311821 Cookie and Cracker Manufacturing[CAN]

This U.S. industry comprises establishments primarily engaged in manufacturing cookies, crackers, and other products, such as ice cream cones.

Cross-References. Establishments primarily engaged in—

- Preparing and selling bakery products (e.g., cookies, pretzels) for immediate consumption—are classified in U.S. Industry 722213, Snack and Nonalcoholic Beverage Bars;
- Retailing bakery products not for immediate consumption made elsewhere—are classified in U.S. Industry 445291, Baked Goods Stores;
- Manufacturing bakery products (e.g., breads, cookies, pies)—are classified in Industry 31181, Bread and Bakery Product Manufacturing; and
- Manufacturing pretzels (except soft)—are classified in U.S. Industry 311919, Other Snack Food Manufacturing.

311822 Flour Mixes and Dough Manufacturing from Purchased Flour[CAN]

This U.S. industry comprises establishments primarily engaged in manufacturing prepared flour mixes or dough mixes from flour ground elsewhere.

Cross-References.

Establishments primarily engaged in milling flour and preparing flour mixes or doughs are classified in U.S. Industry 311211, Flour Milling.

311823 Dry Pasta Manufacturing[CAN]

This U.S. industry comprises establishments primarily engaged in manufacturing dry pasta. The establishments in this industry may package the dry pasta they manufacture with other ingredients.

Cross-References. Establishments primarily engaged in—

- Manufacturing fresh pasta—are classified in U.S. Industry 311991, Perishable Prepared Food Manufacturing;

- Manufacturing pasta specialties—are classified in Industry Group 3114, Fruit and Vegetable Preserving and Specialty Food Manufacturing;

- Mixing purchased dried and/or dehydrated ingredients with purchased dry pasta—are classified in U.S. Industry 311999, All Other Miscellaneous Food Manufacturing; and

- Drying and/or dehydrating ingredients packaged with purchased dry pasta—are classified in U.S. Industry 311423, Dried and Dehydrated Food Manufacturing.

31183 Tortilla Manufacturing
See industry description for 311830 below.

311830 Tortilla Manufacturing

This industry comprises establishments primarily engaged in manufacturing tortillas.

Cross-References. Establishments primarily engaged in—

- Manufacturing canned nationality foods using tortillas—are classified in U.S. Industry 311422, Specialty Canning;

- Manufacturing frozen nationality foods using tortillas—are classified in U.S. Industry 311412, Frozen Specialty Food Manufacturing; and

- Manufacturing tortilla chips—are classified in U.S. Industry 311919, Other Snack Food Manufacturing.

US—United States industry only. CAN—United States and Canadian industries are comparable. MEX—United States and Mexican industries are comparable. Blank—Canadian, Mexican, and United States industries are comparable.

3119 Other Food Manufacturing

This industry group comprises establishments primarily engaged in manufacturing food (except animal food; grain and oilseed milling; sugar and confectionery products; preserved fruit, vegetable, and specialty foods; dairy products; meat products; seafood products; and bakeries and tortillas). The industry group includes industries with different productive processes, such as snack food manufacturing; coffee and tea manufacturing; concentrate, syrup, condiment, and spice manufacturing; and, in general, an entire range of other miscellaneous food product manufacturing.

31191 Snack Food Manufacturing

This industry comprises establishments primarily engaged in one or more of the following: (1) salting, roasting, drying, cooking, or canning nuts; (2) processing grains or seeds into snacks; (3) manufacturing peanut butter; and (4) manufacturing potato chips, corn chips, popped popcorn, pretzels (except soft), pork rinds, and similar snacks.

Cross-References. Establishments primarily engaged in—

- Manufacturing crackers—are classified in Industry 31182, Cookie, Cracker, and Pasta Manufacturing;
- Manufacturing unpopped popcorn—are classified in Industry 31199, All Other Food Manufacturing;
- Manufacturing chocolate or candy-coated nuts and candy-covered popcorn—are classified in Industry Group 3113, Sugar and Confectionery Product Manufacturing; and
- Manufacturing soft pretzels—are classified in Industry 31181, Bread and Bakery Product Manufacturing.

311911 Roasted Nuts and Peanut Butter Manufacturing[CAN]

This U.S. industry comprises establishments primarily engaged in one or more of the following: (1) salting, roasting, drying, cooking, or canning nuts; (2) processing grains or seeds into snacks; and (3) manufacturing peanut butter.

Cross-References.

Establishments primarily engaged in manufacturing chocolate or candy-coated nuts and candy-covered popcorn are classified in Industry Group 3113, Sugar and Confectionery Product Manufacturing.

US—United States industry only. CAN—United States and Canadian industries are comparable. MEX—United States and Mexican industries are comparable. Blank—Canadian, Mexican, and United States industries are comparable.

311919 Other Snack Food Manufacturing^{CAN}

This U.S. industry comprises establishments primarily engaged in manufacturing snack foods (except roasted nuts and peanut butter).

Illustrative Examples:

Corn chips and related corn snacks
manufacturing
Popped popcorn (except candy-covered)
manufacturing

Pork rinds manufacturing
Potato chips manufacturing
Pretzels (except soft) manufacturing
Tortilla chips manufacturing

Cross-References. Establishments primarily engaged in—

- Manufacturing cookies and crackers—are classified in U.S. Industry 311821, Cookie and Cracker Manufacturing;

- Manufacturing candy covered popcorn and nonchocolate granola bars—are classified in Industry 311340, Nonchocolate Confectionery Manufacturing;

- Salting, roasting, drying, cooking, or canning nuts and seeds—are classified in U.S. Industry 311911, Roasted Nuts and Peanut Butter Manufacturing;

- Manufacturing unpopped popcorn—are classified in U.S. Industry 311999, All Other Miscellaneous Food Manufacturing; and

- Manufacturing soft pretzels—are classified in U.S. Industry 311812, Commercial Bakeries.

31192 Coffee and Tea Manufacturing
See industry description for 311920 below.

311920 Coffee and Tea Manufacturing^{CAN}

This industry comprises establishments primarily engaged in one or more of the following: (1) roasting coffee; (2) manufacturing coffee and tea concentrates (including instant and freeze-dried); (3) blending tea; (4) manufacturing herbal tea; and (5) manufacturing coffee extracts, flavorings, and syrups.

Cross-References.

Establishments primarily engaged in bottling and canning iced tea are classified in U.S. Industry 312111, Soft Drink Manufacturing.

31193 Flavoring Syrup and Concentrate Manufacturing
See industry description for 311930 below.

US—United States industry only. CAN—United States and Canadian industries are comparable. MEX—United States and Mexican industries are comparable. Blank—Canadian, Mexican, and United States industries are comparable.

311930 Flavoring Syrup and Concentrate Manufacturing

This industry comprises establishments primarily engaged in manufacturing flavoring syrup drink concentrates and related products for soda fountain use or for the manufacture of soft drinks.

Cross-References. Establishments primarily engaged in—

- Manufacturing chocolate syrup—are classified in Industry 311320, Chocolate and Confectionery Manufacturing from Cacao Beans;

- Manufacturing flavoring extracts (except coffee and meat) and natural food colorings—are classified in U.S. Industry 311942, Spice and Extract Manufacturing;

- Manufacturing coffee extracts—are classified in Industry 311920, Coffee and Tea Manufacturing;

- Manufacturing meat extracts—are classified in Industry 31161, Animal Slaughtering and Processing;

- Manufacturing powdered drink mixes (except coffee, tea, chocolate, or milk-based) and table syrup from corn syrup—are classified in U.S. Industry 311999, All Other Miscellaneous Food Manufacturing;

- Reducing maple sap to maple syrup—are classified in U.S. Industry 111998, All Other Miscellaneous Crop Farming; and

- Manufacturing natural nonfood colorings—are classified in U.S. Industry 325199, All Other Basic Organic Chemical Manufacturing.

31194 Seasoning and Dressing Manufacturing

This industry comprises establishments primarily engaged in one or more of the following: (1) manufacturing dressings and sauces, such as mayonnaise, salad dressing, vinegar, mustard, horseradish, soy sauce, tarter sauce, Worcestershire sauce, and other prepared sauces (except tomato-based and gravies); (2) manufacturing spices, table salt, seasoning, and flavoring extracts (except coffee and meat), and natural food colorings; and (3) manufacturing dry mix food preparations, such as salad dressing mixes, gravy and sauce mixes, frosting mixes, and other dry mix preparations.

Cross-References. Establishments primarily engaged in—

- Manufacturing catsup and other tomato-based sauces—are classified in Industry 31142, Fruit and Vegetable Canning, Pickling, and Drying;

- Mixing purchased dried and/or dehydrated potato, rice, and pasta and packaging them with other purchased ingredients, and manufacturing prepared frosting—are classified in Industry 31199, All Other Food Manufacturing;

- Drying and/or dehydrating ingredients for dry soup mixes and bouillon— are classified in Industry 31142, Fruit and Vegetable Canning, Pickling, and Drying;

- Mixing purchased dried and/or dehydrated ingredients for dry soup mixes and bouillon—are classified in Industry 31199, All Other Food Manufacturing;

- Manufacturing industrial salts—are classified in Industry 32599, Other Chemical Product and Preparation Manufacturing;

- Manufacturing flavoring syrups (except coffee)—are classified in Industry 31193, Flavoring Syrup and Concentrate Manufacturing;

- Manufacturing synthetic food colorings—are classified in Industry 32513, Synthetic Dye and Pigment Manufacturing;

- Manufacturing natural organic colorings for nonfood uses—are classified in Industry 32519, Other Basic Organic Chemical Manufacturing;

- Manufacturing coffee extracts—are classified in Industry 31192, Coffee and Tea Manufacturing;

- Manufacturing meat extracts—are classified in Industry 31161, Animal Slaughtering and Processing; and

- Manufacturing gravies—are classified in Industry 31199, All Other Food Manufacturing.

311941 Mayonnaise, Dressing, and Other Prepared Sauce Manufacturing[US]

This U.S. industry comprises establishments primarily engaged in manufacturing mayonnaise, salad dressing, vinegar, mustard, horseradish, soy sauce, tarter sauce, Worcestershire sauce, and other prepared sauces (except tomato-based and gravy).

Cross-References. Establishments primarily engaged in—

- Manufacturing catsup and similar tomato-based sauces—are classified in U.S. Industry 311421, Fruit and Vegetable Canning;

- Manufacturing dry salad dressing and dry sauce mixes—are classified in U.S. Industry 311942, Spice and Extract Manufacturing; and

- Manufacturing gravies—are classified in U.S. Industry 311999, All Other Miscellaneous Food Manufacturing.

311942 Spice and Extract Manufacturing[US]

This U.S. industry comprises establishments primarily engaged in (1) manufacturing spices, table salt, seasonings, flavoring extracts (except coffee and meat), and natural food colorings and/or (2) manufacturing dry mix food preparations, such as salad dressing mixes, gravy and sauce mixes, frosting mixes, and other dry mix preparations.

Cross-References. Establishments primarily engaged in—

- Manufacturing catsup and other tomato-based sauces—are classified in U.S. Industry 311421, Fruit and Vegetable Canning;
- Manufacturing mayonnaise, dressings, and prepared nontomato-based sauces—are classified in U.S. Industry 311941, Mayonnaise, Dressing, and Other Prepared Sauce Manufacturing;
- Manufacturing industrial salts—are classified in U.S. Industry 325998, All Other Miscellaneous Chemical Product and Preparation Manufacturing;
- Drying and/or dehydrating ingredients for dry soup mixes and bouillon—are classified in U.S. Industry 311423, Dried and Dehydrated Food Manufacturing;
- Mixing purchased dried and/or dehydrated ingredients for dry soup mixes and bouillon—are classified in U.S. Industry 311999, All Other Miscellaneous Food Manufacturing;
- Manufacturing flavoring syrups (except coffee-based syrups)—are classified in Industry 311930, Flavoring Syrup and Concentrate Manufacturing;
- Manufacturing dried and dehydrated potato, rice, or dry pasta packaged with other ingredients, and prepared frostings—are classified in U.S. Industry 311999, All Other Miscellaneous Food Manufacturing;
- Manufacturing coffee extracts and/or coffee-based syrups—are classified in Industry 311920, Coffee and Tea Manufacturing;
- Manufacturing meat extracts—are classified in Industry 31161, Animal Slaughtering and Processing;
- Manufacturing synthetic food colorings—are classified in U.S. Industry 325132, Synthetic Organic Dye and Pigment Manufacturing; and
- Manufacturing natural organic colorings for nonfood uses—are classified in U.S. Industry 325199, All Other Basic Organic Chemical Manufacturing.

31199 All Other Food Manufacturing

This industry comprises establishments primarily engaged in manufacturing food (except animal food; grain and oilseed milling; sugar and confectionery

---

US—United States industry only. CAN—United States and Canadian industries are comparable. MEX—United States and Mexican industries are comparable. Blank—Canadian, Mexican, and United States industries are comparable.

products; preserved fruits, vegetables, and specialties; dairy products; meat products; seafood products; bakeries and tortillas; snack foods; coffee and tea; flavoring syrups and concentrates; seasonings; and dressings). Included in this industry are establishments primarily engaged in mixing purchased dried and/or dehydrated ingredients including those mixing purchased dried and/or dehydrated ingredients for soup mixes and bouillon.

Illustrative Examples:

Baking powder manufacturing
Cut or peeled fresh vegetables
 manufacturing
Dessert puddings manufacturing
Egg substitutes manufacturing
Fresh pasta manufacturing
Fresh pizza manufacturing

Honey processing
Popcorn (except popped) manufacturing
Powdered drink mixes (except chocolate,
 coffee, tea, or milk based)
 manufacturing
Sweetening syrups (except pure maple)
 manufacturing

Cross-References. Establishments primarily engaged in—

- Manufacturing animal foods—are classified in Industry Group 3111, Animal Food Manufacturing;

- Milling grain and oilseed—are classified in Industry Group 3112, Grain and Oilseed Milling;

- Manufacturing sugar and confectionery products—are classified in Industry Group 3113, Sugar and Confectionery Product Manufacturing;

- Preserving fruit, vegetables, and specialty foods—are classified in Industry Group 3114, Fruit and Vegetable Preserving and Specialty Food Manufacturing;

- Manufacturing dairy products—are classified in Industry Group 3115, Dairy Product Manufacturing;

- Manufacturing meat products—are classified in Industry Group 3116, Animal Slaughtering and Processing;

- Manufacturing seafood products—are classified in Industry Group 3117, Seafood Product Preparation and Packaging;

- Manufacturing bakery and tortilla products—are classified in Industry Group 3118, Bakeries and Tortilla Manufacturing;

- Manufacturing snack foods—are classified in Industry 31191, Snack Food Manufacturing;

- Manufacturing coffee and tea—are classified in Industry 31192, Coffee and Tea Manufacturing;

- Manufacturing flavoring syrups and concentrates—are classified in Industry 31193, Flavoring Syrup and Concentrate Manufacturing;

- Manufacturing seasonings and dressings—are classified in Industry 31194, Seasoning and Dressing Manufacturing;

- Milling rice and packaging it with other ingredients—are classified in Industry 31121, Flour Milling and Malt Manufacturing;

- Manufacturing dry pasta and packaging it with other ingredients—are classified in Industry 31182, Cookie, Cracker, and Pasta Manufacturing; and

- Drying and/or dehydrating ingredients and packaging them with other purchased ingredients—are classified in Industry 31142, Fruit and Vegetable Canning, Pickling, and Drying.

311991 Perishable Prepared Food Manufacturing[US]

This U.S. industry comprises establishments primarily engaged in manufacturing perishable prepared foods, such as salads, sandwiches, prepared meals, fresh pizza, fresh pasta, and peeled or cut vegetables.

311999 All Other Miscellaneous Food Manufacturing[US]

This U.S. industry comprises establishments primarily engaged in manufacturing food (except animal food; grain and oilseed milling; sugar and confectionery products; preserved fruits, vegetables, and specialties; dairy products; meat products; seafood products; bakeries and tortillas; snack foods; coffee and tea; flavoring syrups and concentrates; seasonings and dressings; and perishable prepared food). Included in this industry are establishments primarily engaged in mixing purchased dried and/or dehydrated ingredients including those mixing purchased dried and/or dehydrated ingredients for soup mixes and bouillon.

Illustrative Examples:

Baking powder manufacturing
Cake frosting manufacturing
Dessert puddings manufacturing
Egg substitutes manufacturing
Gelatin dessert preparations
  manufacturing
Honey processing

Popcorn (except popped) manufacturing
Powdered drink mixes (except chocolate,
  coffee, tea, or milk based)
  manufacturing Sweetening syrups
  (except pure maple) manufacturing
Yeast manufacturing

Cross-References. Establishments primarily engaged in—

- Manufacturing animal foods—are classified in Industry Group 3111, Animal Food Manufacturing;

- Milling grain and oilseed—are classified in Industry Group 3112, Grain and Oilseed Milling;

- Manufacturing sugar and confectionery products—are classified in Industry Group 3113, Sugar and Confectionery Product Manufacturing;

- Preserving fruit, vegetable, and specialty foods—are classified in Industry Group 3114, Fruit and Vegetable Preserving and Specialty Food Manufacturing;

- Manufacturing dairy products—are classified in Industry Group 3115, Dairy Product Manufacturing;

- Manufacturing meat products—are classified in Industry Group 3116, Meat Product Manufacturing;

- Manufacturing seafood products—are classified in Industry Group 3117, Seafood Product Preparation and Packaging;

- Manufacturing bakery and tortilla products—are classified in Industry Group 3118, Bakeries and Tortilla Manufacturing;

- Manufacturing snack foods—are classified in Industry 31191, Snack Food Manufacturing;

- Manufacturing coffee and tea—are classified in Industry 31192, Coffee and Tea Manufacturing;

- Manufacturing flavoring syrups and concentrates—are classified in Industry 31193, Flavoring Syrup and Concentrate Manufacturing;

- Manufacturing seasonings and dressings—are classified in Industry 31194, Seasoning and Dressing Manufacturing;

- Manufacturing perishable prepared foods—are classified in U.S. Industry 311991, Perishable Prepared Food Manufacturing;

- Milling rice and packaging it with other ingredients—are classified in U.S. Industry 311212, Rice Milling;

- Manufacturing dry pasta and packaging it with ingredients—are classified in U.S. Industry 311823, Dry Pasta Manufacturing; and

- Drying and/or dehydrating ingredients and packaging them with other purchased ingredients—are classified in U.S. Industry 311423, Dried and Dehydrated Food Manufacturing.

312 Beverage and Tobacco Product Manufacturing

Industries in the Beverage and Tobacco Product Manufacturing subsector manufacture beverages and tobacco products. The industry group, Beverage Manufacturing, includes three types of establishments: (1) those that manufacture nonalcoholic beverages; (2) those that manufacture alcoholic beverages through the fermentation process; and (3) those that produce distilled alcoholic beverages. Ice manufacturing,

---

while not a beverage, is included with nonalcoholic beverage manufacturing because it uses the same production process as water purification.

In the case of activities related to the manufacture of beverages, the structure follows the defined productive processes. Brandy, a distilled beverage, was not placed under distillery product manufacturing, but rather under the NAICS class for winery product manufacturing since the productive process used in the manufacturing of alcoholic grape-based beverages produces both wines (fermented beverage) and brandies (distilled beverage).

The industry group, Tobacco Manufacturing, includes two types of establishments: (1) those engaged in redrying and stemming tobacco and, (2) those that manufacture tobacco products, such as cigarettes and cigars.

3121 Beverage Manufacturing

31211 Soft Drink and Ice Manufacturing

This industry comprises establishments primarily engaged in one or more of the following: (1) manufacturing soft drinks; (2) manufacturing ice; and (3) purifying and bottling water.

Cross-References. Establishments primarily engaged in—

- Canning fruit and vegetable juices—are classified in Industry 31142, Fruit and Vegetable Canning, Pickling and Drying;

- Manufacturing soft drink bases—are classified in Industry 31193, Flavoring Syrup and Concentrate Manufacturing;

- Manufacturing nonalcoholic cider—are classified in Industry 31194, Seasoning and Dressing Manufacturing;

- Manufacturing dry ice—are classified in Industry 32512, Industrial Gas Manufacturing;

- Manufacturing milk-based drinks—are classified in Industry 31151, Dairy Product (except Frozen) Manufacturing;

- Manufacturing nonalcoholic beers—are classified in Industry 31212, Breweries;

- Manufacturing nonalcoholic wines—are classified in Industry 31213, Wineries; and

- Bottling purchased purified water—are classified in Industry 42449, Other Grocery and Related Products Merchant Wholesalers.

US—United States industry only. CAN—United States and Canadian industries are comparable. MEX—United States and Mexican industries are comparable. Blank—Canadian, Mexican, and United States industries are comparable.

312111 Soft Drink Manufacturing[MEX]

This U.S. industry comprises establishments primarily engaged in manufacturing soft drinks and artificially carbonated waters.

Cross-References. Establishments primarily engaged in—

- Canning fruit and vegetable juices—are classified in U.S. Industry 311421, Fruit and Vegetable Canning;
- Manufacturing fruit syrups for flavoring—are classified in Industry 31193, Flavoring Syrup and Concentrate Manufacturing;
- Manufacturing nonalcoholic cider—are classified in U.S. Industry 311941, All Other Miscellaneous Food Manufacturing;
- Purifying and bottling water (except artificially carbonated and flavored water)—are classified in U.S. Industry 312112, Bottled Water Manufacturing;
- Manufacturing milk-based drinks—are classified in U.S. Industry 311511, Fluid Milk Manufacturing;
- Manufacturing nonalcoholic beers—are classified in Industry 312120, Breweries; and
- Manufacturing nonalcoholic wines—are classified in Industry 312130, Wineries.

312112 Bottled Water Manufacturing[MEX]

This U.S. industry comprises establishments primarily engaged in purifying and bottling water (including naturally carbonated).

Cross-References. Establishments primarily engaged in—

- Manufacturing artificially carbonated waters—are classified in U.S. Industry 312111, Soft Drink Manufacturing; and
- Bottling purchased purified water— are classified in Industry 424490, Other Grocery and Related Products Merchant Wholesalers.

312113 Ice Manufacturing[MEX]

This U.S. industry comprises establishments primarily engaged in manufacturing ice.

Cross-References.

Establishments primarily engaged in manufacturing dry ice are classified in Industry 325120, Industrial Gas Manufacturing.

31212 Breweries
See industry description for 312120 below.

312120 Breweries

This industry comprises establishments primarily engaged in brewing beer, ale, malt liquors, and nonalcoholic beer.

Cross-References. Establishments primarily engaged in—

- Bottling purchased malt beverages—are classified in Industry 424810, Beer and Ale Merchant Wholesalers; and
- Manufacturing malt—are classified in U.S. Industry 311213, Malt Manufacturing.

31213 Wineries
See industry description for 312130 below.

312130 Wineries^{CAN}

This industry comprises establishments primarily engaged in one or more of the following: (1) growing grapes and manufacturing wine and brandies; (2) manufacturing wine and brandies from grapes and other fruits grown elsewhere; and (3) blending wines and brandies.

Cross-References.

Establishments primarily engaged in bottling purchased wines are classified in Industry 424820, Wine and Distilled Alcoholic Beverage Merchant Wholesalers.

31214 Distilleries
See industry description for 312140 below.

312140 Distilleries^{CAN}

This industry comprises establishments primarily engaged in one or more of the following: (1) distilling potable liquors (except brandies); (2) distilling and blending liquors; and (3) blending and mixing liquors and other ingredients.

US—United States industry only. CAN—United States and Canadian industries are comparable. MEX—United States and Mexican industries are comparable. Blank—Canadian, Mexican, and United States industries are comparable.

Cross-References. Establishments primarily engaged in—

- Manufacturing nonpotable ethyl alcohol—are classified in U.S. Industry 325193, Ethyl Alcohol Manufacturing;
- Bottling liquors made elsewhere—are classified in Industry 424820, Wine and Distilled Alcoholic Beverage Merchant Wholesalers; and
- Manufacturing brandies—are classified in Industry 312130, Wineries.

3122 Tobacco Manufacturing

31221 Tobacco Stemming and Redrying
See industry description for 312210 below.

312210 Tobacco Stemming and Redrying

This industry comprises establishments primarily engaged in the stemming and redrying of tobacco.

Cross-References. Establishments primarily engaged in—

- Reconstituting tobacco—are classified in U.S. Industry 312229, Other Tobacco Product Manufacturing;
- Selling leaf tobacco as merchant wholesalers that also engage in stemming tobacco—are classified in Industry 424940, Tobacco and Tobacco Product Merchant Wholesalers; and
- Selling leaf tobacco as agents or brokers that also engage in stemming tobacco—are classified in Industry 425120, Wholesale Trade Agents and Brokers.

31222 Tobacco Product Manufacturing

This industry comprises establishments primarily engaged in manufacturing cigarettes, cigars, smoking and chewing tobacco, and reconstituted tobacco.

Cross-References.

Establishments primarily engaged in stemming and redrying tobacco are classified in Industry 31221, Tobacco Stemming and Redrying.

312221 Cigarette Manufacturing[MEX]

This U.S. industry comprises establishments primarily engaged in manufacturing cigarettes.

US—United States industry only. CAN—United States and Canadian industries are comparable. MEX—United States and Mexican industries are comparable. Blank—Canadian, Mexican, and United States industries are comparable.

Cross-References.

Establishments primarily engaged in manufacturing cigars, smoking tobacco, chewing tobacco, and reconstituted tobacco are classified in U.S. Industry 312229, Other Tobacco Product Manufacturing.

312229 Other Tobacco Product Manufacturing[US]

This U.S. industry comprises establishments primarily engaged in manufacturing tobacco products (except cigarettes).

Illustrative Examples:

Chewing tobacco manufacturing	Reconstituting tobacco
Cigar manufacturing	Snuff manufacturing
Prepared pipe tobacco manufacturing	

Cross-References. Establishments primarily engaged in—

- Manufacturing cigarettes—are classified in U.S. Industry 312221, Cigarette Manufacturing; and

- Stemming and redrying tobacco—are classified in Industry 312210, Tobacco Stemming and Redrying.

313 Textile Mills

Industries in the Textile Mills subsector group establishments that transform a basic fiber (natural or synthetic) into a product, such as yarn or fabric, that is further manufactured into usable items, such as apparel, sheets towels, and textile bags for individual or industrial consumption. The further manufacturing may be performed in the same establishment and classified in this subsector, or it may be performed at a separate establishment and be classified elsewhere in manufacturing.

The main processes in this subsector include preparation and spinning of fiber, knitting or weaving of fabric, and the finishing of the textile. The NAICS structure follows and captures this process flow. Major industries in this flow, such as preparation of fibers, weaving of fabric, knitting of fabric, and fiber and fabric finishing, are uniquely identified. Texturizing, throwing, twisting, and winding of yarn contains aspects of both fiber preparation and fiber finishing and is classified with preparation of fibers rather than with finishing of fiber.

NAICS separates the manufacturing of primary textiles and the manufacturing of textile products (except apparel) when the textile product is produced from purchased primary textiles, such as fabric. The manufacturing of textile products (except apparel) from purchased fabric is classified in Subsector 314, Textile

Product Mills, and apparel from purchased fabric is classified in Subsector 315, Apparel Manufacturing.

Excluded from this subsector are establishments that weave or knit fabric and make garments. These establishments are included in Subsector 315, Apparel Manufacturing.

3131 Fiber, Yarn, and Thread Mills

31311 Fiber, Yarn, and Thread Mills

This industry comprises establishments primarily engaged in one or more of the following: (1) spinning yarn; (2) manufacturing thread of any fiber; (3) texturizing, throwing, twisting, and winding purchased yarn or manmade fiber filaments; and (4) producing hemp yarn and further processing into rope or bags.

Cross-References.

Establishments primarily engaged in manufacturing artificial and synthetic fibers and filaments and texturizing these filaments are classified in Industry 32522, Artificial and Synthetic Fibers and Filaments Manufacturing.

313111 Yarn Spinning Mills[US]

This U.S. industry comprises establishments primarily engaged in spinning yarn from any fiber and/or producing hemp yarn and further processing into rope or bags.

313112 Yarn Texturizing, Throwing, and Twisting Mills[US]

This U.S. industry comprises establishments primarily engaged in texturizing, throwing, twisting, spooling, or winding purchased yarns or manmade fiber filaments.

Cross-References.

Establishments primarily engaged in manufacturing artificial and synthetic fiber and filament and texturizing these fibers and filaments are classified in Industry 32522, Artificial and Synthetic Fibers and Filaments Manufacturing.

313113 Thread Mills[MEX]

This U.S. industry comprises establishments primarily engaged in manufacturing thread (e.g., sewing, hand-knitting, crochet) of all fibers.

3132 Fabric Mills

31321 Broadwoven Fabric Mills
See industry description for 313210 below.

313210 Broadwoven Fabric Mills

This industry comprises establishments primarily engaged in weaving broadwoven fabrics and felts (except tire fabrics and rugs). Establishments in this industry may weave only, weave and finish, or weave, finish, and further fabricate fabric products.

Cross-References. Establishments primarily engaged in—

- Weaving widths specifically constructed for cutting to narrow widths—are classified in U.S. Industry 313221, Narrow Fabric Mills;
- Weaving or tufting carpet and rugs—are classified in Industry 314110, Carpet and Rug Mills; and
- Making tire cord and tire fabrics—are classified in U.S. Industry 314992, Tire Cord and Tire Fabric Mills.

31322 Narrow Fabric Mills and Schiffli Machine Embroidery

This industry comprises establishments primarily engaged in one or more of the following: (1) weaving or braiding narrow fabrics; (2) manufacturing Schiffli machine embroideries; and (3) making fabric-covered elastic yarn and thread.

313221 Narrow Fabric Mills[US]

This U.S. industry comprises establishments primarily engaged in (1) weaving or braiding narrow fabrics in their final form or initially made in wider widths that are specially constructed for narrower widths and/or (2) making fabric-covered elastic yarn and thread. Establishments in this industry may weave only; weave and finish; or weave, finish, and further fabricate fabric products.

313222 Schiffli Machine Embroidery[US]

This U.S. industry comprises establishments primarily engaged in manufacturing Schiffli machine embroideries.

US—United States industry only. CAN—United States and Canadian industries are comparable. MEX—United States and Mexican industries are comparable. Blank—Canadian, Mexican, and United States industries are comparable.

31323 Nonwoven Fabric Mills

See industry description for 313230 below.

313230 Nonwoven Fabric Mills

This industry comprises establishments primarily engaged in manufacturing nonwoven fabrics and felts. Processes used include bonding and/or interlocking fibers by mechanical, chemical, thermal, or solvent means, or by combinations thereof.

31324 Knit Fabric Mills

This industry comprises establishments primarily engaged in one of the following: (1) knitting weft (i.e., circular) and warp (i.e., flat) fabric; (2) knitting and finishing weft and warp fabric; (3) manufacturing lace; or (4) manufacturing, dyeing, and finishing lace and lace goods. Establishments in this industry may knit only; knit and finish; or knit, finish, and further fabricate fabric products (except apparel).

Cross-References.

Establishments primarily engaged in knitting apparel are classified in Industry Group 3151, Apparel Knitting Mills.

313241 Weft Knit Fabric Mills[US]

This U.S. industry comprises establishments primarily engaged in knitting weft (i.e., circular) fabric or knitting and finishing weft fabric. Establishments in this industry may knit only; knit and finish; or knit, finish, and further fabricate fabric products (except apparel).

Cross-References.

Establishments primarily engaged in knitting apparel are classified in Industry Group 3151, Apparel Knitting Mills.

313249 Other Knit Fabric and Lace Mills[US]

This U.S. industry comprises establishments primarily engaged in one of the following: (1) knitting warp (i.e., flat) fabric; (2) knitting and finishing warp fabric; (3) manufacturing lace; or (4) manufacturing, dyeing, or finishing lace and lace goods. Establishments in this industry may knit only; knit and finish; or knit, finish, and further fabricate fabric products (except apparel).

Cross-References.

Establishments primarily engaged in knitting apparel are classified in Industry Group 3151, Apparel Knitting Mills.

3133 Textile and Fabric Finishing and Fabric Coating Mills

31331 Textile and Fabric Finishing Mills

This industry comprises (1) establishments primarily engaged in finishing of textiles, fabrics, and apparel, and (2) establishments of converters who buy fabric goods in the grey, have them finished on contract, and sell at wholesale. Finishing operations include: bleaching, dyeing, printing (e.g., roller, screen, flock, plisse), stonewashing, and other mechanical finishing, such as preshrinking, shrinking, sponging, calendering, mercerizing, and napping; as well as cleaning, scouring, and the preparation of natural fibers and raw stock.

Cross-References. Establishments primarily engaged in—

- Coating or impregnating fabrics—are classified in Industry 31332, Fabric Coating Mills;

- Knitting or knitting and finishing fabric—are classified in Industry 31324, Knit Fabric Mills;

- Manufacturing and finishing apparel—are classified in Subsector 315, Apparel Manufacturing;

- Weaving and finishing fabrics—are classified in Industry Group 3132, Fabric Mills;

- Manufacturing and finishing rugs and carpets—are classified in Industry 31411, Carpet and Rug Mills; and

- Printing on apparel—are classified in Industry 32311, Printing.

313311 Broadwoven Fabric Finishing Mills[US]

This U.S. industry comprises (1) establishments primarily engaged in finishing broadwoven fabrics, and (2) establishments of converters who buy broadwoven fabrics in the grey, have them finished on contract, and sell at wholesale. Finishing operations include bleaching, dyeing, printing (roller, screen, flock, plisse), and other mechanical finishing, such as preshrinking, shrinking, sponging, calendering, mercerizing and napping.

US—United States industry only. CAN—United States and Canadian industries are comparable. MEX—United States and Mexican industries are comparable. Blank—Canadian, Mexican, and United States industries are comparable.

Cross-References. Establishments primarily engaged in—

- Coating or impregnating fabrics—are classified in Industry 313320, Fabric Coating Mills; and

- Weaving and finishing broadwoven fabrics—are classified in Industry 313210, Broadwoven Fabric Mills.

313312 Textile and Fabric Finishing (except Broadwoven Fabric) Mills[US]

This U.S. industry comprises (1) establishments primarily engaged in dyeing, bleaching, printing, and other finishing of textiles, apparel, and fabrics (except broadwoven) and (2) establishments of converters who buy fabrics (except broadwoven) in the grey, have them finished on contract, and sell at wholesale. Finishing operations include bleaching, dyeing, printing (e.g., roller, screen, flock, plisse), stonewashing, and other mechanical finishing, such as preshrinking, shrinking, sponging, calendering, mercerizing and napping; as well as cleaning, scouring, and the preparation of natural fibers and raw stock.

Cross-References. Establishments primarily engaged in—

- Knitting and finishing fabric—are classified in Industry 31324, Knit Fabric Mills;

- Finishing broadwoven fabric—are classified in U.S. Industry 313311, Broadwoven Fabric Finishing Mills;

- Weaving and finishing narrow woven fabric—are classified in U.S. Industry 313221, Narrow Fabric Mills;

- Manufacturing and finishing apparel—are classified in Subsector 315, Apparel Manufacturing;

- Coating or impregnating fabrics—are classified in Industry 313320, Fabric Coating Mills; and

- Printing on apparel—are classified in Industry 32311, Printing.

31332 Fabric Coating Mills
See industry description for 313320 below.

313320 Fabric Coating Mills

This industry comprises establishments primarily engaged in coating, laminating, varnishing, waxing, and rubberizing textiles and apparel.

Cross-References.

Establishments primarily engaged in dyeing and finishing textiles are classified in Industry 31331, Textile and Fabric Finishing Mills.

314 Textile Product Mills

Industries in the Textile Product Mills subsector group establishments that make textile products (except apparel). With a few exceptions, processes used in these industries are generally cut and sew (i.e., purchasing fabric and cutting and sewing to make nonapparel textile products, such as sheets and towels).

3141 Textile Furnishings Mills

31411 Carpet and Rug Mills
See industry description for 314110 below.

314110 Carpet and Rug Mills

This industry comprises establishments primarily engaged in (1) manufacturing woven, tufted, and other carpets and rugs, such as art squares, floor mattings, needlepunch carpeting, and door mats and mattings, from textile materials or from twisted paper, grasses, reeds, sisal, jute, or rags and/or (2) finishing carpets and rugs.

31412 Curtain and Linen Mills

This industry comprises establishments primarily engaged in manufacturing household textile products, such as curtains, draperies, linens, bedspreads, sheets, tablecloths, towels, and shower curtains, from purchased materials.

Cross-References. Establishments primarily engaged in—

- Weaving broadwoven fabrics—are classified in Industry 31321, Broadwoven Fabric Mills;

- Manufacturing lace curtains on lace machines—are classified in Industry 31324, Knit Fabric Mills;

- Manufacturing textile blanket, wardrobe, and laundry bags—are classified in Industry 31491, Textile Bag and Canvas Mills; and

- Manufacturing mops—are classified in Industry 33999, All Other Miscellaneous Manufacturing.

US—United States industry only. CAN—United States and Canadian industries are comparable. MEX—United States and Mexican industries are comparable. Blank—Canadian, Mexican, and United States industries are comparable.

314121 Curtain and Drapery Mills[US]

This U.S. industry comprises establishments primarily engaged in manufacturing window curtains and draperies from purchased fabrics or sheet goods. The curtains and draperies may be made on a stock or custom basis for sale to individual retail customers.

Cross-References.

Establishments primarily engaged in manufacturing lace curtains on lace machines are classified in U.S. Industry 313249, Other Knit Fabric and Lace Mills.

314129 Other Household Textile Product Mills[US]

This U.S. industry comprises establishments primarily engaged in manufacturing household textile products (except window curtains and draperies), such as bedspreads, sheets, tablecloths, towels, and shower curtains, from purchased materials.

Cross-References. Establishments primarily engaged in—

- Weaving fabrics—are classified in Industry 313210, Broadwoven Fabric Mills;
- Manufacturing blanket, laundry, and wardrobe bags—are classified in U.S. Industry 314911, Textile Bag Mills;
- Manufacturing mops—are classified in U.S. Industry 339994, Broom, Brush, and Mop Manufacturing; and
- Manufacturing window curtains and draperies—are classified in U.S. Industry 314121, Curtain and Drapery Mills.

3149 Other Textile Product Mills

This industry group comprises establishments primarily engaged in making textile products, (except carpets and rugs, curtains and draperies, and other household textile products) from purchased materials.

31491 Textile Bag and Canvas Mills

This industry comprises establishments primarily engaged in manufacturing textile bags, awnings, tents, and related products from purchased textile fabrics.

Cross-References. Establishments primarily engaged in—

- Manufacturing plastic bags—are classified in Industry 32611, Plastics Packaging Materials and Unlaminated Film and Sheet Manufacturing;

- Manufacturing canvas blinds and shades—are classified in Industry 33792, Blind and Shade Manufacturing;

- Manufacturing luggage—are classified in Industry 31699, Other Leather and Allied Product Manufacturing; and

- Manufacturing women's handbags and purses of leather or other material (except precious metal)—are classified in Industry 31699, Other Leather and Allied Product Manufacturing.

314911 Textile Bag Mills[US]

This U.S. industry comprises establishments primarily engaged in manufacturing bags from purchased textile fabrics or yarns.

Illustrative Examples:

Canvas bags manufacturing
Laundry bags made from purchased woven or knitted materials
Seed bags made from purchased woven or knitted materials
Textile bags made from purchased woven or knitted materials

Cross-References. Establishments primarily engaged in—

- Manufacturing plastics bags—are classified in U.S. Industry 326111, Plastics Bag Manufacturing;

- Manufacturing luggage—are classified in U.S. Industry 316991, Luggage Manufacturing; and

- Manufacturing women's handbags and purses of leather or other material, except precious metal—are classified in U.S. Industry 316992, Women's Handbag and Purse Manufacturing.

314912 Canvas and Related Product Mills[US]

This U.S. industry comprises establishments primarily engaged in manufacturing canvas and canvas-like products, such as awnings, sails, tarpaulins, and tents, from purchased fabrics.

Cross-References. Establishments primarily engaged in—

- Manufacturing canvas blinds and shades—are classified in Industry 337920, Blind and Shade Manufacturing; and

- Manufacturing canvas bags—are classified in U.S. Industry 314911, Textile Bag Mills.

US—United States industry only. CAN—United States and Canadian industries are comparable. MEX—United States and Mexican industries are comparable. Blank—Canadian, Mexican, and United States industries are comparable.

31499 All Other Textile Product Mills

This industry comprises establishments primarily engaged in manufacturing nonapparel textile products (except carpet, rugs, curtains, linens, bags, and canvas products) from purchased materials.

Illustrative Examples:

Batts and batting (except nonwoven fabrics) manufacturing

Carpet cutting and binding

Diapers (except disposable) made from purchased fabric

Dust cloths made from purchased fabric apparel) for the trade

Fishing nets made from purchased materials

Sleeping bags manufacturing

Textile fire hoses made from purchased materials

Weatherstripping made from purchased textiles

Cross-References. Establishments primarily engaged in—

- Manufacturing yarns and thread—are classified in Industry 31311, Fiber, Yarn, and Thread Mills;

- Manufacturing carpets and rugs—are classified in Industry 31411, Carpet and Rug Mills;

- Manufacturing apparel—are classified in Subsector 315, Apparel Manufacturing;

- Manufacturing curtains and linens—are classified in Industry 31412, Curtain and Linen Mills; and

- Manufacturing textile bags and canvas products—are classified in Industry 31491, Textile Bag and Canvas Mills.

314991 Rope, Cordage, and Twine Mills[US]

This U.S. industry comprises establishments primarily engaged in manufacturing rope, cable, cordage, twine, and related products from all materials (e.g., abaca, sisal, henequen, hemp, cotton, paper, jute, flax, manmade fibers including glass).

Cross-References.

Establishments primarily engaged in spinning yarns and filaments are classified in U.S. Industry 313111, Yarn Spinning Mills.

314992 Tire Cord and Tire Fabric Mills[US]

This U.S. industry comprises establishments primarily engaged in manufacturing cord and fabric of polyester, rayon, cotton, glass, steel, or other materials for use in reinforcing rubber tires, industrial belting, and similar uses.

US—United States industry only. CAN—United States and Canadian industries are comparable. MEX—United States and Mexican industries are comparable. Blank—Canadian, Mexican, and United States industries are comparable.

314999 All Other Miscellaneous Textile Product Mills[US]

This U.S. industry comprises establishments primarily engaged in manufacturing textile products (except carpets and rugs; curtains and linens; textile bags and canvas products; rope, cordage, and twine; and tire cords and tire fabrics) from purchased materials.

Illustrative Examples:

Batts and batting (except nonwoven fabrics) manufacturing
Carpet cutting and binding
Diapers (except disposable) made from purchased fabricDust cloths made from purchased fabric

Embroidering on textile products (except apparel) for the trade
Sleeping bags manufacturing
Textile fire hose made from purchased materials

Cross-References. Establishments primarily engaged in—

- Manufacturing yarns and thread—are classified in Industry 31311, Fiber, Yarn, and Thread Mills;

- Manufacturing carpets and rugs—are classified in Industry 314110, Carpet and Rug Mills;

- Manufacturing curtains and linens—are classified in Industry 31412, Curtain and Linen Mills;

- Manufacturing textile bags and canvas products—are classified in Industry 31491, Textile Bag and Canvas Mills;

- Manufacturing rope, cordage, and twine—are classified in U.S. Industry 314991, Rope, Cordage, and Twine Mills; and

- Manufacturing tire cords and tire fabrics—are classified in U.S. Industry 314992, Tire Cord and Tire Fabric Mills.

315 Apparel Manufacturing

Industries in the Apparel Manufacturing subsector group establishments with two distinct manufacturing processes: (1) cut and sew (i.e., purchasing fabric and cutting and sewing to make a garment), and (2) the manufacture of garments in establishments that first knit fabric and then cut and sew the fabric into a garment. The Apparel Manufacturing subsector includes a diverse range of establishments manufacturing full lines of ready-to-wear apparel and custom apparel: apparel contractors, performing cutting or sewing operations on materials owned by others; jobbers performing entrepreneurial functions involved in apparel manufacture; and tailors, manufacturing custom garments for individual clients are all included.

US—United States industry only. CAN—United States and Canadian industries are comparable. MEX—United States and Mexican industries are comparable. Blank—Canadian, Mexican, and United States industries are comparable.

Knitting, when done alone, is classified in the Textile Mills subsector, but when knitting is combined with the production of complete garments, the activity is classified in Apparel Manufacturing.

3151 Apparel Knitting Mills

This industry group comprises establishments primarily engaged in knitting apparel or knitting fabric and then manufacturing apparel. This industry group includes jobbers performing entrepreneurial functions involved in knitting apparel and accessories. Knitting fabric, without manufacturing apparel, is classified in Subsector 313, Textile Mills.

31511 Hosiery and Sock Mills

This industry comprises establishments primarily engaged in knitting or knitting and finishing hosiery and socks.

Cross-References. Establishments primarily engaged in—

- Manufacturing orthopedic hosiery—are classified in Industry 33911, Medical Equipment and Supplies Manufacturing;
- Manufacturing slipper socks from purchased socks—are classified in Industry 31621, Footwear Manufacturing; and
- Finishing apparel products only—are classified in Industry 31331, Textile and Fabric Finishing Mills.

315111 Sheer Hosiery Mills[US]

This U.S. industry comprises establishments primarily engaged in knitting or knitting and finishing women's, misses', and girls' full-length and knee-length sheer hosiery (except socks).

Cross-References. Establishments primarily engaged in—

- Knitting or knitting and finishing socks—are classified in U.S. Industry 315119, Other Hosiery and Sock Mills;
- Finishing apparel products only—are classified in U.S. Industry 313312, Textile and Fabric Finishing (except Broadwoven Fabric) Mills; and
- Manufacturing orthopedic hosiery—are classified in U.S. Industry 339113, Surgical Appliance and Supplies Manufacturing.

US—United States industry only. CAN—United States and Canadian industries are comparable. MEX—United States and Mexican industries are comparable. Blank—Canadian, Mexican, and United States industries are comparable.

315119 Other Hosiery and Sock Mills[US]

This U.S. industry comprises establishments primarily engaged in knitting or knitting and finishing hosiery (except women's, misses', and girls' sheer hosiery).

Cross-References. Establishments primarily engaged in—

- Knitting or knitting and finishing women's, misses', and girls' full-length and knee-length sheer hosiery—are classified in U.S. Industry 315111, Sheer Hosiery Mills;

- Manufacturing orthopedic hosiery—are classified in U.S. Industry 339113, Surgical Appliance and Supplies Manufacturing;

- Finishing apparel products only—are classified in U.S. Industry 313312, Textile and Fabric Finishing (except Broadwoven Fabric) Mills; and

- Manufacturing slipper socks from purchased socks—are classified in U.S. Industry 316212, House Slipper Manufacturing.

31519 Other Apparel Knitting Mills

This industry comprises establishments primarily engaged in one of the following: (1) knitting underwear, outerwear, and/or nightwear; (2) knitting fabric and manufacturing underwear, outerwear, and/or nightwear; or (3) knitting, manufacturing, and finishing knit underwear, outerwear, and/or nightwear.

Cross-References. Establishments primarily engaged in—

- Manufacturing outerwear, underwear, and nightwear from purchased fabric—are classified in Industry Group 3152, Cut and Sew Apparel Manufacturing; and

- Finishing apparel products only—are classified in Industry 31331, Textile and Fabric Finishing Mills.

315191 Outerwear Knitting Mills[US]

This U.S. industry comprises establishments primarily engaged in one or more of the following: (1) knitting outerwear; (2) knitting fabric and manufacturing outerwear; and (3) knitting, manufacturing, and finishing knit outerwear. Examples of products made in knit outerwear mills are shirts, shorts, sweat suits, sweaters, gloves, and pants.

Cross-References. Establishments primarily engaged in—

- Manufacturing outerwear from purchased fabric—are classified in Industry Group 3152, Cut and Sew Apparel Manufacturing;

US—United States industry only. CAN—United States and Canadian industries are comparable. MEX—United States and Mexican industries are comparable. Blank—Canadian, Mexican, and United States industries are comparable.

- Finishing apparel products only—are classified in U.S. Industry 313312, Textile and Fabric Finishing (except Broadwoven Fabric) Mills; and

- Knitting underwear and nightwear, knitting fabric and manufacturing underwear and nightwear, or knitting, manufacturing, and finishing knit underwear and nightwear—are classified in U.S. Industry 315192, Underwear and Nightwear Knitting Mills.

315192 Underwear and Nightwear Knitting Mills[US]

This U.S. industry comprises establishments primarily engaged in one of the following: (1) knitting underwear and nightwear; (2) knitting fabric and manufacturing underwear and nightwear; or (3) knitting, manufacturing, and finishing knit underwear and nightwear. Examples of products produced in underwear and nightwear knitting mills are briefs, underwear T-shirts, pajamas, nightshirts, foundation garments, and panties.

Cross-References. Establishments primarily engaged in—

- Manufacturing underwear and nightwear from purchased fabric—are classified in Industry Group 3152, Cut and Sew Apparel Manufacturing; and

- Finishing apparel products only—are classified in U.S. Industry 313312, Textile and Fabric Finishing (except Broadwoven Fabric) Mills.

3152 Cut and Sew Apparel Manufacturing

This industry group comprises establishments primarily engaged in manufacturing cut and sew apparel from woven fabric or purchased knit fabric. Included in this industry group is a diverse range of establishments manufacturing full lines of ready-to-wear apparel and custom apparel: apparel contractors, performing cutting or sewing operations on materials owned by others; jobbers performing entrepreneurial functions involved in apparel manufacture; and tailors, manufacturing custom garments for individual clients. Establishments weaving or knitting fabric, without manufacturing apparel, are classified in Subsector 313, Textile Mills.

31521 Cut and Sew Apparel Contractors[CAN]

This industry comprises establishments commonly referred to as contractors primarily engaged in (1) cutting materials owned by others for apparel and accessories and/or (2) sewing materials owned by others for apparel and accessories.

US—United States industry only. CAN—United States and Canadian industries are comparable. MEX—United States and Mexican industries are comparable. Blank—Canadian, Mexican, and United States industries are comparable.

Cross-References. Establishments primarily engaged in—

- Manufacturing men's and boys' apparel from purchased fabric—are classified in Industry 31522, Men's and Boys' Cut and Sew Apparel Manufacturing;

- Manufacturing women's and girls' apparel from purchased fabric—are classified in Industry 31523, Women's and Girls' Cut and Sew Apparel Manufacturing;

- Manufacturing infants' apparel and all other cut and sew apparel from purchased fabric—are classified in Industry 31529, Other Cut and Sew Apparel Manufacturing; and

- Manufacturing apparel accessories from purchased fabric—are classified in Industry 31599, Apparel Accessories and Other Apparel Manufacturing.

315211 Men's and Boys' Cut and Sew Apparel Contractors[US]

This U.S. industry comprises establishments commonly referred to as contractors primarily engaged in (1) cutting materials owned by others for men's and boys' apparel and/or (2) sewing materials owned by others for men's and boys' apparel.

Cross-References. Establishments primarily engaged in—

- Manufacturing men's and boys' apparel from purchased fabric—are classified in Industry 31522, Men's and Boys' Cut and Sew Apparel Manufacturing;

- Manufacturing infants' apparel from purchased fabric—are classified in U.S. Industry 315291, Infants' Cut and Sew Apparel Manufacturing; and

- Manufacturing men's and boys' apparel accessories from purchased fabric— are classified in Industry 31599, Apparel Accessories and Other Apparel Manufacturing.

315212 Women's, Girls', and Infants' Cut and Sew Apparel Contractors[US]

This U.S. industry comprises establishments commonly referred to as contractors primarily engaged in (1) cutting materials owned by others for women's, girls', and infants' apparel and accessories and/or (2) sewing materials owned by others for women's, girls', and infants' apparel and accessories.

Cross-References. Establishments primarily engaged in—

- Manufacturing women's and girls' apparel from purchased fabric—are classified in Industry 31523, Women's and Girls' Cut and Sew Apparel Manufacturing;

- Manufacturing infants' apparel from purchased fabric—are classified in U.S. Industry 315291, Infants' Cut and Sew Apparel Manufacturing; and

- Manufacturing women's, girls', and infants' apparel accessories from purchased fabric—are classified in Industry 31599, Apparel Accessories and Other Apparel Manufacturing.

31522 Men's and Boys' Cut and Sew Apparel Manufacturing^{CAN}

This industry comprises establishments primarily engaged in manufacturing men's and boys' cut and sew apparel from purchased fabric. Men's and boys' clothing jobbers, who perform entrepreneurial functions involved in apparel manufacture, including buying raw materials, designing and preparing samples, arranging for apparel to be made from their materials, and marketing finished apparel, are included.

Cross-References. Establishments primarily engaged in—

- Cutting and/or sewing materials owned by others for men's and boys' apparel—are classified in Industry 31521, Cut and Sew Apparel Contractors;

- Knitting men's and boys' apparel or knitting fabric and manufacturing men's and boys' apparel—are classified in Industry Group 3151, Apparel Knitting Mills; and

- Manufacturing fur or leather apparel and team athletic uniforms—are classified in Industry 31529, Other Cut and Sew Apparel Manufacturing.

315221 Men's and Boys' Cut and Sew Underwear and Nightwear Manufacturing^{CAN}

This U.S. industry comprises establishments primarily engaged in manufacturing men's and boys' underwear and nightwear from purchased fabric. Men's and boys' underwear and nightwear jobbers, who perform entrepreneurial functions involved in apparel manufacture, including buying raw materials, designing and preparing samples, arranging for apparel to be made from their materials, and marketing finished apparel, are included. Examples of products made by these establishments are briefs, bathrobes, underwear T-shirts and shorts, nightshirts, and pajamas.

Cross-References. Establishments primarily engaged in—

- Knitting men's and boys' underwear and nightwear and/or knitting and manufacturing men's and boys' underwear and nightwear—are classified in U.S. Industry 315192, Underwear and Nightwear Knitting Mills; and

- Cutting and/or sewing materials owned by others for men's and boys' underwear and nightwear—are classified in U.S. Industry 315211, Men's and Boys' Cut and Sew Apparel Contractors.

315222 Men's and Boys' Cut and Sew Suit, Coat, and Overcoat Manufacturing[CAN]

This U.S. industry comprises establishments primarily engaged in manufacturing men's and boys' suits, overcoats, sport coats, tuxedos, dress uniforms, and other tailored apparel (except fur and leather) from purchased fabric. Men's and boys' suit, coat, and overcoat jobbers, who perform entrepreneurial functions involved in apparel manufacture, including buying raw materials, designing and preparing samples, arranging for apparel to be made from their materials, and marketing finished apparel, are included.

Cross-References. Establishments primarily engaged in—

- Manufacturing men's and boys' nontailored coats and jackets such as down coats and windbreakers made from purchased fabric—are classified in U.S. Industry 315228, Men's and Boys' Cut and Sew Other Outerwear Manufacturing;

- Manufacturing fur and leather apparel—are classified in U.S. Industry 315292, Fur and Leather Apparel Manufacturing;

- Manufacturing men's and boys' washable service apparel from purchased fabric—are classified in U.S. Industry 315225, Men's and Boys' Cut and Sew Work Clothing Manufacturing;

- Manufacturing men's and boys' team athletic uniforms from purchased fabric—are classified in U.S. Industry 315299, All Other Cut and Sew Apparel Manufacturing; and

- Cutting and/or sewing materials owned by others for men's and boys' suits, coats, and overcoats—are classified in U.S. Industry 315211, Men's and Boys' Cut and Sew Apparel Contractors.

315223 Men's and Boys' Cut and Sew Shirt (except Work Shirt) Manufacturing[US]

This U.S. industry comprises establishments primarily engaged in manufacturing men's and boys' outerwear shirts from purchased fabric. Men's and boys' shirt (except work shirt) jobbers, who perform entrepreneurial functions involved in apparel manufacture, including buying raw materials, designing and preparing samples, arranging for apparel to be made from their materials, and marketing

US—United States industry only. CAN—United States and Canadian industries are comparable. MEX—United States and Mexican industries are comparable. Blank—Canadian, Mexican, and United States industries are comparable.

finished apparel, are included. Unisex outerwear shirts, such as T-shirts and sweatshirts that are sized without specific reference to gender (i.e., adult S, M, L, XL) are included in this industry.

Cross-References. Establishments primarily engaged in—

- Manufacturing men's and boys' work shirts from purchased fabric—are classified in U.S. Industry 315225, Men's and Boys' Cut and Sew Work Clothing Manufacturing;

- Manufacturing men's and boys' underwear T-shirts and underwear tank tops from purchased fabric—are classified in U.S. Industry 315221, Men's and Boys' Cut and Sew Underwear and Nightwear Manufacturing;

- Cutting and/or sewing materials owned by others for men's and boys' shirts—are classified in U.S. Industry 315211, Men's and Boys' Cut and Sew Apparel Contractors; and

- Knitting men's and boys' outerwear shirts or knitting fabric and manufacturing men's and boys' outerwear shirts—are classified in U.S. Industry 315191, Outerwear Knitting Mills.

315224 Men's and Boys' Cut and Sew Trouser, Slack, and Jean Manufacturing[US]

This U.S. industry comprises establishments primarily engaged in manufacturing men's and boys' jeans, dungarees, and other separate trousers and slacks (except work pants) from purchased fabric. Men's and boys' trouser, slack, and jean jobbers, who perform entrepreneurial functions involved in apparel manufacture, including buying raw materials, designing and preparing samples, arranging for apparel to be made from their materials, and marketing finished apparel, are included.

Cross-References. Establishments primarily engaged in—

- Manufacturing men's and boys' work pants from purchased fabric—are classified in U.S. Industry 315225, Men's and Boys' Cut and Sew Work Clothing Manufacturing;

- Manufacturing fur and leather apparel—are classified in U.S. Industry 315292, Fur and Leather Apparel Manufacturing;

- Manufacturing men's and boys' sweatpants and shorts from purchased fabric—are classified in U.S. Industry 315228, Men's and Boys' Cut and Sew Other Outerwear Manufacturing; and

- Cutting and/or sewing materials owned by others for men's and boys' separate trousers, slacks, and jeans—are classified in U.S. Industry 315211, Men's and Boys' Cut and Sew Apparel Contractors.

315225 Men's and Boys' Cut and Sew Work Clothing Manufacturing[US]

This U.S. industry comprises establishments primarily engaged in manufacturing men's and boys' work shirts, work pants (excluding jeans and dungarees), other work clothing, and washable service apparel from purchased fabric. Men's and boys' work clothing jobbers, who perform entrepreneurial functions involved in apparel manufacture, including buying raw materials, designing and preparing samples, arranging for apparel to be made from their materials, and marketing finished apparel, are included. Examples of products made by these establishments are washable service apparel, laboratory coats, work shirts, work pants (except jeans and dungarees), and hospital apparel.

Cross-References. Establishments primarily engaged in—

- Manufacturing men's and boys' separate trousers, slacks, and pants, including jeans and dungarees from purchased fabric—are classified in U.S. Industry 315224, Men's and Boys' Cut and Sew Trouser, Slack, and Jean Manufacturing; and

- Cutting and/or sewing materials owned by others for men's and boys' work clothing—are classified in U.S. Industry 315211, Men's and Boys' Cut and Sew Apparel Contractors.

315228 Men's and Boys' Cut and Sew Other Outerwear Manufacturing[US]

This U.S. industry comprises establishments primarily engaged in manufacturing men's and boys' cut and sew outerwear from purchased fabric (except underwear, nightwear, shirts, suits, overcoats and tailored coats, separate trousers and slacks, and work clothing). Men's and boys' other outerwear jobbers, who perform entrepreneurial functions involved in apparel manufacture, including buying raw materials, designing and preparing samples, arranging for apparel to be made from their materials, and marketing finished apparel, are included. Unisex sweatpants and similar garments that are sized without specific reference to gender (i.e., adult S, M, L, XL) are also included in this industry. Examples of products made by these establishments are athletic clothing (except athletic uniforms), bathing suits, down coats, outerwear shorts, windbreakers and jackets, and jogging suits.

Cross-References. Establishments primarily engaged in—

- Manufacturing men's and boys' athletic uniforms from purchased fabric— are classified in U.S. Industry 315299, All Other Cut and Sew Apparel Manufacturing;

US—United States industry only. CAN—United States and Canadian industries are comparable. MEX—United States and Mexican industries are comparable. Blank—Canadian, Mexican, and United States industries are comparable.

- Manufacturing leather and fur apparel—are classified in U.S. Industry 315292, Fur and Leather Apparel Manufacturing;

- Knitting men's and boys' apparel or knitting fabric and manufacturing men's and boys' apparel—are classified in Industry Group 3151, Apparel Knitting Mills;

- Cutting and/or sewing materials owned by others for men's and boys' apparel—are classified in U.S. Industry 315211, Men's and Boys' Cut and Sew Apparel Contractors;

- Manufacturing men's and boys' underwear and nightwear from purchased fabric—are classified in U.S. Industry 315221, Men's and Boys' Cut and Sew Underwear and Nightwear Manufacturing;

- Manufacturing men's and boys' tailored suits, coats, and overcoats from purchased fabric—are classified in U.S. Industry 315222, Men's and Boys' Cut and Sew Suit, Coat and Overcoat Manufacturing;

- Manufacturing men's and boys' outerwear shirts (except work shirts) from purchased fabric—are classified in U.S. Industry 315223, Men's and Boys' Cut and Sew Shirt (except Work Shirt) Manufacturing;

- Manufacturing men's and boys' separate pants, trousers, and slacks from purchased fabric—are classified in U.S. Industry 315224, Men's and Boys' Cut and Sew Trouser, Slack, and Jean Manufacturing; and

- Manufacturing men's and boys' work clothing from purchased fabric—are classified in U.S. Industry 315225, Men's and Boys' Cut and Sew Work Clothing Manufacturing.

31523 Women's and Girls' Cut and Sew Apparel Manufacturing[CAN]

This industry comprises establishments primarily engaged in manufacturing women's and girls' apparel from purchased fabric. Women's and girls' clothing jobbers, who perform entrepreneurial functions involved in apparel manufacture, including buying raw materials, designing and preparing samples, arranging for apparel to be made from their materials, and marketing finished apparel, are included.

Cross-References. Establishments primarily engaged in—

- Knitting women's and girls' apparel or knitting fabric and manufacturing women's and girls' apparel—are classified in Industry Group 3151, Apparel Knitting Mills;

- Manufacturing unisex outerwear garments, such as T-shirts, sweatshirts, and sweatpants that are sized without reference to specific gender (i.e., adult S, M, L, XL),—are classified in Industry 31522, Men's and Boys' Cut and Sew Apparel Manufacturing;

- Cutting and/or sewing materials owned by others for women's and girls' apparel—are classified in Industry 31521, Cut and Sew Apparel Contractors; and

- Manufacturing fur or leather apparel and team athletic uniforms—are classified in Industry 31529, Other Cut and Sew Apparel Manufacturing.

315231 Women's and Girls' Cut and Sew Lingerie, Loungewear, and Nightwear Manufacturing[CAN]

This U.S. industry comprises establishments primarily engaged in manufacturing women's and girls' bras, girdles, and other underwear; lingerie; loungewear; and nightwear from purchased fabric. Women's and girls' lingerie, loungewear, and nightwear jobbers, who perform entrepreneurial functions involved in apparel manufacture, including buying raw materials, designing and preparing samples, arranging for apparel to be made from their materials, and marketing finished apparel, are included. Examples of products made by these establishments are bathrobes, foundation garments, nightgowns, pajamas, panties, and slips.

Cross-References. Establishments primarily engaged in—

- Knitting women's and girls' underwear, nightwear, and lingerie or knitting fabric and manufacturing women's and girls' underwear, nightwear, and lingerie—are classified in U.S. Industry 315192, Underwear and Nightwear Knitting Mills; and

- Cutting and/or sewing materials owned by others for women's and girls' underwear, nightwear, and lingerie—are classified in U.S. Industry 315212, Women's, Girls', and Infants' Cut and Sew Apparel Contractors.

315232 Women's and Girls' Cut and Sew Blouse and Shirt Manufacturing[CAN]

This U.S. industry comprises establishments primarily engaged in manufacturing women's and girls' blouses and shirts from purchased fabric. Women's and girls' blouse and shirt jobbers, who perform entrepreneurial functions involved in apparel manufacture, including buying raw materials, designing and preparing samples, arranging for apparel to be made from their materials, and marketing finished apparel, are included.

Cross-References. Establishments primarily engaged in—

- Knitting women's and girls' blouses, shirts, and tops or knitting fabric and manufacturing women's and girls' blouses, shirts, and tops—are classified in U.S. Industry 315191, Outerwear Knitting Mills;

- Manufacturing unisex outerwear shirts, such as T-shirts and sweatshirts that are sized without specific reference to gender (i.e., adult S, M, L, XL),—are classified in U.S. Industry 315223, Men's and Boys' Cut and Sew Shirt (except Work Shirt) Manufacturing; and

- Cutting and/or sewing materials owned by others for women's and girls' shirts and blouses—are classified in U.S. Industry 315212, Women's, Girls', and Infants' Cut and Sew Apparel Contractors.

315233 Women's and Girls' Cut and Sew Dress Manufacturing[CAN]

This U.S. industry comprises establishments primarily engaged in manufacturing women's and girls' dresses from purchased fabric. Women's and girls' dress jobbers, who perform entrepreneurial functions involved in apparel manufacture, including buying raw materials, designing and preparing samples, arranging for apparel to be made from their materials, and marketing finished apparel, are included.

Cross-References. Establishments primarily engaged in—

- Knitting women's and girls' dresses or knitting fabric and manufacturing women's and girls' dresses—are classified in U.S. Industry 315191, Outerwear Knitting Mills; and

- Cutting and/or sewing materials owned by others for women's and girls' dresses—are classified in U.S. Industry 315212, Women's, Girls', and Infants' Cut and Sew Apparel Contractors.

315234 Women's and Girls' Cut and Sew Suit, Coat, Tailored Jacket, and Skirt Manufacturing[CAN]

This U.S. industry comprises establishments primarily engaged in manufacturing women's and girls' suits, pantsuits, skirts, tailored jackets, vests, raincoats, and other tailored coats, (except fur and leather coats) from purchased fabric. Women's and girls' suit, coat, tailored jacket, and skirt jobbers, who perform entrepreneurial functions involved in apparel manufacture, including buying raw materials, designing and preparing samples, arranging for apparel to be made from their materials, and marketing finished apparel, are included.

Cross-References. Establishments primarily engaged in—

- Manufacturing women's and girls' team athletic uniforms from purchased fabric—are classified in U.S. Industry 315299, All Other Cut and Sew Apparel Manufacturing;

- Manufacturing women's and girls' separate slacks, jeans, pants, and nontai-lored coats and jackets, such as down coats and windbreakers from purchased fabric,—are classified in U.S. Industry 315239, Women's and Girls' Cut and Sew Other Outerwear Manufacturing;

- Manufacturing fur and leather apparel—are classified in U.S. Industry 315292, Fur and Leather Apparel Manufacturing;

- Knitting women's and girls' tailored skirts, suits, vests, and coats or knitting fabric and manufacturing women's and girls' tailored skirts, suits, vests, and coats—are classified in U.S. Industry 315191, Outerwear Knitting Mills; and

- Cutting and/or sewing materials owned by others for women's and girls' suits, coats, tailored jackets, and skirts—are classified in U.S. Industry 315212, Women's, Girls', and Infants' Cut and Sew Apparel Contractors.

315239 Women's and Girls' Cut and Sew Other Outerwear Manufacturing[CAN]

This U.S. industry comprises establishments primarily engaged in manufacturing women's and girls' cut and sew apparel from purchased fabric (except underwear, lingerie, nightwear, blouses, shirts, dresses, suits, tailored coats, tailored jackets, and skirts). Women's and girls' other outerwear clothing jobbers, who perform entrepreneurial functions involved in apparel manufacture, including buying raw materials, designing and preparing samples, arranging for apparel to be made from their materials, and marketing finished apparel, are included. Examples of products made by these establishments are bathing suits, down coats, sweaters, jogging suits, outerwear pants and shorts, and windbreakers.

Cross-References. Establishments primarily engaged in—

- Manufacturing women's and girls' team athletic uniforms from purchased fabric—are classified in U.S. Industry 315299, All Other Cut and Sew Apparel Manufacturing;

- Knitting women's and girls' apparel or knitting fabric and manufacturing women's and girls' apparel—are classified in U.S. Industry 315191, Outer-wear Knitting Mills;

- Manufacturing women's and girls' fur and leather apparel—are classified in U.S. Industry 315292, Fur and Leather Apparel Manufacturing;

- Cutting and/or sewing materials owned by others for women's and girls' apparel—are classified in U.S. Industry 315212, Women's, Girls', and Infants' Cut and Sew Apparel Contractors;

- Manufacturing women's and girls' lingerie, loungewear, and nightwear from purchased fabric—are classified in U.S. Industry 315231, Women's and Girls' Cut and Sew Lingerie, Loungewear, and Nightwear Manufacturing;

- Manufacturing women's and girls' blouses and outerwear shirts from purchased fabric—are classified in U.S. Industry 315232, Women's and Girls' Cut and Sew Blouse and Shirt Manufacturing;

- Manufacturing unisex sweatpants and similar outerwear garments that are sized without specific reference to gender (i.e., adult S, M, L, XL)—are classified in U.S. Industry 315228, Men's and Boys' Cut and Sew Other Outerwear Manufacturing;

- Manufacturing women's and girls' dresses from purchased fabric—are classified in U.S. Industry 315233, Women's and Girls' Cut and Sew Dress Manufacturing; and

- Manufacturing women's and girls' suits, skirts, and tailored coats and jackets from purchased fabric—are classified in U.S. Industry 315234, Women's and Girls' Cut and Sew Suit, Coat, Tailored Jacket, and Skirt Manufacturing.

31529 Other Cut and Sew Apparel Manufacturing[CAN]

This industry comprises establishments primarily engaged in manufacturing cut and sew apparel from purchased fabric (except men's, boys', women's, and girls' apparel). This industry includes establishments manufacturing apparel, such as fur apparel, leather apparel, infants' apparel, costumes, and clerical vestments.

Cross-References. Establishments primarily engaged in—

- Manufacturing men's and boys' apparel from purchased fabric—are classified in Industry 31522, Men's and Boys' Cut and Sew Apparel Manufacturing;

- Manufacturing women's and girls' apparel from purchased fabric—are classified in Industry 31523, Women's and Girls' Cut and Sew Apparel Manufacturing;

- Knitting apparel or knitting fabric and manufacturing apparel—are classified in Industry Group 3151, Apparel Knitting Mills;

- Cutting and/or sewing materials owned by others for apparel—are classified in Industry 31521, Cut and Sew Apparel Contractors;

- Manufacturing fur and leather mittens and gloves—are classified in Industry 31599, Apparel Accessories and Other Apparel Manufacturing; and

- Dyeing and dressing furs—are classified in Industry 31611, Leather and Hide Tanning and Finishing.

315291 Infants' Cut and Sew Apparel Manufacturing^{CAN}

This U.S. industry comprises establishments primarily engaged in manufacturing infants' dresses, blouses, shirts, and all other infants' wear from purchased fabric. Infants' clothing jobbers, who perform entrepreneurial functions involved in apparel manufacture, including buying raw materials, designing and preparing samples, arranging for apparel to be made from their materials, and marketing finished apparel, are included. For the purposes of classification, the term "infants' apparel" includes apparel for young children of an age not exceeding 24 months.

Cross-References. Establishments primarily engaged in—

- Knitting infants' apparel or knitting fabric and manufacturing infants' apparel—are classified in U.S. Industry 315191, Outerwear Knitting Mills; and

- Cutting and/or sewing materials owned by others for infants' apparel—are classified in U.S. Industry 315212, Women's, Girls', and Infants' Cut and Sew Apparel Contractors.

315292 Fur and Leather Apparel Manufacturing^{CAN}

This U.S. industry comprises establishments primarily engaged in manufacturing cut and sew fur and leather apparel, and sheep-lined clothing. Fur and leather apparel jobbers, who perform entrepreneurial functions involved in apparel manufacture, including buying raw materials, designing and preparing samples, arranging for apparel to be made from their materials, and marketing finished apparel, are included.

Cross-References. Establishments primarily engaged in—

- Cutting and/or sewing materials owned by others for apparel—are classified in Industry 31521, Cut and Sew Apparel Contractors;

- Dyeing and dressing furs—are classified in Industry 316110, Leather and Hide Tanning and Finishing; and

- Manufacturing fur and leather mittens and gloves—are classified in U.S. Industry 315992, Glove and Mitten Manufacturing.

315299 All Other Cut and Sew Apparel Manufacturing^{CAN}

This U.S. industry comprises establishments primarily engaged in manufacturing cut and sew apparel from purchased fabric (except cut and sew apparel contractors; men's and boys' cut and sew underwear, nightwear, suits, coats, shirts, trousers, work clothing, and other outerwear; women's and girls' lingerie, blouses, shirts, dresses, suits, coats, and other outerwear; infants' apparel; and fur and leather apparel). Clothing jobbers for these products, who perform entrepreneurial functions involved in apparel manufacture, including buying raw materials, designing and preparing samples, arranging for apparel to be made from their materials, and marketing finished apparel, are included. Examples of products made by these establishments are team athletic uniforms, band uniforms, academic caps and gowns, clerical vestments, and costumes.

Cross-References. Establishments primarily engaged in—

- Cutting and/or sewing materials owned by others for apparel—are classified in Industry 31521, Cut and Sew Apparel Contractors;

- Knitting apparel or knitting fabric and manufacturing apparel—are classified in Industry Group 3151, Apparel Knitting Mills;

- Manufacturing men's and boys' underwear and nightwear from purchased fabric—are classified in U.S. Industry 315221, Men's and Boys' Cut and Sew Underwear and Nightwear Manufacturing;

- Manufacturing men's and boys' suits, coats, and overcoats from purchased fabric—are classified in U.S. Industry 315222, Men's and Boys' Cut and Sew Suit, Coat and Overcoat Manufacturing;

- Manufacturing men's and boys' shirts (except work shirts) from purchased fabric—are classified in U.S. Industry 315223, Men's and Boys' Cut and Sew Shirt (except Work Shirt) Manufacturing;

- Manufacturing men's and boys' pants, slacks, trousers, and jeans from purchased fabric—are classified in U.S. Industry 315224, Men's and Boys' Cut and Sew Trouser, Slack, and Jean Manufacturing;

- Manufacturing men's and boys' work clothing from purchased fabric—are classified in U.S. Industry 315225, Men's and Boys' Cut and Sew Work Clothing Manufacturing;

- Manufacturing other men's and boys' outerwear from purchased fabric—are classified in U.S. Industry 315228, Men's and Boys' Cut and Sew Other Outerwear Manufacturing;

- Manufacturing women's and girls' lingerie and nightwear from purchased fabric—are classified in U.S. Industry 315231, Women's and Girls' Cut and Sew Lingerie, Loungewear, and Nightwear Manufacturing;

- Manufacturing women's and girls' blouses and shirts from purchased fabric—are classified in U.S. Industry 315232, Women's and Girls' Cut and Sew Blouse and Shirt Manufacturing;

- Manufacturing women's and girls' dresses from purchased fabric—are classified in U.S. Industry 315233, Women's and Girls' Cut and Sew Dress Manufacturing;

- Manufacturing women's and girls' suits, tailored coats and jackets, and skirts from purchased fabric—are classified in U.S. Industry 315234, Women's and Girls' Cut and Sew Suit, Coat, Tailored Jacket, and Skirt Manufacturing;

- Manufacturing other women's and girls' outerwear from purchased fabric— are classified in U.S. Industry 315239, Women's and Girls' Cut and Sew Other Outerwear Manufacturing;

- Manufacturing infants' apparel from purchased fabric—are classified in U.S. Industry 315291, Infants' Cut and Sew Apparel Manufacturing; and

- Manufacturing fur and leather apparel—are classified in U.S. Industry 315292, Fur and Leather Apparel Manufacturing.

3159 Apparel Accessories and Other Apparel Manufacturing

This industry group comprises establishments primarily engaged in manufacturing apparel accessories and other apparel (except apparel knitting mills, apparel contractors, men's and boys' cut and sew apparel, women's and girls' cut and sew apparel, infants' cut and sew apparel, fur and leather apparel, and all other cut and sew apparel). This industry group includes jobbers performing entrepreneurial functions involved in manufacturing apparel accessories.

31599 Apparel Accessories and Other Apparel Manufacturing

This industry comprises establishments primarily engaged in manufacturing apparel and accessories (except apparel knitting mills, cut and sew apparel contractors, men's and boys' cut and sew apparel, women's and girls' cut and sew apparel, and other cut and sew apparel). Jobbers, who perform entrepreneurial functions involved in apparel accessories manufacture, including buying raw materials, designing and preparing samples, arranging for apparel accessories to be made from their materials, and marketing finished apparel accessories, are included. Examples of products made by these establishments are belts, caps, gloves (except medical, sporting, safety), hats, and neckties.

Cross-References. Establishments primarily engaged in—

- Cutting and/or sewing materials owned by others for apparel accessories— are classified in Industry 31521, Cut and Sew Apparel Contractors;

- Manufacturing paper hats and caps—are classified in Industry 32229, Other Converted Paper Product Manufacturing;

- Manufacturing plastics or rubber hats and caps (except bathing caps)—are classified in Subsector 326, Plastics and Rubber Products Manufacturing;

- Manufacturing athletic gloves, such as boxing gloves, baseball gloves, golf gloves, batting gloves, and racquetball gloves,—are classified in Industry 33992, Sporting and Athletic Goods Manufacturing;

- Manufacturing metal fabric, metal mesh, or rubber gloves—are classified in Industry 33911, Medical Equipment and Supplies Manufacturing;

- Knitting apparel, mittens, gloves, hats, and caps or knitting fabric and manufacturing apparel, mittens, gloves, hats, and caps—are classified in Industry Group 3151, Apparel Knitting Mills;

- Cutting and/or sewing materials owned by others for apparel—are classified in Industry 31521, Cut and Sew Apparel Contractors;

- Manufacturing men's and boys' underwear and outerwear from purchased fabric—are classified in Industry 31522, Men's and Boys' Cut and Sew Apparel Manufacturing;

- Manufacturing women's and girls' underwear and outerwear from purchased fabric—are classified in Industry 31523, Women's and Girls' Cut and Sew Apparel Manufacturing; and

- Manufacturing other apparel from purchased fabric and manufacturing fur and leather apparel, hats, and caps—are classified in Industry 31529, Other Cut and Sew Apparel Manufacturing.

315991 Hat, Cap, and Millinery Manufacturing[MEX]

This U.S. industry comprises establishments primarily engaged in manufacturing cut and sew hats, caps, millinery, and hat bodies from purchased fabric. Jobbers, who perform entrepreneurial functions involved in hat, cap, and millinery manufacture, including buying raw materials, designing and preparing samples, arranging for hats, caps, and millinery to be made from their materials, and marketing finished hats, caps, and millinery, are included.

Cross-References. Establishments primarily engaged in—

- Cutting and/or sewing materials owned by others for hats, caps, and millinery—are classified in Industry 31521, Cut and Sew Apparel Contractors;

- Manufacturing paper hats and caps—are classified in U.S. Industry 322299, All Other Converted Paper Product Manufacturing;

- Manufacturing plastics or rubber hats and caps (except bathing caps)—are classified in Subsector 326, Plastics and Rubber Products Manufacturing; and

- Manufacturing fur and leather hats and caps—are classified in U.S. Industry 315292, Fur and Leather Apparel Manufacturing.

315992 Glove and Mitten Manufacturing[US]

This U.S. industry comprises establishments primarily engaged in manufacturing cut and sew gloves (except rubber, metal, and athletic gloves) and mittens from purchased fabric, fur, leather, or from combinations of fabric, fur, or leather. Jobbers, who perform entrepreneurial functions involved in glove and mitten manufacture, including buying raw materials, designing and preparing samples, arranging for gloves and mittens to be made from their materials, and marketing finished gloves and mittens, are included.

Cross-References. Establishments primarily engaged in—

- Cutting and/or sewing materials owned by others for gloves and mittens—are classified in Industry 31521, Cut and Sew Apparel Contractors;

- Knitting mittens and gloves or knitting fabric and manufacturing mittens and gloves—are classified in U.S. Industry 315191, Outerwear Knitting Mills;

- Manufacturing athletic gloves, such as boxing gloves, baseball gloves, golf gloves, batting gloves, and racquetball gloves—are classified in Industry 339920, Sporting and Athletic Goods Manufacturing; and

- Manufacturing metal fabric, metal mesh, or rubber gloves—are classified in U.S. Industry 339113, Surgical Appliance and Supplies Manufacturing.

315993 Men's and Boys' Neckwear Manufacturing[US]

This U.S. industry comprises establishments primarily engaged in manufacturing men's and boys' cut and sew neckties, scarves, and mufflers from purchased fabric, leather, or from combinations of leather and fabric. Men's and boys' neckwear jobbers, who perform entrepreneurial functions involved in neckwear manufacture, including buying raw materials, designing and preparing samples, arranging for neckwear to be made from their materials, and marketing finished neckwear, are included.

Cross-References.

Establishments primarily engaged in cutting and/or sewing materials owned by others for men's and boys' neckwear are classified in U.S. Industry 315211, Men's and Boys' Cut and Sew Apparel Contractors.

US—United States industry only. CAN—United States and Canadian industries are comparable. MEX—United States and Mexican industries are comparable. Blank—Canadian, Mexican, and United States industries are comparable.

315999 Other Apparel Accessories and Other Apparel Manufacturing[US]

This U.S. industry comprises establishments primarily engaged in manufacturing apparel and apparel accessories (except apparel knitting mills; cut and sew apparel contractors; cut and sew apparel; hats and caps; mittens and gloves; and men's and boys' neckwear). Jobbers for these products, who perform entrepreneurial functions involved in other apparel and accessory manufacture, including buying raw materials, designing and preparing samples, arranging for other apparel and accessories to be made from their materials, and marketing finished other apparel and accessories, are included. Examples of products made by these establishments are apparel trimmings and findings, belts, women's scarves, and suspenders.

Cross-References. Establishments primarily engaged in—

- Knitting apparel or knitting fabric and manufacturing apparel—are classified in Industry Group 3151, Apparel Knitting Mills;
- Cutting and/or sewing materials owned by others for apparel—are classified in Industry 31521, Cut and Sew Apparel Contractors;
- Manufacturing men's and boys' cut and sew underwear and outerwear from purchased fabric—are classified in Industry 31522, Men's and Boys' Cut and Sew Apparel Manufacturing;
- Manufacturing women's and girls' cut and sew underwear and outerwear from purchased fabric—are classified in Industry 31523, Women's and Girls' Cut and Sew Apparel Manufacturing;
- Manufacturing infants' cut and sew apparel from purchased fabric—are classified in U.S. Industry 315291, Infants' Cut and Sew Apparel Manufacturing;
- Manufacturing fur and leather apparel—are classified in U.S. Industry 315292, Fur and Leather Apparel Manufacturing;
- Manufacturing hats, caps, and millinery—are classified in U.S. Industry 315991, Hat, Cap, and Millinery Manufacturing;
- Manufacturing gloves and mittens—are classified in U.S. Industry 315992, Glove and Mitten Manufacturing; and
- Manufacturing men's and boys' neckwear—are classified in U.S. Industry 315993, Men's and Boys' Neckwear Manufacturing.

316 Leather and Allied Product Manufacturing

Establishments in the Leather and Allied Product Manufacturing subsector transform hides into leather by tanning or curing and fabricating the leather into products

---

for final consumption. It also includes the manufacture of similar products from other materials, including products (except apparel) made from "leather substitutes," such as rubber, plastics, or textiles. Rubber footwear, textile luggage, and plastics purses or wallets are examples of "leather substitute" products included in this group. The products made from leather substitutes are included in this subsector because they are made in similar ways leather products are made (e.g., luggage). They are made in the same establishments, so it is not practical to separate them.

The inclusion of leather making in this subsector is partly because leather tanning is a relatively small industry that has few close neighbors as a production process, partly because leather is an input to some of the other products classified in this subsector and partly for historical reasons.

3161 Leather and Hide Tanning and Finishing

31611 Leather and Hide Tanning and Finishing
See industry description for 316110 below.

316110 Leather and Hide Tanning and Finishing

This industry comprises establishments primarily engaged in one or more of the following: (1) tanning, currying, and finishing hides and skins; (2) having others process hides and skins on a contract basis; and (3) dyeing or dressing furs.

3162 Footwear Manufacturing

31621 Footwear Manufacturing

This industry comprises establishments primarily engaged in manufacturing footwear (except orthopedic extension footwear).

Cross-References.

Establishments primarily engaged in manufacturing orthopedic extension footwear are classified in Industry 33911, Medical Equipment and Supplies Manufacturing.

316211 Rubber and Plastics Footwear Manufacturing[US]

This U.S. industry comprises establishments primarily engaged in manufacturing rubber and plastics footwear with vulcanized rubber or plastics soles, molded or cemented to rubber, plastics, or fabric uppers, and rubber and plastics protective footwear.

US—United States industry only. CAN—United States and Canadian industries are comparable. MEX—United States and Mexican industries are comparable. Blank—Canadian, Mexican, and United States industries are comparable.

Cross-References. Establishments primarily engaged in—

- Manufacturing house slippers with fabric uppers and rubber or plastics soles—are classified in U.S. Industry 316212, House Slipper Manufacturing;

- Manufacturing men's footwear (except athletic) with leather or vinyl uppers, regardless of sole material—are classified in U.S. Industry 316213, Men's Footwear (except Athletic) Manufacturing;

- Manufacturing women's footwear (except athletic) with leather or vinyl uppers, regardless of sole material—are classified in U.S. Industry 316214, Women's Footwear (except Athletic) Manufacturing; and

- Manufacturing youths' children's and infants' footwear and athletic footwear with leather or vinyl uppers, regardless of sole material—are classified in U.S. Industry 316219, Other Footwear Manufacturing.

316212 House Slipper Manufacturing[US]

This U.S. industry comprises establishments primarily engaged in manufacturing house slippers and slipper socks, regardless of material.

316213 Men's Footwear (except Athletic) Manufacturing[US]

This U.S. industry comprises establishments primarily engaged in manufacturing men's footwear designed primarily for dress, street, and work. This industry includes men's shoes with rubber or plastics soles and leather or vinyl uppers.

Cross-References. Establishments primarily engaged in—

- Manufacturing men's footwear with fabric uppers and rubber or plastics soles—are classified in U.S. Industry 316211, Rubber and Plastics Footwear Manufacturing;

- Manufacturing orthopedic extension footwear—are classified in U.S. Industry 339113, Surgical Appliance and Supplies Manufacturing; and

- Manufacturing men's leather or vinyl upper athletic footwear and youths' and boys' footwear—are classified in U.S. Industry 316219, Other Footwear Manufacturing.

316214 Women's Footwear (except Athletic) Manufacturing[US]

This U.S. industry comprises establishments primarily engaged in manufacturing women's footwear designed for dress, street, and work. This industry includes women's shoes with rubber or plastics soles and leather or vinyl uppers.

US—United States industry only. CAN—United States and Canadian industries are comparable. MEX—United States and Mexican industries are comparable. Blank—Canadian, Mexican, and United States industries are comparable.

Cross-References. Establishments primarily engaged in—

- Manufacturing women's footwear with fabric uppers and rubber or plastics soles and rubber or plastics sandals—are classified in U.S. Industry 316211, Rubber and Plastics Footwear Manufacturing;

- Manufacturing orthopedic extension footwear—are classified in U.S. Industry 339113, Surgical Appliance and Supplies Manufacturing; and

- Manufacturing women's leather or vinyl upper athletic footwear and youths' and girls' footwear—are classified in U.S. Industry 316219, Other Footwear Manufacturing.

316219 Other Footwear Manufacturing[US]

This U.S. industry comprises establishments primarily engaged in manufacturing other footwear (except rubber and plastics footwear; house slippers; men's footwear (except athletic); and women's footwear (except athletic)).

Illustrative Examples:

Athletic shoes (except rubber-soled, fabric upper) manufacturing
Ballet slippers manufacturing
Children's shoes (except plastics and rubber footwear and orthopedic extension shoes) manufacturing

Cleated athletic shoes manufacturing
Infants' shoes (except plastics and rubber footwear) manufacturing

Cross-References. Establishments primarily engaged in—

- **Manufacturing rubber and plastics footwear with fabric uppers**—are classified in U.S. Industry 316211, Rubber and Plastics Footwear Manufacturing;

- **Manufacturing house slippers**—are classified in U.S. Industry 316212, House Slipper Manufacturing;

- **Manufacturing men's footwear (except athletic)**—are classified in U.S. Industry 316213, Men's Footwear (except Athletic) Manufacturing;

- **Manufacturing orthopedic extension footwear**—are classified in Industry 339113, Surgical Appliance and Supplies Manufacturing; and

- **Manufacturing women's footwear (except athletic)**—are classified in U.S. Industry 316214, Women's Footwear (except Athletic) Manufacturing.

US—United States industry only. CAN—United States and Canadian industries are comparable. MEX—United States and Mexican industries are comparable. Blank—Canadian, Mexican, and United States industries are comparable.

3169 Other Leather and Allied Product Manufacturing

31699 Other Leather and Allied Product Manufacturing

This industry comprises establishments primarily engaged in manufacturing leather products (except footwear and apparel) from purchased leather or leather substitutes (e.g., fabric, plastics).

Illustrative Examples:

Billfolds, all materials, manufacturing	Shoe soles, leather, manufacturing
Boot and shoe cut stock and findings, leather, manufacturing	Toilet kits and cases (except metal) manufacturing
Dog furnishings (e.g., collars, leashes, harnesses, muzzles), manufacturing	Watchbands (except metal) manufacturing
Luggage, all materials, manufacturing	Welders' jackets, leggings, and sleeves, leather, manufacturing
Purses, women's, all materials (except metal), manufacturing	

Cross-References. Establishments primarily engaged in—

- Manufacturing leather apparel—are classified in Industry 31529, Other Cut and Sew Apparel Manufacturing;

- Manufacturing leather gloves, mittens, belts, and apparel accessories— are classified in Industry 31599, Apparel Accessories and Other Apparel Manufacturing;

- Manufacturing footwear—are classified in Industry 31621, Footwear Manufacturing;

- Manufacturing nonleather soles—are classified elsewhere based on the primary input material;

- Manufacturing small articles made of metal carried on or about the person made of metal—are classified in Industry 33991, Jewelry and Silverware Manufacturing; and

- Manufacturing leather gaskets—are classified in Industry 33999, All Other Miscellaneous Manufacturing.

316991 Luggage Manufacturing[US]

This U.S. industry comprises establishments primarily engaged in manufacturing luggage of any material.

316992 Women's Handbag and Purse Manufacturing[US]

This U.S. industry comprises establishments primarily engaged in manufacturing women's handbags and purses of any material (except precious metal).

Cross-References.
Establishments primarily engaged in manufacturing precious metal handbags and purses are classified in U.S. Industry 339911, Jewelry (except Costume) Manufacturing.

316993 Personal Leather Good (except Women's Handbag and Purse) Manufacturing[US]

This U.S. industry comprises establishments primarily engaged in manufacturing personal leather goods (i.e., small articles of any material (except metal) normally carried on or about the person or in a handbag). Examples of personal leather goods made by these establishments are billfolds, coin purses, key cases, toilet kits, and watchbands (except metal).

Cross-References. Establishments primarily engaged in—

- Manufacturing personal goods of precious metal—are classified in U.S. Industry 339911, Jewelry (except Costume) Manufacturing; and
- Manufacturing personal goods of metal (except precious)—are classified in U.S. Industry 339914, Costume Jewelry and Novelty Manufacturing.

316999 All Other Leather Good Manufacturing[US]

This U.S. industry comprises establishments primarily engaged in manufacturing leather goods (except footwear, luggage, handbags, purses, and personal leather goods).

Illustrative Examples:

Boot and shoe cut stock and findings, leather, manufacturing
Dog furnishings (e.g., collars, leashes, harnesses, muzzles) manufacturing
Leather belting for machinery (e.g., flat, solid, twisted, built-up) manufacturing

Shoe soles, leather, manufacturing
Welders' jackets, leggings, and sleeves, leather, manufacturing

Cross-References. Establishments primarily engaged in—

- Manufacturing leather gloves or mittens—are classified in U.S. Industry 315992, Glove and Mitten Manufacturing;

- Manufacturing leather apparel belts—are classified in U.S. Industry 315999, Other Apparel Accessories and Other Apparel Manufacturing;

- Manufacturing footwear—are classified in Industry 31621, Footwear Manufacturing;

- Manufacturing luggage of any material—are classified in U.S. Industry 316991, Luggage Manufacturing;

- Manufacturing handbags and purses—are classified in U.S. Industry 316992, Women's Handbag and Purse Manufacturing;

- Manufacturing personal leather goods, such as wallets and key cases, of all materials (except metal)—are classified in U.S. Industry 316993, Personal Leather Good (except Women's Handbag and Purse) Manufacturing;

- Manufacturing nonleather soles—are classified elsewhere based on the primary input material;

- Manufacturing leather apparel—are classified in U.S. Industry 315292, Fur and Leather Apparel Manufacturing; and

- Manufacturing leather gaskets—are classified in U.S. Industry 339991, Gasket, Packing, and Sealing Device Manufacturing.

321 Wood Product Manufacturing

Industries in the Wood Product Manufacturing subsector manufacture wood products, such as lumber, plywood, veneers, wood containers, wood flooring, wood trusses, manufactured homes (i.e., mobile home), and prefabricated wood buildings. The production processes of the Wood Product Manufacturing subsector include sawing, planing, shaping, laminating, and assembling of wood products starting from logs that are cut into bolts, or lumber that then may be further cut, or shaped by lathes or other shaping tools. The lumber or other transformed wood shapes may also be subsequently planed or smoothed, and assembled into finished products, such as wood containers. The Wood Product Manufacturing subsector includes establishments that make wood products from logs and bolts that are sawed and shaped, and establishments that purchase sawed lumber and make wood products. With the exception of sawmills and wood preservation establishments, the establishments are grouped into industries mainly based on the specific products manufactured.

3211 Sawmills and Wood Preservation

This industry group comprises establishments whose primary production process begins with logs or bolts that are transformed into boards, dimension lumber, beams, timbers, poles, ties, shingles, shakes, siding, and wood chips. Establishments

---

US—United States industry only. CAN—United States and Canadian industries are comparable. MEX—United States and Mexican industries are comparable. Blank—Canadian, Mexican, and United States industries are comparable.

that cut and treat round wood and/or treat wood products made in other establishments to prevent rotting by impregnation with creosote or other chemical compounds are also included in this industry group.

32111 Sawmills and Wood Preservation

This industry comprises establishments primarily engaged in one or more of the following: (1) sawing dimension lumber, boards, beams, timber, poles, ties, shingles, shakes, siding, and wood chips from logs or bolts; (2) sawing round wood poles, pilings, and posts and treating them with preservatives; and (3) treating wood sawed, planed, or shaped in other establishments with creosote or other preservatives to prevent decay and to protect against fire and insects. Sawmills may plane the rough lumber that they make with a planing machine to achieve smoothness and uniformity of size.

Cross-References. Establishments primarily engaged in—

- Operating portable chipper mills in the field—are classified in Industry 11331, Logging;
- Manufacturing wood products (except round wood poles, pilings, and posts) and treating them with preservatives—are classified elsewhere in Subsector 321, Wood Product Manufacturing, based on the related production process;
- Manufacturing veneer from logs and bolts or manufacturing engineered lumber and structural members other than solid wood—are classified in Industry 32121, Veneer, Plywood, and Engineered Wood Product Manufacturing; and
- Planing purchased lumber or manufacturing cut stock or dimension stock (i.e., shapes) from logs or bolts—are classified in Industry 32191, Millwork.

321113 Sawmills[US]

This U.S. industry comprises establishments primarily engaged in sawing dimension lumber, boards, beams, timbers, poles, ties, shingles, shakes, siding, and wood chips from logs or bolts. Sawmills may plane the rough lumber that they make with a planing machine to achieve smoothness and uniformity of size.

Cross-References. Establishments primarily engaged in—

- Planing purchased lumber or manufacturing cut stock or dimension stock (i.e., shapes) from logs or bolts—are classified in Industry 32191, Millwork;
- Manufacturing veneer from logs or bolts—are classified in Industry 32121, Veneer, Plywood, and Engineered Wood Product Manufacturing; and

- Operating portable chipper mills in the field—are classified in Industry 113310, Logging.

321114 Wood Preservation^{CAN}

This U.S. industry comprises establishments primarily engaged in (1) treating wood sawed, planed, or shaped in other establishments with creosote or other preservatives, such as chromated copper arsenate, to prevent decay and to protect against fire and insects and/or (2) sawing round wood poles, pilings, and posts and treating them with preservatives.

Cross-References.

Establishments primarily engaged in manufacturing wood products (except round wood poles, pilings, and posts) and treating them with preservatives are classified elsewhere in Subsector 321, Wood Product Manufacturing, based on the related production process.

3212 Veneer, Plywood, and Engineered Wood Product Manufacturing

32121 Veneer, Plywood, and Engineered Wood Product Manufacturing

This industry comprises establishments primarily engaged in one or more of the following: (1) manufacturing veneer and/or plywood; (2) manufacturing engineered wood members; and (3) manufacturing reconstituted wood products. This industry includes manufacturing plywood from veneer made in the same establishment or from veneer made in other establishments, and manufacturing plywood faced with nonwood materials, such as plastics or metal.

Illustrative Examples:

Fabricated structural wood members manufacturing	Particleboard manufacturing
Laminated structural wood members manufacturing	Plywood manufacturing
Medium density fiberboard (MDF) manufacturing	Reconstituted wood sheets and boards manufacturing
Oriented strandboard (OSB) manufacturing	Roof trusses, wood, manufacturing
	Veneer mills
	Waferboard manufacturing

Cross-References. Establishments primarily engaged in—

- Manufacturing veneer and further processing that veneer into wood containers or wood container parts in the same establishment—are classified in Industry 32192, Wood Container and Pallet Manufacturing;

- Manufacturing prefabricated wood buildings or wood sections, and panels for buildings—are classified in Industry 32199, All Other Wood Product Manufacturing; and
- Manufacturing solid wood structural members, such as dimension lumber and timber from logs or bolts in sawmills—are classified in Industry 32111, Sawmills and Wood Preservation.

321211 Hardwood Veneer and Plywood Manufacturing[CAN]

This U.S. industry comprises establishments primarily engaged in manufacturing hardwood veneer and/or hardwood plywood.

Cross-References. Establishments primarily engaged in—

- Manufacturing veneer and further processing that veneer into wood containers or wood container parts—are classified in Industry 321920, Wood Container and Pallet Manufacturing;
- Manufacturing softwood veneer and softwood plywood—are classified in U.S. Industry 321212, Softwood Veneer and Plywood Manufacturing; and
- Manufacturing reconstituted wood sheets and boards—are classified in U.S. Industry 321219, Reconstituted Wood Product Manufacturing.

321212 Softwood Veneer and Plywood Manufacturing[CAN]

This U.S. industry comprises establishments primarily engaged in manufacturing softwood veneer and/or softwood plywood.

Cross-References. Establishments primarily engaged in—

- Manufacturing veneer and further processing that veneer into wood containers or wood container parts—are classified in Industry 321920, Wood Container and Pallet Manufacturing;
- Manufacturing hardwood veneer and hardwood plywood—are classified in U.S. Industry 321211, Hardwood Veneer and Plywood Manufacturing; and
- Manufacturing reconstituted wood sheets and boards—are classified in U.S. Industry 321219, Reconstituted Wood Product Manufacturing.

321213 Engineered Wood Member (except Truss) Manufacturing[US]

This U.S. industry comprises establishments primarily engaged in manufacturing fabricated or laminated wood arches and/or other fabricated or laminated wood structural members.

US—United States industry only. CAN—United States and Canadian industries are comparable. MEX—United States and Mexican industries are comparable. Blank—Canadian, Mexican, and United States industries are comparable.

Illustrative Examples:

Finger joint lumber manufacturing	Parallel strand lumber manufacturing
I-joists, wood, fabricating	Timbers, structural, glue laminated or
Laminated veneer lumber (LVL) manufacturing	pre-engineered wood, manufacturing

Cross-References. Establishments primarily engaged in—

- Manufacturing prefabricated wood buildings, or wood sections, and panels for buildings—are classified in U.S. Industry 321992, Prefabricated Wood Building Manufacturing;

- Manufacturing wood trusses—are classified in U.S. Industry 321214, Truss Manufacturing; and

- Manufacturing solid wood structural members, such as dimension lumber and timber from logs or bolts,—are classified in U.S. Industry 321113, Sawmills.

321214 Truss Manufacturing^{US}

This U.S. industry comprises establishments primarily engaged in manufacturing laminated or fabricated wood roof and floor trusses.

Cross-References.

Establishments primarily engaged in manufacturing wood I-joists are classified in U.S. Industry 321213, Engineered Wood Member (except Truss) Manufacturing.

321219 Reconstituted Wood Product Manufacturing^{US}

This U.S. industry comprises establishments primarily engaged in manufacturing reconstituted wood sheets and boards.

Illustrative Examples:

Medium density fiberboard (MDF) manufacturing	Reconstituted wood sheets and boards manufacturing
Oriented strandboard (OSB) manufacturing	Waferboard manufacturing
Particleboard manufacturing	

Cross-References. Establishments primarily engaged in—

- Manufacturing softwood plywood—are classified in U.S. Industry 321212, Softwood Veneer and Plywood Manufacturing; and

• Manufacturing hardwood plywood—are classified in U.S. Industry 321211, Hardwood Veneer and Plywood Manufacturing.

3219 Other Wood Product Manufacturing

This industry group comprises establishments primarily engaged in manufacturing wood products (except establishments operating sawmills and wood preservation facilities; and establishments manufacturing veneer, plywood, or engineered wood products).

32191 Millwork

This industry comprises establishments primarily engaged in manufacturing hardwood and softwood cut stock and dimension stock (i.e., shapes); wood windows and wood doors; and other millwork including wood flooring. Dimension stock or cut stock is defined as lumber and worked wood products cut or shaped to specialized sizes. These establishments generally use woodworking machinery, such as jointers, planers, lathes, and routers to shape wood.

Cross-References. Establishments primarily engaged in—

• Manufacturing dimension lumber, boards, beams, timbers, poles, ties, shingles, shakes, siding, and wood chips from logs and bolts—are classified in Industry 32111, Sawmills and Wood Preservation;

• Fabricating millwork at the construction site—are classified in Industry 23835, Finish Carpentry Contractors; and

• Manufacturing wood furniture frames and finished wood furniture parts— are classified in Industry 33721, Office Furniture (including Fixtures) Manufacturing.

321911 Wood Window and Door Manufacturing^{CAN}

This U.S. industry comprises establishments primarily engaged in manufacturing window and door units, sash, window and door frames, and doors from wood or wood clad with metal or plastics.

Cross-References.

Establishments primarily engaged in fabricating wood windows or wood doors at the construction site are classified in Industry 238350, Finish Carpentry Contractors.

321912 Cut Stock, Resawing Lumber, and Planing[US]

This U.S. industry comprises establishments primarily engaged in one or more of the following: (1) manufacturing dimension lumber from purchased lumber; (2) manufacturing dimension stock (i.e., shapes) or cut stock; (3) resawing the output of sawmills; and (4) planing purchased lumber. These establishments generally use woodworking machinery, such as jointers, planers, lathes, and routers to shape wood.

Cross-References. Establishments primarily engaged in—

- Manufacturing dimension lumber, boards, beams, timbers, poles, ties, shingles, shakes, siding, and wood chips from logs or bolts—are classified in U.S. Industry 321113, Sawmills;

- Manufacturing wood stairwork, wood molding, wood trim, and other millwork—are classified in U.S. Industry 321918, Other Millwork (including Flooring); and

- Manufacturing wood furniture frames and finished wood furniture parts— are classified in U.S. Industry 337215, Showcase, Partition, Shelving, and Locker Manufacturing.

321918 Other Millwork (including Flooring)[US]

This U.S. industry comprises establishments primarily engaged in manufacturing millwork (except wood windows, wood doors, and cut stock).

Illustrative Examples:

Clear and finger joint wood moldings manufacturing	Planing mills, millwork
Decorative wood moldings (e.g., base, chair rail, crown, shoe) manufacturing	Stairwork (e.g., newel posts, railings, stairs, staircases), wood, manufacturing
Ornamental woodwork (e.g., cornices, mantel) manufacturing	Wood flooring manufacturing
	Wood shutters manufacturing

Cross-References. Establishments primarily engaged in—

- Manufacturing wood windows and doors—are classified in U.S. Industry 321911, Wood Window and Door Manufacturing; and

- Manufacturing cut stock, resawing lumber, and/or planing purchased lumber—are classified in U.S. Industry 321912, Cut Stock, Resawing Lumber, and Planing.

32192 Wood Container and Pallet Manufacturing

See industry description for 321920 below.

321920 Wood Container and Pallet Manufacturing

This industry comprises establishments primarily engaged in manufacturing wood pallets, wood box shook, wood boxes, other wood containers, and wood parts for pallets and containers.

Cross-References.

Establishments primarily engaged in manufacturing wood burial caskets are classified in U.S. Industry 339995, Burial Casket Manufacturing.

32199 All Other Wood Product Manufacturing

This industry comprises establishments primarily engaged in manufacturing wood products (except establishments operating sawmills and wood preservation facilities; and establishments manufacturing veneer, plywood, engineered wood products, millwork, wood containers, or pallets).

Illustrative Examples:

Mobile home manufacturing
Panels, prefabricated wood building,
  manufacturing
Prefabricated wood buildings
Sections, prefabricated wood building,
  manufacturing

Wood dowels manufacturing
Wood handles (e.g., broom, handtool,
  mop), manufacturing

Cross-References. Establishments primarily engaged in—

- Operating sawmills or preserving wood—are classified in Industry 32111, Sawmills and Wood Preservation;

- Manufacturing veneer, plywood, and engineered wood products—are classified in Industry 32121, Veneer, Plywood, and Engineered Wood Product Manufacturing;

- Manufacturing millwork—are classified in Industry 32191, Millwork;

- Manufacturing wood containers, pallets, and wood container parts—are classified in Industry 32192, Wood Container and Pallet Manufacturing;

- Manufacturing travel trailers with self-contained facilities for storage of water and waste—are classified in Industry 33621, Motor Vehicle Body and Trailer Manufacturing; and

- Fabricating of wood buildings or wood sections and panels for buildings at the construction site—are classified in Sector 23, Construction.

321991 Manufactured Home (Mobile Home) Manufacturing[CAN]

This U.S. industry comprises establishments primarily engaged in making manufactured homes (i.e., mobile homes) and nonresidential mobile buildings. Manufactured homes are designed to accept permanent water, sewer, and utility connections and although equipped with wheels, they are not intended for regular highway movement.

Cross-References. Establishments primarily engaged in—

- Manufacturing prefabricated wood buildings not equipped with wheels— are classified in U.S. Industry 321992, Prefabricated Wood Building Manufacturing; and

- Manufacturing travel trailers with self-contained facilities for storage of water and waste—are classified in U.S. Industry 336214, Travel Trailer and Camper Manufacturing.

321992 Prefabricated Wood Building Manufacturing[CAN]

This U.S. industry comprises establishments primarily engaged in manufacturing prefabricated wood buildings and wood sections and panels for prefabricated wood buildings.

Cross-References. Establishments primarily engaged in—

- Fabricating wood buildings or wood sections and panels for buildings at the construction site—are classified in Sector 23, Construction; and

- Making manufactured homes (i.e., mobile homes)—are classified in U.S. Industry 321991, Manufactured Home (Mobile Home) Manufacturing.

321999 All Other Miscellaneous Wood Product Manufacturing[CAN]

This U.S. industry comprises establishments primarily engaged in manufacturing wood products (except establishments operating sawmills and preservation facilities; establishments manufacturing veneer, engineered wood products, millwork, wood containers, pallets, and wood container parts; and establishments making manufactured homes (i.e., mobile homes) and prefabricated buildings and components).

Illustrative Examples:

Cork products (except gaskets) manufacturing	Wood handles (e.g., broom, handtool, mop), manufacturing
Kiln drying lumber	Wood kitchenware manufacturing
Shoe trees manufacturing	Wood stepladders manufacturing
Wood dowels manufacturing	Wood toilet seats manufacturing
Wood extension ladders manufacturing	Wood toothpicks manufacturing

Cross-References. Establishments primarily engaged in—

- Operating sawmills and preserving wood—are classified in Industry 32111, Sawmills and Wood Preservation;

- Manufacturing veneer and engineered wood products—are classified in Industry 32121, Veneer, Plywood, and Engineered Wood Product Manufacturing;

- Manufacturing millwork—are classified in Industry 32191, Millwork;

- Manufacturing boxes, box shook, wood containers, pallets, and wood parts for containers—are classified in Industry 321920, Wood Container and Pallet Manufacturing;

- Making manufactured homes (i.e., mobile homes)—are classified in U.S. Industry 321991, Manufactured Home (Mobile Home) Manufacturing; and

- Manufacturing prefabricated wood buildings or wood sections and panels for buildings—are classified in U.S. Industry 321992, Prefabricated Wood Building Manufacturing.

322 Paper Manufacturing

Industries in the Paper Manufacturing subsector make pulp, paper, or converted paper products. The manufacturing of these products is grouped together because they constitute a series of vertically connected processes. More than one is often carried out in a single establishment. There are essentially three activities. The manufacturing of pulp involves separating the cellulose fibers from other impurities in wood or used paper. The manufacturing of paper involves matting these fibers into a sheet. Converted paper products are made from paper and other materials by various cutting and shaping techniques and includes coating and laminating activities.

The Paper Manufacturing subsector is subdivided into two industry groups, the first for the manufacturing of pulp and paper and the second for the manufacturing of converted paper products. Paper making is treated as the core activity of the subsector. Therefore, any establishment that makes paper (including paperboard), either alone or in combination with pulp manufacturing or paper converting, is classified as a paper or paperboard mill. Establishments that make pulp without making paper are classified as pulp mills. Pulp mills, paper mills and paperboard mills comprise the first industry group.

Establishments that make products from purchased paper and other materials make up the second industry group, Converted Paper Product Manufacturing. This general activity is then subdivided based, for the most part, on process distinctions. Paperboard container manufacturing uses corrugating, cutting, and shaping machinery to form paperboard into containers. Paper bag and coated and treated paper manufacturing establishments cut and coat paper and foil. Stationery product manufacturing establishments make a variety of paper products used for writing, filing, and similar applications. Other converted paper product manufacturing includes, in particular, the conversion of sanitary paper stock into such things as tissue paper and disposable diapers.

An important process used in the Paper Bag and Coated and Treated Paper Manufacturing industry is lamination, often combined with coating. Lamination and coating makes a composite material with improved properties of strength, impermeability, and so on. The laminated materials may be paper, metal foil, or plastics film. While paper is often one of the components, it is not always. Lamination of plastics film to plastics film is classified in the NAICS Subsector 326, Plastics and Rubber Products Manufacturing, because establishments that do this often first make the film. The same situation holds with respect to bags. The manufacturing of bags from plastics only, whether or not laminated, is classified in Subsector 326, Plastics and Rubber Products Manufacturing, but all other bag manufacturing is classified in this subsector.

Excluded from this subsector are photosensitive papers. These papers are chemically treated and are classified in Industry 32599, All Other Chemical Product and Preparation Manufacturing.

3221 Pulp, Paper, and Paperboard Mills

This industry group comprises establishments primarily engaged in manufacturing pulp, paper, or paperboard.

32211 Pulp Mills

See industry description for 322110 below.

322110 Pulp Mills[MEX]

This industry comprises establishments primarily engaged in manufacturing pulp without manufacturing paper or paperboard. The pulp is made by separating the cellulose fibers from the other impurities in wood or other materials, such as used or recycled rags, linters, scrap paper, and straw.

US—United States industry only. CAN—United States and Canadian industries are comparable. MEX—United States and Mexican industries are comparable. Blank—Canadian, Mexican, and United States industries are comparable.

Cross-References. Establishments primarily engaged in—

- Manufacturing both pulp and paper—are classified in Industry 32212, **Paper Mills;** and

- Manufacturing both pulp and paperboard—are classified in Industry 322130, Paperboard Mills.

32212 Paper Mills

This industry comprises establishments primarily engaged in manufacturing paper from pulp. These establishments may manufacture or purchase pulp. In addition, the establishments may convert the paper they make. The activity of making paper classifies an establishment into this industry regardless of the output.

Cross-References. Establishments primarily engaged in—

- Manufacturing pulp without manufacturing paper—are classified in Industry 32211, Pulp Mills;

- Manufacturing paperboard—are classified in Industry 32213, Paperboard Mills;

- Converting paper without manufacturing paper—are classified in Industry Group 3222, Converted Paper Product Manufacturing; and

- Manufacturing photographic sensitized paper—are classified in Industry 32599, All Other Chemical Product and Preparation Manufacturing.

322121 Paper (except Newsprint) Mills[CAN]

This U.S. industry comprises establishments primarily engaged in manufacturing paper (except newsprint and uncoated groundwood paper) from pulp. These establishments may manufacture or purchase pulp. In addition, the establishments may also convert the paper they make.

Cross-References. Establishments primarily engaged in—

- Manufacturing newsprint and uncoated groundwood paper—are classified in U.S. Industry 322122, Newsprint Mills;

- Converting paper without manufacturing paper—are classified in Industry Group 3222, Converted Paper Product Manufacturing;

- Manufacturing paperboard—are classified in Industry 322130, Paperboard Mills;

- Manufacturing pulp without manufacturing paper—are classified in Industry 322110, Pulp Mills; and

- Manufacturing photographic sensitized paper from purchased paper—are classified in U.S. Industry 325992, Photographic Film, Paper, Plate, and Chemical Manufacturing.

322122 Newsprint Mills^{CAN}

This U.S. industry comprises establishments primarily engaged in manufacturing newsprint and uncoated groundwood paper from pulp. These establishments may manufacture or purchase pulp. In addition, the establishments may also convert the paper they make.

Cross-References. Establishments primarily engaged in—

- Manufacturing paper (except newsprint and uncoated groundwood)—are classified in U.S. Industry 322121, Paper (except Newsprint) Mills;
- Converting paper without manufacturing paper—are classified in Industry Group 3222, Converted Paper Product Manufacturing;
- Manufacturing paperboard—are classified in Industry 322130, Paperboard Mills; and
- Manufacturing pulp without manufacturing paper—are classified in Industry 322110, Pulp Mills.

32213 Paperboard Mills
See industry description for 322130 below.

322130 Paperboard Mills^{CAN}

This industry comprises establishments primarily engaged in manufacturing paperboard from pulp. These establishments may manufacture or purchase pulp. In addition, the establishments may also convert the paperboard they make.

Cross-References. Establishments primarily engaged in—

- Manufacturing pulp without manufacturing paperboard—are classified in Industry 322110, Pulp Mills;
- Converting paperboard without manufacturing paperboard—are classified in Industry Group 3222, Converted Paper Product Manufacturing; and
- Manufacturing insulation board and other reconstituted wood fiberboard—are classified in U.S. Industry 321219, Reconstituted Wood Product Manufacturing.

US—United States industry only. CAN—United States and Canadian industries are comparable. MEX—United States and Mexican industries are comparable. Blank—Canadian, Mexican, and United States industries are comparable.

3222 Converted Paper Product Manufacturing

This industry group comprises establishments primarily engaged in converting paper or paperboard without manufacturing paper or paperboard.

32221 Paperboard Container Manufacturing

This industry comprises establishments primarily engaged in converting paperboard into containers without manufacturing paperboard. These establishments use corrugating, cutting, and shaping machinery to form paperboard into containers. Products made by these establishments include boxes; corrugated sheets, pads, and pallets; paper dishes; and fiber drums and reels.

Cross-References. Establishments primarily engaged in—

- Manufacturing similar items of plastics materials—are classified in Industry Group 3261, Plastics Product Manufacturing;

- Manufacturing paperboard and converting paperboard into containers—are classified in Industry 32213, Paperboard Mills;

- Manufacturing egg cartons, food trays, and other food containers from molded pulp—are classified in Industry 32229, Other Converted Paper Product Manufacturing;

- Manufacturing paper and converting paper into containers—are classified in Industry 32212, Paper Mills; and

- Manufacturing paper bags without manufacturing paper—are classified in Industry 32222, Paper Bag and Coated and Treated Paper Manufacturing.

322211 Corrugated and Solid Fiber Box Manufacturing^{CAN}

This U.S. industry comprises establishments primarily engaged in laminating purchased paper or paperboard into corrugated or solid fiber boxes and related products, such as pads, partitions, pallets, and corrugated paper without manufacturing paperboard. These boxes are generally used for shipping.

Cross-References. Establishments primarily engaged in—

- Manufacturing setup paperboard boxes (except corrugated or laminated solid fiber boxes)—are classified in U.S. Industry 322213, Setup Paperboard Box Manufacturing;

- Manufacturing folding paperboard boxes (except corrugated or laminated solid fiber boxes)—are classified in U.S. Industry 322212, Folding Paperboard Box Manufacturing; and

---

US—United States industry only. CAN—United States and Canadian industries are comparable. MEX—United States and Mexican industries are comparable. Blank—Canadian, Mexican, and United States industries are comparable.

- Manufacturing paperboard and converting paperboard into boxes—are classified in Industry 322130, Paperboard Mills.

322212 Folding Paperboard Box Manufacturing^{CAN}

This U.S. industry comprises establishments primarily engaged in converting paperboard (except corrugated) into folding paperboard boxes without manufacturing paper and paperboard.

Cross-References. Establishments primarily engaged in—

- Manufacturing setup paperboard boxes (except corrugated)—are classified in U.S. Industry 322213, Setup Paperboard Box Manufacturing;

- Manufacturing corrugated and solid fiber boxes—are classified in U.S. Industry 322211, Corrugated and Solid Fiber Box Manufacturing;

- Manufacturing paperboard and converting paperboard into containers—are classified in Industry 322130, Paperboard Mills;

- Manufacturing paper and converting paper into containers—are classified in Industry 32212, Paper Mills;

- Manufacturing milk cartons—are classified in U.S. Industry 322215, Nonfolding Sanitary Food Container Manufacturing; and

- Manufacturing paper bags—are classified in Industry 32222, Paper Bag and Coated and Treated Paper Manufacturing.

322213 Setup Paperboard Box Manufacturing^{US}

This U.S. industry comprises establishments primarily engaged in converting paperboard into setup paperboard boxes (i.e., rigid-sided boxes not shipped flat) without manufacturing paperboard.

Cross-References. Establishments primarily engaged in—

- Manufacturing folding paperboard boxes (except corrugated)—are classified in U.S. Industry 322212, Folding Paperboard Box Manufacturing;

- Manufacturing corrugated and solid fiber boxes—are classified in U.S. Industry 322211, Corrugated and Solid Fiber Box Manufacturing; and

- Manufacturing paperboard and converting paperboard into containers—are classified in Industry 322130, Paperboard Mills.

US—United States industry only. CAN—United States and Canadian industries are comparable. MEX—United States and Mexican industries are comparable. Blank—Canadian, Mexican, and United States industries are comparable.

322214 Fiber Can, Tube, Drum, and Similar Products Manufacturing[US]

This U.S. industry comprises establishments primarily engaged in converting paperboard into fiber cans, tubes, drums, and similar products without manufacturing paperboard.

Cross-References.

Establishments engaged in manufacturing paperboard and converting paperboard into containers are classified in Industry 322130, Paperboard Mills.

322215 Nonfolding Sanitary Food Container Manufacturing[US]

This U.S. industry comprises establishments primarily engaged in converting sanitary foodboard into food containers (except folding).

Cross-References. Establishments primarily engaged in—

- Manufacturing sanitary food containers of solely plastics materials—are classified in Industry Group 3261, Plastics Product Manufacturing;
- Manufacturing egg cartons, food trays, and other food containers from molded pulp—are classified in U.S. Industry 322299, All Other Converted Paper Product Manufacturing; and
- Manufacturing folding sanitary cartons—are classified in U.S. Industry 322212, Folding Paperboard Box Manufacturing.

32222 Paper Bag and Coated and Treated Paper Manufacturing

This industry comprises establishments primarily engaged in one or more of the following: (1) cutting and coating paper and paperboard; (2) cutting and laminating paper and paperboard and other flexible materials (except plastics film to plastics film); (3) manufacturing bags or multiwall bags or sacks of paper, metal foil, coated paper, or laminates or coated combinations of paper and foil with plastics film; (4) manufacturing laminated aluminum and other converted metal foils from purchased foils; and (5) surface coating paper or paperboard.

Cross-References. Establishments primarily engaged in—

- Manufacturing paper from pulp—are classified in Industry 32212, Paper Mills;
- Manufacturing photographic sensitized paper—are classified in Industry 32599, All Other Chemical Product and Preparation Manufacturing;

- Manufacturing textile bags—are classified in Industry 31491, Textile Bag and Canvas Mills;
- Manufacturing single and multiwall plastics bags or plastics laminated bags—are classified in Industry 32611, Plastics Packaging Materials and Unlaminated Film and Sheet Manufacturing;
- Making aluminum and aluminum foil—are classified in Industry 33131, Alumina and Aluminum Production and Processing; and
- Cutting purchased aluminum foil into smaller lengths and widths—are classified in Industry 33299, All Other Fabricated Metal Product Manufacturing.

322221 Coated and Laminated Packaging Paper and Plastics Film Manufacturing[US]

This U.S. industry comprises establishments primarily engaged in performing one or more of the following activities associated with the manufacturing of packaging materials: (1) cutting and coating paper; and (2) cutting and laminating paper with other flexible materials (except plastics to plastics or foil to paper laminates). The products made in this industry are made from purchased sheet materials and may be printed in the same establishment.

Cross-References. Establishments primarily engaged in—

- Manufacturing coated or laminated paper for nonpackaging purposes—are classified in U.S. Industry 322222, Coated and Laminated Paper Manufacturing;
- Manufacturing unsupported plastics film—are classified in U.S. Industry 326113, Unlaminated Plastics Film and Sheet (except Packaging) Manufacturing;
- Manufacturing laminated aluminum foil for flexible packaging uses—are classified in U.S. Industry 322225, Laminated Aluminum Foil Manufacturing for Flexible Packaging Uses;
- Making aluminum and aluminum foil—are classified in Industry 33131, Alumina and Aluminum Production and Processing;
- Cutting purchased aluminum foil into smaller lengths and widths—are classified in U.S. Industry 332999, All Other Miscellaneous Fabricated Metal Product Manufacturing; and
- Manufacturing paper from pulp—are classified in Industry 32212, Paper Mills.

322222 Coated and Laminated Paper Manufacturing[US]

This U.S. industry comprises establishments primarily engaged in performing one or more of the following activities associated with making products designed for purposes other than packaging: (1) cutting and coating paper; (2) cutting and laminating paper and other flexible materials (except plastics film to plastics film); and (3) laminating aluminum and other metal foils for nonpackaging uses from purchased foils. The products made in this industry are made from purchased sheet materials and may be printed in the same establishment.

Illustrative Examples:

Book paper made by coating purchased paper
Gift wrap, laminated, made from purchased paper
Gummed paper products (e.g., labels sheets, tapes) made from purchased paper

Tapes, gummed (e.g., cellophane, masking, pressure sensitive) made from purchased paper or other structures
Wallpaper made from purchased papers or other materials

Cross-References. Establishments primarily engaged in—

- Manufacturing coated and laminated paper for packaging uses—are classified in U.S. Industry 322221, Coated and Laminated Packaging Paper and Plastics Film Manufacturing;

- Manufacturing photographic sensitized paper—are classified in U.S. Industry 325992, Photographic Film, Paper, Plate, and Chemical Manufacturing;

- Making aluminum and aluminum foil—are classified in Industry 33131, Alumina and Aluminum Production and Processing;

- Cutting purchased aluminum foil into smaller lengths and widths—are classified in U.S. Industry 332999, All Other Miscellaneous Fabricated Metal Product Manufacturing; and

- Manufacturing laminated aluminum foil for flexible packaging uses—are classified in U.S. Industry 322225, Laminated Aluminum Foil Manufacturing for Flexible Packaging Uses.

322223 Plastics, Foil, and Coated Paper Bag Manufacturing[US]

This U.S. industry comprises establishments primarily engaged in manufacturing bags of coated paper, of metal foil, or of laminated or coated combinations of plastics, foil, and paper, whether or not printed.

US—United States industry only. CAN—United States and Canadian industries are comparable. MEX—United States and Mexican industries are comparable. Blank—Canadian, Mexican, and United States industries are comparable.

Cross-References. Establishments primarily engaged in—

- Manufacturing uncoated paper bags and multiwall bags and sacks—are classified in U.S. Industry 322224, Uncoated Paper and Multiwall Bag Manufacturing;
- Manufacturing textile bags—are classified in U.S. Industry 314911, Textile Bag Mills; and
- Manufacturing single and multiwall plastics bags—are classified in U.S. Industry 326111, Plastics Bag Manufacturing.

322224   Uncoated Paper and Multiwall Bag Manufacturing[US]

This U.S. industry comprises establishments primarily engaged in manufacturing uncoated paper bags or multiwall bags and sacks.

Cross-References. Establishments primarily engaged in—

- Manufacturing single wall and multiwall bags from plastics unsupported film—are classified in U.S. Industry 326111, Plastics Bag Manufacturing;
- Manufacturing bags of coated paper, of metal foil, or of laminated or coated combinations of plastics, foil, and paper bags—are classified in U.S. Industry 322223, Plastics, Foil, and Coated Paper Bag Manufacturing; and
- Manufacturing textile bags—are classified in U.S. Industry 314911, Textile Bag Mills.

322225   Laminated Aluminum Foil Manufacturing for Flexible Packaging Uses[US]

This U.S. industry comprises establishments primarily engaged in laminating aluminum and other metal foil into products with flexible packaging uses or gift wrap and other packaging wrap applications.

Cross-References. Establishments primarily engaged in—

- Manufacturing plain aluminum foil—are classified in U.S. Industry 331315, Aluminum Sheet, Plate, and Foil Manufacturing;
- Manufacturing laminated aluminum bags and liners—are classified in U.S. Industry 322223, Plastics, Foil, and Coated Paper Bag Manufacturing;
- Manufacturing converted aluminum and other metal foils for nonpackaging uses from purchased foils—are classified in U.S. Industry 322222, Coated and Laminated Paper Manufacturing; and

---

US—United States industry only. CAN—United States and Canadian industries are comparable. MEX—United States and Mexican industries are comparable. Blank—Canadian, Mexican, and United States industries are comparable.

- Manufacturing cookware, dinnerware, and other semirigid metal containers—are classified in U.S. Industry 332999, All Other Miscellaneous Fabricated Metal Product Manufacturing.

322226 Surface-Coated Paperboard Manufacturing[US]

This U.S. industry comprises establishments primarily engaged in laminating, lining, or surface coating purchased paperboard to make other paperboard products.

32223 Stationery Product Manufacturing

This industry comprises establishments primarily engaged in converting paper or paperboard into products used for writing, filing, art work, and similar applications.

Illustrative Examples:

Die-cut paper products for office use made from purchased paper or paperboard
Envelopes (i e., mailing, stationery) made from any material
Tapes (e.g., adding machines, calculator, cash register) made from purchased paper

Stationery made from purchased paper
Tablets (e.g., memo, note, writing) made from purchased paper

Cross-References.

Establishments primarily engaged in manufacturing die-cut paper and paperboard products other than office supplies are classified in U.S. Industry 322299, All Other Converted Paper Product Manufacturing.

322231 Die-Cut Paper and Paperboard Office Supplies Manufacturing[US]

This U.S. industry comprises establishments primarily engaged in converting paper rollstock or paperboard into die-cut paper or paperboard office supplies. For the purpose of this industry, office supplies are defined as office products, such as filing folders, index cards, rolls for adding machines, file separators and dividers, tabulating cards, and other paper and paperboard office supplies.

Cross-References. Establishments primarily engaged in—

- Manufacturing die-cut paper and paperboard products (except office supplies)—are classified in U.S. Industry 322299, All Other Converted Paper Product Manufacturing; and

---

US—United States industry only. CAN—United States and Canadian industries are comparable. MEX—United States and Mexican industries are comparable. Blank—Canadian, Mexican, and United States industries are comparable.

- Manufacturing paper and paperboard products used for writing and similar applications (e.g., looseleaf fillers, notebooks, pads, stationery, tablets)—are classified in U.S. Industry 322233, Stationery, Tablet, and Related Product Manufacturing.

322232 Envelope Manufacturing^{US}

This U.S. industry comprises establishments primarily engaged in manufacturing envelopes for mailing or stationery of any material including combinations.

Cross-References.

Establishments primarily engaged in manufacturing stationery are classified in U.S. Industry 322233, Stationery, Tablet, and Related Product Manufacturing.

322233 Stationery, Tablet, and Related Product Manufacturing^{US}

This U.S. industry comprises establishments primarily engaged in converting paper and paperboard into products used for writing and similar applications (e.g., looseleaf fillers, notebooks, pads, stationery, tablets).

Cross-References. Establishments primarily engaged in—

- Manufacturing envelopes—are classified in U.S. Industry 322232, Envelope Manufacturing; and

- Manufacturing die-cut paper and paperboard office supplies—are classified in U.S. Industry 322231, Die-Cut Paper and Paperboard Office Supplies Manufacturing.

32229 Other Converted Paper Product Manufacturing

This industry comprises establishments primarily engaged in (1) converting paper and paperboard into products (except containers, bags, coated and treated paper and paperboard, and stationery products), or (2) converting pulp into pulp products, such as disposable diapers, or molded pulp egg cartons, food trays, and dishes. Processes used include laminating or lining purchased paper or paperboard.

Illustrative Examples:

Crepe paper made from purchased paper
Die-cut paper products (except for office use) made from purchased paper or paperboard

Paper novelties made from purchased paper

Molded pulp products (e.g., egg cartons, food containers, food trays) manufacturing

Sanitary products made from purchased sanitary paper stock

Cross-References. Establishments primarily engaged in—

- Manufacturing pulp from wood or from other materials—are classified in Industry 32211, Pulp Mills;

- Manufacturing paper from pulp or making pulp and manufacturing paper— are classified in Industry 32212, Paper Mills;

- Manufacturing paperboard from pulp or making pulp and manufacturing paperboard—are classified in Industry 32213, Paperboard Mills;

- Manufacturing paperboard containers—are classified in Industry 32221, Paperboard Container Manufacturing;

- Manufacturing bags of coated, laminated, or uncoated paper, of metal foil, or combinations thereof—are classified in Industry 32222, Paper Bag and Coated and Treated Paper Manufacturing; and

- Manufacturing stationery and other related office supplies—are classified in Industry 32223, Stationery Product Manufacturing.

322291 Sanitary Paper Product Manufacturing[CAN]

This U.S. industry comprises establishments primarily engaged in converting purchased sanitary paper stock or wadding into sanitary paper products, such as facial tissues and handkerchiefs, table napkins, toilet paper, towels, disposable diapers, sanitary napkins, and tampons.

322299 All Other Converted Paper Product Manufacturing[CAN]

This U.S. industry comprises establishments primarily engaged in converting paper or paperboard into products (except containers, bags, coated and treated paper, stationery products, and sanitary paper products) or converting pulp into pulp products, such as egg cartons, food trays, and other food containers from molded pulp.

Illustrative Examples:

Crepe paper made from purchased paper
Die-cut paper products (except for office use) made from purchased paper or paperboard

Molded pulp products (e.g., egg cartons, food containers, food trays) manufacturing
Paper novelties made from purchased paper

Cross-References. Establishments primarily engaged in—

- Manufacturing pulp from wood or from other materials—are classified in Industry 322110, Pulp Mills;
- Manufacturing paper from pulp or making pulp and manufacturing paper—are classified in Industry 32212, Paper Mills;
- Manufacturing paperboard from pulp or making pulp and manufacturing paperboard—are classified in Industry 322130, Paperboard Mills;
- Manufacturing paperboard containers—are classified in Industry 32221, Paperboard Container Manufacturing;
- Manufacturing bags of coated, laminated, or uncoated paper, of metal foil, or combinations thereof—are classified in Industry 32222, Paper Bag and Coated and Treated Paper Manufacturing; and
- Manufacturing stationery and other related office supplies—are classified in Industry 32223, Stationery Product Manufacturing.

323 Printing and Related Support Activities

Industries in the Printing and Related Support Activities subsector print products, such as newspapers, books, labels, business cards, stationery, business forms, and other materials, and perform support activities, such as data imaging, platemaking services, and bookbinding. The support activities included here are an integral part of the printing industry, and a product (a printing plate, a bound book, or a computer disk or file) that is an integral part of the printing industry is almost always provided by these operations.

Processes used in printing include a variety of methods used to transfer an image from a plate, screen, film, or computer file to some medium, such as paper, plastics, metal, textile articles, or wood. The most prominent of these methods is to transfer the image from a plate or screen to the medium (lithographic, gravure, screen, and flexographic printing). A rapidly growing new technology uses a computer file to directly "drive" the printing mechanism to create the image and new electrostatic and other types of equipment (digital or nonimpact printing).

In contrast to many other classification systems that locate publishing of printed materials in manufacturing, NAICS classifies the publishing of printed products in Subsector 511, Publishing Industries (except Internet). Though printing and publishing are often carried out by the same enterprise (a newspaper, for example), it is less and less the case that these distinct activities are carried out in the same establishment. When publishing and printing are done in the same establishment, the establishment is classified in Sector 51, Information, in the appropriate NAICS industry even if the receipts for printing exceed those for publishing.

This subsector includes printing on clothing because the production process for that activity is printing, not clothing manufacturing. For instance, the printing of

---

US—United States industry only. CAN—United States and Canadian industries are comparable. MEX—United States and Mexican industries are comparable. Blank—Canadian, Mexican, and United States industries are comparable.

T-shirts is included in this subsector. In contrast, printing on fabric (or grey goods) is not included. This activity is part of the process of finishing the fabric and is included in the NAICS Textile Mills subsector in Industry 31331, Textile and Fabric Finishing Mills.

3231 Printing and Related Support Activities

32311 Printing

This industry comprises establishments primarily engaged in printing on apparel and textile products, paper, metal, glass, plastics, and other materials, except fabric (grey goods). The printing processes employed include, but are not limited to, lithographic, gravure, screen, flexographic, digital, and letterpress. Establishments in this industry do not manufacture the stock that they print but may perform postprinting activities, such as folding, cutting, or laminating the materials they print, and mailing.

Cross-References. Establishments primarily engaged in—

- Providing photocopying service on nondigital photocopy equipment without performing traditional printing activities—are classified in Industry 56143, Business Service Centers;
- Printing on grey goods—are classified in Industry 31331, Textile and Fabric Finishing Mills;
- Printing and publishing, known as publishers,—are classified in Subsector 511, Publishing Industries (except Internet); and
- Performing prepress or postpress services without performing traditional printing activities—are classified in Industry 32312, Support Services for Printing.

323110 Commercial Lithographic Printing[US]

This U.S. industry comprises establishments primarily engaged in lithographic (i.e., offset) printing without publishing (except books, grey goods, and manifold business forms). This industry includes establishments engaged in lithographic printing on purchased stock materials, such as stationery, letterhead, invitations, labels, and similar items, on a job order basis.

Cross-References. Establishments primarily engaged in—

- Quick printing—are classified in U.S. Industry 323114, Quick Printing;
- Printing on grey goods—are classified in Industry 31331, Textile and Fabric Finishing Mills;

- Printing books and pamphlets—are classified in U.S. Industry 323117, Books Printing;

- Printing manifold business forms including checkbooks—are classified in U.S. Industry 323116, Manifold Business Forms Printing;

- Manufacturing printed stationery, invitations, labels, and similar items—are classified in Subsector 322, Paper Manufacturing; and

- Printing and publishing, known as publishers,—are classified in Subsector 511, Publishing Industries (except Internet).

323111 Commercial Gravure Printing[US]

This U.S. industry comprises establishments primarily engaged in gravure printing without publishing (except books, grey goods, and manifold business forms). This industry includes establishments engaged in gravure printing on purchased stock materials, such as stationery, letterhead, invitations, labels, and similar items, on a job order basis.

Cross-References. Establishments primarily engaged in—

- Printing on grey goods—are classified in Industry 31331, Textile and Fabric Finishing Mills;

- Printing books and pamphlets—are classified in U.S. Industry 323117, Book Printing;

- Printing manifold business forms including checkbooks—are classified in U.S. Industry 323116, Manifold Business Form Printing;

- Manufacturing printed stationery, invitations, labels, and similar items—are classified in Subsector 322, Paper Manufacturing; and

- Printing and publishing, known as publishers,—are classified in Subsector 511, Publishing Industries (except Internet).

323112 Commercial Flexographic Printing[US]

This U.S. industry comprises establishments primarily engaged in flexographic printing without publishing (except books, grey goods, and manifold business forms). This industry includes establishments engaged in flexographic printing on purchased stock materials, such as stationery, invitations, labels, and similar items, on a job order basis.

Cross-References. Establishments primarily engaged in—

- Printing on grey goods—are classified in Industry 31331, Textile and Fabric Finishing Mills;

- Printing books and pamphlets—are classified in U.S. Industry 323117, Books Printing;

- Printing manifold business forms including checkbooks—are classified in U.S. Industry 323116, Manifold Business Forms Printing;

- Manufacturing printed stationery, invitations, labels, and similar items— are classified elsewhere in Subsector 322, Manufacturing; and

- Printing and publishing, known as publishers,—are classified in Subsector 511, Publishing Industries (except Internet).

323113 Commercial Screen Printing[CAN]

This U.S. industry comprises establishments primarily engaged in screen printing without publishing (except books, grey goods, and manifold business forms). This industry includes establishments engaged in screen printing on purchased stock materials, such as stationery, invitations, labels, and similar items, on a job order basis. Establishments primarily engaged in printing on apparel and textile products, such as T-shirts, caps, jackets, towels, and napkins, are included in this industry.

Cross-References. Establishments primarily engaged in—

- Printing on grey goods—are classified in Industry 31331, Textile and Fabric Finishing Mills;

- Printing books and pamphlets—are classified in U.S. Industry 323117, Books Printing;

- Printing manifold business forms including checkbooks—are classified in U.S. Industry 323116, Manifold Business Forms Printing;

- Manufacturing printed stationery, invitations, labels, and similar items— are classified in Subsector 322, Paper Manufacturing; and

- Printing and publishing, known as publishers,—are classified in Subsector 511, Publishing Industries (except Internet).

323114 Quick Printing[CAN]

This U.S. industry comprises establishments primarily engaged in traditional printing activities, such as short-run offset printing or prepress services, in combination with providing document photocopying service. Prepress services include receiving documents in electronic format and directly duplicating from the electronic file and formatting, colorizing, and otherwise modifying the original document to improve presentation. These establishments, known as quick printers, generally provide short-run printing and copying with fast turnaround times.

Cross-References. Establishments primarily engaged in—

- Providing photocopying service on nondigital photocopy equipment without performing traditional printing activities—are classified in U.S. Industry 561439, Other Business Service Centers (including Copy Shops);
- Printing with lithographic equipment known as commercial lithographic printers—are classified in U.S. Industry 323110, Commercial Lithographic Printing; and
- Digital printing on graphical material—are classified in U.S. Industry 323115, Digital Printing.

323115 Digital Printing[CAN]

This U.S. industry comprises establishments primarily engaged in printing graphical materials using digital printing equipment. Establishments known as digital printers typically provide sophisticated prepress services including using scanners to input images and computers to manipulate and format the graphic images prior to printing.

Cross-References.

Establishments primarily engaged in printing with "up front" computer files on conventional-type printing equipment are classified to books, manifold business forms, or based on the type of printing equipment (e.g., lithographic, flexographic, screen) being used.

323116 Manifold Business Forms Printing[CAN]

This U.S. industry comprises establishments primarily engaged in printing special forms, including checkbooks, for use in the operation of a business. The forms may be in single and multiple sets, including carbonized, interleaved with carbon, or otherwise processed for multiple reproduction.

Cross-References.

Establishments primarily engaged in manufacturing single layered continuous computer paper and similar products are classified in U.S. Industry 322231, Die-Cut Paper and Paperboard Office Supplies Manufacturing.

323117 Books Printing[US]

This U.S. industry comprises establishments primarily engaged in printing or printing and binding books and pamphlets without publishing.

Cross-References. Establishments primarily engaged in—

- Printing and publishing, known as book publishers,—are classified in Subsector 511, Publishing Industries (except Internet); and

- Binding books without printing in the same establishment—are classified in U.S. Industry 323121, Tradebinding and Related Work.

323118 Blankbook, Looseleaf Binders, and Devices Manufacturing[US]

This U.S. industry comprises establishments primarily engaged in manufacturing blankbooks, looseleaf devices, and binders. Establishments in this industry may print or print and bind.

Cross-References. Establishments primarily engaged in—

- Checkbook printing—are classified in U.S. Industry 323116, Manifold Business Form Printing; and

- Binding books without printing in the same establishment—are classified in U.S. Industry 323121, Tradebinding and Related Work.

323119 Other Commercial Printing[US]

This U.S. industry comprises establishments primarily engaged in commercial printing (except lithographic, gravure, screen, or flexographic printing) without publishing (except books, grey goods, and manifold business forms). Printing processes included in this industry are letterpress printing and engraving printing. This industry includes establishments engaged in commercial printing on purchased stock materials, such as stationery, invitations, labels, and similar items, on a job order basis.

Cross-References. Establishments primarily engaged in—

- Lithographic, gravure, screen, or flexographic printing on purchased stock materials (except books, grey goods, and manifold business forms)—are classified in Industry 32311, Printing, by printing process employed;

- Printing on grey goods—are classified in Industry 31331, Textile and Fabric Finishing Mills;

US—United States industry only. CAN—United States and Canadian industries are comparable. MEX—United States and Mexican industries are comparable. Blank—Canadian, Mexican, and United States industries are comparable.

- Quick printing—are classified in U.S. Industry 323114, Quick Printing;
- Digital printing on graphical materials—are classified in U.S. Industry 323115, Digital Printing;
- Printing books and pamphlets—are classified in U.S. Industry 323117, Books Printing;
- Printing manifold business forms including checkbooks—are classified in U.S. Industry 323116, Manifold Business Forms Printing;
- Manufacturing printed stationery, invitations, labels, and similar items—are classified in Subsector 322, Paper Manufacturing; and
- Printing and publishing, known as book publishers,—are classified in Subsector 511, Publishing Industries (except Internet).

32312 Support Activities for Printing

This industry comprises establishments primarily engaged in performing prepress (e.g., platemaking, typesetting) and postpress services (e.g., book binding) in support of printing activities.

Cross-References. Establishments primarily engaged in—

- Engraving of the type done on metal—are classified in Industry 33281, Coating, Engraving, Heat Treating, and Allied Activities;
- Manufacturing photosensitive plates for printing—are classified in Industry 32599, All Other Chemical Product and Preparation Manufacturing;
- Manufacturing blank plates for printing—are classified in Industry 33329, Other Industrial Machinery Manufacturing; and
- Printing books or printing and binding books—are classified in Industry 32311, Printing.

323121 Tradebinding and Related Work[US]

This U.S. industry comprises establishments primarily engaged in one or more of the following: (1) tradebinding; (2) sample mounting; and (3) postpress services (e.g., book or paper bronzing, die-cutting, edging, embossing, folding, gilding, gluing, indexing).

Cross-References.

Establishments primarily engaged in printing books or printing and binding books are classified in U.S. Industry 323117, Books Printing.

US—United States industry only. CAN—United States and Canadian industries are comparable. MEX—United States and Mexican industries are comparable. Blank—Canadian, Mexican, and United States industries are comparable.

323122 Prepress Services[US]

This U.S. industry comprises (1) establishments primarily engaged in prepress services, such as imagesetting or typesetting, for printers and (2) establishments primarily engaged in preparing film or plates for printing purposes.

Cross-References. Establishments primarily engaged in—

- Engraving of the type done on metal—are classified in U.S. Industry 332812, Metal Coating, Engraving (except jewelry and silverware), and Allied Services to Manufacturers;
- Manufacturing blank plates (except photosensitive plates) for printing—are classified in U.S. Industry 333293, Printing Machinery and Equipment Manufacturing; and
- Manufacturing photosensitive plates for printing—are classified in U.S. Industry 325992, Photographic Film, Paper, Plate, and Chemical Manufacturing.

324 Petroleum and Coal Products Manufacturing

The Petroleum and Coal Products Manufacturing subsector is based on the transformation of crude petroleum and coal into usable products. The dominant process is petroleum refining that involves the separation of crude petroleum into component products through such techniques as cracking and distillation.

In addition, this subsector includes establishments that primarily further process refined petroleum and coal products and produce products, such as asphalt coatings and petroleum lubricating oils. However, establishments that manufacture petrochemicals from refined petroleum are classified in Industry 32511, Petrochemical Manufacturing.

3241 Petroleum and Coal Products Manufacturing

32411 Petroleum Refineries
See industry description for 324110 below.

324110 Petroleum Refineries

This industry comprises establishments primarily engaged in refining crude petroleum into refined petroleum. Petroleum refining involves one or more of the following activities: (1) fractionation; (2) straight distillation of crude oil; and (3) cracking.

US—United States industry only. CAN—United States and Canadian industries are comparable. MEX—United States and Mexican industries are comparable. Blank—Canadian, Mexican, and United States industries are comparable.

Cross-References. Establishments primarily engaged in—

- Manufacturing asphalt paving, roofing, and saturated materials from refined petroleum—are classified in Industry 32412, Asphalt Paving, Roofing, and Saturated Materials Manufacturing;

- Manufacturing paper mats and felts and saturating them with asphalt or tar into rolls and sheets—are classified in U.S. Industry 322121, Paper (except Newsprint) Mills;

- Blending or compounding refined petroleum to make lubricating oils and greases and/or re-refining used petroleum lubricating oils—are classified in U.S. Industry 324191, Petroleum Lubricating Oil and Grease Manufacturing;

- Manufacturing synthetic lubricating oils and greases—are classified in U.S. Industry 325998, All Other Miscellaneous Chemical Product and Preparation Manufacturing;

- Recovering natural gasoline and/or liquid hydrocarbons from oil and gas field gases—are classified in Industry 21111, Oil and Gas Extraction;

- Manufacturing acyclic and cyclic aromatic hydrocarbons (i.e., petrochemicals) from refined petroleum or liquid hydrocarbons—are classified in Industry 325110, Petrochemical Manufacturing;

- Manufacturing cyclic and acyclic chemicals (except petrochemicals)—are classified in Industry 32519, Other Basic Organic Chemical Manufacturing;

- Manufacturing coke oven products in steel mills—are classified in U.S. Industry 331111, Iron and Steel Mills; and

- Manufacturing coke oven products in coke oven establishments—are classified in U.S. Industry, 324199, All Other Petroleum and Coal Products Manufacturing.

32412 Asphalt Paving, Roofing, and Saturated Materials Manufacturing

This industry comprises establishments primarily engaged in (1) manufacturing asphalt and tar paving mixtures and blocks and roofing cements and coatings from purchased asphaltic materials and/or (2) saturating purchased mats and felts with asphalt or tar from purchased asphaltic materials.

Cross-References. Establishments primarily engaged in—

- Refining crude petroleum and manufacturing asphalt and tar paving, roofing, and saturated materials—are classified in Industry 324110, Petroleum Refineries; and

---

- Manufacturing paper mats and felts and saturating them with asphalt or tar—are classified in Industry 32212, Paper Mills.

324121 Asphalt Paving Mixture and Block Manufacturing^{CAN}

This U.S. industry comprises establishments primarily engaged in manufacturing asphalt and tar paving mixtures and blocks from purchased asphaltic materials.

Cross-References.

Establishments primarily engaged in refining crude petroleum and manufacturing asphalt and tar paving mixtures and blocks are classified in Industry 324110, Petroleum Refineries.

324122 Asphalt Shingle and Coating Materials Manufacturing^{CAN}

This U.S. industry comprises establishments primarily engaged in (1) saturating purchased mats and felts with asphalt or tar from purchased asphaltic materials and (2) manufacturing asphalt and tar and roofing cements and coatings from purchased asphaltic materials.

Cross-References. Establishments primarily engaged in—

- Refining crude petroleum and saturating purchased mats and felts with asphalt or tar into rolls and sheets and/or refining crude petroleum and manufacturing asphalt and tar roofing cements and coatings—are classified in Industry 324110, Petroleum Refineries; and

- Manufacturing paper mats and felts and saturating them with asphalt or tar into rolls and sheets—are classified in U.S. Industry 322121, Paper (except Newsprint) Mills.

32419 Other Petroleum and Coal Products Manufacturing

This industry comprises establishments primarily engaged in manufacturing petroleum products (except asphalt paving, roofing and saturated materials) from refined petroleum or coal products made in coke ovens not integrated with a steel mill.

Illustrative Examples:

Coke oven products (e.g., coke, gases, tars) made in coke oven establishments	Petroleum lubricating oils and greases made from refined petroleum
Petroleum brake fluids made from refined petroleum	Petroleum waxes made from refined petroleum

---

US—United States industry only. CAN—United States and Canadian industries are comparable. MEX—United States and Mexican industries are comparable. Blank—Canadian, Mexican, and United States industries are comparable.

Petroleum briquettes made from refined petroleum	Re-refined used petroleum lubricating oils
Petroleum jelly made from refined petroleum	

Cross-References. Establishments primarily engaged in—

- Manufacturing petroleum products by refining crude petroleum—are classified in Industry 32411, Petroleum Refineries;

- Manufacturing asphalt and tar paving, roofing, and saturated materials from refined petroleum—are classified in Industry 32412, Asphalt Paving, Roofing, and Saturated Materials Manufacturing;

- Manufacturing coke oven products in steel mills—are classified in Industry 33111, Iron and Steel Mills and Ferroalloy Manufacturing;

- Manufacturing acyclic and cyclic aromatic hydrocarbons (i.e., petrochemicals) from refined petroleum or liquid hydrocarbons—are classified in Industry 32511, Petrochemical Manufacturing;

- Manufacturing cyclic and acyclic organic chemicals (except petrochemicals)—are classified in Industry 32519, Other Basic Organic Chemical Manufacturing; and

- Manufacturing synthetic lubricating oils and greases—are classified in Industry 32599, All Other Chemical Product and Preparation Manufacturing.

324191 Petroleum Lubricating Oil and Grease Manufacturing[MEX]

This U.S. industry comprises establishments primarily engaged in blending or compounding refined petroleum to make lubricating oils and greases and/or re-refining used petroleum lubricating oils.

Cross-References. Establishments primarily engaged in—

- Refining crude petroleum and manufacturing lubricating oils and greases— are classified in Industry 324110, Petroleum Refineries; and

- Manufacturing synthetic lubricating oils and greases—are classified in U.S. Industry 325998, All Other Miscellaneous Chemical Product and Preparation Manufacturing.

324199 All Other Petroleum and Coal Products Manufacturing[US]

This U.S. industry comprises establishments primarily engaged in manufacturing petroleum products (except asphalt paving, roofing, and saturated materials and lubricating oils and greases) from refined petroleum and coal products made in coke ovens not integrated with a steel mill.

Illustrative Examples:

Coke oven products (e.g., coke, gases, tars) made in coke oven establishments

Petroleum briquettes made from refined petroleum

Petroleum jelly made from refined petroleum

Petroleum waxes made from refined petroleum

Cross-References. Establishments primarily engaged in—

- Manufacturing petroleum products by refining crude petroleum—are classified in Industry 324110, Petroleum Refineries;

- Manufacturing asphalt paving and roofing materials from refined petroleum—are classified in Industry 32412, Asphalt Paving, Roofing, and Saturated Materials Manufacturing;

- Blending and compounding petroleum lubricating oils and greases and/or re-refining used petroleum lubrication oils and greases—are classified in U.S. Industry 324191, Petroleum Lubricating Oil and Grease Manufacturing;

- Manufacturing coke oven products in steel mills—are classified in U.S. Industry 331111, Iron and Steel Mills;

- Manufacturing acyclic and cyclic aromatic hydrocarbons (i.e., petrochemicals) from refined petroleum or liquid hydrocarbons—are classified in Industry 325110, Petrochemical Manufacturing; and

- Manufacturing cyclic and acyclic organic chemicals (except petrochemicals)—are classified in Industry 32519, Other Basic Organic Chemical Manufacturing.

325 Chemical Manufacturing

The Chemical Manufacturing subsector is based on the transformation of organic and inorganic raw materials by a chemical process and the formulation of products. This subsector distinguishes the production of basic chemicals that comprise the first industry group from the production of intermediate and end products produced by further processing of basic chemicals that make up the remaining industry groups.

This subsector does not include all industries transforming raw materials by a chemical process. It is common for some chemical processing to occur during mining operations. These beneficiating operations, such as copper concentrating, are classified in Sector 21, Mining. Furthermore, the refining of crude petroleum is included in Subsector 324, Petroleum and Coal Products Manufacturing. In addition, the manufacturing of aluminum oxide is included in Subsector 331, Primary Metal Manufacturing; and beverage distilleries are classified in Subsector 312, Beverage and Tobacco Product Manufacturing. As in the case of these two activities, the grouping of industries into subsectors may take into account the association of the activities performed with other activities in the subsector.

3251 Basic Chemical Manufacturing

This industry group comprises establishments primarily engaged in manufacturing chemicals using basic processes, such as thermal cracking and distillation. Chemicals manufactured in this industry group are usually separate chemical elements or separate chemically-defined compounds.

32511 Petrochemical Manufacturing
See industry description for 325110 below.

325110 Petrochemical Manufacturing

This industry comprises establishments primarily engaged in (1) manufacturing acyclic (i.e., aliphatic) hydrocarbons such as ethylene, propylene, and butylene made from refined petroleum or liquid hydrocarbon and/or (2) manufacturing cyclic aromatic hydrocarbons such as benzene, toluene, styrene, xylene, ethyl benzene, and cumene made from refined petroleum or liquid hydrocarbons.

Cross-References. Establishments primarily engaged in—

- Manufacturing petrochemicals by refining crude petroleum—are classified in Industry 324110, Petroleum Refineries;
- Manufacturing acetylene—are classified in Industry 325120, Industrial Gas Manufacturing;
- Manufacturing basic organic chemicals (except petrochemicals)—are classified in Industry 32519, Other Basic Organic Chemical Manufacturing; and
- Recovering liquid hydrocarbons from oil and gas field gases—are classified in Industry 211110, Oil and Gas Extraction.

32512 Industrial Gas Manufacturing
See industry description for 325120 below.

325120 Industrial Gas Manufacturing

This industry comprises establishments primarily engaged in manufacturing industrial organic and inorganic gases in compressed, liquid, and solid forms.

US—United States industry only. CAN—United States and Canadian industries are comparable. MEX—United States and Mexican industries are comparable. Blank—Canadian, Mexican, and United States industries are comparable.

Cross-References. Establishments primarily engaged in—

- Manufacturing chlorine gas—are classified in U.S. Industry 325181, Alkalies and Chlorine Manufacturing; and

- Manufacturing ethane and butane gases made from refined petroleum or liquid hydrocarbons—are classified in Industry 325110, Petrochemical Manufacturing.

32513 Synthetic Dye and Pigment Manufacturing

This industry comprises establishments primarily engaged in manufacturing synthetic organic and inorganic dyes and pigments, such as lakes and toners (except electrostatic and photographic).

Cross-References. Establishments primarily engaged in—

- Manufacturing wood byproducts used as dying materials—are classified in Industry 32519, Other Basic Organic Chemical Manufacturing;

- Manufacturing carbon, bone, and lamp black—are classified in Industry 32518, Other Basic Inorganic Chemical Manufacturing;

- Manufacturing electrostatic and photographic toners—are classified in Industry 32599, All Other Chemical Product and Preparation Manufacturing;

- Manufacturing natural food colorings—are classified in Industry 31193, Flavoring Syrup and Concentrate Manufacturing; and

- Manufacturing natural organic colorings for nonfood uses—are classified in Industry 32519, Other Basic Organic Chemical Manufacturing.

325131 Inorganic Dye and Pigment Manufacturing[US]

This U.S. industry comprises establishments primarily engaged in manufacturing inorganic dyes and pigments.

Cross-References. Establishments primarily engaged in—

- Manufacturing wood byproducts used as dyeing materials—are classified in U.S. Industry 325191, Gum and Wood Chemical Manufacturing;

- Manufacturing organic synthetic dyes and pigments—are classified in U.S. Industry 325132, Synthetic Organic Dye and Pigment Manufacturing;

- Manufacturing carbon, bone, and lamp black—are classified in U.S. Industry 325182, Carbon Black Manufacturing; and

- Manufacturing natural food colorings—are classified in Industry 311930, Flavoring Syrup and Concentrate Manufacturing.

US—United States industry only. CAN—United States and Canadian industries are comparable. MEX—United States and Mexican industries are comparable. Blank—Canadian, Mexican, and United States industries are comparable.

325132 Synthetic Organic Dye and Pigment Manufacturing^{US}

This U.S. industry comprises establishments primarily engaged in manufacturing synthetic organic dyes and pigments, such as lakes and toners (except electrostatic and photographic).

Cross-References. Establishments primarily engaged in—

- Manufacturing wood byproducts used as dyeing materials—are classified in U.S. Industry 325191, Gum and Wood Chemical Manufacturing;

- Manufacturing inorganic dyes and pigments—are classified in U.S. Industry 325131, Inorganic Dye and Pigment Manufacturing;

- Manufacturing electrostatic and photographic toners—are classified in U.S. Industry 325992, Photographic Film, Paper, Plate, and Chemical Manufacturing;

- Manufacturing natural food colorings—are classified in Industry 311930, Flavoring Syrup and Concentrate Manufacturing; and

- Manufacturing natural organic colorings for nonfood uses (except wood byproducts)—are classified in U.S. Industry 325199, All Other Basic Organic Chemical Manufacturing.

32518 Other Basic Inorganic Chemical Manufacturing

This industry comprises establishments primarily engaged in manufacturing basic inorganic chemicals (except industrial gases and synthetic dyes and pigments).

Illustrative Examples:

Alkalies manufacturing	Hydrochloric acid manufacturing
Aluminum compounds, not specified elsewhere by process, manufacturing	Potassium inorganic compounds, not specified elsewhere by process, manufacturing
Carbides (e.g., baron, calcium, silium, tungsten) manufacturing	Radioactive isotopes manufacturing
Carbon black manufacturing	Sulfides and sulfites manufacturing
Chlorine manufacturing	Sulfuric acid manufacturing

Cross-References. Establishments primarily engaged in—

- Manufacturing industrial gases—are classified in Industry 32512, Industrial Gas Manufacturing;

- Manufacturing inorganic dyes and pigments—are classified in Industry 32513, Synthetic Dye and Pigment Manufacturing;

- Manufacturing household bleaches—are classified in Industry 32561, Soap and Cleaning Compound Manufacturing;

- Mining and/or beneficiating alkalies—are classified in Industry 21239, Other Nonmetallic Mineral Mining and Quarrying;
- Manufacturing chlorine preparations (e.g., for swimming pools)—are classified in Industry 32599, All Other Chemical Product and Preparation Manufacturing;
- Manufacturing nitrogenous and phosphoric fertilizers and fertilizer materials—are classified in Industry 32531, Fertilizer Manufacturing;
- Manufacturing aluminum oxide (alumina)—are classified in Industry 33131, Alumina and Aluminum Production and Processing;
- Manufacturing inorganic insecticidal, herbicidal, fungicidal and pesticidal preparations—are classified in Industry 32532, Pesticide and Other Agricultural Chemical Manufacturing; and
- Manufacturing photographic chemicals—are classified in Industry 32599, All Other Chemical Product and Preparation Manufacturing.

325181 Alkalies and Chlorine Manufacturing[CAN]

This U.S. industry comprises establishments primarily engaged in manufacturing chlorine, sodium hydroxide (i.e., caustic soda), and other alkalies often using an electrolysis process.

Cross-References. Establishments primarily engaged in—

- Mining and beneficiating alkalies—are classified in U.S. Industry 212391, Potash, Soda, and Borate Mineral Mining;
- Manufacturing chlorine preparations (e.g., for swimming pools)—are classified in U.S. Industry 325998, All Other Miscellaneous Chemical Product and Preparation Manufacturing;
- Manufacturing industrial bleaches—are classified in U.S. Industry 325188, All Other Basic Inorganic Chemical Manufacturing; and
- Manufacturing household bleaches—are classified in U.S. Industry 325612, Polish and Other Sanitation Good Manufacturing.

325182 Carbon Black Manufacturing[US]

This U.S. industry comprises establishments primarily engaged in manufacturing carbon black, bone black, and lamp black.

Cross-References. Establishments primarily engaged in manufacturing pigments are classified in Industry 32513, Synthetic Dye and Pigment Manufacturing.

US—United States industry only. CAN—United States and Canadian industries are comparable. MEX—United States and Mexican industries are comparable. Blank—Canadian, Mexican, and United States industries are comparable.

325188 All Other Basic Inorganic Chemical Manufacturing[US]

This U.S. industry comprises establishments primarily engaged in manufacturing basic inorganic chemicals (except industrial gases, inorganic dyes and pigments, alkalies and chlorine, and carbon black).

Illustrative Examples:

Aluminum compounds, not specified
  elsewhere by process, manufacturing
Carbides (e.g., baron, calcium, silicon,
  tungsten) manufacturing
Fluorine manufacturing
Hydrochloric acid manufacturing
Potassium inorganic compounds, not
  specified elsewhere by process,
  manufacturing

Sodium inorganic compounds, not
  specified elsewhere by process,
  manufacturing
Sulfides and sulfites manufacturing
Sulfuric acid manufacturing

Cross-References. Establishments primarily engaged in—

- Manufacturing industrial gases—are classified in Industry 325120, Industrial Gas Manufacturing;

- Manufacturing inorganic dyes and pigments—are classified in U.S. Industry 325131, Inorganic Dye and Pigment Manufacturing;

- Manufacturing alkalies and chlorine—are classified in U.S. Industry 325181, Alkalies and Chlorine Manufacturing;

- Manufacturing carbon black—are classified in U.S. Industry 325182, Carbon Black Manufacturing;

- Manufacturing household bleaches—are classified in U.S. Industry 325612, Polish and Other Sanitation Good Manufacturing;

- Manufacturing nitrogenous and phosphoric fertilizers and fertilizer material—are classified in Industry 32531, Fertilizer Manufacturing;

- Manufacturing aluminum oxide (i.e., alumina)—are classified in U.S. Industry 331311, Alumina Refining;

- Manufacturing inorganic insecticidal, herbicidal, fungicidal, and pesticidal preparations—are classified in Industry 325320, Pesticide and Other Agriculture Chemical Manufacturing; and

- Manufacturing photographic chemicals—are classified in U.S. Industry 325992, Photographic Film, Paper, Plate, and Chemical Manufacturing.

US—United States industry only. CAN—United States and Canadian industries are comparable. MEX—United States and Mexican industries are comparable. Blank—Canadian, Mexican, and United States industries are comparable.

32519 Other Basic Organic Chemical Manufacturing

This industry comprises establishments primarily engaged in manufacturing basic organic chemicals (except petrochemicals, industrial gases, and synthetic dyes and pigments).

Illustrative Examples:

Carbon organic compounds, not specified elsewhere by process, manufacturing
Cyclic intermediates made from refined petroleum or natural gas
Enzyme proteins (i.e., basic synthetic chemicals) (except pharmaceutical use) manufacturing
Fatty acids (e.g., margaric, oleic, stearic) manufacturing

Gum and wood chemicals manufacturing
Organo-inorganic compound manufacturing
Plasticizers (i.e., basic synthetic chemical) manufacturing
Silicone (except resins) manufacturing
Synthetic sweeteners (i.e., sweetening agents) manufacturing

Cross-References. Establishments primarily engaged in—

- Manufacturing petrochemicals from refined petroleum or liquid hydrocarbons—are classified in Industry 32511, Petrochemical Manufacturing;

- Manufacturing petrochemicals by refining crude petroleum—are classified in Industry 32411, Petroleum Refineries;

- Manufacturing organic industrial gases—are classified in Industry 32512, Industrial Gas Manufacturing;

- Manufacturing synthetic organic dyes and pigments—are classified in Industry 32513, Synthetic Dye and Pigment Manufacturing;

- Manufacturing natural glycerin—are classified in Industry 32561, Soap and Cleaning Compound Manufacturing;

- Manufacturing activated charcoal—are classified in Industry 32599, All Other Chemical Product and Preparation Manufacturing;

- Manufacturing organic insecticidal, herbicidal, fungicidal, and pesticidal preparations—are classified in Industry 32532, Pesticide and Other Agriculture Chemical Manufacturing;

- Manufacturing elastomers—are classified in Industry 32521, Resin and Synthetic Rubber Manufacturing;

- Manufacturing urea—are classified in Industry 32531, Fertilizer Manufacturing;

- Manufacturing coal tar crudes in integrated steel mills with coke ovens—are classified in Industry 33111, Iron and Steel Mills and Ferroalloy Manufacturing;

US—United States industry only. CAN—United States and Canadian industries are comparable. MEX—United States and Mexican industries are comparable. Blank—Canadian, Mexican, and United States industries are comparable.

- Manufacturing coal tar crudes in coke ovens not integrated with steel mills and fuel briquettes from refined petroleum—are classified in Industry 32419, Other Petroleum and Coal Products Manufacturing; and

- Manufacturing natural food colorings—are classified in Industry 31194, Seasoning and Dressing Manufacturing.

325191 Gum and Wood Chemical Manufacturing^{US}

This U.S. industry comprises establishments primarily engaged in (1) distilling wood or gum into products, such as tall oil and wood distillates, and (2) manufacturing wood or gum chemicals, such as naval stores, natural tanning materials, charcoal briquettes, and charcoal (except activated).

Cross-References. Establishments primarily engaged in—

- Manufacturing activated charcoal—are classified in U.S. Industry 325998, All Other Miscellaneous Chemical Product and Preparation Manufacturing; and

- Manufacturing fuel briquettes from refined petroleum—are classified in U.S. Industry 324199, All Other Petroleum and Coal Products Manufacturing.

325192 Cyclic Crude and Intermediate Manufacturing^{US}

This U.S. industry comprises establishments primarily engaged in (1) distilling coal tars and/or (2) manufacturing cyclic crudes or, cyclic intermediates (i.e., hydrocarbons, except aromatic petrochemicals) from refined petroleum or natural gas.

Cross-References. Establishments primarily engaged in—

- Manufacturing cyclic chemicals (except aromatic and intermediates)—are classified in U.S. Industry 325199, All Other Basic Organic Chemical Manufacturing;

- Manufacturing aromatic petrochemicals from refined petroleum or natural gas—are classified in Industry 325110, Petrochemical Manufacturing;

- Manufacturing aromatic petrochemicals by refining crude petroleum—are classified in Industry 324110, Petroleum Refineries;

- Distilling wood products—are classified in U.S. Industry 325191, Gum and Wood Chemical Manufacturing;

- Manufacturing coal tar crudes in steel mills with coke ovens—are classified in U.S. Industry 331111, Iron and Steel Mills; and

---

US—United States industry only. CAN—United States and Canadian industries are comparable. MEX—United States and Mexican industries are comparable. Blank—Canadian, Mexican, and United States industries are comparable.

• Manufacturing coal tar crudes in coke oven establishments and fuel briquettes from refined petroleum—are classified in U.S. Industry 324199, All Other Petroleum and Coal Products Manufacturing.

325193 Ethyl Alcohol Manufacturing[US]

This U.S. industry comprises establishments primarily engaged in manufacturing nonpotable ethyl alcohol.

Cross-References. Establishments primarily engaged in—

• Distilling liquors (except brandy)—are classified in Industry 312140, Distilleries; and

• Manufacturing brandies—are classified in Industry 312130, Wineries.

325199 All Other Basic Organic Chemical Manufacturing[US]

This U.S. industry comprises establishments primarily engaged in manufacturing basic organic chemical products (except aromatic petrochemicals, industrial gases, synthetic organic dyes and pigments, gum and wood chemicals, cyclic crudes and intermediates, and ethyl alcohol).

Illustrative Examples:

Calcium organic compounds, not specified elsewhere by process, manufacturing
Carbon organic compounds, not specified elsewhere by process, manufacturing
Enzyme proteins (i.e., basic synthetic chemicals) (except pharmaceutical use) manufacturing
Fatty acids (e.g., margaric, oleic, stearic) manufacturing

Organo-inorganic compound manufacturing
Plasticizers (i.e., basic synthetic chemical) manufacturing
Silicone (except resins) manufacturing
Synthetic sweeteners (i.e., sweetening agents) manufacturing

Cross-References. Establishments primarily engaged in—

• Manufacturing aromatic petrochemicals from refined petroleum or natural gas—are classified in Industry 325110, Petrochemical Manufacturing;

• Manufacturing aromatic petrochemicals by refining crude petroleum—are classified in Industry 324110, Petroleum Refineries;

• Manufacturing organic industrial gases—are classified in Industry 325120, Industrial Gas Manufacturing;

- Manufacturing synthetic organic dyes and pigments—are classified in U.S. Industry 325132, Synthetic Organic Dye and Pigment Manufacturing;

- Manufacturing ethyl alcohol—are classified in U.S. Industry 325193, Ethyl Alcohol Manufacturing;

- Manufacturing organic insecticidal, herbicidal, fungicidal, and pesticidal preparations—are classified in Industry 325320, Pesticide and Other Agriculture Chemical Manufacturing;

- Manufacturing elastomers—are classified in Industry 325210, Resin and Synthetic Rubber Manufacturing;

- Manufacturing urea—are classified in U.S. Industry 325311, Nitrogenous Fertilizer Manufacturing;

- Manufacturing natural glycerin—are classified in U.S. Industry 325611, Soap and Other Detergent Manufacturing; and

- Manufacturing natural food colorings—are classified in U.S. Industry 311942, Spice and Extract Manufacturing.

3252 Resin, Synthetic Rubber, and Artificial Synthetic Fibers and Filaments Manufacturing

32521 Resin and Synthetic Rubber Manufacturing

This industry comprises establishments primarily engaged in one or more of the following: (1) manufacturing synthetic resins, plastics materials, and nonvulcanizable elastomers and mixing and blending resins on a custom basis; (2) manufacturing noncustomized synthetic resins; and (3) manufacturing synthetic rubber.

Cross-References. Establishments primarily engaged in—

- Manufacturing plastics resins and converting resins into plastics products—are classified in Industry Group 3261, Plastics Product Manufacturing;

- Processing natural, synthetic, or reclaimed rubber into intermediate or final products—are classified in Industry Group 3262, Rubber Product Manufacturing;

- Custom compounding resins made elsewhere—are classified in Industry 32599, All Other Chemical Product and Preparation Manufacturing; and

- Manufacturing resin adhesives—are classified in Industry 32552, Adhesive Manufacturing.

325211 Plastics Material and Resin Manufacturing[US]

This U.S. industry comprises establishments primarily engaged in (1) manufacturing resins, plastics materials, and nonvulcanizable thermoplastic elastomers and mixing and blending resins on a custom basis and/or (2) manufacturing noncustomized synthetic resins.

Cross-References. Establishments primarily engaged in—

- Manufacturing plastics resins and converting the resins into plastics products—are classified in 3261, Plastics Product Manufacturing;
- Custom compounding resins made elsewhere—are classified in U.S. Industry 325991, Custom Compounding of Purchased Resins; and
- Manufacturing plastics adhesives—are classified in Industry 325520, Adhesive Manufacturing.

325212 Synthetic Rubber Manufacturing[MEX]

This U.S. industry consists of establishments primarily engaged in manufacturing synthetic rubber.

Cross-References. Establishments primarily engaged in—

- Processing natural, synthetic, or reclaimed rubber into intermediate or final products (except adhesives)—are classified in Industry Group 3262, Rubber Product Manufacturing; and
- Manufacturing rubber adhesives—are classified Industry 325520, Adhesive Manufacturing.

32522 Artificial and Synthetic Fibers and Filaments Manufacturing

This industry comprises establishments primarily engaged in (1) manufacturing cellulosic (i.e., rayon and acetate) and noncellulosic (i.e., nylon, polyolefin, and polyester) fibers and filaments in the form of monofilament, filament yarn, staple, or tow or (2) manufacturing and texturing cellulosic and noncellulosic fibers and filaments.

Cross-References. Establishments primarily engaged in—

- Texturizing cellulosic and noncellulosic fiber and filament made elsewhere—are classified in Industry 31311, Fiber, Yarn, and Thread Mills; and
- Manufacturing textile glass fibers—are classified in Industry 32721, Glass and Glass Product Manufacturing.

US—United States industry only. CAN—United States and Canadian industries are comparable. MEX—United States and Mexican industries are comparable. Blank—Canadian, Mexican, and United States industries are comparable.

325221 Cellulosic Organic Fiber Manufacturing[US]

This U.S. industry comprises establishments primarily engaged in (1) manufacturing cellulosic (i.e., rayon and acetate) fibers and filaments in the form of monofilament, filament yarn, staple, or tow or (2) manufacturing and texturizing cellulosic fibers and filaments.

Cross-References. Establishments primarily engaged in—

- Texturizing cellulosic fibers and filaments made elsewhere—are classified in U.S. Industry 313112, Yarn Texturing, Throwing, and Twisting Mills; and

- Manufacturing noncellulosic fibers and filaments—are classified in U.S. Industry 325222, Noncellulosic Organic Fiber Manufacturing.

325222 Noncellulosic Organic Fiber Manufacturing[US]

This U.S. industry consists of establishments primarily engaged in (1) manufacturing noncellulosic (i.e., nylon, polyolefin, and polyester) fibers and filaments in the form of monofilament, filament yarn, staple, or tow, or (2) manufacturing and texturizing noncellulosic fibers and filaments.

Cross-References. Establishments primarily engaged in—

- Texturizing noncellulosic fibers—are classified in U.S. Industry 313112, Yarn Texturing, Throwing, and Twisting Mills;

- Manufacturing cellulose fibers—are classified in U.S. Industry 325221, Cellulosic Organic Fiber Manufacturing; and

- Manufacturing textile glass fibers—are classified in U.S. Industry 327212, Other Pressed and Blown Glass and Glassware Manufacturing.

3253 Pesticide, Fertilizer, and Other Agricultural Chemical Manufacturing

32531 Fertilizer Manufacturing

This industry comprises establishments primarily engaged in one or more of the following: (1) manufacturing nitrogenous or phosphatic fertilizer materials; (2) manufacturing fertilizers from sewage or animal waste; (3) manufacturing nitrogenous or phosphatic materials and mixing with other ingredients into fertilizers; and (4) mixing ingredients made elsewhere into fertilizers.

US—United States industry only. CAN—United States and Canadian industries are comparable. MEX—United States and Mexican industries are comparable. Blank—Canadian, Mexican, and United States industries are comparable.

325311 Nitrogenous Fertilizer Manufacturing[US]

This U.S. industry comprises establishments primarily engaged in one or more of the following: (1) manufacturing nitrogenous fertilizer materials and mixing ingredients into fertilizers; (2) manufacturing fertilizers from sewage or animal waste; and (3) manufacturing nitrogenous materials and mixing them into fertilizers.

Cross-References.

Establishments primarily engaged in mixing ingredients made elsewhere into nitrogenous fertilizers are classified in U.S. Industry 325314, Fertilizer (Mixing Only) Manufacturing.

325312 Phosphatic Fertilizer Manufacturing[US]

This U.S. industry comprises establishments primarily engaged in (1) manufacturing phosphatic fertilizer materials or (2) manufacturing phosphatic materials and mixing them into fertilizers.

Cross-References.

Establishments primarily engaged in mixing ingredients made elsewhere into phosphatic fertilizers are classified in U.S. Industry 325314, Fertilizer (Mixing Only) Manufacturing.

325314 Fertilizer (Mixing Only) Manufacturing[CAN]

This U.S. industry comprises establishments primarily engaged in mixing ingredients made elsewhere into fertilizers.

Cross-References. Establishments primarily engaged in—

- Manufacturing nitrogenous fertilizer materials or fertilizer materials from sewage or animal waste and mixing these ingredients into nitrogenous fertilizers—are classified in U.S. Industry 325311, Nitrogenous Fertilizer Manufacturing; and

- Manufacturing phosphatic fertilizer materials and mixing ingredients into fertilizers—are classified in U.S. Industry 325312, Phosphatic Fertilizer Manufacturing.

32532 Pesticide and Other Agricultural Chemical Manufacturing
See industry description for 325320 below.

325320 Pesticide and Other Agricultural Chemical Manufacturing

This industry comprises establishments primarily engaged in the formulation and preparation of agricultural and household pest control chemicals (except fertilizers).

Cross-References. Establishments primarily engaged in—

- Manufacturing basic chemicals requiring further processing before use as agriculture chemicals—are classified in Industry Group 3251, Basic Chemical Manufacturing;
- Manufacturing fertilizers—are classified in Industry 325310, Fertilizer Manufacturing; and
- Manufacturing agricultural lime products—are classified in Industry 327410, Lime Manufacturing.

3254 Pharmaceutical and Medicine Manufacturing

32541 Pharmaceutical and Medicine Manufacturing

This industry comprises establishments primarily engaged in one or more of the following: (1) manufacturing biological and medicinal products; (2) processing (i.e., grading, grinding, and milling) botanical drugs and herbs; (3) isolating active medicinal principals from botanical drugs and herbs; and (4) manufacturing pharmaceutical products intended for internal and external consumption in such forms as ampoules, tablets, capsules, vials, ointments, powders, solutions, and suspensions.

325411 Medicinal and Botanical Manufacturing[US]

This U.S. industry comprises establishments primarily engaged in (1) manufacturing uncompounded medicinal chemicals and their derivatives (i.e., generally for use by pharmaceutical preparation manufacturers) and/or (2) grading, grinding, and milling uncompounded botanicals.

Cross-References. Establishments primarily engaged in—

- Manufacturing packaged compounded medicinals and botanicals—are classified in U.S. Industry 325412, Pharmaceutical Preparation Manufacturing; and
- Manufacturing vaccines, toxoids, blood fractions, and culture media of plant or animal origin (except for diagnostic use)—are classified in U.S. Industry 325414, Biological Product (except Diagnostic) Manufacturing.

US—United States industry only. CAN—United States and Canadian industries are comparable. MEX—United States and Mexican industries are comparable. Blank—Canadian, Mexican, and United States industries are comparable.

325412 Pharmaceutical Preparation Manufacturing[US]

This U.S. industry comprises establishments primarily engaged in manufacturing in-vivo diagnostic substances and pharmaceutical preparations (except biological) intended for internal and external consumption in dose forms, such as ampoules, tablets, capsules, vials, ointments, powders, solutions, and suspensions.

Cross-References. Establishments primarily engaged in—

- Manufacturing uncompounded medicinal chemicals and their derivatives— are classified in U.S. Industry 325411, Medicinal and Botanical Manufacturing;

- Manufacturing in-vitro diagnostic substances—are classified in U.S. Industry 325413; In-Vitro Diagnostic Substance Manufacturing; and

- Manufacturing vaccines, toxoids, blood fractions, and culture media of plant or animal origin (except for diagnostic use)—are classified in U.S. Industry 325414, Biological Product (except Diagnostic) Manufacturing.

325413 In-Vitro Diagnostic Substance Manufacturing[US]

This U.S. industry comprises establishments primarily engaged in manufacturing in-vitro (i.e., not taken internally) diagnostic substances, such as chemical, biological, or radioactive substances. The substances are used for diagnostic tests that are performed in test tubes, petri dishes, machines, and other diagnostic test-type devices.

Cross-References.

Establishments primarily engaged in manufacturing in-vivo diagnostic substances are classified in U.S. Industry 325412, Pharmaceutical Preparation Manufacturing.

325414 Biological Product (except Diagnostic) Manufacturing[US]

This U.S. industry comprises establishments primarily engaged in manufacturing vaccines, toxoids, blood fractions, and culture media of plant or animal origin (except diagnostic).

Cross-References. Establishments primarily engaged in—

- Manufacturing in-vitro diagnostic substances—are classified in U.S. Industry 325413, In-Vitro Diagnostic Substance Manufacturing; and

- Manufacturing pharmaceutical preparations, (except biological and in-vivo diagnostic substances)—are classified in U.S. Industry 325412, Pharmaceutical Preparation Manufacturing.

3255 Paint, Coating, and Adhesive Manufacturing

32551 Paint and Coating Manufacturing
See industry description for 325510 below.

325510 Paint and Coating Manufacturing

This industry comprises establishments primarily engaged in (1) mixing pigments, solvents, and binders into paints and other coatings, such as stains, varnishes, lacquers, enamels, shellacs, and water repellant coatings for concrete and masonry, and/or (2) manufacturing allied paint products, such as putties, paint and varnish removers, paint brush cleaners, and frit.

Cross-References. Establishments primarily engaged in—

- Manufacturing creosote—are classified in Industry 32519, Other Basic Organic Chemical Manufacturing;
- Manufacturing caulking compounds and sealants—are classified in Industry 325520, Adhesive Manufacturing;
- Manufacturing artists' paints—are classified in U.S. Industry 339942, Lead Pencil and Art Good Manufacturing; and
- Manufacturing turpentine—are classified in U.S. Industry 325191, Gum and Wood Chemical Manufacturing.

32552 Adhesive Manufacturing
See industry description for 325520 below.

325520 Adhesive Manufacturing

This industry comprises establishments primarily engaged in manufacturing adhesives, glues, and caulking compounds.

Cross-References. Establishments primarily engaged in—

- Manufacturing asphalt and tar roofing cements from purchased asphaltic materials—are classified in Industry 324122, Asphalt Shingle and Coating Materials Manufacturing; and

US—United States industry only. CAN—United States and Canadian industries are comparable. MEX—United States and Mexican industries are comparable. Blank—Canadian, Mexican, and United States industries are comparable.

- Manufacturing gypsum based caulking compounds—are classified in Industry 327420, Gypsum Product Manufacturing.

3256 Soap, Cleaning Compound, and Toilet Preparation Manufacturing

32561 Soap and Cleaning Compound Manufacturing

This industry comprises establishments primarily engaged in manufacturing and packaging soap and other cleaning compounds, surface active agents, and textile and leather finishing agents used to reduce tension or speed the drying process.

Cross-References. Establishments primarily engaged in—

- Manufacturing synthetic glycerin—are classified in Industry 32519, Other Basic Organic Chemical Manufacturing;
- Manufacturing industrial bleaches—are classified in Industry 32518 Other Basic Inorganic Chemical Manufacturing; and
- Manufacturing shampoos and shaving preparations—are classified in Industry 32562, Toilet Preparation Manufacturing.

325611 Soap and Other Detergent Manufacturing[US]

This U.S. industry comprises establishments primarily engaged in manufacturing and packaging soaps and other detergents, such as laundry detergents; dishwashing detergents; toothpaste gels, and tooth powders; and natural glycerin.

Cross-References. Establishments primarily engaged in—

- Manufacturing synthetic glycerin—are classified in U.S. Industry 325199, All Other Basic Organic Chemical Manufacturing; and
- Manufacturing shampoos and shaving preparations—are classified in Industry 325620, Toilet Preparation Manufacturing.

325612 Polish and Other Sanitation Good Manufacturing[US]

This U.S. industry comprises establishments primarily engaged in manufacturing and packaging polishes and specialty cleaning preparations.

Cross-References.

Establishments primarily engaged in manufacturing chlorine dioxide (i.e., industrial bleaching agent) are classified in U.S. Industry 325188, All Other Basic Inorganic Chemical Manufacturing.

325613 Surface Active Agent Manufacturing[US]

This U.S. industry comprises establishments primarily engaged in (1) manufacturing bulk surface active agents for use as wetting agents, emulsifiers, and penetrants, and/or (2) manufacturing textiles and leather finishing agents used to reduce tension or speed the drying process.

32562 Toilet Preparation Manufacturing
See industry description for 325620 below.

325620 Toilet Preparation Manufacturing

This industry comprises establishments primarily engaged in preparing, blending, compounding, and packaging toilet preparations, such as perfumes, shaving preparations, hair preparations, face creams, lotions (including sunscreens), and other cosmetic preparations.

Cross-References.
Establishments primarily engaged in manufacturing toothpaste are classified in U.S. Industry 325611, Soap and Other Detergent Manufacturing.

3259 Other Chemical Product and Preparation Manufacturing

This industry group comprises establishments primarily engaged in manufacturing chemical products (except basic chemicals; resins, synthetic rubber, cellulosic and noncellulosic fibers and filaments; pesticides, fertilizers, and other agricultural chemicals; pharmaceuticals and medicines; paints, coatings, and adhesives; soaps and cleaning compounds; and toilet preparations).

32591 Printing Ink Manufacturing
See industry description for 325910 below.

325910 Printing Ink Manufacturing

This industry comprises establishments primarily engaged in manufacturing printing and inkjet inks and inkjet cartridges.

Cross-References. Establishments primarily engaged in—

- Recycling inkjet cartridges—are classified in U.S. Industry 811212, Computer and Office Machine Repair and Maintenance;

- Manufacturing writing, drawing, and stamping ink—are classified in U.S. Industry 325998, All Other Miscellaneous Chemical Product and Preparation Manufacturing; and

- Manufacturing toners and toner cartridges for photocopiers, fax machines, computer printers and similar office machines—are classified in U.S. Industry 325992, Photographic Film, Paper, Plate, and Chemical Manufacturing.

32592 Explosives Manufacturing

See industry description for 325920 below.

325920 Explosives Manufacturing

This industry comprises establishments primarily engaged in manufacturing explosives.

Cross-References. Establishments primarily engaged in—

- Manufacturing ammunition, ammunition detonators, and percussion caps— are classified in U.S. Industry 332992, Small Arms Ammunition Manufacturing; and

- Manufacturing pyrotechnics—are classified in U.S. Industry 325998, All Other Miscellaneous Chemical Product and Preparation Manufacturing.

32599 All Other Chemical Product and Preparation Manufacturing

This industry comprises establishments primarily engaged in manufacturing chemical products (except basic chemicals, resins, and synthetic rubber; cellulosic and noncellulosic fibers and filaments; pesticides, fertilizers, and other agricultural chemicals; pharmaceuticals and medicines; paints, coatings, and adhesives; and soaps, cleaning compounds, and toilet preparations; printing inks; and explosives).

Illustrative Examples:

Activated carbon and charcoal
 manufacturing
Antifreeze preparations manufacturing
Custom compounding (i.e., blending and
 mixing) of purchased plastics resins
Industrial salt manufacturing

Sugar substitutes (i.e., synthetic
 sweeteners blended with other
 ingredients) made from purchased
 synthetic sweeteners
Swimming pool chemical preparations
 manufacturing

US—United States industry only. CAN—United States and Canadian industries are comparable. MEX—United States and Mexican industries are comparable. Blank—Canadian, Mexican, and United States industries are comparable.

Matches and matchbook manufacturing
Photographic chemicals manufacturing
Pyrotechnics (e.g., flares, flashlight
bombs, signals) manufacturing

Writing inks and fluids manufacturing

Cross-References. Establishments primarily engaged in—

- Manufacturing basic chemicals—are classified in Industry Group 3251, Basic Chemical Manufacturing;

- Manufacturing resins, synthetic rubber, and artificial synthetic fibers and filaments—are classified in Industry Group 3252, Resin, Synthetic Rubber, and Artificial Synthetic Fibers and Filaments Manufacturing;

- Manufacturing pesticides, fertilizers, and other agricultural chemicals—are classified in Industry Group 3253, Pesticide, Fertilizer, and Other Agriculture Chemical Manufacturing;

- Manufacturing pharmaceuticals and medicine including medicinal vegetable gelatin (i.e., agar-agar)—are classified in Industry Group 3254, Pharmaceutical and Medicine Manufacturing;

- Manufacturing paints, coatings, and adhesives—are classified in Industry Group 3255, Paint, Coating, and Adhesive Manufacturing;

- Manufacturing soaps and cleaning compounds—are classified in Industry Group 3256, Soap, Cleaning Compound, and Toilet Preparation Manufacturing;

- Manufacturing printing and inkjet inks—are classified in Industry 32591, Printing Ink Manufacturing;

- Manufacturing explosives—are classified in Industry 32592, Explosives Manufacturing;

- Manufacturing photographic paper stock (i.e., unsensitized) and paper mats, mounts, easels, and folders for photographic use—are classified in Subsector 322, Paper Manufacturing;

- Manufacturing dessert gelatins—are classified in Industry 31199, All Other Miscellaneous Food Manufacturing; and

- Manufacturing medicinal gelatins—are classified in Industry 32541, Pharmaceutical and Medicine Manufacturing.

325991 Custom Compounding of Purchased Resins[CAN]

This industry comprises establishments primarily engaged in (1) custom mixing and blending plastics resins made elsewhere or (2) reformulating plastics resins from recycled plastics products.

Cross-References.

Establishments primarily engaged in manufacturing synthetic resins and custom mixing and blending resins are classified in U.S. Industry 325211, Plastics Material and Resin Manufacturing.

325992 Photographic Film, Paper, Plate, and Chemical Manufacturing[MEX]

This U.S. industry comprises establishments primarily engaged in manufacturing sensitized film, sensitized paper, sensitized cloth, sensitized plates, toners (i.e., for photocopiers, laser printers, and similar electrostatic printing devices), toner cartridges, and photographic chemicals.

Cross-References.

Establishments primarily engaged in manufacturing photographic paper stock (i.e., unsensitized) and paper mats, mounts, easels, and folders for photographic use—are classified in Subsector 322, Paper Manufacturing.

325998 All Other Miscellaneous Chemical Product and Preparation Manufacturing[US]

This U.S. industry comprises establishments primarily engaged in manufacturing chemical products (except basic chemicals, resins, synthetic rubber; cellulosic and noncellulosic fiber and filaments; pesticides, fertilizers, and other agricultural chemicals; pharmaceuticals and medicines; paints, coatings and adhesives; soap, cleaning compounds, and toilet preparations; printing inks; explosives; custom compounding of purchased resins; and photographic films, papers, plates, and chemicals).

Illustrative Examples:

Activated carbon and charcoal manufacturing
Antifreeze preparations manufacturing
Industrial salt manufacturing
Lighter fluids (e.g., charcoal, cigarette) manufacturing
Matches and matchbook manufacturing
Pyrotechnics (e.g., flares, flashlight bombs, signals) manufacturing

Sugar substitutes (i.e., synthetic sweeteners blended with other ingredients) made from purchased synthetic sweeteners manufacturing
Swimming pool chemical preparations manufacturing
Writing inks manufacturing

US—United States industry only. CAN—United States and Canadian industries are comparable. MEX—United States and Mexican industries are comparable. Blank—Canadian, Mexican, and United States industries are comparable.

Cross-References. Establishments primarily engaged in—

- Manufacturing basic chemicals—are classified in Industry Group 3251, Basic Chemical Manufacturing;

- Manufacturing resins, synthetic rubber, and artificial synthetic fibers and filaments—are classified in Industry Group 3252, Resin, Synthetic Rubber, and Artificial Synthetic Fibers and Filaments Manufacturing;

- Manufacturing pesticides, fertilizers, and other agricultural chemicals—are classified in Industry Group 3253, Pesticide, Fertilizer, and Other Agriculture Chemical Manufacturing;

- Manufacturing pharmaceuticals and medicines including medicinal vegetable gelatin (i.e., agar-agar)—are classified in Industry Group 3254, Pharmaceutical and Medicine Manufacturing;

- Manufacturing paints, coatings, and adhesives—are classified in Industry Group 3255, Paint, Coating, and Adhesive Manufacturing;

- Manufacturing soaps and cleaning compounds—are classified in Industry Group 3256, Soap, Cleaning Compound, and Toilet Preparation Manufacturing;

- Manufacturing printing and inkjet inks—are classified in Industry 325910, Printing Ink Manufacturing;

- Manufacturing explosives—are classified in Industry 325920, Explosives Manufacturing;

- Custom compounding purchased plastics resins—are classified in U.S. Industry 325991, Custom Compounding of Purchased Resins;

- Manufacturing photographic films, papers, plates, and chemicals—are classified in U.S. Industry 325992, Photographic Film, Paper, Plate, and Chemical Manufacturing; and

- Manufacturing dessert gelatin—are classified in U.S. Industry 311999, All Other Miscellaneous Food Manufacturing.

326 Plastics and Rubber Products Manufacturing

Industries in the Plastics and Rubber Products Manufacturing subsector make goods by processing plastics materials and raw rubber. The core technology employed by establishments in this subsector is that of plastics or rubber product production. Plastics and rubber are combined in the same subsector because plastics are increasingly being used as a substitute for rubber; however the subsector is generally restricted to the production of products made of just one material, either solely plastics or rubber.

US—United States industry only. CAN—United States and Canadian industries are comparable. MEX—United States and Mexican industries are comparable. Blank—Canadian, Mexican, and United States industries are comparable.

Many manufacturing activities use plastics or rubber, for example the manufacture of footwear, or furniture. Typically, the production process of these products involves more than one material. In these cases, technologies that allow disparate materials to be formed and combined are of central importance in describing the manufacturing activity. In NAICS, such activities (the footwear and furniture manufacturing) are not classified in the Plastics and Rubber Products Manufacturing subsector because the core technologies for these activities are diverse and involve multiple materials.

Within the Plastics and Rubber Products Manufacturing subsector, a distinction is made between plastics and rubber products at the industry group level, although it is not a rigid distinction, as can be seen from the definition of Industry 32622, Rubber and Plastics Hoses and Belting Manufacturing. As materials technology progresses, plastics are increasingly being used as a substitute for rubber; and eventually, the distinction may disappear as a basis for establishment classification.

In keeping with the core technology focus of plastics, lamination of plastics film to plastics film as well as the production of bags from plastics only is classified in this subsector. Lamination and bag production involving plastics and materials other than plastics are classified in the NAICS Subsector 322, Paper Manufacturing.

3261 Plastics Product Manufacturing

This industry group comprises establishments primarily engaged in processing new or spent (i.e., recycled) plastics resins into intermediate or final products, using such processes as compression molding; extrusion molding; injection molding; blow molding; and casting. Within most of these industries, the production process is such that a wide variety of products can be made.

32611 Plastics Packaging Materials and Unlaminated Film and Sheet Manufacturing

This industry comprises establishments primarily engaged in (1) converting plastics resins into unsupported plastics film and sheet and/or (2) forming, coating or laminating plastics film and sheet into plastics bags.

Cross-References. Establishments primarily engaged in—

- Laminating plastics sheet (except for packaging)—are classified in Industry 32613, Laminated Plastics Plate, Sheet (except Packaging), and Shape Manufacturing;

- Manufacturing plastics blister and bubble packaging—are classified in Industry 32619, Other Plastics Product Manufacturing; and

- Coating or laminating combinations of plastics, foils and paper (except plastics film to plastics film) into film, sheet or bags—are classified in Industry 32222, Paper Bag and Coated and Treated Paper Manufacturing.

326111 Plastics Bag Manufacturing[CAN]

This U.S. industry comprises establishments primarily engaged in (1) converting plastics resins into plastics bags or (2) forming, coating or laminating plastics film and sheet into single wall or multiwall plastics bags. Establishments in this industry may print on the bags they manufacture.

Cross-References. Establishments primarily engaged in—

- Manufacturing laminated or coated combinations of plastics, foils and paper (except plastics film to plastics film) materials into single wall bags—are classified in U.S. Industry 322223, Plastics, Foil, and Coated Paper Bag Manufacturing; and

- Manufacturing laminated or coated combinations of plastics, foils and paper (except plastics film to plastics film) into multiwalled bags—are classified in U.S. Industry 322224, Uncoated Paper and Multiwall Bag Manufacturing.

326112 Plastics Packaging Film and Sheet (including Laminated) Manufacturing[US]

This U.S. industry comprises establishments primarily engaged in converting plastics resins into plastics packaging (flexible) film and packaging sheet.

Cross-References. Establishments primarily engaged in—

- Converting plastics resins into plastics film and unlaminated sheet (except packaging)—are classified in U.S. Industry 326113, Unlaminated Plastics Film and Sheet (except Packaging) Manufacturing;

- Laminating or coating packaging combinations of plastics, foils and paper (except plastics film to plastics film) film and sheet—are classified in U.S. Industry 322221, Coated and Laminated Packaging Paper and Plastics Film Manufacturing;

- Laminating or coating combinations of plastics, foils, and paper (except plastics film to plastics film) nonpackaging film and sheet—are classified in U.S. Industry 322222, Coated and Laminated Paper Manufacturing;

- Laminating plastics sheet (except for packaging)—are classified in Industry 326130, Laminated Plastics Plate, Sheet (except Packaging), and Shape Manufacturing; and

- Manufacturing plastics bags—are classified in U.S. Industry 326111, Plastics Bag Manufacturing.

326113 Unlaminated Plastics Film and Sheet (except Packaging) Manufacturing[US]

This U.S. industry comprises establishments primarily engaged in converting plastics resins into plastics film and unlaminated sheet (except packaging).

Cross-References. Establishments primarily engaged in—

- Converting plastics resins into plastics packaging film and unlaminated packaging sheet—are classified in U.S. Industry 326112, Plastics Packaging Film and Sheet (including Laminated) Manufacturing;

- Laminating plastics sheet (except for packaging)—are classified in Industry 326130, Laminated Plastics Plate, Sheet (except Packaging), and Shape Manufacturing;

- Laminating or coating a combination of plastics, foils, and paper (except plastics film to plastics film) nonpackaging film and sheet—are classified in U.S. Industry 322222, Coated and Laminated Paper Manufacturing; and

- Manufacturing plastics bags—are classified in U.S. Industry 326111, Plastics Bag Manufacturing.

32612 Plastics Pipe, Pipe Fitting, and Unlaminated Profile Shape Manufacturing

This industry comprises establishments primarily engaged in manufacturing plastics pipes and pipe fittings, and plastics profile shapes such as rod, tube, and sausage casings.

Cross-References. Establishments primarily engaged in—

- Manufacturing plastics hose—are classified in Industry 32622, Rubber and Plastics Hoses and Belting Manufacturing;

- Manufacturing noncurrent carrying plastics conduit—are classified in Industry 33593, Wiring Device Manufacturing;

- Manufacturing plastics plumbing fixtures—are classified in Industry 32619, Other Plastics Product Manufacturing; and

- Manufacturing plastics film, plastics unlaminated sheet, and plastics bags—are classified in Industry 32611, Plastics Packaging Materials and Unlaminated Film and Sheet Manufacturing.

326121 Unlaminated Plastics Profile Shape Manufacturing^{CAN}

This U.S. industry comprises establishments primarily engaged in converting plastics resins into nonrigid plastics profile shapes (except film, sheet and bags), such as rod, tube, and sausage casings.

Cross-References. Establishments primarily engaged in—

- Manufacturing plastics film, plastics unlaminated sheet, and plastics bags—are classified in Industry 32611, Plastics Packaging Materials and Unlaminated Film and Sheet Manufacturing; and

- Manufacturing plastics hoses—are classified in Industry 326220, Rubber and Plastics Hoses and Belting Manufacturing.

326122 Plastics Pipe and Pipe Fitting Manufacturing^{CAN}

This U.S. industry comprises establishments primarily engaged in converting plastics resins into rigid plastics pipes and pipe fittings.

Cross-References. Establishments primarily engaged in—

- Manufacturing plastics hose—are classified in Industry 326220, Rubber and Plastics Hoses and Belting Manufacturing;

- Manufacturing noncurrent-carrying plastics conduit—are classified in U.S. Industry 335932, Noncurrent-Carrying Wiring Device Manufacturing; and

- Manufacturing plastics plumbing fixtures—are classified in U.S. Industry 326191, Plastics Plumbing Fixture Manufacturing.

32613 Laminated Plastics Plate, Sheet (except Packaging), and Shape Manufacturing
See industry description for 326130 below.

326130 Laminated Plastics Plate, Sheet (except Packaging), and Shape Manufacturing

This industry comprises establishments primarily engaged in laminating plastics profile shapes such as plate, sheet (except packaging), and rod. The lamination process generally involves bonding or impregnating profiles with plastics resins and compressing them under heat.

Cross-References. Establishments primarily engaged in—

- Manufacturing plastics film, plastics unlaminated sheet, and plastics bags—are classified in Industry 32611, Plastics Packaging Materials and Unlaminated Film and Sheet Manufacturing;
- Coating or laminating nonplastics film, sheet, or bags with plastics—are classified in Industry 32222, Paper Bag and Coated and Treated Paper Manufacturing; and
- Manufacturing plastics bags—are classified in U.S. Industry 326111, Plastics Bag Manufacturing.

32614 Polystyrene Foam Product Manufacturing
See industry description for 326140 below.

326140 Polystyrene Foam Product Manufacturing

This industry comprises establishments primarily engaged in manufacturing polystyrene foam products.

Cross-References.

Establishments primarily engaged in manufacturing plastics foam products (except polystyrene) are classified in Industry 326150, Urethane and Other Foam Product (except Polystyrene) Manufacturing.

32615 Urethane and Other Foam Product (except Polystyrene) Manufacturing
See industry description for 326150 below.

326150 Urethane and Other Foam Product (except Polystyrene) Manufacturing

This industry comprises establishments primarily engaged in manufacturing plastics foam products (except polystyrene).

Cross-References.

Establishments primarily engaged in manufacturing polystyrene foam products are classified in Industry 326140, Polystyrene Foam Product Manufacturing.

32616 Plastics Bottle Manufacturing

See industry description for 32616 below.

326160 Plastics Bottle Manufacturing

This industry comprises establishments primarily engaged in manufacturing plastics bottles.

Cross-References.

Establishments primarily engaged in manufacturing plastics containers (except bottles) are classified in U.S. Industry 326199, All Other Plastics Product Manufacturing.

32619 Other Plastics Product Manufacturing

This industry comprises establishments primarily engaged in manufacturing resilient floor covering and other plastics products (except film, sheet, bags, profile shapes, pipes, pipe fittings, laminates, foam products, and bottles).

Illustrative Examples:

Inflatable plastics boats manufacturing	Plastics hardware manufacturing
Plastics bowls and bowl covers manufacturing	Plastics or fiberglass plumbing fixtures (e.g., toilets, shower stalls, urinals) manufacturing
Plastics cups (except foam) manufacturing	Plastics siding manufacturing
Plastics dinnerware (except foam) manufacturing	Plastics trash containers manufacturing
Plastics gloves manufacturing	Resilient floor coverings (e.g., sheet, tiles) manufacturing

Cross-References. Establishments primarily engaged in—

- Manufacturing plastics film, plastics unlaminated sheet, and plastics bags—are classified in Industry 32611, Plastics Packaging Materials and Unlaminated Film and Sheet Manufacturing;

- Manufacturing plastics pipes, pipe fittings and plastics profile shapes (except films, sheet, bags)—are classified in Industry 32612, Plastics Pipe, Pipe Fitting, and Unlaminated Profile Shape Manufacturing;

- Laminating plastics profile shapes, such as plate, sheet and rod,—are classified in Industry 32613, Laminated Plastics Plate, Sheet (except packaging) and Shape Manufacturing;

- Manufacturing polystyrene foam products—are classified in Industry 32614, Polystyrene Foam Product Manufacturing;

- Manufacturing foam products (except polystyrene)—are classified in Industry 32615 Urethane and Other Foam Product (except Polystyrene) Manufacturing;

- Manufacturing plastics bottles—are classified in Industry 32616, Plastics Bottle Manufacturing;

- Manufacturing plastics furniture parts—are classified in Industry 33721, Office Furniture (including Fixtures) Manufacturing;

- Assembling plastics components into plumbing fixture fittings, such as faucets,—are classified in Industry 33291, Metal Valve Manufacturing; and

- Manufacturing rubber floor mats and rubber treads—are classified in Industry 32629, Other Rubber Product Manufacturing.

326191 Plastics Plumbing Fixture Manufacturing[CAN]

This U.S. industry comprises establishments primarily engaged in manufacturing plastics or fiberglass plumbing fixtures. Examples of products made by these establishments are plastics or fiberglass bathtubs, hot tubs, portable toilets, and shower stalls.

Cross-References. Establishments primarily engaged in—

- Assembling plastics components into plumbing fixture fittings, such as faucets,—are classified in U.S. Industry 332913, Plumbing Fixture Fitting and Trim Manufacturing; and

- Manufacturing plastics pipe and pipe fittings—are classified in U.S. Industry 326122, Plastics Pipe and Pipe Fitting Manufacturing.

326192 Resilient Floor Covering Manufacturing[US]

This U.S. industry comprises establishments primarily engaged in manufacturing resilient floor coverings for permanent installation.

Cross-References.

Establishments primarily engaged in manufacturing rubber floor mats and rubber treads are classified in U.S. Industry 326299, All Other Rubber Product Manufacturing.

326199 All Other Plastics Product Manufacturing[US]

This U.S. industry comprises establishments primarily engaged in manufacturing plastics products (except film, sheet, bags, profile shapes, pipes, pipe fittings, laminates, foam products, bottles, plumbing fixtures, and resilient floor coverings).

US—United States industry only. CAN—United States and Canadian industries are comparable. MEX—United States and Mexican industries are comparable. Blank—Canadian, Mexican, and United States industries are comparable.

Illustrative Examples:

Inflatable plastics boats manufacturing
Plastics air mattresses manufacturing
Plastics bowls and bowl covers
  manufacturing
Plastics clothes hangers manufacturing
Plastics cups (except foam)
  manufacturing

Plastics dinnerware (except foam)
  manufacturing
Plastics gloves manufacturing
Plastics hardware manufacturing
Plastics siding manufacturing
Plastics trash containers manufacturing

Cross-References. Establishments primarily engaged in—

- Manufacturing plastics film, plastics unlaminated sheet, and plastics bags—are classified in Industry 32611, Plastics Packaging Materials and Unlaminated Film and Sheet Manufacturing;

- Manufacturing plastics pipes, pipe fittings, and plastics profile shapes (except film, sheet, bags)—are classified in Industry 32612, Plastics Pipe, Pipe Fitting, and Unlaminated Profile Shape Manufacturing;

- Manufacturing plastic pipes and pipe fittings—are classified in U.S. Industry 326122, Plastics Pipe and Pipe Fitting Manufacturing;

- Laminating plastics profile shapes, such as plate, sheet, and rod,—are classified in Industry 326130, Laminated Plastics Plate, Sheet (except Packaging), and Shapes Manufacturing;

- Manufacturing polystyrene foam products—are classified in Industry 326140, Polystyrene Foam Product Manufacturing;

- Manufacturing foam (except polystyrene) products—are classified in Industry 326150, Urethane and Other Foam Product (except Polystyrene) Manufacturing;

- Manufacturing plastics bottles—are classified in Industry 326160, Plastics Bottle Manufacturing;

- Manufacturing plastics furniture parts and components—are classified in U.S. Industry 337215, Showcase, Partition, Shelving, and Locker Manufacturing;

- Manufacturing plastics plumbing fixtures—are classified in U.S. Industry 326191, Plastics Plumbing Fixture Manufacturing;

- Manufacturing resilient floor coverings—are classified in U.S. Industry 326192, Resilient Floor Covering Manufacturing; and

- Assembling plastics components into plumbing fixtures fittings such as faucets—are classified in U.S. Industry 332913, Plumbing Fixture Fitting and Trim Manufacturing.

US—United States industry only. CAN—United States and Canadian industries are comparable. MEX—United States and Mexican industries are comparable. Blank—Canadian, Mexican, and United States industries are comparable.

3262 Rubber Product Manufacturing

This industry group comprises establishments primarily engaged in processing natural, and synthetic or reclaimed rubber materials into intermediate or final products using processes such as vulcanizing, cementing, molding, extruding, and lathe-cutting.

32621 Tire Manufacturing

This industry comprises establishments primarily engaged in manufacturing tires and inner tubes from natural and synthetic rubber and retreading or rebuilding tires.

Cross-References. Establishments primarily engaged in—

- Repairing tires, such as plugging,—are classified in Industry 81119, Other Automotive Repair and Maintenance; and

- Retailing tires—are classified in the Industry 44132, Tire Dealers.

326211 Tire Manufacturing (except Retreading)[MEX]

This U.S. industry comprises establishments primarily engaged in manufacturing tires and inner tubes from natural and synthetic rubber.

Cross-References.

Establishments primarily engaged in retreading or rebuilding tires are classified in U.S. Industry 326212, Tire Retreading.

326212 Tire Retreading[MEX]

This U.S. industry comprises establishments primarily engaged in retreading, or rebuilding tires.

Cross-References. Establishments primarily engaged in—

- Repairing tires, such as pluggings—are classified in U.S. Industry 811198, All Other Automotive Repair and Maintenance;

- Retailing tires—are classified in Industry 441320, Tire Dealers; and

- Manufacturing tires and inner tubes from natural and synthetic rubber—are classified in U.S. Industry 326211, Tire Manufacturing (except Retreading).

US—United States industry only. CAN—United States and Canadian industries are comparable. MEX—United States and Mexican industries are comparable. Blank—Canadian, Mexican, and United States industries are comparable.

32622 Rubber and Plastics Hoses and Belting Manufacturing

See industry description for 326220 below.

326220 Rubber and Plastics Hoses and Belting Manufacturing

This industry comprises establishments primarily engaged in manufacturing rubber hose and/or plastics (reinforced) hose and belting from natural and synthetic rubber and/or plastics resins. Establishments manufacturing garden hoses from purchased hose are included in this industry.

Cross-References. Establishments primarily engaged in—

- Manufacturing rubber tubing—are classified in U.S. Industry 326299, All Other Rubber Product Manufacturing;

- Manufacturing plastics tubing—are classified in U.S. Industry 326121, Unlaminated Plastics Profile Shape Manufacturing; and

- Manufacturing fluid power hose assemblies—are classified in U.S. Industry 332912, Fluid Power Valve and Hose Fitting Manufacturing.

32629 Other Rubber Product Manufacturing

This industry comprises establishments primarily engaged in manufacturing rubber products (except tires, hoses, and belting) from natural and synthetic rubber.

Illustrative Examples:

Birth control devices (e.g., diaphragms, prophylactics) manufacturing	Rubberbands manufacturing
Latex foam rubber manufacturing	Rubber floor mats (e.g., door, bath) manufacturing
Mechanical rubber goods (i.e., molded, extruded, lathe-cut) manufacturing	Rubber hair care products (e.g., combs, curlers) manufacturing
Reclaiming rubber from waste and scrap	Rubber tubing (except extruded, lathe-cut, molded) manufacturing
Rubber balloons manufacturing	

Cross-References. Establishments primarily engaged in—

- Manufacturing tires and inner tubes—are classified in Industry 32621, Tire Manufacturing;

- Manufacturing rubber hoses and belting—are classified in Industry 32622, Rubber and Plastics Hoses and Belting Manufacturing;

- Rubberizing fabric—are classified in Industry 31332, Fabric Coating Mills;

- Manufacturing rubber gaskets, packing and sealing devices—are classified in Industry 33999, All Other Miscellaneous Manufacturing;

- Manufacturing rubber gloves—are classified in Industry 33911, Medical Equipment and Supplies Manufacturing;
- Manufacturing rubber clothing accessories (e.g., bathing caps)—are classified in Industry 31599, Apparel Accessories and Other Apparel Manufacturing; and
- Manufacturing rubber toys—are classified in Industry 33993, Doll, Toy, and Game Manufacturing.

326291 Rubber Product Manufacturing for Mechanical Use[US]

This U.S. industry comprises establishments primarily engaged in molding, extruding or lathe- cutting rubber to manufacture rubber goods (except tubing) for mechanical applications. Products of this industry are generally parts for motor vehicles, machinery, and equipment.

Cross-References.

Establishments primarily engaged in manufacturing rubber tubing from natural and synthetic rubber and manufacturing rubber products for mechanical applications using a process other than molding, extruding or lathe-cutting are classified in U.S. Industry 326299, All Other Rubber Product Manufacturing.

326299 All Other Rubber Product Manufacturing[US]

This U.S. industry comprises establishments primarily engaged in manufacturing rubber products (except tires; hoses and belting; and molded, extruded, and lathe-cut rubber goods for mechanical applications) from natural and synthetic rubber.

Illustrative Examples:

Birth control devices (i.e., diaphragms, prophylactics) manufacturing
Inflatable rubber life rafts manufacturing
Latex foam rubber manufacturing
Reclaiming rubber from waste and scrap
Rubber balloons manufacturing
Rubberbands manufacturing

Rubber floor mats (e.g., door, bath) manufacturing
Rubber hair care products (e.g., combs, curlers) manufacturing
Rubber tubing (except extruded, lathe-cut, molded) manufacturing

Cross-References. Establishments primarily engaged in—

- Manufacturing tires and inner tubes and tire rebuilding—are classified in Industry 32621, Tire Manufacturing;
- Manufacturing rubber hoses and belting—are classified in Industry 326220, Rubber and Plastics Hoses and Belting Manufacturing;

- Molding, extruding, and lathe-cutting rubber to manufacture rubber goods (except tubing) for mechanical applications—are classified in Industry 326291, Rubber Product Manufacturing for Mechanical Use;

- Rubberizing fabrics—are classified in Industry 313320, Fabric Coating Mills;

- Manufacturing rubber gaskets, packing and sealing devices—are classified in U.S. Industry 339991, Gasket, Packing, and Sealing Device Manufacturing;

- Manufacturing rubber toys—are classified in Industry 33993, Doll, Toy, and Game Manufacturing;

- Manufacturing rubber gloves—are classified in U.S. Industry 339113, Surgical Appliance and Supplies Manufacturing; and

- Manufacturing rubber clothing accessories (e.g., bathing caps)—are classified in U.S. Industry 315999, Other Apparel Accessories and Other Apparel Manufacturing.

327 Nonmetallic Mineral Product Manufacturing

The Nonmetallic Mineral Product Manufacturing subsector transforms mined or quarried nonmetallic minerals, such as sand, gravel, stone, clay, and refractory materials, into products for intermediate or final consumption. Processes used include grinding, mixing, cutting, shaping, and honing. Heat often is used in the process and chemicals are frequently mixed to change the composition, purity, and chemical properties for the intended product. For example, glass is produced by heating silica sand to the melting point (sometimes combined with cullet or recycled glass) and then drawn, floated, or blow molded to the desired shape or thickness. Refractory materials are heated and then formed into bricks or other shapes for use in industrial applications.

The Nonmetallic Mineral Product Manufacturing subsector includes establishments that manufacture products, such as bricks, refractories, ceramic products, and glass and glass products, such as plate glass and containers. Also included are cement and concrete products, lime, gypsum and other nonmetallic mineral products including abrasive products, ceramic plumbing fixtures, statuary, cut stone products, and mineral wool. The products are used in a wide range of activities from construction and heavy and light manufacturing to articles for personal use.

Mining, beneficiating, and manufacturing activities often occur in a single location. Separate receipts will be collected for these activities whenever possible. When receipts cannot be broken out between mining and manufacturing, establishments that mine or quarry nonmetallic minerals, beneficiate the nonmetallic minerals and further process the nonmetallic minerals into a more finished manufactured product are classified based on the primary activity of the establishment. A mine that manufactures a small amount of finished products will be classified in Sector

21, Mining. An establishment that mines whose primary output is a more-finished manufactured product will be classified in the Manufacturing Sector.

Excluded from the Nonmetallic Mineral Product Manufacturing subsector are establishments that primarily beneficiate mined nonmetallic minerals. Beneficiation is the process whereby the extracted material is reduced to particles that can be separated into mineral and waste, the former suitable for further processing or direct use. Beneficiation establishments are included in Sector 21, Mining.

3271 Clay Product and Refractory Manufacturing

32711 Pottery, Ceramics, and Plumbing Fixture Manufacturing

This industry comprises establishments primarily engaged in shaping, molding, glazing, and firing pottery, ceramics, and plumbing fixtures made entirely or partly of clay or other ceramic materials.

Cross-References. Establishments primarily engaged in—

- Manufacturing ferrite microwave devices and electronic components—are classified in Subsector 334, Computer and Electronic Product Manufacturing;

- Manufacturing enameled iron and steel plumbing fixtures—are classified in Industry 33299, All Other Fabricated Metal Product Manufacturing;

- Manufacturing metal bathroom accessories—are classified in Subsector 332, Fabricated Metal Product Manufacturing;

- Manufacturing plastic bathroom accessories, cultured marble, and other plastic plumbing fixtures—are classified in Industry 32619, Other Plastics Product Manufacturing; and

- Manufacturing clay building materials, such as ceramic tile, bricks, and clay roofing tiles, and refractories—are classified in Industry 32712, Clay Building Material and Refractories Manufacturing.

327111 Vitreous China Plumbing Fixture and China and Earthenware Bathroom Accessories Manufacturing[US]

This U.S. industry comprises establishments primarily engaged in manufacturing vitreous china plumbing fixtures and china and earthenware bathroom accessories, such as faucet handles, towel bars, and soap dishes.

Cross-References. Establishments primarily engaged in—

- Manufacturing enameled iron and steel plumbing fixtures—are classified in U.S. Industry 332998, Enameled Iron and Metal Sanitary Ware Manufacturing;

- Manufacturing metal bathroom accessories—are classified in Subsector 332, Fabricated Metal Product Manufacturing;

- Manufacturing plastic bathroom accessories—are classified in U.S. Industry 326199, All Other Plastics Product Manufacturing;

- Manufacturing cultured marble and other plastic plumbing fixtures—are classified in U.S. Industry 326191, Plastics Plumbing Fixture Manufacturing; and

- Manufacturing china and earthenware products (except bathroom fixtures and accessories)— are classified in U.S. Industry 327112, Vitreous China, Fine Earthenware, and Other Pottery Product Manufacturing.

327112 Vitreous China, Fine Earthenware, and Other Pottery Product Manufacturing[US]

This U.S. industry comprises establishments primarily engaged in manufacturing table and kitchen articles, art and ornamental items, and similar vitreous china, fine earthenware, stoneware, coarse earthenware, and pottery products.

Illustrative Examples:

Chemical stoneware (i.e., pottery products) manufacturing
Clay and ceramic statuary manufacturing
Cooking ware (e.g., stoneware, coarse earthenware, pottery) manufacturing
Earthenware table and kitchen articles, coarse, manufacturing

Florists' articles, red earthenware, manufacturing
Vases, pottery (e.g., china, earthenware, stoneware), manufacturing

Cross-References. Establishments primarily engaged in—

- Manufacturing vitreous china plumbing fixtures—are classified in U.S. Industry 327111, Vitreous China Plumbing Fixture and China and Earthenware Bathroom Accessories Manufacturing;

- Manufacturing porcelain and ceramic electrical products, such as insulators,—are classified in U.S. Industry 327113, Porcelain Electrical Supply Manufacturing; and

- Manufacturing clay building materials, such as ceramic tile, bricks, and clay roofing tiles, and refractories,—are classified in Industry 32712, Clay Building Material and Refractories Manufacturing.

327113 Porcelain Electrical Supply Manufacturing[US]

This U.S. industry comprises establishments primarily engaged in manufacturing porcelain electrical insulators, molded porcelain parts for electrical devices, ferrite

---

or ceramic magnets, and electronic and electrical supplies from nonmetallic minerals, such as clay and ceramic materials.

Cross-References.

Establishments primarily engaged in manufacturing ferrite microwave devices and electronic components are classified in Subsector 334, Computer and Electronic Product Manufacturing.

32712 Clay Building Material and Refractories Manufacturing

This industry comprises establishments primarily engaged in shaping, molding, baking, burning, or hardening clay refractories, nonclay refractories, ceramic tile, structural clay tile, brick, and other structural clay building materials.

Cross-References. Establishments primarily engaged in—

- Manufacturing glass blocks—are classified in Industry 32721, Glass and Glass Product Manufacturing;
- Manufacturing concrete brick and block—are classified in Industry 32733, Concrete Pipe, Brick, and Block Manufacturing; and
- Manufacturing resilient flooring—are classified in Industry 32619, Other Plastics Product Manufacturing.

327121 Brick and Structural Clay Tile Manufacturing[US]

This U.S. industry comprises establishments primarily engaged in manufacturing brick and structural clay tiles.

Cross-References. Establishments primarily engaged in—

- Manufacturing clay fire brick (i.e., refractories)—are classified in U.S. Industry 327124, Clay Refractory Manufacturing;
- Manufacturing nonclay fire brick (i.e., refractories)—are classified in U.S. Industry 327125, Nonclay Refractory Manufacturing;
- Manufacturing glass brick—are classified in Industry 32721, Glass and Glass Product Manufacturing;
- Manufacturing concrete bricks—are classified in U.S. Industry 327331, Concrete Block and Brick Manufacturing; and
- Manufacturing adobe bricks or clay roofing tiles—are classified in U.S. Industry 327123, Other Structural Clay Product Manufacturing.

327122 Ceramic Wall and Floor Tile Manufacturing[US]

This U.S. industry comprises establishments primarily engaged in manufacturing ceramic wall and floor tiles.

Cross-References. Establishments primarily engaged in—

- Manufacturing structural clay tiles—are classified in U.S. Industry 327121, Brick and Structural Clay Tile Manufacturing;
- Manufacturing clay drain tiles—are classified in U.S. Industry 327123, Other Structural Clay Product Manufacturing; and
- Manufacturing resilient flooring and asphalt floor tiles—are classified in U.S. Industry 326192, Resilient Floor Covering Manufacturing.

327123 Other Structural Clay Product Manufacturing[US]

This U.S. industry comprises establishments primarily engaged in manufacturing clay sewer pipe, drain tile, flue lining tile, architectural terra-cotta, and other structural clay products.

Cross-References. Establishments primarily engaged in—

- Manufacturing bricks and structural clay tiles—are classified in U.S. Industry 327121, Brick and Structural Clay Tile Manufacturing;
- Manufacturing ceramic floor and wall tiles—are classified in U.S. Industry 327122, Ceramic Wall and Floor Tile Manufacturing;
- Manufacturing clay refractories—are classified in U.S. Industry 327124, Clay Refractory Manufacturing; and
- Manufacturing nonclay refractories—are classified in U.S. Industry 327125, Nonclay Refractory Manufacturing.

327124 Clay Refractory Manufacturing[US]

This U.S. industry comprises establishments primarily engaged in manufacturing clay refractory, mortar, brick, block, tile, and fabricated clay refractories, such as melting pots. A refractory is a material that will retain its shape and chemical identity when subjected to high temperatures and is used in applications that require extreme resistance to heat, such as furnace linings.

Cross-References.

Establishments primarily engaged in manufacturing nonclay refractories are classified in U.S. Industry 327125, Nonclay Refractory Manufacturing.

US—United States industry only. CAN—United States and Canadian industries are comparable. MEX—United States and Mexican industries are comparable. Blank—Canadian, Mexican, and United States industries are comparable.

327125 Nonclay Refractory Manufacturing^{US}

This U.S. industry comprises establishments primarily engaged in manufacturing nonclay refractory, mortar, brick, block, tile, and fabricated nonclay refractories such as graphite, magnesite, silica, or alumina crucibles. A refractory is a material that will retain its shape and chemical identity when subjected to high temperatures and is used in applications that require extreme resistance to heat, such as furnace linings.

Cross-References.

Establishments primarily engaged in manufacturing clay refractories are classified in U.S. Industry 327124, Clay Refractory Manufacturing.

3272 Glass and Glass Product Manufacturing

32721 Glass and Glass Product Manufacturing

This industry comprises establishments primarily engaged in manufacturing glass and/or glass products. Establishments in this industry may manufacture glass and/or glass products by melting silica sand or cullet, or purchasing glass.

Cross-References. Establishments primarily engaged in—

- Manufacturing glass wool (i.e., fiberglass) insulation products—are classified in Industry 32799, All Other Nonmetallic Mineral Product Manufacturing;

- Manufacturing optical lenses (except ophthalmic), such as magnifying, photographic, and projection lenses,—are classified in Industry 33331, Commercial and Service Industry Machinery Manufacturing;

- Grinding ophthalmic (i.e., eyeglass) lenses for the trade—are classified in Industry 33911, Medical Equipment and Supplies Manufacturing; and

- Manufacturing fiber optic cable from purchased fiber optic strand—are classified in Industry 33592, Communication and Energy Wire and Cable Manufacturing.

327211 Flat Glass Manufacturing^{MEX}

This U.S. industry comprises establishments primarily engaged in (1) manufacturing flat glass by melting silica sand or cullet or (2) manufacturing both flat glass and laminated glass by melting silica sand or cullet.

US—United States industry only. CAN—United States and Canadian industries are comparable. MEX—United States and Mexican industries are comparable. Blank—Canadian, Mexican, and United States industries are comparable.

Cross-References.

Establishments primarily engaged in manufacturing laminated glass from purchased flat glass are classified in U.S. Industry 327215, Glass Product Manufacturing Made of Purchased Glass.

327212 Other Pressed and Blown Glass and Glassware Manufacturing[US]

This U.S. industry comprises establishments primarily engaged in manufacturing glass by melting silica sand or cullet and making pressed, blown, or shaped glass or glassware (except glass packaging containers).

Cross-References. Establishments primarily engaged in—

- Manufacturing flat glass—are classified in U.S. Industry 327211, Flat Glass Manufacturing;
- Manufacturing glass packaging containers in glassmaking operations—are classified in U.S. Industry 327213, Glass Container Manufacturing;
- Manufacturing glass wool (i.e., fiberglass) insulation—are classified in U.S. Industry 327993, Mineral Wool Manufacturing;
- Manufacturing glassware from purchased glass—are classified in U.S. Industry 327215, Glass Product Manufacturing Made of Purchased Glass; and
- Manufacturing fiber optic cable—are classified in U.S. Industry 335921, Fiber Optic Cable Manufacturing.

327213 Glass Container Manufacturing[US]

This U.S. industry comprises establishments primarily engaged in manufacturing glass packaging containers.

327215 Glass Product Manufacturing Made of Purchased Glass[CAN]

This U.S. industry comprises establishments primarily engaged in coating, laminating, tempering, or shaping purchased glass.

Cross-References. Establishments primarily engaged in—

- Manufacturing optical lenses (except ophthalmic), such as magnifying, photographic and projection lenses,—are classified in U.S. Industry 333314, Optical Instrument and Lens Manufacturing;

- Manufacturing ophthalmic (i.e., eyeglass) lenses—are classified in U.S. Industry 339115, Ophthalmic Goods Manufacturing; and
- Manufacturing fiber optic cable from purchased fiber optic strand—are classified in U.S. Industry 335921, Fiber Optic Cable Manufacturing.

3273 Cement and Concrete Product Manufacturing

32731 Cement Manufacturing
See industry description for 327310 below.

327310 Cement Manufacturing

This industry comprises establishments primarily engaged in manufacturing portland, natural, masonry, pozzalanic, and other hydraulic cements. Cement manufacturing establishments may calcine earths or mine, quarry, manufacture, or purchase lime.

Cross-References. Establishments primarily engaged in—

- Mining or quarrying limestone—are classified in U.S. Industry 212312, Crushed and Broken Limestone Mining and Quarrying;
- Manufacturing lime—are classified in Industry 327410, Lime Manufacturing;
- Manufacturing ready-mix concrete—are classified in Industry 327320, Ready-Mix Concrete Manufacturing; and
- Manufacturing dry mix concrete—are classified in U.S. Industry 327999, All Other Miscellaneous Nonmetallic Mineral Product Manufacturing.

32732 Ready-Mix Concrete Manufacturing
See industry description for 327320 below.

327320 Ready-Mix Concrete Manufacturing

This industry comprises establishments, such as batch plants or mix plants, primarily engaged in manufacturing concrete delivered to a purchaser in a plastic and unhardened state. Ready-mix concrete manufacturing establishments may mine, quarry, or purchase sand and gravel.

Cross-References. Establishments primarily engaged in—

- Operating sand or gravel pits—are classified in U.S. Industry 212321, Construction Sand and Gravel Mining; and

---

US—United States industry only. CAN—United States and Canadian industries are comparable. MEX—United States and Mexican industries are comparable. Blank—Canadian, Mexican, and United States industries are comparable.

- Manufacturing dry mix concrete—are classified in U.S. Industry 327999, All Other Miscellaneous Nonmetallic Mineral Product Manufacturing.

32733 Concrete Pipe, Brick, and Block Manufacturing

This industry comprises establishments primarily engaged in manufacturing concrete pipe, brick, and block.

Cross-References.

Establishments primarily engaged in manufacturing concrete products (except brick, block, and pipe) are classified in Industry 32739, Other Concrete Product Manufacturing.

327331 Concrete Block and Brick Manufacturing[US]

This U.S. industry comprises establishments primarily engaged in manufacturing concrete block and brick.

327332 Concrete Pipe Manufacturing[US]

This U.S. industry comprises establishments primarily engaged in manufacturing concrete pipe.

32739 Other Concrete Product Manufacturing
See industry description for 327390 below.

327390 Other Concrete Product Manufacturing[CAN]

This industry comprises establishments primarily engaged in manufacturing concrete products (except block, brick, and pipe).

Cross-References. Establishments primarily engaged in—

- Manufacturing concrete brick and block—are classified in U.S. Industry 327331, Concrete Block and Brick Manufacturing; and
- Manufacturing concrete pipe—are classified in U.S. Industry 327332, Concrete Pipe Manufacturing.

3274 Lime and Gypsum Product Manufacturing

32741 Lime Manufacturing
See industry description for 327410 below.

US—United States industry only. CAN—United States and Canadian industries are comparable. MEX—United States and Mexican industries are comparable. Blank—Canadian, Mexican, and United States industries are comparable.

327410 Lime Manufacturing

This industry comprises establishments primarily engaged in manufacturing lime from calcitic limestone, dolomitic limestone, or other calcareous materials, such as coral, chalk, and shells. Lime manufacturing establishments may mine, quarry, collect, or purchase the sources of calcium carbonate.

Cross-References.

Establishments primarily engaged in manufacturing dolomite refractories are classified in U.S. Industry 327125, Nonclay Refractory Manufacturing.

32742 Gypsum Product Manufacturing
See industry description for 327420 below.

327420 Gypsum Product Manufacturing

This industry comprises establishments primarily engaged in manufacturing gypsum products such as wallboard, plaster, plasterboard, molding, ornamental moldings, statuary, and architectural plaster work. Gypsum product manufacturing establishments may mine, quarry, or purchase gypsum.

Cross-References.

Establishments primarily engaged in operating gypsum mines or quarries are classified in U.S. Industry 212399, All Other Nonmetallic Mineral Mining.

3279 Other Nonmetallic Mineral Product Manufacturing

The Other Nonmetallic Mineral Product Manufacturing industry group comprises establishments manufacturing nonmetallic mineral products (except clay products, refractory products, glass products, cement and concrete products, lime, and gypsum products).

32791 Abrasive Product Manufacturing
See industry description for 327910 below.

327910 Abrasive Product Manufacturing

This industry comprises establishments primarily engaged in manufacturing abrasive grinding wheels of natural or synthetic materials, abrasive-coated products, and other abrasive products.

Illustrative Examples:

Aluminum oxide (fused) abrasives manufacturing	Diamond dressing wheels manufacturing
	Sandpaper manufacturing
Buffing and polishing wheels, abrasive and nonabrasive, manufacturing	Silicon carbide abrasives manufacturing
	Whetstones manufacturing

Cross-References. Establishments primarily engaged in—

- Mining and cutting grindstones, pulpstones, and whetstones—are classified in U.S. Industry 212399, All Other Nonmetallic Mineral Mining;

- Manufacturing plastic scouring pads—are classified in U.S. Industry 326199, All Other Plastics Product Manufacturing; and

- Manufacturing metallic scouring sponges and soap impregnated scouring pads—are classified in U.S. Industry 332999, All Other Miscellaneous Fabricated Metal Product Manufacturing.

32799 All Other Nonmetallic Mineral Product Manufacturing

This industry comprises establishments primarily engaged in manufacturing nonmetallic mineral products (except pottery, ceramics, and plumbing fixtures; clay building materials and refractories; glass and glass products; cement; ready-mix concrete; concrete products; lime; gypsum products; and abrasive products).

Cross-References. Establishments primarily engaged in—

- Manufacturing pottery, ceramics, and plumbing fixtures—are classified in Industry 32711, Pottery, Ceramics, and Plumbing Fixture Manufacturing;

- Mining or quarrying stone, earth, or other nonmetallic minerals—are classified in Industry Group 2123, Nonmetallic Mineral Mining and Quarrying;

- Buying and selling semifinished monuments and tombstones with no work other than polishing, lettering, or shaping to custom order—are classified in Sector 42, Wholesale Trade or Sector 44-45, Retail Trade;

- Manufacturing clay building materials and refractories—are classified in Industry 32712, Clay Building Material and Refractories Manufacturing;

- Manufacturing glass and glass products—are classified in Industry 32721, Glass and Glass Product Manufacturing;

- Manufacturing cement—are classified in Industry 32731, Cement Manufacturing;

- Mixing and delivering ready-mix concrete—are classified in Industry 32732, Ready-Mix Concrete Manufacturing;

- Manufacturing concrete pipe, brick, and block—are classified in Industry 32733, Concrete Pipe, Brick, and Block Manufacturing;

- Manufacturing concrete products (except pipe, brick, and block)—are classified in Industry 32739, Other Concrete Product Manufacturing;

- Manufacturing lime—are classified in Industry 32741, Lime Manufacturing;

- Manufacturing gypsum products—are classified in Industry 32742, Gypsum Product Manufacturing;

- Manufacturing abrasive products—are classified in Industry 32791, Abrasive Product Manufacturing; and

- Manufacturing metallic scouring pads and steel wool—are classified in Industry 33299, All Other Fabricated Metal Product Manufacturing.

327991 Cut Stone and Stone Product Manufacturing^{US}

This U.S. industry comprises establishments primarily engaged in cutting, shaping, and finishing granite, marble, limestone, slate, and other stone for building and miscellaneous uses. Stone product manufacturing establishments may mine, quarry, or purchase stone.

Cross-References. Establishments primarily engaged in—

- Mining or quarrying stone—are classified in Industry Group 2123, Nonmetallic Mineral Mining and Quarrying; and

- Buying and selling semifinished monuments and tombstones with no work other than polishing, lettering, or shaping to custom order—are classified in Sector 42, Wholesale Trade or Sector 44-45, Retail Trade.

327992 Ground or Treated Mineral and Earth Manufacturing^{US}

This U.S. industry comprises establishments primarily engaged in calcining, dead burning, or otherwise processing beyond beneficiation, clays, ceramic and refractory minerals, barite, and miscellaneous nonmetallic minerals.

Cross-References.

Establishments primarily engaged in crushing, grinding, pulverizing, washing, screening, sizing, or otherwise beneficiating mined clays, ceramics and refractory, and other miscellaneous nonmetallic minerals are classified in Industry Group 2123, Nonmetallic Mineral Mining and Quarrying.

327993 Mineral Wool Manufacturing[US]

This U.S. industry comprises establishments primarily engaged in manufacturing mineral wool and mineral wool (i.e., fiberglass) insulation products made of such siliceous materials as rock, slag, and glass or combinations thereof.

Cross-References.

Establishments primarily engaged in manufacturing metallic scouring pads and steel wool are classified in U.S. Industry 332999, All Other Miscellaneous Fabricated Metal Product Manufacturing.

327999 All Other Miscellaneous Nonmetallic Mineral Product Manufacturing[US]

This U.S. industry comprises establishments primarily engaged in manufacturing nonmetallic mineral products (except pottery, ceramics, and plumbing fixtures; clay building materials and refractories; glass and glass products; cement; ready-mix concrete; concrete products; lime; gypsum products; abrasive products; cut stone and stone products; ground and treated minerals and earth; and mineral wool).

Illustrative Examples:

Dry mix concrete manufacturing	Stucco and stucco products
Mica products manufacturing	manufacturing
Synthetic stones, for gem stones and	
industrial use, manufacturing	

Cross-References. Establishments primarily engaged in—

- Manufacturing pottery, ceramics, and plumbing fixtures—are classified in Industry 32711, Pottery, Ceramics, and Plumbing Fixture Manufacturing;

- Manufacturing clay building materials and refractories—are classified in Industry 32712, Clay Building Material and Refractories Manufacturing;

- Manufacturing glass and glass products—are classified in Industry 32721, Glass and Glass Product Manufacturing;

- Manufacturing cement—are classified in Industry 327310, Cement Manufacturing;

- Mixing and delivering ready-mix concrete—are classified in Industry 327320, Ready-Mix Concrete Manufacturing;

- Manufacturing concrete pipe, brick, and block—are classified in Industry 32733, Concrete Pipe, Brick, and Block Manufacturing;

- Manufacturing concrete products (except pipe, brick, and block)—are classified in Industry 327390, Other Concrete Product Manufacturing;

- Manufacturing lime—are classified in Industry 327410, Lime Manufacturing;

- Manufacturing gypsum products—are classified in Industry 327420, Gypsum Product Manufacturing;

- Manufacturing abrasives and abrasive products—are classified in Industry 327910, Abrasive Product Manufacturing;

- Manufacturing cut stone and stone products—are classified in U.S. Industry 327991, Cut Stone and Stone Product Manufacturing;

- Manufacturing ground and treated minerals and earth (i.e., not at the mine site)—are classified in U.S. Industry 327992, Ground or Treated Mineral and Earth Manufacturing; and

- Manufacturing mineral wool and fiberglass insulation products—are classified in U.S. Industry 327993, Mineral Wool Manufacturing.

331 Primary Metal Manufacturing

Industries in the Primary Metal Manufacturing subsector smelt and/or refine ferrous and nonferrous metals from ore, pig or scrap, using electrometallurgical and other process metallurgical techniques. Establishments in this subsector also manufacture metal alloys and superalloys by introducing other chemical elements to pure metals. The output of smelting and refining, usually in ingot form, is used in rolling, drawing, and extruding operations to make sheet, strip, bar, rod, or wire, and in molten form to make castings and other basic metal products.

Primary manufacturing of ferrous and nonferrous metals begins with ore or concentrate as the primary input. Establishments manufacturing primary metals from ore and/or concentrate remain classified in the primary smelting, primary refining, or iron and steel mill industries regardless of the form of their output. Establishments primarily engaged in secondary smelting and/or secondary refining recover ferrous and nonferrous metals from scrap and/or dross. The output of the secondary smelting and/or secondary refining industries is limited to shapes, such as ingot or billet, that will be further processed. Recovery of metals from scrap often occurs in establishments that are primarily engaged in activities, such as rolling, drawing, extruding, or similar processes.

Excluded from the Primary Metal Manufacturing subsector are establishments primarily engaged in manufacturing ferrous and nonferrous forgings (except ferrous forgings made in steel mills) and stampings. Although forging, stamping, and casting are all methods used to make metal shapes, forging and stamping do not use molten metals and are included in Subsector 332, Fabricated Metal Product

US—United States industry only. CAN—United States and Canadian industries are comparable. MEX—United States and Mexican industries are comparable. Blank—Canadian, Mexican, and United States industries are comparable.

Manufacturing. Establishments primarily engaged in operating coke ovens are classified in Industry 32419, Other Petroleum and Coal Products Manufacturing.

3311 Iron and Steel Mills and Ferroalloy Manufacturing

33111 Iron and Steel Mills and Ferroalloy Manufacturing

This industry comprises establishments primarily engaged in one or more of the following: (1) direct reduction of iron ore; (2) manufacturing pig iron in molten or solid form; (3) converting pig iron into steel; (4) manufacturing ferroalloys; (5) making steel; (6) making steel and manufacturing shapes (e.g., bar, plate, rod, sheet, strip, wire); and (7) making steel and forming pipe and tube.

Cross-References. Establishments primarily engaged in—

- Manufacturing nonferrous superalloys, such as cobalt or nickel-based super-alloys,—are classified in Industry 33149, Nonferrous Metal (except Copper and Aluminum) Rolling, Drawing, Extruding, and Alloying; and

- Operating coke ovens—are classified in Industry 32419, Other Petroleum and Coal Products Manufacturing.

331111 Iron and Steel Mills[US]

This U.S. industry comprises establishments primarily engaged in one or more of the following: (1) direct reduction of iron ore; (2) manufacturing pig iron in molten or solid form; (3) converting pig iron into steel; (4) making steel; (5) making steel and manufacturing shapes (e.g., bar, plate, rod, sheet, strip, wire); and (6) making steel and forming tube and pipe.

Cross-References. Establishments primarily engaged in—

- Manufacturing ferroalloys (i.e., alloying elements used to improve, strengthen, or otherwise alter the characteristics of steel)—are classified in U.S. Industry 331112, Electrometallurgical Ferroalloy Product Manufacturing; and

- Operating coke ovens—are classified in U.S. Industry 324199, All Other Petroleum and Coal Products Manufacturing.

331112 Electrometallurgical Ferroalloy Product Manufacturing[US]

This U.S. industry comprises establishments primarily engaged in manufacturing electrometallurgical ferroalloys. Ferroalloys add critical elements, such as silicon and manganese for carbon steel and chromium, vanadium, tungsten, titanium, and molybdenum for low- and high-alloy metals. Ferroalloys include iron-rich alloys and more pure forms of elements added during the steel manufacturing process that alter or improve the characteristics of the metal being made.

Cross-References. Establishments primarily engaged in—

- Manufacturing electrometallurgical steel and iron-based superalloys—are classified in U.S. Industry 331111, Iron and Steel Mills; and
- Manufacturing nonferrous superalloys, such as cobalt or nickel-based superalloys,—are classified in U.S. Industry 331492, Secondary Smelting, Refining, and Alloying of Nonferrous Metal (except Copper and Aluminum).

3312 Steel Product Manufacturing from Purchased Steel

This industry group comprises establishments primarily engaged in manufacturing iron and steel tube and pipe, drawing steel wire, and rolling or drawing shapes from purchased iron or steel.

33121 Iron and Steel Pipe and Tube Manufacturing from Purchased Steel
See industry description for 331210 below.

331210 Iron and Steel Pipe and Tube Manufacturing from Purchased Steel

This industry comprises establishments primarily engaged in manufacturing welded, riveted, or seamless pipe and tube from purchased iron or steel.

Cross-References.
Establishments primarily engaged in making steel and further processing the steel into steel pipe and tube are classified in U.S. Industry 331111, Iron and Steel Mills.

33122 Rolling and Drawing of Purchased Steel

This industry comprises establishments primarily engaged in rolling and/or drawing steel shapes, such as plate, sheet, strip, rod, and bar, from purchased steel.

Cross-References. Establishments primarily engaged in—

- Making steel and rolling and/or drawing steel—are classified in Industry 33111, Iron and Steel Mills and Ferroalloy Manufacturing; and

- Manufacturing wire products from purchased wire—are classified in Industry 33261, Spring and Wire Product Manufacturing.

331221 Rolled Steel Shape Manufacturing^{CAN}

This U.S. industry comprises establishments primarily engaged in rolling or drawing shapes (except wire), such as plate, sheet, strip, rod, and bar, from purchased steel.

Cross-References. Establishments primarily engaged in—

- Making steel and rolling or drawing steel shapes—are classified in U.S. Industry 331111, Iron and Steel Mills; and

- Drawing wire from purchased steel—are classified in U.S. Industry 331222, Steel Wire Drawing.

331222 Steel Wire Drawing^{CAN}

This U.S. industry comprises establishments primarily engaged in drawing wire from purchased steel.

Cross-References. Establishments primarily engaged in—

- Making steel and drawing steel wire—are classified in U.S. Industry 331111, Iron and Steel Mills; and

- Manufacturing wire products, such as nails, spikes, and paper clips, from purchased steel wire—are classified in Industry 33261, Spring and Wire Product Manufacturing.

3313 Alumina and Aluminum Production and Processing

33131 Alumina and Aluminum Production and Processing

This industry comprises establishments primarily engaged in one or more of the following: (1) refining alumina; (2) making (i.e., the primary production) aluminum from alumina; (3) recovering aluminum from scrap or dross; (4) alloying purchased aluminum; and (5) manufacturing aluminum primary forms (e.g., bar, foil, pipe, plate, rod, sheet, tube, wire).

Cross-References. Establishments primarily engaged in—

- Manufacturing aluminum oxide abrasives and refractories—are classified in Subsector 327, Nonmetallic Mineral Product Manufacturing;

- Sorting and breaking up scrap aluminum metal without also smelting or refining—are classified in Sector 42, Wholesale Trade; and
- Operating facilities where commingled recyclable materials, such as paper, plastics, used beverage cans, and metals are sorted into distinct categories without also smelting or refining—are classified in Industry 56292, Materials Recovery Facilities.

331311 Alumina Refining[US]

This U.S. industry comprises establishments primarily engaged in refining alumina (i.e., aluminum oxide) generally from bauxite.

Cross-References. Establishments primarily engaged in—

- Manufacturing aluminum oxide abrasives and refractories—are classified in Subsector 327, Nonmetallic Mineral Product Manufacturing; and
- Making aluminum from alumina—are classified in U.S. Industry 331312, Primary Aluminum Production.

331312 Primary Aluminum Production[US]

This U.S. industry comprises establishments primarily engaged in (1) making aluminum from alumina and/or (2) making aluminum from alumina and rolling, drawing, extruding, or casting the aluminum they make into primary forms (e.g., bar, billet, ingot, plate, rod, sheet, strip). Establishments in this industry may make primary aluminum or aluminum-based alloys from alumina.

Cross-References. Establishments primarily engaged in—

- Refining alumina—are classified in U.S. Industry 331311, Alumina Refining; and
- Recovering aluminum from scrap or alloying purchased aluminum—are classified in U.S. Industry 331314, Secondary Smelting and Alloying of Aluminum.

331314 Secondary Smelting and Alloying of Aluminum[US]

This U.S. industry comprises establishments primarily engaged in (1) recovering aluminum and aluminum alloys from scrap and/or dross (i.e., secondary smelting) and making billet or ingot (except by rolling) and/or (2) **manufac**turing alloys, powder, paste, or flake from purchased aluminum.

US—United States industry only. CAN—United States and Canadian industries are comparable. MEX—United States and Mexican industries are comparable. Blank—Canadian, Mexican, and United States industries are comparable.

Cross-References. Establishments primarily engaged in—

- Making aluminum and/or aluminum alloys from alumina—are classified in U.S. Industry 331312, Primary Aluminum Production;

- Refining alumina—are classified in U.S. Industry 331311, Alumina Refining;

- Manufacturing aluminum sheet, plate, and foil from purchased aluminum or by recovering aluminum from scrap and flat rolling or continuous casting—are classified in U.S. Industry 331315, Aluminum Sheet, Plate, and Foil Manufacturing;

- Manufacturing aluminum extruded products from purchased aluminum or by recovering aluminum from scrap and extruding—are classified in U.S. Industry 331316, Aluminum Extruded Product Manufacturing;

- Manufacturing rolled ingot or billet from purchased aluminum or by recovering aluminum from scrap and rolling or drawing—are classified in U.S. Industry 331319, Other Aluminum Rolling and Drawing;

- Sorting and breaking up scrap metal without also smelting or refining—are classified in Industry 423930, Recyclable Material Merchant Wholesalers; and

- Operating facilities where commingled recyclable materials, such as paper, plastics, used beverage cans, and metals, are sorted into distinct categories without also smelting or refining—are classified in Industry 562920, Materials Recovery Facilities.

331315 Aluminum Sheet, Plate, and Foil Manufacturing[US]

This U.S. industry comprises establishments primarily engaged in (1) flat rolling or continuous casting sheet, plate, foil and welded tube from purchased aluminum; and/or (2) recovering aluminum from scrap and flat rolling or continuous casting sheet, plate, foil, and welded tube in integrated mills.

Cross-References.

Establishments primarily engaged in making aluminum from alumina and flat rolling or continuous casting aluminum sheet, plate, foil, and welded tube are classified in U.S. Industry 331312, Primary Aluminum Production.

331316 Aluminum Extruded Product Manufacturing[US]

This U.S. industry comprises establishments primarily engaged in (1) extruding aluminum bar, pipe, and tube blooms or extruding or drawing tube from purchased aluminum; and/or (2) recovering aluminum from scrap and extruding bar, pipe, and tube blooms or drawing tube in integrated mills.

Cross-References.

Establishments primarily engaged in making aluminum from alumina and extruding aluminum bar, pipe, tube or tube blooms are classified in U.S. Industry 331312, Primary Aluminum Production.

331319 Other Aluminum Rolling and Drawing[US]

This U.S. Industry comprises establishments primarily engaged in (1) rolling, drawing, or extruding shapes (except flat rolled sheet, plate, foil, and welded tube; extruded rod, bar, pipe, and tube blooms; and drawn or extruded tube) from purchased aluminum and/or (2) recovering aluminum from scrap and rolling, drawing or extruding shapes (except flat rolled sheet, plate, foil, and welded tube; extruded rod, bar, pipe, and tube blooms; and drawn or extruded tube) in integrated mills.

Cross-References. Establishments primarily engaged in—

- Flat rolling sheet, plate, foil, and welded tube from either purchased aluminum or by recovering aluminum from scrap and flat rolling or continuous casting—are classified in U.S. Industry 331315, Aluminum Sheet, Plate, and Foil Manufacturing;

- Extruding rod, bar, pipe, tube and tube blooms or drawing tube from purchased aluminum or by recovering aluminum from scrap and extruding—are classified in U.S. Industry 331316, Aluminum Extruded Product Manufacturing; and

- Making aluminum from alumina and making aluminum shapes—are classified in U.S. Industry 331312, Primary Aluminum Production.

3314 Nonferrous Metal (except Aluminum) Production and Processing

33141 Nonferrous Metal (except Aluminum) Smelting and Refining

This industry comprises establishments primarily engaged in (1) smelting ores into nonferrous metals and/or (2) the primary refining of nonferrous metals (except aluminum) using electrolytic or other processes.

US—United States industry only. CAN—United States and Canadian industries are comparable. MEX—United States and Mexican industries are comparable. Blank—Canadian, Mexican, and United States industries are comparable.

Cross-References. Establishments primarily engaged in—

- Making aluminum from alumina or recovery of aluminum from scrap—are classified in Industry 33131, Alumina and Aluminum Production and Processing;

- Recovering copper or copper alloys from scrap or dross and/or alloying, rolling, drawing, and extruding purchased copper—are classified in Industry 33142, Copper Rolling, Drawing, Extruding, and Alloying;

- Recovering nonferrous metals (except copper and aluminum) from scrap and/or alloying, rolling, drawing, and extruding purchased nonferrous metals (except copper and aluminum)—are classified in Industry 33149, Nonferrous Metal (except Copper and Aluminum) Rolling, Drawing, Extruding, and Alloying;

- Mining and making copper and other nonferrous concentrates (including gold and silver bullion) using processes, such as solvent extraction or electrowinning,—are classified in Industry Group 2122, Metal Ore Mining;

- Sorting and breaking up scrap metal without also smelting or refining—are classified in Sector 42, Wholesale Trade; and

- Operating facilities where commingled recyclable materials, such as paper, plastics, used beverage cans, and metals, are sorted into distinct categories without also smelting or refining—are classified in Industry 56292, Materials Recovery Facilities.

331411 Primary Smelting and Refining of Copper[MEX]

This U.S. industry comprises establishments primarily engaged in (1) smelting copper ore and/or (2) the primary refining of copper by electrolytic methods or other processes. Establishments in this industry make primary copper and copper-based alloys, such as brass and bronze, from ore or concentrates.

Cross-References. Establishments primarily engaged in—

- Recovering copper or copper alloys from scrap and making primary forms and/or alloying purchased copper—are classified in U.S. Industry 331423, Secondary Smelting, Refining, and Alloying of Copper;

- Mining and making copper concentrates by processes, such as solvent extraction or electrowinning,—are classified in U.S. Industry 212234, Copper Ore and Nickel Ore Mining;

- Drawing copper wire (except mechanical) from purchased copper or recovering copper from scrap and drawing wire (except mechanical)—are classified in U.S. Industry 331422, Copper Wire (except Mechanical) Drawing; and

---

US—United States industry only. CAN—United States and Canadian industries are comparable. MEX—United States and Mexican industries are comparable. Blank—Canadian, Mexican, and United States industries are comparable.

- Rolling, drawing, or extruding copper shapes (except communication and energy wire) from purchased copper or recovering copper from scrap and rolling, drawing, and extruding copper shapes—are classified in U.S. Industry 331421, Copper Rolling, Drawing, and Extruding.

331419 Primary Smelting and Refining of Nonferrous Metal (except Copper and Aluminum)[MEX]

This U.S. industry comprises establishments primarily engaged in (1) making (i.e., the primary production) nonferrous metals by smelting ore and/or (2) the primary refining of nonferrous metals by electrolytic methods or other processes.

Cross-References. Establishments primarily engaged in—

- Recovering nonferrous metals (except copper and aluminum) from scrap and making primary forms and/or alloying purchased nonferrous metals (except copper and aluminum)—are classified in U.S. Industry 331492, Secondary Smelting, Refining, and Alloying of Nonferrous Metal (except Copper and Aluminum);

- Making aluminum from alumina—are classified in U.S. Industry 331312, Primary Aluminum Production;

- Primary smelting and primary refining of copper—are classified in U.S. Industry 331411, Primary Smelting and Refining of Copper;

- Mining and making copper and other nonferrous concentrates (including gold and silver bullion), by processes, such as solvent extraction or electro-winning,—are classified in Industry Group 2122, Metal Ore Mining; and

- Rolling, drawing, and/or extruding nonferrous metal shapes (except copper and aluminum) from purchased nonferrous metals (except copper and aluminum) or by recovering nonferrous metals (except copper and aluminum) and rolling, drawing, or extruding—are classified in U.S. Industry 331491, Nonferrous Metal (except Copper and Aluminum) Rolling, Drawing, and Extruding.

33142 Copper Rolling, Drawing, Extruding, and Alloying

This industry comprises establishments primarily engaged in one or more of the following: (1) recovering copper or copper alloys from scraps; (2) alloying purchased copper; (3) rolling, drawing, or extruding shapes, (e.g., bar, plate, sheet, strip, tube, wire) from purchased copper; and (4) recovering copper or copper alloys from scrap and rolling drawing, or extruding shapes (e.g., bar, plate, sheet, strip, tube, wire).

Cross-References. Establishments primarily engaged in—

- Smelting copper ore, primary copper refining, and/or rolling, drawing or extruding primary copper made in the same establishment—are classified in Industry 33141, Nonferrous Metal (except Aluminum) Smelting and Refining;

- Manufacturing wire products from purchased wire—are classified in Industry 33261, Spring and Wire Product Manufacturing;

- Insulating purchased copper wire—are classified in Industry 33592, Communication and Energy Wire and Cable Manufacturing;

- Sorting and breaking up scrap metal without also smelting or refining—are classified in Sector 42, Wholesale Trade;

- Operating facilities where commingled recyclable materials, such as paper, plastics, used beverage cans, and metals, are sorted into distinct categories without also smelting or refining—are classified in Industry 56292, Materials Recovery Facilities;

- Die-casting purchased copper—are classified in Industry 33152, Nonferrous Metal Foundries; and

- Recovering nonferrous metals (except copper and aluminum) from scrap, and/or rolling, drawing, extruding, or alloying purchased nonferrous metals (except copper and aluminum)—are classified in Industry 33149, Nonferrous Metal (except Copper and Aluminum) Rolling, Drawing, Extruding, and Alloying.

331421 Copper Rolling, Drawing, and Extruding[US]

This U.S. industry comprises establishments primarily engaged in (1) rolling, drawing, and/or extruding shapes (e.g., bar, plate, sheet, strip, tube (except bare or insulated copper communication or energy wire), from purchased copper; and/or (2) recovering copper from scrap and rolling, drawing, and/or extruding shapes (e.g., bar, plate, sheet, strip, tube (except bare or insulated copper communication or energy wire, in integrated mills.))

Cross-References. Establishments primarily engaged in—

- Recovering copper or copper alloys from scrap and making primary forms and/or alloying purchased copper—are classified in U.S. Industry 331423, Secondary Smelting, Refining, and Alloying of Copper;

- Drawing copper wire (except mechanical) from purchased copper or recovering copper from scrap and drawing copper wire (except mechanical)—are classified in U.S. Industry 331422, Copper Wire (except Mechanical) Drawing;

- Die-casting purchased copper—are classified in U.S. Industry 331522, Nonferrous (except Aluminum) Die-Casting Foundries;
- Making primary copper and rolling, drawing, and/or extruding copper shapes (e.g., bar, plate, rod, sheet, strip)—are classified in U.S. Industry 331411, Primary Smelting and Refining of Copper; and
- Rolling, drawing, or extruding shapes from purchased nonferrous metal (except copper and aluminum) or recovering nonferrous metals (except copper and aluminum) from scrap and rolling, drawing or extruding—are classified in U.S. Industry 331491, Nonferrous Metal (except Copper and Aluminum) Rolling, Drawing, and Extruding.

331422 Copper Wire (except Mechanical) Drawing[US]

This U.S. industry comprises establishments primarily engaged in drawing or drawing and insulating communication and energy wire and cable from purchased copper or in integrated secondary smelting and wire drawing plants.

Cross-References. Establishments primarily engaged in—

- Manufacturing copper mechanical wire from purchased copper or by recovering copper from scrap and drawing or extruding—are classified in U.S. Industry 331421, Copper Rolling, Drawing, and Extruding;
- Insulating purchased copper wire—are classified in U.S. Industry 335929, Other Communication and Energy Wire Manufacturing;
- Making primary copper and drawing copper wire—are classified in U.S. Industry 331411, Primary Smelting and Refining of Copper; and
- Manufacturing wire products from purchased copper wire—are classified in Industry 33261, Spring and Wire Product Manufacturing.

331423 Secondary Smelting, Refining, and Alloying of Copper[US]

This U.S. industry comprises establishments primarily engaged in (1) recovering copper and copper alloys from scrap and/or (2) alloying purchased copper. Establishments in this industry make primary forms, such as ingot, wire bar, cake, and slab from copper or copper alloys, such as brass and bronze.

Cross-References. Establishments primarily engaged in—

- Sorting and breaking up scrap metal without also smelting or refining—are classified in Industry 423930, Recyclable Material Merchant Wholesalers;
- Operating facilities where commingled recyclable materials, such as paper, plastics, used beverage cans, and metals, are sorted into distinct categories

---

US—United States industry only. CAN—United States and Canadian industries are comparable. MEX—United States and Mexican industries are comparable. Blank—Canadian, Mexican, and United States industries are comparable.

without also smelting or refining—are classified in Industry 562920, Materials Recovery Facilities;

- Smelting copper ore and/or the primary refining of copper—are classified in U.S. Industry 331411, Primary Smelting and Refining of Copper;

- Recovering copper and copper alloys from scrap and rolling, drawing, or extruding shapes—are classified in U.S. Industry 331421, Copper Rolling, Drawing, and Extruding;

- Recovering copper and copper alloys from scrap and drawing wire (except mechanical)—are classified in U.S. Industry 331422, Copper Wire (except Mechanical) Drawing; and

- Recovering nonferrous metals (except copper, aluminum) from scrap and making primary forms and/or alloying purchased nonferrous metals (except copper and aluminum)—are classified in U.S. Industry 331492, Secondary Smelting, Refining, and Alloying of Nonferrous Metal (except Copper and Aluminum).

33149 Nonferrous Metal (except Copper and Aluminum) Rolling, Drawing, Extruding, and Alloying

This industry comprises establishments primarily engaged in one or more of the following: (1) recovering nonferrous metals (except copper and aluminum) and nonferrous metal alloys from scrap; (2) alloying purchased nonferrous metals (except copper and aluminum); (3) rolling, drawing, and extruding shapes from purchased nonferrous metals (except copper and aluminum); and (4) recovering nonferrous metals from scrap (except copper and aluminum) and rolling, drawing, or extruding shapes in integrated facilities.

Cross-References. Establishments primarily engaged in—

- Rolling, drawing, and/or extruding aluminum or secondary smelting and alloying of aluminum—are classified in Industry 33131, Alumina and Aluminum Production and Processing;

- Recovering copper and copper alloys from scrap, alloying purchased copper, rolling, drawing, or extruding shapes from purchased copper, and recovering copper or copper alloys from scrap and rolling, drawing, or extruding shapes in integrated mills—are classified in Industry 33142, Copper Rolling, Drawing, Extruding, and Alloying;

- Insulating purchased nonferrous wire—are classified in Industry 33592, Communication and Energy Wire and Cable Manufacturing;

- Making primary nonferrous metals and rolling, drawing, or extruding nonferrous metal shapes—are classified in Industry 33141, Nonferrous Metal (except Aluminum) Smelting and Refining;

- Manufacturing products from purchased wire—are classified in Industry 33261, Spring and Wire Product Manufacturing;
- Sorting and breaking up scrap metal without also smelting or refining— are classified in Sector 42, Wholesale Trade; and
- Operating facilities where commingled recyclable materials, such as paper, plastics, used beverage cans, and metals, are sorted into distinct categories without also smelting or refining—are classified in Industry 56292, Materials Recovery Facilities.

331491 Nonferrous Metal (except Copper and Aluminum) Rolling, Drawing, and Extruding[US]

This U.S. industry comprises establishments primarily engaged in (1) rolling, drawing, or extruding shapes (e.g., bar, plate, sheet, strip, tube) from purchased nonferrous metals) and/or (2) recovering nonferrous metals from scrap and rolling, drawing, and/or extruding shapes (e.g., bar, plate, sheet, strip, tube) in integrated mills.

Cross-References. Establishments primarily engaged in—
- Rolling, drawing, and/or extruding shapes from purchased copper or recovering copper from scrap and rolling, drawing, or extruding shapes—are classified in U.S. Industry 331421, Copper Rolling, Drawing, and Extruding;
- Recovering nonferrous metals (except copper and aluminum) from scrap and making primary forms and/or alloying purchased nonferrous metals— are classified in U.S. Industry 331492, Secondary Smelting, Refining, and Alloying of Nonferrous Metal (except Copper and Aluminum);
- Rolling, drawing, and/or extruding aluminum—are classified in Industry 33131, Alumina and Aluminum Production and Processing;
- Making primary nonferrous metals and rolling, drawing, or extruding nonferrous metal shapes—are classified in U.S. Industry 331419, Primary Smelting and Refining of Nonferrous Metal (except Copper and Aluminum); and
- Insulating purchased nonferrous wire—are classified in U.S. Industry 335929, Other Communication and Energy Wire Manufacturing.

331492 Secondary Smelting, Refining, and Alloying of Nonferrous Metal (except Copper and Aluminum)[US]

This U.S. industry comprises establishments primarily engaged in (1) alloying purchased nonferrous metals and/or (2) recovering nonferrous metals from scrap.

United States industry only. CAN—United States and Canadian industries are comparable. ⁻ited States and Mexican industries are comparable. Blank—Canadian, Mexican, and United ·tries are comparable.

Establishments in this industry make primary forms (e.g., bar, billet, bloom, cake, ingot, slab, slug, wire) using smelting or refining processes.

Cross-References. Establishments primarily engaged in—

- Recovering aluminum and aluminum alloys from scrap and/or alloying purchased aluminum—are classified in U.S. Industry 331314, Secondary Smelting and Alloying of Aluminum;

- Sorting and breaking up scrap metal without also smelting or refining—are classified in Industry 423930, Recyclable Material Merchant Wholesalers;

- Recovering nonferrous metals from scrap and rolling, drawing, or extruding shapes in integrated facilities—are classified in U.S. Industry 331491, Nonferrous Metal (except Copper and Aluminum) Rolling, Drawing, and Extruding;

- Operating facilities where commingled recyclable materials, such as paper, plastics, used beverage cans, and metals, are sorted into distinct categories without also smelting or refining—are classified in Industry 562920, Materials Recovery Facilities; and

- Recovering copper and copper alloys from scrap and making primary forms; and/or alloying purchased copper—are classified in U.S. Industry 331423, Secondary Smelting, Refining, and Alloying of Copper.

3315 Foundries

This industry group comprises establishments primarily engaged in pouring molten metal into molds or dies to form castings. Establishments making castings and further manufacturing, such as machining or assembling, a specific manufactured product are classified in the industry of the finished product. Foundries may perform operations, such as cleaning and deburring, on the castings they manufacture. More involved processes, such as tapping, threading, milling, or machining to tight tolerances, that transform castings into more finished products are classified elsewhere in the manufacturing sector based on the product being made.

Establishments in this industry group make castings from purchased metals or in integrated secondary smelting and casting facilities. When the production of primary metals is combined with making castings, the establishment is classified in 331 with the primary metal being made.

33151 Ferrous Metal Foundries

This industry comprises establishments primarily engaged in pouring molten iron and steel into molds of a desired shape to made castings. Establishments in this industry purchase iron and steel made in other establishments.

US—United States industry only. CAN—United States and Canadian industries are co·
MEX—United States and Mexican industries are comparable. Blank—Canadian, Mexican, ·
States industries are comparable.

Cross-References.

Establishments primarily engaged in manufacturing iron or steel castings and further manufacturing them into finished products are classified based on the specific finished product.

331511 Iron Foundries[CAN]

This U.S. industry comprises establishments primarily engaged in pouring molten pig iron or iron alloys into molds to manufacture castings, (e.g., cast iron manhole covers, cast iron pipe, cast iron skillets). Establishments in this industry purchase iron made in other establishments.

Cross-References.

Establishments primarily engaged in manufacturing iron castings and further manufacturing them into finished products are classified based on the specific finished product.

331512 Steel Investment Foundries[US]

This U.S. industry comprises establishments primarily engaged in manufacturing steel investment castings. Investment molds are formed by covering a wax shape with a refractory slurry. After the refractory slurry hardens, the wax is melted, leaving a seamless mold. Investment molds provide highly detailed, consistent castings. Establishments in this industry purchase steel made in other establishments.

Cross-References. Establishments primarily engaged in—

- Manufacturing steel castings (except steel investment castings)—are classified in U.S. Industry 331513, Steel Foundries (except Investment); and
- Manufacturing steel investment castings and further manufacturing them into finished products—are classified based on the specific finished product.

331513 Steel Foundries (except Investment)[US]

This U.S. industry comprises establishments primarily engaged in manufacturing steel castings (except steel investment castings). Establishments in this industry purchase steel made in other establishments.

Cross-References. Establishments primarily engaged in—

- Manufacturing steel investment castings—are classified in U.S. Industry 331512, Steel Investment Foundries; and

---

US—United States industry only. CAN—United States and Canadian industries are comparable. MEX—United States and Mexican industries are comparable. Blank—Canadian, Mexican, and United States industries are comparable.

- Manufacturing steel castings and further manufacturing them into finished products—are classified based on the specific finished product.

33152 Nonferrous Metal Foundries

This industry comprises establishments primarily engaged in pouring and/or introducing molten nonferrous metal, under high pressure, into metal molds or dies to manufacture castings. Establishments in this industry purchase nonferrous metals made in other establishments.

Cross-References. Establishments primarily engaged in—

- Manufacturing iron or steel castings—are classified in Industry 33151, Ferrous Metal Foundries; and
- Manufacturing nonferrous metal castings and further manufacturing them into finished products—are classified based on the specific finished product.

331521 Aluminum Die-Casting Foundries[US]

This U.S. industry comprises establishments primarily engaged in introducing molten aluminum, under high pressure, into molds or dies to make aluminum die-castings. Establishments in this industry purchase aluminum made in other establishments.

Cross-References. Establishments primarily engaged in—

- Pouring molten aluminum into molds to manufacture aluminum castings—are classified in U.S. Industry 331524, Aluminum Foundries (except Die-Casting); and
- Manufacturing aluminum die-castings and further manufacturing them into finished products—are classified based on the specific finished product.

331522 Nonferrous (except Aluminum) Die-Casting Foundries[US]

This U.S. industry comprises establishments primarily engaged in introducing molten nonferrous metal (except aluminum), under high pressure, into molds to make nonferrous metal die-castings. Establishments in this industry purchase nonferrous metals made in other establishments.

Cross-References. Establishments primarily engaged in—

- Manufacturing aluminum die-castings—are classified in U.S. Industry 331521, Aluminum Die-Casting Foundries;

US—United States industry only. CAN—United States and Canadian industries are comparable. MEX—United States and Mexican industries are comparable. Blank—Canadian, Mexican, and United States industries are comparable.

- Pouring molten aluminum into molds to manufacture aluminum castings—are classified in U.S. Industry 331524, Aluminum Foundries (except Die-Casting);
- Pouring molten copper into molds to manufacture copper castings—are classified in U.S. Industry 331525, Copper Foundries (except Die-Casting);
- Pouring molten nonferrous metal (except copper and aluminum) into molds to manufacture nonferrous (except copper and aluminum) castings—are classified in U.S. Industry 331528, Other Nonferrous Foundries (except Die-Casting); and
- Manufacturing nonferrous die-castings and further manufacturing them into finished products—are classified based on the specific finished product.

331524 Aluminum Foundries (except Die-Casting)[US]

This U.S. industry comprises establishments primarily engaged in pouring molten aluminum into molds to manufacture aluminum castings. Establishments in this industry purchase aluminum made in other establishments.

Cross-References. Establishments primarily engaged in—
- Manufacturing aluminum die-castings—are classified in U.S. Industry 331521, Aluminum Die-Casting Foundries; and
- Manufacturing aluminum or aluminum alloy castings and further manufacturing them into finished products—are classified based on the specific finished product.

331525 Copper Foundries (except Die-Casting)[US]

This U.S. industry comprises establishments primarily engaged in pouring molten copper into molds to manufacture copper castings. Establishments in this industry purchase copper made in other establishments.

Cross-References. Establishments primarily engaged in—
- Manufacturing copper die-castings—are classified in U.S. Industry 331522, Nonferrous (except Aluminum) Die-Casting Foundries; and
- Manufacturing copper castings and further manufacturing them into finished products—are classified based on the specific finished product.

331528 Other Nonferrous Foundries (except Die-Casting)[US]

This U.S. industry comprises establishments primarily engaged in pouring molten nonferrous metals (except aluminum and copper) into molds to manufacture nonferrous castings (except aluminum die-castings, nonferrous (except aluminum) die-castings, aluminum castings, and copper castings). Establishments in this industry purchase nonferrous metals, such as nickel, lead, and zinc, made in other establishments.

Cross-References. Establishments primarily engaged in—

- Manufacturing aluminum die-castings—are classified in U.S. Industry 331521, Aluminum Die-Casting Foundries;

- Manufacturing nonferrous (except aluminum) die-castings—are classified in U.S. Industry 331522, Nonferrous (except Aluminum) Die-Casting Foundries;

- Pouring molten aluminum into molds to manufacture aluminum castings— are classified in U.S. Industry 331524, Aluminum Foundries (except Die-Casting);

- Manufacturing copper castings—are classified in U.S. Industry 331525, Copper Foundries (except Die-Casting); and

- Manufacturing nonferrous castings and further manufacturing them into finished products—are classified based on the specific finished product.

332 Fabricated Metal Product Manufacturing

Industries in the Fabricated Metal Product Manufacturing subsector transform metal into intermediate or end products, other than machinery, computers and electronics, and metal furniture or treating metals and metal formed products fabricated elsewhere. Important fabricated metal processes are forging, stamping, bending, forming, and machining, used to shape individual pieces of metal; and other processes, such as welding and assembling, used to join separate parts together. Establishments in this subsector may use one of these processes or a combination of these processes.

The NAICS structure for this subsector distinguishes the forging and stamping processes in a single industry. The remaining industries, in the subsector, group establishments based on similar combinations of processes used to make products.

The manufacturing performed in the Fabricated Metal Product Manufacturing subsector begins with manufactured metal shapes. The establishments in this sector further fabricate the purchased metal shapes into a product. For instance, the Spring and Wire Product Manufacturing industry starts with wire and fabricates such items.

Within manufacturing there are other establishments that make the same products made by this subsector; only these establishments begin production further back in the production process. These establishments have a more integrated operation. For instance, one establishment may manufacture steel, draw it into wire, and make wire products in the same establishment. Such operations are classified in the Primary Metal Manufacturing subsector.

3321 Forging and Stamping

33211 Forging and Stamping

This industry comprises establishments primarily engaged in one or more of the following: (1) manufacturing forgings from purchased metals; (2) manufacturing metal custom roll forming products; (3) manufacturing metal stamped and spun products (except automotive, cans, coins); and (4) manufacturing powder metallurgy products. Establishments making metal forgings, metal stampings, and metal spun products and further manufacturing (e.g., machining, assembling) a specific manufactured product are classified in the industry of the finished product. Metal forging, metal stamping, and metal spun products establishments may perform surface finishing operations, such as cleaning and deburring, on the products they manufacture.

Cross-References. Establishments primarily engaged in—

- Manufacturing metal forgings in integrated primary metal establishments— are classified in Subsector 331, Primary Metal Manufacturing;

- Stamping automotive stampings—are classified in Industry 33637, Motor Vehicle Metal Stamping;

- Manufacturing and installing rolled formed seamless gutters at construction sites—are classified in Industry 23839, Other Building Finishing Contractors; and

- Stamping coins—are classified in Industry 33991, Jewelry and Silverware Manufacturing.

332111 Iron and Steel Forging[US]

This U.S. industry comprises establishments primarily engaged in manufacturing iron and steel forgings from purchased iron and steel by hammering mill shapes. Establishments making iron and steel forgings and further manufacturing (e.g., machining, assembling) a specific manufactured product are classified in the industry of the finished product. Iron and steel forging establishments may perform surface finishing operations, such as cleaning and deburring, on the forgings they manufacture.

US—United States industry only. CAN—United States and Canadian industries are comparable. MEX—United States and Mexican industries are comparable. Blank—Canadian, Mexican, and United States industries are comparable.

Cross-References. Establishments primarily engaged in—

- Manufacturing iron and steel forgings in integrated iron and steel mills— are classified in U.S. Industry 331111, Iron and Steel Mills; and

- Manufacturing nonferrous forgings—are classified in U.S. Industry 332112, Nonferrous Forging.

332112 Nonferrous Forging^{US}

This U.S. industry comprises establishments primarily engaged in manufacturing nonferrous forgings from purchased nonferrous metals by hammering mill shapes. Establishments making nonferrous forgings and further manufacturing (e.g., machining, assembling) a specific manufactured product are classified in the industry of the finished product. Nonferrous forging establishments may perform surface finishing operations, such as cleaning and deburring, on the forgings they manufacture.

Cross-References. Establishments primarily engaged in—

- Manufacturing iron and steel forgings—are classified in U.S. Industry 332111, Iron and Steel Forging; and

- Manufacturing nonferrous forgings in integrated primary or secondary nonferrous metal production facilities—are classified in Subsector 331, Primary Metal Manufacturing.

332114 Custom Roll Forming^{US}

This U.S. industry comprises establishments primarily engaged in custom roll forming metal products by use of rotary motion of rolls with various contours to bend or shape the products.

Cross-References.

Establishments primarily engaged in manufacturing and installing rolled formed seamless gutters at construction sites are classified in Industry 238390, Other Building Finishing Contractors.

332115 Crown and Closure Manufacturing^{US}

This U.S. industry comprises establishments primarily engaged in stamping metal crowns and closures, such as bottle caps and home canning lids and rings.

332116 Metal Stamping^{US}

This U.S. industry comprises establishments primarily engaged in manufacturing unfinished metal stampings and spinning unfinished metal products (except crowns, cans, closures, automotive, and coins). Establishments making metal stampings and metal spun products and further manufacturing (e.g., machining, assembling) a specific product are classified in the industry of the finished product. Metal stamping and metal spun products establishments may perform surface finishing operations, such as cleaning and deburring, on the products they manufacture.

Cross-References. Establishments primarily engaged in—

- Stamping automotive stampings—are classified in Industry 336370, Motor Vehicle Metal Stamping;
- Stamping metal crowns and closures—are classified in U.S. Industry 332115, Crown and Closure Manufacturing;
- Manufacturing metal cans—are classified in U.S. Industry 332431, Metal Can Manufacturing; and
- Stamping coins—are classified in U.S. Industry 339911, Jewelry (except Costume) Manufacturing.

332117 Powder Metallurgy Part Manufacturing^{US}

This U.S. industry comprises establishments primarily engaged in manufacturing powder metallurgy products by compacting them in a shaped die and sintering. Establishments in this industry generally make a wide range of parts on a job or order basis.

3322 Cutlery and Handtool Manufacturing

33221 Cutlery and Handtool Manufacturing

This industry comprises establishments primarily engaged in one or more of the following: (1) manufacturing nonprecious and precious plated metal cutlery and flatware; (2) manufacturing nonpowered hand and edge tools; (3) manufacturing nonpowered handsaws; (4) manufacturing saw blades, all types (including those for sawing machines); and (5) manufacturing metal kitchen utensils (except cutting-type) and pots and pans (except those manufactured by casting (e.g., cast iron skillets) or stamped without further fabrication).

Cross-References. Establishments primarily engaged in—

- Manufacturing precious (except precious plated) metal cutlery and flatware—are classified in Industry 33991, Jewelry and Silverware Manufacturing;
- Manufacturing electric razors and hair clippers for use on humans—are classified in Industry 33521, Small Electrical Appliance Manufacturing;
- Manufacturing power hedge shears and trimmers and electric hair clippers for use on animals—are classified in Industry 33311, Agricultural Implement Manufacturing;
- Manufacturing metal cutting dies, attachments, and accessories for machine tools—are classified in Industry 33351, Metalworking Machinery Manufacturing;
- Manufacturing handheld power-driven handtools—are classified in Industry 33399, All Other General Purpose Machinery Manufacturing; and
- Manufacturing finished cast iron kitchen utensils (i.e., cast iron skillets) and castings for kitchen utensils, pots, and pans—are classified in Industry Group 3315, Foundries.

332211 Cutlery and Flatware (except Precious) Manufacturing[US]

This U.S. industry comprises establishments primarily engaged in manufacturing nonprecious and precious plated metal cutlery and flatware.

Cross-References. Establishments primarily engaged in—

- Manufacturing precious (except precious plated) metal cutlery and flatware—are classified in U.S. Industry 339912, Silverware and Hollowware Manufacturing;
- Manufacturing electric razors and hair clippers for use on humans and housewares—are classified in U.S. Industry 335211, Electric Housewares and Household Fan Manufacturing;
- Manufacturing power hedge shears and trimmers and electric hair clippers for animal use— are classified in U.S. Industry 333112, Lawn and Garden Tractor and Home Lawn and Garden Equipment Manufacturing; and
- Manufacturing nonelectric hair clippers for use on animals—are classified in U.S. Industry 332212, Hand and Edge Tool Manufacturing.

332212 Hand and Edge Tool Manufacturing[US]

This industry comprises establishments primarily engaged in manufacturing nonpowered hand and edge tools (except saws).

Cross-References. Establishments primarily engaged in—

- Manufacturing saw blades and handsaws—are classified in U.S. Industry 332213, Saw Blade and Handsaw Manufacturing;
- Manufacturing metal cutting dies, attachments, and accessories for machine tools—are classified in Industry 33351, Metalworking Machinery Manufacturing;
- Manufacturing handheld power-driven handtools—are classified in U.S. Industry 333991, Power-Driven Handtool Manufacturing;
- Manufacturing electric razors and hair clippers for use on humans—are classified in U.S. Industry 335211, Electric Housewares and Household Fan Manufacturing;
- Manufacturing electric hair clippers for use on animals—are classified in U.S. Industry 333111, Farm Machinery and Equipment Manufacturing; and
- Manufacturing nonelectric household-type scissors and shears—are classified in U.S. Industry 332211, Cutlery and Flatware (except Precious) Manufacturing.

332213 Saw Blade and Handsaw Manufacturing[US]

This U.S. industry comprises establishments primarily engaged in (1) manufacturing nonpowered handsaws and/or (2) manufacturing saw blades, all types (including those for power sawing machines).

Cross-References.

Establishments primarily engaged in manufacturing handheld powered saws are classified in U.S. Industry 333991, Power-Driven Handtool Manufacturing.

332214 Kitchen Utensil, Pot, and Pan Manufacturing[US]

This U.S. industry comprises establishments primarily engaged in manufacturing metal kitchen utensils (except cutting-type), pots, and pans (except those manufactured by casting (e.g., cast iron skillets) or stamped without further fabrication).

Cross-References. Establishments primarily engaged in—

- Manufacturing finished cast metal kitchen utensils or castings for kitchen utensils—are classified in Industry Group 3315, Foundries;
- Manufacturing stampings for kitchen utensils, pots, and pans—are classified in U.S. Industry 332116, Metal Stamping; and

- Manufacturing metal cutting-type kitchen utensils—are classified in U.S. Industry 332211, Cutlery and Flatware (except Precious) Manufacturing.

3323 Architectural and Structural Metals Manufacturing

33231 Plate Work and Fabricated Structural Product Manufacturing

This industry comprises establishments primarily engaged in manufacturing one or more of the following: (1) prefabricated metal buildings, panels and sections; (2) structural metal products; and (3) metal plate work products.

Cross-References. Establishments primarily engaged in—

- Making manufactured homes (i.e., mobile homes) and prefabricated wood buildings—are classified in Industry 32199, All Other Wood Product Manufacturing;
- Constructing buildings, bridges, and other heavy construction projects on site—are classified in Sector 23, Construction;
- Building ships, boats and barges—are classified in Industry 33661, Ship and Boat Building;
- Manufacturing power boilers and heat exchangers—are classified in Industry 33241, Power Boiler and Heat Exchanger Manufacturing;
- Manufacturing heavy gauge tanks—are classified in Industry 33242, Metal Tank (Heavy Gauge) Manufacturing;
- Manufacturing metal plate cooling towers—are classified in Industry 33341, Ventilation, Heating, Air-Conditioning, and Commercial Refrigeration Equipment Manufacturing; and
- Manufacturing metal windows, doors, and studs—are classified in Industry 33232, Ornamental and Architectural Metal Products Manufacturing.

332311 Prefabricated Metal Building and Component Manufacturing[CAN]

This U.S. industry comprises establishments primarily engaged in manufacturing prefabricated metal buildings, panels, and sections.

Cross-References. Establishments primarily engaged in—

- Making manufactured homes (i.e., mobile homes) and prefabricated wood buildings—are classified in Industry 32199, All Other Wood Product Manufacturing;

- Constructing prefabricated buildings on site—are classified in Subsector 236, Construction of Buildings; and

- Manufacturing metal windows and doors—are classified in U.S. Industry 332321, Metal Window and Door Manufacturing.

332312 Fabricated Structural Metal Manufacturing[US]

This U.S. industry comprises establishments primarily engaged in fabricating structural metal products, such as concrete reinforcing bars and fabricated bar joists.

Cross-References. Establishments primarily engaged in—

- Manufacturing metal windows and doors—are classified in U.S. Industry 332321, Metal Window and Door Manufacturing;

- Manufacturing metal studs—are classified in U.S. Industry 332322, Sheet Metal Work Manufacturing;

- Constructing buildings, bridges, and other heavy construction projects on site—are classified in Sector 23, Construction;

- Building ships, boats and barges—are classified in Industry 33661, Ship and Boat Building; and

- Prefabricating metal buildings, panels, and sections—are classified in U.S. Industry 332311, Prefabricated Metal Building and Component Manufacturing.

332313 Plate Work Manufacturing[US]

This industry comprises establishments primarily engaged in manufacturing fabricated metal plate work by cutting, punching, bending, shaping, and welding purchased metal plate.

Cross-References. Establishments primarily engaged in—

- Manufacturing power boilers and heat exchangers—are classified in Industry 332410, Power Boiler and Heat Exchanger Manufacturing;

- Manufacturing heavy gauge tanks—are classified in Industry 332420, Metal Tank (Heavy Gauge) Manufacturing; and

- Manufacturing metal plate cooling towers—are classified in U.S. Industry 333415, Air-Conditioning and Warm Air Heating Equipment and Commercial and Industrial Refrigeration Equipment Manufacturing.

US—United States industry only. CAN—United States and Canadian industries are comparable. MEX—United States and Mexican industries are comparable. Blank—Canadian, Mexican, and United States industries are comparable.

33232 Ornamental and Architectural Metal Products Manufacturing

This industry comprises establishments primarily engaged in manufacturing one or more of the following: (1) metal framed windows (i.e., typically using purchased glass) and metal doors; (2) sheet metal work; and (3) ornamental and architectural metal products.

Cross-References. Establishments primarily engaged in—

- Manufacturing metal covered (i.e., clad) wood windows and doors—are classified in Industry 32191, Millwork;

- Manufacturing bins, cans, vats, and light tanks of sheet metal—are classified in Industry 33243, Metal Can, Box, and Other Metal Container (Light Gauge) Manufacturing;

- Manufacturing prefabricated metal buildings, panels, and sections—are classified in Industry 33231, Plate Work and Fabricated Structural Product Manufacturing;

- Fabricating sheet metal work on site—are classified in Subsector 238, Specialty Trade Contractors;

- Manufacturing metal stampings (except automotive, coins) and custom roll forming products—are classified in Industry 33211, Forging and Stamping;

- Manufacturing automotive stampings—are classified in Industry 33637, Motor Vehicle Metal Stamping; and

- Stamping coins—are classified in Industry 33991, Jewelry and Silverware Manufacturing.

332321 Metal Window and Door Manufacturing[CAN]

This U.S. industry comprises establishments primarily engaged in manufacturing metal framed windows (i.e., typically using purchased glass) and metal doors. Examples of products made by these establishments are metal door frames; metal framed window and door screens; and metal molding and trim (except automotive).

Cross-References. Establishments primarily engaged in—

- Manufacturing wood or metal covered (i.e., clad) wood framed windows and doors—are classified in U.S. Industry 321911, Wood Window and Door Manufacturing; and

- Manufacturing metal automotive molding and trim—are classified in Industry 336370, Motor Vehicle Metal Stamping.

US—United States industry only. CAN—United States and Canadian industries are comparable. MEX—United States and Mexican industries are comparable. Blank—Canadian, Mexican, and United States industries are comparable.

332322 Sheet Metal Work Manufacturing[US]

This U.S. industry comprises establishments primarily engaged in manufacturing sheet metal work (except stampings).

Cross-References. Establishments primarily engaged in—

- Manufacturing sheet metal bins, vats, and light tanks of sheet metal—are classified in U.S. Industry 332439, Other Metal Container Manufacturing;
- Manufacturing metal cans, lids, and ends—are classified in U.S. Industry 332431, Metal Can Manufacturing;
- Fabricating sheet metal work on site—are classified in Subsector 238, Specialty Trade Contractors;
- Manufacturing metal stampings (except automotive, coins) and custom roll forming products—are classified in Industry 33211, Forging and Stamping;
- Manufacturing automotive stampings—are classified in Industry 336370, Motor Vehicle Metal Stamping; and
- Stamping coins—are classified in U.S. Industry 339911, Jewelry (except Costume) Manufacturing.

332323 Ornamental and Architectural Metal Work Manufacturing[US]

This U.S. industry comprises establishments primarily engaged in manufacturing ornamental and architectural metal work, such as staircases, metal open steel flooring, fire escapes, railings, and scaffolding.

Cross-References.

Establishments primarily engaged in manufacturing prefabricated metal buildings, panels, and sections are classified in U.S. Industry 332311, Prefabricated Metal Building and Component Manufacturing.

3324 Boiler, Tank, and Shipping Container Manufacturing

33241 Power Boiler and Heat Exchanger Manufacturing
See industry description for 332410 below.

332410 Power Boiler and Heat Exchanger Manufacturing

This industry comprises establishments primarily engaged in manufacturing power boilers and heat exchangers. Establishments in this industry may perform installation in addition to manufacturing power boilers and heat exchangers.

Cross-References. Establishments primarily engaged in—

- Manufacturing heavy gauge metal tanks—are classified in Industry 332420, Metal Tank (Heavy Gauge) Manufacturing;
- Manufacturing steam or hot water low pressure heating boilers—are classified in U.S. Industry 333414, Heating Equipment (except Warm Air Furnaces) Manufacturing; and
- Installing power boilers and heat exchanges without manufacturing—are classified in Industry 238220, Plumbing, Heating, and Air-Conditioning Contractors.

33242 Metal Tank (Heavy Gauge) Manufacturing
See industry description for 332420 below.

332420 Metal Tank (Heavy Gauge) Manufacturing

This industry comprises establishments primarily engaged in cutting, forming, and joining heavy gauge metal to manufacture tanks, vessels, and other containers.

Cross-References. Establishments primarily engaged in—

- Manufacturing power boilers—are classified in Industry 332410, Power Boiler and Heat Exchanger Manufacturing;
- Manufacturing light gauge metal containers—are classified in Industry 33243, Metal Can, Box, and Other Metal Container (Light Gauge) Manufacturing; and
- Installing heavy gauge metal tanks without manufacturing—are classified in Industry 238120, Structural Steel and Precast Concrete Contractors.

33243 Metal Can, Box, and Other Metal Container (Light Gauge) Manufacturing

This industry comprises establishments primarily engaged in forming light gauge metal containers.

Cross-References. Establishments primarily engaged in—

- Manufacturing foil containers—are classified in Industry 33299, All Other Fabricated Metal Product Manufacturing;
- Reconditioning barrels and drums—are classified in Industry 81131, Commercial and Industrial Machinery and Equipment (except Automotive and Electronic) Repair and Maintenance; and

---

US—United States industry only. CAN—United States and Canadian industries are comparable. MEX—United States and Mexican industries are comparable. Blank—Canadian, Mexican, and United States industries are comparable.

- Manufacturing heavy gauge metal containers—are classified in Industry 33242, Metal Tank (Heavy Gauge) Manufacturing.

332431 Metal Can Manufacturing[CAN]

This U.S. industry comprises establishments primarily engaged in manufacturing metal cans, lids, and ends.

Cross-References. Establishments primarily engaged in—

- Manufacturing foil containers—are classified in U.S. Industry 332999, All Other Miscellaneous Fabricated Metal Product Manufacturing; and
- Manufacturing light gauge metal containers (except cans)—are classified in U.S. Industry 332439, Other Metal Container Manufacturing.

332439 Other Metal Container Manufacturing[CAN]

This U.S. industry comprises establishments primarily engaged in manufacturing metal (light gauge) containers (except cans).

Illustrative Examples:

Light gauge metal bins manufacturing
Light gauge metal drums manufacturing
Light gauge metal garbage cans manufacturing
Light gauge metal lunch boxes manufacturing
Light gauge metal mailboxes manufacturing
Light gauge metal tool boxes manufacturing
Light gauge metal vats manufacturing
Metal air cargo containers manufacturing
Metal barrels manufacturing
Vacuum bottles and jugs manufacturing

Cross-References. Establishments primarily engaged in—

- Manufacturing foil containers—are classified in U.S. Industry 332999, All Other Miscellaneous Fabricated Metal Product Manufacturing;
- Manufacturing metal cans—are classified in U.S. Industry 332431, Metal Can Manufacturing;
- Reconditioning barrels and drums—are classified in Industry 811310, Commercial and Industrial Machinery and Equipment (except Automotive and Electronic) Repair and Maintenance; and
- Manufacturing heavy gauge metal containers—are classified in Industry 332420, Metal Tank (Heavy Gauge) Manufacturing.

3325 Hardware Manufacturing

33251 Hardware Manufacturing

See industry description for 332510 below.

332510 Hardware Manufacturing

This industry comprises establishments primarily engaged in manufacturing metal hardware, such as metal hinges, metal handles, keys, and locks (except coin-operated, time locks).

Cross-References. Establishments primarily engaged in—

- Manufacturing bolts, nuts, screws, rivets, washers, hose clamps, and turnbuckles—are classified in U.S. Industry 332722, Bolt, Nut, Screw, Rivet, and Washer Manufacturing;
- Manufacturing nails and spikes from wire drawn elsewhere—are classified in U.S. Industry 332618, Other Fabricated Wire Product Manufacturing;
- Manufacturing metal furniture parts (except hardware)—are classified in U.S. Industry 337215, Showcase, Partition, Shelving, and Locker Manufacturing;
- Drawing wire and manufacturing nails and spikes—are classified in Subsector 331, Primary Metal Manufacturing;
- Manufacturing pole line and transmission hardware—are classified in U.S. Industry 335932, Noncurrent-Carrying Wiring Device Manufacturing;
- Manufacturing coin-operated locking mechanisms—are classified in U.S. Industry 333311, Automatic Vending Machine Manufacturing;
- Manufacturing time locks—are classified in U.S. Industry 334518, Watch, Clock, and Part Manufacturing;
- Manufacturing fireplace fixtures and equipment, traps, handcuffs and leg irons, ladder jacks, and other like metal products—are classified in U.S. Industry 332999, All Other Miscellaneous Fabricated Metal Product Manufacturing;
- Manufacturing fire hose nozzles and couplings—are classified in U.S. Industry 332919, Other Metal Valve and Pipe Fitting Manufacturing; and
- Manufacturing luggage and utility racks—are classified in U.S. Industry 336399, All Other Motor Vehicle Parts Manufacturing.

US—United States industry only. CAN—United States and Canadian industries are comparable. MEX—United States and Mexican industries are comparable. Blank—Canadian, Mexican, and United States industries are comparable.

3326 Spring and Wire Product Manufacturing

33261 Spring and Wire Product Manufacturing

This industry comprises establishments primarily engaged in (1) manufacturing steel springs by forming, such as cutting, bending, and heat winding, metal rod or strip stock and/or (2) manufacturing wire springs and fabricated wire products from wire drawn elsewhere (except watch and clock springs).

Cross-References. Establishments primarily engaged in—

- Manufacturing watch and clock springs from purchased wire—are classified in Industry 33451, Navigational, Measuring, Electromedical, and Control Instruments Manufacturing;

- Drawing wire and manufacturing wire products—are classified in Subsector 331, Primary Metal Manufacturing; and

- Manufacturing nonferrous insulated wire from wire drawn elsewhere—are classified in Industry 33592, Communication and Energy Wire and Cable Manufacturing.

332611 Spring (Heavy Gauge) Manufacturing[CAN]

This U.S. industry comprises establishments primarily engaged in manufacturing heavy gauge springs by forming, such as cutting, bending, and heat winding, rod or strip stock.

Cross-References. Establishments primarily engaged in—

- Manufacturing light gauge springs from purchased wire or strip—are classified in U.S. Industry 332612, Spring (Light Gauge) Manufacturing; and

- Drawing wire and manufacturing wire spring—are classified in Subsector 331, Primary Metal Manufacturing.

332612 Spring (Light Gauge) Manufacturing[US]

This U.S. industry comprises establishments primarily engaged in manufacturing light gauge springs from purchased wire or strip.

Cross-References. Establishments primarily engaged in—

- Manufacturing watch and clock springs—are classified in U.S. Industry 334518, Watch, Clock, and Part Manufacturing;

- Manufacturing heavy gauge springs—are classified in U.S. Industry 332611, Spring (Heavy Gauge) Manufacturing; and
- Drawing wire and manufacturing wire spring—are classified in Subsector 331, Primary Metal Manufacturing.

332618 Other Fabricated Wire Product Manufacturing[US]

This U.S. industry comprises establishments primarily engaged in manufacturing fabricated wire products (except springs) made from purchased wire.

Illustrative Examples:

Barbed wire made from purchased wire
Chain link fencing and fence gates made from purchased wire
Metal baskets made from purchased wire
Nails, brads, and staples made from purchased wire

Noninsulated wire cable made from purchased wire
Paper clips made from purchased wire
Woven wire cloth made from purchased wire

Cross-References. Establishments primarily engaged in—

- Drawing wire and manufacturing wire products—are classified in Subsector 331, Primary Metal Manufacturing;
- Manufacturing heavy gauge springs—are classified in U.S. Industry 332611, Spring (Heavy Gauge) Manufacturing;
- Manufacturing light gauge springs from purchased wire or strip—are classified in U.S. Industry 332612, Spring (Light Gauge) Manufacturing; and
- Insulating nonferrous wire from wire drawn elsewhere—are classified in U.S. Industry 335929, Other Communication and Energy Wire Manufacturing.

3327 Machine Shops; Turned Product; and Screw, Nut, and Bolt Manufacturing

33271 Machine Shops
See industry description for 332710 below.

332710 Machine Shops

This industry comprises establishments known as machine shops primarily engaged in machining metal parts on a job or order basis. Generally machine shop jobs are low volume using machine tools, such as lathes (including computer numerically controlled); automatic screw machines; and machines for boring, grinding, and milling.

Cross-References. Establishments primarily engaged in—

- Repairing industrial machinery and equipment—are classified in Industry 811310, Commercial and Industrial Machinery and Equipment (except Automotive and Electronic) Repair and Maintenance; and
- Manufacturing parts (except on a job or order basis) for machinery and equipment—are generally classified in the same manufacturing industry that makes complete machinery and equipment.

33272 Turned Product and Screw, Nut, and Bolt Manufacturing

This industry comprises establishments primarily engaged in (1) machining precision turned products or (2) manufacturing metal bolts, nuts, screws, rivets, and other industrial fasteners. Included in this industry are establishments primarily engaged in manufacturing parts for machinery and equipment on a customized basis.

Cross-References.

Establishments primarily engaged in manufacturing plastics fasteners are classified in Industry 32619, Other Plastics Product Manufacturing.

332721 Precision Turned Product Manufacturing[US]

This U.S. industry comprises establishments known as precision turned manufacturers primarily engaged in machining precision products of all materials on a job or order basis. Generally precision turned product jobs are large volume using machines, such as automatic screw machines, rotary transfer machines, computer numerically controlled (CNC) lathes, or turning centers.

Cross-References.

Establishments primarily engaged in manufacturing metal bolts, nuts, screws, rivets, washers, and other industrial fasteners on machines, such as headers, threaders, and nut forming machines, are classified in U.S. Industry 332722, Bolt, Nut, Screw, Rivet, and Washer Manufacturing.

332722 Bolt, Nut, Screw, Rivet, and Washer Manufacturing[US]

This U.S. industry comprises establishments primarily engaged in manufacturing metal bolts, nuts, screws, rivets, and washers, and other industrial fasteners using machines, such as headers, threaders, and nut forming machines.

Cross-References. Establishments primarily engaged in—

- Manufacturing precision turned products—are classified in U.S. Industry 332721, Precision Turned Product Manufacturing; and

- Plastics fasteners—are classified in U.S. Industry 326199, All Other Plastics Product Manufacturing.

3328   Coating, Engraving, Heat Treating, and Allied Activities

33281   Coating, Engraving, Heat Treating, and Allied Activities

This industry comprises establishments primarily engaged in one or more of the following: (1) heat treating metals and metal products; (2) enameling, lacquering, and varnishing metals and metal products; (3) hot dip galvanizing metals and metal products; (4) engraving, chasing, or etching metals and metal products (except jewelry; personal goods carried on or about the person, such as compacts and cigarette cases; precious metal products (except precious plated flatware and other plated ware); and printing plates); (5) powder coating metals and metal products; (6) electroplating, plating, anodizing, coloring, and finishing metals and metal products; and (7) providing other metal surfacing services for the trade. Establishments in this industry coat engravings and heat treat metals and metal formed products fabricated elsewhere.

Cross-References. Establishments primarily engaged in—

- Engraving, chasing or etching jewelry, metal personal goods, or precious (except precious plated) metal flatware and other plated ware—are classified in Industry 33991, Jewelry and Silverware Manufacturing;

- Engraving, chasing or etching printing plates—are classified in Industry 32312, Support Activities for Printing; and

- Both fabricating and coating, engraving, and heat treating metals and metal products—are classified in manufacturing according to the product made.

332811   Metal Heat Treating[US]

This U.S. industry comprises establishments primarily engaged in heat treating, such as annealing, tempering, and brazing, metals and metal products for the trade.

Cross-References.

Establishments primarily engaged in both fabricating and heat treating metal products are classified in the Manufacturing sector according to the product made.

332812 Metal Coating, Engraving (except Jewelry and Silverware), and Allied Services to Manufacturers[US]

This U.S. industry comprises establishments primarily engaged in one or more of the following: (1) enameling, lacquering, and varnishing metals and metal products; (2) hot dip galvanizing metals and metal products; (3) engraving, chasing, or etching metals and metal products (except jewelry; personal goods carried on or about the person, such as compacts and cigarette cases; precious metal products (except precious plated flatware and other plated ware); and printing plates); (4) powder coating metals and metal products; and (5) providing other metal surfacing services for the trade.

Cross-References. Establishments primarily engaged in—

- Both fabricating and coating and engraving products—are classified in the Manufacturing sector according to the product made;
- Engraving, chasing or etching jewelry, metal personal goods, or precious metal products (except precious plated metal flatware and other plated ware)—are classified in Industry 33991, Jewelry and Silverware Manufacturing; and
- Engraving, chasing or etching printing plates—are classified in U.S. Industry 323122, Prepress Services.

332813 Electroplating, Plating, Polishing, Anodizing, and Coloring[US]

This U.S. industry comprises establishments primarily engaged in electroplating, plating, anodizing, coloring, buffing, polishing, cleaning, and sandblasting metals and metal products for the trade.

Cross-References.

Establishments primarily engaged in both fabricating and electroplating, plating, polishing, anodizing, and coloring products are classified in the Manufacturing sector according to the product made.

3329 Other Fabricated Metal Product Manufacturing

This industry group comprises establishments primarily engaged in manufacturing fabricated metal products (except forgings and stampings, cutlery and handtools, architectural and structural metals, boilers, tanks, shipping containers, hardware, spring and wire products, machine shop products, turned products, screws, and nuts and bolts).

33291 Metal Valve Manufacturing

This industry comprises establishments primarily engaged in manufacturing one or more of the following metal valves: (1) industrial valves; (2) fluid power valves

---

US—United States industry only. CAN—United States and Canadian industries are comparable. MEX—United States and Mexican industries are comparable. Blank—Canadian, Mexican, and United States industries are comparable.

and hose fittings; (3) plumbing fixture fittings and trim; and (4) other metal valves and pipe fittings.

Cross-References. Establishments primarily engaged in—

- Manufacturing fluid power cylinder and pumps—are classified in Industry 33399, All Other General Purpose Machinery Manufacturing;

- Manufacturing intake and exhaust valves for internal combustion engines— are classified in Industry 33631, Motor Vehicle Gasoline Engine and Engine Parts Manufacturing;

- Manufacturing metal shower rods and metal couplings from purchased metal pipe—are classified in Industry 33299, All Other Fabricated Metal Product Manufacturing;

- Manufacturing plastics aerosol spray nozzles—are classified in Industry 32619, Other Plastics Product Manufacturing;

- Casting iron pipe fittings and couplings without machining—are classified in Industry 33151, Ferrous Metal Foundries; and

- Manufacturing plastics pipe fittings and couplings—are classified in Industry 32612, Plastics Pipe, Pipe Fitting, and Unlaminated Profile Shape Manufacturing.

332911 Industrial Valve Manufacturing^{US}

This U.S. industry comprises establishments primarily engaged in manufacturing industrial valves and valves for water works and municipal water systems.

Illustrative Examples:

Complete fire hydrants manufacturing
Industrial-type ball valves manufacturing
Industrial-type butterfly valves manufacturing
Industrial-type check valves manufacturing
Industrial-type gate valves manufacturing
Industrial-type globe valves manufacturing

Industrial-type plug valves manufacturing
Industrial-type solenoid valves (except fluid power) manufacturing
Industrial-type steam traps manufacturing
Valves for nuclear applications manufacturing

Cross-References. Establishments primarily engaged in—

- Manufacturing fluid power valves—are classified in U.S. Industry 332912, Fluid Power Valve and Hose Fitting Manufacturing; and

- Manufacturing plumbing and heating valves—are classified in U.S. Industry 332919, Other Metal Valve and Pipe Fitting Manufacturing.

332912 Fluid Power Valve and Hose Fitting Manufacturing[US]

This U.S. industry comprises establishments primarily engaged in manufacturing fluid power valves and hose fittings.

Illustrative Examples:

Fluid power aircraft subassemblies
Hydraulic and pneumatic hose and tube
Hose assemblies for fluid power systems
  fittings

Hydraulic and pneumatic valves

Cross-References. Establishments primarily engaged in—

- Manufacturing fluid power cylinders—are classified in U.S. Industry 333995, Fluid Power Cylinder and Actuator Manufacturing;
- Manufacturing fluid power pumps—are classified in U.S. Industry 333996, Fluid Power Pump and Motor Manufacturing;
- Manufacturing intake and exhaust valves for internal combustion engines— are classified in U.S. Industry 336311, Carburetor, Piston, Piston Ring, and Valve Manufacturing;
- Manufacturing industrial-type valves—are classified in U.S. Industry 332911, Industrial Valve Manufacturing; and
- Manufacturing plumbing and heating valves—are classified in U.S. Industry 332919, Other Metal Valve and Pipe Fitting Manufacturing.

332913 Plumbing Fixture Fitting and Trim Manufacturing[US]

This U.S. industry comprises establishments primarily engaged in manufacturing metal and plastics plumbing fixture fittings and trim, such as faucets, flush valves, and shower heads.

Cross-References. Establishments primarily engaged in—

- Manufacturing metal shower rods—are classified in U.S. Industry 332999, All Other Miscellaneous Fabricated Metal Product Manufacturing; and
- Manufacturing fire hose nozzles, lawn hose nozzles, water traps, and couplings—are classified in U.S. Industry 332919, Other Metal Valve and Pipe Fitting Manufacturing.

332919 Other Metal Valve and Pipe Fitting Manufacturing[US]

This U.S. industry comprises establishments primarily engaged in manufacturing metal valves (except industrial valves, fluid power valves, fluid power hose fittings, and plumbing fixture fittings and trim).

Illustrative Examples:

Aerosol valves manufacturing
Firefighting nozzles manufacturing
Lawn hose nozzles manufacturing
Lawn sprinklers manufacturing
Metal hose couplings (except fluid power) manufacturing

Metal pipe flanges and flange unions manufacturing
Plumbing and heating in-line valves (e.g., check, cutoff, stop) manufacturing

Cross-References. Establishments primarily engaged in—

- Manufacturing fluid power valves and hose fittings—are classified in U.S. Industry 332912, Fluid Power Valve and Hose Fitting Manufacturing;

- Manufacturing industrial valves—are classified in U.S. Industry 332911, Industrial Valve Manufacturing;

- Manufacturing plastics aerosol spray nozzles—are classified in U.S. Industry 326199, All Other Plastics Product Manufacturing;

- Casting iron pipe fittings and couplings without machining—are classified in U.S. Industry 331511, Iron Foundries;

- Manufacturing metal couplings from purchased metal pipe—are classified in U.S. Industry 332996, Fabricated Pipe and Pipe Fitting Manufacturing; and

- Manufacturing plastics pipe fittings and couplings—are classified in U.S. Industry 326122, Plastics Pipe and Pipe Fitting Manufacturing.

33299 All Other Fabricated Metal Product Manufacturing

This industry comprises establishments primarily engaged in manufacturing fabricated metal products (except forgings and stampings, cutlery and handtools, architectural and structural metal products, boilers, tanks, shipping containers, hardware, spring and wire products, machine shop products, turned products, screws, nuts and bolts, and metal valves).

Illustrative Examples:

Ammunition manufacturing
Ball and roller bearing manufacturing

Industrial pattern manufacturing
Metal safes manufacturing

Enameled iron and metal sanitary ware manufacturing

Fabricated pipe and pipe fittings made from purchased metal pipe

Foil container (except bags) manufacturing

Portable metal ladder manufacturing

Small arms and other ordnance manufacturing

Steel wool manufacturing

Cross-References. Establishments primarily engaged in—

- Manufacturing forging and stamping and powder metallurgy parts—are classified in Industry 33211, Forging and Stamping;

- Manufacturing cutlery and handtools—are classified in Industry 33221, Cutlery and Handtool Manufacturing;

- Manufacturing architectural and structural metals—are classified in Industry Group 3323, Architectural and Structural Metals Manufacturing;

- Manufacturing boilers, tanks, and shipping containers—are classified in Industry Group 3324, Boiler, Tank, and Shipping Container Manufacturing;

- Manufacturing hardware and safe and vault locks—are classified in Industry 33251, Hardware Manufacturing;

- Manufacturing spring and wire products—are classified in Industry 33261, Spring and Wire Product Manufacturing;

- Manufacturing machine shop products, turned products, screws, and nuts and bolts—are classified in Industry Group 3327, Machine Shops; Turned Product; and Screw, Nut, and Bolt Manufacturing;

- Coating, engraving, heat treating and allied activities—are classified in Industry 33281, Coating, Engraving, Heat Treating, and Allied Activities;

- Manufacturing plain bearings—are classified in Industry 33361, Engine, Turbine, and Power Transmission Equipment Manufacturing;

- Manufacturing military tanks—are classified in Industry 33699, Other Transportation Equipment Manufacturing;

- Manufacturing guided missiles—are classified in Industry 33641, Aerospace Product and Parts Manufacturing;

- Manufacturing cast iron pipe and fittings—are classified in Industry 33151, Ferrous Metal Foundries;

- Manufacturing pipe system fittings (except cast iron couplings and couplings made from purchased pipe) and metal aerosol spray nozzles—are classified in Industry 33291, Metal Valve Manufacturing;

- Manufacturing welded and seamless steel pipes from purchased steel—are classified in Industry 33121, Iron and Steel Pipe and Tube Manufacturing from Purchased Steel;

- Manufacturing plastics plumbing fixtures and plastics portable chemical toilets—are classified in Industry 32619, Other Plastics Product Manufacturing;

- Manufacturing vitreous and semivitreous pottery sanitary ware—are classified in Industry 32711, Pottery, Ceramics, and Plumbing Fixture Manufacturing;

- Manufacturing blasting caps, detonating caps, and safety fuses—are classified in Industry 32592, Explosives Manufacturing;

- Manufacturing fireworks—are classified in Industry 32599, All Other Chemical Product and Preparation Manufacturing;

- Manufacturing metal furniture frames—are classified in Industry 33721, Office Furniture (including Fixtures) Manufacturing;

- Manufacturing nonprecious metal trophies—are classified in Industry 33991, Jewelry and Silverware Manufacturing;

- Manufacturing metal mechanically refrigerated drinking fountains—are classified in Industry 33341, Ventilation, Heating, Air-Conditioning, and Commercial Refrigeration Equipment Manufacturing;

- Manufacturing metal foil bags—are classified in Industry 32222, Paper Bag and Coated and Treated Paper Manufacturing;

- Manufacturing aluminum foil—are classified in Industry 33131, Alumina and Aluminum Production and Processing;

- Manufacturing metal foil (except aluminum)—are classified in Industry Group 3314, Nonferrous Metal (except Aluminum) Production and Processing; and

- Manufacturing metal burial vaults—are classified in Industry 33999, All Other Miscellaneous Manufacturing.

332991 Ball and Roller Bearing Manufacturing

This U.S. industry comprises establishments primarily engaged in manufacturing ball and roller bearings of all materials.

Cross-References.

Establishments primarily engaged in manufacturing plain bearings are classified in U.S. Industry 333613, Mechanical Power Transmission Equipment Manufacturing.

332992 Small Arms Ammunition Manufacturing[US]

This U.S. industry comprises establishments primarily engaged in manufacturing small arms ammunition.

US—United States industry only. CAN—United States and Canadian industries are comparable. MEX—United States and Mexican industries are comparable. Blank—Canadian, Mexican, and United States industries are comparable.

Cross-References. Establishments primarily engaged in—

- Manufacturing ammunition (except small arms)—are classified in U.S. Industry 332993, Ammunition (except Small Arms) Manufacturing;
- Manufacturing blasting and detonating caps and safety fuses—are classified in Industry 325920, Explosives Manufacturing; and
- Manufacturing fireworks—are classified in U.S. Industry 325998, All Other Miscellaneous Chemical Product and Preparation Manufacturing.

332993 Ammunition (except Small Arms) Manufacturing^{US}

This U.S. industry comprises establishments primarily engaged in manufacturing ammunition (except small arms). Examples of products made by these establishments are bombs, depth charges, rockets (except guided missiles), grenades, mines, and torpedoes.

Cross-References. Establishments primarily engaged in—

- Manufacturing small arms ammunition—are classified in U.S. Industry 332992, Small Arms Ammunition Manufacturing;
- Manufacturing blasting and detonating caps and safety fuses—are classified in Industry 325920, Explosives Manufacturing;
- Manufacturing fireworks—are classified in U.S. Industry 325998, All Other Miscellaneous Chemical Product and Preparation Manufacturing; and
- Manufacturing guided missiles—are classified in U.S. Industry 336414, Guided Missile and Space Vehicle Manufacturing.

332994 Small Arms Manufacturing^{US}

This U.S. industry comprises establishments primarily engaged in manufacturing small firearms that are carried and fired by the individual.

Cross-References.

Establishments primarily engaged in manufacturing firearms (except small) are classified in U.S. Industry 332995, Other Ordnance and Accessories Manufacturing.

332995 Other Ordnance and Accessories Manufacturing^{US}

This U.S. industry comprises establishments primarily engaged in manufacturing ordnance (except small arms) and accessories.

US—United States industry only. CAN—United States and Canadian industries are comparable. MEX—United States and Mexican industries are comparable. Blank—Canadian, Mexican, and United States industries are comparable.

Cross-References. Establishments primarily engaged in—

- Manufacturing small arms—are classified in U.S. Industry 332994, Small Arms Manufacturing;

- Manufacturing military tanks—are classified in U.S. Industry 336992, Military Armored Vehicle, Tank, and Tank Component Manufacturing; and

- Manufacturing guided missiles—are classified in U.S. Industry 336414, Guided Missile and Space Vehicle Manufacturing.

332996 Fabricated Pipe and Pipe Fitting Manufacturing[US]

This U.S. industry comprises establishments primarily engaged in fabricating, such as cutting, threading and bending metal pipes and pipe fittings made from purchased metal pipe.

Cross-References. Establishments primarily engaged in—

- Manufacturing cast iron pipe and fittings—are classified in U.S. Industry 331511, Iron Foundries;

- Manufacturing pipe system fittings (except cast iron couplings)—are classified in U.S. Industry 332919, Other Metal Valve and Pipe Fitting Manufacturing; and

- Manufacturing welded and seamless steel pipes from purchased steel—are classified in Industry 331210, Iron and Steel Pipe and Tube Manufacturing from Purchased Steel.

332997 Industrial Pattern Manufacturing[US]

This U.S. industry comprises establishments primarily engaged in manufacturing industrial patterns.

332998 Enameled Iron and Metal Sanitary Ware Manufacturing[US]

This U.S. industry comprises establishments primarily engaged in manufacturing enameled iron and metal sanitary ware.

Cross-References. Establishments primarily engaged in—

- Manufacturing plastics plumbing fixtures—are classified in U.S. Industry 326191, Plastics Plumbing Fixture Manufacturing;

- Manufacturing vitreous and semivitreous pottery sanitary ware—are classified in U.S. Industry 327111, Vitreous China Plumbing Fixture and China and Earthenware Bathroom Accessories Manufacturing;

- Manufacturing plastics portable chemical toilets—are classified in U.S. Industry 326199, All Other Plastics Product Manufacturing; and

- Manufacturing metal mechanically refrigerated drinking fountains—are classified in U.S. Industry 333415, Air-Conditioning and Warm Air Heating Equipment and Commercial and Industrial Refrigeration Equipment Manufacturing.

332999 All Other Miscellaneous Fabricated Metal Product Manufacturing[US]

This U.S. industry comprises establishments primarily engaged in manufacturing fabricated metal products (except forgings and stampings, cutlery and handtools, architectural and structural metals, boilers, tanks, shipping containers, hardware, spring and wire products, machine shop products, turned products, screws, nuts and bolts, metal valves, ball and roller bearings, ammunition, small arms and other ordnances, fabricated pipes and pipe fittings, industrial patterns, and enameled iron and metal sanitary ware).

Illustrative Examples:

Foil containers (except bags) manufacturing
Metal hair curlers manufacturing
Metal ironing boards manufacturing
Metal pipe hangers and supports manufacturing
Metal pallets manufacturing

Metal safes manufacturing
Metal vaults (except burial) manufacturing
Permanent metallic magnets manufacturing
Portable metal ladders manufacturing
Steel wool manufacturing

Cross-References. Establishments primarily engaged in—

- Manufacturing forgings and stampings—are classified in Industry 33211, Forging and Stamping;

- Manufacturing cutlery and handtools—are classified in Industry 33221, Cutlery and Handtool Manufacturing;

- Manufacturing architectural and structural metals—are classified in Industry Group 3323, Architectural and Structural Metals Manufacturing;

- Manufacturing boilers, tanks, and shipping containers—are classified in Industry Group 3324, Boiler, Tank, and Shipping Container Manufacturing;

- Manufacturing hardware and safe and vault locks—are classified in Industry 332510, Hardware Manufacturing;

- Manufacturing spring and wire products—are classified in Industry 33261, Spring and Wire Product Manufacturing;

- Manufacturing machine shop products, turned products, screws, and nut and bolt—are classified in Industry Group 3327, Machine Shops; Turned Product; and Screw Nut, and Bolt Manufacturing;

- Coating, engraving, heat treating and allied activities—are classified in Industry 33281, Coating, Engraving, Heat Treating, and Allied Activities;

- Manufacturing ball and roller bearings—are classified in U.S. Industry 332991, Ball and Roller Bearing Manufacturing;

- Manufacturing small arms ammunition—are classified in U.S. Industry 332992, Small Arms Ammunition Manufacturing;

- Manufacturing ammunition (except small arms)—are classified in U.S. Industry 332993, Ammunition (except Small Arms) Manufacturing;

- Manufacturing small firearms that are carried and fired by the individual—are classified in U.S. Industry 332994, Small Arms Manufacturing;

- Manufacturing ordnances (except small) and accessories—are classified in U.S. Industry 332995, Other Ordnance and Accessories Manufacturing;

- Manufacturing metal pipes and pipe fittings from metal pipe produced elsewhere—are classified in U.S. Industry 332996, Fabricated Pipe and Pipe Fitting Manufacturing;

- Manufacturing cast iron pipe and fittings—are classified in U.S. Industry 331511, Iron Foundries;

- Manufacturing welded and seamless steel pipes from purchased steel—are classified in Industry 331210, Iron and Steel Pipe and Tube Manufacturing from Purchased Steel;

- Manufacturing metal furniture frames—are classified in U.S. Industry 337215, Showcase, Partition, Shelving, and Locker Manufacturing;

- Manufacturing powder metallurgy parts—are classified in U.S. Industry 332117, Powder Metallurgy Part Manufacturing;

- Manufacturing metal boxes—are classified in U.S. Industry 332439, Other Metal Container Manufacturing;

- Manufacturing metal nozzles, hose couplings, and aerosol valves—are classified in U.S. Industry 332919, Other Metal Valve and Pipe Fitting Manufacturing;

- Manufacturing nonprecious metal trophies—are classified in U.S. Industry 339914, Costume Jewelry and Novelty Manufacturing;

- Manufacturing metal foil bags—are classified in U.S. Industry 322223, Plastics, Foil, and Coated Paper Bag Manufacturing;

- Manufacturing aluminum foil—are classified in Industry 33131, Alumina and Aluminum Production and Processing;
- Manufacturing metal foil (except aluminum)—are classified in Industry Group 3314, Nonferrous Metal (except Aluminum) Production and Processing; and
- Manufacturing metal burial vaults—are classified in U.S. Industry 339995, Burial Casket Manufacturing.

333 Machinery Manufacturing

Industries in the Machinery Manufacturing subsector create end products that apply mechanical force, for example, the application of gears and levers, to perform work. Some important processes for the manufacture of machinery are forging, stamping, bending, forming, and machining that are used to shape individual pieces of metal. Processes, such as welding and assembling are used to join separate parts together. Although these processes are similar to those used in metal fabricating establishments, machinery manufacturing is different because it typically employs multiple metal forming processes in manufacturing the various parts of the machine. Moreover, complex assembly operations are an inherent part of the production process.

In general, design considerations are very important in machinery production. Establishments specialize in making machinery designed for particular applications. Thus, design is considered to be part of the production process for the purpose of implementing NAICS. The NAICS structure reflects this by defining industries and industry groups that make machinery for different applications. A broad distinction exists between machinery that is generally used in a variety of industrial applications (i.e., general purpose machinery) and machinery that is designed to be used in a particular industry (i.e., special purpose machinery). Three industry groups consist of special purpose machinery—Agricultural, Construction, and Mining Machinery Manufacturing; Industrial Machinery Manufacturing; and Commercial and Service Industry Machinery Manufacturing. The other industry groups make general-purpose machinery: Ventilation, Heating, Air Conditioning, and Commercial Refrigeration Equipment Manufacturing; Metalworking Machinery Manufacturing; Engine, Turbine, and Power Transmission Equipment Manufacturing; and Other General Purpose Machinery Manufacturing.

3331 Agriculture, Construction, and Mining Machinery Manufacturing

33311 Agricultural Implement Manufacturing

This industry comprises establishments primarily engaged in manufacturing farm machinery and equipment, powered mowing equipment and other powered home lawn and garden equipment.

Illustrative Examples:

Combines (i.e., harvester-threshers)
  manufacturing
Cotton ginning machinery manufacturing
Farm tractors and attachments
  manufacturing
Farm-type fertilizing machinery
  manufacturing
Haying machines manufacturing

Milking machines manufacturing
Powered lawnmowers manufacturing
Planting machines, farm-type,
  manufacturing
Poultry brooders, feeders, and waterers
  manufacturing
Residential-type snowblowers and
  throwers manufacturing

Cross-References. Establishments primarily engaged in—

- Manufacturing agricultural handtools and nonpowered lawnmowers—are classified in Industry 33221, Cutlery and Handtool Manufacturing;

- Manufacturing farm conveyors—are classified in Industry 33392, Material Handling Equipment Manufacturing; and

- Manufacturing forestry machinery and equipment, such as brush, limb and log chippers; log splitters; and equipment—are classified in Industry 33312, Construction Machinery Manufacturing.

333111   Farm Machinery and Equipment Manufacturing[US]

This U.S. industry comprises establishments primarily engaged in manufacturing agricultural and farm machinery and equipment, and other turf and grounds care equipment, including planting, harvesting, and grass mowing equipment (except lawn and garden-type).

Illustrative Examples:

Combines (i.e., harvester-threshers)
  manufacturing
Cotton ginning machinery manufacturing
Farm-type feed processing equipment
  manufacturing
Farm-type fertilizing machinery
  manufacturing
Farm-type planting machines
  manufacturing

Farm-type plows manufacturing
Farm-type tractors and attachments
  manufacturing
Haying machines manufacturing
Milking machines manufacturing
Poultry brooders, feeders, and waterers
  manufacturing

Cross-References. Establishments primarily engaged in—

- Manufacturing farm conveyors—are classified in U.S. Industry 333922, Conveyor and Conveying Equipment Manufacturing;

- Manufacturing tractors and lawnmowers for home lawn and garden care— are classified in U.S. Industry 333112, Lawn and Garden Tractor and Home Lawn and Garden Equipment Manufacturing; and

- Manufacturing construction-type tractors—are classified in Industry 333120, Construction Machinery Manufacturing.

333112 Lawn and Garden Tractor and Home Lawn and Garden Equipment Manufacturing[US]

This U.S. industry comprises establishments primarily engaged in manufacturing powered lawnmowers, lawn and garden tractors, and other home lawn and garden equipment, such as tillers, shredders, and yard vacuums and blowers.

Cross-References. Establishments primarily engaged in—

- Manufacturing commercial mowing and other turf and grounds care equipment—are classified in U.S. Industry 333111, Farm Machinery and Equipment Manufacturing; and

- Manufacturing nonpowered lawn and garden shears, edgers, pruners, and lawnmowers— are classified in U.S. Industry 332212, Hand and Edge Tool Manufacturing.

33312 Construction Machinery Manufacturing
See industry description for 333120 below.

333120 Construction Machinery Manufacturing

This industry comprises establishments primarily engaged in manufacturing construction machinery, surface mining machinery, and logging equipment.

Illustrative Examples:

Backhoes manufacturing	Pile-driving equipment manufacturing
Bulldozers manufacturing	Portable crushing, pulverizing, and
Construction and surface mining-type	screening machinery manufacturing
rock drill bits manufacturing	Powered post hole diggers manufacturing
Construction-type tractors and	Road graders manufacturing
attachments manufacturing	Surface mining machinery (except
Off-highway trucks manufacturing	drilling) manufacturing

Cross-References. Establishments primarily engaged in—

- Manufacturing drilling and underground mining machinery and equipment—are classified in Industry 33313, Mining and Oil and Gas Field Machinery Manufacturing;

- Manufacturing industrial plant overhead traveling cranes, hoists, truck-type cranes and hoists, winches, aerial work platforms, and automotive wrecker hoists—are classified in Industry 33392, Material Handling Equipment Manufacturing; and

- Manufacturing rail layers, ballast distributors and other railroad track-laying equipment— are classified in Industry 336510, Railroad Rolling Stock Manufacturing.

33313 Mining and Oil and Gas Field Machinery Manufacturing

This industry comprises establishments primarily engaged in manufacturing oil and gas field and underground mining machinery and equipment.

Illustrative Examples:

Coal breakers, cutters, and pulverizers manufacturing
Core drills, underground mining-type, manufacturing
Mineral processing and beneficiating machinery manufacturing
Mining cars manufacturing
Oil and gas field-type derricks manufacturing

Oil and gas field-type drilling machinery and equipment (except offshore floating platforms) manufacturing
Stationary rock crushing machinery manufacturing
Water well drilling machinery manufacturing

Cross-References. Establishments primarily engaged in—

- Manufacturing offshore oil and gas well drilling and production floating platforms—are classified in Industry 33661, Ship and Boat Building;

- Manufacturing surface mining machinery and equipment—are classified in Industry 33312, Construction Machinery Manufacturing;

- Manufacturing coal and ore conveyors—are classified in Industry 33392, Material Handling Equipment Manufacturing;

- Manufacturing underground mining locomotives—are classified in Industry 33651, Railroad Rolling Stock Manufacturing; and

- Manufacturing pumps and pumping equipment—are classified in Industry 33391, Pump and Compressor Manufacturing.

333131 Mining Machinery and Equipment Manufacturing[US]

This U.S. industry comprises establishments primarily engaged in (1) manufacturing underground mining machinery and equipment, such as coal breakers, mining cars, core drills, coal cutters, rock drills and (2) manufacturing mineral beneficiating machinery and equipment used in surface or underground mines.

Cross-References. Establishments primarily engaged in—

- Manufacturing surface mining machinery and equipment—are classified in Industry 333120, Construction Machinery Manufacturing;
- Manufacturing well-drilling machinery—are classified in U.S. Industry 333132, Oil and Gas Field Machinery and Equipment Manufacturing;
- Manufacturing coal and ore conveyors—are classified in U.S. Industry 333922, Conveyor and Conveying Equipment Manufacturing; and
- Manufacturing underground mining locomotives—are classified in Industry 336510, Railroad Rolling Stock Manufacturing.

333132 Oil and Gas Field Machinery and Equipment Manufacturing[US]

This U.S. industry comprises establishments primarily engaged in (1) manufacturing oil and gas field machinery and equipment, such as oil and gas field drilling machinery and equipment; oil and gas field production machinery and equipment; and oil and gas field derricks and (2) manufacturing water well drilling machinery.

Cross-References. Establishments primarily engaged in—

- Manufacturing offshore oil and gas well drilling and production floating platforms—are classified in U.S. Industry 336611, Ship Building and Repairing;
- Manufacturing underground mining drills—are classified in U.S. Industry 333131, Mining Machinery and Equipment Manufacturing; and
- Manufacturing pumps and pumping equipment—are classified in U.S. Industry 333911, Pump and Pumping Equipment Manufacturing.

3332 Industrial Machinery Manufacturing

33321 Sawmill and Woodworking Machinery Manufacturing
See industry description for 333210 below.

333210 Sawmill and Woodworking Machinery Manufacturing

This industry comprises establishments primarily engaged in manufacturing sawmill and woodworking machinery (except handheld), such as circular and band sawing equipment, planing machinery, and sanding machinery.

US—United States industry only. CAN—United States and Canadian industries are comparable. MEX—United States and Mexican industries are comparable. Blank—Canadian, Mexican, and United States industries are comparable.

Cross-References. Establishments primarily engaged in—

- Manufacturing planes, axes, drawknives, and handsaws—are classified in Industry 33221, Cutlery and Handtool Manufacturing; and
- Manufacturing power-driven handtools—are classified in U.S. Industry 333991, Power-Driven Handtool Manufacturing.

33322 Plastics and Rubber Industry Machinery Manufacturing
See industry description for 333220 below.

333220 Plastics and Rubber Industry Machinery Manufacturing

This industry comprises establishments primarily engaged in manufacturing plastics and rubber products making machinery, such as plastics compression, extrusion and injection molding machinery and equipment, and tire building and recapping machinery and equipment.

Cross-References.

Establishments primarily engaged in manufacturing industrial metal molds for plastics and rubber products making machinery are classified in U.S. Industry 333511, Industrial Mold Manufacturing.

33329 Other Industrial Machinery Manufacturing

This industry comprises establishments primarily engaged in manufacturing industrial machinery (except agricultural and farm-type, construction, mining, sawmill and woodworking, and plastics and rubber products making machinery).

Illustrative Examples:

Bakery ovens manufacturing
Chemical processing machinery and equipment manufacturing
Glass making machinery (e.g., blowing, forming, molding) manufacturing
Paper making machinery manufacturing
Petroleum refinery machinery manufacturing
Printing presses (except textile) manufacturing
Semiconductor making machinery manufacturing
Sewing machines (including household-type) manufacturing
Tannery machinery manufacturing
Textile making machinery (except sewing machines) manufacturing

Cross-References. Establishments primarily engaged in—

- Manufacturing agricultural and farm-type, construction, and mining machinery—are classified in Industry Group 3331, Agriculture, Construction, and Mining Machinery Manufacturing;

- Manufacturing sawmill and woodworking machinery—are classified in Industry 33321, Sawmill and Woodworking Machinery Manufacturing;

- Manufacturing plastics and rubber products making machinery—are classified in Industry 33322, Plastics and Rubber Industry Machinery Manufacturing;

- Manufacturing food and beverage packaging machinery—are classified in Industry 33399, All Other General Purpose Machinery Manufacturing;

- Manufacturing commercial and industrial refrigeration and freezer equipment—are classified in Industry 33341, Ventilation, Heating, Air-Conditioning, and Commercial Refrigeration Equipment Manufacturing;

- Manufacturing commercial-type cooking and food warming equipment, automotive maintenance equipment (except mechanics' handtools) and photocopiers—are classified in Industry 33331, Commercial and Service Industry Machinery Manufacturing; and

- Manufacturing mechanics' handtools—are classified in Industry 33221, Cutlery and Handtool Manufacturing.

333291 Paper Industry Machinery Manufacturing[CAN]

This U.S. industry comprises establishments primarily engaged in manufacturing paper industry machinery for making paper and paper products, such as pulp making machinery, paper and paperboard making machinery, and paper and paperboard converting machinery.

Cross-References.

Establishments primarily engaged in manufacturing printing machinery are classified in U.S. Industry 333293, Printing Machinery and Equipment Manufacturing.

333292 Textile Machinery Manufacturing[MEX]

This U.S. industry comprises establishments primarily engaged in manufacturing textile machinery for making thread, yarn, and fiber.

Illustrative Examples:

Drawing machinery for textiles manufacturing
Extruding machinery for yarn manufacturing
Finishing machinery for textiles manufacturing

Knitting machinery manufacturing
Spinning machinery for textiles manufacturing
Texturizing machinery for textiles manufacturing
Weaving machinery manufacturing

US—United States industry only. CAN—United States and Canadian industries are comparable. MEX—United States and Mexican industries are comparable. Blank—Canadian, Mexican, and United States industries are comparable.

Cross-References.

Establishments primarily engaged in manufacturing sewing machines are classified in U.S. Industry 333298, All Other Industrial Machinery Manufacturing.

333293 Printing Machinery and Equipment Manufacturing[MEX]

This U.S. industry comprises establishments primarily engaged in manufacturing printing and bookbinding machinery and equipment, such as printing presses, typesetting machinery, and bindery machinery.

Cross-References. Establishments primarily engaged in—

- Manufacturing textile printing machinery—are classified in U.S. Industry 333292, Textile Machinery Manufacturing; and

- Manufacturing photocopiers—are classified in U.S. Industry 333315, Photographic and Photocopying Equipment Manufacturing.

333294 Food Product Machinery Manufacturing[US]

This U.S. industry comprises establishments primarily engaged in manufacturing food and beverage manufacturing-type machinery and equipment, such as dairy product plant machinery and equipment (e.g., homogenizers, pasteurizers, ice cream freezers), bakery machinery and equipment (e.g., dough mixers, bake ovens, pastry rolling machines), meat and poultry processing and preparation machinery, and other commercial food products machinery (e.g., slicers, choppers, and mixers).

Cross-References. Establishments primarily engaged in—

- Manufacturing food and beverage packaging machinery—are classified in U.S. Industry 333993, Packaging Machinery Manufacturing;

- Manufacturing commercial and industrial refrigeration and freezer equipment—are classified in U.S. Industry 333415, Air Conditioning and Warm Air Heating Equipment and Commercial and Industrial Refrigeration Equipment Manufacturing; and

- Manufacturing commercial-type cooking and food warming equipment—are classified in U.S. Industry 333319, Other Commercial and Service Industry Machinery Manufacturing.

333295 Semiconductor Machinery Manufacturing[US]

This U.S. industry comprises establishments primarily engaged in manufacturing wafer processing equipment, semiconductor assembly and packaging equipment, and other semiconductor making machinery.

Cross-References. Establishments primarily engaged in—

- Manufacturing printed circuit board manufacturing machinery—are classified in U.S. Industry 333298, All Other Industrial Machinery Manufacturing; and

- Manufacturing semiconductor testing instruments—are classified in U.S. Industry 334515, Instrument Manufacturing for Measuring and Testing Electricity and Electrical Signals.

333298 All Other Industrial Machinery Manufacturing[US]

This U.S. industry comprises establishments primarily engaged in manufacturing industrial machinery (except agricultural and farm-type, construction and mining machinery, sawmill and woodworking machinery, plastics and rubber making machinery, paper and paperboard making machinery, textile machinery, printing machinery and equipment, food manufacturing-type machinery, and semiconductor making machinery).

Illustrative Examples:

Chemical processing machinery and
equipment manufacturing
Cigarette making machinery
manufacturing
Circuit board making machinery
manufacturing
Glass making machinery (e.g., blowing,
forming, molding) manufacturing
Light bulb and tube (i.e., electric lamp)
machinery manufacturing

Petroleum refining machinery
manufacturing
Sewing machines (including household-
type) manufacturing
Shoe making and repairing machinery
manufacturing
Tannery machinery manufacturing
Wire and cable insulating machinery
manufacturing

Cross-References. Establishments primarily engaged in—

- Manufacturing agricultural and farm-type, construction, and mining machinery—are classified in Industry Group 3331, Agriculture, Construction, and Mining Machinery Manufacturing;

- Manufacturing sawmill and woodworking machinery—are classified in Industry 333210, Sawmill and Woodworking Machinery Manufacturing;

- Manufacturing plastics and rubber products making machinery—are classified in Industry 333220, Plastics and Rubber Industry Machinery Manufacturing;

- Manufacturing paper and paperboard making machinery—are classified in U.S. Industry 333291, Paper Industry Machinery Manufacturing;

- Manufacturing textile machinery—are classified in U.S. Industry 333292, Textile Machinery Manufacturing;

- Manufacturing printing and bookbinding machinery and equipment—are classified in U.S. Industry 333293, Printing Machinery and Equipment Manufacturing;

- Manufacturing food and beverage manufacturing-type machinery—are classified in U.S. Industry 333294, Food Product Machinery Manufacturing;

- Manufacturing semiconductor making machinery—are classified in U.S. Industry 333295, Semiconductor Machinery Manufacturing;

- Manufacturing automotive maintenance equipment (except mechanics' handtools)—are classified in U.S. Industry 333319, Other Commercial and Service Industry Machinery Manufacturing; and

- Manufacturing mechanics' handtools—are classified in U.S. Industry 332212, Hand and Edge Tool Manufacturing.

3333 Commercial and Service Industry Machinery Manufacturing

33331 Commercial and Service Industry Machinery Manufacturing

This industry comprises establishments primarily engaged in manufacturing commercial and service machinery, such as automatic vending machinery, commercial laundry and dry-cleaning machinery, office machinery, photographic and photocopying machinery, optical instruments and machinery, automotive maintenance equipment (except mechanic's handtools), industrial vacuum cleaners, and commercial-type cooking equipment.

Cross-References. Establishments primarily engaged in—

- Manufacturing household-type appliances—are classified in Industry Group 3352, Household Appliance Manufacturing;

- Manufacturing computer and peripheral equipment (including point-of-sale terminals and funds transfer devices (ATMs))—are classified in Industry 33411, Computer and Peripheral Equipment Manufacturing;

- Manufacturing facsimile equipment—are classified in Industry 33421, Telephone Apparatus Manufacturing;

- Manufacturing timeclocks, timestamps, and electron and proton microscopes—are classified in Industry 33451, Navigational, Measuring, Electromedical, and Control Instruments Manufacturing;

- Manufacturing pencil sharpeners and staplers—are classified in Industry 33994, Office Supplies (except Paper) Manufacturing;

- Manufacturing sensitized film, paper, cloth, and plates, and prepared photographic chemicals—are classified in Industry 32599, All Other Chemical Product and Preparation Manufacturing;

- Manufacturing ophthalmic focus lenses—are classified in Industry 33911, Medical Equipment and Supplies Manufacturing;
- Manufacturing television, video, and digital cameras—are classified in Subsector 334, Computer and Electronic Product Manufacturing;
- Manufacturing coin-operated arcade games—are classified in Industry 33999, All Other Miscellaneous Manufacturing;
- Manufacturing mechanics' handtools—are classified in Industry 33221, Cutlery and Handtool Manufacturing;
- Manufacturing molded plastics lens blanks—are classified in Industry 32619, Other Plastics Product Manufacturing; and
- Manufacturing molded glass lens blanks—are classified in Industry 32721, Glass and Glass Product Manufacturing.

333311 Automatic Vending Machine Manufacturing^{US}

This U.S. industry comprises establishments primarily engaged in (1) manufacturing coin, token, currency or magnetic card operated vending machines and/or (2) manufacturing coin operated mechanism for machines, such as vending machines, lockers, and laundry machines.

Cross-References.
Establishments primarily engaged in manufacturing coin-operated arcade games are classified in U.S. Industry 339999, All Other Miscellaneous Manufacturing.

333312 Commercial Laundry, Drycleaning, and Pressing Machine Manufacturing^{US}

This U.S. industry comprises establishments primarily engaged in manufacturing commercial and industrial laundry and drycleaning equipment and pressing machines.

Cross-References.
Establishments primarily engaged in manufacturing household-type laundry equipment are classified in U.S. Industry 335224, Household Laundry Equipment Manufacturing.

333313 Office Machinery Manufacturing^{US}

This U.S. industry comprises establishments primarily engaged in manufacturing office machinery (except computers and photocopying equipment), such as mailhandling machinery and equipment, calculators, typewriters, and dedicated word processing equipment.

Cross-References. Establishments primarily engaged in—

- Manufacturing computers and peripheral (including point-of-sale terminals and automatic teller machines (ATMs)) equipment—are classified in Industry 33411, Computer and Peripheral Equipment Manufacturing;

- Manufacturing photocopy equipment—are classified in U.S. Industry 333315, Photographic and Photocopying Equipment Manufacturing;

- Manufacturing facsimile equipment—are classified in Industry 334210, Telephone Apparatus Manufacturing;

- Manufacturing timeclocks and timestamps—are classified in U.S. Industry 334518, Watch, Clock, and Part Manufacturing; and

- Manufacturing pencil sharpeners, staplers, staple removers, hand paper punches, cutters, trimmers, and other hand office equipment—are classified in U.S. Industry 339942, Lead Pencil and Art Good Manufacturing.

333314 Optical Instrument and Lens Manufacturing[US]

This U.S. industry comprises establishments primarily engaged in one or more of the following: (1) manufacturing optical instruments and lens, such as binoculars, microscopes (except electron, proton), telescopes, prisms, and lenses (except ophthalmic); (2) coating or polishing lenses (except ophthalmic); and (3) mounting lenses (except ophthalmic).

Cross-References. Establishments primarily engaged in—

- Manufacturing ophthalmic focus lenses—are classified in U.S. Industry 339115, Ophthalmic Goods Manufacturing;

- Manufacturing electron and proton microscopes—are classified in U.S. Industry 334516, Analytical Laboratory Instrument Manufacturing;

- Manufacturing molded plastics lens blanks—are classified in U.S. Industry 326199, All Other Plastics Product Manufacturing; and

- Manufacturing molded glass lens blanks—are classified in U.S. Industry 327212, Other Pressed and Blown Glass and Glassware Manufacturing.

333315 Photographic and Photocopying Equipment Manufacturing[US]

This U.S. industry comprises establishments primarily engaged in manufacturing photographic and photocopying equipment, such as cameras (except television,

---

US—United States industry only. CAN—United States and Canadian industries are comparable. MEX—United States and Mexican industries are comparable. Blank—Canadian, Mexican, and United States industries are comparable.

video and digital) projectors , film developing equipment, photocopying equipment, and microfilm equipment.

Cross-References. Establishments primarily engaged in—

- Manufacturing sensitized film, paper, cloth, and plates, and prepared photographic chemicals—are classified in U.S. Industry 325992, Photographic Film, Paper, Plate, and Chemical Manufacturing;
- Manufacturing photographic lenses—are classified in U.S. Industry 333314, Optical Instrument and Lens Manufacturing; and
- Manufacturing television, video, and digital cameras—are classified in Subsector 334, Computer and Electronic Product Manufacturing.

333319 Other Commercial and Service Industry Machinery Manufacturing[US]

This U.S. industry comprises establishments primarily engaged in manufacturing commercial and service industry equipment (except automatic vending machines, commercial laundry, drycleaning and pressing machines, office machinery, optical instruments and lenses, and photographic and photocopying equipment).

Illustrative Examples:

Carnival and amusement park rides manufacturing
Carwashing machinery manufacturing
Commercial-type coffee makers and urns manufacturing
Commercial-type cooking equipment (i.e., fryers, microwave ovens, ovens, ranges) manufacturing
Industrial and commercial-type vacuum cleaners manufacturing

Mechanical carpet sweepers manufacturing
Motor vehicle alignment equipment manufacturing
Power washer cleaning equipment manufacturing
Teaching machines (e.g., flight simulators) manufacturing
Water treatment equipment manufacturing

Cross-References. Establishments primarily engaged in—

- Manufacturing automatic vending machines—are classified in U.S. Industry 333311, Automatic Vending Machine Manufacturing;
- Manufacturing commercial laundry drycleaning and pressing machines—are classified in U.S. Industry 333312, Commercial Laundry, Drycleaning, and Pressing Machine Manufacturing;
- Manufacturing office machinery—are classified in U.S. Industry 333313, Office Machinery Manufacturing;

- Manufacturing optical instruments and lenses—are classified in U.S. Industry 333314, Optical Instrument and Lens Manufacturing;

- Manufacturing photographic and photocopying equipment—are classified in U.S. Industry 333315, Photographic and Photocopying Equipment Manufacturing;

- Manufacturing household-type appliances—are classified in Industry Group 3352, Household Appliance Manufacturing; and

- Manufacturing mechanics' handtools—are classified in U.S. Industry 332212, Hand and Edge Tool Manufacturing.

3334 Ventilation, Heating, Air-Conditioning, and Commercial Refrigeration Equipment Manufacturing

33341 Ventilation, Heating, Air-Conditioning, and Commercial Refrigeration Equipment Manufacturing

This industry comprises establishments primarily engaged in manufacturing ventilating, heating, air-conditioning, and commercial and industrial refrigeration and freezer equipment.

Illustrative Examples:

Air-conditioning and warm air heating combination units manufacturing
Air-conditioner filters manufacturing
Attic fans manufacturing
Dust and fume collecting equipment manufacturing
Gas fireplaces manufacturing
Heating boilers manufacturing

Industrial and commercial-type fans manufacturing
Refrigerated counter and display cases manufacturing
Refrigerated drinking fountains manufacturing
Space heaters (except portable electric) manufacturing

Cross-References. Establishments primarily engaged in—

- Manufacturing household-type fans (except attic), portable electric space heaters, humidifiers, dehumidifiers, and air purification equipment—are classified in Industry 33521, Small Electrical Appliance Manufacturing;

- Manufacturing household-type appliances, such as cooking stoves, ranges, refrigerators, and freezers—are classified in Industry 33522, Major Appliance Manufacturing;

- Manufacturing commercial-type cooking equipment—are classified in Industry 33329, Other Industrial Machinery Manufacturing;

- Manufacturing industrial, power, and marine boilers—are classified in Industry 33241, Power Boiler and Heat Exchanger Manufacturing;
- Manufacturing industrial process furnaces and ovens—are classified in Industry 33399, All Other General Purpose Machinery Manufacturing; and
- Manufacturing motor vehicle air-conditioning systems and compressors— are classified in Industry 33639, Other Motor Vehicle Parts Manufacturing.

333411 Air Purification Equipment Manufacturing[US]

This U.S. industry comprises establishments primarily engaged in manufacturing stationary air purification equipment, such as industrial dust and fume collection equipment, electrostatic precipitation equipment, warm air furnace filters, air washers, and other dust collection equipment.

Cross-References. Establishments primarily engaged in—

- Manufacturing air-conditioning units (except motor vehicle)—are classified in U.S. Industry 333415, Air-Conditioning and Warm Air Heating Equipment and Commercial and Industrial Refrigeration Equipment Manufacturing;
- Manufacturing motor vehicle air-conditioning systems and compressors— are classified in U.S. Industry 336391, Motor Vehicle Air-Conditioning Manufacturing;
- Manufacturing household-type fans (except attic) and portable air purification equipment—are classified in U.S. Industry 335211, Electric Housewares and Household Fan Manufacturing; and
- Manufacturing industrial and commercial blowers, industrial and commercial exhaust and ventilating fans, and attic fans—are classified in U.S. Industry 333412, Industrial and Commercial Fan and Blower Manufacturing.

333412 Industrial and Commercial Fan and Blower Manufacturing[US]

This U.S. industry comprises establishments primarily engaged in manufacturing attic fans and industrial and commercial fans and blowers, such as commercial exhaust fans and commercial ventilating fans.

Cross-References. Establishments primarily engaged in—

- Manufacturing air-conditioning units (except motor vehicle)—are classified in U.S. Industry 333415, Air-Conditioning and Warm Air Heating Equipment and Commercial and Industrial Refrigeration Equipment Manufacturing;

US—United States industry only. CAN—United States and Canadian industries are comparable. MEX—United States and Mexican industries are comparable. Blank—Canadian, Mexican, and United States industries are comparable.

- Manufacturing motor vehicle air-conditioning systems and compressors—are classified in U.S. Industry 336391, Motor Vehicle Air-Conditioning Manufacturing;

- Manufacturing household-type fans (except attic) and portable air purification equipment—are classified in U.S. Industry 335211, Electric Housewares and Household Fan Manufacturing; and

- Manufacturing stationary air purification equipment—are classified in U.S. Industry 333411, Air Purification Equipment Manufacturing.

333414 Heating Equipment (except Warm Air Furnaces) Manufacturing[US]

This U.S. industry comprises establishments primarily engaged in manufacturing heating equipment (except electric and warm air furnaces), such as heating boilers, heating stoves, floor and wall furnaces, and wall and baseboard heating units.

Cross-References. Establishments primarily engaged in—

- Manufacturing warm air furnaces—are classified in U.S. Industry 333415, Air-Conditioning and Warm Air Heating Equipment and Commercial and Industrial Refrigeration Equipment Manufacturing;

- Manufacturing electric space heaters—are classified in U.S. Industry 335211, Electric Housewares and Household Fan Manufacturing;

- Manufacturing household-type cooking stoves and ranges—are classified in U.S. Industry 335221, Household Cooking Appliance Manufacturing;

- Manufacturing industrial, power, and marine boilers—are classified in Industry 332410, Power Boiler and Heat Exchanger Manufacturing;

- Manufacturing industrial process furnaces and ovens—are classified in U.S. Industry 333994, Industrial Process Furnace and Oven Manufacturing; and

- Manufacturing commercial-type cooking equipment—are classified in U.S. Industry 333319, Other Commercial and Service Industry Machinery Manufacturing.

333415 Air-Conditioning and Warm Air Heating Equipment and Commercial and Industrial Refrigeration Equipment Manufacturing[US]

This U.S. industry comprises establishments primarily engaged in (1) manufacturing air-conditioning (except motor vehicle) and warm air furnace equipment and/or (2) manufacturing commercial and industrial refrigeration and freezer equipment.

US—United States industry only. CAN—United States and Canadian industries are comparable. MEX—United States and Mexican industries are comparable. Blank—Canadian, Mexican, and United States industries are comparable.

Illustrative Examples:

Air-conditioning and warm air heating combination units manufacturing

Air-conditioning compressors (except motor vehicle) manufacturing

Air-conditioning condensers and condensing units manufacturing

Dehumidifiers (except portable electric) manufacturing

Heat pumps manufacturing

Humidifying equipment (except portable) manufacturing

Refrigerated counter and display cases manufacturing

Refrigerated drinking fountains manufacturing

Soda fountain cooling and dispensing equipment manufacturing

Snow making machinery manufacturing

Cross-References. Establishments primarily engaged in—

- Manufacturing motor vehicle air-conditioning systems and compressors—are classified in U.S. Industry 336391, Motor Vehicle Air-Conditioning Manufacturing;

- **Manufacturing** household-type refrigerators and freezers—are classified in **U.S.** Industry 335222, Household Refrigerator and Home Freezer Manufacturing;

- Manufacturing portable electric space heaters, humidifiers, and dehumidifiers—are classified in U.S. Industry 335211, Electric Housewares and Household Fan Manufacturing;

- Manufacturing heating boilers, heating stoves, floor and wall mount furnaces, and electric wall and baseboard heating units—are classified in U.S. Industry 333414, Heating Equipment (except Warm Air Furnaces) Manufacturing; and

- Manufacturing furnace air filters—are classified in U.S. Industry 333411, Air Purification Equipment Manufacturing.

3335 Metalworking Machinery Manufacturing

33351 Metalworking Machinery Manufacturing

This industry comprises establishments primarily engaged in manufacturing metalworking machinery, such as metal cutting and metal forming machine tools; cutting tools; and accessories for metalworking machinery; special dies, tools, jigs, and fixtures; industrial molds; rolling mill machinery; assembly machinery; coil handling, conversion, or straightening equipment; and wire drawing and fabricating machines.

Cross-References. Establishments primarily engaged in—

- Manufacturing handtools (except power-driven), cutting dies (except metal cutting), sawblades, and handsaws—are classified in Industry 33221, Cutlery and Handtool Manufacturing;

- Manufacturing casting molds for heavy steel ingots—are classified in Industry 33151, Ferrous Metal Foundries; and

- Manufacturing power-driven handtools and welding and soldering equipment—are classified in Industry 33399, All Other General Purpose Machinery Manufacturing.

333511 Industrial Mold Manufacturing^{CAN}

This U.S. industry comprises establishments primarily engaged in manufacturing industrial molds for casting metals or forming other materials, such as plastics, glass, or rubber.

Cross-References.

Establishments primarily engaged in manufacturing casting molds for steel ingots are classified in U.S. Industry 331511, Iron Foundries.

333512 Machine Tool (Metal Cutting Types) Manufacturing^{US}

This U.S. industry comprises establishments primarily engaged in manufacturing metal cutting machine tools (except handtools).

Illustrative Examples:

Home workshop metal cutting machine tools (except handtools, welding equipment) manufacturing
Metalworking boring machines manufacturing
Metalworking buffing and polishing machines manufacturing
Metalworking drilling machines manufacturing
Metalworking grinding machines manufacturing
Metalworking lathes manufacturing
Metalworking milling machines manufacturing

Cross-References. Establishments primarily engaged in—

- Manufacturing welding and soldering equipment—are classified in U.S. Industry 333992, Welding and Soldering Equipment Manufacturing;

- Manufacturing metal-forming machine tools—are classified in U.S. Industry 333513, Machine Tool (Metal Forming Types) Manufacturing;

- Manufacturing power-driven metal cutting handtools—are classified in U.S. Industry 333991, Power-Driven Handtool Manufacturing; and

- Manufacturing accessories and attachments for metal cutting machine tools—are classified in U.S. Industry 333515, Cutting Tool and Machine Tool Accessory Manufacturing.

US—United States industry only. CAN—United States and Canadian industries are comparable. MEX—United States and Mexican industries are comparable. Blank—Canadian, Mexican, and United States industries are comparable.

333513 Machine Tool (Metal Forming Types) Manufacturing[US]

This U.S. industry comprises establishments primarily engaged in manufacturing metal forming machine tools (except handtools), such as punching, sheering, bending, forming, pressing, forging and die-casting machines.

Cross-References. Establishments primarily engaged in—

- Manufacturing welding and soldering equipment—are classified in U.S. Industry 333992, Welding and Soldering Equipment Manufacturing;

- Manufacturing metal-cutting machine tools—are classified in U.S. Industry 333512, Machine Tool (Metal Cutting Types) Manufacturing;

- Manufacturing power-driven handtools—are classified in U.S. Industry 333991, Power-Driven Handtool Manufacturing;

- Manufacturing rolling mill machinery and equipment—are classified in U.S. Industry 333516, Rolling Mill Machinery and Equipment Manufacturing; and

- Manufacturing accessories and attachments for metal forming machine tools—are classified in U.S. Industry 333515, Cutting Tool and Machine Tool Accessory Manufacturing.

333514 Special Die and Tool, Die Set, Jig, and Fixture Manufacturing[US]

This U.S. industry comprises establishments, known as tool and die shops, primarily engaged in manufacturing special tools and fixtures, such as cutting dies and jigs.

Cross-References. Establishments primarily engaged in—

- Manufacturing molds for die-casting and foundry casting; and metal molds for plaster working, rubber working, plastics working, and glass working machinery—are classified in U.S. Industry 333511, Industrial Mold Manufacturing;

- Manufacturing molds for heavy steel ingots—are classified in U.S. Industry 331511, Iron Foundries; and

- Manufacturing cutting dies for materials other than metal—are classified in U.S. Industry 332212, Hand and Edge Tool Manufacturing.

333515 Cutting Tool and Machine Tool Accessory Manufacturing[US]

This U.S. industry comprises establishments primarily engaged in manufacturing accessories and attachments for metal cutting and metal forming machine tools.

US—United States industry only. CAN—United States and Canadian industries are comparable. MEX—United States and Mexican industries are comparable. Blank—Canadian, Mexican, and United States industries are comparable.

Illustrative Examples:

Knives and bits for metalworking lathes, planers, and shapers manufacturing
Measuring attachments (e.g., sine bars) for machine tool manufacturing
Metalworking drill bits
Taps and dies (i.e., machine tool accessories) manufacturing

Cross-References. Establishments primarily engaged in—

- Manufacturing accessories and attachments for cutting and forming machines (except metal cutting, metal forming machinery)—are classified in U.S. Industry 332212, Hand and Edge Tool Manufacturing; and

- Manufacturing saw blades and handsaws—are classified in U.S. Industry 332213, Saw Blade and Handsaw Manufacturing.

333516 Rolling Mill Machinery and Equipment Manufacturing[US]

This U.S. industry comprises establishments primarily engaged in manufacturing rolling mill machinery and equipment for metal production.

333518 Other Metalworking Machinery Manufacturing[US]

This U.S. industry comprises establishments primarily engaged in manufacturing metal working machinery (except industrial molds; metal cutting machine tools; metal forming machine tools; special dies and tools, die sets, jigs, and fixtures; cutting tools and machine tool accessories; and rolling mill machinery and equipment).

Illustrative Examples:

Assembly machines manufacturing
Cradle assemblies machinery (i.e., wire making equipment) manufacturing
Metalworking coil winding and cutting machinery manufacturing
Wire drawing and fabricating machinery and equipment (except dies) manufacturing

Cross-References. Establishments primarily engaged in—

- Manufacturing industrial molds—are classified in U.S. Industry 333511, Industrial Mold Manufacturing;

- Manufacturing metal cutting machinery—are classified in U.S. Industry 333512, Machine Tool (Metal Cutting Types) Manufacturing;

- Manufacturing metal forming machinery—are classified in U.S. Industry 333513, Machine Tool (Metal Forming Types) Manufacturing;

- Manufacturing special dies and tools, die sets, jigs, and fixtures—are classified in U.S. Industry 333514, Special Die and Tool, Die Set, Jig, and Fixture Manufacturing;

- Manufacturing cutting tools and machine tool accessories—are classified in U.S. Industry 333515, Cutting Tool and Machine Tool Accessory Manufacturing; and

- Manufacturing rolling mill machinery—are classified in U.S. Industry 333516, Rolling Mill Machinery and Equipment Manufacturing.

3336 Engine, Turbine, and Power Transmission Equipment Manufacturing

33361 Engine, Turbine, and Power Transmission Equipment Manufacturing

This industry comprises establishments primarily engaged in manufacturing turbines, power transmission equipment, and internal combustion engines (except automotive gasoline and aircraft).

Illustrative Examples:

Clutches and brakes (except electromagnetic industrial controls, motor vehicle) manufacturing
Diesel and semidiesel engines manufacturing
Electric outboard motors manufacturing
Plain bearings (except internal combustion engine) manufacturing
Plain bushings (except internal combustion engine) manufacturing

Power transmission pulleys manufacturing
Speed changers (i.e., power transmission equipment) manufacturing
Speed reducers (i.e., power transmission equipment) manufacturing
Turbine generator set units manufacturing
Universal joints (except aircraft, motor vehicle) manufacturing

Cross-References. Establishments primarily engaged in—

- Manufacturing motor vehicle power transmission equipment—are classified in Industry 33635, Motor Vehicle Transmission and Power Train Parts Manufacturing;

- Manufacturing aircraft engines and aircraft power transmission equipment—are classified in Industry 33641, Aerospace Product and Parts Manufacturing;

- Manufacturing ball and roller bearings—are classified in Industry 33299, All Other Fabricated Metal Product Manufacturing;

US—United States industry only. CAN—United States and Canadian industries are comparable. MEX—United States and Mexican industries are comparable. Blank—Canadian, Mexican, and United States industries are comparable.

- Manufacturing automotive engines (except diesel)—are classified in Industry 33631, Motor Vehicle Gasoline Engine and Engine Parts Manufacturing; and
- Manufacturing electric power transmission, electric power distribution equipment, generators, or prime mover generator sets (except turbines)—are classified in Industry 33531, Electrical Equipment Manufacturing.

333611 Turbine and Turbine Generator Set Units Manufacturing[CAN]

This U.S. industry comprises establishments primarily engaged in manufacturing turbines (except aircraft); and complete turbine generator set units, such as steam, hydraulic, gas, and wind.

Cross-References. Establishments primarily engaged in—

- Manufacturing aircraft turbines—are classified in U.S. Industry 336412, Aircraft Engine and Engine Parts Manufacturing; and
- Manufacturing generators or prime mover generator sets (except turbines)—are classified in U.S. Industry 335312, Motor and Generator Manufacturing.

333612 Speed Changer, Industrial High-Speed Drive, and Gear Manufacturing[US]

This U.S. industry comprises establishments primarily engaged in manufacturing gears, speed changers, and industrial high-speed drives (except hydrostatic).

Cross-References. Establishments primarily engaged in—

- Manufacturing motor vehicle power transmission equipment—are classified in Industry 336350, Motor Vehicle Transmission and Power Train Parts Manufacturing;
- Manufacturing aircraft power transmission equipment—are classified in U.S. Industry 336413, Other Aircraft Parts and Auxiliary Equipment Manufacturing; and
- Manufacturing industrial hydrostatic transmissions—are classified in U.S. Industry 333996, Fluid Power Pump and Motor Manufacturing.

333613 Mechanical Power Transmission Equipment Manufacturing[US]

This U.S. industry comprises establishments primarily engaged in manufacturing mechanical power transmission equipment (except motor vehicle and aircraft), such as plain bearings, clutches (except motor vehicle and electromagnetic industrial control), couplings, joints, and drive chains.

US—United States industry only. CAN—United States and Canadian industries are comparable. MEX—United States and Mexican industries are comparable. Blank—Canadian, Mexican, and United States industries are comparable.

Cross-References. Establishments primarily engaged in—

- Manufacturing motor vehicle power transmission equipment—are classified in Industry 336350, Motor Vehicle Transmission and Power Train Parts Manufacturing;
- Manufacturing aircraft power transmission equipment—are classified in U.S. Industry 336413, Other Aircraft Parts and Auxiliary Equipment Manufacturing;
- Manufacturing ball and roller bearings—are classified in U.S. Industry 332991, Ball and Roller Bearing Manufacturing; and
- Manufacturing gears, speed changers, and industrial high-speed drives (except hydrostatic)—are classified in U.S. Industry 333612, Speed Changer, Industrial High-Speed Drive, and Gear Manufacturing.

333618 Other Engine Equipment Manufacturing[US]

This U.S. industry comprises establishments primarily engaged in manufacturing internal combustion engines (except automotive gasoline and aircraft).

Cross-References. Establishments primarily engaged in—

- Manufacturing gasoline motor vehicle engines and motor vehicle transmissions—are classified in Industry Group 3363, Motor Vehicle Parts Manufacturing;
- Manufacturing gasoline aircraft engines and aircraft transmissions—are classified in Industry 33641, Aerospace Product and Parts Manufacturing;
- Manufacturing turbine and turbine generator sets units—are classified in U.S. Industry 333611, Turbine and Turbine Generator Set Units Manufacturing;
- Manufacturing speed changers and industrial high-speed drivers and gears—are classified in U.S. Industry 333612, Speed Changer, Industrial High-Speed Drive, and Gear Manufacturing; and
- Manufacturing mechanical power transmission equipment (except motor vehicle and aircraft)—are classified in U.S. Industry 333613, Mechanical Power Transmission Equipment Manufacturing.

3339 Other General Purpose Machinery Manufacturing

33391 Pump and Compressor Manufacturing

This industry comprises establishments primarily engaged in manufacturing pumps and compressors, such as general purpose air and gas compressors, nonagricultural spraying and dusting equipment, general purpose pumps and pumping equipment (except fluid power pumps and motors), and measuring and dispensing pumps.

Cross-References. Establishments primarily engaged in—

- Manufacturing fluid power pumps and motors and handheld pneumatic spray guns—are classified in Industry 33399, All Other General Purpose Machinery Manufacturing;
- Manufacturing agricultural spraying and dusting equipment—are classified in Industry 33311, Agricultural Implement Manufacturing;
- Manufacturing laboratory vacuum pumps—are classified in Industry 33911, Medical Equipment and Supplies Manufacturing;
- Manufacturing pumps and air-conditioning systems and compressors for motor vehicles—are classified in Industry Group 3363, Motor Vehicle Parts Manufacturing; and
- Manufacturing air-conditioning systems and compressors (except motor vehicle)—are classified in Industry 33341, Ventilation, Heating, Air-Conditioning, and Commercial Refrigeration Equipment Manufacturing.

333911 Pump and Pumping Equipment Manufacturing[US]

This U.S. industry comprises establishments primarily engaged in manufacturing general purpose pumps and pumping equipment (except fluid power pumps and motors), such as reciprocating pumps, turbine pumps, centrifugal pumps, rotary pumps, diaphragm pumps, domestic water system pumps, oil well and oil field pumps and sump pumps.

Cross-References. Establishments primarily engaged in—

- Manufacturing fluid power pumps and motors—are classified in U.S. Industry 333996, Fluid Power Pump and Motor Manufacturing;
- Manufacturing measuring and dispensing pumps—are classified in U.S. Industry 333913, Measuring and Dispensing Pump Manufacturing;
- Manufacturing vacuum pumps (except laboratory)—are classified in U.S. Industry 333912, Air and Gas Compressor Manufacturing;
- Manufacturing laboratory vacuum pumps—are classified in U.S. Industry 339111, Laboratory Apparatus and Furniture Manufacturing; and
- Manufacturing fluid pumps for motor vehicles, such as oil pumps, water pumps, and power steering pumps—are classified in Industry Group 3363, Motor Vehicle Parts Manufacturing.

333912 Air and Gas Compressor Manufacturing[US]

This U.S. industry comprises establishments primarily engaged in manufacturing general purpose air and gas compressors, such as reciprocating compressors, centrifugal compressors, vacuum pumps (except laboratory), and nonagricultural spraying and dusting compressors and spray gun units.

Cross-References. Establishments primarily engaged in—

- Manufacturing refrigeration and air-conditioning (except motor vehicle) systems and compressors—are classified in U.S. Industry 333415, Air-Conditioning and Warm Air Heating Equipment and Commercial and Industrial Refrigeration Equipment Manufacturing;
- Manufacturing motor vehicle air-conditioning systems and compressors—are classified in U.S. Industry 336391, Motor Vehicle Air-Conditioning Manufacturing;
- Manufacturing fluid power pumps and motors—are classified in U.S. Industry 333996, Fluid Power Pump and Motor Manufacturing;
- Manufacturing agricultural spraying and dusting equipment—are classified in U.S. Industry 333111, Farm Machinery and Equipment Manufacturing;
- Manufacturing laboratory vacuum pumps—are classified in U.S. Industry 339111, Laboratory Apparatus and Furniture Manufacturing; and
- Manufacturing handheld pneumatic spray guns—are classified in U.S. Industry 333991, Power-Driven Handtool Manufacturing.

333913 Measuring and Dispensing Pump Manufacturing[US]

This U.S. industry comprises establishments primarily engaged in manufacturing measuring and dispensing pumps, such as gasoline pumps and lubricating oil measuring and dispensing pumps.

Cross-References.

Establishments primarily engaged in manufacturing pumps and pumping equipment for general industrial use are classified in U.S. Industry 333911, Pump and Pumping Equipment Manufacturing.

33392 Material Handling Equipment Manufacturing

This industry comprises establishments primarily engaged in manufacturing material handling equipment, such as elevators and moving stairs; conveyors and

---

US—United States industry only. CAN—United States and Canadian industries are comparable. MEX—United States and Mexican industries are comparable. Blank—Canadian, Mexican, and United States industries are comparable.

conveying equipment; overhead traveling cranes, hoists, and monorail systems; and industrial trucks, tractors, trailers, and stacker machinery.

Cross-References. Establishments primarily engaged in—

- Manufacturing motor vehicle-type trailers—are classified in Industry 33621, Motor Vehicle Body and Trailer Manufacturing;
- Manufacturing farm-type tractors—are classified in Industry 33311, Agricultural Implement Manufacturing;
- Manufacturing construction-type tractors and cranes—are classified in Industry 33312, Construction Machinery Manufacturing; and
- Manufacturing power transmission pulleys—are classified in Industry 33361, Engine, Turbine, and Power Transmission Equipment Manufacturing.

333921 Elevator and Moving Stairway Manufacturing[US]

This U.S. industry comprises establishments primarily engaged in manufacturing elevators and moving stairways.

Illustrative Examples:

Automobile lifts (i.e., garage-type, service station) manufacturing	Moving walkways manufacturing
Escalators manufacturing	Passenger and freight elevators manufacturing

Cross-References.

Establishments primarily engaged in manufacturing commercial conveyor systems and equipment are classified in U.S. Industry 333922, Conveyor and Conveying Equipment Manufacturing.

333922 Conveyor and Conveying Equipment Manufacturing[US]

This U.S. industry comprises establishments primarily engaged in manufacturing conveyors and conveying equipment, such as gravity conveyors, trolley conveyors, tow conveyors, pneumatic tube conveyors, carousel conveyors, farm conveyors, and belt conveyors.

Cross-References. Establishments primarily engaged in—

- Manufacturing passenger or freight elevators, dumbwaiters, and moving stairways—are classified in U.S. Industry 333921, Elevator and Moving Stairway Manufacturing; and

---

- Manufacturing overhead traveling cranes and monorail systems—are classified in U.S. Industry 333923, Overhead Traveling Crane, Hoist, and Monorail System Manufacturing.

333923 Overhead Traveling Crane, Hoist, and Monorail System Manufacturing[US]

This U.S. industry comprises establishments primarily engaged in manufacturing overhead traveling cranes, hoists, and monorail systems.

Illustrative Examples:

Aerial work platforms manufacturing
Automobile wrecker (i.e., tow truck) hoists manufacturing
Block and tackle manufacturing
Metal pulleys (except power transmission) manufacturing
Winches manufacturing

Cross-References. Establishments primarily engaged in—

- Manufacturing construction-type cranes—are classified in Industry 333120, Construction Machinery Manufacturing;

- Manufacturing aircraft loading hoists—are classified in U.S. Industry 333924, Industrial Truck, Tractor, Trailer, and Stacker Machinery Manufacturing; and

- Manufacturing power transmission pulleys—are classified in U.S. Industry 333613, Mechanical Power Transmission Equipment Manufacturing.

333924 Industrial Truck, Tractor, Trailer, and Stacker Machinery Manufacturing[US]

This U.S. industry comprises establishments primarily engaged in manufacturing industrial trucks, tractors, trailers, and stackers (i.e., truck-type), such as forklifts, pallet loaders and unloaders, and portable loading docks.

Cross-References. Establishments primarily engaged in—

- Manufacturing motor vehicle-type trailers—are classified in U.S. Industry 336212, Truck Trailer Manufacturing;

- Manufacturing farm-type tractors—are classified in U.S. Industry 333111, Farm Machinery and Equipment Manufacturing; and

- Manufacturing construction-type tractors—are classified in Industry 333120, Construction Machinery Manufacturing.

US—United States industry only. CAN—United States and Canadian industries are comparable. MEX—United States and Mexican industries are comparable. Blank—Canadian, Mexican, and United States industries are comparable.

33399 All Other General Purpose Machinery Manufacturing

This industry comprises establishments primarily engaged in manufacturing general purpose machinery (except ventilation, heating, air-conditioning, and commercial refrigeration equipment; metal working machinery; engines, turbines, and power transmission equipment; pumps and compressors; and material handling equipment).

Illustrative Examples:

Automatic fire sprinkler systems
  manufacturing
Bridge and gate lifting machinery
  manufacturing
Fluid power cylinders manufacturing
Fluid power pumps manufacturing
Hydraulic and pneumatic jacks
  manufacturing

Industrial-type furnaces manufacturing
Packaging machinery manufacturing
Power-driven handtools manufacturing
Scales (except laboratory-type)
  manufacturing
Welding equipment manufacturing

Cross-References. Establishments primarily engaged in—

- Manufacturing ventilating, heating, air-conditioning (except motor vehicle), commercial refrigeration, and furnace filters—are classified in Industry 33341, Ventilation, Heating, Air-Conditioning, and Commercial Refrigeration Equipment Manufacturing;

- Manufacturing metalworking machinery—are classified in Industry Group 3335, Metalworking Machinery Manufacturing;

- Manufacturing engine, turbine, and power transmission equipment—are classified in Industry Group 3336, Engine, Turbine, and Power Transmission Equipment Manufacturing;

- Manufacturing pumps and compressors—are classified in Industry 33391, Pump and Compressor Manufacturing;

- Manufacturing material handling equipment—are classified in Industry 33392, Material Handling Equipment Manufacturing;

- Manufacturing motor vehicle air-conditioning systems and compressors, engine filters, and pumps—are classified in Industry Group 3363, Motor Vehicle Parts Manufacturing;

- Manufacturing laboratory scales, balances, ovens, and furnaces—are classified in Industry 33911, Medical Equipment and Supplies Manufacturing;

- Manufacturing metal cutting and metal forming machinery—are classified in Industry 33351, Metalworking Machinery Manufacturing;

- Manufacturing power driven heavy construction and mining hand operated tools, such as tampers and augers—are classified in Industries 33312, Construction Machinery Manufacturing and 33313, Mining and Oil and Gas Field Machinery Manufacturing;
- Manufacturing bakery ovens and industrial kilns, such as cement, wood, and chemical—are classified in Industry 33329, Other Industrial Machinery Manufacturing;
- Manufacturing mechanical jacks, handheld soldering irons, countersink bits, drill bits, router bits, milling cutters, and other machine tools for woodcutting—are classified in Industry 33221, Cutlery and Handtool Manufacturing;
- Manufacturing carnival amusement park equipment, automotive maintenance equipment, and coin-operated vending machines—are classified in Industry 33331, Commercial and Service Industry Machinery Manufacturing; and
- Manufacturing transformers for arc-welding—are classified in Industry 33531, Electrical Equipment Manufacturing.

333991 Power-Driven Handtool Manufacturing[US]

This U.S. industry comprises establishments primarily engaged in manufacturing power-driven (e.g., battery, corded, pneumatic) handtools, such as drills, screwguns, circular saws, chain saws, staplers, and nailers.

Cross-References. Establishments primarily engaged in—
- Manufacturing metal cutting-type and metal forming-type machines (including home workshop)—are classified in Industry 33351, Metalworking Machinery Manufacturing;
- Manufacturing countersink bits, drill bits, router bits, milling cutters, and other machine tools for woodcutting—are classified in U.S. Industry 332212, Hand and Edge Tool Manufacturing;
- Manufacturing power-driven heavy construction or mining hand operated tools, such as tampers, jackhammers, and augers—are classified in Industries 333120, Construction Machinery Manufacturing and 33313, Mining and Oil and Gas Field Machinery Manufacturing; and
- Manufacturing powered home lawn and garden equipment—are classified in U.S. Industry 333112, Lawn and Garden Tractor and Home Lawn and Garden Equipment Manufacturing.

333992 Welding and Soldering Equipment Manufacturing[US]

This U.S. industry comprises establishments primarily engaged in manufacturing welding and soldering equipment and accessories (except transformers), such as arc, resistance, gas, plasma, laser, electron beam, and ultrasonic welding equipment; welding electrodes; coated or cored welding wire; and soldering equipment (except handheld).

Cross-References. Establishments primarily engaged in—

- Manufacturing handheld soldering irons—are classified in U.S. Industry 332212, Hand and Edge Tool Manufacturing; and

- Manufacturing transformers for arc-welding—are classified in U.S. Industry 335311, Power, Distribution, and Specialty Transformer Manufacturing.

333993 Packaging Machinery Manufacturing[US]

This U.S. industry comprises establishments primarily engaged in manufacturing packaging machinery, such as wrapping, bottling, canning, and labeling machinery.

333994 Industrial Process Furnace and Oven Manufacturing[US]

This U.S. Industry comprises establishments primarily engaged in manufacturing industrial process furnaces, ovens, induction and dielectric heating equipment, and kilns (except cement, chemical, wood).

Cross-References. Establishments primarily engaged in—

- Manufacturing bakery ovens—are classified in U.S. Industry 333294, Food Product Machinery Manufacturing;

- Manufacturing cement, wood, and chemical kilns—are classified in U.S. Industry 333298, All Other Industrial Machinery Manufacturing;

- Manufacturing cremating ovens—are classified in U.S. Industry 333999, All Other Miscellaneous General Purpose Machinery Manufacturing; and

- Manufacturing laboratory furnaces and ovens—are classified in U.S. Industry 339111, Laboratory Apparatus and Furniture Manufacturing.

333995 Fluid Power Cylinder and Actuator Manufacturing[US]

This U.S. industry comprises establishments primarily engaged in manufacturing fluid power (i.e., hydraulic and pneumatic) cylinders and actuators.

333996 Fluid Power Pump and Motor Manufacturing[US]

This U.S. industry comprises establishments primarily engaged in manufacturing fluid power (i.e., hydraulic and pneumatic) pumps and motors.

Cross-References. Establishments primarily engaged in—

- Manufacturing fluid pumps for motor vehicles, such as oil pumps, water pumps, and power steering pumps—are classified in Industry Group 3363, Motor Vehicle Parts Manufacturing;
- Manufacturing general purpose pumps (except fluid power)—are classified in U.S. Industry 333911, Pump and Pumping Equipment Manufacturing; and
- Manufacturing air compressors—are classified in U.S. Industry 333912, Air and Gas Compressor Manufacturing.

333997 Scale and Balance (except Laboratory) Manufacturing[US]

This U.S. industry comprises establishments primarily engaged in manufacturing scales and balances (except laboratory).

Cross-References.

Establishments primarily engaged in manufacturing laboratory scales and balances are classified in U.S. Industry 339111, Laboratory Apparatus and Furniture Manufacturing.

333999 All Other Miscellaneous General Purpose Machinery Manufacturing[US]

This U.S. industry comprises establishments primarily engaged in manufacturing general purpose machinery (except ventilating, heating, air-conditioning, and commercial refrigeration equipment; metal working machinery; engines, turbines, and power transmission equipment; pumps and compressors; material handling equipment; power-driven handtools; welding and soldering equipment; packaging machinery; industrial process furnaces and ovens; fluid power cylinders and actuators; fluid power pumps and motors; and scales and balances).

Illustrative Examples:

Automatic fire sprinkler systems manufacturing
Baling machinery (e.g., paper, scrap metal) manufacturing
Bridge and gate lifting machinery manufacturing
Cremating ovens manufacturing
General purpose-type sieves and screening equipment manufacturing

Hydraulic and pneumatic jacks manufacturing
Industrial and general line filters (except internal combustion engine, warm air furnace) manufacturing
Industrial-type centrifuges manufacturing

Cross-References. Establishments primarily engaged in—

- Manufacturing ventilating, heating, air-conditioning (except motor vehicle), and commercial refrigeration—are classified in Industry 33341, Ventilation, Heating, Air-Conditioning, and Commercial Refrigeration Equipment Manufacturing;

- Manufacturing motor vehicle air-conditioning systems and compressors— are classified in U.S. Industry 336391, Motor Vehicle Air-Conditioning Manufacturing;

- Manufacturing metalworking machinery—are classified in Industry Group 3335, Metalworking Machinery Manufacturing;

- Manufacturing engine, turbine, and power transmission equipment—are classified in Industry Group 3336, Engine, Turbine, and Power Transmission Equipment Manufacturing;

- Manufacturing pumps and compressors—are classified in Industry 33391, Pump and Compressor Manufacturing;

- Manufacturing material handling equipment—are classified in Industry 33392, Material Handling Equipment Manufacturing;

- Manufacturing power-driven handtools—are classified in U.S. Industry 333991, Power-Driven Handtool Manufacturing;

- Manufacturing welding and soldering equipment (except handheld soldering irons)—are classified in U.S. Industry 333992, Welding and Soldering Equipment Manufacturing;

- Manufacturing packaging machinery—are classified in U.S. Industry 333993, Packaging Machinery Manufacturing;

- Manufacturing bakery ovens and cement, wood, and chemical kilns—are classified in U.S. Industry 333298, All Other Industrial Machinery Manufacturing;

- Manufacturing industrial process furnaces and ovens (except bakery)—are classified in U.S. Industry 333994, Industrial Process Furnace and Oven Manufacturing;

- Manufacturing fluid power cylinders and actuators—are classified in U.S. Industry 333995, Fluid Power Cylinder and Actuator Manufacturing;

- Manufacturing fluid power pumps and motors—are classified in U.S. Industry 333996, Fluid Power Pump and Motor Manufacturing;

- Manufacturing scales and balances (except laboratory)—are classified in U.S. Industry 333997, Scale and Balance (except Laboratory) Manufacturing;

- Manufacturing carnival and amusement park equipment, automotive maintenance equipment and coin-operated vending machines—are classified in Industry 33331, Commercial and Service Industry Machinery Manufacturing;
- Manufacturing motor vehicle engine filters and pumps—are classified in Industry Group 3363, Motor Vehicle Parts Manufacturing; and
- Manufacturing mechanical jacks—are classified in U.S. Industry 332212, Hand and Edge Tool Manufacturing.

334 Computer and Electronic Product Manufacturing

Industries in the Computer and Electronic Product Manufacturing subsector group establishments that manufacture computers, computer peripherals, communications equipment, and similar electronic products, and establishments that manufacture components for such products. The Computer and Electronic Product Manufacturing industries have been combined in the hierarchy of NAICS because of the economic significance they have attained. Their rapid growth suggests that they will become even more important to the economies of all three North American countries in the future, and in addition their manufacturing processes are fundamentally different from the manufacturing processes of other machinery and equipment. The design and use of integrated circuits and the application of highly specialized miniaturization technologies are common elements in the production technologies of the computer and electronic subsector. Convergence of technology motivates this NAICS subsector. Digitalization of sound recording, for example, causes both the medium (the compact disc) and the equipment to resemble the technologies for recording, storing, transmitting, and manipulating data. Communications technology and equipment have been converging with computer technology. When technologically-related components are in the same sector, it makes it easier to adjust the classification for future changes, without needing to redefine its basic structure. The creation of the Computer and Electronic Product Manufacturing subsector will assist in delineating new and emerging industries because the activities that will serve as the probable sources of new industries, such as computer manufacturing and communications equipment manufacturing, or computers and audio equipment, are brought together. As new activities emerge, they are less likely therefore, to cross the subsector boundaries of the classification.

3341 Computer and Peripheral Equipment Manufacturing

33411 Computer and Peripheral Equipment Manufacturing

This industry comprises establishments primarily engaged in manufacturing and/ or assembling electronic computers, such as mainframes, personal computers, workstations, laptops, and computer servers; and computer peripheral equipment, such as storage devices, printers, monitors, input/output devices and terminals. Computers can be analog, digital, or hybrid. Digital computers, the most common type, are devices that do all of the following: (1) store the processing program or programs and the data immediately necessary for the execution of the program; (2) can be freely programmed in accordance with the requirements of the user; (3) perform arithmetical computations specified by the user; and (4) execute, without human intervention, a processing program that requires the computer to modify its execution by logical decision during the processing run. Analog computers are capable of simulating mathematical models and comprise at least analog, control, and programming elements.

Cross-References. Establishments primarily engaged in—

- Manufacturing digital telecommunications switches, local area network and wide area network communications equipment, such as bridges, routers, and gateways—are classified in Industry 33421, Telephone Apparatus Manufacturing;

- Manufacturing blank magnetic and optical recording media—are classified in Industry 33461, Manufacturing and Reproducing Magnetic and Optical Media;

- Manufacturing machinery or equipment that incorporate electronic computers for operation or control purposes and embedded control applications—are classified in the Manufacturing sector based on the classification of the complete machinery or equipment;

- Manufacturing external audio speakers for computer use—are classified in Industry 33431, Audio and Video Equipment Manufacturing;

- Manufacturing internal loaded printed circuit board devices, such as sound, video, controller, and network interface cards; internal and external computer modems; and semiconductor storage devices—are classified in Industry 33441, Semiconductor and Other Electronic Component Manufacturing; and

- Manufacturing other parts, such as casings, stampings, cable sets, and switches, for computers, storage devices and other peripheral equipment—are classified in the Manufacturing sector based on their associated production processes.

334111 Electronic Computer Manufacturing[US]

This U.S. industry comprises establishments primarily engaged in manufacturing and/or assembling electronic computers, such as mainframes, personal computers, workstations, laptops, and computer servers. Computers can be analog, digital, or

---

hybrid. Digital computers, the most common type, are devices that do all of the following: (1) store the processing program or programs and the data immediately necessary for the execution of the program; (2) can be freely programmed in accordance with the requirements of the user; (3) perform arithmetical computations specified by the user; and (4) execute, without human intervention, a processing program that requires the computer to modify its execution by logical decision during the processing run. Analog computers are capable of simulating mathematical models and contain at least analog, control, and programming elements. The manufacture of computers includes the assembly or integration of processors, coprocessors, memory, storage, and input/output devices into a user-programmable final product.

Cross-References. Establishments primarily engaged in—

- Manufacturing digital telecommunications switches, local area network and wide area network communication equipment, such as bridges, routers, and gateways—are classified in Industry 334210, Telephone Apparatus Manufacturing;

- Manufacturing blank magnetic and optical recording media—are classified in U.S. Industry 334613, Magnetic and Optical Recording Media Manufacturing;

- Manufacturing machinery or equipment that incorporates electronic computers for operation or control purposes and embedded control applications— are classified in the Manufacturing sector based on the classification of the complete machinery or equipment;

- Manufacturing internal, loaded, printed circuit board devices, such as sound, video, controller, and network interface cards; internal and external computer modems; and solid state storage devices for computers—are classified in Industry 33441, Semiconductor and Other Electronic Component Manufacturing;

- Manufacturing other parts, such as casings, stampings, cable sets, and switches, for computers—are classified in the Manufacturing sector based on their associated production processes; and

- Retail sale of computers with on-site assembly is classified in Industry 443120, Computer and Software Stores.

334112 Computer Storage Device Manufacturing[US]

This U.S. industry comprises establishments primarily engaged in manufacturing computer storage devices that allow the storage and retrieval of data from a phase change, magnetic, optical, or magnetic/optical media. Examples of products made

---

US—United States industry only. CAN—United States and Canadian industries are comparable. MEX—United States and Mexican industries are comparable. Blank—Canadian, Mexican, and United States industries are comparable.

by these establishments are CD-ROM drives, floppy disk drives, hard disk drives, and tape storage and backup units.

Cross-References. Establishments primarily engaged in—

- Manufacturing blank magnetic and optical recording media—are classified in U.S. Industry 334613, Magnetic and Optical Recording Media Manufacturing;

- Manufacturing semiconductor storage devices, such as memory chips—are classified in U.S. Industry 334413, Semiconductor and Related Device Manufacturing;

- Manufacturing drive controller cards, internal or external to the storage device—are classified in U.S. Industry 334418, Printed Circuit Assembly (Electronic Assembly) Manufacturing; and

- Manufacturing other parts, such as casings, stampings, cable sets, and switches, for computer storage devices—are classified in the Manufacturing sector based on their associated production processes.

334113 Computer Terminal Manufacturing[US]

This U.S. industry comprises establishments primarily engaged in manufacturing computer terminals. Computer terminals are input/output devices that connect with a central computer for processing.

Cross-References. Establishments primarily engaged in—

- Manufacturing point-of-sale terminals, funds transfer, automatic teller machines, and monitors—are classified in U.S. Industry 334119, Other Computer Peripheral Equipment Manufacturing;

- Manufacturing internal loaded printed circuit board devices, such as sound, video, controller, and network interface cards for computer terminals—are classified in U.S. Industry 334418, Printed Circuit Assembly (Electronic Assembly) Manufacturing; and

- Manufacturing other parts, such as casings, stampings, cable sets, and switches, for computer terminals—are classified in the Manufacturing sector based on their associated production processes.

334119 Other Computer Peripheral Equipment Manufacturing[US]

This U.S. industry comprises establishments primarily engaged in manufacturing computer peripheral equipment (except storage devices and computer terminals).

US—United States industry only. CAN—United States and Canadian industries are comparable. MEX—United States and Mexican industries are comparable. Blank—Canadian, Mexican, and United States industries are comparable.

Illustrative Examples:

Automatic teller machines (ATM)
manufacturing
Joystick devices manufacturing
Keyboards, computer peripheral
equipment, manufacturing
Monitors, computer peripheral
equipment, manufacturing

Mouse devices, computer peripheral
equipment, manufacturing
Optical readers and scanners
manufacturing
Plotters, computer, manufacturing
Point-of-sale terminals, manufacturing
Printers, computer, manufacturing

Cross-References. Establishments primarily engaged in—

- Manufacturing local area network and wide area network communications equipment, such as bridges, routers, and gateways—are classified in Industry 334210, Telephone Apparatus Manufacturing;

- Manufacturing computer storage devices—are classified in U.S. Industry 334112, Computer Storage Device Manufacturing;

- Manufacturing computer terminals—are classified in U.S. Industry 334113, Computer Terminal Manufacturing;

- Manufacturing external audio speakers for computer use—are classified in Industry 334310, Audio and Video Equipment Manufacturing;

- Manufacturing internal, loaded, printed circuit board devices, such as sound, video, controller, and network interface cards; and internal and external computer modems used as computer peripherals—are classified in U.S. Industry 334418, Printed Circuit Assembly (Electronic Assembly) Manufacturing; and

- Manufacturing other parts, such as casings, stampings, cable sets, and switches, for computer peripheral equipment—are classified in the Manufacturing sector based on their associated production processes.

3342 Communications Equipment Manufacturing

33421 Telephone Apparatus Manufacturing
See industry description for 334210 below.

334210 Telephone Apparatus Manufacturing

This industry comprises establishments primarily engaged in manufacturing wire telephone and data communications equipment. These products may be standalone or board-level components of a larger system. Examples of products made by these establishments are central office switching equipment, cordless telephones (except cellular), PBX equipment, telephones, telephone answering machines, LAN

US—United States industry only. CAN—United States and Canadian industries are comparable. MEX—United States and Mexican industries are comparable. Blank—Canadian, Mexican, and United States industries are comparable.

modems, multi-user modems, and other data communications equipment, such as bridges, routers, and gateways.

Cross-References. Establishments primarily engaged in—

- Manufacturing internal and external computer modems, single-user fax/modems and electronic components used in telephone apparatus—are classified in Industry 33441, Semiconductor and Other Electronic Component Manufacturing; and

- Manufacturing cellular telephones—are classified in Industry 334220, Radio and Television Broadcasting and Wireless Communications Equipment Manufacturing.

33422 Radio and Television Broadcasting and Wireless Communications Equipment Manufacturing
See industry description for 334220 below.

334220 Radio and Television Broadcasting and Wireless Communications Equipment Manufacturing

This industry comprises establishments primarily engaged in manufacturing radio and television broadcast and wireless communications equipment. Examples of products made by these establishments are: transmitting and receiving antennas, cable television equipment, GPS equipment, pagers, cellular phones, mobile communications equipment, and radio and television studio and broadcasting equipment.

Cross-References. Establishments primarily engaged in—

- Manufacturing household-type audio and video equipment, such as televisions and radio sets—are classified in Industry 334310, Audio and Video Equipment Manufacturing; and

- Manufacturing wired and nonwired intercommunications equipment (i.e., intercoms)—are classified in Industry 334290, Other Communications Equipment Manufacturing.

33429 Other Communications Equipment Manufacturing
See industry description for 334290 below.

334290 Other Communications Equipment Manufacturing

This industry comprises establishments primarily engaged in manufacturing communications equipment (except telephone apparatus, and radio and television broadcast, and wireless communications equipment).

Illustrative Examples:

Fire detection and alarm systems manufacturing

Intercom systems and equipment manufacturing

Signals (e.g., highway, pedestrian, railway, traffic) manufacturing

Cross-References. Establishments primarily engaged in—

- Manufacturing telephone apparatus—are classified in Industry 334210, Telephone Apparatus Manufacturing;
- Manufacturing radio and television broadcast and wireless communication equipment—are classified in Industry 334220, Radio and Television Broadcasting and Wireless Communications Equipment Manufacturing; and
- Manufacturing automobile audio and related equipment—are classified in Industry 334310, Audio and Video Equipment Manufacturing.

3343 Audio and Video Equipment Manufacturing

33431 Audio and Video Equipment Manufacturing

See industry description for 334310 below.

334310 Audio and Video Equipment Manufacturing

This industry comprises establishments primarily engaged in manufacturing electronic audio and video equipment for home entertainment, motor vehicle, public address and musical instrument amplifications. Examples of products made by these establishments are video cassette recorders, televisions, stereo equipment, speaker systems, household-type video cameras, jukeboxes, and amplifiers for musical instruments and public address systems.

Cross-References. Establishments primarily engaged in—

- Manufacturing telephone answering machines—are classified in Industry 334210, Telephone Apparatus Manufacturing;
- Manufacturing photographic (i.e., still and motion picture) equipment—are classified in U.S. Industry 333315, Photographic and Photocopying Equipment Manufacturing;
- Manufacturing phonograph needles and cartridges—are classified in Industry 33441, Semiconductor and Other Electronic Component Manufacturing;
- Manufacturing auto theft alarms—are classified in Industry 334290, Other Communications Equipment Manufacturing; and

---

US—United States industry only. CAN—United States and Canadian industries are comparable. MEX—United States and Mexican industries are comparable. Blank—Canadian, Mexican, and United States industries are comparable.

- Manufacturing mobile radios, such as citizens band and FM transceivers for household or motor vehicle uses; studio and broadcast video cameras; and cable decoders and satellite television equipment—are classified in Industry 334220, Radio and Television Broadcasting and Wireless Communications Equipment Manufacturing.

3344 Semiconductor and Other Electronic Component Manufacturing

33441 Semiconductor and Other Electronic Component Manufacturing

This industry comprises establishments primarily engaged in manufacturing semiconductors and other components for electronic applications. Examples of products made by these establishments are capacitors, resistors, microprocessors, bare and loaded printed circuit boards, electron tubes, electronic connectors, and computer modems.

Cross-References. Establishments primarily engaged in—

- Manufacturing X-ray tubes—are classified in Industry 33451, Navigational, Measuring, Electromedical, and Control Instruments Manufacturing;
- Manufacturing glass blanks for electron tubes—are classified in Industry 32721, Glass and Glass Product Manufacturing;
- Manufacturing telephone system components or modules—are classified in Industry 33421, Telephone Apparatus Manufacturing;
- Manufacturing finished products that incorporate loaded printed circuit boards—are classified in the Manufacturing sector based on the production process of making the final product;
- Manufacturing communications antennas—are classified in Industry 33422, Radio and Television Broadcasting and Wireless Communications Equipment Manufacturing; and
- Manufacturing coils, switches, transformers, connectors, capacitors, rheostats, and similar devices for electrical applications—are classified in Subsector 335, Electrical Equipment, Appliance, and Component Manufacturing.

334411 Electron Tube Manufacturing[US]

This U.S. industry comprises establishments primarily engaged in manufacturing electron tubes and parts (except glass blanks). Examples of products made by

US—United States industry only. CAN—United States and Canadian industries are comparable. MEX—United States and Mexican industries are comparable. Blank—Canadian, Mexican, and United States industries are comparable.

these establishments are cathode ray tubes (i.e., picture tubes), klystron tubes, magnetron tubes, and traveling wave tubes.

Cross-References. Establishments primarily engaged in—

- Manufacturing X-ray tubes—are classified in U.S. Industry 334517, Irradiation Apparatus Manufacturing; and
- Manufacturing glass blanks for electron tubes—are classified in Industry 32721, Glass and Glass Product Manufacturing.

334412 Bare Printed Circuit Board Manufacturing[US]

This U.S. industry comprises establishments primarily engaged in manufacturing bare (i.e., rigid or flexible) printed circuit boards without mounted electronic components. These establishments print, perforate, plate, screen, etch, or photoprint interconnecting pathways for electric current on laminates.

Cross-References. Establishments primarily engaged in—

- Loading components onto printed circuit boards, or whose output is loaded printed circuit boards—are classified in U.S. Industry 334418, Printed Circuit Assembly (Electronic Assembly) Manufacturing; and
- Manufacturing printed circuit laminates—are classified in U.S. Industry 334419, Other Electronic Component Manufacturing.

334413 Semiconductor and Related Device Manufacturing[US]

This U.S. industry comprises establishments primarily engaged in manufacturing semiconductors and related solid state devices. Examples of products made by these establishments are integrated circuits, memory chips, microprocessors, diodes, transistors, solar cells and other optoelectronic devices.

334414 Electronic Capacitor Manufacturing[US]

This U.S. industry comprises establishments primarily engaged in manufacturing electronic fixed and variable capacitors and condensers.

Cross-References.

Establishments primarily engaged in manufacturing electrical capacitors for power generation and distribution, heavy industrial equipment, induction heating and melting, and similar industrial applications are classified in U.S. Industry

335999, All Other Miscellaneous Electrical Equipment and Component Manufacturing.

334415   Electronic Resistor Manufacturing[US]

This U.S. industry comprises establishments primarily engaged in manufacturing electronic resistors, such as fixed and variable resistors, resistor networks, thermistors, and varistors.

Cross-References.

Establishments primarily engaged in manufacturing electronic rheostats are classified in U.S. Industry 334419, Other Electronic Component Manufacturing.

334416   Electronic Coil, Transformer, and Other Inductor Manufacturing[US]

This U.S. industry comprises establishments primarily engaged in manufacturing electronic inductors, such as coils and transformers.

Cross-References.

Establishments primarily engaged in manufacturing electrical transformers used in the generation, storage, transmission, transformation, distribution, and utilization of electrical energy are classified in U.S. Industry 335311, Power, Distribution, and Specialty Transformer Manufacturing.

334417   Electronic Connector Manufacturing[US]

This U.S. industry comprises establishments primarily engaged in manufacturing electronic connectors, such as coaxial, cylindrical, rack and panel, pin and sleeve, printed circuit and fiber optic.

Cross-References.

Establishments primarily engaged in manufacturing electrical connectors, such as plugs, bus bars, twist on wire connectors and terminals, are classified in U.S. Industry 335931, Current-Carrying Wiring Device Manufacturing.

334418   Printed Circuit Assembly (Electronic Assembly) Manufacturing[US]

This U.S. industry comprises establishments primarily engaged in loading components onto printed circuit boards or who manufacture and ship loaded printed

---

US—United States industry only. CAN—United States and Canadian industries are comparable. MEX—United States and Mexican industries are comparable. Blank—Canadian, Mexican, and United States industries are comparable.

circuit boards. Also known as printed circuit assemblies, electronics assemblies, or modules, these products are printed circuit boards that have some or all of the semiconductor and electronic components inserted or mounted and are inputs to a wide variety of electronic systems and devices.

Cross-References. Establishments primarily engaged in—

- Manufacturing printed circuit laminates—are classified in U.S. Industry 334419, Other Electronic Component Manufacturing;
- Manufacturing bare printed circuit boards—are classified in U.S. Industry 334412, Bare Printed Circuit Board Manufacturing;
- Manufacturing telephone system components or modules— are classified in Industry 334210, Telephone Apparatus Manufacturing; and
- Manufacturing finished products that incorporate loaded printed circuit boards—are classified in the Manufacturing sector based on the production process of making the final product.

334419 Other Electronic Component Manufacturing[US]

This U.S. industry comprises establishments primarily engaged in manufacturing electronic components (except electron tubes; bare printed circuit boards; semiconductors and related devices; electronic capacitors; electronic resistors; coils, transformers and other inductors; connectors; and loaded printed circuit boards).

Illustrative Examples:

Crystals and crystal assemblies, electronic, manufacturing
LCD (liquid crystal display) unit screens manufacturing
Microwave components manufacturing
Piezolelectric devices manufacturing

Printed circuit laminates manufacturing
Switches for electronic applications manufacturing
Transducers (except pressure) manufacturing

Cross-References. Establishments primarily engaged in—

- Manufacturing electron tubes—are classified in U.S. Industry 334411, Electron Tube Manufacturing;
- Manufacturing bare printed circuit boards—are classified in U.S. Industry 334412, Bare Printed Circuit Board Manufacturing;
- Manufacturing semiconductors and related devices—are classified in U.S. Industry 334413, Semiconductor and Related Device Manufacturing;
- Manufacturing electronic capacitors—are classified in U.S. Industry 334414, Electronic Capacitor Manufacturing;

- Manufacturing electronic resistors—are classified in U.S. Industry 334415, Electronic Resistor Manufacturing;

- Manufacturing electronic inductors—are classified in U.S. Industry 334416, Electronic Coil, Transformer, and Other Inductor Manufacturing;

- Manufacturing electronic connectors—are classified in U.S. Industry 334417, Electronic Connector Manufacturing;

- Loading components onto printed circuit boards or whose output is loaded printed circuit boards—are classified in U.S. Industry 334418, Printed Circuit Assembly (Electronic Assembly) Manufacturing; and

- Manufacturing communications antennas—are classified in Industry 334220, Radio and Television Broadcasting and Wireless Communications Equipment Manufacturing.

3345 Navigational, Measuring, Electromedical, and Control Instruments Manufacturing

33451 Navigational, Measuring, Electromedical, and Control Instruments Manufacturing

This industry comprises establishments primarily engaged in manufacturing navigational, measuring, electromedical, and control instruments. Examples of products made by these establishments are aeronautical instruments, appliance regulators and controls (except switches), laboratory analytical instruments, navigation and guidance systems, and physical properties testing equipment.

Cross-References. Establishments primarily engaged in—

- Manufacturing global positioning system (GPS) equipment—are classified in Industry 33422, Radio and Television Broadcasting and Wireless Communications Equipment Manufacturing;

- Manufacturing motor control switches and relays (including timing relays)—are classified in Industry 33531, Electrical Equipment Manufacturing;

- Manufacturing switches for appliances—are classified in Industry 33593, Wiring Device Manufacturing;

- Manufacturing optical instruments—are classified in Industry 33331, Commercial and Service Industry Machinery Manufacturing;

- Manufacturing equipment for measuring and testing communications signals—are classified in Industry Group 3342, Communications Equipment Manufacturing;

- Manufacturing glass watch and clock crystals—are classified in Industry 32721, Glass and Glass Product Manufacturing;

- Manufacturing plastics watch and clock crystals—are classified in Industry 32619, Other Plastics Product Manufacturing; and

- Manufacturing medical thermometers and other nonelectrical medical apparatus—are classified in Industry Group 3391, Medical Equipment and Supplies Manufacturing.

334510 Electromedical and Electrotherapeutic Apparatus Manufacturing[US]

This U.S. industry comprises establishments primarily engaged in manufacturing electromedical and electrotherapeutic apparatus, such as magnetic resonance imaging equipment, medical ultrasound equipment, pacemakers, hearing aids, electrocardiographs, and electromedical endoscopic equipment.

Cross-References. Establishments primarily engaged in—

- Manufacturing medical irradiation apparatus—are classified in U.S. Industry 334517, Irradiation Apparatus Manufacturing; and

- Manufacturing nonelectrical medical and therapeutic apparatus—are classified in Industry Group 3391, Medical Equipment and Supplies Manufacturing.

334511 Search, Detection, Navigation, Guidance, Aeronautical, and Nautical System and Instrument Manufacturing[CAN]

This U.S. industry comprises establishments primarily engaged in manufacturing search, detection, navigation, guidance, aeronautical, and nautical systems and instruments. Examples of products made by these establishments are aircraft instruments (except engine), flight recorders, navigational instruments and systems, radar systems and equipment, and sonar systems and equipment.

Cross-References. Establishments primarily engaged in—

- Manufacturing global positioning system (GPS) equipment—are classified in Industry 334220, Radio and Television Broadcasting and Wireless Communications Equipment Manufacturing; and

- Manufacturing aircraft engine instruments and meteorological systems and equipment—are classified in U.S. Industry 334519, Other Measuring and Controlling Device Manufacturing.

334512 Automatic Environmental Control Manufacturing for Residential, Commercial, and Appliance Use[US]

This U.S. industry comprises establishments primarily engaged in manufacturing automatic controls and regulators for applications, such as heating, air-conditioning, refrigeration and appliances.

Cross-References. Establishments primarily engaged in—

- Manufacturing industrial process controls—are classified in U.S. Industry 334513, Instruments and Related Products Manufacturing for Measuring, Displaying, and Controlling Industrial Process Variables;
- Manufacturing motor control switches and relays—are classified in U.S. Industry 335314, Relay and Industrial Control Manufacturing;
- Manufacturing switches for appliances—are classified in U.S. Industry 335931, Current-Carrying Wiring Device Manufacturing; and
- Manufacturing appliance timers—are classified in U.S. Industry 334518, Watch, Clock, and Part Manufacturing.

334513 Instruments and Related Products Manufacturing for Measuring, Displaying, and Controlling Industrial Process Variables[US]

This U.S. industry comprises establishments primarily engaged in manufacturing instruments and related devices for measuring, displaying, indicating, recording, transmitting, and controlling industrial process variables. These instruments measure, display or control (monitor, analyze, and so forth) industrial process variables, such as temperature, humidity, pressure, vacuum, combustion, flow, level, viscosity, density, acidity, concentration, and rotation.

Cross-References. Establishments primarily engaged in—

- Manufacturing instruments for measuring or testing of electricity and electrical signals—are classified in U.S. Industry 334515, Instrument Manufacturing for Measuring and Testing Electricity and Electrical Signals;
- Manufacturing medical thermometers—are classified in U.S. Industry 339112, Surgical and Medical Instrument Manufacturing;
- Manufacturing glass hydrometers and thermometers for other nonmedical uses—are classified in U.S. Industry 334519, Other Measuring and Controlling Device Manufacturing;
- Manufacturing instruments and instrumentation systems for laboratory analysis of samples—are classified in U.S. Industry 334516, Analytical Laboratory Instrument Manufacturing; and

---

- Manufacturing optical alignment and display instruments, optical comparators, and optical test and inspection equipment—are classified in U.S. Industry 333314, Optical Instrument and Lens Manufacturing.

334514 Totalizing Fluid Meter and Counting Device Manufacturing[US]

This U.S. industry comprises establishments primarily engaged in manufacturing totalizing (i.e., registering) fluid meters and counting devices. Examples of products made by these establishments are gas consumption meters, water consumption meters, parking meters, taxi meters, motor vehicle gauges, and fare collection equipment.

Cross-References. Establishments primarily engaged in—

- Manufacturing integrating meters and counters for measuring the characteristics of electricity and electrical signals—are classified in U.S. Industry 334515, Instrument Manufacturing for Measuring and Testing Electricity and Electrical Signals; and

- Manufacturing instruments and devices that measure, display, or control (i.e., monitor or analyze) related industrial process variables—are classified in U.S. Industry 334513, Instruments and Related Products Manufacturing for Measuring, Displaying, and Controlling Industrial Process Variables.

334515 Instrument Manufacturing for Measuring and Testing Electricity and Electrical Signals[US]

This U.S. industry comprises establishments primarily engaged in manufacturing instruments for measuring and testing the characteristics of electricity and electrical signals. Examples of products made by these establishments are circuit and continuity testers, volt meters, ohm meters, wattmeters, multimeters, and semiconductor test equipment.

Cross-References. Establishments primarily engaged in—

- Manufacturing electronic monitoring, evaluating, and other electronic support equipment for navigational, radar, and sonar systems—are classified in U.S. Industry 334511, Search, Detection, Navigation, Guidance, Aeronautical, and Nautical System and Instrument Manufacturing; and

- Manufacturing equipment for measuring and testing communications signals—are classified in Industry Group 3342, Communications Equipment Manufacturing.

US—United States industry only. CAN—United States and Canadian industries are comparable. MEX—United States and Mexican industries are comparable. Blank—Canadian, Mexican, and United States industries are comparable.

334516 Analytical Laboratory Instrument Manufacturing[US]

This U.S. industry comprises establishments primarily engaged in manufacturing instruments and instrumentation systems for laboratory analysis of the chemical or physical composition or concentration of samples of solid, fluid, gaseous, or composite material.

Cross-References. Establishments primarily engaged in—

- Manufacturing instruments for monitoring and analyzing continuous samples from medical patients—are classified in U.S. Industry 334510, Electromedical and Electrotherapeutic Apparatus Manufacturing; and
- Manufacturing instruments and related devices that measure, display, or control (i.e., monitor or analyze) industrial process variables—are classified in U.S. Industry 334513, Instruments and Related Products Manufacturing for Measuring, Displaying, and Controlling Industrial Process Variables.

334517 Irradiation Apparatus Manufacturing[US]

This U.S. industry comprises establishments primarily engaged in manufacturing irradiation apparatus and tubes for applications, such as medical diagnostic, medical therapeutic, industrial, research and scientific evaluation. Irradiation can take the form of beta-rays, gamma-rays, X-rays, or other ionizing radiation.

334518 Watch, Clock, and Part Manufacturing[US]

This U.S. industry comprises establishments primarily engaged in manufacturing and/or assembling: clocks; watches; timing mechanisms for clockwork operated devices; time clocks; time and date recording devices; and clock and watch parts (except crystals), such as springs, jewels, and modules.

Cross-References. Establishments primarily engaged in—

- Manufacturing glass watch and clock crystals—are classified in Industry 32721, Glass and Glass Product Manufacturing;
- Manufacturing plastics watch and clock crystals—are classified in U.S. Industry 326199, All Other Plastics Product Manufacturing; and
- Manufacturing timing relays—are classified in U.S. Industry 335314, Relay and Industrial Control Manufacturing.

334519 Other Measuring and Controlling Device Manufacturing[US]

This U.S. industry comprises establishments primarily engaged in manufacturing measuring and controlling devices (except search, detection, navigation, guidance, aeronautical, and nautical instruments and systems; automatic environmental controls for residential, commercial, and appliance use; instruments for measurement, display, and control of industrial process variables; totalizing fluid meters and counting devices; instruments for measuring and testing electricity and electrical signals; analytical laboratory instruments; watches, clocks, and parts; irradiation equipment; and electromedical and electrotherapeutic apparatus).

Illustrative Examples:

Aircraft engine instruments manufacturing
Automotive emissions testing equipment
  manufacturing
Meteorological instruments
  manufacturing
Physical properties testing and inspection
  equipment manufacturing

Polygraph machines manufacturing
Radiation detection and monitoring
  instruments manufacturing
Surveying instruments manufacturing
Thermometers liquid-in-glass and
  bimetal types (except medical),
  manufacturing

Cross-References. Establishments primarily engaged in—

- Manufacturing medical thermometers—are classified in U.S. Industry 339112, Surgical and Medical Instrument Manufacturing;

- Manufacturing search, detection, navigation, guidance, aeronautical, and nautical systems and instruments—are classified in U.S. Industry 334511, Search, Detection, Navigation, Guidance, Aeronautical, and Nautical System and Instrument Manufacturing;

- Manufacturing automatic controls and regulators for applications, such as heating, air-conditioning, refrigeration and appliances—are classified in U.S. Industry 334512, Automatic Environmental Control Manufacturing for Residential, Commercial, and Appliance Use;

- Manufacturing instruments and related devices that measure, display, or control (i.e., monitor or analyze) industrial process variables—are classified in U.S. Industry 334513, Instruments and Related Products Manufacturing for Measuring, Displaying, and Controlling Industrial Process Variables;

- Manufacturing totalizing (i.e., registering) fluid meters and counting devices, including motor vehicle gauges—are classified in U.S. Industry 334514, Totalizing Fluid Meter and Counting Device Manufacturing;

- Manufacturing instruments for measuring and testing the characteristics of electricity and electrical signals—are classified in U.S. Industry 334515, Instrument Manufacturing for Measuring and Testing Electricity and Electrical Signals;

- Manufacturing instruments for laboratory analysis of the physical composition or concentration of samples of solid, fluid, gaseous, or composite materials—are classified in U.S. Industry 334516, Analytical Laboratory Instrument Manufacturing;

US—United States industry only. CAN—United States and Canadian industries are comparable. MEX—United States and Mexican industries are comparable. Blank—Canadian, Mexican, and United States industries are comparable.

- Manufacturing and/or assembling watches, clocks, or parts—are classified in U.S. Industry 334518, Watch, Clock, and Part Manufacturing;
- Manufacturing X-ray apparatus, tubes, or related irradiation apparatus—are classified in U.S. Industry 334517, Irradiation Apparatus Manufacturing; and
- Manufacturing electromedical and electrotherapeutic apparatus—are classified in U.S. Industry 334510, Electromedical and Electrotherapeutic Apparatus Manufacturing.

3346 Manufacturing and Reproducing Magnetic and Optical Media

33461 Manufacturing and Reproducing Magnetic and Optical Media

This industry comprises establishments primarily engaged in (1) manufacturing optical and magnetic media, such as blank audio tape, blank video tape, and blank diskettes and/or (2) mass duplicating (i.e., making copies) audio, video, software, and other data on magnetic, optical, and similar media.

Cross-References. Establishments primarily engaged in—

- Designing, developing, and publishing prepackaged software—are classified in Industry 51121, Software Publishers; and
- Audio, motion picture and/or video production and/or distribution—are classified in Subsector 512, Motion Picture and Sound Recording Industries.

334611 Software Reproducing[US]

This U.S. industry comprises establishments primarily engaged in mass reproducing computer software. These establishments do not generally develop any software, they mass reproduce data and programs on magnetic media, such as diskettes, tapes, or cartridges. Establishments in this industry mass reproduce products, such as CD-ROMs and game cartridges.

Cross-References.

Establishments primarily engaged in designing, developing, and publishing prepackaged software are classified in Industry 511210, Software Publishers.

334612 Prerecorded Compact Disc (except Software), Tape, and Record Reproducing[US]

This U.S. industry comprises establishments primarily engaged in mass reproducing audio and video material on magnetic or optical media. Examples of

---

products mass reproduced by these establishments are audio compact discs, prerecorded audio and video cassettes, and laser discs.

Cross-References. Establishments primarily engaged in—

- Designing, developing, and publishing prepackaged software—are classified in Industry 511210, Software Publishers;

- Audio, motion picture and/or video production and/or distribution—are classified in Subsector 512, Motion Picture and Sound Recording Industries; and

- Manufacturing blank audio and video tape, blank diskettes, and blank optical discs—are classified in U.S. Industry 334613, Magnetic and Optical Recording Media Manufacturing.

334613 Magnetic and Optical Recording Media Manufacturing[US]

This U.S. industry comprises establishments primarily engaged in manufacturing magnetic and optical recording media, such as blank magnetic tape, blank diskettes, blank optical discs, hard drive media, and blank magnetic tape cassettes.

Cross-References. Establishments primarily engaged in—

- Mass reproducing computer software—are classified in U.S. Industry 334611, Software Reproducing; and

- Mass reproducing audio and video material—are classified in U.S. Industry 334612, Prerecorded Compact Disc (Except Software), Tape, and Record Reproducing.

335 Electrical Equipment, Appliance, and Component Manufacturing

Industries in the Electrical Equipment, Appliance, and Component Manufacturing subsector manufacture products that generate, distribute and use electrical power. Electric Lighting Equipment Manufacturing establishments produce electric lamp bulbs, lighting fixtures, and parts. Household Appliance Manufacturing establishments make both small and major electrical appliances and parts. Electrical Equipment Manufacturing establishments make goods, such as electric motors, generators, transformers, and switchgear apparatus. Other Electrical Equipment and Component Manufacturing establishments make devices for storing electrical power (e.g., batteries), for transmitting electricity (e.g., insulated wire), and wiring devices (e.g., electrical outlets, fuse boxes, and light switches).

3351 Electric Lighting Equipment Manufacturing

33511 Electric Lamp Bulb and Part Manufacturing
See industry description for 335110 below.

335110 Electric Lamp Bulb and Part Manufacturing

This industry comprises establishments primarily engaged in manufacturing electric light bulbs and tubes, and parts and components (except glass blanks for electric light bulbs).

Cross-References. Establishments primarily engaged in—

- Manufacturing glass blanks for electric light bulbs—are classified in U.S. Industry 327212, Other Pressed and Blown Glass and Glassware Manufacturing;

- Manufacturing vehicular lighting fixtures—are classified in U.S. Industry 336321, Vehicular Lighting Equipment Manufacturing;

- Manufacturing light emitting diodes (LEDs)—are classified in U.S. Industry 334413, Semiconductor and Related Device Manufacturing; and

- Manufacturing other lighting fixtures (except vehicular)—are classified in Industry 33512, Lighting Fixture Manufacturing.

33512 Lighting Fixture Manufacturing

This industry comprises establishments primarily engaged in manufacturing electric lighting fixtures (except vehicular), nonelectric lighting equipment, lamp shades (except glass and plastics), and lighting fixture components (except current-carrying wiring devices).

Cross-References. Establishments primarily engaged in—

- Manufacturing vehicular lighting fixtures—are classified in Industry 33632, Motor Vehicle Electrical and Electronic Equipment Manufacturing;

- Manufacturing electric light bulbs, tubes, and parts—are classified in Industry 33511, Electric Lamp Bulb and Part Manufacturing;

- Manufacturing current-carrying wiring devices for lighting fixtures—are classified in Industry 33593, Wiring Device Manufacturing;

- Manufacturing ceiling fans or bath fans with integrated lighting fixtures—are classified in Industry 33521, Small Electrical Appliance Manufacturing;

- Manufacturing plastics lamp shades—are classified in Industry 32619, Other Plastics Product Manufacturing;

- Manufacturing glassware and glass parts for lighting fixtures—are classified in Industry 32721, Glass and Glass Product Manufacturing; and

- Manufacturing signaling devices that incorporate electric light bulbs, such as traffic and railway signals—are classified in Industry 33429, Other Communications Equipment Manufacturing.

335121 Residential Electric Lighting Fixture Manufacturing^{US}

This U.S. industry comprises establishments primarily engaged in manufacturing fixed or portable residential electric lighting fixtures and lamp shades of metal, paper, or textiles. Residential electric lighting fixtures include those for use both inside and outside the residence.

Illustrative Examples:

Ceiling lighting fixtures, residential, manufacturing
Chandeliers, residential, manufacturing

Table lamps (i.e., lighting fixtures) manufacturing

Cross-References. Establishments primarily engaged in—

- Manufacturing glassware for residential lighting fixtures—are classified in Industry 32721, Glass and Glass Product Manufacturing;

- Manufacturing plastics lamp shades—are classified in U.S. Industry 326199, All Other Plastics Product Manufacturing;

- Manufacturing electric light bulbs, tubes, and parts—are classified in Industry 335110, Electric Lamp Bulb and Part Manufacturing;

- Manufacturing ceiling fans or bath fans with integrated lighting fixtures—are classified in U.S. Industry 335211, Electric Housewares and Household Fan Manufacturing;

- Manufacturing current-carrying wiring devices for lighting fixtures—are classified in U.S. Industry 335931, Current-Carrying Wiring Device Manufacturing;

- Manufacturing commercial, industrial, and institutional electric lighting fixtures—are classified in U.S. Industry 335122, Commercial, Industrial, and Institutional Electric Lighting Fixture Manufacturing; and

- Manufacturing other lighting fixtures, such as street lights, flashlights, and nonelectric lighting fixtures—are classified in U.S. Industry 335129, Other Lighting Equipment Manufacturing.

335122 Commercial, Industrial, and Institutional Electric Lighting Fixture Manufacturing[US]

This U.S. industry comprises establishments primarily engaged in manufacturing commercial, industrial, and institutional electric lighting fixtures.

Cross-References. Establishments primarily engaged in—

- Manufacturing glassware for commercial, industrial, and institutional electric lighting fixtures—are classified in Industry 32721, Glass and Glass Product Manufacturing;
- Manufacturing residential electric lighting fixtures—are classified in U.S. Industry 335121, Residential Electric Lighting Fixture Manufacturing;
- Manufacturing current-carrying wiring devices for lighting fixtures—are classified in U.S. Industry 335931, Current-Carrying Wiring Device Manufacturing;
- Manufacturing vehicular lighting fixtures—are classified in U.S. Industry 336321, Vehicular Lighting Equipment Manufacturing;
- Manufacturing electric light bulbs, tubes, and parts—are classified in Industry 335110, Electric Lamp Bulb and Part Manufacturing; and
- Manufacturing other lighting fixtures, such as street lights, flashlights, and nonelectric lighting equipment—are classified in U.S. Industry 335129, Other Lighting Equipment Manufacturing.

335129 Other Lighting Equipment Manufacturing[US]

This U.S. industry comprises establishments primarily engaged in manufacturing electric lighting fixtures (except residential, commercial, industrial, institutional, and vehicular electric lighting fixtures) and nonelectric lighting equipment.

Illustrative Examples:

Christmas tree lighting sets, electric, manufacturing
Fireplace logs, electric, manufacturing
Flashlights manufacturing
Insect lamps, electric, manufacturing
Lanterns (e.g., carbide, electric, gas, gasoline, kerosene) manufacturing

Spotlights (except vehicular) manufacturing
Street lighting fixtures (except traffic signals) manufacturing

Cross-References. Establishments primarily engaged in—

- Manufacturing glassware for lighting fixtures—are classified in Industry 32721, Glass and Glass Product Manufacturing;

- Manufacturing electric light bulbs, tubes, and parts—are classified in Industry 335110, Electric Lamp Bulb and Part Manufacturing;

- Manufacturing current-carrying wiring devices for lighting fixtures—are classified in U.S. Industry 335931, Current-Carrying Wiring Device Manufacturing;

- Manufacturing residential electric lighting fixtures—are classified in U.S. Industry 335121, Residential Electric Lighting Fixture Manufacturing;

- Manufacturing commercial, industrial, and institutional electric lighting fixtures—are classified in U.S. Industry 335122, Commercial, Industrial, and Institutional Electric Lighting Fixture Manufacturing;

- Manufacturing vehicular lighting fixtures—are classified in U.S. Industry 336321, Vehicular Lighting Equipment Manufacturing; and

- Manufacturing signaling devices that incorporate electric light bulbs, such as traffic and railway signals—are classified in Industry 334290, Other Communications Equipment Manufacturing.

3352 Household Appliance Manufacturing

33521 Small Electrical Appliance Manufacturing

This industry comprises establishments primarily engaged in manufacturing small electric appliances and electric housewares, household-type fans, household-type vacuum cleaners, and other electric household-type floor care machines.

Cross-References. Establishments primarily engaged in—

- Manufacturing room air-conditioners, attic fans, wall and baseboard heating units for permanent installation, and commercial ventilation and exhaust fans—are classified in Industry 33341, Ventilation, Heating, Air-Conditioning, and Commercial Refrigeration Equipment Manufacturing;

- Manufacturing commercial, industrial, and institutional vacuum cleaners, and mechanical carpet sweepers—are classified in Industry 33331, Commercial and Service Industry Machinery Manufacturing;

- Manufacturing major household-type appliances, such as washing machines, dryers, stoves, and hot water heaters—are classified in Industry 33522, Major Appliance Manufacturing; and

- Installing central vacuum cleaning systems—are classified in Industry 23829, Other Building Equipment Contractors.

335211 Electric Housewares and Household Fan Manufacturing^{US}

This U.S. industry comprises establishments primarily engaged in manufacturing small electric appliances and electric housewares for heating, cooking, and other purposes, and electric household-type fans (except attic fans).

Illustrative Examples:

Bath fans, residential, manufacturing
Ceiling fans, residential, manufacturing
Curling irons, household-type electric, manufacturing
Electronic blankets manufacturing
Portable cooking appliances (except microwave, convection ovens), household-type electric, manufacturing
Portable electric space heaters manufacturing
Portable hair dryers, electric, manufacturing
Portable humidifiers and dehumidifiers manufacturing
Scissors, electric, manufacturing
Ventilating and exhaust fans (except attic fans), household-type, manufacturing

Cross-References. Establishments primarily engaged in—

- Manufacturing attic fans—are classified in U.S. Industry 333412, Industrial and Commercial Fan and Blower Manufacturing;

- Manufacturing wall and baseboard heating units for permanent installation—are classified in U.S. Industry 333414, Heating Equipment (except Warm Air Furnaces) Manufacturing;

- Manufacturing room air-conditioners—are classified in U.S. Industry 333415, Air-Conditioning and Warm Air Heating Equipment and Commercial and Industrial Refrigeration Equipment Manufacturing; and

- Manufacturing microwave and convection ovens—are classified in U.S. Industry 335221, Household Cooking Appliance Manufacturing.

335212 Household Vacuum Cleaner Manufacturing^{US}

This U.S. industry comprises establishments primarily engaged in manufacturing electric vacuum cleaners, electric floor waxing machines, and other electric floor care machines typically for household use.

Cross-References. Establishments primarily engaged in—

- Manufacturing electric vacuum cleaners for commercial, industrial, and institutional uses, and mechanical carpet sweepers—are classified in U.S. Industry 333319, Other Commercial and Service Industry Machinery Manufacturing; and

- Installing central vacuum cleaning systems—are classified in Industry 238290, Other Building Equipment Contractors.

33522 Major Appliance Manufacturing

This industry comprises establishments primarily engaged in manufacturing household-type cooking appliances, household-type laundry equipment, household-type refrigerators, upright and chest freezers, and other electrical and nonelectrical major household-type appliances, such as dishwashers, water heaters, and garbage disposal units.

Cross-References. Establishments primarily engaged in—

- Manufacturing small electric appliances and electric housewares, such as hot plates, griddles, toasters, and electric irons—are classified in Industry 33521, Small Electrical Appliance Manufacturing;

- Manufacturing commercial and industrial refrigerators and freezers—are classified in Industry 33341, Ventilation, Heating, Air-Conditioning, and Commercial Refrigeration Equipment Manufacturing;

- Manufacturing commercial-type cooking equipment and commercial-type laundry, drycleaning, and pressing equipment—are classified in Industry 33331, Commercial and Service Industry Machinery Manufacturing; and

- Manufacturing household-type sewing machines—are classified in Industry 33329, Other Industrial Machinery Manufacturing.

335221 Household Cooking Appliance Manufacturing[US]

This U.S. industry comprises establishments primarily engaged in manufacturing household-type electric and nonelectric cooking equipment (except small electric appliances and electric housewares).

Cross-References. Establishments primarily engaged in—

- Manufacturing small electric appliances and electric housewares used for cooking, such as electric skillets, electric hot plates, electric griddles, toasters, and percolators—are classified in U.S. Industry 335211, Electric Housewares and Household Fan Manufacturing; and

- Manufacturing commercial-type cooking equipment—are classified in U.S. Industry 333319, Other Commercial and Service Industry Machinery Manufacturing.

US—United States industry only. CAN—United States and Canadian industries are comparable. MEX—United States and Mexican industries are comparable. Blank—Canadian, Mexican, and United States industries are comparable.

335222 Household Refrigerator and Home Freezer Manufacturing^{US}

This U.S. industry comprises establishments primarily engaged in manufacturing household-type refrigerators and upright and chest freezers.

Cross-References.

Establishments primarily engaged in manufacturing commercial and industrial refrigeration equipment, such as refrigerators and freezers, are classified in U.S. Industry 333415, Air-Conditioning and Warm Air Heating Equipment and Commercial and Industrial Refrigeration Equipment Manufacturing.

335224 Household Laundry Equipment Manufacturing^{US}

This U.S. industry comprises establishments primarily engaged in manufacturing household-type laundry equipment.

Cross-References. Establishments primarily engaged in—

- Manufacturing portable electric irons—are classified in U.S. Industry 335211, Electric Housewares and Household Fan Manufacturing; and

- Manufacturing commercial-type laundry and drycleaning equipment—are classified in U.S. Industry 333312, Commercial Laundry, Dry Cleaning, and Pressing Machine Manufacturing.

335228 Other Major Household Appliance Manufacturing^{US}

This U.S. industry comprises establishments primarily engaged in manufacturing electric and nonelectric major household-type appliances (except cooking equipment, refrigerators, upright and chest freezers, and household-type laundry equipment).

Illustrative Examples:

Dishwashers, household-type, manufacturing	Hot water heaters (including nonelectric), household-type, manufacturing
Garbage disposal units, household-type, manufacturing	Trash and garbage compactors, household-type, manufacturing

Cross-References. Establishments primarily engaged in—

- Manufacturing household-type cooking equipment—are classified in U.S. Industry 335221, Household Cooking Appliance Manufacturing;

- Manufacturing household-type sewing machines—are classified in U.S. Industry 333298, All Other Industrial Machinery Manufacturing;
- Manufacturing household-type refrigerators and upright and chest freezers—are classified in U.S. Industry 335222, Household Refrigerator and Home Freezer Manufacturing; and
- Manufacturing small electric appliances—are classified in U.S. Industry 335211, Electric Housewares and Household Fan Manufacturing.

3353 Electrical Equipment Manufacturing

33531 Electrical Equipment Manufacturing

This industry comprises establishments primarily engaged in manufacturing power, distribution, and specialty transformers; electric motors, generators, and motor generator sets; switchgear and switchboard apparatus; relays; and industrial controls.

Cross-References. Establishments primarily engaged in—

- Manufacturing turbine generator set units and electric outboard motors— are classified in Industry 33361, Engine, Turbine, and Power Transmission Equipment Manufacturing;
- Manufacturing electronic component-type transformers and switches—are classified in Industry 33441, Semiconductor and Other Electronic Component Manufacturing;
- Manufacturing environmental controls and industrial process control instruments—are classified in Industry 33451, Navigational, Measuring, Electromedical, and Control Instruments Manufacturing;
- Manufacturing switches for electrical circuits, such as pushbutton and snap switches—are classified in Industry 33593, Wiring Device Manufacturing;
- Manufacturing complete for welding and soldering equipment—are classified in Industry 33399, All Other General Purpose Machinery Manufacturing; and
- Manufacturing starting motors and generators for internal combustion engines—are classified in Industry 33632, Motor Vehicle Electrical and Electronic Equipment Manufacturing.

335311 Power, Distribution, and Specialty Transformer Manufacturing[CAN]

This U.S. industry comprises establishments primarily engaged in manufacturing power, distribution, and specialty transformers (except electronic components).

Industrial-type and consumer-type transformers in this industry vary (e.g., step up or step down) voltage but do not convert alternating to direct or direct to alternating current.

Illustrative Examples:

Distribution transformers, electric, manufacturing

Fluorescent ballasts (i.e., transformers) manufacturing

Substation transformers, electric power distribution, manufacturing

Transmission and distribution voltage regulators manufacturing

Cross-References.

Establishments primarily engaged in manufacturing electronic component-type transformers are classified in U.S. Industry 334416, Electronic Coil, Transformer, and Other Inductor Manufacturing.

335312 Motor and Generator Manufacturing^{CAN}

This U.S. industry comprises establishments primarily engaged in manufacturing electric motors (except internal combustion engine starting motors), power generators (except battery charging alternators for internal combustion engines), and motor generator sets (except turbine generator set units). This industry includes establishments rewinding armatures on a factory basis.

Cross-References. Establishments primarily engaged in—

- Manufacturing electric outboard motors—are classified in U.S. Industry 333618, Other Engine Equipment Manufacturing;

- Manufacturing gas, steam, or hydraulic turbine generator set units—are classified in U.S. Industry 333611, Turbine and Turbine Generator Set Units Manufacturing;

- Manufacturing starting motors and battery charging alternators for internal combustion engines—are classified in U.S. Industry 336322, Other Motor Vehicle Electrical and Electronic Equipment Manufacturing;

- Rewinding armatures, not on a factory basis—are classified in Industry 811310, Commercial and Industrial Machinery and Equipment (except Automotive and Electronic) Repair and Maintenance; and

- Manufacturing complete welding and soldering equipment—are classified in U.S. Industry 333992, Welding and Soldering Equipment Manufacturing.

335313 Switchgear and Switchboard Apparatus Manufacturing^{US}

This U.S. industry comprises establishments primarily engaged in manufacturing switchgear and switchboard apparatus.

Illustrative Examples:

Circuit breakers, power, manufacturing
Control panels, electric power
  distribution, manufacturing
Duct for electrical switchboard apparatus
  manufacturing
Fuses, electric, manufacturing

Power switching equipment
  manufacturing
Switches, electric power (except
  pushbutton, snap, solenoid, tumbler),
  manufacturing

Cross-References. Establishments primarily engaged in—

- Manufacturing relays—are classified in U.S. Industry 335314, Relay and Industrial Control Manufacturing;
- Manufacturing switches for electronic applications—are classified in U.S. Industry 334419, Other Electronic Component Manufacturing; and
- Manufacturing snap, pushbutton, and similar switches for electrical circuits—are classified in U.S. Industry 335931, Current-Carrying Wiring Device Manufacturing.

335314 Relay and Industrial Control Manufacturing[US]

This U.S. industry comprises establishments primarily engaged in manufacturing relays, motor starters and controllers, and other industrial controls and control accessories.

Cross-References. Establishments primarily engaged in—

- Manufacturing environmental and appliance control equipment—are classified in U.S. Industry 334512, Automatic Environmental Control Manufacturing for Residential, Commercial, and Appliance Use; and
- Manufacturing instruments for controlling industrial process variables— are classified in U.S. Industry 334513, Instruments and Related Products Manufacturing for Measuring, Displaying, and Controlling Industrial Process Variables.

3359 Other Electrical Equipment and Component Manufacturing

This industry group comprises establishments manufacturing electrical equipment and components (except electric lighting equipment, household-type appliances, transformers, switchgear, relays, motors, and generators).

33591 Battery Manufacturing

This industry comprises establishments primarily engaged in manufacturing primary and storage batteries.

335911 Storage Battery Manufacturing^{US}

This U.S. industry comprises establishments primarily engaged in manufacturing storage batteries.

Illustrative Examples:

Lead acid storage batteries
manufacturing

Rechargeable nickel cadmium (NICAD)
batteries manufacturing

Cross-References.

Establishments primarily engaged in manufacturing primary batteries are classified in U.S. Industry 335912, Primary Battery Manufacturing.

335912 Primary Battery Manufacturing^{US}

This U.S. industry comprises establishments primarily engaged in manufacturing wet or dry primary batteries.

Illustrative Examples:

Disposable flashlight batteries
manufacturing
Dry cells, primary (e.g., AAA, AA, C, D
9V), manufacturing

Lithium batteries, primary,
manufacturing
Watch batteries manufacturing

Cross-References.

Establishments primarily engaged in manufacturing storage batteries are classified in U.S. Industry 335911, Storage Battery Manufacturing.

33592 Communication and Energy Wire and Cable Manufacturing

This industry comprises establishments insulating fiber-optic cable, and manufacturing insulated nonferrous wire and cable from nonferrous wire drawn in other establishments.

Cross-References. Establishments primarily engaged in—

- Drawing nonferrous wire—are classified in Subsector 331, Primary Metal Manufacturing;

- Manufacturing cable sets consisting of insulated wire and various connectors for electronic applications—are classified in Industry 33441, Semiconductor and Other Electronic Component Manufacturing;

US—United States industry only. CAN—United States and Canadian industries are comparable. MEX—United States and Mexican industries are comparable. Blank—Canadian, Mexican, and United States industries are comparable.

- Manufacturing extension cords, appliance cords, and similar electrical cord sets from purchased, insulated wire or cable—are classified in Industry 33599, All Other Electrical Equipment and Component Manufacturing; and

- Manufacturing unsheathed fiber-optic materials—are classified in Industry 32721, Glass and Glass Product Manufacturing.

335921 Fiber Optic Cable Manufacturing[US]

This U.S. industry comprises establishments primarily engaged in manufacturing insulated fiber-optic cable from purchased fiber-optic strand.

Cross-References. Establishments primarily engaged in—

- Manufacturing unsheathed fiber-optic materials—are classified in Industry 32721, Glass and Glass Product Manufacturing; and

- Manufacturing insulated nonferrous wire and cable from purchased wire— are classified in U.S. Industry 335929, Other Communication and Energy Wire Manufacturing.

335929 Other Communication and Energy Wire Manufacturing[US]

This U.S. industry comprises establishments primarily engaged in manufacturing insulated wire and cable of nonferrous metals from purchased wire.

Cross-References. Establishments primarily engaged in—

- Manufacturing cable sets consisting of insulated wire and various connectors for electronic applications—are classified in U.S. Industry 334419, Other Electronic Component Manufacturing;

- Manufacturing extension cords, appliance cords, and similar electrical cord sets from purchased insulated wire—are classified in U.S. Industry 335999, All Other Miscellaneous Electrical Equipment and Component Manufacturing;

- Drawing and insulating copper wire in the same establishment—are classified in U.S. Industry 331422, Copper Wire (except Mechanical) Drawing;

- Drawing and insulating aluminum wire in the same establishment—are classified in U.S. Industry 331319, Other Aluminum Rolling and Drawing; and

- Drawing nonferrous wire (except copper and aluminum)—are classified in U.S. Industry 331491, Nonferrous Metal (except Copper and Aluminum) Rolling, Drawing, and Extruding.

US—United States industry only. CAN—United States and Canadian industries are comparable. MEX—United States and Mexican industries are comparable. Blank—Canadian, Mexican, and United States industries are comparable.

33593 Wiring Device Manufacturing

This industry comprises establishments primarily engaged in manufacturing current-carrying wiring devices and noncurrent-carrying wiring devices for wiring electrical circuits.

Cross-References. Establishments primarily engaged in—

- Manufacturing ceramic and glass insulators—are classified in Subsector 327, Nonmetallic Mineral Product Manufacturing; and

- Manufacturing electronic component-type connectors, sockets, and switches—are classified in Industry 33441, Semiconductor and Other Electronic Component Manufacturing.

335931 Current-Carrying Wiring Device Manufacturing[US]

This U.S. industry comprises establishments primarily engaged in manufacturing current-carrying wiring devices.

Illustrative Examples:

Bus bars, electrical conductors (except switchgear-type), manufacturing
GFCI (ground fault circuit interrupters) manufacturing
Lamp holders manufacturing
Lightning arrestors and coils manufacturing

Receptacles (i.e., outlets), electrical, manufacturing
Switches for electrical wiring (e.g., pressure, pushbutton, snap, tumbler) manufacturing

Cross-References. Establishments primarily engaged in—

- Manufacturing electronic component-type connectors—are classified in U.S. Industry 334417, Electronic Connector Manufacturing;

- Manufacturing noncurrent-carrying wiring devices—are classified in U.S. Industry 335932, Noncurrent-Carrying Wiring Device Manufacturing; and

- Manufacturing electronic component-type sockets and switches—are classified in U.S. Industry 334419, Other Electronic Component Manufacturing.

335932 Noncurrent-Carrying Wiring Device Manufacturing[US]

This U.S. industry comprises establishments primarily engaged in manufacturing noncurrent-carrying wiring devices.

Illustrative Examples:

Boxes, electrical wiring (e.g., junction, outlet, switch), manufacturing
Conduits and fittings, electrical, manufacturing

Face plates (i.e., outlet or switch covers) manufacturing
Transmission pole and line hardware manufacturing

Cross-References. Establishments primarily engaged in—

- Manufacturing porcelain and ceramic insulators—are classified in U.S. Industry 327113, Porcelain Electrical Supply Manufacturing;

- Manufacturing current-carrying wiring devices—are classified in U.S. Industry 335931, Current-Carrying Wiring Device Manufacturing; and

- Manufacturing glass insulators—are classified in Industry 32721, Glass and Glass Product Manufacturing.

33599 All Other Electrical Equipment and Component Manufacturing

This industry comprises establishments primarily engaged in manufacturing electrical equipment (except electric lighting equipment, household-type appliances, transformers, motors, generators, switchgear, relays, industrial controls, batteries, communication and energy wire and cable, and wiring devices).

Illustrative Examples:

Carbon and graphite electrodes and brushes manufacturing
Extension cords made from purchased insulated wire

Surge suppressors manufacturing

Cross-References. Establishments primarily engaged in—

- Manufacturing lighting equipment—are classified in Industry Group 3351, Electric Lighting Equipment Manufacturing;

- Manufacturing household-type appliances—are classified in Industry Group 3352, Household Appliance Manufacturing;

- Manufacturing transformers, motors, generators, switchgear, relays, and industrial controls—are classified in Industry 33531, Electrical Equipment Manufacturing;

- Manufacturing batteries—are classified in Industry 33591, Battery Manufacturing;

- Manufacturing communication and energy wire—are classified in Industry 33592, Communication and Energy Wire and Cable Manufacturing;

- Manufacturing current-carrying and noncurrent-carrying wiring devices—are classified in Industry 33593, Wiring Device Manufacturing;

- Manufacturing carbon or graphite gaskets—are classified in Industry 33999, All Other Miscellaneous Manufacturing;

- Manufacturing electronic component-type rectifiers, voltage regulating integrated circuits, power converting integrated circuits, electronic capacitors, electronic resistors, and similar devices—are classified in Industry 33441, Semiconductor and Other Electronic Component Manufacturing; and

- Manufacturing equipment incorporating lasers—are classified in various subsectors of manufacturing based on the associated production process of the finished equipment.

335991 Carbon and Graphite Product Manufacturing^{MEX}

This U.S. industry comprises establishments primarily engaged in manufacturing carbon, graphite, and metal-graphite brushes and brush stock; carbon or graphite electrodes for thermal and electrolytic uses; carbon and graphite fibers; and other carbon, graphite, and metal-graphite products.

Cross-References.

Establishments primarily engaged in manufacturing carbon or graphite gaskets are classified in U.S. Industry 339991, Gasket, Packing, and Sealing Device Manufacturing.

335999 All Other Miscellaneous Electrical Equipment and Component Manufacturing^{MEX}

This U.S. industry comprises establishments primarily engaged in manufacturing industrial and commercial electric apparatus and other equipment (except lighting equipment, household appliances, transformers, motors, generators, switchgear, relays, industrial controls, batteries, communication and energy wire and cable, wiring devices, and carbon and graphite products). This industry includes power converters (i.e., AC to DC and DC to AC), power supplies, surge suppressors, and similar equipment for industrial-type and consumer-type equipment.

Illustrative Examples:

Appliance cords made from purchased insulated wire	Extension cords made from purchased insulated wire
Battery chargers, solid-state, manufacturing	Inverters manufacturing
	Surge suppressers manufacturing

US—United States industry only. CAN—United States and Canadian industries are comparable. MEX—United States and Mexican industries are comparable. Blank—Canadian, Mexican, and United States industries are comparable.

Door opening and closing devices, electrical, manufacturing

Electric bells manufacturing

Uninterruptible power supplies (UPS) manufacturing

Cross-References. Establishments primarily engaged in—

- Manufacturing lighting equipment—are classified in Industry Group 3351, Electric Lighting Equipment Manufacturing;
- Manufacturing household-type appliances—are classified in Industry Group 3352, Household Appliance Manufacturing;
- Manufacturing transformers, motors, generators, switchgear, relays, and industrial controls—are classified in Industry 33531, Electrical Equipment Manufacturing;
- Manufacturing primary and storage batteries—are classified in Industry 33591, Battery Manufacturing;
- Manufacturing communication and energy wire and cable from purchased wire or fiber-optic strand—are classified in Industry 33592, Communication and Energy Wire and Cable Manufacturing;
- Manufacturing current-carrying and noncurrent-carrying wiring devices— are classified in Industry 33593, Wiring Device Manufacturing;
- Manufacturing electronic component-type rectifiers (except semiconductor)—are classified in U.S. Industry 334419, Other Electronic Component Manufacturing;
- Manufacturing semiconductor rectifiers, voltage regulating integrated circuits, power converting integrated circuits, and similar semiconductor devices—are classified in U.S. Industry 334413, Semiconductor and Related Device Manufacturing;
- Manufacturing electronic component-type capacitors and condensers—are classified in U.S. Industry 334414, Electronic Capacitor Manufacturing;
- Manufacturing carbon and graphite products—are classified in U.S. Industry 335991, Carbon and Graphite Product Manufacturing; and
- Manufacturing equipment incorporating lasers—are classified in various manufacturing subsectors based on the associated production process of the finished equipment.

336 Transportation Equipment Manufacturing

Industries in the Transportation Equipment Manufacturing subsector produce equipment for transporting people and goods. Transportation equipment is a type

US—United States industry only. CAN—United States and Canadian industries are comparable. MEX—United States and Mexican industries are comparable. Blank—Canadian, Mexican, and United States industries are comparable.

of machinery. An entire subsector is devoted to this activity because of the significance of its economic size in all three North American countries.

Establishments in this subsector utilize production processes similar to those of other machinery manufacturing establishments—bending, forming, welding, machining, and assembling metal or plastic parts into components and finished products. However, the assembly of components and subassemblies and their further assembly into finished vehicles tends to be a more common production process in this subsector than in the Machinery Manufacturing subsector.

NAICS has industry groups for the manufacture of equipment for each mode of transport—road, rail, air and water. Parts for motor vehicles warrant a separate industry group because of their importance and because parts manufacture requires less assembly, and the establishments that manufacture only parts are not as vertically integrated as those that make complete vehicles.

Land use motor vehicle equipment not designed for highway operation (e.g., agricultural equipment, construction equipment, and materials handling equipment) is classified in the appropriate NAICS subsector based on the type and use of the equipment.

3361 Motor Vehicle Manufacturing

33611 Automobile and Light Duty Motor Vehicle Manufacturing

This industry comprises establishments primarily engaged in (1) manufacturing complete automobile and light duty motor vehicles (i.e., body and chassis or unibody) or (2) manufacturing chassis only.

Cross-References.

Establishments primarily engaged in manufacturing car, truck, and bus bodies and assembling vehicles on a purchased chassis and manufacturing kit cars for highway use are classified in Industry 33621, Motor Vehicle Body and Trailer Manufacturing.

336111 Automobile Manufacturing[US]

This U.S. industry comprises establishments primarily engaged in (1) manufacturing complete automobiles (i.e., body and chassis or unibody) or (2) manufacturing automobile chassis only.

Cross-References.

Establishments primarily engaged in manufacturing car bodies and assembling vehicles on a purchased chassis and manufacturing kit cars for highway use are classified in U.S. Industry 336211, Motor Vehicle Body Manufacturing.

US—United States industry only. CAN—United States and Canadian industries are comparable. MEX—United States and Mexican industries are comparable. Blank—Canadian, Mexican, and United States industries are comparable.

336112 Light Truck and Utility Vehicle Manufacturing[US]

This U.S. industry comprises establishments primarily engaged in (1) manufacturing complete light trucks and utility vehicles (i.e., body and chassis) or (2) manufacturing light truck and utility vehicle chassis only. Vehicles made include light duty vans, pick-up trucks, minivans, and sport utility vehicles.

Cross-References.
Establishments primarily engaged in manufacturing truck and bus bodies and assembling vehicles on a purchased chassis are classified in U.S. Industry 336211, Motor Vehicle Body Manufacturing.

33612 Heavy Duty Truck Manufacturing
See industry description for 336120 below.

336120 Heavy Duty Truck Manufacturing

This industry comprises establishments primarily engaged in (1) manufacturing heavy duty truck chassis and assembling complete heavy duty trucks, buses, heavy duty motor homes, and other special purpose heavy duty motor vehicles for highway use or (2) manufacturing heavy duty truck chassis only.

Cross-References. Establishments primarily engaged in—
- Manufacturing truck and bus bodies and assembling vehicles on a purchased chassis—are classified in U.S. Industry 336211, Motor Vehicle Body Manufacturing;
- Manufacturing motor homes on purchased chassis—are classified in U.S. Industry 336213, Motor Home Manufacturing;
- Manufacturing vans, minivans, and light trucks—are classified in U.S. Industry 336112, Light Truck and Utility Vehicle Manufacturing;
- Manufacturing military armored vehicles—are classified in U.S. Industry 336992, Military Armored Vehicle, Tank, and Tank Component Manufacturing; and
- Manufacturing off highway construction equipment—are classified in Industry 333120, Construction Machinery Manufacturing.

3362 Motor Vehicle Body and Trailer Manufacturing

33621 Motor Vehicle Body and Trailer Manufacturing

This industry comprises establishments primarily engaged in (1) manufacturing motor vehicle bodies and cabs or (2) manufacturing truck, automobile and utility trailers, truck trailer chassis, detachable trailer bodies, and detachable trailer chassis. The products made may be sold separately or may be assembled on purchased chassis and sold as complete vehicles.

Motor homes are units where the motor and the living quarters are contained in the same integrated unit, while travel trailers are designed to be towed by a motor unit, such as an automobile or a light truck.

Illustrative Examples:

Bodies and cabs, truck, manufacturing
Camper unit, slide-in, for pick-up trucks, manufacturing
Motor homes, self-contained, assembling on purchased chassis
Pickup canopies, caps, or covers manufacturing
Travel trailers, recreational, manufacturing
Semitrailer manufacturing

Cross-References. Establishments primarily engaged in—

- Making manufactured homes (i.e., mobile homes)—are classified in Industry 32199, All Other Wood Product Manufacturing;

- Customizing automotive vehicle and trailer interiors (i.e., van conversions) on an individual basis—are classified in Industry 81112, Automotive Body, Paint, Interior, and Glass Repair;

- Manufacturing light duty motor home chassis and assembling complete motor homes—are classified in Industry 33611, Automobile and Light Duty Motor Vehicle Manufacturing; and

- Manufacturing heavy duty truck chassis and assembling heavy duty trucks, buses, motor homes, and other special purpose heavy duty motor vehicles for highway use—are classified in Industry 33612, Heavy Duty Truck Manufacturing.

336211 Motor Vehicle Body Manufacturing[CAN]

This U.S. industry comprises establishments primarily engaged in manufacturing truck and bus bodies and cabs and automobile bodies. The products made may be sold separately or may be assembled on purchased chassis and sold as complete vehicles.

Cross-References.

Establishments primarily engaged in manufacturing heavy duty chassis and assembling heavy duty trucks, buses, motor homes, and other special purpose heavy duty motor vehicles for highway use are classified in Industry 336120, Heavy Duty Truck Manufacturing.

US—United States industry only. CAN—United States and Canadian industries are comparable. MEX—United States and Mexican industries are comparable. Blank—Canadian, Mexican, and United States industries are comparable.

336212 Truck Trailer Manufacturing[CAN]

This U.S. industry comprises establishments primarily engaged in manufacturing truck trailers, truck trailer chassis, cargo container chassis, detachable trailer bodies, and detachable trailer chassis for sale separately.

Cross-References.

Establishments primarily engaged in manufacturing utility trailers, light-truck trailers, and travel trailers are classified in U.S. Industry 336214, Travel Trailer and Camper Manufacturing.

336213 Motor Home Manufacturing[US]

This U.S. industry comprises establishments primarily engaged in (1) manufacturing motor homes on purchased chassis and/or (2) manufacturing conversion vans on an assembly line basis. Motor homes are units where the motor and the living quarters are integrated in the same unit.

Cross-References. Establishments primarily engaged in—

- Manufacturing light duty motor homes chassis and assembling complete motor homes—are classified in U.S. Industry 336112, Light Truck and Utility Vehicle Manufacturing;
- Customizing automotive vehicle and trailer interiors (i.e., van conversions) on an individual basis—are classified in U.S. Industry 811121, Automotive Body, Paint, and Interior Repair and Maintenance; and
- Producing manufactured homes (i.e., mobile homes)—are classified in U.S. Industry 321991, Manufactured Home (Mobile Home) Manufacturing.

336214 Travel Trailer and Camper Manufacturing[US]

This U.S. industry comprises establishments primarily engaged in one or more of the following: (1) manufacturing travel trailers and campers designed to attach to motor vehicles; (2) manufacturing pickup coaches (i.e., campers) and caps (i.e., covers) for mounting on pickup trucks; and (3) manufacturing automobile, utility and light-truck trailers. Travel trailers do not have their own motor but are designed to be towed by a motor unit, such as an automobile or a light truck.

Illustrative Examples:

Automobile transporter trailers, single car, manufacturing

Travel trailers, recreational, manufacturing

Camping trailers and chassis
manufacturing
Horse trailers (except fifth wheel type)
manufacturing

Utility trailers manufacturing

Cross-References.

Establishments primarily engaged in making manufactured homes (i.e., mobile homes) designed to accept permanent water, sewer, and utility connections and equipped with wheels, but not intended for regular highway use, are classified in U.S. Industry 321991, Manufactured Home (Mobile Home) Manufacturing.

3363 Motor Vehicle Parts Manufacturing

33631 Motor Vehicle Gasoline Engine and Engine Parts Manufacturing

This industry comprises establishments primarily engaged in manufacturing and/ or rebuilding motor vehicle gasoline engines, and engine parts, whether or not for vehicular use.

Illustrative Examples:

Carburetors, all types, manufacturing
Crankshaft assemblies, automotive and
truck gasoline engine, manufacturing
Cylinder heads, automotive and truck
gasoline engine, manufacturing
Fuel injection systems and parts,
automotive and truck gasoline engine,
manufacturing
Manifolds (i.e., intake and exhaust),
automotive and truck gasoline engine,
manufacturing

Pistons and piston rings manufacturing
Pumps (e.g., fuel, oil, water), mechanical
automotive and truck gasoline engine
(except power steering), manufacturing
Timing gears and chains, automotive and
truck gasoline engine, manufacturing
Valves, engine, intake and exhaust,
manufacturing

Cross-References. Establishments primarily engaged in—

- Manufacturing wiring harnesses and other vehicular electrical and electronic equipment—are classified in Industry 33632, Motor Vehicle Electrical and Electronic Equipment Manufacturing;

- Manufacturing transmission and power train equipment—are classified in Industry 33635, Motor Vehicle Transmission and Power Train Parts Manufacturing;

- Manufacturing radiators—are classified in Industry 33639, Other Motor Vehicle Parts Manufacturing;

US—United States industry only. CAN—United States and Canadian industries are comparable. MEX—United States and Mexican industries are comparable. Blank—Canadian, Mexican, and United States industries are comparable.

- Manufacturing steering and suspension components—are classified in Industry 33633, Motor Vehicle Steering and Suspension Components (except Spring) Manufacturing;

- Manufacturing parts for machine repair and equipment parts (except electric) on a job or shop basis—are classified in Industry 33271, Machine Shops;

- Manufacturing rubber and plastic belts and hoses without fittings—are classified in Industry 32622, Rubber and Plastics Hoses and Belting Manufacturing; and

- Manufacturing stationary and diesel engines—are classified in Industry 33361, Engine, Turbine, and Power Transmission Equipment Manufacturing.

336311 Carburetor, Piston, Piston Ring, and Valve Manufacturing[US]

This U.S. industry comprises establishments primarily engaged in manufacturing and/or rebuilding carburetors, pistons, piston rings, and engine intake and exhaust valves.

Cross-References.

Establishments primarily engaged in manufacturing parts for machine repair and equipment parts (except electric) on a job or shop basis are classified in Industry 332710, Machine Shops.

336312 Gasoline Engine and Engine Parts Manufacturing[US]

This U.S. industry comprises establishments primarily engaged in manufacturing and/or rebuilding gasoline motor vehicle engines and gasoline motor vehicle engine parts, excluding carburetors, pistons, piston rings, and valves.

Illustrative Examples:

Crankshaft assemblies, automotive and truck gasoline engine, manufacturing
Flywheels and ring gears, automotive and truck gasoline engine, manufacturing
Fuel injection systems and parts, automotive and truck gasoline engine, manufacturing
Manifolds (i.e., intake and exhaust), automotive and truck gasoline engine, manufacturing

Positive crankcase ventilation (PCV) valves, engine, manufacturing
Pumps (e.g., fuel, oil, water), mechanical, automotive and truck gasoline engine (except power steering), manufacturing
Timing gears and chains, automotive and truck gasoline engine, manufacturing

---

US—United States industry only. CAN—United States and Canadian industries are comparable. MEX—United States and Mexican industries are comparable. Blank—Canadian, Mexican, and United States industries are comparable.

Cross-References. Establishments primarily engaged in—

- Manufacturing carburetors, pistons, piston rings, and valves—are classified in U.S. Industry 336311, Carburetor, Piston, Piston Ring, and Valve Manufacturing;
- Manufacturing wiring harnesses and other vehicular electrical and electronic equipment—are classified in U.S. Industry 336322, Other Motor Vehicle Electrical and Electronic Equipment Manufacturing;
- Manufacturing transmission and power train equipment—are classified in Industry 336350, Motor Vehicle Transmission and Power Train Parts Manufacturing;
- Manufacturing radiators—are classified in U.S. Industry 336399, All Other Motor Vehicle Parts Manufacturing;
- Manufacturing steering and suspension components—are classified in Industry 336330, Motor Vehicle Steering and Suspension Components (except Spring) Manufacturing;
- Manufacturing rubber and plastic belts and hoses without fittings—are classified in Industry 326220, Rubber and Plastics Hoses and Belting Manufacturing; and
- Manufacturing stationary and diesel engines—are classified in U.S. Industry 333618, Other Engine Equipment Manufacturing.

33632 Motor Vehicle Electrical and Electronic Equipment Manufacturing

This industry comprises establishments primarily engaged in (1) manufacturing vehicular lighting and/or (2) manufacturing and/or rebuilding motor vehicle electrical and electronic equipment. The products made can be used for all types of transportation equipment (i.e., aircraft, automobiles, trains, ships).

Illustrative Examples:

Alternators and generators for internal combustion engines manufacturing
Automotive lighting fixtures manufacturing
Coils, ignition, internal combustion engines, manufacturing
Distributors for internal combustion engines manufacturing
Electrical ignition cable sets for internal combustion engines manufacturing
Generators for internal combustion engines manufacturing

Ignition wiring harness for internal combustion engines manufacturing
Instrument control panels (i.e., assembling purchased gauges), automotive, truck, and bus, manufacturing
Spark plugs for internal combustion engines manufacturing
Windshield washer pumps, automotive, truck, and bus, manufacturing

---

US—United States industry only. CAN—United States and Canadian industries are comparable. MEX—United States and Mexican industries are comparable. Blank—Canadian, Mexican, and United States industries are comparable.

Cross-References. Establishments primarily engaged in—

- Manufacturing automotive lamps—are classified in Industry 335 1, Electric Lamp Bulb and Part Manufacturing;
- Manufacturing batteries—are classified in Industry 33591, Battery Manufacturing;
- Manufacturing electric motors for motor vehicles (including electric vehicles)—are classified in Industry 33531, Electrical Equipment Manufacturing;
- Manufacturing railway traffic control signals and passenger car alarms— are classified in Industry 33429, Other Communications Equipment Manufacturing; and
- Manufacturing car stereos—are classified in Industry 33431, Audio and Video Equipment Manufacturing.

336321 Vehicular Lighting Equipment Manufacturing[US]

This U.S. industry comprises establishments primarily engaged in manufacturing vehicular lighting fixtures.

Cross-References.

Establishments primarily engaged in manufacturing automotive lamps (i.e., bulbs) are classified in Industry 335110, Electric Lamp Bulb and Part Manufacturing.

336322 Other Motor Vehicle Electrical and Electronic Equipment Manufacturing[US]

This U.S. industry comprises establishments primarily engaged in manufacturing and/or rebuilding electrical and electronic equipment for motor vehicles and internal combustion engines.

Illustrative Examples:

Alternators and generators for internal combustion engines manufacturing

Coils, ignition, internal combustion engines, manufacturing

Distributors for internal combustion engines manufacturing

Electrical ignition cable sets for internal combustion engines manufacturing

Generators for internal combustion engines manufacturing

Ignition wiring harness for internal combustion engines manufacturing

Instrument control panel (i.e., assembling purchased gauges), automotive, truck, and bus, manufacturing

Spark plugs for internal combustion engines manufacturing

Windshield washer pumps, automotive, truck, and bus, manufacturing

---

US—United States industry only. CAN—United States and Canadian industries are comparable. MEX—United States and Mexican industries are comparable. Blank—Canadian, Mexican, and United States industries are comparable.

Cross-References. Establishments primarily engaged in—

- Manufacturing vehicular lighting equipment—are classified in U.S. Industry 336321, Vehicular Lighting Equipment Manufacturing;
- Manufacturing automotive lamps—are classified in Industry 335110, Electric Lamp Bulb and Part Manufacturing;
- Manufacturing batteries—are classified in U.S. Industry 335911, Storage Battery Manufacturing;
- Manufacturing electric motors for electric vehicles—are classified in U.S. Industry 335312, Motor and Generator Manufacturing;
- Manufacturing railway traffic control signals and passenger car alarms—are classified in Industry 334290, Other Communications Equipment Manufacturing; and
- Manufacturing car stereos—are classified in Industry 334310, Audio and Video Equipment Manufacturing.

33633 Motor Vehicle Steering and Suspension Components (except Spring) Manufacturing
See industry description for 336330 below.

336330 Motor Vehicle Steering and Suspension Components (except Spring) Manufacturing

This industry comprises establishments primarily engaged in manufacturing and/or rebuilding motor vehicle steering mechanisms and suspension components (except springs).

Illustrative Examples:

Rack and pinion steering assemblies manufacturing

Shock absorbers, automotive, truck, and bus, manufacturing

Steering columns, automotive, truck, and bus, manufacturing

Steering wheels, automotive, truck, and bus, manufacturing

Struts, automotive, truck, and bus, manufacturing

Cross-References.

Establishments primarily engaged in manufacturing springs are classified in Industry 33261, Spring and Wire Product Manufacturing.

33634 Motor Vehicle Brake System Manufacturing
See industry description for 336340 below.

336340 Motor Vehicle Brake System Manufacturing

This industry comprises establishments primarily engaged in manufacturing and/or rebuilding motor vehicle brake systems and related components.

Illustrative Examples:

Brake cylinders, master and wheel, automotive, truck, and bus, manufacturing

Brake drums, automotive, truck, and bus, manufacturing

Brake hose assemblies manufacturing

Brake pads and shoes, automotive, truck, and bus, manufacturing

Calipers, brake, automotive, truck, and bus, manufacturing

Cross-References.

Establishments primarily engaged in manufacturing rubber and plastics belts and hoses without fittings are classified in Industry 326220, Rubber and Plastics Hoses and Belting Manufacturing.

33635 Motor Vehicle Transmission and Power Train Parts Manufacturing
See industry description for 336350 below.

336350 Motor Vehicle Transmission and Power Train Parts Manufacturing

This industry comprises establishments primarily engaged in manufacturing and/or rebuilding motor vehicle transmission and power train parts.

Illustrative Examples:

Automatic transmissions, automotive, truck, and bus, manufacturing

Axle bearings, automotive, truck, and bus, manufacturing

Constant velocity joints, automotive, truck, and bus, manufacturing

Differential and rear axle assemblies, automotive, truck, and bus, manufacturing

Torque converters, automotive, truck, and bus, manufacturing

Universal joints, automotive, truck, and bus, manufacturing

33636 Motor Vehicle Seating and Interior Trim Manufacturing
See industry description for 336360 below.

336360 Motor Vehicle Seating and Interior Trim Manufacturing

This industry comprises establishments primarily engaged in manufacturing motor vehicle seating, seats, seat frames, seat belts, and interior trimmings.

US—United States industry only. CAN—United States and Canadian industries are comparable. MEX—United States and Mexican industries are comparable. Blank—Canadian, Mexican, and United States industries are comparable.

Cross-References.

Establishments primarily engaged in manufacturing convertible tops for vehicles and those manufacturing air bags are classified in U.S. Industry 336399, All Other Motor Vehicle Parts Manufacturing.

33637 Motor Vehicle Metal Stamping
See industry description for 336370 below.

336370 Motor Vehicle Metal Stamping

This industry comprises establishments primarily engaged in manufacturing motor vehicle stampings, such as fenders, tops, body parts, trim, and molding.

Cross-References. Establishments primarily engaged in—

- Manufacturing stampings and further processing the stampings—are classified according to the process of the specific product made; and

- Manufacturing stampings (except motor vehicle)—are classified in U.S. Industry 332116 Metal Stamping.

33639 Other Motor Vehicle Parts Manufacturing

This industry comprises establishments primarily engaged in manufacturing and/or rebuilding motor vehicle parts and accessories (except motor vehicle gasoline engines and engine parts, motor vehicle electrical and electronic equipment, motor vehicle steering and suspension components, motor vehicle brake systems, motor vehicle transmission and power train parts, motor vehicle seating and interior trim, and motor vehicle stampings).

Illustrative Examples:

Air bag assemblies manufacturing	Mufflers and resonators, motor vehicle, manufacturing
Air-conditioners, motor vehicle, manufacturing	Radiators and cores manufacturing
Catalytic converters, engine exhaust, automotive, truck, and bus, manufacturing	Wheels (i.e., rims), automotive, truck, and bus, manufacturing

Cross-References. Establishments primarily engaged in—

- Manufacturing motor vehicle gasoline engines and engine parts—are classified in Industry 33631, Motor Vehicle Gasoline Engine and Engine Parts Manufacturing;

- Manufacturing motor vehicle electrical and electronic equipment—are classified in Industry 33632, Motor Vehicle Electrical and Electronic Equipment Manufacturing;
- Manufacturing motor vehicle steering and suspension components—are classified in Industry 33633, Motor Vehicle Steering and Suspension Components (except Spring) Manufacturing;
- Manufacturing motor vehicle brake systems—are classified in Industry 33634, Motor Vehicle Brake System Manufacturing;
- Manufacturing motor vehicle transmission and power train parts—are classified in Industry 33635, Motor Vehicle Transmission and Power Train Parts Manufacturing;
- Manufacturing motor vehicle seating and interior trim—are classified in Industry 33636, Motor Vehicle Seating and Interior Trim Manufacturing;
- Manufacturing motor vehicle stampings—are classified in Industry 33637, Motor Vehicle Metal Stamping; and
- Manufacturing air-conditioning systems and compressors (except motor vehicle air-conditioning systems)—are classified in Industry 33341, Ventilation, Heating, Air-Conditioning, and Commercial Refrigeration Equipment Manufacturing.

336391 Motor Vehicle Air-Conditioning Manufacturing[US]

This U.S. industry comprises establishments primarily engaged in manufacturing air-conditioning systems and compressors for motor vehicles, such as automobiles, trucks, buses, aircraft, farm machinery, construction machinery, and other related vehicles.

Cross-References.

Establishments primarily engaged in manufacturing air-conditioning systems and compressors (except motor vehicle air-conditioning systems) are classified in U.S. Industry 333415, Air-Conditioning and Warm Air Heating Equipment and Commercial and Industrial Refrigeration Equipment Manufacturing.

336399 All Other Motor Vehicle Parts Manufacturing[US]

This U.S. industry comprises establishments primarily engaged in manufacturing and/or rebuilding motor vehicle parts and accessories (except motor vehicle gasoline engines and engine parts, motor vehicle electrical and electronic equipment, motor vehicle steering and suspension components, motor vehicle brake systems,

---

US—United States industry only. CAN—United States and Canadian industries are comparable. MEX—United States and Mexican industries are comparable. Blank—Canadian, Mexican, and United States industries are comparable.

motor vehicle transmission and power train parts, motor vehicle seating and interior trim, motor vehicle stampings, and motor vehicle air-conditioning systems and compressors).

Illustrative Examples:

Air bag assemblies manufacturing
Air-filters, automotive, truck, and bus, manufacturing
Catalytic converters, engine exhaust, automotive, truck, and bus, manufacturing

Mufflers and resonators, motor vehicle, manufacturing
Radiators and cores manufacturing
Wheels (i.e., rims), automotive, truck, and bus, manufacturing

Cross-References. Establishments primarily engaged in—

- Manufacturing motor vehicle gasoline engines and engine parts—are classified in Industry 33631, Motor Vehicle Gasoline Engine and Engine Parts Manufacturing;

- Manufacturing motor vehicle electrical and electronic equipment—are classified in Industry 33632, Motor Vehicle Electrical and Electronic Equipment Manufacturing;

- Manufacturing motor vehicle steering and suspension components—are classified in Industry 336330, Motor Vehicle Steering and Suspension Components (except Spring) Manufacturing;

- Manufacturing motor vehicle brake systems—are classified in Industry 336340, Motor Vehicle Brake System Manufacturing;

- Manufacturing motor vehicle transmission and power train parts—are classified in Industry 336350, Motor Vehicle Transmission and Power Train Parts Manufacturing;

- Manufacturing motor vehicle seating and interior trim—are classified in Industry 336360, Motor Vehicle Seating and Interior Trim Manufacturing;

- Manufacturing motor vehicle stampings—are classified in Industry 336370, Motor Vehicle Metal Stamping; and

- Manufacturing motor vehicle air-conditioning systems and compressors— are classified in U.S. Industry 336391, Motor Vehicle Air-Conditioning Manufacturing.

3364 Aerospace Product and Parts Manufacturing

33641 Aerospace Product and Parts Manufacturing

This industry comprises establishments primarily engaged in one or more of the following: (1) manufacturing complete aircraft, missiles, or space vehicles;

US—United States industry only. CAN—United States and Canadian industries are comparable. MEX—United States and Mexican industries are comparable. Blank—Canadian, Mexican, and United States industries are comparable.

(2) manufacturing aerospace engines, propulsion units, auxiliary equipment or parts; (3) developing and making prototypes of aerospace products; (4) aircraft conversion (i.e., major modifications to systems); and (5) complete aircraft or propulsion systems overhaul and rebuilding (i.e., periodic restoration of aircraft to original design specifications).

Cross-References.

- Establishments primarily engaged in manufacturing space satellites are classified in Industry 33422, Radio and Television Broadcasting and Wireless Communications Equipment Manufacturing;
- Establishments primarily engaged in the repair of aircraft or aircraft engines (except overhauling, conversion, and rebuilding) are classified in Industry 48819, Other Support Activities for Air Transportation;
- Research and development establishments primarily engaged in aerospace R&D (except prototype production) are classified in Industry 54171, Research and Development in the Physical, Engineering, and Life Sciences;
- Establishments primarily engaged in manufacturing aircraft engine intake and exhaust valves, pistons, or engine filters are classified in Industry 33631, Motor Vehicle Gasoline Engine and Engine Parts Manufacturing;
- Establishments primarily engaged in manufacturing of aircraft seating are classified in Industry 33636, Motor Vehicle Seating and Interior Trim Manufacturing;
- Establishments primarily engaged in manufacturing aeronautical, navigational, and guidance systems and instruments are classified in Industry 33451, Navigational, Measuring, Electromedical, and Control Instruments Manufacturing;
- Establishment primarily engaged in manufacturing aircraft engine electrical (aeronautical electrical) equipment or aircraft lighting fixtures are classified in Industry 33632, Motor Vehicle Electrical and Electronic Equipment Manufacturing; and
- Establishments primarily engaged in manufacturing of aircraft fluid power subassemblies are classified in Industry 33291, Metal Valve Manufacturing.

336411 Aircraft Manufacturing[US]

This U.S. industry comprises establishments primarily engaged in one or more of the following: (1) manufacturing or assembling complete aircraft; (2) developing and making aircraft prototypes; (3) aircraft conversion (i.e., major modifications to systems); and (4) complete aircraft overhaul and rebuilding (i.e., periodic restoration of aircraft to original design specifications).

Cross-References.

- Establishments primarily engaged in manufacturing guided missiles and space vehicles are classified in U.S. Industry 336414, Guided Missile and Space Vehicle Manufacturing;

- Establishments primarily engaged in the repair of aircraft (except overhauling, conversion, and rebuilding) are classified in Industry 488190, Other Support Activities for Air Transportation; and

- Research and development establishments primarily engaged in aircraft R&D (except prototype production) are classified in Industry 541710, Research and Development in the Physical, Engineering, and Life Sciences.

336412 Aircraft Engine and Engine Parts Manufacturing[US]

This U.S. industry comprises establishments primarily engaged in one or more of the following: (1) manufacturing aircraft engines and engine parts; (2) developing and making prototypes of aircraft engines and engine parts; (3) aircraft propulsion system conversion (i.e., major modifications to systems); and (4) aircraft propulsion systems overhaul and rebuilding (i.e., periodic restoration of aircraft propulsion system to original design specifications).

Cross-References.

- Establishments primarily engaged in manufacturing guided missile and space vehicle propulsion units and parts are classified in U.S. Industry 336415, Guided Missile and Space Vehicle Propulsion Unit and Propulsion Unit Parts Manufacturing;

- Establishments primarily engaged in manufacturing aircraft intake and exhaust valves and pistons are classified in U.S. Industry 336311, Carburetor, Piston, Piston Ring, and Valve Manufacturing;

- Establishments primarily engaged in manufacturing aircraft internal combustion engine filters are classified in U.S. Industry 336312, Gasoline Engine and Engine Parts Manufacturing;

- Establishments primarily engaged in the repair of aircraft engines (except overhauling, conversion, and rebuilding) are classified in Industry 488190, Other Support Activities for Air Transportation;

- Research and development establishments primarily engaged in aircraft engine and engine parts R&D (except prototype production) are classified in Industry 541710, Research and Development in the Physical, Engineering, and Life Sciences; and

- Establishments primarily engaged in manufacturing aeronautical instruments are classified in U.S. Industry 334511, Search, Detection, Navigation,

---

US—United States industry only. CAN—United States and Canadian industries are comparable. MEX—United States and Mexican industries are comparable. Blank—Canadian, Mexican, and United States industries are comparable.

Guidance, Aeronautical, and Nautical System and Instrument Manufacturing.

336413 Other Aircraft Parts and Auxiliary Equipment Manufacturing[US]

This U.S. industry comprises establishment primarily engaged in (1) manufacturing aircraft parts or auxiliary equipment (except engines and aircraft fluid power subassemblies) and/or (2) developing and making prototypes of aircraft parts and auxiliary equipment. Auxiliary equipment includes such items as crop dusting apparatus, armament racks, inflight refueling equipment, and external fuel tanks.

Cross-References.

- Establishments primarily engaged in manufacturing aircraft engines and engine parts are classified in U.S. Industry 336412, Aircraft Engine and Engine Parts Manufacturing;

- Establishments primarily engaged in manufacturing aeronautical instruments are classified in U.S. Industry 334511, Search, Detection, Navigation, Guidance, Aeronautical, and Nautical System and Instrument Manufacturing;

- Establishments primarily engaged in manufacturing aircraft lighting fixtures are classified in U.S. Industry 336321, Vehicular Lighting Equipment Manufacturing;

- Establishments primarily engaged in manufacturing aircraft engine electrical (aeronautical electrical) equipment are classified in U.S. Industry 336322, Other Motor Vehicle Electrical and Electronic Equipment Manufacturing;

- Establishments primarily engaged in manufacturing guided missile and space vehicle parts and auxiliary equipment are classified in U.S. Industry 336419, Other Guided Missile and Space Vehicle Parts and Auxiliary Equipment Manufacturing;

- Establishments primarily engaged in manufacturing of aircraft fluid power subassemblies are classified in U.S. Industry 332912, Fluid Power Valve and Hose Fitting Manufacturing;

- Establishments primarily engaged in manufacturing of aircraft seating are classified in Industry 336360, Motor Vehicle Seating and Interior Trim Manufacturing; and

- Research and development establishments primarily engaged in aircraft parts and auxiliary equipment R&D (except prototype production) are classified in

Industry 541710, Research and Development in the Physical, Engineering, and Life Sciences.

336414 Guided Missile and Space Vehicle Manufacturing[US]

This U.S. industry comprises establishments primarily engaged in (1) manufacturing complete guided missiles and space vehicles and/or (2) developing and making prototypes of guided missile or space vehicles.

Cross-References.

- Establishments primarily engaged in manufacturing space satellites are classified in Industry 334220, Radio and Television Broadcasting and Wireless Communications Equipment Manufacturing; and

- Research and development establishments primarily engaged in guided missile and space vehicle R&D (except prototype production) are classified in Industry 541710, Research and Development in the Physical, Engineering, and Life Sciences.

336415 Guided Missile and Space Vehicle Propulsion Unit and Propulsion Unit Parts Manufacturing[US]

This U.S. industry comprises establishments primarily engaged in (1) manufacturing guided missile and/or space vehicle propulsion units and propulsion unit parts and/or (2) developing and making prototypes of guided missile and space vehicle propulsion units and propulsion unit parts.

Cross-References.

Research and development establishments primarily engaged in guided missile and space propulsion unit and propulsion unit parts R&D (except prototype production) are classified in Industry 541710, Research and Development in the Physical, Engineering, and Life Sciences.

336419 Other Guided Missile and Space Vehicle Parts and Auxiliary Equipment Manufacturing[US]

This U.S. Industry comprises establishments primarily engaged in (1) manufacturing guided missile and space vehicle parts and auxiliary equipment (except guided missile and space vehicle propulsion units and propulsion unit parts) and/or (2) developing and making prototypes of guided missile and space vehicle parts and auxiliary equipment.

Cross-References.

- Establishments primarily engaged in manufacturing navigational and guidance systems are classified in U.S. Industry 334511, Search, Detection, Navigation, Guidance, Aeronautical, and Nautical System and Instrument Manufacturing;

- Establishments primarily engaged in manufacturing guided missile and space vehicle propulsion units and propulsion unit parts are classified in U.S. Industry 336415, Guided Missile and Space Vehicle Propulsion Unit and Propulsion Unit Parts Manufacturing; and

- Research and development establishments primarily engaged in guided missile and space vehicle parts and auxiliary equipment R&D (except prototype production) are classified in Industry 541710, Research and Development in the Physical, Engineering, and Life Sciences.

3365 Railroad Rolling Stock Manufacturing

33651 Railroad Rolling Stock Manufacturing
See industry description for 336510 below.

336510 Railroad Rolling Stock Manufacturing

This industry comprises establishments primarily engaged in one or more of the following: (1) manufacturing and/or rebuilding locomotives, locomotive frames and parts; (2) manufacturing railroad, street, and rapid transit cars and car equipment for operation on rails for freight and passenger service; and (3) manufacturing rail layers, ballast distributors, rail tamping equipment and other railway track maintenance equipment.

Cross-References.

- Establishments primarily engaged in manufacturing mining rail cars are classified in U.S. Industry 333131, Mining Machinery and Equipment Manufacturing;

- Establishments primarily engaged in manufacturing locomotive fuel lubricating or cooling medium pumps are classified in U.S. Industry 333911, Pump and Pumping Equipment Manufacturing;

- Repair establishments of railroad and local transit companies primarily engaged in repairing railroad and transit cars are classified in Industry 488210, Support Activities for Rail Transportation; and

- Establishments not owned by railroad or local transit companies primarily engaged in repairing railroad cars and locomotive engines are classified in

US—United States industry only. CAN—United States and Canadian industries are comparable. MEX—United States and Mexican industries are comparable. Blank—Canadian, Mexican, and United States industries are comparable.

Industry 811310, Commercial and Industrial Machinery and Equipment (except Automotive and Electronic) Repair and Maintenance.

3366 Ship and Boat Building

33661 Ship and Boat Building

This industry comprises establishments primarily engaged in operating shipyards or boat yards (i.e., ship or boat manufacturing facilities). Shipyards are fixed facilities with drydocks and fabrication equipment capable of building a ship, defined as watercraft typically suitable or intended for other than personal or recreational use. Boats are defined as watercraft typically suitable or intended for personal use. Activities of shipyards include the construction of ships, their repair, conversion and alteration, the production of prefabricated ship and barge sections, and specialized services, such as ship scaling.

Illustrative Examples:

Barge building	Drilling and production platforms,
Boat yards (i.e., boat manufacturing	floating, oil and gas, building
facilities)	Passenger ship building
Cargo ship building	Rowboats manufacturing

Cross-References. Establishments primarily engaged in—

- Manufacturing rubber boats—are classified in Industry 32629, Other Rubber Product Manufacturing;

- Manufacturing nonrigid (i.e., inflatable) plastics boats—are classified in Industry 32619, Other Plastics Product Manufacturing;

- Fabricating structural assemblies or components for ships, or subcontractors engaged in ship painting, joinery, carpentry work, and electrical wiring installation—are classified based on the production process used; and

- Ship repairs performed in floating drydocks—are classified in Industry 48839, Other Support Activities for Water Transportation.

336611 Ship Building and Repairing[CAN]

This U.S. industry comprises establishments primarily engaged in operating a shipyard. Shipyards are fixed facilities with drydocks and fabrication equipment capable of building a ship, defined as watercraft typically suitable or intended for other than personal or recreational use. Activities of shipyards include the construction of ships, their repair, conversion and alteration, the production of prefabricated ship and barge sections, and specialized services, such as ship scaling.

Illustrative Examples:

Barge building
Cargo ship building
Drilling and production platforms,
 floating, oil and gas, building

Passenger ship building
Submarine building

Cross-References. Establishments primarily engaged in—

- Fabricating structural assemblies or components for ships, or subcontractors engaged in ship painting, joinery, carpentry work, and electrical wiring installation—are classified based on the production process used; and

- Ship repairs performed in floating drydocks—are classified in Industry 488390, Other Support Activities for Water Transportation.

336612 Boat Building^{CAN}

This U.S. industry comprises establishments primarily engaged in building boats. Boats are defined as watercraft not built in shipyards and typically of the type suitable or intended for personal use.

Illustrative Examples:

Dinghy (except inflatable rubber)
 manufacturing
Motorboats, inboard or outboard,
 building

Rowboats manufacturing
Sailboat building, not done in shipyards
Yacht building, not done in shipyards

Cross-References. Establishments primarily engaged in—

- Ship building or ship repairs performed in a shipyard—are classified in U.S. Industry 336611, Ship Building and Repairing;

- Manufacturing rubber boats and life rafts—are classified in U.S. Industry 326299, All Other Rubber Product Manufacturing; and

- Manufacturing nonrigid (i.e., inflatable) plastics boats—are classified in U.S. Industry 326199, All Other Plastics Product Manufacturing.

3369 Other Transportation Equipment Manufacturing

This industry group comprises establishments primarily engaged in manufacturing transportation equipment (except motor vehicles and parts, aerospace products and parts, railroad rolling stock, ship building, and boat manufacturing).

US—United States industry only. CAN—United States and Canadian industries are comparable. MEX—United States and Mexican industries are comparable. Blank—Canadian, Mexican, and United States industries are comparable.

33699 Other Transportation Equipment Manufacturing

This industry comprises establishments primarily engaged in manufacturing motorcycles, bicycles, metal tricycles, complete military armored vehicles, tanks, self-propelled weapons, vehicles pulled by draft animals, and other transportation equipment (except motor vehicles, boats, ships, railroad rolling stock, and aerospace products), including parts thereof.

Cross-References. Establishments primarily engaged in—

- Manufacturing ships and boats—are classified in Industry 33661, Ship and Boat Building;
- Manufacturing aerospace products and parts—are classified in Industry 33641, Aerospace Product and Parts Manufacturing;
- Manufacturing motor vehicle parts—are classified in Industry Group 3363, Motor Vehicle Parts Manufacturing;
- Manufacturing children's vehicles (except bicycles and metal tricycles)— are classified in Industry 33993, Doll, Toy, and Game Manufacturing;
- Manufacturing railroad rolling stock—are classified in Industry 33651, Railroad Rolling Stock Manufacturing; and
- Manufacturing motor vehicles—are classified in Industry Group 3361, Motor Vehicle Manufacturing.

336991 Motorcycle, Bicycle, and Parts Manufacturing[US]

This U.S. industry comprises establishments primarily engaged in manufacturing motorcycles, bicycles, tricycles and similar equipment, and parts.

Cross-References. Establishments primarily engaged in—

- Manufacturing children's vehicles (except bicycles and metal tricycles)— are classified in U.S. Industry 339932, Game, Toy, and Children's Vehicle Manufacturing; and
- Manufacturing golf carts and other similar personnel carriers—are classified in U.S. Industry 336999, All Other Transportation Equipment Manufacturing.

336992 Military Armored Vehicle, Tank, and Tank Component Manufacturing[US]

This U.S. industry comprises establishments primarily engaged in manufacturing complete military armored vehicles, combat tanks, specialized components for combat tanks, and self-propelled weapons.

Cross-References.

Establishments primarily engaged in manufacturing nonarmored military universal carriers are classified in U.S. Industry 336112, Light Truck and Utility Vehicle Manufacturing.

336999 All Other Transportation Equipment Manufacturing[US]

This U.S. industry comprises establishments primarily engaged in manufacturing transportation equipment (except motor vehicles, motor vehicle parts, boats, ships, railroad rolling stock, aerospace products, motorcycles, bicycles, armored vehicles and tanks).

Illustrative Examples:

All-terrain vehicles (ATVs), wheeled or tracked, manufacturing
Animal-drawn vehicles and parts manufacturing
Gocarts (except children's) manufacturing
Golf carts and similar motorized passenger carriers manufacturing
Race cars manufacturing
Snowmobiles and parts manufacturing

Cross-References. Establishments primarily engaged in—

- Manufacturing motorcycles, bicycles and parts—are classified in U.S. Industry 336991, Motorcycle, Bicycle, and Parts Manufacturing;

- Manufacturing military armored vehicles, tanks, and tank components—are classified in U.S. Industry 336992, Military Armored Vehicle, Tank, and Tank Component Manufacturing;

- Manufacturing ships and boats—are classified in Industry 33661, Ship and Boat Building;

- Manufacturing aerospace products and parts—are classified in Industry 33641, Aerospace Product and Parts Manufacturing;

- Manufacturing motor vehicle parts—are classified in Industry Group 3363, Motor Vehicle Parts Manufacturing;

- Manufacturing railroad rolling stock—are classified in Industry 336510, Railroad Rolling Stock Manufacturing; and

- Manufacturing motor vehicles—are classified in Industry Group 3361, Motor Vehicle Manufacturing.

337 Furniture and Related Product Manufacturing

Industries in the Furniture and Related Product Manufacturing subsector make furniture and related articles, such as mattresses, window blinds, cabinets, and fixtures. The processes used in the manufacture of furniture include the cutting, bending, molding, laminating, and assembly of such materials as wood, metal, glass, plastics, and rattan. However, the production process for furniture is not solely bending metal, cutting and shaping wood, or extruding and molding plastics. Design and fashion trends play an important part in the production of furniture. The integrated design of the article for both esthetic and functional qualities is also a major part of the process of manufacturing furniture. Design services may be performed by the furniture establishment's work force or may be purchased from industrial designers.

Furniture may be made of any material, but the most common ones used in North America are metal and wood. Furniture manufacturing establishments may specialize in making articles primarily from one material. Some of the equipment required to make a wooden table, for example, is different from that used to make a metal one. However, furniture is usually made from several materials. A wooden table might have metal brackets, and a wooden chair a fabric or plastics seat. Therefore, in NAICS, furniture initially is classified based on the type of furniture (application for which it is designed) rather than the material used. For example, an upholstered sofa is treated as household furniture, although it may also be used in hotels or offices.

When classifying furniture according to the component material from which it is made, furniture made from more than one material is classified based on the material used in the frame, or if there is no frame, the predominant component material. Upholstered household furniture (excluding kitchen and dining room chairs with upholstered seats) is classified without regard to the frame material. Kitchen or dining room chairs with upholstered seats are classified according to the frame material.

Furniture may be made on a stock or custom basis and may be shipped assembled or unassembled (i.e., knockdown). The manufacture of furniture parts and frames is included in this subsector.

Some of the processes used in furniture manufacturing are similar to processes that are used in other segments of manufacturing. For example, cutting and assembly occurs in the production of wood trusses that are classified in Subsector 321, Wood Product Manufacturing. However, the multiple processes that distinguish wood furniture manufacturing from wood product manufacturing warrant inclusion of wooden furniture manufacturing in the Furniture and Related Product Manufacturing subsector. Metal furniture manufacturing uses techniques that are also employed in the manufacturing of roll-formed products classified in Subsector 332, Fabricated Metal Product Manufacturing. The molding process for plastics furniture is similar to the molding of other plastics products. However, plastics furniture producing establishments tend to specialize in furniture.

NAICS attempts to keep furniture manufacturing together, but there are two notable exceptions: seating for transportation equipment and laboratory and hospital furniture. These exceptions are related to that fact that some of the aspects of the production process for these products, primarily the design, are highly integrated with that of other manufactured goods, namely motor vehicles and health equipment.

3371 Household and Institutional Furniture and Kitchen Cabinet Manufacturing

This industry group comprises establishments manufacturing household-type furniture, such as living room, kitchen and bedroom furniture and institutional (i.e., public building) furniture, such as furniture for schools, theaters, and churches.

33711 Wood Kitchen Cabinet and Countertop Manufacturing
See industry description for 337110 below.

337110 Wood Kitchen Cabinet and Countertop Manufacturing

This industry comprises establishments primarily engaged in manufacturing wood or plastics laminated on wood kitchen cabinets, bathroom vanities, and countertops (except freestanding). The cabinets and counters may be made on a stock or custom basis.

Cross-References. Establishments primarily engaged in—

- Manufacturing metal kitchen and bathroom cabinets (except freestanding)—are classified in U.S. Industry 337124, Metal Household Furniture Manufacturing;

- Manufacturing plastics countertops—are classified in U.S. Industry 326199, All Other Plastics Product Manufacturing;

- Manufacturing stone countertops—are classified in U.S. Industry 327991, Cut Stone and Stone Product Manufacturing; and

- Manufacturing wood or plastics laminated on wood countertops (except kitchen and bathroom)—are classified in U.S. Industry 337215, Showcase, Partition, Shelving, and Locker Manufacturing.

33712 Household and Institutional Furniture Manufacturing

This industry comprises establishments primarily engaged in manufacturing household-type and public building furniture (i.e., library, school, theater, and church furniture). The furniture may be made on a stock or custom basis and may be assembled or unassembled (i.e., knockdown).

US—United States industry only. CAN—United States and Canadian industries are comparable. MEX—United States and Mexican industries are comparable. Blank—Canadian, Mexican, and United States industries are comparable.

Cross-References. Establishments primarily engaged in—

- Manufacturing laboratory and hospital furniture—are classified in Industry 33911, Medical Equipment and Supplies Manufacturing;
- Manufacturing wood or plastics laminated on wood kitchen cabinets, bathroom vanities, and countertops (except freestanding)—are classified in Industry 33711, Wood Kitchen Cabinet and Countertop Manufacturing;
- Manufacturing office-type furniture and/or office or store fixtures—are classified in Industry 33721, Office Furniture (including Fixtures) Manufacturing; and
- Repairing or refinishing furniture—are classified in Industry 81142, Reupholstery and Furniture Repair.

337121 Upholstered Household Furniture Manufacturing[CAN]

This U.S. industry comprises establishments primarily engaged in manufacturing upholstered household-type furniture. The furniture may be made on a stock or custom basis.

Cross-References. Establishments primarily engaged in—

- Reupholstering furniture or upholstering frames to individual order—are classified in Industry 811420, Reupholstery and Furniture Repair;
- Wood kitchen and dining room chairs with upholstered seats or backs—are classified in U. S. Industry 337122, Nonupholstered Wood Household Furniture Manufacturing;
- Metal kitchen and dining room chairs with upholstered seats or backs—are classified in U.S. Industry 337124, Metal Household Furniture Manufacturing; and
- Kitchen and dining room chairs (except wood and metal) with upholstered seats or backs— are classified in U.S. Industry 337125, Household Furniture (except Wood and Metal) Manufacturing.

337122 Nonupholstered Wood Household Furniture Manufacturing[US]

This U.S. industry comprises establishments primarily engaged in manufacturing nonupholstered wood household-type furniture and freestanding cabinets (except television, radio, and sewing machine cabinets). The furniture may be made on a stock or custom basis and may be assembled or unassembled (i.e., knockdown).

Cross-References. Establishments primarily engaged in—

- Manufacturing reed, rattan, plastics and similar furniture—are classified in U.S. Industry 337125, Household Furniture (except Wood and Metal) Manufacturing;
- Manufacturing wood or plastics laminated on wood kitchen cabinets, bathroom vanities, and countertops (except freestanding)—are classified in Industry 337110, Wood Kitchen Cabinet and Countertop Manufacturing;
- Manufacturing wood television, stereo, loudspeaker, and sewing machine cabinets (i.e., housings)—are classified in U.S. Industry 337129, Wood Television, Radio, and Sewing Machine Cabinet Manufacturing; and
- Repairing or refinishing furniture—are classified in Industry 811420, Reupholstery and Furniture Repair.

337124 Metal Household Furniture Manufacturing[US]

This U.S. industry comprises establishments primarily engaged in manufacturing metal household-type furniture and freestanding cabinets. The furniture may be made on a stock or custom basis and may be assembled or unassembled (i.e., knockdown).

Cross-References.

Establishments primarily engaged in manufacturing metal laboratory and hospital furniture including beds are classified in Industry 33911, Medical Equipment and Supplies Manufacturing.

337125 Household Furniture (except Wood and Metal) Manufacturing[US]

This U.S. industry comprises establishments primarily engaged in manufacturing household-type furniture of materials other than wood or metal, such as plastics, reed, rattan, wicker, and fiberglass. The furniture may be made on a stock or custom basis and may be assembled or unassembled (i.e., knockdown).

Cross-References. Establishments primarily engaged in—

- Manufacturing concrete, ceramic, or stone furniture—are classified in Subsector 327, Nonmetallic Mineral Product Manufacturing, according to the materials used;
- Manufacturing upholstered household-type furniture—are classified in U.S. Industry 337121, Upholstered Household Furniture Manufacturing;

- Manufacturing metal household-type furniture—are classified in U.S. Industry 337124, Metal Household Furniture Manufacturing; and

- Manufacturing nonupholstered wood household-type furniture—are classified in U.S. Industry 337122, Nonupholstered Wood Household Furniture Manufacturing.

337127 Institutional Furniture Manufacturing^{CAN}

This U.S. industry comprises establishments primarily engaged in manufacturing institutional-type furniture (e.g., library, school, theater, and church furniture). The furniture may be made on a stock or custom basis and may be assembled or unassembled (i.e., knockdown).

Cross-References. Establishments primarily engaged in—

- Manufacturing laboratory and hospital furniture—are classified in Industry 33911, Medical Equipment and Supplies Manufacturing;

- Manufacturing wood kitchen cabinets, wood bathroom vanities, and countertops designed for permanent installation—are classified in Industry 337110, Wood Kitchen Cabinet and Countertop Manufacturing;

- Manufacturing office-type furniture and/or office or store fixtures—are classified in Industry 33721, Office Furniture (including Fixtures) Manufacturing; and

- Repairing or refinishing furniture—are classified in Industry 811420, Reupholstery and Furniture Repair.

337129 Wood Television, Radio, and Sewing Machine Cabinet Manufacturing^{US}

This U.S. industry comprises establishments primarily engaged in manufacturing wood cabinets used as housings by television, stereo, loudspeaker, and sewing machine manufacturers.

Cross-References. Establishments primarily engaged in—

- Manufacturing plastics housings used by television, stereo, loudspeaker, and sewing machine manufacturers—are classified in U.S. Industry 326199, All Other Plastics Product Manufacturing;

- Manufacturing metal housings used by television, stereo, loudspeaker, and sewing machine manufacturers—are classified in U.S. Industry 332322, Sheet Metal Work Manufacturing;

US—United States industry only. CAN—United States and Canadian industries are comparable. MEX—United States and Mexican industries are comparable. Blank—Canadian, Mexican, and United States industries are comparable.

- Manufacturing freestanding wood household-type cabinets (e.g., entertainment centers, stands) for consumer electronics—are classified in U.S. Industry 337122, Nonupholstered Wood Household Furniture Manufacturing;

- Manufacturing freestanding metal household-type cabinets (e.g., entertainment centers, stands) for consumer electronics—are classified in U.S. Industry 337124, Metal Household Furniture Manufacturing; and

- Manufacturing freestanding household-type cabinets (e.g., entertainment centers, stands) (except wood and metal) for consumer electronics—are classified in U.S. Industry 337125, Household Furniture (except Wood and Metal) Manufacturing.

3372 Office Furniture (including Fixtures) Manufacturing

33721 Office Furniture (including Fixtures) Manufacturing

This industry comprises establishments primarily engaged in manufacturing office furniture and/or office and store fixtures. The furniture may be made on a stock or custom basis and may be assembled or unassembled (i.e., knockdown).

Cross-References. Establishments primarily engaged in—

- Manufacturing millwork on a factory basis—are classified in Industry 32191, Millwork;

- Manufacturing household-type and institutional-type furniture—are classified in Industry 33712, Household and Institutional Furniture Manufacturing;

- Manufacturing refrigerated cabinets, showcases, and display cases—are classified in Industry 33341, Ventilation, Heating, Air-Conditioning, and Commercial Refrigeration Equipment Manufacturing; and

- Manufacturing metal safes and vaults—are classified in Industry 33299, All Other Fabricated Metal Product Manufacturing.

337211 Wood Office Furniture Manufacturing[US]

This U.S. industry comprises establishments primarily engaged in manufacturing wood office-type furniture. The furniture may be made on a stock or custom basis and may be assembled or unassembled (i.e., knockdown).

337212 Custom Architectural Woodwork and Millwork Manufacturing[US]

This U.S. industry comprises establishments primarily engaged in manufacturing custom designed interiors consisting of architectural woodwork and fixtures utiliz-

---

US—United States industry only. CAN—United States and Canadian industries are comparable. MEX—United States and Mexican industries are comparable. Blank—Canadian, Mexican, and United States industries are comparable.

ing wood, wood products, and plastics laminates. All of the industry output is made to individual order on a job shop basis and requires skilled craftsmen as a labor input. A job might include custom manufacturing of display fixtures, gondolas, wall shelving units, entrance and window architectural detail, sales and reception counters, wall paneling, and matching furniture.

Cross-References. Establishments primarily engaged in—

- Manufacturing millwork on a factory basis—are classified in U.S. Industry 321918, Other Millwork (including Flooring);
- Manufacturing wood office-type furniture on a stock or custom basis—are classified in U.S. Industry 337211, Wood Office Furniture Manufacturing; and
- Manufacturing wood office-type furniture and store fixtures on a stock basis—are classified in U.S. Industry 337215, Showcase, Partition, Shelving, and Locker Manufacturing.

337214 Office Furniture (except Wood) Manufacturing^CAN

This U.S. industry comprises establishments primarily engaged in manufacturing nonwood office-type furniture. The furniture may be made on a stock or custom basis and may be assembled or unassembled (i.e., knockdown).

337215 Showcase, Partition, Shelving, and Locker Manufacturing^CAN

This U.S. industry comprises establishments primarily engaged in manufacturing wood and nonwood office and store fixtures, shelving, lockers, frames, partitions, and related fabricated products of wood and nonwood materials, including plastics laminated fixture tops. The products are made on a stock basis and may be assembled or unassembled (i.e., knockdown). Establishments exclusively making furniture parts (e.g., frames) are included in this industry.

Cross-References. Establishments primarily engaged in—

- Manufacturing refrigerated cabinets, showcases, and display cases—are classified in U.S. Industry 333415, Air-Conditioning and Warm Air Heating Equipment and Commercial and Industrial Refrigeration Equipment Manufacturing;
- Manufacturing metal safes and vaults—are classified in U.S. Industry 332999, All Other Miscellaneous Fabricated Metal Product Manufacturing; and
- Manufacturing wood or plastics laminated kitchen and bathroom countertops—are classified in Industry 337110, Wood Kitchen Cabinet and Countertop Manufacturing.

US—United States industry only. CAN—United States and Canadian industries are comparable. MEX—United States and Mexican industries are comparable. Blank—Canadian, Mexican, and United States industries are comparable.

3379 Other Furniture Related Product Manufacturing

This industry group comprises establishments manufacturing furniture related products, such as mattresses, blinds, and shades.

33791 Mattress Manufacturing
See industry description for 337910 below.

337910 Mattress Manufacturing

This industry comprises establishments primarily engaged in manufacturing innerspring, box spring, and noninnerspring mattresses, including mattresses for waterbeds.

Cross-References. Establishments primarily engaged in—

- Manufacturing individual wire springs—are classified in Industry 33261, Spring and Wire Product Manufacturing; and
- Manufacturing inflatable mattresses—are classified in Subsector 326, Plastics and Rubber Products Manufacturing.

33792 Blind and Shade Manufacturing
See industry description for 337920 below.

337920 Blind and Shade Manufacturing

This industry comprises establishments primarily engaged in manufacturing one or more of the following: venetian blinds, other window blinds, shades; curtain and drapery rods, poles; and/or curtain and drapery fixtures. The blinds and shades may be made on a stock or custom basis and may be made of any material.

Cross-References. Establishments primarily engaged in—

- Manufacturing canvas awnings—are classified in U.S. Industry 314912, Canvas and Related Product Mills; and
- Manufacturing curtains and draperies—are classified in U.S. Industry 314121, Curtain and Drapery Mills.

339 Miscellaneous Manufacturing

Industries in the Miscellaneous Manufacturing subsector make a wide range of products that cannot readily be classified in specific NAICS subsectors in manufacturing. Processes used by these establishments vary significantly, both among and within industries. For example, a variety of manufacturing processes are used in manufacturing sporting and athletic goods that include products, such as tennis racquets and golf balls. The processes for these products differ from each other, and the processes differ significantly from the fabrication processes used in making dolls or toys, the melting and shaping of precious metals to make jewelry, and the bending, forming, and assembly used in making medical products.

The industries in this subsector are defined by what is made rather than how it is made. Although individual establishments might be appropriately classified elsewhere in the NAICS structure, for historical continuity, these product-based industries were maintained. In most cases, no one process or material predominates for an industry.

Establishments in this subsector manufacture products as diverse as medical equipment and supplies, jewelry, sporting goods, toys, and office supplies.

3391 Medical Equipment and Supplies Manufacturing

33911 Medical Equipment and Supplies Manufacturing

This industry comprises establishments primarily engaged in manufacturing medical equipment and supplies. Examples of products made by these establishments are laboratory apparatus and furniture, surgical and medical instruments, surgical appliances and supplies, dental equipment and supplies, orthodontic goods, dentures, and orthodontic appliances.

Cross-References. Establishments primarily engaged in—

- Manufacturing laboratory instruments, X-ray apparatus, electromedical apparatus (including electronic hearing aids), and thermometers (except medical)—are classified in Industry 33451, Navigational, Measuring, Electromedical, and Control Instruments Manufacturing;

- Manufacturing molded glass lens blanks—are classified in Industry 32721, Glass and Glass Product Manufacturing;

- Manufacturing molded plastics lens blanks—are classified in Industry 32619, Other Plastics Product Manufacturing;

- Retailing and grinding prescription eyeglasses—are classified in Industry 44613, Optical Goods Stores; and

- Manufacturing sporting goods helmets and protective equipment—are classified in Industry, 33992 Sporting and Athletic Goods Manufacturing.

339111 Laboratory Apparatus and Furniture Manufacturing[US]

This U.S. industry comprises establishments primarily engaged in manufacturing laboratory apparatus and laboratory and hospital furniture (except dental). Exam-

---

ples of products made by these establishments are hospital beds, operating room tables, laboratory balances and scales, furnaces, ovens, centrifuges, cabinets, cases, benches, tables, and stools.

Cross-References. Establishments primarily engaged in—

- Manufacturing dental laboratory apparatus and furniture—are classified in U.S. Industry 339114, Dental Equipment and Supplies Manufacturing; and

- Manufacturing laboratory instruments—are classified in U.S. Industry 334516, Analytical Laboratory Instrument Manufacturing.

339112 Surgical and Medical Instrument Manufacturing[US]

This U.S. industry comprises establishments primarily engaged in manufacturing medical, surgical, ophthalmic, and veterinary instruments and apparatus (except electrotherapeutic, electromedical and irradiation apparatus). Examples of products made by these establishments are syringes, hypodermic needles, anesthesia apparatus, blood transfusion equipment, catheters, surgical clamps, and medical thermometers.

Cross-References. Establishments primarily engaged in—

- Manufacturing electromedical and electrotherapeutic apparatus—are classified in U.S. Industry 334510, Electromedical and Electrotherapeutic Apparatus Manufacturing;

- Manufacturing irradiation apparatus—are classified in U.S. Industry 334517, Irradiation Apparatus Manufacturing;

- Manufacturing surgical and orthopedic appliances—are classified in U.S. Industry 339113 Surgical Appliance and Supplies Manufacturing;

- Manufacturing dental equipment, dental supplies, dental laboratory apparatus, and dental laboratory furniture—are classified in U.S. Industry 339114, Dental Equipment and Supplies Manufacturing;

- Manufacturing laboratory apparatus and laboratory and hospital furniture (except dental)—are classified in U.S. Industry 339111, Laboratory Apparatus and Furniture Manufacturing; and

- Manufacturing thermometers (except medical)—are classified in U.S. Industry 334519, Other Measuring and Controlling Device Manufacturing.

339113 Surgical Appliance and Supplies Manufacturing[US]

This U.S. industry comprises establishments primarily engaged in manufacturing surgical appliances and supplies. Examples of products made by these establishments are orthopedic devices, prosthetic appliances, surgical dressings, crutches, surgical sutures, and personal industrial safety devices (except protective eyewear).

Cross-References. Establishments primarily engaged in—

- Manufacturing dental equipment, dental supplies, dental laboratory apparatus, and dental laboratory furniture—are classified in U.S. Industry 339114, Dental Equipment and Supplies Manufacturing;

- Manufacturing laboratory apparatus and laboratory and hospital furniture (except dental)—are classified in U.S. Industry 339111, Laboratory Apparatus and Furniture Manufacturing;

- Manufacturing electronic hearing aids—are classified in U.S. Industry 334510, Electromedical and Electrotherapeutic Apparatus Manufacturing;

- Manufacturing industrial protective eyewear—are classified in U.S. Industry 339115, Ophthalmic Goods Manufacturing; and

- Manufacturing sporting goods helmets and protective equipment—are classified in Industry 339920, Sporting and Athletic Goods Manufacturing.

339114 Dental Equipment and Supplies Manufacturing[US]

This U.S. industry comprises establishments primarily engaged in manufacturing dental equipment and supplies used by dental laboratories and offices of dentists, such as dental chairs, dental instrument delivery systems, dental hand instruments, and dental impression material and dental cements.

Cross-References. Establishments primarily engaged in—

- Manufacturing dentures, crowns, bridges, and orthodontic appliances customized for individual application—are classified in U.S. Industry 339116, Dental Laboratories; and

- Manufacturing laboratory apparatus and laboratory and hospital furniture (except dental)—are classified in U.S. Industry 339111, Laboratory Apparatus and Furniture Manufacturing.

339115 Ophthalmic Goods Manufacturing[US]

This U.S. industry comprises establishments primarily engaged in manufacturing ophthalmic goods. Examples of products made by these establishments are prescription eyeglasses (except manufactured in a retail setting), contact lenses, sunglasses, eyeglass frames, and reading glasses made to standard powers, and protective eyewear.

US—United States industry only. CAN—United States and Canadian industries are comparable. MEX—United States and Mexican industries are comparable. Blank—Canadian, Mexican, and United States industries are comparable.

Cross-References. Establishments primarily engaged in—

- Manufacturing molded glass lens blanks—are classified in U.S. Industry 327212, Other Pressed and Blown Glass and Glassware Manufacturing;
- Manufacturing molded plastics lens blanks—are classified in U.S. Industry 326199, All Other Plastics Product Manufacturing; and
- Retailing and grinding prescription eyeglasses—are classified in Industry 446130, Optical Goods Stores.

339116 Dental Laboratories[US]

This U.S. industry comprises establishments primarily engaged in manufacturing dentures, crowns, bridges, and orthodontic appliances customized for individual application.

Cross-References.

Establishments primarily engaged in manufacturing dental equipment and supplies are classified in U.S. Industry 339114, Dental Equipment and Supplies Manufacturing.

3399 Other Miscellaneous Manufacturing

33991 Jewelry and Silverware Manufacturing

This industry comprises establishments primarily engaged in one or more of the following: (1) manufacturing, engraving, chasing, or etching jewelry; (2) manufacturing metal personal goods (i.e., small articles carried on or about the person, such as compacts or cigarette cases); (3) manufacturing, engraving, chasing, or etching precious metal solid, precious metal clad, or pewter cutlery and flatware; (4) manufacturing, engraving, chasing, or etching personal metal goods (i.e., small articles carried on or about the person, such as compacts or cigarette cases); (5) stamping coins; (6) manufacturing unassembled jewelry parts and stock shop products, such as sheet, wire, and tubing; (7) cutting, slabbing, tumbling, carving, engraving, polishing, or faceting precious or semiprecious stones and gems; (8) recutting, repolishing, and setting gem stones; and (9) drilling, sawing, and peeling cultured and costume pearls.

Cross-References. Establishments primarily engaged in—

- Manufacturing nonprecious and precious plated metal cutlery and flatware— are classified in Industry 33221, Cutlery and Handtool Manufacturing;

US—United States industry only. CAN—United States and Canadian industries are comparable. MEX—United States and Mexican industries are comparable. Blank—Canadian, Mexican, and United States industries are comparable.

- Manufacturing nonprecious plated ware (except cutlery, flatware)—are classified in Industry 33299, All Other Fabricated Metal Product Manufacturing;

- Engraving, chasing, or etching nonprecious and precious plated metal flatware and other plated ware and plated jewelry—are classified in Industry 33281, Coating, Engraving, Heat Treating, and Allied Activities;

- Manufacturing synthetic stones or gem stones—are classified in Industry 32799, All Other Nonmetallic Mineral Product Manufacturing; and

- Manufacturing personal goods (except metal) carried on or about the person, such as compacts and cigarette cases—are classified in Industry 31699, Other Leather and Allied Product Manufacturing.

339911   Jewelry (except Costume) Manufacturing[US]

This U.S. industry comprises establishments primarily engaged in one or more of the following: (1) manufacturing, engraving, chasing, or etching precious metal solid or precious metal clad jewelry; (2) manufacturing, engraving, chasing, or etching personal goods (i.e., small articles carried on or about the person, such as compacts or cigarette cases) made of precious solid or clad metal; and (3) stamping coins.

Cross-References. Establishments primarily engaged in—

- Manufacturing, engraving, chasing, or etching costume jewelry and nonprecious metal personal goods—are classified in U.S. Industry 339914, Costume Jewelry and Novelty Manufacturing;

- Manufacturing jewelers' materials or performing lapidary work—are classified in U.S. Industry 339913, Jewelers' Material and Lapidary Work Manufacturing; and

- Plating jewelry—are classified in U.S. Industry 332813, Electroplating, Plating, Polishing, Anodizing and Coloring.

339912   Silverware and Hollowware Manufacturing[US]

This U.S. industry comprises establishments primarily engaged in manufacturing, engraving, chasing, or etching precious metal solid, precious metal clad, or pewter flatware and other hollowware.

Cross-References. Establishments primarily engaged in—

- Manufacturing nonprecious and precious plated metal cutlery and flatware—are classified in U.S. Industry 332211, Cutlery and Flatware (except Precious) Manufacturing;

US—United States industry only. CAN—United States and Canadian industries are comparable. MEX—United States and Mexican industries are comparable. Blank—Canadian, Mexican, and United States industries are comparable.

- Manufacturing nonprecious metal plated ware (except cutlery and flatware)—are classified in U.S. Industry 332999, All Other Miscellaneous Fabricated Metal Product Manufacturing;

- Engraving, chasing, or etching nonprecious and precious plated metal cutlery, flatware and other plated ware—are classified in U.S. Industry 332812, Metal Coating, Engraving (except Jewelry and Silverware), and Allied Services to Manufactures; and

- Manufacturing, engraving, chasing, or etching precious (except precious plated) metal jewelry and personal goods—are classified in U.S. Industry 339911, Jewelry (except Costume) Manufacturing.

339913 Jewelers' Material and Lapidary Work Manufacturing[US]

This U.S. industry comprises establishments primarily engaged in one or more of the following: (1) manufacturing unassembled jewelry parts and stock shop products, such as sheet, wire, and tubing; (2) cutting, slabbing, tumbling, carving, engraving, polishing or faceting precious or semiprecious stones and gems; (3) recutting, repolishing, and setting gem stones; and (4) drilling, sawing, and peeling cultured pearls.

Cross-References. Establishments primarily engaged in—

- Manufacturing synthetic stones—are classified in Industry U.S. 327999, All Other Miscellaneous Nonmetallic Mineral Product Manufacturing; and

- Manufacturing costume pearls—are classified in U.S. Industry 339914, Costume Jewelry and Novelty Manufacturing.

339914 Costume Jewelry and Novelty Manufacturing[US]

This U.S. industry comprises establishments primarily engaged in (1) manufacturing, engraving, chasing, and etching costume jewelry; and/or (2) manufacturing, engraving, chasing, or etching nonprecious metal personal goods (i.e., small articles carried on or about the person, such as compacts or cigarette cases). This industry includes establishments primarily engaged in manufacturing precious plated jewelry and precious plated personal goods.

Cross-References. Establishments primarily engaged in—

- Manufacturing, engraving, chasing, or etching precious (except precious plated) metal jewelry and novelties—are classified in U.S. Industry 339911, Jewelry (except Costume) Manufacturing;

- Manufacturing personal goods (except metal) carried on or about the person, such as compacts and cigarette cases—are classified in U.S. Industry 316993, Personal Leather Goods (except Women's Handbag and Purse) Manufacturing; and

- Manufacturing synthetic stones—are classified in U.S. Industry 327999, All Other Miscellaneous Nonmetallic Mineral Product Manufacturing.

33992 Sporting and Athletic Goods Manufacturing
See industry description for 339920 below.

339920 Sporting and Athletic Goods Manufacturing

This industry comprises establishments primarily engaged in manufacturing sporting and athletic goods (except apparel and footwear).

Cross-References. Establishments primarily engaged in—

- Manufacturing athletic apparel—are classified in Subsector 315, Apparel Manufacturing;

- Manufacturing athletic footwear—are classified in U.S. Industry 316219, Other Footwear Manufacturing; and

- Manufacturing small arms and small arms ammunition—are classified in Industry 33299, All Other Fabricated Metal Product Manufacturing.

33993 Doll, Toy, and Game Manufacturing

This industry comprises establishments primarily engaged in manufacturing dolls, toys, and games, such as complete dolls, doll parts, doll clothes, action figures, toys, games (including electronic), hobby kits, and children's vehicles (except metal bicycles and tricycles).

Cross-References. Establishments primarily engaged in—

- Manufacturing bicycles and metal tricycles—are classified in Industry 33699, Other Transportation Equipment Manufacturing;

- Manufacturing sporting and athletic goods—are classified in Industry 33992, Sporting and Athletic Goods Manufacturing;

- Manufacturing coin-operated game machines—are classified in Industry 33999, All Other Miscellaneous Manufacturing; and

- Manufacturing electronic video game cartridges and reproducing video game software—are classified in Industry 33461, Manufacturing and Reproducing Magnetic and Optical Media.

339931 Doll and Stuffed Toy Manufacturing[US]

This U.S. industry comprises establishments primarily engaged in manufacturing complete dolls, doll parts, and doll clothes, action figures, and stuffed toys.

Cross-References.

Establishments primarily engaged in manufacturing toys (except stuffed) are classified in U.S. Industry 339932, Game, Toy, and Children's Vehicle Manufacturing.

339932 Game, Toy, and Children's Vehicle Manufacturing[US]

This U.S. industry comprises establishments primarily engaged in manufacturing games (including electronic), toys, and children's vehicles (except bicycles and metal tricycles).

Cross-References Establishments primarily engaged in—

- Manufacturing dolls and stuffed toys—are classified in U.S. Industry 339931, Doll and Stuffed Toy Manufacturing;

- Manufacturing metal tricycles and bicycles—are classified in U.S. Industry 336991, Motorcycle, Bicycle, and Parts Manufacturing;

- Manufacturing sporting and athletic goods—are classified in Industry 339920, Sporting and Athletic Goods Manufacturing;

- Manufacturing coin-operated game machines—are classified in U.S. Industry 339999, All Other Miscellaneous Manufacturing; and

- Mass reproducing electronic video game cartridges—are classified in U.S. Industry 334611, Software Reproducing.

33994 Office Supplies (except Paper) Manufacturing

This industry comprises establishments primarily engaged in manufacturing office supplies. Examples of products made by these establishments are pens, pencils, felt tip markers, crayons, chalk, pencil sharpeners, staplers, hand operated stamps, modeling clay, and inked ribbons.

Cross-References. Establishments primarily engaged in—

- Manufacturing writing, drawing, and india inks—are classified in Industry 32599, All Other Chemical Product and Preparation Manufacturing;

US—United States industry only. CAN—United States and Canadian industries are comparable. MEX—United States and Mexican industries are comparable. Blank—Canadian, Mexican, and United States industries are comparable.

- Manufacturing drafting tables and boards—are classified in Industry 33712, Household and Institutional Furniture Manufacturing;
- Manufacturing rubber erasers—are classified in Industry 32629, Other Rubber Product Manufacturing;
- Manufacturing paper office supplies—are classified in Subsector 322, Paper Manufacturing;
- Manufacturing manifold business forms, blankbooks, and looseleaf binders—are classified in Industry 32311, Printing; and
- Manufacturing inkjet cartridges—are classified in Industry 32591, Printing Ink Manufacturing.

339941 Pen and Mechanical Pencil Manufacturing[US]

This U.S. industry comprises establishments primarily engaged in manufacturing pens, ballpoint pen refills and cartridges, mechanical pencils, and felt tipped markers.

Cross-References. Establishments primarily engaged in—

- Manufacturing nonmechanical pencils and pencil leads—are classified in U.S. Industry 339942, Lead Pencil and Art Good Manufacturing;
- Manufacturing writing, drawing, and india inks—are classified in U.S. Industry 325998, All Other Miscellaneous Chemical Product and Preparation Manufacturing; and
- Manufacturing rubber erasers—are classified in U.S. Industry 326299, All Other Rubber Product Manufacturing.

339942 Lead Pencil and Art Good Manufacturing[US]

This U.S. industry comprises establishments primarily engaged in manufacturing nonmechanical pencils, and art goods. Examples of products made by these establishments are pencil leads, crayons, chalk, framed blackboards, pencil sharpeners, staplers, artists' palettes and paints, and modeling clay.

Cross-References. Establishments primarily engaged in—

- Manufacturing mechanical pencils—are classified in U.S. Industry 339941, Pen and Mechanical Pencil Manufacturing;
- Manufacturing writing, drawing, and india inks—are classified in U.S. Industry 325998, All Other Miscellaneous Chemical Product and Preparation Manufacturing;

- Manufacturing rubber erasers—are classified in U.S. Industry 326299, All Other Rubber Product Manufacturing;
- Manufacturing paper office supplies—are classified in Subsector 322, Paper Manufacturing;
- Printing manifold business forms and manufacturing blankbooks and looseleaf binders and devices—are classified in Industry 32311, Printing; and
- Manufacturing drafting tables and boards—are classified in U.S. Industry 337127, Institutional Furniture Manufacturing.

339943 Marking Device Manufacturing[US]

This U.S. industry comprises establishments primarily engaged in manufacturing marking devices, such as hand operated stamps, embossing stamps, stamp pads, and stencils.

Cross-References.
Establishments primarily engaged in manufacturing felt tipped markers are classified in U.S. Industry 339941, Pen and Mechanical Pencil Manufacturing.

339944 Carbon Paper and Inked Ribbon Manufacturing[US]

This U.S. industry comprises establishments primarily engaged in manufacturing carbon paper and inked ribbons.

Cross-References. Establishments primarily engaged in manufacturing inkjet cartridges are classified in Industry 325910, Printing Ink Manufacturing.

33995 Sign Manufacturing
See industry description for 339950 below.

339950 Sign Manufacturing

This industry comprises establishments primarily engaged in manufacturing signs and related displays of all materials (except printing paper and paperboard signs, notices, displays).

Cross-References. Establishments primarily engaged in—
- Printing advertising specialties or printing paper and paperboard signs, notices, and displays—are classified in Industry 32311, Printing;

- Manufacturing and printing advertising specialties—are classified in the manufacturing sector according to products manufactured;
- Manufacturing die-cut paperboard displays—are classified in U.S. Industry 322299, All Other Converted Paper Product Manufacturing; and
- Sign lettering and painting—are classified in Industry 541890, Other Services Related to Advertising.

33999 All Other Miscellaneous Manufacturing

This industry comprises establishments primarily engaged in miscellaneous manufacturing (except medical equipment and supplies, jewelry and flatware, sporting and athletic goods, dolls, toys, games, office supplies (except paper), and signs).

Illustrative Examples:

Artificial Christmas trees manufacturing
Burial caskets and cases manufacturing
Candles manufacturing
Coin-operated amusement machines
 (except jukebox) manufacturing
Fasteners, buttons, needles, and pins
 (except precious metals or precious and
 semiprecious stones and gems)
 manufacturing

Floor and dust mops manufacturing
Gasket, packing, and sealing devices
 manufacturing
Musical instruments (except toy)
 manufacturing
Portable fire extinguishers manufacturing
Umbrellas manufacturing

Cross-References. Establishments primarily engaged in—

- Manufacturing medical equipment and supplies—are classified in Industry Group 3391; Medical Equipment and Supplies Manufacturing;
- Manufacturing jewelry and flatware—are classified in Industry 33991, Jewelry and Silverware Manufacturing;
- Manufacturing sporting and athletic goods—are classified in Industry 33992, Sporting and Athletic Goods Manufacturing;
- Manufacturing dolls, toys, and games—are classified in Industry 33993, Doll, Toy, and Game Manufacturing;
- Manufacturing office supplies (except paper)—are classified in Industry 33994, Office Supplies (except Paper) Manufacturing;
- Manufacturing signs—are classified in Industry 33995, Sign Manufacturing;
- Manufacturing concrete burial vaults—are classified in Industry 32739, Other Concrete Product Manufacturing;

- Manufacturing Christmas tree glass ornaments and glass lamp shades—are classified in Industry 32721, Glass and Glass Product Manufacturing;
- Manufacturing Christmas tree lighting sets—are classified in Industry 33512, Lighting Fixture Manufacturing;
- Manufacturing beauty and barber chairs—are classified in Industry 33712, Household and Institutional Furniture Manufacturing;
- Manufacturing burnt wood articles—are classified in Industry 32199, All Other Wood Product Manufacturing;
- Dressing and bleaching furs—are classified in Industry 31611, Leather and Hide Tanning and Finishing;
- Manufacturing paper, textile, and metal lamp shades—are classified in Industry 33512, Lighting Fixture Manufacturing;
- Manufacturing plastics lamp shades—are classified in Industry 32619, Other Plastics Product Manufacturing;
- Manufacturing matches—are classified in Industry 32599, All Other Chemical Product and Preparation Manufacturing;
- Manufacturing metal products, such as metal combs and hair curlers—are classified in Industry 33299, All Other Fabricated Metal Product Manufacturing;
- Manufacturing plastics products, such as plastics combs and hair curlers—are classified in Industry 32619, Other Plastics Product Manufacturing; and
- Manufacturing electric hair clippers for use on humans—are classified in Industry 33521, Small Electrical Appliance Manufacturing.

339991 Gasket, Packing, and Sealing Device Manufacturing[US]

This U.S. industry comprises establishments primarily engaged in manufacturing gaskets, packing, and sealing devices of all materials.

339992 Musical Instrument Manufacturing[US]

This U.S. industry comprises establishments primarily engaged in manufacturing musical instruments (except toys).

Cross-References.

Establishments primarily engaged in manufacturing toy musical instruments are classified in U.S. Industry 339932, Game, Toy, and Children's Vehicle Manufacturing.

US—United States industry only. CAN—United States and Canadian industries are comparable. MEX—United States and Mexican industries are comparable. Blank—Canadian, Mexican, and United States industries are comparable.

339993 Fastener, Button, Needle, and Pin Manufacturing^{US}

This U.S. industry comprises establishments primarily engaged in manufacturing fasteners, buttons, needles, pins, and buckles (except precious metals or precious and semiprecious stones and gems).

Cross-References. Establishments primarily engaged in—

- Manufacturing buttons, pins, and buckles made of precious metals or precious and semiprecious stones and gems—are classified in U.S. Industry 339911, Jewelry (except Costume) Manufacturing;
- Manufacturing hypodermic and suture needles—are classified in U.S. Industry 339112, Surgical and Medical Instrument Manufacturing; and
- Manufacturing phonograph and styli needles—are classified in U.S. Industry 334419, Other Electronic Component Manufacturing.

339994 Broom, Brush, and Mop Manufacturing^{US}

This U.S. industry comprises establishments primarily engaged in manufacturing brooms, mops, and brushes.

339995 Burial Casket Manufacturing^{MEX}

This U.S. industry comprises establishments primarily engaged in manufacturing burial caskets, cases, and vaults (except concrete).

Cross-References.

Establishments primarily engaged in manufacturing concrete burial vaults are classified in Industry 327390, Other Concrete Product Manufacturing.

339999 All Other Miscellaneous Manufacturing^{US}

This U.S. industry comprises establishments primarily engaged in miscellaneous manufacturing (except medical equipment and supplies, jewelry and flatware, sporting and athletic goods, dolls, toys, games, office supplies (except paper), musical instruments, fasteners, buttons, needles, pins, brooms, brushes, mops, and burial caskets).

Illustrative Examples:

Artificial Christmas trees manufacturing	Hair pieces (e.g., wigs, toupees, wiglets)
Candles manufacturing	manufacturing

US—United States industry only. CAN—United States and Canadian industries are comparable. MEX—United States and Mexican industries are comparable. Blank—Canadian, Mexican, and United States industries are comparable.

Christmas tree ornaments (except glass and electric) manufacturing

Cigarette lighters (except precious metal) manufacturing

Coin-operated amusement machines (except jukebox) manufacturing

Portable fire extinguishers manufacturing

Potpourri manufacturing

Tobacco pipes manufacturing

Umbrellas manufacturing

Cross-References. Establishments primarily engaged in—

- Manufacturing medical equipment and supplies—are classified in Industry Group 3391, Medical Equipment and Supplies Manufacturing;

- Manufacturing jewelry and flatware—are classified in Industry 33991, Jewelry and Silverware Manufacturing;

- Manufacturing sporting and athletic goods—are classified in Industry 339920, Sporting and Athletic Goods Manufacturing;

- Manufacturing dolls, toys, and games—are classified in Industry 33993, Doll, Toy, and Game Manufacturing;

- Manufacturing office supplies (except paper)—are classified in Industry 33994, Office Supplies (except Paper) Manufacturing;

- Manufacturing signs—are classified in Industry 33995, Sign Manufacturing;

- Manufacturing gasket, packing, and sealing devices—are classified in U.S. Industry 339991, Gasket, Packing, and Sealing Device Manufacturing;

- Manufacturing musical instruments—are classified in U.S. Industry 339992, Musical Instrument Manufacturing;

- Manufacturing fasteners, buttons, needles, and pins—are classified in U.S. Industry 339993, Fastener, Button, Needle, and Pin Manufacturing;

- Manufacturing brooms, brushes, and mops—are classified in U.S. Industry 339994, Broom, Brush, and Mop Manufacturing;

- Manufacturing burial caskets—are classified in U.S. Industry 339995, Burial Casket Manufacturing;

- Manufacturing Christmas tree glass ornaments and glass lamp shades—are classified in U.S. Industry 327215, Glass Product Manufacturing Made of Purchased Glass;

- Manufacturing Christmas tree lighting sets—are classified in U.S. Industry 335129, Other Lighting Equipment Manufacturing;

- Manufacturing beauty and barber chairs—are classified in U.S. Industry 337127, Institutional Furniture Manufacturing;

- Manufacturing burnt wood articles—are classified in U.S. Industry 321999, All Other Miscellaneous Wood Product Manufacturing;

US—United States industry only. CAN—United States and Canadian industries are comparable. MEX—United States and Mexican industries are comparable. Blank—Canadian, Mexican, and United States industries are comparable.

- Dressing and bleaching furs—are classified in Industry 316110, Leather and Hide Tanning and Finishing;
- Manufacturing paper, textile, and metal lamp shades—are classified in U.S. Industry 335121, Residential Electric Lighting Fixture Manufacturing;
- Manufacturing plastics lamp shades—are classified in U.S. Industry 326199, All Other Plastics Product Manufacturing;
- Manufacturing matches—are classified in U.S. Industry 325998, All Other Miscellaneous Chemical Product and Preparation Manufacturing;
- Manufacturing metal products, such as metal combs and hair curlers—are classified in U.S. Industry 332999, All Other Miscellaneous Fabricated Metal Product Manufacturing;
- Manufacturing plastics products, such as plastics combs and hair curlers—are classified in U.S. Industry 326199, All Other Plastics Product Manufacturing; and
- Manufacturing electric hair clippers for use on humans—are classified in U.S. Industry 335211, Electric Housewares and Household Fan Manufacturing.

Sector 42—Wholesale Trade

The Sector as a Whole

The Wholesale Trade sector comprises establishments engaged in wholesaling merchandise, generally without transformation, and rendering services incidental to the sale of merchandise. The merchandise described in this sector includes the outputs of agriculture, mining, manufacturing, and certain information industries, such as publishing.

The wholesaling process is an intermediate step in the distribution of merchandise. Wholesalers are organized to sell or arrange the purchase or sale of (a) goods for resale (i.e., goods sold to other wholesalers or retailers), (b) capital or durable nonconsumer goods, and (c) raw and intermediate materials and supplies used in production.

Wholesalers sell merchandise to other businesses and normally operate from a warehouse or office. These warehouses and offices are characterized by having little or no display of merchandise. In addition, neither the design nor the location of the premises is intended to solicit walk-in traffic. Wholesalers do not normally use advertising directed to the general public. Customers are generally reached initially via telephone, in-person marketing, or by specialized advertising that may include Internet and other electronic means. Follow-up orders are either vendor-initiated or client-initiated, generally based on previous sales, and typically exhibit strong ties between sellers and buyers. In fact, transactions are often conducted between wholesalers and clients that have long-standing business relationships.

This sector comprises two main types of wholesalers: merchant wholesalers that sell goods on their own account and business to business electronic markets, agents, and brokers that arrange sales and purchases for others generally for a commission or fee.

(1) Establishments that sell goods on their own account are known as wholesale merchants, distributors, jobbers, drop shippers, and import/export merchants. Also included as wholesale merchants are sales offices and sales branches (but not retail stores) maintained by manufacturing, refining, or mining enterprises apart from their plants or mines for the purpose of marketing their products. Merchant wholesale establishments typically maintain their own warehouse, where they receive and handle goods for their customers. Goods are generally sold without transformation, but may include integral functions, such as sorting, packaging, labeling, and other marketing services.

(2) Establishments arranging for the purchase or sale of goods owned by others or purchasing goods, generally on a commission basis are known as business to business electronic markets, agents and brokers, commission merchants, import/export agents and brokers, auction companies, and manufacturers' representatives. These establishments operate from offices and generally do not own or handle the goods they sell.

US—United States industry only. CAN—United States and Canadian industries are comparable. MEX—United States and Mexican industries are comparable. Blank—Canadian, Mexican, and United States industries are comparable.

Some wholesale establishments may be connected with a single manufacturer and promote and sell the particular manufacturers' products to a wide range of other wholesalers or retailers. Other wholesalers may be connected to a retail chain, or limited number of retail chains, and only provide a variety of products needed by that particular retail operation(s). These wholesalers may obtain the products from a wide range of manufacturers. Still other wholesalers may not take title to the goods, but act as agents and brokers for a commission.

Although, in general, wholesaling normally denotes sales in large volumes, durable nonconsumer goods may be sold in single units. Sales of capital or durable nonconsumer goods used in the production of goods and services, such as farm machinery, medium and heavy duty trucks, and industrial machinery, are always included in wholesale trade.

423 Merchant Wholesalers, Durable Goods[US]

Industries in the Merchant Wholesalers, Durable Goods subsector sell capital or durable goods to other businesses. Merchant wholesalers generally take title to the goods that they sell; in other words, they buy and sell goods on their own account. Durable goods are new or used items generally with a normal life expectancy of three years or more. Durable goods merchant wholesale trade establishments are engaged in wholesaling products, such as motor vehicles, furniture, construction materials, machinery and equipment (including household-type appliances), metals and minerals (except petroleum), sporting goods, toys and hobby goods, recyclable materials, and parts.

Business-to-business electronic markets, agents, and brokers primarily engaged in wholesaling durable goods, generally on a commission or fee basis, are classified in Subsector 425, Wholesale Electronic Markets and Agents and Brokers.

4231 Motor Vehicle and Motor Vehicle Parts and Supplies Merchant Wholesalers[US]

This industry group comprises establishments primarily engaged in the merchant wholesale distribution of automobiles and other motor vehicles, motor vehicle supplies, tires, and new and used parts.

42311 Automobile and Other Motor Vehicle Merchant Wholesalers[US]
See industry description for 423110 below.

423110 Automobile and Other Motor Vehicle Merchant Wholesalers[US]

This industry comprises establishments primarily engaged in the merchant wholesale distribution of new and used passenger automobiles, trucks, trailers, and other motor vehicles, such as motorcycles, motor homes, and snowmobiles.

US—United States industry only. CAN—United States and Canadian industries are comparable. MEX—United States and Mexican industries are comparable. Blank—Canadian, Mexican, and United States industries are comparable.

42312 Motor Vehicle Supplies and New Parts Merchant Wholesalers[US]

See industry description for 423120 below.

423120 Motor Vehicle Supplies and New Parts Merchant Wholesalers[US]

This industry comprises establishments primarily engaged in the merchant wholesale distribution of motor vehicle supplies, accessories, tools, and equipment; and new motor vehicle parts (except new tires and tubes).

Cross-References. Establishments primarily engaged in—

- Merchant wholesale distribution of new and/or used tires and tubes—are classified in Industry 423130, Tire and Tube Merchant Wholesalers;

- Merchant wholesale distribution of automotive chemicals (except lubricating oils and greases)—are classified in Industry 424690, Other Chemical and Allied Products Merchant Wholesalers;

- Merchant wholesale distribution of lubricating oils and greases—are classified in Industry 424720, Petroleum and Petroleum Products Merchant Wholesalers (except Bulk Stations and Terminals); and

- Merchant wholesale distribution of used motor vehicle parts—are classified in Industry 423140, Motor Vehicle Parts (Used) Merchant Wholesalers.

42313 Tire and Tube Merchant Wholesalers[US]

See industry description for 423130 below.

423130 Tire and Tube Merchant Wholesalers[US]

This industry comprises establishments primarily engaged in the merchant wholesale distribution of new and/or used tires and tubes for passenger and commercial vehicles.

Cross-References. Establishments primarily engaged in—

- Merchant wholesale distribution of other new automobile parts and accessories—are classified in Industry 423120, Motor Vehicle Supplies and New Parts Merchant Wholesalers; and

- Merchant wholesale distribution of other used automobile parts and accessories—are classified in Industry 423140, Motor Vehicle Parts (Used) Merchant Wholesalers.

US—United States industry only. CAN—United States and Canadian industries are comparable. MEX—United States and Mexican industries are comparable. Blank—Canadian, Mexican, and United States industries are comparable.

42314 Motor Vehicle Parts (Used) Merchant Wholesalers[US]

See industry description for 423140 below.

423140 Motor Vehicle Parts (Used) Merchant Wholesalers[US]

This industry comprises establishments primarily engaged in the merchant wholesale distribution of used motor vehicle parts (except used tires and tubes) and establishments primarily engaged in dismantling motor vehicles for the purpose of selling the parts.

Cross-References. Establishments primarily engaged in—

- Dismantling motor vehicles for the purpose of selling scrap—are classified in Industry 423930, Recyclable Material Merchant Wholesalers; and
- Merchant wholesale distribution of new and/or used tires and tubes—are classified in Industry 423130, Tire and Tube Merchant Wholesalers.

4232 Furniture and Home Furnishing Merchant Wholesalers[US]

42321 Furniture Merchant Wholesalers[US]

See industry description for 423210 below.

423210 Furniture Merchant Wholesalers[US]

This industry comprises establishments primarily engaged in the merchant wholesale distribution of furniture (except hospital beds, medical furniture, and drafting tables).

Illustrative Examples:

Household-type furniture merchant wholesalers	Outdoor furniture merchant wholesalers
Mattresses merchant wholesalers	Public building furniture merchant wholesalers
Office furniture merchant wholesalers	Religious furniture merchant wholesalers

Cross-References. Establishments primarily engaged in—

- Merchant wholesale distribution of partitions, shelving, lockers, and store fixtures—are classified in Industry 423440, Other Commercial Equipment Merchant Wholesalers;
- Merchant wholesale distribution of hospital beds and medical furniture—are classified in Industry 423450, Medical, Dental, and Hospital Equipment and Supplies Merchant Wholesalers; and

- Merchant wholesale distribution of drafting tables—are classified in Industry 423490, Other Professional Equipment and Supplies Merchant Wholesalers.

42322 Home Furnishing Merchant Wholesalers[US]
See industry description for 423220 below.

423220 Home Furnishing Merchant Wholesalers[US]

This industry comprises establishments primarily engaged in the merchant wholesale distribution of home furnishings and/or housewares.

Illustrative Examples:

Carpet merchant wholesalers
Chinaware merchant wholesalers
Curtain merchant wholesalers
Drapery merchant wholesalers
Floor covering merchant wholesalers
Glassware merchant wholesalers
Household-type cooking utensil merchant wholesalers

Lamp merchant wholesalers
Linen (e.g., bath, bed, table) merchant wholesalers
Window blind and shade merchant wholesalers

Cross-References. Establishments primarily engaged in—

- Merchant wholesale distribution of electrical household-type goods—are classified in Industry 423620, Electrical and Electronic Appliance, Television, and Radio Set Merchant Wholesalers; and

- Merchant wholesale distribution of precious metal flatware—are classified in Industry 423940, Jewelry, Watch, Precious Stone, and Precious Metal Merchant Wholesalers.

4233 Lumber and Other Construction Materials Merchant Wholesalers[US]

42331 Lumber, Plywood, Millwork, and Wood Panel Merchant Wholesalers[US]
See industry description for 423310 below.

423310 Lumber, Plywood, Millwork, and Wood Panel Merchant Wholesalers[US]

This industry comprises establishments primarily engaged in the merchant wholesale distribution of lumber; plywood; reconstituted wood fiber products;

wood fencing; doors and windows and their frames (all materials); wood roofing and siding; and/or other wood or metal millwork.

Cross-References. Establishments primarily engaged in—

- Merchant wholesale distribution of nonwood roofing and siding materials— are classified in Industry 423330, Roofing, Siding, and Insulation Material Merchant Wholesalers; and
- Merchant wholesale distribution of timber and timber products, such as railroad ties, logs, firewood, and pulpwood,—are classified in Industry 423990, Other Miscellaneous Durable Goods Merchant Wholesalers.

42332 Brick, Stone, and Related Construction Material Merchant Wholesalers[US]
See industry description for 423320 below.

423320 Brick, Stone, and Related Construction Material Merchant Wholesalers[US]

This industry comprises establishments primarily engaged in the merchant wholesale distribution of stone, cement, lime, construction sand, and gravel; brick; asphalt and concrete mixtures; and/or concrete, stone, and structural clay products.

Cross-References. Establishments primarily engaged in—

- Merchant wholesale distribution of refractory brick and other refractory products—are classified in Industry 423840, Industrial Supplies Merchant Wholesalers; and
- Selling ready-mix concrete—are classified in Industry 327320, Ready-Mix Concrete Manufacturing.

42333 Roofing, Siding, and Insulation Material Merchant Wholesalers[US]
See industry description for 423330 below.

423330 Roofing, Siding, and Insulation Material Merchant Wholesalers[US]

This industry comprises establishments primarily engaged in the merchant wholesale distribution of nonwood roofing and nonwood siding and insulation materials.

US—United States industry only. CAN—United States and Canadian industries are comparable. MEX—United States and Mexican industries are comparable. Blank—Canadian, Mexican, and United States industries are comparable.

Cross-References.

Establishments primarily engaged in the merchant wholesale distribution of wood roofing and wood siding are classified in Industry 423310, Lumber, Plywood, Millwork, and Wood Panel Merchant Wholesalers.

42339 Other Construction Material Merchant Wholesalers[US]
See industry description for 423390 below.

423390 Other Construction Material Merchant Wholesalers[US]

This industry comprises (1) establishments primarily engaged in the merchant wholesale distribution of manufactured homes (i.e., mobile homes) and/or prefabricated buildings and (2) establishments primarily engaged in the merchant wholesale distribution of construction materials (except lumber, plywood, millwork, wood panels, brick, stone, roofing, siding, electrical and wiring supplies, and insulation materials).

Illustrative Examples:

Flat glass merchant wholesalers
Ornamental ironwork merchant
  wholesalers
Plate glass merchant wholesalers

Prefabricated buildings (except wood)
  merchant wholesalers
Wire fencing and fencing accessories
  merchant wholesalers

Cross-References. Establishments primarily engaged in—

- Merchant wholesale distribution of products of the primary metals industries—are classified in Industry 423510, Metal Service Centers and Other Metal Merchant Wholesalers;

- Merchant wholesale distribution of lumber; plywood; reconstituted wood fiber products; wood fencing; doors, windows, and their frames; wood roofing and wood siding; and other wood or metal millwork—are classified in Industry 423310, Lumber, Plywood, Millwork, and Wood Panel Merchant Wholesalers;

- Merchant wholesale distribution of stone, cement, lime, construction sand and gravel; brick; asphalt and concrete mixtures (except ready-mix concrete); and/or concrete, stone, and structural clay products—are classified in Industry 423320, Brick, Stone, and Related Construction Material Merchant Wholesalers;

- Merchant wholesale distribution of nonwood roofing, nonwood siding and insulation materials—are classified in Industry 423330, Roofing, Siding, and Insulation Material Merchant Wholesalers;

US—United States industry only. CAN—United States and Canadian industries are comparable. MEX—United States and Mexican industries are comparable. Blank—Canadian, Mexican, and United States industries are comparable.

- Merchant wholesale distribution of electrical supplies and wiring supplies—are classified in Industry 423610, Electrical Apparatus and Equipment, Wiring Supplies, and Related Equipment Merchant Wholesalers; and

- Selling ready-mix concrete—are classified in Industry 327320, Ready-Mix Concrete Manufacturing.

4234 Professional and Commercial Equipment and Supplies Merchant Wholesalers[US]

This industry group comprises establishments primarily engaged in the merchant wholesale distribution of photographic equipment and supplies; office, computer, and computer peripheral equipment; and medical, dental, hospital, ophthalmic, and other commercial and professional equipment and supplies.

42341 Photographic Equipment and Supplies Merchant Wholesalers[US]

See industry description for 423410 below.

423410 Photographic Equipment and Supplies Merchant Wholesalers[US]

This industry comprises establishments primarily engaged in the merchant wholesale distribution of photographic equipment and supplies (except office equipment).

Illustrative Examples:

Photofinishing equipment merchant wholesalers

Photographic camera equipment and supplies merchant wholesalers

Photographic film merchant wholesalers

Television cameras merchant wholesalers

Video cameras (except household-type) merchant wholesalers

Cross-References. Establishments primarily engaged in—

- Merchant wholesale distribution of household-type video cameras—are classified in Industry 423620, Electrical and Electronic Appliance, Television, and Radio Set Merchant Wholesalers; and

- Merchant wholesale distribution of office equipment, such as photocopy and microfilm equipment—are classified in Industry 423420, Office Equipment Merchant Wholesalers.

US—United States industry only. CAN—United States and Canadian industries are comparable. MEX—United States and Mexican industries are comparable. Blank—Canadian, Mexican, and United States industries are comparable.

42342 Office Equipment Merchant Wholesalers^{US}

See industry description for 423420 below.

423420 Office Equipment Merchant Wholesalers^{US}

This industry comprises establishments primarily engaged in the merchant wholesale distribution of office machines and related equipment (except computers and computer peripheral equipment).

Illustrative Examples:

Accounting machines merchant
  wholesalers
Calculator and calculating machines
  merchant wholesalers
Cash register merchant wholesalers

Copying machine merchant wholesalers
Mailing machine merchant wholesalers
Microfilm equipment and supplies
  merchant wholesalers
Security safe merchant wholesalers

Cross-References. Establishments primarily engaged in—

- Merchant wholesale distribution of office furniture—are classified in Industry 423210, Furniture Merchant Wholesalers;

- Merchant wholesale distribution of computers and computer peripheral equipment—are classified in Industry 423430, Computer and Computer Peripheral Equipment and Software Merchant Wholesalers; and

- Merchant wholesale distribution of office supplies—are classified in Industry 424120, Stationery and Office Supplies Merchant Wholesalers.

42343 Computer and Computer Peripheral Equipment and Software Merchant Wholesalers^{US}

See industry description for 423430 below.

423430 Computer and Computer Peripheral Equipment and Software Merchant Wholesalers^{US}

This industry comprises establishments primarily engaged in the merchant wholesale distribution of computers, computer peripheral equipment, loaded computer boards, and/or computer software.

Cross-References. Establishments primarily engaged in—

- Merchant wholesale distribution of modems and other electronic communications equipment—are classified in Industry 423690, Other Electronic Parts and Equipment Merchant Wholesalers; and

- Selling, planning, and designing computer systems that integrate computer hardware, software, and communication technologies—are classified in U.S. Industry 541512, Computer Systems Design Services.

42344 Other Commercial Equipment Merchant Wholesalers[US]
See industry description for 423440 below.

423440 Other Commercial Equipment Merchant Wholesalers[US]

This industry comprises establishments primarily engaged in the merchant wholesale distribution of commercial and related machines and equipment (except photographic equipment and supplies; office equipment; and computers and computer peripheral equipment and software) generally used in restaurants and stores.

Illustrative Examples:

Balances and scales (except laboratory) merchant wholesalers
Coin-operated merchandising machine merchant wholesalers
Commercial chinaware merchant wholesalers
Commercial cooking equipment merchant wholesalers
Commercial shelving merchant wholesalers
Electrical sign merchant wholesalers
Partitions merchant wholesalers
Store fixture (except refrigerated) merchant wholesalers

Cross-References. Establishments primarily engaged in—

- Merchant wholesale distribution of photographic equipment and supplies—are classified in Industry 423410, Photographic Equipment and Supplies Merchant Wholesalers;
- Merchant wholesale distribution of office machines and related equipment—are classified in Industry 423420, Office Equipment Merchant Wholesalers;
- Merchant wholesale distribution of computers, computer peripheral equipment, and computer software—are classified in Industry 423430, Computer and Computer Peripheral Equipment and Software Merchant Wholesalers;
- Merchant wholesale distribution of laboratory scales and balances (except medical and dental)—are classified in Industry 423490, Other Professional Equipment and Supplies Merchant Wholesalers; and
- Merchant wholesale distribution of refrigerated store fixtures —are classified in Industry 423740, Refrigeration Equipment and Supplies Merchant Wholesalers.

42345 Medical, Dental, and Hospital Equipment and Supplies Merchant Wholesalers[US]
See industry description for 423450 below.

423450 Medical, Dental, and Hospital Equipment and Supplies Merchant Wholesalers[US]

This industry comprises establishments primarily engaged in the merchant wholesale distribution of professional medical equipment, instruments, and supplies (except ophthalmic equipment and instruments and goods used by ophthalmologists, optometrists, and opticians).

Illustrative Examples:

Dental equipment and supplies merchant wholesalers

Electromedical equipment merchant wholesalers

Hospital beds merchant wholesalers

Hospital furniture merchant wholesalers

Medical and dental X-ray machine merchant wholesalers

Medical dressings merchant wholesalers

Patient monitoring equipment merchant wholesalers

Prosthetic appliance and supplies merchant wholesalers

Surgical instrument and apparatus merchant wholesalers

Cross-References.

Establishments primarily engaged in the merchant wholesale distribution of professional equipment, instruments and/or goods sold, prescribed, or used by ophthalmologists, optometrists, and opticians are classified in Industry 423460, Ophthalmic Goods Merchant Wholesalers.

42346 Ophthalmic Goods Merchant Wholesalers[US]
See industry description for 423460 below.

423460 Ophthalmic Goods Merchant Wholesalers[US]

This industry comprises establishments primarily engaged in the merchant wholesale distribution of professional equipment, instruments, and/or goods sold, prescribed, or used by ophthalmologists, optometrists, and opticians.

Illustrative Examples:

Binocular merchant wholesalers

Ophthalmic frame merchant wholesalers

Ophthalmic lenses merchant wholesalers

Optometric equipment and supplies merchant wholesalers

Sunglasses merchant wholesalers

42349 Other Professional Equipment and Supplies Merchant Wholesalers[US]
See industry description for 423490 below.

US—United States industry only. CAN—United States and Canadian industries are comparable. MEX—United States and Mexican industries are comparable. Blank—Canadian, Mexican, and United States industries are comparable.

423490 Other Professional Equipment and Supplies Merchant Wholesalers[US]

This industry comprises establishments primarily engaged in the merchant wholesale distribution of professional equipment and supplies (except ophthalmic goods and medical, dental, and hospital equipment and supplies).

Illustrative Examples:

Church supplies (except silverware, plated ware) merchant wholesalers

Drafting tables and instruments merchant wholesalers

Laboratory equipment (except medical, dental) merchant wholesalers

School equipment and supplies (except books, furniture) merchant wholesalers

Scientific instruments merchant wholesalers

Surveying equipment and supplies merchant wholesalers

Cross-References. Establishments primarily engaged in—

- Merchant wholesale distribution of professional equipment, instruments, and/or goods sold, prescribed, or used by ophthalmologists, optometrists, and opticians, such as ophthalmic frames and lenses, and sunglasses—are classified in Industry 423460, Ophthalmic Goods Merchant Wholesalers;

- Merchant wholesale distribution of medical professional equipment, instruments, and supplies used by medical and dental practitioners (except ophthalmic equipment, instruments, and goods used by ophthalmologists, optometrists, and opticians) and medical facilities—are classified in Industry 423450, Medical, Dental, and Hospital Equipment and Supplies Merchant Wholesalers;

- Merchant wholesale distribution of silverware and plated flatware—are classified in Industry 423940, Jewelry, Watch, Precious Stone, and Precious Metal Merchant Wholesalers;

- Merchant wholesale distribution of books—are classified in Industry 424920, Book, Periodical, and Newspaper Merchant Wholesalers; and

- Merchant wholesale distribution of school furniture—are classified in Industry 423210, Furniture Merchant Wholesalers.

4235 Metal and Mineral (except Petroleum) Merchant Wholesalers[US]

42351 Metal Service Centers and Other Metal Merchant Wholesalers[US]

See industry description for 423510 below.

US—United States industry only. CAN—United States and Canadian industries are comparable. MEX—United States and Mexican industries are comparable. Blank—Canadian, Mexican, and United States industries are comparable.

423510 Metal Service Centers and Other Metal Merchant Wholesalers[US]

This industry comprises establishments primarily engaged in the merchant wholesale distribution of products of the primary metals industries. Service centers maintain inventory and may perform functions, such as sawing, shearing, bending, leveling, cleaning, or edging, on a custom basis as part of sales transactions.

Illustrative Examples:

Cast iron pipe merchant wholesalers
Metal bars (except precious) merchant wholesalers
Metal ingots (except precious) merchant wholesalers
Metal pipe merchant wholesalers
Metal plate merchant wholesalers
Metal rod merchant wholesalers
Metal sheet merchant wholesalers
Metal spike merchant wholesalers
Nail merchant wholesalers
Noninsulated wire merchant wholesalers

Cross-References. Establishments primarily engaged in—

- Merchant wholesale distribution of gold, silver, and platinum—are classified in Industry 423940, Jewelry, Watch, Precious Stone, and Precious Metal Merchant Wholesalers;

- Merchant wholesale distribution of automotive, industrial, and other recyclable metal scrap—are classified in Industry 423930, Recyclable Material Merchant Wholesalers; and

- Merchant wholesale distribution of insulated wire—are classified in Industry 423610, Electrical Apparatus and Equipment, Wiring Supplies, and Related Equipment Merchant Wholesalers.

42352 Coal and Other Mineral and Ore Merchant Wholesalers[US]
See industry description for 423520 below.

423520 Coal and Other Mineral and Ore Merchant Wholesalers[US]

This industry comprises establishments primarily engaged in the merchant wholesale distribution of coal, coke, metal ores, and/or nonmetallic minerals (except precious and semiprecious stones and minerals used in construction, such as sand and gravel).

Cross-References. Establishments primarily engaged in—

- Merchant wholesale distribution of nonmetallic minerals used in construction, such as sand and gravel—are classified in Industry 423320, Brick, Stone, and Related Construction Material Merchant Wholesalers;

- Merchant wholesale distribution of crude petroleum—are classified in Industry Group 4247, Petroleum and Petroleum Products Merchant Wholesalers; and

- Merchant wholesale distribution of precious and semiprecious stones and metals—are classified in Industry 423940, Jewelry, Watch, Precious Stone, and Precious Metal Merchant Wholesalers.

4236 Electrical and Electronic Goods Merchant Wholesalers[US]

42361 Electrical Apparatus and Equipment, Wiring Supplies, and Related Equipment Merchant Wholesalers[US]
See industry description for 423610 below.

423610 Electrical Apparatus and Equipment, Wiring Supplies, and Related Equipment Merchant Wholesalers[US]

This industry comprises establishments primarily engaged in the merchant wholesale distribution of electrical construction materials; wiring supplies; electric light fixtures; light bulbs; and/or electrical power equipment for the generation, transmission, distribution, or control of electric energy.

42362 Electrical and Electronic Appliance, Television, and Radio Set Merchant Wholesalers[US]
See industry description for 423620 below.

423620 Electrical and Electronic Appliance, Television, and Radio Set Merchant Wholesalers[US]

This industry comprises establishments primarily engaged in the merchant wholesale distribution of household-type electrical appliances, room air-conditioners, gas and electric clothes dryers, and/or household-type audio or video equipment.

Illustrative Examples:

Electric water heater merchant wholesalers	Household-type sewing machine merchant wholesalers
Household-type radio (including automotive) merchant wholesalers	Household-type video camera merchant wholesalers
Household-type refrigerator merchant wholesalers	Television set merchant wholesalers

---

Cross-References. Establishments primarily engaged in—

- Merchant wholesale distribution of gas household-type appliances (except gas clothes dryers)—are classified in Industry 423720, Plumbing and Heating Equipment and Supplies (Hydronics) Merchant Wholesalers; and

- Merchant wholesale distribution of nonhousehold-type video cameras—are classified in Industry 423410, Photographic Equipment and Supplies Merchant Wholesalers.

42369 Other Electronic Parts and Equipment Merchant Wholesalers[US]

See industry description for 423690 below.

423690 Other Electronic Parts and Equipment Merchant Wholesalers[US]

This industry comprises establishments primarily engaged in the merchant wholesale distribution of electronic parts and equipment (except electrical apparatus and equipment, wiring supplies and construction material; and electrical appliances, television and radio sets).

Illustrative Examples:

Blank audio tape merchant wholesalers
Blank diskette merchant wholesalers
Blank video tape merchant wholesalers
Broadcasting equipment merchant wholesalers
Communications equipment merchant wholesalers

Radar equipment merchant wholesalers
Telegraph equipment merchant wholesalers
Telephone equipment merchant wholesalers
Unloaded computer board merchant wholesalers

Cross-References. Establishments primarily engaged in—

- Merchant wholesale distribution of household-type electrical appliances, and television and radio sets—are classified in Industry 423620, Electrical and Electronic Appliance, Television, and Radio Set Merchant Wholesalers;

- Merchant wholesale distribution of computers, computer peripheral equipment, and loaded computer boards—are classified in Industry 423430, Computer and Computer Peripheral Equipment and Software Merchant Wholesalers; and

- Merchant wholesale distribution of electrical construction materials, wiring supplies, electric light fixtures, light bulbs; and/or electrical power equipment for generation, transmission, distribution, or control of electric energy—are classified in Industry 423610, Electrical Apparatus and Equipment, Wiring Supplies, and Related Equipment Merchant Wholesalers.

4237 Hardware, and Plumbing and Heating Equipment and Supplies Merchant Wholesalers[US]

42371 Hardware Merchant Wholesalers[US]
See industry description for 423710 below.

423710 Hardware Merchant Wholesalers[US]

This industry comprises establishments primarily engaged in the merchant wholesale distribution of hardware, knives, or handtools.

Illustrative Examples:

Brads merchant wholesalers
Cutlery merchant wholesalers
Fasteners (e.g., bolts, nuts, rivets, screws) merchant wholesalers
Handtools (except motor vehicle, machinists' precision) merchant wholesalers

Knives (except disposable plastics) merchant wholesalers
Power handtools (e.g., drills, saws, sanders) merchant wholesalers
Staples merchant wholesalers
Tacks merchant wholesalers

Cross-References. Establishments primarily engaged in—

- Merchant wholesale distribution of nails, noninsulated wire, and screening—are classified in Industry 423510, Metal Service Centers and Other Metal Merchant Wholesalers;

- Merchant wholesale distribution of motor vehicle handtools and equipment—are classified in Industry 423120, Motor Vehicle Supplies and New Parts Merchant Wholesalers;

- Merchant wholesale distribution of machinists' precision handtools—are classified in Industry 423830, Industrial Machinery and Equipment Merchant Wholesalers; and

- Merchant wholesale distribution of disposable plastics knives and eating utensils—are classified in Industry 424130, Industrial and Personal Service Paper Merchant Wholesalers.

42372 Plumbing and Heating Equipment and Supplies (Hydronics) Merchant Wholesalers[US]
See industry description for 423720 below.

423720 Plumbing and Heating Equipment and Supplies (Hydronics) Merchant Wholesalers[US]

This industry comprises establishments primarily engaged in the merchant wholesale distribution of plumbing equipment, hydronic heating equipment, household-type gas appliances (except gas clothes dryers), and/or supplies.

Cross-References. Establishments primarily engaged in—

- Selling and installing plumbing, heating and air conditioning equipment—are classified in Industry 238220, Plumbing, Heating, and Air-Conditioning Contractors;

- Merchant wholesale distribution of warm air heating and air-conditioning equipment—are classified in Industry 423730, Warm Air Heating and Air-Conditioning Equipment and Supplies Merchant Wholesalers; and

- Merchant wholesale distribution of household-type electrical appliances, room air-conditioners, gas clothes dryers, and/or household-type audio or video equipment—are classified in Industry 423620, Electrical and Electronic Appliance, Television, and Radio Set Merchant Wholesalers.

42373 Warm Air Heating and Air-Conditioning Equipment and Supplies Merchant Wholesalers[US]
See industry description for 423730 below.

423730 Warm Air Heating and Air-Conditioning Equipment and Supplies Merchant Wholesalers[US]

This industry comprises establishments primarily engaged in the merchant wholesale distribution of warm air heating and air-conditioning equipment and supplies.

Illustrative Examples:

Air pollution control equipment and supplies merchant wholesalers
Air-conditioning equipment (except room units) merchant wholesalers
Automotive air-conditioners merchant wholesalers

Nonportable electric baseboard heaters merchant wholesalers
Warm-air central heating equipment merchant wholesalers

Cross-References. Establishments primarily engaged in—

- Merchant wholesale distribution of household-type electrical appliances and room air-conditioners—are classified in Industry 423620, Electrical and Electronic Appliance, Television, and Radio Set Merchant Wholesalers;

- Merchant wholesale distribution of hydronic heating equipment—are classified in Industry 423720, Plumbing and Heating Equipment and Supplies (Hydronics) Merchant Wholesalers; and

- Selling and installing warm air heating and air-conditioning equipment—are classified in Industry 238220, Plumbing, Heating, and Air-Conditioning Contractors.

42374 Refrigeration Equipment and Supplies Merchant Wholesalers[US]
See industry description for 423740 below.

423740 Refrigeration Equipment and Supplies Merchant Wholesalers[US]

This industry comprises establishments primarily engaged in the merchant wholesale distribution of refrigeration equipment (except household-type refrigerators, freezers, and air-conditioners).

Illustrative Examples:

Cold storage machinery merchant wholesalers	Refrigerated display cases merchant wholesalers
Commercial refrigerators merchant wholesalers	Water coolers merchant wholesalers

Cross-References. Establishments primarily engaged in—

- Merchant wholesale distribution of household-type refrigerators, freezers, and room air-conditioners—are classified in Industry 423620, Electrical and Electronic Appliance, Television, and Radio Set Merchant Wholesalers; and

- Merchant wholesale distribution of air-conditioning equipment (except room units)—are classified Industry 423730, Warm Air Heating and Air-Conditioning Equipment and Supplies Merchant Wholesalers.

4238 Machinery, Equipment, and Supplies Merchant Wholesalers[US]

This industry group comprises establishments primarily engaged in the merchant wholesale distribution of construction, mining, farm, garden, industrial, service establishment, and transportation machinery, equipment and supplies.

42381 Construction and Mining (except Oil Well) Machinery and Equipment Merchant Wholesalers[US]
See industry description for 423810 below.

US—United States industry only. CAN—United States and Canadian industries are comparable. MEX—United States and Mexican industries are comparable. Blank—Canadian, Mexican, and United States industries are comparable.

423810 Construction and Mining (except Oil Well) Machinery and Equipment Merchant Wholesalers[US]

This industry comprises establishments primarily engaged in the merchant wholesale distribution of specialized machinery, equipment, and related parts generally used in construction, mining (except oil well) and logging activities.

Illustrative Examples:

Excavating machinery and equipment
merchant wholesalers
Forestry machinery and equipment
merchant wholesalers

Mining cranes merchant wholesalers
Road construction and maintenance
machinery merchant wholesalers
Scaffolding merchant wholesalers

Cross-References.

Establishments primarily engaged in the merchant wholesale distribution of oil well machinery and equipment are classified in Industry 423830, Industrial Machinery and Equipment Merchant Wholesalers.

42382 Farm and Garden Machinery and Equipment Merchant Wholesalers[US]

See industry description for 423820 below.

423820 Farm and Garden Machinery and Equipment Merchant Wholesalers[US]

This industry comprises establishments primarily engaged in the merchant wholesale distribution of specialized machinery, equipment, and related parts generally used in agricultural, farm, and lawn and garden activities.

Illustrative Examples:

Animal feeders merchant wholesalers
Harvesting machinery and equipment
merchant wholesalers
Lawnmowers merchant wholesalers

Milking machinery and equipment
merchant wholesalers
Planting machinery and equipment
merchant wholesalers

42383 Industrial Machinery and Equipment Merchant Wholesalers[US]

See industry description for 423830 below.

423830 Industrial Machinery and Equipment Merchant Wholesalers^{US}

This industry comprises establishments primarily engaged in the merchant wholesale distribution of specialized machinery, equipment, and related parts generally used in manufacturing, oil well, and warehousing activities.

Illustrative Examples:

Fluid power transmission equipment merchant wholesalers
Food-processing machinery and equipment merchant wholesalers
Materials handling machinery and equipment merchant wholesalers

Metalworking machinery and equipment merchant wholesalers
Oil well machinery and equipment merchant wholesalers

Cross-References. Establishments primarily engaged in—

- Merchant wholesale distribution of specialized machinery, equipment, and related parts generally used in construction, mining (except oil well), and logging activities—are classified in Industry 423810, Construction and Mining (except Oil Well) Machinery and Equipment Merchant Wholesalers; and

- Merchant wholesale distribution of supplies used in machinery and equipment generally used in manufacturing, oil well, and warehousing activities—are classified in Industry 423840, Industrial Supplies Merchant Wholesalers.

42384 Industrial Supplies Merchant Wholesalers^{US}

See industry description for 423840 below.

423840 Industrial Supplies Merchant Wholesalers^{US}

This industry comprises establishments primarily engaged in the merchant wholesale distribution of supplies for machinery and equipment generally used in manufacturing, oil well, and warehousing activities.

Illustrative Examples:

Industrial containers merchant wholesalers
Industrial diamonds merchant wholesalers
Printing inks merchant wholesalers
Refractory materials (e.g., brick, blocks, shapes) merchant wholesalers

Welding supplies (except welding gases) merchant wholesalers

US—United States industry only. CAN—United States and Canadian industries are comparable. MEX—United States and Mexican industries are comparable. Blank—Canadian, Mexican, and United States industries are comparable.

Cross-References. Establishments primarily engaged in—

- Merchant wholesale distribution of hydraulic and pneumatic (fluid power) pumps, motors, pistons, and valves—are classified in Industry 423830, Industrial Machinery and Equipment Merchant Wholesalers; and
- Merchant wholesale distribution of welding gases—are classified in Industry 424690, Other Chemical and Allied Products Merchant Wholesalers.

42385 Service Establishment Equipment and Supplies Merchant Wholesalers[US]

See industry description for 423850 below.

423850 Service Establishment Equipment and Supplies Merchant Wholesalers[US]

This industry comprises establishments primarily engaged in the merchant wholesale distribution of specialized equipment and supplies of the type used by service establishments (except specialized equipment and supplies used in offices, stores, hotels, restaurants, schools, health and medical facilities, photographic facilities, and specialized equipment used in transportation and construction activities).

Illustrative Examples:

Amusement park equipment merchant wholesalers

Beauty parlor equipment and supplies merchant wholesalers

Car wash equipment and supplies merchant wholesalers

Drycleaning equipment and supplies merchant wholesalers

Janitorial equipment and supplies merchant wholesalers

Undertakers' equipment and supplies merchant wholesalers

Upholsterers' equipment and supplies (except fabrics) merchant wholesalers

Cross-References. Establishments primarily engaged in—

- Merchant wholesale distribution of janitorial and automotive chemicals— are classified in Industry 424690, Other Chemical and Allied Products Merchant Wholesalers;
- Merchant wholesale distribution of piece goods, fabrics, knitting yarns (except industrial), thread and other notions—are classified in Industry 424310, Piece Goods, Notions, and Other Dry Goods Merchant Wholesalers; and
- Merchant wholesale distribution of industrial yarns—are classified in Industry 424990, Other Miscellaneous Nondurable Goods Merchant Wholesalers.

US—United States industry only. CAN—United States and Canadian industries are comparable. MEX—United States and Mexican industries are comparable. Blank—Canadian, Mexican, and United States industries are comparable.

42386 Transportation Equipment and Supplies (except Motor Vehicle) Merchant Wholesalers[US]

See industry description for 423860 below.

423860 Transportation Equipment and Supplies (except Motor Vehicle) Merchant Wholesalers[US]

This industry comprises establishments primarily engaged in the merchant wholesale distribution of transportation equipment and supplies (except marine pleasure craft and motor vehicles).

Illustrative Examples:

Aircraft merchant wholesalers	Railroad cars merchant wholesalers
Motorized passenger golf carts merchant wholesalers	Ships merchant wholesalers

Cross-References. Establishments primarily engaged in—

- Merchant wholesale distribution of motor vehicles and motor vehicle parts— are classified in Industry Group 4231, Motor Vehicle and Motor Vehicle Parts and Supplies Merchant Wholesalers; and
- Merchant wholesale distribution of marine pleasure craft—are classified in Industry 423910, Sporting and Recreational Goods and Supplies Merchant Wholesalers.

4239 Miscellaneous Durable Goods Merchant Wholesalers[US]

This industry group comprises establishments primarily engaged in the merchant wholesale distribution of sporting, recreational, toy, hobby, and jewelry goods and supplies, and precious stones and metals.

42391 Sporting and Recreational Goods and Supplies Merchant Wholesalers[US]

See industry description for 423910 below.

423910 Sporting and Recreational Goods and Supplies Merchant Wholesalers[US]

This industry comprises establishments primarily engaged in the merchant wholesale distribution of sporting goods and accessories; billiard and pool supplies; sporting firearms and ammunition; and/or marine pleasure craft, equipment, and supplies.

US—United States industry only. CAN—United States and Canadian industries are comparable. MEX—United States and Mexican industries are comparable. Blank—Canadian, Mexican, and United States industries are comparable.

Cross References. Establishments primarily engaged in—

- Merchant wholesale distribution of motor vehicles and trailers—are classified in Industry 423110, Automobile and Other Motor Vehicle Merchant Wholesalers;

- Merchant wholesale distribution of motorized passenger golf carts—are classified in Industry 423860, Transportation Equipment and Supplies (except Motor Vehicle) Merchant Wholesalers; and

- Merchant wholesale distribution of athletic apparel and athletic footwear—are classified in Industry Group 4243, Apparel, Piece Goods, and Notions Merchant Wholesalers.

42392 Toy and Hobby Goods and Supplies Merchant Wholesalers[US]
See industry description for 423920 below.

423920 Toy and Hobby Goods and Supplies Merchant Wholesalers[US]

This industry comprises establishments primarily engaged in the merchant wholesale distribution of games, toys, fireworks, playing cards, hobby goods and supplies, and/or related goods.

42393 Recyclable Material Merchant Wholesalers[US]
See industry description for 423930 below.

423930 Recyclable Material Merchant Wholesalers[US]

This industry comprises establishments primarily engaged in the merchant wholesale distribution of automotive scrap, industrial scrap, and other recyclable materials. Included in this industry are auto wreckers primarily engaged in dismantling motor vehicles for the purpose of wholesaling scrap.

Cross-References. Establishments primarily engaged in—

- Dismantling motor vehicles for the purpose of selling used parts—are classified in Industry 423140, Motor Vehicle Parts (Used) Merchant Wholesalers; and

- Operating facilities where commingled recyclable materials, such as paper, plastics, used beverage cans, and metals are sorted into distinct categories—are classified in Industry 562920, Materials Recovery Facilities.

42394 Jewelry, Watch, Precious Stone, and Precious Metal Merchant Wholesalers[US]
See industry description for 423940 below.

423940 Jewelry, Watch, Precious Stone, and Precious Metal Merchant Wholesalers[US]

This industry comprises establishments primarily engaged in the merchant wholesale distribution of jewelry, precious and semiprecious stones, precious metals and metal flatware, costume jewelry, watches, clocks, silverware, and/or jewelers' findings.

Cross-References. Establishments primarily engaged in—

- Merchant wholesale distribution of precious metal ores or concentrates— are classified in Industry 423520, Coal and Other Mineral and Ore Merchant Wholesalers; and
- Merchant wholesale distribution of nonprecious flatware—are classified in Industry 423220, Home Furnishing Merchant Wholesalers.

42399 Other Miscellaneous Durable Goods Merchant Wholesalers[US]
See industry description for 423990 below.

423990 Other Miscellaneous Durable Goods Merchant Wholesalers[US]

This industry comprises establishments primarily engaged in the merchant wholesale distribution of durable goods (except motor vehicle and motor vehicle parts and supplies; furniture and home furnishings; lumber and other construction materials; professional and commercial equipment and supplies; metals and minerals (except petroleum); electrical goods; hardware, and plumbing and heating equipment and supplies; machinery, equipment and supplies; sporting and recreational goods and supplies; toy and hobby goods and supplies; recyclable materials; and jewelry, watches, precious stones and precious metals).

Illustrative Examples:

Musical instruments merchant wholesalers
Phonograph records merchant wholesalers
Prerecorded audio and video cassettes merchant wholesalers

Prerecorded audio and video tapes and discs merchant wholesalers
Prerecorded compact discs (CDs) merchant wholesalers
Timber and timber products (except lumber) merchant wholesalers

Cross-References. Establishments primarily engaged in—

- Merchant wholesale distribution of automobiles and other motor vehicles, motor vehicle supplies, tires, and new and used parts—are classified in

---

US—United States industry only. CAN—United States and Canadian industries are comparable. MEX—United States and Mexican industries are comparable. Blank—Canadian, Mexican, and United States industries are comparable.

Industry Group 4231, Motor Vehicle and Motor Vehicle Parts and Supplies Merchant Wholesalers;

- Merchant wholesale distribution of furniture and home furnishings—are classified in Industry Group 4232, Furniture and Home Furnishing Merchant Wholesalers;

- Merchant wholesale distribution of lumber, plywood, millwork, wood panels, brick, stone, roofing, siding, and other nonelectrical construction materials—are classified in Industry Group 4233, Lumber and Other Construction Materials Merchant Wholesalers;

- Merchant wholesale distribution of photographic; office; computer and computer peripheral; medical, dental, hospital, ophthalmic; and other commercial and professional equipment and supplies—are classified in Industry Group 4234, Professional and Commercial Equipment and Supplies Merchant Wholesalers;

- Merchant wholesale distribution of coal and other minerals and ores and semifinished metal products—are classified in Industry Group 4235, Metal and Mineral (except Petroleum) Merchant Wholesalers;

- Merchant wholesale distribution of electrical goods—are classified in Industry Group 4236, Electrical and Electronic Goods Merchant Wholesalers;

- Merchant wholesale distribution of hardware, and plumbing, heating, air conditioning, and refrigeration equipment and supplies—are classified in Industry Group 4237, Hardware, and Plumbing and Heating Equipment and Supplies Merchant Wholesalers;

- Merchant wholesale distribution of construction, mining, farm, garden, industrial, service establishment, and transportation machinery, equipment and supplies—are classified in Industry Group 4238, Machinery, Equipment, and Supplies Merchant Wholesalers;

- Merchant wholesale distribution of sporting goods and accessories; billiard and pool supplies; sporting firearms and ammunition; and/or marine pleasure craft, equipment, and supplies—are classified in Industry 423910, Sporting and Recreational Goods and Supplies Merchant Wholesalers;

- Merchant wholesale distribution of toys, fireworks, playing cards, hobby goods and supplies and/or related goods—are classified in Industry 423920, Toy and Hobby Goods and Supplies Merchant Wholesalers;

- Merchant wholesale distribution of automotive, industrial, and other recyclable materials—are classified in Industry 423930, Recyclable Material Merchant Wholesalers; and

- Merchant wholesale distribution of jewelry, precious and semiprecious stones, precious metals and metal flatware, costume jewelry, watches, clocks, silverware, and/or jewelers' findings—are classified in Industry 423940, Jewelry, Watch, Precious Stone, and Precious Metal Merchant Wholesalers.

424 Merchant Wholesalers, Nondurable Goods[US]

Industries in the Merchant Wholesalers, Nondurable Goods subsector sell nondurable goods to other businesses. Nondurable goods are items generally with a normal life expectancy of less than three years. Nondurable goods merchant wholesale trade establishments are engaged in wholesaling products, such as paper and paper products, chemicals and chemical products, drugs, textiles and textile products, apparel, footwear, groceries, farm products, petroleum and petroleum products, alcoholic beverages, books, magazines, newspapers, flowers and nursery stock, and tobacco products.

The detailed industries within the subsector are organized in the classification structure based on the products sold.

Business to business electronic markets, agents, and brokers primarily engaged in wholesaling nondurable goods, generally on a commission or fee basis, are classified in Subsector 425, Wholesale Electronic Markets and Agents and Brokers.

4241 Paper and Paper Product Merchant Wholesalers[US]

42411 Printing and Writing Paper Merchant Wholesalers[US]
See industry description for 424110 below.

424110 Printing and Writing Paper Merchant Wholesalers[US]

This industry comprises establishments primarily engaged in the merchant wholesale distribution of bulk printing and/or writing paper generally on rolls for further processing.

Illustrative Examples:

Bulk envelope paper merchant wholesalers
Bulk groundwood paper merchant wholesalers

Bulk paper (e.g., fine, printing, writing) merchant wholesalers

Cross-References.

Establishments primarily engaged in the merchant wholesale distribution of stationery are classified in Industry 424120, Stationery and Office Supplies Merchant Wholesalers.

US—United States industry only. CAN—United States and Canadian industries are comparable. MEX—United States and Mexican industries are comparable. Blank—Canadian, Mexican, and United States industries are comparable.

42412 Stationery and Office Supplies Merchant Wholesalers[US]

See industry description for 424120 below.

424120 Stationery and Office Supplies Merchant Wholesalers[US]

This industry comprises establishments primarily engaged in the merchant wholesale distribution of stationery, office supplies and/or gift wrap.

Illustrative Examples:

Computer paper supplies merchant
  wholesalers
Envelope merchant wholesalers
File cards and folders merchant
  wholesalers
Greeting cards merchant wholesalers

Pencils merchant wholesalers
Photocopy supplies merchant wholesalers
Social stationery merchant wholesalers
Typewriter paper merchant wholesalers
Writing pens merchant wholesalers

Cross-References.

Establishments primarily engaged in the merchant wholesale distribution of bulk printing and/or writing paper are classified in Industry 424110, Printing and Writing Paper Merchant Wholesalers.

42413 Industrial and Personal Service Paper Merchant Wholesalers[US]

See industry description for 424130 below.

424130 Industrial and Personal Service Paper Merchant Wholesalers[US]

This industry comprises establishments primarily engaged in the merchant wholesale distribution of kraft wrapping and other coarse paper, paperboard, converted paper (except stationery and office supplies), and/or related disposable plastics products.

Illustrative Examples:

Disposable plastics eating utensils
  merchant wholesalers
Paper and disposable plastics dishes
  merchant wholesalers
Paper and disposable plastics shipping
  supplies merchant wholesalers
Paper bags merchant wholesalers

Paper napkins merchant wholesalers
Paperboard and disposable plastics boxes
  merchant wholesalers
Plastics bags merchant wholesalers
Sanitary paper products merchant
  wholesalers

US—United States industry only. CAN—United States and Canadian industries are comparable. MEX—United States and Mexican industries are comparable. Blank—Canadian, Mexican, and United States industries are comparable.

Cross-References.

Establishments primarily engaged in the merchant wholesale distribution of stationery, office supplies, and/or gift wrap are classified in Industry 424120, Stationery and Office Supplies Merchant Wholesalers.

4242 Drugs and Druggists' Sundries Merchant Wholesalers[US]

42421 Drugs and Druggists' Sundries Merchant Wholesalers[US]
See industry description for 424210 below.

424210 Drugs and Druggists' Sundries Merchant Wholesalers[US]

This industry comprises establishments primarily engaged in the merchant wholesale distribution of biological and medical products; botanical drugs and herbs; and pharmaceutical products intended for internal and external consumption in such forms as ampoules, tablets, capsules, vials, ointments, powders, solutions, and suspensions.

Illustrative Examples:

Antibiotics merchant wholesalers
Blood derivatives merchant wholesalers
Botanicals merchant wholesalers
Cosmetics merchant wholesalers
Endocrine substances merchant
  wholesalers

In-vitro and in-vivo diagnostics merchant
  wholesalers
Vaccines merchant wholesalers
Vitamins merchant wholesalers

Cross-References.

Establishments primarily engaged in the merchant wholesale distribution of surgical, dental, and hospital equipment are classified in Industry 423450, Medical, Dental, and Hospital Equipment and Supplies Merchant Wholesalers.

4243 Apparel, Piece Goods, and Notions Merchant Wholesalers[US]

42431 Piece Goods, Notions, and Other Dry Goods Merchant Wholesalers[US]
See industry description for 424310 below.

424310 Piece Goods, Notions, and Other Dry Goods Merchant Wholesalers[US]

This industry comprises establishments primarily engaged in the merchant wholesale distribution of piece goods, fabrics, knitting yarns (except industrial), thread and other notions, and/or hair accessories.

US—United States industry only. CAN—United States and Canadian industries are comparable. MEX—United States and Mexican industries are comparable. Blank—Canadian, Mexican, and United States industries are comparable.

Cross-References.

- Establishments primarily engaged as converters who buy fabric goods in the grey, have them finished on a contract basis, and sell at wholesale are classified in Industry 31331, Textile and Fabric Finishing Mills.

- Establishments primarily engaged in merchant wholesale distribution of industrial yarns are classified in Industry 424990, Other Miscellaneous Nondurable Goods Merchant Wholesalers.

42432 Men's and Boys' Clothing and Furnishings Merchant Wholesalers^{US}

See industry description for 424320 below.

424320 Men's and Boys' Clothing and Furnishings Merchant Wholesalers^{US}

This industry comprises establishments primarily engaged in the merchant wholesale distribution of men's and/or boys' clothing and furnishings.

Illustrative Examples:

Men's and boys' hosiery merchant wholesalers

Men's and boys' nightwear merchant wholesalers

Men's and boys' sportswear merchant wholesalers

Men's and boys' suits merchant wholesalers

Men's and boys' underwear merchant wholesalers

Men's and boys' work clothing merchant wholesalers

Cross-References.

Establishments primarily engaged in the merchant wholesale distribution of unisex clothing and men's fur clothing are classified in Industry 424330, Women's, Children's, and Infants' Clothing and Accessories Merchant Wholesalers.

42433 Women's, Children's, and Infants' Clothing and Accessories Merchant Wholesalers^{US}

See industry description for 424330 below.

424330 Women's, Children's, and Infants' Clothing and Accessories Merchant Wholesalers^{US}

This industry comprises establishments primarily engaged in the merchant wholesale distribution of (1) women's, children's, infants', and/or unisex clothing and accessories and/or (2) fur clothing.

Illustrative Examples:

Dresses merchant wholesalers	Millinery merchant wholesalers
Fur clothing merchant wholesalers	Women's, children's, and infants'
Lingerie merchant wholesalers	hosiery merchant wholesalers

42434 Footwear Merchant Wholesalers[US]
See industry description for 424340 below.

424340 Footwear Merchant Wholesalers[US]

This industry comprises establishments primarily engaged in the merchant wholesale distribution of footwear (including athletic) of leather, rubber, and other materials.

4244 Grocery and Related Product Merchant Wholesalers[US]

42441 General Line Grocery Merchant Wholesalers[US]
See industry description for 424410 below.

424410 General Line Grocery Merchant Wholesalers[US]

This industry comprises establishments primarily engaged in the merchant wholesale distribution of a general line (wide range) of groceries.

Cross-References.

Establishments primarily engaged in the merchant wholesale distribution of a specialized line of groceries are classified elsewhere in Sector 42, Wholesale Trade, according to the product sold.

42442 Packaged Frozen Food Merchant Wholesalers[US]
See industry description for 424420 below.

424420 Packaged Frozen Food Merchant Wholesalers[US]

This industry comprises establishments primarily engaged in the merchant wholesale distribution of packaged frozen foods (except dairy products).

Illustrative Examples:

Frozen bakery products merchant wholesalers	Packaged frozen meats merchant wholesalers

Frozen juices merchant wholesalers
Frozen vegetables merchant wholesalers
Packaged frozen fish merchant
  wholesalers

Packaged frozen poultry merchant
  wholesalers

Cross-References.

Establishments primarily engaged in the merchant wholesale distribution of frozen dairy products are classified in Industry 424430, Dairy Product (except Dried or Canned) Merchant Wholesalers.

42443 Dairy Product (except Dried or Canned) Merchant Wholesalers[US]
See industry description for 424430 below.

424430 Dairy Product (except Dried or Canned) Merchant Wholesalers[US]

This industry comprises establishments primarily engaged in the merchant wholesale distribution of dairy products (except dried or canned).

Illustrative Examples:

Butter merchant wholesalers
Cheese merchant wholesalers
Cream merchant wholesalers
Fluid milk (except canned) merchant
  wholesalers

Ice cream and ices merchant wholesalers
Yogurt merchant wholesalers

Cross-References. Establishments primarily engaged in—

- Merchant wholesale distribution of dried or canned dairy products and dairy substitutes—are classified in Industry 424490, Other Grocery and Related Products Merchant Wholesalers; and

- Pasteurizing and bottling milk—are classified in U.S. Industry 311511, Fluid Milk Manufacturing.

42444 Poultry and Poultry Product Merchant Wholesalers[US]
See industry description for 424440 below.

424440 Poultry and Poultry Product Merchant Wholesalers[US]

This industry comprises establishments primarily engaged in the merchant wholesale distribution of poultry and/or poultry products (except canned and packaged frozen).

US—United States industry only. CAN—United States and Canadian industries are comparable. MEX—United States and Mexican industries are comparable. Blank—Canadian, Mexican, and United States industries are comparable.

Cross-References. Establishments primarily engaged in—

- Merchant wholesale distribution of packaged frozen poultry—are classified in Industry 424420, Packaged Frozen Food Merchant Wholesalers;
- Merchant wholesale distribution of canned poultry—are classified in Industry 424490, Other Grocery and Related Products Merchant Wholesalers; and
- Slaughtering and dressing poultry—are classified in U.S. Industry 311615, Poultry Processing.

42445 Confectionery Merchant Wholesalers[US]
See industry description for 424450 below.

424450 Confectionery Merchant Wholesalers[US]

This industry comprises establishments primarily engaged in the merchant wholesale distribution of confectioneries; salted or roasted nuts; popcorn; potato, corn, and similar chips; and/or fountain fruits and syrups.

Cross-References. Establishments primarily engaged in—

- Merchant wholesale distribution of frozen pretzels—are classified in Industry 424420, Packaged Frozen Food Merchant Wholesalers; and
- Merchant wholesale distribution of pretzels (except frozen)—are classified in Industry 424490, Other Grocery and Related Products Merchant Wholesalers.

42446 Fish and Seafood Merchant Wholesalers[US]
See industry description for 424460 below.

424460 Fish and Seafood Merchant Wholesalers[US]

This industry comprises establishments primarily engaged in the merchant wholesale distribution of fish and seafood (except canned or packaged frozen).

Cross-References. Establishments primarily engaged in—

- Merchant wholesale distribution of packaged frozen fish and seafood—are classified in Industry 424420, Packaged Frozen Food Merchant Wholesalers;
- Merchant wholesale distribution of canned fish and seafood—are classified in Industry 424490, Other Grocery and Related Products Merchant Wholesalers; and

---

- Canning, smoking, salting, drying, or freezing seafood and shucking and packing fresh shellfish—are classified in Industry 31171, Seafood Product Preparation and Packaging.

42447 Meat and Meat Product Merchant Wholesalers[US]
See industry description for 424470 below.

424470 Meat and Meat Product Merchant Wholesalers[US]

This industry comprises establishments primarily engaged in the merchant wholesale distribution of meats and meat products (except canned and packaged frozen) and/or lard.

Cross-References. Establishments primarily engaged in—

- Merchant wholesale distribution of packaged frozen meats—are classified in Industry 424420, Packaged Frozen Food Merchant Wholesalers;
- Merchant wholesale distribution of canned meats—are classified in Industry 424490, Other Grocery and Related Products Merchant Wholesalers; and
- Preparing boxed beef—are classified in U.S. Industry 311612, Meat Processed from Carcasses.

42448 Fresh Fruit and Vegetable Merchant Wholesalers[US]
See industry description for 424480 below.

424480 Fresh Fruit and Vegetable Merchant Wholesalers[US]

This industry comprises establishments primarily engaged in the merchant wholesale distribution of fresh fruits and vegetables.

42449 Other Grocery and Related Products Merchant Wholesalers[US]
See industry description for 424490 below.

424490 Other Grocery and Related Products Merchant Wholesalers[US]

This industry comprises establishments primarily engaged in the merchant wholesale distribution of groceries and related products (except a general line of groceries; packaged frozen food; dairy products (except dried and canned); poultry products (except canned); confectioneries; fish and seafood (except canned); meat products (except canned); and fresh fruits and vegetables). Included in this industry are establishments primarily engaged in the bottling and merchant wholesale distribution of spring and mineral waters processed by others.

Illustrative Examples:

Bakery products (except frozen) merchant wholesalers	Canned milk merchant wholesalers
	Canned seafood merchant wholesalers
Canned fish merchant wholesalers	Canned vegetables merchant wholesalers
Canned fruits merchant wholesalers	Dried milk merchant wholesalers
Canned meats merchant wholesalers	Soft drinks merchant wholesalers

Cross-References. Establishments primarily engaged in—

- Merchant wholesale distribution of grains, field beans, livestock, and other farm product raw materials—are classified in Industry Group 4245, Farm Product Raw Material Merchant Wholesalers;

- Merchant wholesale distribution of beer, wine, and distilled alcoholic beverages—are classified in Industry Group 4248, Beer, Wine, and Distilled Alcoholic Beverage Merchant Wholesalers;

- Bottling soft drinks—are classified in Industry 31211, Soft Drink and Ice Manufacturing;

- Merchant wholesale distribution of a general line of groceries—are classified in Industry 424410, General Line Grocery Merchant Wholesalers;

- Merchant wholesale distribution of packaged frozen foods (except dairy)—are classified in Industry 424420, Packaged Frozen Food Merchant Wholesalers;

- Merchant wholesale distribution of dairy products—are classified in Industry 424430, Dairy Product (except Dried or Canned) Merchant Wholesalers;

- Merchant wholesale distribution of poultry and poultry products (except canned and packaged frozen)—are classified in Industry 424440, Poultry and Poultry Product Merchant Wholesalers;

- Merchant wholesale distribution of confectioneries; salted or roasted nuts; popcorn; potato, corn, and similar chips; and/or fountain fruits and syrups—are classified in Industry 424450, Confectionery Merchant Wholesalers;

- Merchant wholesale distribution of fish and seafoods (except canned and packaged frozen)—are classified in Industry 424460, Fish and Seafood Merchant Wholesalers;

- Merchant wholesale distribution of meats (except canned and packaged frozen)—are classified in Industry 424470, Meat and Meat Product Merchant Wholesalers;

- Merchant wholesale distribution of fresh fruits and vegetables—are classified in Industry 424480, Fresh Fruit and Vegetable Merchant Wholesalers; and

- Roasting coffee—are classified in Industry 311920, Coffee and Tea Manufacturing.

4245 Farm Product Raw Material Merchant Wholesalers^{US}

This industry group comprises establishments primarily engaged in the merchant wholesale distribution of agricultural products (except raw milk, live poultry, and fresh fruit and vegetables), such as grains, field beans, livestock, and other farm product raw materials (excluding seeds).

42451 Grain and Field Bean Merchant Wholesalers^{US}
See industry description for 424510 below.

424510 Grain and Field Bean Merchant Wholesalers^{US}

This industry comprises establishments primarily engaged in the merchant wholesale distribution of grains, such as corn, wheat, oats, barley, and unpolished rice; dry beans; and soybeans and other inedible beans. Included in this industry are establishments primarily engaged in operating country or terminal grain elevators primarily for the purpose of wholesaling.

Cross-References. Establishments primarily engaged in—

- Merchant wholesale distribution of field and garden seeds—are classified in Industry 424910, Farm Supplies Merchant Wholesalers; and

- Operating grain elevators for storage only—are classified in Industry 493130, Farm Product Warehousing and Storage.

42452 Livestock Merchant Wholesalers^{US}
See industry description for 424520 below.

424520 Livestock Merchant Wholesalers^{US}

This industry comprises establishments primarily engaged in the merchant wholesale distribution of livestock (except horses and mules).

Illustrative Examples:

Cattle merchant wholesalers
Goats merchant wholesalers
Hogs merchant wholesalers
Sheep merchant wholesalers

Cross-References.

Establishments primarily engaged in the merchant wholesale distribution of horses and mules are classified in Industry 424590, Other Farm Product Raw Material Merchant Wholesalers.

42459 Other Farm Product Raw Material Merchant Wholesalers^{US}
See industry description for 424590 below.

424590 Other Farm Product Raw Material Merchant Wholesalers^{US}

This industry comprises establishments primarily engaged in the merchant wholesale distribution of farm products (except grain and field beans, livestock, raw milk, live poultry, and fresh fruits and vegetables).

Illustrative Examples:

Chicks merchant wholesalers	Mules merchant wholesalers
Hides merchant wholesalers	Raw cotton merchant wholesalers
Horses merchant wholesalers	Raw pelts merchant wholesalers
Leaf tobacco merchant wholesalers	

Cross-References. Establishments primarily engaged in—

- Merchant wholesale distribution of raw milk—are classified in **Industry 424430, Dairy Product (except Dried or Canned) Merchant Wholesalers;**

- Merchant wholesale distribution of live poultry (except chicks)—are classified in Industry 424440, Poultry and Poultry Product Merchant Wholesalers;

- Merchant wholesale distribution of grain, dry beans, and soybeans and other inedible beans—are classified in Industry 424510, Grain and Field Bean Merchant Wholesalers;

- Merchant wholesale distribution of livestock (except horses and mules), such as cattle, hogs, sheep, and goats—are classified in Industry 424520, Livestock Merchant Wholesalers; and

- Merchant wholesale distribution of fresh fruits and vegetables—are classified in Industry 424480, Fresh Fruit and Vegetable Merchant Wholesalers.

4246 Chemical and Allied Products Merchant Wholesalers^{US}

This industry group comprises establishments primarily engaged in the merchant wholesale distribution of chemicals; plastics materials and basic forms and shapes; and allied products.

42461 Plastics Materials and Basic Forms and Shapes Merchant Wholesalers[US]
See industry description for 424610 below.

424610 Plastics Materials and Basic Forms and Shapes Merchant Wholesalers[US]

This industry comprises establishments primarily engaged in the merchant wholesale distribution of plastics materials and resins, and unsupported plastics film, sheet, sheeting, rod, tube, and other basic forms and shapes.

42469 Other Chemical and Allied Products Merchant Wholesalers[US]
See industry description for 424690 below.

424690 Other Chemical and Allied Products Merchant Wholesalers[US]

This industry comprises establishments primarily engaged in the merchant wholesale distribution of chemicals and allied products (except agricultural and medicinal chemicals, paints and varnishes, fireworks, and plastics materials and basic forms and shapes).

Illustrative Examples:

Acids merchant wholesalers
Automotive chemicals (except lubricating oils and greases) merchant wholesalers
Dyestuffs merchant wholesalers
Explosives (except ammunition and fireworks) merchant wholesalers
Industrial chemicals merchant wholesalers
Industrial salts merchant wholesalers
Rosins merchant wholesalers
Turpentine merchant wholesalers

Cross-References. Establishments primarily engaged in—

- Merchant wholesale distribution of ammunition—are classified in Industry Group 4239, Miscellaneous Durable Goods Merchant Wholesalers;
- Merchant wholesale distribution of biological and medical products; botanical drugs and herbs; and pharmaceutical products intended for internal and external consumption in such forms as ampoules, tablets, capsules, vials, ointments, powders, solutions, and suspensions—are classified in Industry 424210, Drugs and Druggists' Sundries Merchant Wholesalers;
- Merchant wholesale distribution of farm supplies, such as animal feeds, fertilizers, agricultural chemicals, pesticides, seeds and plant bulbs—are classified in Industry 424910, Farm Supplies Merchant Wholesalers;

- Merchant wholesale distribution of paints, and varnishes and similar coatings, pigments, wallpaper, and supplies, such as paint brushes and rollers—are classified in Industry 424950, Paint, Varnish, and Supplies Merchant Wholesalers;

- Merchant wholesale distribution of lubricating oils and greases—are classified in Industry 424720, Petroleum and Petroleum Products Merchant Wholesalers (except Bulk Stations and Terminals);

- Merchant wholesale distribution of fireworks—are classified in Industry 423920, Toy and Hobby Goods and Supplies Merchant Wholesalers; and

- Merchant wholesale distribution of plastics materials and resins, and unsupported plastics film, sheet, sheeting, rod, tube, and other basic forms and shapes—are classified in Industry 424610, Plastics Materials and Basic Forms and Shapes Merchant Wholesalers.

4247   Petroleum and Petroleum Products Merchant Wholesalers[US]

42471   Petroleum Bulk Stations and Terminals[US]
See industry description for 424710 below.

424710   Petroleum Bulk Stations and Terminals[US]

This industry comprises establishments with bulk liquid storage facilities primarily engaged in the merchant wholesale distribution of crude petroleum and petroleum products, including liquefied petroleum gas.

Cross-References.

Establishments primarily engaged in bulk storage of petroleum are classified in Industry 493190, Other Warehousing and Storage.

42472   Petroleum and Petroleum Products Merchant Wholesalers (except Bulk Stations and Terminals)[US]
See industry description for 424720 below.

424720   Petroleum and Petroleum Products Merchant Wholesalers (except Bulk Stations and Terminals)[US]

This industry comprises establishments primarily engaged in the merchant wholesale distribution of petroleum and petroleum products (except from bulk liquid storage facilities).

Illustrative Examples:

Bottled liquid petroleum gas merchant wholesalers

Fuel oil merchant wholesalers (except bulk stations, terminals)

Gasoline merchant wholesalers (except bulk stations, terminals)

Lubricating oil and grease merchant wholesalers (except bulk stations, terminals)

Cross-References.

Establishments primarily engaged in the merchant wholesale distribution of crude petroleum and petroleum products from bulk liquid storage facilities are classified in Industry 424710, Petroleum Bulk Stations and Terminals.

4248 Beer, Wine, and Distilled Alcoholic Beverage Merchant Wholesalers[US]

42481 Beer and Ale Merchant Wholesalers[US]
See industry description for 424810 below.

424810 Beer and Ale Merchant Wholesalers[US]

This industry comprises establishments primarily engaged in the merchant wholesale distribution of beer, ale, porter, and other fermented malt beverages.

42482 Wine and Distilled Alcoholic Beverage Merchant Wholesalers[US]
See industry description for 424820 below.

424820 Wine and Distilled Alcoholic Beverage Merchant Wholesalers[US]

This industry comprises establishments primarily engaged in the merchant wholesale distribution of wine, distilled alcoholic beverages, and/or neutral spirits and ethyl alcohol used in blended wines and distilled liquors.

4249 Miscellaneous Nondurable Goods Merchant Wholesalers[US]

This industry group comprises establishments primarily engaged in the merchant wholesale distribution of nondurable goods, such as farm supplies; books, periodicals and newspapers; flowers; nursery stock; paints; varnishes; tobacco and tobacco

US—United States industry only. CAN—United States and Canadian industries are comparable. MEX—United States and Mexican industries are comparable. Blank—Canadian, Mexican, and United States industries are comparable.

products; and other miscellaneous nondurable goods, such as cut Christmas trees and pet supplies.

42491 Farm Supplies Merchant Wholesalers[US]
See industry description for 424910 below.

424910 Farm Supplies Merchant Wholesalers[US]

This industry comprises establishments primarily engaged in the merchant wholesale distribution of farm supplies, such as animal feeds, fertilizers, agricultural chemicals, pesticides, plant seeds, and plant bulbs.

Cross-References. Establishments primarily engaged in—

- Merchant wholesale distribution of pet food—are classified in Industry 424490, Other Grocery and Related Products Merchant Wholesalers;
- Merchant wholesale distribution of grains—are classified in Industry 424510, Grain and Field Bean Merchant Wholesalers;
- Merchant wholesale distribution of pet supplies—are classified in Industry 424990, Other Miscellaneous Nondurable Goods Merchant Wholesalers; and
- Merchant wholesale distribution of nursery stock (except seeds and plant bulbs)—are classified in Industry 424930, Flower, Nursery Stock, and Florists' Supplies Merchant Wholesalers.

42492 Book, Periodical, and Newspaper Merchant Wholesalers[US]
See industry description for 424920 below.

424920 Book, Periodical, and Newspaper Merchant Wholesalers[US]

This industry comprises establishments primarily engaged in the merchant wholesale distribution of books, periodicals, and newspapers.

42493 Flower, Nursery Stock, and Florists' Supplies Merchant Wholesalers[US]
See industry description for 424930 below.

424930 Flower, Nursery Stock, and Florists' Supplies Merchant Wholesalers[US]

This industry comprises establishments primarily engaged in the merchant wholesale distribution of flowers, florists' supplies, and/or nursery stock (except plant seeds and plant bulbs).

Cross-References. Establishments primarily engaged in—

- Merchant wholesale distribution of cut Christmas trees—are classified in Industry 424990, Other Miscellaneous Nondurable Goods Merchant Wholesalers; and

- Merchant wholesale distribution of plant seeds and plant bulbs—are classified in Industry 424910, Farm Supplies Merchant Wholesalers.

42494 Tobacco and Tobacco Product Merchant Wholesalers^{US}
See industry description for 424940 below.

424940 Tobacco and Tobacco Product Merchant Wholesalers^{US}

This industry comprises establishments primarily engaged in the merchant wholesale distribution of tobacco products, such as cigarettes, snuff, cigars, and pipe tobacco.

Cross-References.

Establishments primarily engaged in the merchant wholesale distribution of leaf tobacco are classified in Industry 424590, Other Farm Product Raw Material Merchant Wholesalers.

42495 Paint, Varnish, and Supplies Merchant Wholesalers^{US}
See industry description for 424950 below.

424950 Paint, Varnish, and Supplies Merchant Wholesalers^{US}

This industry comprises establishments primarily engaged in the merchant wholesale distribution of paints, varnishes, and similar coatings; pigments; wallpaper; and supplies, such as paint brushes and rollers.

Cross-References.

Establishments primarily engaged in the merchant wholesale distribution of artists' paints are classified in Industry 424990, Other Miscellaneous Nondurable Goods Merchant Wholesalers.

42499 Other Miscellaneous Nondurable Goods Merchant Wholesalers^{US}
See industry description for 424990 below.

424990 Other Miscellaneous Nondurable Goods Merchant WholesalersUS

This industry comprises establishments primarily engaged in the merchant wholesale distribution of nondurable goods (except printing and writing paper; stationery and office supplies; industrial and personal service paper; drugs and druggists' sundries; apparel, piece goods, and notions; grocery and related products; farm product raw materials; chemical and allied products; petroleum and petroleum products; beer, wine, and distilled alcoholic beverages; farm supplies; books, periodicals and newspapers; flower, nursery stock and florists' supplies; tobacco and tobacco products; and paint, varnishes, wallpaper, and supplies).

Illustrative Examples:

Artists' supplies merchant wholesalers
Burlap merchant wholesalers
Christmas trees merchant wholesalers
Pet supplies (except pet food) merchant wholesalers

Statuary goods (except religious) merchant wholesalers
Textile bags merchant wholesalers
Industrial yarn merchant wholesalers

Cross-References. Establishments primarily engaged in—

- Distribution of advertising specialties—are classified in Industry 541890, Other Services Related to Advertising;
- Merchant wholesale distribution of farm supplies—are classified in Industry 424910, Farm Supplies Merchant Wholesalers;
- Merchant wholesale distribution of books, periodicals, and newspapers—are classified in Industry 424920, Book, Periodical, and Newspaper Merchant Wholesalers;
- Merchant wholesale distribution of flowers, nursery stock, and florists' supplies—are classified in Industry 424930, Flower, Nursery Stock, and Florists' Supplies Merchant Wholesalers;
- Merchant wholesale distribution of tobacco and its products—are classified in Industry 424940, Tobacco and Tobacco Product Merchant Wholesalers;
- Merchant wholesale distribution of paints, varnishes, and similar coatings; pigments; wallpaper; and supplies—are classified in Industry 424950, Paint, Varnish, and Supplies Merchant Wholesalers;
- Merchant wholesale distribution of bulk printing and/or writing paper—are classified in Industry 424110, Printing and Writing Paper Merchant Wholesalers;
- Merchant wholesale distribution of stationery, office supplies, and/or gift wrap—are classified in Industry 424120, Stationery and Office Supplies Merchant Wholesalers;

- Merchant wholesale distribution of wrapping and other coarse paper, paper-board, converted paper (except stationery and office supplies), and related disposable plastics products—are classified in Industry 424130, Industrial and Personal Service Paper Merchant Wholesalers;

- Merchant wholesale distribution of biological and medical products; botanical drugs and herbs; and pharmaceutical products intended for internal and external consumption—are classified in Industry 424210, Drugs and Druggists' Sundries Merchant Wholesalers;

- Merchant wholesale distribution of clothing and accessories, footwear, piece goods, yard goods, notions, and/or hair accessories—are classified in Industry Group 4243, Apparel, Piece Goods, and Notions Merchant Wholesalers;

- Merchant wholesale distribution of meat, poultry, seafood, confectioneries, fruits and vegetables; and other groceries—are related products are classified in Industry Group 4244, Grocery and Related Product Merchant Wholesalers;

- Merchant wholesale distribution of grains, field beans, livestock, and other farm product raw materials—are classified in Industry Group 4245, Farm Product Raw Material Merchant Wholesalers;

- Merchant wholesale distribution of chemicals; plastics materials and basic forms and shapes; and allied products—are classified in Industry Group 4246, Chemical and Allied Products Merchant Wholesalers;

- Merchant wholesale distribution of petroleum and petroleum products—are classified in Industry Group 4247, Petroleum and Petroleum Products Merchant Wholesalers;

- Merchant wholesale distribution of beer, ale, wine, and distilled alcoholic beverages—are classified Industry Group 4248, Beer, Wine, and Distilled Alcoholic Beverage Merchant Wholesalers;

- Merchant wholesale distribution of pet foods—are classified in Industry 424490, Other Grocery and Related Products Merchant Wholesalers;

- Merchant wholesale distribution of religious statuary—are classified in Industry 423990, Other Miscellaneous Durable Goods Merchant Wholesalers; and

- Merchant wholesale distribution of knitting yarns (except industrial)—are classified in Industry 424310 Piece Goods, Notions, and Other Dry Goods Merchant Wholesalers.

425 Wholesale Electronic Markets and Agents and Brokers[US]

Industries in the Wholesale Electronic Markets and Agents and Brokers subsector arrange for the sale of goods owned by others, generally on a fee or commission

US—United States industry only. CAN—United States and Canadian industries are comparable. MEX—United States and Mexican industries are comparable. Blank—Canadian, Mexican, and United States industries are comparable.

basis. They act on behalf of the buyers and sellers of goods. This subsector contains agents and brokers as well as business to business electronic markets that facilitate wholesale trade.

4251 Wholesale Electronic Markets and Agents and Brokers^{US}

42511 Business to Business Electronic Markets^{US}
See industry description for 425110 below.

425110 Business to Business Electronic Markets^{US}

This industry comprises business-to-business electronic markets bringing together buyers and sellers of goods using the Internet or other electronic means and generally receiving a commission or fee for the service. Business-to-business electronic markets for durable and nondurable goods are included in this industry.

Cross-References.
Establishments primarily engaged in bringing together buyers and sellers of goods using the Internet in a business-to-consumer or consumer-to-consumer environment are classified in Industry 45411, Electronic Shopping and Mail-Order Houses.

42512 Wholesale Trade Agents and Brokers^{US}
See industry description for 425120 below.

425120 Wholesale Trade Agents and Brokers^{US}

This industry comprises wholesale trade agents and brokers acting on behalf of buyers or sellers in the wholesale distribution of goods. Agents and brokers do not take title to the goods being sold but rather receive a commission or fee for their service. Agents and brokers for all durable and nondurable goods are included in this industry.

Illustrative Examples:

Independent sales representatives   Manufacturers' sales representatives

Cross-References.
Establishments acting in the capacity of agents or brokers that operate using the Internet or other electronic means instead of a sales force are classified in Industry 425110, Business to Business Electronic Markets.

US—United States industry only. CAN—United States and Canadian industries are comparable. MEX—United States and Mexican industries are comparable. Blank—Canadian, Mexican, and United States industries are comparable.

Sector 44-45—Retail Trade

The Sector as a Whole

The Retail Trade sector comprises establishments engaged in retailing merchandise, generally without transformation, and rendering services incidental to the sale of merchandise.

The retailing process is the final step in the distribution of merchandise; retailers are, therefore, organized to sell merchandise in small quantities to the general public. This sector comprises two main types of retailers: store and nonstore retailers.

1. Store retailers operate fixed point-of-sale locations, located and designed to attract a high volume of walk-in customers. In general, retail stores have extensive displays of merchandise and use mass-media advertising to attract customers. They typically sell merchandise to the general public for personal or household consumption, but some also serve business and institutional clients. These include establishments, such as office supply stores, computer and software stores, building materials dealers, plumbing supply stores, and electrical supply stores. Catalog showrooms, gasoline services stations, automotive dealers, and mobile home dealers are treated as store retailers.

   In addition to retailing merchandise, some types of store retailers are also engaged in the provision of after-sales services, such as repair and installation. For example, new automobile dealers, electronic and appliance stores, and musical instrument and supply stores often provide repair services. As a general rule, establishments engaged in retailing merchandise and providing after-sales services are classified in this sector.

   The first eleven subsectors of retail trade are store retailers. The establishments are grouped into industries and industry groups typically based on one or more of the following criteria:

   (a) The merchandise line or lines carried by the store; for example, specialty stores are distinguished from general-line stores.

   (b) The usual trade designation of the establishments. This criterion applies in cases where a store type is well recognized by the industry and the public, but difficult to define strictly in terms of commodity lines carried; for example, pharmacies, hardware stores, and department stores.

   (c) Capital requirements in terms of display equipment; for example, food stores have equipment requirements not found in other retail industries.

   (d) Human resource requirements in terms of expertise; for example, the staff of an automobile dealer requires knowledge in financing, registering, and licensing issues that are not necessary in other retail industries.

US—United States industry only. CAN—United States and Canadian industries are comparable. MEX—United States and Mexican industries are comparable. Blank—Canadian, Mexican, and United States industries are comparable.

2. Nonstore retailers, like store retailers, are organized to serve the general public, but their retailing methods differ. The establishments of this subsector reach customers and market merchandise with methods, such as the broadcasting of "infomercials," the broadcasting and publishing of direct-response advertising, the publishing of paper and electronic catalogs, door-to-door solicitation, in-home demonstration, selling from portable stalls (street vendors, except food), and distribution through vending machines. Establishments engaged in the direct sale (nonstore) of products, such as home heating oil dealers and home delivery newspaper routes are included here.

The buying of goods for resale is a characteristic of retail trade establishments that particularly distinguishes them from establishments in the agriculture, manufacturing, and construction industries. For example, farms that sell their products at or from the point of production are not classified in retail, but rather in agriculture. Similarly, establishments that both manufacture and sell their products to the general public are not classified in retail, but rather in manufacturing. However, establishments that engage in processing activities incidental to retailing are classified in retail. This includes establishments, such as optical goods stores that do in-store grinding of lenses, and meat and seafood markets.

Wholesalers also engage in the buying of goods for resale, but they are not usually organized to serve the general public. They typically operate from a warehouse or office and neither the design nor the location of these premises is intended to solicit a high volume of walk-in traffic. Wholesalers supply institutional, industrial, wholesale, and retail clients; their operations are, therefore, generally organized to purchase, sell, and deliver merchandise in larger quantities. However, dealers of durable nonconsumer goods, such as farm machinery and heavy duty trucks, are included in wholesale trade even if they often sell these products in single units.

441 Motor Vehicle and Parts Dealers[CAN]

Industries in the Motor Vehicle and Parts Dealers subsector retail motor vehicles and parts from fixed point-of-sale locations. Establishments in this subsector typically operate from a showroom and/or an open lot where the vehicles are on display. The display of vehicles and the related parts require little by way of display equipment. The personnel generally include both the sales and sales support staff familiar with the requirements for registering and financing a vehicle as well as a staff of parts experts and mechanics trained to provide repair and maintenance services for the vehicles. Specific industries have been included in this subsector to identify the type of vehicle being retailed.

Sales of capital or durable nonconsumer goods, such as medium and heavy-duty trucks, are always included in wholesale trade. These goods are virtually never sold through retail methods.

US—United States industry only. CAN—United States and Canadian industries are comparable. MEX—United States and Mexican industries are comparable. Blank—Canadian, Mexican, and United States industries are comparable.

4411 Automobile Dealers[CAN]

This industry group comprises establishments primarily engaged in retailing new and used automobiles and light trucks, such as sport utility vehicles, and passenger and cargo vans.

44111 New Car Dealers[CAN]
See industry description for 441110 below.

441110 New Car Dealers[CAN]

This industry comprises establishments primarily engaged in retailing new automobiles and light trucks, such as sport utility vehicles, and passenger and cargo vans, or retailing these new vehicles in combination with activities, such as repair services, retailing used cars, and selling replacement parts and accessories.

Illustrative Examples:

Automobile dealers, new only, or new and used	Light utility truck dealers, new only, or new and used

Cross-References. Establishments primarily engaged in—

- Retailing used automobiles and light trucks without retailing new automobiles and light trucks—are classified in Industry 441120, Used Car Dealers.
- Providing automotive repair services without retailing new automotive vehicles—are classified in Industry Group 8111, Automotive Repair and Maintenance.

44112 Used Car Dealers[CAN]
See industry description for 441120 below.

441120 Used Car Dealers[CAN]

This industry comprises establishments primarily engaged in retailing used automobiles and light trucks, such as sport utility vehicles, and passenger and cargo vans.

Illustrative Examples:

Antique auto dealers	Light truck dealers, used only
Automobile dealers, used only	

US—United States industry only. CAN—United States and Canadian industries are comparable. MEX—United States and Mexican industries are comparable. Blank—Canadian, Mexican, and United States industries are comparable.

Cross-References.

Establishments primarily engaged in retailing new automobiles and light trucks are classified in Industry 441110, New Car Dealers.

4412 Other Motor Vehicle Dealers[CAN]

This industry group comprises establishments primarily engaged in retailing new and used vehicles (except automobiles, light trucks, such as sport utility vehicles, and passenger and cargo vans).

44121 Recreational Vehicle Dealers[CAN]
See industry description for 441210 below.

441210 Recreational Vehicle Dealers[CAN]

This industry comprises establishments primarily engaged in retailing new and/ or used recreational vehicles commonly referred to as RVs or retailing these new vehicles in combination with activities, such as repair services and selling replacement parts and accessories.

Illustrative Examples:

Motor home dealers	Recreational vehicle parts and
Recreational vehicle (RV)	accessories stores
dealers	Travel trailer dealers

Cross-References. Establishments primarily engaged in—

- Retailing new or used boat trailers and utility trailers—are classified in Industry 44122, Motorcycle, Boat, and Other Motor Vehicle Dealers; and
- Retailing manufactured homes (i.e., mobile homes), parts, and equipment— are classified in Industry 453930, Manufactured (Mobile) Home Dealers.

44122 Motorcycle, Boat, and Other Motor Vehicle Dealers[CAN]

This industry comprises establishments primarily engaged in retailing new and used motorcycles, boats, and other vehicles (except automobiles, light trucks, and recreational vehicles), or retailing these new vehicles in combination with activities, such as repair services and selling replacement parts and accessories.

Illustrative Examples:

Aircraft dealers	Motorcycle dealers
All-terrain vehicle (ATV) dealers	Utility trailer dealers
Boat dealers, new and used	

Cross-References. Establishments primarily engaged in—

- Retailing new nonmotorized bicycles, surfboards, or wind sail boards—are classified in Industry 45111, Sporting Goods Stores;

- Retailing used nonmotorized bicycles, surfboards, or wind sail boards— are classified in Industry 45331, Used Merchandise Stores;

- Retailing new or used automobiles and light trucks—are classified in Industry Group 4411, Automotive Dealers;

- Retailing new or used recreational vehicles, such as travel trailers— are classified in Industry 44121, Recreational Vehicle Dealers;

- Providing repair services for vehicles without retailing new vehicles— are classified in the appropriate industry for the repair services and in Sector 81, Other Services (except Public Administration); and

- Retailing fuel and marine supplies at a marina—are classified in Industry 71393, Marinas.

441221 Motorcycle Dealers[US]

This U.S. industry comprises establishments primarily engaged in retailing new and/or used motorcycles, motor scooters, motor bikes, mopeds, off-road all-terrain vehicles, and personal watercraft, or retailing these new vehicles in combination with repair services and selling replacement parts and accessories.

Illustrative Examples:

All-terrain vehicle (ATV) dealers
Moped dealers
Motorcycle dealers
Motorcycle parts and accessories dealers
Personal watercraft dealers

Cross-References. Establishments primarily engaged in—

- Providing motorcycle repair services without retailing new motorcycles— are classified in Industry 811490, Other Personal and Household Goods Repair and Maintenance;

- Retailing new nonmotorized bicycles—are classified in Industry 451110, Sporting Goods Stores;

- Retailing used nonmotorized bicycles—are classified in Industry 453310, Used Merchandise Stores; and

- Retailing new or used boats—are classified in U.S. Industry 441222, Boat Dealers.

441222 Boat Dealers^{US}

This U.S. industry comprises establishments primarily engaged in (1) retailing new and/or used boats or retailing new boats in combination with activities, such as repair services and selling replacement parts and accessories, and/or (2) retailing new and/or used outboard motors, boat trailers, marine supplies, parts, and accessories.

Illustrative Examples:

Boat dealers (e.g., powerboats, rowboats, sailboats)

Marine supply dealers
Outboard motor dealers

Cross-References. Establishments primarily engaged in—

- Retailing new surfboards or wind sail boards—are classified in Industry 451110, Sporting Goods Stores;
- Retailing used surfboards or wind sail boards—are classified in Industry 453310, Used Merchandise Stores;
- Providing boat repair services without retailing new boats—are classified in Industry 811490, Other Personal and Household Goods Repair and Maintenance;
- Retailing new or used personal watercraft—are classified in U.S. Industry 441221, Motorcycle Dealers; and
- Operating docking and/or storage facilities for pleasure craft owners—are classified in Industry 713930, Marinas.

441229 All Other Motor Vehicle Dealers^{US}

This U.S. industry comprises establishments primarily engaged in retailing new and/or used utility trailers and vehicles (except automobiles, light trucks, recreational vehicles, motorcycles, boats, motor scooters, motorbikes, off-road all-terrain vehicles, and personal watercraft) or retailing these new vehicles in combination with activities, such as repair services and selling replacement parts and accessories.

Illustrative Examples:

Aircraft dealers
Powered golf cart dealers

Snowmobile dealers
Utility trailer dealers

Cross-References. Establishments primarily engaged in—

- Retailing new automobiles and light trucks—are classified in Industry 441110, New Car Dealers;

- Retailing used automobiles and light trucks—are classified in Industry 441120, Used Car Dealers;

- Retailing new or used recreational vehicles, such as travel trailers—are classified in Industry 441210, Recreational Vehicle Dealers;

- Retailing new or used motorcycles, motor scooters, motorbikes, off-road all-terrain vehicles, and personal watercraft—are classified in U.S. Industry 441221, Motorcycle Dealers;

- Retailing new or used boats, outboard motors, boat trailers, and marine supplies—are classified in U.S. Industry 441222, Boat Dealers; and

- Providing vehicle repair services without retailing new vehicles—are classified in the appropriate industry for the repair services.

4413 Automotive Parts, Accessories, and Tire Stores^{CAN}

44131 Automotive Parts and Accessories Stores^{CAN}
See industry description for 441310 below.

441310 Automotive Parts and Accessories Stores^{CAN}

This industry comprises one or more of the following: (1) establishments known as automotive supply stores primarily engaged in retailing new, used, and/or rebuilt automotive parts and accessories; (2) automotive supply stores that are primarily engaged in both retailing automotive parts and accessories and repairing automobiles; and (3) establishments primarily engaged in retailing and installing automotive accessories.

Illustrative Examples:

Automotive parts and supply stores	Truck cap stores
Automotive stereo stores	Used automotive parts stores
Speed shops	

Cross-References. Establishments primarily engaged in—

- Retailing automotive parts and accessories via electronic home shopping, mail-order, or direct sale—are classified in Subsector 454, Nonstore Retailers;

- Retailing new or used tires—are classified in Industry 441320, Tire Dealers; and

- Repairing and replacing automotive parts, such as transmissions, mufflers, and brake linings (except establishments known as automotive supply stores)—are classified in Industry 81111, Automotive Mechanical and Electrical Repair and Maintenance.

44132 Tire Dealers^{CAN}

See industry description for 441320 below.

441320 Tire Dealers^{CAN}

This industry comprises establishments primarily engaged in retailing new and/or used tires and tubes or retailing new tires in combination with automotive repair services.

Cross-References. Establishments primarily engaged in—

- Retailing tires via electronic home shopping, mail-order, or direct sale—are classified in Subsector 454, Nonstore Retailers; and

- Providing automotive repair services without retailing new tires—are classified in U.S. Industry 811198, All Other Automotive Repair and Maintenance.

442 Furniture and Home Furnishings Stores^{CAN}

Industries in the Furniture and Home Furnishings Stores subsector retail new furniture and home furnishings from fixed point-of-sale locations. Establishments in this subsector usually operate from showrooms and have substantial areas for the presentation of their products. Many offer interior decorating services in addition to the sale of products.

4421 Furniture Stores^{CAN}

44211 Furniture Stores^{CAN}

See industry description for 442110 below.

442110 Furniture Stores^{CAN}

This industry comprises establishments primarily engaged in retailing new furniture, such as household furniture (e.g., baby furniture box springs and mattresses) and outdoor furniture; office furniture (except those sold in combination with office supplies and equipment); and/or furniture sold in combination with major appliances, home electronics, home furnishings, or floor coverings.

US—United States industry only. CAN—United States and Canadian industries are comparable. MEX—United States and Mexican industries are comparable. Blank—Canadian, Mexican, and United States industries are comparable.

Cross-References. Establishments primarily engaged in—

- Retailing furniture via electronic home shopping, mail-order, or direct sale—are classified in Subsector 454, Nonstore Retailers;
- Retailing used furniture—are classified in Industry 453310, Used Merchandise Stores;
- Retailing custom furniture made on premises—are classified in Subsector 337, Furniture and Related Product Manufacturing; and
- Retailing new office furniture and a range of new office equipment and supplies—are classified in Industry 453210, Office Supplies and Stationery Stores.

4422 Home Furnishings Stores[CAN]

This industry group comprises establishments primarily engaged in retailing new home furnishings (except furniture).

44221 Floor Covering Stores[CAN]
See industry description for 442210 below.

442210 Floor Covering Stores[CAN]

This industry comprises establishments primarily engaged in retailing new floor coverings, such as rugs and carpets, vinyl floor coverings, and floor tile (except ceramic or wood only); or retailing new floor coverings in combination with installation and repair services.

Cross-References. Establishments primarily engaged in—

- Retailing floor coverings via electronic home shopping, mail-order, or direct sale—are classified in Subsector 454, Nonstore Retailers;
- Installing floor coverings without retailing new floor coverings—are classified in Industry 238330, Flooring Contractors;
- Retailing ceramic floor tile or wood floor coverings only—are classified in Industry 444190, Other Building Material Dealers; and
- Retailing used rugs and carpets—are classified in Industry 453310, Used Merchandise Stores.

44229 Other Home Furnishings Stores[CAN]

This industry comprises establishments primarily engaged in retailing new home furnishings (except furniture and floor coverings).

US—United States industry only. CAN—United States and Canadian industries are comparable. MEX—United States and Mexican industries are comparable. Blank—Canadian, Mexican, and United States industries are comparable.

Illustrative Examples:

Bath shops	Kitchenware stores
Chinaware stores	Window treatment stores
Glassware stores	

Cross-References. Establishments primarily engaged in—

- Retailing home furnishings via electronic home shopping, mail-order, or direct sale—are classified in Subsector 454, Nonstore Retailers;

- Retailing custom curtains and draperies made on premises—are classified in Industry 31412, Curtain and Linen Mills;

- Retailing new mirrored glass, lighting fixtures, and new ceramic floor tile or wood floor coverings only—are classified in Industry 44419, Other Building Material Dealers;

- Retailing new furniture—are classified in Industry 44211, Furniture Stores;

- Retailing new floor coverings (except ceramic or wood only)—are classified in Industry 44221, Floor Covering Stores; and

- Retailing used home furnishings—are classified in Industry 45331, Used Merchandise Stores.

442291 Window Treatment Stores^{CAN}

This U.S. industry comprises establishments primarily engaged in retailing new window treatments, such as curtains, drapes, blinds, and shades.

Cross-References. Establishments primarily engaged in—

- Retailing window treatments via electronic home shopping, mail-order, or direct sale—are classified in Subsector 454, Nonstore Retailers; and

- Retailing custom curtains and draperies made on premises—are classified in U.S. Industry 314121, Curtain and Drapery Mills.

442299 All Other Home Furnishings Stores^{US}

This U.S. industry comprises establishments primarily engaged in retailing new home furnishings (except floor coverings, furniture, and window treatments).

Illustrative Examples:

Bath shops	Kitchenware stores
Chinaware stores	Linen stores
Electric lamp shops	Picture frame stores

Glassware stores
Houseware stores

Wood-burning stove stores

Cross-References. Establishments primarily engaged in—

- Selling home furnishings via electronic home shopping, mail-order, or direct sale—are classified in Subsector 454, Nonstore Retailers;
- Retailing new mirrored glass or lighting fixtures—are classified in Industry 444190, Other Building Material Dealers;
- Retailing new furniture—are classified in Industry 442110, Furniture Stores;
- Retailing new floor coverings—are classified in Industry 442210, Floor Covering Stores;
- Retailing new window treatments—are classified in U.S. Industry 442291, Window Treatment Stores; and
- Retailing used home furnishings—are classified in Industry 453310, Used Merchandise Stores.

443 Electronics and Appliance Stores[CAN]

Industries in the Electronics and Appliance Stores subsector retail new electronics and appliances from point-of-sale locations. Establishments in this subsector often operate from locations that have special provisions for floor displays requiring special electrical capacity to accommodate the proper demonstration of the products. The staff includes sales personnel knowledgeable in the characteristics and warranties of the line of goods retailed and may also include trained repair persons to handle the maintenance and repair of the electronic equipment and appliances. The classifications within this subsector are made principally on the type of product and knowledge required to operate each type of store.

4431 Electronics and Appliance Stores[CAN]

This industry group comprises establishments primarily engaged in retailing the following new products: household-type appliances, cameras, computers, and other electronic goods.

44311 Appliance, Television, and Other Electronics Stores[CAN]

This industry comprises establishments primarily engaged in retailing one of the following: (1) retailing an array of new household-type appliances and consumer-type electronic products, such as radios, televisions, and computers; (2) specializing

---

US—United States industry only. CAN—United States and Canadian industries are comparable. MEX—United States and Mexican industries are comparable. Blank—Canadian, Mexican, and United States industries are comparable.

in retailing a single line of new consumer-type electronic products (except computers); and (3) retailing these new products in combination with repair services.

Illustrative Examples:

Appliance stores   Radio and television stores
Consumer electronics stores

Cross-References. Establishments primarily engaged in—

- Retailing new electronic products via electronic home shopping, mail-order, or direct sale—are classified in Subsector 454, Nonstore Retailers;

- Retailing new computers, computer peripherals, and prepackaged computer software without retailing other consumer-type electronic products or office equipment, office furniture, and office supplies; or retailing these products in combination with repair services—are classified in Industry 44312, Computer and Software Stores;

- Retailing new computers, computer peripherals, and prepackaged software in combination with retailing new office equipment, office furniture, and office supplies—are classified in Industry 45321, Office Supplies and Stationery Stores;

- Retailing new sewing machines in combination with selling new sewing supplies, fabrics, patterns, yarns, and other needlework accessories—are classified in Industry 45113, Sewing, Needlework, and Piece Goods Stores;

- Retailing new electronic toys—are classified in Industry 45112, Hobby, Toy, and Game Stores;

- Providing television or other electronic equipment repair services without retailing new televisions or electronic equipment—are classified in Industry 81121, Electronic and Precision Equipment Repair and Maintenance;

- Providing household-type appliance repair services without retailing new appliances—are classified in Industry 81141, Home and Garden Equipment and Appliance Repair and Maintenance;

- Retailing used appliance and electronic products—are classified in Industry 45331, Used Merchandise Stores;

- Retailing new still and motion picture cameras—are classified in Industry 44313, Camera and Photographic Supplies Stores; and

- Retailing automotive electronic sound systems—are classified in Industry 44131, Automotive Parts and Accessories Stores.

443111 Household Appliance Stores[US]

This U.S. industry comprises establishments known as appliance stores primarily engaged in retailing an array of new household appliances, such as refrigerators,

---

US—United States industry only. CAN—United States and Canadian industries are comparable. MEX—United States and Mexican industries are comparable. Blank—Canadian, Mexican, and United States industries are comparable.

dishwashers, ovens, irons, coffeemakers, hair dryers, electric razors, room air-conditioners, microwave ovens, sewing machines, and vacuum cleaners, or retailing new appliances in combination with appliance repair services.

Cross-References. Establishments primarily engaged in—

- Retailing household appliances via electronic home shopping, mail-order, or direct sale—are classified in Subsector 454, Nonstore Retailers;
- Retailing new sewing machines in combination with selling new sewing supplies, fabrics, patterns, yarns, and other needlework accessories—are classified in Industry 451130, Sewing, Needlework, and Piece Goods Stores;
- Providing household-type appliance repair services without retailing new appliances—are classified in U.S. Industry 811412, Appliance Repair and Maintenance; and
- Retailing used appliances—are classified in Industry 453310, Used Merchandise Stores.

443112 Radio, Television, and Other Electronics Stores[US]

This U.S. industry comprises: (1) establishments known as consumer electronics stores primarily engaged in retailing a general line of new consumer-type electronic products; (2) establishments specializing in retailing a single line of consumer-type electronic products (except computers); or (3) establishments primarily engaged in retailing these new electronic products in combination with repair services.

Illustrative Examples:

Consumer electronic stores
Radio and television stores

Stereo stores (except automotive)
Telephone stores (including cellular)

Cross-References. Establishments primarily engaged in—

- Retailing electronic goods via electronic home shopping, mail-order, or direct sale—are classified in Subsector 454, Nonstore Retailers;
- Retailing automotive electronic sound systems—are classified in Industry 441310, Automotive Parts and Accessories Stores;
- Retailing new computers, computer peripherals, and prepackaged computer software without retailing other consumer-type electronic products or office equipment, office furniture and office supplies; or retailing these new computer products in combination with repair services—are classified in Industry 443120, Computer and Software Stores;
- Retailing new computers, computer peripherals, and prepackaged software in combination with retailing new office equipment, office furniture, and

office supplies—are classified in Industry 453210, Office Supplies and Stationery Stores;

- Retailing new still and motion picture cameras—are classified in Industry 443130, Camera and Photographic Supplies Stores;

- Providing television or other electronic equipment repair services without retailing new televisions or electronic products—are classified in Industry 81121, Electronic and Precision Equipment Repair and Maintenance;

- Retailing new electronic toys—are classified in Industry 451120, Hobby, Toy, and Game Stores; and

- Retailing used electronics—are classified in Industry 453310, Used Merchandise Stores.

44312 Computer and Software Stores[CAN]

See industry description for 443120 below.

443120 Computer and Software Stores[CAN]

This industry comprises establishments primarily engaged in retailing new computers, computer peripherals, and prepackaged computer software without retailing other consumer-type electronic products or office equipment, office furniture and office supplies; or retailing these new products in combination with repair and support services.

Cross-References. Establishments primarily engaged in—

- Retailing computers and software via electronic home shopping, mail-order, or direct sale—are classified in Subsector 454, Nonstore Retailers;

- Retailing new electronic toys, such as video games and handheld electronic games—are classified in Industry 451120, Hobby, Toy, and Game Stores;

- Providing computer repair services without retailing new computers—are classified in U.S. Industry 811212, Computer and Office Machine Repair and Maintenance;

- Retailing new computers, computer peripherals, and prepackaged software in combination with retailing new office equipment, office furniture, and office supplies—are classified in Industry 453210, Office Supplies and Stationery Stores;

- Retailing a general line of new electronic products or specializing in retailing a single line of consumer-type electronic products (except computers)—are classified in U.S. Industry 443112, Radio, Television, and Other Electronics Stores; and

---

US—United States industry only. CAN—United States and Canadian industries are comparable. MEX—United States and Mexican industries are comparable. Blank—Canadian, Mexican, and United States industries are comparable.

- Retailing used computers, computer software, video games, and handheld electronic games—are classified in Industry 453310, Used Merchandise Stores.

44313 Camera and Photographic Supplies Stores[CAN]

See industry description for 443130 below.

443130 Camera and Photographic Supplies Stores[CAN]

This industry comprises establishments primarily engaged in either retailing new cameras, photographic equipment, and photographic supplies or retailing new cameras and photographic equipment in combination with activities, such as repair services and film developing.

Cross-References. Establishments primarily engaged in—

- Retailing camera and photographic supplies via electronic home shopping, mail-order, or direct sale—are classified in Subsector 454, Nonstore Retailers;

- Retailing new video cameras—are classified in U.S. Industry 443112, Radio, Television, and Other Electronics Stores;

- One-hour film developing without retailing a range of new photographic equipment and supplies—are classified in U.S. Industry 812922, One-Hour Photofinishing;

- Providing repair services for photographic equipment without retailing new photographic equipment—are classified in U.S. Industry 811211, Consumer Electronics Repair and Maintenance;

- Developing film and/or producing photographic prints, slides, and enlargements (except one-hour photofinishing labs)—are classified in U.S. Industry 812921, Photofinishing Laboratories (except One-Hour); and

- Retailing used cameras and photographic equipment—are classified in Industry 453310, Used Merchandise Stores.

444 Building Material and Garden Equipment and Supplies Dealers[CAN]

Industries in the Building Material and Garden Equipment and Supplies Dealers subsector retail new building material and garden equipment and supplies from fixed point-of-sale locations. Establishments in this subsector have display equipment designed to handle lumber and related products and garden equipment and supplies that may be kept either indoors or outdoors under covered areas. The staff is usually knowledgeable in the use of the specific products being retailed in the construction, repair, and maintenance of the home and associated grounds.

4441 Building Material and Supplies Dealers^{CAN}

This industry group comprises establishments primarily engaged in retailing new building materials and supplies.

44411 Home Centers^{CAN}
See industry description for 444110 below.

444110 Home Centers^{CAN}

This industry comprises establishments known as home centers primarily engaged in retailing a general line of new home repair and improvement materials and supplies, such as lumber, plumbing goods, electrical goods, tools, housewares, hardware, and lawn and garden supplies, with no one merchandise line predominating. The merchandise lines are normally arranged in separate departments.

44412 Paint and Wallpaper Stores^{CAN}
See industry description for 444120 below.

444120 Paint and Wallpaper Stores^{CAN}

This industry comprises establishments known as paint and wallpaper stores primarily engaged in retailing paint, wallpaper, and related supplies.

44413 Hardware Stores^{CAN}
See industry description for 444130 below.

444130 Hardware Stores^{CAN}

This industry comprises establishments known as hardware stores primarily engaged in retailing a general line of new hardware items, such as tools and builders' hardware.

Cross-References. Establishments primarily engaged in—

- Retailing hardware items via electronic home shopping, mail order, or direct sale—are classified in Subsector 454, Nonstore Retailers;

- Retailing a general line of home repair and improvement materials and supplies, known as home centers—are classified in Industry 444110, Home Centers; and

- Retailing used hardware items—are classified in Industry 453310, Used Merchandise Stores.

44419 Other Building Material Dealers^{CAN}

See industry description for 444190 below.

444190 Other Building Material Dealers^{CAN}

This industry comprises establishments (except those known as home centers, paint and wallpaper stores, and hardware stores) primarily engaged in retailing specialized lines of new building materials, such as lumber, fencing, glass, doors, plumbing fixtures and supplies, electrical supplies, prefabricated buildings and kits, and kitchen and bath cabinets and countertops to be installed.

Illustrative Examples:

Electrical supply stores	Garage door dealers
Fencing dealers	Kitchen cabinet (except custom) stores
Floor covering stores, wood or ceramic tile only	Lumber yards, retail
	Plumbing supply stores
Glass stores	Prefabricated building dealers

Cross-References. Establishments primarily engaged in—

- Retailing building materials via electronic home shopping, mail-order, or direct sale—are classified in Subsector 454, Nonstore Retailers;

- Retailing used building materials—are classified in Industry 453310, Used Merchandise Stores;

- Providing carpentry/installation services for products—are classified in Industry 238350, Finish Carpentry Contractors;

- Installing plumbing fixtures and supplies—are classified in Industry 238220, Plumbing, Heating, and Air-Conditioning Contractors;

- Installing electrical supplies, such as lighting fixtures and ceiling fans—are classified in Industry 238210, Electrical Contractors;

- Making custom furniture (e.g., kitchen cabinets)—are classified in Subsector 337, Furniture and Related Product Manufacturing;

- Retailing a general line of new hardware items, known as hardware stores—are classified in Industry 444130, Hardware Stores;

US—United States industry only. CAN—United States and Canadian industries are comparable. MEX—United States and Mexican industries are comparable. Blank—Canadian, Mexican, and United States industries are comparable.

- Retailing paint and wallpaper, known as paint and wallpaper stores—are classified in Industry 444120, Paint and Wallpaper Stores; and
- Retailing a general line of home repair and improvement materials and supplies, known as home centers—are classified in Industry 444110, Home Centers.

4442 Lawn and Garden Equipment and Supplies Stores^{CAN}

This industry group comprises establishments primarily engaged in retailing new lawn and garden equipment and supplies.

44421 Outdoor Power Equipment Stores^{CAN}
See industry description for 444210 below.

444210 Outdoor Power Equipment Stores^{CAN}

This industry comprises establishments primarily engaged in retailing new outdoor power equipment or retailing new outdoor power equipment in combination with activities, such as repair services and selling replacement parts.

Cross-References. Establishments primarily engaged in—

- Retailing outdoor power equipment via electronic home shopping, mail-order, or direct sale—are classified in Subsector 454, Nonstore Retailers;
- Providing outdoor power equipment repair services without retailing new outdoor power equipment—are classified in U.S. Industry 811411, Home and Garden Equipment Repair and Maintenance; and
- Retailing used outdoor power equipment—are classified in Industry 453310, Used Merchandise Stores.

44422 Nursery, Garden Center, and Farm Supply Stores^{CAN}
See industry description for 444220 below.

444220 Nursery, Garden Center, and Farm Supply Stores^{CAN}

This industry comprises establishments primarily engaged in retailing nursery and garden products, such as trees, shrubs, plants, seeds, bulbs, and sod, that are predominantly grown elsewhere. These establishments may sell a limited amount of a product they grow themselves.

US—United States industry only. CAN—United States and Canadian industries are comparable. MEX—United States and Mexican industries are comparable. Blank—Canadian, Mexican, and United States industries are comparable.

Cross-References. Establishments primarily engaged in—

- Retailing nursery and garden products via electronic home shopping, mail-order, or direct sale—are classified in Subsector 454, Nonstore Retailers;
- Providing landscaping services—are classified in Industry 561730, Landscaping Services; and
- Growing and retailing nursery stock—are classified in U.S. Industry 111421, Nursery and Tree Production.

445 Food and Beverage Stores^{CAN}

Industries in the Food and Beverage Stores subsector usually retail food and beverages merchandise from fixed point-of-sale locations. Establishments in this subsector have special equipment (e.g., freezers, refrigerated display cases, refrigerators) for displaying food and beverage goods. They have staff trained in the processing of food products to guarantee the proper storage and sanitary conditions required by regulatory authority.

4451 Grocery Stores^{CAN}

This industry group comprises establishments primarily engaged in retailing a general line of food products.

44511 Supermarkets and Other Grocery (except Convenience) Stores^{CAN}

See industry description for 445110 below.

445110 Supermarkets and Other Grocery (except Convenience) Stores^{CAN}

This industry comprises establishments generally known as supermarkets and grocery stores primarily engaged in retailing a general line of food, such as canned and frozen foods; fresh fruits and vegetables; and fresh and prepared meats, fish, and poultry. Included in this industry are delicatessen-type establishments primarily engaged in retailing a general line of food.

Cross-References. Establishments primarily engaged in—

- Retailing automotive fuels in combination with a convenience store or food mart—are classified in Industry 447110, Gasoline Stations with Convenience Stores;

US—United States industry only. CAN—United States and Canadian industries are comparable. MEX—United States and Mexican industries are comparable. Blank—Canadian, Mexican, and United States industries are comparable.

- Retailing a limited line of goods, known as convenience stores or food marts (except those with fuel pumps)—are classified in Industry 445120, Convenience Stores;
- Retailing frozen food and freezer plans via direct sales to residential customers—are classified in Industry 454390, Other Direct Selling Establishments;
- Providing food services in delicatessen-type establishments—are classified in U.S. Industry 722211, Limited-Service Restaurants; and
- Retailing fresh meat in delicatessen-type establishments—are classified in Industry 445210, Meat Markets.

44512 Convenience Stores[CAN]
See industry description for 445120 below.

445120 Convenience Stores[CAN]

This industry comprises establishments known as convenience stores or food marts (except those with fuel pumps) primarily engaged in retailing a limited line of goods that generally includes milk, bread, soda, and snacks.

Cross-References. Establishments primarily engaged in—
- Retailing a general line of food, known as supermarkets and grocery stores—are classified in Industry 445110, Supermarkets and Other Grocery (except Convenience) Stores; and
- Retailing automotive fuels in combination with a convenience store or food mart—are classified in Industry 447110, Gasoline Stations with Convenience Stores.

4452 Specialty Food Stores[CAN]

This industry group comprises establishments primarily engaged in retailing specialized lines of food.

44521 Meat Markets[CAN]
See industry description for 445210 below.

445210 Meat Markets[CAN]

This industry comprises establishments primarily engaged in retailing fresh, frozen, or cured meats and poultry. Delicatessen-type establishments primarily engaged in retailing fresh meat are included in this industry.

US—United States industry only. CAN—United States and Canadian industries are comparable. MEX—United States and Mexican industries are comparable. Blank—Canadian, Mexican, and United States industries are comparable.

Illustrative Examples:

Baked ham stores	Meat markets
Butcher shops	Poultry dealers
Frozen meat shops	

Cross-References. Establishments primarily engaged in—

- Retailing meat and poultry via electronic home shopping, mail-order, or direct sale—are classified in Subsector 454, Nonstore Retailers;

- Retailing a general line of food, known as supermarkets and grocery stores—are classified in Industry 445110, Supermarkets and Other Grocery (except Convenience) Stores; and

- Providing food services in delicatessen-type establishments—are classified in U.S. Industry 722211, Limited-Service Restaurants.

44522 Fish and Seafood Markets[CAN]

See industry description for 445220 below.

445220 Fish and Seafood Markets[CAN]

This industry comprises establishments primarily engaged in retailing fresh, frozen, or cured fish and seafood products.

Cross-References.

Establishments primarily engaged in retailing fish and seafood products via electronic home shopping, mail-order, or direct sale are classified in Subsector 454, Nonstore Retailers.

44523 Fruit and Vegetable Markets[CAN]

See industry descriptions for 445230 below.

445230 Fruit and Vegetable Markets[CAN]

This industry comprises establishments primarily engaged in retailing fresh fruits and vegetables.

Cross-References. Establishments primarily engaged in—

- Retailing fruits and vegetables via electronic home shopping, mail-order, or direct sale—are classified in Subsector 454, Nonstore Retailers; and

- Growing and selling vegetables and/or fruits at roadside stands—are classified in Subsector 111, Crop Production.

44529 Other Specialty Food Stores^{CAN}

This industry comprises establishments primarily engaged in retailing specialty foods (except meat, fish, seafood, and fruits and vegetables) not for immediate consumption and not made on premises.

Illustrative Examples:

Baked goods stores (except immediate consumption)	Dairy product stores
	Gourmet food stores
Coffee and tea (i.e., packaged) stores	Nut (i.e., packaged) stores
Confectionery (i.e., packaged) stores	

Cross-References. Establishments primarily engaged in—

- Retailing specialty foods via electronic home shopping, mail-order, or direct sale—are classified in Subsector 454, Nonstore Retailers;

- Retailing baked goods made on the premises, but not for immediate consumption—are classified in Industry 31181, Bread and Bakery Product Manufacturing;

- Retailing fresh, frozen, or cured meats and poultry—are classified in Industry 44521, Meat Markets;

- Retailing fresh, frozen, or cured fish and seafood products—are classified in Industry 44522, Fish and Seafood Markets;

- Retailing fresh fruits and vegetables—are classified in Industry 44523, Fruit and Vegetable Markets;

- Retailing candy and confectionery products not for immediate consumption and not made on premises—are classified in Industry Group 3113, Sugar and Confectionery Product Manufacturing; and

- Selling snack foods (e.g., doughnuts, bagels, ice cream, popcorn) for immediate consumption—are classified in Subsector 722, Food Services and Drinking Places.

445291 Baked Goods Stores^{CAN}

This U.S. industry comprises establishments primarily engaged in retailing baked goods not for immediate consumption and not made on the premises.

US—United States industry only. CAN—United States and Canadian industries are comparable. MEX—United States and Mexican industries are comparable. Blank—Canadian, Mexican, and United States industries are comparable.

Cross-References. Establishments primarily engaged in—

- Retailing baked goods via electronic home shopping, mail-order, or direct sale—are classified in Subsector 454, Nonstore Retailers;
- Selling snack foods (e.g., doughnuts, bagels, ice cream, popcorn) for immediate consumption—are classified in U.S. Industry 722213, Snack and Non-alcoholic Beverage Bars; and
- Retailing baked goods made on the premises but not for immediate consumption—are classified in Industry 311811, Retail Bakeries.

445292 Confectionery and Nut Stores^{CAN}

This U.S. industry comprises establishments primarily engaged in retailing candy and other confections, nuts, and popcorn not for immediate consumption and not made on the premises.

Cross-References. Establishments primarily engaged in—

- Retailing confectionery goods and nuts via electronic home shopping, mail-order, or direct sale—are classified in Subsector 454, Nonstore Retailers;
- Retailing confectionery goods and nuts made on premises and not packaged for immediate consumption—are classified in Industry Group 3113, Sugar and Confectionery Product Manufacturing;
- Selling snack foods (e.g., doughnuts, bagels, ice cream, popcorn) for immediate consumption—are classified in U.S. Industry 722213, Snack and Non-alcoholic Beverage Bars; and
- Retailing baked goods made on the premises but not for immediate consumption—are classified in Industry 311811, Retail Bakeries.

445299 All Other Specialty Food Stores^{CAN}

This U.S. industry comprises establishments primarily engaged in retailing miscellaneous specialty foods (except meat, fish, seafood, fruit and vegetables, confections, nuts, popcorn, and baked goods) not for immediate consumption and not made on the premises.

Illustrative Examples:

Coffee and tea (i.e., packaged) stores	Soft drink (i.e., bottled) stores
Dairy product stores	Spice stores
Gourmet food stores	Water (i.e., bottled) stores

Cross-References. Establishments primarily engaged in—

- Retailing specialty foods via electronic home shopping, mail-order, or direct sale—are classified in Subsector 454, Nonstore Retailers;
- Selling snack foods (e.g., doughnuts, bagels, ice cream, popcorn) for immediate consumption—are classified in U.S. Industry 722213, Snack and Non-alcoholic Beverage Bars;
- Retailing fresh, frozen, or cured meats and poultry—are classified in Industry 445210, Meat Markets;
- Retailing fresh, frozen, or cured fish and seafood products—are classified in Industry 445220, Fish and Seafood Markets;
- Retailing fresh fruits and vegetables—are classified in Industry 445230, Fruit and Vegetable Markets;
- Retailing candy and other confections, nuts, and popcorn not for immediate consumption and not made on the premises—are classified in U.S. Industry 445292, Confectionery and Nut Stores; and
- Retailing baked goods not for immediate consumption and not made on the premises—are classified in U.S. Industry 445291, Baked Goods Stores.

4453   Beer, Wine, and Liquor Stores[CAN]

44531   Beer, Wine, and Liquor Stores[CAN]

See industry description for 445310 below.

445310   Beer, Wine, and Liquor Stores[CAN]

This industry comprises establishments primarily engaged in retailing packaged alcoholic beverages, such as ale, beer, wine, and liquor.

Cross-References.

Establishments primarily engaged in retailing packaged liquor in combination with providing prepared drinks for immediate consumption on the premises are classified in Industry 722410, Drinking Places (Alcoholic Beverages).

446   Health and Personal Care Stores[CAN]

Industries in the Health and Personal Care Stores subsector retail health and personal care merchandise from fixed point-of-sale locations. Establishments in this subsector are characterized principally by the products they retail, and some

---

US—United States industry only. CAN—United States and Canadian industries are comparable. MEX—United States and Mexican industries are comparable. Blank—Canadian, Mexican, and United States industries are comparable.

health and personal care stores may have specialized staff trained in dealing with the products. Staff may include pharmacists, opticians, and other professionals engaged in retailing, advising customers, and/or fitting the product sold to the customer's needs.

4461 Health and Personal Care Stores^{CAN}

This industry group comprises establishments primarily engaged in retailing health and personal care products.

44611 Pharmacies and Drug Stores^{CAN}

See industry description for 446110 below.

446110 Pharmacies and Drug Stores^{CAN}

This industry comprises establishments known as pharmacies and drug stores engaged in retailing prescription or nonprescription drugs and medicines.

Cross-References. Establishments primarily engaged in—

- Retailing food supplement products, such as vitamins, nutrition supplements, and body enhancing supplements—are classified in U.S. Industry 446191, Food (Health) Supplement Stores; and

- Retailing prescription and nonprescription drugs via electronic home shopping, mail-order, or direct sale—are classified in Subsector 454, Nonstore Retailers.

44612 Cosmetics, Beauty Supplies, and Perfume Stores^{CAN}

See industry description for 446120 below.

446120 Cosmetics, Beauty Supplies, and Perfume Stores^{CAN}

This industry comprises establishments known as cosmetic or perfume stores or beauty supply shops primarily engaged in retailing cosmetics, perfumes, toiletries, and personal grooming products.

Cross-References. Establishments primarily engaged in—

- Providing beauty parlor services—are classified in U.S. Industry 812112, Beauty Salons; and

- Retailing perfumes, cosmetics, and beauty supplies via electronic home shopping, mail-order, or direct sale—are classified in Subsector 454, Nonstore Retailers.

44613 Optical Goods Stores[CAN]

See industry description for 446130 below.

446130 Optical Goods Stores[CAN]

This industry comprises establishments primarily engaged in one or more of the following: (1) retailing and fitting prescription eyeglasses and contact lenses; (2) retailing prescription eyeglasses in combination with the grinding of lenses to order on the premises; and (3) selling nonprescription eyeglasses.

Cross-References. Establishments primarily engaged in—

- Grinding lenses without retailing lenses—are classified in U.S. Industry 339115, Ophthalmic Goods Manufacturing;

- The private or group practice of optometry, even though glasses and contact lenses are sold at these establishments—are classified in Industry 621320, Offices of Optometrists; and

- Retailing eyeglasses and contact lenses via mail-order—are classified in U.S. Industry 454113, Mail-Order Houses.

44619 Other Health and Personal Care Stores[CAN]

This industry comprises establishments primarily engaged in retailing health and personal care items (except drugs, medicines, optical goods, perfumes, cosmetics, and beauty supplies).

Illustrative Examples:

Convalescent supply stores	Prosthetic stores
Food (i.e., health) supplement stores	Sick room supply stores
Hearing aid stores	

Cross-References. Establishments primarily engaged in—

- Retailing health and personal care items via electronic home shopping, mail-order, or direct sale—are classified in Subsector 454, Nonstore Retailers;

- Retailing orthopedic shoes—are classified in Industry 44821, Shoe Stores;

- Retailing orthopedic and prosthetic appliances that are made on premises—are classified in Industry 33911, Medical Equipment and Supplies Manufacturing;

- Retailing prescription and nonprescription drugs and medicines—are classified in Industry 44611, Pharmacies and Drug Stores;

- Retailing eyeglasses and contact lenses—are classified in Industry 44613, Optical Goods Stores;

- Retailing perfumes, cosmetics, and beauty supplies—are classified in Industry 44612, Cosmetics, Beauty Supplies, and Perfume Stores; and

- Retailing naturally organic foods, such as fruits and vegetables, dairy products, and cereals and grains—are classified in Subsector 445, Food and Beverage Stores.

446191 Food (Health) Supplement Stores[CAN]

This U.S. industry comprises establishments primarily engaged in retailing food supplement products, such as vitamins, nutrition supplements, and body enhancing supplements.

Cross-References. Establishments primarily engaged in—

- Retailing food supplement products via electronic home shopping, mail-order, or direct sale—are classified in Subsector 454, Nonstore Retailers;

- Retailing prescription and nonprescription drugs and medicines—are classified in Industry 446110, Pharmacies and Drug Stores; and

- Retailing naturally organic foods, such as fruits and vegetables, dairy products, and cereals and grains—are classified in Subsector 445, Food and Beverage Stores.

446199 All Other Health and Personal Care Stores[CAN]

This U.S. industry comprises establishments primarily engaged in retailing specialized lines of health and personal care merchandise (except drugs, medicines, optical goods, cosmetics, beauty supplies, perfume, and food supplement products).

Illustrative Examples:

Convalescent supply stores	Prosthetic stores
Hearing aid stores	Sick room supply stores

Cross-References. Establishments primarily engaged in—

- Retailing specialized health and personal care merchandise via electronic home shopping, mail-order, or direct sale—are classified in Subsector 454, Nonstore Retailers;

- Retailing food supplement products—are classified in U.S. Industry 446191, Food (Health) Supplement Stores;

- Retailing prescription or nonprescription drugs and medicines—are classified in Industry 446110, Pharmacies and Drug Stores;

- Retailing eyeglasses and contact lenses—are classified in Industry 446130, Optical Goods Stores;

- Retailing perfumes, cosmetics, and beauty supplies—are classified in Industry 446120, Cosmetics, Beauty Supplies, and Perfume Stores;

- Retailing orthopedic shoes—are classified in Industry 448210, Shoe Stores; and

- Retailing orthopedic and prosthetic appliances that are made on premises— are classified in U.S. Industry 339113, Surgical Appliance and Supplies Manufacturing.

447 Gasoline Stations^{CAN}

Industries in the Gasoline Stations subsector group establishments retailing automotive fuels (e.g., gasoline, diesel fuel, gasohol) and automotive oils and retailing these products in combination with convenience store items. These establishments have specialized equipment for the storage and dispensing of automotive fuels.

4471 Gasoline Stations^{CAN}

44711 Gasoline Stations with Convenience Stores^{CAN}
See industry description for 447110 below.

447110 Gasoline Stations with Convenience Stores^{CAN}

This industry comprises establishments engaged in retailing automotive fuels (e.g., diesel fuel, gasohol, gasoline) in combination with convenience store or food mart items. These establishments can either be in a convenience store (i.e., food mart) setting or a gasoline station setting. These establishments may also provide automotive repair services.

Cross-References. Establishments primarily engaged in—

- Retailing automotive fuels without a convenience store—are classified in Industry 447190, Other Gasoline Stations; and

- Retailing a limited line of goods, known as convenience stores or food marts (except those with fuel pumps)—are classified in Industry 445120, Convenience Stores.

44719 Other Gasoline Stations^{CAN}

See industry description for 447190 below.

447190 Other Gasoline Stations^{CAN}

This industry comprises establishments known as gasoline stations (except those with convenience stores) primarily engaged in one of the following: (1) retailing automotive fuels (e.g., diesel fuel, gasohol, gasoline) or (2) retailing these fuels in combination with activities, such as providing repair services; selling automotive oils, replacement parts, and accessories; and/or providing food services.

Illustrative Examples:

Gasoline stations without convenience
stores

Marine service stations
Truck stops

Cross-References. Establishments primarily engaged in—

- Repairing motor vehicles without retailing automotive fuels—are classified in Industry 81111, Automotive Mechanical and Electrical Repair and Maintenance; and

- Retailing automotive fuels in combination with a convenience store or food mart—are classified in Industry 447110, Gasoline Stations with Convenience Stores.

448 Clothing and Clothing Accessories Stores^{CAN}

Industries in the Clothing and Clothing Accessories Stores subsector retailing new clothing and clothing accessories merchandise from fixed point-of-sale locations. Establishments in this subsector have similar display equipment and staff that is knowledgeable regarding fashion trends and the proper match of styles, colors, and combinations of clothing and accessories to the characteristics and tastes of the customer.

4481 Clothing Stores^{CAN}

This industry group comprises establishments primarily engaged in retailing new clothing.

44811 Men's Clothing Stores^{CAN}
See industry descriptions for 448110 below.

448110 Men's Clothing Stores^{CAN}

This industry comprises establishments primarily engaged in retailing a general line of new men's and boys' clothing. These establishments may provide basic alterations, such as hemming, taking in or letting out seams, or lengthening or shortening sleeves.

Cross-References. Establishments primarily engaged in—

- Retailing men's and boys' clothing via electronic home shopping, mail-order, or direct sale—are classified in Subsector 454, Nonstore Retailers;
- Retailing custom men's clothing made on the premises—are classified in Industry Group 3152, Cut and Sew Apparel Manufacturing;
- Retailing new men's and boys' accessories—are classified in Industry 448150, Clothing Accessories Stores;
- Retailing specialized new apparel, such as raincoats, leather coats, fur apparel, and swimwear—are classified in Industry 448190, Other Clothing Stores;
- Retailing new clothing for all genders and age groups—are classified in Industry 448140, Family Clothing Stores;
- Retailing secondhand clothes—are classified in Industry 453310, Used Merchandise Stores; and
- Providing clothing alterations and repair—are classified in Industry 811490, Other Personal and Household Goods Repair and Maintenance.

44812 Women's Clothing Stores^{CAN}
See industry description for 448120 below.

448120 Women's Clothing Stores^{CAN}

This industry comprises establishments primarily engaged in retailing a general line of new women's, misses'; and juniors' clothing, including maternity wear.

These establishments may provide basic alterations, such as hemming, taking in or letting out seams, or lengthening or shortening sleeves.

Cross-References. Establishments primarily engaged in—

- Retailing women's clothing via electronic home shopping, mail-order, or direct sale—are classified in Subsector 454, Nonstore Retailers;
- Retailing custom women's clothing made on premises—are classified in Industry Group 3152, Cut and Sew Apparel Manufacturing;
- Retailing new women's accessories—are classified in Industry 448150, Clothing Accessories Stores;
- Retailing new clothing for all genders and age groups—are classified in Industry 448140, Family Clothing Stores;
- Retailing specialized new apparel, such as bridal gowns, raincoats, leather coats, fur apparel, and swimwear—are classified in Industry 448190, Other Clothing Stores;
- Retailing secondhand clothes—are classified in Industry 453310, Used Merchandise Stores; and
- Providing clothing alterations and repair—are classified in Industry 811490, Other Personal and Household Goods Repair and Maintenance.

44813 Children's and Infants' Clothing Stores^{CAN}
See industry description for 448130 below.

448130 Children's and Infants' Clothing Stores^{CAN}

This industry comprises establishments primarily engaged in retailing a general line of new children's and infants' clothing. These establishments may provide basic alterations, such as hemming, taking in or letting out seams, or lengthening or shortening sleeves.

Cross-References. Establishments primarily engaged in—

- Retailing children's and infants' clothing via electronic home shopping, mail-order, or direct sale—are classified in Subsector 454, Nonstore Retailers;
- Retailing new children's and infants' accessories—are classified in Industry 448150, Clothing Accessories Stores;
- Retailing new clothing for all genders or age groups—are classified in Industry 448140, Family Clothing Stores;

- Retailing secondhand clothes—are classified in Industry 453310, Used Merchandise Stores; and
- Providing clothing alterations and repair—are classified in Industry 811490, Other Personal and Household Goods Repair and Maintenance.

44814 Family Clothing Stores^{CAN}
See industry description for 448140 below.

448140 Family Clothing Stores^{CAN}

This industry comprises establishments primarily engaged in retailing a general line of new clothing for men, women, and children, without specializing in sales for an individual gender or age group. These establishments may provide basic alterations, such as hemming, taking in or letting out seams, or lengthening or shortening sleeves.

Cross-References. Establishments primarily engaged in—
- Retailing clothing for all genders via electronic home shopping, mail-order, or direct sale—are classified in Subsector 454, Nonstore Retailers;
- Retailing new men's and boys' clothing—are classified in Industry 448110, Men's Clothing Stores;
- Retailing new women's, misses', and juniors' clothing—are classified in Industry 448120, Women's Clothing Stores;
- Retailing new children's and infants' clothing—are classified in Industry 448130, Children's and Infants' Clothing Stores;
- Retailing specialized new apparel, such as raincoats, bridal gowns, leather coats, fur apparel, and swimwear—are classified in Industry 448190, Other Clothing Stores;
- Providing clothing alterations and repair—are classified in Industry 811490, Other Personal and Household Goods Repair and Maintenance; and
- Retailing secondhand clothes—are classified in Industry 453310, Used Merchandise Stores.

44815 Clothing Accessories Stores^{CAN}
See industry descriptions for 448150 below.

448150 Clothing Accessories Stores^{CAN}

This industry comprises establishments primarily engaged in retailing single or combination lines of new clothing accessories, such as hats and caps, costume jewelry, gloves, handbags, ties, wigs, toupees, and belts.

US—United States industry only. CAN—United States and Canadian industries are comparable. MEX—United States and Mexican industries are comparable. Blank—Canadian, Mexican, and United States industries are comparable.

Illustrative Examples:

Costume jewelry stores   Wig and hairpiece stores
Neckwear stores

Cross-References. Establishments primarily engaged in—

- Retailing specialized lines of clothing via electronic home shopping, mail-order, or direct sale—are classified in Subsector 454, Nonstore Retailers;

- Retailing precious jewelry and watches—are classified in Industry 448310, Jewelry Stores;

- Retailing used clothing accessories—are classified in Industry 453310, Used Merchandise Stores;

- Retailing luggage, briefcases, trunks, or these products in combination with a general line of leather items (except leather apparel), known as luggage and leather goods stores—are classified in Industry 448320, Luggage and Leather Goods Stores; and

- Retailing leather apparel—are classified in Industry 448190, Other Clothing Stores.

44819 Other Clothing Stores[CAN]

See industry description for 448190 below.

448190 Other Clothing Stores[US]

This industry comprises establishments primarily engaged in retailing specialized lines of new clothing (except general lines of men's, women's, children's, infants', and family clothing). These establishments may provide basic alterations, such as hemming, taking in or letting out seams, or lengthening or shortening sleeves.

Illustrative Examples:

Bridal gown (except custom) shops   Leather coat stores
Costume shops   Lingerie stores
Fur apparel stores   Swimwear stores
Hosiery stores   Uniform (except athletic) stores

Cross-References. Establishments primarily engaged in—

- Retailing specialized apparel via electronic home shopping, mail-order, or direct sale—are classified in Subsector 454, Nonstore Retailers;

- Retailing custom apparel and accessories made on the premises—are classified in Subsector 315, Apparel Manufacturing;

- Retailing new men's and boys' clothing—are classified in Industry 448110, Men's Clothing Stores;
- Retailing new women's, misses', and juniors' clothing, including maternity wear—are classified in Industry 448120, Women's Clothing Stores;
- Retailing new children's and infants' clothing—are classified in Industry 448130, Children's and Infants' Clothing Stores;
- Retailing new clothing for all genders or age groups—are classified in Industry 448140, Family Clothing Stores;
- Retailing athletic uniforms—are classified in Industry 451110, Sporting Goods Stores;
- Retailing secondhand clothes—are classified in Industry 453310, Used Merchandise Stores;
- Retailing luggage, briefcases, trunks, or these products in combination with a general line of leather items (except leather apparel), known as luggage and leather good stores—are classified in Industry 448320, Luggage and Leather Goods Stores; and
- Providing clothing alterations and repair—are classified in Industry 811490, Other Personal Household Goods Repair and Maintenance.

4482 Shoe Stores^{CAN}

44821 Shoe Stores^{CAN}
See industry description for 448210 below.

448210 Shoe Stores^{CAN}

This industry comprises establishments primarily engaged in retailing all types of new footwear (except hosiery and specialty sports footwear, such as golf shoes, bowling shoes, and spiked shoes). Establishments primarily engaged in retailing new tennis shoes or sneakers are included in this industry.

Cross-References. Establishments primarily engaged in—

- Retailing footwear via electronic home shopping, mail-order, or direct sale—are classified in Subsector 454, Nonstore Retailers;
- Retailing hosiery—are classified in Industry 448190, Other Clothing Stores;
- Retailing new specialty sports footwear (e.g., bowling shoes, golf shoes, spiked shoes)—are classified in Industry 451110, Sporting Goods Stores; and

- Retailing used footwear—are classified in Industry 453310, Used Merchandise Stores.

4483 Jewelry, Luggage, and Leather Goods Stores^{CAN}

This industry group comprises establishments primarily engaged in retailing new jewelry (except costume jewelry); new silver and plated silverware; new watches and clocks; and new luggage with or without a general line of new leather goods and accessories, such as hats, gloves, handbags, ties, and belts.

44831 Jewelry Stores^{CAN}
See industry descriptions for 448310 below.

448310 Jewelry Stores^{CAN}

This industry comprises establishments primarily engaged in retailing one or more of the following items: (1) new jewelry (except costume jewelry); (2) new sterling and plated silverware; and (3) new watches and clocks. Also included are establishments retailing these new products in combination with lapidary work and/or repair services.

Cross-References. Establishments primarily engaged in—

- Retailing new costume jewelry—are classified in Industry 448150, Clothing Accessories Stores;
- Retailing jewelry via electronic home shopping, mail-order, or direct sale— are classified in Subsector 454, Nonstore Retailers;
- Retailing antiques or used jewelry, silverware, and watches and clocks— are classified in Industry 453310, Used Merchandise Stores;
- Providing jewelry or watch and clock repair without retailing new jewelry or watches and clocks—are classified in Industry 811490, Other Personal and Household Goods Repair and Maintenance; and
- Cutting and setting gem stones—are classified in U.S. Industry 339913, Jewelers' Material and Lapidary Work Manufacturing.

44832 Luggage and Leather Goods Stores^{CAN}
See industry descriptions for 448320 below.

448320 Luggage and Leather Goods Stores^{CAN}

This industry comprises establishments known as luggage and leather goods stores primarily engaged in retailing new luggage, briefcases, trunks, or these new

---

products in combination with a general line of leather items (except leather apparel), such as belts, gloves, and handbags.

Cross-References. Establishments primarily engaged in—

- Retailing luggage and leather goods via electronic home shopping, mail-order, or direct sale—are classified in Subsector 454, Nonstore Retailers;
- Retailing used luggage and leather goods—are classified in Industry 453310, Used Merchandise Stores;
- Retailing single or combination lines of new clothing accessories (e.g., gloves, handbags, or leather belts)—are classified in Industry 448150, Clothing Accessories Stores; and
- Retailing new leather coats—are classified in Industry 448190, Other Clothing Stores.

451 Sporting Goods, Hobby, Book, and Music Stores^{CAN}

Industries in the Sporting Goods, Hobby, Book, and Music Stores subsector are engaged in retailing and providing expertise on use of sporting equipment or other specific leisure activities, such as needlework and musical instruments. Book stores are also included in this subsector.

4511 Sporting Goods, Hobby, and Musical Instrument Stores^{CAN}

This industry group comprises establishments primarily engaged in retailing new sporting goods, games and toys, and musical instruments.

45111 Sporting Goods Stores^{CAN}
See industry description for 451110 below.

451110 Sporting Goods Stores^{CAN}

This industry comprises establishments primarily engaged in retailing new sporting goods, such as bicycles and bicycle parts; camping equipment; exercise and fitness equipment; athletic uniforms; specialty sports footwear; and sporting goods, equipment, and accessories.

Illustrative Examples:

Athletic uniform supply stores	Golf pro shops
Bicycle (except motorized) shops	Saddlery stores

Bowling equipment and supply stores
Diving equipment stores
Exercise equipment stores
Fishing supply stores

Sporting goods (e.g., scuba, skiing, outdoor) stores
Sporting gun shops

Cross-References. Establishments primarily engaged in—

- Retailing sporting goods via electronic home shopping, mail order, or direct sale—are classified in Subsector 454, Nonstore Retailers;

- Retailing new or used campers (pickup coaches) and camping trailers—are classified in Industry 441210, Recreational Vehicle Dealers;

- Retailing new or used snowmobiles, motorized bicycles, and motorized golf carts—are classified in Industry 44122, Motorcycle, Boat, and Other Motor Vehicle Dealers;

- Retailing new shoes (except specialty sports footwear, such as golf shoes, bowling shoes, and spiked shoes)—are classified in Industry 448210, Shoe Stores;

- Repairing or servicing sporting goods, without retailing new sporting goods—are classified in Industry 811490, Other Personal and Household Goods Repair and Maintenance; and

- Retailing used sporting goods and used bicycles—are classified in Industry 453310, Used Merchandise Stores.

45112 Hobby, Toy, and Game Stores[CAN]

See industry description for 451120 below.

451120 Hobby, Toy, and Game Stores[CAN]

This industry comprises establishments primarily engaged in retailing new toys, games, and hobby and craft supplies (except needlecraft).

Cross-References. Establishments primarily engaged in—

- Retailing toys, games, and hobby and craft supplies via electronic home shopping, mail-order, or direct sale—are classified in Subsector 454, Nonstore Retailers;

- Retailing artists' supplies or collectors' items, such as coins, stamps, autographs, and cards—are classified in U.S. Industry 453998, All Other Miscellaneous Store Retailers (except Tobacco Stores);

- Retailing new computer software (e.g., game software)—are classified in Industry 443120, Computer and Software Stores;

US—United States industry only. CAN—United States and Canadian industries are comparable. MEX—United States and Mexican industries are comparable. Blank—Canadian, Mexican, and United States industries are comparable.

- Retailing used toys, games, and hobby supplies—are classified in Industry 453310, Used Merchandise Stores; and

- Retailing new sewing supplies, fabrics, and needlework accessories—are classified in Industry 451130, Sewing, Needlework, and Piece Goods Stores.

45113 Sewing, Needlework, and Piece Goods Stores[CAN]

See industry description for 451130 below.

451130 Sewing, Needlework, and Piece Goods Stores[CAN]

This industry comprises establishments primarily engaged in retailing new sewing supplies, fabrics, patterns, yarns, and other needlework accessories or retailing these products in combination with selling new sewing machines.

Illustrative Examples:

Fabric shops

Needlecraft sewing supply stores

Sewing supply stores

Upholstery materials stores

Cross-References. Establishments primarily engaged in—

- Retailing sewing supplies via electronic home shopping, mail-order, or direct sale—are classified in Subsector 454, Nonstore Retailers;

- Retailing new sewing machines only and in combination with retailing other new appliances—are classified in U.S. Industry 443111, Household Appliance Stores; and

- Retailing used sewing, needlework, and piece goods—are classified in Industry 453310, Used Merchandise Stores.

45114 Musical Instrument and Supplies Stores[CAN]

See industry description for 451140 below.

451140 Musical Instrument and Supplies Stores[CAN]

This industry comprises establishments primarily engaged in retailing new musical instruments, sheet music, and related supplies; or retailing these new products in combination with musical instrument repair, rental, or music instruction.

Illustrative Examples:

Music instrument stores

Piano stores

Sheet music stores

Cross-References. Establishments primarily engaged in—

- Retailing musical instruments, sheet music, and related supplies via electronic home shopping, mail-order, or direct sale—are classified in Subsector 454, Nonstore Retailers;

- Retailing new musical recordings—are classified in Industry 451220, Prerecorded Tape, Compact Disc, and Record Stores; and

- Retailing used musical instruments, sheet music, and related supplies—are classified in Industry 453310, Used Merchandise Stores.

4512 Book, Periodical, and Music Stores[CAN]

This industry group comprises establishments primarily engaged in retailing new books, newspapers, magazines, and prerecorded audio and video media.

45121 Book Stores and News Dealers[CAN]

This industry comprises establishments primarily engaged in retailing new books, newspapers, magazines, and other periodicals.

Cross-References. Establishments primarily engaged in—

- Retailing newspapers, magazines, and other periodicals via electronic home shopping, mail-order, or direct sale—are classified in Subsector 454, Nonstore Retailers;

- Home delivery of newspapers—are classified in Industry 45439, Other Direct Selling Establishments; and

- Retailing used books, newspapers, magazines, and other periodicals—are classified in Industry 45331, Used Merchandise Stores.

451211 Book Stores[US]

This U.S. industry comprises establishments primarily engaged in retailing new books.

Cross-References. Establishments primarily engaged in—

- Retailing books via electronic home shopping, mail-order, or direct sale—are classified in Subsector 454, Nonstore Retailers; and

- Retailing used books—are classified in Industry 453310, Used Merchandise Stores.

451212 News Dealers and Newsstands^{US}

This U.S. industry comprises establishments primarily engaged in retailing current newspapers, magazines, and other periodicals.

Cross-References. Establishments primarily engaged in—

- Home delivery of newspapers—are classified in Industry 454390, Other Direct Selling Establishments;
- Retailing newspapers and periodicals by mail-order—are classified in Industry 454113, Mail-Order Houses; and
- Retailing used newspapers, magazines, and other periodicals—are classified in Industry 453310, Used Merchandise Stores.

45122 Prerecorded Tape, Compact Disc, and Record Stores^{CAN}
See industry description for 451220 below.

451220 Prerecorded Tape, Compact Disc, and Record Stores^{CAN}

This industry comprises establishments primarily engaged in retailing new prerecorded audio and video tapes, compact discs (CDs), digital video discs (DVDs), and phonograph records.

Cross-References. Establishments primarily engaged in—

- Retailing new computer software—are classified in Industry 443120, Computer and Software Stores;
- Retailing prerecorded tapes, compact discs, digital video discs (DVDs), and records by mail-order—are classified in Industry 454113, Mail-Order Houses;
- Retailing used phonograph records and prerecorded audio and video tapes and discs—are classified in Industry 453310, Used Merchandise Stores; and
- Retailing new audio sound equipment (except automotive)—are classified in U.S. Industry 443112, Radio, Television, and Other Electronics Stores.

452 General Merchandise Stores^{CAN}

Industries in the General Merchandise Stores subsector retail new general merchandise from fixed point-of-sale locations. Establishments in this subsector are unique in that they have the equipment and staff capable of retailing a large variety

---

of goods from a single location. This includes a variety of display equipment and staff trained to provide information on many lines of products.

4521 Department Stores[CAN]

45211 Department Stores[CAN]

This industry comprises establishments known as department stores primarily engaged in retailing a wide range of the following new products with no one merchandise line predominating: apparel, furniture, appliances and home furnishings; and selected additional items, such as paint, hardware, toiletries, cosmetics, photographic equipment, jewelry, toys, and sporting goods. Merchandise lines are normally arranged in separate departments.

Cross-References. Establishments primarily engaged in—

- Retailing packaged grocery items in combination with general lines of merchandise with no one merchandise line predominating—are classified in Industry 45291, Warehouse Clubs and Supercenters;

- Retailing apparel without a significant amount of housewares or general merchandise—are classified in Subsector 448, Clothing and Clothing Accessories Stores;

- Retailing general lines of merchandise via electronic home shopping, mail-order, or direct sale—are classified in Subsector 454, Nonstore Retailers; and

- Retailing used merchandise—are classified in Industry 45331, Used Merchandise Stores.

452111 Department Stores (except Discount Department Stores)[US]

This U.S. industry comprises establishments known as department stores that have separate departments for various merchandise lines, such as apparel, jewelry, home furnishings, and linens, each with separate cash registers and sales associates. Department stores in this industry generally do not have central customer checkout and cash register facilities.

Cross-References. Establishments primarily engaged in—

- Retailing apparel without a significant amount of housewares or general merchandise—are classified in Subsector 448, Clothing and Clothing Accessories Stores;

US—United States industry only. CAN—United States and Canadian industries are comparable. MEX—United States and Mexican industries are comparable. Blank—Canadian, Mexican, and United States industries are comparable.

- Retailing a wide variety of general merchandise in department stores with central customer checkout and cash register facilities—are classified in U.S. Industry 452112, Discount Department Stores; and

- Retailing a wide variety of general merchandise in combination with a general line of perishable groceries, such as fresh meat, vegetable, and dairy products—are classified in Industry 452910, Warehouse Clubs and Supercenters.

452112 Discount Department Stores[US]

This U.S. industry comprises establishments known as department stores that have central customer checkout areas, generally in the front of the store, and that may have additional cash registers located in one or more individual departments. Department stores in this industry sell a wide range of general merchandise (except fresh, perishable foods).

Cross-References. Establishments primarily engaged in—

- Retailing apparel without a significant amount of housewares or general merchandise—are classified in Subsector 448, Clothing and Clothing Accessories Stores;

- Retailing a wide variety of general merchandise in department stores with separate cash registers and sales associates for each department—are classified in U.S. Industry 452111, Department Stores (except Discount Department Stores); and

- Retailing a wide variety of general merchandise in combination with a general line of perishable groceries, such as fresh meat, vegetable, and dairy products—are classified in Industry 452910, Warehouse Clubs and Supercenters.

4529 Other General Merchandise Stores[CAN]

This industry group comprises establishments primarily engaged in retailing new goods in general merchandise stores (except department stores).

45291 Warehouse Clubs and Supercenters[CAN]
See industry description for 452910 below.

452910 Warehouse Clubs and Supercenters[CAN]

This industry comprises establishments known as warehouse clubs, superstores or supercenters primarily engaged in retailing a general line of groceries in combina-

---

tion with general lines of new merchandise, such as apparel, furniture, and appliances.

Cross-References. Establishments primarily engaged in—

- Retailing general lines of merchandise via electronic home shopping, mail-order, or direct sale—are classified in Subsector 454, Nonstore Retailers;
- Retailing a general line of food, generally known as supermarkets and grocery stores—are classified in Industry 445110, Supermarkets and Other Grocery (except Convenience) Stores;
- Retailing general lines of new merchandise with little grocery item sales—are classified in Industry 452990, All Other General Merchandise Stores;
- Retailing new merchandise in discount department stores—are classified in U.S. Industry 452112, Discount Department Stores; and
- Retailing new merchandise in department stores other than discount department stores—are classified in U.S. Industry 452111, Department Stores (except Discount Department Stores); and
- Retailing used merchandise—are classified in Industry 453310, Used Merchandise Stores.

45299 All Other General Merchandise Stores^{CAN}

See industry description for 452990 below.

452990 All Other General Merchandise Stores^{US}

This industry comprises establishments primarily engaged in retailing new goods in general merchandise stores (except department stores, warehouse clubs, super-stores, and supercenters). These establishments retail a general line of new merchandise, such as apparel, automotive parts, dry goods, hardware, groceries, housewares or home furnishings, and other lines in limited amounts, with none of the lines predominating.

Illustrative Examples:

Dollar stores	General merchandise trading posts
General merchandise catalog showrooms (except catalog mail-order)	Home and auto supply stores
	Variety stores
General stores	

Cross-References. Establishments primarily engaged in—

- Retailing general lines of merchandise via electronic home shopping, mail-order, or direct sale—are classified in Subsector 454, Nonstore Retailers;

- Retailing automotive parts—are classified in Industry 441310, Automotive Parts and Accessories Stores;
- Retailing merchandise in department stores—are classified in U.S. Industry 452111, Department Stores (except Discount Department Stores);
- Retailing merchandise in warehouse clubs, superstores, or supercenters—are classified in Industry 452910, Warehouse Clubs and Supercenters;
- Retailing merchandise in catalogue showrooms of mail-order houses—are classified in U.S. Industry 454113, Mail-Order Houses;
- Retailing a general line of new hardware items, known as hardware stores—are classified in Industry 444130, Hardware Stores;
- Retailing a general line of new home repair and improvement materials and supplies, known as home centers—are classified in Industry 444110, Home Centers; and
- Retailing used merchandise—are classified in Industry 453310, Used Merchandise Stores.

453 Miscellaneous Store Retailers[CAN]

Industries in the Miscellaneous Store Retailers subsector retail merchandise from fixed point-of-sale locations (except new or used motor vehicles and parts; new furniture and house furnishings; new appliances and electronic products; new building materials; and garden equipment and supplies; food and beverages; health and personal care goods; gasoline; new clothing and accessories; and new sporting goods, hobby goods, books, and music). Establishments in this subsector include stores with unique characteristics like florists, used merchandise stores, and pet and pet supply stores as well as other store retailers.

4531 Florists[CAN]

45311 Florists[CAN]
See industry description for 453110 below.

453110 Florists[CAN]

This industry comprises establishments known as florists primarily engaged in retailing cut flowers, floral arrangements, and potted plants purchased from others. These establishments usually prepare the arrangements they sell.

Cross-References. Establishments primarily engaged in—

- Retailing flowers or nursery stock grown on premises—are classified in Industry 11142, Nursery and Floriculture Production;

- Retailing trees, shrubs, plants, seeds, bulbs, and sod grown elsewhere—are classified in Industry 444220, Nursery, Garden Center and Farm Supply Stores; and

- Retailing flowers via electronic home shopping, mail-order, or direct sale—are classified in Subsector 454, Nonstore Retailers.

4532 Office Supplies, Stationery, and Gift Stores[CAN]

45321 Office Supplies and Stationery Stores[CAN]
See industry description for 453210 below.

453210 Office Supplies and Stationery Stores[CAN]

This industry comprises establishments primarily engaged in one or more of the following: (1) retailing new stationery, school supplies, and office supplies; (2) selling a combination of new office equipment, furniture, and supplies; and (3) selling new office equipment, furniture, and supplies in combination with selling new computers.

Cross-References. Establishments primarily engaged in—

- Retailing stationery, school supplies, and office supplies via electronic shopping, mail-order, or direct sale—are classified in Subsector 454, Nonstore Retailers;

- Retailing greeting cards—are classified in Industry 453220, Gift, Novelty, and Souvenir Stores;

- Retailing new typewriters—are classified in U.S. Industry 443112, Radio, Television, and Other Electronics Stores;

- Retailing new computers without retailing other consumer-type electronic products or office equipment, furniture, and supplies—are classified in Industry 443120, Computer and Software Stores;

- Printing business forms—are classified in Industry 32311, Printing;

- Retailing new office furniture—are classified in Industry 442110, Furniture Stores; and

- Retailing used office supplies—are classified in Industry 453310, Used Merchandise Stores.

45322 Gift, Novelty, and Souvenir Stores[CAN]
See industry description for 453220 below.

US—United States industry only. CAN—United States and Canadian industries are comparable. MEX—United States and Mexican industries are comparable. Blank—Canadian, Mexican, and United States industries are comparable.

453220 Gift, Novelty, and Souvenir Stores^{CAN}

This industry comprises establishments primarily engaged in retailing new gifts, novelty merchandise, souvenirs, greeting cards, seasonal and holiday decorations, and curios.

Illustrative Examples:

Balloon shops	Greeting card shops
Christmas stores	Novelty shops
Curio shops	Souvenir shops
Gift shops	

Cross-References. Establishments primarily engaged in—

- Retailing gifts and novelties via electronic home shopping, mail-order, or direct sale—are classified in Subsector 454, Nonstore Retailers;
- Retailing stationery—are classified in Industry 453210, Office Supplies and Stationery Stores; and
- Retailing used curios and novelties—are classified in Industry 453310, Used Merchandise Stores.

4533 Used Merchandise Stores^{CAN}

45331 Used Merchandise Stores^{CAN}
See industry description for 453310 below.

453310 Used Merchandise Stores^{CAN}

This industry comprises establishments primarily engaged in retailing used merchandise, antiques, and secondhand goods (except motor vehicles, such as automobiles, RVs, motorcycles, and boats; motor vehicle parts; tires; and mobile homes).

Illustrative Examples:

Antique shops	Used household-type appliance stores
Used book stores	Used merchandise thrift shops
Used clothing stores	Used sporting goods stores

Cross-References. Establishments primarily engaged in—

- Retailing used merchandise via electronic home shopping, mail-order, or direct sale—are classified in Subsector 454, Nonstore Retailers;

US—United States industry only. CAN—United States and Canadian industries are comparable. MEX—United States and Mexican industries are comparable. Blank—Canadian, Mexican, and United States industries are comparable.

- Operating pawnshops—are classified in U.S. Industry 522298, All Other Nondepository Credit Intermediation;

- Retailing used automobiles—are classified in Industry 441120, Used Car Dealers;

- Retailing used automobile parts (except tires and tubes)—are classified in Industry 441310, Automotive Parts and Accessories Stores;

- Retailing used tires—are classified in Industry 441320, Tire Dealers;

- Retailing used mobile homes—are classified in Industry 453930, Manufactured (Mobile) Home Dealers;

- Retailing used motorcycles—are classified in U.S. Industry 441221, Motorcycle Dealers;

- Retailing used recreational vehicles—are classified in Industry 441210, Recreational Vehicle Dealers;

- Retailing used boats—are classified in U.S. Industry 441222, Boat Dealers;

- Retailing used aircraft, snowmobiles, and utility trailers—are classified in U.S. Industry 441229, All Other Motor Vehicle Dealers; and

- Retailing a general line of used merchandise on an auction basis (except electronic auctions)—are classified in U.S. Industry 453998, All Other Miscellaneous Store Retailers (except Tobacco Stores).

4539 Other Miscellaneous Store Retailers[CAN]

This industry group comprises establishments primarily engaged in retailing new miscellaneous specialty store merchandise (except motor vehicle and parts dealers; furniture and home furnishings stores; consumer-type electronics and appliance stores; building material and garden equipment and supplies dealers; food and beverage stores; health and personal care stores; gasoline stations; clothing and clothing accessories stores; sporting goods, hobby, book, and music stores; general merchandise stores; florists; office supplies, stationery, and gift stores; and used merchandise stores).

45391 Pet and Pet Supplies Stores[CAN]
See industry descriptions for 453910 below.

453910 Pet and Pet Supplies Stores[CAN]

This industry comprises establishments primarily engaged in retailing pets, pet foods, and pet supplies.

US—United States industry only. CAN—United States and Canadian industries are comparable. MEX—United States and Mexican industries are comparable. Blank—Canadian, Mexican, and United States industries are comparable.

Cross References. Establishments primarily engaged in—

- Retailing pets, pet foods, and pet supplies via electronic home shopping, mail-order, or direct sale—are classified in Subsector 454, Nonstore Retailers;
- Providing pet grooming and boarding services—are classified in Industry 812910, Pet Care (except Veterinary) Services; and
- Providing veterinary services—are classified in Industry 541940, Veterinary Services.

45392 Art Dealers^{CAN}

See industry descriptions for 453920 below.

453920 Art Dealers^{CAN}

This industry comprises establishments primarily engaged in retailing original and limited edition art works. Included in this industry are establishments primarily engaged in displaying works of art for retail sale in art galleries.

Cross-References. Establishments primarily engaged in—

- Retailing original and limited edition art works via electronic home shopping, mail-order, or direct sale—are classified in Subsector 454, Nonstore Retailers;
- Retailing art reproductions (except limited editions)—are classified in U.S. Industry 442299, All Other Home Furnishings Stores;
- Retailing artists' supplies—are classified in U.S. Industry 453998, All Other Miscellaneous Store Retailers (except Tobacco Stores); and
- Displaying works of art not for retail sale in art galleries—are classified in Industry 712110, Museums.

45393 Manufactured (Mobile) Home Dealers^{CAN}

See industry description for 453930 below.

453930 Manufactured (Mobile) Home Dealers^{CAN}

This industry comprises establishments primarily engaged in retailing new and/ or used manufactured homes (i.e.; mobile homes), parts, and equipment.

Cross-References. Establishments primarily engaged in—

- Retailing new or used motor homes, campers, and travel trailers—are classified in Industry 441210, Recreational Vehicle Dealers; and

---

US—United States industry only. CAN—United States and Canadian industries are comparable. MEX—United States and Mexican industries are comparable. Blank—Canadian, Mexican, and United States industries are comparable.

- Retailing prefabricated buildings and kits without construction—are classified in Industry 444190, Other Building Material Dealers.

45399 All Other Miscellaneous Store Retailers^{CAN}

This industry comprises establishments primarily engaged in retailing specialized lines of merchandise (except motor vehicle and parts dealers; furniture and home furnishings stores; electronic and appliance stores; building material and garden equipment and supplies dealers; food and beverage stores; health and personal care stores; gasoline stations; clothing and clothing accessories stores; sporting goods, hobby, book, and music stores; general merchandise stores; florists; office supplies, stationery and gift stores; used merchandise stores; pet and pet supplies; art dealers; and manufactured home (i.e., mobile home) dealers). This industry also includes establishments primarily engaged in retailing a general line of new and used merchandise on an auction basis (except electronic auctions).

Illustrative Examples:

Art supply stores	Cigar stores
Cemetery memorial (e.g., markers,	Swimming pool supply stores, new
headstones, vaults) dealers	· Tobacco stores

Cross-References. Establishments primarily engaged in—

- Retailing merchandise via electronic home shopping, mail-order, or direct sale—are classified in Subsector 454, Nonstore Retailers;

- Auctioning on the location of others as independent auctioneers—are classified in Industry 56199, All Other Support Services;

- Retailing pets and pet supplies—are classified in Industry 45391, Pet and Pet Supplies Stores;

- Retailing original and limited edition art works—are classified in Industry 45392, Art Dealers;

- Retailing manufactured homes (i.e., mobile homes)—are classified in Industry 45393, Manufactured (Mobile) Home Dealers;

- Retailing new books—are classified in Industry 45121, Book Stores and News Dealers;

- Retailing new jewelry (except costume jewelry)—are classified in Industry 44831, Jewelry Stores;

- Retailing new costume jewelry—are classified in Industry 44815, Clothing Accessories Stores; and

US—United States industry only. CAN—United States and Canadian industries are comparable. MEX—United States and Mexican industries are comparable. Blank—Canadian, Mexican, and United States industries are comparable.

- Retailing used merchandise (except automobiles, RVs, mobile homes, motorcycles, boats, motor vehicle parts, and tires)—are classified in Industry 453310, Used Merchandise Stores.

453991 Tobacco Stores[US]

This U.S. industry comprises establishments primarily engaged in retailing cigarettes, cigars, tobacco, pipes, and other smokers' supplies.

Illustrative Examples:

Cigar stores	Smokers' supply stores
Cigarette stands (i.e., permanent)	Tobacco stores

Cross-References.

Establishments primarily engaged in retailing tobacco products and supplies via electronic home shopping, mail-order, or direct sale are classified in Subsector 454, Nonstore Retailers.

453998 All Other Miscellaneous Store Retailers (except Tobacco Stores)[US]

This U.S. industry comprises establishments primarily engaged in retailing specialized lines of merchandise (except motor vehicle and parts dealers; furniture and home furnishings stores; electronic and appliance stores; building material and garden equipment and supplies dealers; food and beverage stores; health and personal care stores; gasoline stations; clothing and clothing accessories stores; sporting goods, hobby, book and music stores; general merchandise stores; florists; office supplies, stationery and gift stores; used merchandise stores; pet and pet supplies stores; art dealers; manufactured home (i.e., mobile homes) dealers; and tobacco stores). This industry also includes establishments primarily engaged in retailing a general line of new and used merchandise on an auction basis.

Illustrative Examples:

Art supply stores	Flower shops, artificial or dried
Candle shops	General merchandise auction houses
Cemetery memorial (e.g., headstones, markers, vaults) dealers	Home security equipment stores
	Hot tub stores
Collectors' items (e.g., autograph, coin, card, stamp) shops	Swimming pool supply stores
	Trophy (e.g., awards and plaques) shops
Fireworks shops (permanent location)	

US—United States industry only. CAN—United States and Canadian industries are comparable. MEX—United States and Mexican industries are comparable. Blank—Canadian, Mexican, and United States industries are comparable.

Cross-References. Establishments primarily engaged in—

- Retailing specialized lines of merchandise via electronic home shopping, mail-order, or direct sale—are classified in Subsector 454, Nonstore Retailers;
- Retailing merchandise via electronic auctions—are classified in Industry 454112, Electronic Auctions;
- Auctioning (i.e., on the location of others as independent auctioneers)—are classified in Industry 561990, All Other Support Services;
- Retailing pets and pet supplies—are classified in Industry 453910, Pet and Pet Supplies Stores;
- Retailing original and limited edition art works—are classified in Industry 453920, Art Dealers;
- Retailing manufactured homes (i.e., mobile homes)—are classified in Industry 453930, Manufactured (Mobile) Home Dealers;
- Retailing cigarettes, cigars, tobacco, pipes, and other smokers' supplies—are classified in U.S. Industry 453991, Tobacco Stores;
- Retailing antiques—are classified in Industry 453310, Used Merchandise Stores;
- Retailing new books—are classified in Industry 451211, Book Stores;
- Retailing new jewelry (except costume jewelry)—are classified in Industry 448310, Jewelry Stores; and
- Retailing new costume jewelry—are classified in Industry 448150, Clothing Accessories Stores.

454 Nonstore Retailers^{CAN}

Industries in the Nonstore Retailers subsector retail merchandise using methods, such as the broadcasting of infomercials, the broadcasting and publishing of direct-response advertising, the publishing of paper and electronic catalogs, door-to-door solicitation, in-home demonstration, selling from portable stalls and distribution through vending machines. Establishments in this subsector include mail-order houses, vending machine operators, home delivery sales, door-to-door sales, party plan sales, electronic shopping, and sales through portable stalls (e.g., street vendors, except food). Establishments engaged in the direct sale (i.e., nonstore) of products, such as home heating oil dealers and newspaper delivery are included in this subsector.

4541 Electronic Shopping and Mail-Order Houses^{CAN}

45411 Electronic Shopping and Mail-Order Houses^{CAN}

This industry comprises establishments primarily engaged in retailing all types of merchandise using non-store means, such as catalogs, toll free telephone numbers, or electronic media, such as interactive television or computer. Included in this industry are establishments primarily engaged in retailing from catalog showrooms of mail-order houses.

Illustrative Examples:

Catalog (i.e., order-taking) office of
  mail- order house
Collectors' items, mail-order houses
Computer software, mail-order houses
Home shopping television orders

Mail-order book clubs (not publishing)
Mail-order houses
Web retailers
Internet auction sites, retail

Cross-References. Establishments primarily engaged in—

- Store retailing or a combination of store retailing and non-store retailing in the same establishment—are classified in Sector 44-45, Retail Trade, based on the classification of the store portion of the activity;

- Facilitating business to business electronic sales of new and used merchandise on an auction basis using the Internet—are classified in Industry 42511, Business to Business Electronic Markets; and

- Providing telemarketing (e.g., telephone marketing) services for others—are classified in Industry 56142, Telephone Call Centers.

454111 Electronic Shopping[US]

This U.S. Industry comprises establishments engaged in retailing all types of merchandise using the Internet.

Cross-References. Establishments primarily engaged in—

- Store retailing or a combination of store retailing and Internet retailing in the same establishment—are classified in NAICS 44-45, Retail Trade, based on the classification of the store portion of the activity; and

- Retailing all types of merchandise using catalogs or television to generate clients and display merchandise—are classified in U.S. Industry 454113, Mail-Order Houses.

454112 Electronic Auctions[US]

This U.S. Industry comprises establishments engaged in providing sites for and facilitating consumer-to-consumer or business-to-consumer trade in new and used goods, on an auction basis, using the Internet. Establishments in this industry provide the electronic location for retail auctions, but do not take title to the goods being sold.

US—United States industry only. CAN—United States and Canadian industries are comparable. MEX—United States and Mexican industries are comparable. Blank—Canadian, Mexican, and United States industries are comparable.

Cross-References. Establishments primarily engaged in—

- Retailing a general line of new and used merchandise on an auction basis from physical auction sites—are classified in U.S. Industry 453998, All Other Miscellaneous Store Retailers (except Tobacco Stores);
- Facilitating business-to-business sales of new and used merchandise on an auction basis using the Internet—are classified in U.S. Industry 425110, Business to Business Electronic Markets; and
- A combination of Internet auction and auction house sales in the same establishment—are classified in NAICS 44-45, Retail Trade, based on the classification of the auction house portion of the activity

454113 Mail-Order Houses^{US}

This U.S. industry comprises establishments primarily engaged in retailing all types of merchandise using mail catalogs or television to generate clients and display merchandise. Included in this industry are establishments primarily engaged in retailing from catalog showrooms of mail-order houses as well as establishments providing a combination of Internet and mail-order sales.

Illustrative Examples:

Catalog (i.e., order-taking) offices of
  mail-order houses
Home shopping television orders
Mail-order book clubs (not publishing)

Collectors' items, mail-order houses
Mail-order houses
Computer software, mail-order houses

Cross-References. Establishments primarily engaged in—

- Providing telemarketing (e.g., telephone marketing) services for others— are classified in U.S. Industry 561422, Telemarketing Bureaus; and
- Retailing merchandise using store and nonstore methods at the same establishment—are classified in Store retail activities based on the store portion of the activity.

4542 Vending Machine Operators^{CAN}

45421 Vending Machine Operators^{CAN}
See industry description for 454210 below.

454210 Vending Machine Operators^{CAN}

This industry comprises establishments primarily engaged in retailing merchandise through vending machines that they service.

Cross-References. Establishments primarily engaged in—

- Selling insurance policies through vending machines—are classified in Subsector 524, Insurance Carriers and Related Activities;
- Supplying and servicing coin-operated photobooths, restrooms, and lockers—are classified in Industry 812990, All Other Personal Services; and
- Supplying and servicing coin-operated amusement and gambling devices in places of business operated by others—are classified in Subsector 713, Amusement, Gambling, and Recreation Industries.

4543 Direct Selling Establishments^{CAN}

This industry group comprises establishments primarily engaged in nonstore retailing (except electronic, mail-order, or vending machine sales). These establishments typically go to the customers' location rather than the customer coming to them (e.g., door-to-door sales, home parties). Examples of establishments in this industry are home delivery newspaper routes; home delivery of heating oil, liquefied petroleum (LP) gas, and other fuels; locker meat provisioners; frozen food and freezer plan providers; coffee-break services providers; and bottled water or water softener services.

45431 Fuel Dealers^{CAN}

This industry comprises establishments primarily engaged in retailing heating oil, liquefied petroleum (LP) gas, and other fuels via direct selling.

Cross-References. Establishments primarily engaged in—

- Providing oil burner repair services—are classified in Industry 81141, Home and Garden Equipment and Appliance Repair and Maintenance; and
- Installing oil burners—are classified in Industry 23822, Plumbing, Heating, and Air-Conditioning Contractors.

454311 Heating Oil Dealers^{US}

This U.S. industry comprises establishments primarily engaged in retailing heating oil via direct selling.

Cross-References. Establishments primarily engaged in—

- Providing oil burner repair services—are classified in U.S. Industry 811411, Home and Garden Equipment Repair and Maintenance; and

- Installing oil burners—are classified in Industry 238220, Plumbing, Heating, and Air-Conditioning Contractors.

454312 Liquefied Petroleum Gas (Bottled Gas) Dealers[US]

This U.S. industry comprises establishments primarily engaged in retailing liquefied petroleum (LP) gas via direct selling.

454319 Other Fuel Dealers[US]

This U.S. industry comprises establishments primarily engaged in retailing fuels (except liquefied petroleum gas and heating oil) via direct selling.

45439 Other Direct Selling Establishments[CAN]
See industry description for 454390 below.

454390 Other Direct Selling Establishments[CAN]

This industry comprises establishments primarily engaged in retailing merchandise (except food for immediate consumption and fuel) via direct sale to the customer by means, such as in-house sales (i.e., party plan merchandising), truck or wagon sales, and portable stalls (i.e., street vendors).

Illustrative Examples:

Direct selling bottled water providers
Direct selling coffee-break service providers
Direct selling frozen food and freezer plan providers
Direct selling home delivery newspaper routes
Direct selling party plan merchandisers
Direct selling locker meat provisioners

Cross-References. Establishments primarily engaged in—

- Preparing and selling meals and snacks for immediate consumption from motorized vehicles or nonmotorized carts catering a route—are classified in Industry 722330, Mobile Food Services;
- Retailing heating oil via direct sale—are classified in U.S. Industry 454311, Heating Oil Dealers;
- Retailing liquefied petroleum (LP) gas via direct sale—are classified in U.S. Industry 454312, Liquefied Petroleum Gas (Bottled Gas) Dealers; and
- Retailing other fuels, such as coal or wood, via direct sale—are classified in U.S. Industry 454319, Other Fuel Dealers.

US—United States industry only. CAN—United States and Canadian industries are comparable. MEX—United States and Mexican industries are comparable. Blank—Canadian, Mexican, and United States industries are comparable.

Sector 48-49—Transportation and Warehousing

The Sector as a Whole

The Transportation and Warehousing sector includes industries providing transportation of passengers and cargo, warehousing and storage for goods, scenic and sightseeing transportation, and support activities related to modes of transportation. Establishments in these industries use transportation equipment or transportation related facilities as a productive asset. The type of equipment depends on the mode of transportation. The modes of transportation are air, rail, water, road, and pipeline.

The Transportation and Warehousing sector distinguishes three basic types of activities: subsectors for each mode of transportation, a subsector for warehousing and storage, and a subsector for establishments providing support activities for transportation. In addition, there are subsectors for establishments that provide passenger transportation for scenic and sightseeing purposes, postal services, and courier services.

A separate subsector for support activities is established in the sector because, first, support activities for transportation are inherently multimodal, such as freight transportation arrangement, or have multimodal aspects. Secondly, there are production process similarities among the support activity industries.

One of the support activities identified in the support activity subsector is the routine repair and maintenance of transportation equipment (e.g., aircraft at an airport, railroad rolling stock at a railroad terminal, or ships at a harbor or port facility). Such establishments do not perform complete overhauling or rebuilding of transportation equipment (i.e., periodic restoration of transportation equipment to original design specifications) or transportation equipment conversion (i.e., major modification to systems). An establishment that primarily performs factory (or shipyard) overhauls, rebuilding, or conversions of aircraft, railroad rolling stock, or a ship is classified in Subsector 336, Transportation Equipment Manufacturing according to the type of equipment.

Many of the establishments in this sector often operate on networks, with physical facilities, labor forces, and equipment spread over an extensive geographic area.

Warehousing establishments in this sector are distinguished from merchant wholesaling in that the warehouse establishments do not sell the goods.

Excluded from this sector are establishments primarily engaged in providing travel agent services that support transportation and other establishments, such as hotels, businesses, and government agencies. These establishments are classified in Sector 56, Administrative and Support and Waste Management and Remediation Services. Also, establishments primarily engaged in providing rental and leasing of transportation equipment without operator are classified in Subsector 532, Rental and Leasing Services.

US—United States industry only. CAN—United States and Canadian industries are comparable. MEX—United States and Mexican industries are comparable. Blank—Canadian, Mexican, and United States industries are comparable.

481 Air Transportation

Industries in the Air Transportation subsector provide air transportation of passengers and/or cargo using aircraft, such as airplanes and helicopters. The subsector distinguishes scheduled from nonscheduled air transportation. Scheduled air carriers fly regular routes on regular schedules and operate even if flights are only partially loaded. Nonscheduled carriers often operate during nonpeak time slots at busy airports. These establishments have more flexibility with respect to choice of airport, hours of operation, load factors, and similar operational characteristics. Nonscheduled carriers provide chartered air transportation of passengers, cargo, or specialty flying services. Specialty flying services establishments use general-purpose aircraft to provide a variety of specialized flying services.

Scenic and sightseeing air transportation and air courier services are not included in this subsector but are included in Subsector 487, Scenic and Sightseeing Transportation and in Subsector 492, Couriers and Messengers. Although these activities may use aircraft, they are different from the activities included in air transportation. Air sightseeing does not usually involve place-to-place transportation; the passenger's flight (e.g., balloon ride, aerial sightseeing) typically starts and ends at the same location. Courier services (individual package or cargo delivery) include more than air transportation; road transportation is usually required to deliver the cargo to the intended recipient.

4811 Scheduled Air Transportation

48111 Scheduled Air Transportation

This industry comprises establishments primarily engaged in providing air transportation of passengers and/or cargo over regular routes and on regular schedules. Establishments in this industry operate flights even if partially loaded. Establishments primarily engaged in providing scheduled air transportation of mail on a contract basis are included in this industry.

Illustrative Examples:

Air commuter carriers, scheduled   Scheduled air passenger carriers
Scheduled air cargo carriers (except air Scheduled helicopter passenger carriers
couriers)

Cross-References. Establishments primarily engaged in—

- Providing air courier services—are classified in Industry 49211, Couriers;

- Providing air transportation of passengers, cargo, or specialty flying services with no regular routes and regular schedules—are classified in Industry 48121, Nonscheduled Air Transportation; and

---

- Providing helicopter rides for scenic and sightseeing transportation—are classified in Industry 48799, Scenic and Sightseeing Transportation, Other.

481111 Scheduled Passenger Air Transportation[US]

This U.S. industry comprises establishments primarily engaged in providing air transportation of passengers or passengers and freight over regular routes and on regular schedules. Establishments in this industry operate flights even if partially loaded. Scheduled air passenger carriers including commuter and helicopter carriers (except scenic and sightseeing) are included in this industry.

Cross-References. Establishments primarily engaged in—

- Providing air transportation of passengers or passengers and cargo with no regular routes and regular schedules—are classified in U.S. Industry 481211, Nonscheduled Chartered Passenger Air Transportation;

- Providing helicopter rides for scenic and sightseeing transportation—are classified in Industry 487990, Scenic and Sightseeing Transportation, Other; and

- Providing air transportation of cargo (without transporting passengers) over regular routes and on regular schedules—are classified in U.S. Industry 481112, Scheduled Freight Air Transportation.

481112 Scheduled Freight Air Transportation[US]

This U.S. industry comprises establishments primarily engaged in providing air transportation of cargo without transporting passengers over regular routes and on regular schedules. Establishments in this industry operate flights even if partially loaded. Establishments primarily engaged in providing scheduled air transportation of mail on a contract basis are included in this industry.

Cross-References. Establishments primarily engaged in—

- Providing air courier services—are classified in Industry 492110, Couriers;

- Providing air transportation of cargo with no regular routes and regular schedules—are classified in U.S. Industry 481212, Nonscheduled Chartered Freight Air Transportation; and

- Providing air transportation of passengers or passengers and cargo over regular routes and on regular schedules—are classified in U.S. Industry 481111, Scheduled Passenger Air Transportation.

US—United States industry only. CAN—United States and Canadian industries are comparable. MEX—United States and Mexican industries are comparable. Blank—Canadian, Mexican, and United States industries are comparable.

4812 Nonscheduled Air Transportation

48121 Nonscheduled Air Transportation

This industry comprises establishments primarily engaged in (1) providing air transportation of passengers and/or cargo with no regular routes and regular schedules or (2) providing specialty flying services with no regular routes and regular schedules using general purpose aircraft. These establishments have more flexibility with respect to choice of airports, hours of operation, load factors, and similar operational characteristics.

Illustrative Examples:

Air taxi services	Aircraft charter services
Nonscheduled air freight transportation services	Nonscheduled air passenger transportation services

Cross-References. Establishments primarily engaged in—

- Crop dusting using specialized aircraft—are classified in Industry 11511, Support Activities for Crop Production;
- Fighting forest fires using specialized water bombers—are classified in Industry 11531, Support Activities for Forestry;
- Providing air transportation of passengers and/or cargo over regular routes and on regular schedules—are classified in Industry 48111, Scheduled Air Transportation;
- Providing specialized air sightseeing services—are classified in Industry 48799, Scenic and Sightseeing Transportation, Other;
- Aerial gathering of geophysical data—are classified in Industry 54136, Geophysical Surveying and Mapping Services;
- Providing aerial and/or other surveying and mapping services—are classified in Industry 54137, Surveying and Mapping (except Geophysical) Services;
- Providing air ambulance services using specialized equipment—are classified in Industry 62191, Ambulance Services;
- Operating specialized flying schools, including all training for commercial pilots—are classified in Industry 61151, Technical and Trade Schools;
- Operating recreation aviation clubs—are classified in Industry 71399, All Other Amusement and Recreation Industries;
- Operating advocacy aviation clubs—are classified in U.S. Industry 81331, Social Advocacy Organizations; and
- Providing air courier services—are classified in Industry 49211, Couriers.

481211 Nonscheduled Chartered Passenger Air Transportation[US]

This U.S. industry comprises establishments primarily engaged in providing air transportation of passengers or passengers and cargo with no regular routes and regular schedules.

Cross-References. Establishments primarily engaged in—

- Providing specialty air transportation or flying services with no regular routes and regular schedules using general purpose aircraft—are classified in U.S. Industry 481219, Other Nonscheduled Air Transportation;
- Providing specialized air sightseeing services—are classified in Industry 487990, Scenic and Sightseeing Transportation, Other;
- Providing air transportation of passengers or passengers and cargo over regular routes and on regular schedules—are classified in U.S. Industry 481111, Scheduled Passenger Air Transportation; and
- Providing air transportation of cargo (without transporting passengers) with no regular routes and schedules—are classified in U.S. Industry 481212, Nonscheduled Chartered Freight Air Transportation.

481212 Nonscheduled Chartered Freight Air Transportation[US]

This U.S. industry comprises establishments primarily engaged in providing air transportation of cargo without transporting passengers with no regular routes and regular schedules.

Cross-References. Establishments primarily engaged in—

- Providing specialty air transportation or flying services with no regular routes and regular schedules using general purpose aircraft—are classified in U.S. Industry 481219, Other Nonscheduled Air Transportation;
- Providing air courier services—are classified in Industry 492110, Couriers;
- Providing air transportation of cargo without transporting passengers over regular routes and on regular schedules—are classified in U.S. Industry 481112, Scheduled Freight Air Transportation; and
- Providing air transportation of cargo and passengers with no regular routes and schedules—are classified in U.S. Industry 481211, Nonscheduled Chartered Passenger Air Transportation.

481219 Other Nonscheduled Air Transportation[US]

This U.S. industry comprises establishments primarily engaged in providing air transportation with no regular routes and regular schedules (except nonscheduled chartered passenger and/or cargo air transportation). These establishments provide a variety of specialty air transportation or flying services based on individual customer needs using general purpose aircraft.

Illustrative Examples:

Aircraft charter services (i.e., general purpose aircraft used for a variety of specialty air and flying services)

Aviation clubs providing a variety of air transportation activities to the general public

Cross-References. Establishments primarily engaged in—

- Providing air transportation of passengers or passengers and cargo with no regular routes and regular schedules—are classified in U.S. Industry 481211, Nonscheduled Chartered Passenger Air Transportation;

- Providing air transportation of cargo without transporting passengers with no regular routes and regular schedules—are classified in U.S. Industry 481212, Nonscheduled Chartered Freight Air Transportation;

- Crop dusting using specialized aircraft—are classified in U.S. Industry 115112, Soil Preparation, Planting, and Cultivating;

- Fighting forest fires using specialized water bombers—are classified in Industry 115310, Support Activities for Forestry;

- Providing specialized air sightseeing services—are classified in Industry 487990, Scenic and Sightseeing Transportation, Other;

- Operating specialized flying schools, including all training for commercial pilots—are classified in U.S. Industry 611512, Flight Training;

- Providing specialized air ambulance services using specialized equipment— are classified in U.S. Industry 621999, All Other Miscellaneous Ambulatory Health Care Services;

- Operating recreation aviation clubs—are classified in Industry 713990, All Other Amusement and Recreation Industries;

- Operating advocacy aviation clubs—are classified in U.S. Industry 813319, Other Social Advocacy Organizations;

- Aerial gathering of geophysical data for surveying and mapping—are classified in Industry 541360, Geophysical Surveying and Mapping Services; and

- Providing aerial and/or other surveying and mapping services—are classified in Industry 541370, Surveying and Mapping (except Geophysical) Services.

US—United States industry only. CAN—United States and Canadian industries are comparable. MEX—United States and Mexican industries are comparable. Blank—Canadian, Mexican, and United States industries are comparable.

482 Rail Transportation

Industries in the Rail Transportation subsector provide rail transportation of passengers and/or cargo using railroad rolling stock. The railroads in this subsector primarily either operate on networks, with physical facilities, labor force, and equipment spread over an extensive geographic area, or operate over a short distance on a local rail line.

Scenic and sightseeing rail transportation and street railroads, commuter rail, and rapid transit are not included in this subsector but are included in Subsector 487, Scenic and Sightseeing Transportation, and Subsector 485, Transit and Ground Passenger Transportation, respectively. Although these activities use railroad rolling stock, they are different from the activities included in rail transportation. Sightseeing and scenic railroads do not usually involve place-to-place transportation; the passenger's trip typically starts and ends at the same location. Commuter railroads operate in a manner more consistent with local and urban transit and are often part of integrated transit systems.

4821 Rail Transportation

48211 Rail Transportation

This industry comprises establishments primarily engaged in operating railroads (except street railroads, commuter rail, urban rapid transit, and scenic and sightseeing trains). Line-haul rail roads and short line railroads are included in this industry.

Cross-References. Establishments primarily engaged in—

- Operating street railroads, commuter rail, and urban rapid transit systems— are classified in Industry Group 4851, Urban Transit Systems;

- Operating scenic and sightseeing trains—are classified in Industry 48711, Scenic and Sightseeing Transportation, Land; and

- Operating switching and terminal facilities as separate establishments—are classified in Industry 48821, Support Activities for Rail Transportation.

482111 Line-Haul Railroads[US]

This U.S. industry comprises establishments known as line-haul railroads primarily engaged in operating railroads for the transport of passengers and/or cargo over a long distance within a rail network. These establishments provide for the intercity movement of trains between the terminals and stations on main and branch lines of a line-haul rail network (except for local switching services).

US—United States industry only. CAN—United States and Canadian industries are comparable. MEX—United States and Mexican industries are comparable. Blank—Canadian, Mexican, and United States industries are comparable.

Cross-References. Establishments primarily engaged in—

- Operating switching and terminal facilities as separate establishments—are classified in Industry 488210, Support Activities for Rail Transportation;
- Operating railroads over a short distance on local rail lines—are classified in U.S. Industry 482112, Short Line Railroads; and
- Operating commuter rail systems—are classified in U.S. Industry 485112, Commuter Rail Systems.

482112 Short Line Railroads[CAN]

This U.S. industry comprises establishments known as short line railroads primarily engaged in operating railroads for the transport of cargo over a short distance on local rail lines not part of a rail network.

Cross-References. Establishments primarily engaged in—

- Operating street railroads, commuter rail, and urban rapid transit systems— are classified in Industry Group 4851, Urban Transit Systems;
- Operating scenic and sightseeing trains—are classified in Industry 487110, Scenic and Sightseeing Transportation, Land;
- Operating switching and terminal facilities as separate establishments— are classified in Industry 488210, Support Activities for Rail Transportation; and
- Operating railroads for the transport of passengers and/or cargo over a long distance—are classified in U.S. Industry 482111, Line-Haul Railroads.

483 Water Transportation

Industries in the Water Transportation subsector provide water transportation of passengers and cargo using water craft, such as ships, barges, and boats.

The subsector is composed of two industry groups: (1) one for deep sea, coastal, and Great Lakes; and (2) one for inland water transportation. This split typically reflects the difference in equipment used.

Scenic and sightseeing water transportation services are not included in this subsector but are included in Subsector 487, Scenic and Sightseeing Transportation. Although these activities use water craft, they are different from the activities included in water transportation. Water sightseeing does not usually involve place-to-place transportation; the passenger's trip starts and ends at the same location.

US—United States industry only. CAN—United States and Canadian industries are comparable. MEX—United States and Mexican industries are comparable. Blank—Canadian, Mexican, and United States industries are comparable.

4831 Deep Sea, Coastal, and Great Lakes Water Transportation

48311 Deep Sea, Coastal, and Great Lakes Water Transportation

This industry comprises establishments primarily engaged in providing deep sea, coastal, Great Lakes, and St. Lawrence Seaway water transportation. Marine transportation establishments using the facilities of the St. Lawrence Seaway Authority Commission are considered to be using the Great Lakes Water Transportation System.

Cross-References. Establishments primarily engaged in—

- Providing inland water transportation on lakes, rivers, or intracoastal waterways (except on the Great Lakes System)—are classified in Industry 48321, Inland Water Transportation;
- Providing scenic and sightseeing water transportation, such as harbor cruises—are classified in Industry 48721, Scenic and Sightseeing Transportation, Water; and
- Operating floating casinos (i.e., gambling cruises, river boat gambling casinos)—are classified in Industry 71321, Casinos (except Casino Hotels).

483111 Deep Sea Freight Transportation^{US}

This U.S. industry comprises establishments primarily engaged in providing deep sea transportation of cargo to or from foreign ports.

Cross-References.

Establishments primarily engaged in providing deep sea transportation of cargo to and from domestic ports are classified in U.S. Industry 483113, Coastal and Great Lakes Freight Transportation.

483112 Deep Sea Passenger Transportation^{US}

This U.S. industry comprises establishments primarily engaged in providing deep sea transportation of passengers to or from foreign ports.

Cross-References. Establishments primarily engaged in—

- Providing deep sea transportation of passengers to and from domestic ports—are classified in U.S. Industry 483114, Coastal and Great Lakes Passenger Transportation; and

US—United States industry only. CAN—United States and Canadian industries are comparable. MEX—United States and Mexican industries are comparable. Blank—Canadian, Mexican, and United States industries are comparable.

- Operating floating casinos (i.e., gambling cruises)—are classified in Industry 713210, Casinos (except Casino Hotels).

483113   Coastal and Great Lakes Freight Transportation^{US}

This U.S. industry comprises establishments primarily engaged in providing water transportation of cargo in coastal waters, on the Great Lakes System, or deep seas between ports of the United States, Puerto Rico, and United States island possessions or protectorates. Marine transportation establishments using the facilities of the St. Lawrence Seaway Authority Commission are considered to be using the Great Lakes Water Transportation System. Establishments primarily engaged in providing coastal and/or Great Lakes barge transportation services are included in this industry.

Cross-References. Establishments primarily engaged in—

- Providing deep sea transportation of cargo to or from foreign ports—are classified in U.S. Industry 483111, Deep Sea Freight Transportation; and

- Providing inland water transportation of cargo on lakes, rivers, or intra-coastal waterways (except on the Great Lakes System)—are classified in U.S. Industry 483211, Inland Water Freight Transportation.

483114   Coastal and Great Lakes Passenger Transportation^{US}

This U.S. industry comprises establishments primarily engaged in providing water transportation of passengers in coastal waters, the Great Lakes System, or deep seas between ports of the United States, Puerto Rico, and United States island possessions and protectorates. Marine transportation establishments using the facilities of the St. Lawrence Seaway Authority Commission are considered to be using the Great Lakes Water Transportation System.

Cross-References. Establishments primarily engaged in—

- Providing inland water transportation of passengers on lakes, rivers, or intracoastal waterways (except on the Great Lakes System)—are classified in U.S. Industry 483212, Inland Water Passenger Transportation;

- Providing scenic and sightseeing water transportation, such as harbor cruises—are classified in Industry 487210, Scenic and Sightseeing Transportation, Water; and

- Operating floating casinos (i.e., gambling cruises)—are classified in Industry 713210, Casinos (except Casino Hotels).

US—United States industry only. CAN—United States and Canadian industries are comparable. MEX—United States and Mexican industries are comparable. Blank—Canadian, Mexican, and United States industries are comparable.

4832 Inland Water Transportation

48321 Inland Water Transportation

This industry comprises establishments primarily engaged in providing inland water transportation of passengers and/or cargo on lakes, rivers, or intracoastal waterways (except on the Great Lakes System).

Cross-References. Establishments primarily engaged in—

- Providing water transportation in deep sea, coastal, or on the Great Lakes System—are classified in Industry Group 4831, Deep Sea, Coastal and Great Lakes Water Transportation;
- Providing scenic and sightseeing water transportation, such as harbor cruises—are classified in Industry 48721, Scenic and Sightseeing Transportation, Water; and
- Operating floating casinos (i.e., gambling cruises, river boat gambling casinos)—are classified in Industry 71321, Casinos (except Casino Hotels).

483211 Inland Water Freight Transportation[US]

This U.S. industry comprises establishments primarily engaged in providing inland water transportation of cargo on lakes, rivers, or intracoastal waterways (except on the Great Lakes System).

Cross-References. Establishments primarily engaged in—

- Providing deep sea transportation of cargo to and from foreign ports—are classified in U.S. Industry 483111, Deep Sea Freight Transportation; and
- Providing water transportation of cargo in coastal waters or on the Great Lakes System—are classified in U.S. Industry 483113, Coastal and Great Lakes Freight Transportation.

483212 Inland Water Passenger Transportation[US]

This U.S. industry comprises establishments primarily engaged in providing inland water transportation of passengers on lakes, rivers, or intracoastal waterways (except on the Great Lakes System).

Cross-References. Establishments primarily engaged in—

- Providing deep sea transportation of passengers to and from foreign ports—are classified in U.S. Industry 483112, Deep Sea Passenger Transportation;

- Operating cruise ships or ferries in coastal waters or on the Great Lakes System—are classified in U.S. Industry 483114, Coastal and Great Lakes Passenger Transportation; and

- Providing scenic and sightseeing water transportation, such as harbor cruises—are classified in Industry 487210, Scenic and Sightseeing Transportation, Water.

484 Truck Transportation

Industries in the Truck Transportation subsector provide over-the-road transportation of cargo using motor vehicles, such as trucks and tractor trailers. The subsector is subdivided into general freight trucking and specialized freight trucking. This distinction reflects differences in equipment used, type of load carried, scheduling, terminal, and other networking services. General freight transportation establishments handle a wide variety of general commodities, generally palletized, and transported in a container or van trailer. Specialized freight transportation is the transportation of cargo that, because of size, weight, shape, or other inherent characteristics require specialized equipment for transportation.

Each of these industry groups is further subdivided based on distance traveled. Local trucking establishments primarily carry goods within a single metropolitan area and its adjacent nonurban areas. Long distance trucking establishments carry goods between metropolitan areas.

The Specialized Freight Trucking industry group includes a separate industry for Used Household and Office Goods Moving. The household and office goods movers are separated because of the substantial network of establishments that has developed to deal with local and long-distance moving and the associated storage. In this area, the same establishment provides both local and long-distance services, while other specialized freight establishments generally limit their services to either local or long-distance hauling.

4841 General Freight Trucking

This industry group comprises establishments primarily engaged in providing general freight trucking. General freight establishments handle a wide variety of commodities, generally palletized, and transported in a container or van trailer. The establishments of this industry group provide a combination of the following network activities: local pickup, local sorting and terminal operations, line-haul, destination sorting and terminal operations, and local delivery.

48411 General Freight Trucking, Local
See industry description for 484110 below.

US—United States industry only. CAN—United States and Canadian industries are comparable. MEX—United States and Mexican industries are comparable. Blank—Canadian, Mexican, and United States industries are comparable.

484110 General Freight Trucking, Local^{CAN}

This industry comprises establishments primarily engaged in providing local general freight trucking. General freight establishments handle a wide variety of commodities, generally palletized and transported in a container or van trailer. Local general freight trucking establishments usually provide trucking within a metropolitan area which may cross state lines. Generally the trips are same-day return.

Cross-References. Establishments primarily engaged in—

- Operating independent trucking terminals—are classified in Industry 488490, Other Support Activities for Road Transportation; and
- Providing general freight long—distance trucking including all North American international travel—are classified in Industry 48412, General Freight Trucking, Long-Distance.

48412 General Freight Trucking, Long-Distance

This industry comprises establishments primarily engaged in providing long-distance general freight trucking. General freight establishments handle a wide variety of commodities, generally palletized and transported in a container or van trailer. Long-distance general freight trucking establishments usually provide trucking between metropolitan areas which may cross North American country borders. Included in this industry are establishments operating as truckload (TL) or less than truckload (LTL) carriers.

Cross-References. Establishments primarily engaged in—

- Providing courier services—are classified in Industry 49211, Couriers;
- Providing warehousing services of general freight—are classified in Industry 49311, General Warehousing and Storage;
- Providing specialized freight trucking—are classified in Industry Group 4842, Specialized Freight Trucking;
- Operating independent trucking terminals—are classified in Industry 48849, Other Support Activities for Road Transportation; and
- Providing local general freight trucking services—are classified in Industry 48411, General Freight Trucking, Local.

484121 General Freight Trucking, Long-Distance, Truckload^{CAN}

This U.S. industry comprises establishments primarily engaged in providing long-distance general freight truckload (TL) trucking. These long-distance general

---

US—United States industry only. CAN—United States and Canadian industries are comparable. MEX—United States and Mexican industries are comparable. Blank—Canadian, Mexican, and United States industries are comparable.

freight truckload carrier establishments provide full truck movement of freight from origin to destination. The shipment of freight on a truck is characterized as a full single load not combined with other shipments.

Cross-References. Establishments primarily engaged in—

- Providing general freight long-distance, less than truckload trucking—are classified in U.S. Industry 484122, General Freight Trucking, Long-Distance, Less Than Truckload;

- Providing specialized freight trucking—are classified in Industry Group 4842, Specialized Freight Trucking;

- Operating independent trucking terminals—are classified in Industry 488490, Other Support Activities for Road Transportation; and

- Providing local general freight trucking services—are classified in Industry 484110, General Freight Trucking, Local.

484122 General Freight Trucking, Long-Distance, Less Than Truckload[CAN]

This U.S. industry comprises establishments primarily engaged in providing long-distance, general freight, less than truckload (LTL) trucking. LTL carriage is characterized as multiple shipments combined onto a single truck for multiple deliveries within a network. These establishments are generally characterized by the following network activities: local pickup, local sorting and terminal operations, line-haul, destination sorting and terminal operations, and local delivery.

Cross-References. Establishments primarily engaged in—

- Providing courier services—are classified in Industry 492110, Couriers;

- Providing warehousing services of general freight—are classified in Industry 493110, General Warehousing and Storage;

- Providing specialized freight trucking—are classified in Industry Group 4842, Specialized Freight Trucking;

- Operating independent trucking terminals—are classified in Industry 488490, Other Support Activities for Road Transportation;

- Providing general freight long-distance truckload trucking—are classified in U.S. Industry 484121, General Freight Trucking, Long-Distance, Truckload; and

- Providing local general freight trucking services—are classified in Industry 484110, General Freight Trucking, Local.

4842 Specialized Freight Trucking

This industry group comprises establishments primarily engaged in providing local or long-distance specialized freight trucking. The establishments of this industry are primarily engaged in the transportation of freight which, because of size, weight, shape, or other inherent characteristics, requires specialized equipment, such as flatbeds, tankers, or refrigerated trailers. This industry includes the transportation of used household, institutional, and commercial furniture and equipment.

48421 Used Household and Office Goods Moving
See industry description for 484210 below.

484210 Used Household and Office Goods Moving

This industry comprises establishments primarily engaged in providing local or long-distance trucking of used household, used institutional, or used commercial furniture and equipment. Incidental packing and storage activities are often provided by these establishments.

48422 Specialized Freight (except Used Goods) Trucking, Local
See industry description for 484220 below.

484220 Specialized Freight (except Used Goods) Trucking, Local[US]

This industry comprises establishments primarily engaged in providing local, specialized trucking. Local trucking establishments provide trucking within a metropolitan area that may cross state lines. Generally the trips are same-day return.

Illustrative Examples:

Local agricultural products trucking	Local dump trucking (e.g., gravel, sand,
Local boat hauling	top-soil)
Local bulk liquids trucking	Local livestock trucking

Cross-References. Establishments primarily engaged in—

- Providing long-distance specialized freight (except used goods) trucking including all North American international travel—are classified in Industry 48423, Specialized Freight (except Used Goods) Trucking, Long-Distance;

- Providing local general freight trucking—are classified in U.S. Industry 484110, General Freight Trucking, Local;

- Providing trucking of used household and office goods—are classified in Industry 484210, Used Household and Office Goods Moving; and
- Providing waste collection—are classified in Industry Group 5621, Waste Collection.

48423 Specialized Freight (except Used Goods) Trucking, Long-Distance

See industry description for 484230 below.

484230 Specialized Freight (except Used Goods) Trucking, Long-Distance[US]

This industry comprises establishments primarily engaged in providing long-distance specialized trucking. These establishments provide trucking between metropolitan areas that may cross North American country borders.

Illustrative Examples:

Long-distance automobile carrier trucking

Long-distance bulk liquid trucking

Long-distance hazardous material trucking

Long-distance refrigerated product trucking

Long-distance trucking of waste

Cross-References. Establishments primarily engaged in—

- Providing local specialized freight trucking (except used goods)—are classified in Industry 484220, Specialized Freight (except Used Goods) Trucking, Local;
- Providing long-distance general freight trucking including all North American international travel—are classified in Industry 48412, General Freight Trucking, Long-Distance;
- Providing trucking of used household and office goods—are classified in Industry 484210, Used Household and Office Goods Moving; and
- Collecting and/or hauling hazardous waste, nonhazardous waste, and/or recyclable materials within a local area—are classified in Industry 56211, Waste Collection.

485 Transit and Ground Passenger Transportation

Industries in the Transit and Ground Passenger Transportation subsector include a variety of passenger transportation activities, such as urban transit systems; chartered bus, school bus, and interurban bus transportation; and taxis. These activities are distinguished based primarily on such production process factors as vehicle types, routes, and schedules.

In this subsector, the principal splits identify scheduled transportation as separate from nonscheduled transportation. The scheduled transportation industry groups are Urban Transit Systems, Interurban and Rural Bus Transportation, and School and Employee Bus Transportation. The nonscheduled industry groups are the Charter Bus Industry and Taxi and Limousine Service. The Other Transit and Ground Passenger Transportation Industry group includes both scheduled and nonscheduled transportation.

Scenic and sightseeing ground transportation services are not included in this subsector but are included in Subsector 487, Scenic and Sightseeing Transportation. Sightseeing does not usually involve place-to-place transportation; the passenger's trip starts and ends at the same location.

4851 Urban Transit Systems

48511 Urban Transit Systems

This industry comprises establishments primarily engaged in operating local and suburban passenger transit systems over regular routes and on regular schedules within a metropolitan area and its adjacent nonurban areas. Such transportation systems involve the use of one or more modes of transport including light rail, commuter rail, subways, streetcars, as well as buses and other motor vehicles.

Cross-References. Establishments primarily engaged in—

- Providing scenic and sightseeing transportation—are classified in Industry 48711, Scenic and Sightseeing Transportation, Land;

- Providing support services to transit and ground transportation—are classified in Industry Group 4884, Support Activities for Road Transportation; and

- Providing interurban and rural bus transportation—are classified in Industry 48521, Interurban and Rural Bus Transportation.

485111 Mixed Mode Transit Systems[US]

This U.S. industry comprises establishments primarily engaged in operating local and suburban ground passenger transit systems using more than one mode of transport over regular routes and on regular schedules within a metropolitan area and its adjacent nonurban areas.

US—United States industry only. CAN—United States and Canadian industries are comparable. MEX—United States and Mexican industries are comparable. Blank—Canadian, Mexican, and United States industries are comparable.

Cross-References. Establishments primarily engaged in—

- Operating local and suburban passenger transit systems using only one mode of transportation—are classified according to the mode of transport; and

- Providing support services to transit and ground passenger transportation— are classified in Industry Group 4884, Support Activities for Road Transportation.

485112 Commuter Rail Systems^{US}

This U.S. industry comprises establishments primarily engaged in operating local and suburban commuter rail systems over regular routes and on a regular schedule within a metropolitan area and its adjacent nonurban areas. Commuter rail is usually characterized by reduced fares, multiple ride, and commutation tickets and mostly used by passengers during the morning and evening peak periods.

Cross-References. Establishments primarily engaged in—

- Operating local and suburban mass passenger transit systems using both commuter rail and another mode of transport—are classified in U.S. Industry 485111, Mixed Mode Transit Systems;

- Operating a subway system—are classified in U.S. Industry 485119, Other Urban Transit Systems; and

- Providing scenic and sightseeing transportation on land—are classified in Industry 487110, Scenic and Sightseeing Transportation, Land.

485113 Bus and Other Motor Vehicle Transit Systems^{US}

This U.S. industry comprises establishments primarily engaged in operating local and suburban passenger transportation systems using buses or other motor vehicles over regular routes and on regular schedules within a metropolitan area and its adjacent nonurban areas.

Cross-References. Establishments primarily engaged in—

- Operating local and suburban passenger transportation systems using both a bus or other motor vehicle and another mode of transport—are classified in U.S. Industry 485111, Mixed Mode Transit Systems;

- Providing interurban and rural bus transportation—are classified in Industry 485210, Interurban and Rural Bus Transportation; and

- Providing scenic and sightseeing transportation using buses or other motor vehicles—are classified in Industry 487110, Scenic and Sightseeing Transportation, Land.

US—United States industry only. CAN—United States and Canadian industries are comparable. MEX—United States and Mexican industries are comparable. Blank—Canadian, Mexican, and United States industries are comparable.

485119 Other Urban Transit Systems^{US}

This U.S. industry comprises establishments primarily engaged in operating local and suburban ground passenger transit systems (except mixed mode transit systems, commuter rail systems, and buses and other motor vehicles) over regular routes and on regular schedules within a metropolitan area and its adjacent nonurban areas.

Illustrative Examples:

Commuter cable car systems
(i.e., stand-alone)
Commuter tramway systems
(i.e., stand-alone)

Commuter trolley systems (i.e., stand-alone)
Light rail systems (i.e., stand-alone)
Monorail transit systems (i.e., stand-alone)

Cross-References. Establishment primarily engaged in—

- Operating local and suburban ground passenger transit systems using more than one mode of transport—are classified in U.S. Industry 485111, Mixed Mode Transit Systems;
- Providing local and suburban passenger transportation using commuter rail systems—are classified in U.S. Industry 485112, Commuter Rail Systems; and
- Operating local and suburban bus transit systems—are classified in U.S. Industry 485113, Bus and Other Motor Vehicle Transit Systems.

4852 Interurban and Rural Bus Transportation

48521 Interurban and Rural Bus Transportation
See industry description for 485210 below.

485210 Interurban and Rural Bus Transportation

This industry comprises establishments primarily engaged in providing bus passenger transportation over regular routes and on regular schedules, principally outside a single metropolitan area and its adjacent nonurban areas.

Cross-References. Establishments primarily engaged in—

- Providing scenic and sightseeing transportation using buses—are classified in Industry 487110, Scenic and Sightseeing Transportation, Land;
- Providing buses for charter—are classified in Industry 485510, Charter Bus Industry;

US—United States industry only. CAN—United States and Canadian industries are comparable. MEX—United States and Mexican industries are comparable. Blank—Canadian, Mexican, and United States industries are comparable.

- Operating local and suburban bus transit systems—are classified in U.S. Industry 485113, Bus and Other Motor Vehicle Transit Systems; and

- Operating independent bus terminals—are classified in Industry 488490, Other Support Activities for Road Transportation.

4853 Taxi and Limousine Service

48531 Taxi Service
See industry description for 485310 below.

485310 Taxi Service[CAN]

This industry comprises establishments primarily engaged in providing passenger transportation by automobile or van, not operated over regular routes and on regular schedules. Establishments of taxicab owner/operators, taxicab fleet operators, or taxicab organizations are included in this industry.

Cross-References. Establishments primarily engaged in—

- Providing special needs transportation services (except to and from school or work) for the infirm, elderly, or handicapped—are classified in U.S. Industry 485991, Special Needs Transportation;

- Providing limousine services—are classified in Industry 485320, Limousine Service; and

- Providing scheduled shuttle services between hotels, airports, or other destination points—are classified in U.S. Industry 485999, All Other Transit and Ground Passenger Transportation.

48532 Limousine Service
See industry description for 485320 below.

485320 Limousine Service

This industry comprises establishments primarily engaged in providing an array of specialty and luxury passenger transportation services via limousine or luxury sedans generally on a reserved basis. These establishments do not operate over regular routes and on regular schedules.

Cross-References. Establishments primarily engaged in—

- Providing taxi services—are classified in Industry 485310, Taxi Service; and

- Providing scheduled shuttle services between hotels, airports, or other destination points—are classified in U.S. Industry 485999, All Other Transit and Ground Passenger Transportation.

4854 School and Employee Bus Transportation

48541 School and Employee Bus Transportation
See industry description for 485410 below.

485410 School and Employee Bus Transportation

This industry comprises establishments primarily engaged in providing buses and other motor vehicles to transport pupils to and from school or employees to and from work.

Cross-References. Establishments primarily engaged in—

- Operating local and suburban bus transit systems—are classified in U.S. Industry, 485113 Bus and Other Motor Vehicle Transit Systems;
- Providing interurban and rural bus transportation—are classified in Industry 485210, Interurban and Rural Bus Transportation; and
- Providing buses for charter—are classified in Industry 485510, Charter Bus Industry.

4855 Charter Bus Industry

48551 Charter Bus Industry
See industry description for 485510 below.

485510 Charter Bus Industry

This industry comprises establishments primarily engaged in providing buses for charter. These establishments provide bus services to meet customers' road transportation needs and generally do not operate over fixed routes and on regular schedules.

Cross-References. Establishments primarily engaged in—

- Providing scenic and local sightseeing transportation using buses—are classified in Industry 487110, Scenic and Sightseeing Transportation, Land; and

- Providing interurban and rural bus transportation—are classified in Industry 485210, Interurban and Rural Bus Transportation.

4859 Other Transit and Ground Passenger Transportation

48599 Other Transit and Ground Passenger Transportation

This industry comprises establishments primarily engaged in providing other transit and ground passenger transportation (except urban transit systems, interurban and rural bus transportation, taxi services, school and employee bus transportation, charter bus services, and limousine services (except shuttle services)). Shuttle services (except employee bus) and special needs transportation services are included in this industry. Shuttle services establishments generally travel within a metropolitan area and its adjacent nonurban areas on regular routes, on regular schedules and provide services between hotels, airports, or other destination points. Special needs transportation establishments provide passenger transportation to the infirm, elderly, or handicapped. These establishments may use specially equipped vehicles to provide passenger transportation.

Cross-References. Establishments primarily engaged in—

- Providing school or employee bus transportation for the infirm, elderly, or handicapped—are classified in Industry 48541, School and Employee Bus Transportation;
- Providing ambulance services for emergency and medical purposes—are classified in Industry 62191, Ambulance Services;
- Operating urban transit systems—are classified in Industry Group 4851, Urban Transit Systems;
- Providing interurban and rural bus transportation—are classified in Industry 48521, Interurban and Rural Bus Transportation;
- Providing taxi services and/or limousine services (except shuttle services)—are classified in Industry Group 4853; Taxi and Limousine Service; and
- Providing buses for charter—are classified in Industry 48551, Charter Bus Industry.

485991 Special Needs Transportation[US]

This U.S. industry comprises establishments primarily engaged in providing special needs transportation (except to and from school or work) to the infirm, elderly, or handicapped. These establishments may use specially equipped vehicles to provide passenger transportation.

US—United States industry only. CAN—United States and Canadian industries are comparable. MEX—United States and Mexican industries are comparable. Blank—Canadian, Mexican, and United States industries are comparable.

Cross-References. Establishments primarily engaged in—

- Providing school or employee bus transportation for the infirm, elderly, or handicapped—are classified in Industry 485410, School and Employee Bus Transportation; and

- Providing ambulance services for emergency and medical purposes—are classified in Industry 62191, Ambulance Services.

485999 All Other Transit and Ground Passenger Transportation[US]

This U.S. industry comprises establishments primarily engaged in providing ground passenger transportation (except urban transit systems; interurban and rural bus transportation, taxi and/or limousine services (except shuttle services), school and employee bus transportation, charter bus services, and special needs transportation). Establishments primarily engaged in operating shuttle services and vanpools are included in this industry. Shuttle services establishments generally provide travel on regular routes and on regular schedules between hotels, airports, or other destination points.

Cross-References. Establishments primarily engaged in—

- Providing urban transit systems—are classified in Industry Group 4851, Urban Transit Systems;

- Providing interurban and rural bus transportation—are classified in Industry 485210, Interurban and Rural Bus Transportation;

- Providing taxi and/or limousine services (except shuttle services)—are classified in Industry Group 4853, Taxi and Limousine Service;

- Providing school and employee bus transportation (including for the infirm, elderly, or handicapped)—are classified in Industry 485410, School and Employee Bus Transportation;

- Providing buses for charter—are classified in Industry 485510, Charter Bus Industry;

- Providing special needs transportation (except to and from school or work) for the infirm, elderly, or handicapped—are classified in Industry 485991, Special Needs Transportation; and

- Providing ambulance services for emergency and medical purposes—are classified in Industry 621910, Ambulance Services.

486 Pipeline Transportation

Industries in the Pipeline Transportation subsector use transmission pipelines to transport products, such as crude oil, natural gas, refined petroleum products, and slurry. Industries are identified based on the products transported (i.e., pipeline transportation of crude oil, natural gas, refined petroleum products, and other products).

The Pipeline Transportation of Natural Gas industry includes the storage of natural gas because the storage is usually done by the pipeline establishment and because a pipeline is inherently a network in which all the nodes are interdependent.

4861 Pipeline Transportation of Crude Oil

48611 Pipeline Transportation of Crude Oil
See industry description for 486110 below.

486110 Pipeline Transportation of Crude Oil

This industry comprises establishments primarily engaged in the pipeline transportation of crude oil.

Cross-References. Establishments primarily engaged in—

- Providing the pipeline transportation of natural gas—are classified in Industry 486210, Pipeline Transportation of Natural Gas; and
- Providing the pipeline transportation of refined petroleum products—are classified in Industry 486910, Pipeline Transportation of Refined Petroleum Products.

4862 Pipeline Transportation of Natural Gas

48621 Pipeline Transportation of Natural Gas
See industry description for 486210 below.

486210 Pipeline Transportation of Natural Gas

This industry comprises establishments primarily engaged in the pipeline transportation of natural gas from processing plants to local distribution systems.

Cross-References.

Establishments primarily engaged in providing natural gas to the end consumer are classified in Industry 221210, Natural Gas Distribution.

US—United States industry only. CAN—United States and Canadian industries are comparable. MEX—United States and Mexican industries are comparable. Blank—Canadian, Mexican, and United States industries are comparable.

4869 Other Pipeline Transportation

This industry group comprises establishments primarily engaged in the pipeline transportation of products (except crude oil and natural gas).

48691 Pipeline Transportation of Refined Petroleum Products
See industry description for 486910 below.

486910 Pipeline Transportation of Refined Petroleum Products

This industry comprises establishments primarily engaged in the pipeline transportation of refined petroleum products.

48699 All Other Pipeline Transportation
See industry description for 486990 below.

486990 All Other Pipeline Transportation

This industry comprises establishments primarily engaged in the pipeline transportation of products except crude oil, natural gas, and refined petroleum products.

Cross-References. Establishments primarily engaged in—

- Providing pipeline transportation of crude oil—are classified in Industry 486110, Pipeline Transportation of Crude Oil;

- Providing pipeline transportation of natural gas—are classified in Industry 486210, Pipeline Transportation of Natural Gas;

- Providing pipeline transportation of refined petroleum products—are classified in Industry 486910, Pipeline Transportation of Refined Petroleum Products; and

- Providing pipeline transportation of water—are classified in Industry 221310, Water Supply and Irrigation Systems.

487 Scenic and Sightseeing Transportation

Industries in the Scenic and Sightseeing Transportation subsector utilize transportation equipment to provide recreation and entertainment. These activities have a production process distinct from passenger transportation carried out for the purpose of other types of for-hire transportation. This process does not emphasize efficient transportation; in fact, such activities often use obsolete vehicles, such as steam trains, to provide some extra ambience. The activity is local in nature, usually involving a same-day return to the point of departure.

The Scenic and Sightseeing Transportation subsector is separated into three industries based on the mode: land, water, and other.

Activities that are recreational in nature and involve participation by the customer,such as white-water rafting, are generally excluded from this subsector, unless they impose an impact on part of the transportation system. Charter boat fishing, for example, is included in the Scenic and Sightseeing Transportation, Water industry.

4871 Scenic and Sightseeing Transportation, Land

48711 Scenic and Sightseeing Transportation, Land
See industry description for 487110 below.

487110 Scenic and Sightseeing Transportation, Land

This industry comprises establishments primarily engaged in providing scenic and sightseeing transportation on land, such as sightseeing buses and trolleys, steam train excursions, and horse-drawn sightseeing rides. The services provided are usually local and involve same-day return to place of origin.

Cross-References. Establishments primarily engaged in—

- Operating aerial trams or aerial cable cars—are classified in Industry 487990, Scenic and Sightseeing Transportation, Other;
- Providing sporting services, such as pack trains—are classified in Industry 713990, All Other Amusement and Recreation Industries;
- Providing intercity and rural bus transportation—are classified in Industry 485210, Interurban and Rural Bus Transportation;
- Providing buses for charter—are classified in Industry 485510, Charter Bus Industry;
- Operating local and suburban passenger transit systems—are classified in Industry 48511, Urban Transit Systems; and
- Providing passenger travel arrangements and tours—are classified in Industry Group 5615, Travel Arrangement and Reservation Services.

4872 Scenic and Sightseeing Transportation, Water

48721 Scenic and Sightseeing Transportation, Water
See industry description for 487210 below.

487210 Scenic and Sightseeing Transportation, Water

This industry comprises establishments primarily engaged in providing scenic and sightseeing transportation on water. The services provided are usually local and involve same-day return to place of origin.

Illustrative Examples:

Airboat (i.e., swamp buggy) operation
Charter fishing boat services
Dinner cruises

Excursion boat operation
Harbor sightseeing tours

Cross-References. Establishments primarily engaged in—

- Providing recreation services, such as fishing guides, white-water rafting, parasailing, and water skiing—are classified in Industry 713990, All Other Amusement and Recreation Industries;
- Providing water taxi services—are classified in Industry 48321, Inland Water Transportation;
- Providing water transportation of passengers—are classified in Subsector 483, Water Transportation;
- Operating floating casinos (i.e., gambling cruises or river boat casinos)— are classified in Industry 713210, Casinos (except Casino Hotels); and
- Providing boat rental without operators—are classified in U.S. Industry 532292, Recreational Goods Rental.

4879 Scenic and Sightseeing Transportation, Other

48799 Scenic and Sightseeing Transportation, Other
See industry description for 487990 below.

487990 Scenic and Sightseeing Transportation, Other

This industry comprises establishments primarily engaged in providing scenic and sightseeing transportation (except on land and water). The services provided are usually local and involve same-day return to place of departure.

Illustrative Examples:

Aerial tramways, scenic and sightseeing operation
Aerial cablecars, scenic and sightseeing operation
Glider excursions

Helicopter rides, scenic and sightseeing operation
Hot air balloon rides, scenic and sightseeing operation

Cross-References. Establishments primarily engaged in—

- Providing recreational activities, such as hang gliding—are classified in Industry 713990, All Other Amusement and Recreation Industries; and
- Providing scheduled or nonscheduled air transportation of passengers or specialty flying services—are classified in Subsector 481, Air Transportation.

488 Support Activities for Transportation

Industries in the Support Activities for Transportation subsector provide services which support transportation. These services may be provided to transportation carrier establishments or to the general public. This subsector includes a wide array of establishments, including air traffic control services, marine cargo handling, and motor vehicle towing.

The Support Activities for Transportation subsector includes services to transportation but is separated by type of mode serviced. The Support Activities for Rail Transportation industry includes services to the rail industry (e.g., railroad switching and terminal establishments).

Ship repair and maintenance not done in a shipyard are included in Other Support Activities for Water Transportation. An example would be floating drydock services in a harbor.

Excluded from this subsector are establishments primarily engaged in providing factory conversion and overhaul of transportation equipment, which are classified in Subsector 336, Transportation Equipment Manufacturing. Also, establishments primarily engaged in providing rental and leasing of transportation equipment without operator are classified in Subsector 532, Rental and Leasing Services.

4881 Support Activities for Air Transportation

This industry group comprises establishments primarily engaged in providing services to the air transportation industry. These services include airport operation, servicing, repairing (except factory conversion and overhaul of aircraft), maintaining and storing aircraft, and ferrying aircraft.

48811 Airport Operations

This industry comprises establishments primarily engaged in (1) operating international, national, or civil airports or public flying fields or (2) supporting airport operations (except special food services contractors), such as rental of hangar space, air traffic control services, baggage handling services, and cargo handling services.

US—United States industry only. CAN—United States and Canadian industries are comparable. MEX—United States and Mexican industries are comparable. Blank—Canadian, Mexican, and United States industries are comparable.

Cross-References. Establishments primarily engaged in—

- Providing factory conversion, overhaul, and rebuilding of ai craft—are classified in Industry 33641, Aerospace Product and Parts Manufacturing;
- Wholesaling fuel at airports—are classified in Industry 424720, Petroleum and Petroleum Products Merchant Wholesalers (except Bulk Stations and Terminals);
- Providing airport janitorial services—are classified in Industry 56172, Janitorial Services; and
- Providing food services at airports on a contractual arrangement (i.e., food service contractors)—are classified in Industry 72231, Food Service Contractors.

488111 Air Traffic Control

This U.S. industry comprises establishments primarily engaged in providing air traffic control services to regulate the flow of air traffic.

488119 Other Airport Operations^{CAN}

This U.S. industry comprises establishments primarily engaged in (1) operating international, national, or civil airports, or public flying fields or (2) supporting airport operations, such as rental of hangar space, and providing baggage handling and/or cargo handling services.

Cross-References. Establishments primarily engaged in—

- Providing air traffic control services—are classified in U.S. Industry 488111, Air Traffic Control;
- Providing factory conversion, overhaul, and rebuilding of aircraft—are classified in Industry 33641, Aerospace Product and Parts Manufacturing;
- Wholesaling fuel at airports—are classified in Industry 424720, Petroleum and Petroleum Products Merchant Wholesalers (except Bulk Stations and Terminals);
- Providing airport janitorial services—are classified in Industry 561720, Janitorial Services; and
- Providing food services at airports on a contractual arrangement—are classified in Industry 722310, Food Service Contractors.

48819 Other Support Activities for Air Transportation
See industry description for 488190 below.

488190 Other Support Activities for Air Transportation

This industry comprises establishments primarily engaged in providing specialized services for air transportation (except air traffic control and other airport operations).

Illustrative Examples:

Aircraft services

Aircraft maintenance and repair services
(except factory conversions, overhauls,
rebuilding

Aircraft testing services

Cross-References. Establishments primarily engaged in—

- Wholesaling fuel at airports—are classified in Industry 424720, Petroleum and Petroleum Products Merchant Wholesalers (except Bulk Stations and Terminals);
- Providing aircraft janitorial services—are classified in Industry 561720, Janitorial Services;
- Providing air traffic control services—are classified in U.S. Industry 488111, Air Traffic Control;
- Providing airport operations (except air traffic control)—are classified in U.S. Industry 488119, Other Airport Operations;
- Providing factory conversion, overhaul, and rebuilding of aircraft—are classified in Industry 33641, Aerospace Product and Parts Manufacturing; and
- Providing food services to airlines on a contractual arrangement—are classified in Industry 722310, Food Service Contractors.

4882 Support Activities for Rail Transportation

48821 Support Activities for Rail Transportation
See industry description for 488210 below.

488210 Support Activities for Rail Transportation

This industry comprises establishments primarily engaged in providing specialized services for railroad transportation including servicing, routine repairing (except factory conversion, overhaul or rebuilding of rolling stock), and maintaining rail cars; loading and unloading rail cars; and operating independent terminals.

Cross-References. Establishments primarily engaged in—

- Providing railroad car rental—are classified in U.S. Industry 532411, Commercial Air, Rail, and Water Transportation Equipment Rental and Leasing;
- Factory conversion, overhaul, or rebuilding of railroad rolling stock—are classified in Industry 336510, Railroad Rolling Stock Manufacturing;
- Providing rail car janitorial services—are classified in Industry 561720, Janitorial Services; and
- Providing dredging services—are classified in Industry 237990, Other Heavy and Civil Engineering Construction.

4883 Support Activities for Water Transportation

48831 Port and Harbor Operations
See industry description for 488310 below.

488310 Port and Harbor Operations

This industry comprises establishments primarily engaged in operating ports, harbors (including docking and pier facilities), or canals.

Cross-References. Establishments primarily engaged in—

- Providing stevedoring and other marine cargo handling services—are classified in Industry 488320, Marine Cargo Handling;
- Providing navigational services to shipping—are classified in Industry 488330, Navigational Services to Shipping; and
- Operating docking and/or storage facilities and commonly known as marinas—are classified in Industry 713930, Marinas.

48832 Marine Cargo Handling
See industry description for 488320 below.

488320 Marine Cargo Handling

This industry comprises establishments primarily engaged in providing stevedoring and other marine cargo handling services (except warehousing).

Cross-References. Establishments primarily engaged in—

- Preparing freight for transportation—are classified in U.S. Industry 488991, Packing and Crating;

US—United States industry only. CAN—United States and Canadian industries are comparable. MEX—United States and Mexican industries are comparable. Blank—Canadian, Mexican, and United States industries are comparable.

- Operating general merchandise, refrigerated, or other warehousing and storage facilities—are classified in Subsector 493, Warehousing and Storage; and

- Operating docking and pier facilities—are classified in Industry 488310, Port and Harbor Operations.

48833 Navigational Services to Shipping
See industry description for 488330 below.

488330 Navigational Services to Shipping^{MEX}

This industry comprises establishments primarily engaged in providing navigational services to shipping. Marine salvage establishments are included in this industry.

Illustrative Examples:

Docking and undocking marine vessel services

Marine vessel traffic reporting services

Piloting services, water transportation

Tugboat services, harbor operation

Cross-References. Establishments primarily engaged in—

- Providing water transportation of barges (except coastal or Great Lakes barge transportation services)—are classified in U.S. Industry 483211, Inland Water Freight Transportation; and

- Providing coastal and/or Great Lakes barge transportation services—are classified in U.S. Industry 483113, Coastal and Great Lakes Freight Transportation.

48839 Other Support Activities for Water Transportation
See industry description for 488390 below.

488390 Other Support Activities for Water Transportation

This industry comprises establishments primarily engaged in providing services to water transportation (except port and harbor operations; marine cargo handling services; and navigational services to shipping).

Illustrative Examples:

Floating drydocks (i.e., maintenance and routine repairs for ships)

Marine cargo checkers and surveyors

Ship scaling services

Cross-References. Establishments primarily engaged in—

- Ship painting—are classified in Industry 238320, Painting and Wall Covering Contractors;
- Providing ship janitorial services—are classified in Industry 561720, Janitorial Services;
- Operating port, harbor, or canal facilities—are classified in Industry 488310, Port and Harbor Operations;
- Providing stevedoring and other marine cargo handling services—are classified in Industry 488320, Marine Cargo Handling;
- Providing navigational services to shipping—are classified in Industry 488330, Navigational Services to Shipping; and
- Providing ship overhauling or repairs in a shipyard—are classified in U.S. Industry 336611, Ship Building and Repairing.

4884 Support Activities for Road Transportation

48841 Motor Vehicle Towing
See industry description for 488410 below.

488410 Motor Vehicle Towing

This industry comprises establishments primarily engaged in towing light or heavy motor vehicles, both local and long distance. These establishments may provide incidental services, such as storage and emergency road repair services.

Cross-References. Establishments primarily engaged in—

- Operating gasoline stations—are classified in Industry Group 4471, Gasoline Stations;
- Providing automotive repair and maintenance—are classified in Industry Group 8111, Automotive Repair and Maintenance; and
- Both retailing automotive parts and accessories, and repairing automobiles and known as automotive supply stores—are classified in Industry 441310, Automotive Parts and Accessories Stores.

48849 Other Support Activities for Road Transportation
See industry description for 488490 below.

488490 Other Support Activities for Road Transportation^{CAN}

This industry comprises establishments primarily engaged in providing services (except motor vehicle towing) to road network users.

Illustrative Examples:

Bridge, tunnel, and highway operations
Driving services (e.g., automobile, truck delivery)

Pilot car services (i.e., wide load warning services)
Truck or weighing station operations

Cross-References. Establishments primarily engaged in—

- Providing automotive repair and maintenance—are classified in Industry Group 8111, Automotive Repair and Maintenance;
- Providing towing services to motor vehicles—are classified in Industry 488410, Motor Vehicle Towing;
- Providing a network for busing in combination with providing terminal services—are classified in Industry 485210, Interurban and Rural Bus Transportation; and
- Providing a network for trucking in combination with providing terminal services—are classified in Subsector 484, Truck Transportation.

4885 Freight Transportation Arrangement

48851 Freight Transportation Arrangement

See industry description for 488510 below.

488510 Freight Transportation Arrangement^{US}

This industry comprises establishments primarily engaged in arranging transportation of freight between shippers and carriers. These establishments are usually known as freight forwarders, marine shipping agents, or customs brokers and offer a combination of services spanning transportation modes.

Cross-References.

Establishments primarily engaged in tariff and freight rate consulting services are classified in U.S. Industry 541614, Process, Physical Distribution, and Logistics Consulting Services.

US—United States industry only. CAN—United States and Canadian industries are comparable. MEX—United States and Mexican industries are comparable. Blank—Canadian, Mexican, and United States industrie· are comparable.

4889 Other Support Activities for Transportation

48899 Other Support Activities for Transportation

This industry comprises establishments primarily engaged in providing support activities to transportation (except for air transportation; rail transportation; water transportation; road transportation; and freight transportation arrangement).

Illustrative Examples:

Arrangement of vanpools or carpools
Independent pipeline terminal facilities
Stockyards (i.e., not for fattening or selling livestock)

Cross-References. Establishments primarily engaged in—

- Providing support activities for air transportation—are classified in Industry Group 4881, Support Activities for Air Transportation;
- Providing support activities for rail transportation—are classified in Industry Group 4882, Support Activities for Rail Transportation;
- Providing support activities for water transportation—are classified in Industry Group 4883, Support Activities for Water Transportation;
- Providing support activities for road transportation—are classified in Industry Group 4884, Support Activities for Road Transportation;
- Arranging transportation of freight between shippers and carriers—are classified in Industry 48851, Freight Transportation Arrangement;
- Providing tariff and freight rate consulting services—are classified in Industry 54161, Management Consulting Services;
- Operating stockyards for fattening livestock—are classified in Subsector 112, Animal Production; and
- Providing packaging and labeling services—are classified in Industry 56191, Packaging and Labeling Services.

488991 Packing and Crating[US]

This U.S. industry comprises establishments primarily engaged in packing, crating, and otherwise preparing goods for transportation.

Cross-References.

Establishments primarily engaged in providing packaging and labeling services are classified in Industry 561910, Packaging and Labeling Services.

US—United States industry only. CAN—United States and Canadian industries are comparable. MEX—United States and Mexican industries are comparable. Blank—Canadian, Mexican, and United States industries are comparable.

488999   All Other Support Activities for Transportation^{US}

This U.S. industry comprises establishments primarily engaged in providing support activities to transportation (except for air transportation; rail transportation; water transportation; road transportation; freight transportation arrangement; and packing and crating).

Illustrative Examples:

Arrangement of vanpools or carpools	Stockyards (i.e., not for fattening or
Independent pipeline terminal facilities	selling livestock)

Cross-References. Establishments primarily engaged in—

- Operating stockyards for fattening livestock—are classified in Subsector 112, Animal Production;
- Providing tariff and freight rate consulting services—are classified in U.S. Industry 541614, Process, Physical Distribution, and Logistics Consulting Services;
- Providing packing and crating services for transportation—are classified in U.S. Industry 488991, Packing and Crating;
- Providing support activities for air transportation—are classified in Industry Group 4881, Support Activities for Air Transportation;
- Providing support activities for rail transportation—are classified in Industry 488210, Support Activities for Rail Transportation;
- Providing support activities for water transportation—are classified in Industry Group 4883, Support Activities for Water Transportation;
- Providing support activities for road transportation—are classified in Industry Group 4884, Support Activities for Road Transportation; and
- Arranging transportation of freight between shippers and carriers—are classified in Industry 488510, Freight Transportation Arrangement.

491   Postal Service

The Postal Service subsector includes the activities of the National Post Office and its subcontractors in delivering letters and small parcels, normally without pick-up at the sender's location. These articles can be described as those that can be handled by one person without using special equipment. This allows the collection, pick-up, and delivery operations to be done with limited labor costs and minimal equipment. Sorting and transportation activities, where necessary, are generally mechanized. The restriction to small parcels distinguishes these establishments from those in the transportation industries.

US—United States industry only. CAN—United States and Canadian industries are comparable. MEX—United States and Mexican industries are comparable. Blank—Canadian, Mexican, and United States industries are comparable.

The traditional activity of the National Postal Service is described in this subsector. Subcontractors include rural Post Offices on contract to the Postal Service.

Bulk transportation of mail on contract to the Postal Service is not included here, because it is usually done by transportation establishments that carry other customers' cargo as well.

4911 Postal Service

49111 Postal Service
See industry description for 491110 below.

491110 Postal Service

This industry comprises establishments primarily engaged in operating the National Postal Service. Establishments primarily engaged in performing one or more postal services, such as sorting, routing, and/or delivery, on a contract basis (except the bulk transportation of mail) are included in this industry.

Cross-References. Establishments primarily engaged in—

- Providing bulk transportation of mail on a contract basis to and from postal service establishments—are classified in Industry Group 4841, General Freight Trucking;
- Providing courier services—are classified in Industry 492110, Couriers;
- Providing mailbox services along with other business services—are classified in U.S. Industry 561431, Private Mail Centers; and
- Providing local messenger and delivery services—are classified in Industry 492210, Local Messengers and Local Delivery.

492 Couriers and Messengers

Industries in the Couriers and Messengers subsector provide intercity and/or local delivery of parcels. These articles can be described as those that may be handled by one person without using special equipment. This allows the collection, pick-up, and delivery operations to be done with limited labor costs and minimal equipment. Sorting and transportation activities, where necessary, are generally mechanized. The restriction to small parcels partly distinguishes these establishments from those in the transportation industries. The complete network of courier services establishments also distinguishes these transportation services from local messenger and delivery establishments in this subsector. This includes the establishments that perform intercity transportation as well as establishments that, under contract to them, perform local pick-up and delivery. Messengers, which usually deliver within a metropolitan or single urban area, may use bicycle, foot, small truck, or van.

4921 Couriers

49211 Couriers
See industry description for 492110 below.

492110 Couriers

This industry comprises establishments primarily engaged in providing air, surface, or combined courier delivery services of parcels generally between metropolitan areas or urban centers. The establishments of this industry form a network including courier local pick-up and delivery to serve their customers' needs.

Cross-References. Establishments primarily engaged in—

- Providing messenger and delivery services within a metropolitan area or within an urban center—are classified in Industry 492210, Local Messengers and Local Delivery; and
- Providing the truck transportation of palletized general freight—are classified in Industry Group 4841, General Freight Trucking.

4922 Local Messengers and Local Delivery

49221 Local Messengers and Local Delivery
See industry description for 492210 below.

492210 Local Messengers and Local Delivery

This industry comprises establishments primarily engaged in providing local messenger and delivery services of small items within a single metropolitan area or within an urban center. These establishments generally provide point-to-point pickup and delivery and do not operate as part of an intercity courier network.

Illustrative Examples:

Alcoholic beverages delivery services
Grocery delivery services (i.e.,
  independent service from grocery store)
Letters, documents, or small parcel local
  delivery services

Restaurant meals delivery services (i.e.,
independent service from restaurant)

US—United States industry only. CAN—United States and Canadian industries are comparable. MEX—United States and Mexican industries are comparable. Blank—Canadian, Mexican, and United States industries are comparable.

Cross-References. Establishments primarily engaged in—

- Providing local letter and parcel delivery services as part of an intercity courier network—are classified in Industry 492110, Couriers;
- Operating the National Postal Service or providing postal services on a contract basis (except the bulk transportation of mail)—are classified in Industry 491110, Postal Service; and
- Providing the bulk transportation of mail on a contract basis to and from Postal Service establishments—are classified in Industry Group 4841, General Freight Trucking.

493 Warehousing and Storage

Industries in the Warehousing and Storage subsector are primarily engaged in operating warehousing and storage facilities for general merchandise, refrigerated goods, and other warehouse products. These establishments provide facilities to store goods. They do not sell the goods they handle. These establishments take responsibility for storing the goods and keeping them secure. They may also provide a range of services, often referred to as logistics services, related to the distribution of goods. Logistics services can include labeling, breaking bulk, inventory control and management, light assembly, order entry and fulfillment, packaging, pick and pack, price marking and ticketing, and transportation arrangement. However, establishments in this industry group always provide warehousing or storage services in addition to any logistic services. Furthermore, the warehousing or storage of goods must be more than incidental to the performance of services, such as price marking.

Bonded warehousing and storage services and warehouses located in free trade zones are included in the industries of this subsector.

4931 Warehousing and Storage

49311 General Warehousing and Storage
See industry description for 493110 below.

493110 General Warehousing and Storage[CAN]

This industry comprises establishments primarily engaged in operating merchandise warehousing and storage facilities. These establishments generally handle goods in containers, such as boxes, barrels, and/or drums, using equipment, such as forklifts, pallets, and racks. They are not specialized in handling bulk products of any particular type, size, or quantity of goods or products.

US—United States industry only. CAN—United States and Canadian industries are comparable. MEX—United States and Mexican industries are comparable. Blank—Canadian, Mexican, and United States industries are comparable.

Cross-References. Establishments primarily engaged in—

- Renting or leasing space for self storage—are classified in Industry 531130, Lessors of Miniwarehouses and Self-Storage Units; and

- Selling in combination with handling and/or distributing goods to other wholesale or retail establishments—are classified in Sector 42, Wholesale Trade.

49312 Refrigerated Warehousing and Storage
See industry description for 493120 below.

493120 Refrigerated Warehousing and Storage

This industry comprises establishments primarily engaged in operating refrigerated warehousing and storage facilities. Establishments primarily engaged in the storage of furs for the trade are included in this industry. The services provided by these establishments include blast freezing, tempering, and modified atmosphere storage services.

Cross-References.

Establishments primarily engaged in storing furs (except for the trade) and garments are classified in Industry 812320, Drycleaning and Laundry Services (except Coin-Operated).

49313 Farm Product Warehousing and Storage
See industry description for 493130 below.

493130 Farm Product Warehousing and Storage

This industry comprises establishments primarily engaged in operating bulk farm product warehousing and storage facilities (except refrigerated). Grain elevators primarily engaged in storage are included in this industry.

Cross-References. Establishments primarily engaged in—

- Operating refrigerated warehousing and storage facilities—are classified in Industry 493120, Refrigerated Warehousing and Storage; and

- Storing grains and field beans (i.e., grain elevators) as an incidental activity to sales—are classified in Industry 424510, Grain and Field Bean Merchant Wholesalers.

US—United States industry only. CAN—United States and Canadian industries are comparable. MEX—United States and Mexican industries are comparable. Blank—Canadian, Mexican, and United States industries are comparable.

49319 Other Warehousing and Storage
See industry description for 493190 below.

493190 Other Warehousing and Storage

This industry comprises establishments primarily engaged in operating warehousing and storage facilities (except general merchandise, refrigerated, and farm product warehousing and storage).

Illustrative Examples:

Bulk petroleum storage
Lumber storage terminals

Whiskey warehousing

Cross-References. Establishments primarily engaged in—

- Renting or leasing space for self storage—are classified in Industry 531130, Lessors of Miniwarehouses and Self-Storage Units;

- Storing hazardous materials for treatment and disposal—are classified in U.S. Industry 562211, Hazardous Waste Treatment and Disposal;

- Operating general warehousing and storage facilities—are classified in Industry 493110, General Warehousing and Storage;

- Operating refrigerated warehousing and storage facilities—are classified in Industry 493120, Refrigerated Warehousing and Storage; and

- Operating farm product warehousing and storage facilities—are classified in Industry 493130, Farm Product Warehousing and Storage.

3. The value of these products to the consumer lies in their informational, educational, cultural, or entertainment content, not in the format in which they are distributed. Most of these products are protected from unlawful reproduction by copyright laws.

4. The intangible property aspect of information and cultural products makes the processes involved in their production and distribution very different from goods and services. Only those possessing the rights to these works are authorized to reproduce, alter, improve, and distribute them. Acquiring and using these rights often involves significant costs. In addition, technology is revolutionizing the distribution of these products. It is possible to distribute them in a physical form, via broadcast, or on-line.

5. Distributors of information and cultural products can easily add value to the products they distribute. For instance, broadcasters add advertising not contained in the original product. This capacity means that unlike traditional distributors, they derive revenue not from sale of the distributed product to the final consumer, but from those who pay for the privilege of adding information to the original product. Similarly, a directory and mailing list publisher can acquire the rights to thousands of previously published newspaper and periodical articles and add new value by providing search and software and organizing the information in a way that facilitates research and retrieval. These products often command a much higher price than the original information.

The distribution modes for information commodities may either eliminate the necessity for traditional manufacture, or reverse the conventional order of manufacture-distribute: A newspaper distributed on-line, for example, can be printed locally or by the final consumer. Similarly, it is anticipated that packaged software, which today is mainly bought through the traditional retail channels, will soon be available mainly on-line. The NAICS Information sector is designed to make such economic changes transparent as they occur, or to facilitate designing surveys that will monitor the new phenomena and provide data to analyze the changes.

Many of the industries in the NAICS Information sector are engaged in producing products protected by copyright law, or in distributing them (other than distribution by traditional wholesale and retail methods). Examples are traditional publishing industries, software and directory and mailing list publishing industries, and film and sound industries. Broadcasting and telecommunications industries and information providers and processors are also included in the Information sector, because their technologies are so closely linked to other industries in the Information sector.

511 Publishing Industries (except Internet)

Industries in the Publishing Industries (except Internet) subsector group establishments engaged in the publishing of newspapers, magazines, other periodicals, and books, as well as directory and mailing list and software publishing. In general, these establishments, which are known as publishers, issue copies of works for which they usually possess copyright. Works may be in one or more formats including traditional print form, CD-ROM, or proprietary electronic networks. Publishers may publish works originally created by others for which they have obtained the rights and/or works that they have created in-house. Software publishing is included here because the activity, creation of a copyrighted product and bringing it to market, is equivalent to the creation process for other types of intellectual products.

In NAICS, publishing—the reporting, writing, editing, and other processes that are required to create an edition of a newspaper—is treated as a major economic activity in its own right, rather than as a subsidiary activity to a manufacturing activity, printing. Thus, publishing is classified in the Information sector; whereas, printing remains in the NAICS Manufacturing sector. In part, the NAICS classification reflects the fact that publishing increasingly takes place in establishments that are physically separate from the associated printing establishments. More crucially, the NAICS classification of book and newspaper publishing is intended to portray their roles in a modern economy, in which they do not resemble manufacturing activities.

Music publishers are not included in the Publishing Industries (except Internet) subsector, but are included in the Motion Picture and Sound Recording Industries subsector. Reproduction of prepackaged software is treated in NAICS as a manufacturing activity; on-line distribution of software products is in the Information sector, and custom design of software to client specifications is included in the Professional, Scientific, and Technical Services sector. These distinctions arise because of the different ways that software is created, reproduced, and distributed.

The Publishing Industries (except Internet) subsector does not include establishments that publish exclusively on the Internet. Establishments publishing exclusively on the Internet are included in Subsector 516, Internet Publishing and Broadcasting. The Publishing Industries (except Internet) subsector also excludes products, such as manifold business forms. Information is not the essential component of these items. Establishments producing these items are included in Subsector 323, Printing and Related Support Activities.

5111 Newspaper, Periodical, Book, and Directory Publishers

This industry group comprises establishments primarily engaged in publishing newspapers, magazines, other periodicals, books, directories and mailing lists, and other works, such as calendars, greeting cards, and maps. These works are characterized by the intellectual creativity required in their development and are usually protected by copyright. Publishers distribute or arrange for the distribution of these works.

US—United States industry only. CAN—United States and Canadian industries are comparable. MEX—United States and Mexican industries are comparable. Blank—Canadian, Mexican, and United States industries are comparable.

Publishing establishments may create the works in-house, contract for, purchase, or compile works that were originally created by others. These works may be published in one or more formats, such as print and/or electronic form, including proprietary electronic networks. Establishments in this industry may print, reproduce, or offer direct access to the works themselves or may arrange with others to carry out such functions.

Establishments that both print and publish may fill excess capacity with commercial or job printing. However, the publishing activity is still considered to be the primary activity of these establishments.

51111 Newspaper Publishers

See industry description for 511110 below.

511110 Newspaper Publishers^{CAN}

This industry comprises establishments known as newspaper publishers. Establishments in this industry carry out operations necessary for producing and distributing newspapers, including gathering news; writing news columns, feature stories, and editorials; and selling and preparing advertisements. These establishments may publish newspapers in print or electronic form.

Cross-References.

- Establishments publishing newspapers exclusively on the Internet are classified in Industry 516110, Internet Publishing and Broadcasting;

- Establishments primarily engaged in printing newspapers without publishing are classified in Industry 32311, Printing;

- Establishments, such as trade associations, schools and universities, and social welfare organizations that publish newsletters for distribution to their membership, but that are not commonly known as newspaper publishers, are classified according to their primary activity designation;

- Establishments primarily engaged in supplying the news media with information, such as news, reports, and pictures, are classified in Industry 519110, News Syndicates; and

- Establishments of independent representatives primarily engaged in selling advertising space are classified in Industry 541840, Media Representatives.

51112 Periodical Publishers

See industry description for 511120 below.

US—United States industry only. CAN—United States and Canadian industries are comparable. MEX—United States and Mexican industries are comparable. Blank—Canadian, Mexican, and United States industries are comparable.

511120 Periodical Publishers^{CAN}

This industry comprises establishments known either as magazine publishers or periodical publishers. These establishments carry out the operations necessary for producing and distributing magazines and other periodicals, such as gathering, writing, and editing articles, and selling and preparing advertisements. These establishments may publish magazines and other periodicals in print or electronic form.

Illustrative Examples:

Comic book publishers (except Internet)
Magazine publishers (except Internet)
Newsletter publishers (except Internet)
Radio and television guide publishers
  (except Internet)
Scholarly journal publishers (except
  Internet)
Trade journal publishers (except Internet)

Cross-References.

- Establishments publishing periodicals exclusively on the Internet are classified in Industry 516110, Internet Publishing and Broadcasting;

- Establishments primarily engaged in printing periodicals without publishing are classified in Industry 32311, Printing;

- Establishments, such as trade associations, schools and universities, and social welfare organizations, that publish magazines and periodicals for distribution to their membership, but that are not commonly known as periodical publishers, are classified according to their primary activity designation;

- Establishments primarily engaged in publishing directories and mailing lists are classified in Industry 511140, Directory and Mailing List Publishers; and

- Establishments of independent representatives primarily engaged in selling advertising space are classified in Industry 541840, Media Representatives.

51113 Book Publishers
See industry description for 511130 below.

511130 Book Publishers^{CAN}

This industry comprises establishments known as book publishers. Establishments in this industry carry out design, editing, and marketing activities necessary for producing and distributing books. These establishments may publish books in print, electronic, or audio form.

US—United States industry only. CAN—United States and Canadian industries are comparable. MEX—United States and Mexican industries are comparable. Blank—Canadian, Mexican, and United States industries are comparable.

Illustrative Examples:

Atlas publishers (except Internet)	School textbook publishers (except
Book publishers (except Internet)	Internet)
Encyclopedia publishers (except Internet)	Technical manual publishers (except
Map publishers (except Internet)	Internet)
Religious book publishers (except	Travel guide book publishers (except
Internet)	Internet)

Cross-References.

- Establishments publishing books on the Internet exclusively are classified in Industry 516110, Internet Publishing and Broadcasting;

- Establishments primarily engaged in printing books without publishing are classified in Industry 32311, Printing;

- Establishments known as music publishers are classified in Industry 512230, Music Publishers;

- Establishments, such as trade associations, schools and universities, and social welfare organizations, that publish books for distribution to their membership, that are not commonly known as book publishers, are classified according to their primary activity designation; and

- Book clubs primarily engaged in direct sales activities without publishing are classified in Industry 454390, Other Direct Selling Establishments.

51114 Directory and Mailing List Publishers

See industry description for 511140 below.

511140 Directory and Mailing List Publishers^{CAN}

This industry comprises establishments primarily engaged in publishing directories, mailing lists, and collections or compilations of fact. The products are typically protected in their selection, arrangement and/or presentation. Examples are lists of mailing addresses, telephone directories, directories of businesses, collections or compilations of proprietary drugs or legal case results, compilations of public records, etc. These establishments may publish directories and mailing lists in print or electronic form.

Illustrative Examples:

Business directory publishers (except	Mailing list publishers (except Internet)
Internet)	Telephone directory publishers (except
Directory publishers (except Internet)	Internet)

Cross-References. Establishments primarily engaged in—

- Developing and publishing, exclusively on the Internet, collections or compilations of creative works or facts—are classified in Industry 516110, Internet Publishing and Broadcasting;

- Compiling mailing lists in conjunction with providing direct mail advertising services—are classified in Industry 541860, Direct Mail Advertising;

- Printing without publishing directories and mailing lists—are classified in Industry 32311, Printing;

- Operating Web search portals—are classified in U.S. Industry 518112, Web Search Portals;

- Publishing computer software—are classified in Industry 511210, Software Publishers;

- Creating and publishing encyclopedias and similar collections of creative works in print and/or electronic media—are classified in Industry 511130, Book Publishers; and

- Creating and publishing collections of creative works that are periodically updated—are classified in Industry 511120, Periodical Publishers.

51119 Other Publishers

This industry comprises establishments known as publishers (except newspaper, magazine, book, directory, mailing list, and music publishers). These establishments may publish works in print or electronic form.

Illustrative Examples:

Art print publishers (except Internet)
Calendar publishers (except Internet)

Greeting card publishers (except Internet)

Cross-References.

- Establishments publishing exclusively on the Internet are classified in Industry 51611, Internet Publishing and Broadcasting;

- Establishments known as newspaper publishers are classified in Industry 51111, Newspaper Publishers;

- Establishments known as magazine and other periodical publishers are classified in Industry 51112, Periodical Publishers;

- Establishments known as book publishers are classified in Industry 51113, Book Publishers;

- Establishments primarily engaged in publishing directories and mailing lists are classified in Industry 51114, Directory and Mailing List Publishers;

- Establishments known as music publishers are classified in Industry 51223, Music Publishers; and
- Establishments primarily engaged in manufacturing manifold business forms are classified in Industry 32311, Printing.

511191 Greeting Card Publishers[US]

This U.S. industry comprises establishments primarily engaged in publishing greeting cards.

Cross-References. Establishments primarily engaged in—

- Publishing greeting cards exclusively on the Internet—are classified in Industry 516110, Internet Publishing and Broadcasting; and
- Printing greeting cards without publishing—are classified in Industry 32311, Printing.

511199 All Other Publishers[US]

This U.S. industry comprises establishments generally known as publishers (except newspaper, magazine, book, directory, database, music, and greeting card publishers). These establishments may publish works in print or electronic form.

Illustrative Examples:

Art print publishers (except Internet)   Calendar publishers (except Internet)

Cross-References.

- Establishments publishing exclusively on the Internet are classified in Industry 516110, Internet Publishing and Broadcasting;
- Establishments known as newspaper publishers are classified in Industry 511110, Newspaper Publishers;
- Establishments known as magazine or other periodical publishers are classified in Industry 511120, Periodical Publishers;
- Establishments known as book publishers are classified in Industry 511130, Book Publishers;
- Establishments primarily engaged in publishing directories and mailing lists are classified in Industry 511140, Directory and Mailing List Publishers;
- Establishments primarily engaged in greeting card publishing are classified in U.S. Industry 511191, Greeting Card Publishers;

- Establishments known as music publishers are classified in Industry 512230, Music Publishers;

- Establishments primarily engaged in manufacturing manifold business forms are classified in U.S. Industry 323116, Manifold Business Forms Printing; and

- Establishments primarily engaged in manufacturing day schedulers are classified in U.S. Industry 323118, Blankbooks, Looseleaf Binders, and Devices Manufacturing.

5112 Software Publishers

51121 Software Publishers
See industry description for 511210 below.

511210 Software Publishers^{CAN}

This industry comprises establishments primarily engaged in computer software publishing or publishing and reproduction. Establishments in this industry carry out operations necessary for producing and distributing computer software, such as designing, providing documentation, assisting in installation, and providing support services to software purchasers. These establishments may design, develop, and publish, or publish only.

Cross-References. Establishments primarily engaged in—

- Reselling packaged software—are classified in Sector 42, Wholesale Trade or Sector 44-45, Retail Trade;

- Providing access to software for clients from a central host site—are classified in Industry 518210, Data Processing, Hosting, and Related Services;

- Designing software to meet the needs of specific users—are classified in U.S. Industry 541511, Custom Computer Programming Services; and

- Mass duplication of software—are classified in U.S. Industry 334611, Software Reproducing.

512 Motion Picture and Sound Recording Industries

Industries in the Motion Picture and Sound Recording Industries subsector group establishments involved in the production and distribution of motion pictures and sound recordings. While producers and distributors of motion pictures and sound recordings issue works for sale as traditional publishers do, the processes are

---

sufficiently different to warrant placing establishments engaged in these activities in a separate subsector. Production is typically a complex process that involves several distinct types of establishments that are engaged in activities, such as contracting with performers, creating the film or sound content, and providing technical postproduction services. Film distribution is often to exhibitors, such as theaters and broadcasters, rather than through the wholesale and retail distribution chain. When the product is in a mass-produced form, NAICS treats production and distribution as the major economic activity as it does in the Publishing Industries subsector, rather than as a subsidiary activity to the manufacture of such products.

This subsector does not include establishments primarily engaged in the wholesale distribution of videocassettes and sound recordings, such as compact discs and audio tapes; these establishments are included in the Wholesale Trade sector. Reproduction of videocassettes and sound recordings that is carried out separately from establishments engaged in production and distribution is treated in NAICS as a manufacturing activity.

5121 Motion Picture and Video Industries

This industry group comprises establishments primarily engaged in the production and/or distribution of motion pictures, videos, television programs, or commercials; in the exhibition of motion pictures; or in the provision of postproduction and related services.

51211 Motion Picture and Video Production
See industry description for 512110 below.

512110 Motion Picture and Video Production^{CAN}

This industry comprises establishments primarily engaged in producing, or producing and distributing motion pictures, videos, television programs, or television commercials.

Cross-References. Establishments primarily engaged in—

- Producing motion pictures and videos on contract as independent producers—are classified in Industry 711510, Independent Artists, Writers, and Performers;
- Providing teleproduction and other postproduction services—are classified in U.S. Industry 512191, Teleproduction and Other Postproduction Services;
- Providing video taping of weddings, special events, and/or business inventories—are classified in Industry 54192, Photographic Services;

US—United States industry only. CAN—United States and Canadian industries are comparable. MEX—United States and Mexican industries are comparable. Blank—Canadian, Mexican, and United States industries are comparable.

- Providing motion picture laboratory services—are classified in U.S. Industry 512199, Other Motion Picture and Video Industries;
- Providing mass duplication and packaging of video tapes—are classified in U.S. Industry 334612, Prerecorded Compact Disc (except Software), Tape, and Record Reproducing; and
- Acquiring distribution rights and distributing motion pictures and videos— are classified in Industry 512120, Motion Picture and Video Distribution.

51212 Motion Picture and Video Distribution

See industry description for 512120 below.

512120 Motion Picture and Video Distribution[CAN]

This industry comprises establishments primarily engaged in acquiring distribution rights and distributing film and video productions to motion picture theaters, television networks and stations, and exhibitors.

Cross-References. Establishments primarily engaged in—

- Producing and distributing motion pictures and videos—are classified in Industry 512110, Motion Picture and Video Production;
- Merchant wholesale distribution of blank video cassette tapes and discs— are classified in Industry 423690, Other Electronic Parts and Equipment Merchant Wholesalers;
- Merchant wholesale distribution of prerecorded video cassette tapes and discs—are classified in Industry 423990, Other Miscellaneous Durable Goods Merchant Wholesalers;
- Providing mass duplication and packaging of video tapes—are classified in U.S. Industry 334612, Prerecorded Compact Disc (except Software), Tape, and Record Reproducing;
- Providing motion picture footage (via film libraries) to producers—are classified in U.S. Industry 512199, Other Motion Picture and Video Industries;
- Renting video tapes and discs to the general public—are classified in Industry 532230, Video Tape and Disc Rental; and
- Selling video cassettes and discs to the general public—are classified in Industry 451220, Prerecorded Tape, Compact Disc and Record Stores.

51213 Motion Picture and Video Exhibition

This industry comprises establishments primarily engaged in operating motion picture theaters and/or exhibiting motion pictures or videos at film festivals, and so forth.

US—United States industry only. CAN—United States and Canadian industries are comparable. MEX—United States and Mexican industries are comparable. Blank—Canadian, Mexican, and United States industries are comparable.

512131 Motion Picture Theaters (except Drive-Ins)^{US}

This U.S. industry comprises establishments primarily engaged in operating motion picture theaters (except drive-ins) and/or exhibiting motion pictures or videos at film festivals, and so forth.

512132 Drive-In Motion Picture Theaters^{US}

This U.S. industry comprises establishments primarily engaged in operating drive-in motion picture theaters.

51219 Postproduction Services and Other Motion Picture and Video Industries

This industry comprises establishments primarily engaged in providing postproduction services and other services to the motion picture industry, including specialized motion picture or video postproduction services, such as editing, film/tape transfers, titling, subtitling, credits, closed captioning, and computer-produced graphics, animation and special effects, as well as developing and processing motion picture film.

Illustrative Examples:

Motion picture film laboratories	Stock footage film libraries
Postproduction facilities	Teleproduction services

Cross-References. Establishments primarily engaged in—

- Mass duplicating video tapes and film—are classified in Industry 33461, Manufacturing and Reproducing Magnetic and Optical Media;
- Providing audio services for film, television, and video productions—are classified in Industry 51224, Sound Recording Studios;
- Renting wardrobes and costumes for motion picture production—are classified in Industry 53222, Formal Wear and Costume Rental;
- Renting studio equipment—are classified in Industry 53249, Other Commercial and Industrial Machinery and Equipment Rental and Leasing; and
- Casting actors and actresses with production companies—are classified in Industry 56131, Employment Placement Agencies.

512191 Teleproduction and Other Postproduction Services^{US}

This U.S. industry comprises establishments primarily engaged in providing specialized motion picture or video postproduction services, such as editing, film/

tape transfers, subtitling, credits, closed captioning, and animation and special effects.

Cross-References. Establishments primarily engaged in—

- Mass duplicating video tapes and film—are classified in Industry 33461, Manufacturing and Reproducing Magnetic and Optical Media;
- Developing and processing motion picture film—are classified in U.S. Industry 512199, Other Motion Picture and Video Industries;
- Providing audio services for film, television, and video productions—are classified in Industry 512240, Sound Recording Studios; and
- Acquiring distribution rights and distributing film and video productions to motion picture theaters, television networks and stations, and exhibitors—are classified in Industry 512120, Motion Picture and Video Distribution.

512199 Other Motion Picture and Video Industries[US]

This U.S. industry comprises establishments primarily engaged in providing motion picture and video services (except motion picture and video production, distribution, exhibition, and teleproduction and other postproduction services).

Illustrative Examples:

Motion picture film laboratories   Stock footage film libraries

Cross-References. Establishments primarily engaged in—

- Renting wardrobes and costumes for motion picture production—are classified in Industry 532220, Formal Wear and Costume Rental;
- Renting studio equipment—are classified in Industry 532490, Other Commercial and Industrial Machinery and Equipment Rental and Leasing;
- Casting actors and actresses with production companies—are classified in Industry 561310, Employment Placement Agencies;
- Motion picture and video production—are classified in Industry 512110, Motion Picture and Video Production;
- Motion picture and video distribution—are classified in Industry 512120, Motion Picture and Video Distribution;
- Teleproduction and other postproduction services—are classified in U.S. Industry 512191, Teleproduction and Other Postproduction Services; and
- Motion picture and video exhibition—are classified in Industry 51213, Motion Picture and Video Exhibition.

US—United States industry only. CAN—United States and Canadian industries are comparable. MEX—United States and Mexican industries are comparable. Blank—Canadian, Mexican, and United States industries are comparable.

5122 Sound Recording Industries

This industry group comprises establishments primarily engaged in producing and distributing musical recordings, in publishing music, or in providing sound recording and related services.

51221 Record Production

See industry description for 512210 below.

512210 Record Production^{CAN}

This industry comprises establishments primarily engaged in record production (e.g., tapes, CDs). These establishments contract with artists and arrange and finance the production of original master recordings. Establishments in this industry hold the copyright to the master recording and derive most of their revenues from the sales, leasing, and licensing of master recordings. Establishments in this industry do not have their own duplication or distribution capabilities.

Cross-References. Establishments primarily engaged in—

- Releasing, promoting, and distributing recordings—are classified in Industry 512220, Integrated Record Production/Distribution;
- Promoting and authorizing the use of musical works in various media—are classified in Industry 512230, Music Publishers;
- Mass duplication services—are classified in U.S. Industry 334612, Prerecorded Compact Disc (except Software), Tape, and Record Reproducing;
- Merchant wholesale distribution of blank audio cassettes, tapes, and discs—are classified in Industry 423690, Other Electronic Parts and Equipment Merchant Wholesalers;
- Merchant wholesale distribution of prerecorded audio cassettes, tapes, and discs—are classified in Industry 423990, Other Miscellaneous Durable Goods Merchant Wholesalers;
- Managing the careers of artists—are classified in Industry 711410, Agents and Managers for Artists, Athletes, Entertainers and Other Public Figures;
- Providing facilities and technical expertise for recording musical performances—are classified in Industry 512240, Sound Recording Studios; and
- Producing albums on contract as independent producers—are classified in Industry 711510, Independent Artists, Writers, and Performers.

51222 Integrated Record Production/Distribution

See industry description for 512220 below.

512220 Integrated Record Production/Distribution^{CAN}

This industry comprises establishments primarily engaged in releasing, promoting, and distributing sound recordings. These establishments manufacture or arrange for the manufacture of recordings, such as audio tapes/cassettes and compact discs, and promote and distribute these products to wholesalers, retailers, or directly to the public. Establishments in this industry produce master recordings themselves, or obtain reproduction and distribution rights to master recordings produced by record production companies or other integrated record companies.

Cross-References. Establishments primarily engaged in—

- Contracting with musical artists, arranging for the production of master recordings, and marketing the reproduction rights—are classified in Industry 512210, Record Production;

- Providing facilities and technical expertise for recording musical performances—are classified in Industry 512240, Sound Recording Studios;

- Mass duplication of recorded products—are classified in U.S. Industry 334612, Prerecorded Compact Disc (except Software), Tape, and Record Reproducing;

- Merchant wholesale distribution of prerecorded audio cassettes, tapes, and discs—are classified in Industry 423990, Other Miscellaneous Durable Goods Merchant Wholesalers; and

- Retailing records, tapes, and compact discs without producing recordings—are classified in Sector 44-45, Retail Trade.

51223 Music Publishers

See industry description for 512230 below.

512230 Music Publishers^{CAN}

This industry comprises establishments primarily engaged in acquiring and registering copyrights for musical compositions in accordance with law and promoting and authorizing the use of these compositions in recordings, radio, television, motion pictures, live performances, print, or other media. Establishments in this industry represent the interests of the songwriter or other owners of musical compositions to produce revenues from the use of such works, generally through licensing agreements. These establishments may own the copyright or act as administrator of the music copyrights on behalf of copyright owners. Publishers of music books and sheet music are included in this industry.

US—United States industry only. CAN—United States and Canadian industries are comparable. MEX—United States and Mexican industries are comparable. Blank—Canadian, Mexican, and United States industries are comparable.

Cross-References.

Establishments primarily engaged as independent songwriters who act as their own publishers are classified in Industry 711510, Independent Artists, Writers, and Performers.

51224 Sound Recording Studios
See industry description for 512240 below.

512240 Sound Recording Studios^{CAN}

This industry comprises establishments primarily engaged in providing the facilities and technical expertise for sound recording in a studio. This industry includes establishments that provide audio production and postproduction services to produce master recordings. These establishments may provide audio services for film, television, and video productions.

Cross-References. Establishments primarily engaged in—

* Releasing, promoting, and distributing sound recordings—are classified in Industry 512220, Integrated Record Production/Distribution;

* Providing mass duplication of recorded products—are classified in U.S. Industry 334612, Prerecorded Compact Disc (except Software), Tape, and Record Reproducing; and

* Contracting with musical artists, arranging for the production of master recordings, and marketing the reproduction rights—are classified in Industry 512210, Record Production.

51229 Other Sound Recording Industries
See industry description for 512290 below.

512290 Other Sound Recording Industries^{CAN}

This industry comprises establishments primarily engaged in providing sound recording services (except record production, distribution, music publishing, and sound recording in a studio). Establishments in this industry provide services, such as the audio recording of meetings and conferences.

Cross-References. Establishments primarily engaged in—

* Producing records, including contracting with musical artists, arranging and financing the production of master recordings, and marketing the reproduction rights—are classified in Industry 512210, Record Production;

- Releasing, promoting, and distributing sound recordings—are classified in Industry 512220, Integrated Record Production/Distribution;

- Promoting and authorizing the use of musical works in various media—are classified in Industry 512230, Music Publishers;

- Providing facilities and expertise for recording musical performance—are classified in Industry 512240, Sound Recording Studios;

- Providing mass duplication of recorded products—are classified in U.S. Industry 334612, Prerecorded Compact Disc (except Software), Tape, and Record Reproducing; and

- Organizing and promoting the presentation of performing arts productions—are classified in Industry Group 7113, Promoters of Performing Arts, Sports and Similar Events.

515 Broadcasting (except Internet)

Industries in the Broadcasting (except Internet) subsector include establishments that create content or acquire the right to distribute content and subsequently broadcast the content. The industry groups (Radio and Television Broadcasting and Cable and Other Subscription Programming) are based on differences in the methods of communication and the nature of services provided. The Radio and Television Broadcasting industry group includes establishments that operate broadcasting studios and facilities for over the air or satellite delivery of radio and television programs of entertainment, news, talk, and the like. These establishments are often engaged in the production and purchase of programs and generating revenues from the sale of air time to advertisers and from donations, subsidies, and/or the sale of programs. The Cable and Other Subscription Programming industry group includes establishments operating studios and facilities for the broadcasting of programs that are typically narrowcast in nature (limited format, such as news, sports, education, and youth-oriented programming) on a subscription or fee basis.

The distribution of cable and other subscription programming is included in Subsector 517, Telecommunications. Establishments that broadcast exclusively on the Internet are included in Subsector 516, Internet Publishing and Broadcasting.

5151 Radio and Television Broadcasting

This industry group comprises establishments primarily engaged in operating broadcast studios and facilities for over-the-air or satellite delivery of radio and television programs. These establishments are often engaged in the production or purchase of programs or generate revenues from the sale of air time to advertisers, from donations and subsidies, or from the sale of programs.

51511 Radio Broadcasting

This industry comprises establishments primarily engaged in broadcasting audio signals. These establishments operate radio broadcasting studios and facilities for the transmission of aural programming by radio to the public, to affiliates, or to subscribers. The radio programs may include entertainment, news, talk shows, business data, or religious services.

Cross-References. Establishments primarily engaged in—

- Broadcasting exclusively on the Internet—are classified in Industry 51611, Internet Publishing and Broadcasting; and
- Producing taped radio programming—are classified in Industry 51229, Other Sound Recording Industries.

515111 Radio Networks^{US}

This U.S. industry comprises establishments primarily engaged in assembling and transmitting aural programming to their affiliates or subscribers via over-the-air broadcasts, cable, or satellite. The programming covers a wide variety of material, such as news services, religious programming, weather, sports, or music.

Cross-References. Establishments primarily engaged in—

- Broadcasting exclusively on the Internet—are classified in Industry 516110, Internet Publishing and Broadcasting; and
- Producing taped radio programming—are classified in Industry 512290, Other Sound Recording Industries.

515112 Radio Stations^{US}

This U.S. industry comprises establishments primarily engaged in broadcasting aural programs by radio to the public. Programming may originate in their own studio, from an affiliated network, or from external sources.

51512 Television Broadcasting
See industry description for 515120 below.

515120 Television Broadcasting^{CAN}

This industry comprises establishments primarily engaged in broadcasting images together with sound. These establishments operate television broadcasting

---

studios and facilities for the programming and transmission of programs to the public. These establishments also produce or transmit visual programming to affiliated broadcast television stations, which in turn broadcast the programs to the public on a predetermined schedule. Programming may originate in their own studio, from an affiliated network, or from external sources.

Cross-References. Establishments primarily engaged in—

- Broadcasting exclusively on the Internet—are classified in Industry 516110, Internet Publishing and Broadcasting;

- Producing taped television program materials—are classified in Industry 512110, Motion Picture and Video Production;

- Furnishing cable and other pay television services—are classified in Industry 517510, Cable and Other Program Distribution; and

- Producing and broadcasting television programs for cable and satellite television systems—are classified in Industry 515210, Cable and Other Subscription Programming.

5152 Cable and Other Subscription Programming

51521 Cable and Other Subscription Programming
See industry description for 515210 below.

515210 Cable and Other Subscription Programming[CAN]

This industry comprises establishments primarily engaged in operating studios and facilities for the broadcasting of programs on a subscription or fee basis. The broadcast programming is typically narrowcast in nature (e.g., limited format, such as news, sports, education, or youth-oriented). These establishments produce programming in their own facilities or acquire programming from external sources. The programming material is usually delivered to a third party, such as cable systems or direct-to-home satellite systems, for transmission to viewers.

Cross-References. Establishments primarily engaged in—

- Producing taped television program material—are classified in Industry 512110, Motion Picture and Video Production;

- Producing and transmitting television programs to affiliated stations—are classified in Industry 515120, Television Broadcasting;

- Furnishing cable and other pay television services—are classified in Industry 517510, Cable and Other Program Distribution; and

---

US—United States industry only. CAN—United States and Canadian industries are comparable. MEX—United States and Mexican industries are comparable. Blank—Canadian, Mexican, and United States industries are comparable.

- Retailing merchandise by electronic media, such as television—are classified in Industry 45411, Electronic Shopping and Mail-Order Houses.

516 Internet Publishing and Broadcasting

Industries in the Internet Publishing and Broadcasting subsector group establishments that publish and/or broadcast content exclusively for the Internet. The unique combination of text, audio, video, and interactive features present in informational or cultural products on the Internet justifies the separation of Internet publishers and broadcasters from more traditional publishers included in subsector 511, Publishing Industries (except Internet) and subsector 515, Broadcasting (except Internet).

5161 Internet Publishing and Broadcasting

51611 Internet Publishing and Broadcasting
See industry description for 516110 below.

516110 Internet Publishing and Broadcasting^{CAN}

This industry comprises establishments engaged in publishing and/or broadcasting content on the Internet exclusively. These establishments do not provide traditional (non-Internet) versions of the content that they publish or broadcast. Establishments in this industry provide textual, audio, and/or video content of general or specific interest on the Internet.

Illustrative Examples:

Internet book publishers	Internet periodical publishers
Internet entertainment sites	Internet radio stations
Internet game sites	Internet sports sites
Internet news publishers	Internet video broadcast sites

Cross-References. Establishments primarily engaged in—

- Providing Internet access, known as Internet Service Providers—are classified in U.S. Industry 518111, Internet Service Providers;

- Providing both Internet publishing and other print or electronic (e.g., CD-ROM, diskette) editions in the same establishment or using proprietary networks to distribute content—are classified in Subsector 511, Publishing Industries (except Internet) based on the materials produced;

- Operating web search portals—are classified in U.S. Industry 518112, Web Search Portals;

- Providing streaming services on content owned by others—are classified in Industry 518210, Data Processing, Hosting, and Related Services;

- Wholesaling goods on the Internet—are classified in Sector 42, Wholesale Trade;

- Retailing goods on the Internet—are classified in Sector 44-45, Retail Trade; and

- Operating stock brokerages, travel reservation systems, purchasing services, and similar activities using the Internet rather than traditional methods—are classified with the more traditional establishments providing these services.

517 Telecommunications

Industries in the Telecommunications subsector include establishments providing telecommunications and the services related to that activity. The Telecommunications subsector is primarily engaged in operating, maintaining, and/or providing access to facilities for the transmission of voice, data, text, sound, and video. A transmission facility may be based on a single technology or a combination of technologies. Establishments primarily engaged as independent contractors in the maintenance and installation of broadcasting and telecommunications systems are classified in Sector 23, Construction.

5171 Wired Telecommunications Carriers

This industry group comprises establishments primarily engaged in operating, maintaining or providing access to facilities for the transmission of voice, data, text, sound, and video using wired telecommunications networks. Transmission facilities may be based on a single technology or a combination of technologies.

51711 Wired Telecommunications Carriers
See industry description for 517110 below.

517110 Wired Telecommunications Carriers^{CAN}

This industry comprises establishments engaged in (1) operating and maintaining switching and transmission facilities to provide point-to-point communications via landlines, microwave, or a combination of landlines and satellite linkups or (2) furnishing telegraph and other non-vocal communications using their own facilities.

US—United States industry only. CAN—United States and Canadian industries are comparable. MEX—United States and Mexican industries are comparable. Blank—Canadian, Mexican, and United States industries are comparable.

Cross-References. Establishments primarily engaged in—

- Distributing scheduled television programs via cable or satellite facilities on a subscription or fee basis—are classified in Industry 517510, Cable and Other Program Distribution;
- Providing coin-operated pay telephones—are classified in Industry 812990, All Other Personal Services;
- Operating and maintaining wireless networks—are classified in Industry 51721, Wireless Telecommunications Carriers (except Satellite);
- Reselling telecommunications, without operating a network—are classified in Industry 517310, Telecommunications Resellers;
- Publishing telephone directories—are classified in Industry 511140, Directory and Mailing List Publishers; and
- Maintaining and installing wired telecommunication systems as independent contractors—are classified in Sector 23, Construction.

5172 Wireless Telecommunications Carriers (except Satellite)

This industry group comprises establishments primarily engaged in operating, maintaining or providing access to facilities for the transmission of voice, data, text, sound, and video using wireless telecommunications networks. Transmission facilities may be based on a single technology or a combination of technologies.

51721 Wireless Telecommunications Carriers (except Satellite)

This industry comprises establishments primarily engaged in operating and maintaining switching and transmission facilities that provide omni-directional communications via airwaves. Included in this industry are establishments providing wireless telecommunications network services, such as cellular telephone or paging services.

Cross-Reference.

Establishments primarily engaged in providing telephone answering services using pagers are classified in Industry 56142, Telephone Call Centers.

517211 Paging[US]

This U.S. industry comprises establishments primarily engaged in operating paging networks. The establishments of this industry may also supply and maintain equipment used to receive signals.

Cross-Reference.

Establishments primarily engaged in providing telephone answering services using pagers are classified in U.S. Industry 561421, Telephone Answering Services.

517212 Cellular and Other Wireless Telecommunications[US]

This U.S. industry comprises establishments primarily engaged in operating cellular telecommunications and other wireless telecommunications networks (except paging).

Cross-Reference.

Establishments primarily engaged in operating paging networks are classified in U.S. Industry 517211, Paging.

5173 Telecommunications Resellers

51731 Telecommunications Resellers

See industry description for 517310 below.

517310 Telecommunications Resellers[CAN]

This industry comprises establishments primarily engaged in purchasing access and network capacity from owners and operators of the networks and reselling wired and wireless telecommunications services (except satellite) to businesses and households. Establishments in this industry resell telecommunications; they do not operate and maintain telecommunications switching and transmission facilities.

Cross-References. Establishments primarily engaged in—

- Operating and maintaining wired telecommunications networks—are classified in Industry 517110, Wired Telecommunications Carriers;
- Reselling satellite telecommunications services—are classified in Industry 517410, Satellite Telecommunications; and
- Operating and maintaining wireless telecommunications—are classified in Industry 51721, Wireless Telecommunications Carriers (except Satellite).

5174 Satellite Telecommunications

51741 Satellite Telecommunications

See industry description for 517410 below.

US—United States industry only. CAN—United States and Canadian industries are comparable. MEX—United States and Mexican industries are comparable. Blank—Canadian, Mexican, and United States industries are comparable.

517410 Satellite Telecommunications[CAN]

This industry comprises establishments primarily engaged in providing point-to-point telecommunications services to other establishments in the telecommunications and broadcasting industries by forwarding and receiving communications signals via a system of satellites or reselling satellite telecommunications.

Cross-Reference.

Establishments primarily engaged in providing direct-to-home satellite television systems to individual households or consumers are classified in Industry 517510, Cable and Other Program Distribution.

5175 Cable and Other Program Distribution

51751 Cable and Other Program Distribution
See industry description for 517510 below.

517510 Cable and Other Program Distribution[CAN]

This industry comprises establishments primarily engaged as third-party distribution systems for broadcast programming. The establishments of this industry deliver visual, aural, or textual programming received from cable networks, local television stations, or radio networks to consumers via cable or direct-to-home satellite systems on a subscription or fee basis. These establishments do not generally originate programming material.

Cross-References. Establishments primarily engaged in—

- Producing and broadcasting television programs for cable and satellite television systems—are classified in Industry 515210, Cable and Other Subscription Programming; and

- Maintenance and installation of cable systems as independent contractors—are classified in Sector 23, Construction.

5179 Other Telecommunications

51791 Other Telecommunications
See industry description for 517910 below.

517910 Other Telecommunications^{CAN}

This industry comprises establishments primarily engaged in (1) providing specialized telecommunications applications, such as satellite tracking, communications telemetry, and radar station operations; or (2) providing satellite terminal stations and associated facilities operationally connected with one or more terrestrial communications systems and capable of transmitting telecommunications to or receiving telecommunications from satellite systems.

Cross-References. Establishments primarily engaged in—

- Providing satellite telecommunications—are classified in Industry 517410, Satellite Telecommunications; and

- Providing custom design, programming, or facilities management services for integrated computer and telecommunications systems or operations— are classified in Industry 54151, Computer Systems Design and Related Services.

518 Internet Service Providers, Web Search Portals, and Data Processing Services

Industries in the Internet Service Providers, Web Search Portals, and Data Processing Services subsector group establishments that provide: (1) access to the Internet; (2) search facilities for the Internet; and (3) data processing, hosting, and related services. The industry groups (Internet Service Providers and Web Search Portals, Data Processing Hosting, and Related Services) are based on differences in the processes used to access information and process information. The Internet Service Providers and Web Search Portals industry group includes establishments that are providing access to the Internet or aiding in navigation on the Internet. The Data Processing, Hosting, and Related Services industry group includes establishments that process data. These establishments can transform data, prepare data for dissemination, or place data or content on the Internet for others. In addition, the shared use of computer resources is included in the Data Processing, Hosting, and Related Services industry group.

Establishments that are publishing exclusively on the Internet are included in Subsector 516, Internet Publishing and Broadcasting and establishments that are retailing goods using the Internet are included in Sector 44-45, Retail Trade.

5181 Internet Service Providers and Web Search Portals

51811 Internet Service Providers and Web Search Portals

This industry comprises establishments known as Internet service providers or known as Web search portals. Establishments in this industry provide clients access

---

to the Internet or operate Web sites that use a search engine to provide Internet search services. Establishments in this industry generally provide related services, such as Web hosting, Web page design, and related advice and assistance. Web search portals often provide additional Internet services, such as e-mail, connections to other Web sites, auctions, news, and other limited content, and serve as a home base for Internet users.

Cross-References. Establishments primarily engaged in—

- Publishing or broadcasting exclusively on the Internet—are classified in Industry 51611, Internet Publishing and Broadcasting;
- Web hosting—are classified in Industry 51821, Data Processing, Hosting, and Related Services;
- Designing Web sites for others on a fee basis—are classified in Industry 54151, Computer Systems Design and Related Services;
- Providing telecommunications related consulting services—are classified in Industry 54161, Management Consulting Services;
- Wholesaling goods on the Internet—are classified in Sector 42, Wholesale Trade;
- Retailing goods on the Internet—are classified in Sector 44-45, Retail Trade; and
- Operating stock brokerages, travel reservation systems, purchasing services, and similar activities using the Internet rather than traditional methods—are classified with the more traditional establishments providing these services.

518111 Internet Service Providers[US]

This U.S. industry comprises establishments known as Internet service providers. Establishments in this industry provide clients access to the Internet and generally provide related services such as Web hosting, Web page designing, and hardware or software consulting related to Internet connectivity. Establishments in this industry may provide local, regional, or national coverage for clients or provide backbone services (except telecommunications carriers) for other Internet service providers. Internet service providers have the equipment and telecommunication network access required for a point-of-presence on the Internet.

Cross References. Establishments primarily engaged in—

- Publishing or broadcasting exclusively on the Internet—are classified in Industry 516110;
- Web hosting—are classified in Industry 518210, Data Processing, Hosting, and Related Services;

- Designing Web sites for others on a fee basis—are classified in U.S. Industry 541511, Custom Computer Programming Services; and

- Providing telecommunications related consulting services—are classified in U.S. Industry 541618, Other Management Consulting Services.

518112 Web Search Portals[US]

This U.S. industry comprises establishments known as Web search portals. Establishments in this industry operate Web sites that use a search engine to generate and maintain extensive databases of Internet addresses and content in an easily searchable format. Web search portals often provide additional Internet services, such as e-mail, connections to other Web sites, auctions, news, and other limited content, and serve as a home base for Internet users.

Cross-References. Establishments primarily engaged in—

- Publishing or broadcasting exclusively on the Internet—are classified in Industry 516110;

- Providing Internet access, known as Internet Service Providers—are classified in U.S. Industry 518111, Internet Service Providers;

- Wholesaling goods on the Internet—are classified in Sector 42, Wholesale Trade;

- Retailing goods on the Internet—are classified in Sector 44-45, Retail Trade; and

- Operating stock brokerages, travel reservation systems, purchasing services, and similar activities using the Internet rather than traditional methods—are classified with the more traditional establishments providing these services.

5182 Data Processing, Hosting, and Related Services

51821 Data Processing, Hosting, and Related Services
See industry description for 518210 below

518210 Data Processing, Hosting, and Related Services[CAN]

This industry comprises establishments primarily engaged in providing infrastructure for hosting or data processing services. These establishments may provide specialized hosting activities, such as Web hosting, streaming services or application hosting, provide application service provisioning, or may provide general time-share mainframe facilities to clients. Data processing establishments provide complete processing and specialized reports from data supplied by clients or provide automated data processing and data entry services.

Illustrative Examples:

Application hosting
Application service providers
Computer input preparation services
Computer time rental

Microfilm imaging services
Optical scanning services
Web hosting

Cross-References. Establishments primarily engaged in—

- Providing text processing and related document preparation activities—are classified in Industry 561410, Document Preparation Services;

- Providing on-site management and operation of a clients' data-processing facilities—are classified in U.S. Industry 541513, Computer Facilities Management Services;

- Providing Internet access services in combination with Web hosting—are classified in U.S. Industry 518111, Internet Service Providers;

- Operating Web search portals—are classified in U.S. Industry 518112, Web Search Portals;

- Providing access to computers and office equipment, as well as other office support services—are classified in Industry 56143, Business Service Centers;

- Processing financial transactions, such as credit card transactions—are classified in Industry 522320, Financial Transactions Processing, Reserve, and Clearinghouse Activities; and

- Providing payroll processing services—are classified in U.S. Industry 541214, Payroll Services.

519 Other Information Services

Industries in the Other Information Services subsector group establishments supplying information, storing information, providing access to information, and searching and retrieving information. The main components of the subsector are news syndicates, libraries, and archives.

5191 Other Information Services

51911 News Syndicates
See industry description for 519110 below.

519110 News Syndicates^{CAN}

This industry comprises establishments primarily engaged in supplying information, such as news reports, articles, pictures, and features, to the news media.

Cross-Reference.

Independent writers and journalists (including photojournalists) are classified in Industry 711510, Independent Artists, Writers, and Performers.

51912 Libraries and Archives
See industry description for 519120 below.

519120 Libraries and Archives^{US}

This industry comprises establishments primarily engaged in providing library or archive services. These establishments are engaged in maintaining collections of documents (e.g., books, journals, newspapers, and music) and facilitating the use of such documents (recorded information regardless of its physical form and characteristics) as are required to meet the informational, research, educational, or recreational needs of their user. These establishments may also acquire, research, store, preserve, and generally make accessible to the public historical documents, photographs, maps, audio material, audiovisual material, and other archival material of historical interest. All or portions of these collections may be accessible electronically.

Cross-References. Establishments primarily engaged in—

* Providing stock footage (via motion picture and video tape libraries) to the media, multimedia, and advertising industries—are classified in U.S. Industry 512199, Other Motion Picture and Video Industries; and

* Distributing film and video productions to motion picture theaters, television networks and stations, and exhibitors—are classified in Industry 512120, Motion Picture and Video Distribution.

51919 All Other Information Services
See industry description for 519190 below.

519190 All Other Information Services^{CAN}

This industry comprises establishments primarily engaged in providing other information services (except news syndicates and libraries and archives).

Illustrative Examples:

News clipping services	Telephone-based information services
Stock photo agencies	

Cross-References. Establishments primarily engaged in—

- Providing Internet access—are classified in U.S. Industry 518111, Internet Service Providers;

- Operating Web search portals—are classified in U.S. Industry 518112, Web Search Portals,

- Publishing (except exclusively on the Internet)—are classified in Subsector 511, Publishing Industries (except Internet)

- Publishing or broadcasting exclusively on the Internet—are classified in Industry 516110, Internet Publishing and Broadcasting;

- Operating news syndicates—are classified in Industry 519110, News Syndicates; and

- Operating libraries and archives—are classified in Industry 519120, Libraries and Archives.

Sector 52—Finance and Insurance

The Sector as a Whole

The Finance and Insurance sector comprises establishments primarily engaged in financial transactions (transactions involving the creation, liquidation, or change in ownership of financial assets) and/or in facilitating financial transactions. Three principal types of activities are identified:

1. Raising funds by taking deposits and/or issuing securities and, in the process, incurring liabilities. Establishments engaged in this activity use raised funds to acquire financial assets by making loans and/or purchasing securities. Putting themselves at risk, they channel funds from lenders to borrowers and transform or repackage the funds with respect to maturity, scale, and risk. This activity is known as financial intermediation.

2. Pooling of risk by underwriting insurance and annuities. Establishments engaged in this activity collect fees, insurance premiums, or annuity considerations; build up reserves; invest those reserves; and make contractual payments. Fees are based on the expected incidence of the insured risk and the expected return on investment.

3. Providing specialized services facilitating or supporting financial intermediation, insurance, and employee benefit programs.

In addition, monetary authorities charged with monetary control are included in this sector.

The subsectors, industry groups, and industries within the NAICS Finance and Insurance sector are defined on the basis of their unique production processes. As with all industries, the production processes are distinguished by their use of specialized human resources and specialized physical capital. In addition, the way in which these establishments acquire and allocate financial capital, their source of funds, and the use of those funds provides a third basis for distinguishing characteristics of the production process. For instance, the production process in raising funds through deposit-taking is different from the process of raising funds in bond or money markets. The process of making loans to individuals also requires different production processes than does the creation of investment pools or the underwriting of securities.

Most of the Finance and Insurance subsectors contain one or more industry groups of (1) intermediaries with similar patterns of raising and using funds and (2) establishments engaged in activities that facilitate, or are otherwise related to, that type of financial or insurance intermediation. Industries within this sector are defined in terms of activities for which a production process can be specified, and many of these activities are not exclusive to a particular type of financial institution.

To deal with the varied activities taking place within existing financial institutions, the approach is to split these institutions into components performing specialized services. This requires defining the units engaged in providing those services and developing procedures that allow for their delineation. These units are the equivalents for finance and insurance of the establishments defined for other industries.

The output of many financial services, as well as the inputs and the processes by which they are combined, cannot be observed at a single location and can only be defined at a higher level of the organizational structure of the enterprise. Additionally, a number of independent activities that represent separate and distinct production processes may take place at a single location belonging to a multiloca-tion financial firm. Activities are more likely to be homogeneous with respect to production characteristics than are locations, at least in financial services. The classification defines activities broadly enough that it can be used both by those classifying by location and by those employing a more top-down approach to the delineation of the establishment.

Establishments engaged in activities that facilitate, or are otherwise related to, the various types of intermediation have been included in individual subsectors, rather than in a separate subsector dedicated to services alone because these services are performed by intermediaries, as well as by specialist establishments, the extent to which the activity of the intermediaries can be separately identified is not clear.

The Finance and Insurance sector has been defined to encompass establishments primarily engaged in financial transactions; that is, transactions involving the creation, liquidation, change in ownership of financial assets; or in facilitating financial transactions. Financial industries are extensive users of electronic means for facilitating the verification of financial balances, authorizing transactions, trans-ferring funds to and from transactors' accounts, notifying banks (or credit card issuers) of the individual transactions, and providing daily summaries. Since these transaction processing activities are integral to the production of finance and insurance services, establishments that principally provide a financial transaction processing service are classified to this sector, rather than to the data processing industry in the Information sector.

Legal entities that hold portfolios of assets on behalf of others are significant and data on them are required for a variety of purposes. Thus for NAICS, these funds, trusts, and other financial vehicles are the fifth subsector of the Finance and Insurance sector. These entities earn interest, dividends, and other property income, but have little or no employment and no revenue from the sale of services. Separate establishments and employees devoted to the management of funds are classified in Industry Group 5239, Other Financial Investment Activities.

521 Monetary Authorities-Central Bank

The Monetary Authorities-Central Bank subsector groups establishments that engage in performing central banking functions, such as issuing currency, managing the Nation's money supply and international reserves, holding deposits that represent the reserves of other banks and other central banks, and acting as a fiscal agent for the central government.

5211 Monetary Authorities-Central Bank

52111 Monetary Authorities-Central Bank
See industry description for 521110 below.

521110 Monetary Authorities-Central Bank

This industry comprises establishments primarily engaged in performing central banking functions, such as issuing currency, managing the Nation's money supply and international reserves, holding deposits that represent the reserves of other banks and other central banks, and acting as a fiscal agent for the central government.

Cross-References.

Establishments of the Board of Governors of the Federal Reserve System are classified in Industry 921130, Public Finance Activities.

522 Credit Intermediation and Related Activities

Industries in the Credit Intermediation and Related Activities subsector group establishments that (1) lend funds raised from depositors; (2) lend funds raised from credit market borrowing; or (3) facilitate the lending of funds or issuance of credit by engaging in such activities as mortgage and loan brokerage, clearinghouse and reserve services, and check cashing services.

5221 Depository Credit Intermediation^CAN

This industry group comprises establishments primarily engaged in accepting deposits (or share deposits) and in lending funds from these deposits. Within this group, industries are defined on the basis of differences in the types of deposit liabilities assumed and in the nature of the credit extended.

52211 Commercial Banking^US
See industry description for 522110 below.

US—United States industry only. CAN—United States and Canadian industries are comparable. MEX—United States and Mexican industries are comparable. Blank—Canadian, Mexican, and United States industries are comparable.

522110 Commercial Banking[US]

This industry comprises establishments primarily engaged in accepting demand and other deposits and making commercial, industrial, and consumer loans. Commercial banks and branches of foreign banks are included in this industry.

Cross-References.

- Establishments primarily engaged in credit card banking are classified in Industry 522210, Credit Card Issuing;
- Establishments known as industrial banks and primarily engaged in accepting deposits are classified in Industry 522190, Other Depository Credit Intermediation; and
- Establishments of depository institutions primarily engaged in trust activities are classified in U.S. Industry 523991, Trust, Fiduciary, and Custody Activities.

52212 Savings Institutions[US]
See industry description for 522120 below.

522120 Savings Institutions[US]

This U.S. industry comprises establishments primarily engaged in accepting time deposits, making mortgage and real estate loans, and investing in high-grade securities. Savings and loan associations and savings banks are included in this industry.

Cross-References.

Establishments primarily engaged in accepting demand and other deposits and making all types of loans are classified in Industry 522110, Commercial Banking.

52213 Credit Unions[CAN]
See industry description for 522130 below.

522130 Credit Unions[CAN]

This industry comprises establishments primarily engaged in accepting members' share deposits in cooperatives that are organized to offer consumer loans to their members.

US—United States industry only. CAN—United States and Canadian industries are comparable. MEX—United States and Mexican industries are comparable. Blank—Canadian, Mexican, and United States industries are comparable.

52219 Other Depository Credit Intermediation^{CAN}

See industry description for 522190 below.

522190 Other Depository Credit Intermediation^{CAN}

This industry comprises establishments primarily engaged in accepting deposits and lending funds (except commercial banking, savings institutions, and credit unions). Establishments known as industrial banks or Morris Plans and primarily engaged in accepting deposits, and private banks (i.e., unincorporated banks) are included in this industry.

Cross-References.

- Establishments primarily engaged in accepting demand and other deposits and making all types of loans are classified in Industry 522110, Commercial Banking;
- Establishments primarily engaged in accepting time deposits are classified in Industry 522120, Savings Institutions;
- Establishments primarily engaged in accepting members' share deposits in cooperatives are classified in Industry 522130, Credit Unions; and
- Establishments known as industrial banks and Morris Plans and are primarily engaged in providing nondepository credit are classified in U.S. Industry 522298, All Other Nondepository Credit Intermediation.

5222 Nondepository Credit Intermediation^{CAN}

This industry group comprises establishments, both public (government-sponsored enterprises) and private, primarily engaged in extending credit or lending funds raised by credit market borrowing, such as issuing commercial paper or other debt instruments or by borrowing from other financial intermediaries. Within this group, industries are defined on the basis of the type of credit being extended.

52221 Credit Card Issuing^{CAN}

See industry description for 522210 below.

522210 Credit Card Issuing^{CAN}

This industry comprises establishments primarily engaged in providing credit by issuing credit cards. Credit card issuance provides the funds required to purchase goods and services in return for payment of the full balance or payments on an installment basis. Credit card banks are included in this industry.

US—United States industry only. CAN—United States and Canadian industries are comparable. MEX—United States and Mexican industries are comparable. Blank—Canadian, Mexican, and United States industries are comparable.

Cross-References.

Establishments primarily engaged in issuing cards that contain a stored prepaid value are classified with the industry providing the service represented by the cards, such as transit fare cards, in Subsector 482, Rail Transportation, and long-distance telephone cards in Subsector 517, Telecommunications.

52222 Sales Financing^{CAN}

See industry description for 522220 below.

522220 Sales Financing^{CAN}

This industry comprises establishments primarily engaged in sales financing or sales financing in combination with leasing. Sales financing establishments are primarily engaged in lending money for the purpose of providing collateralized goods through a contractual installment sales agreement, either directly from or through arrangements with dealers.

Cross-References.

Establishments not engaged in sales financing, but primarily engaged in providing leases for equipment and other assets are classified in Subsector 532, Rental and Leasing Services.

52229 Other Nondepository Credit Intermediation^{CAN}

This industry comprises establishments primarily engaged in making cash loans or extending credit through credit instruments (except credit cards and sales finance agreements).

Illustrative Examples:

Consumer finance companies (i.e., unsecured cash loans) International trade financing	Mortgage companies Secondary market financing

Cross-References. Establishments primarily engaged in—

- Providing credit sales by issuing credit cards—are classified in Industry 52221, Credit Card Issuing;
- Providing leases for equipment and other assets without sales financing—are classified in Subsector 532, Rental and Leasing Services;
- Accepting deposits and lending funds from these deposits—are classified in Industry Group 5221, Depository Credit Intermediation;

US—United States industry only. CAN—United States and Canadian industries are comparable. MEX—United States and Mexican industries are comparable. Blank—Canadian, Mexican, and United States industries are comparable.

- Arranging loans for others on a commission or fee basis—are classified Industry 52231, Mortgage and Nonmortgage Loan Brokers; and

- Guaranteeing international trade loans—are classified in Industry 52412, Direct Insurance (except Life, Health, and Medical) Carriers.

522291 Consumer Lending[CAN]

This U.S. industry comprises establishments primarily engaged in making unsecured cash loans to consumers.

Illustrative Examples:

Finance companies (i.e., unsecured cash loans)
Loan companies (i.e., consumer, personal, student, small)

Personal credit institutions (i.e., unsecured cash loans)
Student loans companies

Cross-References. Establishments primarily engaged in—

- Accepting deposits and lending funds from these deposits—are classified in Industry Group 5221, Depository Credit Intermediation; and

- Arranging loans for others on a commission or fee basis—are classified Industry 522310, Mortgage and Nonmortgage Loan Brokers.

522292 Real Estate Credit[US]

This U.S. industry comprises establishments primarily engaged in lending funds with real estate as collateral.

Illustrative Examples:

Home equity credit lending
Mortgage banking (i.e., nondepository mortgage lending)

Mortgage companies

Cross-References. Establishments primarily engaged in—

- Servicing loans—are classified in Industry 522390, Other Activities Related to Credit Intermediation;

- Arranging loans for others on a commission or fee basis—are classified in Industry 522310, Mortgage and Nonmortgage Loan Brokers; and

- Accepting deposits and lending funds secured by real estate—are classified in Industry Group 5221, Depository Credit Intermediation.

US—United States industry only. CAN—United States and Canadian industries are comparable. MEX—United States and Mexican industries are comparable. Blank—Canadian, Mexican, and United States industries are comparable.

522293 International Trade Financing^{US}

This U.S. industry comprises establishments primarily engaged in providing one or more of the following: (1) working capital funds to U.S. exporters; (2) lending funds to foreign buyers of U.S. goods; and/or (3) lending funds to domestic buyers of imported goods.

Illustrative Examples:

Agreement corporations (i.e., international trade financing)
Edge Act corporations (i.e., international trade financing)

Export-Import banks
Trade banks (i.e., international trade financing)

Cross-References. Establishments primarily engaged in—

- Guaranteeing international trade loans—are classified in U.S. Industry 524126, Direct Property and Casualty Insurance Carriers;

- Brokering international trade loans—are classified in Industry 522310, Mortgage and Nonmortgage Loan Brokers; and

- Accepting deposits and lending funds from these deposits—are classified in Industry Group 5221, Depository Credit Intermediation.

522294 Secondary Market Financing^{US}

This U.S. industry comprises establishments primarily engaged in buying, pooling, and repackaging loans for sale to others on the secondary market.

Illustrative Examples:

Federal Home Loan Mortgage Corporation (FHLMC)
Federal National Mortgage Association (FNMA)

Government National Mortgage Association (GNMA)
Student Loan Marketing Association (SLMA)

522298 All Other Nondepository Credit Intermediation^{US}

This U.S. industry comprises establishments primarily engaged in providing nondepository credit (except credit card issuing, sales financing, consumer lending, real estate credit, international trade financing, and secondary market financing). Examples of types of lending in this industry are: short-term inventory credit, agricultural lending (except real estate and sales financing) and consumer cash lending secured by personal property.

Illustrative Examples:

Commodity Credit Corporation	Morris Plans (i.e., known as),
Factoring accounts receivable	nondepository
Industrial banks (i.e., known as),	Pawnshops
nondepository	

Cross-References.

- Establishments primarily engaged in providing credit sales funding are classified in Industry 522210, Credit Card Issuing;
- Establishments primarily engaged in sales financing or sales financing in combination with leasing are classified in Industry 522220, Sales Financing;
- Establishments primarily engaged in making unsecured cash loans to consumers are classified in U.S. Industry 522291, Consumer Lending;
- Establishments primarily engaged in lending funds with real estate as collateral are classified in U.S. Industry 522292, Real Estate Credit;
- Establishments primarily engaged in international trade financing are classified in U.S. Industry 522293, International Trade Financing;
- Establishments primarily engaged in buying, pooling, and repackaging loans for sale to others on the secondary market are classified in U.S. Industry 522294, Secondary Market Financing; and
- Establishments known as industrial banks or Morris Plans and are primarily engaged in accepting deposits are classified in Industry 522190, Other Depository Credit Intermediation.

5223 Activities Related to Credit Intermediation[CAN]

This industry group comprises establishments primarily engaged in facilitating credit intermediation by performing activities, such as arranging loans by bringing borrowers and lenders together and clearing checks and credit card transactions.

52231 Mortgage and Nonmortgage Loan Brokers[CAN]
See industry description for 522310 below.

522310 Mortgage and Nonmortgage Loan Brokers[CAN]

This industry comprises establishments primarily engaged in arranging loans by bringing borrowers and lenders together on a commission or fee basis.

Cross-References. Establishments primarily engaged in—

- Lending funds with real estate as collateral—are classified in U.S. Industry 522292, Real Estate Credit; and

---

US—United States industry only. CAN—United States and Canadian industries are comparable. MEX—United States and Mexican industries are comparable. Blank—Canadian, Mexican, and United States industries are comparable.

- Servicing loans—are classified in Industry 522390, Other Activities Related to Credit Intermediation.

52232 Financial Transactions Processing, Reserve, and Clearinghouse Activities[CAN]
See industry description for 522320 below.

522320 Financial Transactions Processing, Reserve, and Clearinghouse Activities[US]

This industry comprises establishments primarily engaged in providing one or more of the following: (1) financial transaction processing (except central bank); (2) reserve and liquidity services (except central bank); and/or (3) check or other financial instrument clearinghouse services (except central bank).

Illustrative Examples:

Automated clearinghouses, bank or check (except central bank)	Credit card processing services
Check clearing services (except central bank)	Electronic funds transfer services

Cross-References.

- Establishments primarily engaged in nonfinancial data and electronic transaction processing are classified in Industry Group 5182, Data Processing, Hosting, and Related Services; and
- Establishments of the central bank primarily engaged in check clearing and other financial transaction processing are classified in Industry 521110, Monetary Authorities-Central Bank.

52239 Other Activities Related to Credit Intermediation[CAN]
See industry description for 522390 below.

522390 Other Activities Related to Credit Intermediation[CAN]

This industry comprises establishments primarily engaged in facilitating credit intermediation (except mortgage and loan brokerage; and financial transactions processing, reserve, and clearinghouse activities).

Illustrative Examples:

Check cashing services	Money order issuance services
Loan servicing	Travelers' check issuance services

Cross-References. Establishments primarily engaged in—

- Arranging loans for others on a commission or fee basis—are classified in Industry 522310, Mortgage and Nonmortgage Loan Brokers;

- Providing financial transactions processing, reserve, and clearinghouse activities—are classified in Industry 522320, Financial Transactions Processing, Reserve, and Clearinghouse Activities;

- Foreign currency exchange dealing—are classified in Industry 523130, Commodity Contracts Dealing; and

- Providing escrow services (except real estate)—are classified in U.S. Industry 523991, Trust, Fiduciary, and Custody Activities.

523 Securities, Commodity Contracts, and Other Financial Investments and Related Activities

Industries in the Securities, Commodity Contracts, and Other Financial Investments and Related Activities subsector group establishments that are primarily engaged in one of the following: (1) underwriting securities issues and/or making markets for securities and commodities; (2) acting as agents (i.e., brokers) between buyers and sellers of securities and commodities; (3) providing securities and commodity exchange services; and (4) providing other services, such as managing portfolios of assets; providing investment advice; and trust, fiduciary, and custody services.

5231 Securities and Commodity Contracts Intermediation and Brokerage

This industry group comprises establishments primarily engaged in putting capital at risk in the process of underwriting securities issues or in making markets for securities and commodities; and those acting as agents and/or brokers between buyers and sellers of securities and commodities, usually charging a commission.

52311 Investment Banking and Securities Dealing[CAN]
See industry description for 523110 below.

523110 Investment Banking and Securities Dealing[CAN]

This industry comprises establishments primarily engaged in underwriting, originating, and/or maintaining markets for issues of securities. Investment bankers act as principals (i.e., investors who buy or sell on their own account) in firm commit-

---

US—United States industry only. CAN—United States and Canadian industries are comparable. MEX—United States and Mexican industries are comparable. Blank—Canadian, Mexican, and United States industries are comparable.

ment transactions or act as agents in best effort and standby commitments. This industry also includes establishments acting as principals in buying or selling securities generally on a spread basis, such as securities dealers or stock option dealers.

Illustrative Examples:

Bond dealing (i.e., acting as a principal in dealing securities to investors)

Securities underwriting
Stock option dealing

Cross-References.

- Establishments primarily engaged in acting as agents (i.e., brokers) in buying or selling securities on a commission or transaction fee basis are classified in Industry 523120, Securities Brokerage; and
- Investment clubs or individual investors primarily engaged in buying or selling financial contracts (e.g., securities) on their own account are classified in Industry 523910, Miscellaneous Intermediation.

52312 Securities Brokerage^{CAN}

See industry description for 523120 below.

523120 Securities Brokerage^{CAN}

This industry comprises establishments primarily engaged in acting as agents (i.e., brokers) between buyers and sellers in buying or selling securities on a commission or transaction fee basis.

Illustrative Examples:

Mutual fund agencies (i.e., brokerages)
Securities brokerages

Stock brokerages

Cross-References.

Establishments primarily engaged in investment banking and securities dealing (i.e., buying or selling securities on their own account) are classified in Industry 523110, Investment Banking and Securities Dealing.

52313 Commodity Contracts Dealing^{CAN}

See industry description for 523130 below.

523130 Commodity Contracts Dealing^{CAN}

This industry comprises establishments primarily engaged in acting as principals (i.e., investors who buy or sell for their own account) in buying or selling spot or futures commodity contracts or options, such as precious metals, foreign currency, oil, or agricultural products, generally on a spread basis.

Cross-References. Establishments primarily engaged in—

- Acting as agents (i.e., brokers) in buying or selling spot or future commodity contracts on a commission or transaction fee basis—are classified in Industry 523140, Commodity Contracts Brokerage; and
- Buying and selling physical commodities for resale to other than the general public—are classified in Sector 42, Wholesale Trade.

52314 Commodity Contracts Brokerage^{CAN}
See industry description for 523140 below.

523140 Commodity Contracts Brokerage^{CAN}

This industry comprises establishments primarily engaged in acting as agents (i.e., brokers) in buying or selling spot or future commodity contracts or options on a commission or transaction fee basis.

Illustrative Examples:

Commodity contracts brokerages   Financial futures brokerages
Commodity futures brokerages

Cross-References. Establishments primarily engaged in—

- Acting as principals in buying or selling spot or futures commodity contracts generally on a spread basis—are classified in Industry 523130, Commodity Contracts Dealing; and
- Buying and selling physical commodities for resale to other than the general public—are classified in Sector 42, Wholesale Trade.

5232 Securities and Commodity Exchanges

52321 Securities and Commodity Exchanges
See industry description for 523210 below.

523210 Securities and Commodity Exchanges

This industry comprises establishments primarily engaged in furnishing physical or electronic marketplaces for the purpose of facilitating the buying and selling of stocks, stock options, bonds, or commodity contracts.

US—United States industry only. CAN—United States and Canadian industries are comparable. MEX—United States and Mexican industries are comparable. Blank—Canadian, Mexican, and United States industries are comparable.

Cross-References.

Establishments primarily engaged in investment banking, and securities dealing, securities brokering commodity contracts dealing, or commodity contracts brokering are classified in Industry Group 5231, Securities and Commodity Contracts Intermediation and Brokerage.

5239 Other Financial Investment Activities

This industry group comprises establishments primarily engaged in one of the following: (1) acting as principals in buying or selling financial contracts (except investment bankers, securities dealers, and commodity contracts dealers); (2) acting as agents (i.e., brokers) (except securities brokerages and commodity contracts brokerages) in buying or selling financial contracts; or (3) providing other investment services (except securities and commodity exchanges), such as portfolio management; investment advice; and trust, fiduciary, and custody services.

52391 Miscellaneous Intermediation^CAN
See industry description for 523910 below.

523910 Miscellaneous Intermediation^CAN

This industry comprises establishments primarily engaged in acting as principals (except investment bankers, securities dealers, and commodity contracts dealers) in buying or selling of financial contracts generally on a spread basis. Principals are investors that buy or sell for their own account.

Illustrative Examples:

Investment clubs
Mineral royalties or leases dealing (i.e., acting as a principal in dealing royalties or leases to investors)

Tax liens dealing (i.e., acting as a principal in dealing tax liens to investors)
Venture capital companies

Cross-References.

Establishments primarily engaged in investment banking, securities dealing, securities brokering, commodity contracts dealing, or commodity contracts brokering are classified in Industry Group 5231, Securities and Commodity Contracts Intermediation and Brokerage.

52392 Portfolio Management^CAN
See industry description for 523920 below.

523920 Portfolio Management^{CAN}

This industry comprises establishments primarily engaged in managing the portfolio assets (i.e., funds) of others on a fee or commission basis. Establishments in this industry have the authority to make investment decisions, and they derive fees based on the size and/or overall performance of the portfolio.

Illustrative Examples:

Managing trusts   Pension fund managing
Mutual fund managing   Portfolio fund managing

Cross-References.

Establishments primarily engaged in investment banking and securities dealing, securities brokering, commodity contracts dealing, or commodity contracts brokering are classified in Industry Group 5231, Securities and Commodity Contracts Intermediation and Brokerage.

52393 Investment Advice^{CAN}
See industry description for 523930 below.

523930 Investment Advice^{CAN}

This industry comprises establishments primarily engaged in providing customized investment advice to clients on a fee basis, but do not have the authority to execute trades. Primary activities performed by establishments in this industry are providing financial planning advice and investment counseling to meet the goals and needs of specific clients.

Illustrative Examples:

Financial investment advice services,   Investment advisory services,
  customized, fees paid by client   customized, fees paid by client
Financial planning services, customized,
  fees paid by client

Cross-References.

- Establishments providing investment advice in conjunction with their primary activity, such as portfolio management, or the sale of stocks, bonds, annuities, and real estate, are classified according to their primary activity; and

---

US—United States industry only. CAN—United States and Canadian industries are comparable. MEX—United States and Mexican industries are comparable. Blank—Canadian, Mexican, and United States industries are comparable.

- Establishments known as publishers providing generalized investment information to subscribers are classified in Subsector 511, Publishing Industries (except Internet) or Subsector 516, Internet Publishing and Broadcasting.

52399 All Other Financial Investment Activities[CAN]

This industry comprises establishments primarily engaged in acting as agents or brokers (except securities brokerages and commodity contracts brokerages) in buying and selling financial contracts providing financial investment activities (except securities and commodity exchanges, portfolio management, and investment advice).

Illustrative Examples:

Bank trust offices	Fiduciary agencies (except real estate)
Escrow agencies (except real estate)	Stock quotation services

Cross-References. Establishments primarily engaged in—

- Investment banking and securities dealing, securities brokerage, commodity contracts dealing, or commodity contracts brokering—are classified in Industry Group 5231, Securities and Commodity Contracts Intermediation and Brokerage;
- Acting as principals (except investment bankers, securities dealers, and commodity contracts dealers) in buying or selling financial contracts (except securities or commodity contracts)—are classified in Industry 52391, Miscellaneous Intermediation;
- Furnishing physical or electronic marketplaces for the purpose of facilitating the buying and selling of securities and commodities—are classified in Industry 52321, Securities and Commodity Exchanges;
- Managing the portfolio assets (i.e., funds) of others—are classified in Industry 52392, Portfolio Management;
- Providing customized investment advice—are classified in Industry 52393, Investment Advice;
- Awarding grants from trust funds—are classified in Industry 81321, Grantmaking and Giving Services;
- Performing real estate escrow or real estate fiduciary activities—are classified in Industry 53139, Other Activities Related to Real Estate; and
- Financial transactions processing, reserve, and clearinghouse activities—are classified in Industry 52232, Financial Transactions Processing, Reserve, and Clearinghouse Activities.

US—United States industry only. CAN—United States and Canadian industries are comparable. MEX—United States and Mexican industries are comparable. Blank—Canadian, Mexican, and United States industries are comparable.

523991 Trust, Fiduciary, and Custody Activities[US]

This U.S. industry comprises establishments primarily engaged in providing trust, fiduciary, and custody services to others, as instructed, on a fee or contract basis, such as bank trust offices and escrow agencies (except real estate).

Cross-References. Establishments primarily engaged in—

- Managing the portfolio assets (i.e., funds) of others—are classified in Industry 523920, Portfolio Management;
- Performing real estate escrow or real estate fiduciary activities—are classified in Industry 531390, Other Activities Related to Real Estate; and
- Awarding grants from trust funds—are classified in Industry 81321, Grantmaking and Giving Services.

523999 Miscellaneous Financial Investment Activities[US]

This U.S. industry comprises establishments primarily engaged in acting as agents and/or brokers (except securities brokerages and commodity contracts brokerages) in buying or selling financial contracts and those providing financial investment services (except securities and commodity exchanges; portfolio management; investment advice; and trust, fiduciary, and custody services) on a fee or commission basis.

Illustrative Examples:

Exchange clearinghouses, commodities or securities	Gas lease brokers' offices
	Stock quotation services

Cross-References. Establishments primarily engaged in—

- Investment banking and securities dealing, securities brokering, commodity contracts dealing, or commodity contracts brokering—are classified in Industry Group 5231, Securities and Commodity Contracts Intermediation and Brokerage;
- Acting as principals (except investment bankers, securities dealers, and commodity contracts dealers) in buying or selling financial contracts—are classified in Industry 523910, Miscellaneous Intermediation;
- Furnishing physical or electrical marketplaces for the purpose of facilitating the buying and selling of securities and commodities—are classified in Industry 523210, Securities and Commodity Exchanges;
- Managing the portfolio assets (i.e., funds) of others—are classified in Industry 523920, Portfolio Management;

US—United States industry only. CAN—United States and Canadian industries are comparable. MEX—United States and Mexican industries are comparable. Blank—Canadian, Mexican, and United States industries are comparable.

52412 Direct Insurance (except Life, Health, and Medical) Carriers[CAN]

This industry comprises establishments primarily engaged in initially underwriting (i.e., assuming the risk and assigning premiums) various types of insurance policies (except life, disability income, accidental death and dismemberment, and health and medical insurance policies).

Illustrative Examples:

Automobile insurance carriers, direct	Title insurance carriers, real estate, direct
Bank deposit insurance carriers, direct	Warranty insurance carriers (e.g.,
Mortgage guaranty insurance carriers, direct	appliance, automobile, homeowners, product), direct
Property and casualty insurance carriers, direct	

Cross-References.

- Establishments primarily engaged in reinsuring insurance policies are classified in Industry 524130, Reinsurance Carriers;

- Legal entities (i.e., funds, plans, and/or programs) organized to provide insurance and employee benefits exclusively for the sponsor, firm, or its employees or members are classified in Industry Group 5251, Insurance and Employee Benefit Funds; and

- Establishments primarily engaged in initially underwriting annuities and life insurance policies, disability income insurance policies, accidental death and dismemberment insurance policies, and health and medical insurance policies are classified in Industry 52411, Direct Life, Health, and Medical Insurance Carriers.

524126 Direct Property and Casualty Insurance Carriers[US]

This U.S. industry comprises establishments primarily engaged in initially underwriting (i.e., assuming the risk and assigning premiums) insurance policies that protect policyholders against losses that may occur as a result of property damage or liability.

Illustrative Examples:

Automobile insurance carriers, direct	Malpractice insurance carriers, direct
Fidelity insurance carriers, direct	Mortgage guaranty insurance carriers, direct
Homeowners insurance carriers, direct	
Liability insurance carriers, direct	Surety insurance carriers, direct

Cross-References.

Establishments primarily engaged in reinsuring property and casualty insurance policies are classified in Industry 524130, Reinsurance Carriers.

524127 Direct Title Insurance Carriers[US]

This U.S. industry comprises establishments primarily engaged in initially underwriting (i.e., assuming the risk and assigning premiums) insurance policies to protect the owners of real estate or real estate creditors against loss sustained by reason of any title defect to real property.

Cross-References.

Establishments primarily engaged in reinsuring title insurance policies are classified in Industry 524130, Reinsurance Carriers.

524128 Other Direct Insurance (except Life, Health, and Medical) Carriers[US]

This U.S. industry comprises establishments primarily engaged in initially underwriting (e.g., assuming the risk, assigning premiums) insurance policies (except life, disability income, accidental death and dismemberment, health and medical, property and casualty, and title insurance policies).

Illustrative Examples:

Bank deposit insurance carriers, direct
Deposit or share insurance carriers, direct
Product warranty insurance carriers, direct
Warranty insurance carriers (e.g., appliance, automobile, homeowners, product), direct

Cross-References. Establishments primarily engaged in—

- Reinsuring insurance policies—are classified in Industry 524130, Reinsurance Carriers;
- Initially underwriting annuities and life insurance policies, disability income insurance policies, and accidental death and dismemberment insurance policies—are classified in U.S. Industry 524113, Direct Life Insurance Carriers;
- Initially underwriting health and medical insurance policies—are classified in U.S. Industry 524114, Direct Health and Medical Insurance Carriers;
- Initially underwriting property and casualty insurance policies—are classified in U.S. Industry 524126, Direct Property and Casualty Insurance Carriers; and

- Initially underwriting title insurance policies—are classified in U.S. Industry 524127, Direct Title Insurance Carriers.

52413 Reinsurance Carriers^{CAN}
See industry description for 524130 below.

524130 Reinsurance Carriers^{US}

This industry comprises establishments primarily engaged in assuming all or part of the risk associated with existing insurance policies originally underwritten by other insurance carriers.

Cross-References. Establishments primarily engaged in—
- Initially underwriting annuities and life insurance policies, disability income insurance policies, accidental death and dismemberment insurance policies, and health and medical insurance policies—are classified in Industry 52411, Direct Life, Health, and Medical Insurance Carriers; and
- Initially underwriting various types of insurance policies (except life, disability income, accidental death and dismemberment, and health and medical insurance policies)—are classified in Industry 52412, Direct Insurance (except Life, Health, and Medical) Carriers.

5242 Agencies, Brokerages, and Other Insurance Related Activities

This industry group comprises establishments primarily engaged in (1) acting as agents (i.e., brokers) in selling annuities and insurance policies or (2) providing other employee benefits and insurance related services, such as claims adjustment and third party administration.

52421 Insurance Agencies and Brokerages^{CAN}
See industry description for 524210 below.

524210 Insurance Agencies and Brokerages^{CAN}

This industry comprises establishments primarily engaged in acting as agents (i.e., brokers) in selling annuities and insurance policies.

Cross-References.
Establishments primarily engaged in underwriting annuities and insurance policies are classified in Industry Group 5241, Insurance Carriers.

US—United States industry only. CAN—United States and Canadian industries are comparable. MEX—United States and Mexican industries are comparable. Blank—Canadian, Mexican, and United States industries are comparable.

52429 Other Insurance Related Activities^{CAN}

This industry comprises establishments primarily engaged in providing services related to insurance (except insurance agencies and brokerages).

Illustrative Examples:

Claims adjusting
Insurance adjusting

Insurance plan administrative services

Cross-References. Establishments primarily engaged in—

- Managing the portfolio assets (i.e., funds) of others—are classified in Industry 52392, Portfolio Management;

- Acting as agents (i.e., brokers) in selling annuities and insurance policies—are classified in Industry 52421, Insurance Agencies and Brokerages; and

- Providing actuarial consulting services—are classified in Industry 54161, Management Consulting Services.

524291 Claims Adjusting^{CAN}

This industry comprises establishments primarily engaged in investigating, appraising, and settling insurance claims.

524292 Third Party Administration of Insurance and Pension Funds^{US}

This U.S. industry comprises establishments primarily engaged in providing third party administration services of insurance and pension funds, such as claims processing and other administrative services to insurance carriers, employee-benefit plans, and self-insurance funds.

Cross-References. Establishments primarily engaged in—

- Managing the portfolio assets (i.e., funds) of others—are classified in Industry 523920, Portfolio Management; and

- Providing actuarial consulting services—are classified in U.S. Industry 541612, Human Resources and Executive Search Consulting Services.

524298 All Other Insurance Related Activities^{US}

This U.S. industry comprises establishments primarily engaged in providing insurance services on a contract or fee basis (except insurance agencies and broker-

US—United States industry only. CAN—United States and Canadian industries are comparable. MEX—United States and Mexican industries are comparable. Blank—Canadian, Mexican, and United States industries are comparable.

ages, claims adjusting, and third party administration). Insurance advisory services and insurance ratemaking services are included in this industry.

Cross-References. Establishments primarily engaged in—

- Providing actuarial consulting services—are classified in U.S. Industry 541612, Human Resources Management and Executive Search Consulting Services;

- Acting as agents (i.e., brokers) in selling annuities and insurance policies— are classified in Industry 524210, Insurance Agencies and Brokerages;

- Insurance claims adjusting—are classified in U.S. Industry 524291, Claims Adjusting; and

- Third party administration services of insurance and pension funds—are classified in U.S. Industry 524292, Third Party Administration of Insurance and Pension Funds.

525 Funds, Trusts, and Other Financial Vehicles[US]

Industries in the Funds, Trusts, and Other Financial Vehicles subsector are comprised of legal entities (i.e., funds, plans, and/or programs) organized to pool securities or other assets on behalf of shareholders or beneficiaries of employee benefit or other trust funds. The portfolios are customized to achieve specific investment characteristics, such as diversification, risk, rate of return, and price volatility. These entities earn interest, dividends, and other property income, but have little or no employment and no revenue from the sale of services. Establishments with employees devoted to the management of funds are classified in Industry Group 5239, Other Financial Investment Activities.

Establishments primarily engaged in holding the securities of (or other equity interests in) other firms are classified in Sector 55, Management of Companies and Enterprises.

5251 Insurance and Employee Benefit Funds[US]

This industry group comprises legal entities (i.e., funds, plans, and/or programs) organized to provide insurance and employee benefits exclusively for the sponsor, firm, or its employees or members.

52511 Pension Funds[US]

See industry description for 525110 below.

US—United States industry only. CAN—United States and Canadian industries are comparable. MEX—United States and Mexican industries are comparable. Blank—Canadian, Mexican, and United States industries are comparable.

525110 Pension Funds[US]

This industry comprises legal entities (i.e., funds, plans, and/or programs) organized to provide retirement income benefits exclusively for the sponsor's employees or members.

Illustrative Examples:

Employee benefit plans
Pension funds and plans

Retirement plans

Cross-References. Establishments primarily engaged in—

- Managing portfolios of pension funds—are classified in Industry 523920, Portfolio Management; and
- Initially underwriting annuities—are classified in U.S. Industry 524113, Direct Life Insurance Carriers.

52512 Health and Welfare Funds[US]
See industry description for 525120 below.

525120 Health and Welfare Funds[US]

This industry comprises legal entities (i.e., funds, plans, and/or programs) organized to provide medical, surgical, hospital, vacation, training, and other health- and welfare-related employee benefits exclusively for the sponsor's employees or members.

Cross-References. Establishments primarily engaged in—

- Managing portfolios of health and welfare funds—are classified in Industry 523920, Portfolio Management; and
- Third party claims administration of health and welfare plans—are classified in U.S. Industry 524292, Third Party Administration of Insurance and Pension Funds.

52519 Other Insurance Funds[US]
See industry description for 525190 below.

525190 Other Insurance Funds[US]

This industry comprises legal entities (i.e., funds (except pension, and health- and welfare-related employee benefit funds)) organized to provide insurance exclu-

---

US—United States industry only. CAN—United States and Canadian industries are comparable. MEX—United States and Mexican industries are comparable. Blank—Canadian, Mexican, and United States industries are comparable.

sively for the sponsor, firm, or its employees or members. Self-insurance funds (except employee benefit funds) and workers' compensation insurance funds are included in this industry.

Cross-References.

- Legal entities (i.e., funds, plans, and/or programs) organized to provide retirement income benefits exclusively for the sponsor's employees or members are classified in Industry 525110, Pension Funds;

- Legal entities (i.e., funds, plans, and/or programs) organized to provide health- and welfare-related employee benefits exclusively for the sponsor's employees or members are classified in Industry 525120, Health and Welfare Funds;

- Establishments primarily engaged in managing portfolios of insurance funds are classified in Industry 523920, Portfolio Management;

- Establishments primarily engaged in third party claims administration of insurance, and other employee benefit funds are classified in U.S. Industry 524292, Third Party Administration of Insurance and Pension Funds; and

- Establishments primarily engaged in providing insurance on a fee or contract basis are classified in Industry Group 5241, Insurance Carriers.

5259 Other Investment Pools and Funds[US]

This industry group comprises legal entities (i.e., investment pools and/or funds) organized to pool securities or other assets (except insurance and employee-benefit funds) on behalf of shareholders, unitholders, or beneficiaries.

52591 Open-End Investment Funds[US]

See industry description for 525910 below.

525910 Open-End Investment Funds[US]

This industry comprises legal entities (i.e., open-end investment funds) organized to pool assets that consist of securities or other financial instruments. Shares in these pools are offered to the public in an initial offering with additional shares offered continuously and perpetually and redeemed at a specific price determined by the net asset value.

Illustrative Examples:

Investment funds, open-ended   Money market mutual funds, open-ended

---

US—United States industry only. CAN—United States and Canadian industries are comparable. MEX—United States and Mexican industries are comparable. Blank—Canadian, Mexican, and United States industries are comparable.

52592 Trusts, Estates, and Agency Accounts^{US}
See industry description for 525920 below.

525920 Trusts, Estates, and Agency Accounts^{US}

This industry comprises legal entities, trusts, estates, or agency accounts, administered on behalf of the beneficiaries under the terms of a trust agreement, will, or agency agreement.

Illustrative Examples:

Bankruptcy estates
Personal investment trusts
Private estates (i.e., administering on
behalf of beneficiaries)

Testamentary trusts

Cross-References. Establishments primarily engaged in—

- Managing portfolios of trusts—are classified in Industry 523920, Portfolio Management;
- Administering personal estates—are classified in U.S. Industry 523991, Trust, Fiduciary, and Custody Activities; and
- Operating businesses of trusts and bankruptcy estates—are classified according to the kind of business operated.

52593 Real Estate Investment Trusts^{US}
See industry description for 525930 below.

525930 Real Estate Investment Trusts^{US}

This industry comprises legal entities that are Real Estate Investment Trusts (REITs).

Cross-References.

- Legal entities of mortgage-backed investment funds that are not REITs are classified elsewhere in the Funds, Trusts, and Other Financial Vehicles subsector based on the types of funds; and
- Legal entities of investments in real estate that are not REITs are classified in Industry Group 5311, Lessors of Real Estate.

52599 Other Financial Vehicles^{US}
See industry description for 525990 below.

US—United States industry only. CAN—United States and Canadian industries are comparable. MEX—United States and Mexican industries are comparable. **Blank**—Canadian, Mexican, and United States industries are comparable.

525990 Other Financial Vehicles[US]

This industry comprises legal entities (i.e., funds (except insurance and employee benefit funds; open-end investment funds; trusts, estates, and agency accounts; and Real Estate Investment Trusts (REITs)).

Illustrative Examples:

Closed-end investment funds (except REITs)

Collateralized Mortgage Obligations (CMOs)

Face-amount certificate funds

Real Estate Mortgage Investment Conduits (REMICs)

Special purpose vehicles

Unit investment trust funds

Cross-References.

- Legal entities (i.e., funds, plans, and programs) that provide insurance and employee benefits exclusively for the sponsor, firm, or its employees or members are classified in Industry Group 5251, Insurance and Employee Benefit Funds;

- Legal entities (i.e., open-end investment funds) organized to pool assets that consist of securities or other financial instruments, where the pools are offered to the public in an initial offering with additional shares offered continuously and perpetually at a specific price determined by the net asset value, are classified in Industry 525910, Open-End Investment Funds;

- Legal entities (i.e., trusts, estates, or agency accounts) administered on behalf of the beneficiaries under the terms of a trust agreement, will, or agency agreement are classified in Industry 525920, Trusts, Estates, and Agency Accounts; and

- Legal entities that are Real Estate Investment Trusts (REITs) are classified in Industry 525930, Real Estate Investment Trusts.

Sector 53—Real Estate and Rental and Leasing

The Sector as a Whole

The Real Estate and Rental and Leasing sector comprises establishments primarily engaged in renting, leasing, or otherwise allowing the use of tangible or intangible assets, and establishments providing related services. The major portion of this sector comprises establishments that rent, lease, or otherwise allow the use of their own assets by others. The assets may be tangible, as is the case of real estate and equipment, or intangible, as is the case with patents and trademarks.

This sector also includes establishments primarily engaged in managing real estate for others, selling, renting and/or buying real estate for others, and appraising real estate. These activities are closely related to this sector's main activity, and it was felt that from a production basis they would best be included here. In addition, a substantial proportion of property management is self-performed by lessors.

The main components of this sector are the real estate lessors industries; equipment lessors industries (including motor vehicles, computers, and consumer goods); and lessors of nonfinancial intangible assets (except copyrighted works).

Excluded from this sector are real estate investment trusts (REITS) and establishments primarily engaged in renting or leasing equipment with operators. REITS are classified in Subsector 525, Funds, Trusts, and Other Financial Vehicles, because they are considered investment vehicles. Establishments renting or leasing equipment with operators are classified in various subsectors of NAICS depending on the nature of the services provided (e.g., transportation, construction, agriculture). These activities are excluded from this sector because the client is paying for the expertise and knowledge of the equipment operator, in addition to the rental of the equipment. In many cases, such as the rental of heavy construction equipment, the operator is essential to operate the equipment.

531 Real Estate

Industries in the Real Estate subsector group establishments that are primarily engaged in renting or leasing real estate to others; managing real estate for others; selling, buying, or renting real estate for others; and providing other real estate related services, such as appraisal services.

Establishments primarily engaged in subdividing and developing unimproved real estate and constructing buildings for sale are classified in Subsector 236, Construction of Buildings. Establishments primarily engaged in subdividing and improving raw land for subsequent sale to builders are classified in Subsector 237, Heavy and Civil Engineering Construction.

Real Estate Investment Trusts (REITS) are classified in Subsector 525, Funds, Trusts, and Other Financial Vehicles, because they are considered investment vehicles.

5311 Lessors of Real Estate

53111 Lessors of Residential Buildings and Dwellings^{CAN}
See industry description for 531110 below.

531110 Lessors of Residential Buildings and Dwellings^{US}

This industry comprises establishments primarily engaged in acting as lessors of buildings used as residences or dwellings, such as single-family homes, apartment buildings, and town homes. Included in this industry are owner-lessors and establishments renting real estate and then acting as lessors in subleasing it to others. The establishments in this industry may manage the property themselves or have another establishment manage it for them.

Cross-References.

Establishments primarily engaged in managing residential real estate for others are classified in U.S. Industry 531311, Residential Property Managers.

53112 Lessors of Nonresidential Buildings (except Miniwarehouses)^{CAN}
See industry description for 531120 below.

531120 Lessors of Nonresidential Buildings (except Miniwarehouses)^{CAN}

This industry comprises establishments primarily engaged in acting as lessors of buildings (except miniwarehouses and self-storage units) that are not used as residences or dwellings. Included in this industry are: (1) owner-lessors of nonresidential buildings; (2) establishments renting real estate and then acting as lessors in subleasing it to others; and (3) establishments providing full service office space, whether on a lease or service contract basis. The establishments in this industry may manage the property themselves or have another establishment manage it for them.

Cross-References. Establishments primarily engaged in—

- Acting as lessors of buildings used as residences or dwellings—are classified in Industry 531110, Lessors of Residential Buildings and Dwellings;
- Renting or leasing space for self-storage—are classified in Industry 531130, Lessors of Miniwarehouses and Self-Storage Units;

- Managing nonresidential real estate for others—are classified in U.S. Industry 531312, Nonresidential Property Managers;

- Providing a range of office support services, such as mailbox rental, other postal and mailing (except direct mail advertising) services, document copying services, facsimile services, word processing services or on-site personal computer rental, that are not providing office space—are classified in Industry 56143, Business Service Centers;

- Managing and operating arenas, stadiums, theaters, or other related facilities and promoting and organizing performing arts productions, sports events, and similar events at those facilities—are classified in Industry 711310, Promoters of Performing Arts, Sports, and Similar Events with Facilities; and

- Operating public and contract general merchandise warehousing and storage facilities—are classified in Industry 493110, General Warehousing and Storage.

53113 Lessors of Miniwarehouses and Self-Storage Units[CAN]
See industry description for 531130 below.

531130 Lessors of Miniwarehouses and Self-Storage Units[CAN]

This industry comprises establishments primarily engaged in renting or leasing space for self-storage. These establishments provide secure space (i.e., rooms, compartments, lockers, containers, or outdoor space) where clients can store and retrieve their goods.

Cross-References. Establishments primarily engaged in—

- Operating public and contract general merchandise warehousing and storage facilities—are classified in Industry 493110, General Warehousing and Storage; and

- Operating coin-operated lockers—are classified in Industry 812990, All Other Personal Services.

53119 Lessors of Other Real Estate Property[CAN]
See industry description for 531190 below.

531190 Lessors of Other Real Estate Property[CAN]

This industry comprises establishments primarily engaged in acting as lessors of real estate (except buildings), such as manufactured home (i.e., mobile home) sites, vacant lots, and grazing land.

Cross-References. Establishments primarily engaged in—

- Acting as lessors of buildings used as residences or dwellings including manufactured (mobile) homes on-site—are classified in Industry 531110, Lessors of Residential Buildings and Dwellings;

- Acting as lessors of buildings (except miniwarehouses and self-storage units) that are not used as residences or dwellings—are classified in Industry 531120, Lessors of Nonresidential Buildings (except Miniwarehouses); and

- Renting or leasing space for self-storage—are classified in Industry 531130, Lessors of Miniwarehouses and Self-Storage Units.

5312 Offices of Real Estate Agents and Brokers

53121 Offices of Real Estate Agents and Brokers
See industry description for 531210 below.

531210 Offices of Real Estate Agents and Brokers

This industry comprises establishments primarily engaged in acting as agents and/or brokers in one or more of the following: (1) selling real estate for others; (2) buying real estate for others; and (3) renting real estate for others.

5313 Activities Related to Real Estate

This industry group comprises establishments primarily engaged in providing real estate services (except lessors of real estate and offices of real estate agents and brokers). Included in this industry group are establishments primarily engaged in activities, such as managing real estate for others and appraising real estate.

53131 Real Estate Property Managers^{CAN}

This industry comprises establishments primarily engaged in managing real property for others. Management includes ensuring that various activities associated with the overall operation of the property are performed, such as collecting rents, and overseeing other services (e.g., maintenance, security, trash removal.)

Cross-References.

- Establishments primarily engaged in acting as lessors of real estate are classified in Industry Group 5311, Lessors of Real Estate; and

---

US—United States industry only. CAN—United States and Canadian industries are comparable. MEX—United States and Mexican industries are comparable. Blank—Canadian, Mexican, and United States industries are comparable.

- Establishments formed on behalf of individual condominium owners or homeowners are classified in Industry 81399, Other Similar Organizations (except Business, Professional, Labor, and Political Organizations).

531311 Residential Property Managers[US]

This U.S. industry comprises establishments primarily engaged in managing residential real estate for others.

Cross-References.

- Establishments primarily engaged in managing nonresidential real estate for others are classified in U.S. Industry 531312, Nonresidential Property Managers;
- Establishments primarily engaged in acting as lessors of buildings used as residences or dwellings are classified in Industry 531110, Lessors of Residential Buildings and Dwellings; and
- Establishments formed on behalf of individual residential condominium owners or homeowners are classified in Industry 81399, Other Similar Organizations (except Business, Professional, Labor, and Political Organizations).

531312 Nonresidential Property Managers[US]

This U.S. industry comprises establishments primarily engaged in managing nonresidential real estate for others.

Cross-References.

- Establishments primarily engaged in managing residential real estate for others are classified in U.S. Industry 531311, Residential Property Managers;
- Establishments primarily engaged in acting as lessors of buildings (except miniwarehouses and self storage units) that are not used as residences or dwellings are classified in Industry 531120, Lessors of Nonresidential Buildings (except Miniwarehouses);
- Establishments primarily engaged in renting or leasing space for self-storage are classified in Industry 531130, Lessors of Miniwarehouses and Self-Storage Units; and
- Establishments formed on behalf of individual nonresidential condominium owners are classified in Industry 81399, Other Similar Organizations (except Business, Professional, Labor, and Political Organizations).

US—United States industry only. CAN—United States and Canadian industries are comparable. MEX—United States and Mexican industries are comparable. Blank—Canadian, Mexican, and United States industries are comparable.

53132 Offices of Real Estate Appraisers[CAN]
See industry description for 531320 below.

531320 Offices of Real Estate Appraisers[CAN]

This industry comprises establishments primarily engaged in estimating the fair market value of real estate.

53139 Other Activities Related to Real Estate[CAN]
See industry description for 531390 below.

531390 Other Activities Related to Real Estate[CAN]

This industry comprises establishments primarily engaged in performing real estate related services (except lessors of real estate, offices of real estate agents and brokers, real estate property managers, and offices of real estate appraisers).

Illustrative Examples:

Real estate escrow agencies   Real estate listing services
Real estate fiduciaries' offices

Cross-References. Establishments primarily engaged in—

- Acting as lessors of real estate—are classified in Industry Group 5311, Lessors of Real Estate;
- Selling, buying, and/or renting real estate for others—are classified in Industry 531210, Offices of Real Estate Agents and Brokers;
- Managing real estate for others—are classified in Industry 53131, Real Estate Property Managers;
- Estimating fair market value of real estate—are classified in Industry 531320, Offices of Real Estate Appraisers; and
- Researching public land records for ownership of titles and/or conveying real estate titles—are classified in U.S. Industry 541191, Title Abstract and Settlement Offices.

532 Rental and Leasing Services

Industries in the Rental and Leasing Services subsector include establishments that provide a wide array of tangible goods, such as automobiles, computers, consumer goods, and industrial machinery and equipment, to customers in return for a periodic rental or lease payment.

The subsector includes two main types of establishments: (1) those that are engaged in renting consumer goods and equipment and (2) those that are engaged in leasing machinery and equipment often used for business operations. The first type typically operates from a retail-like or store-front facility and maintains inventories of goods that are rented for short periods of time. The latter type typically does not operate from retail-like locations or maintain inventories, and offers longer term leases. These establishments work directly with clients to enable them to acquire the use of equipment on a lease basis, or they work with equipment vendors or dealers to support the marketing of equipment to their customers under lease arrangements. Equipment lessors generally structure lease contracts to meet the specialized needs of their clients and use their remarketing expertise to find other users for previously leased equipment. Establishments that provide operating and capital (i.e., finance) leases are included in this subsector.

Establishments primarily engaged in leasing in combination with providing loans are classified in Sector 52, Finance and Insurance. Establishments primarily engaged in leasing real property are classified in Subsector 531, Real Estate. Those establishments primarily engaged in renting or leasing equipment with operators are classified in various subsectors of NAICS depending on the nature of the services provided (e.g., Transportation, Construction, Agriculture). These activities are excluded from this subsector since the client is paying for the expertise and knowledge of the equipment operator, in addition to the rental of the equipment. In many cases, such as the rental of heavy construction equipment, the operator is essential to operate the equipment. Likewise, since the provision of crop harvesting services includes both the equipment and operator, it is included in the agriculture subsector. The rental or leasing of copyrighted works is classified in Sector 51, Information, and the rental or leasing of assets, such as patents, trademarks, and/ or licensing agreements is classified in Subsector 533, Lessors of Nonfinancial Intangible Assets (except Copyrighted Works).

5321 Automotive Equipment Rental and Leasing

This industry group comprises establishments primarily engaged in renting or leasing the following types of vehicles: passenger cars and trucks without drivers, and utility trailers. These establishments generally operate from a retail-like facility. Some establishments offer only short-term rental, others only longer-term leases, and some provide both type of services.

53211 Passenger Car Rental and Leasing

This industry comprises establishments primarily engaged in renting or leasing passenger cars without drivers.

US—United States industry only. CAN—United States and Canadian industries are comparable. MEX—United States and Mexican industries are comparable. Blank—Canadian, Mexican, and United States industries are comparable.

Cross-References. Establishments primarily engaged in—

- Renting or leasing passenger cars with drivers (e.g., limousines, hearses, taxis)—are classified in Industry Group 4853, Taxi and Limousine Service;
- Retailing passenger cars through sales or lease arrangements—are classified in Industry Group 4411, Automobile Dealers; and
- Leasing passenger cars in combination with providing loans to buyers of such vehicles—are classified in Sector 52, Finance and Insurance.

532111 Passenger Car Rental^{CAN}

This industry comprises establishments primarily engaged in renting passenger cars without drivers, generally for short periods of time.

Cross-References. Establishments primarily engaged in—

- Leasing passenger cars without drivers, generally for long periods of time—are classified in U.S. Industry 532112, Passenger Car Leasing; and
- Renting or leasing passenger cars with drivers (e.g., limousines, hearses, taxis)—are classified in Industry Group 4853, Taxi and Limousine Service.

532112 Passenger Car Leasing^{CAN}

This industry comprises establishments primarily engaged in leasing passenger cars without drivers, generally for long periods of time.

Cross-References. Establishments primarily engaged in—

- Renting passenger cars without drivers, generally for short periods of time—are classified in U.S. Industry 532111, Passenger Car Rental;
- Renting or leasing passenger cars with drivers (e.g., limousines, hearses, taxis)—are classified in Industry Group 4853, Taxi and Limousine Service;
- Retailing passenger cars through sales or lease arrangements—are classified in Industry Group 4411, Automobile Dealers; and
- Leasing passenger cars in combination with providing loans to buyers of such vehicles—are classified in Sector 52, Finance and Insurance.

53212 Truck, Utility Trailer, and RV (Recreational Vehicle) Rental and Leasing
See industry description for 532120 below.

US—United States industry only. CAN—United States and Canadian industries are comparable. MEX—United States and Mexican industries are comparable. Blank—Canadian, Mexican, and United States industries are comparable.

532120 Truck, Utility Trailer, and RV (Recreational Vehicle) Rental and Leasing^{CAN}

This industry comprises establishments primarily engaged in renting or leasing, without drivers, one or more of the following: trucks, truck tractors or buses: semitrailers, utility trailers, or RVs (recreational vehicles).

Cross-References. Establishments primarily engaged in—

- Renting recreational goods, such as pleasure boats, canoes, motorcycles, mopeds, or bicycles—are classified in Industry 53229, Other Consumer Goods Rental;

- Renting or leasing farm tractors, industrial equipment, and industrial trucks, such as forklifts and other materials handling equipment—are classified in Industry 532490, Other Commercial and Industrial Machinery Equipment Rental and Leasing;

- Renting or leasing mobile home sites—are classified in Industry 53119, Lessors of Other Real Estate Property;

- Retailing vehicles commonly referred to as RVs through sales or lease arrangements—are classified in Industry 44121, Recreational Vehicle Dealers; and

- Leasing trucks, utility trailers, and RVs in combination with providing loans to buyers of such vehicles—are classified in Sector 52, Finance and Insurance.

5322 Consumer Goods Rental

This industry group comprises establishments primarily engaged in renting personal and household-type goods. Establishments classified in this industry group generally provide short-term rental although in some instances, the goods may be leased for longer periods of time. These establishments often operate from a retail-like or store-front facility.

53221 Consumer Electronics and Appliances Rental
See industry description for 532210 below.

532210 Consumer Electronics and Appliances Rental

This industry comprises establishments primarily engaged in renting consumer electronics equipment and appliances, such as televisions, stereos, and refrigerators. Included in this industry are appliance rental centers.

US—United States industry only. CAN—United States and Canadian industries are comparable. MEX—United States and Mexican industries are comparable. Blank—Canadian, Mexican, and United States industries are comparable.

Cross-References. Establishments primarily engaged in—

- Renting or leasing computers—are classified in Industry 532420, Office Machinery and Equipment Rental and Leasing; and
- Renting a range of consumer, commercial, and industrial equipment, such as lawn and garden equipment, home repair tools, and party and banquet equipment—are classified in Industry 532310, General Rental Centers.

53222 Formal Wear and Costume Rental
See industry description for 532220 below.

532220 Formal Wear and Costume Rental

This industry comprises establishments primarily engaged in renting clothing, such as formal wear, costumes (e.g., theatrical), or other clothing (except laundered uniforms and work apparel).

Cross-References.

Establishments primarily engaged in laundering and supplying uniforms and other work apparel are classified in Industry 81233, Linen and Uniform Supply.

53223 Video Tape and Disc Rental
See industry description for 532230 below.

532230 Video Tape and Disc Rental

This industry comprises establishments primarily engaged in renting prerecorded video tapes and discs for home electronic equipment.

Cross-References. Establishments primarily engaged in—

- Theatrical distribution of motion pictures and videos—are classified in Subsector 512, Motion Picture and Sound Recording Industries;
- Renting video recorders and players—are classified in Industry 532210, Consumer Electronics and Appliances Rental; and
- Retailing prerecorded video tapes and discs—are classified in Industry 451220, Prerecorded Tape, Compact Disc, and Record Stores.

53229 Other Consumer Goods Rental

This industry comprises establishments primarily engaged in renting consumer goods (except consumer electronics and appliances, formal wear and costumes, and prerecorded video tapes).

US—United States industry only. CAN—United States and Canadian industries are comparable. MEX—United States and Mexican industries are comparable. Blank—Canadian, Mexican, and United States industries are comparable.

Illustrative Examples:

Furniture rental centers	Sporting goods rental
Party rental supply centers	

Cross-References. Establishments primarily engaged in—

- Renting consumer electronics and appliances—are classified in Industry 53221, Consumer Electronics and Appliances Rental;

- Renting formal wear and costumes—are classified in Industry 53222, Formal Wear and Costume Rental;

- Renting prerecorded video tapes and discs—are classified in Industry 53223, Video Tape and Disc Rental;

- Renting a general line of products, such as lawn and garden equipment, home repair tools, and party and banquet equipment—are classified in Industry 53231, General Rental Centers;

- Renting medical equipment (except home health equipment), such as electro-medical and electrotherapeutic apparatus—are classified in Industry 53249, Other Commercial and Industrial Machinery and Equipment Rental and Leasing;

- Providing home health care services and home health equipment—are classified in Industry 62161, Home Health Care Services; and

- Retailing and renting musical instruments—are classified in Industry 45114, Musical Instrument and Supplies Stores.

532291 Home Health Equipment Rental[US]

This U.S. industry comprises establishments primarily engaged in renting home-type health and invalid equipment, such as wheel chairs, hospital beds, oxygen tanks, walkers, and crutches.

Cross-References. Establishments primarily engaged in—

- Renting medical equipment (except home health equipment), such as electro-medical and electrotherapeutic apparatus—are classified in Industry 532490, Other Commercial and Industrial Machinery and Equipment Rental and Leasing; and

- Providing home health care services and home health equipment—are classified in Industry 62161, Home Health Care Services.

532292 Recreational Goods Rental[US]

This U.S. industry comprises establishments primarily engaged in renting recreational goods, such as bicycles, canoes, motorcycles, skis, sailboats, beach chairs, and beach umbrellas.

532299 All Other Consumer Goods Rental[US]

This U.S. industry comprises establishments primarily engaged in renting consumer goods and products (except consumer electronics and appliances; formal wear and costumes; prerecorded video tapes and discs for home electronic equipment; home health furniture and equipment; and recreational goods). Included in this industry are furniture rental centers and party rental supply centers.

Cross-References. Establishments primarily engaged in—

- Renting consumer electronics and appliances—are classified in Industry 532210, Consumer Electronics and Appliances Rental;
- Renting formal wear and costumes—are classified in Industry 532220, Formal Wear and Costume Rental;
- Renting video tapes and discs—are classified in Industry 532230, Video Tape and Disc Rental;
- Renting home health furniture and equipment—are classified in U.S. Industry 532291, Home Health Equipment Rental;
- Renting recreational goods—are classified in U.S. Industry 532292, Recreational Goods Rental;
- Retailing and renting musical instruments—are classified in Industry 451140, Musical Instrument and Supplies Stores; and
- Renting a range of consumer, commercial, and industrial equipment, such as lawn and garden equipment, home repair tools, and party and banquet equipment—are classified in Industry 532310, General Rental Centers.

5323 General Rental Centers

53231 General Rental Centers
See industry description for 532310 below.

532310 General Rental Centers

This industry comprises establishments primarily engaged in renting a range of consumer, commercial, and industrial equipment. Establishments in this industry typically operate from conveniently located facilities where they maintain inventories of goods and equipment that they rent for short periods of time. The type of equipment that establishments in this industry provide often includes, but is not limited to: audio visual equipment, contractors' and builders' tools and equipment, home repair tools, lawn and garden equipment, moving equipment and supplies, and party and banquet equipment and supplies.

US—United States industry only. CAN—United States and Canadian industries are comparable. MEX—United States and Mexican industries are comparable. Blank—Canadian, Mexican, and United States industries are comparable.

Cross-References. Establishments primarily engaged in—

- Renting trucks and trailers without drivers—are classified in Industry 532120, Truck, Utility Trailer, and RV (Recreational Vehicle) Rental and Leasing;
- Renting party and banquet equipment—are classified in Industry 53229, Other Consumer Goods Rental;
- Renting heavy construction equipment without operators—are classified in U.S. Industry 532412, Construction, Mining, and Forestry Machinery and Equipment Rental and Leasing; and
- Renting specialized types of commercial and industrial equipment, such as garden tractors or public address systems—are classified in Industry 532490, Other Commercial and Industrial Machinery and Equipment Rental and Leasing.

5324 Commercial and Industrial Machinery and Equipment Rental and Leasing

This industry group comprises establishments primarily engaged in renting or leasing commercial-type and industrial-type machinery and equipment. The types of establishments included in this industry group are generally involved in providing capital or investment-type equipment that clients use in their business operations. These establishments typically cater to a business clientele and do not generally operate a retail-like or store-front facility.

53241 Construction, Transportation, Mining, and Forestry Machinery and Equipment Rental and Leasing

This industry comprises establishments primarily engaged in renting or leasing one or more of the following without operators: heavy construction, off-highway transportation, mining, and forestry machinery and equipment. Establishments in this industry may rent or lease products, such as aircraft, railroad cars, steamships, tugboats, bulldozers, earthmoving equipment, well-drilling machinery and equipment, or cranes.

Cross-References. Establishments primarily engaged in—

- Renting or leasing automobiles or trucks without operators—are classified in Industry Group 5321, Automotive Equipment Rental and Leasing;
- Renting or leasing air, rail, highway, and water transportation equipment with operators—are classified in Sector 48-49, Transportation and Warehousing, based on their primary activity;

- Renting or leasing heavy construction equipment with operators—are classified in Industry 2389, Other Specialty Trade Contractors;
- Renting or leasing heavy equipment for mining with operators—are classified in Industry 21311, Support Activities for Mining;
- Renting or leasing heavy equipment for forestry with operators—are classified in Industry Group 1153, Support Activities for Forestry; and
- Leasing heavy equipment in combination with providing loans to buyers of such equipment—are classified in Sector 52, Finance and Insurance.

532411 Commercial Air, Rail, and Water Transportation Equipment Rental and Leasing[US]

This U.S. industry comprises establishments primarily engaged in renting or leasing off-highway transportation equipment without operators, such as aircraft, railroad cars, steamships, or tugboats.

Cross-References. Establishments primarily engaged in—

- Renting or leasing air, rail, highway, and water transportation equipment with operators—are classified in Sector 48-49, Transportation and Warehousing, based on their primary activity;
- Renting pleasure boats—are classified in U.S. Industry 532292, Recreational Goods Rental; and
- Renting or leasing automobiles or trucks without drivers—are classified in Industry Group 5321, Automotive Equipment Rental and Leasing.

532412 Construction, Mining, and Forestry Machinery and Equipment Rental and Leasing[US]

This U.S. industry comprises establishments primarily engaged in renting or leasing heavy equipment without operators that may be used for construction, mining, or forestry, such as bulldozers, earthmoving equipment, well-drilling machinery and equipment, or cranes.

Cross-References. Establishments primarily engaged in—

- Renting or leasing heavy construction equipment with operators—are classified in Industry 23499, All Other Heavy Construction;
- Renting or leasing heavy equipment for mining with operators—are classified in Industry 21311, Support Activities for Mining;
- Renting or leasing heavy equipment for forestry with operators—are classified in Industry Group 1153, Support Activities for Forestry; and

- Leasing heavy equipment in combination with providing loans to buyers of such equipment—are classified in Sector 52, Finance and Insurance.

53242 Office Machinery and Equipment Rental and Leasing
See industry description for 532420 below.

532420 Office Machinery and Equipment Rental and Leasing

This industry comprises establishments primarily engaged in renting or leasing office machinery and equipment, such as computers, office furniture, duplicating machines (i.e., copiers), or facsimile machines.

Cross-References. Establishments primarily engaged in—

- Renting or leasing residential furniture—are classified in Industry 53229, Other Consumer Goods Rental; and
- Leasing office machinery and equipment in combination with providing loans to buyers of such equipment—are classified in Sector 52, Finance and Insurance.

53249 Other Commercial and Industrial Machinery and Equipment Rental and Leasing
See industry description for 532490 below.

532490 Other Commercial and Industrial Machinery and Equipment Rental and Leasing[CAN]

This industry comprises establishments primarily engaged in renting or leasing nonconsumer-type machinery and equipment (except heavy construction, transportation, mining, and forestry machinery and equipment without operators; and office machinery and equipment). Establishments in this industry rent or lease products, such as manufacturing equipment; metalworking, telecommunications, motion picture, or theatrical machinery and equipment; institutional (i.e., public building) furniture, such as furniture for schools, theaters, or buildings; or agricultural equipment without operators.

Cross-References. Establishments primarily engaged in—

- Renting or leasing heavy equipment without operators—are classified in Industry 53241, Construction, Transportation, Mining, and Forestry Machinery and Equipment Rental and Leasing;

US—United States industry only. CAN—United States and Canadian industries are comparable. MEX—United States and Mexican industries are comparable. Blank—Canadian, Mexican, and United States industries are comparable.

- Renting or leasing office machinery and equipment—are classified in Industry 532420, Office Machinery and Equipment Rental and Leasing;
- Renting or leasing agricultural machinery and equipment with operators—are classified in Subsector 115, Support Activities for Agriculture and Forestry;
- Renting home furniture or medical equipment for home use—are classified in Industry 53229, Other Consumer Goods Rental; and
- Leasing nonconsumer machinery and equipment in combination with providing loans to buyers of such equipment—are classified in Sector 52, Finance and Insurance.

533 Lessors of Nonfinancial Intangible Assets (except Copyrighted Works)

Industries in the Lessors of Nonfinancial Intangible Assets (except Copyrighted Works) subsector include establishments that are primarily engaged in assigning rights to assets, such as patents, trademarks, brand names, and/or franchise agreements for which a royalty payment or licensing fee is paid to the asset holder. Establishments in this subsector own the patents, trademarks, and/or franchise agreements that they allow others to use or reproduce for a fee and may or may not have created those assets.

Establishments that allow franchisees the use of the franchise name, contingent on the franchisee buying products or services from the franchisor, are classified elsewhere.

Excluded from this subsector are establishments primarily engaged in leasing real property and establishments primarily engaged in leasing tangible assets, such as automobiles, computers, consumer goods, and industrial machinery and equipment. These establishments are classified in Subsector 531, Real Estate and Subsector 532, Rental and Leasing Services, respectively.

5331 Lessors of Nonfinancial Intangible Assets (except Copyrighted Works)

53311 Lessors of Nonfinancial Intangible Assets (except Copyrighted Works)
See industry description for 533110 below.

533110 Lessors of Nonfinancial Intangible Assets (except Copyrighted Works)

This industry comprises establishments primarily engaged in assigning rights to assets, such as patents, trademarks, brand names, and/or franchise agreements for which a royalty payment or licensing fee is paid to the asset holder.

US—United States industry only. CAN—United States and Canadian industries are comparable. MEX—United States and Mexican industries are comparable. Blank—Canadian, Mexican, and United States industries are comparable.

Cross-References.

- Establishments primarily engaged in producing, reproducing, and/or distributing copyrighted works are classified in Sector 51, Information;

- Independent artists, writers, and performers primarily engaged in creating copyrighted works are classified in Industry 711510, Independent Artists, Writers, and Performers;

- Establishments primarily engaged in leasing real property are classified in Subsector 531, Real Estate;

- Establishments primarily engaged in leasing tangible assets, such as automobiles, computers, consumer goods, and industrial machinery and equipment, are classified in Subsector 532, Rental and Leasing Services; and

- Establishments that allow franchisees the use of the franchise name, contingent on the franchisee buying products or services from the franchisor are classified elsewhere.

Sector 54—Professional, Scientific, and Technical Services

The Sector as a Whole

The Professional, Scientific, and Technical Services sector comprises establishments that specialize in performing professional, scientific, and technical activities for others. These activities require a high degree of expertise and training. The establishments in this sector specialize according to expertise and provide these services to clients in a variety of industries and, in some cases, to households. Activities performed include: legal advice and representation; accounting, bookkeeping, and payroll services; architectural, engineering, and specialized design services; computer services; consulting services; research services; advertising services; photographic services; translation and interpretation services; veterinary services; and other professional, scientific, and technical services.

This sector excludes establishments primarily engaged in providing a range of day-to-day office administrative services, such as financial planning, billing and recordkeeping, personnel, and physical distribution and logistics. These establishments are classified in Sector 56, Administrative and Support and Waste Management and Remediation Services.

541 Professional, Scientific, and Technical Services

Industries in the Professional, Scientific, and Technical Services subsector group establishments engaged in processes where human capital is the major input. These establishments make available the knowledge and skills of their employees, often on an assignment basis, where an individual or team is responsible for the delivery of services to the client. The individual industries of this subsector are defined on the basis of the particular expertise and training of the services provider.

The distinguishing feature of the Professional, Scientific, and Technical Services subsector is the fact that most of the industries grouped in it have production processes that are almost wholly dependent on worker skills. In most of these industries, equipment and materials are not of major importance, unlike health care, for example, where "high tech" machines and materials are important collaborating inputs to labor skills in the production of health care. Thus, the establishments classified in this subsector sell expertise. Much of the expertise requires degrees, though not in every case.

5411 Legal Services

54111 Offices of Lawyers
See industry description for 541110 below.

541110 Offices of Lawyers

This industry comprises offices of legal practitioners known as lawyers or attorneys (i.e., counselors-at-law) primarily engaged in the practice of law. Establishments in this industry may provide expertise in a range or in specific areas of law, such as criminal law, corporate law, family and estate law, patent law, real estate law, or tax law.

Cross-References.

Establishments of legal practitioners (except lawyers or attorneys) primarily engaged in providing specialized legal or paralegal services are classified in Industry 54119, Other Legal Services.

54112 Offices of Notaries
See industry description for 541120 below.

541120 Offices of Notaries

This industry comprises establishments (except offices of lawyers and attorneys) primarily engaged in drafting, approving, and executing legal documents, such as real estate transactions, wills, and contracts; and in receiving, indexing, and storing such documents.

Cross-References.

- Establishments of lawyers and attorneys primarily engaged in the practice of law are classified in Industry 541110, Offices of Lawyers; and

- Establishments of notaries public engaged in activities, such as administering oaths and taking affidavits and depositions, witnessing and certifying signatures on documents, but not empowered to draw and approve legal documents and contracts, are classified in U.S. Industry 541199, All Other Legal Services

54119 Other Legal Services

This industry comprises establishments of legal practitioners (except lawyers and attorneys) primarily engaged in providing specialized legal or paralegal services.

Illustrative Examples:

Notary public services	Process serving services
Paralegal services	Real estate settlement offices

US—United States industry only. CAN—United States and Canadian industries are comparable. MEX—United States and Mexican industries are comparable. Blank—Canadian, Mexican, and United States industries are comparable.

Patent agent services (i.e., patent filing   Real estate title abstract companies
and searching services)

Cross-References.

- Establishments of lawyers and attorneys primarily engaged in the practice of law are classified in Industry 54111, Offices of Lawyers; and

- Establishments (except offices of lawyers, attorneys, and paralegals) primarily engaged in providing arbitration and conciliation services are classified in Industry 54199, All Other Professional, Scientific, and Technical Services.

541191 Title Abstract and Settlement Offices[US]

This U.S. industry comprises establishments (except offices of lawyers and attorneys) primarily engaged in one or more of the following activities: (1) researching public land records to gather information relating to real estate titles; (2) preparing documents necessary for the transfer of the title, financing, and settlement; (3) conducting final real estate settlements and closings; and (4) filing legal and other documents relating to the sale of real estate. Real estate settlement offices, title abstract companies, and title search companies are included in this industry.

Cross-References.

Establishments of lawyers and attorneys primarily engaged in the practice of law are classified in Industry 541110, Offices of Lawyers.

541199 All Other Legal Services[US]

This U.S. industry comprises establishments of legal practitioners (except offices of lawyers and attorneys, settlement offices, and title abstract offices). These establishments are primarily engaged in providing specialized legal or paralegal services.

Illustrative Examples:

Notary public services   Process serving services
Paralegal services
Patent agent services (i.e., patent filing
and searching services)

Cross-References.

- Establishments of lawyers and attorneys primarily engaged in the practice of law are classified in Industry 541110, Offices of Lawyers;

- Establishments (except offices of lawyers and attorneys) primarily engaged in researching public land records for ownership or title; preparing documents necessary for the transfer of the title, financing, and settlement; conducting final real estate settlements and closings; and/or filing legal and other documents relating to the sale of real estate are classified in U.S. Industry 541191, Title Abstract and Settlement Offices; and

- Establishments (except offices of lawyers, attorneys, and paralegals) primarily engaged in providing arbitration and conciliation services are classified in Industry 541990, All Other Professional, Scientific, and Technical Services.

5412 Accounting, Tax Preparation, Bookkeeping, and Payroll Services

54121 Accounting, Tax Preparation, Bookkeeping, and Payroll Services

This industry comprises establishments primarily engaged in providing services, such as auditing of accounting records, designing accounting systems, preparing financial statements, developing budgets, preparing tax returns, processing payrolls, bookkeeping, and billing.

Illustrative Examples:

Accountants' offices	Payroll processing services
Bookkeeping services	Tax return preparation services

541211 Offices of Certified Public Accountants[US]

This U.S. industry comprises establishments of accountants that are certified to audit the accounting records of public and private organizations and to attest to compliance with generally accepted accounting practices. Offices of certified public accountants (CPAs) may provide one or more of the following accounting services: (1) auditing financial statements; (2) designing accounting systems; (3) preparing financial statements; (4) developing budgets; and (5) providing advice on matters related to accounting. These establishments may also provide related services, such as bookkeeping, tax return preparation, and payroll processing.

Cross-References. Establishments of non-CPAs engaged in—

- Providing tax return preparation services only—are classified in U.S. Industry 541213, Tax Preparation Services;

- Providing payroll processing services only—are classified in U.S. Industry 541214, Payroll Services; and

---

US—United States industry only. CAN—United States and Canadian industries are comparable. MEX—United States and Mexican industries are comparable. Blank—Canadian, Mexican, and United States industries are comparable.

- Providing accounting, bookkeeping, and billing services—are classified in U.S. Industry 541219, Other Accounting Services.

541213 Tax Preparation Services[CAN]

This U.S. industry comprises establishments (except offices of CPAs) engaged in providing tax return preparation services without also providing accounting, bookkeeping, billing, or payroll processing services. Basic knowledge of tax law and filing requirements is required.

Cross-References.

- Establishments of CPAs are classified in U.S. Industry 541211, Offices of Certified Public Accountants;
- Establishments of non-CPAs providing payroll services along with tax return preparation services are classified in U.S. Industry 541214, Payroll Services;
- Establishments of non-CPAs providing accounting, bookkeeping, or billing services along with tax return preparation services are classified in U.S. Industry 541219, Other Accounting Services; and
- Establishments providing computer data processing services at their own facility for others are classified in Industry 518210, Data Processing, Hosting, and Related Services.

541214 Payroll Services[US]

This U.S. industry comprises establishments (except offices of CPAs) engaged in the following without also providing accounting, bookkeeping, or billing services: (1) collecting information on hours worked, pay rates, deductions, and other payroll-related data from their clients and (2) using that information to generate paychecks, payroll reports, and tax filings. These establishments may use data processing and tabulating techniques as part of providing their services.

Cross-References.

- Establishments of CPAs are classified in U.S. Industry 541211, Offices of Certified Public Accountants;
- Establishments of non-CPAs providing tax return preparation services only are classified in U.S. Industry 541213, Tax Preparation Services; and
- Establishments of non-CPAs providing accounting, bookkeeping, or billing services along with payroll services are classified in U.S. Industry 541219, Other Accounting Services.

US—United States industry only. CAN—United States and Canadian industries are comparable. MEX—United States and Mexican industries are comparable. Blank—Canadian, Mexican, and United States industries are comparable.

541219 Other Accounting Services[US]

This U.S. industry comprises establishments (except offices of CPAs) engaged in providing accounting services (except tax return preparation services only or payroll services only). These establishments may also provide tax return preparation or payroll services. Accountant (except CPA) offices, bookkeeper offices, and billing offices are included in this industry.

Cross-References.

- Establishments of CPAs are classified in U.S. Industry 541211, Offices of Certified Public Accountants;

- Establishments of non-CPAs engaged in providing tax return preparation services only are classified in U.S. Industry 541213, Tax Preparation Services; and

- Establishments of non-CPAs engaged in providing payroll services only are classified in U.S. Industry 541214, Payroll Services.

5413 Architectural, Engineering, and Related Services

54131 Architectural Services
See industry description for 541310 below.

541310 Architectural Services

This industry comprises establishments primarily engaged in planning and designing residential, institutional, leisure, commercial, and industrial buildings and structures by applying knowledge of design, construction procedures, zoning regulations, building codes, and building materials.

Cross-References. Establishments primarily engaged in—

- Planning and designing the development of land areas—are classified in Industry 541320, Landscape Architectural Services; and

- Both the design and construction of buildings, highways, or other structures or in managing construction projects—are classified Sector 23, Construction, according to the type of project.

54132 Landscape Architectural Services
See industry description for 541320 below.

US—United States industry only. CAN—United States and Canadian industries are comparable. MEX—United States and Mexican industries are comparable. Blank—Canadian, Mexican, and United States industries are comparable.

541320 Landscape Architectural Services

This industry comprises establishments primarily engaged in planning and designing the development of land areas for projects, such as parks and other recreational areas; airports; highways; hospitals; schools; land subdivisions; and commercial, industrial, and residential areas, by applying knowledge of land characteristics, location of buildings and structures, use of land areas, and design of landscape projects.

Illustrative Examples:

Garden planning services
Golf course or ski area design services
Industrial land use planning services

Landscape architects' offices
Landscape consulting services
Landscape design services

Cross-References.

Establishments primarily engaged in providing landscape care and maintenance services and/or installing trees, shrubs, plants, lawns, or gardens along with the design of landscape plans are classified in Industry 561730, Landscaping Services.

54133 Engineering Services
See industry description for 541330 below.

541330 Engineering Services

This industry comprises establishments primarily engaged in applying physical laws and principles of engineering in the design, development, and utilization of machines, materials, instruments, structures, processes, and systems. The assignments undertaken by these establishments may involve any of the following activities: provision of advice, preparation of feasibility studies, preparation of preliminary and final plans and designs, provision of technical services during the construction or installation phase, inspection and evaluation of engineering projects, and related services.

Illustrative Examples:

Civil engineering services
Construction engineering services
Engineers' offices

Environmental engineering services
Mechanical engineering services

Cross-References. Establishments primarily engaged in—

- Planning and designing computer systems that integrate computer hardware, software, and communication technologies—are classified in U.S. Industry 541512, Computer Systems Design Services;

- Performing surveying and mapping services of the surface of the earth, including the sea floor—are classified in Industry 541370, Surveying and Mapping (except Geophysical) Services;
- Gathering, interpreting, and mapping geophysical data—are classified in Industry 541360, Geophysical Surveying and Mapping Services;
- Creating and developing designs and specifications that optimize the use, value, and appearance of products—are classified in Industry 541420, Industrial Design Services;
- Providing advice and assistance to others on environmental issues, such as the control of environmental contamination from pollutants, toxic substances, and hazardous materials—are classified in Industry 541620, Environmental Consulting Services; and
- Both the design and construction of buildings, highways, and other structures or in managing construction projects—are classified in Sector 23, Construction, according to the type of project.

54134 Drafting Services

See industry description for 541340 below.

541340 Drafting Services

This industry comprises establishments primarily engaged in drawing detailed layouts, plans, and illustrations of buildings, structures, systems, or components from engineering and architectural specifications.

54135 Building Inspection Services

See industry description for 541350 below.

541350 Building Inspection Services

This industry comprises establishments primarily engaged in providing building inspection services. These establishments typically evaluate all aspects of the building structure and component systems and prepare a report on the physical condition of the property, generally for buyers or others involved in real estate transactions. Building inspection bureaus and establishments providing home inspection services are included in this industry.

Cross-References. Establishments primarily engaged in—

- Inspecting buildings for termites and other pests—are classified in Industry 561710, Exterminating and Pest Control Services;

US—United States industry only. CAN—United States and Canadian industries are comparable. MEX—United States and Mexican industries are comparable. Blank—Canadian, Mexican, and United States industries are comparable.

- Inspecting buildings for hazardous materials—are classified in Industry 541620, Environmental Consulting Services; and

- Conducting inspections and enforcing public building codes and standards— are classified in Industry 925110, Administration of Housing Programs.

54136 Geophysical Surveying and Mapping Services

See industry description for 541360 below.

541360 Geophysical Surveying and Mapping Services

This industry comprises establishments primarily engaged in gathering, interpreting, and mapping geophysical data. Establishments in this industry often specialize in locating and measuring the extent of subsurface resources, such as oil, gas, and minerals but they may also conduct surveys for engineering purposes. Establishments in this industry use a variety of surveying techniques depending on the purpose of the survey, including magnetic surveys, gravity surveys, seismic surveys, or electrical and electromagnetic surveys.

Cross-References.

Establishments primarily engaged in taking core samples, drilling test wells, or other mine development activities (except geophysical surveying and mapping) on a contract basis for others are classified in Industry 21311, Support Activities for Mining.

54137 Surveying and Mapping (except Geophysical) Services

See industry description for 541370 below.

541370 Surveying and Mapping (except Geophysical) Services

This industry comprises establishments primarily engaged in performing surveying and mapping services of the surface of the earth, including the sea floor. These services may include surveying and mapping of areas above or below the surface of the earth, such as the creation of view easements or segregating rights in parcels of land by creating underground utility easements.

Illustrative Examples:

Cadastral surveying services	Mapping (except geophysical) services
Cartographic surveying services	Topographic surveying services
Geodetic surveying services	

Cross-References. Establishments primarily engaged in—

- Providing geophysical surveying and mapping services—are classified in Industry 541360, Geophysical Surveying and Mapping Services; and
- Publishing atlases and maps, except for exclusive Internet publishing—are classified in U.S. Industry 511130, Book Publishers; and
- Publishing atlases and maps exclusively on the Internet—are classified in U.S. Industry 516110, Internet Publishing and Broadcasting.

54138 Testing Laboratories
See industry description for 541380 below.

541380 Testing Laboratories

This industry comprises establishments primarily engaged in performing physical, chemical, and other analytical testing services, such as acoustics or vibration testing, assaying, biological testing (except medical and veterinary), calibration testing, electrical and electronic testing, geotechnical testing, mechanical testing, nondestructive testing, or thermal testing. The testing may occur in a laboratory or on-site.

Cross-References. Establishments primarily engaged in—

- Laboratory testing for the medical profession—are classified in Industry 62151, Medical and Diagnostic Laboratories;
- Veterinary testing services—are classified in Industry 541940, Veterinary Services; and
- Auto emissions testing—are classified in U.S. Industry 811198, All Other Automotive Repair and Maintenance.

5414 Specialized Design Services

This industry group comprises establishments providing specialized design services (except architectural, engineering, and computer systems design).

54141 Interior Design Services
See industry description for 541410 below.

541410 Interior Design Services

This industry comprises establishments primarily engaged in planning, designing, and administering projects in interior spaces to meet the physical and aesthetic

---

needs of people using them, taking into consideration building codes, health and safety regulations, traffic patterns and floor planning, mechanical and electrical needs, and interior fittings and furniture. Interior designers and interior design consultants work in areas, such as hospitality design, health care design, institutional design, commercial and corporate design, and residential design. This industry also includes interior decorating consultants engaged exclusively in providing aesthetic services associated with interior spaces.

54142 Industrial Design Services

See industry description for 541420 below.

541420 Industrial Design Services

This industry comprises establishments primarily engaged in creating and developing designs and specifications that optimize the use, value, and appearance of their products. These services can include the determination of the materials, construction, mechanisms, shape, color, and surface finishes of the product, taking into consideration human characteristics and needs, safety, market appeal, and efficiency in production, distribution, use, and maintenance. Establishments providing automobile or furniture industrial design services or industrial design consulting services are included in this industry.

Cross-References. Establishments primarily engaged in—

- Applying physical laws and principles of engineering in the design, development, and utilization of machines, materials, instruments, structures, processes, and systems—are classified in Industry 541330, Engineering Services; and

- Designing clothing, shoes, or jewelry—are classified in Industry 541490, Other Specialized Design Services.

54143 Graphic Design Services

See industry description for 541430 below.

541430 Graphic Design Services

This industry comprises establishments primarily engaged in planning, designing, and managing the production of visual communication in order to convey specific messages or concepts, clarify complex information, or project visual identities. These services can include the design of printed materials, packaging, advertising, signage systems, and corporate identification (logos). This industry also includes commercial artists engaged exclusively in generating drawings and illustrations requiring technical accuracy or interpretative skills.

Illustrative Examples:

Commercial art studios
Corporate identification (i.e., logo)
  design services
Graphic design consulting services

Independent commercial or graphic
  artists
Medical art or illustration services

Cross-References.

- Establishments primarily engaged in creating and/or placing public display advertising material are classified in Industry 541850, Display Advertising; and

- Independent artists primarily engaged in creating and selling visual artwork for noncommercial use and independent cartoonists are classified in Industry 711510, Independent Artists, Writers, and Performers.

54149 Other Specialized Design Services
See industry description for 541490 below.

541490 Other Specialized Design Services

This industry comprises establishments primarily engaged in providing professional design services (except architectural, landscape architecture, engineering, interior, industrial, graphic, and computer system design).

Illustrative Examples:

Costume design services (except
  independent theatrical costume
  designers)
Fashion design services
Float design services

Fur design services
Jewelry design services
Shoe design services
Textile design services

Cross-References. Establishments primarily engaged in—

- Providing architectural design services—are classified in Industry 541310, Architectural Services;

- Providing landscape architecture design services—are classified in Industry 541320, Landscape Architectural Services;

- Providing engineering design services—are classified in Industry 541330, Engineering Services;

US—United States industry only. CAN—United States and Canadian industries are comparable. MEX—United States and Mexican industries are comparable. Blank—Canadian, Mexican, and United States industries are comparable.

- Providing interior design services—are classified in Industry 541410, Interior Design Services;
- Providing industrial design services—are classified in Industry 541420, Industrial Design Services;
- Providing graphic design services—are classified in Industry 541430, Graphic Design Services;
- Providing computer systems design services—are classified in U.S. Industry 541512, Computer Systems Design Services; and
- Operating as independent theatrical designers—are classified in Industry 711510, Independent Artists, Writers, and Performers.

5415 Computer Systems Design and Related Services
See industry description for 54151 below.

54151 Computer Systems Design and Related Services

This industry comprises establishments primarily engaged in providing expertise in the field of information technologies through one or more of the following activities: (1) writing, modifying, testing, and supporting software to meet the needs of a particular customer; (2) planning and designing computer systems that integrate computer hardware, software, and communication technologies; (3) on-site management and operation of clients' computer systems and/or data processing facilities; and (4) other professional and technical computer-related advice and services.

Illustrative Examples:

Computer facilities management services
Computer hardware or software
  consulting services
Computer systems integration design
  services

Custom computer programming services
Software installation services

Cross-References. Establishments primarily engaged in—

- Selling computer hardware or software products from retail-like locations and providing supporting services, such as customized assembly of personal computers—are classified in Industry 44312, Computer and Software Stores;
- Wholesaling computer hardware or software products and providing supporting services, such as customized assembly of personal computers—are classified in Industry 423430, Computer and Computer Peripheral Equipment and Software Merchant Wholesalers;

US—United States industry only. CAN—United States and Canadian industries are comparable. MEX—United States and Mexican industries are comparable. Blank—Canadian, Mexican, and United States industries are comparable.

- Publishing packaged software—are classified in Industry 51121, Software Publishers; and
- Providing computer data processing services at their own facility for others—are classified in Industry 518210, Data Processing, Hosting, and Related Services.

541511 Custom Computer Programming Services[US]

This U.S. industry comprises establishments primarily engaged in writing, modifying, testing, and supporting software to meet the needs of a particular customer.

Cross-References. Establishments primarily engaged in—

- Publishing packaged software—are classified in Industry 511210, Software Publishers; and
- Planning and designing computer systems that integrate computer hardware, software, and communication technologies, even though such establishments may provide custom software as an integral part of their services—are classified in U.S. Industry 541512, Computer Systems Design Services.

541512 Computer Systems Design Services[US]

This U.S. industry comprises establishments primarily engaged in planning and designing computer systems that integrate computer hardware, software, and communication technologies. The hardware and software components of the system may be provided by this establishment or company as part of integrated services or may be provided by third parties or vendors. These establishments often install the system and train and support users of the system.

Illustrative Examples:

Computer systems integration design
   consulting services
Information management computer
   systems integration design services

Local area network (LAN) computer
   systems integration design services
Office automation computer systems
   integration design services

Cross-References. Establishments primarily engaged in—

- Selling computer hardware or software products and systems from retail-like locations, and providing supporting services, such as customized assembly of personal computers—are classified in Industry 443120, Computer and Software Stores; and
- Wholesaling computer hardware or software products and providing supporting services, such as customized assembly of personal computers—

are classified in Industry 423430, Computer and Computer Peripheral Equipment and Software Merchant Wholesalers.

541513 Computer Facilities Management Services[US]

This U.S. industry comprises establishments primarily engaged in providing on-site management and operation of clients' computer systems and/or data processing facilities. Establishments providing computer systems or data processing facilities support services are included in this industry.

Cross-References.

Establishments primarily engaged in providing computer data processing services at their own facility for others are classified in Industry 518210, Data Processing, Hosting, and Related Services.

541519 Other Computer Related Services[US]

This U.S. industry comprises establishments primarily engaged in providing computer related services (except custom programming, systems integration design, and facilities management services). Establishments providing computer disaster recovery services or software installation services are included in this industry.

Cross-References. Establishments primarily engaged in—

- Providing custom computer programming services—are classified in U.S. Industry 541511, Custom Computer Programming Services;
- Providing computer systems integration design services—are classified in U.S. Industry 541512, Computer Systems Design Services; and
- Providing computer systems and/or data processing facilities management services—are classified in U.S. Industry 541513, Computer Facilities Management Services.

5416 Management, Scientific, and Technical Consulting Services

54161 Management Consulting Services

This industry comprises establishments primarily engaged in providing advice and assistance to businesses and other organizations on management issues, such as strategic and organizational planning; financial planning and budgeting; marketing objectives and policies; human resource policies, practices, and planning; production scheduling; and control planning.

Illustrative Examples:

Actuarial, benefit, and compensation
consulting services
Administrative and general management
consulting services
Human resources and executive search
consulting services

Marketing consulting services
Process, physical distribution, and
logistics consulting services

Cross-References.

- Establishments primarily engaged in providing a range of day-to-day office administrative services, such as financial planning, billing and recordkeeping, personnel, and physical distribution and logistics, are classified in Industry 56111, Office Administrative Services;

- Establishments primarily engaged in administering, overseeing, and managing other establishments of the company or enterprise (except government establishments) are classified in Industry 55111, Management of Companies and Enterprises;

- Government establishments primarily engaged in administering, overseeing, and managing governmental programs are classified in Sector 92, Public Administration;

- Establishments primarily engaged in professional and management development training are classified in Industry 61143, Professional and Management Development Training;

- Establishments primarily engaged in listing employment vacancies and in selecting, referring, and placing applicants in employment are classified in Industry 56131, Employment Placement Agencies;

- Establishments primarily engaged in developing and implementing public relations plans are classified in Industry 54182, Public Relations Agencies;

- Establishments primarily engaged in developing and conducting marketing research or public opinion polling are classified in Industry 54191, Marketing Research and Public Opinion Polling;

- Establishments primarily engaged in planning and designing industrial processes and systems are classified in Industry 54133, Engineering Services;

- Establishments primarily engaged in planning and designing computer systems are classified in Industry 54151, Computer Systems Design and Related Services; and

- Establishments primarily engaged in providing financial investment advice services are classified in Industry 52393, Investment Advice.

541611 Administrative Management and General Management Consulting Services[CAN]

This U.S. industry comprises establishments primarily engaged in providing operating advice and assistance to businesses and other organizations on administrative management issues, such as financial planning and budgeting, equity and asset management, records management, office planning, strategic and organizational planning, site selection, new business startup, and business process improvement. This industry also includes establishments of general management consultants that provide a full range of administrative; human resource; marketing; process, physical distribution, and logistics; or other management consulting services to clients.

Illustrative Examples:

Administrative management consulting services

Financial management (except investment advice) consulting services

General management consulting services

Site selection consulting services

Strategic planning consulting services

Cross-References.

- Establishments primarily engaged in providing a range of day-to-day office administrative services, such as financial planning, billing and recordkeeping, personnel, and physical distribution and logistics, are classified in Industry 561110, Office Administrative Services;

- Establishments primarily engaged in administering, overseeing, and managing other establishments of the company or enterprise (except government establishments) are classified in U.S. Industry 551114, Corporate, Subsidiary, and Regional Managing Offices;

- Government establishments primarily engaged in administering, overseeing, and managing governmental programs are classified in Sector 92, Public Administration; and

- Establishments primarily engaged in providing investment advice are classified in Industry 523930, Investment Advice.

541612 Human Resources and Executive Search Consulting Services[CAN]

This U.S. industry comprises establishments primarily engaged in providing advice and assistance to businesses and other organizations in one or more of the following areas: (1) human resource and personnel policies, practices, and procedures; (2) employee benefits planning, communication, and administration;

(3) compensation systems planning; (4) wage and salary administration; and (5) executive search and recruitment.

Illustrative Examples:

Benefit or compensation consulting services

Employee assessment consulting services

Executive placement or search consulting services

Human resources consulting services

Personnel management consulting services

Cross-References. Establishments primarily engaged in—

- Professional and management development training—are classified in Industry 611430, Professional and Management Development Training; and
- Listing employment vacancies and in selecting, referring, and placing applicants in employment—are classified in Industry 561310, Employment Placement Agencies.

541613 Marketing Consulting Services[US]

This U.S. industry comprises establishments primarily engaged in providing operating advice and assistance to businesses and other organizations on marketing issues, such as developing marketing objectives and policies, sales forecasting, new product developing and pricing, licensing and franchise planning, and marketing planning and strategy.

Illustrative Examples:

Customer services management consulting services

Marketing management consulting services

New product development consulting services

Sales management consulting services

Cross-References. Establishment primarily engaged in—

- Developing and implementing public relations plans—are classified in Industry 541820, Public Relations Agencies; and
- Developing and conducting marketing research or public opinion polling—are classified in Industry 541910, Marketing Research and Public Opinion Polling.

541614 Process, Physical Distribution, and Logistics Consulting Services[US]

This U.S. industry comprises establishments primarily engaged in providing operating advice and assistance to businesses and other organizations in areas,

---

such as: (1) manufacturing operations improvement; (2) productivity improvement; (3) production planning and control; (4) quality assurance and quality control; (5) inventory management; (6) distribution networks; (7) warehouse use, operations, and utilization; (8) transportation and shipment of goods and materials; and (9) materials management and handling.

Illustrative Examples:

Freight rate or tariff rate consulting services

Inventory planning and control management consulting services

Manufacturing management consulting services

Productivity improvement consulting services

Transportation management consulting services

Cross-References. Establishments primarily engaged in—

- Planning and designing industrial processes and systems—are classified in Industry 541330, Engineering Services; and

- Providing computer systems integration design services—are classified in U.S. Industry 541512, Computer Systems Design Services.

541618 Other Management Consulting Services[US]

This U.S. industry comprises establishments primarily engaged in providing management consulting services (except administrative and general management consulting; human resources consulting; marketing consulting; or process, physical distribution, and logistics consulting). Establishments providing telecommunications or utilities management consulting services are included in this industry.

Cross-References. Establishments primarily engaged in—

- Providing administrative and general management consulting services—are classified in U.S. Industry 541611, Administrative Management and General Management Consulting Services;

- Providing human resources and executive search consulting services—are classified in U.S. Industry 541612, Human Resources and Executive Search Consulting Services;

- Providing marketing consulting services—are classified in U.S. Industry 541613, Marketing Consulting Services; and

- Providing process, physical distribution, and logistics consulting services—are classified in U.S. Industry 541614, Process, Physical Distribution, and Logistics Consulting Services.

US—United States industry only. CAN—United States and Canadian industries are comparable. MEX—United States and Mexican industries are comparable. Blank—Canadian, Mexican, and United States industries are comparable.

54162 Environmental Consulting Services
See industry description for 541620 below.

541620 Environmental Consulting Services

This industry comprises establishments primarily engaged in providing advice and assistance to businesses and other organizations on environmental issues, such as the control of environmental contamination from pollutants, toxic substances, and hazardous materials. These establishments identify problems (e.g., inspect buildings for hazardous materials), measure and evaluate risks, and recommend solutions. They employ a multidisciplined staff of scientists, engineers, and other technicians with expertise in areas, such as air and water quality, asbestos contamination, remediation, and environmental law. Establishments providing sanitation or site remediation consulting services are included in this industry.

Cross-References. Establishments primarily engaged in—

* Environmental remediation—are classified in Industry 562910, Remediation Services; and

* Providing environmental engineering services—are classified in Industry 541330, Engineering Services.

54169 Other Scientific and Technical Consulting Services
See industry description for 541690 below.

541690 Other Scientific and Technical Consulting Services

This industry comprises establishments primarily engaged in providing advice and assistance to businesses and other organizations on scientific and technical issues (except environmental).

Illustrative Examples:

Agricultural consulting services	Motion picture consulting services
Biological consulting services	Physics consulting services
Chemical consulting services	Radio consulting services
Economic consulting services	Safety consulting services
Energy consulting services	Security consulting services

Cross-References.

Establishments primarily engaged in environmental consulting are classified in Industry 541620, Environmental Consulting Services.

5417 Scientific Research and Development Services

This industry group comprises establishments engaged in conducting original investigation undertaken on a systematic basis to gain new knowledge (research) and/or the application of research findings or other scientific knowledge for the creation of new or significantly improved products or processes (experimental development). The industries within this industry group are defined on the basis of the domain of research; that is, on the scientific expertise of the establishment.

54171 Research and Development in the Physical, Engineering, and Life Sciences
See industry description for 541710 below.

541710 Research and Development in the Physical, Engineering, and Life Sciences[CAN]

This industry comprises establishments primarily engaged in conducting research and experimental development in the physical, engineering, and life sciences, such as agriculture, electronics, environmental, biology, botany, biotechnology, computers, chemistry, food, fisheries, forests, geology, health, mathematics, medicine, oceanography, pharmacy, physics, veterinary, and other allied subjects.

Cross-References. Establishments primarily engaged in—

- Providing physical, chemical, or other analytical testing services (except medical or veterinary)—are classified in Industry 541380, Testing Laboratories;

- Providing medical laboratory testing for humans—are classified in U.S. Industry 621511, Medical Laboratories; and

- Providing veterinary testing services—are classified in Industry 541940, Veterinary Services.

54172 Research and Development in the Social Sciences and Humanities
See industry description for 541720 below.

541720 Research and Development in the Social Sciences and Humanities[CAN]

This industry comprises establishments primarily engaged in conducting research and analyses in cognitive development, sociology, psychology, language, behavior, economic, and other social science and humanities research.

Cross-References.

Establishments primarily engaged in marketing research are classified in Industry 541910, Marketing Research and Public Opinion Polling.

5418 Advertising and Related Services

54181 Advertising Agencies
See industry description for 541810 below.

541810 Advertising Agencies

This industry comprises establishments primarily engaged in creating advertising campaigns and placing such advertising in periodicals, newspapers, radio and television, or other media. These establishments are organized to provide a full range of services (i.e., through in-house capabilities or subcontracting), including advice, creative services, account management, production of advertising material, media planning, and buying (i.e., placing advertising).

Cross-References. Establishments primarily engaged in—

- Purchasing advertising space from media outlets and reselling it directly to advertising agencies or individual companies—are classified in Industry 541830, Media Buying Agencies;
- Conceptualizing and producing artwork or graphic designs without providing other advertising agency services—are classified in Industry 541430, Graphic Design Services;
- Creating direct mail advertising campaigns—are classified in Industry 541860, Direct Mail Advertising;
- Providing marketing consulting services—are classified in U.S. Industry 541613, Marketing Consulting Services; and
- Selling media time or space for media owners as independent representatives—are classified in Industry 541840, Media Representatives.

54182 Public Relations Agencies
See industry description for 541820 below.

541820 Public Relations Agencies

This industry comprises establishments primarily engaged in designing and implementing public relations campaigns. These campaigns are designed to pro-

---

mote the interests and image of their clients. Establishments providing lobbying, political consulting, or public relations consulting are included in this industry.

54183 Media Buying Agencies
See industry description for 541830 below.

541830 Media Buying Agencies

This industry comprises establishments primarily engaged in purchasing advertising time or space from media outlets and reselling it to advertising agencies or individual companies directly.

Cross-References. Establishments primarily engaged in—

- Selling time and space to advertisers for media owners as independent representatives—are classified in Industry 541840, Media Representatives; and

- Creating advertising campaigns and placing such advertising in media— are classified in Industry 541810, Advertising Agencies.

54184 Media Representatives
See industry description for 541840 below.

541840 Media Representatives

This industry comprises establishments of independent representatives primarily engaged in selling media time or space for media owners.

Illustrative Examples:

Newspaper advertising representatives (i.e., independent of media owners)
Publishers' advertising representatives (i.e., independent of media owners)

Radio advertising representatives (i.e., independent of media owners)
Television advertising representatives (i.e., independent of media owners)

Cross-References. Establishments primarily engaged in—

- Purchasing advertising time or space from media outlets and reselling it directly to advertising agencies or individual companies—are classified in Industry 541830, Media Buying Agencies; and

- Creating advertising campaigns and placing such advertising in media— are classified in Industry 541810, Advertising Agencies.

54185 Display Advertising

See industry description for 541850 below.

541850 Display Advertising

This industry comprises establishments primarily engaged in creating and designing public display advertising, campaign materials, such as printed, painted, or electronic displays, and/or placing such displays on indoor or outdoor billboards and panels, or on or within transit vehicles or facilities, shopping malls, retail (in-store) displays, and other display structures or sites.

Cross-References. Establishments primarily engaged in—

- Providing sign lettering and painting services—are classified in Industry 541890, Other Services Related to Advertising;
- Printing paper on paperboard signs—are classified in Industry 32311, Printing;
- Erecting display boards—are classified in Sector 238990, All Other Specialty Trade Contractors; and
- Manufacturing electrical, mechanical, or plate signs and point-of-sale advertising displays—are classified in Industry 339950, Sign Manufacturing.

54186 Direct Mail Advertising

See industry description for 541860 below.

541860 Direct Mail Advertising

This industry comprises establishments primarily engaged in (1) creating and designing advertising campaigns for the purpose of distributing advertising materials (e.g., coupons, flyers, samples) or specialties (e.g., key chains, magnets, pens with customized messages imprinted) by mail or other direct distribution; and/or (2) preparing advertising materials or specialties for mailing or other direct distribution. These establishments may also compile, maintain, sell, and rent mailing lists.

Cross-References. Establishments primarily engaged in—

- The direct distribution or delivery (e.g., door-to-door, windshield placement) of advertisements or samples—are classified in Industry 541870, Advertising Material Distribution Services;

US—United States industry only. CAN—United States and Canadian industries are comparable. MEX—United States and Mexican industries are comparable. Blank—Canadian, Mexican, and United States industries are comparable.

- Distributing advertising specialties for clients who wish to use such materials for promotional purposes—are classified in Industry 541890, Other Services Related to Advertising;

- Creating advertising campaigns and placing such advertising in media— are classified in Industry 541810, Advertising Agencies;

- Compiling and selling mailing lists without providing direct mail advertising services—are classified in Industry 511140, Directory and Mailing List Publishers; and

- Broadcasting exclusively on the Internet—are classified in Industry 516110, Internet Publishing and Broadcasting.

54187 Advertising Material Distribution Services
See industry description for 541870 below.

541870 Advertising Material Distribution Services

This industry comprises establishments primarily engaged in the direct distribution or delivery of advertisements (e.g., circulars, coupons, handbills) or samples. Establishments in this industry use methods, such as delivering advertisements or samples door-to-door, placing flyers or coupons on car windshields in parking lots, or handing out samples in retail stores.

Cross-References. Establishments primarily engaged in—

- Creating and designing advertising campaigns for the purpose of distributing advertising materials or samples through the mail—are classified in Industry 541860, Direct Mail Advertising;

- Publishing newspapers or operating television stations or on-line information services—are classified in Sector 51, Information; and

- Distributing advertising specialties (e.g., key chains, magnets, or pens with customized messages imprinted) to clients who wish to use such materials for promotional purposes—are classified in Industry 541890, Other Services Related to Advertising.

54189 Other Services Related to Advertising
See industry description for 541890 below.

541890 Other Services Related to Advertising^{MEX}

This industry comprises establishments primarily engaged in providing advertising services (except advertising agency services, public relations agency services, media buying agency services, media representative services, display advertising services, direct mail advertising services, advertising material distribution services, and marketing consulting services).

Illustrative Examples:

Advertising specialties (e.g., key chains, magnets, pens) distribution services (except direct mail)

Display lettering services

Mannequin decorating services

Merchandise demonstration services

Sign lettering and painting services

Store window dressing or trimming services

Welcoming services (i.e., advertising services)

Cross-References. Establishments primarily engaged in—

- Creating advertising campaigns and placing such advertising in newspapers, television, or other media—are classified in Industry 541810, Advertising Agencies;
- Designing and implementing public relations campaigns—are classified in Industry 541820, Public Relations Agencies;
- Purchasing advertising time or space from media outlets and reselling it directly to advertising agencies or individual companies—are classified in Industry 541830, Media Buying Agencies;
- Selling media time or space for media owners as independent representatives—are classified in Industry 541840, Media Representatives;
- Providing display advertising services (except aerial)—are classified in Industry 541850, Display Advertising;
- Providing direct distribution or delivery (e.g., door-to-door, windshield placement) of advertisements or samples—are classified in Industry 541870, Advertising Material Distribution Services;
- Providing direct mail advertising services—are classified in Industry 541860, Direct Mail Advertising;
- Publishing newspapers or operating television stations or on-line information services—are classified in Sector 51, Information; and
- Providing marketing consulting services—are classified in U.S. Industry 541613, Marketing Consulting Services.

5419 Other Professional, Scientific, and Technical Services

This industry group comprises establishments engaged in professional, scientific, and technical services (except legal services; accounting, tax preparation, bookkeeping, and related services; architectural, engineering, and related services; specialized design services; computer systems design and related services; management, scientific, and technical consulting services; scientific research and development services; and advertising and related services).

54191 Marketing Research and Public Opinion Polling
See industry description for 541910 below.

541910 Marketing Research and Public Opinion Polling

This industry comprises establishments primarily engaged in systematically gathering, recording, tabulating, and presenting marketing and public opinion data.

Illustrative Examples:

Broadcast media rating services
Marketing analysis or research services
Opinion research services

Political opinion polling services
Statistical sampling services

Cross-References. Establishments primarily engaged in—

- Providing research and analysis in economics, sociology, and related fields—are classified in Industry 541720, Research and Development in the Social Sciences and Humanities; and

- Providing advice and counsel on marketing strategies—are classified in U.S. Industry 541613, Marketing Consulting Services.

54192 Photographic Services

This industry comprises establishments primarily engaged in providing still, video, or digital photography services. These establishments may specialize in a particular field of photography, such as commercial and industrial photography, portrait photography, and special events photography. Commercial or portrait photography studios are included in this industry.

Cross-References. Establishments primarily engaged in—

- Producing film and videotape for commercial exhibition or sale—are classified in Industry 51211, Motion Picture and Video Production;

- Developing still photographs—are classified in Industry 81292, Photofinishing;

- Developing motion picture film—are classified in Industry 51219, Postproduction Services and Other Motion Picture and Video Industries;

- Taking, developing, and selling artistic, news, or other types of photographs on a freelance basis, such as photojournalists—are classified in Industry 71151, Independent Artists, Writers, and Performers; and
- Supplying and servicing automatic photography machines in places of business operated by others—are classified in Industry 81299, All Other Personal Services.

541921 Photography Studios, Portrait[US]

This U.S. industry comprises establishments known as portrait studios primarily engaged in providing still, video, or digital portrait photography services.

Illustrative Examples:

Home photography services
Passport photography services
School photography services

Videotaping services for special events (e.g., weddings)

Cross-References. Establishments primarily engaged in—

- Producing film and videotape for commercial exhibition or sale—are classified in Industry 512110, Motion Picture and Video Production;
- Developing still photographs—are classified in Industry 81292, Photofinishing;
- Developing motion picture film—are classified in U.S. Industry 512199, Other Motion Picture and Video Industries;
- Taking, developing, and selling artistic, news, or other types of photographs on a freelance basis, such as photojournalists—are classified in Industry 711510, Independent Artists, Writers, and Performers; and
- Supplying and servicing automatic photography machines in places of business operated by others—are classified in Industry 812990, All Other Personal Services.

541922 Commercial Photography[US]

This U.S. industry comprises establishments primarily engaged in providing commercial photography services, generally for advertising agencies, publishers, and other business and industrial users.

Cross-References. Establishments primarily engaged in—

- Producing film and videotape for commercial exhibition or sale—are classified in Industry 512110, Motion Picture and Video Production;

- Developing still photographs—are classified in Industry 81292, Photofinishing;

- Developing motion picture film—are classified in U.S. Industry 512199, Other Motion Picture and Video Industries;

- Taking, developing, and selling artistic, news, or other types of photographs on a freelance basis, such as photojournalists—are classified in Industry 711510, Independent Artists, Writers, and Performers; and

- Supplying and servicing coin-operated photography machines in places of business operated by others—are classified in Industry 812990, All Other Personal Services.

54193 Translation and Interpretation Services
See industry description for 541930 below.

541930 Translation and Interpretation Services

This industry comprises establishments primarily engaged in translating written material and interpreting speech from one language to another and establishments primarily engaged in providing sign language services.

Cross-References. Establishments primarily engaged in—

- Providing transcription services—are classified in Industry 561410, Document Preparation Services;

- Providing real-time (i.e., simultaneous) closed captioning services for live television performances, at meetings and conferences—are classified in U.S. Industry 561492, Court Reporting and Stenotype Services;

- Providing film or tape closed captioning services—are classified in U.S. Industry 512191, Teleproduction and Other Postproduction Services; and

- Analyzing handwriting—are classified in Industry 541990, All Other Professional, Scientific, and Technical Services.

54194 Veterinary Services
See industry description for industry 541940 below.

541940 Veterinary Services[CAN]

This industry comprises establishments of licensed veterinary practitioners primarily engaged in the practice of veterinary medicine, dentistry, or surgery for animals; and establishments primarily engaged in providing testing services for licensed veterinary practitioners.

Illustrative Examples:

Animal hospitals
Veterinarians' offices

Veterinary clinics
Veterinary testing laboratories

Cross-References. Establishments primarily engaged in—

- Providing veterinary research and development services—are classified in Industry 541710, Research and Development in the Physical, Engineering, and Life Sciences;

- Providing nonveterinary pet care services, such as boarding or grooming pets—are classified in Industry 812910, Pet Care (except Veterinary) Services;

- Providing animal breeding services or boarding horses—are classified in Industry 115210, Support Activities for Animal Production; and

- Transporting pets—are classified in U.S. Industry 485991, Special Needs Transportation.

54199   All Other Professional, Scientific, and Technical Services
See industry description for 541990 below.

541990   All Other Professional, Scientific, and Technical Services

This industry comprises establishments primarily engaged in the provision of professional, scientific, or technical services (except legal services; accounting, tax preparation, bookkeeping, and related services; architectural, engineering, and related services; specialized design services; computer systems design and related services; management, scientific, and technical consulting services; scientific research and development services; advertising and related services; market research and public opinion polling; photographic services; translation and interpretation services; and veterinary services).

Illustrative Examples:

Appraisal (except real estate) services
Arbitration and conciliation services
  (except by lawyer, attorney, or
  paralegal offices)
Commodity inspector services
Consumer credit counseling services
Handwriting analysis services

Marine surveyor (i.e., appraiser) services
Patent broker services (i.e., patent
  marketing services)
Pipeline or power line inspection (i.e.,
  visual) services
Weather forecasting services

US—United States industry only. CAN—United States and Canadian industries are comparable. MEX—United States and Mexican industries are comparable. Blank—Canadian, Mexican, and United States industries are comparable.

Cross-References. Establishments primarily engaged in—

- Providing legal services—are classified in Industry Group 5411, Legal Services;

- Providing accounting, tax preparation, bookkeeping, and payroll services— are classified in Industry Group 5412, Accounting, Tax Preparation, Book- keeping, and Payroll Services;

- Providing architectural, engineering, and related services—are classified in Industry Group 5413, Architectural, Engineering, and Related Services;

- Providing specialized design services—are classified in Industry Group 5414, Specialized Design Services;

- Providing computer systems design and related services—are classified in Industry Group 5415, Computer Systems Design and Related Services;

- Providing management, scientific, and technical consulting services—are classified in Industry Group 5416, Management, Scientific, and Technical Consulting Services;

- Providing scientific research and development services—are classified in Industry Group 5417, Scientific Research and Development Services;

- Providing advertising and related services—are classified in Industry Group 5418, Advertising and Related Services;

- Providing marketing research and public opinion polling—are classified in Industry 541910, Marketing Research and Public Opinion Polling;

- Providing photographic services—are classified in Industry 54192, Photo- graphic Services;

- Providing translation and interpretation services—are classified in Industry 541930, Translation and Interpretation Services;

- Providing veterinary services—are classified in Industry 541940, Veterinary Services; and

- Providing real estate appraisal services—are classified in Industry 531320, Offices of Real Estate Appraisers.

Sector 55—Management of Companies and Enterprises

The Sector as a Whole

The Managen.ent of Companies and Enterprises sector comprises (1) establishments that hold the securities of (or other equity interests in) companies and enterprises for the purpose of owning a controlling interest or influencing management decisions or (2) establishments (except government establishments) that administer, oversee, and manage establishments of the company or enterprise and that normally undertake the strategic or organizational planning and decisionmaking role of the company or enterprise. Establishments that administer, oversee, and manage may hold the securities of the company or enterprise.

Establishments in this sector perform essential activities that are often undertaken, in-house, by establishments in many sectors of the economy. By consolidating the performance of these activities of the enterprise at one establishment, economies of scale are achieved.

Government establishments primarily engaged in administering, overseeing, and managing governmental programs are classified in Sector 92, Public Administration. Establishments primarily engaged in providing a range of day-to-day office administrative services, such as financial planning, billing and recordkeeping, personnel, and physical distribution and logistics are classified in Industry 56111, Office Administrative Services.

551 Management of Companies and Enterprises

Industries in the Management of Companies and Enterprises subsector include three main types of establishments: (1) those that hold the securities of (or other equity interests in) companies and enterprises; (2) those (except government establishments) that administer, oversee, and manage other establishments of the company or enterprise but do not hold the securities of these establishments; and (3) those that both administer, oversee, and manage other establishments of the company or enterprise and hold the securities of (or other equity interests in) these establishments. Those establishments that administer, oversee, and manage normally undertake the strategic or organizational planning and decisionmaking role of the company or enterprise.

5511 Management of Companies and Enterprises

55111 Management of Companies and Enterprises

This industry comprises (1) establishments primarily engaged in holding the securities of (or other equity interests in) companies and enterprises for the purpose of owning a controlling interest or influencing the management decisions or (2) establishments (except government establishments) that administer, oversee, and manage other establishments of the company or enterprise and that normally undertake the strategic or organizational planning and decisionmaking role of the company or enterprise. Establishments that administer, oversee, and manage may hold the securities of the company or enterprise.

Cross-References.

- Establishments primarily engaged in holding the securities of companies or enterprises and operating these entities are classified according to the business operated;

- Establishments primarily engaged in holding the securities of depository banks and operating these entities are classified in Industry Group 5221, Depository Credit Intermediation;

- Establishments primarily engaged in providing a single service to other establishments of the company or enterprise, such as trucking, warehousing, research and development, and data processing are classified according to the service provided; and

- Government establishments primarily engaged in administering, overseeing, and managing governmental programs are classified in Sector 92, Public Administration.

551111 Offices of Bank Holding Companies[US]

This U.S. industry comprises legal entities known as bank holding companies primarily engaged in holding the securities of (or other equity interests in) companies and enterprises for the purpose of owning a controlling interest or influencing the management decisions of these firms. The holding companies in this industry do not administer, oversee, and manage other establishments of the company or enterprise whose securities they hold.

Cross-References. Establishments primarily engaged in—

- Holding the securities of (or other equity interests in) a company or enterprise and administering, overseeing, and managing establishments of the company or enterprise whose securities they hold—are classified in U.S. Industry 551114, Corporate, Subsidiary, and Regional Managing Offices; and

- Holding the securities of depository banks and operating these entities— are classified in Industry Group 5221, Depository Credit Intermediation.

551112 Offices of Other Holding Companies[US]

This U.S. industry comprises legal entities known as holding companies (except bank holding) primarily engaged in holding the securities of (or other equity interests in) companies and enterprises for the purpose of owning a controlling interest or influencing the management decisions of these firms. The holding companies in this industry do not administer, oversee, and manage other establishments of the company or enterprise whose securities they hold.

Cross-References. Establishments primarily engaged in—

- Holding the securities of (or other equity interests in) depository banks for the purpose of owning a controlling interest or influencing the management decisions of these firms—are classified in U.S. Industry 551111, Offices of Bank Holding Companies;

- Holding the securities of (or other equity interests in) a company or enterprise and administering, overseeing, and managing establishments of the company or enterprise whose securities they hold—are classified in U.S. Industry 551114, Corporate, Subsidiary, and Regional Managing Offices; and

- Holding the securities of companies or enterprises and operating these entities—are classified according to the business operated.

551114 Corporate, Subsidiary, and Regional Managing Offices[CAN]

This U.S. industry comprises establishments (except government establishments) primarily engaged in administering, overseeing, and managing other establishments of the company or enterprise. These establishments normally undertake the strategic or organizational planning and decisionmaking role of the company or enterprise. Establishments in this industry may hold the securities of the company or enterprise.

Illustrative Examples:

Centralized administrative offices	Head offices
Corporate offices	Holding companies that manage
District and regional offices	Subsidiary management offices

Cross-References.

- Government establishments primarily engaged in administering, overseeing, and managing governmental programs are classified in Sector 92, Public Administration;

- Legal entities known as bank holding companies that do not administer, oversee, and manage other establishments of the companies or enterprises

US—United States industry only. CAN—United States and Canadian industries are comparable. MEX—United States and Mexican industries are comparable. Blank—Canadian, Mexican, and United States industries are comparable.

The industries in this subsector cannot be viewed as strictly "support." The Travel Arrangement and Reservation Services industry group, includes travel agents, tour operators, and providers of other travel arrangement services, such as hotel and restaurant reservations and arranging the purchase of tickets, serves many types of clients, including individual consumers. This group was placed in this subsector because the services are often of the "support" nature (e.g., travel arrangement) and businesses and other organizations are increasingly the ones purchasing such services.

The administrative and management activities performed by establishments in this sector are typically on a contract or fee basis. These activities may also be performed by establishments that are part of the company or enterprise. However, establishments involved in administering, overseeing, and managing other establishments of the company or enterprise, are classified in Sector 55, Management of Companies and Enterprises. These establishments normally undertake the strategic and organizational planning and decisionmaking role of the company or enterprise. Government establishments engaged in administering, overseeing and managing governmental programs are classified in Sector 92, Public Administration.

5611 Office Administrative Services

56111 Office Administrative Services

See industry description for 561110 below.

561110 Office Administrative Services

This industry comprises establishments primarily engaged in providing a range of day-to-day office administrative services, such as financial planning; billing and recordkeeping; personnel; and physical distribution and logistics for others on a contract or fee basis. These establishments do not provide operating staff to carry out the complete operations of a business.

Cross-References. Establishments primarily engaged in—

- Holding the securities or financial assets of companies and enterprises for the purpose of controlling them and influencing their management decisions—are classified in U.S. Industry 551111, Offices of Bank Holding Companies or U.S. Industry 551112, Offices of Other Holding Companies;

- Administering, overseeing, and managing other establishments of the company or enterprise (except government establishments)—are classified in U.S. Industry 551114, Corporate, Subsidiary, and Regional Managing Offices;

US—United States industry only. CAN—United States and Canadian industries are comparable. MEX—United States and Mexican industries are comparable. Blank—Canadian, Mexican, and United States industries are comparable.

- Government establishments primarily engaged in administering, overseeing, and managing governmental programs—are classified in Sector 92, Public Administration;

- Providing computer facilities management—are classified in U.S. Industry 541513, Computer Facilities Management Services;

- Providing construction management—are classified in Sector 23, Construction, by type of construction project managed;

- Providing farm management—are classified in U.S. Industry 115116, Farm Management Services;

- Managing real property for others—are classified in Industry 53131, Real Estate Property Managers;

- Providing food services management at institutional, governmental, commercial, or industrial locations—are classified in Industry 722310, Food Service Contractors;

- Providing management advice without day-to-day management—are classified in Industry 54161, Management Consulting Services;

- Providing both management and operating staff for the complete operation of a client's business, such as a hotel, restaurant, mine site, or hospital—are classified according to the industry of the establishment operated; and

- Providing only one of the support services (e.g., accounting services) that establishments in this industry provide—are classified in the appropriate industry according to the service provided.

5612 Facilities Support Services

56121 Facilities Support Services
See industry description for 561210 below.

561210 Facilities Support Services

This industry comprises establishments primarily engaged in providing operating staff to perform a combination of support services within a client's facilities. Establishments in this industry typically provide a combination of services, such as janitorial; maintenance; trash disposal; guard and security; mail routing; reception; laundry; and related services to support operations within facilities. These establishments provide operating staff to carry out these support activities; but, are not involved with or responsible for the core business or activities of the client. Establishments providing facilities (except computer and/or data processing) operation support services and establishments operating correctional facilities (i.e., jails) on a contract or fee basis are included in this industry.

Cross-References.

- Establishments primarily engaged in providing only one of the support services (e.g., janitorial services) that establishments in this industry provide are classified in the appropriate industry according to the service provided;

- Establishments primarily engaged in providing management and operating staff for the complete operation of a client's establishment, such as a hotel, restaurant, mine, or hospital, are classified according to the industry of the establishment operated;

- Establishments primarily engaged in providing on-site management and operation of a client's computer systems and/or data processing facilities are classified in U.S. Industry 541513, Computer Facilities Management Services; and

- Government correctional institutions are classified in Industry 922140, Correctional Institutions.

5613 Employment Services

56131 Employment Placement Agencies
See industry description for 561310 below.

561310 Employment Placement Agencies

This industry comprises establishments primarily engaged in listing employment vacancies and in referring or placing applicants for employment. The individuals referred or placed are not employees of the employment agencies.

Illustrative Examples:

Babysitting bureaus (i.e., registries)	Employment agencies
Casting agencies or bureaus (i.e., motion picture, theatrical, video)	Employment registries
	Model registries

Cross-References. Establishments primarily engaged in—

- Providing executive search consulting services—are classified in U.S. Industry 541612, Human Resources and Executive Search Consulting Services;

- Supplying their own employees for limited periods of time to supplement the working force of a client's business—are classified in Industry 561320, Temporary Help Services;

- Providing human resources and human resource management services to clients—are classified in Industry 561330, Professional Employer Organizations; and

- Representing models, entertainers, athletes, and other public figures as their agent or manager—are classified in Industry 711410, Agents and Managers for Artists, Athletes, Entertainers, and Other Public Figures.

56132 Temporary Help Services

See industry description for 561320 below.

561320 Temporary Help Services

This industry comprises establishments primarily engaged in supplying workers to clients' businesses for limited periods of time to supplement the working force of the client. The individuals provided are employees of the temporary help service establishment. However, these establishments do not provide direct supervision of their employees at the clients' work sites.

Illustrative Examples:

Help supply services
Labor (except farm) contractors (i.e., personnel suppliers)
Manpower pools

Model supply services
Temporary employment or temporary staffing services

Cross-References. Establishments primarily engaged in—

- Providing human resources and human resource management services to clients—are classified in Industry 561330, Professional Employer Organizations;

- Supplying farm labor—are classified in U.S. Industry 115115, Farm Labor Contractors and Crew Leaders;

- Providing operating staff to perform a combination of services to support operations within a client's facilities—are classified in Industry 561210, Facilities Support Services;

- Listing employment vacancies and referring or placing applicants for employment—are classified in Industry 561310, Employment Placement Agencies; and

- Representing models, entertainers, athletes, and other public figures as their agent or manager—are classified in Industry 711410, Agents and Managers for Artists, Athletes, Entertainers, and Other Public Figures.

56133 Professional Employer Organizations
See industry description for 561330 below.

561330 Professional Employer Organizations

This industry comprises establishments primarily engaged in providing human resources and human resource management services to staff client businesses. Establishments in this industry operate in a coemployment relationship with client businesses or organizations and are specialized in performing a wide range of human resource and personnel management duties, such as payroll accounting, payroll tax return preparation, benefits administration, recruiting, and managing labor relations. Employee leasing establishments typically acquire and lease back some or all of the employees of their clients and serve as the employer of the leased employees for payroll, benefits, and related purposes. Employee leasing establishments exercise varying degrees of decisionmaking relating to their human resource or personnel management role, but do not have management accountability for the work of their clients' operations with regard to strategic planning, output, or profitability. Professional employer organizations (PEO) and establishments providing labor or staff leasing services are included in this industry.

Cross-References. Establishments primarily engaged in—

- Supplying their own employees for limited periods of time to supplement the working force of a client's business—are classified in Industry 561320, Temporary Help Services; and

- Listing employment vacancies and in referring or placing applicants for employment—are classified in Industry 561310, Employment Placement Agencies.

5614 Business Support Services

This industry group comprises establishments engaged in performing activities that are ongoing routine business support functions that businesses and organizations traditionally do for themselves.

56141 Document Preparation Services
See industry description for 561410 below.

561410 Document Preparation Services

This industry comprises establishments primarily engaged in one or more of the following: (1) letter or resume writing; (2) document editing or proofreading;

US—United States industry only. CAN—United States and Canadian industries are comparable. MEX—United States and Mexican industries are comparable. Blank—Canadian, Mexican, and United States industries are comparable.

(3) typing, word processing, or desktop publishing; and (4) stenographic (except court reporting or stenotype recording), transcription, and other secretarial services.

Cross-References. Establishments primarily engaged in—

- Providing verbatim reporting and stenotype recording of live legal proceedings and transcribing subsequent recorded materials—are classified in U.S. Industry 561492, Court Reporting and Stenotype Services;
- Performing prepress and postpress services in support of printing activities—are classified in Industry 32312, Support Activities for Printing;
- Providing document translation services—are classified in Industry 541930, Translation and Interpretation Services;
- Photocopying, duplicating, and other document copying services, with or without a range of other office support services (except printing)—are classified in U.S. Industry 561439, Other Business Service Centers (including Copy Shops); and
- Providing document copying services in combination with printing services, with or without a range of other office support services, and establishments known as quick or digital printers—are classified in Industry 32311, Printing.

56142 Telephone Call Centers

This industry comprises (1) establishments primarily engaged in answering telephone calls and relaying messages to clients and (2) establishments primarily engaged in providing telemarketing services on a contract or fee basis for others, such as promoting clients' products or services by telephone; taking orders for clients by telephone; and soliciting contributions or providing information for clients by telephone. Telemarketing establishments never own the product or provide the service that they are representing and generally can originate and/or receive calls for others.

Cross-References. Establishments primarily engaged in—

- Providing paging and beeper transmission services—are classified in Industry 51721, Wireless Telecommunications Carriers (except Satellite);
- Organizing and conducting fundraising campaigns on a contract or fee basis, that may include telephone solicitation services—are classified in Industry 56149, Other Business Support Services; and
- Gathering, recording, tabulating, and presenting marketing and public opinion data, that may include telephone canvassing services—are classified in Industry 54191, Marketing Research and Public Opinion Polling.

561421 Telephone Answering Services[US]

This U.S. industry comprises establishments primarily engaged in answering telephone calls and relaying messages to clients.

Cross-References.

Establishments primarily engaged in providing paging or beeper transmission services are classified in Industry 517211, Paging.

561422 Telemarketing Bureaus[MEX]

This U.S. industry comprises establishments primarily engaged in providing telemarketing services on a contract or fee basis for others, such as: (1) promoting clients' products or services by telephone, (2) taking orders for clients by telephone, and (3) soliciting contributions or providing information for clients by telephone. These establishments never own the product or provide the services they are representing and generally can originate and/or receive calls for others.

Cross-References. Establishments primarily engaged in—

- Organizing and conducting fundraising campaigns on a contract or fee basis, that may include telephone solicitation services—are classified in U.S. Industry 561499, All Other Business Support Services; and
- Gathering, recording, tabulating, and presenting marketing and public opinion data, that may include telephone canvassing services—are classified in Industry 541910, Marketing Research and Public Opinion Polling.

56143 Business Service Centers

This industry comprises (1) establishments primarily engaged in providing mailbox rental and other postal and mailing services (except direct mail advertising); (2) establishments, generally known as copy centers or shops, primarily engaged in providing photocopying, duplicating, blueprinting, and other document copying services without also providing printing services (i.e., offset printing, quick printing, digital printing, prepress services); and (3) establishments that provide a range of office support services (except printing services), such as mailing services, document copying services, facsimile services, word processing services, on-site PC rental services, and office product sales.

Cross-References. Establishments primarily engaged in—

- Operating contract post offices—are classified in Industry 49111, Postal Service;

US—United States industry only. CAN—United States and Canadian industries are comparable. MEX—United States and Mexican industries are comparable. Blank—Canadian, Mexican, and United States industries are comparable.

- Delivering letters and parcels—are classified in Subsector 492, Couriers and Messengers;

- Providing voice mailbox services—are classified in Industry 56142, Telephone Call Centers;

- Providing direct mail advertising services—are classified in Industry 54186, Direct Mail Advertising;

- Providing document copying services in combination with printing services, with or without a range of other office support services, and establishments known as quick or digital printers—are classified in Industry 32311, Printing; and

- Providing only one of the support services (e.g., word processing services) that establishments in this industry provide—are classified in the appropriate industry according to the service provided.

561431 Private Mail Centers^{US}

This U.S. industry comprises (1) establishments primarily engaged in providing mailbox rental and other postal and mailing (except direct mail advertising) services or (2) establishments engaged in providing these mailing services along with one or more other office support services, such as facsimile services, word processing services, on-site PC rental services, and office product sales.

Cross-References. Establishments primarily engaged in—

- Operating contract post offices—are classified in Industry 491110, Postal Service;

- Delivering letters and parcels—are classified in Subsector 492, Couriers and Messengers;

- Providing voice mailbox services—are classified in U.S. Industry 561421, Telephone Answering Services;

- Providing direct mail advertising services—are classified in Industry 541860, Direct Mail Advertising; and

- Providing only one of the support services (e.g., word processing services) that establishments in this industry provide—are classified in the appropriate industry according to the service provided.

- Establishments engaged in providing full service office space, whether on a lease or service contract basis—are classified in Industry 531120, Lessors of Nonresidential Buildings (except Miniwarehouses).

US—United States industry only. CAN—United States and Canadian industries are comparable. MEX—United States and Mexican industries are comparable. Blank—Canadian, Mexican, and United States industries are comparable.

561439 Other Business Service Centers (including Copy Shops)[US]

This U.S. industry comprises (1) establishments generally known as copy centers or shops primarily engaged in providing photocopying, duplicating, blueprinting, and other document copying services, without also providing printing services (e.g., offset printing, quick printing, digital printing, prepress services) and (2) establishments (except private mail centers) engaged in providing a range of office support services (except printing services), such as document copying services, facsimile services, word processing services, on-site PC rental services, and office product sales.

Cross-References.

- Establishments engaged in providing document copying services in combination with printing services, with or without a range of other office support services, and establishments known as quick or digital printers are classified in Industry 32311, Printing;

- Establishments engaged in providing mailbox rental and other postal and mailing services with or without one or more other office support services (except printing) are classified in U.S. Industry 561431, Private Mail Centers; and

- Establishments exclusively engaged in providing a single office support service (except document copying) to clients, but not the range of office support services that establishments in this industry may provide, are classified according to the service provided.

- Establishments engaged in providing full service office space, whether on a lease or service contract basis, are classified in Industry 531120, Lessors of Nonresidential Buildings (except Miniwarehouses).

56144 Collection Agencies

See industry description for 561440 below.

561440 Collection Agencies

This industry comprises establishments primarily engaged in collecting payments for claims and remitting payments collected to their clients.

Illustrative Examples:

Account or delinquent account collection services	Tax collection services on a contract or fee basis
Bill or debt collection services	

Cross-References. Establishments primarily engaged in—

- Repossessing tangible assets—are classified in U.S. Industry 561491, Repossession Services; and
- Providing financing to others by factoring accounts receivables (i.e., assuming the risk of collection and credit losses)—are classified in U.S. Industry 522298, All Other Nondepository Credit Intermediation.

56145 Credit Bureaus

See industry description for 561450 below.

561450 Credit Bureaus

This industry comprises establishments primarily engaged in compiling information, such as credit and employment histories on individuals and credit histories on businesses, and providing the information to financial institutions, retailers, and others who have a need to evaluate the creditworthiness of these persons and businesses.

Illustrative Examples:

Credit agencies
Credit investigation services

Credit rating services
Credit reporting bureaus

56149 Other Business Support Services

This industry comprises establishments primarily engaged in providing business support services (except secretarial and other document preparation services; telephone answering or telemarketing services; private mail services or document copying services conducted as separate activities or in conjunction with other office support services; monetary debt collection services; and credit reporting services).

Illustrative Examples:

Address bar coding services
Bar code imprinting services
Court reporting services
Fundraising organization services on
a contract or fee basis

Mail presorting services
Real-time (i.e., simultaneous) closed
captioning of live television
performances, meetings, conferences
Repossession services

Cross-References. Establishments primarily engaged in—

- Providing secretarial and other document preparation services—are classified in Industry 56141, Document Preparation Services;

- Providing telephone answering or telemarketing services—are classified in Industry 56142, Telephone Call Centers;

- Providing private mail services; document copying services (except printing services); and/or a range of office support services (except printing)—are classified in Industry 56143, Business Service Centers;

- Providing document copying services in combination with printing services, with or without a range of other office support services, and establishments known as quick or digital printers—are classified in Industry 32311, Printing;

- Providing monetary debt collection services—are classified in Industry 56144, Collection Agencies;

- Providing credit reporting services—are classified in Industry 56145, Credit Bureaus; and

- Providing film or tape captioning or subtitling services—are classified in Industry 51219, Postproduction Services and Other Motion Picture and Video Industries.

561491 Repossession Services[US]

This U.S. industry comprises establishments primarily engaged in repossessing tangible assets (e.g., automobiles, boats, equipment, planes, furniture, appliances) for the creditor as a result of delinquent debts.

Cross-References.

Establishments primarily engaged in providing monetary debt collection services are classified in Industry 561440, Collection Agencies.

561492 Court Reporting and Stenotype Services[US]

This U.S. industry comprises establishments primarily engaged in providing verbatim reporting and stenotype recording of live legal proceedings and transcribing subsequent recorded materials.

Illustrative Examples:

Court reporting or stenotype recording services	Real-time (i.e., simultaneous) closed captioning of live television perform-
Public stenography services	ances of meetings, conferences

US—United States industry only. CAN—United States and Canadian industries are comparable. MEX—United States and Mexican industries are comparable. Blank—Canadian, Mexican, and United States industries are comparable.

Cross-References. Establishments primarily engaged in—

- Providing stenotype recording of correspondence, reports, and other documents or in providing document transcription services—are classified in Industry 561410, Document Preparation Services; and

- Providing film or tape captioning or subtitling services—are classified in U.S. Industry 512191, Teleproduction and Other Postproduction Services.

561499 All Other Business Support Services[US]

This U.S. industry comprises establishments primarily engaged in providing business support services (except secretarial and other document preparation services; telephone answering and telemarketing services; private mail services or document copying services conducted as separate activities or in conjunction with other office support services; monetary debt collection services; credit reporting services; repossession services; and court reporting and stenotype recording services).

Illustrative Examples:

Address bar coding services
Bar code imprinting services
Fundraising organization services on a
    contract or fee basis

Mail presorting services

Cross-References. Establishments primarily engaged in—

- Providing secretarial and other document preparation services—are classified in Industry 561410, Document Preparation Services;

- Providing telephone answering or telemarketing services—are classified in Industry 56142, Telephone Call Centers;

- Providing private mail services, document copying services without printing services and/or a range of office support services—are classified in Industry 56143, Business Service Centers;

- Providing document copying services in combination with printing services (with or without one or more other office support services) and establishments known as quick or digital printers—are classified in Industry 32311, Printing;

- Providing monetary debt collection services—are classified in Industry 561440, Collection Agencies;

- Providing credit reporting services—are classified in Industry 561450, Credit Bureaus;

- Providing repossession services—are classified in U.S. Industry 561491, Repossession Services; and

- Providing court reporting and stenotype services—are classified in U.S. Industry 561492, Court Reporting and Stenotype Services.

5615 Travel Arrangement and Reservation Services

56151 Travel Agencies
See industry description for 561510 below.

561510 Travel Agencies

This industry comprises establishments primarily engaged in acting as agents in selling travel, tour, and accommodation services to the general public and commercial clients.

Cross-References. Establishments primarily engaged in—

- Arranging and assembling tours that they generally sell through travel agencies or on their own account—are classified in Industry 561520, Tour Operators;

- Providing guide services, such as archeological, museum, tourist, hunting, or fishing—are classified in Industry 713990, All Other Amusement and Recreation Industries; and

- Providing reservation services (e.g., accommodations, entertainment events, travel)—are classified in U.S. Industry 561599, All Other Travel Arrangement and Reservation Services.

56152 Tour Operators
See industry description for 561520 below.

561520 Tour Operators

This industry comprises establishments primarily engaged in arranging and assembling tours. The tours are sold through travel agencies or tour operators. Travel or wholesale tour operators are included in this industry.

Cross-References. Establishments primarily engaged in—

- Acting as agents in selling travel, tour, and accommodation services to the general public and commercial clients—are classified in Industry 561510, Travel Agencies;

- Conducting scenic and sightseeing tours—are classified in Subsector 487, Scenic and Sightseeing Transportation; and

- Providing guide services, such as archeological, museum, tourist, hunting, or fishing—are classified in Industry 713990, All Other Amusement and Recreation Industries.

56159 Other Travel Arrangement and Reservation Services

This industry comprises establishments (except travel agencies and tour operators) primarily engaged in providing travel arrangement and reservation services.

Illustrative Examples:

Condominium time-share exchange services
Convention or visitors bureaus
Reservation (e.g., airline, car rental, hotel, restaurant) services

Road and travel services automobile clubs
Ticket (e.g., airline, bus, cruise ship, sports, theatrical) offices
Ticket (e.g., amusement, sports, theatrical) agencies

Cross-References.

- Establishments primarily engaged in arranging the rental of vacation properties are classified in Industry 53121, Offices of Real Estate Agents and Brokers;

- Travel agencies are classified in Industry 56151, Travel Agencies;

- Tour operators are classified in Industry 56152, Tour Operators;

- Automobile clubs (i.e., enthusiasts' clubs) (except road and travel services) are classified in Industry 81341, Civic and Social Organizations; and

- Establishments primarily engaged in organizing, promoting, and/or managing events, such as business and trade shows, conventions, conferences, and meetings (whether or not they manage and provide the staff to operate the facilities in which these events take place), are classified in Industry 56192, Convention and Trade Show Organizers.

561591 Convention and Visitors Bureaus[US]

This U.S. industry comprises establishments primarily engaged in marketing and promoting communities and facilities to businesses and leisure travelers through a range of activities, such as assisting organizations in locating meeting and convention sites; providing travel information on area attractions, lodging accommodations, restaurants; providing maps; and organizing group tours of local historical, recreational, and cultural attractions.

US—United States industry only. CAN—United States and Canadian industries are comparable. MEX—United States and Mexican industries are comparable. Blank—Canadian, Mexican, and United States industries are comparable.

Cross-References.

Establishments primarily engaged in organizing, promoting, and/or managing events, such as business and trade shows, conventions, conferences, and meetings (whether or not they manage and provide the staff to operate the facilities in which these events take place), are classified in Industry 561920, Convention and Trade Show Organizers.

561599 All Other Travel Arrangement and Reservation Services[US]

This U.S. industry comprises establishments (except travel agencies, tour operators, and convention and visitors bureaus) primarily engaged in providing travel arrangement and reservation services.

Illustrative Examples:

Condominium time-share exchange services

Reservation (e.g., airline, car rental, hotel, restaurant) services

Road and travel services automobile clubs

Ticket (e.g., airline, bus, cruise ship, sports, theatrical) offices

Ticket (e.g., amusement, sports, theatrical) agencies

Cross-References.

- Establishments primarily engaged in arranging the rental of vacation properties are classified in Industry 531210, Offices of Real Estate Agents and Brokers;
- Travel agencies are classified in Industry 561510, Travel Agencies;
- Tour operators are classified in Industry 561520, Tour Operators;
- Convention and visitors bureaus are classified in U.S. Industry 561591, Convention and Visitors Bureaus;
- Establishments primarily engaged in organizing, promoting, and/or managing events, such as business and trade shows, conventions, conferences, and meetings (whether or not they manage and provide the staff to operate the facilities in which these events take place), are classified in Industry 561920, Convention and Trade Show Organizers; and
- Automobile clubs (i.e., enthusiasts' clubs) (except road and travel services) are classified in Industry 813410, Civic and Social Organizations.

5616 Investigation and Security Services

56161 Investigation, Guard, and Armored Car Services

This industry comprises establishments primarily engaged in providing one or more of the following: (1) investigation and detective services; (2) guard and patrol services; and (3) picking up and delivering money, receipts, or other valuable items with personnel and equipment to protect such properties while in transit.

Illustrative Examples:

Armored car services
Bodyguard services
Polygraph services

Private detective services
Security guard services

Cross-References. Establishments primarily engaged in—

- Providing credit checks—are classified in Industry 56145, Credit Bureaus; and

- Selling, installing, monitoring, and maintaining security systems and devices (e.g., burglar and fire alarm systems)—are classified in Industry 56162, Security Systems Services.

561611 Investigation Services[CAN]

This U.S. industry comprises establishments primarily engaged in providing investigation and detective services.

Illustrative Examples:

Fingerprinting services
Polygraph services

Private detective services
Private investigative services

Cross-References.

Establishments primarily engaged in providing credit checks are classified in Industry 561450, Credit Bureaus.

561612 Security Guards and Patrol Services[CAN]

This U.S. industry comprises establishments primarily engaged in providing guard and patrol services, such as bodyguard, guard dog, and parking security services.

Cross-References.

Establishments primarily engaged in selling, installing, monitoring, and maintaining security systems and devices, such as burglar and fire alarms and locking devices, are classified in Industry 56162, Security Systems Services.

US—United States industry only. CAN—United States and Canadian industries are comparable. MEX—United States and Mexican industries are comparable. Blank—Canadian, Mexican, and United States industries are comparable.

561613 Armored Car Services[CAN]

This U.S. industry comprises establishments primarily engaged in picking up and delivering money, receipts, or other valuable items. These establishments maintain personnel and equipment to protect such properties while in transit.

56162 Security Systems Services

This industry comprises establishments engaged in (1) selling security systems, such as burglar and fire alarms and locking devices, along with installation, repair, or monitoring services or (2) remote monitoring of electronic security alarm systems.

Cross-References. Establishments primarily engaged in—

- Selling security systems for buildings without installation, repair, or monitoring services—are classified in Sector 42, Wholesale Trade or Sector 44-45, Retail Trade;
- Retailing motor vehicle security systems with or without installation or repair services—are classified in Industry 44131, Automotive Parts and Accessories Stores; and
- Providing key duplication services—are classified in Industry 81149, Other Personal and Household Goods Repair and Maintenance.

561621 Security Systems Services (except Locksmiths)[CAN]

This U.S. industry comprises establishments primarily engaged in (1) selling security alarm systems, such as burglar and fire alarms, along with installation, repair, or monitoring services or (2) remote monitoring of electronic security alarm systems.

Cross-References. Establishments primarily engaged in—

- Selling security alarm systems for buildings, without installation, repair, or monitoring services—are classified in Sector 42, Wholesale Trade or Sector 44-45, Retail Trade; and
- Retailing motor vehicle security systems with or without installation or repair services—are classified in Industry 441310, Automotive Parts and Accessories Stores.

561622 Locksmiths[CAN]

This U.S. industry comprises establishments primarily engaged in (1) selling mechanical or electronic locking devices, safes, and security vaults, along with installation, repair, rebuilding, or adjusting services or (2) installing, repairing, rebuilding, and adjusting mechanical or electronic locking devices, safes, and security vaults.

Cross-References. Establishments primarily engaged in—

- Selling security systems, such as locking devices, safes, and vaults, without installation or maintenance services—are classified in Sector 42, Wholesale Trade or Sector 44-45, Retail Trade; and
- Providing key duplication services—are classified in Industry 811490, Other Personal and Household Goods Repair and Maintenance.

5617 Services to Buildings and Dwellings

56171 Exterminating and Pest Control Services
See industry description for 561710 below.

561710 Exterminating and Pest Control Services

This industry comprises establishments primarily engaged in exterminating and controlling birds, mosquitoes, rodents, termites, and other insects and pests (except for crop production and forestry production). Establishments providing fumigation services are included in this industry.

Cross-References.

Establishments primarily engaged in providing pest control for crop or forestry production are classified in Subsector 115, Support Activities for Agriculture and Forestry.

56172 Janitorial Services
See industry description for 561720 below.

561720 Janitorial Services[MEX]

This industry comprises establishments primarily engaged in cleaning building interiors, interiors of transportation equipment (e.g., aircraft, rail cars, ships), and/ or windows.

Illustrative Examples:

Custodial services
Housekeeping (i.e., cleaning) services
Maid (i.e., cleaning) services

Service station cleaning and degreasing services
Washroom sanitation services

US—United States industry only. CAN—United States and Canadian industries are comparable. MEX—United States and Mexican industries are comparable. Blank—Canadian, Mexican, and United States industries are comparable.

Cross-References. Establishments primarily engaged in—

- Cleaning building exteriors (except sandblasting and window cleaning) or chimneys—are classified in Industry 561790, Other Services to Buildings and Dwellings; and
- Sandblasting building exteriors—are classified in Industry 238990, All Other Specialty Trade Contractors.

56173 Landscaping Services
See industry description for 561730 below.

561730 Landscaping Services

This industry comprises (1) establishments primarily engaged in providing landscape care and maintenance services and/or installing trees, shrubs, plants, lawns, or gardens and (2) establishments primarily engaged in providing these services along with the design of landscape plans and/or the construction (i.e., installation) of walkways, retaining walls, decks, fences, ponds, and similar structures.

Cross-References. Establishments primarily engaged in—

- Installing artificial turf or in constructing (i.e., installing) walkways, retaining walls, decks, fences, ponds, or similar structures—are classified in Sector 23, Construction;
- Planning and designing the development of land areas for projects, such as parks and other recreational areas; airports; highways; hospitals; schools; land subdivisions; and commercial, industrial, and residential areas (without also installing trees, shrubs, plants, lawns/gardens, walkways, retaining walls, decks, and similar items or structures)—are classified in Industry 541320, Landscape Architectural Services; and
- Retailing landscaping materials and providing the installation and maintenance of these materials—are classified in Industry 444220, Nursery, Garden Center, and Farm Supply Stores.

56174 Carpet and Upholstery Cleaning Services
See industry description for 561740 below.

561740 Carpet and Upholstery Cleaning Services

This industry comprises establishments primarily engaged in cleaning and dyeing used rugs, carpets, and upholstery.

US—United States industry only. CAN—United States and Canadian industries are comparable. MEX—United States and Mexican industries are comparable. Blank—Canadian, Mexican, and United States industries are comparable.

Cross-References. Establishments primarily engaged in—

- Rug repair not associated with rug cleaning—are classified in Industry 811490, Other Personal and Household Goods Repair and Maintenance; and
- Reupholstering and repairing furniture—are classified in Industry 811420, Reupholstery and Furniture Repair.

56179 Other Services to Buildings and Dwellings
See industry description for 561790 below.

561790 Other Services to Buildings and Dwellings[MEX]

This industry comprises establishments primarily engaged in providing services to buildings and dwellings (except exterminating and pest control; janitorial; landscaping care and maintenance; and carpet and upholstery cleaning).

Illustrative Examples:

Building exterior cleaning services (except sandblasting and window cleaning)
Chimney cleaning services

Drain or gutter cleaning services
Swimming pool cleaning and maintenance services
Ventilation duct cleaning services

Cross-References. Establishments primarily engaged in—

- Providing exterminating and pest control services—are classified in Industry 561710, Exterminating and Pest Control Services;
- Providing janitorial services—are classified in Industry 561720, Janitorial Services;
- Providing landscaping care and maintenance—are classified in Industry 561730, Landscaping Services;
- Providing carpet and upholstery cleaning services—are classified in Industry 561740, Carpet and Upholstery Cleaning Services; and
- Sandblasting building exteriors—are classified in Industry 238990, All Other Specialty Trade Contractors.

5619 Other Support Services

This industry group comprises establishments primarily engaged in providing day-to-day business and other organizational support services (except office administrative services; facilities support services; employment services; business support services; travel arrangement and reservation services; security and investigation services; and services to buildings and dwellings).

56191 Packaging and Labeling Services

See industry description for 561910 below.

561910 Packaging and Labeling Services

This industry comprises establishments primarily engaged in packaging client-owned materials. The services may include labeling and/or imprinting the package.

Illustrative Examples:

Apparel and textile folding and
  packaging services
Blister packaging services

Gift wrapping services
Kit assembling and packaging services
Shrink-wrapping services

Cross-References. Establishments primarily engaged in—

- Processing client-owned materials into a different product, such as mixing water and concentrate to produce soft drinks—are classified in Sector 31-33, Manufacturing;

- Providing aerosol packaging services—are classified in U.S. Industry 325998, All Other Miscellaneous Chemical Product and Preparation Manufacturing;

- Providing packing and crating services incidental to transportation—are classified in U.S. Industry 488991, Packing and Crating;

- Providing warehousing services, as well as packaging or other logistics services—are classified in Industry Group 4931, Warehousing and Storage; and

- Providing packing and crating services for agricultural products—are classified in U.S. Industry 115114, Postharvest Crop Activities (except Cotton Ginning).

56192 Convention and Trade Show Organizers

See industry description for 561920 below.

561920 Convention and Trade Show Organizers

This industry comprises establishments primarily engaged in organizing, promoting, and/or managing events, such as business and trade shows, conventions, conferences, and meetings (whether or not they manage and provide the staff to operate the facilities in which these events take place).

US—United States industry only. CAN—United States and Canadian industries are comparable. MEX—United States and Mexican industries are comparable. Blank—Canadian, Mexican, and United States industries are comparable.

Cross-References.

Establishments primarily engaged in organizing, promoting, and/or managing live performing arts productions, sports events, and similar events, such as festivals (whether or not they manage and provide the staff to operate the facilities in which these events take place), are classified in Industry Group 7113, Promoters of Performing Arts, Sports, and Similar Events.

56199 All Other Support Services
See industry description for 561990 below.

561990 All Other Support Services

This industry comprises establishments primarily engaged in providing day-to-day business and other organizational support services (except office administrative services, facilities support services, employment services, business support services, travel arrangement and reservation services, security and investigation services, services to buildings and other structures, packaging and labeling services, and convention and trade show organizing services).

Illustrative Examples:

Bartering services
Bottle exchanges
Cloth cutting, bolting, or winding for the trade
Contract meter reading services

Diving services on a contract or fee basis
Flagging (i.e., traffic control) services
Float decorating services
Inventory taking services
Lumber grading services

Cross-References. Establishments primarily engaged in—

- Providing office administrative services—are classified in Industry 561110, Office Administrative Services;

- Providing facilities support services—are classified in Industry 561210, Facilities Support Services;

- Providing employment services—are classified in Industry Group 5613, Employment Services;

- Providing business support services—are classified in Industry Group 5614, Business Support Services;

- Providing travel arrangement and reservation services—are classified in Industry Group 5615, Travel Arrangement and Reservation Services;

- Providing security and investigation services—are classified in Industry Group 5616, Investigation and Security Services;

- Providing services to buildings and other structures—are classified in Industry Group 5617, Services to Buildings and Dwellings;

- Providing packaging and labeling services—are classified in Industry 561910, Packaging and Labeling Services; and

- Organizing, promoting, and/or managing conferences, conventions, and trade shows (whether or not they manage and provide the staff to operate the facilities in which these events take place)—are classified in Industry 561920, Convention and Trade Show Organizers.

562 Waste Management and Remediation Services

Industries in the Waste Management and Remediation Services subsector group establishments engaged in the collection, treatment, and disposal of waste materials. This includes establishments engaged in local hauling of waste materials; operating materials recovery facilities (i.e., those that sort recyclable materials from the trash stream); providing remediation services (i.e., those that provide for the cleanup of contaminated buildings, mine sites, soil, or ground water); and providing septic pumping and other miscellaneous waste management services. There are three industry groups within the subsector that separate these activities into waste collection, waste treatment and disposal, and remediation and other waste management.

Excluded from this subsector are establishments primarily engaged in collecting, treating, and disposing waste through sewer systems or sewage treatment facilities that are classified in Industry 22132, Sewage Treatment Facilities and establishments primarily engaged in long-distance hauling of waste materials that are classified in Industry 48423, Specialized Freight (except Used Goods) Trucking, Long-Distance. Also, there are some activities that appear to be related to waste management, but that are not included in this subsector. For example, establishments primarily engaged in providing waste management consulting services are classified in Industry 54162, Environmental Consulting Services.

5621 Waste Collection^{CAN}

56211 Waste Collection^{CAN}

This industry comprises establishments primarily engaged in (1) collecting and/or hauling hazardous waste, nonhazardous waste, and/or recyclable materials within a local area and/or (2) operating hazardous or nonhazardous waste transfer stations. Hazardous waste collection establishments may be responsible for the identification, treatment, packaging, and labeling of waste for the purposes of transport.

US—United States industry only. CAN—United States and Canadian industries are comparable. MEX—United States and Mexican industries are comparable. Blank—Canadian, Mexican, and United States industries are comparable.

Cross-References. Establishments primarily engaged in—

- Long-distance trucking of waste—are classified in Industry 48423, Specialized Freight (except Used Goods) Trucking, Long-Distance;
- Operating facilities for separating and sorting recyclable materials from nonhazardous waste streams (i.e., garbage) and/or for sorting commingled recyclable materials, such as paper, plastics, and metal cans, into distinct categories—are classified in Industry 56292, Materials Recovery Facilities; and
- Collecting and/or hauling in combination with disposal of waste materials— are classified in Industry 56221, Waste Treatment and Disposal.

562111 Solid Waste Collection[US]

This U.S. industry comprises establishments primarily engaged in one or more of the following: (1) collecting and/or hauling nonhazardous solid waste (i.e., garbage) within a local area; (2) operating nonhazardous solid waste transfer stations; and (3) collecting and/or hauling mixed recyclable materials within a local area.

Cross-References. Establishments primarily engaged in—

- Long-distance trucking of waste—are classified in Industry 484230, Specialized Freight (except Used Goods) Trucking, Long-Distance;
- Collecting and/or hauling in combination with disposal of nonhazardous waste materials—are classified in Industry 56221, Waste Treatment and Disposal;
- Collecting and/or hauling hazardous waste within a local area and/or operating hazardous waste transfer stations—are classified in U.S. Industry 562112, Hazardous Waste Collection;
- Collecting and removing debris, such as brush or rubble, within a local area—are classified in U.S. Industry 562119, Other Waste Collection; and
- Operating facilities for separating and sorting recyclable materials from nonhazardous waste streams (i.e., garbage) and/or for sorting commingled recyclable materials, such as paper, plastics, and metal cans, into distinct categories—are classified in Industry 562920, Materials Recovery Facilities.

562112 Hazardous Waste Collection[US]

This U.S. industry comprises establishments primarily engaged in collecting and/or hauling hazardous waste within a local area and/or operating hazardous

---

US—United States industry only. CAN—United States and Canadian industries are comparable. MEX—United States and Mexican industries are comparable. Blank—Canadian, Mexican, and United States industries are comparable.

waste transfer stations. Hazardous waste collection establishments may be responsible for the identification, treatment, packaging, and labeling of waste for the purposes of transport.

Cross-References. Establishments primarily engaged in—

- Long-distance trucking of waste—are classified in Industry 484230, Specialized Freight (except Used Goods) Trucking, Long-Distance;
- Collecting and/or hauling in combination with disposal of hazardous waste materials—are classified in U.S. Industry 562211, Hazardous Waste Treatment and Disposal;
- Collecting and/or hauling nonhazardous solid waste (i.e., garbage) and/or recyclable materials within a local area and/or operating nonhazardous solid waste transfer stations—are classified in U.S. Industry 562111, Solid Waste Collection; and
- Collecting and removing debris, such as brush or rubble, within a local area—are classified in U.S. Industry 562119, Other Waste Collection.

562119 Other Waste Collection[US]

This U.S. industry comprises establishments primarily engaged in collecting and/or hauling waste (except nonhazardous solid waste and hazardous waste) within a local area. Establishments engaged in brush or rubble removal services are included in this industry.

Cross-References. Establishments primarily engaged in—

- Long-distance trucking of waste—are classified in Industry 484230, Specialized Freight (except Used Goods) Trucking, Long-Distance;
- Collecting and/or hauling in combination with disposal of waste materials—are classified in Industry Group 5622, Waste Treatment and Disposal;
- Collecting and/or hauling nonhazardous solid waste (i.e., garbage) or mixed recyclable materials within a local area or operating nonhazardous solid waste transfer stations—are classified in U.S. Industry 562111, Solid Waste Collection;
- Collecting and/or hauling hazardous waste within a local area or operating hazardous waste transfer stations—are classified in U.S. Industry 562112, Hazardous Waste Collection; and
- Operating facilities for separating and sorting recyclable materials from nonhazardous waste streams (i.e., garbage) and/or for sorting commingled

recyclable materials, such as paper, plastics, and metal cans, into distinct categories—are classified in Industry 562920, Materials Recovery Facilities.

5622 Waste Treatment and Disposal[CAN]

56221 Waste Treatment and Disposal[CAN]

This industry comprises establishments primarily engaged in (1) operating waste treatment or disposal facilities (except sewer systems or sewage treatment facilities) or (2) the combined activity of collecting and/or hauling of waste materials within a local area and operating waste treatment or disposal facilities. Waste combustors or incinerators (including those that may produce byproducts, such as electricity), solid waste landfills, and compost dumps are included in this industry.

Cross-References. Establishments primarily engaged in—

- Collecting, treating, and disposing waste through sewer systems or sewage treatment facilities—are classified in Industry 22132, Sewage Treatment Facilities; and

- Manufacturing compost—are classified in Industry 32531, Fertilizer Manufacturing.

562211 Hazardous Waste Treatment and Disposal[US]

This U.S. industry comprises establishments primarily engaged in (1) operating treatment and/or disposal facilities for hazardous waste or (2) the combined activity of collecting and/or hauling of hazardous waste materials within a local area and operating treatment or disposal facilities for hazardous waste.

Cross-References. Establishments primarily engaged in—

- Operating landfills for the disposal of nonhazardous solid waste—are classified in U.S. Industry 562212, Solid Waste Landfill;

- Operating combustors and incinerators for the disposal of nonhazardous solid waste—are classified in U.S. Industry 562213, Solid Waste Combustors and Incinerators;

- Collecting, treating, and disposing waste through sewer systems or sewage treatment facilities—are classified in Industry 221320, Sewage Treatment Facilities; and

- Operating nonhazardous waste treatment and disposal facilities (except landfills, combustors, incinerators, and sewer systems or sewage treatment facilities)—are classified in U.S. Industry 562219, Other Nonhazardous Waste Treatment and Disposal.

562212 Solid Waste Landfill[US]

This U.S. industry comprises establishments primarily engaged in (1) operating landfills for the disposal of nonhazardous solid waste or (2) the combined activity of collecting and/or hauling nonhazardous waste materials within a local area and operating landfills for the disposal of nonhazardous solid waste.

Cross-References. Establishments primarily engaged in—

- Operating treatment and/or disposal facilities for hazardous waste—are classified in U.S. Industry 562211, Hazardous Waste Treatment and Disposal;

- Operating combustors and incinerators for the disposal of nonhazardous solid waste—are classified in U.S. Industry 562213, Solid Waste Combustors and Incinerators;

- Collecting, treating, and disposing waste through sewer systems or sewage treatment facilities—are classified in Industry 221320, Sewage Treatment Facilities;

- Operating nonhazardous waste treatment and disposal facilities (except landfills, combustors, incinerators, and sewer systems or sewage treatment facilities)—are classified in U.S. Industry 562219, Other Nonhazardous Waste Treatment and Disposal; and

- Manufacturing compost—are classified in U.S. Industry 325314, Fertilizer (Mixing Only) Manufacturing.

562213 Solid Waste Combustors and Incinerators[US]

This U.S. industry comprises establishments primarily engaged in operating combustors and incinerators for the disposal of nonhazardous solid waste. These establishments may produce byproducts, such as electricity and steam.

Cross-References. Establishments primarily engaged in—

- Operating treatment and/or disposal facilities for hazardous waste—are classified in U.S. Industry 562211, Hazardous Waste Treatment and Disposal;

- Operating landfills for the disposal of nonhazardous solid waste—are classified in U.S. Industry 562212, Solid Waste Landfill;

- Collecting, treating, and disposing waste through sewer systems or sewage treatment facilities—are classified in Industry 221320, Sewage Treatment Facilities; and

- Operating nonhazardous waste treatment and disposal facilities (except landfills, combustors, incinerators, and sewer systems or sewage treatment facilities)—are classified in U.S. Industry 562219, Other Nonhazardous Waste Treatment and Disposal.

562219 Other Nonhazardous Waste Treatment and Disposal[US]

This U.S. industry comprises establishments primarily engaged in (1) operating nonhazardous waste treatment and disposal facilities (except landfills, combustors, incinerators and sewer systems or sewage treatment facilities) or (2) the combined activity of collecting and/or hauling of nonhazardous waste materials within a local area and operating waste treatment or disposal facilities (except landfills, combustors, incinerators and sewer systems, or sewage treatment facilities). Compost dumps are included in this industry.

Cross-References. Establishments primarily engaged in—

- Operating landfills for the disposal of nonhazardous solid waste—are classified in U.S. Industry 562212, Solid Waste Landfill;

- Operating combustors and incinerators for the disposal of nonhazardous solid waste—are classified in U.S. Industry 562213, Solid Waste Combustors and Incinerators;

- Collecting, treating, and disposing waste through sewer systems or sewage treatment facilities—are classified in Industry 221320, Sewage Treatment Facilities; and

- Manufacturing compost—are classified in U.S. Industry 325314, Fertilizer (Mixing Only) Manufacturing.

5629 Remediation and Other Waste Management Services[CAN]

This industry group comprises establishments primarily engaged in remediation and other waste management services (except waste collection, waste treatment and disposal, and waste management consulting services).

56291 Remediation Services[CAN]
See industry description for 562910 below.

562910 Remediation Services^{CAN}

This industry comprises establishments primarily engaged in one or more of the following: (1) remediation and cleanup of contaminated buildings, mine sites, soil, or ground water; (2) integrated mine reclamation activities, including demolition, soil remediation, waste water treatment, hazardous material removal, contouring land, and revegetation; and (3) asbestos, lead paint, and other toxic material abatement.

Cross-References. Establishments primarily engaged in—

- Developing remedial action plans—are classified in Industry 541620, Environmental Consulting Services;
- Excavating soil—are classified in Industry 238910, Site Preparation Contractors;
- Individual activities as part of a reclamation or remediation project—are classified according to the primary activity;
- Building modifications to alleviate radon gas—are classified in Industry 238990, All Other Specialty Trade Contractors; and
- Collecting, treating, and disposing waste water through sewer systems or sewage treatment facilities—are classified in Industry 221320, Sewage Treatment Facilities.

56292 Materials Recovery Facilities^{CAN}
See industry description for 562920 below.

562920 Materials Recovery Facilities^{CAN}

This industry comprises establishments primarily engaged in (1) operating facilities for separating and sorting recyclable materials from nonhazardous waste streams (i.e., garbage) and/or (2) operating facilities where commingled recyclable materials, such as paper, plastics, used beverage cans, and metals are sorted into distinct categories.

Cross-References.

Establishments primarily engaged in merchant wholesaling automotive, industrial, and other recyclable materials are classified in Industry 423930, Recyclable Material Merchant Wholesalers.

56299 All Other Waste Management Services^{CAN}

This industry comprises establishments primarily engaged in waste management services (except waste collection, waste treatment and disposal, remediation, operation of materials recovery facilities, and waste management consulting services).

US—United States industry only. CAN—United States and Canadian industries are comparable. MEX—United States and Mexican industries are comparable. Blank—Canadian, Mexican, and United States industries are comparable.

Illustrative Examples:

Beach cleaning and maintenance services	Sewer cleaning and rodding services
Cesspool cleaning services	Sewer or storm basin cleanout services
Portable toilet renting and/or servicing	
Pumping (i.e., cleaning) cesspools, portable toilets, or septic tanks	

Cross-References. Establishments primarily engaged in—

- Collecting and/or hauling waste within a local area—are classified in Industry 56211, Waste Collection;

- Long-distance trucking of waste—are classified in Industry 48423, Specialized Freight (except Used Goods) Trucking, Long-Distance;

- Operating treatment or disposal facilities (except sewer systems or sewage treatment facilities) for waste—are classified in Industry 56221, Waste Treatment and Disposal;

- Collecting, treating, and disposing waste through sewer systems or sewage treatment facilities—are classified in Industry 22132, Sewage Treatment Facilities;

- Remediation and cleanup of contaminated buildings, mine sites, soil, or ground water—are classified in Industry 56291, Remediation Services;

- Operating facilities for separating and sorting recyclable materials from nonhazardous waste streams (i.e., garbage) or where commingled recyclable materials, such as paper, plastics, and metal cans—are sorted into distinct categories are classified in Industry 56292, Materials Recovery Facilities;

- Installing septic tanks—are classified in Industry 23822, Plumbing, Heating, and Air-Conditioning Contractors; and

- Providing waste management consulting services, such as developing remedial action plans—are classified in Industry 54162, Environmental Consulting Services.

562991 Septic Tank and Related Services[US]

This U.S. industry comprises establishments primarily engaged in (1) pumping (i.e., cleaning) septic tanks and cesspools and/or (2) renting and/or servicing portable toilets.

Cross-References. Establishments primarily engaged in—

- Installing septic tanks—are classified in Industry 23822, Plumbing, Heating, and Air-Conditioning Contractors; and

- Cleaning and rodding sewers and catch basins—are classified in U.S. Industry 562998, All Other Miscellaneous Waste Management Services.

562998 All Other Miscellaneous Waste Management Services[US]

This U.S. industry comprises establishments primarily engaged in providing waste management services (except waste collection, waste treatment and disposal, remediation, operation of materials recovery facilities, septic tank pumping and related services, and waste management consulting services).

Illustrative Examples:

Beach cleaning and maintenance services	Sewer or storm basin cleanout services
Catch basin cleaning services	Tank cleaning and disposal services,
Sewer cleaning and rodding services	commercial or industrial

Cross-References. Establishments primarily engaged in—

- Collecting and/or hauling waste within a local area—are classified in Industry 56211, Waste Collection;

- Long-distance trucking of waste—are classified in Industry 484230, Specialized Freight (except Used Goods) Trucking, Long-Distance;

- Operating treatment or disposal facilities (except sewer systems or sewage treatment facilities) for waste—are classified in Industry 56221 Waste Treatment and Disposal;

- Collecting, treating, and disposing waste through sewer systems or sewage treatment facilities—are classified in Industry 221320, Sewage Treatment Facilities;

- The remediation and cleanup of contaminated buildings, mine sites, soil, or ground water—are classified in Industry 562910, Remediation Services;

- Operating facilities for separating and sorting recyclable materials from nonhazardous waste streams (i.e., garbage) or for sorting commingled recyclable materials, such as paper, plastics, and metal cans, into distinct categories—are classified in Industry 562920, Materials Recovery Facilities;

- Pumping (i.e., cleaning) cesspools, portable toilets, and septic tanks or renting portable toilets—are classified in U.S. Industry 562991, Septic Tank and Related Services; and

- Providing waste management consulting services, such as developing remedial action plans—are classified in Industry 541620, Environmental Consulting Services.

US—United States industry only. CAN—United States and Canadian industries are comparable. MEX—United States and Mexican industries are comparable. Blank—Canadian, Mexican, and United States industries are comparable.

Sector 61—Educational Services

The Sector as a Whole

The Educational Services sector comprises establishments that provide instruction and training in a wide variety of subjects. This instruction and training is provided by specialized establishments, such as schools, colleges, universities, and training centers. These establishments may be privately owned and operated for profit or not for profit, or they may be publicly owned and operated. They may also offer food and accommodation services to their students.

Educational services are usually delivered by teachers or instructors that explain, tell, demonstrate, supervise, and direct learning. Instruction is imparted in diverse settings, such as educational institutions, the workplace, or the home through correspondence, television, or other means. It can be adapted to the particular needs of the students, for example sign language can replace verbal language for teaching students with hearing impairments. All industries in the sector share this commonality of process, namely, labor inputs of instructors with the requisite subject matter expertise and teaching ability.

611 Educational Services

Industries in the Educational Services subsector provide instruction and training in a wide variety of subjects. The instruction and training is provided by specialized establishments, such as schools, colleges, universities, and training centers.

The subsector is structured according to level and type of educational services. Elementary and secondary schools, junior colleges and colleges, universities, and professional schools correspond to a recognized series of formal levels of education designated by diplomas, associate degrees (including equivalent certificates), and degrees. The remaining industry groups are based more on the type of instruction or training offered and the levels are not always as formally defined. The establishments are often highly specialized, many offering instruction in a very limited subject matter, for example ski lessons or one specific computer software package. Within the sector, the level and types of training that are required of the instructors and teachers vary depending on the industry.

Establishments that manage schools and other educational establishments on a contractual basis are classified in this subsector if they both manage the operation and provide the operating staff. Such establishments are classified in the educational services subsector based on the type of facility managed and operated.

6111 Elementary and Secondary Schools

61111 Elementary and Secondary Schools^{CAN}

See industry description for 611110 below.

US—United States industry only. CAN—United States and Canadian industries are comparable. MEX—United States and Mexican industries are comparable. Blank—Canadian, Mexican, and United States industries are comparable.

611110 Elementary and Secondary Schools[CAN]

This industry comprises establishments primarily engaged in furnishing academic courses and associated course work that comprise a basic preparatory education. A basic preparatory education ordinarily constitutes kindergarten through 12th grade. This industry includes school boards and school districts.

Illustrative Examples:

Elementary schools	Parochial schools, elementary or
High schools	secondary
Kindergartens	Primary schools
Military academies, elementary or	Schools for the physically disabled,
secondary	elementary or secondary

Cross-References.

- Establishments primarily engaged in providing preschool or prekindergarten education are classified in Industry 624410, Child Day Care Services; and

- Military academies, college level are classified in Industry 611310, Colleges, Universities, and Professional Schools.

6112 Junior Colleges

61121 Junior Colleges
See industry description for 611210 below.

611210 Junior Colleges[CAN]

This industry comprises establishments primarily engaged in furnishing academic, or academic and technical, courses and granting associate degrees, certificates, or diplomas below the baccalaureate level. The requirement for admission to an associate or equivalent degree program is at least a high school diploma or equivalent general academic training. Instruction may be provided in diverse settings, such as the establishment's or client's training facilities, educational institutions, the workplace, or the home, and through correspondence, television, Internet, or other means.

6113 Colleges, Universities, and Professional Schools

61131 Colleges, Universities, and Professional Schools
See industry description for 611310 below.

US—United States industry only. CAN—United States and Canadian industries are comparable. MEX—United States and Mexican industries are comparable. Blank—Canadian, Mexican, and United States industries are comparable.

611310 Colleges, Universities, and Professional Schools[CAN]

This industry comprises establishments primarily engaged in furnishing academic courses and granting degrees at baccalaureate or graduate levels. The requirement for admission is at least a high school diploma or equivalent general academic training. Instruction may be provided in diverse settings, such as the establishment's or client's training facilities, educational institutions, the workplace, or the home, and through correspondence, television, Internet, or other means.

Illustrative Examples:

Colleges (except junior colleges)
Military academies, college level
Professional schools (e.g.,business
 administration, dental, law, medical)

Theological seminaries offering
 baccalaureate or graduate degrees
Universities

Cross-References.

Establishments primarily engaged in furnishing academic, or academic and technical, courses and granting associate degrees, certificates, or diplomas below the baccalaureate level are classified in Industry 611210, Junior Colleges.

6114 Business Schools and Computer and Management Training

61141 Business and Secretarial Schools
See industry description for 611410 below.

611410 Business and Secretarial Schools[CAN]

This industry comprises establishments primarily engaged in offering courses in office procedures and secretarial and stenographic skills and may offer courses in basic office skills, such as word processing. In addition, these establishments may offer such classes as office machine operation, reception, communications, and other skills designed for individuals pursuing a clerical or secretarial career. Instruction may be provided in diverse settings, such as the establishment's or client's training facilities, educational institutions, the workplace, or the home, and through correspondence, television, Internet, or other means.

Cross-References. Establishments primarily engaged in—

- Offering computer training (except computer repair)—are classified in Industry 611420, Computer Training;

US—United States industry only. CAN—United States and Canadian industries are comparable. MEX—United States and Mexican industries are comparable. Blank—Canadian, Mexican, and United States industries are comparable.

- Offering academic degrees (e.g., baccalaureate, graduate level) in business education—are classified in Industry 611310, Colleges, Universities, and Professional Schools; and

- Offering training in the maintenance and repair of computers—are classified in Industry 611519, Other Technical and Trade Schools.

61142 Computer Training

See industry description for 611420 below.

611420 Computer Training[CAN]

This industry comprises establishments primarily engaged in conducting computer training (except computer repair), such as computer programming, software packages, computerized business systems, computer electronics technology, computer operations, and local area network management. Instruction may be provided in diverse settings, such as the establishment's or client's training facilities, educational institutions, the workplace, or the home, and through correspondence, television, Internet, or other means.

Cross-References. Establishments primarily engaged in—

- Offering training in the maintenance and repair of computers—are classified in Industry 611519, Other Technical and Trade Schools; and

- Computer retailing, wholesaling, or computer system designing that may also provide computer training—are classified in their appropriate industries.

61143 Professional and Management Development Training

See industry description for 611430 below.

611430 Professional and Management Development Training[CAN]

This industry comprises establishments primarily engaged in offering an array of short duration courses and seminars for management and professional development. Training for career development may be provided directly to individuals or through employers' training programs; and courses may be customized or modified to meet the special needs of customers. Instruction may be provided in diverse settings, such as the establishment's or client's training facilities, educational institutions, the workplace, or the home, and through correspondence, television, Internet, or other means.

US—United States industry only. CAN—United States and Canadian industries are comparable. MEX—United States and Mexican industries are comparable. Blank—Canadian, Mexican, and United States industries are comparable.

Cross-References. Establishments primarily engaged in—

- Advising clients on human resource and training issues without providing the training—are classified in U.S. Industry 541612, Human Resources and Executive Search Consulting Services; and
- Offering academic degrees (e.g., baccalaureate, graduate level)—are classified in Industry 611310, Colleges, Universities and Professional Schools.

6115 Technical and Trade Schools

61151 Technical and Trade Schools

This industry comprises establishments primarily engaged in offering vocational and technical training in a variety of technical subjects and trades. The training often leads to job-specific certification. Instruction may be provided in diverse settings, such as the establishment's or client's training facilities, educational institutions, the workplace, or the home, and through correspondence, television, Internet, or other means.

Illustrative Examples:

Apprenticeship training programs
Aviation and flight training instruction
  schools
Computer repair training
Cosmetology schools
Electronic equipment repair training

Graphic arts schools
Modeling schools
Nursing schools (except academic)
Real estate schools
Truck driving schools

Cross-References. Establishments primarily engaged in—

- Offering courses in office procedures and secretarial and stenographic skills—are classified in Industry 61141, Business and Secretarial Schools;
- Offering computer training (except computer repair)—are classified in Industry 61142, Computer Training;
- Offering professional and management development training—are classified in Industry 61143, Professional and Management Development Training;
- Offering academic courses that may also offer technical and trade courses— are classified according to the type of school;
- Specialty air transportation services which may also provide flight training— are classified in Industry 48121, Nonscheduled Air Transportation; and
- Offering registered nursing training—are classified in Industry 61121, Junior Colleges or Industry 61131, Colleges, Universities and Professional Schools.

US—United States industry only. CAN—United States and Canadian industries are comparable. MEX—United States and Mexican industries are comparable. Blank—Canadian, Mexican, and United States industries are comparable.

611511 Cosmetology and Barber Schools[US]

This U.S. industry comprises establishments primarily engaged in offering training in barbering, hair styling, or the cosmetic arts, such as makeup or skin care. These schools provide job-specific certification.

611512 Flight Training[US]

This U.S. industry comprises establishments primarily engaged in offering aviation and flight training. These establishments may offer vocational training, recreational training, or both.

Cross-References.

Establishments primarily engaged in specialty air transportation services which may also provide flight training are classified in U.S. Industry 481219, Other Nonscheduled Air Transportation.

611513 Apprenticeship Training[US]

This U.S. industry comprises establishments primarily engaged in offering apprenticeship training programs. These programs involve applied training as well as course work.

611519 Other Technical and Trade Schools[US]

This U.S. industry comprises establishments primarily engaged in offering job or career vocational or technical courses (except cosmetology and barber training, aviation and flight training, and apprenticeship training). The curriculums offered by these schools are highly structured and specialized and lead to job-specific certification.

Illustrative Examples:

Bartending schools	Modeling schools
Broadcasting schools	Real estate schools
Computer repair training	Truck driving schools
Graphic arts schools	

Cross-References. Establishments primarily engaged in—

- Offering courses in office procedures and secretarial and stenographic skills—are classified in Industry 611410, Business and Secretarial Schools;

- Offering computer training (except computer repair)—are classified in Industry 611420, Computer Training;

- Offering professional and management development training—are classified in Industry 611430, Professional and Management Development Training;

- Offering registered nursing training with academic degrees (e.g., associate baccalaureate)—are classified in Industry 611210, Junior Colleges or Industry 611310, Colleges, Universities and Professional Schools;

- Offering aviation and flight training—are classified in U.S. Industry 611512, Flight Training;

- Offering cosmetology and barber training—are classified in U.S. Industry 611511, Cosmetology and Barber Schools;

- Offering academic courses that may also offer technical and trade courses—are classified according to the type of school; and

- Offering apprenticeship training programs—are classified in U.S. Industry 611513, Apprenticeship Training.

6116 Other Schools and Instruction

This industry group comprises establishments primarily engaged in offering or providing instruction (except academic schools, colleges, and universities; and business, computer, management, technical, or trade instruction). Instruction may be provided in diverse settings, such as the establishment's or client's training facilities, educational institutions, the workplace, or the home, and through correspondence, television, Internet, or other means.

61161 Fine Arts Schools
See industry description for 611610 below.

611610 Fine Arts Schools^{CAN}

This industry comprises establishments primarily engaged in offering instruction in the arts, including dance, art, drama, and music.

Illustrative Examples:

Art (except commercial and graphic) instruction
Dance instruction
Dance studios
Drama schools (except academic)
Fine arts schools (except academic)

Music instruction (e.g., piano, guitar)
Music schools (except academic)
Performing arts schools (except academic)
Photography schools (except commercial photography)

US—United States industry only. CAN—United States and Canadian industries are comparable. MEX—United States and Mexican industries are comparable. Blank—Canadian, Mexican, and United States industries are comparable.

Cross-References.

- Establishments offering high school diplomas or academic degrees (i.e., even if they specialize in fine arts) are classified elsewhere in this subsector according to the type of school; and
- Establishments primarily engaged in offering courses in commercial and graphic arts and commercial photography are classified in U.S. Industry 611519, Other Technical and Trade Schools.

61162 Sports and Recreation Instruction
See industry description for 611620 below.

611620 Sports and Recreation Instruction^{CAN}

This industry comprises establishments, such as camps and schools, primarily engaged in offering instruction in athletic activities to groups of individuals. Overnight and day sports instruction camps are included in this industry.

Illustrative Examples:

Camps, sports instruction	Riding instruction academies or schools
Cheerleading instruction	Sports (e.g., baseball, basketball,
Gymnastics instruction	football, golf)
Martial arts instruction, camps or schools	Swimming instruction
Professional sports instructors (i.e., not	
participating in sporting events)	

Cross-References.

- Establishments primarily engaged in operating overnight recreational camps that may offer some athletic instruction in addition to other activities are classified in U.S. Industry 721214, Recreation and Vacation Camps (except Campgrounds);
- Establishments primarily engaged in operating sports and recreation establishments that also offer athletic instruction are classified in Sector 71, Arts, Entertainment, and Recreation;
- Independent (i.e., freelance) athletes engaged in providing sports instruction and participating in spectator sporting events are classified in U.S. Industry 711219, Other Spectator Sports; and
- Offering academic courses that may also offer athletic instruction are classified according to the type of school.

61163 Language Schools
See industry description for 611630 below.

611630 Language Schools^{CAN}

This industry comprises establishments primarily engaged in offering foreign language instruction (including sign language). These establishments are designed to offer language instruction ranging from conversational skills for personal enrichment to intensive training courses for career or educational opportunities.

Cross-References. Establishments primarily engaged in—

- Offering academic courses that may also offer language instruction—are classified according to type of school; and

- Providing translation and interpretation services—are classified in Industry 541930, Translation and Interpretation Services.

61169 All Other Schools and Instruction

This industry comprises establishments primarily engaged in offering instruction (except business, computer, management, technical, trade, fine arts, athletic, and language instruction). Also excluded from this industry are academic schools, colleges, and universities.

Illustrative Examples:

Academic tutoring services   Public speaking training
Automobile driving schools   Speed reading instruction
Exam preparation services

Cross-References. Establishments primarily engaged in—

- Offering elementary and secondary school instruction—are classified in Industry 61111, Elementary and Secondary Schools;

- Offering junior college instruction—are classified in Industry 61121, Junior Colleges;

- Offering college, university, and professional school instruction with academic degrees (e.g., baccalaureate, graduate)—are classified in Industry 61131, Colleges, Universities and Professional Schools;

- Offering business, computer (except computer repair), and management training—are classified in Industry Group 6114, Business Schools and Computer and Management Training;

- Offering technical and trade school instruction (e.g., computer repair and maintenance)—are classified in Industry 61151, Technical and Trade Schools;

- Offering fine arts instruction—are classified in Industry 61161, Fine Arts Schools;
- Offering sports and recreation instruction—are classified in Industry 61162, Sports and Recreation Instruction; and
- Offering language instruction—are classified in Industry 61163, Language Schools.

611691 Exam Preparation and Tutoring[US]

This U.S. industry comprises establishments primarily engaged in offering preparation for standardized examinations and/or academic tutoring services.

llustrative Examples:

Academic tutoring services
College board preparation centers
Learning centers offering remedial
   courses

Professional examination review
   instruction

611692 Automobile Driving Schools[US]

This U.S. industry comprises establishments primarily engaged in offering automobile driving instruction.

Cross-References.

Establishments primarily engaged in offering truck and bus driving instruction are classified in U.S. Industry 611519, Other Technical and Trade Schools.

611699 All Other Miscellaneous Schools and Instruction[US]

This U.S. industry comprises establishments primarily engaged in offering instruction (except business, computer, management, technical, trade, fine arts, athletic, language instruction, tutoring, and automobile driving instruction). Also excluded from this industry are academic schools, colleges, and universities.

Illustrative Examples:

Public speaking training
Speed reading instruction

Survival training

Cross-References. Establishments primarily engaged in—

- Offering elementary and secondary school instruction—are classified in Industry 611110, Elementary and Secondary Schools;

US—United States industry only. CAN—United States and Canadian industries are comparable. MEX—United States and Mexican industries are comparable. Blank—Canadian, Mexican, and United States industries are comparable.

- Offering junior college instruction—are classified in Industry 611210, Junior Colleges;

- Offering college, university, and professional school instruction with academic degrees (e.g., baccalaureate, graduate)—are classified in Industry 611310, Colleges, Universities and Professional Schools;

- Offering business, computer (except computer repair), and management training—are classified in Industry Group 6114, Business Schools and Computer and Management Training;

- Offering technical and trade school instruction (e.g., computer repair and maintenance)—are classified in Industry 61151, Technical and Trade Schools;

- Offering fine arts instruction—are classified in Industry 611610, Fine Arts Schools;

- Offering sports and recreation instruction—are classified in Industry 611620, Sports and Recreation Instruction;

- Offering language instruction—are classified in Industry 611630, Language Schools;

- Offering exam preparation and tutoring services—are classified in U.S. Industry 611691, Exam Preparation and Tutoring; and

- Offering automobile driving instruction—are classified in U.S. Industry 611692, Automobile Driving Schools.

6117 Educational Support Services

61171 Educational Support Services
See industry description for 611710 below.

611710 Educational Support Services

This industry comprises establishments primarily engaged in providing noninstructional services that support educational processes or systems.

Illustrative Examples:

Educational consultants

Educational guidance counseling services

Educational testing evaluation services

Educational testing services

Student exchange programs

Cross-References. Establishments primarily engaged in—

- Providing job training for the unemployed, underemployed, physically disabled, and persons who have a job market disadvantage because of lack of education or job skills—are classified in Industry 624310, Vocational Rehabilitation Services; and

- Conducting research and analyses in cognitive development—are classified in Industry 541720, Research and Development in the Social Sciences and Humanities.

Sector 62—Health Care and Social Assistance

The Sector as a Whole

The Health Care and Social Assistance sector comprises establishments providing health care and social assistance for individuals. The sector includes both health care and social assistance because it is sometimes difficult to distinguish between the boundaries of these two activities. The industries in this sector are arranged on a continuum starting with those establishments providing medical care exclusively, continuing with those providing health care and social assistance, and finally finishing with those providing only social assistance. The services provided by establishments in this sector are delivered by trained professionals. All industries in the sector share this commonality of process, namely, labor inputs of health practitioners or social workers with the requisite expertise. Many of the industries in the sector are defined based on the educational degree held by the practitioners included in the industry.

Excluded from this sector are aerobic classes in Subsector 713, Amusement, Gambling and Recreation Industries and nonmedical diet and weight reducing centers in Subsector 812, Personal and Laundry Services. Although these can be viewed as health services, these services are not typically delivered by health practitioners.

621 Ambulatory Health Care Services

Industries in the Ambulatory Health Care Services subsector provide health care services directly or indirectly to ambulatory patients and do not usually provide inpatient services. Health practitioners in this subsector provide outpatient services, with the facilities and equipment not usually being the most significant part of the production process.

6211 Offices of Physicians

62111 Offices of Physicians

This industry comprises establishments of health practitioners having the degree of M.D. (Doctor of medicine) or D.O. (Doctor of osteopathy) primarily engaged in the independent practice of general or specialized medicine (e.g., anesthesiology, oncology, ophthalmology, psychiatry) or surgery. These practitioners operate private or group practices in their own offices (e.g., centers, clinics) or in the facilities of others, such as hospitals or HMO medical centers.

US—United States industry only. CAN—United States and Canadian industries are comparable. MEX—United States and Mexican industries are comparable. Blank—Canadian, Mexican, and United States industries are comparable.

Cross-References.

- Medical centers primarily engaged in providing emergency medical care for accident or trauma victims and ambulatory surgical centers primarily engaged in providing surgery on an outpatient basis are classified in Industry 62149, Other Outpatient Care Centers;

- Establishments of oral pathologists are classified in Industry 62121, Offices of Dentists; and

- Establishments of speech or voice pathologists are classified in Industry 62134, Offices of Physical, Occupational and Speech Therapists, and Audiologists.

621111 Offices of Physicians (except Mental Health Specialists)[US]

This U.S. industry comprises establishments of health practitioners having the degree of M.D. (Doctor of medicine) or D.O. (Doctor of osteopathy) primarily engaged in the independent practice of general or specialized medicine (except psychiatry or psychoanalysis) or surgery. These practitioners operate private or group practices in their own offices (e.g., centers, clinics) or in the facilities of others, such as hospitals or HMO medical centers.

Cross-References.

- Establishments of physicians primarily engaged in the independent practice of psychiatry or psychoanalysis are classified in U.S. Industry 621112, Offices of Physicians, Mental Health Specialists;

- Freestanding medical centers primarily engaged in providing emergency medical care for accident or catastrophe victims and freestanding ambulatory surgical centers primarily engaged in providing surgery on an outpatient basis are classified in U.S. Industry 621493, Freestanding Ambulatory Surgical and Emergency Centers;

- Establishments of oral pathologists are classified in Industry 621210, Offices of Dentists; and

- Establishments of speech or voice pathologists are classified in Industry 621340, Offices of Physical, Occupational and Speech Therapists, and Audiologists.

621112 Offices of Physicians, Mental Health Specialists[US]

This U.S. industry comprises establishments of health practitioners having the degree of M.D. (Doctor of medicine) or D.O. (Doctor of osteopathy) primarily engaged in the independent practice of psychiatry or psychoanalysis. These practitioners operate private or group practices in their own offices (e.g., centers, clinics) or in the facilities of others, such as hospitals or HMO medical centers.

6212 Offices of Dentists

62121 Offices of Dentists
See industry description for 621210 below.

621210 Offices of Dentists[CAN]

This industry comprises establishments of health practitioners having the degree of D.M.D. (Doctor of dental medicine), D.D.S. (Doctor of dental surgery), or D.D.Sc. (Doctor of dental science) primarily engaged in the independent practice of general or specialized dentistry or dental surgery. These practitioners operate private or group practices in their own offices (e.g., centers, clinics) or in the facilities of others, such as hospitals or HMO medical centers. They can provide either comprehensive preventive, cosmetic, or emergency care, or specialize in a single field of dentistry.

Cross-References.
- Establishments known as dental laboratories primarily engaged in making dentures, artificial teeth, and orthodontic appliances to order for dentists are classified U.S. Industry 339116, Dental Laboratories; and
- Establishments of dental hygienists primarily engaged in cleaning teeth and gums or establishments of denturists primarily engaged in taking impressions for and fitting dentures are classified in U.S. Industry 621399, Offices of All Other Miscellaneous Health Practitioners.

6213 Offices of Other Health Practitioners

This industry group comprises establishments of independent health practitioners (except physicians and dentists).

62131 Offices of Chiropractors
See industry description for 621310 below.

621310 Offices of Chiropractors[CAN]

This industry comprises establishments of health practitioners having the degree of D.C. (Doctor of chiropractic) primarily engaged in the independent practice of chiropractic. These practitioners provide diagnostic and therapeutic treatment of neuromusculoskeletal and related disorders through the manipulation and adjustment of the spinal column and extremities, and operate private or group practices in their own offices (e.g., centers, clinics) or in the facilities of others, such as hospitals or HMO medical centers.

62132 Offices of Optometrists
See industry description for 621320 below.

621320 Offices of Optometrists

This industry comprises establishments of health practitioners having the degree of O.D. (Doctor of optometry) primarily engaged in the independent practice of optometry. These practitioners provide eye examinations to determine visual acuity or the presence of vision problems and to prescribe eyeglasses, contact lenses, and eye exercises. They operate private or group practices in their own offices (e.g., centers, clinics) or in the facilities of others, such as hospitals or HMO medical centers, and may also provide the same service as opticians, such as selling and fitting prescription eyeglasses and contact lenses.

Cross-References. Establishments of—

- Opticians primarily engaged in selling and fitting prescription eyeglasses and contact lenses—are classified in Industry 446130, Optical Goods Stores; and

- Physicians primarily engaged in the independent practice of ophthalmology—are classified in U.S. Industry 621111, Offices of Physicians (except Mental Health Specialists).

62133 Offices of Mental Health Practitioners (except Physicians)
See industry description for 621330 below.

621330 Offices of Mental Health Practitioners (except Physicians)[CAN]

This industry comprises establishments of independent mental health practitioners (except physicians) primarily engaged in (1) the diagnosis and treatment of mental, emotional, and behavioral disorders and/or (2) the diagnosis and treatment of individual or group social dysfunction brought about by such causes as mental illness, alcohol and substance abuse, physical and emotional trauma, or stress. These practitioners operate private or group practices in their own offices (e.g., centers, clinics) or in the facilities of others, such as hospitals or HMO medical centers.

US—United States industry only. CAN—United States and Canadian industries are comparable. MEX—United States and Mexican industries are comparable. Blank—Canadian, Mexican, and United States industries are comparable.

Cross-References.

Establishments of psychiatrists, psychoanalysts, and psychotherapists having the degree of M.D. (Doctor of medicine) or D.O. (Doctor of osteopathy) are classified in U.S. Industry 621112, Offices of Physicians, Mental Health Specialists.

62134 Offices of Physical, Occupational and Speech Therapists, and Audiologists

See industry description for 621340 below.

621340 Offices of Physical, Occupational and Speech Therapists, and Audiologists[CAN]

This industry comprises establishments of independent health practitioners primarily engaged in one of the following: (1) administering medically prescribed physical therapy treatment for patients suffering from injuries or muscle, nerve, joint, and bone disease; (2) planning and administering educational, recreational, and social activities designed to help patients or individuals with disabilities, regain physical or mental functioning or to adapt to their disabilities; and (3) diagnosing and treating speech, language, or hearing problems. These practitioners operate private or group practices in their own offices (e.g., centers, clinics) or in the facilities of others, such as hospitals or HMO medical centers.

Illustrative Examples:

Audiologists' offices
Industrial therapists' offices

Recreational (e.g., art, dance, music) therapists' offices

62139 Offices of All Other Health Practitioners

This industry comprises establishments of independent health practitioners (except physicians; dentists; chiropractors; optometrists; mental health specialists; physical, occupational, and speech therapists; and audiologists). These practitioners operate private or group practices in their own offices (e.g., centers, clinics) or in the facilities of others, such as hospitals or HMO medical centers.

Illustrative Examples:

Acupuncturists' (except MDs or DOs) offices
Dental hygienists' offices
Denturists' offices
Dietitians' offices
Homeopaths' offices

Inhalation or respiratory therapists' offices
Midwives' offices
Naturopaths' offices
Podiatrists' offices
Registered or licensed practical nurses' offices

US—United States industry only. CAN—United States and Canadian industries are comparable. MEX—United States and Mexican industries are comparable. Blank—Canadian, Mexican, and United States industries are comparable.

Cross-References. Establishments primarily engaged in—

- The independent practice of medicine (i.e., physicians)—are classified in Industry 62111, Offices of Physicians;

- The independent practice of dentistry—are classified in Industry 62121, Offices of Dentists;

- The independent practice of chiropractic—are classified in Industry 62131, Offices of Chiropractors;

- The independent practice of optometry—are classified in Industry 62132, Offices of Optometrists;

- The independent practice of mental health (except physicians)—are classified in Industry 62133, Offices of Mental Health Practitioners (except Physicians); and

- The independent practice of physical, occupational, and speech therapy and audiology—are classified in Industry 62134, Offices of Physical, Occupational and Speech Therapists, and Audiologists.

621391 Offices of Podiatrists[US]

This U.S. industry comprises establishments of health practitioners having the degree of D.P. (Doctor of podiatry) primarily engaged in the independent practice of podiatry. These practitioners diagnose and treat diseases and deformities of the foot and operate private or group practices in their own offices (e.g., centers, clinics) or in the facilities of others, such as hospitals or HMO medical centers.

621399 Offices of All Other Miscellaneous Health Practitioners[US]

This U.S. industry comprises establishments of independent health practitioners (except physicians; dentists; chiropractors; optometrists; mental health specialists; physical, occupational, and speech therapists; audiologists; and podiatrists). These practitioners operate private or group practices in their own offices (e.g., centers, clinics) or in the facilities of others, such as hospitals or HMO medical centers.

Illustrative Examples:

Acupuncturists' (except MDs or DOs) offices	Inhalation or respiratory therapists' offices
Hypnotherapists' offices	Midwives' offices
Dental hygienists' offices	Naturopaths' offices
Denturists' offices	Registered or licensed practical nurses' offices
Dietitians' offices	
Homeopaths' offices	

Cross-References. Establishments primarily engaged in—

- The independent practice of medicine (i.e., physicians)—are classified in Industry 62111, Offices of Physicians;

- The independent practice of dentistry—are classified in Industry 621210, Offices of Dentists;

- The independent practice of chiropractic—are classified in Industry 621310, Offices of Chiropractors;

- The independent practice of optometry—are classified in Industry 621320, Offices of Optometrists;

- The independent practice of mental health (except physicians)—are classified in Industry 621330, Offices of Mental Health Practitioners (except Physicians);

- The independent practice of physical, occupational, and speech therapy, and audiology—are classified in Industry 621340, Offices of Physical, Occupational and Speech Therapists, and Audiologists; and

- The independent practice of podiatry—are classified in U.S. Industry 621391, Offices of Podiatrists.

6214 Outpatient Care Centers

62141 Family Planning Centers

See industry description for 621410 below.

621410 Family Planning Centers^{CAN}

This industry comprises establishments with medical staff primarily engaged in providing a range of family planning services on an outpatient basis, such as contraceptive services, genetic and prenatal counseling, voluntary sterilization, and therapeutic and medically indicated termination of pregnancy.

Illustrative Examples:

Birth control clinics
Childbirth preparation classes

Fertility clinics
Pregnancy counseling centers

62142 Outpatient Mental Health and Substance Abuse Centers

See industry description for 621420 below.

621420 Outpatient Mental Health and Substance Abuse Centers[CAN]

This industry comprises establishments with medical staff primarily engaged in providing outpatient services related to the diagnosis and treatment of mental health disorders and alcohol and other substance abuse. These establishments generally treat patients who do not require inpatient treatment. They may provide a counseling staff and information regarding a wide range of mental health and substance abuse issues and/or refer patients to more extensive treatment programs, if necessary.

Illustrative Examples:

Outpatient alcoholism treatment centers and clinics (except hospitals)
Outpatient detoxification centers and clinics (except hospitals)
Outpatient drug addiction treatment centers and clinics (except hospitals)

Outpatient mental health centers and clinics (except hospitals)
Outpatient substance abuse treatment (except hospitals)

Cross-References.

- Establishments known and licensed as hospitals primarily engaged in the inpatient treatment of mental health and substance abuse illnesses with an emphasis on medical treatment and monitoring are classified in Industry 622210, Psychiatric and Substance Abuse Hospitals; and

- Establishments primarily engaged in the inpatient treatment of mental health and substance abuse illness with an emphasis on residential care and counseling rather than medical treatment are classified in Industry 623220, Residential Mental Health and Substance Abuse Facilities.

62149 Other Outpatient Care Centers

This industry comprises establishments with medical staff primarily engaged in providing general or specialized outpatient care (except family planning centers and outpatient mental health and substance abuse centers). Centers or clinics of health practitioners with different degrees from more than one industry practicing within the same establishment (i.e., Doctor of medicine and Doctor of dental medicine) are included in this industry.

Illustrative Examples:

Dialysis centers and clinics
Freestanding ambulatory surgical centers and clinics
Freestanding emergency medical centers and clinics
Health maintenance organization (HMO) medical centers and clinics

Outpatient community health centers and clinics
Outpatient biofeedback centers and clinics
Outpatient sleep disorder centers and clinics

US—United States industry only. CAN—United States and Canadian industries are comparable. MEX—United States and Mexican industries are comparable. Blank—Canadian, Mexican, and United States industries are comparable.

Cross-References.

- Physician walk-in centers are classified in Industry 62111, Offices of Physicians;

- Centers and clinics of health practitioners from the same industry primarily engaged in the independent practice of their profession are classified in Industry 62111, Offices of Physicians; Industry 62121, Offices of Dentists; and Industry Group 6213, Offices of Other Health Practitioners;

- Family planning centers are classified in Industry 62141, Family Planning Centers;

- Outpatient mental health and substance abuse centers are classified in Industry 62142, Outpatient Mental Health and Substance Abuse Centers;

- HMO establishments (except those providing health care services) primarily engaged in underwriting health and medical insurance policies are classified in Industry 52411, Direct Life, Health, and Medical Insurance Carriers; and

- Establishments known and licensed as hospitals that also perform ambulatory surgery and emergency room services are classified in Subsector 622, Hospitals.

621491 HMO Medical Centers[US]

This U.S. industry comprises establishments with physicians and other medical staff primarily engaged in providing a range of outpatient medical services to the health maintenance organization (HMO) subscribers with a focus generally on primary health care. These establishments are owned by the HMO. Included in this industry are HMO establishments that both provide health care services and underwrite health and medical insurance policies.

Cross-References.

- Health practitioners or health practitioner groups contracting to provide their services to subscribers of prepaid health plans are classified in Industry 62111, Offices of Physicians; Industry 621210, Offices of Dentists; and Industry Group 6213, Offices of Other Health Practitioners; and

- HMO establishments (except those providing health care services) primarily engaged in underwriting and administering health and medical insurance policies are classified in U.S. Industry 524114, Direct Health and Medical Insurance Carriers.

621492 Kidney Dialysis Centers[US]

This U.S. industry comprises establishments with medical staff primarily engaged in providing outpatient kidney or renal dialysis services.

621493 Freestanding Ambulatory Surgical and Emergency Centers[US]

This U.S. industry comprises establishments with physicians and other medical staff primarily engaged in (1) providing surgical services (e.g., orthoscopic and cataract surgery) on an outpatient basis or (2) providing emergency care services (e.g., setting broken bones, treating lacerations, or tending to patients suffering injuries as a result of accidents, trauma, or medical conditions necessitating immediate medical care) on an outpatient basis. Outpatient surgical establishments have specialized facilities, such as operating and recovery rooms, and specialized equipment, such as anesthetic or X-ray equipment.

Illustrative Examples:

Freestanding ambulatory surgical centers and clinics	Freestanding trauma centers except hospitals
Freestanding emergency medical centers and clinics	Urgent medical care centers and clinics (except hospitals)

Cross-References.

- Physician walk-in centers are classified in U.S. Industry 621111, Offices of Physicians (except Mental Health Specialists); and

- Establishments known and licensed as hospitals that also perform ambulatory surgery and emergency room services are classified in Subsector 622, Hospitals.

621498 All Other Outpatient Care Centers[US]

This U.S. industry comprises establishments with medical staff primarily engaged in providing general or specialized outpatient care (except family planning centers, outpatient mental health and substance abuse centers, HMO medical centers, kidney dialysis centers, and freestanding ambulatory surgical and emergency centers). Centers or clinics of health practitioners with different degrees from more than one industry practicing within the same establishment (i.e., Doctor of medicine and Doctor of dental medicine) are included in this industry.

Illustrative Examples:

Outpatient biofeedback centers and clinics	Outpatient pain therapy centers and clinics
Outpatient community health centers and clinics	Outpatient sleep disorder centers and clinics

---

US—United States industry only. CAN—United States and Canadian industries are comparable. MEX—United States and Mexican industries are comparable. Blank—Canadian, Mexican, and United States industries are comparable.

Cross-References.

- Physician walk-in centers are classified in U.S. Industry 621111, Offices of Physicians (except Mental Health Specialists);
- Centers and clinics of health practitioners from the same industry primarily engaged in the independent practice of their profession are classified in Industry 62111, Offices of Physicians; Industry 621210, Offices of Dentists; and Industry Group 6213, Offices of Other Health Practitioners;
- Family planning centers are classified in Industry 621410, Family Planning Centers;
- Outpatient mental health and substance abuse centers are classified in Industry 621420, Outpatient Mental Health and Substance Abuse Centers;
- HMO medical centers are classified in U.S. Industry 621491, HMO Medical Centers;
- Dialysis centers are classified in U.S. Industry 621492, Kidney Dialysis Centers; and
- Freestanding ambulatory surgical and emergency centers are classified in U.S. Industry 621493, Freestanding Ambulatory Surgical and Emergency Centers.

6215 Medical and Diagnostic Laboratories

62151 Medical and Diagnostic Laboratories

This industry comprises establishments known as medical and diagnostic laboratories primarily engaged in providing analytic or diagnostic services, including body fluid analysis and diagnostic imaging, generally to the medical profession or to the patient on referral from a health practitioner.

Illustrative Examples:

Dental or medical X-ray laboratories
Diagnostic imaging centers
Medical forensic laboratories

Medical pathology laboratories
Medical testing laboratories

Cross-References.

Establishments, such as dental, optical, and orthopedic laboratories, primarily engaged in providing the following activities to the medical profession, respectively: making dentures, artificial teeth, and orthodontic appliances to prescription; grinding of lenses to prescription; and making orthopedic or prosthetic appliances to prescription are classified in Industry 33911, Medical Equipment and Supplies Manufacturing.

621511   Medical Laboratories[US]

This U.S. industry comprises establishments known as medical laboratories primarily engaged in providing analytic or diagnostic services, including body fluid analysis, generally to the medical profession or to the patient on referral from a health practitioner.

Illustrative Examples:

Blood analysis laboratories
Medical bacteriological laboratories
Medical forensic laboratories

Medical pathology laboratories
Medical testing laboratories

Cross-References.

- Establishments known as dental laboratories primarily engaged in making dentures, artificial teeth, and orthodontic appliances to prescription are classified in U.S. Industry 339116, Dental Laboratories;

- Establishments known as optical laboratories primarily engaged in grinding of lenses to prescription are classified in U.S. Industry 339115, Ophthalmic Goods Manufacturing; and

- Establishments known as orthopedic laboratories primarily engaged in making orthopedic or prosthetic appliances to prescription are classified in U.S. Industry 339113, Surgical Appliance and Supplies Manufacturing.

621512   Diagnostic Imaging Centers[US]

This U.S. industry comprises establishments known as diagnostic imaging centers primarily engaged in producing images of the patient generally on referral from a health practitioner.

Illustrative Examples:

Computer tomography (CT-scan) centers
Dental or medical X-ray laboratories
Medical radiological laboratories

Magnetic resonance imaging (MRI)
  centers
Ultrasound imaging centers

6216   Home Health Care Services

62161   Home Health Care Services

See industry description for 621610 below.

621610 Home Health Care Services

This industry comprises establishments primarily engaged in providing skilled nursing services in the home, along with a range of the following: personal care services; homemaker and companion services; physical therapy; medical social services; medications; medical equipment and supplies; counseling; 24-hour home care; occupation and vocational therapy; dietary and nutritional services; speech therapy; audiology; and high-tech care, such as intravenous therapy.

Illustrative Examples:

Home health care agencies
In-home hospice care services

Visiting nurse associations

Cross-References.

- In-home health services provided by establishments of health practitioners and others primarily engaged in the independent practice of their profession are classified in Industry 62111, Offices of Physicians; Industry 621210, Offices of Dentists; and Industry Group 6213, Offices of Other Health Practitioners; and U.S. Industry 621999, All Other Miscellaneous Ambulatory Health Care Services; and

- Establishments primarily engaged in renting or leasing products for home health care are classified in U.S. Industry 532291, Home Health Equipment Rental.

6219 Other Ambulatory Health Care Services

This industry group comprises establishments primarily engaged in providing ambulatory health care services (except offices of physicians, dentists, and other health practitioners; outpatient care centers; medical laboratories and diagnostic imaging centers; and home health care providers).

62191 Ambulance Services
See industry description for 621910 below.

621910 Ambulance Services[MEX]

This industry comprises establishments primarily engaged in providing transportation of patients by ground or air, along with medical care. These services are often provided during a medical emergency but are not restricted to emergencies. The vehicles are equipped with lifesaving equipment operated by medically trained personnel.

US—United States industry only. CAN—United States and Canadian industries are comparable. MEX—United States and Mexican industries are comparable. Blank—Canadian, Mexican, and United States industries are comparable.

Cross-References.

Establishments primarily engaged in providing transportation of the disabled or elderly (without medical care) are classified in U.S. Industry 485991, Special Needs Transportation.

62199 All Other Ambulatory Health Care Services

This industry comprises establishments primarily engaged in providing ambulatory health care services (except office physicians, dentists, and other health practitioners; outpatient care centers; medical and diagnostic laboratories; home health care providers; and ambulances).

Illustrative Examples:

Blood or body organ banks
Blood donor stations
Health screening services (except by health practitioner offices)
Hearing testing services (except by audiologist offices)

Pacemaker monitoring services
Physical fitness evaluation services (except by health practitioner offices)
Smoking cessation programs

Cross-References.

- Establishments primarily engaged in the independent practice of medicine are classified in Industry 62111, Offices of Physicians;

- Establishments primarily engaged in the independent practice of dentistry are classified in Industry 62121, Offices of Dentists;

- Establishments primarily engaged in the independent practice of health care (except offices of physicians and dentists) are classified in Industry Group 6213, Offices of Other Health Practitioners;

- Establishments primarily engaged in providing general or specialized outpatient care services are classified in Industry Group 6214, Outpatient Care Centers;

- Establishments primarily engaged in providing home health care services are classified in Industry 62161, Home Health Care Services;

- Establishments primarily engaged in transportation of patients by ground or air, along with medical care are classified in Industry 62191, Ambulance Services; and

- Establishments known as medical and diagnostic laboratories primarily engaged in providing analytic or diagnostic services are classified in Industry 62151, Medical and Diagnostic Laboratories.

US—United States industry only. CAN—United States and Canadian industries are comparable. MEX—United States and Mexican industries are comparable. Blank—Canadian, Mexican, and United States industries are comparable.

621991 Blood and Organ Banks[US]

This U.S. industry comprises establishments primarily engaged in collecting, storing, and distributing blood and blood products and storing and distributing body organs.

621999 All Other Miscellaneous Ambulatory Health Care Services[US]

This U.S. industry comprises establishments primarily engaged in providing ambulatory health care services (except offices of physicians, dentists, and other health practitioners; outpatient care centers; medical and diagnostic laboratories; home health care providers; ambulances; and blood and organ banks).

Illustrative Examples:

Health screening services (except by offices of health practitioners)
Hearing testing services (except by offices of audiologists)
Pacemaker monitoring services

Physical fitness evaluation services (except by offices of health practitioners)
Smoking cessation programs

Cross-References.

- Establishments primarily engaged in the independent practice of medicine are classified in Industry 62111, Offices of Physicians;

- Establishments primarily engaged in the independent practice of dentistry are classified in Industry 621210, Offices of Dentists;

- Establishments primarily engaged in the independent practice of health care (except offices of physicians and dentists) are classified in Industry Group 6213, Offices of Other Health Practitioners;

- Establishments primarily engaged in providing general or specialized outpatient care services are classified in Industry Group 6214, Outpatient Care Centers;

- Establishments primarily engaged in providing home health care services are classified in Industry 621610, Home Health Care Services;

- Establishments primarily engaged in the transportation of patients by ground or air, along with medical care are classified in Industry 621910, Ambulance Services;

- Establishments known as medical and diagnostic laboratories primarily engaged in providing analytic or diagnostic services are classified in Industry 62151, Medical and Diagnostic Laboratories; and

- Blood and organ banks are classified in U.S. Industry 621991, Blood and Organ Banks.

622 Hospitals

Industries in the Hospitals subsector provide medical, diagnostic, and treatment services that include physician, nursing, and other health services to inpatients and the specialized accommodation services required by inpatients. Hospitals may also provide outpatient services as a secondary activity. Establishments in the Hospitals subsector provide inpatient health services, many of which can only be provided using the specialized facilities and equipment that form a significant and integral part of the production process.

6221 General Medical and Surgical Hospitals

62211 General Medical and Surgical Hospitals
See industry description for 622110 below.

622110 General Medical and Surgical Hospitals[US]

This industry comprises establishments known and licensed as general medical and surgical hospitals primarily engaged in providing diagnostic and medical treatment (both surgical and nonsurgical) to inpatients with any of a wide variety of medical conditions. These establishments maintain inpatient beds and provide patients with food services that meet their nutritional requirements. These hospitals have an organized staff of physicians and other medical staff to provide patient care services. These establishments usually provide other services, such as outpatient services, anatomical pathology services, diagnostic X-ray services, clinical laboratory services, operating room services for a variety of procedures, and pharmacy services.

6222 Psychiatric and Substance Abuse Hospitals

62221 Psychiatric and Substance Abuse Hospitals
See industry description for 622210 below.

622210 Psychiatric and Substance Abuse Hospitals[CAN]

This industry comprises establishments known and licensed as psychiatric and substance abuse hospitals primarily engaged in providing diagnostic, medical treatment, and monitoring services for inpatients who suffer from mental illness or substance abuse disorders. The treatment often requires an extended stay in the hospital. These establishments maintain inpatient beds and provide patients with food services that meet their nutritional requirements. They have an organized staff of physicians and other medical staff to provide patient care services. Psychiatric, psychological, and social work services are available at the facility. These hospitals usually provide other services, such as outpatient services, clinical laboratory services, diagnostic X-ray services, and electroencephalograph services.

Cross-References.

- Establishments primarily engaged in providing treatment of mental health and substance abuse illnesses on an exclusively outpatient basis are classified in Industry 621420, Outpatient Mental Health and Substance Abuse Centers;

- Establishments referred to as hospitals but are primarily engaged in providing inpatient treatment of mental health and substance abuse illness with the emphasis on counseling rather than medical treatment are classified in Industry 623220, Residential Mental Health and Substance Abuse Facilities; and

- Establishments referred to as hospitals but are primarily engaged in providing residential care for persons diagnosed with mental retardation are classified in Industry 623210, Residential Mental Retardation Facilities.

6223 Specialty (except Psychiatric and Substance Abuse) Hospitals

62231 Specialty (except Psychiatric and Substance Abuse) Hospitals
See industry description for 622310 below.

622310 Specialty (except Psychiatric and Substance Abuse) Hospitals[CAN]

This industry consists of establishments known and licensed as specialty hospitals primarily engaged in providing diagnostic and medical treatment to inpatients with a specific type of disease or medical condition (except psychiatric or substance abuse). Hospitals providing long-term care for the chronically ill and hospitals providing rehabilitation, restorative, and adjustive services to physically challenged or disabled people are included in this industry. These establishments maintain inpatient beds and provide patients with food services that meet their nutritional requirements. They have an organized staff of physicians and other medical staff to provide patient care services. These hospitals may provide other services, such as outpatient services, diagnostic X-ray services, clinical laboratory services, operating room services, physical therapy services, educational and vocational services, and psychological and social work services.

Cross-References.

- Establishments known and licensed as hospitals primarily engaged in providing diagnostic and therapeutic inpatient services for a variety of medical conditions, both surgical and nonsurgical, are classified in Industry 622110, General Medical and Surgical Hospitals;

- Establishments known and licensed as hospitals primarily engaged in providing diagnostic and treatment services for inpatients with psychiatric or substance abuse illnesses are classified in Industry 622210, Psychiatric and Substance Abuse Hospitals;

- Establishments referred to as hospitals but are primarily engaged in providing inpatient nursing and rehabilitative services to persons requiring convalescence are classified in Industry 623110, Nursing Care Facilities;

- Establishments referred to as hospitals but are primarily engaged in providing residential care of persons diagnosed with mental retardation are classified in Industry 623210, Residential Mental Retardation Facilities; and

- Establishments referred to as hospitals but are primarily engaged in providing inpatient treatment for mental health and substance abuse illnesses with the emphasis on counseling rather than medical treatment are classified in Industry 623220, Residential Mental Health and Substance Abuse Facilities.

623 Nursing and Residential Care Facilities

Industries in the Nursing and Residential Care Facilities subsector provide residential care combined with either nursing, supervisory, or other types of care as required by the residents. In this subsector, the facilities are a significant part of the production process and the care provided is a mix of health and social services with the health services being largely some level of nursing services.

6231 Nursing Care Facilities

62311 Nursing Care Facilities
See industry description for 623110 below.

623110 Nursing Care Facilities^CAN

This industry comprises establishments primarily engaged in providing inpatient nursing and rehabilitative services. The care is generally provided for an extended

---

US—United States industry only. CAN—United States and Canadian industries are comparable. MEX—United States and Mexican industries are comparable. Blank—Canadian, Mexican, and United States industries are comparable.

period of time to individuals requiring nursing care. These establishments have a permanent core staff of registered or licensed practical nurses who, along with other staff, provide nursing and continuous personal care services.

Illustrative Examples:

Convalescent homes or convalescent hospitals (except psychiatric)
Homes for the elderly with nursing care
Inpatient care hospices
Nursing homes
Rest homes with nursing care

Cross-References.

- Assisted-living facilities with on-site nursing care facilities are classified in U.S. Industry 623311, Continuing Care Retirement Communities; and

- Psychiatric convalescent homes are classified in Industry 623220, Residential Mental Health and Substance Abuse Facilities.

6232 Residential Mental Retardation, Mental Health and Substance Abuse Facilities

This industry group comprises establishments primarily engaged in providing residential care (but not licensed hospital care) to people with mental retardation, mental illness, or substance abuse problems.

62321 Residential Mental Retardation Facilities
See industry description for 623210 below.

623210 Residential Mental Retardation Facilities[CAN]

This industry comprises establishments (e.g., group homes, hospitals, intermediate care facilities) primarily engaged in providing residential care services for persons diagnosed with mental retardation. These facilities may provide some health care, though the focus is room, board, protective supervision, and counseling.

Cross-References.

- Establishments primarily engaged in providing inpatient treatment of mental health and substance abuse illnesses with an emphasis on counseling rather than medical treatment are classified in Industry 623220, Residential Mental Health and Substance Abuse Facilities;

- Establishments primarily engaged in providing treatment of mental health and substance abuse illnesses on an exclusively outpatient basis are classified in Industry 621420, Outpatient Mental Health and Substance Abuse Centers; and

- Establishments known and licensed as hospitals primarily engaged in providing inpatient treatment of mental health and substance abuse illnesses with an emphasis on medical treatment and monitoring are classified in Industry 622210, Psychiatric and Substance Abuse Hospitals.

62322 Residential Mental Health and Substance Abuse Facilities
See industry description for 623220 below.

623220 Residential Mental Health and Substance Abuse Facilities[US]

This industry comprises establishments primarily engaged in providing residential care and treatment for patients with mental health and substance abuse illnesses. These establishments provide room, board, supervision, and counseling services. Although medical services may be available at these establishments, they are incidental to the counseling, mental rehabilitation, and support services offered. These establishments generally provide a wide range of social services in addition to counseling.

Illustrative Examples:

Alcoholism or drug addiction rehabilitation facilities (except licensed hospitals)

Mental health halfway houses

Psychiatric convalescent homes or hospitals

Residential group homes for the emotionally disturbed

Cross-References.

- Establishments primarily engaged in providing treatment of mental health and substance abuse illnesses on an exclusively outpatient basis are classified in Industry 621420, Outpatient Mental Health and Substance Abuse Centers;

- Establishments primarily engaged in providing residential care for persons diagnosed with mental retardation are classified in Industry 623210, Residential Mental Retardation Facilities; and

- Establishments known and licensed as hospitals primarily engaged in providing inpatient treatment of mental health and substance abuse illnesses with an emphasis on medical treatment and monitoring are classified in Industry 622210, Psychiatric and Substance Abuse Hospitals.

6233 Community Care Facilities for the Elderly

62331 Community Care Facilities for the Elderly

This industry comprises establishments primarily engaged in providing residential and personal care services for (1) the elderly and other persons who are unable to fully care for themselves and/or (2) the elderly and other persons who do not desire to live independently. The care typically includes room, board, supervision, and assistance in daily living, such as housekeeping services. In some instances these establishments provide skilled nursing care for residents in separate on-site facilities.

Illustrative Examples:

Assisted-living facilities

Continuing care retirement communities

Homes for the elderly without nursing care

Rest homes without nursing care

Cross-References.

- Establishments primarily engaged in providing inpatient nursing and rehabilitative services are classified in Industry 62311, Nursing Care Facilities; and

- Apartment or condominium complexes where people live independently in rented housing units are classified in Industry 53111, Lessors of Residential Buildings and Dwellings.

623311 Continuing Care Retirement Communities[US]

This U.S. industry comprises establishments primarily engaged in providing a range of residential and personal care services with on-site nursing care facilities for (1) the elderly and other persons who are unable to fully care for themselves and/or (2) the elderly and other persons who do not desire to live independently. Individuals live in a variety of residential settings with meals, housekeeping, social, leisure, and other services available to assist residents in daily living. Assisted-living facilities with on-site nursing care facilities are included in this industry.

Cross-References.

- Establishments primarily engaged in providing inpatient nursing and rehabilitative services are classified in Industry 623110, Nursing Care Facilities;

- Assisted-living facilities without on-site nursing care facilities are classified in U.S. Industry 623312, Homes for the Elderly; and

- Apartment or condominium complexes where people live independently in rented housing units are classified in Industry 531110, Lessors of Residential Buildings and Dwellings.

623312 Homes for the Elderly[US]

This U.S. industry comprises establishments primarily engaged in providing residential and personal care services (i.e., without on-site nursing care facilities)

US—United States industry only. CAN—United States and Canadian industries are comparable. MEX—United States and Mexican industries are comparable. Blank—Canadian, Mexican, and United States industries are comparable.

for (1) the elderly or other persons who are unable to fully care for themselves and/or (2) the elderly or other persons who do not desire to live independently. The care typically includes room, board, supervision, and assistance in daily living, such as housekeeping services.

Illustrative Examples:

Assisted-living facilities without on-site nursing care facilities	Homes for the elderly without nursing care
	Rest homes without nursing care

Cross-References.

- Assisted-living facilities with on-site nursing care facilities are classified in U.S. Industry 623311, Continuing Care Retirement Communities;

- Homes for the elderly with nursing care or rest homes with nursing care are classified in Industry 623110, Nursing Care Facilities; and

- Apartment or condominium complexes where people live independently in rented or owned housing units are classified in Industry 53111, Lessors of Residential Buildings and Dwellings.

6239 Other Residential Care Facilities

This industry group comprises establishments of residential care facilities (except residential mental retardation, mental health, and substance abuse facilities and community care facilities for the elderly).

62399 Other Residential Care Facilities

See industry description for 623990 below.

623990 Other Residential Care Facilities[US]

This industry comprises establishments primarily engaged in providing residential care (except residential mental retardation facilities, residential health and substance abuse facilities, continuing care retirement communities, and homes for the elderly). These establishments also provide supervision and personal care services.

Illustrative Examples:

Boot or disciplinary camps (except correctional) for delinquent youth	Group homes for the disabled without nursing care
Child group foster homes	Halfway group homes for delinquents or ex-offenders
Delinquent youth halfway group homes	

Group homes for the hearing or visually impaired

Homes for unwed mothers
Orphanages

Cross-References.

- Residential mental retardation facilities are classified in Industry 623210, Residential Mental Retardation Facilities;
- Continuing care retirement communities are classified in U.S. Industry 623311, Continuing Care Retirement Communities;
- Residential mental health and substance abuse facilities are classified in 623220, Residential Mental Health and Substance Abuse Facilities;
- Homes for the elderly without nursing care are classified in U.S. Industry 623312, Homes for the Elderly;
- Establishments primarily engaged in providing inpatient nursing and rehabilitative services are classified in Industry 623110, Nursing Care Facilities;
- Establishments primarily engaged in providing temporary shelter are classified in U.S. Industry 624221, Temporary Shelters; and
- Correctional camps are classified in Industry 922140, Correctional Institutions.

624 Social Assistance

Industries in the Social Assistance subsector provide a wide variety of social assistance services directly to their clients. These services do not include residential or accommodation services, except on a short stay basis.

6241 Individual and Family Services

62411 Child and Youth Services
See industry description for 624110 below.

624110 Child and Youth Services^{CAN}

This industry comprises establishments primarily engaged in providing nonresidential social assistance services for children and youth. These establishments provide for the welfare of children in such areas as adoption and foster care, drug prevention, life skills training, and positive social development.

Illustrative Examples:

Adoption agencies
Child guidance organizations
Foster care placement services

Youth centers (except recreational only)
Youth self-help organizations

US—United States industry only. CAN—United States and Canadian industries are comparable. MEX—United States and Mexican industries are comparable. Blank—Canadian, Mexican, and United States industries are comparable.

Cross-References.

- Youth recreational centers are classified in Industry 713940, Fitness and Recreational Sports Centers;
- Youth recreational sports teams and leagues are classified in Industry 713990, All Other Amusement and Recreation Industries;
- Scouting organizations are classified in Industry 813410, Civic and Social Organizations; and
- Establishments primarily engaged in providing day care services for children are classified in Industry 624410, Child Day Care Services.

62412 Services for the Elderly and Persons with Disabilities
See industry description for 624120 below.

624120 Services for the Elderly and Persons with Disabilities^{CAN}

This industry comprises establishments primarily engaged in providing nonresidential social assistance services to improve the quality of life for the elderly, persons diagnosed with mental retardation, or persons with disabilities. These establishments provide for the welfare of these of individuals in such areas as day care, nonmedical home care or homemaker services, social activities, group support, and companionship.

Cross-References. Establishments primarily engaged in—

- Providing job training for persons diagnosed with mental retardation or persons with disabilities—are classified in Industry 624310, Vocational Rehabilitation Services;
- Providing residential care for the elderly, persons diagnosed with mental retardation, or persons with disabilities—are classified in Subsector 623, Nursing and Residential Care Facilities; and
- Providing in-home health care services—are classified in Subsector 621, Ambulatory Health Care Services.

62419 Other Individual and Family Services
See industry description for 624190 below.

624190 Other Individual and Family Services^{CAN}

This industry comprises establishments primarily engaged in providing nonresidential individual and family social assistance services (except those specifically

---

directed toward children, the elderly, persons diagnosed with mental retardation, or persons with disabilities).

Illustrative Examples:

Community action services agencies

Crisis intervention centers

Family social services agencies

Family welfare services

Hotline centers

Marriage counseling services (except by offices of mental health practitioners)

Multipurpose social services centers

Self-help organizations (except for disabled persons, the elderly, persons diagnosed with mental retardation)

Suicide crisis centers

Telephone counseling services

Cross-References. Establishments primarily engaged in—

- Providing clinical psychological and psychiatric social counseling services—are classified in Industry 621330, Offices of Mental Health Practitioners (except Physicians);

- Providing child and youth social assistance services (except day care)—are classified in Industry 624110, Child and Youth Services;

- Providing child day care services—are classified in Industry 624410, Child Day Care Services;

- Providing social assistance services for the elderly, persons diagnosed with mental retardation, and persons with disabilities—are classified in Industry 624120, Services for the Elderly and Persons with Disabilities;

- Community action advocacy—are classified in U.S. Industry 813319, Other Social Advocacy Organizations; and

- Providing in-home health care services—are classified in Subsector 621, Ambulatory Health Care Services.

6242 Community Food and Housing, and Emergency and Other Relief Services

62421 Community Food Services
See industry description for 624210 below.

624210 Community Food Services[CAN]

This industry comprises establishments primarily engaged in the collection, preparation, and delivery of food for the needy. Establishments in this industry may also distribute clothing and blankets to the poor. These establishments may prepare and deliver meals to persons who by reason of age, disability, or illness are unable to prepare meals for themselves; collect and distribute salvageable or donated food; or prepare and provide meals at fixed or mobile locations. Food banks, meal delivery programs, and soup kitchens are included in this industry.

62422 Community Housing Services

This industry comprises establishments primarily engaged in providing one or more of the following community housing services: (1) short term emergency shelter for victims of domestic violence, sexual assault, or child abuse; (2) temporary residential shelter for the homeless, runaway youths, and patients and families caught in medical crises; (3) transitional housing for low-income individuals and families; (4) volunteer construction or repair of low cost housing, in partnership with the homeowner who may assist in construction or repair work; and (5) repair of homes for elderly or disabled homeowners. These establishments may operate their own shelter; or may subsidize housing using existing homes, apartments, hotels, or motels; or may require a low-cost mortgage or work (sweat) equity.

Cross-References.

Central offices of government housing programs are classified in Industry 92511, Administration of Housing Programs.

624221 Temporary Shelters[US]

This U.S. industry comprises establishments primarily engaged in providing (1) short term emergency shelter for victims of domestic violence, sexual assault, or child abuse and/or (2) temporary residential shelter for homeless individuals or families, runaway youth, and patients and families caught in medical crises. These establishments may operate their own shelters or may subsidize housing using existing homes, apartments, hotels, or motels.

Cross-References.

Establishments primarily engaged in providing emergency shelter for victims of domestic or international disasters or conflicts are classified in Industry 624230, Emergency and Other Relief Services.

624229 Other Community Housing Services[US]

This U.S. industry comprises establishments primarily engaged in providing one or more of the following community housing services: (1) transitional housing to low-income individuals and families; (2) volunteer construction or repair of low-cost housing, in partnership with the homeowner who may assist in the construction or repair work; and (3) the repair of homes for elderly or disabled homeowners. These establishments may subsidize housing using existing homes, apartments, hotels, or motels or may require a low-cost mortgage or sweat equity. These establishments may also provide low-income families with furniture and household supplies.

Cross-References.

Central offices of government housing programs are classified in Industry 925110, Administration of Housing Programs.

62423 Emergency and Other Relief Services
See industry description for 624230 below.

624230 Emergency and Other Relief Services[CAN]

This industry comprises establishments primarily engaged in providing food, shelter, clothing, medical relief, resettlement, and counseling to victims of domestic or international disasters or conflicts (e.g., wars).

6243 Vocational Rehabilitation Services

62431 Vocational Rehabilitation Services
See industry description for 624310 below.

624310 Vocational Rehabilitation Services[CAN]

This industry comprises (1) establishments primarily engaged in providing vocational rehabilitation or habilitation services, such as job counseling, job training, and work experience, to unemployed and underemployed persons, persons with disabilities, and persons who have a job market disadvantage because of lack of education, job skill, or experience and (2) establishments primarily engaged in providing training and employment to persons with disabilities. Vocational rehabilitation job training facilities (except schools) and sheltered workshops (i.e., work experience centers) are included in this industry.

Cross-References.

- Schools (except high schools) primarily engaged in providing vocational training are classified in Industry 61151, Technical and Trade Schools;

- Vocational high schools are classified in Industry 611110, Elementary and Secondary Schools; and
- Establishments primarily engaged in providing career and vocational counseling (except rehabilitative) are classified in Industry 611710, Educational Support Services.

6244 Child Day Care Services

62441 Child Day Care Services
See industry description for 624410 below.

624410 Child Day Care Services[CAN]

This industry comprises establishments primarily engaged in providing day care of infants or children. These establishments generally care for preschool children, but may care for older children when they are not in school and may also offer prekindergarten educational programs.

Illustrative Examples:

Child day care babysitting services   Nursery schools
Child or infant day care centers   Preschool centers

Cross-References.

Establishments primarily engaged in offering kindergarten educational programs are classified in Industry 611110, Elementary and Secondary Schools.

Sector 71—Arts, Entertainment, and Recreation

The Sector as a Whole

The Arts, Entertainment, and Recreation sector includes a wide range of establishments that operate facilities or provide services to meet varied cultural, entertainment, and recreational interests of their patrons. This sector comprises (1) establishments that are involved in producing, promoting, or participating in live performances, events, or exhibits intended for public viewing; (2) establishments that preserve and exhibit objects and sites of historical, cultural, or educational interest; and (3) establishments that operate facilities or provide services that enable patrons to participate in recreational activities or pursue amusement, hobby, and leisure-time interests.

Some establishments that provide cultural, entertainment, or recreational facilities and services are classified in other sectors. Excluded from this sector are: (1) establishments that provide both accommodations and recreational facilities, such as hunting and fishing camps and resort and casino hotels are classified in Subsector 721, Accommodation; (2) restaurants and night clubs that provide live entertainment in addition to the sale of food and beverages are classified in Subsector 722, Food Services and Drinking Places; (3) motion picture theaters, libraries and archives, and publishers of newspapers, magazines, books, periodicals, and computer software are classified in Sector 51, Information; and (4) establishments using transportation equipment to provide recreational and entertainment services, such as those operating sightseeing buses, dinner cruises, or helicopter rides are classified in Subsector 487, Scenic and Sightseeing Transportation.

711 Performing Arts, Spectator Sports, and Related Industries

Industries in the Performing Arts, Spectator Sports, and Related Industries subsector group establishments that produce or organize and promote live presentations involving the performances of actors and actresses, singers, dancers, musical groups and artists, athletes, and other entertainers, including independent (i.e., freelance) entertainers and the establishments that manage their careers. The classification recognizes four basic processes: (1) producing (i.e., presenting) events; (2) organizing, managing, and/or promoting events; (3) managing and representing entertainers; and (4) providing the artistic, creative and technical skills necessary to the production of these live events. Also, this subsector contains four industries for performing arts companies. Each is defined on the basis of the particular skills of the entertainers involved in the presentations.

The industry structure for this subsector makes a clear distinction between performing arts companies and performing artists (i.e., independent or freelance).

US—United States industry only. CAN—United States and Canadian industries are comparable. MEX—United States and Mexican industries are comparable. Blank—Canadian, Mexican, and United States industries are comparable.

Although not unique to arts and entertainment, freelancing is a particularly important phenomenon in this Performing Arts, Spectator Sports, and Related Industries subsector. Distinguishing this activity from the production activity is a meaningful process differentiation. This approach, however, is difficult to implement in the case of musical groups (i.e., companies) and artists, especially pop groups. These establishments tend to be more loosely organized and it can be difficult to distinguish companies from freelancers. For this reason, NAICS includes one industry that covers both musical groups and musical artists.

This subsector contains two industries for Industry Group 7113, Promoters of Performing Arts, Sports, and Similar Events, one for those that operate facilities and another for those that do not. This is because there are significant differences in cost structures between those promoters that manage and provide the staff to operate facilities and those that do not. In addition to promoters without facilities, other industries in this subsector include establishments that may operate without permanent facilities. These types of establishments include: performing arts companies, musical groups and artists, spectator sports, and independent (i.e., freelance) artists, writers, and performers.

Excluded from this subsector are nightclubs. Some nightclubs promote live entertainment on a regular basis and it can be argued that they could be classified in Industry Group 7113, Promoters of Performing Arts, Sports, and Similar Events. However, since most of these establishments function as any other drinking place when they do not promote entertainment and because most of their revenue is derived from sale of food and beverages, they are classified in Subsector 722, Food Services and Drinking Places.

7111 Performing Arts Companies

This industry group comprises establishments primarily engaged in producing live presentations involving the performances of actors and actresses, singers, dancers, musical groups and artists, and other performing artists.

71111 Theater Companies and Dinner Theaters
See industry description for 711110 below.

711110 Theater Companies and Dinner Theaters[US]

This industry comprises (1) companies, groups, or theaters primarily engaged in producing the following live theatrical presentations: musicals; operas; plays; and comedy, improvisational, mime, and puppet shows and (2) establishments, commonly known as dinner theaters, engaged in producing live theatrical productions and in providing food and beverages for consumption on the premises. Theater

---

US—United States industry only. CAN—United States and Canadian industries are comparable. MEX—United States and Mexican industries are comparable. Blank—Canadian, Mexican, and United States industries are comparable.

groups or companies may or may not operate their own theater or other facility for staging their shows.

Illustrative Examples:

Comedy troupes	Opera companies
Live theatrical production (except dance)	Theatrical stock or repertory companies
Musical theater companies	

Cross-References.

- Establishments, such as nightclubs, primarily engaged in providing food and beverages for consumption on the premises and that also present live nontheatrical entertainment, are classified in Subsector 722, Food Services and Drinking Places;

- Establishments primarily engaged in organizing, managing, and/or promoting performing arts productions without producing their own shows are classified in Industry Group 7113, Promoters of Performing Arts, Sports, and Similar Events;

- Companies, groups, or theaters primarily engaged in producing all types of live theatrical dance presentations are classified in Industry 711120, Dance Companies;

- Freelance producers and performing artists (except musicians and vocalists) primarily engaged in theatrical activities independent of a company or group are classified in Industry 711510, Independent Artists, Writers, and Performers; and

- Musicians and vocalists are classified in Industry 711130, Musical Groups and Artists.

71112 Dance Companies

See industry description for 711120 below.

711120 Dance Companies^{CAN}

This industry comprises companies, groups, or theaters primarily engaged in producing all types of live theatrical dance (e.g., ballet, contemporary dance, folk dance) presentations. Dance companies or groups may or may not operate their own theater or other facility for staging their shows.

Cross-References.

- Establishments, such as exotic dance clubs, primarily engaged in providing food and beverages for consumption on the premises and that also present live dance entertainment, are classified in Subsector 722, Food Services and Drinking Places;

- Establishments primarily engaged in organizing, promoting, and/or managing dance productions without producing their own shows are classified in Industry Group 7113, Promoters of Performing Arts, Sports, and Similar Events; and

  - Freelance producers and dancers primarily engaged in theatrical activities independent of a company or group are classified in Industry 711510, Independent Artists, Writers, and Performers.

71113 Musical Groups and Artists
See industry description for 711130 below.

711130 Musical Groups and Artists^{CAN}

This industry comprises (1) groups primarily engaged in producing live musical entertainment (except theatrical musical or opera productions) and (2) independent (i.e., freelance) artists primarily engaged in providing live musical entertainment. Musical groups and artists may perform in front of a live audience or in a studio, and may or may not operate their own facilities for staging their shows.

Illustrative Examples:

Bands	Drum and bugle corps (i.e., drill teams)
Musical groups (except theatrical musical groups)	Independent musicians or vocalists
	Orchestras

Cross-References.

- Establishments primarily engaged in organizing, promoting, and/or managing concerts and other musical performances without producing their own shows are classified in Industry Group 7113, Promoters of Performing Arts, Sports, and Similar Events;

- Companies, groups, or theaters primarily engaged in producing theatrical musicals and opera productions are classified in Industry 711110, Theater Companies and Dinner Theaters; and

- Freelance producers (except musical groups and artists) primarily engaged in musical activities independent of a company or group are classified in Industry 711510, Independent Artists, Writers, and Performers.

71119 Other Performing Arts Companies
See industry description for 711190 below.

711190 Other Performing Arts Companies[CAN]

This industry comprises companies or groups (except theater companies, dance companies, musical groups, and artists) primarily engaged in producing live theatrical presentations.

Illustrative Examples:

Carnival traveling shows
Circuses

Ice skating companies
Magic shows

Cross-References.

- Establishments, such as comedy clubs or nightclubs, primarily engaged in providing food and beverages for consumption on the premises and that also present live nontheatrical entertainment are classified in Subsector 722, Food Services and Drinking Places;

- Establishments primarily engaged in organizing, promoting, and/or managing ice skating shows, circuses, and other live performing arts presentations without producing their own shows are classified in Industry Group 7113, Promoters of Performing Arts, Sports, and Similar Events;

- Theater companies and groups (except dance) or dinner theaters engaged in producing musicals; plays; operas; and comedy, improvisational, mime, and puppet shows are classified in Industry 711110, Theater Companies and Dinner Theaters;

- Dance companies or groups are classified in Industry 711120, Dance Companies;

- Freelance producers and performing artists (except musicians and vocalists) are classified in Industry 711510, Independent Artists, Writers, and Performers; and

- Musical groups and independent musicians and vocalists are classified in Industry 711130, Musical Groups and Artists.

7112 Spectator Sports

71121 Spectator Sports

This industry comprises (1) sports teams or clubs primarily participating in live sporting events before a paying audience; (2) establishments primarily engaged in operating racetracks; (3) independent athletes engaged in participating in live sporting or racing events before a paying audience; (4) owners of racing participants, such as cars, dogs, and horses, primarily engaged in entering them in racing events or other spectator sports events; and (5) establishments, such as sports trainers, primarily engaged in providing specialized services to support participants in sports events or competitions. The sports teams and clubs included in this industry may or may not operate their own arena, stadium, or other facility for presenting their games or other spectator sports events.

Cross-References.

- Establishments primarily engaged in promoting sporting events without participating in sporting events are classified in Industry Group 7113, Promoters of Performing Arts, Sports, and Similar Events;

- Establishments, such as youth league baseball teams, primarily engaged in participating in sporting events for recreational purposes without playing before a paying audience are classified in Industry 71399, All Other Amusement and Recreation Industries;

- Amateur, semiprofessional, or professional athletic associations or leagues are classified in Industry 81399, Other Similar Organizations (except Business, Professional, Labor, and Political Organizations);

- Establishments primarily engaged in representing or managing the careers of sports figures are classified in Industry 71141, Agents and Managers for Artists, Athletes, Entertainers, and Other Public Figures;

- Independent athletes engaged in providing sports instruction without participating in sporting events before a paying audience are classified in Industry 61162, Sports and Recreation Instruction;

- Independent athletes exclusively engaged in endorsing products or making speeches are classified in Industry 71151, Independent Artists, Writers, and Performers; and

- Establishments primarily engaged in raising horses, mules, donkeys, and other equines are classified in Industry 11292, Horses and Other Equine Production.

711211 Sports Teams and Clubs[CAN]

This U.S. industry comprises professional or semiprofessional sports teams or clubs primarily engaged in participating in live sporting events, such as baseball, basketball, football, hockey, soccer, and jai alai games, before a paying audience. These establishments may or may not operate their own arena, stadium, or other facility for presenting these events.

US—United States industry only. CAN—United States and Canadian industries are comparable. MEX—United States and Mexican industries are comparable. Blank—Canadian, Mexican, and United States industries are comparable.

Cross-References.

- Establishments primarily engaged in promoting sporting events without participating in sporting events are classified in Industry Group 7113, Promoters of Performing Arts, Sports, and Similar Events;

- Establishments, such as youth league baseball teams, primarily engaged in participating in sporting events for recreational purposes without playing before a paying audience are classified in Industry 713990, All Other Amusement and Recreation Industries; and

- Amateur, semiprofessional, or professional athletic associations or leagues are classified in Industry 813990, Other Similar Organizations (except Business, Professional, Labor, and Political Organizations).

711212 Racetracks[US]

This U.S. industry comprises establishments primarily engaged in operating racetracks. These establishments may also present and /or promote the events, such as auto, dog, and horse races, held in these facilities.

Cross-References.

Owners of racing participants, such as cars, dogs, and horses, primarily engaged in entering them in racing events; trainers of racing participants; and independent athletes, such as jockeys and race car drivers, primarily engaged in participating in racing events are classified in U.S. Industry 711219, Other Spectator Sports.

711219 Other Spectator Sports[US]

This U.S. industry comprises (1) independent athletes, such as professional or semiprofessional golfers, boxers, and race car drivers, primarily engaged in participating in live sporting or racing events before a paying audience; (2) owners of racing participants, such as cars, dogs, and horses, primarily engaged in entering them in racing events or other spectator events; and (3) establishments, such as sports trainers, primarily engaged in providing specialized services required to support participants in sports events or competitions.

Cross-References.

- Establishments primarily engaged in operating racetracks are classified in U.S. Industry 711212, Racetracks;

- Establishments primarily engaged in representing or managing the careers of sports figures are classified in Industry 711410, Agents and Managers for Artists, Athletes, Entertainers, and Other Public Figures;

US—United States industry only. CAN—United States and Canadian industries are comparable. MEX—United States and Mexican industries are comparable. Blank—Canadian, Mexican, and United States industries are comparable.

- Independent athletes engaged in providing sports instruction without participating in sporting events before a paying audience are classified in Industry 611620, Sports and Recreation Instruction;

- Independent athletes exclusively engaged in endorsing products or making speeches are classified in Industry 711510, Independent Artists, Writers, and Performers; and

- Establishments primarily engaged in raising horses, mules, donkeys, and other equines are classified in Industry 112920, Horses and Other Equine Production.

7113 Promoters of Performing Arts, Sports, and Similar Events

71131 Promoters of Performing Arts, Sports, and Similar Events with Facilities
See industry description for 711310 below.

711310 Promoters of Performing Arts, Sports, and Similar Events with Facilities[US]

This industry comprises establishments primarily engaged in (1) organizing, promoting, and/or managing live performing arts productions, sports events, and similar events, such as state fairs, county fairs, agricultural fairs, concerts, and festivals, held in facilities that they manage and operate and/or (2) managing and providing the staff to operate arenas, stadiums, theaters, or other related facilities for rent to other promoters.

Cross-References. Establishments primarily engaged in—

- Producing live performances (but may also promote the performances and/or operate the facilities where the performances take place)—are classified in Industry Group 7111, Performing Arts Companies;

- Operating racetracks (but may also promote the events held in these facilities)—are classified in U.S. Industry 711212, Racetracks;

- Presenting sporting events (but may also promote these sporting events and/or operate the stadiums or arenas where the sporting events take place)—are classified in U.S. Industry 711211, Sports Teams and Clubs;

- Organizing, promoting, and/or managing conventions, conferences, and trade shows (but may also operate the facilities where these events take place)—are classified in Industry 561920, Convention and Trade Show Organizers;

US—United States industry only. CAN—United States and Canadian industries are comparable. MEX—United States and Mexican industries are comparable. Blank—Canadian, Mexican, and United States industries are comparable.

- Organizing, promoting, and/or managing performing arts productions, sports events, and similar events in facilities managed and operated by others—are classified in Industry 711320 Promoters of Performing Arts, Sports, and Similar Events without Facilities; and

- Leasing stadiums, arenas, theaters, and other related facilities to others without operating the facilities—are classified in Industry 531120, Lessors of Nonresidential Buildings (except Miniwarehouses).

71132 Promoters of Performing Arts, Sports, and Similar Events without Facilities

See industry description for 711320 below.

711320 Promoters of Performing Arts, Sports, and Similar Events without Facilities[MEX]

This industry comprises promoters primarily engaged in organizing, promoting, and/or managing live performing arts productions, sports events, and similar events, such as state fairs, county fairs, agricultural fairs, concerts, and festivals, in facilities that are managed and operated by others. Theatrical (except motion picture) booking agencies are included in this industry.

Cross-References. Establishments primarily engaged in—

- Booking motion pictures or videos—are classified in U.S. Industry 512199, Other Motion Picture and Video Industries;

- Producing live performances (but may also promote the performances)—are classified in Industry Group 7111, Performing Arts Companies;

- Operating racetracks (but may also promote the events held in these facilities)—are classified in U.S. Industry 711212, Racetracks;

- Presenting sporting events (but may also promote these events)—are classified in U.S. Industry 711211, Sports Teams and Clubs;

- Organizing, promoting, and/or managing conventions, conferences, and trade shows (but may also operate the facilities where these events take place)—are classified in Industry 561920, Convention and Trade Show Organizers;

- Organizing, promoting, and/or managing performing arts, sports, and similar events in facilities they manage or operate—are classified in Industry 711310, Promoters of Performing Arts, Sports, and Similar Events with Facilities; and

- Operating amateur, semiprofessional, or professional athletic associations or leagues—are classified in Industry 813990, Other Similar Organizations (except Business, Professional, Labor, and Political Organizations).

7114 Agents and Managers for Artists, Athletes, Entertainers, and Other Public Figures

71141 Agents and Managers for Artists, Athletes, Entertainers, and Other Public Figures
See industry description for 711410 below.

711410 Agents and Managers for Artists, Athletes, Entertainers, and Other Public Figures

This industry comprises establishments of agents and managers primarily engaged in representing and/or managing creative and performing artists, sports figures, entertainers, and other public figures. The representation and management includes activities, such as representing clients in contract negotiations; managing or organizing client's financial affairs; and generally promoting the careers of their clients.

Illustrative Examples:

Celebrity agents or managers
Literary agents
Modeling agents

Sports figure agents or managers
Talent agents

Cross-References.
- Establishments primarily engaged in supplying models to clients are classified in Industry 561320, Temporary Help Services; and
- Establishments known as model registries primarily engaged in recruiting and placing models for clients are classified in Industry 561310, Employment Placement Agencies.

7115 Independent Artists, Writers, and Performers

71151 Independent Artists, Writers, and Performers
See industry description for 711510 below.

711510 Independent Artists, Writers, and Performers

This industry comprises independent (i.e., freelance) individuals primarily engaged in performing in artistic productions, in creating artistic and cultural works or productions, or in providing technical expertise necessary for these productions. This industry also includes athletes and other celebrities exclusively engaged in endorsing products and making speeches or public appearances for which they receive a fee.

Illustrative Examples:

Independent actors or actresses
Independent art restorers
Independent artists (except musical, commercial, or medical)
Independent cartoonists
Independent dancers
Independent journalists

Independent producers
Independent recording technicians
Independent speakers
Independent theatrical costume designers
Independent theatrical lighting technicians

Cross-References.

- Freelance musicians and vocalists—are classified in Industry 711130, Musical Groups and Artists;
- Independent commercial artists and graphic designers—are classified in Industry 541430, Graphic Design Services; and
- Artisans and craftspersons—are classified in the Sector 31-33, Manufacturing.

712 Museums, Historical Sites, and Similar Institutions

Industries in the Museums, Historical Sites, and Similar Institutions subsector engage in the preservation and exhibition of objects, sites, and natural wonders of historical, cultural, and/or educational value.

7121 Museums, Historical Sites, and Similar Institutions

71211 Museums
See industry description for 712110 below.

712110 Museums^{US}

This industry comprises establishments primarily engaged in the preservation and exhibition of objects of historical, cultural, and/or educational value.

Illustrative Examples:

Art galleries (except retail)
Art museums
Halls of fame

Planetariums
Science or technology museums
Wax museums

US—United States industry only. CAN—United States and Canadian industries are comparable. MEX—United States and Mexican industries are comparable. Blank—Canadian, Mexican, and United States industries are comparable.

Cross-References.

Commercial art galleries primarily engaged in selling art objects are classified in Industry 453920, Art Dealers.

71212 Historical Sites
See industry description for 712120 below.

712120 Historical Sites

This industry comprises establishments primarily engaged in the preservation and exhibition of sites, buildings, forts, or communities that describe events or persons of particular historical interest. Archeological sites, battlefields, historical ships, and pioneer villages are included in this industry.

71213 Zoos and Botanical Gardens
See industry description for 712130 below.

712130 Zoos and Botanical Gardens^{CAN}

This industry comprises establishments primarily engaged in the preservation and exhibition of live plant and animal life displays.

Illustrative Examples:

Aquariums	Wild animal parks
Arboreta	Zoological gardens
Aviaries	

71219 Nature Parks and Other Similar Institutions
See industry description for 712190 below.

712190 Nature Parks and Other Similar Institutions

This industry comprises establishments primarily engaged in the preservation and exhibition of natural areas or settings.

Illustrative Examples:

Bird or wildlife sanctuaries	Nature centers or preserves
Conservation areas	National parks
Natural wonder (e.g., cavern, waterfall) tourist attractions	

US—United States industry only. CAN—United States and Canadian industries are comparable. MEX—United States and Mexican industries are comparable. Blank—Canadian, Mexican, and United States industries are comparable.

Cross-References.

Establishments primarily engaged in operating commercial hunting or fishing preserves (e.g., game farms) are classified in Industry 114210, Hunting and Trapping.

713 Amusement, Gambling, and Recreation Industries

Industries in the Amusement, Gambling, and Recreation Industries subsector (1) operate facilities where patrons can primarily engage in sports, recreation, amusement, or gambling activities and/or (2) provide other amusement and recreation services, such as supplying and servicing amusement devices in places of business operated by others; operating sports teams, clubs, or leagues engaged in playing games for recreational purposes; and guiding tours without using transportation equipment.

This subsector does not cover all establishments providing recreational services. Other sectors of NAICS also provide recreational services. Providers of recreational services are often engaged in processes classified in other sectors of NAICS. For example, operators of resorts and hunting and fishing camps provide both accommodation and recreational facilities and services. These establishments are classified in Subsector 721, Accommodation, partly to reflect the significant costs associated with the provision of accommodation services and partly to ensure consistency with international standards. Likewise, establishments using transportation equipment to provide recreational and entertainment services, such as those operating sightseeing buses, dinner cruises, or helicopter rides, are classified in Subsector 48-49, Transportation and Warehousing.

The industry groups in this subsector highlight particular types of activities: amusement parks and arcades, gambling industries, and other amusement and recreation industries. The groups, however, are not all inclusive of the activity. The Gambling Industries industry group does not provide for full coverage of gambling activities. For example, casino hotels are classified in Subsector 721, Accommodation; and horse and dog racing tracks are classified in Industry Group 7112, Spectator Sports.

7131 Amusement Parks and Arcades

This industry group comprises establishments primarily engaged in operating amusement parks and amusement arcades and parlors.

71311 Amusement and Theme Parks

See industry description for 713110 below.

713110 Amusement and Theme Parks^{CAN}

This industry comprises establishments, known as amusement or theme parks, primarily engaged in operating a variety of attractions, such as mechanical rides, water rides, games, shows, theme exhibits, refreshment stands, and picnic grounds. These establishments may lease space to others on a concession basis.

Cross-References. Establishments primarily engaged in—

- Operating mechanical or water rides on a concession basis in amusement parks, fairs, and carnivals or in operating a single attraction, such as a waterslide—are classified in Industry 713990, All Other Amusement and Recreation Industries;

- Operating refreshment stands on a concession basis—are classified in Industry Group 7222, Limited-Service Eating Places;

- Supplying and servicing coin-operated amusement (except gambling) devices in other's facilities—are classified in Industry 713990, All Other Amusement and Recreation Industries;

- Supplying and servicing coin-operated gambling devices (e.g., slot machines) in places of business operated by others—are classified in Industry 713290, Other Gambling Industries; and

- Organizing, promoting, and/or managing events, such as carnivals and fairs, with or without facilities—are classified in Industry Group 7113, Promoters of Performing Arts, Sports, and Similar Events.

71312 Amusement Arcades
See industry description for 713120 below.

713120 Amusement Arcades

This industry comprises establishments primarily engaged in operating amusement (except gambling, billiard, or pool) arcades and parlors.

Cross-References. Establishments primarily engaged in—

- Supplying and servicing coin-operated amusement (except gambling) devices in places of business operated by others or in operating billiard or pool parlors—are classified in Industry 713990, All Other Amusement and Recreation Industries;

- Operating bingo, off-track betting, or slot machine parlors or in supplying and servicing coin-operated gambling devices (e.g., slot machines or video

---

gambling terminals) in places of business operated by others—are classified in Industry 713290, Other Gambling Industries;

- Operating casinos (except casino hotels)—are classified in Industry 713210, Casinos (except Casino Hotels); and
- Operating casino hotels—are classified in Industry 721120, Casino Hotels.

7132 Gambling Industries

This industry group comprises establishments (except casino hotels) primarily engaged in operating gambling facilities, such as casinos, bingo halls, and video gaming terminals, or in the provision of gambling services, such as lotteries and off-track betting. Casino hotels are classified in Industry 72112, Casino Hotels.

71321 Casinos (except Casino Hotels)
See industry description for 713210 below.

713210 Casinos (except Casino Hotels)

This industry comprises establishments primarily engaged in operating gambling facilities that offer table wagering games along with other gambling activities, such as slot machines and sports betting. These establishments often provide food and beverage services. Included in this industry are floating casinos (i.e., gambling cruises, riverboat casinos).

Cross-References. Establishments primarily engaged in—

- Operating bingo, off-track betting, or slot machine parlors or in supplying and servicing coin-operated gambling devices, such as slot machines and video gaming terminals in places of business operated by others—are classified in Industry 713290, Other Gambling Industries; and
- Operating casino hotels—are classified in Industry 721120, Casino Hotels.

71329 Other Gambling Industries
See industry description for 713290 below.

713290 Other Gambling Industries[US]

This industry comprises establishments primarily engaged in operating gambling facilities (except casinos or casino hotels) or providing gambling services.

US—United States industry only. CAN—United States and Canadian industries are comparable. MEX—United States and Mexican industries are comparable. Blank—Canadian, Mexican, and United States industries are comparable.

Illustrative Examples:

Bingo, off-track betting, or slot
machine parlors
Bookmakers
Card rooms (e.g., poker rooms)
Coin-operated gambling device
concession operators (i.e., supplying
and servicing in other's facilities)

Lottery ticket sales agents (except
retail stores)

Cross-References. Establishments primarily engaged in—

- Operating casinos—are classified in Industry 713210, Casinos (except Casino Hotels);

- Operating casino hotels—are classified in Industry 721120, Casino Hotels;

- Operating facilities with coin-operated nongambling amusement devices— are classified in Industry 713120, Amusement Arcades;

- Supplying and servicing coin-operated nongambling amusement devices in places of business operated by others—are classified in Industry 713990, All Other Amusement and Recreation Industries; and

- Operating racetracks or presenting live racing or sporting events—are classified in Industry 71121, Spectator Sports.

7139 Other Amusement and Recreation Industries

71391 Golf Courses and Country Clubs
See industry description for 713910 below.

713910 Golf Courses and Country Clubs

This industry comprises (1) establishments primarily engaged in operating golf courses (except miniature) and (2) establishments primarily engaged in operating golf courses, along with dining facilities and other recreational facilities that are known as country clubs. These establishments often provide food and beverage services, equipment rental services, and golf instruction services.

Cross-References. Establishments primarily engaged in—

- Operating driving ranges and miniature golf courses—are classified in Industry 713990, All Other Amusement and Recreation Industries; and

- Operating resorts where golf facilities are combined with accommodations—are classified in Industry Group 7211, Traveler Accommodation.

71392 Skiing Facilities

See industry description for 713920 below.

713920 Skiing Facilities

This industry comprises establishments engaged in (1) operating downhill, cross-country, or related skiing areas and/or (2) operating equipment, such as ski lifts and tows. These establishments often provide food and beverage services, equipment rental services, and ski instruction services. Four-season resorts without accommodations are included in this industry.

Cross-References.

Establishments primarily engaged in operating resorts where skiing facilities are combined with accommodations are classified in Industry Group 7211, Traveler Accommodation.

71393 Marinas

See industry description for 713930 below.

713930 Marinas

This industry comprises establishments, commonly known as marinas, engaged in operating docking and/or storage facilities for pleasure craft owners, with or without one or more related activities, such as retailing fuel and marine supplies; and repairing, maintaining, or renting pleasure boats.

Cross-References. Establishments primarily engaged in—

- Renting pleasure boats—are classified in U.S. Industry 532292, Recreational Goods Rental;
- Repairing pleasure boats—are classified in Industry 811490, Other Personal and Household Goods Repair and Maintenance;
- Retailing marine supplies—are classified in U.S. Industry 441222, Boat Dealers; and
- Retailing fuel for boats—are classified in Industry 447190, Other Gasoline Stations.

71394 Fitness and Recreational Sports Centers

See industry description for 713940 below.

US—United States industry only. CAN—United States and Canadian industries are comparable. MEX—United States and Mexican industries are comparable. Blank—Canadian, Mexican, and United States industries are comparable.

713940 Fitness and Recreational Sports Centers[CAN]

This industry comprises establishments primarily engaged in operating fitness and recreational sports facilities featuring exercise and other active physical fitness conditioning or recreational sports activities, such as swimming, skating, or racquet sports.

Illustrative Examples:

Aerobic dance or exercise centers	Ice or roller skating rinks
Gymnasiums	Physical fitness centers
Handball, racquetball, or tennis club facilities	Swimming or wave pools

Cross-References.

- Establishments primarily engaged in providing nonmedical services to assist clients in attaining or maintaining a desired weight are classified in U.S. Industry 812191, Diet and Weight Reducing Centers;

- Establishments primarily engaged in operating health resorts and spas where recreational facilities—are combined with accommodations are classified in Industry 721110, Hotels (except Casino Hotels) and Motels; and

- Recreational sports clubs (i.e., sports teams) not operating sports facilities—instructional) are classified in Industry 713990, All Other Amusement and Recreation Industries.

71395 Bowling Centers
See industry description for 713950 below.

713950 Bowling Centers

This industry comprises establishments engaged in operating bowling centers. These establishments often provide food and beverage services.

71399 All Other Amusement and Recreation Industries
See industry description for 713990 below.

713990 All Other Amusement and Recreation Industries[CAN]

This industry comprises establishments (except amusement parks and arcades; gambling industries; golf courses and country clubs; skiing facilities; marinas;

---

fitness and recreational sports centers; and bowling centers) primarily engaged in providing recreational and amusement services.

Illustrative Examples:

Amusement ride or coin-operated nongambling amusement device concession operators (i.e., supplying or servicing in others facilities)	Miniature golf courses
	Recreational day camps (except instructional)
Archery or shooting ranges	Recreational or youth sports teams and leagues
Billiard or pool parlors	Recreational sports clubs (i.e., sports teams) not operating facilities
Boating clubs (without marinas)	
Dance halls	Riding stables

Cross-References.

- Establishments primarily engaged in operating amusement parks and arcades are classified in Industry Group 7131, Amusement Parks and Arcades;

- Establishments primarily engaged in operating gambling facilities (except casino hotels) or providing gambling services are classified in Industry Group 7132, Gambling Industries;

- Establishments primarily engaged in operating casino hotels are classified in Industry 721120, Casino Hotels;

- Establishments primarily engaged in operating golf courses (except miniature) and country clubs are classified in Industry 713910, Golf Courses and Country Clubs;

- Establishments primarily engaged in operating skiing facilities without hotel accommodation are classified in Industry 713920, Skiing Facilities;

- Establishments primarily engaged in operating resorts where recreational facilities are combined with lodging are classified in Industry Group 7211, Traveler Accommodation;

- Establishments primarily engaged in operating marinas are classified in Industry 713930, Marinas;

- Establishments primarily engaged in operating fitness and recreational sports centers are classified in Industry 713940, Fitness and Recreational Sports Centers;

- Establishments primarily engaged in operating bowling centers are classified in Industry 713950, Bowling Centers;

- Establishments primarily engaged in operating instructional camps, such as sports camps, fine arts camps, and computer camps, are classified in Sector 61, Educational Services, based on the nature of instruction;

- Independent athletes engaged in participating in sporting events before a paying audience are classified in U.S. Industry 711219, Other Spectator Sports;

- Independent athletes engaged in providing sports instruction without participating in sporting events before a paying audience are classified in Industry 611620, Sports and Recreation Instruction;

- Independent athletes exclusively engaged in endorsing products or making speeches are classified in Industry 711510, Independent Artists, Writers, and Performers;

- Establishments primarily engaged in providing scenic and sightseeing transportation are classified in Subsector 487, Scenic and Sightseeing Transportation;

- Aviation clubs primarily engaged in providing specialty air and flying services are classified in U.S. Industry 481219, Other Nonscheduled Air Transportation;

- Aviation clubs primarily engaged in advocating social and political causes are classified in U.S. Industry 813319, Other Social Advocacy Organizations; and

- Amateur, semiprofessional, or professional athletic associations or leagues are classified in Industry 813990, Other Similar Organizations (except Business, Professional, Labor, and Political Organizations).

Sector 72—Accommodation and Food Services

The Sector as a Whole

The Accommodation and Food Services sector comprises establishments providing customers with lodging and/or preparing meals, snacks, and beverages for immediate consumption. The sector includes both accommodation and food services establishments because the two activities are often combined at the same establishment.

Excluded from this sector are civic and social organizations; amusement and recreation parks; theaters; and other recreation or entertainment facilities providing food and beverage services.

721 Accommodation

Industries in the Accommodation subsector provide lodging or short-term accommodations for travelers, vacationers, and others. There is a wide range of establishments in these industries. Some provide lodging only; while others provide meals, laundry services, and recreational facilities, as well as lodging. Lodging establishments are classified in this subsector even if the provision of complementary services generates more revenue. The types of complementary services provided vary from establishment to establishment.

The subsector is organized into three industry groups: (1) traveler accommodation, (2) recreational accommodation, and (3) rooming and boarding houses. The Traveler Accommodation industry group includes establishments that primarily provide traditional types of lodging services. This group includes hotels, motels, and bed and breakfast inns. In addition to lodging, these establishments may provide a range of other services to their guests. The RV (Recreational Vehicle) Parks and Recreational Camps industry group includes establishments that operate lodging facilities primarily designed to accommodate outdoor enthusiasts. Included are travel trailer campsites, recreational vehicle parks, and outdoor adventure retreats. The Rooming and Boarding Houses industry group includes establishments providing temporary or longer-term accommodations, which for the period of occupancy, may serve as a principal residence. Board (i.e., meals) may be provided but is not essential.

Establishments that manage short-stay accommodation establishments (e.g., hotels and motels) on a contractual basis are classified in this subsector if they both manage the operation and provide the operating staff. Such establishments are classified based on the type of facility managed and operated.

7211 Traveler Accommodation

72111 Hotels (except Casino Hotels) and Motels
See industry description for 721110 below.

721110 Hotels (except Casino Hotels) and Motels[US]

This industry comprises establishments primarily engaged in providing short-term lodging in facilities known as hotels, motor hotels, resort hotels, and motels. The establishments in this industry may offer food and beverage services, recreational services, conference rooms and convention services, laundry services, parking, and other services.

Cross-References. Establishments primarily engaged in—

- Providing short-term lodging with a casino on the premises—are classified in Industry 721120, Casino Hotels; and

- Providing short-term lodging in facilities known as bed-and-breakfast inns, youth hostels, housekeeping cabins and cottages, and tourist homes—are classified in Industry 72119, Other Traveler Accommodation.

72112 Casino Hotels
See industry description for 721120 below.

721120 Casino Hotels

This industry comprises establishments primarily engaged in providing short-term lodging in hotel facilities with a casino on the premises. The casino on premises includes table wagering games and may include other gambling activities, such as slot machines and sports betting. These establishments generally offer a range of services and amenities, such as food and beverage services, entertainment, valet parking, swimming pools, and conference and convention facilities.

Cross-References. Establishments primarily engaged in—

- Providing short-term lodging in facilities known as hotels and motels that provide limited gambling activities, such as slot machines, without a casino on the premises—are classified in Industry 721110, Hotels (except Casino Hotels) and Motels; and

- Operating as stand-alone casinos—are classified in Industry 713210, Casinos (except Casino Hotels).

72119 Other Traveler Accommodation

This industry comprises establishments primarily engaged in providing short-term lodging (except hotels, motels, and casino hotels).

US—United States industry only. CAN—United States and Canadian industries are comparable. MEX—United States and Mexican industries are comparable. Blank—Canadian, Mexican, and United States industries are comparable.

Illustrative Examples:

Bed-and-breakfast inns	Tourist homes
Guest houses	Youth hostels
Housekeeping cabins and cottages	

Cross-References. Establishments primarily engaged in—

- Providing short-term lodging in facilities known as hotels without a casino on the premises—are classified in Industry 72111, Hotels (except Casino Hotels) and Motels; and

- Providing short-term lodging in facilities known as hotels with a casino on the premises—are classified in Industry 72112, Casino Hotels.

721191 Bed-and-Breakfast Inns[CAN]

This U.S. industry comprises establishments primarily engaged in providing short-term lodging in facilities known as bed-and-breakfast inns. These establishments provide short-term lodging in private homes or small buildings converted for this purpose. Bed-and-breakfast inns are characterized by a highly personalized service and inclusion of a full breakfast in a room rate.

721199 All Other Traveler Accommodation[US]

This U.S. industry comprises establishments primarily engaged in providing short-term lodging (except hotels, motels, casino hotels, and bed-and-breakfast inns).

Illustrative Examples:

Guest houses	Tourist homes
Housekeeping cabins and cottages	Youth hostels

Cross-References. Establishments primarily engaged in—

- Providing short-term lodging in facilities known as hotels without a casino on the premises—are classified in Industry 721110, Hotels (except Casino Hotels) and Motels;

- Providing short-term lodging in facilities known as hotels with a casino on the premises—are classified in Industry 721120, Casino Hotels; and

- Providing short-term lodging in establishments known as bed-and-breakfast inns—are classified in U.S. Industry 721191, Bed-and-Breakfast Inns.

7212 RV (Recreational Vehicle) Parks and Recreational Camps

72121 RV (Recreational Vehicle) Parks and Recreational Camps

This industry comprises establishments primarily engaged in operating recreational vehicle parks and campgrounds and recreational and vacation camps. These establishments cater to outdoor enthusiasts and are characterized by the type of accommodation and by the nature and the range of recreational facilities and activities provided to their clients.

Illustrative Examples:

Fishing and hunting camps	Travel trailer campsites
Outdoor adventure retreats	Vacation camps (except instructional,
Recreational vehicle parks	day)

Cross-References. Establishments primarily engaged in—

- Operating recreational facilities without accommodations—are classified in Subsector 713, Amusement, Gambling, and Recreation Industries;
- Operating instructional camps, such as sports camps, fine arts camps, and computer camps—are classified in Sector 61, Educational Services, based on the nature of instruction;
- Operating children's day camps (except instructional)—are classified in Industry 71399, All Other Amusement and Recreation Industries; and
- Acting as lessors of residential mobile home sites (i.e., trailer parks)—are classified in Industry 53119, Lessors of Other Real Estate Property.

721211 RV (Recreational Vehicle) Parks and Campgrounds[CAN]

This U.S. industry comprises establishments primarily engaged in operating sites to accommodate campers and their equipment, including tents, tent trailers, travel trailers, and RVs (recreational vehicles). These establishments may provide access to facilities, such as washrooms, laundry rooms, recreation halls and playgrounds, stores, and snack bars.

Cross-References. Establishments primarily engaged in—

- Operating recreational facilities without accommodations—are classified in Subsector 713, Amusement, Gambling, and Recreation Industries; and
- Acting as lessors of residential mobile home sites (i.e., trailer parks)—are classified in Industry 531190, Lessors of Other Real Estate Property.

US—United States industry only. CAN—United States and Canadian industries are comparable. MEX—United States and Mexican industries are comparable. Blank—Canadian, Mexican, and United States industries are comparable.

721214 Recreational and Vacation Camps (except Campgrounds)[US]

This U.S. industry comprises establishments primarily engaged in operating overnight recreational camps, such as children's camps, family vacation camps, hunting and fishing camps, and outdoor adventure retreats that offer trail riding, white-water rafting, hiking, and similar activities. These establishments provide accommodation facilities, such as cabins and fixed campsites, and other amenities, such as food services, recreational facilities and equipment, and organized recreational activities.

Illustrative Examples:

Fishing camps
Hunting camps
Outdoor adventure retreats

Vacation camps (except instructional, day)
Wilderness camps

Cross-References. Establishments primarily engaged in—

- Operating instructional camps, such as sports camps, fine arts camps, and computer camps—are classified in Sector 61, Educational Services, based on the nature of instruction; and

- Operating children's day camps (except instructional)—are classified in Industry 713990, All Other Amusement and Recreation Industries.

7213 Rooming and Boarding Houses

72131 Rooming and Boarding Houses
See industry description for 721310 below.

721310 Rooming and Boarding Houses[CAN]

This industry comprises establishments primarily engaged in operating rooming and boarding houses and similar facilities, such as fraternity houses, sorority houses, off-campus dormitories, residential clubs, and workers' camps. These establishments provide temporary or longer-term accommodations which, for the period of occupancy, may serve as a principal residence. These establishments also may provide complementary services, such as housekeeping, meals, and laundry services.

Illustrative Examples:

Dormitories (off campus)
Fraternity houses
Rooming houses

Sorority houses
Workers' camps

US—United States industry only. CAN—United States and Canadian industries are comparable. MEX—United States and Mexican industries are comparable. Blank—Canadian, Mexican, and United States industries are comparable.

722 Food Services and Drinking Places

Industries in the Food Services and Drinking Places subsector prepare meals, snacks, and beverages to customer order for immediate on-premises and off-premises consumption. There is a wide range of establishments in these industries. Some provide food and drink only; while others provide various combinations of seating space, waiter/waitress services and incidental amenities, such as limited entertainment. The industries in the subsector are grouped based on the type and level of services provided. The industry groups are full-service restaurants; limited-service eating places; special food services, such as food service contractors, caterers, and mobile food services; and drinking places.

Food services and drink activities at hotels and motels; amusement parks, theaters, casinos, country clubs, and similar recreational facilities; and civic and social organizations are included in this subsector only if these services are provided by a separate establishment primarily engaged in providing food and beverage services.

Excluded from this subsector are establishments operating dinner cruises. These establishments are classified in Subsector 487, Scenic and Sightseeing Transportation because those establishments utilize transportation equipment to provide scenic recreational entertainment.

7221 Full-Service Restaurants

This industry group comprises establishments primarily engaged in providing food services to patrons who order and are served while seated (i.e., waiter/waitress service) and pay after eating. Establishments that provide these types of food services to patrons with any combination of other services, such as takeout services, are classified in this industry.

72211 Full-Service Restaurants
See industry description for 722110 below.

722110 Full-Service Restaurants^{CAN}

This industry comprises establishments primarily engaged in providing food services to patrons who order and are served while seated (i.e. waiter/waitress service) and pay after eating. These establishments may provide this type of food services to patrons in combination with selling alcoholic beverages, providing carry out services, or presenting live nontheatrical entertainment.

Cross-References. Establishments primarily engaged in—

- Providing food services where patrons generally order or select items and pay before eating—are classified in U.S. Industry 722211, Limited-Service Restaurants;

US—United States industry only. CAN—United States and Canadian industries are comparable. MEX—United States and Mexican industries are comparable. Blank—Canadian, Mexican, and United States industries are comparable.

- Selling a specialty snack or nonalcoholic beverage for consumption on or near the premises—are classified in U.S. Industry 722213, Snack and Nonalcoholic Beverage Bars;

- Preparing and serving alcoholic beverages and known as bars, taverns, or nightclubs—are classified in Industry 722410, Drinking Places (Alcoholic Beverages); and

- Presenting live theatrical productions and providing food and beverages for consumption on the premises—are classified in Industry 711110, Theater Companies and Dinner Theaters.

7222 Limited-Service Eating Places

This industry group comprises establishments primarily engaged in providing food services where patrons generally order or select items and pay before eating. Most establishments do not have waiter/waitress service, but some provide limited service, such as cooking to order (i.e., per special request), bringing food to seated customers, or providing off-site delivery.

72221 Limited-Service Eating Places

This industry comprises establishments primarily engaged in (1) providing food services where patrons generally order or select items and pay before eating or (2) selling a specialty snack or nonalcoholic beverage for consumption on or near the premises. Food and drink may be consumed on the premises, taken out, or delivered to the customer's location. Some establishments (except snack and nonalcoholic beverage bars) in this industry may provide these food services in combination with selling alcoholic beverages.

Illustrative Examples:

Cafeterias
Fast-food restaurants
Nonalcoholic beverage bars
Pizza delivery establishments

Snack bars (e.g., cookies, pretzels, popcorn)
Takeout eating places

Cross-References. Establishments primarily engaged in—

- Providing food services to patrons who order and are served while seated and pay after eating in combination with providing takeout service—are classified in Industry 72211, Full-Service Restaurants;

- Retailing confectionery goods and nuts not packaged for immediate consumption—are classified in Industry 44529, Other Specialty Food Stores;

- Retailing baked goods (e.g., pretzels, doughnuts, cookies, and bagels) not baked on the premises and not for immediate consumption—are classified in Industry 44529, Other Specialty Food Stores;

- Retailing baked goods (e.g., doughnuts and bagels) and providing food services to patrons who order and are served while seated and pay after eating—are classified in Industry 72211, Full-Service Restaurants;

- Selling snacks and nonalcoholic beverages from mobile vehicles—are classified in Industry 72233, Mobile Food Services; and

- Preparing and serving alcoholic beverages and known as bars, taverns, or nightclubs—are classified in Industry 72241, Drinking Places (Alcoholic Beverages).

722211 Limited-Service Restaurants[US]

This U.S. industry comprises establishments primarily engaged in providing food services (except snack and nonalcoholic beverage bars) where patrons generally order or select items and pay before eating. Food and drink may be consumed on premises, taken out, or delivered to the customer's location. Some establishments in this industry may provide these food services in combination with selling alcoholic beverages.

Illustrative Examples:

Delicatessen restaurants	Pizza delivery shops
Family restaurants, limited service	Takeout eating places
Fast-food restaurants	Takeout sandwich shops
Limited-service pizza parlors	

Cross-References. Establishments primarily engaged in—

- Preparing and serving meals for immediate consumption using cafeteria—style serving equipment, known as cafeterias—are classified in U.S. Industry 722212, Cafeterias;

- Providing food services to patrons who order and are served while seated and pay after eating—are classified in Industry 722110, Full-Service Restaurants;

- Selling a specialty snack (e.g., ice cream, frozen yogurt, candy, cookies) or nonalcoholic beverages, for consumption on or near the premises—are classified in U.S. Industry 722213, Snack and Nonalcoholic Beverage Bars;

- Retailing confectionery goods and nuts not packaged for immediate consumption—are classified in U.S. Industry 445292, Confectionery and Nut Stores;

- Retailing baked goods (e.g., pretzels, doughnuts, cookies, and bagels) not baked on the premises and not for immediate consumption—are classified in U.S. Industry 445291, Baked Goods Stores;
- Preparing and serving alcoholic beverages, known as bars, taverns, or night-clubs—are classified in Industry 722410, Drinking Places (Alcoholic Beverages); and
- Selling baked goods (e.g., doughnuts and bagels) and providing food services to patrons who order and are served while seated and pay after eating—are classified in Industry 722110, Full-Service Restaurants.

722212 Cafeterias[US]

This U.S. industry comprises establishments, known as cafeterias, primarily engaged in preparing and serving meals for immediate consumption using cafeteria-style serving equipment, such as steam tables, a refrigerated area, and self-service nonalcoholic beverage dispensing equipment. Patrons select from food and drink items on display in a continuous cafeteria line.

Cross-References. Establishments primarily engaged in—

- Providing food services to patrons who order and are served while seated and pay after eating—are classified in Industry 722110, Full-Service Restaurants; and
- Providing food services where patrons generally order or select items and pay before eating—are classified in U.S. Industry 722211, Limited-Service Restaurants.

722213 Snack and Nonalcoholic Beverage Bars[US]

This U.S. industry comprises establishments primarily engaged in (1) preparing and/or serving a specialty snack, such as ice cream, frozen yogurt, cookies, or popcorn or (2) serving nonalcoholic beverages, such as coffee, juices, or sodas for consumption on or near the premises. These establishments may carry and sell a combination of snack, nonalcoholic beverage, and other related products (e.g., coffee beans, mugs, coffee makers) but generally promote and sell a unique snack or nonalcoholic beverage.

Illustrative Examples:

Beverage bars
Carryout service bagel shops with on-premises baking
Carryout service cookie shops with on-premises baking

Carryout service donut shops with on-premises baking
Carryout service pretzel shops with on-premises baking
Ice cream parlors

US—United States industry only. CAN—United States and Canadian industries are comparable. MEX—United States and Mexican industries are comparable. Blank—Canadian, Mexican, and United States industries are comparable.

Cross-References. Establishments primarily engaged in—

- Selling one or more of the following food specialties: hamburgers, hot dogs, pizza, chicken, specialty cuisines—are classified in U.S. Industry 722211, Limited-Service Restaurants or Industry 722110, Full-Service Restaurants, based on type of food services provided to patrons;

- Preparing and serving snacks and nonalcoholic beverages from mobile vehicles—are classified in Industry 722330, Mobile Food Services;

- Retailing confectionery goods and nuts not packaged for immediate consumption—are classified in U.S. Industry 445292, Confectionery and Nut Stores;

- Retailing baked goods (e.g., pretzels, doughnuts, cookies, and bagels) not baked on the premises and not for immediate consumption—are classified in U.S. Industry 445291, Baked Goods Stores; and

- Retailing baked goods (e.g., doughnuts and bagels) and providing food services to patrons who order and are served while seated and pay after eating—are classified in Industry 722110, Full-Service Restaurants.

7223 Special Food Services

This industry group comprises establishments primarily engaged in providing food services at one or more of the following: (1) the customer's location; (2) a location designated by the customer; or (3) from motorized vehicles or nonmotorized carts.

72231 Food Service Contractors
See industry description for 722310 below.

722310 Food Service Contractors

This industry comprises establishments primarily engaged in providing food services at institutional, governmental, commercial, or industrial locations of others based on contractual arrangements with these type of organizations for a specified period of time. The establishments of this industry provide food services for the convenience of the contracting organization or the contracting organization's customers. The contractual arrangement of these establishments with contracting organizations may vary from type of facility operated (e.g., cafeteria, restaurant, fast-food eating place), revenue sharing, cost structure, to providing personnel. Management staff is always provided by the food service contractors.

US—United States industry only. CAN—United States and Canadian industries are comparable. MEX—United States and Mexican industries are comparable. Blank—Canadian, Mexican, and United States industries are comparable.

Illustrative Examples:

Airline food service contractors

Cafeteria food service contractors (e.g., at schools, hospitals, government offices)

Food concession contractors (e.g., at sporting, entertainment, convention facilities)

Cross-References. Establishments primarily engaged in—

- Providing food services on a single-event basis—are classified in Industry 722320, Caterers; and

- Supplying and servicing food vending machines—are classified in Industry 454210, Vending Machine Operators.

72232 Caterers

See industry description for 722320 below.

722320 Caterers

This industry comprises establishments primarily engaged in providing single event-based food services. These establishments generally have equipment and vehicles to transport meals and snacks to events and/or prepare food at an off-premise site. Banquet halls with catering staff are included in this industry. Examples of events catered by establishments in this industry are graduation parties, wedding receptions, business or retirement luncheons, and trade shows.

Cross-References. Establishments primarily engaged in—

- Preparing and serving meals and snacks for immediate consumption from motorized vehicles or nonmotorized carts—are classified in Industry 722330, Mobile Food Services;

- Providing food services at institutional, governmental, commercial, or industrial locations of others (e.g., airline contractors, industrial caterers) or providing food services based on contractual arrangements for a specified period of time—are classified in Industry 722310, Food Service Contractors; and

- Renting out facilities without providing catering staff—are classified in Industry 531120, Lessors of Nonresidential Buildings (except Miniwarehouses).

72233 Mobile Food Services

See industry description for 722330 below.

US—United States industry only. CAN—United States and Canadian industries are comparable. MEX—United States and Mexican industries are comparable. Blank—Canadian, Mexican, and United States industries are comparable.

722330 Mobile Food Services

This industry comprises establishments primarily engaged in preparing and serving meals and snacks for immediate consumption from motorized vehicles or nonmotorized carts. The establishment is the central location from which the caterer route is serviced, not each vehicle or cart. Included in this industry are establishments primarily engaged in providing food services from vehicles, such as hot dog carts, and ice cream trucks.

Illustrative Examples:

Ice cream truck vendors   Mobile food concession stands
Mobile canteens   Mobile refreshment stands
Mobile food carts   Mobile snack stand

Cross-References. Establishments primarily engaged in—

- Providing food services where patrons generally order or select items and pay before eating—are classified in U.S. Industry 722211, Limited-Service Restaurants;

- Selling unprepared foods, such as vegetables, melons, and nuts or fruit from carts—are classified in Industry 454390, Other Direct Selling Establishments;

- Selling specialty snacks (e.g., ice cream, frozen yogurt, cookies, popcorn) or nonalcoholic beverages in nonmobile facilities for consumption on or near the premises—are classified in U.S. Industry 722213, Snack and Nonalcoholic Beverage Bars;

- Selling food specialties, such as hamburgers, hot dogs, chicken, pizza, or specialty cuisines from nonmobile facilities—are classified in U.S. Industry 722211, Limited-Service Restaurants or Industry 722110, Full-Service Restaurants based on type of food services provided to patrons; and

- Operating as street vendors (except food)—are classified in Industry 454390, Other Direct Selling Establishments.

7224 Drinking Places (Alcoholic Beverages)

This industry group comprises establishments primarily engaged in preparing and serving alcoholic beverages for immediate consumption.

72241 Drinking Places (Alcoholic Beverages)

See industry description for 722410 below.

US—United States industry only. CAN—United States and Canadian industries are comparable. MEX—United States and Mexican industries are comparable. Blank—Canadian, Mexican, and United States industries are comparable.

722410 Drinking Places (Alcoholic Beverages)^{CAN}

This industry comprises establishments known as bars, taverns, nightclubs, or drinking places primarily engaged in preparing and serving alcoholic beverages for immediate consumption. These establishments may also provide limited food services.

Cross-References. Establishments primarily engaged in—

- Preparing and serving alcoholic beverages (i.e. not known as bars or taverns) and providing food services to patrons who order and are served while seated and pay after eating—are classified in Industry 722110, Full-Service Restaurants

- Preparing and serving alcoholic beverages (i.e. not known as bars or taverns) and providing food services to patrons who generally order or select items and pay before eating—are classified in Industry 722211, Limited-Service Restaurants

- Operating a civic or social association with a bar for the association members—are classified in Industry 81341, Civic and Social Organizations;

- Retailing packaged alcoholic beverages not for immediate consumption on the premises—are classified in Industry 445310, Beer, Wine, and Liquor Stores; and

- Operating discotheques or dance clubs without selling alcoholic beverages—are classified in Industry 713990, All Other Amusement and Recreation Industries.

Sector 81—Other Services (except Public Administration)

The Sector as a Whole

The Other Services (except Public Administration) sector comprises establishments engaged in providing services not specifically provided for elsewhere in the classification system. Establishments in this sector are primarily engaged in activities, such as equipment and machinery repairing, promoting or administering religious activities, grantmaking, advocacy, and providing drycleaning and laundry services, personal care services, death care services, pet care services, photofinishing services, temporary parking services, and dating services.

Private households that engage in employing workers on or about the premises in activities primarily concerned with the operation of the household are included in this sector.

Excluded from this sector are establishments primarily engaged in retailing new equipment and also performing repairs and general maintenance on equipment. These establishments are classified in Sector 44-45, Retail Trade.

811 Repair and Maintenance

Industries in the Repair and Maintenance subsector restore machinery, equipment, and other products to working order. These establishments also typically provide general or routine maintenance (i.e., servicing) on such products to ensure they work efficiently and to prevent breakdown and unnecessary repairs.

The NAICS structure for this subsector brings together most types of repair and maintenance establishments and categorizes them based on production processes (i.e., on the type of repair and maintenance activity performed, and the necessary skills, expertise, and processes that are found in different repair and maintenance establishments). This NAICS classification does not delineate between repair services provided to businesses versus those that serve households. Although some industries primarily serve either businesses or households, separation by class of customer is limited by the fact that many establishments serve both. Establishments repairing computers and consumer electronics products are two examples of such overlap.

The Repair and Maintenance subsector does not include all establishments that do repair and maintenance. For example, a substantial amount of repair is done by establishments that also manufacture machinery, equipment, and other goods. These establishments are included in the Manufacturing sector in NAICS. In addition, repair of transportation equipment is often provided by or based at transportation facilities, such as airports, seaports, and these activities are included

US—United States industry only. CAN—United States and Canadian industries are comparable. MEX—United States and Mexican industries are comparable. Blank—Canadian, Mexican, and United States industries are comparable.

in the Transportation and Warehousing sector. A particularly unique situation exists with repair of buildings. Plumbing, electrical installation and repair, painting and decorating, and other construction-related establishments are often involved in performing installation or other work on new construction as well as providing repair services on existing structures. While some specialize in repair, it is difficult to distinguish between the two types and all have been included in the Construction sector.

Excluded from this subsector are establishments primarily engaged in rebuilding or remanufacturing machinery and equipment. These are classified in Sector 31-33, Manufacturing. Also excluded are retail establishments that provide after-sale services and repair. These are classified in Sector 44-45, Retail Trade.

8111 Automotive Repair and Maintenance

This industry group comprises establishments involved in providing repair and maintenance services for automotive vehicles, such as passenger cars, trucks, and vans, and all trailers. Establishments in this industry group employ mechanics with specialized technical skills to diagnose and repair the mechanical and electrical systems for automotive vehicles, repair automotive interiors, and paint or repair automotive exteriors.

81111 Automotive Mechanical and Electrical Repair and Maintenance

This industry comprises establishments primarily engaged in providing mechanical or electrical repair and maintenance services for automotive vehicles, such as passenger cars, trucks and vans, and all trailers. These establishments specialize in or may provide a wide range of these services.

Cross-References. Establishments primarily engaged in—

- Retailing automotive vehicles and automotive parts and accessories and also providing automotive repair services—are classified in Subsector 441, Motor Vehicle and Parts Dealers;

- Retailing motor fuels and also providing automotive vehicle repair services—are classified in Industry Group 4471, Gasoline Stations;

- Changing motor oil and lubricating the chassis of automotive vehicles—are classified in Industry 81119, Other Automotive Repair and Maintenance;

- Providing automotive vehicle air-conditioning repair—are classified in Industry 81119, Other Automotive Repair and Maintenance; and

- Motorcycle repair and maintenance services—are classified in Industry 81149, Other Personal and Household Goods Repair and Maintenance.

US—United States industry only. CAN—United States and Canadian industries are comparable. MEX—United States and Mexican industries are comparable. Blank—Canadian, Mexican, and United States industries are comparable.

811111 General Automotive Repair[CAN]

This U.S. industry comprises establishments primarily engaged in providing (1) a wide range of mechanical and electrical repair and maintenance services for automotive vehicles, such as passenger cars, trucks, and vans, and all trailers or (2) engine repair and replacement.

Illustrative Examples:

Automobile repair garages (except gasoline service stations)

Automotive engine repair and replacement shops

General automotive repair shops

Cross-References. Establishments primarily engaged in—

- Retailing new automotive parts and accessories and also providing automotive repair services—are classified in Industry 441310, Automotive Parts and Accessories Stores;
- Changing motor oil and lubricating the chassis of automotive vehicles— are classified in U.S. Industry 811191, Automotive Oil Change and Lubrication Shops;
- Replacing and repairing automotive vehicle exhaust systems—are classified in U.S. Industry 811112, Automotive Exhaust System Repair;
- Replacing and repairing automotive vehicle transmissions—are classified in U.S. Industry 811113, Automotive Transmission Repair;
- Retailing motor fuels and also providing automotive vehicle repair services—are classified in Industry Group 4471, Gasoline Stations;
- Retailing automobiles and light trucks for highway use and also providing automotive repair services—are classified in Industry Group 4411, Automobile Dealers; and
- Motorcycle repair and maintenance services—are classified in Industry 811490, Other Personal and Household Goods Repair and Maintenance.

811112 Automotive Exhaust System Repair[CAN]

This U.S. industry comprises establishments primarily engaged in replacing or repairing exhaust systems of automotive vehicles, such as passenger cars, trucks, and vans.

Illustrative Examples:

Automotive exhaust system replacement and repair shops

Automotive muffler replacement and repair shops

US—United States industry only. CAN—United States and Canadian industries are comparable. MEX—United States and Mexican industries are comparable. Blank—Canadian, Mexican, and United States industries are comparable.

Cross-References.

Establishments primarily engaged in motorcycle repair and maintenance services are classified in Industry 811490, Other Personal and Household Goods Repair and Maintenance.

811113 Automotive Transmission Repair[US]

This U.S. industry comprises establishments primarily engaged in replacing or repairing transmissions of automotive vehicles, such as passenger cars, trucks, and vans.

Cross-References.

Establishments primarily engaged in motorcycle repair and maintenance services are classified in Industry 811490, Other Personal and Household Goods Repair and Maintenance.

811118 Other Automotive Mechanical and Electrical Repair and Maintenance[US]

This U.S. industry comprises establishments primarily engaged in providing specialized mechanical or electrical repair and maintenance services (except engine repair and replacement, exhaust systems repair, and transmission repair) for automotive vehicles, such as passenger cars, trucks, and vans, and all trailers.

Illustrative Examples:

Automotive brake repair shops	Automotive radiator repair shops
Automotive electrical repair shops	Automotive tune-up shops

Cross-References. Establishments primarily engaged in—

- Providing a wide range of mechanical and electrical automotive vehicle repair or specializing in engine repair or replacement—are classified in U.S. Industry 811111, General Automotive Repair;

- Replacing and repairing automotive vehicle exhaust systems—are classified in U.S. Industry 811112, Automotive Exhaust System Repair;

- Replacing and repairing automotive vehicle transmissions—are classified in U.S. Industry 811113, Automotive Transmission Repair;

- Providing automotive vehicle air-conditioning repair—are classified in U.S. Industry 811198, All Other Automotive Repair and Maintenance; and

- Motorcycle repair and maintenance services—are classified in Industry 811490, Other Personal and Household Goods Repair and Maintenance.

US—United States industry only. CAN—United States and Canadian industries are comparable. MEX—United States and Mexican industries are comparable. Blank—Canadian, Mexican, and United States industries are comparable.

81112 Automotive Body, Paint, Interior, and Glass Repair

This industry comprises establishments primarily engaged in providing one or more of the following: (1) repairing or customizing automotive vehicles, such as passenger cars, trucks, and vans, and all trailer bodies and interiors; (2) painting automotive vehicle and trailer bodies; (3) replacing, repairing, and/or tinting automotive vehicle glass; and (4) customizing automobile, truck, and van interiors for the physically disabled or other customers with special requirements.

Illustrative Examples:

Automotive body shops
Automotive glass shops

Automotive paint shops

Cross-References. Establishments primarily engaged in—

- Manufacturing automotive vehicles and trailers or customizing these vehicles on an assembly-line basis—are classified in Subsector 336, Transportation Equipment Manufacturing;

- Motorcycle repair and maintenance services—are classified in Industry 81149, Other Personal and Household Goods Repair and Maintenance.

811121 Automotive Body, Paint, and Interior Repair and Maintenance[CAN]

This U.S. industry comprises establishments primarily engaged in repairing or customizing automotive vehicles, such as passenger cars, trucks, and vans, and all trailer bodies and interiors; and/or painting automotive vehicles and trailer bodies.

Illustrative Examples:

Automotive body shops
Automotive paint shops

Automotive upholstery shops

Cross-References. Establishments primarily engaged in—

- Automotive glass replacement, repair and/or tinting—are classified in U.S. Industry 811122, Automotive Glass Replacement Shops;

- Manufacturing automotive vehicles and trailers or customizing these vehicles on an assembly-line basis—are classified in Subsector 336, Transportation Equipment Manufacturing; and

- Motorcycle repair and maintenance services—are classified in Industry 811490, Other Personal and Household Goods Repair and Maintenance.

811122 Automotive Glass Replacement Shops[CAN]

This U.S. industry comprises establishments primarily engaged in replacing, repairing, and/or tinting automotive vehicle, such as passenger car, truck, and van, glass.

Cross-References.

Establishments primarily engaged in motorcycle repair and maintenance service are classified in Industry 811490, Other Personal and Household Goods Repair and Maintenance.

81119 Other Automotive Repair and Maintenance

This industry comprises establishments primarily engaged in providing automotive repair and maintenance services (except mechanical and electrical repair and maintenance; transmission repair; and body, paint, interior, and glass repair) for automotive vehicles, such as passenger cars, trucks, and vans, and all trailers.

Illustrative Examples:

Automotive air-conditioning repair shops
Automotive oil change and lubrication
  shops
Automotive rustproofing and
  undercoating shops

Automotive tire repair shops
Car washes

Cross-References. Establishments primarily engaged in—

- Tire retreading or recapping—are classified in Industry 32621, Tire Manufacturing;
- Automotive vehicle mechanical and electrical repair and maintenance—are classified in Industry 81111, Automotive Mechanical and Electrical Repair and Maintenance;
- Automotive body, paint, interior, and glass repair—are classified in Industry 81112, Automotive Body, Paint, Interior, and Glass Repair; and
- Motorcycle repair and maintenance services—are classified in Industry 81149, Other Personal and Household Goods Repair and Maintenance.

811191 Automotive Oil Change and Lubrication Shops[US]

This U.S. industry comprises establishments primarily engaged in changing motor oil and lubricating the chassis of automotive vehicles, such as passenger cars, trucks, and vans.

Cross-References.

Establishments primarily engaged in motorcycle repair and maintenance services are classified in Industry 811490, Other Personal and Household Goods Repair and Maintenance.

811192 Car Washes[CAN]

This U.S. industry comprises establishments primarily engaged in cleaning, washing, and/or waxing automotive vehicles, such as passenger cars, trucks, and vans, and trailers.

Illustrative Examples:

Automotive detail shops
Car washes

Mobile car and truck washes

811198 All Other Automotive Repair and Maintenance[US]

This U.S. industry comprises establishments primarily engaged in providing automotive repair and maintenance services (except mechanical and electrical repair and maintenance; body, paint, interior, and glass repair; motor oil change and lubrication; and car washing) for automotive vehicles, such as passenger cars, trucks, and vans, and all trailers.

Illustrative Examples:

Automotive air-conditioning repair shops
Automotive tire repair (except retreading) shops

Automotive rustproofing and undercoating shops

Cross-References. Establishments primarily engaged in—

- Tire retreading or recapping—are classified in U.S. Industry 326212, Tire Retreading;

- Providing a range of mechanical and electrical automotive vehicle repair or specializing in engine repair or replacement—are classified in U.S. Industry 811111, General Automotive Repair;

- Replacing and repairing automotive vehicle exhaust systems—are classified in U.S. Industry 811112, Automotive Exhaust System Repair;

- Replacing and repairing automotive vehicle transmissions—are classified in U.S. Industry 811113, Automotive Transmission Repair;

- Repairing or customizing automotive vehicle bodies and interiors—are classified in U.S. Industry 811121, Automotive Body, Paint, and Interior Repair and Maintenance;
- Replacing, repairing, and/or tinting automotive glass—are classified in U.S. Industry 811122, Automotive Glass Replacement Shops;
- Changing motor oil and lubricating the chassis of automotive vehicles—are classified in U.S. Industry 811191, Automotive Oil Change and Lubrication Shops;
- Cleaning, washing, and/or waxing automotive vehicles and trailers—are classified in U.S. Industry 811192, Car Washes;
- Motorcycle repair and maintenance services—are classified in Industry 811490, Other Personal and Household Goods Repair and Maintenance; and
- Retailing and installing audio equipment—are classified in Industry 441310, Automotive Parts and Accessories Stores.

8112 Electronic and Precision Equipment Repair and Maintenance

This industry group comprises establishments primarily engaged in repairing electronic equipment, such as computers and communications equipment, and highly specialized precision instruments. Establishments in this industry group typically have staff skilled in repairing items having complex, electronic components.

81121 Electronic and Precision Equipment Repair and Maintenance

This industry comprises establishments primarily engaged in repairing and maintaining one or more of the following: (1) consumer electronic equipment; (2) computers; (3) office machines; (4) communication equipment; and (5) other electronic and precision equipment and instruments, without retailing these products as new. Establishments in this industry repair items, such as microscopes, radar and sonar equipment, televisions, stereos, video recorders, computers, fax machines, photocopying machines, two-way radios and other communications equipment, scientific instruments, and medical equipment.

Cross-References. Establishments primarily engaged in—

- Installing and monitoring home security systems—are classified in Industry 56162, Security Systems Services;
- Retailing new radios, televisions, and other consumer electronics and also providing repair services—are classified in Industry 44311, Appliance, Television, and Other Electronics Stores;

US—United States industry only. CAN—United States and Canadian industries are comparable. MEX—United States and Mexican industries are comparable. Blank—Canadian, Mexican, and United States industries are comparable.

- Retailing new computers and computer peripherals and also providing repair services—are classified in Industry 44312, Computer and Software Stores; and
- Rewinding armatures and rebuilding electric motors on a factory basis— are classified in Industry 33531, Electrical Equipment Manufacturing.

811211 Consumer Electronics Repair and Maintenance[MEX]

This U.S. industry comprises establishments primarily engaged in repairing and maintaining consumer electronics, such as televisions, stereos, speakers, video recorders, CD players, radios, and cameras, without retailing new consumer electronics.

Cross-References. Establishments primarily engaged in—

- Repairing computers and peripheral equipment—are classified in U.S. Industry 811212, Computer and Office Machine Repair and Maintenance;
- Installing and monitoring home security systems—are classified in U.S. Industry 561621, Security Systems Services (except Locksmiths);
- Retailing new radios, televisions, and other consumer electronics and also providing repair services—are classified in U.S. Industry 443112, Radio, Television, and Other Electronics Stores; and
- Repairing two-way radios—are classified in U.S. Industry 811213, Communication Equipment Repair and Maintenance.

811212 Computer and Office Machine Repair and Maintenance[US]

This U.S. industry comprises establishments primarily engaged in repairing and maintaining computers and office machines without retailing new computers and office machines, such as photocopying machines; and computer terminals, storage devices, printers; and CD-ROM drives.

Cross-References. Establishments primarily engaged in—

- Retailing new computers and computer peripherals and also providing repair services—are classified in Industry 443120, Computer and Software Stores; and
- Repairing and servicing fax machines—are classified in Industry 811213, Communication Equipment Repair and Maintenance.

811213 Communication Equipment Repair and Maintenance[US]

This U.S. industry comprises establishments primarily engaged in repairing and maintaining communications equipment without retailing new communication

---

US—United States industry only. CAN—United States and Canadian industries are comparable. MEX—United States and Mexican industries are comparable. Blank—Canadian, Mexican, and United States industries are comparable.

equipment, such as telephones, fax machines, communications transmission equipment, and two-way radios.

Cross-References. Establishments primarily engaged in—
- Retailing new telephones and also providing repair services—are classified in U.S. Industry 443112, Radio, Television, and Other Electronics Stores; and
- Repairing stereo and other consumer electronic equipment—are classified in U.S. Industry 811211, Consumer Electronics Repair and Maintenance.

811219 Other Electronic and Precision Equipment Repair and Maintenance[US]

This U.S. industry comprises establishments primarily engaged in repairing and maintaining (without retailing) electronic and precision equipment (except consumer electronics, computers and office machines, and communications equipment). Establishments in this industry repair and maintain equipment, such as medical diagnostic imaging equipment, measuring and surveying instruments, laboratory instruments, and radar and sonar equipment.

Cross-References. Establishments primarily engaged in—
- Rewinding armatures and rebuilding electric motors on a factory basis— are classified in U.S. Industry 335312, Motor and Generator Manufacturing;
- Repairing stereo and other consumer electronic equipment—are classified in U.S. Industry 811211, Consumer Electronics Repair and Maintenance;
- Repairing computers and office machines—are classified in U.S. Industry 811212, Computer and Office Machine Repair and Maintenance; and
- Repairing communications equipment—are classified in U.S. Industry 811213, Communication Equipment Repair and Maintenance.

8113 Commercial and Industrial Machinery and Equipment (except Automotive and Electronic) Repair and Maintenance

81131 Commercial and Industrial Machinery and Equipment (except Automotive and Electronic) Repair and Maintenance
See industry description for 811310 below.

811310 Commercial and Industrial Machinery and Equipment (except Automotive and Electronic) Repair and Maintenance[CAN]

This industry comprises establishments primarily engaged in the repair and maintenance of commercial and industrial machinery and equipment. Establishments in this industry either sharpen/install commercial and industrial machinery blades and saws or provide welding (e.g., automotive, general) repair services; or repair agricultural and other heavy and industrial machinery and equipment (e.g., forklifts and other materials handling equipment, machine tools, commercial refrigeration equipment, construction equipment, and mining machinery).

Cross-References. Establishments primarily engaged in—

- Automotive repair (except welding) and maintenance are—classified in Industry Group 8111, Automotive Repair and Maintenance;
- Repairing and maintaining electronic and precision equipment—are classified in Industry 81121, Electronic and Precision Equipment Repair and Maintenance;
- Repairing and servicing aircraft—are classified in Industry 488190, Other Support Activities for Air Transportation;
- Converting, rebuilding, and overhauling aircraft—are classified in Industry 336410, Aerospace Product and Parts Manufacturing;
- Repairing and servicing railroad cars and engines—are classified in Industry 488210, Support Activities for Rail Transportation;
- Rebuilding or remanufacturing railroad engines and cars—are classified in Industry 336510, Railroad Rolling Stock Manufacturing;
- Repairing and overhauling ships at floating dry docks—are classified in Industry 488390, Other Support Activities for Water Transportation;
- Repairing and overhauling ships at shipyards—are classified in U.S. Industry 336611, Ship Building and Repairing;
- Rewinding armatures or rebuilding electric motors on a factory basis—are classified in U.S. Industry 335312, Motor and Generator Manufacturing; and
- Repairing and maintaining home and garden equipment (e.g., sharpening or installing blades and saws)—are classified in Industry 811411, Home and Garden Equipment Repair and Maintenance.

8114 Personal and Household Goods Repair and Maintenance

81141 Home and Garden Equipment and Appliance Repair and Maintenance

This industry comprises establishments primarily engaged in repairing and servicing home and garden equipment and/or household-type appliances without retailing new equipment or appliances. Establishments in this industry repair and maintain items, such as lawnmowers, edgers, snow- and leaf-blowers, washing machines, clothes dryers, and refrigerators.

Cross-References. Establishments primarily engaged in—

- Retailing outdoor power equipment and also providing repair services— are classified in Industry 44421, Outdoor Power Equipment Stores;
- Retailing an array of new appliances and also providing repair services— are classified in Industry 44311, Appliance, Television, and Other Electronics Stores;
- Repairing, servicing, or installing central heating and air-conditioning equipment—are classified in Industry 23822, Plumbing, Heating, and Air-Conditioning Contractors; and
- Repairing commercial refrigeration equipment—are classified in Industry 81131, Commercial and Industrial Machinery and Equipment (except Automotive and Electronic) Repair and Maintenance.

811411 Home and Garden Equipment Repair and Maintenance[CAN]

This U.S. industry comprises establishments primarily engaged in repairing and servicing home and garden equipment without retailing new home and garden equipment, such as lawnmowers, handheld power tools, edgers, snow- and leaf-blowers, and trimmers.

Cross-References.

Establishments primarily engaged in retailing new outdoor power equipment and also providing repair services are classified in Industry 444210, Outdoor Power Equipment Stores.

811412 Appliance Repair and Maintenance[CAN]

This U.S. industry comprises establishments primarily engaged in repairing and servicing household appliances without retailing new appliances, such as refrigerators, stoves, washing machines, clothes dryers, and room air-conditioners.

Cross-References. Establishments primarily engaged in—

- Installing central heating and air-conditioning equipment—are classified in Industry 238220, Plumbing, Heating, and Air-Conditioning Contractors;
- Repairing commercial refrigeration equipment—are classified in Industry 811310, Commercial and Industrial Machinery and Equipment (except Automotive and Electronic) Repair and Maintenance; and

---

US—United States industry only. CAN—United States and Canadian industries are comparable. MEX—United States and Mexican industries are comparable. Blank—Canadian, Mexican, and United States industries are comparable.

- Retailing an array of new appliances and also providing repair services—are classified in U.S. Industry 443111, Household Appliance Stores.

81142 Reupholstery and Furniture Repair
See industry description for 811420 below.

811420 Reupholstery and Furniture Repair

This industry comprises establishments primarily engaged in one or more of the following: (1) reupholstering furniture; (2) refinishing furniture; (3) repairing furniture; and (4) repairing and restoring furniture.

Cross-References. Establishments primarily engaged in—

- Automotive vehicle and trailer upholstery repair—are classified in U.S. Industry 811121, Automotive Body, Paint, and Interior Repair and Maintenance; and
- The restoration of museum pieces—are classified in Industry 711510, Independent Artists, Writers, and Performers.

81143 Footwear and Leather Goods Repair
See industry description for 811430 below.

811430 Footwear and Leather Goods Repair

This industry comprises establishments primarily engaged in repairing footwear and/or repairing other leather or leather-like goods without retailing new footwear and leather or leather-like goods, such as handbags and briefcases.

Cross-References. Establishments primarily engaged in—

- Retailing new luggage and leather goods and also providing repair services—are classified in Industry 448320, Luggage and Leather Goods Stores;
- Shining shoes—are classified in Industry 812990, All Other Personal Services; and
- Repairing leather clothing—are classified in Industry 811490, Other Personal and Household Goods Repair and Maintenance.

81149 Other Personal and Household Goods Repair and Maintenance
See industry description for 811490 below.

US—United States industry only. CAN—United States and Canadian industries are comparable. MEX—United States and Mexican industries are comparable. Blank—Canadian, Mexican, and United States industries are comparable.

811490 Other Personal and Household Goods Repair and Maintenance[CAN]

This industry comprises establishments primarily engaged in repairing and servicing personal or household-type goods without retailing new personal and household-type goods (except home and garden equipment, appliances, furniture, and footwear and leather goods). Establishments in this industry repair items, such as garments; watches; jewelry; musical instruments; bicycles and motorcycles; motorboats, canoes, sailboats, and other recreational boats.

Cross-References. Establishments primarily engaged in—

- Repairing home and garden equipment—are classified in U.S. Industry 811411, Home and Garden Equipment Repair and Maintenance;

- Repairing appliances—are classified in U.S. Industry 811412, Appliance Repair and Maintenance;

- Reupholstering and repairing furniture—are classified in Industry 811420, Reupholstery and Furniture Repair;

- Repairing footwear and leather goods—are classified in Industry 811430, Footwear and Leather Goods Repair;

- Operating marinas and providing a range of other services including boat cleaning and repair—are classified in Industry 713930, Marinas; and

- Drycleaning garments—are classified in Industry Group 8123, Drycleaning and Laundry Services.

812 Personal and Laundry Services

Industries in the Personal and Laundry Services subsector group establishments that provide personal and laundry services to individuals, households, and businesses. Services performed include: personal care services; death care services; laundry and drycleaning services; and a wide range of other personal services, such as pet care (except veterinary) services, photofinishing services, temporary parking services, and dating services.

The Personal and Laundry Services subsector is by no means all-inclusive of the services that could be termed personal services (i.e., those provided to individuals rather than businesses). There are many other subsectors, as well as sectors, that provide services to persons. Establishments providing legal, accounting, tax preparation, architectural, portrait photography, and similar professional services are classified in Sector 54, Professional, Scientific, and Technical Services; those providing job placement, travel arrangement, home security, interior and exterior house cleaning, exterminating, lawn and garden care, and similar support services

---

are classified in Sector 56, **Administrative and Support, Waste Management and Remediation Services**; those providing health and social services are classified in Sector 62, Health Care and Social Assistance; those providing amusement and recreation services are classified in Sector 71, Arts, Entertainment and Recreation; those providing educational instruction are classified in Sector 61, Educational Services; those providing repair services are classified in Subsector 811, Repair and Maintenance; and those providing spiritual, civic, and advocacy services are classified in Subsector 813, Religious, Grantmaking, Civic, Professional, and Similar Organizations.

8121 Personal Care Services[CAN]

This industry group comprises establishments, such as barber and beauty shops, that provide appearance care services to individual consumers.

81211 Hair, Nail, and Skin Care Services[CAN]

This industry comprises establishments primarily engaged in one or more of the following: (1) providing hair care services; (2) providing nail care services; and (3) providing facials or applying makeup (except permanent makeup).

Illustrative Examples:

Barber shops
Beauty salons
Cosmetology salons
Hair stylist shops
Nail salons

Cross-References. Establishments primarily engaged in—

- Offering training in barbering, hair styling, or the cosmetic arts—are classified in Industry 61151, Technical and Trade Schools;

- Providing massage, electrolysis (i.e., hair removal), permanent makeup, or tanning services—are classified in Industry 81219, Other Personal Care Services; and

- Providing medical skin care services (e.g., cosmetic surgery, dermatology)—are classified in Sector 62, Health Care and Social Assistance.

812111 Barber Shops[US]

This U.S. industry comprises establishments known as barber shops or men's hair stylist shops primarily engaged in cutting, trimming, and styling boys' and men's hair; and/or shaving and trimming men's beards.

Cross-References. Establishments primarily engaged in—

- Offering training in barbering—are classified in U.S. Industry 611511, Cosmetology and Barber Schools; and
- Providing hair care services (except establishments known as barber shops or men's hair stylists)—are classified in U.S. Industry 812112, Beauty Salons.

812112 Beauty Salons[US]

This U.S. industry comprises establishments (except those known as barber shops or men's hair stylist shops) primarily engaged in one or more of the following: (1) cutting, trimming, shampooing, weaving, coloring, waving, or styling hair; (2) providing facials; and (3) applying makeup (except permanent makeup).

Illustrative Examples:

Beauty parlors or shops
Combined beauty and barber shops
Cosmetology salons or shops

Facial salons or shops
Hairdressing salons or shops
Unisex or women's hair stylist shops

Cross-References. Establishments primarily engaged in—

- Cutting, trimming, and styling men's and boys' hair (known as barber shops or men's hair stylist shops)—are classified in U.S. Industry 812111, Barber Shops;
- Offering training in hair styling or the cosmetic arts—are classified in U.S. Industry 611511, Cosmetology and Barber Schools;
- Providing nail care services—are classified in U.S. Industry 812113, Nail Salons;
- Providing massage, electrolysis (i.e., hair removal), permanent makeup, or tanning services—are classified in U.S. Industry 812199, All Other Personal Care Services; and
- Providing medical skin care services (e.g., cosmetic surgery, dermatology)—are classified in Sector 62, Health Care and Social Assistance.

812113 Nail Salons[US]

This U.S. industry comprises establishments primarily engaged in providing nail care services, such as manicures, pedicures, and nail extensions.

81219 Other Personal Care Services[CAN]

This industry comprises establishments primarily engaged in providing personal care services (except hair, nail, facial, or nonpermanent makeup services).

US—United States industry only. CAN—United States and Canadian industries are comparable. MEX—United States and Mexican industries are comparable. Blank—Canadian, Mexican, and United States industries are comparable.

Illustrative Examples:

Depilatory or electrolysis (i.e., hair removal) salons

Ear piercing services

Hair replacement (except by offices of physicians) or weaving services

Massage parlors

Nonmedical diet and weight reducing centers

Permanent makeup salons

Steam or turkish baths

Tanning salons

Tattoo parlors

Cross-References. Establishments primarily engaged in—

- Providing hair, nail, facial, or nonpermanent makeup services—are classified in Industry 81211, Hair, Nail, and Skin Care Services;

- Operating physical fitness facilities—are classified in Industry 71394, Fitness and Recreational Sports Centers;

- Operating health resorts and spas that provide lodging—are classified in Industry 72111, Hotels (except Casino Hotels) and Motels; and

- Providing medical or surgical hair replacement or weight reduction—are classified in Sector 62, Health Care and Social Assistance.

812191 Diet and Weight Reducing Centers[US]

This U.S. industry comprises establishments primarily engaged in providing nonmedical services to assist clients in attaining or maintaining a desired weight. The sale of weight reduction products, such as food supplements, may be an integral component of the program. These services typically include individual or group counseling, menu and exercise planning, and weight and body measurement monitoring.

Cross-References. Establishments primarily engaged in—

- Operating physical fitness facilities—are classified in Industry 713940, Fitness and Recreational Sports Centers;

- Operating health resorts and spas that provide lodging—are classified in Industry 721110, Hotels (except Casino Hotels) and Motels; and

- Providing medical or surgical weight reduction—are classified in Sector 62, Health Care and Social Assistance.

812199 Other Personal Care Services[US]

This U.S. industry comprises establishments primarily engaged in providing personal care services (except hair, nail, facial, nonpermanent makeup, or nonmedical diet and weight reducing services).

Illustrative Examples:

Depilatory or electrolysis (i.e., hair removal) salons
Ear piercing services
Hair replacement (except by offices of physicians) or weaving services
Massage parlors
Permanent makeup salons
Saunas
Steam or turkish baths
Tanning salons
Tattoo parlors

Cross-References. Establishments primarily engaged in—

- Cutting, trimming, and styling men's and boys' hair (known as barber shops or men's hair stylist shops)—are classified in U. S. Industry 812111, Barber Shops;

- Providing hair, facial, or nonpermanent makeup services (except establishments known as barber shops or men's hair stylist shops)—are classified in U.S. Industry 812112, Beauty Shops;

- Nail care services—are classified in U.S. Industry 812113, Nail Salons;

- Providing nonmedical diet and weight reducing services—are classified in U.S. Industry 812191, Diet and Weight Reducing Centers; and

- Providing medical or surgical hair replacement or weight reduction services—are classified in Sector 62, Health Care and Social Assistance.

8122 Death Care Services CAN

81221 Funeral Homes and Funeral Services CAN
See industry description for 812210 below.

812210 Funeral Homes and Funeral Services CAN

This industry comprises establishments primarily engaged in preparing the dead for burial or interment and conducting funerals (i.e., providing facilities for wakes, arranging transportation for the dead, selling caskets and related merchandise). Funeral homes combined with crematories are included in this industry.

Cross-References.

Establishments (except funeral homes) primarily engaged in cremating the dead are classified in Industry 812220, Cemeteries and Crematories.

81222 Cemeteries and Crematories CAN
See industry description for 812220 below.

US—United States industry only. CAN—United States and Canadian industries are comparable. MEX—United States and Mexican industries are comparable. Blank—Canadian, Mexican, and United States industries are comparable.

812220 Cemeteries and Crematories^{CAN}

This industry comprises establishments primarily engaged in operating sites or structures reserved for the interment of human or animal remains and/or cremating the dead.

Illustrative Examples:

Cemetery associations (i.e., operators of cemeteries)
Crematories (except combined with funeral homes)
Mausoleums
Memorial gardens (i.e., burial places)
Pet cemeteries

Cross-References.

Crematories combined with funeral homes are classified in Industry 812210, Funeral Homes and Funeral Services.

8123 Drycleaning and Laundry Services^{CAN}

81231 Coin-Operated Laundries and Drycleaners^{CAN}
See industry description for 812310 below.

812310 Coin-Operated Laundries and Drycleaners^{CAN}

This industry comprises (1) establishments primarily engaged in operating facilities with coin-operated or similar self-service laundry and drycleaning equipment for customer use on the premises and (2) establishments primarily engaged in supplying and servicing coin-operated or similar self-service laundry and drycleaning equipment for customer use in places of business operated by others, such as apartments and dormitories.

81232 Drycleaning and Laundry Services (except Coin-Operated)^{CAN}
See industry description for 812320 below.

812320 Drycleaning and Laundry Services (except Coin-Operated)^{CAN}

This industry comprises establishments primarily engaged in one or more of the following: (1) providing drycleaning services (except coin-operated); (2) providing laundering services (except linen and uniform supply or coin-operated); (3) providing dropoff and pickup sites for laundries and/or drycleaners; and

(4) providing specialty cleaning services for specific types of garments and other textile items (except carpets and upholstery), such as fur, leather, or suede garments; wedding gowns; hats; draperies; and pillows. These establishments may provide all, a combination of, or none of the cleaning services on the premises.

Cross-References. Establishments primarily engaged in—

- Supplying laundered linens and uniforms on a rental or contract basis— are classified in Industry 81233, Linen and Uniform Supply;

- Operating coin-operated or similar self-service laundry or drycleaning facilities—are classified in Industry 812310, Coin-Operated Laundries and Drycleaners; and

- Cleaning used carpets and upholstery—are classified in Industry 561740, Carpet and Upholstery Cleaning Services.

81233 Linen and Uniform Supply[CAN]

This industry comprises establishments primarily engaged in supplying, on a rental or contract basis, laundered items, such as uniforms, gowns and coats, table linens, bed linens, towels, clean room apparel, and treated mops or shop towels.

812331 Linen Supply[US]

This U.S. industry comprises establishments primarily engaged in supplying, on a rental or contract basis, laundered items, such as table and bed linens; towels; diapers; and uniforms, gowns, or coats of the type used by doctors, nurses, barbers, beauticians, and waitresses.

Cross-References.

Establishments primarily engaged in supplying, on a rental or contract basis, laundered industrial work uniforms and related work clothing are classified in U.S. Industry 812332, Industrial Launderers.

812332 Industrial Launderers[US]

This U.S. industry comprises establishments primarily engaged in supplying, on a rental or contract basis, laundered industrial work uniforms and related work clothing, such as protective apparel (flame and heat resistant) and clean room apparel; dust control items, such as treated mops, rugs, mats, dust tool covers, cloths, and shop or wiping towels.

US—United States industry only. CAN—United States and Canadian industries are comparable. MEX—United States and Mexican industries are comparable. Blank—Canadian, Mexican, and United States industries are comparable.

Cross-References.

Establishments primarily engaged in supplying, on a rental or contract basis, laundered uniforms, gowns or coats of the type used by doctors, nurses, barbers, beauticians, and waitresses are classified in U.S. Industry 812331, Linen Supply.

8129 Other Personal Services[CAN]

The industry group comprises establishments primarily engaged in providing personal services (except personal care services, death care services, or drycleaning and laundry services).

81291 Pet Care (except Veterinary) Services[CAN]

See industry description for 812910 below.

812910 Pet Care (except Veterinary) Services[CAN]

This industry comprises establishments primarily engaged in providing pet care services (except veterinary), such as boarding, grooming, sitting, and training pets.

Cross-References. Establishments primarily engaged in—

- Practicing veterinary medicine—are classified in Industry 541940, Veterinary Services;

- Boarding horses—are classified in Industry 115210, Support Activities for Animal Production; and

- Transporting pets—are classified in U.S. Industry 485991, Special Needs Transportation.

81292 Photofinishing[CAN]

This industry comprises establishments primarily engaged in developing film and/or making photographic slides, prints, and enlargements.

Cross-References.

Establishments primarily engaged in processing motion picture film for the motion picture and television industries are classified in Industry 51219, Postproduction Services and Other Motion Picture and Video Industries.

812921 Photofinishing Laboratories (except One-Hour)^{CAN}

This U.S. industry comprises establishments (except those known as "one-hour" photofinishing labs) primarily engaged in developing film and/or making photographic slides, prints, and enlargements.

Cross-References.

- Establishments primarily engaged in processing motion picture film for the motion picture and television industries are classified in U.S. Industry 512199, Other Motion Picture and Video Industries; and

- Establishments known as "one-hour" photofinishing labs are classified in U.S. Industry 812922, One-Hour Photofinishing.

812922 One-Hour Photofinishing^{CAN}

This U.S. industry comprises establishments known as "one-hour" photofinishing labs primarily engaged in developing film and/or making photographic slides, prints, and enlargements on a short turnaround or while-you-wait basis.

Cross-References.

Photofinishing laboratories (except those known as "one-hour" photofinishing labs) are classified in U.S. Industry 812921, Photofinishing Laboratories (except One-Hour).

81293 Parking Lots and Garages^{CAN}
See industry description for 812930 below.

812930 Parking Lots and Garages^{CAN}

This industry comprises establishments primarily engaged in providing parking space for motor vehicles, usually on an hourly, daily, or monthly basis and/or valet parking services.

Cross-References.

Establishments primarily engaged in providing extended or dead storage of motor vehicles are classified in Industry 493190, Other Warehousing and Storage.

81299 All Other Personal Services^{CAN}
See industry description for 812990 below.

812990 All Other Personal Services^{CAN}

This industry comprises establishments primarily engaged in providing personal services (except personal care services, death care services, drycleaning and laundry services, pet care services, photofinishing services, or parking space and/or valet parking services).

Illustrative Examples:

Bail bonding or bondsperson services
Coin-operated personal services machine
  (e.g., blood pressure, locker,
  photographic, scale, shoeshine)
  concession operators

Consumer buying services
Dating services
Shoeshine services
Social escort services
Wedding planning services

Cross-References. Establishments primarily engaged in—

- Providing personal care services—are classified in Industry Group 8121, Personal Care Services;

- Providing death care services—are classified in Industry Group 8122, Death Care Services;

- Providing drycleaning and laundry services—are classified in Industry Group 8123, Drycleaning and Laundry Services;

- Providing pet care (except veterinary) services—are classified in Industry 812910, Pet Care (except Veterinary) Services;

- Practicing veterinary medicine—are classified in Industry 541940, Veterinary Services;

- Providing photofinishing services—are classified in Industry 81292, Photofinishing; and

- Providing parking space for motor vehicles and/or valet parking services—are classified in Industry 812930, Parking Lots and Garages.

813 Religious, Grantmaking, Civic, Professional, and Similar Organizations

Industries in the Religious, Grantmaking, Civic, Professional, and Similar Organizations subsector group establishments that organize and promote religious activities; support various causes through grantmaking; advocate various social and political causes; and promote and defend the interests of their members.

The industry groups within the subsector are defined in terms of their activities, such as establishments that provide funding for specific causes or for a variety of charitable causes; establishments that advocate and actively promote causes and beliefs for the public good; and establishments that have an active membership structure to promote causes and represent the interests of their members. Establishments in this subsector may publish newsletters, books, and periodicals for distribution to their membership.

8131 Religious Organizations^{CAN}

81311 Religious Organizations^{CAN}
See industry description for 813110 below.

813110 Religious Organizations^{CAN}

This industry comprises (1) establishments primarily engaged in operating religious organizations, such as churches, religious temples, and monasteries and/or (2) establishments primarily engaged in administering an organized religion or promoting religious activities.

Illustrative Examples:

Churches	Shrines, religious
Monasteries (except schools)	Temples, religious
Mosques, religious	Synagogues

Cross-References.

- Schools, colleges, or universities operated by religious organizations are classified in Sector 61, Educational Services;
- Radio and television stations operated by religious organizations are classified in Subsector 515, Broadcasting (except Internet);
- Publishing houses operated by religious organizations are classified in Subsector 511, Publishing Industries (except Internet);
- Establishments operated by religious organizations primarily engaged in health and social assistance for individuals are classified in Sector 62, Health Care and Social Assistance; and
- Used merchandise stores operated by religious organizations are classified in Industry 453310, Used Merchandise Stores.

8132 Grantmaking and Giving Services^{CAN}

81321 Grantmaking and Giving Services^{CAN}

This industry comprises (1) establishments known as grantmaking foundations or charitable trusts and (2) establishments primarily engaged in raising funds for

---

a wide range of social welfare activities, such as health, educational, scientific, and cultural activities.

Cross-References. Establishments primarily engaged in—

- Providing trust management services for others—are classified in Industry 52392, Portfolio Management;
- Organizing and conducting fundraising campaigns on a contract or fee basis—are classified in Industry 56149, Other Business Support Services;
- Providing telemarketing services for others—are classified in Industry 56142, Telephone Call Centers;
- Raising funds for political purposes—are classified in Industry 81394, Political Organizations;
- Advocating social causes or issues—are classified in Industry 81331, Social Advocacy Organizations; and
- Conducting health research—are classified in Industry 54171, Research and Development in the Physical, Engineering, and Life Sciences.

813211 Grantmaking Foundations[US]

This U.S. industry comprises establishments known as grantmaking foundations or charitable trusts. Establishments in this industry award grants from trust funds based on a competitive selection process or the preferences of the foundation managers and grantors; or fund a single entity, such as a museum or university.

Illustrative Examples:

Community foundations
Corporate foundations, awarding grants
Grantmaking foundations

Philanthropic trusts
Scholarship trusts

Cross-References.

Establishments primarily engaged in providing trust management services for others are classified in Industry 523920, Portfolio Management.

813212 Voluntary Health Organizations[US]

This U.S. industry comprises establishments primarily engaged in raising funds for health related research, such as disease (e.g., heart, cancer, diabetes) prevention, health education, and patient services.

US—United States industry only. CAN—United States and Canadian industries are comparable. MEX—United States and Mexican industries are comparable. Blank—Canadian, Mexican, and United States industries are comparable.

Illustrative Examples:

Disease awareness fundraising organizations

Disease research (e.g., heart, cancer) fundraising organizations

Health research fundraising organizations

Voluntary health organizations

Cross-References.

- Establishments primarily engaged in raising funds for a wide range of social welfare activities, such as educational, scientific, cultural, and health, are classified in U.S. Industry 813219, Other Grantmaking and Giving Services;

- Establishments primarily engaged in organizing and conducting fundraising campaigns on a contract or fee basis are classified in U.S. Industry 561499, All Other Business Support Services;

- Establishments primarily engaged in providing telemarketing services for others are classified in U.S. Industry 561422, Telemarketing Bureaus;

- Establishments known as grantmaking foundations or charitable trusts are classified in U.S. Industry 813211, Grantmaking Foundations; and

- Establishments primarily engaged in conducting health research are classified in Industry 541710, Research and Development in the Physical, Engineering, and Life Sciences.

813219 Other Grantmaking and Giving Services[US]

This U.S. industry comprises establishments (except voluntary health organizations) primarily engaged in raising funds for a wide range of social welfare activities, such as educational, scientific, cultural, and health.

Illustrative Examples:

Community chests

Federated charities

United fund councils

United funds for colleges

Cross-References.

- Establishments primarily engaged in raising funds for health related research are classified in U.S. Industry 813212, Voluntary Health Organizations;

- Establishments known as grantmaking foundations or charitable trusts are classified in U.S. Industry 813211, Grantmaking Foundations;

- Establishments primarily engaged in organizing and conducting fundraising campaigns on a contract or fee basis are classified in U.S. Industry 561499, All Other Business Support Services;

- Establishments primarily engaged in providing telemarketing services for others are classified in U.S. Industry 561422, Telemarketing Bureaus;
- Establishments primarily engaged in raising funds for political purposes are classified in Industry 813940, Political Organizations; and
- Establishments primarily engaged in advocating social causes or issues are classified in Industry 81331, Social Advocacy Organizations.

8133 Social Advocacy Organizations^{CAN}

81331 Social Advocacy Organizations^{CAN}

This industry comprises establishments primarily engaged in promoting a particular cause or working for the realization of a specific social or political goal to benefit a broad or specific constituency. These organizations may solicit contributions and offer memberships to support these goals.

Illustrative Examples:

Conservation advocacy organizations
Community action advocacy
 organizations
Environmental advocacy organizations

Firearms advocacy organizations
Human rights advocacy organizations
Wildlife preservation organizations

Cross-References. Establishments primarily engaged in—

- Promoting the civic and social interests of their members—are classified in Industry 81341, Civic and Social Organizations;
- Promoting the interests of the organized labor and union employees—are classified in Industry 81393, Labor Unions and Similar Labor Organizations; and
- Providing legal services for social advocacy organizations—are classified in Industry Group 5411, Legal Services.

813311 Human Rights Organizations^{US}

This U.S. industry comprises establishments primarily engaged in promoting causes associated with human rights either for a broad or specific constituency. Establishments in this industry address issues, such as protecting and promoting the broad constitutional rights and civil liberties of individuals and those suffering from neglect, abuse, or exploitation; promoting the interests of specific groups, such as children, women, senior citizens, or persons with disabilities; improving relations between racial, ethnic, and cultural groups; and promoting voter education

---

and registration. These organizations may solicit contributions and offer memberships to support these causes.

Illustrative Examples:

Civil liberties organizations   Senior citizens' advocacy organizations
Human rights advocacy organizations   Veterans' rights organizations

Cross-References. Establishments primarily engaged in—

- Promoting the interests of organized labor and union employees—are classified in Industry 813930, Labor Unions and Similar Labor Organizations; and
- Providing legal services for human rights organizations—are classified in Industry Group 5411, Legal Services.

813312 Environment, Conservation and Wildlife Organizations[US]

This U.S. industry comprises establishments primarily engaged in promoting the preservation and protection of the environment and wildlife. Establishments in this industry address issues, such as clean air and water; global warming; conserving and developing natural resources, including land, plant, water, and energy resources; and protecting and preserving wildlife and endangered species. These organizations may solicit contributions and offer memberships to support these causes.

Illustrative Examples:

Animal rights organizations   Natural resource preservation
Conservation advocacy organizations   organizations
Humane societies   Wildlife preservation organizations

Cross-References.

Establishments primarily engaged in providing legal services for environment, conservation, and wildlife organizations are classified in Industry Group 5411, Legal Services.

813319 Other Social Advocacy Organizations[US]

This U.S. industry comprises establishments primarily engaged in social advocacy (except human rights and environmental protection, conservation, and wildlife preservation). Establishments in this industry address issues, such as peace and international understanding; community action (excluding civic organizations); or advancing social causes, such as firearms safety, drunk driving prevention, drug abuse awareness. These organizations may solicit contributions and offer memberships to support these causes.

Illustrative Examples:

Community action advocacy organizations	Substance abuse prevention advocacy organizations
Firearms advocacy organizations	Taxpayers' advocacy organizations
Peace advocacy organizations	

Cross-References. Establishments primarily engaged in—

- Advocating human rights issues—are classified in U.S. Industry 813311, Human Rights Organizations;
- Promoting the preservation and protection of the environment and wildlife—are classified in U.S. Industry 813312, Environment, Conservation and Wildlife Organizations;
- Promoting the civic and social interests of their members—are classified in Industry 813410, Civic and Social Organizations;
- Providing legal services for social advocacy organizations—are classified in Industry Group 5411, Legal Services; and
- Providing community action services, such as community action services agencies—are classified in Industry 624190, Other Individual and Family Services.

8134 Civic and Social Organizations^{CAN}

81341 Civic and Social Organizations^{CAN}
See industry description for 813410 below.

813410 Civic and Social Organizations^{CAN}

This industry comprises establishments primarily engaged in promoting the civic and social interests of their members. Establishments in this industry may operate bars and restaurants for their members.

Illustrative Examples:

Alumni associations	Granges
Automobile clubs (except travel)	Parent-teacher associations
Booster clubs	Scouting organizations
Ethnic associations	Social clubs
Fraternal lodges	Veterans' membership organizations

US—United States industry only. CAN—United States and Canadian industries are comparable. MEX—United States and Mexican industries are comparable. Blank—Canadian, Mexican, and United States industries are comparable.

Cross-References.

- Establishments of insurance offices operated by fraternal benefit organizations are classified in Subsector 524, Insurance Carriers and Related Activities;
- Establishments primarily engaged in operating residential fraternity and sorority houses are classified in Industry 721310, Rooming and Boarding Houses; and
- Establishments primarily engaged in providing travel arrangements and reservation services, such as automobile travel clubs or motor travel clubs are classified in U.S. Industry 561599, All Other Travel Arrangement and Reservation Services.

8139 Business, Professional, Labor, Political, and Similar Organizations[CAN]

This industry group comprises establishments primarily engaged in promoting the interests of their members (except religious organizations, social advocacy organizations, and civic and social organizations). Examples of establishments in this industry are business associations, professional organizations, labor unions, and political organizations.

81391 Business Associations[CAN]

See industry description for 813910 below.

813910 Business Associations[CAN]

This industry comprises establishments primarily engaged in promoting the business interests of their members. These establishments may conduct research on new products and services; develop market statistics; sponsor quality and certification standards; lobby public officials; or publish newsletters, books, or periodicals for distribution to their members.

Illustrative Examples:

Agricultural organizations (except youth farming organizations, farm granges)
Chambers of commerce

Manufacturers' associations
Real estate boards
Trade associations

Cross-References.

- Establishments owned by their members but organized to perform a specific business function, such as common marketing of crops, joint advertising, or buying cooperatives, are classified according to their primary activity;

- Establishments primarily engaged in promoting the professional interests of their members and the profession as a whole are classified in Industry 813920, Professional Organizations;

- Establishments primarily engaged in promoting the interests of organized labor and union employees, such as trade unions, are classified in Industry 813930, Labor Unions and Similar Labor Organizations; and

- Establishments primarily engaged in lobbying public officials (i.e., lobbyists) are classified in Industry 541820, Public Relations Agencies.

81392 Professional Organizations^{CAN}

See industry description for 813920 below.

813920 Professional Organizations^{CAN}

This industry comprises establishments primarily engaged in promoting the professional interests of their members and the profession as a whole. These establishments may conduct research; develop statistics; sponsor quality and certification standards; lobby public officials; or publish newsletters, books, or periodicals for distribution to their members.

Illustrative Examples:

Bar associations
Dentists' associations
Engineers' associations
Health professionals' associations

Learned societies
Peer review boards
Professional standards review boards
Scientists' associations

Cross-References. Establishments primarily engaged in—

- Promoting the business interests of their members—are classified in Industry 813910, Business Associations; and

- Lobbying public officials (i.e., lobbyists)—are classified in Industry 541820, Public Relations Agencies.

81393 Labor Unions and Similar Labor Organizations^{CAN}

See industry description for 813930 below.

813930 Labor Unions and Similar Labor Organizations^{CAN}

This industry comprises establishments primarily engaged in promoting the interests of organized labor and union employees.

81394   Political Organizations^{CAN}

81394   Political Organizations[CAN]
See industry description for 813940 below.

813940   Political Organizations[CAN]

This industry comprises establishments primarily engaged in promoting the interests of national, state, or local political parties or candidates. Included are political groups organized to raise funds for a political party or individual candidates.

Illustrative Examples:

Campaign organizations, political
Political action committees (PACs)
Political campaign organizations

Political organizations or clubs
Political parties

Cross-References. Establishments primarily engaged in—

- Organizing and conducting fundraising campaigns on a contract or fee basis—are classified in U.S. Industry 561499, All Other Business Support Services; and

- Providing telemarketing services for others—are classified in U.S. Industry 561422, Telemarketing Bureaus.

81399   Other Similar Organizations (except Business, Professional, Labor, and Political Organizations)[CAN]
See industry description for 813990 below.

813990   Other Similar Organizations (except Business, Professional, Labor, and Political Organizations)[CAN]

This industry comprises establishments (except religious organizations, social advocacy organizations, civic and social organizations, business associations, professional organizations, labor unions, and political organizations) primarily engaged in promoting the interest of their members.

Illustrative Examples:

Athletic associations, regulatory or administrative
Condominium and homeowners' associations

Cooperative owners' associations
Property owners' associations
Tenant associations (except advocacy)

Cross-References. Establishments primarily engaged in—

- Operating religious organizations, such as churches, religious temples, and monasteries—are classified in Industry 813110, Religious Organizations;

- Raising funds for a wide range of social welfare activities and establishments known as grantmaking foundations or charitable trusts—are classified in Industry 81321, Grantmaking and Giving Services;

- Advocating social causes or issues—are classified in Industry 81331, Social Advocacy Organizations;

- Promoting the civic and social interests of their members—are classified in Industry 813410, Civic and Social Organizations;

- Promoting the business interests of their members—are classified in Industry 813910, Business Associations;

- Promoting the professional interests of their members and the profession as a whole—are classified in Industry 813920, Professional Organizations;

- Promoting the interests of organized labor and union employees—are classified in Industry 813930, Labor Unions and Similar Labor Organizations;

- Promoting the interests of national, state, or local political parties or candidates—are classified in Industry 813940, Political Organizations; and

- Providing recreational and amusement services, such as recreational or youth sports teams and leagues—are classified in Industry 713990, All Other Amusement and Recreation Industries.

814 Private Households

Industries in the Private Households subsector include private households that engage in employing workers on or about the premises in activities primarily concerned with the operation of the household. These private households may employ individuals, such as cooks, maids, and butlers, and outside workers, such as gardeners, caretakers, and other maintenance workers.

8141 Private Households

81411 Private Households
See industry description for 814110 below.

814110 Private Households

This industry comprises private households primarily engaged in employing workers on or about the premises in activities primarily concerned with the operation of the household. These private households may employ individuals, such as cooks, maids, nannies, and butlers, and outside workers, such as gardeners, caretakers, and other maintenance workers.

US—United States industry only. CAN—United States and Canadian industries are comparable. MEX—United States and Mexican industries are comparable. Blank—Canadian, Mexican, and United States industries are comparable.

Sector 92—Public Administration

The Sector as a Whole

The Public Administration sector consists of establishments of federal, state, and local government agencies that administer, oversee, and manage public programs and have executive, legislative, or judicial authority over other institutions within a given area. These agencies also set policy, create laws, adjudicate civil and criminal legal cases, provide for public safety and for national defense. In general, government establishments in the Public Administration sector oversee governmental programs and activities that are not performed by private establishments. Establishments in this sector typically are engaged in the organization and financing of the production of public goods and services, most of which are provided for free or at prices that are not economically significant.

Government establishments also engage in a wide range of productive activities covering not only public goods and services but also individual goods and services similar to those produced in sectors typically identified with private-sector establishments. In general, ownership is not a criterion for classification in NAICS. Therefore, government establishments engaged in the production of private-sector-like goods and services should be classified in the same industry as private-sector establishments engaged in similar activities.

As a practical matter, it is difficult to identify separate establishment detail for many government agencies. To the extent that separate establishment records are available, the administration of governmental programs is classified in Sector 92, Public Administration, while the operation of that same governmental program is classified elsewhere in NAICS based on the activities performed. For example, the governmental administrative authority for an airport is classified in Industry 92612, Regulation and Administration of Transportation Programs, while operating the airport is classified in Industry 48811, Airport Operations. When separate records are not available to distinguish between the administration of a governmental program and the operation of it, the establishment is classified in Sector 92, Public Administration.

Examples of government-provided goods and services that are classified in sectors other than Public Administration include: schools, classified in Sector 61, Educational Services; hospitals, classified in Subsector 622, Hospitals; establishments operating transportation facilities, classified in Sector 48-49, Transportation and Warehousing; the operation of utilities, classified in Sector 22, Utilities; and the Government Printing Office, classified in Subsector 323, Printing and Related Support Activities.

921 Executive, Legislative, and Other General Government Support[US]

The Executive, Legislative, and Other General Government Support subsector groups offices of government executives, legislative bodies, public finance and general government support.

US—United States industry only. CAN—United States and Canadian industries are comparable. MEX—United States and Mexican industries are comparable. Blank—Canadian, Mexican, and United States industries are comparable.

9211 Executive, Legislative, and Other General Government Support[US]

92111 Executive Offices[US]
See industry description for 921110 below.

921110 Executive Offices[US]

This industry comprises government establishments serving as offices of chief executives and their advisory committees and commissions. This industry includes offices of the president, governors, and mayors, in addition to executive advisory commissions.

92112 Legislative Bodies[US]
See industry description for 921120 below.

921120 Legislative Bodies[US]

This industry comprises government establishments serving as legislative bodies and their advisory committees and commissions. Included in this industry are legislative bodies, such as Congress, state legislatures, and advisory and study legislative commissions.

92113 Public Finance Activities[US]
See industry description for 921130 below.

921130 Public Finance Activities[US]

This industry comprises government establishments primarily engaged in public finance, taxation and monetary policy. Included are financial administration activities, such as monetary policy; tax administration and collection; custody and disbursement of funds; debt and investment administration; auditing activities; and government employee retirement trust fund administration.

Cross-References. Government establishments primarily engaged in—

- Administering income maintenance programs—are classified in Industry 923130, Administration of Human Resource Programs (except Education, Public Health, and Veterans' Affairs Programs);
- Regulating insurance and banking institutions—are classified in Industry 926150, Regulation, Licensing, and Inspection of Miscellaneous Commercial Sectors; and

- Performing central banking functions, such as issuing currency and acting as the fiscal agent for the central government—are classified in Industry 521110, Monetary Authorities-Central Bank.

92114 Executive and Legislative Offices, Combined[US]

See industry description for 921140 below.

921140 Executive and Legislative Offices, Combined[US]

This industry comprises government establishments serving as councils and boards of commissioners or supervisors and such bodies where the chief executive (e.g., county executive or city mayor) is a member of the legislative body (e.g., county or city council) itself.

Cross-References. Government establishments primarily engaged in—

- Serving as offices of chief executives—are classified in Industry 921110, Executive Offices; and

- Serving as legislative bodies—are classified in Industry 921120, Legislative Bodies.

92115 American Indian and Alaska Native Tribal Governments[US]

See industry description for 921150 below.

921150 American Indian and Alaska Native Tribal Governments[US]

This industry comprises American Indian and Alaska Native governing bodies. Establishments in this industry perform legislative, judicial, and administrative functions for their American Indian and Alaska Native lands. Included in this industry are American Indian and Alaska Native councils, courts, and law enforcement bodies.

Cross-References.

- Establishments primarily engaged in providing funding for American Indian and Alaska Native tribal programs through commercial activities, such as gaming, are classified in the industry of the commercial activity; and

- Government establishments providing public administration of American Indian and Alaska Native affairs are classified in Industry 921190, Other General Government Support.

US—United States industry only. CAN—United States and Canadian industries are comparable. MEX—United States and Mexican industries are comparable. Blank—Canadian, Mexican, and United States industries are comparable.

92119 Other General Government Support[US]
See industry description for 921190 below.

921190 Other General Government Support[US]

This industry comprises government establishments primarily engaged in providing general support for government. Such support services include personnel services, election boards, and other general government support establishments that are not classified elsewhere in public administration.

Illustrative Examples:

Civil rights commissions
Civil service commissions
General services departments, government

Personnel offices, government
Supply agencies, government

Cross-References.

- Government establishments primarily engaged in serving as offices of chief executives and their advisory committees and commissions are classified in Industry 921110, Executive Offices;
- Government establishments primarily engaged in serving as legislative bodies and their advisory committees and commissions are classified in Industry 921120, Legislative bodies;
- Government establishments primarily engaged in providing administration of public finance, tax collection, and monetary policy programs are classified in Industry 921130, Public Finance Activities;
- Government establishments primarily engaged in serving as combined executive and legislative offices are classified in Industry 921140, Executive and Legislative Offices, Combined; and
- Establishments primarily engaged in serving as American Indian or Alaska Native tribal leadership are classified in Industry 921150, American Indian and Alaska Native Tribal Governments.

922 Justice, Public Order, and Safety Activities[US]

The Justice, Public Order, and Safety Activities subsector groups government establishments engaged in the administration of justice, public order, and safety programs.

9221 Justice, Public Order, and Safety Activities[US]

92211 Courts[US]
See industry description for 922110 below.

US—United States industry only. CAN—United States and Canadian industries are comparable. MEX—United States and Mexican industries are comparable. Blank—Canadian, Mexican, and United States industries are comparable.

922110 Courts^{US}

This industry comprises civilian courts of law (except Indian tribal and Alaska Native courts). Included in this industry are civilian courts, courts of law, and sheriffs' offices conducting court functions only.

Cross-References.

- Government establishments primarily engaged in operating military courts are classified in Industry 928110, National Security; and
- Establishments primarily engaged in operating Indian tribal or Alaska Native courts are classified in Industry 921150, American Indian and Alaska Native Tribal Governments.

92212 Police Protection^{US}
See industry description for 922120 below.

922120 Police Protection^{US}

This industry comprises government establishments primarily engaged in criminal and civil law enforcement, police, traffic safety, and other activities related to the enforcement of the law and preservation of order. Combined police and fire departments are included in this industry.

Cross-References.

- Government establishments primarily engaged in prosecution are classified in Industry 922130, Legal Counsel and Prosecution;
- Government establishments primarily engaged in collection of law enforcement statistics are classified in Industry 922190, Other Justice, Public Order, and Safety Activities;
- Government establishments primarily engaged in providing police service for the military or National Guard are classified in Industry 928110, National Security;
- Government establishments primarily engaged in providing police service for tribal governments are classified in Industry 921150, American Indian and Alaska Native Tribal Governments;
- Government establishments primarily engaged in enforcing immigration laws are classified in Industry 928120, International Affairs;
- Sheriffs' offices conducting court functions only are classified in Industry 922110, Courts; and

---

US—United States industry only. CAN—United States and Canadian industries are comparable. MEX—United States and Mexican industries are comparable. Blank—Canadian, Mexican, and United States industries are comparable.

- Private establishments primarily engaged in providing security and investigation services are classified in Industry 56161, Investigation, Guard, and Armored Car Services.

92213 Legal Counsel and Prosecution[US]
See industry description for 922130 below.

922130 Legal Counsel and Prosecution[US]

This industry comprises government establishments primarily engaged in providing legal counsel or prosecution services for the government.

Illustrative Examples:

Attorney generals' offices   Public defenders' offices
District attorneys' offices   Public prosecutors' offices

Cross-References.

Government establishments primarily engaged in collecting criminal justice statistics are classified in Industry 922190, Other Justice, Public Order, and Safety Activities.

92214 Correctional Institutions[US]
See industry description for 922140 below.

922140 Correctional Institutions[US]

This industry comprises government establishments primarily engaged in managing and operating correctional institutions. The facility is generally designed for the confinement, correction, and rehabilitation of adult and/or juvenile offenders sentenced by a court.

Illustrative Examples:

Correctional institutions, public   Jails, public administration
  administration   Penitentiaries, public administration
Detention centers, public administration Prisons, public administration

Cross-References.

- Government establishments primarily engaged in operating half-way houses for ex-criminal offenders and delinquent youths are classified in Industry 623990, Other Residential Care Facilities; and

---

US—United States industry only. CAN—United States and Canadian industries are comparable. MEX—United States and Mexican industries are comparable. Blank—Canadian, Mexican, and United States industries are comparable.

- Establishments primarily engaged in managing or operating correctional facilities owned by others are classified in Industry 561210, Facilities Support Services.

92215 Parole Offices and Probation Offices[US]
See industry description for 922150 below.

922150 Parole Offices and Probation Offices[US]

This industry comprises government establishments primarily engaged in judicially administering probation offices, parole offices and boards, and pardon boards.

Cross-References.

Government establishments primarily engaged in providing probation, parole, and pardon activities as an integral part of a central administrative corrections' office are classified in Industry 922140, Correctional Institutions.

92216 Fire Protection[US]
See industry description for 922160 below.

922160 Fire Protection[US]

This industry comprises government establishments primarily engaged in fire fighting and other related fire protection activities. Government establishments providing combined fire protection and ambulance or rescue services are classified in this industry.

Cross-References. Government establishments primarily engaged in—

- Forest fire fighting—are classified in Industry 115310, Support Activities for Forestry;
- Providing combined police and fire protection services—are classified in Industry 922120, Police Protection;
- Providing fire fighting services as a commercial activity—are classified in Industry 561990, All Other Support Services; and
- Providing ambulance services without fire protection service—are classified in Industry 621910, Ambulance Services.

92219 Other Justice, Public Order, and Safety Activities[US]
See industry description for 922190 below.

US—United States industry only. CAN—United States and Canadian industries are comparable. MEX—United States and Mexican industries are comparable. Blank—Canadian, Mexican, and United States industries are comparable.

922190 Other Justice, Public Order, and Safety Activities[US]

This industry comprises government establishments primarily engaged in public order and safety (except courts, police protection, legal counsel and prosecution, correctional institutions, parole offices, probation offices, pardon boards, and fire protection). These establishments include the general administration of public order and safety programs. Government establishments responsible for the collection of statistics on public safety are included in this industry.

Illustrative Examples:

Consumer product safety commissions, public administration	Emergency planning and management offices, government
Disaster preparedness and management offices, government	Public safety bureaus and statistics centers, government

Cross-References. Government establishments primarily engaged in—

- Serving as civilian courts of law (except Indian tribal and Alaska Native)—are classified in Industry 922110, Courts;
- Criminal and civil law enforcement, police, traffic safety and similar activities related to the enforcement of law—are classified in Industry 922120, Police Protection;
- Providing legal counsel to or prosecution services for their governments—are classified in Industry 922130, Legal Counsel and Prosecution;
- The confinement, correction, and rehabilitation of adult and juvenile offenders sentenced by a court—are classified in Industry 922140, Correctional Institutions;
- Judicially administering probation offices, parole offices and boards, and pardon boards—are classified in Industry 922150, Parole Offices and Probation Offices; and
- Fire fighting and other related fire protection activities—are classified in Industry 922160, Fire Protection.

923 Administration of Human Resource Programs[US]

The Administration of Human Resource Programs subsector groups government establishments primarily engaged in the administration of human resource programs.

9231 Administration of Human Resource Programs[US]

92311 Administration of Education Programs[US]
See industry description for 923110 below.

923110 Administration of Education Programs[US]

This industry comprises government establishments primarily engaged in the central coordination, planning, supervision and administration of funds, policies, intergovernmental activities, statistical reports and data collection, and centralized programs for educational administration. Government scholarship programs are included in this industry.

Illustrative Examples:

Education offices, nonoperating, public administration

Education statistics centers, government

State education departments

University regents or boards, government

Cross-References.

Schools and local school boards are classified in Subsector 611, Educational Services.

92312 Administration of Public Health Programs[US]

See industry description for 923120 below.

923120 Administration of Public Health Programs[US]

This industry comprises government establishments primarily engaged in the planning, administration, and coordination of public health programs and services, including environmental health activities, mental health, categorical health programs, health statistics, and immunization services. Government establishments primarily engaged in conducting public health-related inspections are included in this industry.

Illustrative Examples:

Communicable disease program administration, public administration

Coroners' offices, public administration

Health program administration, public administration

Mental health program administration, public administration

Public health program administration, nonoperating, public administration

Cross-References. Government establishments primarily engaged in—

- Operating hospitals (i.e., government or military)—are classified in Subsector 622, Hospitals;

- Providing health care in a clinical setting (i.e., military or government clinics)—are classified in Subsector 621, Ambulatory Health Care Services; and

---

US—United States industry only. CAN—United States and Canadian industries are comparable. MEX—United States and Mexican industries are comparable. Blank—Canadian, Mexican, and United States industries are comparable.

- Inspecting food, plants, animals, and other agriculture products—are classified in Industry 926140, Regulation of Agricultural Marketing and Commodities.

92313 Administration of Human Resource Programs (except Education, Public Health, and Veterans' Affairs Programs)[US]
See industry description for 923130 below.

923130 Administration of Human Resource Programs (except Education, Public Health, and Veterans' Affairs Programs)[US]

This industry comprises government establishments primarily engaged in the planning, administration, and coordination of programs for public assistance, social work, and welfare activities. The administration of Social Security, disability insurance, Medicare, unemployment insurance, and workers' compensation programs are included in this industry.

Cross-References. Government establishments primarily engaged in—

- Administering veterans' programs—are classified in Industry 923140, Administration of Veterans' Affairs;
- Operating state employment job service offices—are classified in Industry 561310, Employment Placement Agencies; and
- Operating programs for public assistance, social work, and welfare—are classified in Subsector 624, Social Assistance.

92314 Administration of Veterans' Affairs[US]
See industry description for 923140 below.

923140 Administration of Veterans' Affairs[US]

This industry comprises government establishments primarily engaged in the administration of programs of assistance, training, counseling, and other services to veterans and their dependents, heirs or survivors. Included in this industry are Veterans' Affairs offices that maintain liaison and coordinate activities with other service organizations and governmental agencies.

Cross-References.

- Government establishments operating veterans' hospitals are classified in Subsector 622, Hospitals;

US—United States industry only. CAN—United States and Canadian industries are comparable. MEX—United States and Mexican industries are comparable. Blank—Canadian, Mexican, and United States industries are comparable.

- Establishments providing veterans' insurance are classified in Subsector 524, Insurance Carriers and Related Activities; and

- Establishments operating civic and social organizations for veterans are classified in Industry 813410, Civic and Social Organizations.

924 Administration of Environmental Quality Programs[US]

The Administration of Environmental Quality Programs subsector groups government establishments primarily engaged in the administration of environmental quality.

9241 Administration of Environmental Quality Programs[US]

92411 Administration of Air and Water Resource and Solid Waste Management Programs[US]

See industry description for 924110 below.

924110 Administration of Air and Water Resource and Solid Waste Management Programs[US]

This industry comprises government establishments primarily engaged in one or more of the following: (1) the administration, regulation, and enforcement of air and water resource programs; (2) the administration and regulation of solid waste management programs; (3) the administration and regulation of water and air pollution control and prevention programs; (4) the administration and regulation of flood control programs; (5) the administration and regulation of drainage development and water resource consumption programs; (6) the administration and regulation of toxic waste removal and cleanup programs; and (7) coordination of these activities at intergovernmental levels.

Illustrative Examples:

Environmental protection program
  administration, public administration
Pollution control program administration,
  public administration
Waste management program (except
  sanitation districts), administration,
  public administration

Water control and quality program
  administration, public administration

Cross-References. Government establishments primarily engaged in—

- Operating water and irrigation systems—are classified in Industry 221310, Water Supply and Irrigation Systems;

US—United States industry only. CAN—United States and Canadian industries are comparable. MEX—United States and Mexican industries are comparable. Blank—Canadian, Mexican, and United States industries are comparable.

- Administering sanitation districts—are classified in Industry 926130, Regulation and Administration of Communications, Electric, Gas, and Other Utilities;
- Operating sewage treatment facilities—are classified in Industry 221320, Sewage Treatment Facilities; and
- Providing waste collection, treatment, disposal, and/or remediation—are classified in Subsector 562, Waste Management and Remediation Services.

92412 Administration of Conservation Programs[US]
See industry description for 924120 below.

924120 Administration of Conservation Programs[US]

This industry comprises government establishments primarily engaged in the administration, regulation, supervision and control of land use, including recreational areas; conservation and preservation of natural resources; erosion control; geological survey program administration; weather forecasting program administration; and the administration and protection of publicly and privately owned forest lands. Government establishments responsible for planning, management, regulation and conservation of game, fish, and wildlife populations, including wildlife management areas and field stations; and other administrative matters relating to the protection of fish, game, and wildlife are included in this industry.

Cross-References. Government establishments primarily engaged in—

- Operating parks—are classified in Industry 712190, Nature Parks and Other Similar Institutions;
- Operating forest property—are classified in Subsector 113, Forestry and Logging;
- Geophysical surveying and/or mapping—are classified in Industry 541360, Geophysical Surveying and Mapping Services;
- Surveying and/or mapping (except geophysical)—are classified in Industry 541370, Surveying and Mapping (except Geophysical) Services;
- Weather forecasting—are classified in Industry 541990, All Other Professional, Scientific and Technical Services;
- Operating fish and game preserves—are classified in Industry 712130, Zoos and Botanical Gardens; and
- Serving as urban planning commissions—are classified in Industry 925120, Administration of Urban Planning and Community and Rural Development.

US—United States industry only. CAN—United States and Canadian industries are comparable. MEX—United States and Mexican industries are comparable. Blank—Canadian, Mexican, and United States industries are comparable.

925 Administration of Housing Programs, Urban Planning, and Community Development[US]

The Administration of Housing Programs, Urban Planning, and Community Development subsector groups government establishments primarily engaged in the administration of housing, urban planning, and community development.

9251 Administration of Housing Programs, Urban Planning, and Community Development[US]

92511 Administration of Housing Programs[US]
See industry description for 925110 below.

925110 Administration of Housing Programs[US]

This industry comprises government establishments primarily engaged in the administration and planning of housing programs.

Cross-References. Government establishments primarily engaged in—

- Operating government rental housing—are classified in Subsector 531, Real Estate;
- Conducting building inspections and enforcing building codes and standards—are classified in Industry 926150, Regulation, Licensing, and Inspection of Miscellaneous Commercial Sectors; and
- Buying, pooling, and repackaging mortgages or home loans for sale to others on the secondary market—are classified in U.S. Industry 522294, Secondary Market Financing.

92512 Administration of Urban Planning and Community and Rural Development[US]
See industry description for 925120 below.

925120 Administration of Urban Planning and Community and Rural Development[US]

This industry comprises government establishments primarily engaged in the administration and planning of the development of urban and rural areas. Included in this industry are government zoning boards and commissions.

US—United States industry only. CAN—United States and Canadian industries are comparable. MEX—United States and Mexican industries are comparable. Blank—Canadian, Mexican, and United States industries are comparable.

Illustrative Examples:

Land redevelopment agencies, government

Regional planning and development program administration, public administration

Urban planning commissions, government

Zoning boards and commissions, public administration

926 Administration of Economic Programs^{US}

This subsector comprises government establishments primarily engaged in the administration of economic programs.

9261 Administration of Economic Program^{US}

92611 Administration of General Economic Programs^{US}
See industry description for 926110 below.

926110 Administration of General Economic Programs^{US}

This industry comprises government establishments primarily engaged in the administration, promotion and development of economic resources, including business, industry, and tourism. Included in this industry are government establishments responsible for the development of general statistical data and analyses and promotion of the general economic well-being of the governed area.

Illustrative Examples:

Consumer protection offices, public administration

Economic development agencies, government

General economics statistical agencies, public administration

Small business development agencies, public administration

Trade commissions, government

92612 Regulation and Administration of Transportation Programs^{US}
See industry description for 926120 below.

926120 Regulation and Administration of Transportation Program^{US}

This industry comprises government establishments primarily engaged in the administration, regulation, licensing, planning, inspection, and investigation of transportation services and facilities. Included in this industry are government

---

establishments responsible for motor vehicle and operator licensing, the Coast Guard (except the Coast Guard Academy), and parking authorities.

Cross-References. Government establishments primarily engaged in—

- Operating airports, railroads, depots, ports, toll roads and bridges, and other transportation facilities—are classified in Sector 48-49, Transportation and Warehousing;
- Operating parking lots and parking garages—are classified in Industry 812930, Parking Lots and Garages;
- Operating automobile safety inspection and emission testing facilities—are classified in Industry Group 8111, Automotive Repair and Maintenance;
- Building and/or maintaining roads and highways—are classified in Industry 237310, Highway, Street and Bridge Construction;
- Providing air traffic control services—are classified in U.S. Industry 488111, Air Traffic Control; and
- Operating weigh stations—are classified in Industry 488490, Other Support Activities for Road Transportation.

92613 Regulation and Administration of Communications, Electric, Gas, and Other Utilities US

See industry description for 926130 below.

926130 Regulation and Administration of Communications, Electric, Gas, and Other Utilities US

This industry comprises government establishments primarily engaged in the administration, regulation, licensing and inspection of utilities, such as communications, electric power (including fossil, nuclear, solar, water, and wind), gas and water supply, and sewerage.

Cross-References.

Government establishments primarily engaged in operating utilities are classified in Subsector 221, Utilities.

92614 Regulation of Agricultural Marketing and Commodities US

See industry description for 926140 below.

926140 Regulation of Agricultural Marketing and Commodities US

This industry comprises government establishments primarily engaged in the planning, administration, and coordination of agricultural programs for production,

US—United States industry only. CAN—United States and Canadian industries are comparable. MEX—United States and Mexican industries are comparable. Blank—Canadian, Mexican, and United States industries are comparable.

marketing, and utilization, including educational and promotional activities. Included in this industry are government establishments responsible for regulating and controlling the grading and inspection of food, plants, animals, and other agricultural products.

Cross-References. Government establishments primarily engaged in—

- Administering programs for developing economic data about agricultural and trade in agricultural products—are classified in Industry 926110, Administration of General Economic Programs;

- Administering programs for the conservation of natural resources—are classified in Industry Group 9241, Administration of Environmental Quality Programs; and

- Administering food stamp programs—are classified in Industry 923130, Administration Human Resource Programs (except Education, Public Health, and Veterans' Affairs Programs).

92615 Regulation, Licensing, and Inspection of Miscellaneous Commercial Sectors[US]

See industry description for 926150 below.

926150 Regulation, Licensing, and Inspection of Miscellaneous Commercial Sectors[US]

This industry comprises government establishments primarily engaged in the regulation, licensing, and inspection of commercial sectors, such as retail trade, professional occupations, manufacturing, mining, construction, and services. Included in this industry are government establishments maintaining physical standards, regulating hazardous conditions not elsewhere classified, and enforcing alcoholic beverage control regulations.

Illustrative Examples:

Alcoholic beverage control boards, public administration
Banking regulatory agencies, public administration
Building inspections, government
Insurance commissions, government
Labor management negotiations boards, government

Licensing and permit issuance for professional occupations, government
Licensing and permit issuance for business operations, government
Securities regulation commissions, public administration

Cross-References. Government establishments primarily engaged in—

- Regulating, administering, and inspecting transportation services and facilities—are classified in Industry 926120, Regulation and Administration of Transportation Programs; and

- Regulating, administering, and inspecting communications, electric, gas, and other utilities—are classified in Industry 926130, Regulation and Administration of Communications, Electric, Gas, and Other Utilities.

927 Space Research and Technology[US]

This subsector group comprises government establishments that conduct space research.

9271 Space Research and Technology[US]

92711 Space Research and Technology[US]

See industry description for 927110 below.

927110 Space Research and Technology[US]

This industry comprises government establishments primarily engaged in the administration and operations of space flights, space research, and space exploration. Included in this industry are government establishments operating space flight centers.

Cross-References.

- Private establishments primarily engaged in providing space freight transportation are classified in U.S. Industry 481212, Nonscheduled Chartered Freight Air Transportation;

- Government establishments primarily engaged in manufacturing aerospace vehicles and parts are classified in Industry 33641, Aerospace Product and Parts Manufacturing; and

- Government establishments primarily engaged in manufacturing space satellites are classified in Industry 334220, Radio and Television Broadcasting and Wireless Communications Equipment Manufacturing.

928 National Security and International Affairs[US]

This subsector comprises government establishments primarily engaged in national security and international affairs.

9281 National Security and International Affairs[US]

92811 National Security[US]
See industry description for 928110 below.

928110 National Security[US]

This industry comprises government establishments of the Armed Forces, including the National Guard, primarily engaged in national security and related activities.

Illustrative Examples:

Air Force	Military training schools (except military
Army	service academies)
Marine Corps	National Guard
Military courts	Navy
Military police	

Cross-References. Government establishments primarily engaged in—

- Operating military service academies—are classified in Industry 611310, Colleges, Universities, and Professional Schools; and

- Regulating and administering water transportation, such as the U.S. Coast Guard and the Merchant Marine—are classified in Industry 926120, Regulation and Administration of Transportation Programs.

92812 International Affairs[US]
See industry description for 928120 below.

928120 International Affairs[US]

This industry comprises establishments of U.S. and foreign governments primarily engaged in international affairs and programs relating to other nations and peoples.

Cross-References.

- Private sector trade associations and councils are classified in Industry 813910, Business Associations; and

- Government establishments administering international trade, such as trade commissions and councils are classified in Industry 926110, Administration of General Economic Programs.

Part II

List of Short Titles

List of Short Titles

Standard Short Titles for NAICS United States are shown below. They have been created for the use of those who find that space limitations preclude the use of the full title for the dissemination of data classified to NAICS. The adoptions of these titles is recommended in all cases when the full title cannot be used.

The standard short titles are limited to 45 spaces. If the official full title falls within 45 spaces it remains unchanged.

Note: For definitions of abbreviations and acronyms see page 964.

Code	Short title	Code	Short title
11	**AGRICULTURE, FORESTRY, FISHING AND HUNTING**	1114	Greenhouse and nursery production
		11141	Food crops grown under cover
		111411	Mushroom production
111	**Crop production**	111419	Other food crops grown under cover
1111	Oilseed and grain farming		
11111	Soybean farming	11142	Nursery and floriculture production
111110	Soybean farming		
11112	Oilseed, except soybean, farming	111421	Nursery and tree production
		111422	Floriculture production
111120	Oilseed, except soybean, farming	1119	Other crop farming
		11191	Tobacco farming
11113	Dry pea and bean farming	111910	Tobacco farming
111130	Dry pea and bean farming	11192	Cotton farming
11114	Wheat farming	111920	Cotton farming
111140	Wheat farming	11193	Sugarcane farming
11115	Corn farming	111930	Sugarcane farming
111150	Corn farming	11194	Hay farming
11116	Rice farming	111940	Hay farming
111160	Rice farming	11199	All other crop farming
11119	Other grain farming	111991	Sugar beet farming
111191	Oilseed and grain combination farming	111992	Peanut farming
		111998	All other miscellaneous crop farming
111199	All other grain farming		
1112	**Vegetable and melon farming**	**112**	**Animal production**
11121	Vegetable and melon farming		
111211	Potato farming	1121	Cattle ranching and farming
111219	Other vegetable and melon farming	11211	Beef cattle ranching, farming, and feedlots
1113	Fruit and tree nut farming	112111	Beef cattle ranching and farming
11131	Orange groves		
111310	Orange groves	112112	Cattle feedlots
11132	Citrus, except orange, groves	11212	Dairy cattle and milk production
111320	Citrus, except orange, groves		
11133	Noncitrus fruit and tree nut farming	112120	Dairy cattle and milk production
111331	Apple orchards	11213	Dual-purpose cattle ranching and farming
111332	Grape vineyards		
111333	Strawberry farming	112130	Dual-purpose cattle ranching and farming
111334	Berry, except strawberry, farming		
		1122	Hog and pig farming
111335	Tree nut farming	11221	Hog and pig farming
111336	Fruit and tree nut combination farming	112210	Hog and pig farming
		1123	Poultry and egg production
111339	Other noncitrus fruit farming	11231	Chicken egg production

Note: For definitions of abbreviations and acronyms see page 964.

Code	Short title
112310	Chicken egg production
11232	Broilers and meat type chicken production
112320	Broilers and meat type chicken production
11233	Turkey production
112330	Turkey production
11234	Poultry hatcheries
112340	Poultry hatcheries
11239	Other poultry production
112390	Other poultry production
1124	Sheep and goat farming
11241	Sheep farming
112410	Sheep farming
11242	Goat farming
112420	Goat farming
1125	Animal aquaculture
11251	Animal aquaculture
112511	Finfish farming and fish hatcheries
112512	Shellfish farming
112519	Other animal aquaculture
1129	Other animal production
11291	Apiculture
112910	Apiculture
11292	Horses and other equine production
112920	Horses and other equine production
11293	Fur-bearing animal and rabbit production
112930	Fur-bearing animal and rabbit production
11299	All other animal production
112990	All other animal production

113 Forestry and logging

Code	Short title
1131	Timber tract operations
11311	Timber tract operations
113110	Timber tract operations
1132	Forest nursery and gathering forest products
11321	Forest nursery and gathering forest products

Code	Short title
113210	Forest nursery and gathering forest products
1133	Logging
11331	Logging
113310	Logging

114 Fishing, hunting and trapping

Code	Short title
1141	Fishing
11411	Fishing
114111	Finfish fishing
114112	Shellfish fishing
114119	Other marine fishing
1142	Hunting and trapping
11421	Hunting and trapping
114210	Hunting and trapping

115 Agriculture and forestry support activities

Code	Short title
1151	Support activities for crop production
11511	Support activities for crop production
115111	Cotton ginning
115112	Soil preparation, planting, and cultivating
115113	Crop harvesting, primarily by machine
115114	Other postharvest crop activities
115115	Farm labor contractors and crew leaders
115116	Farm management services
1152	Support activities for animal production
11521	Support activities for animal production
115210	Support activities for animal production
1153	Support activities for forestry
11531	Support activities for forestry
115310	Support activities for forestry

21 MINING

211 Oil and gas extraction

Code	Short title
2111	Oil and gas extraction
21111	Oil and gas extraction

Note: For definitions of abbreviations and acronyms see page 964.

Code	Short title
211111	Crude petroleum and natural gas extraction
211112	Natural gas liquid extraction
212	Mining, except oil and gas
2121	Coal mining
21211	Coal mining
212111	Bituminous coal and lignite surface mining
212112	Bituminous coal underground mining
212113	Anthracite mining
2122	Metal ore mining
21221	Iron ore mining
212210	Iron ore mining
21222	Gold ore and silver ore mining
212221	Gold ore mining
212222	Silver ore mining
21223	Copper, nickel, lead, and zinc mining
212231	Lead ore and zinc ore mining
212234	Copper ore and nickel ore mining
21229	Other metal ore mining
212291	Uranium-radium-vanadium ore mining
212299	All other metal ore mining
2123	Nonmetallic mineral mining and quarrying
21231	Stone mining and quarrying
212311	Dimension stone mining and quarrying
212312	Crushed and broken limestone mining
212313	Crushed and broken granite mining
212319	Other crushed and broken stone mining
21232	Sand, gravel, clay, and refractory mining
212321	Construction sand and gravel mining
212322	Industrial sand mining
212324	Kaolin and ball clay mining
212325	Clay, ceramic, and refractory minerals mining

Code	Short title
21239	Other nonmetallic mineral mining
212391	Potash, soda, and borate mineral mining
212392	Phosphate rock mining
212393	Other chemical and fertilizer mineral mining
212399	All other nonmetallic mineral mining
213	**Support activities for mining**
2131	Support activities for mining
21311	Support activities for mining
213111	Drilling oil and gas wells
213112	Support activities for oil and gas operations
213113	Support activities for coal mining
213114	Support activities for metal mining
213115	Support activities for nonmetallic minerals
22	**UTILITIES**
221	**Utilities**
2211	Power generation and supply
22111	Electric power generation
221111	Hydroelectric power generation
221112	Fossil fuel electric power generation
221113	Nuclear electric power generation
221119	Other electric power generation
22112	Electric power transmission and distribution
221121	Electric bulk power transmission and control
221122	Electric power distribution
2212	Natural gas distribution
22121	Natural gas distribution
221210	Natural gas distribution
2213	Water, sewage and other systems
22131	Water supply and irrigation systems

Note: For definitions of abbreviations and acronyms see page 964.

Code	Short title	Code	Short title
221310	Water supply and irrigation systems	2372	Land subdivision
22132	Sewage treatment facilities	23721	Land subdivision
221320	Sewage treatment facilities	237210	Land subdivision
22133	Steam and air-conditioning supply	2373	Highway, street, and bridge construction
221330	Steam and air-conditioning supply	23731	Highway, street, and bridge construction
23	**CONSTRUCTION**	237310	Highway, street, and bridge construction
236	**Construction of buildings**	2379	Other heavy construction
2361	Residential building construction	23799	Other heavy construction
23611	Residential building construction	237990	Other heavy construction
236115	New single-family general contractors	**238**	**Specialty trade contractors**
236116	New multifamily general contractors	2381	Building foundation and exterior contractors
236117	New housing operative builders	23811	Poured concrete structure contractors
236118	Residential remodelers	238110	Poured concrete structure contractors
2362	Nonresidential building construction	23812	Steel and precast concrete contractors
23621	Industrial building construction	238120	Steel and precast concrete contractors
236210	Industrial building construction	23813	Framing contractors
23622	Commercial building construction	238130	Framing contractors
236220	Commercial building construction	23814	Masonry contractors
		238140	Masonry contractors
237	**Heavy and civil engineering construction**	23815	Glass and glazing contractors
		238150	Glass and glazing contractors
2371	Utility system construction	23816	Roofing contractors
23711	Water and sewer system construction	238160	Roofing contractors
		23817	Siding contractors
237110	Water and sewer system construction	238170	Siding contractors
23712	Oil and gas pipeline construction	23819	Other building exterior contractors
237120	Oil and gas pipeline construction	238190	Other building exterior contractors
		2382	Building equipment contractors
23713	Power and communication system construction	23821	Electrical contractors
		238210	Electrical contractors
237130	Power and communication system construction	23822	Plumbing and HVAC contractors
		238220	Plumbing and HVAC contractors

Note: For definitions of abbreviations and acronyms see page 964.

Code	Short title	Code	Short title
23829	Other building equipment contractors	31122	Starch and vegetable oil manufacturing
238290	Other building equipment contractors	311221	Wet corn milling
2383	Building finishing contractors	311222	Soybean processing
23831	Drywall and insulation contractors	311223	Other oilseed processing
		311225	Fats and oils refining and blending
238310	Drywall and insulation contractors	31123	Breakfast cereal manufacturing
23832	Painting and wall covering contractors	311230	Breakfast cereal manufacturing
		3113	Sugar and confectionery product manufacturing
238320	Painting and wall covering contractors	31131	Sugar manufacturing
23833	Flooring contractors	311311	Sugarcane mills
238330	Flooring contractors	311312	Cane sugar refining
23834	Tile and terrazzo contractors	311313	Beet sugar manufacturing
238340	Tile and terrazzo contractors	31132	Confectionery manufacturing from cacao beans
23835	Finish carpentry contractors	311320	Confectionery manufacturing from cacao beans
238350	Finish carpentry contractors	31133	Confectionery mfg. from purchased chocolate
23839	Other building finishing contractors	311330	Confectionery mfg. from purchased chocolate
238390	Other building finishing contractors	31134	Nonchocolate confectionery manufacturing
2389	Other specialty trade contractors	311340	Nonchocolate confectionery manufacturing
23891	Site preparation contractors	3114	Fruit and vegetable preserving and specialty
238910	Site preparation contractors	31141	Frozen food manufacturing
23899	All other specialty trade contractors	311411	Frozen fruit and vegetable manufacturing
238990	All other specialty trade contractors	311412	Frozen specialty food manufacturing
31-33	**MANUFACTURING**	31142	Fruit and vegetable canning and drying
311	**Food manufacturing**	311421	Fruit and vegetable canning
3111	Animal food manufacturing	311422	Specialty canning
31111	Animal food manufacturing	311423	Dried and dehydrated food manufacturing
311111	Dog and cat food manufacturing	3115	Dairy product manufacturing
311119	Other animal food manufacturing	31151	Dairy product, except frozen, manufacturing
3112	Grain and oilseed milling	311511	Fluid milk manufacturing
31121	Flour milling and malt manufacturing	311512	Creamery butter manufacturing
311211	Flour milling		
311212	Rice milling		
311213	Malt manufacturing		

Note: For definitions of abbreviations and acronyms see page 964.

Code	Short title
311513	Cheese manufacturing
311514	Dry, condensed, and evaporated dairy products
31152	Ice cream and frozen dessert manufacturing
311520	Ice cream and frozen dessert manufacturing
3116	Animal slaughtering and processing
31161	Animal slaughtering and processing
311611	Animal, except poultry, slaughtering
311612	Meat processed from carcasses
311613	Rendering and meat byproduct processing
311615	Poultry processing
3117	Seafood product preparation and packaging
31171	Seafood product preparation and packaging
311711	Seafood canning
311712	Fresh and frozen seafood processing
3118	Bakeries and tortilla manufacturing
31181	Bread and bakery product manufacturing
311811	Retail bakeries
311812	Commercial bakeries
311813	Frozen cakes and other pastries manufacturing
31182	Cookie, cracker, and pasta manufacturing
311821	Cookie and cracker manufacturing
311822	Mixes and dough made from purchased flour
311823	Dry pasta manufacturing
31183	Tortilla manufacturing
311830	Tortilla manufacturing
3119	Other food manufacturing
31191	Snack food manufacturing
311911	Roasted nuts and peanut butter manufacturing

Code	Short title
311919	Other snack food manufacturing
31192	Coffee and tea manufacturing
311920	Coffee and tea manufacturing
31193	Flavoring syrup and concentrate manufacturing
311930	Flavoring syrup and concentrate manufacturing
31194	Seasoning and dressing manufacturing
311941	Mayonnaise, dressing, and sauce manufacturing
311942	Spice and extract manufacturing
31199	All other food manufacturing
311991	Perishable prepared food manufacturing
311999	All other miscellaneous food manufacturing
312	**Beverage and tobacco product manufacturing**
3121	Beverage manufacturing
31211	Soft drink and ice manufacturing
312111	Soft drink manufacturing
312112	Bottled water manufacturing
312113	Ice manufacturing
31212	Breweries
312120	Breweries
31213	Wineries
312130	Wineries
31214	Distilleries
312140	Distilleries
3122	Tobacco manufacturing
31221	Tobacco stemming and redrying
312210	Tobacco stemming and redrying
31222	Tobacco product manufacturing
312221	Cigarette manufacturing
312229	Other tobacco product manufacturing
313	**Textile mills**
3131	Fiber, yarn, and thread mills
31311	Fiber, yarn, and thread mills
313111	Yarn spinning mills

Note: For definitions of abbreviations and acronyms see page 964.

Code	Short title
313112	Yarn texturizing and twisting mills
313113	Thread mills
3132	Fabric mills
31321	Broadwoven fabric mills
313210	Broadwoven fabric mills
31322	Narrow fabric mills and schiffli embroidery
313221	Narrow fabric mills
313222	Schiffli machine embroidery
31323	Nonwoven fabric mills
313230	Nonwoven fabric mills
31324	Knit fabric mills
313241	Weft knit fabric mills
313249	Other knit fabric and lace mills
3133	Textile and fabric finishing mills
31331	Textile and fabric finishing mills
313311	Broadwoven fabric finishing mills
313312	Other textile and fabric finishing mills
31332	Fabric coating mills
313320	Fabric coating mills

314 **Textile product mills**

Code	Short title
3141	Textile furnishings mills
31411	Carpet and rug mills
314110	Carpet and rug mills
31412	Curtain and linen mills
314121	Curtain and drapery mills
314129	Other household textile product mills
3149	Other textile product mills
31491	Textile bag and canvas mills
314911	Textile bag mills
314912	Canvas and related product mills
31499	All other textile product mills
314991	Rope, cordage, and twine mills
314992	Tire cord and tire fabric mills
314999	All other miscellaneous textile product mills

315 **Apparel manufacturing**

Code	Short title
3151	Apparel knitting mills
31511	Hosiery and sock mills
315111	Sheer hosiery mills
315119	Other hosiery and sock mills
31519	Other apparel knitting mills
315191	Outerwear knitting mills
315192	Underwear and nightwear knitting mills
3152	Cut and sew apparel manufacturing
31521	Cut and sew apparel contractors
315211	Men's cut and sew apparel contractors
315212	Women's cut and sew apparel contractors
31522	Men's cut and sew apparel manufacturing
315221	Men's underwear and nightwear manufacturing
315222	Men's suit, coat, and overcoat manufacturing
315223	Men's shirt, except work shirt, manufacturing
315224	Men's pants, except work pants, manufacturing
315225	Men's work clothing manufacturing
315228	Other men's outerwear manufacturing
31523	Women's cut and sew apparel manufacturing
315231	Women's lingerie and nightwear manufacturing
315232	Women's blouse and shirt manufacturing
315233	Women's dress manufacturing
315234	Women's suit, coat, jacket, and skirt mfg.
315239	Other women's outerwear manufacturing
31529	Other cut and sew apparel manufacturing
315291	Infants' cut and sew apparel manufacturing

Note: For definitions of abbreviations and acronyms see page 964.

Code	Short title
315292	Fur and leather apparel manufacturing
315299	All other cut and sew apparel manufacturing
3159	Accessories and other apparel manufacturing
31599	Accessories and other apparel manufacturing
315991	Hat, cap, and millinery manufacturing
315992	Glove and mitten manufacturing
315993	Men's and boys' neckwear manufacturing
315999	All other accessory and apparel manufacturing
316	**Leather and allied product manufacturing**
3161	Leather and hide tanning and finishing
31611	Leather and hide tanning and finishing
316110	Leather and hide tanning and finishing
3162	Footwear manufacturing
31621	Footwear manufacturing
316211	Rubber and plastics footwear manufacturing
316212	House slipper manufacturing
316213	Men's nonathletic footwear manufacturing
316214	Women's nonathletic footwear manufacturing
316219	Other footwear manufacturing
3169	Other leather product manufacturing
31699	Other leather product manufacturing
316991	Luggage manufacturing
316992	Women's handbag and purse manufacturing
316993	Other personal leather good manufacturing
316999	All other leather good manufacturing

Code	Short title
321	**Wood product manufacturing**
3211	Sawmills and wood preservation
32111	Sawmills and wood preservation
321113	Sawmills
321114	Wood preservation
3212	Plywood and engineered wood product mfg.
32121	Plywood and engineered wood product mfg.
321211	Hardwood veneer and plywood manufacturing
321212	Softwood veneer and plywood manufacturing
321213	Engineered wood member manufacturing
321214	Truss manufacturing
321219	Reconstituted wood product manufacturing
3219	Other wood product manufacturing
32191	Millwork
321911	Wood window and door manufacturing
321912	Cut stock, resawing lumber, and planing
321918	Other millwork, including flooring
32192	Wood container and pallet manufacturing
321920	Wood container and pallet manufacturing
32199	All other wood product manufacturing
321991	Manufactured home, mobile home, manufacturing
321992	Prefabricated wood building manufacturing
321999	Miscellaneous wood product manufacturing
322	**Paper manufacturing**
3221	Pulp, paper, and paperboard mills
32211	Pulp mills
322110	Pulp mills

Note: For definitions of abbreviations and acronyms see page 964.

Code	Short title	Code	Short title
32212	Paper mills	**323**	**Printing and related support activities**
322121	Paper, except newsprint, mills		
322122	Newsprint mills	3231	Printing and related support activities
32213	Paperboard mills		
322130	Paperboard mills	32311	Printing
3222	Converted paper product manufacturing	323110	Commercial lithographic printing
32221	Paperboard container manufacturing	323111	Commercial gravure printing
322211	Corrugated and solid fiber box manufacturing	323112	Commercial flexographic printing
322212	Folding paperboard box manufacturing	323113	Commercial screen printing
		323114	Quick printing
322213	Setup paperboard box manufacturing	323115	Digital printing
		323116	Manifold business forms printing
322214	Fiber can, tube, and drum manufacturing	323117	Books printing
322215	Nonfolding sanitary food container mfg.	323118	Blankbook and looseleaf binder manufacturing
32222	Paper bag and coated and treated paper mfg.	323119	Other commercial printing
		32312	Support activities for printing
322221	Coated and laminated packaging materials mfg.	323121	Tradebinding and related work
		323122	Prepress services
322222	Coated and laminated paper manufacturing	**324**	**Petroleum and coal products manufacturing**
322223	Plastics, foil, and coated paper bag mfg.		
		3241	Petroleum and coal products manufacturing
322224	Uncoated paper and multiwall bag mfg.		
		32411	Petroleum refineries
322225	Flexible packaging foil manufacturing	324110	Petroleum refineries
		32412	Asphalt paving and roofing materials mfg.
322226	Surface-coated paperboard manufacturing		
		324121	Asphalt paving mixture and block mfg.
32223	Stationery product manufacturing		
		324122	Asphalt shingle and coating materials mfg.
322231	Die-cut paper office supplies manufacturing		
		32419	Other petroleum and coal products mfg.
322232	Envelope manufacturing		
322233	Stationery and related product manufacturing	324191	Petroleum lubricating oil and grease mfg.
32229	Other converted paper product manufacturing	324199	All other petroleum and coal products mfg.
322291	Sanitary paper product manufacturing	**325**	**Chemical manufacturing**
322299	All other converted paper product mfg.	3251	Basic chemical manufacturing
		32511	Petrochemical manufacturing

Note: For definitions of abbreviations and acronyms see page 964.

Code	Short title	Code	Short title
325110	Petrochemical manufacturing	325314	Fertilizer, mixing only, manufacturing
32512	Industrial gas manufacturing		
325120	Industrial gas manufacturing	32532	Pesticide and other ag. chemical mfg.
32513	Synthetic dye and pigment manufacturing	325320	Pesticide and other ag. chemical mfg.
325131	Inorganic dye and pigment manufacturing	3254	Pharmaceutical and medicine manufacturing
325132	Synthetic organic dye and pigment mfg.	32541	Pharmaceutical and medicine manufacturing
32518	Other basic inorganic chemical manufacturing	325411	Medicinal and botanical manufacturing
325181	Alkalies and chlorine manufacturing	325412	Pharmaceutical preparation manufacturing
325182	Carbon black manufacturing	325413	In-vitro diagnostic substance manufacturing
325188	All other basic inorganic chemical mfg.	325414	Other biological product manufacturing
32519	Other basic organic chemical manufacturing	3255	Paint, coating, and adhesive manufacturing
325191	Gum and wood chemical manufacturing	32551	Paint and coating manufacturing
325192	Cyclic crude and intermediate manufacturing	325510	Paint and coating manufacturing
325193	Ethyl alcohol manufacturing	32552	Adhesive manufacturing
325199	All other basic organic chemical mfg.	325520	Adhesive manufacturing
3252	Resin, rubber, and artificial fibers mfg.	3256	Soap, cleaning compound, and toiletry mfg.
32521	Resin and synthetic rubber manufacturing	32561	Soap and cleaning compound manufacturing
325211	Plastics material and resin manufacturing	325611	Soap and other detergent manufacturing
325212	Synthetic rubber manufacturing	325612	Polish and other sanitation good mfg.
32522	Artificial fibers and filaments manufacturing	325613	Surface active agent manufacturing
325221	Cellulosic organic fiber manufacturing	32562	Toilet preparation manufacturing
325222	Noncellulosic organic fiber manufacturing	325620	Toilet preparation manufacturing
3253	Agricultural chemical manufacturing	3259	Other chemical product and preparation mfg.
32531	Fertilizer manufacturing	32591	Printing ink manufacturing
325311	Nitrogenous fertilizer manufacturing	325910	Printing ink manufacturing
		32592	Explosives manufacturing
325312	Phosphatic fertilizer manufacturing	325920	Explosives manufacturing
		32599	All other chemical preparation manufacturing

Note: For definitions of abbreviations and acronyms see page 964.

Code	Short title
325991	Custom compounding of purchased resins
325992	Photographic film and chemical manufacturing
325998	Other miscellaneous chemical product mfg.

326   Plastics and rubber products manufacturing

Code	Short title
3261	Plastics product manufacturing
32611	Plastics packaging materials, film and sheet
326111	Plastics bag manufacturing
326112	Plastics packaging film and sheet mfg.
326113	Nonpackaging plastics film and sheet mfg.
32612	Plastics pipe, fittings, and profile shapes
326121	Unlaminated plastics profile shape mfg.
326122	Plastics pipe and pipe fitting manufacturing
32613	Laminated plastics plate, sheet, and shapes
326130	Laminated plastics plate, sheet, and shapes
32614	Polystyrene foam product manufacturing
326140	Polystyrene foam product manufacturing
32615	Urethane and other foam product manufacturing
326150	Urethane and other foam product manufacturing
32616	Plastics bottle manufacturing
326160	Plastics bottle manufacturing
32619	Other plastics product manufacturing
326191	Plastics plumbing fixture manufacturing
326192	Resilient floor covering manufacturing
326199	All other plastics product manufacturing

Code	Short title
•3262	Rubber product manufacturing
32621	Tire manufacturing
326211	Tire manufacturing, except retreading
326212	Tire retreading
32622	Rubber and plastics hose and belting mfg.
326220	Rubber and plastics hose and belting mfg.
32629	Other rubber product manufacturing
326291	Rubber product mfg. for mechanical use
326299	All other rubber product manufacturing

327   Nonmetallic mineral product manufacturing

Code	Short title
3271	Clay product and refractory manufacturing
32711	Pottery, ceramics, and plumbing fixture mfg.
327111	Vitreous china plumbing fixture manufacturing
327112	Vitreous china and earthenware articles mfg.
327113	Porcelain electrical supply manufacturing
32712	Clay building material and refractories mfg.
327121	Brick and structural clay tile manufacturing
327122	Ceramic wall and floor tile manufacturing
327123	Other structural clay product manufacturing
327124	Clay refractory manufacturing
327125	Nonclay refractory manufacturing
3272	Glass and glass product manufacturing
32721	Glass and glass product manufacturing
327211	Flat glass manufacturing
327212	Other pressed and blown glass and glassware

Note: For definitions of abbreviations and acronyms see page 964.

Code	Short title	Code	Short title
327213	Glass container manufacturing	331111	Iron and steel mills
327215	Glass product mfg. made of purchased glass	331112	Ferroalloy and related product manufacturing
3273	Cement and concrete product manufacturing	3312	Steel product mfg. from purchased steel
32731	Cement manufacturing	33121	Iron, steel pipe and tube from purchase steel
327310	Cement manufacturing	331210	Iron, steel pipe and tube from purchase steel
32732	Ready-mix concrete manufacturing		
327320	Ready-mix concrete manufacturing	33122	Rolling and drawing of purchased steel
32733	Concrete pipe, brick, and block manufacturing	331221	Rolled steel shape manufacturing
327331	Concrete block and brick manufacturing	331222	Steel wire drawing
327332	Concrete pipe manufacturing	3313	Alumina and aluminum production
32739	Other concrete product manufacturing	33131	Alumina and aluminum production
327390	Other concrete product manufacturing	331311	Alumina refining
		331312	Primary aluminum production
3274	Lime and gypsum product manufacturing	331314	Secondary smelting and alloying of aluminum
32741	Lime manufacturing	331315	Aluminum sheet, plate, and foil manufacturing
327410	Lime manufacturing		
32742	Gypsum product manufacturing	331316	Aluminum extruded product manufacturing
327420	Gypsum product manufacturing		
3279	Other nonmetallic mineral products	331319	Other aluminum rolling and drawing
32791	Abrasive product manufacturing	3314	Other nonferrous metal production
327910	Abrasive product manufacturing	33141	Other nonferrous metal production
32799	All other nonmetallic mineral products mfg.	331411	Primary smelting and refining of copper
327991	Cut stone and stone product manufacturing	331419	Primary nonferrous metal, except Cu and Al
327992	Ground or treated minerals and earths mfg.	33142	Rolled, drawn, extruded, and alloyed copper
327993	Mineral wool manufacturing	331421	Copper rolling, drawing, and extruding
327999	Miscellaneous nonmetallic mineral products		
		331422	Copper wire, except mechanical, drawing
331	**Primary metal manufacturing**		
3311	Iron and steel mills and ferroalloy mfg.	331423	Secondary processing of copper
33111	Iron and steel mills and ferroalloy mfg.	33149	Nonferrous metal, except Cu and Al, shaping

Note: For definitions of abbreviations and acronyms see page 964.

Code	Short title
331491	Nonferrous metal, except Cu and Al, shaping
331492	Secondary processing of other nonferrous
3315	Foundries
33151	Ferrous metal foundries
331511	Iron foundries
331512	Steel investment foundries
331513	Steel foundries, except investment
33152	Nonferrous metal foundries
331521	Aluminum die-casting foundries
331522	Nonferrous, except Al, die-casting foundries
331524	Aluminum foundries, except die-casting
331525	Copper foundries, except die-casting
331528	Other nonferrous foundries, exc. die-casting
332	**Fabricated metal product manufacturing**
3321	Forging and stamping
33211	Forging and stamping
332111	Iron and steel forging
332112	Nonferrous forging
332114	Custom roll forming
332115	Crown and closure manufacturing
332116	Metal stamping
332117	Powder metallurgy part manufacturing
3322	Cutlery and handtool manufacturing
33221	Cutlery and handtool manufacturing
332211	Cutlery and flatware, except precious, mfg.
332212	Hand and edge tool manufacturing
332213	Saw blade and handsaw manufacturing
332214	Kitchen utensil, pot, and pan manufacturing

Code	Short title
3323	Architectural and structural metals mfg.
33231	Plate work and fabricated structural products
332311	Prefabricated metal buildings and components
332312	Fabricated structural metal manufacturing
332313	Plate work manufacturing
33232	Ornamental and architectural metal products
332321	Metal window and door manufacturing
332322	Sheet metal work manufacturing
332323	Ornamental and architectural metal work mfg.
3324	Boiler, tank, and shipping container mfg.
33241	Power boiler and heat exchanger manufacturing
332410	Power boiler and heat exchanger manufacturing
33242	Metal tank, heavy gauge, manufacturing
332420	Metal tank, heavy gauge, manufacturing
33243	Metal can, box, and other container mfg.
332431	Metal can manufacturing
332439	Other metal container manufacturing
3325	Hardware manufacturing
33251	Hardware manufacturing
332510	Hardware manufacturing
3326	Spring and wire product manufacturing
33261	Spring and wire product manufacturing
332611	Spring, heavy gauge, manufacturing
332612	Spring, light gauge, manufacturing
332618	Other fabricated wire product manufacturing
3327	Machine shops and threaded product mfg.

Note: For definitions of abbreviations and acronyms see page 964.

Code	Short title	Code	Short title
33271	Machine shops	**333**	**Machinery manufacturing**
332710	Machine shops	3331	Ag., construction, and mining machinery mfg.
33272	Turned product and screw, nut, and bolt mfg.	33311	Agricultural implement manufacturing
332721	Precision turned product manufacturing	333111	Farm machinery and equipment manufacturing
332722	Bolt, nut, screw, rivet, and washer mfg.	333112	Lawn and garden equipment manufacturing
3328	Coating, engraving, and heat treating metals	33312	Construction machinery manufacturing
33281	Coating, engraving, and heat treating metals	333120	Construction machinery manufacturing
332811	Metal heat treating	33313	Mining and oil and gas field machinery mfg.
332812	Metal coating and nonprecious engraving	333131	Mining machinery and equipment manufacturing
332813	Electroplating, anodizing, and coloring metal	333132	Oil and gas field machinery and equipment
3329	Other fabricated metal product manufacturing	3332	Industrial machinery manufacturing
33291	Metal valve manufacturing	33321	Sawmill and woodworking machinery
332911	Industrial valve manufacturing	333210	Sawmill and woodworking machinery
332912	Fluid power valve and hose fitting mfg.	33322	Plastics and rubber industry machinery
332913	Plumbing fixture fitting and trim mfg.	333220	Plastics and rubber industry machinery
332919	Other metal valve and pipe fitting mfg.	33329	Other industrial machinery manufacturing
33299	All other fabricated metal product mfg.	333291	Paper industry machinery manufacturing
332991	Ball and roller bearing manufacturing	333292	Textile machinery manufacturing
332992	Small arms ammunition manufacturing	333293	Printing machinery and equipment mfg.
332993	Ammunition, except small arms, manufacturing	333294	Food product machinery manufacturing
332994	Small arms manufacturing	333295	Semiconductor machinery manufacturing
332995	Other ordnance and accessories manufacturing	333298	All other industrial machinery manufacturing
332996	Fabricated pipe and pipe fitting mfg.	3333	Commercial and service industry machinery
332997	Industrial pattern manufacturing		
332998	Enameled iron and metal sanitary ware mfg.		
332999	Miscellaneous fabricated metal product mfg.		

Note: For definitions of abbreviations and acronyms see page 964.

Code	Short title
33331	Commercial and service industry machinery
333311	Automatic vending machine manufacturing
333312	Commercial laundry and drycleaning machinery
333313	Office machinery manufacturing
333314	Optical instrument and lens manufacturing
333315	Photographic and photocopying equipment mfg.
333319	Other commercial and service machinery mfg.
3334	HVAC and commercial refrigeration equipment
33341	HVAC and commercial refrigeration equipment
333411	Air purification equipment manufacturing
333412	Industrial and commercial fan and blower mfg.
333414	Heating equipment, except warm air furnaces
333415	AC, refrigeration, and forced air heating
3335	Metalworking machinery manufacturing
33351	Metalworking machinery manufacturing
333511	Industrial mold manufacturing
333512	Metal cutting machine tool manufacturing
333513	Metal forming machine tool manufacturing
333514	Special tool, die, jig, and fixture mfg.
333515	Cutting tool and machine tool accessory mfg.
333516	Rolling mill machinery and equipment mfg.
333518	Other metalworking machinery manufacturing
3336	Turbine and power transmission equipment mfg.
33361	Turbine and power transmission equipment mfg.

Code	Short title
333611	Turbine and turbine generator set units mfg.
333612	Speed changer, drive, and gear manufacturing
333613	Mechanical power transmission equipment mfg.
333618	Other engine equipment manufacturing
3339	Other general purpose machinery manufacturing
33391	Pump and compressor manufacturing
333911	Pump and pumping equipment manufacturing
333912	Air and gas compressor manufacturing
333913	Measuring and dispensing pump manufacturing
33392	Material handling equipment manufacturing
333921	Elevator and moving stairway manufacturing
333922	Conveyor and conveying equipment mfg.
333923	Overhead cranes, hoists, and monorail systems
333924	Industrial truck, trailer, and stacker mfg.
33399	All other general purpose machinery mfg.
333991	Power-driven handtool manufacturing
333992	Welding and soldering equipment manufacturing
333993	Packaging machinery manufacturing
333994	Industrial process furnace and oven mfg.
333995	Fluid power cylinder and actuator mfg.
333996	Fluid power pump and motor manufacturing
333997	Scale and balance, except laboratory, mfg.
333999	Miscellaneous general purpose machinery mfg.

Note: For definitions of abbreviations and acronyms see page 964.

Code	Short title	Code	Short title
334	**Computer and electronic product manufacturing**	334415	Electronic resistor manufacturing
3341	Computer and peripheral equipment mfg.	334416	Electronic coils, transformers, and inductors
33411	Computer and peripheral equipment mfg.	334417	Electronic connector manufacturing
334111	Electronic computer manufacturing	334418	Printed circuit assembly manufacturing
334112	Computer storage device manufacturing	334419	Other electronic component manufacturing
334113	Computer terminal manufacturing	3345	Electronic instrument manufacturing
334119	Other computer peripheral equipment mfg.	33451	Electronic instrument manufacturing
3342	Communications equipment manufacturing	334510	Electromedical apparatus manufacturing
33421	Telephone apparatus manufacturing	334511	Search, detection, and navigation instruments
334210	Telephone apparatus manufacturing	334512	Automatic environmental control manufacturing
33422	Broadcast and wireless communications equip.	334513	Industrial process variable instruments
334220	Broadcast and wireless communications equip.	334514	Totalizing fluid meters and counting devices
33429	Other communications equipment manufacturing	334515	Electricity and signal testing instruments
334290	Other communications equipment manufacturing	334516	Analytical laboratory instrument mfg.
3343	Audio and video equipment manufacturing	334517	Irradiation apparatus manufacturing
33431	Audio and video equipment manufacturing	334518	Watch, clock, and part manufacturing
334310	Audio and video equipment manufacturing	334519	Other measuring and controlling device mfg.
3344	Semiconductor and electronic component mfg.	3346	Magnetic media manufacturing and reproducing
33441	Semiconductor and electronic component mfg.	33461	Magnetic media manufacturing and reproducing
334411	Electron tube manufacturing	334611	Software reproducing
334412	Bare printed circuit board manufacturing	334612	Audio and video media reproduction
334413	Semiconductors and related device mfg.	334613	Magnetic and optical recording media mfg.
334414	Electronic capacitor manufacturing		

Note: For definitions of abbreviations and acronyms see page 964.

Code	Short title
335	**Electrical equipment and appliance mfg.**
3351	Electric lighting equipment manufacturing
33511	Electric lamp bulb and part manufacturing
335110	Electric lamp bulb and part manufacturing
33512	Lighting fixture manufacturing
335121	Residential electric lighting fixture mfg.
335122	Nonresidential electric lighting fixture mfg.
335129	Other lighting equipment manufacturing
3352	Household appliance manufacturing
33521	Small electrical appliance manufacturing
335211	Electric housewares and household fan mfg.
335212	Household vacuum cleaner manufacturing
33522	Major appliance manufacturing
335221	Household cooking appliance manufacturing
335222	Household refrigerator and home freezer mfg.
335224	Household laundry equipment manufacturing
335228	Other major household appliance manufacturing
3353	Electrical equipment manufacturing
33531	Electrical equipment manufacturing
335311	Electric power and specialty transformer mfg.
335312	Motor and generator manufacturing
335313	Switchgear and switchboard apparatus mfg.
335314	Relay and industrial control manufacturing

Code	Short title
3359	Other electrical equipment and component mfg.
33591	Battery manufacturing
335911	Storage battery manufacturing
335912	Primary battery manufacturing
33592	Communication and energy wire and cable mfg.
335921	Fiber optic cable manufacturing
335929	Other communication and energy wire mfg.
33593	Wiring device manufacturing
335931	Current-carrying wiring device manufacturing
335932	Noncurrent-carrying wiring device mfg.
33599	Other electrical equipment and component mfg.
335991	Carbon and graphite product manufacturing
335999	Miscellaneous electrical equipment mfg.
336	**Transportation equipment manufacturing**
3361	Motor vehicle manufacturing
33611	Automobile and light truck manufacturing
336111	Automobile manufacturing
336112	Light truck and utility vehicle manufacturing
33612	Heavy duty truck manufacturing
336120	Heavy duty truck manufacturing
3362	Motor vehicle body and trailer manufacturing
33621	Motor vehicle body and trailer manufacturing
336211	Motor vehicle body manufacturing
336212	Truck trailer manufacturing
336213	Motor home manufacturing
336214	Travel trailer and camper manufacturing
3363	Motor vehicle parts manufacturing
33631	Motor vehicle gasoline engine and parts mfg.

Note: For definitions of abbreviations and acronyms see page 964.

Code	Short title
336311	Carburetor, piston, ring, and valve mfg.
336312	Gasoline engine and engine parts mfg.
33632	Motor vehicle electric equipment
336321	Vehicular lighting equipment manufacturing
336322	Other motor vehicle electric equipment mfg.
33633	Motor vehicle steering and suspension parts
336330	Motor vehicle steering and suspension parts
33634	Motor vehicle brake system manufacturing
336340	Motor vehicle brake system manufacturing
33635	Motor vehicle power train components mfg.
336350	Motor vehicle power train components mfg.
33636	Motor vehicle seating and interior trim mfg.
336360	Motor vehicle seating and interior trim mfg.
33637	Motor vehicle metal stamping
336370	Motor vehicle metal stamping
33639	Other motor vehicle parts manufacturing
336391	Motor vehicle air-conditioning manufacturing
336399	All other motor vehicle parts manufacturing
3364	Aerospace product and parts manufacturing
33641	Aerospace product and parts manufacturing
336411	Aircraft manufacturing
336412	Aircraft engine and engine parts mfg.
336413	Other aircraft parts and equipment
336414	Guided missile and space vehicle mfg.

Code	Short title
336415	Space vehicle propulsion units and parts mfg.
336419	Other guided missile and space vehicle parts
3365	Railroad rolling stock manufacturing
33651	Railroad rolling stock manufacturing
336510	Railroad rolling stock manufacturing
3366	Ship and boat building
33661	Ship and boat building
336611	Ship building and repairing
336612	Boat building
3369	Other transportation equipment manufacturing
33699	Other transportation equipment manufacturing
336991	Motorcycle, bicycle, and parts manufacturing
336992	Military armored vehicles and tank parts mfg.
336999	All other transportation equipment mfg.
337	**Furniture and related product manufacturing**
3371	Household and institutional furniture mfg.
33711	Wood kitchen cabinet and countertop mfg.
337110	Wood kitchen cabinet and countertop mfg.
33712	Other household and institutional furniture
337121	Upholstered household furniture manufacturing
337122	Nonupholstered wood household furniture mfg.
337124	Metal household furniture manufacturing
337125	Household furniture, exc. wood or metal, mfg.
337127	Institutional furniture manufacturing

Note: For definitions of abbreviations and acronyms see page 964.

Code	Short title
337129	Wood TV, radio, and sewing machine housings
3372	Office furniture and fixtures manufacturing
33721	Office furniture and fixtures manufacturing
337211	Wood office furniture manufacturing
337212	Custom architectural woodwork and millwork
337214	Office furniture, except wood, manufacturing
337215	Showcases, partitions, shelving, and lockers
3379	Other furniture related product manufacturing
33791	Mattress manufacturing
337910	Mattress manufacturing
33792	Blind and shade manufacturing
337920	Blind and shade manufacturing
339	**Miscellaneous manufacturing**
3391	Medical equipment and supplies manufacturing
33911	Medical equipment and supplies manufacturing
339111	Laboratory apparatus and furniture mfg.
339112	Surgical and medical instrument manufacturing
339113	Surgical appliance and supplies manufacturing
339114	Dental equipment and supplies manufacturing
339115	Ophthalmic goods manufacturing
339116	Dental laboratories
3399	Other miscellaneous manufacturing
33991	Jewelry and silverware manufacturing
339911	Jewelry, except costume, manufacturing
339912	Silverware and hollowware manufacturing

Code	Short title
339913	Jewelers' material and lapidary work mfg.
339914	Costume jewelry and novelty manufacturing
33992	Sporting and athletic goods manufacturing
339920	Sporting and athletic goods manufacturing
33993	Doll, toy, and game manufacturing
339931	Doll and stuffed toy manufacturing
339932	Game, toy, and children's vehicle mfg.
33994	Office supplies, except paper, manufacturing
339941	Pen and mechanical pencil manufacturing
339942	Lead pencil and art good manufacturing
339943	Marking device manufacturing
339944	Carbon paper and inked ribbon manufacturing
33995	Sign manufacturing
339950	Sign manufacturing
33999	All other miscellaneous manufacturing
339991	Gasket, packing, and sealing device mfg.
339992	Musical instrument manufacturing
339993	Fastener, button, needle, and pin mfg.
339994	Broom, brush, and mop manufacturing
339995	Burial casket manufacturing
339999	All other miscellaneous manufacturing
42	**WHOLESALE TRADE**
423	**Merchant wholesalers, durable goods**
4231	Motor vehicle and parts merchant wholesalers

Note: For definitions of abbreviations and acronyms see page 964.

Code	Short title	Code	Short title
42311	Motor vehicle merchant wholesalers	423410	Photographic equip. merchant wholesalers
423110	Motor vehicle merchant wholesalers	42342	Office equipment merchant wholesalers
42312	New motor vehicle parts merchant wholesalers	423420	Office equipment merchant wholesalers
423120	New motor vehicle parts merchant wholesalers	42343	Computer and software merchant wholesalers
42313	Tire and tube merchant wholesalers	423430	Computer and software merchant wholesalers
423130	Tire and tube merchant wholesalers	42344	Other commercial equip. merchant wholesalers
42314	Used motor vehicle parts merchant wholesalers	423440	Other commercial equip. merchant wholesalers
423140	Used motor vehicle parts merchant wholesalers	42345	Medical equipment merchant wholesalers
4232	Furniture and furnishing merchant wholesalers	423450	Medical equipment merchant wholesalers
42321	Furniture merchant wholesalers	42346	Ophthalmic goods merchant wholesalers
423210	Furniture merchant wholesalers	423460	Ophthalmic goods merchant wholesalers
42322	Home furnishing merchant wholesalers	42349	Other professional equip. merchant wholesaler
423220	Home furnishing merchant wholesalers	423490	Other professional equip. merchant wholesaler
4233	Lumber and const. supply merchant wholesalers	4235	Metal and mineral merchant wholesalers
42331	Lumber and wood merchant wholesalers	42351	Metal merchant wholesalers
423310	Lumber and wood merchant wholesalers	423510	Metal merchant wholesalers
42332	Masonry material merchant wholesalers	42352	Coal and other mineral merchant wholesalers
423320	Masonry material merchant wholesalers	423520	Coal and other mineral merchant wholesalers
42333	Roofing and siding merchant wholesalers	4236	Electric goods merchant wholesalers
423330	Roofing and siding merchant wholesalers	42361	Elec. equip. and wiring merchant wholesalers
42339	Other const. material merchant wholesalers	423610	Elec. equip. and wiring merchant wholesalers
423390	Other const. material merchant wholesalers	42362	Electric appliance merchant wholesalers
4234	Commercial equip. merchant wholesalers	423620	Electric appliance merchant wholesalers
42341	Photographic equip. merchant wholesalers	42369	Other electronic parts merchant wholesalers

Note: For definitions of abbreviations and acronyms see page 964.

Code	Short title
423690	Other electronic parts merchant wholesalers
4237	Hardware and plumbing merchant wholesalers
42371	Hardware merchant wholesalers
423710	Hardware merchant wholesalers
42372	Plumbing equip. merchant wholesalers
423720	Plumbing equip. merchant wholesalers
42373	HVAC equip. merchant wholesalers
423730	HVAC equip. merchant wholesalers
42374	Refrigeration equip. merchant wholesalers
423740	Refrigeration equip. merchant wholesalers
4238	Machinery and supply merchant wholesalers
42381	Construction equipment merchant wholesalers
423810	Construction equipment merchant wholesalers
42382	Farm and garden equip. merchant wholesalers
423820	Farm and garden equip. merchant wholesalers
42383	Industrial machinery merchant wholesalers
423830	Industrial machinery merchant wholesalers
42384	Industrial supplies merchant wholesalers
423840	Industrial supplies merchant wholesalers
42385	Service estab. equip. merchant wholesalers
423850	Service estab. equip. merchant wholesalers
42386	Other transport. goods merchant wholesalers
423860	Other transport. goods merchant wholesalers
4239	Misc. durable goods merchant wholesalers

Code	Short title
42391	Sporting goods merchant wholesalers
423910	Sporting goods merchant wholesalers
42392	Toy and hobby goods merchant wholesalers
423920	Toy and hobby goods merchant wholesalers
42393	Recyclable material merchant wholesalers
423930	Recyclable material merchant wholesalers
42394	Jewelry merchant wholesalers
423940	Jewelry merchant wholesalers
42399	All other durable goods merchant wholesalers
423990	All other durable goods merchant wholesalers
424	**Merchant wholesalers, nondurable goods**
4241	Paper and paper product merchant wholesalers
42411	Printing and writing paper merch. whls.
424110	Printing and writing paper merch. whls.
42412	Office supplies merchant wholesalers
424120	Office supplies merchant wholesalers
42413	Industrial paper merchant wholesalers
424130	Industrial paper merchant wholesalers
4242	Druggists' goods merchant wholesalers
42421	Druggists' goods merchant wholesalers
424210	Druggists' goods merchant wholesalers
4243	Apparel and piece goods merchant wholesalers
42431	Piece goods merchant wholesalers

Note: For definitions of abbreviations and acronyms see page 964.

Code	Short title	Code	Short title
424310	Piece goods merchant wholesalers	42449	Other grocery product merchant wholesalers
42432	Men's and boys' clothing merchant wholesalers	424490	Other grocery product merchant wholesalers
424320	Men's and boys' clothing merchant wholesalers	4245	Farm product raw material merch. whls.
42433	Women's and children's clothing merch. whls.	42451	Grain and field bean merchant wholesalers
424330	Women's and children's clothing merch. whls.	424510	Grain and field bean merchant wholesalers
42434	Footwear merchant wholesalers	42452	Livestock merchant wholesalers
424340	Footwear merchant wholesalers	424520	Livestock merchant wholesalers
4244	Grocery and related product wholesalers	42459	Other farm product raw material merch. whls.
42441	General line grocery merchant wholesalers	424590	Other farm product raw material merch. whls.
424410	General line grocery merchant wholesalers	4246	Chemical merchant wholesalers
42442	Packaged frozen food merchant wholesalers	42461	Plastics materials merchant wholesalers
424420	Packaged frozen food merchant wholesalers	424610	Plastics materials merchant wholesalers
42443	Dairy product merchant wholesalers	42469	Other chemicals merchant wholesalers
424430	Dairy product merchant wholesalers	424690	Other chemicals merchant wholesalers
42444	Poultry product merchant wholesalers	4247	Petroleum merchant wholesalers
424440	Poultry product merchant wholesalers	42471	Petroleum bulk stations and terminals
42445	Confectionery merchant wholesalers	424710	Petroleum bulk stations and terminals
424450	Confectionery merchant wholesalers	42472	Other petroleum merchant wholesalers
42446	Fish and seafood merchant wholesalers	424720	Other petroleum merchant wholesalers
424460	Fish and seafood merchant wholesalers	4248	Alcoholic beverage merchant wholesalers
42447	Meat and meat product merchant wholesalers	42481	Beer and ale merchant wholesalers
424470	Meat and meat product merchant wholesalers	424810	Beer and ale merchant wholesalers
42448	Fruit and vegetable merchant wholesalers	42482	Wine and spirit merchant wholesalers
424480	Fruit and vegetable merchant wholesalers	424820	Wine and spirit merchant wholesalers
		4249	Misc. nondurable goods merchant wholesalers

Note: For definitions of abbreviations and acronyms see page 964.

Code	Short title
42491	Farm supplies merchant wholesalers
424910	Farm supplies merchant wholesalers
42492	Book and periodical merchant wholesalers
424920	Book and periodical merchant wholesalers
42493	Nursery and florist merchant wholesalers
424930	Nursery and florist merchant wholesalers
42494	Tobacco and tobacco product merch. whls.
424940	Tobacco and tobacco product merch. whls.
42495	Paint and supplies merchant wholesalers
424950	Paint and supplies merchant wholesalers
42499	Other nondurable goods merchant wholesalers
424990	Other nondurable goods merchant wholesalers
425	**Electronic markets and agents and brokers**
4251	Electronic markets and agents and brokers
42511	Business to business electronic markets
425110	Business to business electronic markets
42512	Wholesale trade agents and brokers
425120	Wholesale trade agents and brokers
44-45	**RETAIL TRADE**
441	**Motor vehicle and parts dealers**
4411	Automobile dealers
44111	New car dealers
441110	New car dealers
44112	Used car dealers

Code	Short title
441120	Used car dealers
4412	Other motor vehicle dealers
44121	Recreational vehicle dealers
441210	Recreational vehicle dealers
44122	Motorcycle, boat, and other vehicle dealers
441221	Motorcycle dealers
441222	Boat dealers
441229	All other motor vehicle dealers
4413	Auto parts, accessories, and tire stores
44131	Automotive parts and accessories stores
441310	Automotive parts and accessories stores
44132	Tire dealers
441320	Tire dealers
442	**Furniture and home furnishings stores**
4421	Furniture stores
44211	Furniture stores
442110	Furniture stores
4422	Home furnishings stores
44221	Floor covering stores
442210	Floor covering stores
44229	Other home furnishings stores
442291	Window treatment stores
442299	All other home furnishings stores
443	**Electronics and appliance stores**
4431	Electronics and appliance stores
44311	Appliance, TV, and other electronics stores
443111	Household appliance stores
443112	Radio, TV, and other electronics stores
44312	Computer and software stores
443120	Computer and software stores
44313	Camera and photographic supplies stores
443130	Camera and photographic supplies stores

Note: For definitions of abbreviations and acronyms see page 964.

Code	Short title
444	**Building material and garden supply stores**
4441	Building material and supplies dealers
44411	Home centers
444110	Home centers
44412	Paint and wallpaper stores
444120	Paint and wallpaper stores
44413	Hardware stores
444130	Hardware stores
44419	Other building material dealers
444190	Other building material dealers
4442	Lawn and garden equipment and supplies stores
44421	Outdoor power equipment stores
444210	Outdoor power equipment stores
44422	Nursery, garden, and farm supply stores
444220	Nursery, garden, and farm supply stores
445	**Food and beverage stores**
4451	Grocery stores
44511	Supermarkets and other grocery stores
445110	Supermarkets and other grocery stores
44512	Convenience stores
445120	Convenience stores
4452	Specialty food stores
44521	Meat markets
445210	Meat markets
44522	Fish and seafood markets
445220	Fish and seafood markets
44523	Fruit and vegetable markets
445230	Fruit and vegetable markets
44529	Other specialty food stores
445291	Baked goods stores
445292	Confectionery and nut stores
445299	All other specialty food stores
4453	Beer, wine, and liquor stores
44531	Beer, wine, and liquor stores
445310	Beer, wine, and liquor stores

Code	Short title
446	**Health and personal care stores**
4461	Health and personal care stores
44611	Pharmacies and drug stores
446110	Pharmacies and drug stores
44612	Cosmetic and beauty supply stores
446120	Cosmetic and beauty supply stores
44613	Optical goods stores
446130	Optical goods stores
44619	Other health and personal care stores
446191	Food, health, supplement stores
446199	All other health and personal care stores
447	**Gasoline stations**
4471	Gasoline stations
44711	Gasoline stations with convenience stores
447110	Gasoline stations with convenience stores
44719	Other gasoline stations
447190	Other gasoline stations
448	**Clothing and clothing accessories stores**
4481	Clothing stores
44811	Men's clothing stores
448110	Men's clothing stores
44812	Women's clothing stores
448120	Women's clothing stores
44813	Children's and infants' clothing stores
448130	Children's and infants' clothing stores
44814	Family clothing stores
448140	Family clothing stores
44815	Clothing accessories stores
448150	Clothing accessories stores
44819	Other clothing stores
448190	Other clothing stores
4482	Shoe stores
44821	Shoe stores

Note: For definitions of abbreviations and acronyms see page 964.

Code	Short title
448210	Shoe stores
4483	Jewelry, luggage, and leather goods stores
44831	Jewelry stores
448310	Jewelry stores
44832	Luggage and leather goods stores
448320	Luggage and leather goods stores

451   **Sporting goods, hobby, book and music stores**

Code	Short title
4511	Sporting goods and musical instrument stores
45111	Sporting goods stores
451110	Sporting goods stores
45112	Hobby, toy, and game stores
451120	Hobby, toy, and game stores
45113	Sewing, needlework, and piece goods stores
451130	Sewing, needlework, and piece goods stores
45114	Musical instrument and supplies stores
451140	Musical instrument and supplies stores
4512	Book, periodical, and music stores
45121	Book stores and news dealers
451211	Book stores
451212	News dealers and newsstands
45122	Prerecorded tape, CD, and record stores
451220	Prerecorded tape, CD, and record stores

452   **General merchandise stores**

Code	Short title
4521	Department stores
45211	Department stores
452111	Department stores, except discount
452112	Discount department stores
4529	Other general merchandise stores
45291	Warehouse clubs and supercenters
452910	Warehouse clubs and supercenters
45299	All other general merchandise stores
452990	All other general merchandise stores

453   **Miscellaneous store retailers**

Code	Short title
4531	Florists
45311	Florists
453110	Florists
4532	Office supplies, stationery, and gift stores
45321	Office supplies and stationery stores
453210	Office supplies and stationery stores
45322	Gift, novelty, and souvenir stores
453220	Gift, novelty, and souvenir stores
4533	Used merchandise stores
45331	Used merchandise stores
453310	Used merchandise stores
4539	Other miscellaneous store retailers
45391	Pet and pet supplies stores
453910	Pet and pet supplies stores
45392	Art dealers
453920	Art dealers
45393	Manufactured, mobile, home dealers
453930	Manufactured, mobile, home dealers
45399	All other miscellaneous store retailers
453991	Tobacco stores
453998	Store retailers not specified elsewhere

454   **Nonstore retailers**

Code	Short title
4541	Electronic shopping and mail-order houses
45411	Electronic shopping and mail-order houses

Note: For definitions of abbreviations and acronyms see page 964.

Code	Short title
454111	Electronic shopping
454112	Electronic auctions
454113	Mail-order houses
4542	Vending machine operators
45421	Vending machine operators
454210	Vending machine operators
4543	Direct selling establishments
45431	Fuel dealers
454311	Heating oil dealers
454312	Liquefied petroleum gas, bottled gas, dealers
454319	Other fuel dealers
45439	Other direct selling establishments
454390	Other direct selling establishments

48-49 TRANSPORTATION AND WAREHOUSING

481 Air transportation

Code	Short title
4811	Scheduled air transportation
48111	Scheduled air transportation
481111	Scheduled passenger air transportation
481112	Scheduled freight air transportation
4812	Nonscheduled air transportation
48121	Nonscheduled air transportation
481211	Nonscheduled air passenger chartering
481212	Nonscheduled air freight chartering
481219	Other nonscheduled air transportation

482 Rail transportation

Code	Short title
4821	Rail transportation
48211	Rail transportation
482111	Line-haul railroads
482112	Short line railroads

483 Water transportation

Code	Short title
4831	Sea, coastal, and Great Lakes transportation
48311	Sea, coastal, and Great Lakes transportation
483111	Deep sea freight transportation
483112	Deep sea passenger transportation
483113	Coastal and Great Lakes freight transport.
483114	Coastal and Great Lakes passenger transport.
4832	Inland water transportation
48321	Inland water transportation
483211	Inland water freight transportation
483212	Inland water passenger transportation

484 Truck transportation

Code	Short title
4841	General freight trucking
48411	General freight trucking, local
484110	General freight trucking, local
48412	General freight trucking, long-distance
484121	General freight trucking, long-distance TL
484122	General freight trucking, long-distance LTL
4842	Specialized freight trucking
48421	Used household and office goods moving
484210	Used household and office goods moving
48422	Other specialized trucking, local
484220	Other specialized trucking, local
48423	Other specialized trucking, long-distance
484230	Other specialized trucking, long-distance

485 Transit and ground passenger transportation

Code	Short title
4851	Urban transit systems
48511	Urban transit systems
485111	Mixed mode transit systems
485112	Commuter rail systems
485113	Bus and other motor vehicle transit systems

Note: For definitions of abbreviations and acronyms see page 964.

Code	Short title
485119	Other urban transit systems
4852	Interurban and rural bus transportation
48521	Interurban and rural bus transportation
485210	Interurban and rural bus transportation
4853	Taxi and limousine service
48531	Taxi service
485310	Taxi service
48532	Limousine service
485320	Limousine service
4854	School and employee bus transportation
48541	School and employee bus transportation
485410	School and employee bus transportation
4855	Charter bus industry
48551	Charter bus industry
485510	Charter bus industry
4859	Other ground passenger transportation
48599	Other ground passenger transportation
485991	Special needs transportation
485999	All other ground passenger transportation

486   Pipeline transportation

Code	Short title
4861	Pipeline transportation of crude oil
48611	Pipeline transportation of crude oil
486110	Pipeline transportation of crude oil
4862	Pipeline transportation of natural gas
48621	Pipeline transportation of natural gas
486210	Pipeline transportation of natural gas
4869	Other pipeline transportation
48691	Refined petroleum product pipeline transport.

Code	Short title
486910	Refined petroleum product pipeline transport.
48699	All other pipeline transportation
486990	All other pipeline transportation

487   Scenic and sightseeing transportation

Code	Short title
4871	Scenic and sightseeing transportation, land
48711	Scenic and sightseeing transportation, land
487110	Scenic and sightseeing transportation, land
4872	Scenic and sightseeing transportation, water
48721	Scenic and sightseeing transportation, water
487210	Scenic and sightseeing transportation, water
4879	Scenic and sightseeing transportation, other
48799	Scenic and sightseeing transportation, other
487990	Scenic and sightseeing transportation, other

488   Support activities for transportation

Code	Short title
4881	Support activities for air transportation
48811	Airport operations
488111	Air traffic control
488119	Other airport operations
48819	Other support activities for air transport.
488190	Other support activities for air transport.
4882	Support activities for rail transportation
48821	Support activities for rail transportation
488210	Support activities for rail transportation
4883	Support activities for water transportation

Note: For definitions of abbreviations and acronyms see page 964.

Code	Short title
48831	Port and harbor operations
488310	Port and harbor operations
48832	Marine cargo handling
488320	Marine cargo handling
48833	Navigational services to shipping
488330	Navigational services to shipping
48839	Other support activities for water transport.
488390	Other support activities for water transport.
4884	Support activities for road transportation
48841	Motor vehicle towing
488410	Motor vehicle towing
48849	Other support activities for road transport.
488490	Other support activities for road transport.
4885	Freight transportation arrangement
48851	Freight transportation arrangement
488510	Freight transportation arrangement
4889	Other support activities for transportation
48899	Other support activities for transportation
488991	Packing and crating
488999	All other support activities for transport.
491	**Postal service**
4911	Postal service
49111	Postal service
491110	Postal service
492	**Couriers and messengers**
4921	Couriers
49211	Couriers
492110	Couriers
4922	Local messengers and local delivery

Code	Short title
49221	Local messengers and local delivery
492210	Local messengers and local delivery
493	**Warehousing and storage**
4931	Warehousing and storage
49311	General warehousing and storage
493110	General warehousing and storage
49312	Refrigerated warehousing and storage
493120	Refrigerated warehousing and storage
49313	Farm product warehousing and storage
493130	Farm product warehousing and storage
49319	Other warehousing and storage
493190	Other warehousing and storage
51	**INFORMATION**
511	**Publishing industries, except Internet**
5111	Newspaper, book, and directory publishers
51111	Newspaper publishers
511110	Newspaper publishers
51112	Periodical publishers
511120	Periodical publishers
51113	Book publishers
511130	Book publishers
51114	Directory and mailing list publishers
511140	Directory and mailing list publishers
51119	Other publishers
511191	Greeting card publishers
511199	All other publishers,
5112	Software publishers
51121	Software publishers
511210	Software publishers

Note: For definitions of abbreviations and acronyms see page 964.

Code	Short title
512	**Motion picture and sound recording industries**
5121	Motion picture and video industries
51211	Motion picture and video production
512110	Motion picture and video production
51212	Motion picture and video distribution
512120	Motion picture and video distribution
51213	Motion picture and video exhibition
512131	Motion picture theaters, except drive-ins
512132	Drive-in motion picture theaters
51219	Postproduction and other related industries
512191	Teleproduction and postproduction services
512199	Other motion picture and video industries
5122	Sound recording industries
51221	Record production
512210	Record production
51222	Integrated record production and distribution
512220	Integrated record production and distribution
51223	Music publishers
512230	Music publishers
51224	Sound recording studios
512240	Sound recording studios
51229	Other sound recording industries
512290	Other sound recording industries
515	**Broadcasting, except Internet**
5151	Radio and television broadcasting
51511	Radio broadcasting
515111	Radio networks
515112	Radio stations

Code	Short title
51512	Television broadcasting
515120	Television broadcasting
5152	Cable and other subscription programming
51521	Cable and other subscription programming
515210	Cable and other subscription programming
516	**Internet publishing and broadcasting**
5161	Internet publishing and broadcasting
51611	Internet publishing and broadcasting
516110	Internet publishing and broadcasting
517	**Telecommunications**
5171	Wired telecommunications carriers
51711	Wired telecommunications carriers
517110	Wired telecommunications carriers
5172	Wireless telecommunications carriers
51721	Wireless telecommunications carriers
517211	Paging
517212	Cellular and other wireless carriers
5173	Telecommunications resellers
51731	Telecommunications resellers
517310	Telecommunications resellers
5174	Satellite telecommunications
51741	Satellite telecommunications
517410	Satellite telecommunications
5175	Cable and other program distribution
51751	Cable and other program distribution
517510	Cable and other program distribution
5179	Other telecommunications

Note: For definitions of abbreviations and acronyms see page 964.

Code	Short title
51791	Other telecommunications
517910	Other telecommunications

518 **ISPs, search portals, and data processing**

Code	Short title
5181	ISPs and Web search portals
51811	ISPs and Web search portals
518111	Internet service providers
518112	Web search portals
5182	Data processing and related services
51821	Data processing and related services
518210	Data processing and related services

519 **Other information services**

Code	Short title
5191	Other information services
51911	News syndicates
519110	News syndicates
51912	Libraries and archives
519120	Libraries and archives
51919	All other information services
519190	All other information services

52 **FINANCE AND INSURANCE**

521 **Monetary authorities—central bank**

Code	Short title
5211	Monetary authorities—central bank
52111	Monetary authorities—central bank
521110	Monetary authorities—central bank

522 **Credit intermediation and related activities**

Code	Short title
5221	Depository credit intermediation
52211	Commercial banking
522110	Commercial banking
52212	Savings institutions
522120	Savings institutions
52213	Credit unions
522130	Credit unions
52219	Other depository credit intermediation
522190	Other depository credit intermediation
5222	Nondepository credit intermediation
52221	Credit card issuing
522210	Credit card issuing
52222	Sales financing
522220	Sales financing
52229	Other nondepository credit intermediation
522291	Consumer lending
522292	Real estate credit
522293	International trade financing
522294	Secondary market financing
522298	All other nondepository credit intermediation
5223	Activities related to credit intermediation
52231	Mortgage and nonmortgage loan brokers
522310	Mortgage and nonmortgage loan brokers
52232	Financial transaction processing and clearing
522320	Financial transaction processing and clearing
52239	Other credit intermediation activities
522390	Other credit intermediation activities

523 **Securities, commodity contracts, investments**

Code	Short title
5231	Securities and commodity contracts brokerage
52311	Investment banking and securities dealing
523110	Investment banking and securities dealing
52312	Securities brokerage
523120	Securities brokerage
52313	Commodity contracts dealing
523130	Commodity contracts dealing

Note: For definitions of abbreviations and acronyms see page 964.

Code	Short title
52314	Commodity contracts brokerage
523140	Commodity contracts brokerage
5232	Securities and commodity exchanges
52321	Securities and commodity exchanges
523210	Securities and commodity exchanges
5239	Other financial investment activities
52391	Miscellaneous intermediation
523910	Miscellaneous intermediation
52392	Portfolio management
523920	Portfolio management
52393	Investment advice
523930	Investment advice
52399	All other financial investment activities
523991	Trust, fiduciary, and custody activities
523999	Miscellaneous financial investment activities
524	**Insurance carriers and related activities**
5241	Insurance carriers
52411	Direct life and health insurance carriers
524113	Direct life insurance carriers
524114	Direct health and medical insurance carriers
52412	Direct insurers, except life and health
524126	Direct property and casualty insurers
524127	Direct title insurance carriers
524128	Other direct insurance carriers
52413	Reinsurance carriers
524130	Reinsurance carriers
5242	Insurance agencies and brokerages
52421	Insurance agencies and brokerages
524210	Insurance agencies and brokerages

Code	Short title
52429	Other insurance related activities
524291	Claims adjusting
524292	Third party administration of insurance funds
524298	All other insurance related activities
525	**Funds, trusts, and other financial vehicles**
5251	Insurance and employee benefit funds
52511	Pension funds
525110	Pension funds
52512	Health and welfare funds
525120	Health and welfare funds
52519	Other insurance funds
525190	Other insurance funds
5259	Other investment pools and funds
52591	Open-end investment funds
525910	Open-end investment funds
52592	Trusts, estates, and agency accounts
525920	Trusts, estates, and agency accounts
52593	Real estate investment trusts
525930	Real estate investment trusts
52599	Other financial vehicles
525990	Other financial vehicles
53	**REAL ESTATE AND RENTAL AND LEASING**
531	**Real estate**
5311	Lessors of real estate
53111	Lessors of residential buildings
531110	Lessors of residential buildings
53112	Lessors of nonresidential buildings
531120	Lessors of nonresidential buildings
53113	Miniwarehouse and self-storage unit operators
531130	Miniwarehouse and self-storage unit operators

Note: For definitions of abbreviations and acronyms see page 964.

Code	Short title
53119	Lessors of other real estate property
531190	Lessors of other real estate property
5312	Offices of real estate agents and brokers
53121	Offices of real estate agents and brokers
531210	Offices of real estate agents and brokers
5313	Activities related to real estate
53131	Real estate property managers
531311	Residential property managers
531312	Nonresidential property managers
53132	Offices of real estate appraisers
531320	Offices of real estate appraisers
53139	Other activities related to real estate
531390	Other activities related to real estate
532	**Rental and leasing services**
5321	Automotive equipment rental and leasing
53211	Passenger car rental and leasing
532111	Passenger car rental
532112	Passenger car leasing
53212	Truck, trailer, and RV rental and leasing
532120	Truck, trailer, and RV rental and leasing
5322	Consumer goods rental
53221	Consumer electronics and appliances rental
532210	Consumer electronics and appliances rental
53222	Formal wear and costume rental
532220	Formal wear and costume rental
53223	Video tape and disc rental
532230	Video tape and disc rental
53229	Other consumer goods rental
532291	Home health equipment rental
532292	Recreational goods rental
532299	All other consumer goods rental

Code	Short title
5323	General rental centers
53231	General rental centers
532310	General rental centers
5324	Machinery and equipment rental and leasing
53241	Heavy machinery rental and leasing
532411	Transportation equipment rental and leasing
532412	Other heavy machinery rental and leasing
53242	Office equipment rental and leasing
532420	Office equipment rental and leasing
53249	Other machinery rental and leasing
532490	Other machinery rental and leasing
533	**Lessors of nonfinancial intangible assets**
5331	Lessors of nonfinancial intangible assets
53311	Lessors of nonfinancial intangible assets
533110	Lessors of nonfinancial intangible assets
54	**PROFESSIONAL AND TECHNICAL SERVICES**
541	**Professional and technical services**
5411	Legal services
54111	Offices of lawyers
541110	Offices of lawyers
54112	Offices of notaries
541120	Offices of notaries
54119	Other legal services
541191	Title abstract and settlement offices
541199	All other legal services
5412	Accounting and bookkeeping services

Note: For definitions of abbreviations and acronyms **see page 964.**

Code	Short title	Code	Short title
54121	Accounting and bookkeeping services	541511	Custom computer programming services
541211	Offices of certified public accountants	541512	Computer systems design services
541213	Tax preparation services	541513	Computer facilities management services
541214	Payroll services		
541219	Other accounting services	541519	Other computer related services
5413	Architectural and engineering services	5416	Management and technical consulting services
54131	Architectural services	54161	Management consulting services
541310	Architectural services	541611	Administrative management consulting services
54132	Landscape architectural services	541612	Human resource consulting services
541320	Landscape architectural services		
54133	Engineering services	541613	Marketing consulting services
541330	Engineering services	541614	Process and logistics consulting services
54134	Drafting services		
541340	Drafting services	541618	Other management consulting services
54135	Building inspection services		
541350	Building inspection services	54162	Environmental consulting services
54136	Geophysical surveying and mapping services	541620	Environmental consulting services
541360	Geophysical surveying and mapping services		
		54169	Other technical consulting services
54137	Other surveying and mapping services	541690	Other technical consulting services
541370	Other surveying and mapping services		
		5417	Scientific research and development services
54138	Testing laboratories	54171	Physical, engineering and biological research
541380	Testing laboratories		
5414	Specialized design services	541710	Physical, engineering and biological research
54141	Interior design services		
541410	Interior design services	54172	Social science and humanities research
54142	Industrial design services		
541420	Industrial design services	541720	Social science and humanities research
54143	Graphic design services		
541430	Graphic design services		
54149	Other specialized design services	5418	Advertising and related services
		54181	Advertising agencies
541490	Other specialized design services	541810	Advertising agencies
		54182	Public relations agencies
5415	Computer systems design and related services	541820	Public relations agencies
		54183	Media buying agencies
54151	Computer systems design and related services	541830	Media buying agencies
		54184	Media representatives

Note: For definitions of abbreviations and acronyms see page 964.

Code	Short title	Code	Short title
541840	Media representatives	551112	Offices of other holding companies
54185	Display advertising		
541850	Display advertising	551114	Managing offices
54186	Direct mail advertising	**56**	**ADMINISTRATIVE AND WASTE SERVICES**
541860	Direct mail advertising		
54187	Advertising material distribution services		
541870	Advertising material distribution services	**561**	**Administrative and support services**
54189	Other services related to advertising	5611	Office administrative services
		56111	Office administrative services
541890	Other services related to advertising	561110	Office administrative services
		5612	Facilities support services
5419	Other professional and technical services	56121	Facilities support services
		561210	Facilities support services
54191	Marketing research and public opinion polling	5613	Employment services
		56131	Employment placement agencies
541910	Marketing research and public opinion polling	561310	Employment placement agencies
54192	Photographic services	56132	Temporary help services
541921	Photography studios, portrait	561320	Temporary help services
541922	Commercial photography	56133	Professional employer organizations
54193	Translation and interpretation services	561330	Professional employer organizations
541930	Translation and interpretation services	5614	Business support services
		56141	Document preparation services
54194	Veterinary services	561410	Document preparation services
541940	Veterinary services	56142	Telephone call centers
54199	All other professional and technical services	561421	Telephone answering services
		561422	Telemarketing bureaus
541990	All other professional and technical services	56143	Business service centers
		561431	Private mail centers
55	**MANAGEMENT OF COMPANIES AND ENTERPRISES**	561439	Other business service centers
		56144	Collection agencies
		561440	Collection agencies
551	**Management of companies and enterprises**	56145	Credit bureaus
		561450	Credit bureaus
5511	Management of companies and enterprises	56149	Other business support services
		561491	Repossession services
55111	Management of companies and enterprises	561492	Court reporting and stenotype services
551111	Offices of bank holding companies	561499	All other business support services

Note: For definitions of abbreviations and acronyms see page 964.

Code	Short title
5615	Travel arrangement and reservation services
56151	Travel agencies
561510	Travel agencies
56152	Tour operators
561520	Tour operators
56159	Other travel arrangement services
561591	Convention and visitors bureaus
561599	All other travel arrangement services
5616	Investigation and security services
56161	Security and armored car services
561611	Investigation services
561612	Security guards and patrol services
561613	Armored car services
56162	Security systems services
561621	Security systems services, except locksmiths
561622	Locksmiths
5617	Services to buildings and dwellings
56171	Exterminating and pest control services
561710	Exterminating and pest control services
56172	Janitorial services
561720	Janitorial services
56173	Landscaping services
561730	Landscaping services
56174	Carpet and upholstery cleaning services
561740	Carpet and upholstery cleaning services
56179	Other services to buildings and dwellings
561790	Other services to buildings and dwellings
5619	Other support services
56191	Packaging and labeling services
561910	Packaging and labeling services

Code	Short title
56192	Convention and trade show organizers
561920	Convention and trade show organizers
56199	All other support services
561990	All other support services
562	**Waste management and remediation services**
5621	Waste collection
56211	Waste collection
562111	Solid waste collection
562112	Hazardous waste collection
562119	Other waste collection
5622	Waste treatment and disposal
56221	Waste treatment and disposal
562211	Hazardous waste treatment and disposal
562212	Solid waste landfill
562213	Solid waste combustors and incinerators
562219	Other nonhazardous waste disposal
5629	Remediation and other waste services
56291	Remediation services
562910	Remediation services
56292	Materials recovery facilities
562920	Materials recovery facilities
56299	All other waste management services
562991	Septic tank and related services
562998	Miscellaneous waste management services
61	**EDUCATIONAL SERVICES**
611	**Educational services**
6111	Elementary and secondary schools
61111	Elementary and secondary schools
611110	Elementary and secondary schools
6112	Junior colleges
61121	Junior colleges

Note: For definitions of abbreviations and acronyms see page 964.

Code	Short title
611210	Junior colleges
6113	Colleges and universities
61131	Colleges and universities
611310	Colleges and universities
6114	Business, computer and management training
61141	Business and secretarial schools
611410	Business and secretarial schools
61142	Computer training
611420	Computer training
61143	Management training
611430	Management training
6115	Technical and trade schools
61151	Technical and trade schools
611511	Cosmetology and barber schools
611512	Flight training
611513	Apprenticeship training
611519	Other technical and trade schools
6116	Other schools and instruction
61161	Fine arts schools
611610	Fine arts schools
61162	Sports and recreation instruction
611620	Sports and recreation instruction
61163	Language schools
611630	Language schools
61169	All other schools and instruction
611691	Exam preparation and tutoring
611692	Automobile driving schools
611699	Miscellaneous schools and instruction
6117	Educational support services
61171	Educational support services
611710	Educational support services
62	**HEALTH CARE AND SOCIAL ASSISTANCE**
621	**Ambulatory health care services**
6211	Offices of physicians
62111	Offices of physicians
621111	Offices of physicians, except mental health

Code	Short title
621112	Offices of mental health physicians
6212	Offices of dentists
62121	Offices of dentists
621210	Offices of dentists
6213	Offices of other health practitioners
62131	Offices of chiropractors
621310	Offices of chiropractors
62132	Offices of optometrists
621320	Offices of optometrists
62133	Offices of mental health practitioners
621330	Offices of mental health practitioners
62134	Offices of specialty therapists
621340	Offices of specialty therapists
62139	Offices of all other health practitioners
621391	Offices of podiatrists
621399	Offices of miscellaneous health practitioners
6214	Outpatient care centers
62141	Family planning centers
621410	Family planning centers
62142	Outpatient mental health centers
621420	Outpatient mental health centers
62149	Other outpatient care centers
621491	HMO medical centers
621492	Kidney dialysis centers
621493	Freestanding emergency medical centers
621498	All other outpatient care centers
6215	Medical and diagnostic laboratories
62151	Medical and diagnostic laboratories
621511	Medical laboratories
621512	Diagnostic imaging centers
6216	Home health care services
62161	Home health care services
621610	Home health care services
6219	Other ambulatory health care services
62191	Ambulance services

Note: For definitions of abbreviations and acronyms see page 964.

Code	Short title
621910	Ambulance services
62199	All other ambulatory health care services
621991	Blood and organ banks
621999	Miscellaneous ambulatory health care services

622   Hospitals

Code	Short title
6221	General medical and surgical hospitals
62211	General medical and surgical hospitals
622110	General medical and surgical hospitals
6222	Psychiatric and substance abuse hospitals
62221	Psychiatric and substance abuse hospitals
622210	Psychiatric and substance abuse hospitals
6223	Other hospitals
62231	Other hospitals
622310	Other hospitals

623   Nursing and residential care facilities

Code	Short title
6231	Nursing care facilities
62311	Nursing care facilities
623110	Nursing care facilities
6232	Residential mental health facilities
62321	Residential mental retardation facilities
623210	Residential mental retardation facilities
62322	Residential mental and substance abuse care
623220	Residential mental and substance abuse care
6233	Community care facilities for the elderly
62331	Community care facilities for the elderly
623311	Continuing care retirement communities

Code	Short title
623312	Homes for the elderly
6239	Other residential care facilities
62399	Other residential care facilities
623990	Other residential care facilities

624   Social assistance

Code	Short title
6241	Individual and family services
62411	Child and youth services
624110	Child and youth services
62412	Services for the elderly and disabled
624120	Services for the elderly and disabled
62419	Other individual and family services
624190	Other individual and family services
6242	Emergency and other relief services
62421	Community food services
624210	Community food services
62422	Community housing services
624221	Temporary shelters
624229	Other community housing services
62423	Emergency and other relief services
624230	Emergency and other relief services
6243	Vocational rehabilitation services
62431	Vocational rehabilitation services
624310	Vocational rehabilitation services
6244	Child day care services
62441	Child day care services
624410	Child day care services

71   ARTS, ENTERTAINMENT, AND RECREATION

711   Performing arts and spectator sports

Code	Short title
7111	Performing arts companies

Note: For definitions of abbreviations and acronyms see page 964.

Code	Short title
71111	Theater companies and dinner theaters
711110	Theater companies and dinner theaters
71112	Dance companies
711120	Dance companies
71113	Musical groups and artists
711130	Musical groups and artists
71119	Other performing arts companies
711190	Other performing arts companies
7112	Spectator sports
71121	Spectator sports
711211	Sports teams and clubs
711212	Racetracks
711219	Other spectator sports
7113	Promoters of performing arts and sports
71131	Promoters with facilities
711310	Promoters with facilities
71132	Promoters without facilities
711320	Promoters without facilities
7114	Agents and managers for public figures
71141	Agents and managers for public figures
711410	Agents and managers for public figures
7115	Independent artists, writers, and performers
71151	Independent artists, writers, and performers
711510	Independent artists, writers, and performers
712	**Museums, historical sites, zoos, and parks**
7121	Museums, historical sites, zoos, and parks
71211	Museums
712110	Museums
71212	Historical sites
712120	Historical sites
71213	Zoos and botanical gardens

Code	Short title
712130	Zoos and botanical gardens
71219	Nature parks and other similar institutions
712190	Nature parks and other similar institutions
713	**Amusements, gambling, and recreation**
7131	Amusement parks and arcades
71311	Amusement and theme parks
713110	Amusement and theme parks
71312	Amusement arcades
713120	Amusement arcades
7132	Gambling industries
71321	Casinos, except casino hotels
713210	Casinos, except casino hotels
71329	Other gambling industries
713290	Other gambling industries
7139	Other amusement and recreation industries
71391	Golf courses and country clubs
713910	Golf courses and country clubs
71392	Skiing facilities
713920	Skiing facilities
71393	Marinas
713930	Marinas
71394	Fitness and recreational sports centers
713940	Fitness and recreational sports centers
71395	Bowling centers
713950	Bowling centers
71399	All other amusement and recreation industries
713990	All other amusement and recreation industries
72	**ACCOMMODATION AND FOOD SERVICES**
721	**Accommodation**
7211	Traveler accommodation
72111	Hotels and motels, except casino hotels
721110	Hotels and motels, except casino hotels

Note: For definitions of abbreviations and acronyms see page 964.

Code	Short title	Code	Short title
72112	Casino hotels	**81**	**OTHER SERVICES,**
721120	Casino hotels		**EXCEPT PUBLIC**
72119	Other traveler accommodation		**ADMINISTRATION**
721191	Bed-and-breakfast inns	**811**	**Repair and maintenance**
721199	All other traveler accommodation	8111	Automotive repair and maintenance
7212	RV parks and recreational camps	81111	Automotive mechanical and electrical repair
72121	RV parks and recreational camps	811111	General automotive repair
721211	RV parks and campgrounds	811112	Automotive exhaust system repair
721214	Recreational and vacation camps	811113	Automotive transmission repair
7213	Rooming and boarding houses	811118	Other automotive mechanical and elec. repair
72131	Rooming and boarding houses	81112	Automotive body, interior, and glass repair
721310	Rooming and boarding houses	811121	Automotive body and interior repair
722	**Food services and drinking places**	811122	Automotive glass replacement shops
7221	Full-service restaurants	81119	Other automotive repair and maintenance
72211	Full-service restaurants	811191	Automotive oil change and lubrication shops
722110	Full-service restaurants	811192	Car washes
7222	Limited-service eating places	811198	All other automotive repair and maintenance
72221	Limited-service eating places	8112	Electronic equipment repair and maintenance
722211	Limited-service restaurants	81121	Electronic equipment repair and maintenance
722212	Cafeterias	811211	Consumer electronics repair and maintenance
722213	Snack and nonalcoholic beverage bars	811212	Computer and office machine repair
7223	Special food services	811213	Communication equipment repair
72231	Food service contractors	811219	Other electronic equipment repair
722310	Food service contractors	8113	Commercial machinery repair and maintenance
72232	Caterers	811131	Commercial machinery repair and maintenance
722320	Caterers	811310	Commercial machinery repair and maintenance
72233	Mobile food services		
722330	Mobile food services		
7224	Drinking places, alcoholic beverages		
72241	Drinking places, alcoholic beverages		
722410	Drinking places, alcoholic beverages		

Note: For definitions of abbreviations and acronyms see page 964.

Code	Short title	Code	Short title
8114	Household goods repair and maintenance	81232	Drycleaning and laundry services
81141	Home and garden equip. and appliance repair	812320	Drycleaning and laundry services
811411	Home and garden equipment repair	81233	Linen and uniform supply
811412	Appliance repair and maintenance	812331	Linen supply
		812332	Industrial launderers
81142	Reupholstery and furniture repair	8129	Other personal services
		81291	Pet care, except veterinary, services
811420	Reupholstery and furniture repair	812910	Pet care, except veterinary, services
81143	Footwear and leather goods repair	81292	Photofinishing
		812921	Photofinishing laboratories, except one-hour
811430	Footwear and leather goods repair	812922	One-hour photofinishing
81149	Other household goods repair and maintenance	81293	Parking lots and garages
		812930	Parking lots and garages
811490	Other household goods repair and maintenance	81299	All other personal services
		812990	All other personal services
812	**Personal and laundry services**	**813**	**Membership associations and organizations**
8121	Personal care services		
81211	Hair, nail, and skin care services	8131	Religious organizations
		81311	Religious organizations
812111	Barber shops	813110	Religious organizations
812112	Beauty salons	8132	Grantmaking and giving services
812113	Nail salons		
81219	Other personal care services	81321	Grantmaking and giving services
812191	Diet and weight reducing centers		
812199	Other personal care services	813211	Grantmaking foundations
8122	Death care services	813212	Voluntary health organizations
81221	Funeral homes and funeral services	813219	Other grantmaking and giving services
812210	Funeral homes and funeral services	8133	Social advocacy organizations
		81331	Social advocacy organizations
81222	Cemeteries and crematories	813311	Human rights organizations
812220	Cemeteries and crematories	813312	Environment and conservation organizations
8123	Drycleaning and laundry services		
		813319	Other social advocacy organizations
81231	Coin-operated laundries and drycleaners	8134	Civic and social organizations
		81341	Civic and social organizations
812310	Coin-operated laundries and drycleaners	813410	Civic and social organizations

Note: For definitions of abbreviations and acronyms see page 964.

Code	Short title	Code	Short title
8139	Professional and similar organizations	92211	Courts
81391	Business associations	922110	Courts
813910	Business associations	92212	Police protection
81392	Professional organizations	922120	Police protection
813920	Professional organizations	92213	Legal counsel and prosecution
81393	Labor unions and similar labor organizations	922130	Legal counsel and prosecution
813930	Labor unions and similar labor organizations	92214	Correctional institutions
		922140	Correctional institutions
81394	Political organizations	92215	Parole offices and probation offices
813940	Political organizations		
81399	Other similar organizations	922150	Parole offices and probation offices
813990	Other similar organizations	92216	Fire protection
814	**Private households**	922160	Fire protection
8141	Private households	92219	Other justice and safety activities
81411	Private households		
814110	Private households	922190	Other justice and safety activities
92	**PUBLIC ADMINISTRATION**	**923**	**Administration of human resource programs**
921	**Executive, legislative and general government**	9231	Administration of human resource programs
9211	Executive, legislative and general government	92311	Administration of education programs
92111	Executive offices	923110	Administration of education programs
921110	Executive offices		
92112	Legislative bodies	92312	Administration of public health programs
921120	Legislative bodies		
92113	Public finance activities	923120	Administration of public health programs
921130	Public finance activities		
92114	Executive and legislative offices, combined	92313	Other human resource programs administration
921140	Executive and legislative offices, combined	923130	Other human resource programs administration
92115	Tribal governments	92314	Administration of veterans' affairs
921150	Tribal governments		
92119	Other general government support	923140	Administration of veterans' affairs
921190	Other general government support	**924**	**Administration of environmental programs**
922	**Justice, public order, and safety activities**	9241	Administration of environmental programs
9221	Justice, public order, and safety activities	92411	Air, water, and waste program administration

Code	Short title	Code	Short title
924110	Air, water, and waste program administration	926120	Transportation program administration
92412	Administration of conservation programs	92613	Utility regulation and administration
924120	Administration of conservation programs	926130	Utility regulation and administration
925	**Community and housing program administration**	92614	Agricultural market and commodity regulation
9251	Community and housing program administration	926140	Agricultural market and commodity regulation
92511	Administration of housing programs	92615	Licensing and regulating commercial sectors
925110	Administration of housing programs	926150	Licensing and regulating commercial sectors
92512	Urban and rural development administration	**927**	**Space research and technology**
925120	Urban and rural development administration	9271	Space research and technology
926	**Administration of economic programs**	92711	Space research and technology
		927110	Space research and technology
9261	Administration of economic programs	**928**	**National security and international affairs**
92611	Administration of general economic programs	9281	National security and international affairs
926110	Administration of general economic programs	92811	National security
		928110	National security
92612	Transportation program administration	92812	International affairs
		928120	International affairs

Note: For definitions of abbreviations and acronyms see page 964.

Code	Short title	Code	Short title

Abbreviations and Acronyms Used in Short Titles

Abbreviation/Acronym	Word
AC	air conditioning
ag.	agriculture
Al	aluminum
CD	compact disc
const.	construction
Cu	copper
elec.	electrical
equip.	equipment
estab.	establishment
exc.	except
HVAC	heating, ventilation, and air-conditioning
ISPs	Internet service providers
LTL	less than truckload
merch.	merchant
mfg.	manufacturing
misc.	miscellaneous
RV	recreational vehicle
TL	truckload
transport.	transportation
TV	television
whls.	wholesalers

Part III

Appendixes

Appendixes A and B map the changes for 2002 NAICS to the 1997 NAICS in 2002 NAICS sequence (Appendix A) and 1997 NAICS sequence (Appendix B). The tables do not provide a comprehensive guide to all economic activities, but rather provide a map for the largest and most important changes from 1997 to 2002.

Full concordances for 1997 NAICS to 2002 NAICS and 1987 SIC to 2002 NAICS are available on the Census Bureau's Website at www.census.gov/naics.

Appendix A
2002 NAICS U.S. Matched to
1997 NAICS U.S.

2002 NAICS Code	2002 NAICS U.S. Description	1997 NAICS Code	1997 NAICS U.S. Description
236	Construction of Buildings		
2361	Residential Building Construction		
23611	Residential Building Construction		
US 236115	New Single-Family Housing Construction (except Operative Builders)	*233210	Single Family Housing Construction (except operative builders and remodeling contractors)
US 236116	New Multifamily Housing Construction (except Operative Builders)	*233220	Multifamily Housing Construction (except barrack and dormitory construction, operative builders, and remodeling contractors)
US 236117	New Housing Operative Builders	*233210	Single Family Housing Construction (operative builders)
		*233220	Multifamily Housing Construction (operative builders)
US 236118	Residential Remodelers	*233210	Single Family Housing Construction (remodeling contractors)
		*233220	Multifamily Housing Construction (remodeling contractors)
2362	Nonresidential Building Construction		
23621	Industrial Building Construction	*233310	Manufacturing and Industrial Building Construction (except grain elevators, dry cleaning plants, and manufacturing and industrial warehouses)

US—United States industry only. CAN—United States and Canadian industries are comparable. MEX—United States and Mexican industries are comparable. Blank—Canadian, Mexican, and United States industries are comparable. *—Part of.

2002 NAICS Code	2002 NAICS U.S. Description	1997 NAICS Code	1997 NAICS U.S. Description
		*234930	Industrial Nonbuilding Structure Construction (process batch plants, incinerators, industrial furnaces and kilns, mining appurtenance, and construction management of these projects)
		*234990	All Other Heavy Construction (waste disposal plant construction)
23622	Commercial and Institutional Building Construction	*233220	Multifamily Housing Construction (barrack and dormitory construction)
		*233310	Manufacturing and Industrial Building Construction (grain elevators, dry cleaning plants, and manufacturing and industrial warehouses)
		233320	Commercial and Institutional Building Construction
		*235990	All Other Special Trade Contractors (indoor swimming pools)
237	Heavy and Civil Engineering Construction		
2371	Utility System Construction		
23711	Water and Sewer Line and Related Structures Construction	*234910	Water, Sewer, and Pipeline Construction (water/sewer pumping stations, sewage collection and disposal lines, storm sewers, sewer/water mains and lines, water storage tanks and towers, and construction management of these projects)
		*234990	All Other Heavy Construction (irrigation systems, sewage treatment and water treatment plants, construction management of these projects)
		235810	Water Well Drilling Contractors

US—United States industry only. CAN—United States and Canadian industries are comparable. MEX—United States and Mexican industries are comparable. Blank—Canadian, Mexican, and United States industries are comparable. *—Part of.

2002 NAICS Code	2002 NAICS U.S. Description	1997 NAICS Code	1997 NAICS U.S. Description
23712	Oil and Gas Pipeline and Related Structures Construction	*213112	Support Activities for Oil and Gas Operations (construction of field gathering lines on a contract basis)
		*234910	Water, Sewer, and Pipeline Construction (gas and oil pumping stations, gas and oil pipeline construction, gas mains, gas and oil storage tank construction, and construction management of these projects)
		*234930	Industrial Nonbuilding Structure Construction (petrochemical plants, refineries, and construction management of these projects)
23713	Power and Communication Line and Related Structures Construction	234920	Power and Communication Transmission Line Construction
		*234930	Industrial Nonbuilding Structure Construction (power generation plants (excluding hydroelectric dams), transmission and distribution transformer stations, and construction management of these projects)
2372	Land Subdivision		
23721	Land Subdivision	233110	Land Subdivision and Land Development
2373	Highway, Street, and Bridge Construction		
23731	Highway, Street, and Bridge Construction	234110	Highway and Street Construction
		*234120	Bridge and Tunnel Construction (bridge construction)
		*235210	Painting and Wall Covering Contractors (highway and traffic line painting)
2379	Other Heavy and Civil Engineering Construction		

2002 NAICS Code	2002 NAICS U.S. Description	1997 NAICS Code	1997 NAICS U.S. Description
23799	Other Heavy and Civil Engineering Construction	*234120	Bridge and Tunnel Construction (tunnel construction)
		*234990	All Other Heavy Construction (except waste disposal plant construction, irrigation systems, sewage treatment and water treatment plants, right-of-way clearing and line slashing, blasting, trenching, and equipment rental with operator)
		*235990	All Other Special Trade Contractors (anchored earth retention contractors)
238	Specialty Trade Contractors		
2381	Foundation, Structure, and Building Exterior Contractors		
23811	Poured Concrete Foundation and Structure Contractors	*235710	Concrete Contractors (except residential and commercial asphalt, brick, and concrete paving)
23812	Structural Steel and Precast Concrete Contractors	*235910	Structural Steel Erection Contractors (except curtain walls, metal furring installation, and cooling tower installation)
CAN 23813	Framing Contractors	*235510	Carpentry Contractors (framing carpentry)
CAN 23814	Masonry Contractors	235410	Masonry and Stone Contractors
		*235420	Drywall, Plastering, Acoustical, and Insulation Contractors (stucco contractors)
CAN 23815	Glass and Glazing Contractors	235920	Glass and Glazing Contractors
CAN 23816	Roofing Contractors	*235610	Roofing, Siding, and Sheet Metal Contractors (roofing contractors)
CAN 23817	Siding Contractors	*235610	Roofing, Siding, and Sheet Metal Contractors (siding contractors)
CAN 23819	Other Foundation, Structure, and Building Exterior Contractors	*235910	Structural Steel Erection Contractors (curtain walls and metal furring installation)

US—United States industry only. CAN—United States and Canadian industries are comparable. MEX—United States and Mexican industries are comparable. Blank—Canadian, Mexican, and United States industries are comparable. *—Part of.

2002 NAICS Code	2002 NAICS U.S. Description	1997 NAICS Code	1997 NAICS U.S. Description
		*235990	All Other Special Trade Contractors (forming contractors, ornamental metal work installation)
2382	Building Equipment Contractors		
23821	Electrical Contractors	*235110	Plumbing, Heating, and Air-Conditioning Contractors (environmental controls installation contractors)
		235310	Electrical Contractors
23822	Plumbing, Heating, and Air-Conditioning Contractors	*235110	Plumbing, Heating, and Air-Conditioning Contractors (except environmental controls installation contractors and septic tank, cesspool, and dry well construction)
		*235910	Structural Steel Erection Contractors (cooling tower installation)
		*235950	Building Equipment and Other Machinery Installation Contractors (scrubber, dust collection, and other industrial ventilation installation)
23829	Other Building Equipment Contractors	*235950	Building Equipment and Other Machinery Installation Contractors (except scrubber, dust collection, and other industrial ventilation installation)
		*235990	All Other Special Trade Contractors (service station equipment installation; boiler, duct, and pipe insulation; lightning rod installation; bowling alley installation; household-type antenna installation; church bell installation; and tower clock installation)
2383	Building Finishing Contractors		

2002 NAICS Code	2002 NAICS U.S. Description	1997 NAICS Code	1997 NAICS U.S. Description
23831	Drywall and Insulation Contractors	*235420	Drywall, Plastering, Acoustical, and Insulation Contractors (except stucco contractors)
23832	Painting and Wall Covering Contractors	*235210	Painting and Wall Covering Contractors (except highway and traffic line painting)
23833	Flooring Contractors	235520	Floor Laying and Other Floor Contractors
23834	Tile and Terrazzo Contractors	235430	Tile, Marble, Terrazzo, and Mosaic Contractors
23835	Finish Carpentry Contractors	*235510	Carpentry Contractors (finish carpentry)
23839	Other Building Finishing Contractors	*235610	Roofing, Siding, and Sheet Metal Contractors (metal ceiling, panel, and shelving installation)
		*235990	All Other Special Trade Contractors (weather stripping and damp-proofing, modular furniture installation, bathtub refinishing, window covering fixture installation, trade show exhibit installation and dismantling, and spectator seating installation)
2389	Other Specialty Trade Contractors		
23891	Site Preparation Contractors	*213112	Support Activities for Oil and Gas Operations (site preparation and related construction activities on a contract basis)
		*213113	Support Activities for Coal Mining (site preparation and related construction activities on a contract basis)
		*213114	Support Activities for Metal Mining (site preparation and related construction activities on a contract basis)

2002 NAICS Code	2002 NAICS U.S. Description	1997 NAICS Code	1997 NAICS U.S. Description
		*213115	Support Activities for Nonmetallic Minerals (except Fuels) (site preparation and related construction activities on a contract basis)
		*234990	All Other Heavy Construction (right-of-way clearing and line slashing, blasting, trenching, and equipment rental (except cranes) with operator)
		*235110	Plumbing, Heating, and Air-Conditioning Contractors (septic tank, cesspool, and dry well construction contractors)
		235930	Excavation Contractors
		235940	Wrecking and Demolition Contractors
		*235990	All Other Special Trade Contractors (dewatering contractors, core drilling for construction, and test drilling for construction)
23899	All Other Specialty Trade Contractors	*234990	All Other Heavy Construction (rental of cranes with operator)
		*235710	Concrete Contractors (residential and commercial asphalt, brick, and concrete paving)
		*235990	All Other Special Trade Contractors (except indoor swimming pools, earth retention contractors, forming contractors, ornamental metal work, building equipment contractors, building finishing contractors, dewatering contractors, core drilling for construction, and test boring for construction)
		*561720	Janitorial Services (cleaning buildings during and immediately after construction)

2002 NAICS Code	2002 NAICS U.S. Description	1997 NAICS Code	1997 NAICS U.S. Description
42	Wholesale Trade		
US 423	Merchant Wholesalers, Durable Goods		
US 4231	Motor Vehicle and Motor Vehicle Parts and Supplies Merchant Wholesalers		
US 42311	Automobile and Other Motor Vehicle Merchant Wholesalers	*421110	Automobile and Other Motor Vehicle Wholesalers (merchant wholesalers)
US 42312	Motor Vehicle Supplies and New Parts Merchant Wholesalers	*421120	Motor Vehicle Supplies and New Parts Wholesalers (merchant wholesalers)
US 42313	Tire and Tube Merchant Wholesalers	*421130	Tire and Tube Wholesalers (merchant wholesalers)
US 42314	Motor Vehicle Parts (Used) Merchant Wholesalers	*421140	Motor Vehicle Parts (Used) Wholesalers (merchant wholesalers)
US 4232	Furniture and Home Furnishing Merchant Wholesalers		
US 42321	Furniture Merchant Wholesalers	*421210	Furniture Wholesalers (merchant wholesalers)
US 42322	Home Furnishing Merchant Wholesalers	*421220	Home Furnishing Wholesalers (merchant wholesalers)
US 4233	Lumber and Other Construction Materials Merchant Wholesalers		
US 42331	Lumber, Plywood, Millwork, and Wood Panel Merchant Wholesalers	*421310	Lumber, Plywood, Millwork, and Wood Panel Wholesalers (merchant wholesalers)
US 42332	Brick, Stone, and Related Construction Material Merchant Wholesalers	*421320	Brick, Stone, and Related Construction Material Wholesalers (merchant wholesalers)
US 42333	Roofing, Siding, and Insulation Material Merchant Wholesalers	*421330	Roofing, Siding, and Insulation Material Wholesalers (merchant wholesalers)
US 42339	Other Construction Material Merchant Wholesalers	*421390	Other Construction Material Wholesalers (merchant wholesalers)

US—United States industry only. CAN—United States and Canadian industries are comparable. MEX—United States and Mexican industries are comparable. Blank—Canadian, Mexican, and United States industries are comparable. *—Part of.

2002 NAICS Code	2002 NAICS U.S. Description	1997 NAICS Code	1997 NAICS U.S. Description
US 4234	Professional and Commercial Equipment and Supplies Merchant Wholesalers		
US 42341	Photographic Equipment and Supplies Merchant Wholesalers	*421410	Photographic Equipment and Supplies Wholesalers (merchant wholesalers)
US 42342	Office Equipment Merchant Wholesalers	*421420	Office Equipment Wholesalers (merchant wholesalers)
US 42343	Computer and Computer Peripheral Equipment and Software Merchant Wholesalers	*421430	Computer and Computer Peripheral Equipment and Software Wholesalers (merchant wholesalers)
US 42344	Other Commercial Equipment Merchant Wholesalers	*421440	Other Commercial Equipment Wholesalers (merchant wholesalers)
US 42345	Medical, Dental, and Hospital Equipment and Supplies Merchant Wholesalers	*421450	Medical, Dental, and Hospital Equipment and Supplies Wholesalers (merchant wholesalers)
US 42346	Ophthalmic Goods Merchant Wholesalers	*421460	Ophthalmic Goods Wholesalers (merchant wholesalers)
US 42349	Other Professional Equipment and Supplies Merchant Wholesalers	*421490	Other Professional Equipment and Supplies Wholesalers (merchant wholesalers)
US 4235	Metal and Mineral (except Petroleum) Merchant Wholesalers		
US 42351	Metal Service Centers and Other Metal Merchant Wholesalers	*421510	Metal Service Centers and Offices (merchant wholesalers)
US 42352	Coal and Other Mineral and Ore Merchant Wholesalers	*421520	Coal and Other Mineral and Ore Wholesalers (merchant wholesalers)
US 4236	Electrical and Electronic Goods Merchant Wholesalers		
US 42361	Electrical Apparatus and Equipment, Wiring Supplies, and Related Equipment Merchant Wholesalers	*421610	Electrical Apparatus and Equipment, Wiring Supplies, and Construction Material Wholesalers (merchant wholesalers)

US—United States industry only. CAN—United States and Canadian industries are comparable. MEX—United States and Mexican industries are comparable. Blank—Canadian, Mexican, and United States industries are comparable. *—Part of.

2002 NAICS Code	2002 NAICS U.S. Description	1997 NAICS Code	1997 NAICS U.S. Description
US 42362	Electrical and Electronic Appliance, Television, and Radio Set Merchant Wholesalers	*421620	Electrical Appliance, Television, and Radio Set Wholesalers (merchant wholesalers)
US 42369	Other Electronic Parts and Equipment Merchant Wholesalers	*421690	Other Electronic Parts and Equipment Wholesalers (merchant wholesalers)
US 4237	Hardware, and Plumbing and Heating Equipment and Supplies Merchant Wholesalers		
US 42371	Hardware Merchant Wholesalers	*421710	Hardware Wholesalers (merchant wholesalers)
US 42372	Plumbing and Heating Equipment and Supplies (Hydronics) Merchant Wholesalers	*421720	Plumbing and Heating Equipment and Supplies (Hydronics) Wholesalers (merchant wholesalers)
US 42373	Warm Air Heating and Air-Conditioning Equipment and Supplies Merchant Wholesalers	*421730	Warm Air Heating and Air-Conditioning Equipment and Supplies Wholesalers (merchant wholesalers)
US 42374	Refrigeration Equipment and Supplies Merchant Wholesalers	*421740	Refrigeration Equipment and Supplies Wholesalers (merchant wholesalers)
US 4238	Machinery, Equipment, and Supplies Merchant Wholesalers		
US 42381	Construction and Mining (except Oil Well) Machinery and Equipment Merchant Wholesalers	*421810	Construction and Mining (except Oil Well) Machinery and Equipment Wholesalers (merchant wholesalers)
US 42382	Farm and Garden Machinery and Equipment Merchant Wholesalers	*421820	Farm and Garden Machinery and Equipment Wholesalers (merchant wholesalers)
US 42383	Industrial Machinery and Equipment Merchant Wholesalers	*421830	Industrial Machinery and Equipment Wholesalers (merchant wholesalers)
US 42384	Industrial Supplies Merchant Wholesalers	*421840	Industrial Supplies Wholesalers (merchant wholesalers)

US—United States industry only. CAN—United States and Canadian industries are comparable. MEX—United States and Mexican industries are comparable. Blank—Canadian, Mexican, and United States industries are comparable. *—Part of.

2002 NAICS Code	2002 NAICS U.S. Description	1997 NAICS Code	1997 NAICS U.S. Description
US 42385	Service Establishment Equipment and Supplies Merchant Wholesalers	*421850	Service Establishment Equipment and Supplies Wholesalers (merchant wholesalers)
US 42386	Transportation Equipment and Supplies (except Motor Vehicle) Merchant Wholesalers	*421860	Transportation Equipment and Supplies (except Motor Vehicle) Wholesalers (merchant wholesalers)
US 4239	Miscellaneous Durable Goods Merchant Wholesalers		
US 42391	Sporting and Recreational Goods and Supplies Merchant Wholesalers	*421910	Sporting and Recreational Goods and Supplies Wholesalers (merchant wholesalers)
US 42392	Toy and Hobby Goods and Supplies Merchant Wholesalers	*421920	Toy and Hobby Goods and Supplies Wholesalers (merchant wholesalers)
US 42393	Recyclable Material Merchant Wholesalers	*421930	Recyclable Material Wholesalers (merchant wholesalers)
US 42394	Jewelry, Watch, Precious Stone, and Precious Metal Merchant Wholesalers	*421940	Jewelry, Watch, Precious Stone, and Precious Metal Wholesalers (merchant wholesalers)
US 42399	Other Miscellaneous Durable Goods Merchant Wholesalers	*421990	Other Miscellaneous Durable Goods Wholesalers (merchant wholesalers)
US 424	Merchant Wholesalers, Nondurable Goods		
US 4241	Paper and Paper Product Merchant Wholesalers		
US 42411	Printing and Writing Paper Merchant Wholesalers	*422110	Printing and Writing Paper Wholesalers (merchant wholesalers)
US 42412	Stationary and Office Supplies Merchant Wholesalers	*422120	Stationary and Office Supplies Wholesalers (merchant wholesalers)
US 42413	Industrial and Personal Service Paper Merchant Wholesalers	*422130	Industrial and Personal Service Paper Wholesalers (merchant wholesalers)

2002 NAICS Code	2002 NAICS U.S. Description	1997 NAICS Code	1997 NAICS U.S. Description
US 4242	Drugs and Druggists' Sundries Merchant Wholesalers		
US 42421	Drugs and Druggists' Sundries Merchant Wholesalers	*422210	Drugs and Druggists' Sundries Wholesalers (merchant wholesalers)
US 4243	Apparel, Piece Goods, and Notions Merchant Wholesalers		
US 42431	Piece Goods, Notions, and Other Dry Goods Merchant Wholesalers	*422310	Piece Goods, Notions, and Other Dry Goods Wholesalers (merchant wholesalers)
US 42432	Men's and Boys' Clothing and Furnishings Merchant Wholesalers	*422320	Men's and Boys' Clothing and Furnishings Wholesalers (merchant wholesalers)
US 42433	Women's, Children's, and Infants' Clothing and Accessories Merchant Wholesalers	*422330	Women's, Children's, and Infants' Clothing and Accessories Wholesalers (merchant wholesalers)
US 42434	Footwear Merchant Wholesalers	*422340	Footwear Wholesalers (merchant wholesalers)
US 4244	Grocery and Related Product Merchant Wholesalers		
US 42441	General Line Grocery Merchant Wholesalers	*422410	General Line Grocery Wholesalers (merchant wholesalers)
US 42442	Packaged Frozen Food Merchant Wholesalers	*422420	Packaged Frozen Food Wholesalers (merchant wholesalers)
US 42443	Dairy Product (except Dried or Canned) Merchant Wholesalers	*422430	Dairy Product (except Dried or Canned) Wholesalers (merchant wholesalers)
US 42444	Poultry and Poultry Product Merchant Wholesalers	*422440	Poultry and Poultry Product Wholesalers (merchant wholesalers)
US 42445	Confectionery Merchant Wholesalers	*422450	Confectionery Wholesalers (merchant wholesalers)
US 42446	Fish and Seafood Merchant Wholesalers	*422460	Fish and Seafood Wholesalers (merchant wholesalers)

US—United States industry only. CAN—United States and Canadian industries are comparable. MEX—United States and Mexican industries are comparable. Blank—Canadian, Mexican, and United States industries are comparable. *—Part of.

2002 NAICS Code	2002 NAICS U.S. Description	1997 NAICS Code	1997 NAICS U.S. Description
US 42447	Meat and Meat Product Merchant Wholesalers	*422470	Meat and Meat Product Wholesalers (merchant wholesalers)
US 42448	Fresh Fruit and Vegetable Merchant Wholesalers	*422480	Fresh Fruit and Vegetable Wholesalers (merchant wholesalers)
US 42449	Other Grocery and Related Products Merchant Wholesalers	*422490	Other Grocery and Related Products Wholesalers (merchant wholesalers)
US 4245	Farm Product Raw Material Merchant Wholesalers		
US 42451	Grain and Field Bean Merchant Wholesalers	*422510	Grain and Field Bean Wholesalers (merchant wholesalers)
US 42452	Livestock Merchant Wholesalers	*422520	Livestock Wholesalers (merchant wholesalers)
US 42459	Other Farm Product Raw Material Merchant Wholesalers	*422590	Other Farm Product Raw Material Wholesalers (merchant wholesalers)
US 4246	Chemical and Allied Products Merchant Wholesalers		
US 42461	Plastics Materials and Basic Forms and Shapes Merchant Wholesalers	*422610	Plastics Materials and Basic Forms and Shapes Wholesalers (merchant wholesalers)
US 42469	Other Chemical and Allied Products Merchant Wholesalers	*422690	Other Chemical and Allied Products Wholesalers (merchant wholesalers)
US 4247	Petroleum and Petroleum Products Merchant Wholesalers		
US 42471	Petroleum Bulk Stations and Terminals	422710	Petroleum Bulk Stations and Terminals
US 42472	Petroleum and Petroleum Products Merchant Wholesalers (except Bulk Stations and Terminals)	*422720	Petroleum and Petroleum Products Wholesalers (except Bulk Stations and Terminals) (merchant wholesalers)
US 4248	Beer, Wine, and Distilled Alcoholic Beverage Merchant Wholesalers		

2002 NAICS Code	2002 NAICS U.S. Description	1997 NAICS Code	1997 NAICS U.S. Description
US 42481	Beer and Ale Merchant Wholesalers	*422810	Beer and Ale Wholesalers (merchant wholesalers)
US 42482	Wine and Distilled Alcoholic Beverage Merchant Wholesalers	*422820	Wine and Distilled Alcoholic Beverage Wholesalers (merchant wholesalers)
US 4249	Miscellaneous Nondurable Goods Merchant Wholesalers		
US 42491	Farm Supplies Merchant Wholesalers	*422910	Farm Supplies Wholesalers (merchant wholesalers)
US 42492	Book, Periodical, and Newspaper Merchant Wholesalers	*422920	Book, Periodical, and Newspaper Wholesalers (merchant wholesalers)
US 42493	Flower, Nursery Stock, and Florists' Supplies Merchant Wholesalers	*422930	Flower, Nursery Stock, and Florists' Supplies Wholesalers (merchant wholesalers)
US 42494	Tobacco and Tobacco Product Merchant Wholesalers	*422940	Tobacco and Tobacco Product Wholesalers (merchant wholesalers)
US 42495	Paint, Varnish, and Supplies Merchant Wholesalers	*422950	Paint, Varnish, and Supplies Wholesalers (merchant wholesalers)
US 42499	Other Miscellaneous Nondurable Goods Merchant Wholesalers	*422990	Other Miscellaneous Nondurable Goods Wholesalers (merchant wholesalers)
US 425	Wholesale Electronic Markets and Agents and Brokers		
US 4251	Wholesale Electronic Markets and Agents and Brokers		
US 42511	Business to Business Electronic Markets	*421110	Automobile and Other Motor Vehicle Wholesalers (electronic markets)
		*421120	Motor Vehicle Supplies and New Parts Wholesalers (electronic markets)
		*421130	Tire and Tube Wholesalers (electronic markets)

2002 NAICS Code	2002 NAICS U.S. Description	1997 NAICS Code	1997 NAICS U.S. Description
		*421140	Motor Vehicle Parts (Used) Wholesalers (electronic markets)
		*421210	Furniture Wholesalers (electronic markets)
		*421220	Home Furnishing Wholesalers (electronic markets)
		*421310	Lumber, Plywood, Millwork, and Wood Panel Wholesalers (electronic markets)
		*421320	Brick, Stone, and Related Construction Material Wholesalers (electronic markets)
		*421330	Roofing, Siding, and Insulation Material Wholesalers (electronic markets)
		*421390	Other Construction Material Wholesalers (electronic markets)
		*421410	Photographic Equipment and Supplies Wholesalers (electronic markets)
		*421420	Office Equipment Wholesalers (electronic markets)
		*421430	Computer and Computer Peripheral Equipment and Software Wholesalers (electronic markets)
		*421440	Other Commercial Equipment Wholesalers (electronic markets)
		*421450	Medical, Dental, and Hospital Equipment and Supplies Wholesalers (electronic markets)
		*421460	Ophthalmic Goods Wholesalers (electronic markets)
		*421490	Other Professional Equipment and Supplies Wholesalers (electronic markets)
		*421510	Metal Service Centers and Offices (electronic markets)

US—United States industry only. CAN—United States and Canadian industries are comparable. MEX—United States and Mexican industries are comparable. Blank—Canadian, Mexican, and United States industries are comparable. *—Part of.

2002 NAICS Code	2002 NAICS U.S. Description	1997 NAICS Code	1997 NAICS U.S. Description
		*421520	Coal and Other Mineral and Ore Wholesalers (electronic markets)
		*421610	Electrical Apparatus and Equipment, Wiring Supplies, and Construction Material Wholesalers (electronic markets)
		*421620	Electrical Appliance, Television, and Radio Set Wholesalers (electronic markets)
		*421690	Other Electronic Parts and Equipment Wholesalers (electronic markets)
		*421710	Hardware Wholesalers (electronic markets)
		*421720	Plumbing and Heating Equipment and Supplies (Hydronics) Wholesalers (electronic markets)
		*421730	Warm Air Heating and Air-Conditioning Equipment and Supplies Wholesalers (electronic markets)
		*421740	Refrigeration Equipment and Supplies Wholesalers (electronic markets)
		*421810	Construction and Mining (except Oil Well) Machinery and Equipment Wholesalers (electronic markets)
		*421820	Farm and Garden Machinery and Equipment Wholesalers (electronic markets)
		*421830	Industrial Machinery and Equipment Wholesalers (electronic markets)
		*421840	Industrial Supplies Wholesalers (electronic markets)
		*421850	Service Establishment Equipment and Supplies Wholesalers (electronic markets)

US—United States industry only. CAN—United States and Canadian industries are comparable. MEX—United States and Mexican industries are comparable. Blank—Canadian, Mexican, and United States industries are comparable. *—Part of.

2002 NAICS Code	2002 NAICS U.S. Description	1997 NAICS Code	1997 NAICS U.S. Description
		*421860	Transportation Equipment and Supplies (except Motor Vehicle) Wholesalers (electronic markets)
		*421910	Sporting and Recreational Goods and Supplies Wholesalers (electronic markets)
		*421920	Toy and Hobby Goods and Supplies Wholesalers (electronic markets)
		*421930	Recyclable Material Wholesalers (electronic markets)
		*421940	Jewelry, Watch, Precious Stone, and Precious Metal Wholesalers (electronic markets)
		*421990	Other Miscellaneous Durable Goods Wholesalers (electronic markets)
		*422110	Printing and Writing Paper Wholesalers (electronic markets)
		*422120	Stationary and Office Supplies Wholesalers (electronic markets)
		*422130	Industrial and Personal Service Paper Wholesalers (electronic markets)
		*422210	Drugs and Druggists' Sundries Wholesalers (electronic markets)
		*422310	Piece Goods, Notions, and Other Dry Goods Wholesalers (electronic markets)
		*422320	Men's and Boys' Clothing and Furnishings Wholesalers (electronic markets)
		*422330	Women's, Children's, and Infants' Clothing and Accessories Wholesalers (electronic markets)

2002 NAICS Code	2002 NAICS U.S. Description	1997 NAICS Code	1997 NAICS U.S. Description
		*422340	Footwear Wholesalers (electronic markets)
		*422410	General Line Grocery Wholesalers (electronic markets)
		*422420	Packaged Frozen Food Wholesalers (electronic markets)
		*422430	Dairy Product (except Dried or Canned) Wholesalers (electronic markets)
		*422440	Poultry and Poultry Product Wholesalers (electronic markets)
		*422450	Confectionery Wholesalers (electronic markets)
		*422460	Fish and Seafood Wholesalers (electronic markets)
		*422470	Meat and Meat Product Wholesalers (electronic markets)
		*422480	Fresh Fruit and Vegetable Wholesalers (electronic markets)
		*422490	Other Grocery and Related Products Wholesalers (electronic markets)
		*422510	Grain and Field Bean Wholesalers (electronic markets)
		*422520	Livestock Wholesalers (electronic markets)
		*422590	Other Farm Product Raw Material Wholesalers (electronic markets)
		*422610	Plastics Materials and Basic Forms and Shapes Wholesalers (electronic markets)
		*422690	Other Chemical and Allied Products Wholesalers (electronic markets)

2002 NAICS Code	2002 NAICS U.S. Description	1997 NAICS Code	1997 NAICS U.S. Description
		*422720	Petroleum and Petroleum Products Wholesalers (except Bulk Stations and Terminals) (electronic markets)
		*422810	Beer and Ale Wholesalers (electronic markets)
		*422820	Wine and Distilled Alcoholic Beverage Wholesalers (electronic markets)
		*422910	Farm Supplies Wholesalers (electronic markets)
		*422920	Book, Periodical, and Newspaper Wholesalers (electronic markets)
		*422930	Flower, Nursery Stock, and Florists' Supplies Wholesalers (electronic markets)
		*422940	Tobacco and Tobacco Product Wholesalers (electronic markets)
		*422950	Paint, Varnish, and Supplies Wholesalers (electronic markets)
		*422990	Other Miscellaneous Nondurable Goods Wholesalers (electronic markets)
US 42512	Wholesale Trade Agents and Brokers	*421110	Automobile and Other Motor Vehicle Wholesalers (agents and brokers)
		*421120	Motor Vehicle Supplies and New Parts Wholesalers (agents and brokers)
		*421130	Tire and Tube Wholesalers (agents and brokers)
		*421140	Motor Vehicle Parts (Used) Wholesalers (agents and brokers)

US—United States industry only. CAN—United States and Canadian industries are comparable. MEX—United States and Mexican industries are comparable. Blank—Canadian, Mexican, and United States industries are comparable. *—Part of.

2002 NAICS Code	2002 NAICS U.S. Description	1997 NAICS Code	1997 NAICS U.S. Description
		*421210	Furniture Wholesalers (agents and brokers)
		*421220	Home Furnishing Wholesalers (agents and brokers)
		*421310	Lumber, Plywood, Millwork, and Wood Panel Wholesalers (agents and brokers)
		*421320	Brick, Stone, and Related Construction Material Wholesalers (agents and brokers)
		*421330	Roofing, Siding, and Insulation Material Wholesalers (agents and brokers)
		*421390	Other Construction Material Wholesalers (agents and brokers)
		*421410	Photographic Equipment and Supplies Wholesalers (agents and brokers)
		*421420	Office Equipment Wholesalers (agents and brokers)
		*421430	Computer and Computer Peripheral Equipment and Software Wholesalers (agents and brokers)
		*421440	Other Commercial Equipment Wholesalers (agents and brokers)
		*421450	Medical, Dental, and Hospital Equipment and Supplies Wholesalers (agents and brokers)
		*421460	Ophthalmic Goods Wholesalers (agents and brokers)
		*421490	Other Professional Equipment and Supplies Wholesalers (agents and brokers)
		*421510	Metal Service Centers and Offices (agents and brokers)
		*421520	Coal and Other Mineral and Ore Wholesalers (agents and brokers)

US—United States industry only. CAN—United States and Canadian industries are comparable. MEX—United States and Mexican industries are comparable. Blank—Canadian, Mexican, and United States industries are comparable. *—Part of.

2002 NAICS Code	2002 NAICS U.S. Description	1997 NAICS Code	1997 NAICS U.S. Description
		*421610	Electrical Apparatus and Equipment, Wiring Supplies, and Construction Material Wholesalers (agents and brokers)
		*421620	Electrical Appliance, Television, and Radio Set Wholesalers (agents and brokers)
		*421690	Other Electronic Parts and Equipment Wholesalers (agents and brokers)
		*421710	Hardware Wholesalers (agents and brokers)
		*421720	Plumbing and Heating Equipment and Supplies (Hydronics) Wholesalers (agents and brokers)
		*421730	Warm Air Heating and Air-Conditioning Equipment and Supplies Wholesalers (agents and brokers)
		*421740	Refrigeration Equipment and Supplies Wholesalers (agents and brokers)
		*421810	Construction and Mining (except Oil Well) Machinery and Equipment Wholesalers (agents and brokers)
		*421820	Farm and Garden Machinery and Equipment Wholesalers (agents and brokers)
		*421830	Industrial Machinery and Equipment Wholesalers (agents and brokers)
		*421840	Industrial Supplies Wholesalers (agents and brokers)
		*421850	Service Establishment Equipment and Supplies Wholesalers (agents and brokers)

2002 NAICS Code	2002 NAICS U.S. Description	1997 NAICS Code	1997 NAICS U.S. Description
		*421860	Transportation Equipment and Supplies (except Motor Vehicle) Wholesalers (agents and brokers)
		*421910	Sporting and Recreational Goods and Supplies Wholesalers (agents and brokers)
		*421920	Toy and Hobby Goods and Supplies Wholesalers (agents and brokers)
		*421930	Recyclable Material Wholesalers (agents and brokers)
		*421940	Jewelry, Watch, Precious Stone, and Precious Metal Wholesalers (agents and brokers)
		*421990	Other Miscellaneous Durable Goods Wholesalers (agents and brokers)
		*422110	Printing and Writing Paper Wholesalers (agents and brokers)
		*422120	Stationary and Office Supplies Wholesalers (agents and brokers)
		*422130	Industrial and Personal Service Paper Wholesalers (agents and brokers)
		*422210	Drugs and Druggists' Sundries Wholesalers (agents and brokers)
		*422310	Piece Goods, Notions, and Other Dry Goods Wholesalers (agents and brokers)
		*422320	Men's and Boys' Clothing and Furnishings Wholesalers (agents and brokers)

2002 NAICS Code	2002 NAICS U.S. Description	1997 NAICS Code	1997 NAICS U.S. Description
		*422330	Women's, Children's, and Infants' Clothing and Accessories Wholesalers (agents and brokers)
		*422340	Footwear Wholesalers (agents and brokers)
		*422410	General Line Grocery Wholesalers (agents and brokers)
		*422420	Packaged Frozen Food Wholesalers (agents and brokers)
		*422430	Dairy Product (except Dried or Canned) Wholesalers (agents and brokers)
		*422440	Poultry and Poultry Product Wholesalers (agents and brokers)
		*422450	Confectionery Wholesalers (agents and brokers)
		*422460	Fish and Seafood Wholesalers (agents and brokers)
		*422470	Meat and Meat Product Wholesalers (agents and brokers)
		*422480	Fresh Fruit and Vegetable Wholesalers (agents and brokers)
		*422490	Other Grocery and Related Products Wholesalers (agents and brokers)
		*422510	Grain and Field Bean Wholesalers (agents and brokers)
		*422520	Livestock Wholesalers (agents and brokers)
		*422590	Other Farm Product Raw Material Wholesalers (agents and brokers)
		*422610	Plastics Materials and Basic Forms and Shapes Wholesalers (agents and brokers)

US—United States industry only. CAN—United States and Canadian industries are comparable. MEX—United States and Mexican industries are comparable. Blank—Canadian, Mexican, and United States industries are comparable. *—Part of.

2002 NAICS Code	2002 NAICS U.S. Description	1997 NAICS Code	1997 NAICS U.S. Description
		*422690	Other Chemical and Allied Products Wholesalers (agents and brokers)
		*422720	Petroleum and Petroleum Products Wholesalers (except Bulk Stations and Terminals) (agents and brokers)
		*422810	Beer and Ale Wholesalers (agents and brokers)
		*422820	Wine and Distilled Alcoholic Beverage Wholesalers (agents and brokers)
		*422910	Farm Supplies Wholesalers (agents and brokers)
		*422920	Book, Periodical, and Newspaper Wholesalers (agents and brokers)
		*422930	Flower, Nursery Stock, and Florists' Supplies Wholesalers (agents and brokers)
		*422940	Tobacco and Tobacco Product Wholesalers (agents and brokers)
		*422950	Paint, Varnish, and Supplies Wholesalers (agents and brokers)
		*422990	Other Miscellaneous Nondurable Goods Wholesalers (agents and brokers)
CAN 4521	Department Stores		
CAN 45211	Department Stores		
US 452111	Department Stores (except Discount Department Stores)	*452110	Department Stores (except discount department stores)
US 452112	Discount Department Stores	*452110	Department Stores (discount department stores)
CAN 4541	Electronic Shopping and Mail-Order Houses		
CAN 45411	Electronic Shopping and Mail-Order Houses		
US 454111	Electronic Shopping	*454110	Electronic Shopping and Mail-Order Houses (electronic shopping)

2002 NAICS Code	2002 NAICS U.S. Description	1997 NAICS Code	1997 NAICS U.S. Description
US 454112	Electronic Auctions	*454110	Electronic Shopping and Mail-Order Houses (Internet auctions)
US 454113	Mail-Order Houses	*454110	Electronic Shopping and Mail-Order Houses (except electronic shopping and Internet auctions)
51	Information		
511	Publishing Industries (except Internet)		
5111	Newspaper, Periodical, Book, and Directory Publishers		
51111	Newspaper Publishers	*511110	Newspaper Publishers (except Internet publishing)
51112	Periodical Publishers	*511120	Periodical Publishers (except Internet publishing)
51113	Book Publishers	*511130	Book Publishers (except Internet publishing)
		*511199	All Other Publishers (atlas and map publishing, except Internet publishing)
51114	Directory and Mailing List Publishers	*511140	Database and Directory Publishers (except Internet publishing)
51119	Other Publishers		
US 511191	Greeting Card Publishers	*511191	Greeting Card Publishers (except Internet publishing)
US 511199	All Other Publishers	*511199	All Other Publishers (except atlas and map publishing and Internet publishing)
5112	Software Publishers		
51121	Software Publishers	511210	Software Publishers
512	Motion Picture and Sound Recording Industries		
5121	Motion Picture and Video Industries		
51211	Motion Picture and Video Production	512110	Motion Picture and Video Production
51212	Motion Picture and Video Distribution	512120	Motion Picture and Video Distribution
51213	Motion Picture and Video Exhibition		

2002 NAICS Code	2002 NAICS U.S. Description	1997 NAICS Code	1997 NAICS U.S. Description
US 512131	Motion Picture Theaters (except Drive-Ins)	512131	Motion Picture Theaters (except Drive-Ins)
US 512132	Drive-In Motion Picture Theaters	512132	Drive-In Motion Picture Theaters
51219	Post Production Services and Other Motion Picture and Video Industries		
US 512191	Teleproduction and Other Postproduction Services	512191	Teleproduction and Other Postproduction Services
US 512199	Other Motion Picture and Video Industries	512199	Other Motion Picture and Video Industries
5122	Sound Recording Industries		
51221	Record Production	512210	Record Production
51222	Integrated Record Production/Distribution	512220	Integrated Record Production/Distribution
51223	Music Publishers	512230	Music Publishers
51224	Sound Recording Studios	512240	Sound Recording Studios
51229	Other Sound Recording Industries	512290	Other Sound Recording Industries
515	Broadcasting (except Internet)		
5151	Radio and Television Broadcasting		
US 515111	Radio Networks	513111	Radio Networks
US 515112	Radio Stations	513112	Radio Stations
51512	Television Broadcasting	513120	Television Broadcasting
5152	Cable and Other Subscription Programming		
51521	Cable and Other Subscription Programming	513210	Cable Networks
516	Internet Publishing and Broadcasting		
5161	Internet Publishing and Broadcasting		
51611	Internet Publishing and Broadcasting	*511110	Newspaper Publishers (Internet newspaper publishers)

US—United States industry only. CAN—United States and Canadian industries are comparable. MEX—United States and Mexican industries are comparable. Blank—Canadian, Mexican, and United States industries are comparable. *—Part of.

2002 NAICS Code	2002 NAICS U.S. Description	1997 NAICS Code	1997 NAICS U.S. Description
		*511120	Periodical Publishers (Internet periodical publishers)
		*511130	Book Publishers (Internet book publishers)
		*511140	Database and Directory Publishers (Internet directory publishers)
		*511191	Greeting Card Publishers (Internet greeting card publishers)
		*511199	All Other Publishers (All other Internet publishers)
		*514199	All Other Information Services (Internet broadcasting)
517	Telecommunications		
5171	Wired Telecommunications Carriers		
51711	Wired Telecommunications Carriers	513310	Wired Telecommunications Carriers
5172	Wireless Telecommunications Carriers (except Satellite)		
51721	Wireless Telecommunications Carriers (except Satellite)		
US 517211	Paging	513321	Paging
US 517212	Cellular and Other Wireless Telecommunications	513322	Cellular and Other Wireless Telecommunications
5173	Telecommunications Resellers		
51731	Telecommunications Resellers	513330	Telecommunications Resellers
5174	Satellite Telecommunications		
51741	Satellite Telecommunications	513340	Satellite Telecommunications
5175	Cable and Other Program Distribution		

US—United States industry only. CAN—United States and Canadian industries are comparable. MEX—United States and Mexican industries are comparable. Blank—Canadian, Mexican, and United States industries are comparable. *—Part of.

2002 NAICS Code	2002 NAICS U.S. Description	1997 NAICS Code	1997 NAICS U.S. Description
51751	Cable and Other Program Distribution	513220	Cable and Other Program Distribution
5179	Other Telecommunications		
51791	Other Telecommunications	513390	Other Telecommunications
518	Internet Service Providers, Web Search Portals, and Data Processing Services		
5181	Internet Service Providers and Web Search Portals		
51811	Internet Service Providers and Web Search Portals		
US 518111	Internet Service Providers	514191	On-Line Information Services
US 518112	Web Search Portals	*514199	All Other Information Services (Internet search portals)
5182	Data Processing, Hosting, and Related Services		
51821	Data Processing, Hosting, and Related Services	514210	Data Processing Services
519	Other Information Services		
5191	Other Information Services		
51911	News Syndicates	514110	News Syndicates
51912	Libraries and Archives	514120	Libraries and Archives
51919	All Other Information Services	*514199	All Other Information Services (except Internet search portals and Internet Broadcasting)

Appendix B
1997 NAICS U.S. Matched to 2002 NAICS U.S.

1997 NAICS Code	1997 NAICS U.S. Description	2002 NAICS Code	2002 NAICS U.S. Description
213112	Support Activities for Oil and Gas Operations		
	Construction of Field Gathering Lines On A Contract Basis	237120	Oil and Gas Pipeline and Related Structures Construction (pt)
	Site Preparation and Related Construction Activities On A Contract Basis	238910	Site Preparation Contractors (pt)
	Support Activities For Oil and Gas Operations Except Site Preparation and Related Construction Activities	213112	Support Activities for Oil and Gas Operations
213113	Support Activities for Coal Mining		
	Site Preparation and Related Construction Activities On A Contract Basis	238910	Site Preparation Contractors (pt)
	Support Activities For Coal Mining Except Site Preparation and Related Construction Activities	213113	Support Activities for Coal Mining
213114	Support Activities for Metal Mining		
	Site Preparation and Related Construction Activities On A Contract Basis	238910	Site Preparation Contractors (pt)
	Support Activities For Metal Mining Except Site Preparation and Related Construction Activities	213114	Support Activities for Metal Mining
213115	Support Activities for Nonmetallic Minerals (except Fuels)		
	Site Preparation and Related Construction Activities On A Contract Basis	238910	Site Preparation Contractors (pt)

(pt)—Part of.

1997 NAICS Code	1997 NAICS U.S. Description	2002 NAICS Code	2002 NAICS U.S. Description
	Support Activities For Nonmetallic Mineral (Except Fuel) Mining Except Site Preparation and Related Construction Activities	213115	Support Activities for Nonmetallic Minerals (except Fuels)
233110	Land Subdivision and Land Development	237210	Land Subdivision
233210	Single Family Housing Construction		
	General Contractors	236115	New Single-Family Housing Construction (except Operative Builders)
	Operative Builders	236117	New Housing Operative Builders (pt)
	Remodeling Contractors	236118	Residential Remodelers (pt)
233220	Multifamily Housing Construction		
	General Contractors	236116	New Multifamily Housing Construction (except Operative Builders)
	Operative Builders	236117	New Housing Operative Builders (pt)
	Remodeling Contractors	236118	Residential Remodelers (pt)
	Barrack and Dormitory Construction	236220	Commercial and Institutional Building Construction (pt)
233310	Manufacturing and Industrial Building Construction		
	Grain Elevators, Dry Cleaning Plants, and Manufacturing and Industrial Warehouses	236220	Commercial and Institutional Building Construction (pt)
	Except Grain Elevators, Dry Cleaning Plants, and Manufacturing and Industrial Warehouses	236210	Industrial Building Construction (pt)
233320	Commercial and Institutional Building Construction	236220	Commercial and Institutional Building Construction (pt)
234110	Highway and Street Construction	237310	Highway, Street, and Bridge Construction (pt)
234120	Bridge and Tunnel Construction		
	Bridge Construction	237310	Highway, Street, and Bridge Construction (pt)
	Tunnel Construction	237990	Other Heavy and Civil Engineering Construction (pt)

(pt)—Part of.

1997 NAICS Code	1997 NAICS U.S. Description	2002 NAICS Code	2002 NAICS U.S. Description
234910	Water, Sewer, and Pipeline Construction		
	Water/Sewer Pumping Stations, Sewage Collection and Disposal Lines, Storm Sewers, Sewer/Water Mains and Lines, and Water Storage Tanks and Towers, and Construction Management of these Projects	237110	Water and Sewer Line and Related Structures Construction (pt)
	Gas and Oil Pumping Stations, Gas and Oil Pipeline Construction, Gas Mains, Gas and Oil Storage Tank Construction, and Construction Management of these Projects	237120	Oil and Gas Pipeline and Related Structures Construction (pt)
234920	Power and Communication Transmission Line Construction	237130	Power and Communication Line and Related Structures Construction (pt)
234930	Industrial Nonbuilding Structure Construction		
	Petrochemical Plants, Refineries, and Construction Management of these Projects	237120	Oil and Gas Pipeline and Related Structures Construction (pt)
	Power Generation Plants (excluding Hydroelectric Dams), Transmission and Distribution Transformer Stations, and Construction Management of these Projects	237130	Power and Communication Line and Related Structures Construction (pt)
	Process Batch Plants, Incinerators, Industrial Furnaces and Kilns, Mining Appurtenance, and Construction Management of these Projects	236210	Industrial Building Construction (pt)
234990	All Other Heavy Construction		
	Waste Disposal Plant Construction	236210	Industrial Building Construction (pt)
	Irrigation Systems, Sewage Treatment and Water Treatment Plants, Construction Management of these Projects	237110	Water and Sewer Line and Related Structures Construction (pt)

(pt)—Part of.

1997 NAICS Code	1997 NAICS U.S. Description	2002 NAICS Code	2002 NAICS U.S. Description
	Right-of-Way Clearing and Line Slashing, Blasting, Trenching, and Equipment Rental (except cranes) with Operator	238910	Site Preparation Contractors (pt)
	Crane Rental with Operator	238990	All Other Specialty Trade Contractors (pt)
	Except Waste Disposal Plant Construction, Irrigation Systems, Sewage Treatment and Water Treatment Plants, Right-of-Way Clearing and Line Slashing, Blasting, Trenching, and Equipment Rental with Operator	237990	Other Heavy and Civil Engineering Construction (pt)
235110	Plumbing, Heating, and Air-Conditioning Contractors		
	Environmental Controls Installation Contractors	238210	Electrical Contractors (pt)
	Septic Tank, Cesspool, and Dry Well Construction Contractors	238910	Site Preparation Contractors (pt)
	Except Environmental Controls Installation Contractors and Septic Tank, Cesspool, and Dry Well Construction Contractors	238220	Plumbing, Heating, and Air-Conditioning Contractors (pt)
235210	Painting and Wall Covering Contractors		
	Highway and Traffic Line Painting	237310	Highway, Street, and Bridge Construction (pt)
	Except Highway and Traffic Line Painting	238320	Painting and Wall Covering Contractors
235310	Electrical Contractors	238210	Electrical Contractors (pt)
235410	Masonry and Stone Contractors	238140	Masonry Contractors (pt)
235420	Drywall, Plastering, Acoustical, and Insulation Contractors		
	Stucco Contractors	238140	Masonry Contractors (pt)
	Except Stucco Contractors	238310	Drywall and Insulation Contractors
235430	Tile, Marble, Terrazzo, and Mosaic Contractors	238340	Tile and Terrazzo and Tile Contractors
235510	Carpentry Contractors		
	Framing Carpentry	238130	Framing Contractors

(pt)—Part of.

1997 NAICS Code	1997 NAICS U.S. Description	2002 NAICS Code	2002 NAICS U.S. Description
	Finish Carpentry	238350	Finish Carpentry Contractors
235520	Floor Laying and Other Floor Contractors	238330	Flooring Contractors
235610	Roofing, Siding, and Sheet Metal Contractors		
	Roofing Contractors	238160	Roofing Contractors
	Siding Contractors	238170	Siding Contractors
	Metal Ceiling, Panel, and Shelving Installation	238390	Other Building Finishing Contractors (pt)
235710	Concrete Contractors		
	Residential and Commercial Asphalt, Brick, and Concrete Paving	238990	All Other Specialty Trade Contractors (pt)
	Except Residential and Commercial Asphalt, Brick, and Concrete Paving	238110	Poured Concrete Foundation and Structure Contractors
235810	Water Well Drilling Contractors	237110	Water and Sewer Line and Related Structures Construction (pt)
235910	Structural Steel Erection Contractors		
	Curtain Walls and Metal Furring Installation	238190	Other Foundation, Structure, and Building Exterior Contractors (pt)
	Cooling Tower Installation	238220	Plumbing, Heating, and Air-Conditioning Contractors (pt)
	Except Curtain Walls, Metal Furring Installation, and Cooling Tower Installation	238120	Structural Steel and Precast Concrete Contractors
235920	Glass and Glazing Contractors	238150	Glass and Glazing Contractors
235930	Excavation Contractors	238910	Site Preparation Contractors (pt)
235940	Wrecking and Demolition Contractors	238910	Site Preparation Contractors (pt)
235950	Building Equipment and Other Machinery Installation Contractors		
	Scrubber, Dust Collection, and Other Industrial Ventilation Installation	238220	Plumbing, Heating, and Air-Conditioning Contractors (pt)
	Except Scrubber, Dust Collection, and Other Industrial Ventilation Installation	238290	Other Building Equipment Contractors (pt)

(pt)—Part of.

1997 NAICS Code	1997 NAICS U.S. Description	2002 NAICS Code	2002 NAICS U.S. Description
235990	All Other Special Trade Contractors		
	Indoor Swimming Pool Contractors	236220	Commercial and Institutional Building Construction (pt)
	Anchored Earth Retention Contractors	237990	Other Heavy and Civil Engineering Construction (pt)
	Forming Contractors, Ornamental Metal Work Installation	238190	Other Foundation, Structure, and Building Exterior Contractors (pt)
	Service Station Equipment Installation Contractors; Boiler, Duct, and Pipe Insulation; Lightning Rod Installation; Bowling Alley Installation; Household- Type Antenna Installation; Church Bell Installation; and Tower Clock Installation	238290	Other Building Equipment Contractors (pt)
	Weather Stripping and Damp-Proofing, Modular Furniture Installation, Bathtub Refinishing, Window Covering Fixture Installation, Trade Show Exhibit Installation and Dismantling, and Spectator Seating Installation	238390	Other Building Finishing Contractors (pt)
	Dewatering Contractors, Core Drilling For Construction, and Test Boring for Construction	238910	Site Preparation Contractors (pt)
	Except Indoor Swimming Pool Contractors, Anchored Earth Retention Contractors, Forming Contractors, Ornamental Metal Work Installation, Building Equipment Contractors, Building Finishing Contractors, Dewatering Contractors, Test Boring For Construction, and Core Drilling For Construction	238990	All Other Specialty Trade Contractors (pt)
421110	Automobile and Other Motor Vehicle Wholesalers		
	Merchant Wholesalers	423110	Automobile and Other Motor Vehicle Merchant Wholesalers

---

(pt)—Part of.

1997 NAICS Code	1997 NAICS U.S. Description	2002 NAICS Code	2002 NAICS U.S. Description
	Business to Business Electronic Markets	425110	Business to Business Electronic Markets (pt)
	Agents and Brokers	425120	Wholesale Trade Agents and Brokers (pt)
421120	Motor Vehicle Supplies and New Parts Wholesalers		
	Merchant Wholesalers	423120	Motor Vehicle Supplies and New Parts Merchant Wholesalers
	Business to Business Electronic Markets	425110	Business to Business Electronic Markets (pt)
	Agents and Brokers	425120	Wholesale Trade Agents and Brokers (pt)
421130	Tire and Tube Wholesalers		
	Merchant Wholesalers	423130	Tire and Tube Merchant Wholesalers
	Business to Business Electronic Markets	425110	Business to Business Electronic Markets (pt)
	Agents and Brokers	425120	Wholesale Trade Agents and Brokers (pt)
421140	Motor Vehicle Parts (Used) Wholesalers		
	Merchant Wholesalers	423140	Motor Vehicle Parts (Used) Merchant Wholesalers
	Business to Business Electronic Markets	425110	Business to Business Electronic Markets (pt)
	Agents and Brokers	425120	Wholesale Trade Agents and Brokers (pt)
421210	Furniture Wholesalers		
	Merchant Wholesalers	423210	Furniture Merchant Wholesalers
	Business to Business Electronic Markets	425110	Business to Business Electronic Markets (pt)
	Agents and Brokers	425120	Wholesale Trade Agents and Brokers (pt)
421220	Home Furnishing Wholesalers		
	Merchant Wholesalers	423220	Home Furnishing Merchant Wholesalers
	Business to Business Electronic Markets	425110	Business to Business Electronic Markets
	Agents and Brokers	425120	Wholesale Trade Agents and Brokers
421310	Lumber, Plywood, Millwork, and Wood Panel Wholesalers		

(pt)—Part of.

1997 NAICS Code	1997 NAICS U.S. Description	2002 NAICS Code	2002 NAICS U.S. Description
	Merchant Wholesalers	423310	Lumber, Plywood, Millwork, and Wood Panel Merchant Wholesalers
	Business to Business Electronic Markets	425110	Business to Business Electronic Markets (pt)
	Agents and Brokers	425120	Wholesale Trade Agents and Brokers (pt)
421320	Brick, Stone, and Related Construction Material Wholesalers		
	Merchant Wholesalers	423320	Brick, Stone, and Related Construction Material Merchant Wholesalers
	Business to Business Electronic Markets	425110	Business to Business Electronic Markets (pt)
	Agents and Brokers	425120	Wholesale Trade Agents and Brokers (pt)
421330	Roofing, Siding, and Insulation Material Wholesalers		
	Merchant Wholesalers	423330	Roofing, Siding, and Insulation Material Merchant Wholesalers
	Business to Business Electronic Markets	425110	Business to Business Electronic Markets (pt)
	Agents and Brokers	425120	Wholesale Trade Agents and Brokers (pt)
421390	Other Construction Material Wholesalers		
	Merchant Wholesalers	423390	Other Construction Material Merchant Wholesalers
	Business to Business Electronic Markets	425110	Business to Business Electronic Markets (pt)
	Agents and Brokers	425120	Wholesale Trade Agents and Brokers (pt)
421410	Photographic Equipment and Supplies Wholesalers		
	Merchant Wholesalers	423410	Photographic Equipment and Supplies Merchant Wholesalers
	Business to Business Electronic Markets	425110	Business to Business Electronic Markets (pt)
	Agents and Brokers	425120	Wholesale Trade Agents and Brokers (pt)
421420	Office Equipment Wholesalers		
	Merchant Wholesalers	423420	Office Equipment Merchant Wholesalers

(pt)—Part of.

1997 NAICS Code	1997 NAICS U.S. Description	2002 NAICS Code	2002 NAICS U.S. Description
	Business to Business Electronic Markets	425110	Business to Business Electronic Markets (pt)
	Agents and Brokers	425120	Wholesale Trade Agents and Brokers (pt)
421430	Computer and Computer Peripheral Equipment and Software Wholesalers		
	Merchant Wholesalers	423430	Computer and Computer Peripheral Equipment and Software Merchant Wholesalers
	Business to Business Electronic Markets	425110	Business to Business Electronic Markets (pt)
	Agents and Brokers	425120	Wholesale Trade Agents and Brokers (pt)
421440	Other Commercial Equipment Wholesalers		
	Merchant Wholesalers	423440	Other Commercial Equipment Merchant Wholesalers
	Business to Business Electronic Markets	425110	Business to Business Electronic Markets (pt)
	Agents and Brokers	425120	Wholesale Trade Agents and Brokers (pt)
421450	Medical, Dental, and Hospital Equipment and Supplies Wholesalers		
	Merchant Wholesalers	423450	Medical, Dental, and Hospital Equipment and Supplies Merchant Wholesalers
	Business to Business Electronic Markets	425110	Business to Business Electronic Markets (pt)
	Agents and Brokers	425120	Wholesale Trade Agents and Brokers (pt)
421460	Ophthalmic Goods Wholesalers		
	Merchant Wholesalers	423460	Ophthalmic Goods Merchant Wholesalers
	Business to Business Electronic Markets	425110	Business to Business Electronic Markets (pt)
	Agents and Brokers	425120	Wholesale Trade Agents and Brokers (pt)
421490	Other Professional Equipment and Supplies Wholesalers		
	Merchant Wholesalers	423490	Other Professional Equipment and Supplies Merchant Wholesalers

___
(pt)—Part of.

1997 NAICS Code	1997 NAICS U.S. Description	2002 NAICS Code	2002 NAICS U.S. Description
	Business to Business Electronic Markets	425110	Business to Business Electronic Markets (pt)
	Agents and Brokers	425120	Wholesale Trade Agents and Brokers (pt)
421510	Metal Service Centers and Offices		
	Merchant Wholesalers	423510	Metal Service Centers and Other Metal Merchant Wholesalers
	Business to Business Electronic Markets	425110	Business to Business Electronic Markets (pt)
	Agents and Brokers	425120	Wholesale Trade Agents and Brokers (pt)
421520	Coal and Other Mineral and Ore Wholesalers		
	Merchant Wholesalers	423520	Coal and Other Mineral and Ore Merchant Wholesalers
	Business to Business Electronic Markets	425110	Business to Business Electronic Markets (pt)
	Agents and Brokers	425120	Wholesale Trade Agents and Brokers (pt)
421610	Electrical Apparatus and Equipment, Wiring Supplies, and Construction Material Wholesalers		
	Merchant Wholesalers	423610	Electrical Apparatus and Equipment, Wiring Supplies, and Related Equipment Merchant Wholesalers
	Business to Business Electronic Markets	425110	Business to Business Electronic Markets (pt)
	Agents and Brokers	425120	Wholesale Trade Agents and Brokers (pt)
421620	Electrical Appliance, Television, and Radio Set Wholesalers		
	Merchant Wholesalers	423620	Electrical and Electronic Appliance, Television, and Radio Set Merchant Wholesalers
	Business to Business Electronic Markets	425110	Business to Business Electronic Markets (pt)
	Agents and Brokers	425120	Wholesale Trade Agents and Brokers (pt)
421690	Other Electronic Parts and Equipment Wholesalers		

(pt)—Part of.

1997 NAICS Code	1997 NAICS U.S. Description	2002 NAICS Code	2002 NAICS U.S. Description
	Merchant Wholesalers	423690	Other Electronic Parts and Equipment Merchant Wholesalers
	Business to Business Electronic Markets	425110	Business to Business Electronic Markets (pt)
	Agents and Brokers	425120	Wholesale Trade Agents and Brokers (pt)
421710	Hardware Wholesalers		
	Merchant Wholesalers	423710	Hardware Merchant Wholesalers
	Business to Business Electronic Markets	425110	Business to Business Electronic Markets (pt)
	Agents and Brokers	425120	Wholesale Trade Agents and Brokers (pt)
421720	Plumbing and Heating Equipment and Supplies (Hydronics) Wholesalers		
	Merchant Wholesalers	423720	Plumbing and Heating Equipment and Supplies (Hydronics) Merchant Wholesalers
	Business to Business Electronic Markets	425110	Business to Business Electronic Markets (pt)
	Agents and Brokers	425120	Wholesale Trade Agents and Brokers (pt)
421730	Warm Air Heating and Air-Conditioning Equipment and Supplies Wholesalers		
	Merchant Wholesalers	423730	Warm Air Heating and Air-Conditioning Equipment and Supplies Merchant Wholesalers
	Business to Business Electronic Markets	425110	Business to Business Electronic Markets (pt)
	Agents and Brokers	425120	Wholesale Trade Agents and Brokers (pt)
421740	Refrigeration Equipment and Supplies Wholesalers		
	Merchant Wholesalers	423740	Refrigeration Equipment and Supplies Merchant Wholesalers
	Business to Business Electronic Markets	425110	Business to Business Electronic Markets (pt)
	Agents and Brokers	425120	Wholesale Trade Agents and Brokers (pt)

(pt)—Part of.

1997 NAICS Code	1997 NAICS U.S. Description	2002 NAICS Code	2002 NAICS U.S. Description
421810	Construction and Mining (except Oil Well) Machinery and Equipment Wholesalers Merchant Wholesalers	423810	Construction and Mining (except Oil Well) Machinery and Equipment Merchant Wholesalers
	Business to Business Electronic Markets	425110	Business to Business Electronic Markets (pt)
	Agents and Brokers	425120	Wholesale Trade Agents and Brokers (pt)
421820	Farm and Garden Machinery and Equipment Wholesalers Merchant Wholesalers	423820	Farm and Garden Machinery and Equipment Merchant Wholesalers
	Business to Business Electronic Markets	425110	Business to Business Electronic Markets (pt)
	Agents and Brokers	425120	Wholesale Trade Agents and Brokers (pt)
421830	Industrial Machinery and Equipment Wholesalers Merchant Wholesalers	423830	Industrial Machinery and Equipment Merchant Wholesalers
	Business to Business Electronic Markets	425110	Business to Business Electronic Markets (pt)
	Agents and Brokers	425120	Wholesale Trade Agents and Brokers (pt)
421840	Industrial Supplies Wholesalers Merchant Wholesalers	423840	Industrial Supplies Merchant Wholesalers
	Business to Business Electronic Markets	425110	Business to Business Electronic Markets (pt)
	Agents and Brokers	425120	Wholesale Trade Agents and Brokers (pt)
421850	Service Establishment Equipment and Supplies Wholesalers Merchant Wholesalers	423850	Service Establishment Equipment and Supplies Merchant Wholesalers
	Business to Business Electronic Markets	425110	Business to Business Electronic Markets (pt)

(pt)—Part of.

1997 NAICS Code	1997 NAICS U.S. Description	2002 NAICS Code	2002 NAICS U.S. Description
	Agents and Brokers	425120	Wholesale Trade Agents and Brokers (pt)
421860	Transportation Equipment and Supplies (except Motor Vehicle) Wholesalers		
	Merchant Wholesalers	423860	Transportation Equipment and Supplies (except Motor Vehicle) Merchant Wholesalers
	Business to Business Electronic Markets	425110	Business to Business Electronic Markets (pt)
	Agents and Brokers	425120	Wholesale Trade Agents and Brokers (pt)
421910	Sporting and Recreational Goods and Supplies Wholesalers		
	Merchant Wholesalers	423910	Sporting and Recreational Goods and Supplies Merchant Wholesalers
	Business to Business Electronic Markets	425110	Business to Business Electronic Markets (pt)
	Agents and Brokers	425120	Wholesale Trade Agents and Brokers (pt)
421920	Toy and Hobby Goods and Supplies Wholesalers		
	Merchant Wholesalers	423920	Toy and Hobby Goods and Supplies Merchant Wholesalers
	Business to Business Electronic Markets	425110	Business to Business Electronic Markets (pt)
	Agents and Brokers	425120	Wholesale Trade Agents and Brokers (pt)
421930	Recyclable Material Wholesalers		
	Merchant Wholesalers	423930	Recyclable Material Merchant Wholesalers
	Business to Business Electronic Markets	425110	Business to Business Electronic Markets (pt)
	Agents and Brokers	425120	Wholesale Trade Agents and Brokers (pt)
421940	Jewelry, Watch, Precious Stone, and Precious Metal Wholesalers		
	Merchant Wholesalers	423940	Jewelry, Watch, Precious Stone, and Precious Metal Merchant Wholesalers
	Business to Business Electronic Markets	425110	Business to Business Electronic Markets (pt)

(pt)—Part of.

1997 NAICS Code	1997 NAICS U.S. Description	2002 NAICS Code	2002 NAICS U.S. Description
	Agents and Brokers	425120	Wholesale Trade Agents and Brokers (pt)
421990	Other Miscellaneous Durable Goods Wholesalers		
	Merchant Wholesalers	423990	Other Miscellaneous Durable Goods Merchant Wholesalers
	Business to Business Electronic Markets	425110	Business to Business Electronic Markets (pt)
	Agents and Brokers	425120	Wholesale Trade Agents and Brokers (pt)
422110	Printing and Writing Paper Wholesalers		
	Merchant Wholesalers	424110	Printing and Writing Paper Merchant Wholesalers
	Business to Business Electronic Markets	425110	Business to Business Electronic Markets (pt)
	Agents and Brokers	425120	Wholesale Trade Agents and Brokers (pt)
422120	Stationary and Office Supplies Wholesalers		
	Merchant Wholesalers	424120	Stationary and Office Supplies Merchant Wholesalers
	Business to Business Electronic Markets	425110	Business to Business Electronic Markets (pt)
	Agents and Brokers	425120	Wholesale Trade Agents and Brokers (pt)
422130	Industrial and Personal Service Paper Wholesalers		
	Merchant Wholesalers	424130	Industrial and Personal Service Paper Merchant Wholesalers
	Business to Business Electronic Markets	425110	Business to Business Electronic Markets (pt)
	Agents and Brokers	425120	Wholesale Trade Agents and Brokers (pt)
422210	Drugs and Druggists' Sundries Wholesalers		
	Merchant Wholesalers	424210	Drugs and Druggists' Sundries Merchant Wholesalers
	Business to Business Electronic Markets	425110	Business to Business Electronic Markets (pt)
	Agents and Brokers	425120	Wholesale Trade Agents and Brokers (pt)
422310	Piece Goods, Notions, and Other Dry Goods Wholesalers		

(pt)—Part of.

1997 NAICS Code	1997 NAICS U.S. Description	2002 NAICS Code	2002 NAICS U.S. Description
	Merchant Wholesalers	424310	Piece Goods, Notions, and Other Dry Goods Merchant Wholesalers
	Business to Business Electronic Markets	425110	Business to Business Electronic Markets (pt)
	Agents and Brokers	425120	Wholesale Trade Agents and Brokers (pt)
422320	Men's and Boys' Clothing and Furnishings Wholesalers		
	Merchant Wholesalers	424320	Men's and Boys' Clothing and Furnishings Merchant Wholesalers
	Business to Business Electronic Markets	425110	Business to Business Electronic Markets (pt)
	Agents and Brokers	425120	Wholesale Trade Agents and Brokers (pt)
422330	Women's, Children's, and Infants' Clothing and Accessories Wholesalers		
	Merchant Wholesalers	424330	Women's, Children's, and Infants' Clothing and Accessories Merchant Wholesalers
	Business to Business Electronic Markets	425110	Business to Business Electronic Markets (pt)
	Agents and Brokers	425120	Wholesale Trade Agents and Brokers (pt)
422340	Footwear Wholesalers		
	Merchant Wholesalers	424340	Footwear Merchant Wholesalers
	Business to Business Electronic Markets	425110	Business to Business Electronic Markets (pt)
	Agents and Brokers	425120	Wholesale Trade Agents and Brokers (pt)
422410	General Line Grocery Wholesalers		
	Merchant Wholesalers	424410	General Line Grocery Merchant Wholesalers
	Business to Business Electronic Markets	425110	Business to Business Electronic Markets (pt)
	Agents and Brokers	425120	Wholesale Trade Agents and Brokers (pt)
422420	Packaged Frozen Food Wholesalers		
	Merchant Wholesalers	424420	Packaged Frozen Food Merchant Wholesalers

(pt)—Part of.

1997 NAICS Code	1997 NAICS U.S. Description	2002 NAICS Code	2002 NAICS U.S. Description
	Business to Business Electronic Markets	425110	Business to Business Electronic Markets (pt)
	Agents and Brokers	425120	Wholesale Trade Agents and Brokers (pt)
422430	Dairy Product (except Dried or Canned) Wholesalers		
	Merchant Wholesalers	424430	Dairy Product (except Dried or Canned) Merchant Wholesalers
	Business to Business Electronic Markets	425110	Business to Business Electronic Markets (pt)
	Agents and Brokers	425120	Wholesale Trade Agents and Brokers (pt)
422440	Poultry and Poultry Product Wholesalers		
	Merchant Wholesalers	424440	Poultry and Poultry Product Merchant Wholesalers
	Business to Business Electronic Markets	425110	Business to Business Electronic Markets (pt)
	Agents and Brokers	425120	Wholesale Trade Agents and Brokers (pt)
422450	Confectionery Wholesalers		
	Merchant Wholesalers	424450	Confectionery Merchant Wholesalers
	Business to Business Electronic Markets	425110	Business to Business Electronic Markets (pt)
	Agents and Brokers	425120	Wholesale Trade Agents and Brokers (pt)
422460	Fish and Seafood Wholesalers		
	Merchant Wholesalers	424460	Fish and Seafood Merchant Wholesalers
	Business to Business Electronic Markets	425110	Business to Business Electronic Markets (pt)
	Agents and Brokers	425120	Wholesale Trade Agents and Brokers (pt)
422470	Meat and Meat Product Wholesalers		
	Merchant Wholesalers	424470	Meat and Meat Product Merchant Wholesalers
	Business to Business Electronic Markets	425110	Business to Business Electronic Markets (pt)
	Agents and Brokers	425120	Wholesale Trade Agents and Brokers (pt)
422480	Fresh Fruit and Vegetable Wholesalers		

(pt)—Part of.

1997 NAICS Code	1997 NAICS U.S. Description	2002 NAICS Code	2002 NAICS U.S. Description
	Merchant Wholesalers	424480	Fresh Fruit and Vegetable Merchant Wholesalers
	Business to Business Electronic Markets	425110	Business to Business Electronic Markets (pt)
	Agents and Brokers	425120	Wholesale Trade Agents and Brokers (pt)
422490	Other Grocery and Related Products Wholesalers		
	Merchant Wholesalers	424490	Other Grocery and Related Products Merchant Wholesalers
	Business to Business Electronic Markets	425110	Business to Business Electronic Markets (pt)
	Agents and Brokers	425120	Wholesale Trade Agents and Brokers (pt)
422510	Grain and Field Bean Wholesalers		
	Merchant Wholesalers	424510	Grain and Field Bean Merchant Wholesalers
	Business to Business Electronic Markets	425110	Business to Business Electronic Markets (pt)
	Agents and Brokers	425120	Wholesale Trade Agents and Brokers (pt)
422520	Livestock Wholesalers		
	Merchant Wholesalers	424520	Livestock Merchant Wholesalers
	Business to Business Electronic Markets	425110	Business to Business Electronic Markets (pt)
	Agents and Brokers	425120	Wholesale Trade Agents and Brokers (pt)
422590	Other Farm Product Raw Material Wholesalers		
	Merchant Wholesalers	424590	Other Farm Product Raw Material Merchant Wholesalers
	Business to Business Electronic Markets	425110	Business to Business Electronic Markets (pt)
	Agents and Brokers	425120	Wholesale Trade Agents and Brokers (pt)
422610	Plastics Materials and Basic Forms and Shapes Wholesalers		
	Merchant Wholesalers	424610	Plastics Materials and Basic Forms and Shapes Merchant Wholesalers
	Business to Business Electronic Markets	425110	Business to Business Electronic Markets (pt)

(pt)—Part of.

1997 NAICS Code	1997 NAICS U.S. Description	2002 NAICS Code	2002 NAICS U.S. Description
	Agents and Brokers	425120	Wholesale Trade Agents and Brokers (pt)
422690	Other Chemical and Allied Products Wholesalers		
	Merchant Wholesalers	424690	Other Chemical and Allied Products Merchant Wholesalers
	Business to Business Electronic Markets	425110	Business to Business Electronic Markets (pt)
	Agents and Brokers	425120	Wholesale Trade Agents and Brokers (pt)
422710	Petroleum Bulk Stations and Terminals	424710	Petroleum Bulk Stations and Terminals
422720	Petroleum and Petroleum Products Wholesalers (except Bulk Stations and Terminals)		
	Merchant Wholesalers	424720	Petroleum and Petroleum Products Merchant Wholesalers (except Bulk Stations and Terminals)
	Business to Business Electronic Markets	425110	Business to Business Electronic Markets (pt)
	Agents and Brokers	425120	Wholesale Trade Agents and Brokers (pt)
422810	Beer and Ale Wholesalers		
	Merchant Wholesalers	424810	Beer and Ale Merchant Wholesalers
	Business to Business Electronic Markets	425110	Business to Business Electronic Markets (pt)
	Agents and Brokers	425120	Wholesale Trade Agents and Brokers (pt)
422820	Wine and Distilled Alcoholic Beverage Wholesalers		
	Merchant Wholesalers	424820	Wine and Distilled Alcoholic Beverage Merchant Wholesalers
	Business to Business Electronic Markets	425110	Business to Business Electronic Markets (pt)
	Agents and Brokers	425120	Wholesale Trade Agents and Brokers (pt)
422910	Farm Supplies Wholesalers		
	Merchant Wholesalers	424910	Farm Supplies Merchant Wholesalers
	Business to Business Electronic Markets	425110	Business to Business Electronic Markets (pt)
	Agents and Brokers	425120	Wholesale Trade Agents and Brokers (pt)

(pt)—Part of.

1997 NAICS Code	1997 NAICS U.S. Description	2002 NAICS Code	2002 NAICS U.S. Description
422920	Book, Periodical, and Newspaper Wholesalers Merchant Wholesalers	424920	Book, Periodical, and Newspaper Merchant Wholesalers
	Business to Business Electronic Markets	425110	Business to Business Electronic Markets (pt)
	Agents and Brokers	425120	Wholesale Trade Agents and Brokers (pt)
422930	Flower, Nursery Stock, and Florists' Supplies Wholesalers Merchant Wholesalers	424930	Flower, Nursery Stock, and Florists' Supplies Merchant Wholesalers
	Business to Business Electronic Markets	425110	Business to Business Electronic Markets (pt)
	Agents and Brokers	425120	Wholesale Trade Agents and Brokers (pt)
422940	Tobacco and Tobacco Product Wholesalers Merchant Wholesalers	424940	Tobacco and Tobacco Product Merchant Wholesalers
	Business to Business Electronic Markets	425110	Business to Business Electronic Markets (pt)
	Agents and Brokers	425120	Wholesale Trade Agents and Brokers (pt)
422950	Paint, Varnish, and Supplies Wholesalers Merchant Wholesalers	424950	Paint, Varnish, and Supplies Merchant Wholesalers
	Business to Business Electronic Markets	425110	Business to Business Electronic Markets (pt)
	Agents and Brokers	425120	Wholesale Trade Agents and Brokers (pt)
422990	Other Miscellaneous Nondurable Goods Wholesalers Merchant Wholesalers	424990	Other Miscellaneous Nondurable Goods Merchant Wholesalers
	Business to Business Electronic Markets	425110	Business to Business Electronic Markets (pt)
	Agents and Brokers	425120	Wholesale Trade Agents and Brokers (pt)
452110	Department Stores		

(pt)—Part of.

1997 NAICS Code	1997 NAICS U.S. Description	2002 NAICS Code	2002 NAICS U.S. Description
	Department Stores (except Discount Department Stores)	452111	Department Stores (except Discount Department Stores)
	Discount Department Stores	452112	Discount Department Stores
454110	Electronic Shopping and Mail Order Houses		
	Electronic Shopping	454111	Electronic Shopping
	Electronic Auctions	454112	Electronic Auctions
	Mail-Order Houses	454113	Mail-Order Houses
511110	Newspaper Publishers		
	Newspaper Publishers (except Internet Publishers)	511110	Newspaper Publishers
	Internet Newspaper Publishers	516110	Internet Publishers (pt.)
511120	Periodical Publishers		
	Periodical Publishers (except Internet Publishers)	511120	Periodical Publishers
	Internet Periodical Publishers	516110	Internet Publishers (pt.)
511130	Book Publishers		
	Book Publishers (except Internet Publishers)	511130	Book Publishers
	Internet Book Publishers	516110	Internet Publishers (pt.)
511140	Database and Directory Publishers		
	Database and Directory Publishers (except Internet Publishers)	511140	Directory and Mailing List Publishers
	Internet Database and Directory Publishers	516110	Internet Publishers (pt.)
511191	Greeting Card Publishers		
	Greeting Card Publishers (except Internet Publishers)	511191	Greeting Card Publishers
	Internet Greeting Card Publishers	516110	Internet Publishers (pt.)
511199	All Other Publishers		
	Atlas and Map Publishers (except Internet Publishers)	511130	Book Publishers (pt.)
	All Other Publishers (except Internet Publishers)	511199	All Other Publishers
	Atlas and Map Publishers (Internet Publishers) and All Other Internet Publishers	516110	Internet Publishers (pt.)
511210	Software Publishers	511210	Software Publishers

1997 NAICS Code	1997 NAICS U.S. Description	2002 NAICS Code	2002 NAICS U.S. Description
512110	Motion Picture and Video Production	512110	Motion Picture and Video Production
512120	Motion Picture and Video Distribution	512120	Motion Picture and Video Distribution
512131	Motion Picture Theaters (except Drive-Ins)	512131	Motion Picture Theaters (except Drive-Ins)
512132	Drive-In Motion Picture Theaters	512132	Drive-In Motion Picture Theaters
512191	Teleproduction and Other Postproduction Services	512191	Teleproduction and other Postproduction Services
512199	Other Motion Picture and Video Industries	512199	Other Motion Picture and Video Industries
512210	Record Production	512210	Record Production
512220	Integrated Record Production/ Distribution	512220	Integrated Record Production/ Distribution
512230	Music Publishers	512230	Music Publishers
512240	Sound Recording Studios	512240	Sound Recording Studios
512290	Other Sound Recording Industries	512290	Other Sound Recording Industries
513111	Radio Networks	515111	Radio Networks
513112	Radio Stations	515112	Radio Stations
513120	Television Broadcasting	515120	Television Broadcasting
513210	Cable Networks	515210	Cable and Other Subscription Programming
513220	Cable and Other Program Distribution	517510	Cable and Other Program Distribution
513310	Wired Telecommunications Carriers	517110	Wired Telecommunications Carriers
513321	Paging	517211	Paging
513322	Cellular and Other Wireless Telecommunications	517212	Cellular and Other Wireless Telecommunications
513330	Telecommunications Resellers	517310	Telecommunications Resellers
513340	Satellite Telecommunications	517410	Satellite Telecommunications
513390	Other Telecommunications	517910	Other Telecommunications
514110	News Syndicates	519110	News Syndicates
514120	Libraries and Archives	519120	Libraries and Archives
514191	On-Line Information Services	518111	Internet Service Providers
514199	All Other Information Services Internet Broadcasting	516110	Internet Publishing and Broadcasting (pt.)
	Web Search Portals	518112	Web Search Portals
	All Other Information Services	519190	All Other Information Services

1997 NAICS Code	1997 NAICS U.S. Description	2002 NAICS Code	2002 NAICS U.S. Description
514210	Data Processing Services	518210	Data Processing, Hosting, and Related Services
561720	Janitorial Services		
	Cleaning Buildings During and Immediately After Construction	238990	All Other Specialty Trade Contractors (pt)
	Except Cleaning Buildings During and Immediately After Construction	561720	Janitorial Services

Part IV

Alphabetic Index

Alphabetic Index

325191	Acetone, natural, manufacturing
325199	Acetone, synthetic, manufacturing
332420	Acetylene cylinders, heavy gauge metal, manufacturing
325120	Acetylene manufacturing
325411	Acetylsalicylic acid manufacturing
325132	Acid dyes, synthetic organic, manufacturing
325199	Acid esters, not specified elsewhere by process, manufacturing
324110	Acid oils made in petroleum refineries
236210	Acid plant construction
562211	Acid waste disposal facilities
562211	Acid waste treatment facilities
334513	Acidity (i.e., pH) instruments, industrial process type, manufacturing
334516	Acidity (i.e., pH) measuring equipment, laboratory analysis-type, manufacturing
213112	Acidizing oil and gas field wells on a contract basis
311511	Acidophilus milk manufacturing
424690	Acids merchant wholesalers
325199	Acids, organic, not specified elsewhere by process, manufacturing
111219	Acorn squash farming, field, bedding plant and seed production
238310	Acoustical ceiling tile and panel installation
541330	Acoustical engineering consulting services
238310	Acoustical foam (i.e., sound barrier) installation
332323	Acoustical suspension systems, metal, manufacturing
541330	Acoustical system engineering design services
541380	Acoustics testing laboratories or services
325199	Acrolein manufacturing
325212	Acrylate rubber manufacturing
325212	Acrylate-butadiene rubber manufacturing

313112	Acrylic and modacrylic filament yarn throwing, twisting, texturizing, or winding purchased yarn
325222	Acrylic fibers and filaments manufacturing
326113	Acrylic film and unlaminated sheet (except packaging) manufacturing
325211	Acrylic resins manufacturing
325212	Acrylic rubber manufacturing
313111	Acrylic spun yarns made from purchased fiber
325222	Acrylonitrile fibers and filaments manufacturing
325199	Acrylonitrile manufacturing
325211	Acrylonitrile-butadiene-styrene (ABS) resins manufacturing
334519	Actinometers, meteorological, manufacturing
339931	Action figures manufacturing
325998	Activated carbon or charcoal manufacturing
624120	Activity centers for disabled persons, the elderly, and persons diagnosed with mental retardation
711510	Actors, independent
711510	Actresses, independent
541612	Actuarial consulting services
524298	Actuaries
333995	Actuators, fluid power, manufacturing
621399	Acupuncturists' (except MDs or DOs) offices (e.g., centers, clinics)
621111	Acupuncturists' (MDs or DOs) offices (e.g., centers, clinics)
325110	Acyclic hydrocarbons (e.g., butene, ethylene, propene) (except acetylene) made from refined petroleum or liquid hydrocarbons
332993	Adapters, bombcluster, manufacturing
333313	Adding machines manufacturing
236118	Addition, alteration and renovation (i.e., construction), multifamily building

322222	Adhesive tape (except medical) made from purchased materials
339113	Adhesive tape, medical, manufacturing
325520	Adhesives (except asphalt, dental, gypsum base) manufacturing
424690	Adhesives and sealants merchant wholesalers
325199	Adipic acid esters or amines manufacturing
325199	Adipic acid manufacturing
325199	Adiponitrile manufacturing
236220	Administration building construction
922110	Administrative courts
541611	Administrative management consulting services
561110	Administrative management services
523991	Administrators of private estates
327123	Adobe bricks manufacturing
624110	Adoption agencies
624110	Adoption services, child
325411	Adrenal derivatives, uncompounded, manufacturing
325412	Adrenal medicinal preparations manufacturing
611691	Adult literacy instruction
541810	Advertising agencies
541810	Advertising agency consulting services
541870	Advertising material (e.g., coupons, flyers, samples) direct distribution services
541860	Advertising material preparation services for mailing or other direct distribution
323110	Advertising materials (e.g., coupons, flyers) lithographic (offset) printing without publishing
541840	Advertising media representatives (i.e., independent of media owners)
511120	Advertising periodical publishers (except exclusive Internet publishing)
511120	Advertising periodical publishers and printing combined
516110	Advertising periodical publishers, exclusively on Internet
541850	Advertising services, indoor or outdoor display
541890	Advertising specialty (e.g., keychain, magnet, pen) distribution services
541850	Advertising, aerial
921110	Advisory commissions, executive government
921120	Advisory commissions, legislative
487990	Aerial cable car, scenic and sightseeing, operation
333315	Aerial cameras manufacturing
115112	Aerial dusting or spraying (i.e., using specialized or dedicated aircraft)
541360	Aerial geophysical surveying services
238910	Aerial or picker truck, construction, rental with operator
541370	Aerial surveying (except geophysical) services
487990	Aerial tramway, scenic and sightseeing, operation
333923	Aerial work platforms manufacturing
713940	Aerobic dance and exercise centers
423860	Aeronautical equipment and supplies merchant wholesalers
334511	Aeronautical systems and instruments manufacturing
325998	Aerosol can filling on a job order or contract basis
332431	Aerosol cans, light gauge metal, manufacturing
325998	Aerosol packaging services
332919	Aerosol valves manufacturing
332410	Aftercoolers (i.e., heat exchangers) manufacturing
325620	After-shave preparations manufacturing

323119	Agricultural magazines and periodicals printing (except flexographic, gravure, lithographic, quick, screen) without publishing
323113	Agricultural magazines and periodicals screen printing without publishing
926140	Agricultural marketing services government
813910	Agricultural organizations (except youth farming organizations, farm granges)
926140	Agricultural pest and weed regulation, government
484220	Agricultural products trucking, local
531190	Agricultural property rental leasing
926140	Agriculture fair boards administration
115115	Agriculture production or harvesting crews
541710	Agriculture research and development laboratories or services
541690	Agrology consulting services
541690	Agronomy consulting services
624110	Aid to families with dependent children (AFDC)
621910	Air ambulance services
336399	Air bag assemblies manufacturing
336612	Air boat building
336340	Air brake systems and parts, automotive, truck, and bus, manufacturing
481212	Air cargo carriers (except air couriers), nonscheduled
481112	Air cargo carriers (except air couriers), scheduled
332439	Air cargo containers, light gauge metal, manufacturing
335313	Air circuit breakers manufacturing
481111	Air commuter carriers, scheduled
333912	Air compressors manufacturing
492110	Air courier services

332322	Air cowls, sheet metal (except stampings), manufacturing
336399	Air filters, automotive, truck, and bus, manufacturing
334512	Air flow controllers (except valves), air-conditioning and refrigeration, manufacturing
928110	Air Force
313230	Air laid nonwoven fabrics manufacturing
481211	Air passenger carriers, nonscheduled
481111	Air passenger carriers, scheduled
423730	Air pollution control equipment and supplies merchant wholesalers
335211	Air purification equipment, portable, manufacturing
333411	Air purification equipment, stationary, manufacturing
332420	Air receiver tanks, heavy gauge metal, manufacturing
333411	Air scrubbing systems manufacturing
711310	Air show managers with facilities
711320	Air show managers without facilities
711310	Air show organizers with facilities
711320	Air show organizers without facilities
711310	Air show promoters with facilities
711320	Air show promoters without facilities
238220	Air system balancing and testing
481211	Air taxi services
334511	Air traffic control radar systems and equipment manufacturing
611519	Air traffic control schools
488111	Air traffic control services (except military)
928110	Air traffic control, military
238220	Air vent installation
333411	Air washers (i.e., air scrubbers) manufacturing

488190 Aircraft maintenance and repair services (except factory conversion, factory overhaul, factory rebuilding)
336411 Aircraft manufacturing
423860 Aircraft merchant wholesalers
336411 Aircraft overhauling
488119 Aircraft parking service
336413 Aircraft propellers and parts manufacturing
336411 Aircraft rebuilding (i.e., restoration to original design specifications)
532411 Aircraft rental and leasing
336360 Aircraft seats manufacturing
488190 Aircraft testing services
314999 Aircraft tie down strap assemblies (except leather) manufacturing
326211 Aircraft tire manufacturing
336412 Aircraft turbines manufacturing
811420 Aircraft upholstery repair
333412 Aircurtains manufacturing
336413 Airframe assemblies (except for guided missiles) manufacturing
336419 Airframe assemblies for guided missiles manufacturing
334511 Airframe equipment instruments manufacturing
325612 Airfreshners manufacturing
722310 Airline food services contractors
561599 Airline reservation services
561599 Airline ticket offices
332313 Airlocks, fabricated metal plate work, manufacturing
481112 Airmail carriers, scheduled
532411 Airplane rental or leasing
488119 Airport baggage handling services
236220 Airport building construction
488119 Airport cargo handling services
531190 Airport leasing, not operating airport, rental or leasing
335311 Airport lighting transformers manufacturing
485999 Airport limousine services (i.e., shuttle)
488119 Airport operators (e.g., civil, international, national)

237310 Airport runway construction
238210 Airport runway lighting contractors
237310 Airport runway line painting (e.g., striping)
488119 Airport runway maintenance services
485999 Airport shuttle services
236220 Airport terminal construction
488119 Airports, civil, operation and maintenance
334511 Airspeed instruments (aeronautical) manufacturing
212399 Alabaster mining and/or beneficiating
423610 Alarm apparatus, electric, merchant wholesalers
334518 Alarm clocks manufacturing
238210 Alarm system (e.g., fire, burglar), electric, installation only
334290 Alarm system central monitoring equipment manufacturing
561621 Alarm system monitoring services
334290 Alarm systems and equipment manufacturing
561621 Alarm systems sales combined with installation, repair, or monitoring services
323118 Albums (e.g., photo, scrap) and refills manufacturing
424120 Albums, photo, merchant wholesalers
424690 Alcohol, industrial, merchant wholesalers
922120 Alcohol, tobacco, and firearms control
926150 Alcoholic beverage control boards
492210 Alcoholic beverage delivery service
722410 Alcoholic beverage drinking places
312140 Alcoholic beverages (except brandy) distilling
424810 Alcoholic beverages (except distilled spirits, wine) merchant wholesalers

312130 Alcoholic beverages, brandy, distilling

424820 Alcoholic beverages, wine and distilled spirits merchant wholesalers

624190 Alcoholism and drug addiction self-help organizations

624190 Alcoholism counseling (except medical treatment), nonresidential

623220 Alcoholism rehabilitation facilities (except licensed hospitals), residential

622210 Alcoholism rehabilitation hospitals

624190 Alcoholism self-help organizations

621420 Alcoholism treatment centers and clinics (except hospitals), outpatient

325199 Aldehydes manufacturing

312120 Ale brewing

424810 Ale merchant wholesalers

111940 Alfalfa hay farming

311119 Alfalfa meal, dehydrated, manufacturing

424910 Alfalfa merchant wholesalers

311119 Alfalfa prepared as feed for animals

111998 Alfalfa seed farming

111419 Alfalfa sprout farming, grown under cover

311119 Alfalfa, cubed, manufacturing

111998 Algae farming

325199 Alginates (e.g., calcium, potassium, sodium) manufacturing

325199 Alginic acid manufacturing

334519 Alidades, surveying, manufacturing

333319 Alignment equipment, motor vehicle, manufacturing

325110 Aliphatic (e.g., hydrocarbons) (except acetylene) made from refined petroleum or liquid hydrocarbons

324110 Aliphatic chemicals (i.e., acyclic) made in petroleum refineries

325181 Alkalies manufacturing

424690 Alkalies merchant wholesalers

335912 Alkaline cell primary batteries manufacturing

335911 Alkaline cell storage batteries (i.e., nickel-cadmium, nickel-iron, silver oxide-zinc) manufacturing

335912 Alkaline manganese primary batteries manufacturing

325211 Alkyd resins manufacturing

324110 Alkylates made in petroleum refineries

423110 All terrain vehicle (ATV's) merchant wholesalers

336999 All terrain vehicles (ATV's), wheeled or tracked, manufacturing

325414 Allergenic extracts (except diagnostic substances) manufacturing

325414 Allergens manufacturing

621111 Allergists' offices (e.g., centers, clinics)

112519 Alligator production, farm raising

331513 Alloy steel castings (except investment), unfinished, manufacturing

331314 Alloying purchased aluminum metals

331423 Alloying purchased copper

331423 Alloying purchased copper metals

331492 Alloying purchased nonferrous metals (except aluminum, copper)

441221 All-terrain vehicle (ATV) dealers

325211 Allyl resins manufacturing

323121 Almanac binding without printing

511130 Almanac publishers (except exclusive Internet publishing)

511130 Almanac publishers and printing combined

516110 Almanac publishers, exclusively on Internet

323117 Almanacs printing and binding without publishing

323117   Almanacs printing without publishing

111335   Almond farming

115114   Almond hulling and shelling

311999   Almond pastes manufacturing

111998   Aloe farming

112990   Alpaca production

721110   Alpine skiing facilities with accommodations (i.e., ski resort)

713920   Alpine skiing facilities without accommodations

237130   Alternative energy (e.g., geothermal, ocean wave, solar, wind) structure construction

334515   Alternator and generator testers manufacturing

336322   Alternators and generators for internal combustion engines manufacturing

334511   Altimeters, aeronautical, manufacturing

212391   Alum, natural, mining and/or beneficiating

327125   Alumina fused refractories manufacturing

327113   Alumina porcelain insulators manufacturing

331311   Alumina refining

327125   Aluminous refractory cement manufacturing

331312   Aluminum alloys made from bauxite or alumina producing primary aluminum and manufacturing

331314   Aluminum alloys made from scrap or dross

331316   Aluminum bar made by extruding purchased aluminum

331316   Aluminum bar made in integrated secondary smelting and extruding mills

331314   Aluminum billet made from purchased aluminum

331314   Aluminum billet made in integrated secondary smelting and rolling mills

332431   Aluminum cans, light gauge metal, manufacturing

331524   Aluminum castings (except die-castings), unfinished, manufacturing

325188   Aluminum chloride manufacturing

332812   Aluminum coating of metal products for the trade

325188   Aluminum compounds, not specified elsewhere by process, manufacturing

331521   Aluminum die-casting foundries

331521   Aluminum die-castings, unfinished, manufacturing

238350   Aluminum door and window, residential-type, installation

331314   Aluminum extrusion ingot (i.e., billet), secondary

331314   Aluminum flakes made from purchased aluminum

331315   Aluminum foil made by flat rolling purchased aluminum

331315   Aluminum foil made in integrated secondary smelting and flat rolling mills

332112   Aluminum forgings made from purchased metals, unfinished

331524   Aluminum foundries (except die-casting)

332999   Aluminum freezer foil not made in rolling mills

325188   Aluminum hydroxide (i.e., alumina trihydrate) manufacturing

331312   Aluminum ingot and other primary aluminum production shapes made from bauxite or alumina

331314   Aluminum ingot made from purchased aluminum

331314   Aluminum ingot, secondary smelting of aluminum and manufacturing

331314   Aluminum ingot, secondary, manufacturing

332999   Aluminum ladders manufacturing

327910   Aluminum oxide (fused) abrasives manufacturing

331311   Aluminum oxide refining

921150	American Indian or Alaska Native tribal courts
921150	American Indian or Alaska Native, tribal chief's or chairman's office
212399	Amethyst mining and/or beneficiating
334516	Amino acid analyzers, laboratory-type, manufacturing
325211	Amino resins manufacturing
325211	Amino-aldehyde resins manufacturing
325192	Aminoanthraquinone manufacturing
325192	Aminoazobenzene manufacturing
325192	Aminoazotoluene manufacturing
325192	Aminophenol manufacturing
424690	Ammonia (except fertilizer material) merchant wholesalers
325311	Ammonia, anhydrous and aqueous, manufacturing
424910	Ammonia, fertilizer material, merchant wholesalers
325612	Ammonia, household-type, manufacturing
325188	Ammonium chloride manufacturing
325188	Ammonium compounds, not specified elsewhere by process, manufacturing
325188	Ammonium hydroxide manufacturing
325188	Ammonium molybdate manufacturing
325311	Ammonium nitrate manufacturing
325188	Ammonium perchlorate manufacturing
325312	Ammonium phosphates manufacturing
236210	Ammonium plant construction
325311	Ammonium sulfate manufacturing
325188	Ammonium thiosulfate manufacturing
423990	Ammunition (except sporting) merchant wholesalers
332993	Ammunition (i.e., more than 30 mm., more than 1.18 inch) manufacturing
321920	Ammunition boxes, wood, manufacturing
332439	Ammunition boxes, light gauge metal, manufacturing
332994	Ammunition carts (i.e., 30 mm or less, 1.18 inch or less) manufacturing
332995	Ammunition carts (i.e., more than 30 mm., more than 1.18 inch) manufacturing
332993	Ammunition loading and assembling plants
332992	Ammunition, small arms (i.e., 30 mm. or less, 1.18 inch or less), manufacturing
423910	Ammunition, sporting, merchant wholesalers
334515	Ampere-hour meters manufacturing
325411	Amphetamines, uncompounded, manufacturing
334310	Amplifiers (e.g., auto, home, musical instrument, public address) manufacturing
334220	Amplifiers, (e.g., RF power and IF), broadcast and studio equipment, manufacturing
335999	Amplifiers, magnetic, pulse, and maser, manufacturing
713120	Amusement arcades
713990	Amusement device (except gambling) concession operators (i.e., supplying and servicing in others' facilities)
713120	Amusement device (except gambling) parlors, coin-operated
713120	Amusement devices (except gambling) operated in own facilities
236220	Amusement facility construction
339999	Amusement machines, coin-operated, manufacturing
423850	Amusement park equipment merchant wholesalers
713110	Amusement parks (e.g., theme, water)

315119	Anklets, sheer hosiery or socks, knitting or knitting and finishing
325191	Annato extract manufacturing
332811	Annealing metals and metal products for the trade
332420	Annealing vats, heavy gauge metal, manufacturing
711510	Announcers, independent radio and television
524113	Annuities underwriting
332991	Annular ball bearings manufacturing
334513	Annunciators, relay and solid-state types, industrial display, manufacturing
333298	Anodizing equipment manufacturing
332813	Anodizing metals and metal products for the trade
423620	Answering machines, telephone, merchant wholesalers
561421	Answering services, telephone
325320	Ant poisons manufacturing
325412	Antacid preparations manufacturing
238290	Antenna, household-type, installation
423690	Antennas merchant wholesalers
334220	Antennas, satellite, manufacturing
334220	Antennas, transmitting and receiving, manufacturing
325412	Anthelmintic preparations manufacturing
325192	Anthracene manufacturing
212113	Anthracite beneficiating (e.g., crushing, screening, washing, cleaning, sizing)
213113	Anthracite mine tunneling on a contract basis
212113	Anthracite mining and/or beneficiating
213113	Anthracite mining services (except site preparation and related construction contractor activities) on a contract basis
325132	Anthraquinone dyes manufacturing

332995	Antiaircraft artillery manufacturing
325412	Antibacterial preparations manufacturing
325412	Antibiotic preparations manufacturing
424210	Antibiotics merchant wholesalers
325411	Antibiotics, uncompounded, manufacturing
325411	Anticholinergics, uncompounded, manufacturing
325411	Anticonvulsants, uncompounded, manufacturing
325412	Antidepressant preparations manufacturing
325411	Antidepressants, uncompounded, manufacturing
424690	Antifreeze merchant wholesalers
325998	Antifreeze preparations manufacturing
325414	Antigens manufacturing
325412	Antihistamine preparations manufacturing
325131	Antimony based pigments manufacturing
212299	Antimony concentrates mining and/or beneficiating
212299	Antimony ores mining and/or beneficiating
325188	Antimony oxide (except pigments) manufacturing
331419	Antimony refining, primary
325412	Antineoplastic preparations manufacturing
325620	Antiperspirants, personal, manufacturing
813319	Antipoverty advocacy organizations
325412	Antipyretic preparations manufacturing
811121	Antique and classic automotive restoration
441120	Antique auto dealers
424920	Antique book merchant wholesalers
453310	Antique dealers (except motor vehicles)
423210	Antique furniture merchant wholesalers

811420 Antique furniture repair and restoration shops
423220 Antique homefurnishing merchant wholesalers
423220 Antique houseware merchant wholesalers
423940 Antique jewelry merchant wholesalers
453310 Antique shops
332913 Antiscald bath and shower valves, plumbing, manufacturing
325998 Antiscaling compounds manufacturing
325412 Antiseptic preparations manufacturing
424210 Antiseptics merchant wholesalers
325414 Antiserums manufacturing
325412 Antispasmodic preparations manufacturing
332995 Antisubmarine projectors manufacturing
332995 Antitank rocket launchers manufacturing
325414 Antitoxins manufacturing
325414 Antivenoms manufacturing
236116 Apartment building construction general contractors
236117 Apartment building operative builders
531110 Apartment building rental or leasing
531110 Apartment hotel rental or leasing
531311 Apartment managers' offices
531110 Apartment rental or leasing
212392 Apatite mining and/or beneficiating
212325 Aplite mining and/or beneficiating
446110 Apothecaries
331491 Apparatus wire and cord (except aluminum, copper) made from purchased nonferrous metals (except aluminum, copper) in wire drawing plants

331422 Apparatus wire or cord made from purchased copper in wire drawing plants
331319 Apparatus wire or cord made in aluminum wire drawing plants
448150 Apparel accessory stores
314999 Apparel fillings (e.g., cotton mill waste, kapok) manufacturing
315999 Apparel findings and trimmings cut and sewn from purchased fabric (except apparel contractors)
561910 Apparel folding and packaging services
812320 Apparel pressing services
448130 Apparel stores, children's and infants' clothing
448110 Apparel stores, men's and boys' clothing
453310 Apparel stores, used clothing
448120 Apparel stores, women's and girls' clothing
315211 Apparel trimmings and findings, men's and boys', cut and sew apparel contractors
315212 Apparel trimmings and findings, women's, girls', and infants', cut and sew apparel contractors
424310 Apparel trimmings merchant wholesalers
313221 Apparel webbings manufacturing
315292 Apparel, fur (except apparel contractors), manufacturing
315211 Apparel, fur, men's and boys', cut and sew apparel contractors
315212 Apparel, fur, women's, girls', and infants', cut and sew apparel contractors
315211 Apparel, men's and boys', cut and sew apparel contractors
315212 Apparel, women's, girls', and infants', cut and sew contractors
111331 Apple orchards
312130 Applejack distilling

334512 Appliance controls manufacturing

335999 Appliance cords made from purchased insulated wire

332510 Appliance hardware, metal, manufacturing

334512 Appliance regulators (except switches) manufacturing

532210 Appliance rental

443111 Appliance stores, household-type

453310 Appliance stores, household-type, used

334518 Appliance timers manufacturing

811412 Appliance, household-type, repair and maintenance services without retailing new appliances

423720 Appliances, gas (except dryers, freezers, refrigerators), merchant wholesalers

423620 Appliances, household-type (except gas ranges, gas water heaters), merchant wholesalers

423450 Appliances, surgical, merchant wholesalers

518210 Application hosting

518210 Application service providers (ASPs)

541511 Applications software programming services, custom computer

511210 Applications software, computer, packaged

321999 Applicators, wood, manufacturing

315211 Appliqueing on men's and boys' apparel

314999 Appliqueing on textile products (except apparel)

315212 Appliqueing on women's, girls', and infants' apparel

323118 Appointment books and refills manufacturing

541990 Appraisal (except real estate) services

531320 Appraisal services, real estate

531320 Appraisers' offices, real estate

611513 Apprenticeship training programs

111339 Apricot farming

812331 Apron supply services

316999 Aprons for textile machinery, leather, manufacturing

316999 Aprons, leather (e.g., blacksmith's, welder's), manufacturing

315999 Aprons, waterproof (e.g., plastics, rubberized fabric), rubberizing fabric and manufacturing aprons

315212 Aprons, waterproof (including plastics, rubberized fabric), woman's, girls', and infants', cut and sew apparel contractors

315999 Aprons, waterproof (including rubberized fabric, plastics), cut and sewn from purchased fabric (except apparel contractors)

315211 Aprons, waterproof (including rubberized fabric, plastics), men's and boys', cut and sew apparel contractors

315211 Aprons, work (except leather), men's and boys, cut and sew apparel contractors

315212 Aprons, work (except leather), women's, girls', and infants', cut and sew apparel contractors

315225 Aprons, work (except leather, waterproof), men's and boys', cut and sewn from purchased fabric (except apparel contractors)

315239 Aprons, work (except waterproof, leather), women's, misses', and girls', cut and sewn from purchased fabric (except apparel contractors)

332999 Aquarium accessories, metal, manufacturing

712130 Aquariums

327215 Aquariums made from purchased glass

237110 Aqueduct construction

541990 Arbitration and conciliation services (except by attorney, paralegal)

333513 Arbor presses, metalworking, manufacturing

712130 Arboreta

712130 Arboretums

561730 Arborist services

333515 Arbors (i.e., a machine tool accessory) manufacturing

334510 Arc lamp units, electrotherapeutic (except infrared, ultraviolet), manufacturing

335129 Arc lighting fixtures (except electrotherapeutic), electric, manufacturing

333992 Arc welding equipment manufacturing

713120 Arcades, amusement

339113 Arch supports, orthopedic, manufacturing

541720 Archeological research and development services

712120 Archeological sites (i.e., public display)

339920 Archery equipment manufacturing

423910 Archery equipment merchant wholesalers

713990 Archery ranges

321213 Arches, glue laminated or pre-engineered wood, manufacturing

541310 Architects' (except landscape) offices

541310 Architects' (except landscape) private practices

813920 Architects' associations

423490 Architect's equipment and supplies merchant wholesalers

541320 Architects' offices, landscape

541320 Architects' private practices, landscape

541310 Architectural (except landscape) consultants' offices

541310 Architectural (except landscape) design services

541310 Architectural (except landscape) services

327331 Architectural block, concrete (e.g., fluted, ground face, screen, slump, split), manufacturing

325510 Architectural coatings (i.e., paint) manufacturing

332323 Architectural metalwork manufacturing

423390 Architectural metalwork merchant wholesalers

327112 Architectural sculptures, clay, manufacturing

327991 Architectural sculptures, stone, manufacturing

541320 Architectural services, landscape

327123 Architectural terra cotta manufacturing

327390 Architectural wall panels, precast concrete, manufacturing

337212 Architectural woodwork and fixtures (i.e., custom designed interiors) manufacturing

519120 Archives

316211 Arctics, plastics or plastics soled fabric upper, manufacturing

316211 Arctics, rubber or rubber soled fabric, manufacturing

335311 Arc-welding transformers, separate solid-state, manufacturing

335129 Area and sports luminaries (e.g., stadium lighting fixtures), electric, manufacturing

236220 Arena construction

711310 Arena operators

531120 Arena, no promotion of events, rental or leasing

212311 Argillite mining or quarrying

325120 Argon manufacturing

315999 Arm bands, elastic, cut and sewn from purchased fabric (except apparel contractors)

315211 Arm bands, elastic, men's and boys', cut and sew apparel contractors

315212 Arm bands, elastic, women's, girls', and infants', cut and sew apparel contractors

335314 Armature relays manufacturing

335312 Armature rewinding on a factory basis

811310 Armature rewinding services (except on an assembly line or factory basis)

335312 Armatures, industrial, manufacturing

928110 Armed forces

332993 Arming and fusing devices, missile, manufacturing

331111 Armor plate made in iron and steel mills

331422 Armored cable made from purchased copper in wire drawing plants

331422 Armored cable, copper, made in integrated secondary smelting and drawing plants

561613 Armored car services

336992 Armored military vehicles (except tanks) and parts manufacturing

236220 Armory construction

928110 Army

424690 Aromatic chemicals merchant wholesalers

113210 Aromatic wood gathering

488999 Arrangement of car pools and vanpools

335931 Arrestors and coils, lighting, manufacturing

325320 Arsenate insecticides manufacturing

325188 Arsenates (except insecticides) manufacturing

325131 Arsenic based pigments manufacturing

325188 Arsenic compounds, not specified elsewhere by process, manufacturing

212393 Arsenic mineral mining and/or beneficiating

325320 Arsenite insecticides manufacturing

325188 Arsenites manufacturing

611610 Art (except commercial or graphic) instruction

453920 Art auctions

453920 Art dealers

712110 Art galleries (except retail)

453920 Art galleries retailing art

327420 Art goods (e.g., gypsum, plaster of paris) manufacturing

424990 Art goods merchant wholesalers

712110 Art museums

315211 Art needlework contractors on men's and boys' apparel

315212 Art needlework contractors on women's, girls', and infants' apparel

314999 Art needlework on clothing for the trade

511199 Art print (except exclusive Internet publishing) publishers

323111 Art print gravure printing without publishing

511199 Art print publishers and printing combined

323112 Art prints flexographic printing without publishing

323110 Art prints lithographic (offset) printing without publishing

323119 Art prints printing (except flexographic, digital, gravure, lithographic, quick, screen) without publishing

323113 Art prints screen printing without publishing

511199 Art publishers (except exclusive Internet publishing)

516110 Art publishers, exclusively on Internet

711510 Art restorers, independent

611610 Art schools (except academic), fine

611519 Art schools, commercial or graphic

541430 Art services, commercial

541430 Art services, graphic

541430 Art studios, commercial

453998 Art supply stores

621340 Art therapists' offices (e.g., centers, clinics)

237110 Artesian well construction

238330	Asphalt flooring, installation only
322121	Asphalt paper made in paper mills
237310	Asphalt paving (i.e., highway, road, street, public sidewalk)
324121	Asphalt paving blocks made from purchased asphaltic materials
324121	Asphalt paving mixtures made from purchased asphaltic materials
324110	Asphalt paving mixtures made in petroleum refineries
324121	Asphalt road compounds made from purchased asphaltic materials
212399	Asphalt rock mining and/or beneficiating
238160	Asphalt roof shingle installation
324122	Asphalt roofing cements made from purchased asphaltic materials
324122	Asphalt roofing coatings made from purchased asphaltic materials
333120	Asphalt roofing construction machinery manufacturing
423330	Asphalt roofing shingles merchant wholesalers
324122	Asphalt saturated boards made from purchased asphaltic materials
324122	Asphalt saturated mats and felts made from purchased asphaltic materials and paper
324122	Asphalt shingles made from purchased asphaltic materials
212399	Asphalt, native, mining and/or beneficiating
238990	Asphalting, residential and commercial driveway and parking area
518210	ASPs (Application Service Providers)
541380	Assaying services
336213	Assembly line conversions of purchased vans and mini-vans
336312	Assembly line rebuilding of automotive and truck gasoline engines
336350	Assembly line rebuilding of automotive, truck, and bus transmissions
333518	Assembly machines manufacturing
236210	Assembly plant construction
336120	Assembly plants, heavy trucks, and buses on chassis of own manufacture
336112	Assembly plants, light trucks on chassis of own manufacture
336112	Assembly plants, mini-vans on chassis of own manufacture
336111	Assembly plants, passenger car, on chassis of own manufacture
336112	Assembly plants, sport utility vehicles on chassis of own manufacture
921130	Assessor's offices, tax
325613	Assistants, textile and leather finishing, manufacturing
623311	Assisted-living facilities with on-site nursing facilities
623312	Assisted-living facilities without on-site nursing care facilities
813311	Associations for retired persons, advocacy
522120	Associations, savings and loan
325412	Astringent preparations manufacturing
812990	Astrology services
711219	Athletes, amateur, independent
711219	Athletes, independent (i.e., participating in live sports events)
813990	Athletic associations, regulatory
315228	Athletic clothing (except team athletic uniforms), men's, boys' and unisex (i.e., sized without regard to gender), cut and sewn from purchased fabric (except apparel contractors)

315239 Athletic clothing (except team athletic uniforms), women's, misses', and girls', cut and sewn from purchased fabric (except apparel contractors)

315191 Athletic clothing made in apparel knitting mills

315211 Athletic clothing, men's and boys', cut and sew apparel contractors

315212 Athletic clothing, women's, girls', and infants', cut and sew apparel contractors

713940 Athletic club facilities, physical fitness

713990 Athletic clubs (i.e., sports teams) not operating sports facilities, recreational

236220 Athletic court, indoor, construction

451110 Athletic equipment and supply stores (including uniforms)

237990 Athletic field (except stadium) construction

424340 Athletic footwear merchant wholesalers

339920 Athletic goods (except ammunition, clothing, footwear, small arms) manufacturing

423910 Athletic goods (except apparel, footwear, nonspecialty) merchant wholesalers

813990 Athletic leagues (i.e., regulating bodies)

448210 Athletic shoe (except bowling, golf, spiked) stores

316219 Athletic shoes (except rubber or plastics soled with fabric upper) manufacturing

316211 Athletic shoes, plastics or plastics soled fabric upper (except cleated), manufacturing

316211 Athletic shoes, rubber or rubber soled fabric uppers (except cleated), manufacturing

315119 Athletic socks, knitting or knitting and finishing

423910 Athletic uniforms merchant wholesalers

315299 Athletic uniforms, team, cut and sewn from purchased fabric (except apparel contractors)

315211 Athletic uniforms, team, men's and boys', cut and sew apparel contractors

315212 Athletic uniforms, team, women's, girls', and infants, cut and sew apparel contractors

511130 Atlas publishers (except exclusive Internet publishing)

511130 Atlas publishers and printing combined

516110 Atlas publishers, exclusively on Internet

323112 Atlases flexographic printing without publishing

323111 Atlases gravure printing without publishing

323110 Atlases lithographic (offset) printing without publishing

323119 Atlases printing (except flexographic, digital, gravure, lithographic, quick, screen) without publishing

323113 Atlases screen printing without publishing

238290 ATM (automated teller machine) installation

334119 ATM's (automatic teller machines) manufacturing

335999 Atom smashers (i.e., particle accelerators) manufacturing

339999 Atomizers (e.g., perfumes) manufacturing

325411 Atropine and derivatives manufacturing

316991 Attache cases, all materials, manufacturing

333112 Attachments, powered lawn and garden equipment, manufacturing

333412 Attic fans manufacturing

238310 Attic space insulating

922130 Attorney generals' offices

541110 Attorneys' offices

541110 Attorneys' private practices

453998	Auction houses (general merchandise)
424590	Auction markets, tobacco, horses, mules
561990	Auctioneers, independent
454112	Auctions, Internet retail
423990	Audio and video tapes and disks, prerecorded, merchant wholesalers
337129	Audio cabinets (i.e., housings), wood, manufacturing
238210	Audio equipment installation (except automotive) contractors
443112	Audio equipment stores (except automotive)
423620	Audio equipment, household-type, merchant wholesalers
512290	Audio recording of meetings or conferences
512240	Audio recording post-production services
532490	Audio visual equipment rental or leasing
334515	Audiofrequency oscillators manufacturing
334510	Audiological equipment, electromedical, manufacturing
621340	Audiologists' offices (e.g., centers, clinics)
334515	Audiometers (except medical) manufacturing
334613	Audiotape, blank, manufacturing
423690	Audiotapes, blank, merchant wholesalers
541211	Auditing accountants' (i.e., CPAs) offices
541211	Auditing accountants' (i.e., CPAs) private practices
541211	Auditing services (i.e., CPA services), accounts
236220	Auditorium construction
531120	Auditorium rental or leasing
541211	Auditors' (i.e., CPAs) offices, accounts
541211	Auditors' (i.e., CPAs) private practices, accounts
921190	Auditor's offices, government

213113	Auger coal mining services (except site preparation and related construction contractor activities) on a contract basis
333120	Augers (except mining-type) manufacturing
333131	Augers, mining-type, manufacturing
332212	Augers, nonpowered, manufacturing
711410	Authors' agents or managers
711510	Authors, independent
423120	Auto body shop supplies, merchant wholesalers
721110	Auto courts, lodging
441310	Auto supply stores
339114	Autoclaves, dental, manufacturing
332420	Autoclaves, industrial-type, heavy gauge metal, manufacturing
339111	Autoclaves, laboratory-type (except dental), manufacturing
336411	Autogiros manufacturing
238290	Automated and revolving door installation
334510	Automated blood and body fluid analyzers (except laboratory) manufacturing
522320	Automated clearinghouses, bank or check (except central bank)
518210	Automated data processing services
332911	Automatic (i.e., controlling-type, regulating) valves, industrial-type, manufacturing
334516	Automatic chemical analyzers, laboratory-type, manufacturing
238290	Automatic gate (e.g., garage, parking lot) installation
812310	Automatic laundries, coin-operated
454210	Automatic merchandising machine operators
333512	Automatic screw machines, metal cutting type, manufacturing
334119	Automatic teller machines (ATM) manufacturing

441310	Automotive audio equipment stores
811121	Automotive body shops
811118	Automotive brake repair shops
424690	Automotive chemicals (except lubricating greases, lubrication oils) merchant wholesalers
811192	Automotive detailing services (i.e., cleaning, polishing)
334515	Automotive electrical engine diagnostic equipment manufacturing
811118	Automotive electrical repair shops
335931	Automotive electrical switches manufacturing
334519	Automotive emissions testing equipment manufacturing
811198	Automotive emissions testing services
811111	Automotive engine repair and replacement shops
811112	Automotive exhaust system repair and replacement shops
811118	Automotive front end alignment shops
811122	Automotive glass shops
336322	Automotive harness and ignition sets manufacturing
335110	Automotive light bulbs manufacturing
336321	Automotive lighting fixtures manufacturing
336399	Automotive mirrors, framed, manufacturing
811191	Automotive oil change and lubrication shops
331319	Automotive or aircraft wire and cable made in aluminum wire drawing plants
811121	Automotive paint shops
441310	Automotive parts and supply stores
441310	Automotive parts dealers, used
423120	Automotive parts, new, merchant wholesalers
811118	Automotive radiator repair shops
423620	Automotive radios merchant wholesalers
811111	Automotive repair and replacement shops, general
811198	Automotive rustproofing and undercoating shops
811198	Automotive safety inspection services
334290	Automotive theft alarm systems manufacturing
441320	Automotive tire dealers
811198	Automotive tire repair (except retreading) shops
811113	Automotive transmission repair shops
811118	Automotive tune-up shops
811121	Automotive upholstery shops
811192	Automotive washing and polishing
336330	Automotive, truck and bus steering assemblies and parts manufacturing
336330	Automotive, truck and bus suspension assemblies and parts (except springs) manufacturing
339992	Autophones (organs with perforated music rolls) manufacturing
335311	Autotransformers for switchboards (except telephone switchboards) manufacturing
335311	Autotransformers manufacturing
237990	Avalanche protection, construction
712130	Aviaries
112990	Aviaries (i.e., raising birds for sale)
813319	Aviation advocacy organizations
481219	Aviation clubs providing a variety of air transportation activities to the general public
488119	Aviation clubs, primarily providing flying field services to the general public
713990	Aviation clubs, recreational
324110	Aviation fuels manufacturing
611512	Aviation schools
111339	Avocado farming
332212	Awls manufacturing
238190	Awning installation

313111 Bags, hemp, made from purchased fiber

322224 Bags, multiwall, made from purchased uncoated paper

424130 Bags, paper and disposable plastics, merchant wholesalers

322224 Bags, paper, uncoated, made from purchased paper

326111 Bags, plastics film, single wall or multiwall, manufacturing

314911 Bags, plastics, made from purchased woven plastics

339920 Bags, punching, manufacturing

314911 Bags, rubberized fabric, manufacturing

314999 Bags, sleeping, manufacturing

314911 Bags, textile, made from purchased woven or knitted materials

424990 Bags, textile, merchant wholesalers

322224 **Bags, uncoated paper, made from purchased paper**

812990 **Bail bonding** services

339920 Bait, artificial, fishing, manufacturing

423910 Bait, artificial, merchant wholesalers

424990 Bait, live, merchant wholesalers

112511 Baitfish production, farm raising

311422 Baked beans canning

311813 Baked goods (except bread, bread-type rolls), frozen, manufacturing

445210 Baked ham stores

311811 Bakeries with baking from flour on the premises, retailing not for immediate consumption

315211 Bakers' service apparel, washable, men's and boys', cut and sew apparel contractors

315225 Bakers' service apparel, washable, men's and boys', cut and sewn from purchased fabric (except apparel contractors)

315212 Bakers' service apparel, washable, women's, cut and sew apparel contractors

315239 Bakers' service apparel, washable, women's, misses', and girls, cut and sewn from purchased fabric (except apparel contractors)

333294 Bakery machinery and equipment manufacturing

423830 Bakery machinery and equipment merchant wholesalers

333294 Bakery ovens manufacturing

424490 Bakery products (except frozen) merchant wholesalers

311821 Bakery products, dry (e.g., biscuits, cookies, crackers), manufacturing

311812 Bakery products, fresh (i.e., bread, cakes, doughnuts, pastries), made in commercial bakeries

424420 Bakery products, frozen, merchant wholesalers

445291 Bakery stores, retailing only (except immediate consumption)

311320 Baking chocolate made from cacao beans

311330 Baking chocolate made from purchased chocolate

311999 Baking powder manufacturing

333997 Balances (except laboratory-type) manufacturing

423440 Balances and scales (except laboratory) merchant wholesalers

423490 Balances and scales, laboratory, merchant wholesalers

339111 Balances and scales, laboratory-type, manufacturing

333319 Balancing equipment, motor vehicle, manufacturing

332323 Balcony railings, metal, manufacturing

238190 Balcony, metal, installation

238120 Balcony, precast concrete, installation

333111 Bale throwers manufacturing

332618 Bale ties made from purchased wire

333111 Balers, farm-type (e.g., cotton, hay, straw), manufacturing

333999 Baling machinery (e.g., paper, scrap metal) manufacturing

332991 Ball bearings manufacturing

212324 Ball clay mining and/or beneficiating

333613 Ball joints (except aircraft, motor vehicle) manufacturing

339941 Ball point pens manufacturing

332911 Ball valves, industrial-type, manufacturing

335311 Ballasts (i.e., transformers) manufacturing

711120 Ballet companies

711510 Ballet dancers, independent

711120 Ballet productions, live theatrical

611610 Ballet schools (except academic)

316219 Ballet slippers manufacturing

453220 Balloon shops

812990 Balloon-o-gram services

326199 Balloons, plastics, manufacturing

326299 Balloons, rubber, manufacturing

713990 Ballrooms

339920 Balls, baseball, basketball, football, golf, tennis, pool, and bowling, manufacturing

339932 Balls, rubber (except athletic equipment), manufacturing

331111 Balls, steel, made in iron and steel mills

113210 Balsam needles gathering

111339 Banana farming

115114 Banana ripening

315299 Band uniforms cut and sewn from purchased fabric (except apparel contractors)

315211 Band uniforms, men's and boys', cut and sew apparel contractors

315212 Band uniforms, women's, girls', and infants', cut and sew apparel contractors

339113 Bandages and dressings, surgical and orthopedic, manufacturing

424210 Bandages merchant wholesalers

315212 Bandeaux, women's and girls', cut and sew apparel contractors

315231 Bandeaux, women's, misses', and girls', cut and sewn from purchased fabric (except apparel contractors)

711130 Bands

711130 Bands, dance

711130 Bands, musical

333210 Bandsaws, woodworking-type, manufacturing

339992 Banjos and parts manufacturing

334511 Bank and turn indicators and components (aeronautical instruments) manufacturing

236220 Bank building construction

531120 Bank building rental or leasing

332999 Bank chests, metal, manufacturing

522320 Bank clearinghouse associations

524128 Bank deposit insurance carriers, direct

332323 Bank fixtures, ornamental metal, manufacturing

551111 Bank holding companies (except managing)

523991 Bank trust offices

813910 Bankers' associations

926150 Banking regulatory agencies

611519 Banking schools (training in banking)

521110 Banking, central

523110 Banking, investment

525920 Bankruptcy estates

522110 Banks, commercial

522210 Banks, credit card

521110 Banks, Federal Reserve

522190 Banks, industrial (i.e., known as), depository

522298 Banks, industrial (i.e., known as), nondepository

522190 Banks, private (i.e., unincorporated)

522120 Banks, savings

522293 Banks, trade (i.e., international trade financing)

314999 Banners made from purchased fabrics

332323	Bannisters, metal, manufacturing
531120	Banquet hall rental or leasing
722320	Banquet halls with catering staff
327991	Baptismal fonts, cut stone, manufacturing
813920	Bar associations
561499	Bar code imprinting services
331316	Bar made by extruding purchased aluminum
331319	Bar made by rolling purchased aluminum
333516	Bar mill machinery, metalworking, manufacturing
325611	Bar soaps manufacturing
331316	Bar, aluminum, made in integrated secondary smelting and extruding mills
331319	Bar, aluminum, made in integrated secondary smelting and rolling mills
331421	Bar, copper and copper alloy, made from purchased copper or in integrated secondary smelting and rolling, drawing or extruding plants
331491	Bar, nonferrous metals (except aluminum, copper), made from purchased metals in wire drawing plants or in integrated secondary smelting and rolling, drawing, or extruding plants
311421	Barbecue sauce manufacturing
335221	Barbecues, grills, and braziers manufacturing
331222	Barbed and twisted wire made in wire drawing plants
332618	Barbed wire made from purchased wire
611511	Barber colleges
236220	Barber shop construction
423850	Barber shop equipment and supplies merchant wholesalers
812111	Barber shops
332211	Barber's scissors, manufacturing
315211	Barbers' service apparel, washable, men's and boys', cut and sew apparel contractors

315225	Barbers' service apparel, washable, men's and boys', cut and sewn from purchased fabric (except apparel contractors)
325412	Barbiturate preparations manufacturing
325411	Barbiturates, uncompounded, manufacturing
325411	Barbituric acid manufacturing
336611	Barge building
532411	Barge rental or leasing
332312	Barge sections, prefabricated metal, manufacturing
483211	Barge transportation, canal (freight)
483113	Barge transportation, coastal or Great Lakes (including St. Lawrence Seaway)
212393	Barite mining and/or beneficiating
327992	Barite processing beyond beneficiation
325188	Barium compounds, not specified elsewhere by process, manufacturing
325188	Barium hydroxide manufacturing
325412	Barium in-vivo diagnostic substances manufacturing
212393	Barium ores mining and/or beneficiating
327992	Barium processing beyond beneficiation
113210	Bark gathering
111199	Barley farming, field and seed production
311119	Barley feed, chopped, crushed or ground, manufacturing
311211	Barley flour manufacturing
311213	Barley, malt, manufacturing
332323	Barn stanchions and standards manufacturing
334519	Barographs manufacturing
334519	Barometers manufacturing
332410	Barometric condensers manufacturing
236220	Barrack construction
321920	Barrel heading and staves manufacturing

332994 Barrels, gun (i.e., 30 mm. or less, 1.18 inch or less), manufacturing
332995 Barrels, gun (i.e., more than 30 mm., more than 1.18 inch), manufacturing
332439 Barrels, light gauge metal, manufacturing
423840 Barrels, new and reconditioned, merchant wholesalers
321920 Barrels, wood, coopered, manufacturing
332999 Barricades, metal, manufacturing
541110 Barristers' offices
541110 Barristers' private practices
722410 Bars (i.e., drinking places), alcoholic beverage
331411 Bars made in primary copper smelting and refining mills
332312 Bars, concrete reinforcing, manufacturing
331111 Bars, iron, made in iron and steel mills
423510 Bars, metal (except precious), merchant wholesalers
331221 Bars, steel, made in cold rolling mills made from purchased steel
331111 Bars, steel, made in iron and steel mills
611519 Bartending schools
561990 Bartering services
325131 Barytes based pigments manufacturing
212393 Barytes mining and/or beneficiating
212319 Basalt crushed and broken stone mining and/or beneficiating
212311 Basalt mining or quarrying
561210 Base facilities operation support services
315211 Baseball caps (except plastics), men's and boys', cut and sew apparel contractors
315212 Baseball caps (except plastics), women's, girls', and infants', cut and sew apparel contractors

315991 Baseball caps cut and sewn from purchased fabric (except apparel contractors)
711211 Baseball clubs, professional or semiprofessional
713990 Baseball clubs, recreational
339920 Baseball equipment and supplies (except footwear, uniforms) manufacturing
423910 Baseball equipment and supplies merchant wholesalers
611620 Baseball instruction, camps, or schools
711211 Baseball teams, professional or semiprofessional
315299 Baseball uniforms cut and sewn from purchased fabric (except apparel contractors)
315211 Baseball uniforms, men's and boys', cut and sew apparel contractors
315212 Baseball uniforms, women's and girls', cut and sew apparel contractors
423730 Baseboard heaters, electric, non-portable, merchant wholesalers
333414 Baseboard heating equipment manufacturing
321918 Baseboards, floor, wood, manufacturing
332321 Baseboards, metal, manufacturing
711211 Basketball clubs, professional or semiprofessional
713990 Basketball clubs, recreational
339920 Basketball equipment and supplies (except footwear, uniforms) manufacturing
611620 Basketball instruction, camps, or schools
711211 Basketball teams, professional or semiprofessional
315299 Basketball uniforms cut and sewn from purchased fabric (except apparel contractors)
315211 Basketball uniforms, men's and boys', cut and sew apparel contractors

315212 Basketball uniforms, women's and girls', cut and sew apparel contractors

424990 Baskets merchant wholesalers

331222 Baskets, iron or steel, made in wire drawing plants

332618 Baskets, metal, made from purchased wire

321920 Baskets, wood (e.g., round stave, veneer), manufacturing

337125 Bassinets, reed and rattan, manufacturing

339992 Bassoons manufacturing

212299 Bastnaesite mining and/or beneficiating

335211 Bath fans with integral lighting fixture, residential, manufacturing

335211 Bath fans, residential, manufacturing

314110 Bath mats and bath sets made in carpet mills

326299 Bath mats, rubber, manufacturing

325620 Bath salts manufacturing

442299 Bath shops

238390 Bath tub refinishing on site

713990 Bathing beaches

315999 Bathing caps, rubber, manufacturing

315191 Bathing suits made in apparel knitting mills

315291 Bathing suits, infants', cut and sewn from purchased fabric (except apparel contractors)

315211 Bathing suits, men's and boys', cut and sew apparel contractors

315228 Bathing suits, men's and boys', cut and sewn from purchased fabric (except apparel contractors)

315212 Bathing suits, women's, girls', and infants', cut and sew apparel contractors

315239 Bathing suits, women's, misses', and girls', cut and sewn from purchased fabric (except apparel contractors)

315192 Bathrobes made in apparel knitting mills

315291 Bathrobes, infants', cut and sewn from purchased fabric (except apparel contractors)

315211 Bathrobes, men's and boys', cut and sew apparel contractors

315221 Bathrobes, men's and boys', cut and sewn from purchased fabric (except apparel contractors)

315212 Bathrobes, women's, girls', and infants', cut and sew apparel contractors

315231 Bathrobes, women's, misses', and girls', cut and sewn from purchased fabric (except apparel contractors)

423220 Bathroom accessories merchant wholesalers

327111 Bathroom accessories, vitreous china and earthenware, manufacturing

326199 Bathroom and toilet accessories, plastics, manufacturing

332998 Bathroom fixtures, metal, manufacturing

238220 Bathroom plumbing fixture and sanitary ware installation

333997 Bathroom scales manufacturing

337110 Bathroom vanities (except freestanding), stock or custom wood, manufacturing

812199 Baths, steam or turkish

332998 Bathtubs, metal, manufacturing

326191 Bathtubs, plastics, manufacturing

611620 Baton instruction

624221 Battered women's shelters

423610 Batteries (except automotive) merchant wholesalers

423120 Batteries, automotive, merchant wholesalers

335912 Batteries, primary, dry or wet, manufacturing

335911 Batteries, rechargeable, manufacturing

335911 Batteries, storage, manufacturing

711320   Beauty pageant promoters without facilities
423850   Beauty parlor equipment and supplies merchant wholesalers
812112   Beauty parlors
424210   Beauty preparations merchant wholesalers
236220   Beauty salon construction
812112   Beauty salons
812112   Beauty shops
424210   Beauty supplies merchant wholesalers
446120   Beauty supply stores
721191   Bed and breakfast inns
337122   Bed frames, wood household-type, manufacturing
812331   Bed linen supply services
442110   Bed stores, retail
335211   Bedcoverings, electric, manufacturing
111422   Bedding plant growing (except vegetable and melon bedding plants)
315212   Bedjackets, women's, girls' and infants', cut and sew apparel contractors
315231   Bedjackets, women's, misses', juniors', and girls', cut and sewn from purchased fabric (except apparel contractors)
337122   Bedroom furniture (except upholstered), wood household-type, manufacturing
337122   Beds (except hospital), wood household-type, manufacturing
337124   Beds (including cabinet and folding), metal household-type (except hospital), manufacturing
339111   Beds, hospital, manufacturing
423450   Beds, hospital, merchant wholesalers
337910   Beds, sleep-system ensembles (i.e., flotation, adjustable), manufacturing
337122   Beds, wood dormitory-type, manufacturing
337122   Beds, wood hotel-type, manufacturing

314129   Bedspreads and bed sets made from purchased fabrics
313249   Bedspreads and bed sets made in lace mills
313249   Bedspreads and bed sets made in warp knitting mills
313241   Bedspreads and bed sets made in weft knitting mills
112910   Bee production (i.e., apiculture)
311611   Beef carcasses, half carcasses, primal and sub-primal cuts, produced in slaughtering plants
112112   Beef cattle feedlots (except stockyards for transportation)
112111   Beef cattle ranching or farming
311611   Beef produced in slaughtering plants
311612   Beef stew made from purchased carcasses
311612   Beef, primal and sub-primal cuts, made from purchased carcasses
424910   Beekeeping supplies merchant wholesalers
517211   Beeper (i.e., radio pager) communication carriers
327213   Beer bottles, glass, manufacturing
312120   Beer brewing
332431   Beer cans, light gauge metal, manufacturing
333415   Beer cooling and dispensing equipment manufacturing
332439   Beer kegs, light gauge metal, manufacturing
424810   Beer merchant wholesalers
445310   Beer stores, packaged
325612   Beeswax polishes and waxes manufacturing
112910   Beeswax production
111219   Beet farming (except sugar beets), field, bedding plant and seed production
311313   Beet pulp, dried, manufacturing
311313   Beet sugar refining
541720   Behavioral research and development services
325412   Belladonna preparations manufacturing

332999 Bellows, hand, manufacturing
333999 Bellows, industrial type, manufacturing
339992 Bells (musical instruments) manufacturing
335999 Bells, electric, manufacturing
424310 Belt and buckle assembly kits merchant wholesalers
333922 Belt conveyor systems manufacturing
316999 Belt laces, leather, manufacturing
316110 Belting butts, curried or rough, manufacturing
313221 Belting fabrics, narrow woven
316999 Belting for machinery, leather, manufacturing
316110 Belting leather, manufacturing
314999 Belting made from purchased fabrics
423840 Belting, industrial, merchant wholesalers
326220 Belting, rubber (e.g., conveyor, elevator, transmission), manufacturing
482112 Beltline railroads
315999 Belts, apparel (e.g., fabric, leather, vinyl), cut and sewn from purchased fabric (except apparel contractors)
315211 Belts, apparel (e.g., fabric, leather, vinyl), men's and boys', cut and sew apparel contractors
315212 Belts, apparel (e.g., fabric, leather, vinyl), women's, girls', and infants', cut and sew apparel contractors
332618 Belts, conveyor, made from purchased wire
332618 Belts, drying, made from purchased wire
316999 Belts, leather safety, manufacturing
332994 Belts, machine gun (i.e., 30 mm. or less, 1.18 inch or less), manufacturing
332995 Belts, machine gun (i.e., more than 30 mm., more than 1.18 inch), manufacturing

315999 Belts, money, any material, cut and sewn from purchased fabric (except apparel contractors)
315211 Belts, money, any material, men's and boys', cut and sew apparel contractors
315212 Belts, money, any material, women's and girls', cut and sew apparel contractors
339111 Benches, laboratory-type, manufacturing
337127 Benches, park-type (except concrete, stone), manufacturing
337127 Benches, public building-type, manufacturing
337127 Benches, work, manufacturing
333513 Bending and forming machines, metalworking, manufacturing
332996 Bends, pipe, made from purchased metal pipe
541612 Benefit consulting services
111998 Bentgrass seed farming
212325 Bentonite mining and/or beneficiating
321999 Bentwood (steam bent) products (except furniture) manufacturing
325192 Benzaldehyde manufacturing
325320 Benzene hexachloride (BHC) insecticides manufacturing
325110 Benzene made from refined petroleum or liquid hydrocarbons
324110 Benzene made in petroleum refineries
325192 Benzoic acid manufacturing
311421 Berries, canned, manufacturing
424480 Berries, fresh, merchant wholesalers
115113 Berries, machine harvesting
111334 Berry (except strawberry) farming
321920 Berry crates, wood, wirebound, manufacturing
321920 Berry cups, veneer and splint, manufacturing
333111 Berry harvesting machines manufacturing

212299 Beryl mining and/or beneficiating

327113 Beryllia porcelain insulators manufacturing

331528 Beryllium castings (except die-castings), unfinished manufacturing

212299 Beryllium concentrates beneficiating

331522 Beryllium die-castings, unfinished, manufacturing

212299 Beryllium ores mining and/or beneficiating

325188 Beryllium oxide manufacturing

331419 Beryllium refining, primary

334517 Beta-ray irradiation equipment manufacturing

335999 Betatrons manufacturing

813910 Better business bureaus

722213 Beverage (e.g., coffee, juice, soft drink) bars, nonalcoholic, fixed location

311930 Beverage bases manufacturing

424490 Beverage bases merchant wholesalers

423830 Beverage bottling machinery merchant wholesalers

424490 Beverage concentrates merchant wholesalers

327213 Beverage containers, glass, manufacturing

423740 Beverage coolers, mechanical, merchant wholesalers

311930 Beverage flavorings (except coffee based) manufacturing

722330 Beverage stands, nonalcoholic, mobile

311930 Beverage syrups (except coffee based) manufacturing

424810 Beverages, alcoholic (except distilled spirits, wine), merchant wholesalers

312120 Beverages, beer, ale, and malt liquors, manufacturing

311514 Beverages, dietary, dairy and nondairy based

312111 Beverages, fruit and vegetable drinks, cocktails, and ades, manufacturing

311421 Beverages, fruit and vegetable juice, manufacturing

312140 Beverages, liquors (except brandies), manufacturing

311511 Beverages, milk based (except dietary), manufacturing

312112 Beverages, naturally carbonated bottled water, manufacturing

312111 Beverages, soft drink (including artificially carbonated waters), manufacturing

424820 Beverages, wine and distilled spirits, merchant wholesalers

312130 Beverages, wines and brandies, manufacturing

314999 Bias bindings made from purchased fabrics

313221 Bias bindings, woven, manufacturing

611699 Bible schools (except degree granting)

813110 Bible societies

315999 Bibs and aprons, waterproof (e.g., plastics, rubber, similar materials), cut and sewn from purchased fabric (except apparel contractors)

315211 Bibs and aprons, waterproof (e.g., plastics, rubber, similar materials), men's and boys', cut and sew apparel contractors

315999 Bibs and aprons, waterproof (e.g., plastics, rubber, similar materials), rubberizing fabric and manufacturing bibs and aprons

315212 Bibs and aprons, waterproof (e.g., plastics, rubber, similar materials), women's, girls', and infants', cut and sew apparel contractors

315212 Bibs, waterproof, cut and sew apparel contractors

451110 Bicycle (except motorized) shops

453310 Bicycle (except motorized) shops, used

492210 Bicycle courier

333912 Bicycle pumps manufacturing

333515	Bits, drill, metalworking, manufacturing
332212	Bits, edge tool, woodworking, manufacturing
333120	Bits, rock drill, construction and surface mining-type, manufacturing
333132	Bits, rock drill, oil and gas field-type, manufacturing
333131	Bits, rock drill, underground mining-type, manufacturing
212399	Bitumens, native, mining and/or beneficiating
212111	Bituminous coal and lignite surface mine site development for own account
212111	Bituminous coal cleaning plants
212111	Bituminous coal crushing
213113	Bituminous coal mining services (except site preparation and related construction contractor activities) on a contract basis
212111	Bituminous coal or lignite beneficiating (e.g., cleaning, crushing, screening, washing)
213113	Bituminous coal or lignite surface mine site development (except site preparation and related construction contractor activities) on a contract basis
212111	Bituminous coal screening plants
212111	Bituminous coal stripping (except on a contract, fee, or other basis)
213113	Bituminous coal stripping service on a contract basis
212111	Bituminous coal surface mining and/or beneficiating
212112	Bituminous coal underground mine site development for own account
212112	Bituminous coal underground mining or mining and beneficiating
212111	Bituminous coal washeries
212319	Bituminous limestone mining and/or beneficiating
213113	Bituminous or lignite auger mining service on a contract basis
212319	Bituminous sandstone mining and/or beneficiating
325131	Black pigments (except carbon black, bone black, lamp black) manufacturing
423510	Black plate merchant wholesalers
111334	Blackberry farming
423490	Blackboards merchant wholesalers
339942	Blackboards, framed, manufacturing
327991	Blackboards, unframed, slate, manufacturing
331111	Blackplate made in iron and steel mills
316999	Blacksmith's aprons, leather, manufacturing
311312	Blackstrap invert made from purchased raw cane sugar
311311	Blackstrap molasses made in sugarcane mill
238990	Blacktop work, residential and commercial driveway and parking area
811310	Blade sharpening, commercial and industrial machinery and equipment
423710	Blades (e.g., knife, saw) merchant wholesalers
333120	Blades for graders, scrapers, bulldozers, and snowplows manufacturing
332211	Blades, knife and razor, manufacturing
424210	Blades, razor, merchant wholesalers
332213	Blades, saw, all types, manufacturing
325131	Blanc fixe (i.e., barium sulfate, precipitated) manufacturing
332992	Blank cartridges (i.e., 30 mm. or less, 1.18 inch or less) manufacturing
423690	Blank diskette merchant wholesalers

324121 Blocks, asphalt paving, made from purchased asphaltic materials

327331 Blocks, concrete and cinder, manufacturing

327124 Blocks, fire clay, manufacturing

327212 Blocks, glass, made in glass making plants

321999 Blocks, tackle, wood, manufacturing

321999 Blocks, tailors' pressing wood, manufacturing

621511 Blood analysis laboratories

334516 Blood bank process equipment manufacturing

621991 Blood banks

325413 Blood derivative in-vitro diagnostic substances manufacturing

325414 Blood derivatives manufacturing

424210 Blood derivatives merchant wholesalers

621991 Blood donor stations

325414 Blood fractions manufacturing

325413 Blood glucose test kits manufacturing

424210 Blood plasma merchant wholesalers

339112 Blood pressure apparatus manufacturing

621999 Blood pressure screening facilities

621999 Blood pressure screening services

812990 Blood pressure testing machine concession operators, coin-operated

339111 Blood testing apparatus, laboratory-type, manufacturing

339112 Blood transfusion equipment manufacturing

333516 Blooming and slabbing mill machinery, metalworking, manufacturing

331111 Blooms, steel, made in iron and steel mills

315191 Blouses made in apparel knitting mills

315291 Blouses, infants', manufacturing

315212 Blouses, women's, girls', and infants', cut and sew apparel contractors

315232 Blouses, women's, misses', and girls', cut and sewn from purchased fabric (except apparel contractors)

335211 Blow dryers, household-type electric, manufacturing

333220 Blow molding machinery for plastics manufacturing

332212 Blow torches manufacturing

238220 Blower and fan, cooling and dry heating, installation

333412 Blower filter units manufacturing

333111 Blowers, forage, manufacturing

423830 Blowers, industrial, merchant wholesalers

333112 Blowers, leaf, manufacturing

238310 Blown-in insulation (e.g., cellulose, vermiculite) installation

221210 Blue gas, carbureted, production and distribution

111334 Blueberry farming

114111 Bluefish fishing

111998 Bluegrass-Kentucky seed farming

541340 Blueprint drafting services

333315 Blueprint equipment manufacturing

423420 Blueprinting equipment merchant wholesalers

561439 Blueprinting services

212311 Bluestone mining or quarrying

325620 Blushes, face, manufacturing

921130 Board of Governors, Federal Reserve

321219 Board, bagasse, manufacturing

327420 Board, gypsum, manufacturing

321219 Board, particle, manufacturing

115210 Boarding horses

721310 Boarding houses

611110 Boarding schools, elementary or secondary

812910 Boarding services, pet

921120 Boards of supervisors, county and local

813910 Boards of trade

324122 Boards, asphalt saturated, made from purchased asphaltic materials

321999 Boards, bulletin, wood and cork, manufacturing

321999 Boards, wood (e.g., clip, ironing, meat, pastry), manufacturing

321113 Boards, wood, made from logs or bolts

321912 Boards, wood, resawing purchased lumber

336321 Boat and ship lighting fixtures manufacturing

441222 Boat dealers, new and used

541330 Boat engineering design services

484220 Boat hauling, truck, local

484230 Boat hauling, truck, long-distance

238990 Boat lift installation

333923 Boat lifts manufacturing

532411 Boat rental (except pleasure)

532411 Boat rental or leasing, commercial

532292 Boat rental, pleasure

332312 Boat sections, prefabricated metal, manufacturing

441222 Boat trailer dealers

336212 Boat transporter trailers, multi-unit, manufacturing

336214 Boat transporter trailers, single-unit, manufacturing

336612 Boat yards (i.e., boat manufacturing facilities)

487210 Boat, fishing charter, operation

811490 Boat, pleasure, repair and maintenance services without retailing new boats

713930 Boating clubs with marinas

713990 Boating clubs without marinas

423860 Boats (except pleasure) merchant wholesalers

336612 Boats (i.e., suitable or intended for personal use) manufacturing

326199 Boats, inflatable plastics, manufacturing

423910 Boats, pleasure (e.g., canoes, motorboats, sailboats), merchant wholesalers

321912 Bobbin blocks and blanks, wood, manufacturing

322214 Bobbins, fiber, made from purchased paperboard

333292 Bobbins, textile machinery, manufacturing

339920 Bobsleds manufacturing

812320 Bobtailers, laundry and drycleaning

713990 Boccie ball courts

423110 Bodies, motor vehicle, merchant wholesalers

713940 Body building studios, physical fitness

561612 Body guard services

811121 Body shops, automotive

315191 Body stockings made in apparel knitting mills

315212 Body stockings, women's, girls', and infants', cut and sew apparel contractors

315239 Body stockings, women's, misses', and girls', cut and sewn from purchased fabric (except apparel contractors)

332995 Bofors guns manufacturing

238290 Boiler and pipe insulation installation

332410 Boiler casings manufacturing

238220 Boiler chipping, cleaning and scaling

334513 Boiler controls, industrial, power, and marine-type, manufacturing

332919 Boiler couplings and drains, plumbing and heating-type, manufacturing

238290 Boiler covering installation

332911 Boiler gauge cocks, industrial-type, manufacturing

331210 Boiler tubes, wrought, made from purchased iron

238220 Boiler, heating, installation

423720 Boilers (e.g., heating, hot water, power, steam) merchant wholesalers

333414 Boilers, heating, manufacturing

332410 Boilers, power, manufacturing
311612 Bologna made from purchased carcasses
332722 Bolts, metal, manufacturing
326199 Bolts, nuts, and rivets, plastics, manufacturing
333924 Bomb lifts manufacturing
332993 Bomb loading and assembling plants
332993 Bombcluster adapters manufacturing
332993 Bombs manufacturing
523120 Bond brokerages
523110 Bond dealing (i.e., acting as a principal in dealing securities to investors)
322233 Bond paper made from purchased paper
322121 Bond paper made in paper mills
493190 Bonded warehousing (except farm products, general merchandise, refrigerated)
493130 Bonded warehousing, farm products (except refrigerated)
493110 Bonded warehousing, general merchandise
493120 Bonded warehousing, refrigerated
313230 Bonded-fiber fabrics manufacturing
332812 Bonderizing metal and metal products for the trade
524126 Bonding, fidelity or surety insurance, direct
812990 Bondsperson services
325182 Bone black manufacturing
327112 Bone china manufacturing
339112 Bone drills manufacturing
311119 Bone meal prepared as feed for animals and fowls
339999 Bone novelties manufacturing
339112 Bone plates and screws manufacturing
339112 Bone rongeurs manufacturing
311613 Bones, fat, rendering
511130 Book (e.g., hardback, paperback, tape) publishers (except exclusive Internet publishing)
323121 Book binding shops
323121 Book binding without printing
454113 Book clubs, not publishing, mail-order
813410 Book discussion clubs
332999 Book ends, metal, manufacturing
322222 Book paper made by coating purchased paper
322222 Book paper, coated, made from purchased paper
322121 Book paper, coated, made in paper mills
511130 Book publishers and printing combined
516110 Book publishers, exclusively on Internet
511130 Book publishers, university press (except exclusive Internet publishing)
451211 Book stores
453310 Book stores, used
316110 Bookbinder's leather manufacturing
333293 Bookbinding machines manufacturing
323121 Bookbinding without printing
337125 Bookcases (except wood and metal), household-type, manufacturing
337214 Bookcases (except wood), office-type, manufacturing
337124 Bookcases, metal household-type, manufacturing
337122 Bookcases, wood household-type, manufacturing
337211 Bookcases, wood office-type, manufacturing
713290 Bookies
512199 Booking agencies, motion picture
512199 Booking agencies, motion picture or video productions
711320 Booking agencies, theatrical (except motion picture)
541219 Bookkeepers' offices
541219 Bookkeepers' private practices
423420 Bookkeeping machines merchant wholesalers
541219 Bookkeeping services
713290 Bookmakers

325320   Botanical insecticides manufacturing
424210   Botanicals merchant wholesalers
541710   Botany research and development laboratories or services
326199   Bottle caps and lids, plastics, manufacturing
332115   Bottle caps and tops, metal, stamping
321999   Bottle corks manufacturing
321999   Bottle covers, willow, rattan, and reed, manufacturing
561990   Bottle exchanges
335211   Bottle warmers, household-type electric, manufacturing
333993   Bottle washers, packaging machinery, manufacturing
454312   Bottled gas dealers, direct selling
424490   Bottled water (except water treating) merchant wholesalers
454390   Bottled water providers, direct selling
423840   Bottles (except waste) merchant wholesalers
327213   Bottles (i.e., bottling, canning, packaging), glass, manufacturing
326160   Bottles, plastics, manufacturing
332439   Bottles, vacuum, light gauge metal, manufacturing
423930   Bottles, waste, merchant wholesalers
333993   Bottling machinery (e.g., capping, filling, labeling, sterilizing, washing) manufacturing
423830   Bottling machinery and equipment merchant wholesalers
335121   Boudoir lamp fixtures manufacturing
311422   Bouillon canning
311423   Bouillon made in dehydration plants
212319   Boulder crushed and broken mining and/or beneficiating

324199   Boulets (i.e., fuel bricks) made from refined petroleum
424590   Bovine semen merchant wholesalers
315211   Bow ties, men's and boys', cut and sew apparel contractors
315993   Bow ties, men's and boys', cut and sewn from purchased fabric (except apparel contractors)
238290   Bowling alley equipment installation
713950   Bowling alleys
337127   Bowling center furniture manufacturing
713950   Bowling centers
423910   Bowling equipment and supplies merchant wholesalers
451110   Bowling equipment and supply stores
611620   Bowling instruction
713990   Bowling leagues or teams, recreational
321912   Bowling pin blanks manufacturing
339920   Bowling pin machines, automatic, manufacturing
326199   Bowls and bowl covers, plastics, manufacturing
321999   Bowls, wood, turned and shaped, manufacturing
314999   Bows made from purchased fabrics
339920   Bows, archery, manufacturing
316999   Bows, shoe, leather, manufacturing
321920   Box cleats, wood, manufacturing
311991   Box lunches (for sale off premises) manufacturing
321920   Box shook manufacturing
337910   Box springs, assembled, made from purchased spring
316999   Box toes (i.e., shoe cut stock), leather, manufacturing
311612   Boxed beef made from purchased carcasses
311611   Boxed beef produced in slaughtering plants

311612 Boxed meat produced from purchased carcasses
311611 Boxed meats produced in slaughtering plants
711219 Boxers, independent professional
423840 Boxes and crates, industrial (except disposable plastics, paperboard, waste), merchant wholesalers
321920 Boxes, cigar, wood or part wood, manufacturing
322211 Boxes, corrugated and solid fiber, made from purchased paper or paperboard
335932 Boxes, electrical wiring (e.g., junction, outlet, switch), manufacturing
322212 Boxes, folding (except corrugated), made from purchased paperboard
316991 Boxes, hat (except paper or paperboard), manufacturing
321920 Boxes, jewelry, wood or part wood, manufacturing
316999 Boxes, leather, manufacturing
332439 Boxes, light gauge metal, manufacturing
424130 Boxes, paperboard and disposable plastics, merchant wholesalers
322215 Boxes, sanitary food (except folding), made from purchased paper or paperboard
322213 Boxes, setup (i.e., not shipped flat), made from purchased paperboard
322211 Boxes, shipping, laminated paper and paperboard, made from purchased paperboard
336211 Boxes, truck (e.g., cargo, dump, utility, van), assembled on purchased chassis
423930 Boxes, waste, merchant wholesalers
321920 Boxes, wood, manufacturing
321920 Boxes, wood, plain or fabric covered, nailed or lock corner, manufacturing

711211 Boxing clubs, professional or semiprofessional
713990 Boxing clubs, recreational
339920 Boxing equipment manufacturing
711310 Boxing event managers with facilities
711320 Boxing event managers without facilities
711310 Boxing event organizers with facilities
711320 Boxing event organizers without facilities
711310 Boxing event promoters with facilities
711320 Boxing event promoters without facilities
337215 Boxspring frames manufacturing
813410 Boy guiding organizations
623990 Boys' and girls' residential facilities (e.g., homes, ranches, villages)
721214 Boys' camps (except day, instructional)
611620 Boys' camps, sports instruction
611620 Boys' camps, sports instructor
713990 Boys' day camps (except instructional)
315119 Boys' socks manufacturing
111334 Boysenberry farming
339911 Bracelets, precious metal, manufacturing
115112 Bracing of orchard trees and vines
332510 Brackets (i.e., builder's hardware-type), metal, manufacturing
332618 Brackets made from purchased wire
321918 Brackets, wood, manufacturing
423710 Brads merchant wholesalers
331222 Brads, iron or steel, wire or cut, made in wire drawing plants
332618 Brads, metal, made from purchased wire
333292 Braiding machinery for textiles manufacturing
313221 Braiding narrow fabrics

336340 Brake and brake parts, automotive, truck, and bus, manufacturing

336340 Brake caliper assemblies, automotive, truck, and bus, manufacturing

336340 Brake cylinders, master and wheel, automotive, truck, and bus, manufacturing

336340 Brake discs (rotor), automotive, truck, and bus, manufacturing

336340 Brake drums, automotive, truck, and bus, manufacturing

325998 Brake fluid, synthetic, manufacturing

324191 Brake fluids, petroleum, made from refined petroleum

336340 Brake hose assemblies manufacturing

336340 Brake lining, automotive, truck, and bus, manufacturing

336340 Brake pads and shoes, automotive, truck, and bus, manufacturing

811118 Brake repair shops, automotive

333319 Brake service equipment (except mechanic's hand tools), motor vehicle, manufacturing

336340 Brake shoes and pads, asbestos, manufacturing

335314 Brakes and clutches, electromagnetic, manufacturing

336510 Brakes and parts for railroad rolling stock manufacturing

335314 Brakes, electromagnetic, manufacturing

333513 Brakes, press, metalworking, manufacturing

311212 Bran and other residues of milling rice

522110 Branches of foreign banks

521110 Branches, Federal Reserve Bank

533110 Brand name licensing

115210 Branding

339943 Branding irons (i.e., marking irons) manufacturing

424820 Brandy and brandy spirits merchant wholesalers

312130 Brandy distilling

315212 Bra-slips, women's and girls', cut and sew apparel contractors

315231 Bra-slips, women's, misses', and juniors', cut and sewn from purchased fabric (except apparel contractors)

331522 Brass die-castings, unfinished, manufacturing

331525 Brass foundries (except die-casting)

423720 Brass goods, plumbers', merchant wholesalers

325612 Brass polishes manufacturing

331421 Brass products, rolling, drawing, or extruding, made from purchased copper or in integrated secondary smelting and rolling, drawing or extruding plants

315212 Brassieres cut and sew apparel contractors

315231 Brassieres cut and sewn from purchased fabric (except apparel contractors)

332323 Brasswork, ornamental, manufacturing

335221 Braziers, barbecue, manufacturing

111335 Brazil nut farming

325191 Brazilwood extract manufacturing

332811 Brazing (i.e., hardening) metals and metal products for the trade

311822 Bread and bread-type roll mixes made from purchased flour

311812 Bread and bread-type rolls made in commercial bakeries

311999 Bread crumbs not made in bakeries

335211 Bread machines, household-type electric, manufacturing

333294 Bread slicing machinery manufacturing

333993 Bread wrapping machines manufacturing

212113 Breakers, anthracite mining and/or beneficiating

333131 Breakers, coal, manufacturing
332919 Breakers, vacuum, plumbing, manufacturing
311340 Breakfast bars, nonchocolate covered, manufacturing
311230 Breakfast cereals manufacturing
424490 Breakfast cereals merchant wholesalers
237990 Breakwater construction
332313 Breechings, fabricated metal plate work, manufacturing
112990 Breeding of pets (e.g., birds, cats, dogs)
115210 Breeding, animal, services
312120 Breweries
311211 Brewers' and distillers' flakes and grits, corn, manufacturing
311213 Brewers' malt manufacturing
325191 Brewers' pitch made by distillation of wood
311212 Brewers' rice manufacturing
424490 Brewers' yeast merchant wholesalers
333294 Brewery machinery manufacturing
238990 Brick driveway contractors
238990 Brick paver (e.g., driveways, patios, sidewalks) installation
238140 Brick veneer, installation
238140 Bricklaying contractors
423320 Bricks (except refractory) merchant wholesalers
327121 Bricks (i.e., common, face, glazed, hollow, vitrified), clay, manufacturing
327123 Bricks, adobe, manufacturing
327124 Bricks, clay refractory, manufacturing
327331 Bricks, concrete, manufacturing
327215 Bricks, glass, made from purchased glass
327212 Bricks, glass, made in glass making plants
327125 Bricks, nonclay refractory, manufacturing
315233 Bridal dresses or gowns, custom made

315233 Bridal dresses or gowns, women's, misses', and girls', cut and sewn from purchased fabric (except apparel contractors)
315212 Bridal dresses or gowns, women's, misses', and juniors', apparel contractors
448190 Bridal gown shops (except custom)
532220 Bridal wear rental
333999 Bridge and gate lifting machinery manufacturing
611699 Bridge and other card game instruction
321114 Bridge and trestle parts, wood, treating
237310 Bridge approach construction
713990 Bridge clubs, recreational
237310 Bridge construction
237310 Bridge decking construction
238320 Bridge painting
332312 Bridge sections, prefabricated metal, manufacturing
488490 Bridge, tunnel, and highway operations
339116 Bridges, custom made in dental laboratories
334515 Bridges, electrical (e.g., Kelvin, megohm, vacuum tube, Wheatstone), manufacturing
316110 Bridle leather manufacturing
237990 Bridle path construction
316991 Briefcases, all materials, manufacturing
315291 Briefs, infants', cut and sewn from purchased fabric (except apparel contractors)
315192 Briefs, underwear, made in apparel knitting mills
315211 Briefs, underwear, men's and boys', cut and sew apparel contractors
315221 Briefs, underwear, men's and boys', cut and sewn from purchased fabric (except apparel contractors)
315231 Briefs, underwear, women's, misses', and girls', cut and sewn from purchased fabric (except apparel contractors)

315212	Briefs, women's, girls', and infants', cut and sew apparel contractors
212393	Brimstone mining and/or beneficiating
311421	Brining of fruits and vegetables
212210	Briquets, iron, mining and/or beneficiating
324199	Briquettes, petroleum, made from refined petroleum
424590	Bristles merchant wholesalers
322130	Bristols board stock manufacturing
322121	Bristols paper stock manufacturing
333515	Broaches (i.e., a machine tool accessory) manufacturing
333512	Broaching machines, metalworking, manufacturing
334220	Broadcast equipment (including studio), for radio and television, manufacturing
541910	Broadcast media rating services
423690	Broadcasting equipment merchant wholesalers
516110	Broadcasting exclusively on Internet, audio
516110	Broadcasting exclusively on Internet, video
515111	Broadcasting networks, radio
515120	Broadcasting networks, television
611519	Broadcasting schools
236220	Broadcasting station construction
515112	Broadcasting stations (except exclusively on Internet), radio
515120	Broadcasting stations, television
515112	Broadcasting studio, radio station
711110	Broadway theaters
313210	Broadwoven fabrics (except rugs, tire fabrics) weaving
313311	Broadwoven fabrics finishing
313210	Brocades weaving
111219	Broccoli farming, field, bedding plant and seed production
112320	Broiler chicken production
523140	Brokerages, commodity contracts
524210	Brokerages, insurance
522310	Brokerages, loan
522310	Brokerages, mortgage
531210	Brokerages, real estate
523120	Brokerages, securities
524210	Brokers' offices, insurance
522310	Brokers' offices, loan
522310	Brokers' offices, mortgage
531210	Brokers' offices, real estate
325188	Bromine manufacturing
325199	Bromochloromethane manufacturing
339112	Bronchoscopes (except electromedical) manufacturing
334510	Bronchoscopes, electromedical, manufacturing
331522	Bronze die-castings, unfinished, manufacturing
331525	Bronze foundries (except die-casting)
325910	Bronze printing inks manufacturing
331421	Bronze products, rolling, drawing, or extruding, made from purchased copper or in integrated secondary smelting and rolling, drawing or extruding plants
111199	Broomcorn farming
424590	Broomcorn merchant wholesalers
423220	Brooms and brushes, household-type, merchant wholesalers
339994	Brooms, hand and machine, manufacturing
311422	Broth (except seafood) canning
311313	Brown beet sugar refining
212111	Brown coal mining and/or beneficiating
212210	Brown ore mining and/or beneficiating
311313	Brown sugar made from beet sugar
311312	Brown sugar made from purchased raw cane sugar
311311	Brown sugar made in sugarcane mill
325411	Brucine manufacturing

212325 Brucite mining and/or beneficiating

335991 Brush blocks, carbon or molded graphite, manufacturing

321912 Brush blocks, wood, turned and shaped

562119 Brush collection services

562119 Brush hauling, local

562119 Brush removal services

335991 Brushes and brush stock contacts, electric, carbon and graphite, manufacturing

339942 Brushes, artists', manufacturing

339994 Brushes, household-type and industrial, manufacturing

339994 Brushes, paint (except artists'), manufacturing

326299 Brushes, rubber, manufacturing

333512 Brushing machines, metalworking, manufacturing

335991 Brushplates, carbon or graphite, manufacturing

111219 Brussel sprout farming, field, bedding plant and seed production

325620 Bubble bath preparations manufacturing

326199 Bubble packaging materials, plastics, manufacturing

333120 Bucket and scarifier teeth manufacturing

333922 Buckets, elevator or conveyor, manufacturing

333120 Buckets, excavating (e.g., clamshell, concrete, drag scraper, dragline, shovel), manufacturing

321920 Buckets, wood, coopered, manufacturing

339993 Buckles and buckle parts (including shoe) manufacturing

111199 Buckwheat farming

311211 Buckwheat flour manufacturing

921130 Budget agencies, government

112990 Buffalo production

722212 Buffet eating places

337122 Buffets (furniture), wood, manufacturing

333512 Buffing and polishing machines, metalworking, manufacturing

327910 Buffing and polishing wheels, abrasive and nonabrasive, manufacturing

325612 Buffing compounds manufacturing

333991 Buffing machines, handheld power-driven, manufacturing

332813 Buffing metals and metal products for the trade

316110 Buffings, russet, manufacturing

332510 Builder's hardware, metal, manufacturing

541310 Building architectural design services

238210 Building automation system installation contractors

423320 Building blocks (e.g., cinder, concrete) merchant wholesalers

423310 Building board (e.g., fiber, flake, particle) merchant wholesalers

561720 Building cleaning services, interior

561720 Building cleaning services, janitorial

238910 Building demolition

561790 Building exterior cleaning services (except sand blasting, window cleaning)

238390 Building fixture and fitting (except mechanical equipment) installation

238130 Building framing (except structural steel)

541350 Building inspection bureaus

541350 Building inspection services

926150 Building inspections, government

238310 Building insulation contractors

237210 Building lot subdividing

326199 Building materials (e.g., fascia, panels, siding, soffit), plastics, manufacturing

444190 Building materials supply dealers

423390 Building materials, fiberglass (except insulation, roofing, siding), merchant wholesalers
213112 Building oil and gas well foundations on a contract basis
326199 Building panels, corrugated and flat, plastics, manufacturing
423390 Building paper merchant wholesalers
322121 Building paper stock manufacturing
334512 Building services monitoring controls, automatic, manufacturing
925110 Building standards agencies, government
423320 Building stone merchant wholesalers
327121 Building tile, clay, manufacturing
531110 Building, apartment, rental or leasing
213112 Building, erecting, repairing, and dismantling oil and gas field rigs and derricks on a contract basis
531120 Building, nonresidential (except miniwarehouse), rental or leasing
236118 Building, residential, addition, alteration and renovation
531110 Building, residential, rental or leasing
321991 Buildings, mobile, commercial use, manufacturing
332311 Buildings, prefabricated metal, manufacturing
423390 Buildings, prefabricated nonwood, merchant wholesalers
423310 Buildings, prefabricated wood, merchant wholesalers
321992 Buildings, prefabricated, wood, manufacturing
238350 Built-in wood cabinets constructed on site
327999 Built-up mica manufacturing
335110 Bulbs, electric light, complete, manufacturing

311211 Bulgur (flour) manufacturing
424710 Bulk gasoline stations
484220 Bulk liquids trucking, local
484230 Bulk liquids trucking, long-distance
484110 Bulk mail truck transportation, contract, local
484121 Bulk mail truck transportation, contract, long-distance (TL)
493190 Bulk petroleum storage
424710 Bulk stations, petroleum
332420 Bulk storage tanks, heavy gauge metal, manufacturing
237990 Bulkhead wall construction
115210 Bull testing stations
532412 Bulldozer rental or leasing without operator
238910 Bulldozer rental with operator
333120 Bulldozers manufacturing
332992 Bullet jackets and cores (i.e., 30 mm. or less, 1.18 inch or less) manufacturing
321999 Bulletin boards, wood and cork, manufacturing
339113 Bulletproof vests manufacturing
212221 Bullion, gold, produced at the mine
212222 Bullion, silver, produced at the mine
336399 Bumpers and bumperettes assembled, automotive, truck, and bus, manufacturing
333313 Bundling machinery (e.g., box strapping, mail, newspaper) manufacturing
321999 Bungs, wood, manufacturing
236220 Bunkhouse construction
339111 Bunsen burners manufacturing
315212 Buntings, infants', cut and sew apparel contractors
315291 Buntings, infants', cut and sewn from purchased fabric (except apparel contractors)
334513 Buoyancy instruments, industrial process-type, manufacturing
321999 Buoys, cork, manufacturing
332313 Buoys, fabricated plate work metal, manufacturing

561621 Burglar alarm monitoring services
561621 Burglar alarm sales combined with installation, repair, or monitoring services
238210 Burglar alarm system, electric, installation only
334290 Burglar alarm systems and equipment manufacturing
524126 Burglary and theft insurance carriers, direct
339995 Burial caskets and cases manufacturing
423850 Burial caskets merchant wholesalers
315299 Burial garments cut and sewn from purchased fabric (except apparel contractors)
315211 Burial garments, men's and boys', cut and sew apparel contractors
315212 Burial garments, women's, girls' and infants', cut and sew apparel contractors
524128 Burial insurance carriers, direct
339995 Burial vaults (except concrete, stone) manufacturing
327390 Burial vaults, concrete and precast terrazzo, manufacturing
327991 Burial vaults, stone, manufacturing
424990 Burlap merchant wholesalers
711110 Burlesque companies
212325 Burley mining and/or beneficiating
313311 Burling and mending broadwoven fabrics
313312 Burling and mending fabrics (except broadwoven)
335311 Burner ignition transformers manufacturing
423720 Burners, fuel oil and distillate oil, merchant wholesalers
333414 Burners, heating, manufacturing
332811 Burning metals and metal products for the trade
333512 Burnishing machines, metalworking, manufacturing

321999 Burnt wood articles manufacturing
314999 Burnt-out laces manufacturing
112920 Burro production
212399 Burrstones, natural, mining and/or beneficiating
335313 Bus bar structures, switchgear-type, manufacturing
335931 Bus bars, electrical conductors (except switchgear-type), manufacturing
336211 Bus bodies assembling on purchased chassis
336211 Bus bodies manufacturing
541850 Bus card advertising services
485510 Bus charter services (except scenic, sightseeing)
541850 Bus display advertising services
611519 Bus driver training
485210 Bus line operation, intercity
485113 Bus line, local (except mixed mode)
423110 Bus merchant wholesalers
485410 Bus operation, school and employee
532120 Bus rental or leasing
485113 Bus services, urban and suburban (except mixed mode)
236220 Bus shelter construction
236220 Bus terminal construction
488490 Bus terminal operation, independent
561599 Bus ticket offices
485113 Bus transit systems (except mixed mode)
336120 Buses (except trackless trolley) assembling on chassis of own manufacture
487110 Buses, scenic and sightseeing operation
336510 Buses, trackless trolley, manufacturing
333613 Bushings, plain (except internal combustion engine), manufacturing
326199 Bushings, plastics, manufacturing
321999 Bushings, wood, manufacturing
813910 Business associations

541990   Business brokers (except real estate brokers)

611410   Business colleges or schools not offering academic degrees

611310   Business colleges or schools offering baccalaureate or graduate degrees

323112   Business directories flexographic printing without publishing

323111   Business directories gravure printing without publishing

323110   Business directories lithographic (offset) printing without publishing

323119   Business directories printing (except flexographic, gravure, lithographic, quick, screen) without publishing

323113   Business directories screen printing without publishing

511140   Business directory publishers (except exclusive Internet publishing)

511140   Business directory publishers and printing combined

516110   Business directory publishers, exclusively on Internet

323112   Business forms (except manifold) flexographic printing without publishing

323111   Business forms (except manifold) gravure printing without publishing

323110   Business forms (except manifold) lithographic printing

323119   Business forms (except manifold) printing (except flexographic, gravure, lithographic, quick, screen) without publishing

323113   Business forms (except manifold) screen printing without publishing

323116   Business forms, manifold, printing

423420   Business machines and equipment (except computers) merchant wholesalers

541611   Business management consulting services

561110   Business management services

541720   Business research and development services

611410   Business schools not offering academic degrees

561439   Business service centers (except private mail centers)

561439   Business service centers (except private mail centers) providing range of office support services (except printing)

541611   Business start-up consulting services

425110   Business to business electronic markets, durable goods, wholesale trade

425110   Business to business electronic markets, nondurable goods, wholesale trade

454111   Business to Consumer retail sales Internet sites

325211   Butadiene copolymers containing less than 50 percent butadiene manufacturing

325212   Butadiene copolymers containing more than 50 percent butadiene manufacturing

325199   Butadiene made from alcohol

325110   Butadiene made from refined petroleum or liquid hydrocarbons

325212   Butadiene rubber (i.e., polybutadiene) manufacturing

325110   Butane made from refined petroleum or liquid hydrocarbons

211112   Butane, natural, mining

445210   Butcher shops

332211   Butcher's knives manufacturing

311512   Butter manufacturing

424430   Butter merchant wholesalers

333294   Butter processing machinery manufacturing

311512   Butter, creamery and whey, manufacturing

332911 Butterfly valves, industrial-type, manufacturing
311511 Buttermilk manufacturing
111219 Butternut squash farming, field, bedding plant and seed production
335912 Button cells, primary batteries, manufacturing
333298 Buttonhole and eyelet machinery manufacturing
315211 Buttonhole making apparel contractors, men's and boys'
315212 Buttonhole making apparel contractors, women's, misses', girls', and infants' (except fur)
315212 Buttonhole making, fur goods, women's, girls', and infants', cut and sew apparel contractors
315211 Buttonholing and button covering apparel contractors, men's and boys'
315212 Buttonholing and button covering apparel contractors, women's, misses', and girls'
339993 Buttons (except precious metal, precious stones, semiprecious stones) manufacturing
339911 Buttons, precious metal, precious stones, semiprecious stones, manufacturing
325199 Butyl acetate manufacturing
325212 Butyl rubber manufacturing
324110 Butylene (i.e., butene) made in petroleum refineries
325110 Butylene made from refined petroleum or liquid hydrocarbons
531210 Buyers' agents, real estate, offices
531210 Buying agencies, real estate
531210 Buying real estate for others (i.e., agents, brokers)
485310 Cab (i.e., taxi) services
336112 Cab and chassis, light trucks and vans, manufacturing
111219 Cabbage farming, field, bedding plant and seed production
236115 Cabin construction general contractors

336612 Cabin cruiser
334511 Cabin environment indicators, transmitters, and sensors manufacturing
236117 Cabin operative builders
332510 Cabinet hardware, metal, manufacturing
444190 Cabinet stores, kitchen (except custom), to be installed
238350 Cabinet work performed at the construction site
238350 Cabinetry work performed at the construction site
337214 Cabinets (except wood), office-type, freestanding, manufacturing
337129 Cabinets (i.e., housings), wood (e.g., sewing machines, stereo, television), manufacturing
337110 Cabinets, kitchen (except freestanding), stock or custom wood, manufacturing
423310 Cabinets, kitchen, built in, merchant wholesalers
423210 Cabinets, kitchen, free standing, merchant wholesalers
337124 Cabinets, metal (i.e., bathroom, kitchen) (except freestanding), manufacturing
337124 Cabinets, metal household-type, freestanding, manufacturing
337124 Cabinets, metal, radio and television, manufacturing
238350 Cabinets, wood built-in, constructed on site
337122 Cabinets, wood household-type, freestanding, manufacturing
337211 Cabinets, wood office-type, freestanding, manufacturing
721199 Cabins, housekeeping
515210 Cable broadcasting networks
485119 Cable car systems (except mixed mode), commuter
487110 Cable car, land, scenic and sightseeing operation
334220 Cable decoders manufacturing
237130 Cable laying (e.g., cable television, electricity, marine, telephone), including underground

517510   Cable program distribution operators
238990   Cable splicing (except electrical or fiber optic)
238210   Cable splicing, electrical or fiber optic
238210   Cable television hookup contractors
515210   Cable television networks
334220   Cable television transmission and receiving equipment manufacturing
517510   Cable TV providers (except networks)
331422   Cable, copper (e.g., armored, bare, insulated), made from purchased copper in wire drawing plants
331422   Cable, copper (e.g., armored, bare, insulated), made in integrated secondary smelting and wire drawing plants
331222   Cable, iron or steel, insulated or armored, made in wire drawing plants
335929   Cable, nonferrous, insulated, or armored, made from purchased nonferrous wire
332618   Cable, noninsulated wire, made from purchased wire
423510   Cable, wire (except insulated), merchant wholesalers
333111   Cabs for agricultural machinery manufacturing
333120   Cabs for construction machinery manufacturing
333924   Cabs for industrial trucks manufacturing
111339   Cactus fruit farming
541512   CAD (computer-aided design) systems integration design services
541370   Cadastral surveying services
339920   Caddy carts manufacturing
331419   Cadmium refining, primary
541512   CAE (computer-aided engineering) systems integration design services
337215   Cafeteria fixtures manufacturing

722310   Cafeteria food services contractors (e.g., government office cafeterias, hospital cafeterias, school cafeterias)
337127   Cafeteria furniture manufacturing
337127   Cafeteria tables and benches manufacturing
722212   Cafeterias
325411   Caffeine and derivatives (i.e., basic chemicals) manufacturing
315291   Caftans, infants', cut and sewn from purchased fabric (except apparel contractors)
315211   Caftans, men's and boys', cut and sew apparel contractors
315223   Caftans, men's and boys', cut and sewn from purchased fabric (except apparel contractors)
315212   Caftans, women's, girls', and infants', cut and sew apparel contractors
315231   Caftans, women's, misses' and girls', cut and sewn from purchased fabric (except apparel contractors)
332618   Cages made from purchased wire
238910   Caisson (i.e., drilled building foundations) construction
237990   Caisson (i.e., marine or pneumatic structures) construction
332420   Caissons, underwater work, heavy gauge metal, manufacturing
311999   Cake frosting manufacturing
311999   Cake frosting mixes manufacturing
311822   Cake mixes made from purchased flour
311340   Cake ornaments, confectionery, manufacturing
311813   Cake, frozen, manufacturing
311812   Cakes, baking (except frozen), made in commercial bakeries
212231   Calamine mining and/or beneficiating

212221 Calaverite mining and/or beneficiating

212312 Calcareous tufa crushed and broken stone mining and/or beneficiating

212311 Calcareous tufa mining or quarrying

325510 Calcimines manufacturing

424950 Calcimines, merchant wholesalers

212392 Calcined phosphate rock mining and/or beneficiating

324199 Calcining petroleum coke from refined petroleum

212399 Calcite mining and/or beneficiating

325188 Calcium carbide, chloride, and hypochlorite manufacturing

325199 Calcium citrate manufacturing

327410 Calcium hydroxide (i.e., hydrated lime) manufacturing

325188 Calcium hypochlorite manufacturing

325188 Calcium inorganic compounds, not specified elsewhere by process, manufacturing

325199 Calcium organic compounds, not specified elsewhere by process, manufacturing

325199 Calcium oxalate manufacturing

327410 Calcium oxide (i.e., quicklime) manufacturing

423420 Calculators and calculating machines merchant wholesalers

333313 Calculators manufacturing

511199 Calendar publishers (except exclusive Internet publishing)

511199 Calendar publishers and printing combined

516110 Calendar publishers, exclusively on Internet

453998 Calendar shops

323112 Calendars flexographic printing without publishing

323111 Calendars gravure printing without publishing

323110 Calendars lithographic (offset) printing without publishing

323119 Calendars printing (except flexographic, digital, lithographic, gravure, quick, screen) without publishing

323113 Calendars screen printing without publishing

313311 Calendering broadwoven fabrics

333220 Calendering machinery for plastics manufacturing

333292 Calendering machinery for textiles manufacturing

313312 Calendering textile products, apparel, and fabrics (except broadwoven)

112111 Calf (e.g., feeder, stocker, veal) production

315119 Calf high sheer hosiery knitting or knitting and finishing

541380 Calibration and certification testing laboratories or services

332212 Calipers and dividers, machinists' precision tools, manufacturing

336340 Calipers, brake, automotive, truck, and bus, manufacturing

339992 Calliopes (steam organs) manufacturing

541512 CAM (computer-aided manufacturing) systems integration design services

532210 Camcorder rental

334310 Camcorders manufacturing

326211 Camelback (i.e., retreading material) manufacturing

333220 Camelback (i.e., retreading materials) machinery manufacturing

316991 Camera carrying bags, all materials, manufacturing

423410 Camera equipment and supplies, photographic, merchant wholesalers

333314 Camera lenses manufacturing

811211 Camera repair shops without retailing new cameras

443130 Camera shops, photographic

423410 Camera, television, merchant wholesalers

423410 Camera, video (except household-type) merchant wholesalers

711510 Cameramen, independent (freelance)

333315 Cameras (except digital, television, video) manufacturing

334220 Cameras, television, manufacturing

315212 Camisoles, women's and girls', cut and sew apparel contractors

315231 Camisoles, women's, misses' and girls', cut and sewn from purchased fabric (except apparel contractors)

337124 Camp furniture, metal, manufacturing

337125 Camp furniture, reed and rattan, manufacturing

337122 Camp furniture, wood, manufacturing

813940 Campaign organizations, political

441210 Camper dealers, recreational

532120 Camper rental

336214 Camper units, slide-in, for pick-up trucks, manufacturing

721211 Campgrounds

325191 Camphor, natural, manufacturing

325199 Camphor, synthetic, manufacturing

423910 Camping equipment and supplies merchant wholesalers

423110 Camping trailer merchant wholesalers

336214 Camping trailers and chassis manufacturing

721214 Camps (except day, instructional)

713990 Camps (except instructional), day

623990 Camps, boot or disciplinary (except correctional), for delinquent youth

611620 Camps, sports instruction

333515 Cams (i.e., a machine tool accessory) manufacturing

333513 Can forming machines, metalworking, manufacturing

332618 Can keys made from purchased wire

332431 Can lids and ends, light gauge metal, manufacturing

332212 Can openers (except electric) manufacturing

335211 Can openers, household-type electric, manufacturing

483211 Canal barge transportation (freight)

237990 Canal construction

488310 Canal maintenance services (except dredging)

488310 Canal operation

483212 Canal passenger transportation

221310 Canal, irrigation

333313 Canceling machinery, postal office-type, manufacturing

923120 Cancer detection program administration

622310 Cancer hospitals

541710 Cancer research laboratories or services

311340 Candied fruits and fruit peel manufacturing

713950 Candle pin bowling alleys

713950 Candle pin bowling centers

453998 Candle shops

339999 Candles manufacturing

424990 Candles merchant wholesalers

311320 Candy bars, chocolate (including chocolate covered), made from cacao beans

311340 Candy bars, nonchocolate, manufacturing

424450 Candy merchant wholesalers

311330 Candy stores, chocolate, candy made on premises not for immediate consumption

311340 Candy stores, nonchocolate, candy made on premises, not for immediate consumption

445292 Candy stores, packaged, retailing only

311320 Candy, chocolate, made from cacao beans

111930 Cane farming, sugar, field production

315299 Capes, waterproof (e.g., plastics, rubber, similar materials), cut and sewn from purchased fabric (except apparel contractors)

237110 Capping of water wells

333993 Capping, sealing, and lidding packaging machinery manufacturing

325199 Caprolactam manufacturing

315991 Caps (except fur, leather) cut and sewn from purchased fabric (except apparel contractors)

315991 Caps (i.e., apparel accessory) cut and sewn from purchased fabric (except fur, leather, apparel contractors)

315211 Caps (i.e., apparel accessory), men's and boys', cut and sew apparel contractors

315212 Caps (i.e., apparel accessory), women's, girls', and infants', cut and sew apparel contractors

315299 Caps and gowns, academic, cut and sewn from purchased fabric (except apparel contractors)

315211 Caps and gowns, academic, men's and boys', cut and sew apparel contractors

315212 Caps and gowns, academic, women's and girls', cut and sew apparel contractors

335931 Caps and plugs, attachment, electric, manufacturing

332115 Caps and tops, bottle, metal, stamping

336214 Caps for pick-up trucks manufacturing

325998 Caps for toy pistols manufacturing

315191 Caps made in apparel knitting mills

325920 Caps, blasting and detonating, manufacturing

332993 Caps, bomb, manufacturing

315292 Caps, fur (except apparel contractors), manufacturing

316999 Caps, heel and toe, leather, manufacturing

315292 Caps, leather (except apparel contractors), manufacturing

315991 Caps, textiles, straw, fur-felt, and wool-felt, cut and sewn from purchased fabric (except apparel contractors)

315211 Caps, textiles, straw, fur-felt, and wool-felt, men's and boys', cut and sew apparel contractors

315212 Caps, textiles, straw, fur-felt, and wool-felt, women's, girls', and infants', cut and sew apparel contractors

325998 Capsules, gelatin, empty, manufacturing

334290 Car alarm manufacturing

336211 Car bodies, kit, manufacturing

811192 Car detailers

532112 Car leasing

483212 Car lighters (i.e., ferries), inland waters (except on Great Lakes system)

485999 Car pool operation

488999 Car pools, arrangement of

532111 Car rental

532111 Car rental agencies

561599 Car rental reservation services

811111 Car repair shops, general

332999 Car seals, metal, manufacturing

337125 Car seats, infant (except metal), manufacturing

334310 Car stereos manufacturing

423850 Car wash equipment and supplies merchant wholesalers

811192 Car washes

331111 Car wheels, rolled steel, made in iron and steel mills

325188 Carbides (e.g., boron, calcium, silicon, tungsten) manufacturing

332994 Carbines manufacturing

325199 Carbinol manufacturing

325211 Carbohydrate plastics manufacturing

334510 Carbon arc lamp units, electrotherapeutic (except infrared and ultraviolet), manufacturing
325182 Carbon black manufacturing
424690 Carbon black merchant wholesalers
327125 Carbon brick manufacturing
325120 Carbon dioxide manufacturing
325188 Carbon disulfide manufacturing
335991 Carbon electrodes and contacts, electric, manufacturing
325188 Carbon inorganic compounds manufacturing
334290 Carbon monoxide detectors manufacturing
423690 Carbon monoxide detectors, electronic, merchant wholesalers
325199 Carbon organic compounds, not specified elsewhere by process, manufacturing
339944 Carbon paper manufacturing
335991 Carbon specialties for aerospace use (except gaskets) manufacturing
335991 Carbon specialties for electrical use manufacturing
335991 Carbon specialties for mechanical use (except gaskets) manufacturing
325199 Carbon tetrachloride manufacturing
325998 Carbon, activated, manufacturing
312111 Carbonated soda manufacturing
312111 Carbonated soft drinks manufacturing
325188 Carbonic acid manufacturing
333292 Carbonizing equipment for processing wool manufacturing
313312 Carbonizing textile fibers
335991 Carbons, electric, manufacturing
335991 Carbons, lighting, manufacturing
325998 Carburetor cleaners manufacturing
336311 Carburetors, all types, manufacturing

316993 Card cases (except metal) manufacturing
339911 Card cases, precious metal, manufacturing
713290 Card rooms (e.g., poker rooms)
453220 Card shops, greeting
337122 Card table sets (furniture), wood, manufacturing
337124 Card table sets, metal, manufacturing
424130 Cardboard products merchant wholesalers
322130 Cardboard stock manufacturing
322226 Cardboard, laminated or surface coated, made from purchased paperboard
313230 Carded nonwoven fabrics manufacturing
313111 Carded yarn manufacturing
325412 Cardiac preparations manufacturing
333292 Carding machinery for textiles manufacturing
313312 Carding textile fibers
334510 Cardiodynameter manufacturing
334510 Cardiographs manufacturing
621111 Cardiologists' offices (e.g., centers, clinics)
334510 Cardiophone, electric, manufacturing
334510 Cardioscope manufacturing
334510 Cardiotachometer manufacturing
323119 Cards (e.g., business, greeting, playing, postcards, trading) engraving printing without publishing
323112 Cards (e.g., business, greeting, playing, postcards, trading) flexographic printing without publishing
323111 Cards (e.g., business, greeting, playing, postcards, trading) gravure printing without publishing
323119 Cards (e.g., business, greeting, playing, postcards, trading) letterpress printing without publishing

323110 Cards (e.g., business, greeting, playing, postcards, trading) lithographic (offset) printing without publishing

323119 Cards (e.g., business, greeting, playing, postcards, trading) printing (except flexographic, gravure, lithographic, quick, screen) without publishing

323113 Cards (e.g., business, greeting, playing, postcards, trading) screen printing without publishing

322299 Cards, die-cut (except office supply) made from purchased paper or paperboard

322231 Cards, die-cut office supply (e.g., index, library, time recording), made from purchased paper or paperboard

424120 Cards, greeting, merchant wholesalers

****** Cards, publishing—see specific product

481112 Cargo carriers, air, scheduled

488390 Cargo checkers, marine

488330 Cargo salvaging, marine

336611 Cargo ship building

488390 Cargo surveyors, marine

488490 Cargo surveyors, truck transportation

333319 Carnival and amusement park rides manufacturing

333319 Carnival and amusement park shooting gallery machinery manufacturing

423850 Carnival equipment merchant wholesalers

713990 Carnival ride concession operators (i.e., supplying and servicing in others' facilities)

711190 Carnival traveling shows

212291 Carnotite mining and/or beneficiating

333922 Carousel conveyors (e.g., luggage) manufacturing

333319 Carousels (i.e., merry-go-rounds) manufacturing

238350 Carpenters (except framing)

611513 Carpenters' apprenticeship training

332212 Carpenter's handtools, nonelectric (except saws), manufacturing

532490 Carpentry equipment rental or leasing

238350 Carpentry work (except framing)

238130 Carpentry, framing

333319 Carpet and floor cleaning equipment, electric commercial-type, manufacturing

335212 Carpet and floor cleaning equipment, household-type electric, manufacturing

532490 Carpet and rug cleaning equipment rental or leasing

313111 Carpet and rug yarn spinning

532299 Carpet and rug, residential, rental

561740 Carpet cleaning on customers' premises

561740 Carpet cleaning plants

561740 Carpet cleaning services

314999 Carpet cutting and binding

313210 Carpet linings (except felt) weaving

423220 Carpet merchant wholesalers

313230 Carpet paddings, nonwoven, manufacturing

442210 Carpet stores

333319 Carpet sweepers, mechanical, manufacturing

238330 Carpet, installation only

314110 Carpets and rugs made from textile materials

321999 Carpets, cork, manufacturing

332311 Carports, prefabricated metal, manufacturing

487110 Carriage, horse-drawn, operation

339932 Carriages, baby, manufacturing

339932 Carriages, doll, manufacturing

334210 Carrier equipment (i.e., analog, digital), telephone, manufacturing

111219 Carrot farming, field, bedding plant and seed production

311991 Carrots, cut, peeled or sliced fresh, manufacturing
722211 Carryout restaurants
336111 Cars, electric, for highway use, assembling on chassis of own manufacture
333131 Cars, mining, manufacturing
541370 Cartographic surveying services
333993 Carton filling machinery manufacturing
322299 Cartons, egg, molded pulp manufacturing
322212 Cartons, folding (except milk), made from purchased paperboard
322215 Cartons, milk, made from purchased paper or paperboard
424130 Cartons, paper and paperboard, merchant wholesalers
711510 Cartoonists, independent
333991 Cartridge (i.e., powder) handheld power-driven tools manufacturing
332992 Cartridge cases for ammunition (i.e., 30 mm.or less, 1.18 inch or less) manufacturing
331421 Cartridge cups, discs, and sheets, copper and copper alloy, made from purchased copper or in integrated secondary smelting and rolling, drawing or extruding plants
424120 Cartridge toner merchant wholesalers
332992 Cartridges (i.e., 30 mm. or less, 1.18 inch or less) manufacturing
339920 Carts, caddy, manufacturing
423860 Carts, golf, motorized passenger merchant wholesalers
333924 Carts, grocery, made from purchased wire
333112 Carts, lawn and garden-type, manufacturing
332211 Carving sets manufacturing
333319 Carwashing machinery manufacturing

111219 Casaba melon farming, field, bedding plant and seed production
316110 Case leather manufacturing
325222 Casein fibers and filaments manufacturing
325211 Casein plastics manufacturing
311514 Casein, dry and wet, manufacturing
332321 Casements, metal, manufacturing
316993 Cases, jewelry (except metal), manufacturing
339914 Cases, jewelry, metal (except precious), manufacturing
339911 Cases, jewelry, precious metal, manufacturing
316991 Cases, luggage, manufacturing
316991 Cases, musical instrument, manufacturing
321920 Cases, shipping, wood, wirebound, manufacturing
321920 Cases, wood packing, nailed or lock corner, manufacturing
321920 Cases, wood shipping, nailed or lock corner, manufacturing
332439 Cash boxes, light gauge metal, manufacturing
532420 Cash register rental or leasing
333313 Cash registers (except point of sales terminals) manufacturing
423420 Cash registers merchant wholesalers
111335 Cashew farming
211112 Casing-head butane and propane production
326121 Casings, sausage, nonrigid plastics, manufacturing
332313 Casings, scroll, fabricated metal plate work, manufacturing
332322 Casings, sheet metal (except stampings), manufacturing
236220 Casino construction
721120 Casino hotels
713210 Casinos (except casino hotels)
332510 Casket hardware, metal, manufacturing
339995 Caskets, burial, manufacturing
423850 Caskets, burial, merchant wholesalers

321920   Casks, wood, coopered, manufacturing

111219   Cassava farming, field and seed casava production

335211   Casseroles, household-type electric, manufacturing

334612   Cassette tapes, pre-recorded audio, mass reproducing

532230   Cassette, prerecorded video, rental

423990   Cassettes, prerecorded audio and video, merchant wholesalers

331511   Cast iron brake shoes, railroad, manufacturing

331511   Cast iron pipe and pipe fittings manufacturing

423510   Cast iron pipe merchant wholesalers

331511   Cast iron railroad car wheels manufacturing

331513   Cast steel railroad car wheels, unfinished, manufacturing

327390   Cast stone, concrete (except structural), manufacturing

327124   Castable refractories, clay, manufacturing

327125   Castable refractories, nonclay, manufacturing

332510   Casters, furniture, metal manufacturing

332510   Casters, industrial, metal, manufacturing

561310   Casting agencies (i.e., motion picture, theatrical, video)

561310   Casting agencies, motion picture or video

561310   Casting agencies, theatrical

561310   Casting bureaus (e.g., motion picture, theatrical, video)

561310   Casting bureaus, motion picture or video

561310   Casting bureaus, theatrical

331528   Castings (except die-castings), nonferrous metals (except aluminum, copper), unfinished manufacturing

331524   Castings (except die-castings), unfinished, aluminum, manufacturing

331525   Castings (except die-castings), unfinished, copper, manufacturing

331511   Castings, compacted graphite iron, unfinished, manufacturing

331511   Castings, malleable iron, unfinished, manufacturing

331513   Castings, steel (except investment), unfinished, manufacturing

331511   Castings, unfinished iron (e.g., ductile, gray, malleable, semisteel), manufacturing

311223   Castor oil and pomace made in crushing mills

316213   Casual shoes (except athletic, plastics, rubber), men's, manufacturing

316214   Casual shoes (except athletic, rubber, plastics), women's, manufacturing

316219   Casual shoes (except rubber, plastics), children's and infants', manufacturing

524126   Casualty insurance carriers, direct

621512   CAT (computerized axial tomography) scanner centers

311111   Cat food manufacturing

325998   Cat litter manufacturing

112990   Cat production

511199   Catalog (i.e., mail order, store merchandise) publishers (except exclusive Internet publishing)

511199   Catalog (i.e., mail order, store merchandise) publishers and printing combined

454113   Catalog (i.e., order taking) offices of mail-order houses

511140   Catalog of collections publishers (except exclusive Internet publishing)

511140   Catalog of collections publishers and printing combined

516110   Catalog of collections publishers, exclusively on Internet

335121	Ceiling lighting fixtures, residential, manufacturing
321912	Ceiling lumber, dressed, resawing purchased lumber
321113	Ceiling lumber, made from logs or bolts
238310	Ceiling tile installation
238390	Ceiling, metal, installation
334519	Ceilometers manufacturing
711410	Celebrities' agents or managers
711510	Celebrity spokespersons, independent
111219	Celery farming, field, bedding plant and seed production
212393	Celestite mining and/or beneficiating
325221	Cellophane film or sheet manufacturing
424120	Cellophane tape merchant wholesalers
339992	Cellos and parts manufacturing
237130	Cellular phone tower construction
517212	Cellular telephone communication carriers
517212	Cellular telephone services
443112	Cellular telephone stores
334220	Cellular telephones manufacturing
423690	Cellular telephones merchant wholesalers
325199	Cellulose acetate (except resins) manufacturing
325211	Cellulose acetate resins manufacturing
325211	Cellulose nitrate resins manufacturing
325211	Cellulose propionate resins manufacturing
325211	Cellulose resins manufacturing
325211	Cellulose xanthate (viscose) manufacturing
238310	Cellulosic fiber insulation installation
325221	Cellulosic fibers and filaments manufacturing
325221	Cellulosic filament yarn manufacturing
326113	Cellulosic plastics film and unlaminated sheet (except packaging) manufacturing
325221	Cellulosic staple fibers manufacturing
327310	Cement (e.g., hydraulic, masonry, portland, pozzolana) manufacturing
238140	Cement block laying
327310	Cement clinker manufacturing
333298	Cement kilns manufacturing
423320	Cement merchant wholesalers
236210	Cement plant construction
212312	Cement rock crushed and broken stone mining and/or beneficiating
327124	Cement, clay refractory, manufacturing
327420	Cement, Keene's (i.e., tiling plaster), manufacturing
325520	Cement, rubber, manufacturing
213112	Cementing oil and gas well casings on a contract basis
423830	Cement-making machinery merchant wholesalers
324122	Cements, asphalt roofing, made from purchased asphaltic materials
339114	Cements, dental, manufacturing
812220	Cemeteries
812220	Cemetery associations (i.e., operators)
812220	Cemetery management services
453998	Cemetery memorial dealers (e.g., headstones, markers, vaults)
561730	Cemetery plot care services
333512	Centering machines, metalworking, manufacturing
519120	Centers for documentation (i.e., archives)
624120	Centers, senior citizens'
238220	Central air-conditioning equipment installation
521110	Central bank, monetary authorities
238220	Central cooling equipment and piping installation
238220	Central heating equipment and piping installation

423730	Central heating equipment, warm-air, merchant wholesalers
325412	Central nervous system stimulant preparations manufacturing
334210	Central office and switching equipment, telephone, manufacturing
333319	Central vacuuming systems, commercial-type, manufacturing
335212	Central vacuuming systems, household-type, manufacturing
551114	Centralized administrative offices
327320	Central-mixed concrete manufacturing
333911	Centrifugal pumps manufacturing
333999	Centrifuges, industrial-type, manufacturing
325411	Cephalosporin, uncompounded, manufacturing
325131	Ceramic colors manufacturing
423320	Ceramic construction materials (except refractory) merchant wholesalers
327999	Ceramic fiber manufacturing
333994	Ceramic kilns and furnaces manufacturing
238340	Ceramic tile installation
444190	Ceramic tile stores
327122	Ceramic tiles, floor and wall, manufacturing
611610	Ceramics instruction
311211	Cereal grain flour manufacturing
311211	Cereal grain germ manufacturing
424490	Cereal products merchant wholesalers
541710	Cerebral palsy research laboratories or services
212299	Cerium concentrates mining and/or beneficiating
212299	Cerium ores mining and/or beneficiating
325188	Cerium salts manufacturing

523120	Certificate of deposit (CD) brokers' offices
923110	Certification of schools and teachers
541211	Certified accountants' offices
523930	Certified financial planners, customized, fees paid by client
541211	Certified public accountants' (CPAs) offices
212231	Cerussite mining and/or beneficiating
339113	Cervical collars manufacturing
325188	Cesium and cesium compounds, not specified elsewhere by process, manufacturing
562991	Cesspool cleaning services
238910	Cesspool construction
325199	Cetyl alcohol manufacturing
335211	Chafing dishes, household-type electric, manufacturing
332999	Chain fittings manufacturing
333923	Chain hoists manufacturing
332323	Chain ladders, metal, manufacturing
238990	Chain link fence installation
332618	Chain link fencing and fence gates made from purchased wire
331222	Chain link fencing, iron or steel, made in wire drawing plants
332618	Chain made from purchased wire
332213	Chain saw blades manufacturing
333991	Chain saws, handheld power-driven, manufacturing
332618	Chain, welded, made from purchased wire
339911	Chains or necklace, precious metal, manufacturing
333613	Chains, power transmission, manufacturing
334519	Chains, surveyor's, manufacturing
423830	Chainsaws merchant wholesalers
337121	Chair and couch springs, assembled, manufacturing
337215	Chair glides manufacturing

337215 Chair seats for furniture manufacturing

337122 Chairs (except upholstered), wood household-type, manufacturing

337214 Chairs (except wood), office-type, manufacturing

337127 Chairs, barber and beauty (i.e., hydraulic), manufacturing

337127 Chairs, barber, beauty shop (i.e., hydraulic), manufacturing

337125 Chairs, cane, wood household-type, manufacturing

339114 Chairs, dentist's, manufacturing

337124 Chairs, metal household-type (except upholstered), manufacturing

337127 Chairs, portable folding, auditorium-type, manufacturing

337127 Chairs, stacking, auditorium-type, manufacturing

337121 Chairs, upholstered household-type (except dining room, kitchen), manufacturing

337211 Chairs, wood office-type, manufacturing

212234 Chalcocite mining and/or beneficiating

212234 Chalcopyrite mining and/or beneficiating

339942 Chalk (e.g., artist's, blackboard, carpenter's, marking, tailor's), manufacturing

212312 Chalk crushed and broken stone mining and/or beneficiating

212312 Chalk, ground or otherwise treated, mining and/or beneficiating

339942 Chalkboards, framed, manufacturing

711130 Chamber musical groups

711130 Chamber orchestras

813910 Chambers of commerce

313210 Chambrays weaving

333512 Chamfering machines, metalworking, manufacturing

316110 Chamois leather manufacturing

424990 Chamois, leather, merchant wholesalers

312130 Champagne method sparkling wine, manufacturing

335122 Chandeliers, commercial, industrial, and institutional electric, manufacturing

335121 Chandeliers, residential, manufacturing

333311 Change making machines manufacturing

325182 Channel black manufacturing

237990 Channel construction

332323 Channels, furring metal, manufacturing

325191 Charcoal (except activated) manufacturing

325191 Charcoal briquettes, wood, manufacturing

424990 Charcoal merchant wholesalers

325998 Charcoal, activated, manufacturing

522210 Charge card issuing

813211 Charitable trusts, awarding grants

611699 Charm schools

481212 Charter air freight services

481211 Charter air passenger services

485510 Charter bus services (except scenic, sightseeing)

487210 Charter fishing boat operation

333515 Chasers (i.e., a machine tool accessory) manufacturing

212399 Chasers mining and/or beneficiating

332812 Chasing metals and metal products for the trade

336111 Chassis, automobile, manufacturing

336120 Chassis, heavy truck, with or without cabs, manufacturing

336112 Chassis, light truck and utility, manufacturing

423110 Chassis, motor vehicle, merchant wholesalers

561310 Chauffeur registries

611519 Chauffeur training

315991 Chauffeurs' hats and caps cut and sewn from purchased fabric (except apparel contractors)

315211 Chauffeurs' hats and caps, men's, cut and sew apparel contractors

315212 Chauffeurs' hats and caps, women's, cut and sew apparel contractors

522390 Check cashing services

521110 Check clearing activities of the central bank

522320 Check clearing services (except central banks)

522320 Check clearinghouse services (except central banks)

423420 Check handling machines merchant wholesalers

812990 Check room services

522320 Check validation services

332911 Check valves, industrial-type, manufacturing

333313 Check writing machines manufacturing

316993 Checkbook covers, (except metal), manufacturing

339911 Checkbook covers, precious metal, manufacturing

323116 Checkbooks and refills printing

339932 Checkers and checkerboards manufacturing

611620 Cheerleading instruction, camps, or schools

311513 Cheese (except cottage cheese) manufacturing

311513 Cheese analogs manufacturing

311941 Cheese based salad dressing manufacturing

424450 Cheese confections (e.g., curls, puffs) merchant wholesalers

311919 Cheese curls and puffs manufacturing

424430 Cheese merchant wholesalers

333294 Cheese processing machinery manufacturing

311513 Cheese products, imitation or substitute, manufacturing

311513 Cheese spreads manufacturing

311511 Cheese, cottage, manufacturing

311513 Cheese, imitation or substitute, manufacturing

311513 Cheese, natural (except cottage cheese), manufacturing

313210 Cheesecloths weaving

236210 Chemical (except petrochemical process type) plant construction

424690 Chemical additives (e.g., concrete, food, fuel, oil) merchant wholesalers

541690 Chemical consulting services

541330 Chemical engineering services

313311 Chemical finishing (e.g., fire, mildew, water resistance) broadwoven fabrics

313312 Chemical finishing (e.g., fire, mildew, water resistance) fabrics (except broadwoven and textile products)

424690 Chemical gases merchant wholesalers

423830 Chemical industries machinery and equipment merchant wholesalers

333298 Chemical kilns manufacturing

332710 Chemical milling job shops

333512 Chemical milling machines, metalworking, manufacturing

333298 Chemical processing machinery and equipment manufacturing

541710 Chemical research and development laboratories or services

327112 Chemical stoneware (i.e., pottery products) manufacturing

326191 Chemical toilets, plastics, manufacturing

115112 Chemical treatment of soil for crops

213112 Chemically treating oil and gas wells (e.g., acidizing, bailing, swabbing) on a contract basis

424690 Chemicals (except agriculture) (e.g., automotive, household, industrial, photographic) merchant wholesalers

424910 Chemicals, agricultural, merchant wholesalers

315191 Chemises made in apparel knitting mills

315212 Chemises, women's and girls', cut and sew apparel contractors

315231 Chemises, women's, misses' and girls', cut and sewn from purchased fabric (except apparel contractors)

111339 Cherry farming

113210 Cherry gum, gathering

339932 Chessmen and chessboards manufacturing

325191 Chestnut extract manufacturing

113210 Chestnut gum, gathering

321920 Chests for tools, wood, manufacturing

332999 Chests, fire or burglary resistive, metal, manufacturing

332999 Chests, money, metal, manufacturing

332999 Chests, safe deposit, metal, manufacturing

311340 Chewing gum base manufacturing

333294 Chewing gum machinery manufacturing

311340 Chewing gum manufacturing

424450 Chewing gum merchant wholesalers

312229 Chewing tobacco manufacturing

424940 Chewing tobacco merchant wholesalers

424440 Chicken and chicken products (except canned and packaged frozen) merchant wholesalers

333111 Chicken brooders manufacturing

321920 Chicken coops (i.e., crates), wood, wirebound for shipping poultry, manufacturing

321992 Chicken coops, prefabricated, wood, manufacturing

112310 Chicken egg production

112310 Chicken eggs (table, hatching) production

333111 Chicken feeders manufacturing

311119 Chicken feeds, prepared, manufacturing

112340 Chicken hatcheries

332618 Chicken netting made from purchased wire

112320 Chicken production (except egg laying)

311615 Chickens, processing, fresh, frozen, canned, or cooked (except baby and pet food)

311615 Chickens, slaughtering and dressing

424590 Chicks merchant wholesalers

111998 Chicory farming

624410 Child day care centers

624410 Child day care services

624410 Child day care services in provider's own home

624410 Child day care, before or after school, separate from schools

623990 Child group foster homes

624110 Child guidance agencies

624110 Child welfare services

621410 Childbirth preparation classes

622210 Children's hospitals, psychiatric or substance abuse

622310 Children's hospitals, specialty (except psychiatric, substance abuse)

721214 Children's camps (except day, instructional)

424330 Children's clothing merchant wholesalers

511199 Children's coloring book publishers (except exclusive Internet publishing)

516110 Children's coloring book publishers, exclusively on Internet

622110 Children's hospitals, general

316219 Children's shoes (except orthopedic extension, plastics, rubber) manufacturing

315119 Children's socks manufacturing

423920 Children's vehicles (except bicycles) merchant wholesalers

623990 Children's villages

311422 Chili con carne canning

311942 Chili pepper or powder manufacturing

311421 Chili sauce manufacturing

238220 Chilled water system installation

339992 Chimes and parts (musical instruments) manufacturing
335999 Chimes, electric, manufacturing
327390 Chimney caps, concrete, manufacturing
561790 Chimney cleaning services
238220 Chimney liner installation
561790 Chimney sweep (i.e., cleaning) services
238140 Chimney, brick, block or stone, contractors
238110 Chimney, concrete, construction
212324 China clay mining and/or beneficiating
337122 China closets, wood, manufacturing
327112 China cooking ware manufacturing
811490 China repair services
327112 China tableware, vitreous, manufacturing
442299 Chinaware stores
423440 Chinaware, commercial, merchant wholesalers
423220 Chinaware, household-type, merchant wholesalers
112930 Chinchilla production
311422 Chinese foods canning
311999 Chinese noodles, fried, manufacturing
111219 Chinese pea farming, bedding plant and seed production
313210 Chintzes weaving
333298 Chip placement machinery manufacturing
322130 Chipboard (i.e., paperboard) stock manufacturing
321219 Chipboard (i.e., particle core, wood chip face), manufacturing
322226 Chipboard, laminated or surface coated, made from purchased paperboard
321113 Chipper mills (except portable)
333112 Chippers (i.e., shredders), lawn and garden-type, manufacturing
333120 Chippers, portable, commercial (e.g., brush, limb, log), manufacturing

333291 Chippers, stationary (e.g., log), manufacturing
424450 Chips (e.g., corn, potato) merchant wholesalers
621310 Chiropractors' offices (e.g., centers, clinics)
332212 Chisels manufacturing
333991 Chissels, handheld power-driven, manufacturing
111219 Chive farming, field, bedding plant and seed production
325199 Chloral manufacturing
325320 Chlordane insecticides manufacturing
325188 Chloride of lime manufacturing
325212 Chlorinated rubber, synthetic, manufacturing
325188 Chlorine compounds, not specified elsewhere by process, manufacturing
325188 Chlorine dioxide manufacturing
325181 Chlorine manufacturing
325199 Chloroacetic acid manufacturing
325192 Chlorobenzene manufacturing
325120 Chlorodifluoromethane manufacturing
325120 Chlorofluorocarbon gases manufacturing
325199 Chloroform manufacturing
325192 Chloronaphthalene manufacturing
325192 Chlorophenol manufacturing
325199 Chloropicrin manufacturing
325212 Chloroprene rubber manufacturing
325212 Chlorosulfonated polyethylenes manufacturing
325188 Chlorosulfonic acid manufacturing
325192 Chlorotoluene manufacturing
311330 Chocolate (coating, instant, liquor, syrups) made from purchased chocolate
311320 Chocolate (e.g., coatings, instant, liquor, syrups) made from cacao beans
424490 Chocolate (except candy) merchant wholesalers
311320 Chocolate bars made from cocoa beans

424450 Chocolate candy merchant wholesalers
311330 Chocolate coatings and syrups made from purchased chocolate
311330 Chocolate covered candy bars made from purchased chocolate
311330 Chocolate covered granola bars made from purchased chocolate
311511 Chocolate drink (milk based) manufacturing
311511 Chocolate milk manufacturing
333294 Chocolate processing machinery manufacturing
311320 Chocolate, confectionery, made from cacao beans
711130 Choirs
334416 Chokes for electronic circuitry manufacturing
325414 Cholera serums manufacturing
325320 Cholinesterse inhibitors used as insecticides manufacturing
311412 Chop suey, frozen, manufacturing
115113 Chopping and silo filling
711510 Choreographers, independent
311412 Chow mein, frozen, manufacturing
311711 Chowders, fish and seafood, canning
311712 Chowders, frozen fish and seafood, manufacturing
621399 Christian Science practitioners' offices (e.g., centers, clinics)
424990 Christmas ornaments merchant wholesalers
453220 Christmas stores
333132 Christmas tree assemblies, oil and gas field-type, manufacturing
111421 Christmas tree growing
335129 Christmas tree lighting sets, electric, manufacturing
339999 Christmas tree ornaments (except electric, glass) manufacturing
327215 Christmas tree ornaments made from purchased glass

327212 Christmas tree ornaments, glass, made in glass making plants
424990 Christmas trees (e.g., artificial, cut) merchant wholesalers
339999 Christmas trees, artificial, manufacturing
454390 Christmas trees, cut, direct selling
334516 Chromatographic instruments, laboratory-type, manufacturing
334513 Chromatographs, industrial process-type, manufacturing
325131 Chrome pigments (e.g., chrome green, chrome orange, chrome yellow) manufacturing
332813 Chrome plating metals and metal products for the trade
325188 Chromic acid manufacturing
212299 Chromite mining and/or beneficiating
325188 Chromium compounds, not specified elsewhere by process, manufacturing
212299 Chromium concentrates beneficiating
212299 Chromium ore mining and/or beneficiating
325188 Chromium oxide manufacturing
331419 Chromium refining, primary
325188 Chromium salts manufacturing
622310 Chronic disease hospitals
334518 Chronographs manufacturing
334518 Chronometers manufacturing
334516 Chronoscopes manufacturing
333512 Chucking machines, automatic, metalworking, manufacturing
333515 Chucks (i.e., a machine tool accessory) manufacturing
238290 Church bell and tower clock installation
337127 Church furniture (except concrete, stone) manufacturing
423490 Church supplies (except plated ware, silverware) merchant wholesalers
813110 Churches
332313 Chutes, fabricated metal plate work, manufacturing
333294 Cider presses manufacturing
311941 Cider vinegar manufacturing

541320	City planning services
813410	Civic associations
236220	Civic center construction
541330	Civil engineering services
813311	Civil liberties organizations
921190	Civil rights commissions
921190	Civil service commissions
524291	Claims adjusting, insurance
524292	Claims processing services, insurance, third-party
114112	Clam digging
112512	Clam production, farm raising
333515	Clamps (i.e., a machine tool accessory) manufacturing
339112	Clamps, surgical, manufacturing
339992	Clarinets and parts manufacturing
316999	Clasps, shoe (leather), manufacturing
813410	Classic car clubs
711120	Classical dance companies
711130	Classical musical artists, independent
711130	Classical musical groups
212325	Clay (except kaolin, ball) mining and/or beneficiating
327112	Clay and ceramic statuary manufacturing
212325	Clay bleaching
423320	Clay construction materials (except refractory) merchant wholesalers
327124	Clay refractories (e.g., mortar, brick, tile, block) manufacturing
212324	Clay, ball, mining and/or beneficiating
212325	Clay, ceramic and refractory minerals, mining and/or beneficiating
212325	Clay, fire, mining and/or beneficiating
339942	Clay, modeling, manufacturing
212324	Clay, natural, mining and/or beneficiating
333298	Clayworking and tempering machinery manufacturing
812332	Clean room apparel supply services
236210	Clean room construction
339113	Clean room suits and accessories manufacturing
812320	Cleaners, drycleaning and laundry service (except coin-operated)
335212	Cleaners, household-type electric vacuum, manufacturing
561790	Cleaning (e.g., power sweeping, washing) driveways and parking lots
332813	Cleaning and descaling metals and metal products for the trade
812320	Cleaning and dyeing plants (except rug cleaning plants)
311212	Cleaning and polishing rice
561790	Cleaning building exteriors (except sand blasting, window cleaning)
238990	Cleaning building interiors during and immediately after construction
561740	Cleaning carpets
424690	Cleaning compounds and preparations merchant wholesalers
335999	Cleaning equipment, ultrasonic (except dental, medical), manufacturing
561720	Cleaning homes
333131	Cleaning machinery, mining-type, manufacturing
238990	Cleaning new building interiors immediately after construction
561720	Cleaning offices
213112	Cleaning oil and gas field lease tanks on a contract basis
213112	Cleaning out (e.g., bailing out, steam cleaning, swabbing) wells on a contract basis
212113	Cleaning plants, anthracite coal
212111	Cleaning plants, bituminous coal
561740	Cleaning plants, carpet and rug
115210	Cleaning poultry houses
561740	Cleaning rugs
561740	Cleaning services, carpet and rug
561720	Cleaning shopping centers

561790 Cleaning swimming pools
213112 Cleaning wells on a contract basis
213112 Cleaning, repairing, and dismantling oil and gas field lease tanks on a contract basis
321918 Clear and finger joint wood moldings manufacturing
522320 Clearinghouses, bank or check
523999 Clearinghouses, commodity exchange or securities exchange
316219 Cleated athletic shoes manufacturing
332211 Cleavers manufacturing
315299 Clerical vestments cut and sewn from purchased fabric (except apparel contractors)
315191 Clerical vestments made in apparel knitting mills
315211 Clerical vestments, men's and boys, cut and sew apparel contractors
315212 Clerical vestments, women's and girls', cut and sew apparel contractors
316211 Climbing shoes, plastics or plastics soled fabric upper, manufacturing
316211 Climbing shoes, rubber or rubber soled fabric upper, manufacturing
236220 Clinic construction
621111 Clinical pathologists' offices (e.g., centers, clinics)
621330 Clinical psychologists' offices (e.g., centers, clinics)
****** Clinics, medical—see type
621498 Clinics/centers of health practitioners from more than one industry practicing within the same establishment
621498 Clinics/centers of health practitioners with multi-industry degrees
321999 Clipboards, wood, manufacturing
332212 Clippers for animal use, nonelectric, manufacturing

332211 Clippers, fingernail and toenail, manufacturing
519190 Clipping services, news
332994 Clips, gun (i.e., 30 mm. or less, 1.18 inch or less), manufacturing
332995 Clips, gun (i.e., more than 30 mm., more than 1.18 inch), manufacturing
334518 Clock materials and parts (except crystals) manufacturing
334518 Clock or watch springs, precision, made from purchased wire
334310 Clock radios manufacturing
811490 Clock repair shops without retailing new clocks
448310 Clock shops
334518 Clocks assembling
334518 Clocks assembling from purchased components
423940 Clocks merchant wholesalers
561492 Closed captioning services, real-time (i.e., simultaneous)
512191 Closed captioning services, taped material
517510 Closed circuit television (CCTV)
334220 Closed circuit television equipment manufacturing
525990 Closed-end investment funds (except REITs)
453998 Closet organizer stores
238390 Closet organizer system installation
332115 Closures, metal, stamping
424130 Closures, paper and disposable plastics, merchant wholesalers
327910 Cloth (e.g., aluminum oxide, garnet, emery, silicon carbide) coated manufacturing
561990 Cloth cutting, bolting, or winding for the trade
333292 Cloth spreading machinery manufacturing
321999 Cloth winding reels, wood
332618 Cloth, woven wire, made from purchased wire

334512   Clothes dryer controls, including dryness controls, manufacturing

423620   Clothes dryer, gas and electric, merchant wholesalers

811412   Clothes dryer, household-type, repair and maintenance services without retailing new clothes dryers

321999   Clothes dryers (clothes horses), wood manufacturing

424990   Clothes hangers merchant wholesalers

326199   Clothes hangers, plastics, manufacturing

321999   Clothes poles, wood, manufacturing

326199   Clothespins, plastics, manufacturing

321999   Clothespins, wood, manufacturing

448150   Clothing accessories stores

424330   Clothing accessories, women's, children's, and infants', merchant wholesalers

541490   Clothing design services

532220   Clothing rental (except industrial launderer, linen supply)

811490   Clothing repair shops, alterations only

448130   Clothing stores, children's and infants'

448140   Clothing stores, family

448110   Clothing stores, men's and boys'

453310   Clothing stores, used

448120   Clothing stores, women's and girls'

339931   Clothing, doll, manufacturing

315292   Clothing, fur (except apparel contractors), manufacturing

315211   Clothing, fur, men's and boys', cut and sew apparel contractors

315212   Clothing, fur, women's, girls', and infants', cut and sew apparel contractors

315292   Clothing, leather or sheep-lined (except apparel contractors), manufacturing

315211   Clothing, leather or sheep-lined, men's and boys', cut and sew apparel contractors

315212   Clothing, leather or sheep-lined, women's, girls', and infants', cut and sew apparel contractors

424320   Clothing, men's and boys', merchant wholesalers

315291   Clothing, water resistant, infants', cut and sewn from purchased fabric (except apparel contractors)

315211   Clothing, water resistant, men's and boy's, cut and sew apparel contractors

315228   Clothing, water resistant, not specified elsewhere, men's and boys', cut and sewn from purchased fabric (except apparel contractors)

315239   Clothing, water resistant, not specified elsewhere, women's, misses', and girls', cut and sewn from purchased fabric (except apparel contractors)

315212   Clothing, water resistant, women's, girls' and infants', cut and sew apparel contractors

315299   Clothing, waterproof, cut and sewn from purchased fabric (except apparel contractors)

315211   Clothing, waterproof, men's and boys', cut and sew apparel contractors

315212   Clothing, waterproof, women's, girls', and infants', cut and sew apparel contractors

315291   Clothing, water-repellent, infants', cut and sewn from purchased fabric (except apparel contractors)

315211   Clothing, water-repellent, men's and boys', cut and sew apparel contractors

315228 Clothing, water-repellent, not specified elsewhere, men's and boys', cut and sewn from purchased fabric (except apparel contractors)

315239 Clothing, water-repellent, not specified elsewhere, women's, misses', and girls', cut and sewn from purchased fabric (except apparel contractors)

315212 Clothing, water-repellent, women's, girls', and infants', cut and sew apparel contractors

424330 Clothing, women's, children's, and infants', merchant wholesalers

339994 Cloths (except chemically treated), dusting and polishing, manufacturing

325612 Cloths, dusting and polishing, chemically treated, manufacturing

325998 Clove oil manufacturing

111940 Clover hay farming

111998 Clover seed farming

721310 Clubs, residential

339920 Clubs, sporting goods (e.g., golf, Indian), manufacturing

336350 Clutches and clutch facings, asbestos, manufacturing

525990 CMOs (collateralized mortgage obligations)

325413 Coagulation in-vitro diagnostic substances manufacturing

325412 Coagulation in-vivo diagnostic substances manufacturing

333922 Coal and ore conveyors manufacturing

212113 Coal beneficiating plants, anthracite

212111 Coal beneficiating plants, bituminous or lignite (surface or underground)

333131 Coal breakers, cutters, and pulverizers manufacturing

332322 Coal chutes, sheet metal (except stampings), manufacturing

454319 Coal dealers, direct selling

211111 Coal gasification at mine site

484220 Coal hauling, truck, local

211111 Coal liquefaction at mine site

423520 Coal merchant wholesalers

213113 Coal mining services (except site preparation and related construction contractor activities)

213113 Coal mining support services (tunneling, blasting, training, overburden removal)(except site preparation and related construction contractor activities)

486990 Coal pipeline transportation

211111 Coal pyrolysis

325192 Coal tar distillates manufacturing

324121 Coal tar paving materials made from purchased coal tar

424690 Coal tar products, primary and intermediate, merchant wholesalers

325211 Coal tar resins manufacturing

212113 Coal, anthracite, mining and/or beneficiating

212111 Coal, bituminous, beneficiating

212112 Coal, bituminous, underground mining or mining and beneficiating

212111 Coal, brown, mining and/or beneficiating

926120 Coast Guard (except academy)

483113 Coastal freight transportation to and from domestic ports

483114 Coastal passenger transportation to and from domestic ports

483113 Coastal shipping of freight to and from domestic ports

812331 Coat (e.g., barber's, beautician's, doctor's, nurse's) supply services

332618 Coat hangers made from purchased wire

315292 Coat linings, fur (except apparel contractors), manufacturing

315211 Coat linings, fur, men's and boys', cut and sew apparel contractors

315212   Coat linings, fur, women's, girls', and infants', cut and sew apparel contractors

448190   Coat stores

315999   Coat trimmings fabric cut and sewn from purchased fabric (except apparel contractors)

315211   Coat trimmings, fabric, men's and boys', cut and sew apparel contractors

315212   Coat trimmings, fabric, women's, girls', and infants', cut and sew apparel contractors

322226   Coated board made from purchased paperboard

322130   Coated board made in paperboard mills

324122   Coating compounds, tar, made from purchased asphaltic materials

238390   Coating concrete structures with plastics

332812   Coating metals and metal products for the trade

332812   Coating of metal and metal products with plastics for the trade

335110   Coating purchased light bulbs

322222   Coating purchased papers for nonpackaging applications (except photosensitive paper)

322221   Coating purchased papers for packaging applications

311320   Coatings, chocolate, made from cacao beans

315239   Coats (except fur, leather, tailored, waterproof), women's, misses', and girls', cut and sewn from purchased fabric (except apparel contractors)

315228   Coats (except fur, leather, tailored, waterproof, work), men's and boys', cut and sewn from purchased fabric (except apparel contractors)

315292   Coats (including tailored), leather or sheep-lined (except apparel contractors), manufacturing

315212   Coats (including tailored, leather, or sheep-lined), women's, girls', and infants', cut and sew apparel contractors

315292   Coats, artificial leather, cut and sewn from purchased fabric (except apparel contractors)

315211   Coats, artificial leather, men's and boys', cut and sew apparel contractors

315212   Coats, artificial leather, women's, girls', and infants', cut and sew apparel contractors

315292   Coats, fur (except apparel contractors), manufacturing

315211   Coats, fur, men's and boys', cut and sew apparel contractors

315212   Coats, fur, women's, girls', and infants', cut and sew apparel contractors

315291   Coats, infants' (except waterproof), cut and sewn from purchased fabric (except apparel contractors)

315292   Coats, leather, (except apparel contractors)

315211   Coats, leather, men's and boys', cut and sew apparel contractors

315212   Coats, leather, women's, girls', and infants', cut and sew apparel contractors

315211   Coats, men's and boys', cut and sew apparel contractors

315211   Coats, nontailored service apparel (e.g., laboratory, mechanics', medical), men's and boys', cut and sew apparel contractors

315225   Coats, nontailored service apparel (e.g., laboratory, mechanics', medical), men's and boys', cut and sewn from purchased fabric (except apparel contractors)

315212 Coats, nontailored service apparel (e.g., laboratory, medical, mechanics'), women's and girls', cut and sew apparel contractors

315239 Coats, nontailored service apparel (e.g., laboratory, medical, mechanics'), women's, misses', and girls', cut and sewn from purchased fabric (except apparel contractors)

315222 Coats, tailored (except fur, leather), men's and boys', cut and sewn from purchased fabric (except apparel contractors)

315234 Coats, tailored (except fur, leather), women's, misses', and girls', cut and sewn from purchased fabric

315299 Coats, waterproof (e.g., plastics, rubberized fabric, similar materials) rubberizing fabric and manufacturing coats

315211 Coats, waterproof (i.e., plastic, rubberized fabric, similar materials), men's and boy's, cut and sew apparel contractors

315212 Coats, waterproof (i.e., plastics, rubberized fabric, similar materials), women's, girls', and infants', cut and sew apparel contractors

315299 Coats, waterproof, (e.g., plastics, rubberized fabric, similar materials) cut and sewn from purchased fabric (except apparel contractors)

315212 Coats, women's, girls', and infants', cut and sew apparel contractors

331319 Coaxial cable made in aluminum wire drawing plants

423610 Coaxial cable merchant wholesalers

331422 Coaxial cable, copper, made from purchased copper in wire drawing plants

331491 Coaxial cable, nonferrous metals (except aluminum, copper), made from purchased nonferrous metals (except aluminum, copper) in wire drawing plants

335929 Coaxial cable, nonferrous, made from purchased nonferrous wire

334417 Coaxial connectors manufacturing

339991 Coaxial mechanical face seals manufacturing

325188 Cobalt 60 (i.e., radioactive cobalt) manufacturing

325188 Cobalt chloride manufacturing

325188 Cobalt compounds, not specified elsewhere by process, manufacturing

212299 Cobalt concentrates beneficiating

212299 Cobalt ores mining and/or beneficiating

331419 Cobalt refining, primary

325188 Cobalt sulfate manufacturing

325411 Cocaine and derivatives (i.e., basic chemicals) manufacturing

332913 Cocks, drain, plumbing, manufacturing

722410 Cocktail lounges

311999 Cocktail mixes, dry, manufacturing

424820 Cocktails, alcoholic, premixed, merchant wholesalers

311320 Cocoa (e.g., instant, mix, mixed with other ingredients, powder drink, powdered) made from cacao beans

424590 Cocoa beans merchant wholesalers

311320 Cocoa butter made from cocoa beans

311330 Cocoa, powdered drink, prepared, made from purchased chocolate

311330 Cocoa, powdered, made from purchased chocolate

311330   Cocoa, powdered, mixed with other ingredients, made from purchased chocolate
311225   Coconut oil made from purchased oils
311223   Coconut oil made in crushing mills
111339   Coconut tree farming
311999   Coconut, desiccated and shredded, manufacturing
114111   Cod catching
114111   Cod fishing
311711   Cod liver oil extraction, crude, produced in a cannery
311712   Cod liver oil extraction, crude, produced in a fresh and frozen seafood plant
325411   Cod liver oil, medicinal, uncompounded, manufacturing
325411   Codeine and derivatives (i.e., basic chemicals) manufacturing
333993   Coding, dating, and imprinting packaging machinery manufacturing
445299   Coffee and tea (i.e., packaged) stores
722330   Coffee carts, mobile
311920   Coffee concentrates (i.e., instant coffee) manufacturing
311920   Coffee extracts manufacturing
111339   Coffee farming
322299   Coffee filters made from purchased paper
311920   Coffee flavoring and syrups (i.e., made from coffee) manufacturing
333319   Coffee makers and urns, commercial-type, manufacturing
335211   Coffee makers, household-type electric, manufacturing
424490   Coffee merchant wholesalers
311920   Coffee roasting
333294   Coffee roasting and grinding machinery (i.e., food manufacturing-type) manufacturing
722213   Coffee shops, on premise brewing

311920   Coffee substitute manufacturing
337122   Coffee tables, wood, manufacturing
311920   Coffee, blended, manufacturing
312111   Coffee, iced, manufacturing
311920   Coffee, instant and freeze dried, manufacturing
454390   Coffee-break service providers, direct selling
237990   Cofferdam construction
487110   Cog railway, scenic and sightseeing, operation
237130   Co-generation plant construction
541720   Cognitive research and development services
811310   Coil rewinding (except on an assembly line or factory basis)
333518   Coil winding and cutting machinery, metalworking, manufacturing
332612   Coiled springs (except clock, watch), light gauge, made from purchased wire or strip, manufacturing
332611   Coiled springs, heavy gauge metal, manufacturing
335312   Coils for motors and generators manufacturing
336322   Coils, ignition, internal combustion engines, manufacturing
332996   Coils, pipe, made from purchased metal pipe
333313   Coin counting machinery manufacturing
561990   Coin pick-up services, parking meter
316993   Coin purses (except metal) manufacturing
339911   Coin purses, precious metal, manufacturing
423420   Coin sorting machines merchant wholesalers
333313   Coin wrapping machines manufacturing
339999   Coin-operated amusement machines (except jukebox) manufacturing
812310   Coin-operated drycleaners and laundries

713290 Coin-operated gambling device concession operators (i.e., supplying and servicing in others' facilities)

339999 Coin-operated gambling devices manufacturing

423990 Coin-operated game machines merchant wholesalers

334310 Coin-operated jukebox manufacturing

812310 Coin-operated laundry and drycleaning routes (i.e., concession operators)

423440 Coin-operated merchandising machine merchant wholesalers

713990 Coin-operated nongambling amusement device concession operators (i.e., supplying and servicing in others' facilities)

812990 Coin-operated personal service machine (e.g., blood pressure, locker, photographic, scale, shoeshine) concession operators

423440 Coin-operated phonographs and vending machines merchant wholesalers

333311 Coin-operated vending machines manufacturing

423940 Coins merchant wholesalers

423520 Coke merchant wholesalers

221210 Coke oven gas, production and distribution

324199 Coke oven products (e.g., coke, gases, tars) made in coke oven establishments

331111 Coke oven products made in iron and steel mills

324110 Coke, petroleum, made in petroleum refineries

335110 Cold cathode fluorescent lamp tubes manufacturing

332111 Cold forgings made from purchased iron or steel, unfinished

332112 Cold forgings made from purchased nonferrous metals, unfinished

325412 Cold remedies manufacturing

333516 Cold rolling mill machinery, metalworking, manufacturing

331221 Cold rolling steel shapes (e.g., bar, plate, rod, sheet, strip) made from purchased steel

493120 Cold storage locker services

423740 Cold storage machinery merchant wholesalers

236220 Cold storage plant construction

493120 Cold storage warehousing

311991 Cole slaw, fresh, manufacturing

212391 Colemanite mining and/or beneficiating

311612 Collagen sausage casings made from purchased hides

332439 Collapsible tubes (e.g., toothpaste, glue), light gauge metal, manufacturing

315191 Collar and cuff sets made in apparel knitting mills

315212 Collar and cuff sets, women's, girls' and infants', cut and sew apparel contractors

315239 Collar and cuff sets, women's, misses' and girls', cut and sewn from purchased fabric (except apparel contractors)

316110 Collar leather, manufacturing

111219 Collard farming, field, bedding plant and seed production

333515 Collars (i.e., a machine tool accessory) manufacturing

316999 Collars and collar pads (i.e., harness) manufacturing

316999 Collars, dog, manufacturing

333613 Collars, shaft for power transmission equipment, manufacturing

525990 Collateralized mortgage obligations (CMOs)

333293 Collating machinery for printing and bookbinding manufacturing

333313 Collating machinery, office-type, manufacturing

453220 Collectible gift shops (e.g., crystal, pewter, porcelain)

812320 Collecting and distributing agents, laundry and drycleaning

561440　Collection agencies
561440　Collection agencies, accounts
221320　Collection, treatment, and disposal of waste through a sewer system
335312　Collector rings for motors and generators manufacturing
453998　Collector's items shops (e.g., autograph, card, coin, stamp)
454113　Collector's items, mail-order houses
611691　College board preparation centers
611691　College entrance exam preparation instruction
611710　College selection services
611310　Colleges (except junior colleges)
611511　Colleges, barber and beauty
611210　Colleges, community
611210　Colleges, junior
611310　Colleges, universities, and professional schools
333515　Collets (i.e., a machine tool accessory) manufacturing
325620　Colognes manufacturing
424210　Colognes merchant wholesalers
334510　Colonscopes, electromedical, manufacturing
812199　Color consulting services (i.e., personal care services)
325131　Color pigments, inorganic (except bone black, carbon black, lamp black), manufacturing
325132　Color pigments, organic (except animal black, bone black), manufacturing
323122　Color separation services, for the printing trade
334516　Colorimeters, laboratory-type, manufacturing
423920　Coloring books merchant wholesalers
316110　Coloring leather
332813　Coloring metals and metal products (except coating) for the trade
339113　Colostomy appliances manufacturing

812220　Columbariums
212299　Columbite mining and/or beneficiating
212299　Columbium ores mining and/or beneficiating
327420　Columns, architectural or ornamental plaster work, manufacturing
332420　Columns, fractionating, heavy gauge metal, manufacturing
321918　Columns, porch, wood, manufacturing
316993　Comb cases (except metal) manufacturing
339911　Comb cases, precious metal, manufacturing
334512　Combination limit and fan controls manufacturing
112990　Combination livestock farming (except dairy, poultry)
334512　Combination oil and hydronic controls manufacturing
333111　Combines (i.e., harvester-threshers) manufacturing
313312　Combing and converting top
333292　Combing machinery for textiles manufacturing
313312　Combing textile fibers
115113　Combining, agricultural
332999　Combs, metal, manufacturing
326199　Combs, plastics, manufacturing
326299　Combs, rubber, manufacturing
334513　Combustion control instruments (except commercial, household furnace-type) manufacturing
541330　Combustion engineering consulting services
562211　Combustors, hazardous waste
562213　Combustors, nonhazardous solid waste
711510　Comedians, independent
711110　Comedy troupes
812990　Comfort station operation
314129　Comforters made from purchased fabrics
511120　Comic book publishers (except exclusive Internet publishing)

523140 Commodity contracts floor brokers

523130 Commodity contracts floor traders (i.e., acting as a principal in dealing commodities to investors)

523130 Commodity contracts floor trading (i.e., acting as a principal in dealing commodities to investors)

523140 Commodity contracts options brokerages

523130 Commodity contracts options dealing (i.e., acting as a principal in dealing commodities to investors)

523130 Commodity contracts traders (i.e., acting as a principal in dealing commodities to investors)

522298 Commodity Credit Corporation

523140 Commodity futures brokerages

541990 Commodity inspection services

212325 Common clay mining and/or beneficiating

212321 Common sand quarrying and/or beneficiating

212325 Common shale mining and/or beneficiating

923120 Communicable disease program administration

237130 Communication antenna construction

541430 Communication design services, visual

238210 Communication equipment installation

811213 Communication equipment repair and maintenance services

237130 Communication tower construction

926130 Communications commissions

423690 Communications equipment merchant wholesalers

334220 Communications equipment, mobile and microwave, manufacturing

334210 Communications headgear, telephone, manufacturing

926130 Communications licensing commissions and agencies

335929 Communications wire and cable, nonferrous, made from purchased nonferrous wire

331319 Communications wire or cable made in aluminum wire drawing plants

331422 Communications wire or cable, copper, made from purchased copper in wire drawing plants

331491 Communications wire or cable, nonferrous metals (except aluminum, copper), made from purchased nonferrous metals (except aluminum, copper) in wire drawing plants

311812 Communion wafer manufacturing

813319 Community action advocacy organizations

624190 Community action service agencies

624120 Community centers (except recreational only), adult

624110 Community centers (except recreational only), youth

813219 Community chests

611210 Community colleges

611210 Community colleges offering a wide variety of academic and technical training

925120 Community development agencies, government

813211 Community foundations

621498 Community health centers and clinics, outpatient

923120 Community health programs administration

624210 Community meals, social services

712110 Community museums

924120 Community recreation programs, government

923130 Community social service program administration

711110 Community theaters

335312 Commutators, electric motor, manufacturing

481111   Commuter air carriers, scheduled
485113   Commuter bus operation (except mixed mode)
485112   Commuter rail systems (except mixed mode)
485111   Commuter transit systems, mixed mode (e.g., bus, commuter rail, subway combination)
334310   Compact disc players (e.g., automotive, household-type) manufacturing
423990   Compact discs (CDs), prerecorded, merchant wholesalers
334611   Compact discs (i.e., CD-ROM), software, mass reproducing
334612   Compact discs, prerecorded audio, mass reproducing
334613   Compact discs, recordable or rewritable, blank, manufacturing
335110   Compact fluorescent light bulbs manufacturing
339911   Compacts, precious metal, manufacturing
316993   Compacts, solid leather, manufacturing
112990   Companion animals production (e.g., cats, dogs, parakeets, parrots)
624120   Companion services for disabled persons, the elderly, and persons diagnosed with mental retardation
333314   Comparators, optical, manufacturing
334511   Compasses, gyroscopic and magnetic (except portable), manufacturing
334519   Compasses, portable magnetic-type, manufacturing
541612   Compensation consulting services
541612   Compensation planning services
525190   Compensation, workers, insurance funds
311119   Complete feed, livestock, manufacturing

711510   Composers, independent
322214   Composite cans (i.e., foil-fiber and other combinations) manufacturing
562219   Compost dumps
325314   Compost manufacturing
325120   Compressed and liquefied industrial gas manufacturing
332911   Compressed gas cylinder valves manufacturing
424690   Compressed gases (except LP gas) merchant wholesalers
321219   Compression modified wood manufacturing
333220   Compression molding machinery for plastics manufacturing
339991   Compression packings manufacturing
532490   Compressor, air and gas, rental or leasing
237120   Compressor, metering and pumping station, gas and oil pipeline, construction
423830   Compressors (except air-conditioning, refrigeration) merchant wholesalers
333912   Compressors, air and gas, general purpose-type, manufacturing
423730   Compressors, air-conditioning, merchant wholesalers
336391   Compressors, motor vehicle air-conditioning, manufacturing
423740   Compressors, refrigeration, merchant wholesalers
238210   Computer and network cable installation
541710   Computer and related hardware research and development laboratories or services
423430   Computer boards, loaded, merchant wholesalers
423690   Computer boards, unloaded, merchant wholesalers
334419   Computer cable (e.g., monitor, printer) manufacturing
423690   Computer chips merchant wholesalers

541519 Computer disaster recovery services

813410 Computer enthusiasts clubs

811212 Computer equipment repair and maintenance services without retailing new computers

443120 Computer equipment stores

238330 Computer flooring installation

323116 Computer forms (manifold or continuous) printing

337124 Computer furniture, metal household-type, manufacturing

337122 Computer furniture, wood household-type, manufacturing

541512 Computer hardware consulting services or consultants

518210 Computer input preparation services

334119 Computer input/output equipment (except terminals) manufacturing

611420 Computer operator training

424120 Computer paper supplies merchant wholesalers

322231 Computer paper, single layered continuous, die-cut, made from purchased paper

423430 Computer peripheral equipment merchant wholesalers

532420 Computer peripheral equipment rental or leasing

811212 Computer peripheral equipment repair and maintenance, without retailing new computer peripheral equipment

325992 Computer printer toner cartridges manufacturing

423430 Computer printers merchant wholesalers

541511 Computer program or software development, custom

611420 Computer programming schools

541511 Computer programming services, custom

532420 Computer rental or leasing

811212 Computer repair and maintenance services, without retailing new computers

611519 Computer repair training

334111 Computer servers manufacturing

541511 Computer software analysis and design services, custom

541512 Computer software consulting services or consultants

541511 Computer software programming services, custom

511210 Computer software publishers, packaged

511210 Computer software publishing and reproduction

541511 Computer software support services, custom

334613 Computer software tapes and disks, blank, rigid and floppy, manufacturing

611420 Computer software training

454113 Computer software, mail-order houses

423430 Computer software, packaged, merchant wholesalers

443120 Computer stores

541513 Computer systems facilities (i.e., clients' facilities) management and operation services

541512 Computer systems integration analysis and design services

541512 Computer systems integration design consulting services

541512 Computer systems integrator services

334113 Computer terminals manufacturing

518210 Computer time leasing

518210 Computer time rental

518210 Computer time sharing services

621512 Computer tomography (CT-SCAN) centers

611420 Computer training (except repair)

532230 Computer video game rental

541512 Computer-aided design (CAD) systems integration design services

541512 Computer-aided engineering (CAE) systems integration design services

332312	Concrete reinforcing bars manufacturing
423510	Concrete reinforcing bars merchant wholesalers
332618	Concrete reinforcing mesh made from purchased wire
238110	Concrete repair
238110	Concrete resurfacing
238990	Concrete sawing and drilling (except demolition)
327390	Concrete tanks manufacturing
327999	Concrete, dry mixture, manufacturing
211112	Condensate, cycle, natural gas production
333294	Condensed and evaporated milk machinery manufacturing
311514	Condensed milk manufacturing
311514	Condensed, evaporated or powdered whey, manufacturing
332410	Condenser boxes, metal, manufacturing
335999	Condensers (except electronic), fixed and variable, manufacturing
334414	Condensers, electronic, manufacturing
423690	Condensers, electronic, merchant wholesalers
332410	Condensers, steam, manufacturing
335312	Condensers, synchronous, electric, manufacturing
423830	Condensing units (except air-conditioning, refrigeration) merchant wholesalers
423730	Condensing units, air-conditioning, merchant wholesalers
423740	Condensing units, refrigeration, merchant wholesalers
326299	Condom manufacturing
813990	Condominium corporations
531312	Condominium managers' offices, commercial
531311	Condominium managers' offices, residential
236117	Condominium operative builders
813990	Condominium owners' associations
561599	Condominium time share exchange services
236116	Condominium, multifamily, construction general contractors
236115	Condominium, single-family, construction general contractors
335931	Conductor connectors, solderless connectors, sleeves, or soldering lugs, manufacturing
327123	Conduit, vitrified clay, manufacturing
331210	Conduit, welded and lock joint, made from purchased iron or steel
335932	Conduits and fittings, electrical, manufacturing
327332	Conduits, concrete, manufacturing
322214	Cones (e.g., winding yarn, string, ribbon, cloth), fiber, made from purchased paperboard
311821	Cones, ice cream, manufacturing
327112	Cones, pyrometric, earthenware, manufacturing
311313	Confectioner's beet sugar manufacturing
311312	Confectioner's powdered sugar made from purchased raw cane sugar
311320	Confectionery chocolate made from cacao beans
333294	Confectionery machinery manufacturing
424450	Confectionery merchant wholesalers
722213	Confectionery snack shops, made on premises with carryout services
445292	Confectionery stores, packaged, retailing only
311340	Confectionery, nonchocolate, manufacturing

237110   Construction management, water and sewage treatment plant

237110   Construction management, water and sewer line

423610   Construction materials, electrical, merchant wholesalers

322233   Construction paper, school and art, made from purchased paper

322121   Construction paper, school and art, made in paper mills

212321   Construction sand and gravel beneficiating (e.g., grinding, screening, washing)

212321   Construction sand or gravel dredging

238990   Construction site cleanup contractors

333120   Construction-type tractors and attachments manufacturing

928120   Consulates

******   Consultants—see specific activity

813920   Consultants' associations

531390   Consultants', real estate (except appraisers), offices

541330   Consulting engineers' offices

541330   Consulting engineers' private practices

812990   Consumer buying services

541990   Consumer credit counseling services

561450   Consumer credit reporting bureaus

423620   Consumer electronics merchant wholesalers

532210   Consumer electronics rental

811211   Consumer electronics repair and maintenance services without retailing new consumer electronics

522291   Consumer finance companies (i.e., unsecured cash loans)

522291   Consumer lending

922190   Consumer product safety commissions

926110   Consumer protection offices

443112   Consumer-type electronic stores (e.g., radio, television, video camera)

334514   Consumption meters (e.g., gas, water) manufacturing

524128   Contact lens insurance, direct

339115   Contact lenses manufacturing

423460   Contact lenses merchant wholesalers

335931   Contacts, electrical (except carbon and graphite), manufacturing

335991   Contacts, electrical, carbon and graphite, manufacturing

322130   Container board stock manufacturing

336611   Container ship building

484110   Container trucking services, local

484121   Container trucking services, long-distance (TL)

327213   Containers for packaging, bottling, and canning, glass, manufacturing

332439   Containers, air cargo, light gauge metal, manufacturing

332999   Containers, foil (except bags), manufacturing

423840   Containers, industrial, merchant wholesalers

332439   Containers, light gauge metal (except cans), manufacturing

424130   Containers, paper and disposable plastics, merchant wholesalers

321920   Containers, wood, manufacturing

712110   Contemporary art museums

711120   Contemporary dance companies

623311   Continuing care retirement communities

325412   Contraceptive preparations manufacturing

213112   Contract services (except site preparation and related construction contractor activities) for oil and gas fields

******   Contractors—see specific activity

722213 Cookie shops, on premise baking and carryout service
311821 Cookies manufacturing
424490 Cookies merchant wholesalers
311821 Cookies, filled, manufacturing
335211 Cooking appliances (except convection, microwave ovens), household-type electric portable, manufacturing
311320 Cooking chocolate made from cacao beans
333319 Cooking equipment (i.e., fryers, microwave ovens, ovens, ranges), commercial-type, manufacturing
423440 Cooking equipment, commercial, merchant wholesalers
423620 Cooking equipment, electric household-type, merchant wholesalers
423720 Cooking equipment, gas, household-type, merchant wholesalers
424490 Cooking oils merchant wholesalers
611519 Cooking schools
331511 Cooking utensils, cast iron, manufacturing
332214 Cooking utensils, fabricated metal, manufacturing
327212 Cooking utensils, glass and glass ceramic, made in glass making plants
423220 Cooking utensils, household-type, merchant wholesalers
327112 Cooking ware (e.g., stoneware, coarse earthenware, pottery), manufacturing
327215 Cooking ware made from purchased glass
327212 Cooking ware made in glass making plants
327112 Cooking ware, china, manufacturing
327112 Cooking ware, fine earthenware, manufacturing
221330 Cooled air distribution
326199 Coolers or ice chests, plastics (except foam), manufacturing

326140 Coolers or ice chests, polystyrene foam, manufacturing
333415 Coolers, refrigeration, manufacturing
333415 Coolers, water, manufacturing
238220 Cooling tower installation
333415 Cooling towers manufacturing
321920 Cooperage manufacturing
321920 Cooperage stock (e.g., heading, hoops, staves) manufacturing
423840 Cooperage stock merchant wholesalers
321920 Cooperage stock mills
531311 Cooperative apartment managers' offices
236117 Cooperative apartment operative builders
236116 Cooperative apartment, construction general contractors
812331 Cooperative hospital laundries (i.e., linen supply services)
524113 Cooperative life insurance organizations
813990 Cooperative owners' associations
321920 Coopered tubs manufacturing
332212 Coordinate and contour measuring machines, machinists' precision tools, manufacturing
532420 Copier rental or leasing
327123 Coping, wall, clay, manufacturing
327390 Copings, concrete, manufacturing
331525 Copper alloy castings (except die-castings), unfinished, manufacturing
331423 Copper alloys (e.g., brass, bronze) made from purchased metal or scrap
331411 Copper alloys made in primary copper smelting and refining mills
331423 Copper and copper-based shapes (e.g., cake, ingot, slag, wire bar) made from purchased metal or scrap

333994   Core baking and mold drying ovens manufacturing
213112   Core cutting in oil and gas wells, on a contract basis
238910   Core drilling and test boring for construction
213112   Core drilling, exploration services, oil and gas field
333131   Core drills, underground mining-type, manufacturing
322214   Cores (i.e., all-fiber, nonfiber ends of any material), fiber, made from purchased paperboard
332992   Cores, bullet (i.e., 30 mm. or less, 1.18 inch or less), manufacturing
332997   Cores, sand foundry, manufacturing
423840   Cork merchant wholesalers
321999   Cork products (except gaskets) manufacturing
321999   Corks, bottle, manufacturing
111421   Corms farming
311230   Corn breakfast foods manufacturing
311919   Corn chips and related corn snacks manufacturing
424450   Corn chips and related corn snacks merchant wholesalers
311340   Corn confections manufacturing
321992   Corn cribs, prefabricated, wood, manufacturing
311221   Corn dextrin manufacturing
115114   Corn drying
111150   Corn farming (except sweet corn), field and seed production
311211   Corn flour manufacturing
311221   Corn gluten feed manufacturing
311221   Corn gluten meal manufacturing
333111   Corn heads for combines manufacturing
311211   Corn meal made in flour mills
311221   Corn oil cake and meal manufacturing
311225   Corn oil made from purchased oils
311221   Corn oil mills

311221   Corn oil, crude and refined, made by wet milling corn
333111   Corn pickers and shellers manufacturing
335211   Corn poppers, household-type electric, manufacturing
333294   Corn popping machinery (i.e., food manufacturing-type) manufacturing
333319   Corn popping machines, commercial-type, manufacturing
339113   Corn remover and bunion pad manufacturing
115114   Corn shelling
311221   Corn starch manufacturing
311221   Corn sweeteners (e.g., dextrose, fructose, glucose) made by wet milling corn
311999   Corn syrups made from purchased sweeteners
311213   Corn, malt, manufacturing
339112   Corneal microscopes manufacturing
311612   Corned meats made from purchases carcasses
316999   Corners, luggage, leather, manufacturing
339992   Cornets and parts manufacturing
332322   Cornices, sheet metal (except stampings), manufacturing
321918   Cornices, wood, manufacturing
112320   Cornish hen production
424490   Cornmeal, edible, merchant wholesalers
212325   Cornwall stone mining and/or beneficiating
923120   Coroners' offices
522130   Corporate credit unions
813211   Corporate foundations, awarding grants
541430   Corporate identification (i.e., logo) design services
541110   Corporate law offices
551114   Corporate offices
115210   Corralling, drovers
332323   Corrals, metal, manufacturing
325998   Correction fluids (i.e., typewriter) manufacturing
922140   Correctional boot camps

561210 Correctional facility operation on a contract or fee basis
922140 Correctional institutions
237120 Corrosion protection, underground pipeline and oil storage tank
322211 Corrugated and solid fiber boxes made from purchased paper or paperboard
322211 Corrugated and solid fiberboard pads made from purchased paper or paperboard
238160 Corrugated metal roofing installation
322211 Corrugated paper made from purchased paper or paperboard
331221 Corrugating iron or steel in cold rolling mills made from purchased iron or steel
315212 Corselets cut and sew apparel contractors
315231 Corselets, women's, misses', and girls', cut and sewn from purchased fabric (except apparel contractors)
315212 Corsets and allied garments (except surgical), women's, cut and sew apparel contractors
315231 Corsets and allied garments (except surgical), women's, misses', and girls', cut and sewn from purchased fabric (except apparel contractors)
339113 Corsets, surgical, manufacturing
325411 Cortisone, uncompounded, manufacturing
212399 Corundum mining and/or beneficiating
316993 Cosmetic bags (except metal) manufacturing
339911 Cosmetic bags, precious metal, manufacturing
325620 Cosmetic creams, lotions, and oils manufacturing
561910 Cosmetic kit assembling and packaging services
424210 Cosmetics merchant wholesalers
446120 Cosmetics stores
812112 Cosmetology salons or shops
611511 Cosmetology schools
541490 Costume design services (except independent theatrical costume designers)
711510 Costume designers, independent theatrical
339914 Costume jewelry manufacturing
423940 Costume jewelry merchant wholesalers
448150 Costume jewelry stores
532220 Costume rental
448190 Costume stores (including theatrical)
315299 Costumes (e.g., lodge, masquerade, theatrical) cut and sewn from purchased fabric (except apparel contractors)
315212 Costumes (e.g., lodge, masquerade, theatrical) women's, girls' and infants', cut and sew apparel contractors
315211 Costumes (e.g., lodge, masquerade, theatrical), men's and boys', cut and sew apparel contractors
337121 Cot springs, assembled, manufacturing
337124 Cots, metal household-type, manufacturing
337122 Cots, wood household-type, manufacturing
311511 Cottage cheese manufacturing
236115 Cottage construction general contractors
236117 Cottage operative builders
531110 Cottage rental or leasing
721199 Cottages, housekeeping
332722 Cotter pins, metal, manufacturing
424990 Cotton (except raw) merchant wholesalers
339113 Cotton and cotton balls, absorbent, manufacturing
333111 Cotton balers and presses manufacturing
314999 Cotton battings (except nonwoven batting) manufacturing

313111	Cotton cordage spun yarns made from purchased fiber
313210	Cotton fabrics, broadwoven, weaving
313221	Cotton fabrics, narrow woven weaving
111920	Cotton farming, field and seed production
322121	Cotton fiber paper stock manufacturing
115111	Cotton ginning
333111	Cotton ginning machinery manufacturing
333111	Cotton picker and stripper harvesting machinery manufacturing
313111	Cotton spun yarns made from purchased fiber
313113	Cotton thread manufacturing
339113	Cotton tipped applicators manufacturing
115113	Cotton, machine harvesting
424590	Cotton, raw, merchant wholesalers
111920	Cottonseed farming
311225	Cottonseed oil made from purchased oils
311223	Cottonseed oil, cake and meal, made in crushing mills
337121	Couch springs, assembled, manufacturing
337121	Couches, upholstered, manufacturing
311340	Cough drops (except medicated) manufacturing
325412	Cough drops, medicated, manufacturing
325412	Cough medicines manufacturing
334513	Coulometric analyzers, industrial process-type, manufacturing
334516	Coulometric analyzers, laboratory-type, manufacturing
325199	Coumarin manufacturing
325211	Coumarone-indene resins manufacturing
926110	Councils of Economic Advisers
624190	Counseling services
621410	Counseling services, family planning
541110	Counselors' at law offices
541110	Counselors' at law private practices
334519	Count rate meters, nuclear radiation, manufacturing
238350	Counter top, residential-type, installation
334514	Counter type registers manufacturing
337215	Counter units (except refrigerated) manufacturing
333515	Counterbores (i.e., a machine tool accessory), metalworking, manufacturing
332212	Counterbores and countersinking bits, woodworking, manufacturing
334511	Countermeasure sets (e.g., active countermeasures, jamming equipment) manufacturing
334514	Counters (e.g., electrical, electronic, mechanical), totalizing, manufacturing
316999	Counters (i.e., shoe cut stock), leather, manufacturing
333415	Counters and display cases, refrigerated, manufacturing
334514	Counters, revolution, manufacturing
333515	Countersinks (i.e., a machine tool accessory) manufacturing
238390	Countertop and cabinet, metal (except residential-type), installation
337215	Countertops (except kitchen and bathroom), wood or plastics laminated on wood, manufacturing
337110	Countertops (i.e., kitchen, bathroom), wood or plastics laminated on wood, manufacturing
326199	Countertops, plastics, manufacturing
327991	Countertops, stone, manufacturing
337110	Countertops, wood, manufacturing
334514	Counting devices manufacturing

532412	Crane rental or leasing without operator
238990	Crane rental with operator
423810	Cranes (except industrial) merchant wholesalers
333120	Cranes, construction-type, manufacturing
333924	Cranes, industrial truck, manufacturing
423830	Cranes, industrial, merchant wholesalers
423810	Cranes, mining, merchant wholesalers
333923	Cranes, overhead traveling, manufacturing
325998	Crankcase additive preparations manufacturing
336312	Crankshaft assemblies, automotive and truck gasoline engine, manufacturing
333512	Crankshaft grinding machines metal cutting type, manufacturing
321920	Crates (e.g., berry, butter, fruit, vegetable) made of wood, wirebound, manufacturing
488991	Crating goods for shipping
112512	Crawfish production, farm raising
238910	Crawler tractor rental with operator
114112	Crayfish fishing
339942	Crayons manufacturing
311511	Cream manufacturing
424430	Cream merchant wholesalers
325199	Cream of tartar manufacturing
333111	Cream separators, farm-type, manufacturing
333294	Cream separators, industrial, manufacturing
424430	Cream stations merchant wholesalers
311514	Cream, dried and powdered, manufacturing
311512	Creamery butter manufacturing
424430	Creamery products (except canned) merchant wholesalers
424490	Creamery products, canned, merchant wholesalers

313311	Crease resistant finishing of broadwoven fabric
313312	Crease resistant finishing of fabrics (except broadwoven)
561450	Credit agencies
323119	Credit and identification card imprinting and embossing
326199	Credit and identification card stock, plastics, manufacturing
524126	Credit and other financial responsibility insurance carriers, direct
561450	Credit bureaus
522210	Credit card banks
522210	Credit card issuing
812990	Credit card notification services (i.e., lost or stolen card reporting)
522320	Credit card processing services
561450	Credit investigation services
524113	Credit life insurance carriers, direct
561450	Credit rating services
541990	Credit repair (i.e., counseling) services, consumer
561450	Credit reporting bureaus
522130	Credit unions
333999	Cremating ovens manufacturing
812220	Crematories (except combined with funeral homes)
111219	Crenshaw melon farming, field, bedding plant and seed production
325192	Creosote made by distillation of coal tar
325191	Creosote made by distillation of wood tar
321114	Creosoting of wood
322299	Crepe paper made from purchased paper
325211	Cresol resins manufacturing
325211	Cresol-furfural resins manufacturing
325192	Cresols made by distillation of coal tar
325192	Cresylic acids made from refined petroleum or natural gas
115115	Crew leaders, farm labor

339113 Crutches and walkers manufacturing
423450 Crutches merchant wholesalers
532291 Crutches, invalid, rental
332420 Cryogenic tanks, heavy gauge metal, manufacturing
212399 Cryolite mining and/or beneficiating
311340 Crystallized fruits and fruit peel manufacturing
334419 Crystals and crystal assemblies, electronic, manufacturing
334517 CT/CAT (computerized axial tomography) scanners manufacturing
621512 CT-SCAN (computer tomography) centers
335313 Cubicles (i.e., electric switchboard equipment) manufacturing
111219 Cucumber farming (except under cover), field, bedding plant and seed production
111419 Cucumber farming, grown under cover
339993 Cuff links (except precious) manufacturing
339911 Cuff links, precious metal, manufacturing
332999 Cuffs, leg, iron, manufacturing
611519 Culinary arts schools
112310 Cull hen production
212113 Culm bank recovery, anthracite (except on a contract basis)
213113 Culm bank recovery, anthracite, on a contract basis
212111 Culm bank recovery, bituminous coal or lignite (except on a contract basis)
213113 Culm bank recovery, coal, on a contract basis
315212 Culottes, women's, girls' and infants', cut and sew apparel contractors
315239 Culottes, women's, misses', and girls', cut and sewn from purchased fabric (except apparel contractors)
111422 Cultivated florist greens growing

423820 Cultivating machinery and equipment merchant wholesalers
115112 Cultivation services
333111 Cultivators, farm-type, manufacturing
333112 Cultivators, powered, lawn and garden-type, manufacturing
926110 Cultural and arts development support program administration
325414 Culture media manufacturing
326191 Cultured marble plumbing fixtures manufacturing
326199 Cultured marble products (except plumbing fixtures) manufacturing
112512 Cultured pearl production, farm raising
326199 Cultured stone products (except plumbing fixtures) manufacturing
327332 Culvert pipe, concrete, manufacturing
238990 Culvert, concrete, residential and commercial paved area
332313 Culverts, fabricated metal plate work, manufacturing
237310 Culverts, highway, road and street, construction
332322 Culverts, sheet metal (except stampings), manufacturing
325110 Cumene made from refined petroleum or liquid hydrocarbons
324110 Cumene made in petroleum refineries
315999 Cummerbunds cut and sewn from purchased fabric (except apparel contractors)
315211 Cummerbunds, men's and boys', cut and sew apparel contractors
332313 Cupolas, fabricated metal plate work, manufacturing
212234 Cuprite mining and/or beneficiating
322299 Cups, molded pulp, manufacturing

325991   Custom compounding (i.e., blending and mixing) of purchased plastics resins

337212   Custom design interiors (i.e., coordinated furniture, architectural woodwork, fixtures), manufacturing

311119   Custom milling of animal feed

442299   Custom picture frame shops

333513   Custom roll forming machines, metalworking, manufacturing

332114   Custom roll forming metal products

321113   Custom sawmills

311611   Custom slaughtering

315223   Custom tailors, men's and boys' dress shirts, cut and sewn from purchased fabric

315222   Custom tailors, men's and boys' suits, cut and sewn from purchased fabric

315233   Custom tailors, women's, misses' and girls' dresses cut and sewn from purchased fabric (except apparel contractors)

541613   Customer service management consulting services

488510   Customs brokers

921130   Customs bureaus

541614   Customs consulting services

327215   Cut and engraved glassware made from purchased glass

315211   Cut and sew apparel contractors, men's and boys'

315212   Cut and sew apparel contractors, women's, girls', and infants'

111422   Cut flower growing

111422   Cut rose growing

316999   Cut stock for boots and shoes manufacturing

321912   Cut stock manufacturing

327991   Cut stone bases (e.g., desk sets pedestals, lamps, plaques and similar small particles) manufacturing

327991   Cut stone products (e.g., blocks, statuary) manufacturing

811490   Cutlery (e.g., knives, scissors) sharpening, household-type

423710   Cutlery merchant wholesalers

332211   Cutlery, nonprecious and precious plated metal, manufacturing

339912   Cutlery, precious metal (except precious plated), manufacturing

333512   Cut-off machines, metalworking, manufacturing

335931   Cutouts, switch and fuse, manufacturing

333131   Cutters, coal, manufacturing

332212   Cutters, glass, manufacturing

333515   Cutters, metal milling, manufacturing

113310   Cutting and transporting timber

213112   Cutting cores in oil and gas wells on a contract basis

332212   Cutting dies (e.g., paper, leather, textile) manufacturing

332212   Cutting dies (except metal cutting) manufacturing

333514   Cutting dies, metalworking, manufacturing

315211   Cutting fabric owned by others for men's and boys' apparel

315212   Cutting fabric owned by others for women's, girls', and infants' apparel

339114   Cutting instruments, dental, manufacturing

333512   Cutting machines, metalworking, manufacturing

238910   Cutting new rights of way

316110   Cutting of leather

424470   Cutting of purchased carcasses (except boxed meat cut on an assembly-line basis) merchant wholesalers

324191   Cutting oils made from refined petroleum

325998   Cutting oils, synthetic, manufacturing

113310   Cutting timber

327215   Cutting, engraving, etching, painting or polishing purchased glass

111422 Cuttings farming
325188 Cyanides manufacturing
212325 Cyanite mining and/or beneficiating
211112 Cycle condensate production
325110 Cyclic aromatic hydrocarbons made from refined petroleum or liquid hydrocarbons
324110 Cyclic aromatic hydrocarbons made in petroleum refineries
424690 Cyclic crudes and intermediates merchant wholesalers
325192 Cyclic crudes made by distillation of coal tar
325212 Cyclo rubber, synthetic, manufacturing
325192 Cyclohexane manufacturing
332313 Cyclones, industrial, fabricated metal plate work, manufacturing
325192 Cyclopentane made from refined petroleum or natural gas
325192 Cyclopropane made from refined petroleum or natural gas
325412 Cyclopropane medicinal preparations manufacturing
325191 Cycloterpenes manufacturing
335999 Cyclotrons manufacturing
333512 Cylinder boring machines metal cutting type, manufacturing
336312 Cylinder heads, automotive and truck gasoline engine, manufacturing
327332 Cylinder pipe, prestressed concrete, manufacturing
332618 Cylinder wire cloth made from purchased wire
332994 Cylinders and clips, gun (i.e., 30 mm. or less, 1.18 inch or less), manufacturing
332995 Cylinders and clips, gun (i.e., more than 30 mm., more than 1.18 inch), manufacturing
333995 Cylinders, fluid power, manufacturing
336340 Cylinders, master brake (new and rebuilt), manufacturing

332420 Cylinders, pressure, heavy gauge metal, manufacturing
334417 Cylindrical connectors, electronic, manufacturing
332991 Cylindrical roller bearings manufacturing
339992 Cymbals and parts manufacturing
339112 Cystoscopes (except electromedical) manufacturing
334510 Cystoscopes, electromedical, manufacturing
325413 Cytology and histology in-vitro diagnostic substances manufacturing
621511 Cytology health laboratories
112120 Dairy cattle farming
311119 Dairy cattle feeds supplements, concentrates, and premixes, manufacturing
424430 Dairy depots merchant wholesalers
311514 Dairy food canning
112420 Dairy goat farming
112111 Dairy heifer replacement production
541690 Dairy herd consulting services
115210 Dairy herd improvement associations
445299 Dairy product stores
424430 Dairy products (except canned, dried) merchant wholesalers
424490 Dairy products, dried or canned, merchant wholesalers
424430 Dairy products, frozen, merchant wholesalers
112410 Dairy sheep farming
237990 Dam construction
332312 Dam gates, metal plate, manufacturing
334512 Damper operators (e.g., electric, pneumatic, thermostatic) manufacturing
332322 Dampers, sheet metal (except stampings), manufacturing
238390 Dampproofing contractors
711130 Dance bands
713940 Dance centers, aerobic
711120 Dance companies

711310	Dance festival managers with facilities
711320	Dance festival managers without facilities
711310	Dance festival organizers with facilities
711320	Dance festival organizers without facilities
711310	Dance festival promoters with facilities
711320	Dance festival promoters without facilities
531120	Dance hall rental or leasing
713990	Dance halls
611610	Dance instruction
711120	Dance productions, live theatrical
611610	Dance schools
611610	Dance studios
711120	Dance theaters
621340	Dance therapists' offices (e.g., centers, clinics)
711120	Dance troupes
711510	Dancers, independent
313113	Darning thread (e.g., cotton, manmade fibers, silk, wool) manufacturing
332994	Dart guns manufacturing
339932	Darts and dart games manufacturing
518210	Data capture imaging services
334210	Data communications equipment (e.g., bridges, gateways, routers) manufacturing
518210	Data entry services
334513	Data loggers, industrial process-type, manufacturing
518210	Data processing computer services
541513	Data processing facilities (i.e., clients' facilities) management and operation services
423430	Data processing machines, computer, merchant wholesalers
518210	Data processing services (except payroll services, financial transition processing services)
323112	Databases flexographic printing without publishing
323111	Databases gravure printing without publishing
323110	Databases lithographic (offset) printing without publishing
323119	Databases printing (except flexographic, gravure, lithographic, quick, screen) without publishing
323113	Databases screen printing without publishing
111339	Date farming
339943	Date stamps, hand operated, manufacturing
311423	Dates, dried, made in dehydration plant
311340	Dates, sugared and stuffed, manufacturing
334518	Dating devices and machines (except rubber stamps) manufacturing
812990	Dating services
333923	Davits manufacturing
******	Day camps, instructional—see type of instruction
624120	Day care centers for disabled persons, the elderly, and persons diagnosed with mental retardation
624120	Day care centers, adult
624410	Day care centers, child or infant
624410	Day care services, child or infant
621310	DCs' (doctors of chiropractic) offices (e.g., centers, clinics)
621210	DDSs' (doctors of dental surgery) offices (e.g., centers, clinics)
325320	DDT (dichlorodiphenyltrichloroethane) insecticides manufacturing
922120	DEA (Drug Enforcement Administration)
332510	Dead bolts, metal, manufacturing
******	Dealers—see type
561440	Debt collection services
333512	Deburring machines, metalworking, manufacturing

332618	Delivery cases made from purchased wire
492210	Delivery service (except as part of intercity carrier network, U.S. Postal Service)
334515	Demand meters, electric, manufacturing
541720	Demographic research and development services
238910	Demolition contractor
238910	Demolition, building and structure
541890	Demonstration services, merchandise
336212	Demountable cargo containers manufacturing
325193	Denatured alcohol manufacturing
313210	Denims weaving
321219	Densified wood manufacturing
333315	Densitometers (except laboratory analytical) manufacturing
334516	Densitometers, laboratory analytical, manufacturing
334513	Density and specific gravity instruments, industrial process-type, manufacturing
339114	Dental alloys for amalgams manufacturing
339114	Dental chairs manufacturing
423450	Dental chairs merchant wholesalers
339114	Dental equipment and instruments manufacturing
423450	Dental equipment and supplies merchant wholesalers
811219	Dental equipment repair and maintenance services
325620	Dental floss manufacturing
339114	Dental glues and cements manufacturing
339114	Dental hand instruments (e.g., forceps) manufacturing
611519	Dental hygienist schools
621399	Dental hygienists' offices (e.g., centers, clinics)
339114	Dental impression materials manufacturing

339114	Dental instrument delivery systems manufacturing
524114	Dental insurance carriers, direct
339116	Dental laboratories
339114	Dental laboratory equipment manufacturing
541710	Dental research and development laboratories or services
611310	Dental schools
621210	Dental surgeons' offices (e.g., centers, clinics)
611519	Dental technician schools
339114	Dental wax manufacturing
621512	Dental X-ray laboratories
325611	Dentifrices manufacturing
424210	Dentifrices merchant wholesalers
813920	Dentists' associations
621210	Dentists' offices (e.g., centers, clinics)
423450	Dentists' professional supplies merchant wholesalers
325620	Denture adhesives manufacturing
325620	Denture cleaners, effervescent, manufacturing
339114	Denture materials manufacturing
339116	Dentures, custom made in dental laboratories
621399	Denturists' offices (e.g., centers, clinics)
561720	Deodorant servicing of rest rooms
325612	Deodorants (except personal) manufacturing
424690	Deodorants (except personal) merchant wholesalers
325620	Deodorants, personal, manufacturing
424210	Deodorants, personal, merchant wholesalers
238290	Deodorization (i.e., air filtration) system installation
561720	Deodorizing services
452111	Department stores (except discount department stores)
452112	Department stores, discount

926110 Development assistance program administration

813311 Developmentally disabled advocacy organizations

238910 Dewatering contractors

111334 Dewberry farming

325520 Dextrin glues manufacturing

311221 Dextrin made by wet milling corn

212319 Diabase crushed and broken stone mining and/or beneficiating

212311 Diabase mining or quarrying

325412 Diagnostic biological preparations (except in-vitro) manufacturing

811198 Diagnostic centers without repair, automotive

334510 Diagnostic equipment, electromedical, manufacturing

423450 Diagnostic equipment, medical, merchant wholesalers

334510 Diagnostic equipment, MRI (magnetic resonance imaging), manufacturing

621512 Diagnostic imaging centers (medical)

811219 Diagnostic imaging equipment repair and maintenance services

424210 Diagnostic reagents merchant wholesalers

325413 Diagnostic substances, in-vitro, manufacturing

424210 Diagnostics, in-vitro and in-vivo, merchant wholesalers

332212 Dial indicators, machinists' precision tools, manufacturing

621492 Dialysis centers and clinics

334510 Dialysis equipment, electromedical, manufacturing

325312 Diammonium phosphates manufacturing

332618 Diamond cloths made from purchased wire

339913 Diamond cutting and polishing

333514 Diamond dies, metalworking, manufacturing

327910 Diamond dressing wheels manufacturing

423940 Diamonds (except industrial) merchant wholesalers

423840 Diamonds, industrial, merchant wholesalers

212399 Diamonds, industrial, mining and/or beneficiating

315212 Diaper covers, water resistant and waterproof, cut and sew apparel contractors

315291 Diaper covers, waterproof, infants', cut and sewn from purchased fabric (except apparel contractors)

812331 Diaper supply services

314999 Diapers (except disposable) made from purchased fabrics

424330 Diapers (except paper) merchant wholesalers

322291 Diapers, disposable, made from purchased paper or textile fiber

322121 Diapers, disposable, made in paper mills

424130 Diapers, paper, merchant wholesalers

326299 Diaphragms (i.e., birth control device), rubber, manufacturing

323118 Diaries manufacturing

511199 Diary and time scheduler publishers (except exclusive Internet publishing)

516110 Diary and time scheduler publishers, exclusively on Internet

212325 Diaspore mining and/or beneficiating

334510 Diathermy apparatus, electromedical, manufacturing

334510 Diathermy units manufacturing

212399 Diatomaceous earth mining and/or beneficitating

327992 Diatomaceous earth processing beyond beneficiation

212399 Diatomite mining and/or beneficiating

325992 Diazo (i.e., whiteprint) paper and cloth, sensitized, manufacturing

325120 Dichlorodifluoromethane manufacturing

325188 Dichromates manufacturing

315212 Dickeys, women's, girls', and infants', cut and sew apparel contractors

315239 Dickeys, women's, misses' and girls', cut and sewn from purchased fabric (except apparel contractors)

333313 Dictating machines manufacturing

423420 Dictating machines merchant wholesalers

561410 Dictation services

611699 Diction schools

323117 Dictionaries printing and binding without publishing

323117 Dictionaries printing without publishing

323121 Dictionary binding without printing

511130 Dictionary publishers (except exclusive Internet publishing)

511130 Dictionary publishers and printing combined

516110 Dictionary publishers, exclusively on Internet

325211 Dicyandiamine resins manufacturing

333514 Die sets for metal stamping presses manufacturing

333512 Die sinking machines, metalworking, manufacturing

333511 Die-casting dies manufacturing

333513 Die-casting machines, metalworking, manufacturing

331521 Die-castings, aluminum, unfinished, manufacturing

331522 Die-castings, nonferrous metals (except aluminum), unfinished, manufacturing

322299 Die-cut paper products (except for office use) made from purchased paper or paperboard

322231 Die-cut paper products for office use made from purchased paper or paperboard

333994 Dielectric industrial heating equipment manufacturing

333514 Dies and die holders for metal cutting and forming (except threading) manufacturing

333515 Dies and taps (i.e., a machine tool accessory) manufacturing

332212 Dies, cutting (except metal cutting), manufacturing

333514 Dies, metalworking (except threading), manufacturing

333514 Dies, plastics forming, manufacturing

332212 Dies, steel rule (except metal cutting), manufacturing

333514 Dies, steel rule, metal cutting, manufacturing

333618 Diesel and semidiesel engines manufacturing

324110 Diesel fuels manufacturing

812191 Diet centers, non-medical

812191 Diet workshops

311514 Dietary drinks, dairy and nondairy based, manufacturing

325192 Diethylcyclohexane manufacturing

325199 Diethylene glycol manufacturing

813920 Dietitians' associations

621399 Dietitians' offices (e.g., centers, clinics)

336350 Differential and rear axle assemblies, automotive, truck, and bus, manufacturing

334513 Differential pressure instruments, industrial process-type, manufacturing

334516 Differential thermal analysis instruments, laboratory-type, manufacturing

332420 Digesters, industrial-type, heavy gauge metal, manufacturing

325412 Digestive system preparations manufacturing

238910 Digging foundations

334119 Digital cameras manufacturing

334111 Digital computers manufacturing

334513 Digital displays of process variables manufacturing

334515 Digital panel meters, electricity measuring, manufacturing

323115   Digital printing (e.g., billboards, other large format graphic materials)

323115   Digital printing (e.g., graphics, high resolution)

333293   Digital printing presses manufacturing

334515   Digital test equipment (e.g., electronic and electrical circuits and equipment testing) manufacturing

334310   Digital video disc players manufacturing

325412   Digitalis medicinal preparations manufacturing

325411   Digitoxin, uncompounded, manufacturing

325211   Diisocyanate resins manufacturing

237990   Dike and other flood control structure construction

111219   Dill farming, field and seed production

321113   Dimension lumber, hardwood, made from logs or bolts

321912   Dimension lumber, hardwood, resawing purchased lumber

321113   Dimension lumber, made from logs or bolts

321912   Dimension lumber, resawing purchased lumber

321113   Dimension lumber, softwood, made from logs or bolts

321912   Dimension lumber, softwood, resawing purchased lumber

321912   Dimension stock, hardwood, manufacturing

321912   Dimension stock, softwood, manufacturing

321912   Dimension stock, wood, manufacturing

327991   Dimension stone dressing and manufacturing

327991   Dimension stone for buildings manufacturing

212311   Dinension stone mining or quarrying

325199   Dimethyl divinyl acetylene (di-isopropenyl acetylene) manufacturing

325199   Dimethylhydrazine manufacturing

335931   Dimmer switches, outlet box mounting-type, manufacturing

722110   Diners, full service

337124   Dinette sets, metal household-type, manufacturing

326299   Dinghies, inflatable rubber, manufacturing

336612   Dinghy (except inflatable rubber) manufacturing

337124   Dining room chairs (including upholstered), metal, manufacturing

337125   Dining room chairs (including upholstered), plastics manufacturing

337122   Dining room chairs (including upholstered), wood, manufacturing

337124   Dining room furniture, metal household-type, manufacturing

337122   Dining room furniture, wood household-type, manufacturing

487210   Dinner cruises

711110   Dinner theaters

311412   Dinners, frozen (except seafood-based), manufacturing

311712   Dinners, frozen seafood, manufacturing

424420   Dinners, frozen, merchant wholesalers

326199   Dinnerware, plastics (except polystyrene foam), manufacturing

326140   Dinnerware, polystyrene foam, manufacturing

334515   Diode and transistor testers manufacturing

423690   Diodes merchant wholesalers

334413   Diodes, solid-state (e.g., germanium, silicon), manufacturing

212313   Diorite crushed and broken stone mining and/or beneficiating

212311   Diorite mining or quarrying

325192   Diphenylamine manufacturing

928120   Diplomatic services

813212	Disease awareness fundraising organizations
115112	Disease control for crops
813212	Disease research (e.g., cancer, heart) fundraising organizations
541940	Disease testing services, veterinary
313249	Dishcloths made in warp knitting mills
313241	Dishcloths made in weft knitting mills
423220	Dishes, household-type (except disposable plastics, paper), merchant wholesalers
424130	Dishes, paper and disposable plastics, merchant wholesalers
327112	Dishes, pottery, manufacturing
339932	Dishes, toy, manufacturing
321999	Dishes, wood, manufacturing
325611	Dishwasher detergents manufacturing
335228	Dishwashers, household-type, manufacturing
423620	Dishwashers, household-type, merchant wholesalers
423440	Dishwashing equipment, commercial-type, merchant wholesalers
333319	Dishwashing machines, commercial-type, manufacturing
335228	Dishwashing machines, household-type, manufacturing
325612	Disinfectants, household-type and industrial, manufacturing
518210	Disk and diskette conversion services
518210	Disk and diskette recertification services
332611	Disk and ring springs, heavy gauge metal, manufacturing
334112	Disk drives, computer, manufacturing
423430	Disk drives, computer, merchant wholesalers
334613	Diskettes, blank, manufacturing
423690	Diskettes, blank, merchant wholesalers
238910	Dismantling engineering structures (e.g., oil storage tank)
238290	Dismantling large-scale machinery and equipment
213112	Dismantling of oil well rigs on a contract basis
333913	Dispensing and measuring pumps (e.g., gasoline, lubricants) manufacturing
325132	Disperse dyes manufacturing
325510	Dispersions, pigment, manufacturing
541850	Display advertising services
423440	Display cases (except refrigerated) merchant wholesalers
337215	Display cases and fixtures (except refrigerated) manufacturing
333415	Display cases, refrigerated, manufacturing
423740	Display cases, refrigerated, merchant wholesalers
334513	Display instruments, industrial process control-type, manufacturing
541890	Display lettering services
339950	Displays (e.g., counter, floor, point-of-purchase) manufacturing
335912	Disposable flashlight batteries manufacturing
424130	Disposable plastics products (e.g., boxes, cups, cutlery, dishes, sanitary food containers) merchant wholesalers
334511	Distance measuring equipment (DME), aeronautical, manufacturing
325191	Distillates, wood, manufacturing
333994	Distillation ovens, charcoal and coke, manufacturing
424820	Distilled alcoholic beverages merchant wholesalers
325998	Distilled water manufacturing
312140	Distilleries
311213	Distiller's malt manufacturing

423830 Distillery machinery merchant wholesalers
312140 Distilling alcoholic beverages (except brandy)
312130 Distilling brandy
333298 Distilling equipment (except beverage) manufacturing
333294 Distilling equipment, beverage, manufacturing
312140 Distilling potable liquor (except brandy)
334515 Distortion meters and analyzers manufacturing
335313 Distribution boards, electric, manufacturing
335313 Distribution cutouts manufacturing
423610 Distribution equipment, electrical, merchant wholesalers
237120 Distribution line, gas and oil, construction
237110 Distribution line, sewer and water, construction
221330 Distribution of cooled air
221122 Distribution of electric power
221330 Distribution of heated air
221210 Distribution of manufactured gas
221210 Distribution of natural gas
221330 Distribution of steam heat
335311 Distribution transformers, electric, manufacturing
336322 Distributor cap and rotor for internal combustion engines manufacturing
813910 Distributors' associations
336322 Distributors for internal combustion engines manufacturing
551114 District and regional offices
922130 District attorneys' offices
333120 Ditchers and trenchers, self-propelled, manufacturing
325412 Diuretic preparations manufacturing
332212 Dividers, machinists' precision tools, manufacturing
451110 Diving equipment stores

561990 Diving services on a contract or fee basis
621210 DMDs' (doctors of dental medicine) offices (e.g., centers, clinics)
621511 DNA testing laboratories
531120 Dock and associated building rental or leasing
237990 Dock construction
488330 Docking and undocking marine vessel services
488310 Docking facility operations
621310 Doctors of chiropractic (DCs) offices (e.g., centers, clinics)
621210 Doctors of dental medicine (DMDs) offices (e.g., centers, clinics)
621210 Doctors of dental surgery (DDSs) offices (e.g., centers, clinics)
621320 Doctors of optometry (ODs) offices (e.g., centers, clinics)
621112 Doctors of osteopathy (DOs), mental health, offices (e.g., centers, clinics)
621111 Doctors of osteopathy (DOs, except mental health) offices (e.g., centers, clinics)
621391 Doctors of podiatry (DPs) offices (e.g., centers, clinics)
621330 Doctors of psychology offices (e.g., centers, clinics)
561439 Document copying services (except combined with printing services)
561439 Document duplicating services (except combined with printing services)
561410 Document preparation services
561990 Document shredding services
561410 Document transcription services
325110 Dodecene made from refined petroleum or liquid hydrocarbons
311111 Dog and cat food (e.g., canned, dry, frozen, semimoist), manufacturing
311111 Dog food manufacturing

316999   Dog furnishings (e.g., collars, harnesses, leashes, muzzles), manufacturing
711219   Dog owners, race (i.e., racing dogs)
812910   Dog pounds
112990   Dog production
711212   Dog racetracks
711219   Dog racing kennels
424990   Dogs merchant wholesalers
322299   Doilies, paper, made from purchased paper
339932   Doll carriages and carts manufacturing
339931   Doll clothing manufacturing
452990   Dollar stores
333924   Dollies manufacturing
423920   Dolls merchant wholesalers
339931   Dolls, doll parts, and doll clothing (except wigs) manufacturing
212312   Dolomite crushed and broken stone mining and/or beneficiating
212311   Dolomite mining or quarrying
327410   Dolomite, dead-burned, manufacturing
327410   Dolomitic lime manufacturing
212319   Dolomitic marble crushed and broken stone mining and/or beneficiating
212311   Dolomitic marble mining or quarrying
114111   Dolphin fishing
112920   Donkey production
332321   Door and jamb assemblies, metal, manufacturing
238350   Door and window frame construction
238350   Door and window, prefabricated, installation
332321   Door frames and sash, metal, manufacturing
321911   Door frames and sash, wood and covered wood, manufacturing
332322   Door hoods, sheet metal (except stampings), manufacturing
321911   Door jambs, wood, manufacturing

332510   Door locks, metal, manufacturing
332510   Door opening and closing devices (except electrical), metal, manufacturing
335999   Door opening and closing devices, electrical, manufacturing
321918   Door shutters, wood, manufacturing
444190   Door stores
321918   Door trim, wood molding, manufacturing
321911   Door units, prehung, wood and covered wood, manufacturing
238290   Door, commercial- or industrial-type, installation
238350   Door, folding, installation
314110   Doormats, all materials (except entirely of rubber or plastics), manufacturing
326199   Doormats, plastics, manufacturing
326299   Doormats, rubber, manufacturing
423310   Doors and door frames merchant wholesalers
326199   Doors and door frames, plastics, manufacturing
321911   Doors, combination screen-storm, wood, manufacturing
332321   Doors, metal, manufacturing
332999   Doors, safe and vault, metal, manufacturing
327215   Doors, unframed glass, made from purchased glass
321911   Doors, wood and covered wood, manufacturing
541870   Door-to-door distribution of advertising materials (e.g., coupons, flyers, samples)
454390   Door-to-door retailing of merchandise, direct selling
325510   Dopes, paint, and laquer, manufacturing
336612   Dories building
721310   Dormitories, off campus
236220   Dormitory construction

621112 DOs' (doctors of osteopathy), mental health, offices (e.g., centers, clinics)

621111 DOs' (doctors of osteopathy, except mental health) offices (e.g., centers, clinics)

334519 Dosimetry devices manufacturing

333294 Dough mixing machinery (i.e., food manufacturing-type) manufacturing

722110 Doughnut shops, full service

722213 Doughnut shops, on premise baking and carryout service

311812 Doughnuts (except frozen) made in commercial bakeries

311813 Doughnuts, frozen, manufacturing

424420 Doughs, frozen, merchant wholesalers

311211 Doughs, prepared, made in flour mills

311822 Doughs, refrigerated or frozen, made from purchased flour

333210 Dovetailing machines, woodworking-type, manufacturing

332722 Dowel pins, metal, manufacturing

321999 Dowels, wood, manufacturing

315291 Down-filled clothing, infants', cut and sewn from purchased fabric (except apparel contractors)

315211 Down-filled clothing, men's and boys', cut and sew apparel contractors

315228 Down-filled clothing, men's and boys', cut and sewn from purchased fabric (except apparel contractors)

315212 Down-filled clothing, women's, girls' and infants' cut and sew apparel contractors

315239 Down-filled clothing, women's, misses', and girls', cut and sewn from purchased fabric (except apparel contractors)

713920 Downhill skiing facilities without accommodations

238170 Downspout, gutter, and gutter guard installation

332322 Downspouts, sheet metal (except stampings), manufacturing

621391 DPs' (doctors of podiatry) offices (e.g., centers, clinics)

334513 Draft gauges, industrial process-type, manufacturing

334519 Drafting instruments manufacturing

423490 Drafting instruments merchant wholesalers

339942 Drafting materials (except instruments and tables) manufacturing

541340 Drafting services

337127 Drafting tables and boards manufacturing

423490 Drafting tables merchant wholesalers

541340 Draftsmen's offices

711212 Drag strips

333120 Draglines, crawler, manufacturing

325191 Dragon's blood manufacturing

333111 Drags, farm-type equipment, manufacturing

333120 Drags, road construction and road maintenance equipment, manufacturing

212399 Dragstones mining and/or beneficiating

561790 Drain cleaning services

332913 Drain cocks, plumbing, manufacturing

325612 Drain pipe cleaners manufacturing

332999 Drain plugs, magnetic, metal, manufacturing

327123 Drain tile, clay, manufacturing

238220 Drain, waste and vent system installation

237990 Drainage canal and ditch construction

237990 Drainage project construction

238910 Drainage system (e.g., cesspool, septic tank) installation

337110 Drainboards, wood or plastics laminated on wood, manufacturing

213113 Draining or pumping coal mines on a contract basis

213114 Draining or pumping of metal mines on a contract basis

213115 Draining or pumping of nonmetallic mineral mines (except fuels) on a contract basis

611610 Drama schools (except academic)

314121 Draperies made from purchased fabrics or sheet goods

423220 Draperies merchant wholesalers

812320 Drapery cleaning services

238390 Drapery fixture (e.g., hardware, rods, tracks) installation

339113 Drapes, surgical, disposable, manufacturing

333518 Draw bench machines manufacturing

315192 Drawers, apparel, made in apparel knitting mills

315211 Drawers, men's and boys', cut and sew apparel contractors

315221 Drawers, men's and boys', cut and sewn from purchased fabric (except apparel contractors)

315212 Drawers, women's, girls', and infants', cut and sew apparel contractors

315231 Drawers, women's, misses', and girls', cut and sewn from purchased fabric (except apparel contractors)

325998 Drawing inks manufacturing

331222 Drawing iron or steel wire from purchased iron or steel

331222 Drawing iron or steel wire from purchased iron or steel and fabricating wire products

333292 Drawing machinery for textiles manufacturing

337127 Drawing tables and boards, artist's, manufacturing

332212 Drawknives manufacturing

336611 Dredge building

237990 Dredging (e.g., canal, channel, ditch, waterway)

333120 Dredging machinery manufacturing

315992 Dress and semidress gloves cut and sewn from purchased fabric (except apparel contractors)

315191 Dress and semidress gloves made in apparel knitting mills

315211 Dress and semidress gloves, men's and boys', cut and sew apparel contractors

315212 Dress and semidress gloves, women's, girls', and infants', cut and sew apparel contractors

316219 Dress shoes, children's and infants', manufacturing

316213 Dress shoes, men's, manufacturing

316214 Dress shoes, women's, manufacturing

448190 Dress shops

532220 Dress suit rental

315999 Dress trimmings cut and sewn from purchased fabric (except apparel contractors)

315212 Dress trimmings, women's, girls', and infants', cut and sew apparel contractors

424990 Dressed furs and skins merchant wholesalers

337124 Dressers, metal, manufacturing

337122 Dressers, wood, manufacturing

315191 Dresses made in apparel knitting mills

424330 Dresses merchant wholesalers

315191 Dresses, hand-knit, manufacturing

315291 Dresses, infants', cut and sewn from purchased fabric (except apparel contractors)

315233 Dresses, women's, misses', and girls', cut and sewn from purchased fabric (except apparel contractors)

315212 Dresses, women's, misses', girls', and infants', cut and sew apparel contractors

316110 Dressing (i.e., bleaching, blending, currying, scraping, tanning) furs

315212 Dressing gowns, women's, girls', and infants', cut and sew apparel contractors

315231 Dressing gowns, women's, misses', and girls', cut and sewn from purchased fabric (except apparel contractors)

316110 Dressing hides

311615 Dressing small game

337124 Dressing tables, metal, manufacturing

337122 Dressing tables, wood, manufacturing

423450 Dressings, medical, merchant wholesalers

339113 Dressings, surgical, manufacturing

424490 Dried foods (e.g., fruits, milk, vegetables) merchant wholesalers

311612 Dried meats made from purchased carcasses

212392 Dried phosphate rock mining and/or beneficiating

325510 Driers, paint, and varnish, manufacturing

325992 Driers, photographic chemical, manufacturing

333315 Driers, photographic, manufacturing

334511 Driftmeters, aeronautical, manufacturing

333515 Drill bits, metalworking, manufacturing

332212 Drill bits, woodworking, manufacturing

333512 Drill presses, metalworking, manufacturing

333210 Drill presses, woodworking-type, manufacturing

332999 Drill stands, metal, manufacturing

238910 Drilled pier (i.e., for building foundations) contractors

238910 Drilled shaft (i.e., drilled building foundations) construction

339913 Drilling pearls

336611 Drilling and production platforms, floating, oil and gas, building

213111 Drilling directional oil and gas field wells on a contract basis

333132 Drilling equipment, oil and gas field-type, manufacturing

333131 Drilling equipment, underground mining-type, manufacturing

213111 Drilling for gas on a contract basis

213111 Drilling for oil on a contract basis

213111 Drilling gas and oil field wells on a contract basis

333512 Drilling machines, metalworking, manufacturing

325998 Drilling mud compounds, conditioners, and additives (except bentonites) manufacturing

424690 Drilling muds merchant wholesalers

213111 Drilling oil and gas field service wells on a contract basis

213112 Drilling rat holes and mouse holes at oil and gas fields on a contract basis

333132 Drilling rigs, oil and gas field-type, manufacturing

213113 Drilling services for coal mining on a contract basis

213114 Drilling services for metal mining on a contract basis

213115 Drilling services for nonmetallic mineral (except fuels) mining on a contract basis

213112 Drilling shot holes at oil and gas fields on a contract basis

213112 Drilling site preparation at oil and gas fields on a contract basis

213111 Drilling water intake wells, oil and gas field on a contract basis

237110 Drilling water wells (except water intake wells in oil and gas fields)

313210   Drills weaving
333131   Drills, core, underground mining-type, manufacturing
339114   Drills, dental, manufacturing
332212   Drills, hand held, nonelectric, manufacturing
333991   Drills, handheld power-driven (except heavy construction and mining type), manufacturing
333131   Drills, rock, underground mining-type, manufacturing
213112   Drill-stem testing in oil, gas, dry, and service well drilling on a contract basis
311999   Drink powder mixes (except chocolate, coffee, milk based, tea) manufacturing
311320   Drink powdered mixes, cocoa, made from cacao
311330   Drink powdered mixes, cocoa, made from purchased cocoa
311511   Drink, chocolate milk, manufacturing
238220   Drinking fountain installation
332998   Drinking fountains (except mechanically refrigerated), metal, manufacturing
326191   Drinking fountains (except mechanically refrigerated), plastics, manufacturing
333415   Drinking fountains, refrigerated, manufacturing
327111   Drinking fountains, vitreous china, non-refrigerated, manufacturing
722410   Drinking places (i.e., bars, lounges, taverns), alcoholic
312111   Drinks, fruit (except juice), manufacturing
333613   Drive chains, bicycle and motorcycle, manufacturing
336350   Drive shafts and half shafts, automotive, truck, and bus, manufacturing
512132   Drive-in motion picture theaters
237990   Drive-in movie facility construction
722211   Drive-in restaurants
611692   Driver education
611692   Driver training schools (except bus, heavy equipment, truck)
711219   Drivers, harness or race car
333612   Drives, high-speed industrial (except hydrostatic), manufacturing
561790   Driveway cleaning (e.g., power sweeping, washing) services
238990   Driveway paving or sealing
713990   Driving ranges, golf
488490   Driving services (e.g., automobile, truck delivery)
238310   Drop ceiling installation
332111   Drop forgings made from purchased iron or steel, unfinished
333513   Drop hammers, metal forging and shaping, manufacturing
812320   Drop-off and pick-up sites for laundries and drycleaners
813319   Drug abuse prevention advocacy organizations
623220   Drug addiction rehabilitation facilities (except licensed hospitals), residential
622210   Drug addiction rehabilitation hospitals
624190   Drug addiction self-help organizations
621420   Drug addiction treatment centers and clinics (except hospitals), outpatient
922120   Drug enforcement agencies and offices
424210   Drug proprietaries merchant wholesalers
446110   Drug stores
424210   Druggists' sundries merchant wholesalers
424210   Drugs merchant wholesalers
711130   Drum and bugle corps (i.e., drill teams)
333924   Drum cradles manufacturing
339992   Drums (musical instruments), parts, and accessories manufacturing
332439   Drums, light gauge metal, manufacturing
423840   Drums, new and reconditioned, merchant wholesalers

112390	Duck production
313210	Ducks weaving
311615	Ducks, processing, fresh, frozen, canned, or cooked
311615	Ducks, slaughtering and dressing
561790	Duct cleaning services
238290	Duct insulation installation
322222	Duct tape made from purchased materials
238220	Duct work (e.g., cooling, dust collection, exhaust, heating, ventilation) installation
331511	Ductile iron castings, unfinished, manufacturing
331511	Ductile iron foundries
332313	Ducting, fabricated metal plate work, manufacturing
335313	Ducts for electrical switchboard apparatus manufacturing
332322	Ducts, sheet metal, manufacturing
721214	Dude ranches
339920	Dumbbells manufacturing
238290	Dumbwaiter installation
333921	Dumbwaiters manufacturing
212325	Dumortierite mining and/or beneficiating
336212	Dump trailer manufacturing
484220	Dump trucking (e.g., gravel, sand, top soil)
562119	Dump trucking of rubble or brush with collection or disposal
333131	Dumpers, mining car, manufacturing
562219	Dumps, compost
562212	Dumps, nonhazardous solid waste (e.g., trash)
336211	Dump-truck lifting mechanisms manufacturing
315291	Dungarees, infants', cut and sewn from purchased fabric (except apparel contractors)
315211	Dungarees, men's and boys', cut and sew apparel contractors
315224	Dungarees, men's and boys', cut and sewn from purchased fabric (except apparel contractors)
315212	Dungarees, women's girls' and infants', cut and sew apparel contractors
315239	Dungarees, women's, misses', and girls', cut and sewn from pruchased fabric (except apparel contractors)
236116	Duplex (i.e., one unit above the other), construction general contractors
236115	Duplex (i.e., side-by-side) construction general contractors
531110	Duplex houses (i.e., single family) rental or leasing
236117	Duplex operative builders
335931	Duplex receptacles, electrical, manufacturing
325910	Duplicating inks manufacturing
532420	Duplicating machine (e.g., copier) rental or leasing
333512	Duplicating machines (e.g., key cutting), metalworking, manufacturing
425120	Durable goods agents and brokers, wholesale trade
425110	Durable goods business to business electronic markets, wholesale trade
311211	Durum flour manufacturing
333411	Dust and fume collecting equipment manufacturing
314999	Dust cloths made from purchased fabrics
238220	Dust collecting and bag house equipment installation
423730	Dust collection equipment merchant wholesalers
812332	Dust control textile item (e.g., cloths, mats, mops, rugs, shop towels) supply services
315212	Dusters (i.e., apparel), women's and girls', cut and sew apparel contractors

333315   Editing equipment, motion picture (e.g., rewinders, splicers, titlers, viewers), manufacturing
561410   Editing services
923110   Education offices, nonoperating
923110   Education program administration
923110   Education statistics centers, government
236220   Educational building construction
611710   Educational consultants
611710   Educational guidance counseling services
611710   Educational support services
611710   Educational testing evaluation services
611710   Educational testing services
813211   Educational trusts, awarding grants
813920   Educators' associations
114111   Eel fishing
325412   Effervescent salts manufacturing
541614   Efficiency management (i.e., efficiency expert) consulting services
321920   Egg cases, wood, manufacturing
335211   Egg cookers, household-type electric, manufacturing
112340   Egg hatcheries, poultry
311823   Egg noodles, dry, manufacturing
311991   Egg noodles, fresh, manufacturing
112310   Egg production, chicken
112330   Egg production, turkey
311999   Egg substitutes manufacturing
312140   Eggnog, alcoholic, manufacturing
311514   Eggnog, canned, nonalcoholic, manufacturing
311511   Eggnog, fresh, nonalcoholic, manufacturing
311511   Eggnog, nonalcoholic (except canned), manufacturing
111219   Eggplant farming (except under cover), field, bedding plant and seed production

111419   Eggplant farming, grown under cover
424440   Eggs merchant wholesalers
112310   Eggs, chicken (table, hatching) production
311999   Eggs, processed, manufacturing
334515   Elapsed time meters, electronic, manufacturing
313210   Elastic fabrics, more than 12 inches in width, weaving
313221   Elastic fabrics, narrow woven, manufacturing
339113   Elastic hosiery, orthopedic, manufacturing
325222   Elastomeric fibers and filaments manufacturing
325211   Elastomers (except synthetic rubber) manufacturing
325212   Elastomers, synthetic rubber, manufacturing
332322   Elbows for conductor pipe, hot air ducts, and stovepipe, sheet metal (except stampings), manufacturing
332919   Elbows, pipe, metal (except made from purchased pipe), manufacturing
921190   Election boards
334512   Electric air cleaner controls, automatic, manufacturing
334513   Electric and electronic controllers, industrial process-type, manufacturing
336111   Electric automobiles for highway use manufacturing
335999   Electric bells manufacturing
335211   Electric blankets manufacturing
423620   Electric blankets merchant wholesalers
335211   Electric comfort heating equipment, portable, manufacturing
238210   Electric contracting
335999   Electric fence chargers manufacturing
335311   Electric furnace transformers manufacturing
334512   Electric heat proportioning controls, modulating controls, manufacturing

335999   Electrochemical generators (i.e., fuel cells) manufacturing

333512   Electrochemical milling machines, metalworking, manufacturing

333512   Electrode discharge metal cutting machines manufacturing

333992   Electrode holders, welding, manufacturing

335991   Electrodes for thermal and electrolytic uses, carbon and graphite, manufacturing

334513   Electrodes used in industrial process measurement manufacturing

335110   Electrodes, cold cathode fluorescent lamp, manufacturing

333992   Electrodes, welding, manufacturing

334510   Electroencephalographs manufacturing

334510   Electrogastrograph manufacturing

332912   Electrohydraulic servo valves, fluid power, manufacturing

812199   Electrolysis (i.e., hair removal) salons

325412   Electrolyte in-vivo diagnostic substances manufacturing

334513   Electrolytic conductivity instruments, industrial process-type, manufacturing

334516   Electrolytic conductivity instruments, laboratory-type, manufacturing

333512   Electrolytic metal cutting machines manufacturing

334513   Electromagnetic flowmeters manufacturing

541360   Electromagnetic geophysical surveying services

334514   Electromechanical counters manufacturing

334510   Electromedical diagnostic equipment manufacturing

334510   Electromedical equipment manufacturing

423450   Electromedical equipment merchant wholesalers

334510   Electromedical therapy equipment manufacturing

331112   Electrometallurgical ferroalloy manufacturing

331111   Electrometallurgical steel manufacturing

334510   Electromyographs manufacturing

333992   Electron beam welding equipment manufacturing

335999   Electron linear accelerators manufacturing

334516   Electron microprobes, laboratory-type, manufacturing

334516   Electron microscopes manufacturing

334516   Electron paramagnetic spin-type apparatus manufacturing

333298   Electron tube machinery manufacturing

334411   Electron tube parts (e.g., bases, getters, guns) (except glass blanks) manufacturing

327215   Electron tube parts, glass blanks, made from purchased glass

327212   Electron tube parts, glass blanks, made in glass making plants

334515   Electron tube test equipment manufacturing

334411   Electron tubes manufacturing

333512   Electron-discharge metal cutting machines manufacturing

454112   Electronic auctions, retail

238210   Electronic containment fencing for pets, installation

238210   Electronic control installation and service

238210   Electronic control system installation

518210   Electronic data processing services

511140   Electronic directory publishers (except exclusive Internet publishing)

516110   Electronic directory publishers, exclusively on Internet

333292	Embroidery machinery manufacturing
424310	Embroidery products merchant wholesalers
313111	Embroidery spun yarns (e.g., cotton, manmade fiber, silk, wool) made from purchased fiber
313113	Embroidery thread (e.g., cotton, manmade fibers, silk, wool) manufacturing
335122	Emergency lighting (i.e., battery backup) manufacturing
621493	Emergency medical centers and clinics, freestanding
621910	Emergency medical transportation services, air or ground
922190	Emergency planning and management offices, government
453998	Emergency preparedness supply stores
624230	Emergency relief services
488410	Emergency road services (i.e., tow service)
624221	Emergency shelters (except for victims of domestic or international disasters or conflicts)
624230	Emergency shelters for victims of domestic or international disasters or conflicts
212399	Emery mining and/or beneficiating
811198	Emissions testing without repair, automotive
541612	Employee assessment consulting services
541612	Employee benefit consulting services
525110	Employee benefit pension plans
525120	Employee benefit plans (except pension)
524292	Employee benefit plans, third-party administrative processing services
485410	Employee bus services
541612	Employee compensation consulting services

561330	Employee leasing services
813930	Employees' associations for improvement of wages and working conditions
561310	Employment agencies
561310	Employment agencies, motion picture or video
561310	Employment agencies, radio or television
561310	Employment agencies, theatrical
561310	Employment placement agencies or services
561310	Employment referral agencies or services
561310	Employment registries
335932	EMTs (electrical metallic tube) manufacturing
112390	Emu production
325613	Emulsifiers (i.e., surface-active agents) manufacturing
325510	Enamel paints manufacturing
212322	Enamel sand quarrying and/or beneficiating
332214	Enameled metal cutting utensils
332812	Enameling metals and metal products for the trade
333994	Enameling ovens manufacturing
424950	Enamels merchant wholesalers
339114	Enamels, dental, manufacturing
323121	Encyclopedia binding without printing
511130	Encyclopedia publishers (except exclusive Internet publishing)
511130	Encyclopedia publishers and printing combined
516110	Encyclopedia publishers, exclusively on Internet
323117	Encyclopedias printing and binding without publishing
323117	Encyclopedias printing without publishing
337124	End tables, metal, manufacturing
337122	End tables, wood, manufacturing
111219	Endive farming (except under cover), field, bedding plant and seed production
111419	Endive farming, grown under cover

325411 Endocrine products, uncompounded, manufacturing

424210 Endocrine substances merchant wholesalers

621210 Endodontists' offices (e.g., centers, clinics)

334510 Endoscopic equipment, electromedical (e.g., bronchoscopes, colonoscopes, cystoscopes), manufacturing

325320 Endrin insecticides manufacturing

624229 Energy assistance programs

541690 Energy consulting services

334512 Energy cutoff controls, residential and commercial types, manufacturing

926110 Energy development and conservation agencies, nonoperating

926130 Energy development and conservation programs, government

334515 Energy measuring equipment, electrical, manufacturing

926110 Energy program administration

331319 Energy wire or cable made in aluminum wire drawing plants

331422 Energy wire or cable, copper, made from purchased copper in wire drawing plants

331491 Energy wire or cable, nonferrous metals (except aluminum, copper), made from purchased nonferrous metals (except aluminum, copper) in wire drawing plants

924110 Enforcement of environmental and pollution control regulations

336312 Engine block assemblies, automotive and truck gasoline, manufacturing

325998 Engine degreasers manufacturing

336311 Engine intake and exhaust valves manufacturing

811310 Engine repair (except automotive, small engine)

811111 Engine repair and replacement shops, automotive

811411 Engine repair, small engine

325998 Engine starting fluids manufacturing

423120 Engine testing equipment, motor vehicle, merchant wholesalers

541330 Engineering consulting services

541330 Engineering design services

541710 Engineering research and development laboratories or services

541330 Engineering services

238320 Engineering structure (e.g., oil storage tank, water tower) painting

813920 Engineers' associations

423490 Engineers' equipment and supplies merchant wholesalers

541330 Engineers' offices

541330 Engineers' private practices

336412 Engines and engine parts, aircraft (except carburetors, pistons, piston rings, valves), manufacturing

336312 Engines and parts (except diesel), automotive and truck, manufacturing

423860 Engines and parts, aircraft, merchant wholesalers

423120 Engines and parts, automotive, new, merchant wholesalers

423860 Engines and turbines, marine, merchant wholesalers

333618 Engines, diesel and semidiesel, manufacturing

333618 Engines, diesel locomotive, manufacturing

423830 Engines, internal combustion (except aircraft, automotive), merchant wholesalers

333618 Engines, internal combustion (except aircraft, nondiesel automotive), manufacturing

333618 Engines, natural gas, manufacturing

111219 English pea farming (except under cover), field, bedding plant and seed production

111419 English pea farming, grown under cover

332212 Engraver's handtools, nonpowered, manufacturing

339911 Engraving and etching precious metal (except precious plated) jewelry and flatware

339912 Engraving and etching precious metal flatware

339914 Engraving and/or etching costume jewelry

423830 Engraving machinery merchant wholesalers

332812 Engraving metals and metal products (except printing plates) for the trade

323122 Engraving printing plate, for the printing trade

333315 Enlargers, photographic, manufacturing

315191 Ensemble dresses made in apparel knitting mills

315212 Ensemble dresses, women's, girls', and infants', cut and sew apparel contractors

315233 Ensemble dresses, women's, misses', and girls', cut and sewn from purchased fabric (except apparel contractors)

711130 Ensembles, musical

926110 Enterprise development program administration

711410 Entertainers' agents or managers

711510 Entertainers, independent

516110 Entertainment sites, Internet

541710 Entomological research and development laboratories or services

115112 Entomological service, agricultural

541690 Entomology consulting services

333291 Envelope making machinery manufacturing

424110 Envelope paper, bulk, merchant wholesalers

333313 Envelope stuffing, sealing, and addressing machinery manufacturing

322232 Envelopes (i.e., mailing, stationery) made from any material

424120 Envelopes merchant wholesalers

813312 Environmental advocacy organizations

541620 Environmental consulting services

238210 Environmental control system installation

541330 Environmental engineering services

923120 Environmental health program administration

924110 Environmental protection program administration

562910 Environmental remediation services

541710 Environmental research and development laboratories or services

541380 Environmental testing laboratories or services

325413 Enzyme and isoenzyme in-vitro diagnostic substances manufacturing

325199 Enzyme proteins (i.e., basic synthetic chemicals) (except pharmaceutical use) manufacturing

325411 Enzyme proteins (i.e., basic synthetic chemicals), pharmaceutical use, manufacturing

325132 Eosin dyes manufacturing

325411 Ephedrine and derivatives (i.e., basic chemicals) manufacturing

325211 Epichlorohydrin bisphenol manufacturing

325211 Epichlorohydrin diphenol manufacturing

325212 Epichlorohydrin elastomers manufacturing

325520 Epoxy adhesives manufacturing

238190 Epoxy application contractors

325510 Epoxy coatings made from purchased resins

325211 Epoxy resins manufacturing

324110	Ethylene made in petroleum refineries
325199	Ethylene oxide manufacturing
325212	Ethylene-propylene rubber manufacturing
325212	Ethylene-propylene-nonconjugated diene (EPDM) rubber manufacturing
325211	Ethylene-vinyl acetate resins manufacturing
325998	Eucalyptus oil manufacturing
311514	Evaporated milk manufacturing
334519	Evaporation meters manufacturing
333415	Evaporative condensers (i.e., heat transfer equipment) manufacturing
611691	Exam preparation services
423810	Excavating machinery and equipment merchant wholesalers
213112	Excavating mud pits, slush pits, and cellars at oil and gas fields on a contract basis
238910	Excavating, earthmoving or land clearing, agricultural
238910	Excavating, earthmoving or land clearing, mining (except overburden removal at open pit mine sites or quarries)
238910	Excavating, earthmoving, or land clearing contractors
238910	Excavation contractors
333120	Excavators (e.g., power shovels) manufacturing
321999	Excelsior (e.g., pads, wrappers) manufacturing
523999	Exchange clearinghouses, commodities or securities
332410	Exchangers, heat, manufacturing
523210	Exchanges, commodity contracts
523210	Exchanges, securities
335312	Exciter assemblies, motor and generator, manufacturing
531210	Exclusive buyers' agencies
531210	Exclusive buyers' agents, offices of
487210	Excursion boat operation
921140	Executive and legislative office combinations
561110	Executive management services
921110	Executive offices, federal, state, and local (e.g., governor, mayor, president)
541612	Executive placement consulting services
541612	Executive search consulting services
531120	Executive suites (i.e., full service office space provision)
713940	Exercise centers
532292	Exercise equipment rental
451110	Exercise equipment stores
339920	Exercise machines manufacturing
621340	Exercise physiologists' offices (e.g., centers, clinics)
336399	Exhaust and tail pipes, automotive, truck, and bus, manufacturing
333412	Exhaust fans, industrial and commercial-type, manufacturing
238220	Exhaust system (e.g., kitchens, industrial work areas) installation
811112	Exhaust system repair and replacement shops, automotive
336399	Exhaust systems and parts, automotive, truck, and bus, manufacturing
531120	Exhibition hall, no promotion of events, rental or leasing
624190	Exoffender rehabilitation agencies
624190	Exoffender self-help organizations
316110	Exotic leathers manufacturing
332312	Expansion joints, metal, manufacturing
541710	Experimental farms
213113	Exploration services for coal (except geophysical surveying and mapping) on a contract basis
213114	Exploration services for metal (except geophysical surveying and mapping) on a contract basis

451130	Fabric shops
325612	Fabric softeners manufacturing
238310	Fabric wall system, noise insulating, installation
332312	Fabricated bar joists manufacturing
332996	Fabricated pipe and pipe fittings made from purchased pipe
332313	Fabricated plate work manufacturing
314991	Fabricated rope products (e.g., nets, slings) made in cordage or twine mills
332312	Fabricated structural metal manufacturing
321213	Fabricated structural wood members (except trusses) manufacturing
238390	Fabrication, metal cabinet or countertop, on site
313210	Fabrics (except rug, tire fabrics), broadwoven, weaving
314992	Fabrics for reinforcing rubber tires, industrial belting, and fuel cells manufacturing
313311	Fabrics, broadwoven, finishing
313311	Fabrics, broadwoven, mercerizing
313249	Fabrics, knit, made in warp knit fabric mills
313241	Fabrics, knit, made in weft knit fabric mills
313249	Fabrics, lace, made in lace mills
313221	Fabrics, narrow woven, weaving
313230	Fabrics, nonwoven, manufacturing
424310	Fabrics, textile (except burlap, felt), merchant wholesalers
332618	Fabrics, woven wire, made from purchased wire
325620	Face creams (e.g., cleansing, moisturizing) manufacturing
335932	Face plates (i.e., outlet or switch covers) manufacturing
525990	Face-amount certificate funds
812112	Facial salons
424130	Facial tissue merchant wholesalers
322291	Facial tissues made from purchased paper
322121	Facial tissues made in paper mills
561210	Facilities (except computer operation) support services
541513	Facilities (i.e., clients' facilities) management and operation services, computer systems or data processing
541513	Facilities (i.e., clients' facilities) support services, computer systems or data processing
517110	Facilities-based telecommunication carriers (except wireless)
333512	Facing machines, metalworking, manufacturing
334210	Facsimile equipment, standalone, manufacturing
532420	Facsimile machine rental or leasing
811213	Facsimile machine repair and maintenance services
423690	Facsimile machines merchant wholesalers
325992	Facsimile toner cartridges manufacturing
522298	Factoring accounts receivable
236210	Factory construction
711310	Fair managers with facilities, agricultural
711320	Fair managers without facilities, agricultural
711310	Fair organizers with facilities, agricultural
711320	Fair organizers without facilities, agricultural
711310	Fair promoters with facilities
711310	Fair promoters with facilities, agricultural
711320	Fair promoters without facilities
711320	Fair promoters without facilities, agricultural
238190	Falsework construction
448140	Family clothing stores
621210	Family dentists' offices (e.g., centers, clinics)
713120	Family fun centers
541110	Family law offices
621111	Family physicians' offices (e.g., centers, clinics)

327111 Faucet handles, vitreous china and earthenware, manufacturing

332913 Faucets, plumbing, manufacturing

532420 Fax machine rental or leasing

811213 Fax machine repair and maintenance services

339999 Feather dusters manufacturing

315291 Feather-filled clothing, infants', cut and sewn from purchased fabric (except apparel contractors)

315239 Feather-filled clothing, jackets, and vests, women's, misses', and juniors', cut and sewn from purchased fabric (except apparel contractors)

315211 Feather-filled clothing, men's and boys', cut and sew apparel contractors

315228 Feather-filled clothing, men's and boys', cut and sewn from purchased fabric (except apparel contractors)

315212 Feather-filled clothing, women's, girls', and infants', cut and sew apparel contractors

424590 Feathers merchant wholesalers

339999 Feathers, preparing (i.e., for use in apparel and textile products)

519110 Feature syndicates (i.e., advice columns, comic, news)

522294 Federal Agricultural Mortgage Corporation

926120 Federal Aviation Administration (except air traffic control)

922120 Federal Bureau of Investigation (FBI)

926130 Federal Communications Commission (FCC)

522130 Federal credit unions

522298 Federal Home Loan Banks (FHLB)

522294 Federal Home Loan Mortgage Corporation (FHLMC)

522294 Federal Intermediate Credit Bank

522292 Federal Land Banks

522294 Federal National Mortgage Association (FNMA)

922120 Federal police services

521110 Federal Reserve Banks or Branches

921130 Federal Reserve Board of Governors

522120 Federal savings and loan associations (S&L)

522120 Federal savings banks

813219 Federated charities

813930 Federation of workers, labor organizations

813930 Federations of labor

424910 Feed additives merchant wholesalers

316999 Feed bags for horses manufacturing

314911 Feed bags made from purchased woven or knitted materials

311119 Feed concentrates, animal, manufacturing

311514 Feed grade dry milk products manufacturing

311119 Feed premixes, animal, manufacturing

333111 Feed processing equipment, farm-type, manufacturing

444220 Feed stores (except pet)

453910 Feed stores, pet

311119 Feed supplements, animal (except cat, dog), manufacturing

311111 Feed supplements, dog and cat, manufacturing

112112 Feed yards (except stockyards for transportation), cattle

112111 Feeder calf production

112210 Feeder pig farming

335311 Feeder voltage regulators and boosters (i.e., electrical transformers) manufacturing

423820 Feeders, animal, merchant wholesalers

333131 Feeders, mineral beneficiating-type, manufacturing

112112 Feedlots (except stockyards for transportation), cattle

212393 Fertilizer minerals, natural, mining and/or beneficiating

325314 Fertilizers, mixed, made in plants not manufacturing fertilizer materials

325311 Fertilizers, mixed, made in plants producing nitrogenous fertilizer materials

325312 Fertilizers, mixed, made in plants producing phosphatic fertilizer materials

325311 Fertilizers, natural organic (except compost), manufacturing

325311 Fertilizers, of animal waste origin, manufacturing

325311 Fertilizers, of sewage origin, manufacturing

561730 Fertilizing lawns

333111 Fertilizing machinery, farm-type, manufacturing

111998 Fescue seed farming

711310 Festival managers with facilities

711320 Festival managers without facilities

711310 Festival of arts managers with facilities

711320 Festival of arts managers without facilities

711310 Festival of arts organizers with facilities

711320 Festival of arts organizers without facilities

711310 Festival of arts promoters with facilities

711320 Festival of arts promoters without facilities

711310 Festival organizers with facilities

711320 Festival organizers without facilities

711310 Festival promoters with facilities

711320 Festival promoters without facilities

325412 Fever remedy preparations manufacturing

522294 FHLMC (Federal Home Loan Mortgage Corporation)

322214 Fiber cans and drums (i.e., all-fiber, nonfiber ends of any material) made from purchased paperboard

424130 Fiber cans and drums merchant wholesalers

322214 Fiber drums made from purchased paperboard

337125 Fiber furniture (except upholstered), household-type, manufacturing

313221 Fiberglasses, narrow woven, weaving

238210 Fiber optic cable (except transmission lines) installation

335921 Fiber optic cable manufacturing

237130 Fiber optic cable transmission line construction

334417 Fiber optic connectors manufacturing

322214 Fiber spools, reels, blocks made from purchased paperboard

322214 Fiber tubes made from purchased paperboard

314999 Fiber, textile recovery from textile mill waste and rags

321219 Fiberboard manufacturing

423310 Fiberboard merchant wholesalers

423390 Fiberglass building materials (except insulation, roofing, siding) merchant wholesalers

424310 Fiberglass fabrics merchant wholesalers

313210 Fiberglass fabrics weaving

327993 Fiberglass insulation products manufacturing

325221 Fibers and filaments, cellulosic, manufacturing and texturizing

325222 Fibers and filaments, noncellulosic, manufacturing and texturizing

335991 Fibers, carbon and graphite, manufacturing

327212 Fibers, glass, textile, made in glass making plants

424690 Fibers, manmade, merchant wholesalers

424590 Fibers, vegetable, merchant wholesalers

325992 Film, sensitized (e.g., camera, motion picture, X-ray), manufacturing

512110 Films, motion picture production

512110 Films, motion picture production and distribution

424130 Filter papers merchant wholesalers

327112 Filtering media, pottery, manufacturing

336399 Filters (e.g., air, engine oil, fuel) automotive, truck, and bus, manufacturing

333411 Filters, air-conditioner, manufacturing

334419 Filters, electronic component-type, manufacturing

333411 Filters, furnace, manufacturing

333999 Filters, industrial and general line (except internal combustion engine, warm air furnace), manufacturing

322299 Filters, paper, made from purchased paper

221310 Filtration plant, water

212322 Filtration sand quarrying and/or beneficiating

332993 Fin assemblies, mortar, manufacturing

332993 Fin assemblies, torpedo and bomb, manufacturing

522291 Finance companies (i.e., unsecured cash loans)

523140 Financial futures brokerages

551112 Financial holding companies

523930 Financial investment advice services, customized, fees paid by client

511120 Financial magazine and periodical publishers (except exclusive Internet publishing)

511120 Financial magazine and periodical publishers and printing combined

516110 Financial magazine and periodical publishers, exclusively on Internet

323112 Financial magazines and periodicals flexographic printing without publishing

323111 Financial magazines and periodicals gravure printing without publishing

323110 Financial magazines and periodicals lithographic (offset) printing without publishing

323119 Financial magazines and periodicals printing (except flexographic, gravure, lithographic, quick, screen) without publishing

323113 Financial magazines and periodicals screen printing without publishing

541611 Financial management consulting (except investment advice) services

523930 Financial planning services, customized, fees paid by client

522320 Financial transactions processing (except central bank)

521110 Financial transactions processing of the central bank

522220 Financing, sales

522294 Financing, secondary market

316999 Findings, boot and shoe, manufacturing

339913 Findings, jeweler's, manufacturing

315212 Findings, suit and coat (e.g., coat fronts, pockets), women's, girls', and infants', cut and sew apparel contractors

315999 Findings, suit and coat (e.g., coat fronts, pockets), cut and sewn from purchased fabric (except apparel contractors)

315211 Findings, suit and coat (e.g., coat fronts, pockets), men's and boys', cut and sew apparel contractors

712110 Fine arts museums

336611	Fireboat building
327124	Firebrick, clay refractories, manufacturing
315211	Firefighters' dress uniforms, men's, cut and sew apparel contractors
315222	Firefighters' dress uniforms, men's, cut and sewn from purchased fabric (except apparel contractors)
315212	Firefighters' dress uniforms, women's, cut and sew apparel contractors
315234	Firefighters' dress uniforms, women's, cut and sewn from purchased fabric (except apparel contractors)
922160	Firefighting (except forest), government and volunteer (except private)
423850	Firefighting equipment and supplies merchant wholesalers
922160	Firefighting services (except forest and private)
339113	Firefighting suits and accessories manufacturing
115310	Firefighting, forest
332999	Fireplace fixtures and equipment manufacturing
333414	Fireplace inserts (i.e., heat directing) manufacturing
335129	Fireplace logs, electric, manufacturing
238140	Fireplace, masonry, installation
238220	Fireplace, natural gas, installation
423720	Fireplaces, gas, merchant wholesalers
238330	Fireproof flooring installation
238190	Fireproofing buildings
321999	Firewood and fuel wood containing fuel binder manufacturing
454319	Firewood dealers, direct selling
423990	Firewood merchant wholesalers
713990	Fireworks display services
325998	Fireworks manufacturing
423920	Fireworks merchant wholesalers
453998	Fireworks shops (i.e., permanent location)

327112	Firing china for the trade
321920	Firkins and kits, wood, coopered, manufacturing
611699	First aid instruction
339113	First aid, snake bite, or burn kits manufacturing
423450	First-aid kits merchant wholesalers
424210	First-aid supplies merchant wholesalers
424460	Fish (except canned, packaged frozen) merchant wholesalers
924120	Fish and game agencies
311711	Fish and marine animal oils produced in a cannery
311712	Fish and marine animal oils produced in a fresh and frozen seafood plant
311711	Fish and seafood chowder canning
924120	Fish and wildlife conservation program administration
311711	Fish egg bait canning
112511	Fish farms, finfish
112512	Fish farms, shellfish
334511	Fish finders (i.e., sonar) manufacturing
311119	Fish food for feeding fish manufacturing
311712	Fish freezing (e.g., blocks, fillets, ready-to-serve products)
325411	Fish liver oils, medicinal, uncompounded, manufacturing
445220	Fish markets
311711	Fish meal produced in a cannery
311712	Fish meal produced in a fresh and frozen seafood plant
236210	Fish processing plant construction
332212	Fish wire (i.e., electrical wiring tool) manufacturing
311711	Fish, canned and cured, manufacturing
424490	Fish, canned, merchant wholesalers
311711	Fish, curing, drying, pickling, salting, and smoking

315291　Flannel shirts, infants', cut and sewn from purchased fabric (except apparel contractors)

315211　Flannel shirts, men's and boys', cut and sew apparel contractors

315212　Flannel shirts, women's, girls', and infants', cut and sew apparel contractors

315232　Flannel shirts, women's, misses', and girls', cut and sewn from purchased fabric (except apparel contrctors)

315225　Flannel shirts, work, men's and boys', cut and sewn from purchased fabric (except apparel contractors)

313210　Flannels, broadwoven, weaving

325998　Flares manufacturing

333315　Flash apparatus, photographic, manufacturing

335110　Flash bulbs, photographic, manufacturing

238170　Flashing contractors

335912　Flashlight batteries, disposable, manufacturing

335110　Flashlight bulb manufacturing

335129　Flashlights manufacturing

423610　Flashlights merchant wholesalers

313249　Flat (i.e., warp) fabrics knitting

331221　Flat bright steel strip made in cold rolling mills made from purchased steel

327211　Flat glass (e.g., float, plate) manufacturing

423390　Flat glass merchant wholesalers

334119　Flat panel displays (i.e., complete units), computer peripheral equipment, manufacturing

332612　Flat springs (except clock, watch), light gauge, made from purchased wire or strip, manufacturing

332611　Flat springs, heavy gauge metal, manufacturing

336212　Flatbed trailers, commercial, manufacturing

484220　Flatbed trucking, local

484230　Flatbed trucking, long-distance

331111　Flats, iron or steel, made in iron and steel mills

321920　Flats, wood, greenhouse, manufacturing

423220　Flatware (except plated, precious) merchant wholesalers

332211　Flatware, nonprecious and precious plated metal, manufacturing

423940　Flatware, precious and plated, merchant wholesalers

311942　Flavor extracts (except coffee) manufacturing

311511　Flavored milk drinks manufacturing

312111　Flavored water manufacturing

311930　Flavoring concentrates (except coffee based) manufacturing

424490　Flavoring extracts (except for fountain use) merchant wholesalers

325199　Flavoring materials (i.e., basic synthetic chemicals such as coumarin) manufacturing

311930　Flavoring pastes, powders, and syrups for soft drink manufacturing

313111　Flax spun yarns made from purchased fiber

111120　Flaxseed farming, field and seed production

311225　Flaxseed oil made from purchased oils

311223　Flaxseed oil made in crushing mills

531190　Flea market space (except under roof) rental or leasing

531120　Flea market space, under roof, rental or leasing

454390　Flea markets, temporary location, direct selling

453310　Flea markets, used merchandise, permanent

325320　Flea powders or sprays manufacturing

532112　Fleet leasing, passenger vehicle

316110　Fleshers, leather (i.e., flesh side of split leather), manufacturing

334112 Flexible (i.e., floppy) magnetic disk drives manufacturing

332999 Flexible metal hose and tubing manufacturing

322221 Flexible packaging sheet materials (except foil-paper laminates) made by coating or laminating purchased paper

322225 Flexible packaging sheet materials made by laminating purchased foil

326112 Flexible packaging, plastics film, manufacturing

334412 Flexible wiring boards, bare, manufacturing

325910 Flexographic inks manufacturing

323122 Flexographic plate preparation services

323112 Flexographic printing (except books, manifold business forms, printing grey goods)

333293 Flexographic printing presses manufacturing

339920 Flies, artificial fishing, manufacturing

334511 Flight and navigation sensors, transmitters, and displays manufacturing

611519 Flight attendant schools

334511 Flight recorders (i.e., black boxes) manufacturing

333319 Flight simulation machinery manufacturing

611512 Flight training schools

212325 Flint clay mining and/or beneficiating

327992 Flint processing beyond beneficiation

339999 Flints, lighter, manufacturing

321113 Flitches (i.e., veneer stock) made in sawmills

334512 Float controls, residential and commercial types, manufacturing

561990 Float decorating services

541490 Float design services

327124 Floaters, glasshouse, clay, manufacturing

713210 Floating casinos (i.e., gambling cruises, riverboat casinos)

332313 Floating covers, fabricated metal plate work, manufacturing

311711 Floating factory ships seafood processing

332812 Flocking metals and metal products for the trade

237990 Flood control project construction

332312 Flood gates, metal plate, manufacturing

335129 Floodlights (i.e., lighting fixtures) manufacturing

237990 Floodway canal and ditch construction

321918 Floor baseboards, wood, manufacturing

442210 Floor covering stores (except wood or ceramic tile only)

444190 Floor covering stores, wood or ceramic tile only

423220 Floor coverings merchant wholesalers

326192 Floor coverings, linoleum, manufacturing

326192 Floor coverings, resilient, manufacturing

326192 Floor coverings, rubber, manufacturing

326192 Floor coverings, vinyl, manufacturing

332312 Floor jacks, metal, manufacturing

335121 Floor lamps (i.e., lighting fixtures), residential, manufacturing

238330 Floor laying, scraping, finishing and refinishing

423850 Floor maintenance equipment merchant wholesalers

326299 Floor mats (e.g., bath, door), rubber, manufacturing

325612 Floor polishes and waxes manufacturing

332312 Floor posts, adjustable metal, manufacturing

532490 Floor sanding machine rental or leasing

333319   Floor sanding, washing, and polishing machines, commercial-type, manufacturing

335212   Floor scrubbing and shampooing machines, household-type electric, manufacturing

335211   Floor standing fans, household-type electric, manufacturing

238330   Floor tile and sheets, installation only

327122   Floor tile, ceramic, manufacturing

321214   Floor trusses, wood, manufacturing

335212   Floor waxers and polishers, household-type electric, manufacturing

532490   Floor waxing equipment rental or leasing

332323   Flooring, open steel (i.e., grating), manufacturing

332322   Flooring, sheet metal (except stampings), manufacturing

321114   Flooring, wood block, treating

321918   Flooring, wood, manufacturing

423310   Flooring, wood, merchant wholesalers

334112   Floppy disk drives manufacturing

561422   Floral wire services (i.e., telemarketing services)

453110   Florists

327112   Florists' articles, red earthenware, manufacturing

424930   Florist's supplies merchant wholesalers

333131   Flotation machinery, mining-type, manufacturing

114111   Flounder fishing

314911   Flour bags made from purchased woven or knitted materials

424490   Flour merchant wholesalers

333294   Flour milling machinery manufacturing

311230   Flour mills, breakfast cereal, manufacturing

311211   Flour mills, cereals grains (except breakfast cereals, rice)

311211   Flour mixes made in flour mills

311822   Flour, blended or self-rising, made from purchased flour

311211   Flour, blended, prepared, or self-rising (except rice), made in flour mills

311213   Flour, malt, manufacturing

311212   Flour, rice, manufacturing

321999   Flour, wood, manufacturing

335314   Flow actuated electrical switches manufacturing

334513   Flow instruments, industrial process-type, manufacturing

327420   Flower boxes, plaster of paris, manufacturing

111421   Flower bulb growing

424910   Flower bulbs merchant wholesalers

111422   Flower growing

327112   Flower pots, red earthenware, manufacturing

111422   Flower seed production

453998   Flower shops, artificial or dried

453110   Flower shops, fresh

561920   Flower show managers

561920   Flower show organizers

561920   Flower show promoters

424930   Flowers merchant wholesalers

339999   Flowers, artificial (except glass, plastics), manufacturing

327123   Flue lining, clay, manufacturing

423320   Flue pipe and linings merchant wholesalers

332322   Flues, stove and furnace, sheet metal (except stampings), manufacturing

332439   Fluid milk shipping containers, light gauge metal, manufacturing

311511   Fluid milk substitutes processing

333995   Fluid power actuators manufacturing

332912   Fluid power aircraft subassemblies manufacturing

333995   Fluid power cylinders manufacturing

332912 Fluid power hose assemblies manufacturing

333996 Fluid power motors manufacturing

333996 Fluid power pumps manufacturing

332912 Fluid power valves and hose fittings manufacturing

334513 Fluidic devices, circuits, and systems for process control, manufacturing

423830 Fluid-power transmission equipment merchant wholesalers

332313 Flumes, fabricated metal plate work, manufacturing

332322 Flumes, sheet metal (except stampings), manufacturing

325188 Fluoboric acid manufacturing

335311 Fluorescent ballasts (i.e., transformers) manufacturing

325132 Fluorescent dyes manufacturing

335110 Fluorescent lamp tubes, electric, manufacturing

335122 Fluorescent lighting fixtures, commercial, institutional, and industrial electric, manufacturing

335121 Fluorescent lighting fixtures, residential, manufacturing

335311 Fluorescent lighting transformers manufacturing

325120 Fluorinated hydrocarbon gases manufacturing

325188 Fluorine manufacturing

212393 Fluorite mining and/or beneficiating

325212 Fluoro rubbers manufacturing

325212 Fluorocarbon derivative rubbers manufacturing

325222 Fluorocarbon fibers and filaments manufacturing

325120 Fluorocarbon gases manufacturing

325211 Fluorohydrocarbon resins manufacturing

325211 Fluoro-polymer resins manufacturing

334517 Fluoroscopes manufacturing

334517 Fluoroscopic X-ray apparatus and tubes manufacturing

212393 Fluorspar mining and/or beneficiating

335110 Fluroescent lamp electrodes, cold cathode, manufacturing

332998 Flush tanks, metal, manufacturing

332913 Flush valves, plumbing, manufacturing

339992 Flutes and parts manufacturing

325998 · Fluxes (e.g., brazing, galvanizing, soldering, welding) manufacturing

325320 Fly sprays manufacturing

339999 Fly swatters manufacturing

541870 Flyer direct distribution (except direct mail) services

713990 Flying clubs, recreational

488119 Flying field operators

611512 Flying instruction

335129 Flytraps, electrical, manufacturing

336312 Flywheels and ring gears, automotive and truck gasoline engine, manufacturing

515112 FM radio stations

522294 FNMA (Federal National Mortgage Association)

238310 Foam insulation installation

326150 Foam plastics products (except polystrene) manufacturing

326140 Foam polystyrene products manufacturing

424990 Foam rubber merchant wholesalers

424610 Foam, plastics, resins and shapes, merchant wholesalers

322223 Foil bags made from purchased foil

332999 Foil containers (except bags) manufacturing

332999 Foil not made in rolling mills

322225 Foil sheet, laminating purchased foil sheets for packaging applications

331315 Foil, aluminum, made by flat rolling purchased aluminum

331315   Foil, aluminum, made in integrated secondary smelting and flat rolling mills

331421   Foil, copper, made from purchased metal or scrap

331491   Foil, gold, made by rolling purchased metals or scrap

331491   Foil, nickel, made by rolling purchased metals or scrap

331491   Foil, silver, made by rolling purchased metals or scrap

424120   Folders, file, merchant wholesalers

561910   Folding and packaging services, textile and apparel

322130   Folding boxboard stock manufacturing

322212   Folding boxes (except corrugated) made from purchased paperboard

322212   Folding paper and paperboard containers (except corrugated) made from purchased paperboard

111422   Foliage growing

711120   Folk dance companies

711510   Folk dancers, independent

445110   Food (i.e., groceries) stores

446191   Food (i.e., health) supplement stores

336999   Food (vendor) carts on wheels manufacturing

624210   Food banks

722330   Food carts, mobile

333294   Food choppers, grinders, mixers, and slicers (i.e., food manufacturing-type) manufacturing

325132   Food coloring, synthetic, manufacturing

311942   Food coloring, natural, manufacturing

722310   Food concession contractors (e.g., convention facilities, entertainment facilities, sporting facilities)

722330   Food concession stands, mobile

322299   Food containers made from molded pulp

326140   Food containers, polystyrene foam, manufacturing

322215   Food containers, sanitary (except folding), made from purchased paper or paperboard

322212   Food containers, sanitary, folding, made from purchased paperboard

333294   Food dehydrating equipment (except household-type) manufacturing

923130   Food distribution program administration, government

311942   Food extracts (except coffee, meat) manufacturing

926140   Food inspection agencies

811310   Food machinery repair and maintenance services

335211   Food mixers, household-type electric, manufacturing

333993   Food packaging machinery manufacturing

327213   Food packaging, glass, manufacturing

236210   Food processing plant construction

541710   Food research and development laboratories or services

722310   Food service contractors, airline

722310   Food service contractors, cafeteria

722310   Food service contractors, concession operator (e.g., convention facilities, entertainment facilities, sporting facilities)

423440   Food service equipment (except refrigerated), commercial, merchant wholesalers

923120   Food service health inspections

326111   Food storage bags, plastics film, single wall or multiwall, manufacturing

541380   Food testing laboratories or services

322299   Food trays, molded pulp, manufacturing

333319   Food warming equipment, commercial-type, manufacturing

484230 Forest products trucking, long-distance

423810 Forestry machinery and equipment merchant wholesalers

532412 Forestry machinery and equipment rental or leasing

811310 Forestry machinery and equipment repair and maintenance services

541710 Forestry research and development laboratories or services

115310 Forestry services

333513 Forging machinery and hammers manufacturing

332111 Forgings made from purchased iron or steel, unfinished

331111 Forgings, iron or steel, made in iron and steel mills

811310 Forklift repair and maintenance services

423830 Forklift trucks (except log) merchant wholesalers

333924 Forklifts manufacturing

332212 Forks, handtools (e.g., garden, hay, manure), manufacturing

332211 Forks, table, nonprecious and precious plated metal, manufacturing

331222 Form ties made in wire drawing plants

315211 Formal jackets, men's and boys', cut and sew apparel contractors

315222 Formal jackets, men's and boys', cut and sewn from purchased fabric (except apparel contractors)

532220 Formal wear rental

325199 Formaldehyde manufacturing

325199 Formalin manufacturing

325199 Formic acid manufacturing

238190 Forming contractor

333513 Forming machines (except drawing), metalworking, manufacturing

327112 Forms for dipped rubber products, pottery, manufacturing

238190 Forms for poured concrete, erecting and dismantling

423420 Forms handling machines merchant wholesalers

332322 Forms, concrete, sheet metal (except stampings), manufacturing

321999 Forms, display, boot and shoe, all materials, manufacturing

424120 Forms, paper (e.g., business, office, sales), merchant wholesalers

312130 Fortified wines manufacturing

812990 Fortune-telling services

624110 Foster care placement agencies

624110 Foster home placement services

238140 Foundation (e.g., brick, block, stone), building, contractors

238390 Foundation dampproofing (including installing rigid foam insulation)

238910 Foundation digging (i.e., excavation)

238910 Foundation drilling contractors

315212 Foundation garments, women's and girls', cut and sew apparel contractors

315231 Foundation garments, women's, misses', and girls', cut and sewn from purchased fabric (except apparel contractors)

238110 Foundation, building, poured concrete, contractors

238130 Foundation, building, wood, contractors

325620 Foundations (i.e., make-up) manufacturing

331528 Foundries (except die-casting), nonferrous metals (except aluminum, copper)

331524 Foundries, aluminum (except die-casting)

331525 Foundries, brass, bronze, and copper (except die-casting) manufacturing

331525 Foundries, copper (except die-casting)

331521 Foundries, die-casting, aluminum

331522 Foundries, die-casting, nonferrous metals (except aluminum)
331511 Foundries, iron (i.e., ductile, gray, malleable, semisteel)
331513 Foundries, steel (except investment)
331512 Foundries, steel investment
333511 Foundry casting molds manufacturing
236210 Foundry construction
325998 Foundry core oil, wash, and wax manufacturing
332997 Foundry cores manufacturing
423830 Foundry machinery and equipment merchant wholesalers
811310 Foundry machinery and equipment repair and maintenance services
332997 Foundry pattern making
423510 Foundry products merchant wholesalers
212322 Foundry sand quarrying and/or beneficiating
424450 Fountain fruits and syrups merchant wholesalers
335129 Fountain lighting fixtures manufacturing
339941 Fountain pens manufacturing
332999 Fountains (except drinking), metal, manufacturing
332998 Fountains, drinking (except mechanically refrigerated), metal, manufacturing
423720 Fountains, drinking (except refrigerated), merchant wholesalers
423740 Fountains, drinking, refrigerated, merchant wholesalers
327420 Fountains, plaster of paris, manufacturing
333415 Fountains, refrigerated drinking, manufacturing
713920 Four season ski resorts without accommodations
333291 Fourdrinier machinery manufacturing

332618 Fourdrinier wire cloth made from purchased wire
112930 Fox production
335312 Fractional horsepower electric motors manufacturing
333298 Fractionating equipment, chemical, manufacturing
211112 Fractionating natural gas liquids
333319 Frame and body alignment equipment, motor vehicle, manufacturing
332999 Frames and handles, handbag and luggage, metal, manufacturing
423220 Frames and pictures merchant wholesalers
339942 Frames for artist's canvases (i.e., stretchers) manufacturing
333292 Frames for textile making machinery manufacturing
332321 Frames, door and window, metal, manufacturing
321911 Frames, door and window, wood, manufacturing
332999 Frames, metal, lamp shade, manufacturing
332999 Frames, metal, umbrella and parasol, manufacturing
339999 Frames, mirror and picture, all materials, manufacturing
423460 Frames, ophthalmic, merchant wholesalers
238130 Framework, house, contractors
238130 Framing contractors
533110 Franchise agreements, leasing, selling or licensing, without providing other services
813410 Fraternal associations or lodges, social or civic
524113 Fraternal life insurance organizations
813410 Fraternal lodges
813410 Fraternal organizations
813410 Fraternities (except residential)
721310 Fraternity houses
621493 Freestanding ambulatory surgical centers and clinics
621493 Freestanding emergency medical centers and clinics

311423	Freeze-dried, food processing, fruits and vegetables
811310	Freezer, commercial, repair and maintenance services
335222	Freezers, chest and upright household-type, manufacturing
423620	Freezers, household-type, merchant wholesalers
333415	Freezing equipment, industrial and commercial-type, manufacturing
311712	Freezing fish (e.g., blocks, fillets, ready-to-serve products)
488210	Freight car cleaning services
481112	Freight carriers (except air couriers), air, scheduled
481212	Freight charter services, air
488510	Freight forwarding
482111	Freight railways, line-haul
482112	Freight railways, short-line or beltline
541614	Freight rate auditor services
541614	Freight rate consulting services
483113	Freight shipping on the Great Lakes system (including St. Lawrence Seaway)
541614	Freight traffic consulting services
481212	Freight transportation, air, charter services
481212	Freight transportation, air, nonscheduled
483113	Freight transportation, deep sea, to and from domestic ports
483111	Freight transportation, deep sea, to or from foreign ports
483211	Freight transportation, inland waters (except on Great Lakes system)
311411	French fries, frozen, pre-cooked, manufacturing
311412	French toast, frozen, manufacturing
335312	Frequency converters (i.e., electric generators) manufacturing
334515	Frequency meters (e.g., electrical, electronic, mechanical) manufacturing
334515	Frequency synthesizers manufacturing
238310	Fresco (i.e., decorative plaster finishing) contractors
424460	Fresh fish merchant wholesalers
424480	Fresh fruits, vegetables and berries merchant wholesalers
424470	Fresh meats merchant wholesalers
424440	Fresh poultry merchant wholesalers
424460	Fresh seafood merchant wholesalers
339992	Fretted instruments and parts manufacturing
313221	Fringes weaving
325510	Frit manufacturing
114119	Frog fishing
112519	Frog production, farm raising
331111	Frogs, iron or steel, made in iron and steel mills
811118	Front end alignment shops, automotive
423820	Frost protection machinery merchant wholesalers
311999	Frosting, prepared, manufacturing
311411	Frozen ades, drinks and cocktail mixes, manufacturing
311812	Frozen bread and bread-type rolls, made in commercial bakeries
311813	Frozen cake manufacturing
311411	Frozen citrus pulp manufacturing
311520	Frozen custard manufacturing
722213	Frozen custard stands, fixed location
311520	Frozen desserts (except bakery) manufacturing
311412	Frozen dinners (except seafood-based) manufacturing
311822	Frozen doughs made from purchased flour
424460	Frozen fish (except packaged) merchant wholesalers
454390	Frozen food and freezer plan providers, direct selling

424480	Fruits, fresh, merchant wholesalers
311411	Fruits, frozen, manufacturing
424420	Fruits, frozen, merchant wholesalers
112320	Fryer chicken production
335211	Fryers, household-type electric, manufacturing
311320	Fudge, chocolate, made from cacao beans
311330	Fudge, chocolate, made from purchased chocolate
311340	Fudge, nonchocolate, manufacturing
326299	Fuel bladders, rubber, manufacturing
324199	Fuel briquettes or boulets made from refined petroleum
335999	Fuel cells, electrochemical generators, manufacturing
334413	Fuel cells, solid-state, manufacturing
334519	Fuel densitometers, aircraft engine, manufacturing
336312	Fuel injection systems and parts, automotive and truck gasoline engine, manufacturing
334519	Fuel mixture indicators, aircraft engine, manufacturing
454311	Fuel oil (i.e., heating) dealers, direct selling
424710	Fuel oil bulk stations and terminals
238220	Fuel oil burner installation
424720	Fuel oil merchant wholesalers (except bulk stations, terminals)
424720	Fuel oil truck jobbers
324110	Fuel oils manufacturing
325188	Fuel propellants, solid inorganic, not specified elsewhere by process, manufacturing
325199	Fuel propellants, solid organic, not specified elsewhere by process, manufacturing
336322	Fuel pumps, electric, automotive, truck, and bus, manufacturing
336312	Fuel pumps, mechanical, automotive and truck gasoline engine, manufacturing
334519	Fuel system instruments, aircraft, manufacturing
334519	Fuel totalizers, aircraft engine, manufacturing
423520	Fuel, coal and coke, merchant wholesalers
424720	Fueling aircraft (except on a contract or fee basis)
488190	Fueling aircraft on a contract or fee basis
324110	Fuels, jet, manufacturing
321113	Fuelwood made from sawmill waste
531120	Full service office space provision
722110	Full service restaurants
212325	Fuller's earth mining and/or beneficiating
327992	Fuller's earth processing beyond beneficiating
332313	Fumigating chambers, fabricated metal plate work, manufacturing
115114	Fumigating grain
561710	Fumigating services (except crop fumigating)
334515	Function generators manufacturing
561499	Fundraising campaign organization services on a contract or fee basis
334119	Funds transfer devices manufacturing
525110	Funds, employee benefit pension
525120	Funds, health and welfare
525990	Funds, mutual, closed-end
525910	Funds, mutual, open-ended
525110	Funds, pension
525190	Funds, self-insurance (except employee benefit funds)
812210	Funeral director services
812210	Funeral homes
812210	Funeral homes combined with crematories
524128	Funeral insurance carriers, direct
812210	Funeral parlors

333415 Furnaces, warm air (i.e., forced air), manufacturing

423730 Furnaces, warm air (i.e., forced air), merchant wholesalers

333994 Furnances and ovens for drying and redrying, industrial process-type, manufacturing

424320 Furnishings (except shoes), men's and boys', merchant wholesalers

424330 Furnishings (except shoes), women's, girls' and infants', merchant wholesalers

448150 Furnishings stores, men's and boys'

448150 Furnishings stores, women's and girls'

423210 Furniture (except drafting tables, hospital beds, medical furniture) merchant wholesalers

337124 Furniture (except upholstered), metal household-type, manufacturing

337214 Furniture (except wood), office-type, padded, upholstered, or plain, manufacturing

337125 Furniture (except wood, metal, upholstered) indoor and outdoor household-type, manufacturing

532299 Furniture (i.e., residential) rental centers

442110 Furniture and appliance stores (i.e., primarily retailing furniture)

561740 Furniture cleaning on customers' premises

561740 Furniture cleaning services

541420 Furniture design services

321912 Furniture dimension stock, hardwood, unfinished, manufacturing

321912 Furniture dimension stock, softwood, unfinished, manufacturing

321912 Furniture dimension stock, unfinished wood, manufacturing

337215 Furniture frames and parts, metal, manufacturing

337215 Furniture frames, wood, manufacturing

332510 Furniture hardware, metal, manufacturing

321999 Furniture inlays manufacturing

484210 Furniture moving, used

423210 Furniture parts merchant wholesalers

337215 Furniture parts, finished metal, manufacturing

337215 Furniture parts, finished plastics, manufacturing

337215 Furniture parts, finished wood, manufacturing

325612 Furniture polishes and waxes manufacturing

811420 Furniture refinishing shops

811420 Furniture repair shops

811420 Furniture reupholstering shops

332612 Furniture springs, light gauge, unassembled, made from purchased wire or strip

321912 Furniture squares, unfinished hardwood, manufacturing

442110 Furniture stores (e.g., household, office, outdoor)

453310 Furniture stores, used

327215 Furniture tops, glass (e.g., beveled, cut, polished), made from purchased glass

314999 Furniture trimmings made from purchased fabrics

327991 Furniture, cut stone (i.e., benches, tables, church), manufacturing

337127 Furniture, factory-type (e.g., cabinets, stools, tool stands, work benches), manufacturing

532291 Furniture, home health, rental

339111 Furniture, hospital (e.g., hospital beds, operating room furniture), manufacturing

337121 Furniture, household-type, upholstered on frames of any material, manufacturing

532490 Furniture, institutional (i.e. public building), rental or leasing

334515 Galvanometers (except geophysical) manufacturing
334519 Galvanometers, geophysical, manufacturing
325191 Gambier extract manufacturing
921130 Gambling control boards, nonoperating
713290 Gambling control boards, operating gambling activities
713210 Gambling cruises
713290 Gambling device arcades or parlors, coin-operated
713290 Gambling device concession operators (i.e., supplying and servicing in others' facilities), coin-operated
924120 Game and inland fish agencies
334611 Game cartridge software, mass reproducing
114210 Game preserves, commercial
114210 Game propagation
114210 Game retreats
516110 Game sites, Internet
423430 Game software merchant wholesalers
451120 Game stores (including electronic)
924120 Game wardens
339932 Games (except coin-operated), children's and adult, manufacturing
423920 Games (except coin-operated) merchant wholesalers
339999 Games, coin-operated, manufacturing
423990 Games, coin-operated, merchant wholesalers
334611 Games, computer software, mass reproducing
511210 Games, computer software, publishing
334517 Gamma ray irradiation equipment manufacturing
212319 Ganister crushed and broken stone mining and/or beneficiating
236220 Garage and service station, commercial, construction
444190 Garage door dealers

335999 Garage door openers manufacturing
238290 Garage door, commercial- or industrial-type, installation
238350 Garage door, residential-type, installation
332321 Garage doors, metal, manufacturing
321911 Garage doors, wood, manufacturing
812930 Garages, automobile parking
811198 Garages, do-it-yourself automotive repair
811111 Garages, general automotive repair (except gasoline service stations)
332311 Garages, prefabricated metal, manufacturing
321992 Garages, prefabricated wood, manufacturing
332439 Garbage cans, light gauge metal, manufacturing
562111 Garbage collection services
562213 Garbage disposal combustors or incinerators
562212 Garbage disposal landfills
236210 Garbage disposal plant construction
333319 Garbage disposal units, commercial-type, manufacturing
423440 Garbage disposal units, commercial-type, merchant wholesalers
335228 Garbage disposal units, household-type, manufacturing
423620 Garbage disposal units, household-type, merchant wholesalers
562212 Garbage dumps
562111 Garbage hauling, local
333994 Garbage incinerators (except precast concrete) manufacturing
327390 Garbage incinerators, precast concrete, manufacturing
562111 Garbage pick-up services
336211 Garbage truck bodies manufacturing

336120   Garbage trucks assembling on chassis of own manufacture
336211   Garbage trucks assembling on purchased chassis
111130   Garbanzo farming, dry, field and seed production
236116   Garden apartment construction general contractors
236117   Garden apartment operative builders
444220   Garden centers
813410   Garden clubs
811411   Garden equipment repair and maintenance services without retailing new garden equipment
327390   Garden furniture, precast concrete, manufacturing
327991   Garden furniture, stone, manufacturing
337122   Garden furniture, wood, manufacturing
326220   Garden hose, rubber or plastics, manufacturing
423820   Garden machinery and equipment merchant wholesalers
333112   Garden machinery and equipment, powered, manufacturing
561730   Garden maintenance services
541320   Garden planning services
327112   Garden pottery manufacturing
444210   Garden power equipment stores
424910   Garden supplies (e.g., fertilizers, pesticides) merchant wholesalers
811411   Garden tool sharpening and repair services
532490   Garden tractor rental or leasing
339999   Garden umbrellas manufacturing
712130   Gardens, zoological or botanical
111219   Garlic farming (except under cover), field, bedding plant and seed production
111419   Garlic farming, grown under cover

811490   Garment alteration and/or repair shops without retailing new garments
812320   Garment cleaning (e.g., fur, leather, suede) services
321999   Garment hangers, wood, manufacturing
316110   Garment leather manufacturing
314911   Garment storage bags manufacturing
315292   Garments, leather or sheep-lined (except apparel contractors), manufacturing
315211   Garments, leather or sheep-lined, men's and boys', cut and sew apparel contractors
315212   Garments, leather or sheep-lined, women's, girls', and infants', cut and sew apparel contractors
313320   Garments, oiling (i.e., waterproofing)
212399   Garnet mining and/or beneficiating
333292   Garnetting machinery for textiles manufacturing
314999   Garnetting of textile waste and rags
315212   Garter belts cut and sew apparel contractors
315231   Garter belts cut and sewn from purchased fabric (except apparel contractors)
315212   Garters, women's, cut and sew apparel contractors
315231   Garters, women's, misses', and girls', cut and sewn from purchased fabric (except apparel contractors)
334513   Gas analyzers, industrial process-type, manufacturing
334516   Gas analyzers, laboratory-type, manufacturing
334513   Gas and liquid analysis instruments, industrial process-type, manufacturing
334512   Gas burner automatic controls (except valves) manufacturing
333414   Gas burners, heating, manufacturing

334513 Gas chromatographic instruments, industrial process-type, manufacturing

334516 Gas chromatographic instruments, laboratory-type, manufacturing

333414 Gas fireplaces manufacturing

423720 Gas fireplaces merchant wholesalers

238220 Gas fitting contractor

334513 Gas flow instrumentation, industrial process-type, manufacturing

333999 Gas generating machinery, general purpose-type, manufacturing

423720 Gas hot water heaters merchant wholesalers

334519 Gas leak detectors manufacturing

523999 Gas lease brokers' offices

335129 Gas lighting fixtures manufacturing

423990 Gas lighting fixtures merchant wholesalers

238220 Gas line installation, individual hookup, contractors

333298 Gas liquefying machinery manufacturing

237120 Gas main construction

339113 Gas masks manufacturing

561990 Gas meter reading services, contract

423720 Gas ranges merchant wholesalers

333319 Gas ranges, commercial-type, manufacturing

335221 Gas ranges, household-type, manufacturing

333999 Gas separating machinery manufacturing

333414 Gas space heaters manufacturing

332420 Gas storage tanks, heavy gauge metal, manufacturing

336399 Gas tanks assembled, automotive, truck, and bus, manufacturing

333611 Gas turbine generator set units manufacturing

333611 Gas turbines (except aircraft) manufacturing

336412 Gas turbines, aircraft, manufacturing

332911 Gas valves, industrial-type, manufacturing

333992 Gas welding equipment manufacturing

333992 Gas welding rods, coated or cored, manufacturing

213111 Gas well drilling on a contract basis

333132 Gas well machinery and equipment manufacturing

213112 Gas well rig building, repairing, and dismantling on a contract basis

213112 Gas, compressing natural, in the field on a contract basis

221210 Gas, manufactured, production and distribution

221210 Gas, mixed natural and manufactured, production and distribution

211112 Gas, natural liquefied petroleum, extraction

221210 Gas, natural, distribution

211111 Gas, natural, extraction

211112 Gas, natural, liquids, extraction

486210 Gas, natural, pipeline operation

211112 Gas, residue, extraction

424690 Gases, compressed and liquefied (except liquefied petroleum gas), merchant wholesalers

325120 Gases, industrial (i.e., compressed, liquefied, solid), manufacturing

211112 Gases, petroleum, liquefied, extraction

339991 Gasket, packing, and sealing devices manufacturing

339991 Gaskets manufacturing

423840 Gaskets merchant wholesalers

334514 Gasmeters, consumption registering, manufacturing

334514 Gasmeters, large capacity, domestic and industrial, manufacturing

333414 Gas-oil burners, combination, manufacturing

336350 Gears (e.g., crown, pinion, spider), automotive, truck, and bus, manufacturing

333612 Gears, power transmission (except aircraft, motor vehicle), manufacturing

112390 Geese production

311615 Geese, processing, fresh, frozen, canned, or cooked

311615 Geese, slaughtering and dressing

334519 Geiger counters manufacturing

325998 Gelatin capsules, empty, manufacturing

311999 Gelatin dessert preparations manufacturing

311999 Gelatin for cooking manufacturing

424490 Gelatin, edible, merchant wholesalers

424690 Gelatin, inedible, merchant wholesalers

212399 Gem stone (e.g., amethyst, garnet, agate, ruby, sapphire, jade) mining and/or beneficiating

423940 Gem stones merchant wholesalers

333298 Gemstone processing machinery manufacturing

325414 Gene therapy preparations manufacturing

812990 Genealogical investigation services

921190 General accounting offices, government

811111 General automotive repair shops

112990 General combination animal farming

111998 General combination crop farming (except fruit and nut combinations, oilseed and grain, vegetable)

926110 General economics statistical agencies

484110 General freight trucking, local

484122 General freight trucking, long-distance, less-than-truckload (LTL)

484121 General freight trucking, long-distance, truckload (TL)

541611 General management consulting services

622110 General medical and surgical hospitals

423990 General merchandise, durable goods, merchant wholesalers

424990 General merchandise, nondurable goods, merchant wholesalers

921190 General public administration

532310 General rental centers

921190 General services departments, government

452990 General stores

493110 General warehousing and storage

424210 General-line drugs merchant wholesalers

424410 General-line groceries merchant wholesalers

423840 General-line industrial supplies merchant wholesalers

423930 General-line scrap merchant wholesalers

423830 General-purpose industrial machinery and equipment merchant wholesalers

336322 Generating apparatus and parts for internal combustion engines manufacturing

335312 Generating apparatus and parts, electrical (except internal combustion engine and welding), manufacturing

333992 Generating apparatus and parts, welding, electrical, manufacturing

335313 Generator control and metering panels, switchgear-type, manufacturing

532490 Generator rental or leasing

335312 Generator sets, prime mover (except turbine generator sets), manufacturing

333611 Generator sets, turbine (e.g., gas, hydraulic, steam), manufacturing

335311 Generator voltage regulators, electric induction and step-type (except engine electrical equipment), manufacturing

335312 Generators and sets, electric (except internal combustion engine, welding, turbine generator sets), manufacturing

335312 Generators for gas-electric and oil-electric vehicles, manufacturing

336322 Generators for internal combustion engines manufacturing

335312 Generators for storage battery chargers (except internal combustion engine and aircraft) manufacturing

423610 Generators, electrical (except motor vehicle), merchant wholesalers

423120 Generators, motor vehicle electrical, new, merchant wholesalers

423140 Generators, motor vehicle electrical, used, merchant wholesalers

332995 Generators, smoke, manufacturing

334517 Generators, X-ray, manufacturing

621511 Genetic testing laboratories

541710 Genetics research and development laboratories or services

541690 Geochemical consulting services

321992 Geodesic domes, prefabricated, wood, manufacturing

541370 Geodetic surveying services

541370 Geographic information system (GIS) base mapping services

541330 Geological engineering services

213112 Geological exploration (except surveying) for oil and gas on a contract basis

541710 Geological research and development laboratories or services

924120 Geological research program administration

541360 Geological surveying services

541330 Geophysical engineering services

213112 Geophysical exploration (except surveying) for oil and gas on a contract basis

334519 Geophysical instruments manufacturing

541360 Geophysical mapping services

541360 Geophysical surveying services

541370 Geospatial mapping services

541380 Geotechnical testing laboratories or services

237110 Geothermal drilling

221330 Geothermal steam production

325199 Geraniol manufacturing

331492 Germanium recovering from scrap and/or alloying purchased metals

331419 Germanium refining, primary

335931 GFCI (ground fault circuit interrupters) manufacturing

711510 Ghost writers, independent

453220 Gift shops

453220 Gift stands, permanent location

322222 Gift wrap made from purchased materials

424120 Gift wrapping paper merchant wholesalers

561910 Gift wrapping services

212399 Gilsonite mining and/or beneficiating

111219 Gingerroot farming (except under cover), field, bedding plant and seed production

111419 Gingerroot farming, grown under cover

115111 Ginning cotton

111219 Ginseng farming (except under cover), field, bedding plant and seed production

111419 Ginseng farming, grown under cover

113210 Ginseng gathering

327390 Girders and beams, prestressed concrete, manufacturing

327390 Girders, prestressed concrete, manufacturing

315192	Girdles and other foundation garments made in apparel knitting mills
315212	Girdles, women's, cut and sew apparel contractors
315231	Girdles, women's, misses', and girls', cut and sewn from purchased fabric (except apparel contractors)
813410	Girl guiding organizations
721214	Girls' camps (except day, instructional)
611620	Girls' camps, sports instruction
713990	Girls' day camps (except instructional)
315111	Girls' hosiery, sheer, full length or knee length, knitting and finishing
315119	Girls' socks manufacturing
325411	Glandular derivatives, uncompounded, manufacturing
325412	Glandular medicinal preparations manufacturing
325612	Glass and tile cleaning preparations manufacturing
327215	Glass blanks for electric light bulbs made from purchased glass
327212	Glass blanks for electric light bulbs made in glass making plants
238140	Glass block laying
334290	Glass breakage detection and signaling devices
313210	Glass broadwoven fabrics weaving
238150	Glass cladding (i.e., curtain wall), installation
238150	Glass coating and tinting (except automotive) contractors
313221	Glass fabrics, narrow woven weaving
238310	Glass fiber insulation installation
327212	Glass fiber, optical, made in glass making plants
327212	Glass fiber, textile type, made in glass making plants

238150	Glass installation (except automotive) contractors
811122	Glass installation, automotive repair
327212	Glass making and blowing by hand
333298	Glass making machinery (e.g., blowing, forming, molding) manufacturing
327213	Glass packaging containers manufacturing
238150	Glass partitions, installation
327215	Glass products (except packaging containers) made from purchased glass
327212	Glass products (except packaging containers) made in a glass making plants
212322	Glass sand quarrying and/or beneficiating
423930	Glass scrap merchant wholesalers
811122	Glass shops, automotive
444190	Glass stores
811122	Glass tinting, automotive
238140	Glass unit (i.e., glass block) masonry
811122	Glass work, automotive
327215	Glass, automotive, made from purchased glass
423120	Glass, automotive, merchant wholesalers
327211	Glass, plate, made in glass making plants
423390	Glass, plate, merchant wholesalers
333314	Glasses, field or opera, manufacturing
327124	Glasshouse refractories manufacturing
322299	Glassine wrapping paper made from purchased paper
322121	Glassine wrapping paper made in paper mills
327215	Glassware for industrial, scientific, and technical use made from purchased glass

315211	Gloves, leather (except athletic), men's and boys', cut and sew apparel contractors
315212	Gloves, leather (except athletic), women's, girls', and infants', cut and sew apparel contractors
315992	Gloves, leather (except athletic, cut and sewn apparel contractors), manufacturing
424320	Gloves, men's and boys', merchant wholesalers
326199	Gloves, plastics, manufacturing
339113	Gloves, rubber (e.g., electrician's, examination, household-type, surgeon's), manufacturing
339920	Gloves, sport and athletic (e.g., baseball, boxing, racketball, handball), manufacturing
424330	Gloves, women's, children's, and infants', merchant wholesalers
335110	Glow lamp bulbs manufacturing
339114	Glue, dental, manufacturing
325520	Glues (except dental) manufacturing
424690	Glues merchant wholesalers
311221	Gluten feed, flour, and meal, made by wet milling corn
311221	Gluten manufacturing
325611	Glycerin (i.e., glycerol), natural, manufacturing
325199	Glycerin (i.e., glycerol), synthetic, manufacturing
325411	Glycosides, uncompounded, manufacturing
212313	Gneiss crushed and broken stone mining and/or beneficiating
212311	Gneiss mining or quarrying
522294	GNMA (Government National Mortgage Association)
112420	Goat farming (e.g., meat, milk, mohair production)
424520	Goats merchant wholesalers
713990	Gocart raceways (i.e., amusement rides)
713990	Gocart tracks (i.e., amusement rides)
336999	Gocarts (except children's) manufacturing
423910	Gocarts merchant wholesalers
339932	Go-carts, children's, manufacturing
339115	Goggles (e.g., industrial, safety, sun, underwater) manufacturing
331491	Gold and gold alloy bar, sheet, strip, and tubing made from purchased metals or scrap
332813	Gold and silver plating metals and metal products for the trade
332999	Gold beating (i.e., foil, leaf)
331419	Gold bullion or dore bar produced at primary metal refineries
332999	Gold foil and leaf not made in rolling mills
331491	Gold foil made by rolling purchased metals or scrap
212221	Gold lode mining and/or beneficiating
212221	Gold ore mine site development for own account
212221	Gold ore mining ard/or beneficiating plants
212221	Gold ores, concentrates, bullion, and/or precipitates mining and/or beneficiating
212221	Gold placer mining and/or beneficiating
325910	Gold printing inks manufacturing
331492	Gold recovering from scrap and/or alloying purchased metals
331419	Gold refining, primary
331491	Gold rolling and drawing purchased metals or scrap
323121	Gold stamping books for the trade
813410	Golden age clubs
112511	Goldfish production, farm raising
713910	Golf and country clubs
441229	Golf cart dealers, powered
532292	Golf cart rental

423910 Golf carts (except motorized passenger) merchant wholesalers
336999 Golf carts and similar motorized passenger carriers manufacturing
423860 Golf carts, motorized passenger, merchant wholesalers
336999 Golf carts, powered, manufacturing
237990 Golf course construction
541320 Golf course design services
713910 Golf courses (except miniature, pitch-n-putt)
713990 Golf courses, miniature
713990 Golf courses, pitch-n-putt
713990 Golf driving ranges
423910 Golf equipment and supplies merchant wholesalers
611620 Golf instruction, camps, or schools
713990 Golf practice ranges
451110 Golf pro shops
316219 Golf shoes, men's cleated, manufacturing
316219 Golf shoes, women's cleated, manufacturing
711219 Golfers, independent professional (i.e., participating in sports events)
339920 Golfing equipment (e.g., bags, balls, caddy carts, clubs, tees) manufacturing
335999 Gongs, electric, manufacturing
111334 Gooseberry farming
332212 Gouges, woodworking, manufacturing
445299 Gourmet food stores
561210 Government base facilities operation support services
522294 Government National Mortgage Association (GNMA)
522294 Government-sponsored enterprises providing secondary market financing
336312 Governors for automotive gasoline engines manufacturing
921110 Governors' offices

333618 Governors, diesel engine, manufacturing
333618 Governors, gasoline engine (except automotive), manufacturing
333611 Governors, steam, manufacturing
812331 Gown (e.g., doctors, nurses, hospital, beauticians) supply services
532220 Gown rental
315299 Gowns (e.g., academic, choir, clerical) cut and sewn from purchased fabric (except apparel contractors)
315211 Gowns (e.g., academic, choir, clerical), men's and boys', cut and sew apparel contractors
315212 Gowns (e.g., academic, choir, clerical), women's, and girls', cut and sew apparel contractors
315212 Gowns, formal, women's and girls', cut and sew apparel contractors
315233 Gowns, formal, women's, misses', and girls', cut and sewn from purchased fabric (except apparel contractors)
315299 Gowns, hospital, surgical and patient, cut and sewn from purchased fabric (except apparel contractors)
315211 Gowns, hospital, surgical and patient, men's and boys', cut and sew apparel contractors
315212 Gowns, hospital, surgical and patient, women's, girls', and infants', cut and sew apparel contractors
315212 Gowns, wedding, women's, cut and sew apparel contractors
315233 Gowns, wedding, women's, misses', and girls', cut and sewn from purchased fabric (except apparel contractors)
334220 GPS (global positioning system) equipment manufacturing
333120 Grader attachments manufacturing

333120	Graders, road, manufacturing
238910	Grading construction sites
333294	Grading, cleaning, and sorting machinery (i.e., food manufacturing-type) manufacturing
333111	Grading, cleaning, and sorting machinery, farm-type, manufacturing
237310	Grading, highway, road, street and airport runway
334512	Gradual switches, pneumatic, manufacturing
532220	Graduation cap and gown rental
315299	Graduation caps and gowns cut and sewn from purchased fabric (except apparel contractors)
315211	Graduation caps and gowns, men's and boys', cut and sew apparel contractors
315212	Graduation caps and gowns, women's and girls', cut and sew apparel contractors
311211	Graham flour manufacturing
311821	Graham wafers manufacturing
212399	Grahamite mining and/or beneficiating
312140	Grain alcohol, beverage, manufacturing
325193	Grain alcohol, nonpotable, manufacturing
115114	Grain cleaning
333111	Grain drills manufacturing
115114	Grain drying
236220	Grain elevator construction
424510	Grain elevators merchant wholesalers grain
493130	Grain elevators, storage only
115114	Grain fumigation
115114	Grain grinding (except custom grinding for animal feed)
311119	Grain grinding, custom, for animal feed
484220	Grain hauling, local
484230	Grain hauling, long-distance
488210	Grain leveling and trimming in railroad cars
321999	Grain measures, wood, turned and shaped, manufacturing

424510	Grain merchant wholesalers
333294	Grain milling machinery manufacturing
311211	Grain mills (except animal feed, breakfast cereal, rice)
311119	Grain mills, animal feed
311230	Grain mills, breakfast cereal
311212	Grain mills, rice
333111	Grain stackers manufacturing
311230	Grain, breakfast cereal, manufacturing
312120	Grain, brewers' spent, manufacturing
115113	Grain, machine harvesting
327910	Grains, abrasive, natural and artificial, manufacturing
813410	Granges
212313	Granite beneficiating plants (e.g., grinding or pulverizing)
212313	Granite crushed and broken stone mining and/or beneficiating
212311	Granite mining or quarrying
238140	Granite, exterior, contractors
238340	Granite, interior, installation
311320	Granola bars and clusters, chocolate, made from cacao beans
311330	Granola bars and clusters, chocolate, made from purchased chocolate
311340	Granola bars and clusters, nonchocolate, manufacturing
311230	Granola, cereal (except bars and clusters), manufacturing
813211	Grantmaking foundations
311313	Granulated beet sugar manufacturing
311312	Granulated cane sugar made from purchased raw cane sugar
311311	Granulated cane sugar made from sugar cane
333220	Granulator and pelletizer machinery for plastics manufacturing
212319	Granules, slate, mining and/or beneficiating
312130	Grape farming and making wine

511191 Greeting card publishers (except exclusive Internet publishing)
511191 Greeting card publishers and printing combined
516110 Greeting card publishers, exclusively on Internet
453220 Greeting card shops
323112 Greeting cards (e.g., birthday, holiday, sympathy) flexographic printing without publishing
323111 Greeting cards (e.g., birthday, holiday, sympathy) gravure printing without publishing
323110 Greeting cards (e.g., birthday, holiday, sympathy) lithographic (offset) printing without publishing
323119 Greeting cards (e.g., birthday, holiday, sympathy) printing (except flexographic, gravure, lithographic, quick, screen) without publishing
323113 Greeting cards (e.g., birthday, holiday, sympathy) screen printing without publishing
323119 Greeting cards engraving printing without publishing
323119 Greeting cards letterpress printing without publishing
424120 Greeting cards merchant wholesalers
332994 Grenade launchers manufacturing
332993 Grenades, hand or projectile, manufacturing
711212 Greyhound dog racetracks
335211 Griddles and grills, household-type portable electric, manufacturing
332618 Grilles and grillwork made from purchased wire
332323 Grills and grillwork, sheet metal, manufacturing
332323 Grillwork, ornamental metal, manufacturing
333991 Grinders, handheld power-driven, manufacturing
325411 Grinding and milling botanicals (i.e., for medicinal use)

327910 Grinding balls, ceramic, manufacturing
333512 Grinding machines, metalworking, manufacturing
332813 Grinding metal castings for the trade
324191 Grinding oils, petroleum, made from refined petroleum
212399 Grinding pebbles mining and/or beneficiating
212322 Grinding sand quarrying and/or beneficiating
311942 Grinding spices
327910 Grinding wheels manufacturing
212399 Grindstones mining and/or beneficiating
326299 Grips and handles, rubber, manufacturing
311211 Grits and flakes, corn brewer's, manufacturing
212319 Grits crushed and broken stone mining and/or beneficiating
424410 Groceries, general-line, merchant wholesalers
322224 Grocers' bags and sacks made from purchased uncoated paper
326111 Grocery bags, plastics film, single wall or multiwall, manufacturing
333924 Grocery carts made from purchased wire
492210 Grocery delivery services (i.e., independent service from grocery store)
445110 Grocery stores
423840 Grommets merchant wholesalers
326299 Grommets, rubber, manufacturing
812910 Grooming services, animal
335931 Ground clamps (i.e., electric wiring devices) manufacturing
335931 Ground fault circuit interrupters (GFCI) manufacturing
238910 Ground thawing for construction site digging
322122 Groundwood paper products (e.g., publication and printing paper, tablet stock, wallpaper base) made in newsprint mills

323113   Guides, street map, screen printing without publishing

339992   Guitars and parts, electric and nonelectric, manufacturing

113210   Gum (i.e., forest product) gathering

325191   Gum and wood chemicals manufacturing

424690   Gum and wood chemicals merchant wholesalers

311340   Gum, chewing, manufacturing

424450   Gum, chewing, merchant wholesalers

322222   Gummed paper products (e.g., labels, sheets, tapes) made from purchased paper

424130   Gummed tapes (except cellophane) merchant wholesalers

424120   Gummed tapes, cellophane, merchant wholesalers

332994   Gun barrels (i.e., 30 mm. or less, 1.18 inch or less) manufacturing

332995   Gun barrels (i.e., more than 30 mm., more than 1.18 inch) manufacturing

713990   Gun clubs, recreational

813319   Gun control organizations

332111   Gun forgings made from purchased iron or steel, unfinished

331111   Gun forgings made in iron and steel mills

332994   Gun magazines (i.e., 30 mm. or less, 1.18 inch or less) manufacturing

332995   Gun magazines (i.e., more than 30 mm., more than 1.18 inch) manufacturing

811490   Gun repair and maintenance shops without retailing new guns

451110   Gun shops

333314   Gun sighting and fire control equipment and instruments, optical, manufacturing

333314   Gun sights, optical, manufacturing

332612   Gun springs, light gauge, made from purchased wire or strip, manufacturing

321912   Gun stock blanks manufacturing

332510   Gun trigger locks, metal, manufacturing

332995   Gun turrets (i.e., more than 30 mm., more than 1.18 inch) manufacturing

238110   Gunite contractors

334413   Gunn effect devices manufacturing

238110   Gunning shotcrete

325920   Gunpowder manufacturing

423990   Guns (except sporting) merchant wholesalers

332994   Guns (i.e., 30 mm. or less, 1.18 inch or less) manufacturing

332995   Guns (i.e., more than 30 mm., more than 1.18 inch) manufacturing

332994   Guns, BB and pellet, manufacturing

332212   Guns, caulking, nonpowered, manufacturing

423910   Guns, sporting equipment, merchant wholesalers

451110   Gunsmith shops retailing new guns

811490   Gunsmith shops without retailing new guns

238170   Gutter and downspout contractors

561790   Gutter cleaning services

423330   Gutters and down spouts (except wood) merchant wholesalers

332114   Gutters and down spouts sheet metal, custom roll formed, manufacturing

326199   Gutters and down spouts, plastics, manufacturing

238170   Gutters, seamless roof, formed and installed on site

332322   Gutters, sheet metal (except custom roll formed), manufacturing

339920   Gymnasium and playground equipment, manufacturing

713940   Gymnasiums
611620   Gymnastics instruction, camps,
         or schools
339113   Gynecological supplies and
         appliances manufacturing
621111   Gynecologists' offices (e.g.,
         centers, clinics)
212399   Gypsite mining and/or
         beneficiating
238310   Gypsum board installation
327420   Gypsum building products
         manufacturing
423390   Gypsum building products
         merchant wholesalers
212399   Gypsum mining and/or
         beneficiating
327420   Gypsum products (e.g., block,
         board, plaster, lath, rock, tile)
         manufacturing
334511   Gyrocompasses manufacturing
334511   Gyrogimbals manufacturing
334511   Gyroscopes manufacturing
624310   Habilitation job counseling and
         training, vocational
114111   Haddock fishing
212299   Hafnium mining and/or
         beneficiating
424310   Hair accessories merchant
         wholesalers
326299   Hair care products (e.g., combs,
         curlers), rubber, manufacturing
333111   Hair clippers for animal use,
         electric, manufacturing
332212   Hair clippers for animal use,
         nonelectric, manufacturing
335211   Hair clippers for human use,
         electric, manufacturing
332211   Hair clippers for human use,
         nonelectric, manufacturing
325620   Hair coloring preparations
         manufacturing
335211   Hair curlers, household-type
         electric, manufacturing
332999   Hair curlers, metal,
         manufacturing
335211   Hair driers, electric (except
         equipment designed for beauty
         parlor use), manufacturing
423620   Hair dryers merchant
         wholesalers

333319   Hair dryers, beauty parlor-type,
         manufacturing
339999   Hair nets made from purchased
         netting
325620   Hair preparations (e.g.,
         conditioners, dyes, rinses,
         shampoos) manufacturing
424210   Hair preparations (except
         professional) merchant
         wholesalers
423850   Hair preparations, professional,
         merchant wholesalers
812199   Hair removal (i.e., dipilatory,
         electrolysis) services
812199   Hair replacement services
         (except by offices of
         physicians)
325620   Hair sprays manufacturing
812112   Hair stylist salons or shops,
         unisex or women's
812111   Hair stylist services, men's
812112   Hair stylist services, unisex or
         women's
812111   Hair stylist shops, men's
812199   Hair weaving services
339994   Hairbrushes manufacturing
424990   Hairbrushes merchant
         wholesalers
812112   Hairdresser services
812112   Hairdressing salons or shops,
         unisex or women's
339999   Hairpieces (e.g., toupees, wigs,
         wiglets) manufacturing
424990   Hairpieces (e.g., toupees, wigs,
         wiglets) merchant wholesalers
339993   Hairpins (except rubber)
         manufacturing
326299   Hairpins, rubber, manufacturing
332612   Hairsprings (except clock,
         watch), light gauge, made
         from purchased wire or strip,
         manufacturing
114111   Hake fishing
623990   Halfway group homes for
         delinquents and ex-offenders
623220   Halfway houses for patients
         with mental health illnesses
623220   Halfway houses, substance
         abuse (e.g., alcoholism, drug
         addiction)

114111 Halibut fishing
531120 Hall and banquet room, nonresidential, rental or leasing
334413 Hall effect devices manufacturing
531120 Hall, nonresidential, rental or leasing
339912 Hallowware, precious metal, manufacturing
712110 Halls of fame
335110 Halogen light bulbs manufacturing
325192 Halogenated aromatic hydrocarbon derivatives manufacturing
325199 Halogenated hydrocarbon derivatives (except aromatic) manufacturing
311340 Halvah manufacturing
332111 Hammer forgings made from purchased iron or steel, unfinished
332112 Hammer forgings made from purchased nonferrous metals, unfinished
333120 Hammer mill machinery (i.e., rock and ore crushing machines), portable, manufacturing
333131 Hammer mill machinery (i.e., rock and ore crushing machines), stationary, manufacturing
332212 Hammers, handtools, manufacturing
339992 Hammers, piano, manufacturing
321999 Hammers, wood, meat, manufacturing
314999 Hammocks, fabric, manufacturing
337124 Hammocks, metal framed, manufacturing
337122 Hammocks, wood framed, manufacturing
326199 Hampers, laundry, plastics, manufacturing
337125 Hampers, laundry, reed, wicker, rattan, manufacturing

332322 Hampers, laundry, sheet metal (except stampings), manufacturing
311611 Hams (except poultry) produced in slaughtering plants
311612 Hams, canned, made from purchased carcasses
311615 Hams, poultry, manufacturing
311612 Hams, preserved (except poultry), made from purchased carcasses
327215 Hand blowing purchased glass
334111 Hand held computers (e.g., PDAs) manufacturing
313249 Hand knitting lace or warp fabric products
812320 Hand laundries
325620 Hand lotions manufacturing
339943 Hand operated stamps (e.g., canceling, postmark, shoe, textile marking) manufacturing
325611 Hand soaps (e.g., hard, liquid, soft) manufacturing
334518 Hand stamps (e.g., date, time), timing mechanism operated, manufacturing
333924 Hand trucks manufacturing
313221 Hand weaving fabric, 12 inches or less (30cm)
313210 Hand weaving fabrics, more than 12 inches (30 cm) in width
316110 Handbag leather manufacturing
448150 Handbag stores
316993 Handbags (except metal), men's, manufacturing
424330 Handbags merchant wholesalers
339911 Handbags, precious metal, manufacturing
316992 Handbags, women's, all materials (except precious metal), manufacturing
713940 Handball club facilities
541870 Handbill direct distribution services
332999 Handcuffs manufacturing
332212 Handheld edge tools (except saws, scissors-type), nonelectric, manufacturing

313210 Hard fiber fabrics, broadwoven, weaving

313111 Hard fiber spun yarns made from purchased fiber

313113 Hard fiber thread manufacturing

313221 Hard fiber, narrow woven, weaving

339113 Hard hats manufacturing

321219 Hardboard manufacturing

332811 Hardening (i.e., heat treating) metals and metal products for the trade

334519 Hardness testing equipment manufacturing

423710 Hardware (except motor vehicle) merchant wholesalers

332618 Hardware cloth, woven wire, made from purchased wire

444130 Hardware stores

423120 Hardware, motor vehicle, merchant wholesalers

326199 Hardware, plastics, manufacturing

335932 Hardware, transmission pole and line, manufacturing

423610 Hardware, transmission pole and line, merchant wholesalers

321912 Hardwood dimension lumber and stock, resawing purchased lumber

325191 Hardwood distillates manufacturing

444190 Hardwood flooring dealers

238330 Hardwood flooring, installation only

321211 Hardwood plywood composites manufacturing

321211 Hardwood veneer or plywood manufacturing

339992 Harmonicas manufacturing

334419 Harness assemblies for electronic use manufacturing

711219 Harness drivers

424910 Harness equipment merchant wholesalers

316110 Harness leather manufacturing

332999 Harness parts, metal, manufacturing

711212 Harness racetracks

316999 Harnesses and harness parts, leather, manufacturing

316999 Harnesses, dog, manufacturing

339992 Harps and parts manufacturing

339992 Harpsichords manufacturing

333111 Harrows (e.g., disc, spring, tine) manufacturing

315991 Harvest hats, straw, manufacturing

113210 Harvesting berries or nuts from native and non-cultivated plants

333111 Harvesting machinery and equipment, agriculture, manufacturing

423820 Harvesting machinery and equipment, agriculture, merchant wholesalers

335211 Hassock fans, electric, manufacturing

448150 Hat and cap stores

339999 Hat blocks manufacturing

315991 Hat bodies (e.g., fur-felt, straw, wool-felt) cut and sewn from purchased fabric (except apparel contractors)

315211 Hat bodies (e.g., fur-felt, straw, wool-felt), men's and boys', cut and sew apparel contractors

315212 Hat bodies (e.g., fur-felt, straw, wool-felt), women's, girls', and infants', cut and sew apparel contractors

812320 Hat cleaning services

315999 Hat findings cut and sewn from purchased fabric (except apparel contractors)

315211 Hat findings, men's and boys', cut and sew apparel contractors

315212 Hat findings, women's, girls', and infants', cut and sew apparel contractors

315999 Hat linings and trimmings cut and sewn from purchased fabric (except apparel contractors)

315211 Hat linings and trimmings, men's and boys', cut and sew apparel contractors

315212 Hat linings and trimmings, women's, girls', and infants', cut and sew apparel contractors

112511 Hatcheries, finfish

112340 Hatcheries, poultry

112512 Hatcheries, shellfish

332212 Hatchets manufacturing

315991 Hats (except fur, knitting mill products, leather) cut and sewn from purchased fabric (except apparel contractors)

424320 Hats and caps, men's and boys', merchant wholesalers

424330 Hats and caps, women's, girls' and infants', merchant wholesalers

322299 Hats made from purchased paper

315191 Hats made in apparel knitting mills

315991 Hats, cloth, cut and sewn from purchased fabric (except apparel contractors)

315211 Hats, cloth, men's and boys', cut and sew apparel contractors

315212 Hats, cloth, women's, girls', and infants', cut and sew apparel contractors

315292 Hats, fur (except apparel contractors), manufacturing

315211 Hats, fur, men's and boys', cut and sew apparel contractors

315212 Hats, fur, women's, girls', and infants', cut and sew apparel contractors

315991 Hats, fur-felt, straw, and wool-felt, cut and sewn from purchased fabric (except apparel contractors)

315211 Hats, fur-felt, straw, and wool-felt, men's and boys', cut and sew apparel contractors

315212 Hats, fur-felt, straw, and wool-felt, women's, girls', and infants', cut and sew apparel contractors

315292 Hats, leather (except apparel contractors), manufacturing

315211 Hats, leather, men's and boys', cut and sew apparel contractors

315212 Hats, leather, women's, girls', and infants', cut and sew apparel contractors

315211 Hats, men's and boys', cut and sew apparel contractors

315991 Hats, trimmed, cut and sewn from purchased fabric (except apparel contractors)

315211 Hats, trimmed, men's and boys', cut and sew apparel contractors

315212 Hats, trimmed, women's, girls', and infants', cut and sew apparel contractors

315212 Hats, women's, girls', and infants', cut and sew apparel contractors

333111 Hay balers and presses manufacturing

111940 Hay farming (e.g., alfalfa hay, clover hay, grass hay)

424910 Hay merchant wholesalers

115113 Hay mowing, raking, baling, and chopping

111998 Hay seed farming

311119 Hay, cubed, manufacturing

333111 Haying machines manufacturing

423820 Haying machines merchant wholesalers

562112 Hazardous waste collection services

562211 Hazardous waste disposal facilities

562211 Hazardous waste disposal facilities combined with collection and/or local hauling of hazardous waste

562211 Hazardous waste material disposal facilities

562211 Hazardous waste material treatment facilities

562211 Hazardous waste treatment facilities

562211 Hazardous waste treatment facilities combined with collection and/or local hauling of hazardous waste
111335 Hazelnut farming
334613 Head cleaners for magnetic tape equipment, manufacturing
551114 Head offices
311212 Head rice manufacturing
624410 Head start programs, separate from schools
315999 Headbands, women's and girls', cut and sewn from purchased fabric (except apparel contractors)
315212 Headbands, women's, girls', and infants', cut and sew apparel contractors
337122 Headboards, wood, manufacturing
321920 Heading, barrel (i.e., cooperage stock), wood, manufacturing
334419 Heads (e.g., recording, read/write) manufacturing
334511 Heads-up display (HUD) systems, aeronautical, manufacturing
236220 Health and athletic club construction
525120 Health and welfare funds
713940 Health club facilities, physical fitness
424490 Health foods (except fresh fruits, vegetables) merchant wholesalers
424480 Health foods, fresh fruits and vegetables, merchant wholesalers
524114 Health insurance carriers, direct
335110 Health lamp bulbs, infrared and ultraviolet radiation, manufacturing
621491 Health maintenance organization (HMO) medical centers and clinics
923120 Health planning and development agencies, government
813920 Health professionals' associations

926150 Health professions licensure agencies
923120 Health program administration
541710 Health research and development laboratories or services
813212 Health research fundraising organizations
621999 Health screening services (except by offices of health practitioners)
621111 Health screening services in physicians' offices
721110 Health spas (i.e., physical fitness facilities) with accommodations
713940 Health spas without accommodations, physical fitness
923120 Health statistics centers, government
713940 Health studios, physical fitness
446199 Hearing aid stores
423450 Hearing aids merchant wholesalers
334510 Hearing aids, electronic, manufacturing
621999 Hearing testing services (except by offices of audiologists)
621340 Hearing testing services by offices of audiologists
336211 Hearse bodies manufacturing
532111 Hearse rental
485320 Hearse rental with driver
336111 Hearses assembling on chassis of own manufacture
336211 Hearses assembling on purchased chassis
334510 Heart-lung machine, manufacturing
332410 Heat exchangers manufacturing
238220 Heat pump installation
333415 Heat pumps manufacturing
423730 Heat pumps merchant wholesalers
325992 Heat sensitized (i.e., thermal) paper made from purchased paper
335991 Heat shields, carbon or graphite, manufacturing

332811 Heat treating metals and metal products for the trade
333994 Heat treating ovens, industrial process-type, manufacturing
221330 Heat, steam, distribution
221330 Heated air distribution
335211 Heaters, portable electric space, manufacturing
423620 Heaters, portable electric, merchant wholesalers
333414 Heaters, space (except portable electric), manufacturing
333414 Heaters, swimming pool, manufacturing
335211 Heaters, tape, manufacturing
333415 Heating and air conditioning combination units manufacturing
238220 Heating and cooling duct work installation
334512 Heating and cooling system controls, residential and commercial, manufacturing
238220 Heating and ventilation system component (e.g., air registers, diffusers, filters, grilles, sound attenuators) installation
238220 Heating boiler installation
423720 Heating boilers, steam and hot water, merchant wholesalers
238220 Heating contractors
541330 Heating engineering consulting services
238220 Heating equipment installation
333414 Heating equipment, hot water (except hot water heaters), manufacturing
423720 Heating equipment, hot water, merchant wholesalers
423730 Heating equipment, warm air (i.e. forced air), merchant wholesalers
333415 Heating equipment, warm air (i.e., forced air), manufacturing
454311 Heating oil dealers, direct selling
324110 Heating oils made in petroleum refineries

335211 Heating pads, electric, manufacturing
334512 Heating regulators manufacturing
221330 Heating steam (suppliers of heat) providers
335211 Heating units for electric appliances manufacturing
333414 Heating units, baseboard, manufacturing
238220 Heating, ventilation and air-conditioning (HVAC) contractors
532412 Heavy construction equipment rental without operator
611519 Heavy equipment operation schools
611519 Heavy equipment repair training
811310 Heavy machinery and equipment repair and maintenance services
336120 Heavy trucks assembling on chassis of own manufacture
336211 Heavy trucks assembling on purchased chassis
325188 Heavy water (i.e., deuterium oxide) manufacturing
332212 Hedge shears and trimmers, nonelectric, manufacturing
333112 Hedge trimmers, powered, manufacturing
316999 Heel caps, leather or metal, manufacturing
316999 Heel lifts, leather, manufacturing
321999 Heels, boot and shoe, finished wood, manufacturing
316999 Heels, boot and shoe, leather, manufacturing
332611 Helical springs, hot wound heavy gauge metal, manufacturing
332612 Helical springs, light gauge, made from purchased wire or strip, manufacturing
481212 Helicopter carriers, freight, nonscheduled
481112 Helicopter freight carriers, scheduled

481211 Helicopter passenger carriers (except scenic, sightseeing), nonscheduled
481111 Helicopter passenger carriers, scheduled
487990 Helicopter ride, scenic and sightseeing, operation
336411 Helicopters manufacturing
325120 Helium manufacturing
325120 Helium recovery from natural gas
339113 Helmets (except athletic), safety (e.g., motorized vehicle crash helmets, space helmets), manufacturing
339920 Helmets, athletic (except motorized vehicle crash helmets), manufacturing
561320 Help supply services
212210 Hematite mining and/or beneficiating
334516 Hematology instruments manufacturing
325413 Hematology in-vitro diagnostic substances manufacturing
325412 Hematology in-vivo diagnostic substances manufacturing
325414 Hematology products (except diagnostic substances) manufacturing
325191 Hemlock extract manufacturing
113210 Hemlock gum gathering
621492 Hemodialysis centers and clinics
313111 Hemp bags made from purchased fiber
313111 Hemp ropes made from purchased fiber
313111 Hemp spun yarns made from purchased fiber
315211 Hemstitching apparel contractors on men's and boys' apparel
315212 Hemstitching apparel contractors on women's, girls', and infants' apparel
325110 Heptanes made from refined petroleum or liquid hydrocarbons

325110 Heptenes made from refined petroleum or liquid hydrocarbons
111419 Herb farming, grown under cover
111998 Herb farming, open field
111421 Herbaceous perennial growing
621399 Herbalists' offices (e.g., centers, clinics)
712110 Herbariums
325320 Herbicides manufacturing
711310 Heritage festival managers with facilities
711320 Heritage festival managers without facilities
711310 Heritage festival organizers with facilities
711320 Heritage festival organizers without facilities
711310 Heritage festival promoters with facilities
711320 Heritage festival promoters without facilities
712120 Heritage villages
238150 Hermetically sealed window unit, commercial type, installation
238350 Hermetically sealed window unit, residential-type, installation
114111 Herring fishing
325199 Heterocyclic chemicals, not specified elsewhere by process, manufacturing
325199 Hexadecanol manufacturing
325199 Hexamethylenediamine manufacturing
325199 Hexamethylenetetramine manufacturing
325199 Hexanol manufacturing
311221 HFCS (high fructose corn syrup) manufacturing
311611 Hides and skins produced in slaughtering plants
316110 Hides and skins, finishing on a contract basis
424590 Hides merchant wholesalers
316110 Hides, tanning, currying, dressing, and finishing

551111	Holding companies, bank (except managing)
333313	Holepunchers (except hand operated), office-type, manufacturing
339942	Holepunchers, hand operated, manufacturing
332999	Hollowware, precious plated metal, manufacturing
316999	Holsters, leather, manufacturing
452990	Home and auto supply stores
532310	Home and garden equipment rental centers
238210	Home automation system installation
236116	Home builders (except operative), multifamily
236115	Home builders (except operative), single-family
236117	Home builders, operative
332115	Home canning lids and rings, metal stamping
621610	Home care of elderly, medical
624120	Home care of elderly, non-medical
444110	Home centers, building materials
624229	Home construction organizations, work (sweat) equity
454390	Home delivery newspaper routes, direct selling
337124	Home entertainment centers, metal, manufacturing
337122	Home entertainment centers, wood, manufacturing
522292	Home equity credit lending
621610	Home health agencies
611519	Home health aid schools
621610	Home health care agencies
532291	Home health furniture and equipment rental
236118	Home improvement (e.g., adding on, remodeling, renovating)
236118	Home improvement (e.g., adding on, remodeling, renovating), multifamily building, general contractors
236118	Home improvement (e.g., adding on, remodeling, renovating), multifamily building, operative builders
236118	Home improvement (e.g., adding on, remodeling, renovating), single-family housing, general contractors
236118	Home improvement (e.g., adding on, remodeling, renovating), single-family housing, operative builders
444110	Home improvement centers
541350	Home inspection services
621610	Home nursing services (except private practices)
621399	Home nursing services, private practice
236118	Home renovation
453998	Home security equipment stores
561920	Home show managers
561920	Home show organizers
561920	Home show promoters
334310	Home stereo systems manufacturing
334310	Home tape recorders and players (e.g., cartridge, cassette, reel) manufacturing
334310	Home theater audio and video equipment manufacturing
238210	Home theater installation
333512	Home workshop metal cutting machine tools (except handtools, welding equipment) manufacturing
423220	Homefurnishings merchant wholesalers
442299	Homefurnishings stores
624221	Homeless shelters
624120	Homemaker's service for elderly or disabled persons, non-medical
621399	Homeopaths' offices (e.g., centers, clinics)
813990	Homeowners' associations
813990	Homeowners' associations, condominium
524126	Homeowners' insurance carriers, direct

524128 Homeowners' warranty insurance carriers, direct

623990 Homes for children with health care incidental

623220 Homes for emotionally disturbed adults or children

623110 Homes for the aged with nursing care

623312 Homes for the aged without nursing care

623110 Homes for the elderly with nursing care

623312 Homes for the elderly without nursing care

623990 Homes for unwed mothers

623210 Homes with or without health care, mental retardation

623220 Homes, psychiatric convalescent

311211 Hominy grits (except breakfast food), manufacturing

311230 Hominy grits, prepared as cereal breakfast food, manufacturing

311421 Hominy, canned, manufacturing

333294 Homogenizing machinery, food, manufacturing

311511 Homogenizing milk

212399 Hones mining and/or beneficiating

112910 Honey bee production

424490 Honey merchant wholesalers

311999 Honey processing

111219 Honeydew melon farming, field, bedding plant and seed production

333512 Honing and lapping machines, metal cutting type, manufacturing

333515 Honing heads (i.e., a machine tool accessory) manufacturing

922140 Honor camps, correctional

332313 Hoods, industrial, fabricated metal plate work, manufacturing

332322 Hoods, range (except household-type), sheet metal (except stampings), manufacturing

335211 Hoods, range, household-type, manufacturing

115210 Hoof trimming

339993 Hook and eye fasteners (i.e., sewing accessories) manufacturing

332722 Hook and eye latches, metal, manufacturing

313221 Hook and loop fastener fabric manufacturing

332722 Hooks (i.e., general purpose fasteners), metal, manufacturing

339920 Hooks, fishing, manufacturing

332212 Hooks, handtools (e.g., baling, bush, grass, husking), manufacturing

332722 Hooks, metal screw, manufacturing

331111 Hoops made in iron and steel mills

331111 Hoops, galvanized, made in iron and steel mills

332999 Hoops, metal (except wire), fabricated from purchased metal

321920 Hoops, sawed or split wood for tight or slack cooperage, manufacturing

311942 Hop extract manufacturing

424490 Hop extract merchant wholesalers

111998 Hop farming

333515 Hopper feed devices (i.e., a machine tool accessory) manufacturing

332313 Hoppers, fabricated metal plate work, manufacturing

332439 Hoppers, light gauge metal, manufacturing

424590 Hops merchant wholesalers

334511 Horizon situation instrumentation manufacturing

237990 Horizontal drilling (e.g., underground cable, pipeline, sewer installation)

325413 Hormone in-vitro diagnostic substances manufacturing

325412 Hormone preparations (except in-vitro diagnostics) manufacturing

325411	Hormones and derivatives, uncompounded, manufacturing
112920	Horse (including thoroughbreds) production
332999	Horse bits manufacturing
316999	Horse boots and muzzles manufacturing
711212	Horse racetracks
711219	Horse racing stables
713990	Horse rental services, recreational saddle
711310	Horse show managers with facilities
711320	Horse show managers without facilities
711310	Horse show organizers with facilities
711320	Horse show organizers without facilities
711310	Horse show promoters with facilities
711320	Horse show promoters without facilities
336214	Horse trailers (except fifth-wheel-type) manufacturing
336212	Horse trailers, fifth-wheel-type, manufacturing
713990	Horseback riding, recreational
487110	Horse-drawn carriage operation
311611	Horsemeat produced in slaughtering plants
311111	Horsemeat, processing, for dog and cat food
311421	Horseradish (except sauce) canning
311941	Horseradish, prepared sauce, manufacturing
115210	Horses (except racehorses), boarding
424590	Horses merchant wholesalers
115210	Horses, training (except racehorses)
331222	Horseshoe nails, iron or steel, made in wire drawing plants
115210	Horseshoeing
332111	Horseshoes, ferrous forged, made from purchased iron or steel
541690	Horticultural consulting services
332912	Hose assemblies for fluid power systems manufacturing
332722	Hose clamps, metal, manufacturing
332912	Hose couplings and fittings, fluid power, manufacturing
332919	Hose couplings, metal (except fluid power), manufacturing
313221	Hose fabrics, tubular, weaving
332999	Hose, flexible metal, manufacturing
423840	Hose, industrial, merchant wholesalers
326220	Hoses, reinforced, made from purchased rubber or plastics manufacturing
326220	Hoses, rubberized fabric, manufacturing
315119	Hosiery (except sheer), women's, girls' and infants', manufacturing
333292	Hosiery machines manufacturing
448190	Hosiery stores
424320	Hosiery, men's and boys', merchant wholesalers
339113	Hosiery, orthopedic support, manufacturing
315111	Hosiery, sheer, women's, misses', and girls' full-length and knee-length, knitting or knitting and finishing
424330	Hosiery, women's and girls', merchant wholesalers
424330	Hosiery, women's, children's, and infants', merchant wholesalers
621610	Hospice care services, in home
623110	Hospices, inpatient care
813920	Hospital administrators' associations
524114	Hospital and medical service plans, direct, without providing health care services
813910	Hospital associations
532291	Hospital bed rental and leasing (i.e. home use)
339111	Hospital beds manufacturing
423450	Hospital beds merchant wholesalers

335228 Hot water heaters (including nonelectric), household-type, manufacturing

238220 Hot water heating system installation

238220 Hot water tank installation

531120 Hotel building, rental or leasing, not operating hotel

236220 Hotel construction

423440 Hotel equipment and supplies (except furniture) merchant wholesalers

423210 Hotel furniture merchant wholesalers

561110 Hotel management services (except complete operation of client's business)

721110 Hotel management services (i.e., providing management and operating staff to run hotel)

561599 Hotel reservation services

327112 Hotel tableware and kitchen articles, vitreous china, manufacturing

721110 Hotels (except casino hotels)

721110 Hotels (except casino hotels) with golf courses, tennis courts, and/or other health spa facilities (i.e., resorts)

721120 Hotels, casino

721110 Hotels, membership

721120 Hotels, resort, with casinos

721110 Hotels, resort, without casinos

721120 Hotels, seasonal, with casinos

721110 Hotels, seasonal, without casinos

624190 Hotline centers

333319 Hotplates, commercial-type, manufacturing

335211 Hotplates, household-type electric, manufacturing

331111 Hot-rolling iron or steel products in iron and steel mills

333516 Hot-rolling mill machinery, metalworking, manufacturing

331221 Hot-rolling purchased steel

238910 House demolishing

238130 House framing

238990 House moving (i.e., raising from one site, moving, and placing on a new foundation)

238320 House painting

111422 House plant growing

238910 House razing

812990 House sitting services

316212 House slippers manufacturing

316212 House slippers, plastics or plastics soled fabric upper, manufacturing

316212 House slippers, rubber or rubber soled fabric upper, manufacturing

532292 Houseboat rental

315191 Housecoats made in apparel knitting mills

315291 Housecoats, infants', cut and sewn from purchased fabric (except apparel contractors)

315212 Housecoats, women's, girls', and infants', cut and sew apparel contractors

315231 Housecoats, women's, misses', and girls', cut and sewn from purchased fabric (except apparel contractors)

315212 Housedresses, women's and girls', cut and sew apparel contractors

315233 Housedresses, women's, misses', and girls', cut and sewn from purchased fabric (except apparel contractors)

238220 Household oil storage tank installation

814110 Households, private, employing (e.g., cooks, maids, chauffeurs, gardeners)

814110 Households, private, employing domestic personnel

443111 Household-type appliance stores

423620 Household-type appliances, electrical, merchant wholesalers

327112 Household-type earthenware, semivitreous, manufacturing

334512	Humidity controls, air-conditioning-type, manufacturing
334519	Humidity instruments (except industrial process and air-conditioning type) manufacturing
334513	Humidity instruments, industrial process-type, manufacturing
212399	Humus, peat, mining and/or beneficiating
721214	Hunting camps with accommodation facilities
713990	Hunting clubs, recreational
315211	Hunting coats and vests, men's and boys', cut and sew apparel contractors
315228	Hunting coats and vests, men's and boys', cut and sewn from purchased fabric (except apparel contractors)
423910	Hunting equipment and supplies merchant wholesalers
713990	Hunting guide services
332211	Hunting knives manufacturing
114210	Hunting preserves
238220	HVAC (heating, ventilation and air-conditioning) contractors
334111	Hybrid computers manufacturing
334413	Hybrid integrated circuits manufacturing
112511	Hybrid striped bass production
327410	Hydrated lime (i.e., calcium hydroxide) manufacturing
332912	Hydraulic aircraft subassemblies manufacturing
333995	Hydraulic cylinders, fluid power, manufacturing
811310	Hydraulic equipment repair and maintenance services
324110	Hydraulic fluids made in petroleum refineries
324191	Hydraulic fluids, petroleum, made from refined petroleum
325998	Hydraulic fluids, synthetic, manufacturing
213112	Hydraulic fracturing wells on a contract basis
332912	Hydraulic hose fittings, fluid power, manufacturing
326220	Hydraulic hoses (without fitting), rubber or plastics, manufacturing
423830	Hydraulic power transmission equipment merchant wholesalers
423830	Hydraulic pumps and parts merchant wholesalers
333996	Hydraulic pumps, fluid power, manufacturing
336340	Hydraulic slave cylinders, automotive, truck, and bus clutch, manufacturing
333611	Hydraulic turbine generator set units manufacturing
333611	Hydraulic turbines manufacturing
332912	Hydraulic valves, fluid power, manufacturing
325188	Hydrazine manufacturing
325188	Hydrochloric acid manufacturing
325188	Hydrocyanic acid manufacturing
238910	Hydrodemolition (i.e., demolition with pressurized water) contractors
237990	Hydroelectric generating facility construction
221111	Hydroelectric power generation
325188	Hydrofluoric acid manufacturing
325188	Hydrofluosilicic acid manufacturing
336611	Hydrofoil vessel building and repairing in shipyard
325120	Hydrogen manufacturing
325188	Hydrogen peroxide manufacturing
325188	Hydrogen sulfide manufacturing
311225	Hydrogenating purchased oil
541370	Hydrographic mapping services
541370	Hydrographic surveying services
541690	Hydrology consulting services
334519	Hydrometers (except industrial process-type) manufacturing
334513	Hydrometers, industrial process-type, manufacturing

334512 Hydronic circulator control, automatic, manufacturing
423720 Hydronic heating equipment and supplies merchant wholesalers
333414 Hydronic heating equipment manufacturing
238220 Hydronic heating system installation
334512 Hydronic limit control manufacturing
334512 Hydronic limit, pressure, and temperature controls, manufacturing
334511 Hydrophones manufacturing
111419 Hydroponic crop farming
325192 Hydroquinone manufacturing
561730 Hydroseeding services (e.g., decorative, erosion control purposes)
333996 Hydrostatic drives manufacturing
541380 Hydrostatic testing laboratories or services
333996 Hydrostatic transmissions manufacturing
325188 Hydrosulfites manufacturing
339113 Hydrotherapy equipment manufacturing
334519 Hygrometers (except industrial process-type) manufacturing
334513 Hygrometers, industrial process-type, manufacturing
334519 Hygrothermographs manufacturing
621399 Hypnotherapists' offices (e.g., centers, clinics)
325411 Hypnotic drugs, uncompounded, manufacturing
325188 Hypochlorites manufacturing
339112 Hypodermic needles and syringes manufacturing
325188 Hypophosphites manufacturing
312113 Ice (except dry ice) manufacturing
424990 Ice (except dry ice) merchant wholesalers
238170 Ice apron, roof, installation
334512 Ice bank controls manufacturing

335222 Ice boxes, household-type, manufacturing
326199 Ice buckets, plastics (except foam), manufacturing
326140 Ice buckets, polystyrene foam, manufacturing
326150 Ice buckets, urethane or other plastics foam (except polystyrene), manufacturing
332439 Ice chests or coolers, light gauge metal, manufacturing
326199 Ice chests or coolers, plastics (except plastics foam) manufacturing
326140 Ice chests or coolers, polystyrene foam, manufacturing
326150 Ice chests or coolers, urethane or other plastics foam (except polystyrene) manufacturing
445299 Ice cream (i.e., packaged) stores
424430 Ice cream and ices merchant wholesalers
311821 Ice cream cones manufacturing
424490 Ice cream cones merchant wholesalers
333294 Ice cream making machinery manufacturing
311520 Ice cream manufacturing
424430 Ice cream merchant wholesalers
311514 Ice cream mix manufacturing
722213 Ice cream parlors
311520 Ice cream specialties manufacturing
722330 Ice cream truck vendors
333311 Ice cream vending machines manufacturing
335211 Ice crushers, household-type electric, manufacturing
333999 Ice crushers, industrial and commercial-type, manufacturing
711211 Ice hockey clubs, professional or semiprofessional
713990 Ice hockey clubs, recreational
334512 Ice maker controls manufacturing
333415 Ice making machinery manufacturing

423740	Ice making machines merchant wholesalers
311520	Ice milk manufacturing
311514	Ice milk mix manufacturing
311520	Ice milk specialties manufacturing
237990	Ice rink (except indoor) construction
236220	Ice rink, indoor, construction
339920	Ice skates manufacturing
711190	Ice skating companies
713940	Ice skating rinks
711190	Ice skating shows
312130	Ice wine
325120	Ice, dry, manufacturing
424690	Ice, dry, merchant wholesalers
312111	Iced coffee manufacturing
312111	Iced tea manufacturing
212399	Iceland spar (i.e., optical grade calcite), mining and/or beneficiating
311520	Ices, flavored sherbets, manufacturing
332999	Identification plates, metal, manufacturing
423410	Identity recorders merchant wholesalers
332993	Igniters, ammunition tracer (i.e., more than 30 mm., more than 1.18 inch), manufacturing
334512	Ignition controls for gas appliances and furnaces, automatic, manufacturing
336322	Ignition points and condensers for internal combustion engines manufacturing
334515	Ignition testing instruments manufacturing
336322	Ignition wiring harness for internal combustion engines manufacturing
321213	I-joists, wood, fabricating
335122	Illuminated indoor lighting fixtures (e.g., directional, exit) manufacturing
541430	Illustrators, independent commercial
212299	Ilmenite ores mining and/or beneficiating

327420	Images, small gypsum, manufacturing
327999	Images, small papier-mache, manufacturing
323122	Imagesetting services, prepress
312221	Imitation tobacco cigarettes, manufacturing
335211	Immersion heaters, household-type electric, manufacturing
624230	Immigrant resettlement services
928120	Immigration services
923120	Immunization program administration
621111	Immunologists' offices (e.g., centers, clinics)
334516	Immunology instruments, laboratory, manufacturing
333991	Impact wrenches, handheld power-driven, manufacturing
334515	Impedance measuring equipment manufacturing
334514	Impeller and counter driven flow meters manufacturing
339113	Implants, surgical, manufacturing
213112	Impounding and storing salt water in connection with petroleum production
221310	Impounding reservoirs, irrigation
339114	Impression material, dental, manufacturing
711110	Improvisational theaters
334512	In-built thermostats, filled system and bimetal types, manufacturing
335110	Incandescent filament lamp bulbs, complete, manufacturing
325998	Incense manufacturing
334512	Incinerator control systems, residential and commercial-type, manufacturing
236210	Incinerator, mass-burn type, construction
236210	Incinerator, municipal waste disposal, construction
333994	Incinerators (except precast concrete) manufacturing

238290   Incinerators, building equipment type, installation
562211   Incinerators, hazardous waste, operating
562213   Incinerators, nonhazardous solid waste
327390   Incinerators, precast concrete, manufacturing
541213   Income tax compilation services
541213   Income tax return preparation services
333313   Incoming mail handling equipment (e.g., opening, scanning, sorting) manufacturing
339113   Incubators, infant, manufacturing
339111   Incubators, laboratory-type, manufacturing
333111   Incubators, poultry, manufacturing
325998   Indelible inks manufacturing
488190   Independent pilot, air (except owner-operators)
488490   Independent truck driver (except owner-operators)
333515   Indexing, rotary tables (i.e., a machine tool accessory) manufacturing
325998   India inks manufacturing
921190   Indian affairs programs, government
334515   Indicating instruments, electric, manufacturing
334519   Indicator testers, turntable, manufacturing
334513   Indicators, industrial process control-type, manufacturing
325188   Indium chloride manufacturing
624190   Individual and family social services, multi-purpose
523910   Individuals investing in financial contracts on own account
541850   Indoor display advertising services
713120   Indoor play areas
236220   Indoor swimming pool construction

333994   Induction heating equipment, industrial process-type, manufacturing
334416   Inductors, electronic component-type (e.g., chokes, coils, transformers), manufacturing
813910   Industrial associations
522190   Industrial banks (i.e., known as), depository
522298   Industrial banks (i.e., known as), nondepository
314992   Industrial belting reinforcement, cord and fabric, manufacturing
236210   Industrial building (except warehouses) construction
236210   Industrial building (except warehouses) construction, general contractors
236210   Industrial building (except warehouses) construction, operative builders
531120   Industrial building rental or leasing
722310   Industrial caterers (i.e., providing food services on a contractual arrangement (except single-event basis))
424690   Industrial chemicals merchant wholesalers
423840   Industrial containers merchant wholesalers
335314   Industrial controls (e.g., push button, selector, and pilot switches, manufacturing
423610   Industrial controls, electrical, merchant wholesalers
541420   Industrial design consulting services
533110   Industrial design licensing
541420   Industrial design services
926110   Industrial development program administration
423840   Industrial diamonds merchant wholesalers
541330   Industrial engineering services
811310   Industrial equipment and machinery repair and maintenance services

315211	Industrial garments, men's and boys', cut and sew apparel contractors
315225	Industrial garments, men's and boys', cut and sewn from purchased fabric (except apparel contractors)
315212	Industrial garments, women's and girls', cut and sew apparel contractors
315239	Industrial garments, women's, misses', and girls', cut and sewn from purchased fabric (except apparel contractors)
325120	Industrial gases manufacturing
424690	Industrial gases merchant wholesalers
327212	Industrial glassware and glass products, pressed or blown, made in glass making plants
327215	Industrial glassware made from purchased glass
813930	Industrial labor unions
541320	Industrial land use planning services
812332	Industrial launderers
335122	Industrial lighting fixtures, electric, manufacturing
522298	Industrial loan companies, nondepository
336510	Industrial locomotives and parts manufacturing
423830	Industrial machinery and equipment (except electrical) merchant wholesalers
335122	Industrial mercury lighting fixtures, electric, manufacturing
333511	Industrial molds (except steel ingot) manufacturing
331511	Industrial molds, steel ingot, manufacturing
332997	Industrial pattern manufacturing
334513	Industrial process control instruments manufacturing
238220	Industrial process piping installation
325510	Industrial product finishes and coatings (i.e., paint) manufacturing
541710	Industrial research and development laboratories or services
423450	Industrial safety devices (e.g., eye shields, face shields, first-aid kits) merchant wholesalers
325998	Industrial salt manufacturing
424690	Industrial salts merchant wholesalers
212322	Industrial sand beneficiating (e.g., screening, washing)
212322	Industrial sand sandpits and dredging
333997	Industrial scales manufacturing
423840	Industrial supplies (except disposable plastics, paper) merchant wholesalers
424130	Industrial supplies, disposable plastics, paper, merchant wholesalers
541380	Industrial testing laboratories or services
621340	Industrial therapists' offices (e.g., centers, clinics)
811310	Industrial truck (e.g., forklifts) repair and maintenance services
532490	Industrial truck rental or leasing
333924	Industrial trucks and tractors manufacturing
423830	Industrial trucks, tractors, or trailers merchant wholesalers
812332	Industrial uniform supply services
423930	Industrial wastes to be reclaimed merchant wholesalers
311611	Inedible products (e.g., hides, skins, pulled wool, wool grease) produced in slaughtering plants
334511	Inertial navigation systems, aeronautical, manufacturing
311422	Infant and junior food canning
311230	Infant cereals, dry, manufacturing
624410	Infant day care centers
624410	Infant day care services
339113	Infant incubators manufacturing

315291 Infants' apparel cut and sewn from purchased fabric (except apparel contractors)

424330 Infants' clothing merchant wholesalers

315212 Infants' cut and sew apparel contractors

311514 Infant's formulas manufacturing

316219 Infant's shoes (except plastics, rubber), manufacturing

315291 Infants water resistant outerwear cut and sewn from purchased fabric (except apparel contractors)

518111 Information access services, on-line

541512 Information management computer systems integration design services

334516 Infrared analytical instruments, laboratory-type, manufacturing

334511 Infrared homing systems, aeronautical, manufacturing

334513 Infrared instruments, industrial process-type, manufacturing

335110 Infrared lamp bulbs manufacturing

335129 Infrared lamp fixtures manufacturing

333994 Infrared ovens, industrial, manufacturing

334413 Infrared sensors, solid-state, manufacturing

621498 Infusion therapy centers and clinics, outpatient

331319 Ingot made by rolling purchased aluminum

331111 Ingot made in iron and steel mills

331319 Ingot, aluminum, made in integrated secondary smelting and rolling mills

331492 Ingot, nonferrous metals (except aluminum, copper), secondary smelting and refining

331312 Ingot, primary aluminum, manufacturing

331419 Ingot, primary, nonferrous metals (except aluminum, copper), manufacturing

423510 Ingots (except precious) merchant wholesalers

423940 Ingots, precious, merchant wholesalers

621399 Inhalation therapists' offices (e.g., centers, clinics)

339112 Inhalation therapy equipment manufacturing

339112 Inhalators, surgical and medical, manufacturing

325998 Inhibitors (e.g., corrosion, oxidation, polymerization) manufacturing

454390 In-home sales of merchandise, direct selling

333220 Injection molding machinery for plastics manufacturing

325612 Ink eradicators manufacturing

424120 Ink, writing, merchant wholesalers

339944 Inked ribbons manufacturing

424120 Inked ribbons merchant wholesalers

325910 Inkjet cartridges manufacturing

325910 Inkjet inks manufacturing

325910 Inks, printing, manufacturing

423840 Inks, printing, merchant wholesalers

325998 Inks, writing, manufacturing

316999 Inner soles, leather, manufacturing

326211 Inner tubes manufacturing

337910 Innerspring cushions manufacturing

721191 Inns, bed and breakfast

424690 Inorganic chemicals merchant wholesalers

325131 Inorganic pigments (except bone black, carbon black, lamp black) manufacturing

334119 Input/output equipment, computer (except terminals), manufacturing

115112 Insect control for crops

335129 Insect lamps, electric, manufacturing

332618 Insect screening made from purchased wire

325320 Insecticides manufacturing

333515	Inserts, cutting tool, manufacturing
541350	Inspection bureaus, building
926150	Inspection for labor standards
488490	Inspection or weighing services, truck transportation
488190	Inspection services, aircraft
541350	Inspection services, building or home
213112	Installing production equipment at the oil or gas field on a contract basis
522220	Installment sales financing
311920	Instant coffee manufacturing
311230	Instant hot cereals manufacturing
323114	Instant printing (i.e., quick printing)
311920	Instant tea manufacturing
236220	Institutional building construction
236220	Institutional building construction general contractors
236220	Institutional building construction operative builders
337127	Institutional furniture manufacturing
335122	Institutional lighting fixtures, electric, manufacturing
522120	Institutions, savings
******	Instruction—see type of training
512110	Instructional video production
336322	Instrument control panels (i.e., assembling purchased gauges), automotive, truck, and bus, manufacturing
334511	Instrument landing system instrumentation, airborne or airport, manufacturing
333314	Instrument lenses manufacturing
334514	Instrument panels, assembling gauges made in the same establishment
334515	Instrument shunts manufacturing

332612	Instrument springs, precision (except clock, watch), light gauge, made from purchased wire or strip, manufacturing
335311	Instrument transformers (except complete instruments) for metering or protective relaying use manufacturing
334519	Instrumentation for reactor controls, auxiliary, manufacturing
423830	Instruments (except electrical) (e.g., controlling, indicating, recording) merchant wholesalers
334513	Instruments for industrial process control manufacturing
334515	Instruments for measuring electrical quantities manufacturing
334511	Instruments, aeronautical, manufacturing
334515	Instruments, electric (i.e., testing electrical characteristics), manufacturing
339112	Instruments, mechanical microsurgical, manufacturing
339992	Instruments, musical, manufacturing
423990	Instruments, musical, merchant wholesalers
423490	Instruments, professional and scientific, merchant wholesalers
331422	Insulated wire or cable made from purchased copper in wire drawing plants
331319	Insulated wire or cable made in aluminum wire drawing plants
423610	Insulated wire or cable merchant wholesalers
331422	Insulated wire or cable, copper, made in integrated secondary smelting and wire drawing plants
322299	Insulating batts, fills, or blankets made from purchased paper

335312   Integral horsepower electric motors manufacturing
423690   Integrated circuits merchant wholesalers
334413   Integrated microcircuits manufacturing
512220   Integrated record companies (i.e., releasing, promoting, distributing)
512220   Integrated record production and distribution
334515   Integrated-circuit testers manufacturing
334515   Integrating electricity meters manufacturing
334514   Integrating meters, nonelectric, manufacturing
712110   Interactive museums
485210   Intercity bus line operation
483113   Intercoastal freight transportation to and from domestic ports
483114   Intercoastal transportation of passengers to and from domestic ports
334290   Intercom systems and equipment manufacturing
238210   Intercommunication (intercom) system installation
332410   Intercooler shells manufacturing
333314   Interferometers manufacturing
541410   Interior decorating consultant services
541410   Interior decorating consulting services
541410   Interior design consulting services
541410   Interior design services
541410   Interior designer services
811121   Interior repair shops, automotive
238990   Interlocking brick and block installation
623210   Intermediate care facilities, mental retardation
334515   Internal combustion engine analyzers (i.e., testing electrical characteristics) manufacturing

333618   Internal combustion engines (except aircraft, nondiesel automotive, nondiesel truck) manufacturing
423830   Internal combustion engines (except aircraft, nondiesel automotive, nondiesel truck) merchant wholesalers
336412   Internal combustion engines, aircraft, manufacturing
336312   Internal combustion engines, automotive and truck gasoline, manufacturing
921130   Internal Revenue Service
928120   International Monetary Fund
522293   International trade financing
518111   Internet access providers
454112   Internet auctions, retail
516110   Internet book publishers
516110   Internet broadcasting
516110   Internet comic book publishing
516110   Internet entertainment sites
516110   Internet game sites
516110   Internet magazine publishing
516110   Internet news publishers
516110   Internet newsletter publishing
516110   Internet newspaper publishing
516110   Internet periodical publishers
516110   Internet radio stations
454111   Internet retail sales sites
518112   Internet search Web sites
518111   Internet service providers (ISP)
516110   Internet sports sites
516110   Internet video broadcast sites
621111   Internists' offices (e.g., centers, clinics)
541940   Internists' offices, veterinary
541930   Interpretation services, language
712190   Interpretive centers, nature
711120   Interpretive dance companies
711510   Interpretive dancers, independent
485210   Interstate bus line operation
485210   Interurban bus line operation
339113   Intra ocular lenses manufacturing
483211   Intracoastal transportation of freight
483212   Intracoastal transportation of passengers

339113 Intrauterine devices manufacturing

325412 Intravenous (IV) solution preparations manufacturing

812990 Introduction services, social

532291 Invalid equipment rental (i.e., home use)

561990 Inventory computing services

541614 Inventory planning and control management consulting services

561990 Inventory taking services

311312 Invert sugar made from purchased raw cane sugar

335312 Inverters, rotating electrical, manufacturing

335999 Inverters, solid-state, manufacturing

561611 Investigation services (except credit), private

561450 Investigation services, credit

561611 Investigators, private

523930 Investment advice consulting services, customized, fees paid by client

523930 Investment advice counseling services, customized, fees paid by client

523930 Investment advisory services, customized, fees paid by client

523110 Investment banking

331524 Investment castings, aluminum, unfinished, manufacturing

331525 Investment castings, copper (except die-castings), unfinished, manufacturing

331528 Investment castings, nonferrous metal (except alumninum, copper), unfinished, manufacturing

331512 Investment castings, steel, unfinished, manufacturing

523910 Investment clubs

525990 Investment funds, closed-end

525910 Investment funds, open-ended

523920 Investment management

325413 In-vitro diagnostic substances manufacturing

325412 In-vivo diagnostic substances manufacturing

325188 Iodides manufacturing

325412 Iodinated in-vivo diagnostic substances manufacturing

325188 Iodine, crude or resublimed, manufacturing

334519 Ion chambers manufacturing

325211 Ion exchange resins manufacturing

325211 Ionomer resins manufacturing

325199 Ionone manufacturing

331491 Iridium bar, rod, sheet, strip and tubing made from purchased metals or scrap

212299 Iridium mining and/or beneficiating

331492 Iridium recovering from scrap and/or alloying purchased metals

331419 Iridium refining, primary

423390 Iron and steel architectural shapes merchant wholesalers

325131 Iron based pigments manufacturing

331511 Iron castings, unfinished, manufacturing

325188 Iron compounds, not specified elsewhere by process, manufacturing

332111 Iron forgings made from purchased iron, unfinished

331511 Iron foundries

339113 Iron lungs manufacturing

212210 Iron ore (e.g., hematite, magnetite, siderite, taconite) mining and/or beneficiating

212210 Iron ore agglomerates mining and/or beneficiating

212210 Iron ore beneficiating plants (e.g., agglomeration, sintering)

212210 Iron ore mine site development for own account

331111 Iron ore recovery from open hearth slag

212210 Iron ore, blocked, mining and/or beneficiating

331111 Iron sinter made in iron and steel mills

325188 Iron sulphate manufacturing

238120 Iron work, structural, contractors
331111 Iron, pig, manufacturing
335224 Ironers and mangles, household-type (except portable irons), manufacturing
332999 Ironing boards, metal, manufacturing
321999 Ironing boards, wood, manufacturing
335211 Irons, household-type electric, manufacturing
334517 Irradiation apparatus and tubes (e.g., industrial, medical diagnostic, medical therapeutic, research, scientific), manufacturing
334517 Irradiation equipment manufacturing
115114 Irradiation of fruits and vegetables
926130 Irrigation districts, nonoperating
423820 Irrigation equipment merchant wholesalers
333111 Irrigation equipment, agriculture, manufacturing
327332 Irrigation pipe, concrete, manufacturing
332322 Irrigation pipe, sheet metal (except stampings), manufacturing
237110 Irrigation system construction
221310 Irrigation system operation
325110 Isobutane made from refined petroleum or liquid hydrocarbons
211112 Isobutane recovered from oil and gas field gases
325110 Isobutene made from refined petroleum or liquid hydrocarbons
325211 Isobutylene polymer resins manufacturing
325212 Isobutylene-isoprene rubber manufacturing
325212 Isocyanate rubber manufacturing
325192 Isocyanates manufacturing
335311 Isolation transformers manufacturing

211112 Isopentane recovered from oil and gas field gases
325110 Isoprene made from refined petroleum or liquid hydrocarbons
325199 Isopropyl alcohol manufacturing
518111 ISP (internet service providers)
522210 Issuing, credit card
311422 Italian foods canning
339112 IV apparatus manufacturing
333120 Jack hammers manufacturing
315191 Jackets made in apparel knitting mills
332992 Jackets, bullet (i.e., 30 mm. or less, 1.18 inch or less), manufacturing
315292 Jackets, fur (except apparel contractors), manufacturing
315211 Jackets, fur, men's and boys', cut and sew apparel contractors
315212 Jackets, fur, women's, girls', and infants', cut and sew apparel contractors
332313 Jackets, industrial, fabricated metal plate work, manufacturing
315291 Jackets, infants', cut and sewn from purchased fabric (except apparel contractors)
315292 Jackets, leather (except welders') or sheep-lined (except apparel contractors), manufacturing
315211 Jackets, leather (except welders') or sheep-lined, men's and boys', cut and sew apparel contractors
315212 Jackets, leather (except welders') or sheep-lined, women's, girls', and infants', cut and sew apparel contractors
315211 Jackets, men's and boys', cut and sew apparel contractors
315225 Jackets, nontailored work, men's and boys', cut and sewn from purchased fabric (except apparel contractors)

315239 Jackets, nontailored work, women's, misses', and girls', cut and sewn from purchased fabric (except apparel contractors)

315239 Jackets, nontailored, women's, misses', and girls', cut and sewn from purchased fabric (except apparel contractors)

315228 Jackets, not tailored (except work), men's and boys', cut and sewn from purchased fabric (except apparel contractors)

315211 Jackets, service apparel (e.g., laboratory, medical), men's and boys', cut and sew apparel contractors

315225 Jackets, service apparel (e.g., laboratory, medical), men's and boys', cut and sewn from purchased fabric (except apparel contractors)

315212 Jackets, service apparel (e.g., laboratory, medical), women's and girls', cut and sew apparel contractors

315239 Jackets, service apparel (e.g., laboratory, medical), women's, misses', and girls', cut and sewn from purchased fabric (except apparel contractors)

315291 Jackets, ski, infants', cut and sewn from purchased fabric (except apparel contractors)

315211 Jackets, ski, men's and boys', cut and sew apparel contractors

315228 Jackets, ski, men's and boys', cut and sewn from purchased fabric (except apparel contractors)

315212 Jackets, ski, women's, girls', and infants', cut and sew apparel contractors

315239 Jackets, ski, women's, misses', and girls', cut and sewn from purchased fabric (except apparel contractors)

315222 Jackets, tailored (except fur, leather, sheep-lined), men's and boys', cut and sewn from purchased fabric (except apparel contractors)

315234 Jackets, tailored (except fur, sheep-lined), women's, misses', and girls', cut and sewn from purchased fabric (except apparel contractors)

315211 Jackets, tailored, men's and boys', cut and sew apparel contractors

315212 Jackets, tailored, women's, girls', and infants', cut and sew apparel contractors

316999 Jackets, welder's, leather, manufacturing

315212 Jackets, women's, girls', and infants', cut and sew apparel contractors

332212 Jacks (except hydraulic, pneumatic) manufacturing

333999 Jacks, hydraulic and pneumatic, manufacturing

333292 Jacquard card cutting machinery manufacturing

313210 Jacquard woven fabrics weaving

212399 Jade mining and/or beneficiating

611620 Jai alai instruction, camps, or schools

711211 Jai alai teams, professional or semiprofessional

236220 Jail construction

561210 Jail operation on a contract or fee basis

922140 Jails (except private operation of)

561210 Jails, privately operated

332321 Jalousies, metal, manufacturing

424690 Janitorial chemicals merchant wholesalers

423850 Janitorial equipment and supplies merchant wholesalers

453998 Janitorial equipment and supplies stores

561720 Janitorial services

561720 Janitorial services, aircraft

332812 Japanning metals and metal products for the trade

316110 Japanning of leather

333994 Japanning ovens manufacturing

327213 Jars for packaging, bottling, and canning, glass, manufacturing
326199 Jars, plastics, manufacturing
711120 Jazz dance companies
711510 Jazz dancers, independent
711130 Jazz musical artists, independent
711130 Jazz musical groups
315211 Jean-cut casual slacks, men's and boys', cut and sew apparel contractors
315224 Jean-cut casual slacks, men's and boys', cut and sewn from purchased fabric (except apparel contractors)
315212 Jean-cut casual slacks, women's, girls, and infants', cut and sew apparel contractors
315239 Jean-cut casual slacks, women's, misses', and girls', cut and sewn from purchased fabric (except apparel contractors)
315291 Jeans, infants', cut and sewn from purchased fabric (except apparel contractors)
315211 Jeans, men's and boys', cut and sew apparel contractors
315239 Jeans, women's, misses', and girls', cut and sewn from purchased fabric (except apparel contractors)
315212 Jeans, women's, misses', girls', and infants', cut and sew apparel contractors
311421 Jellies and jams manufacturing
424490 Jellies and jams merchant wholesalers
311340 Jelly candies manufacturing
315191 Jerseys made in apparel knitting mills
315211 Jerseys, men's and boys', cut and sew apparel contractors
315223 Jerseys, men's and boys', cut and sewn from purchased fabric (except apparel contractors)
315212 Jerseys, women's, girls', and infants', cut and sew apparel contractors
315232 Jerseys, women's, misses', and girls', cut and sewn from purchased fabric (except apparel contractors)
324110 Jet fuels manufacturing
336412 Jet propulsion and internal combustion engines and parts, aircraft, manufacturing
332993 Jet propulsion projectiles (except guided missiles) manufacturing
237990 Jetty construction
339911 Jewel settings and mountings, precious metal, manufacturing
339913 Jeweler's findings and materials manufacturing
423940 Jewelers' findings merchant wholesalers
332212 Jeweler's handtools, nonelectric, manufacturing
424990 Jewelry boxes merchant wholesalers
541490 Jewelry design services
423940 Jewelry merchant wholesalers
811490 Jewelry repair shops without retailing new jewelry
448150 Jewelry stores, costume
448310 Jewelry stores, precious
339914 Jewelry, costume, manufacturing
339911 Jewelry, natural or cultured pearls, manufacturing
339911 Jewelry, precious metal, manufacturing
333514 Jigs (e.g., checking, gauging, inspection) manufacturing
333514 Jigs and fixtures for use with machine tools manufacturing
333991 Jigsaws, handheld power-driven, manufacturing
333210 Jigsaws, woodworking-type, stationary, manufacturing
624310 Job counseling, vocational rehabilitation or habilitation
323119 Job printing (except flexographic, digital, gravure, lithographic, quick, screen)

611210 Junior colleges
611210 Junior colleges offering a wide variety of academic and technical training
611110 Junior high schools
313210 Jute bags made in broadwoven mills
424310 Jute piece goods (except burlap) merchant wholesalers
337124 Juvenile furniture (except upholstered), metal manufacturing
337122 Juvenile furniture (except upholstered), wood, manufacturing
337125 Juvenile furniture, rattan and reed, manufacturing
337121 Juvenile furniture, upholstered, manufacturing
623990 Juvenile halfway group homes
511120 Juvenile magazine and periodical publishers (except exclusive Internet publishing)
511120 Juvenile magazine and periodical publishers and printing combined
516110 Juvenile magazine and periodical publishers, exclusively on Internet
323112 Juvenile magazines and periodicals flexographic printing without publishing
323111 Juvenile magazines and periodicals gravure printing without publishing
323110 Juvenile magazines and periodicals lithographic (offset) printing without publishing
323119 Juvenile magazines and periodicals printing (except flexographic, gravure, lithographic, quick, screen) without publishing
323113 Juvenile magazines and periodicals screen printing without publishing
111219 Kale farming, field, bedding plant and seed production

212324 Kaolin mining and/or beneficiating
327992 Kaolin, processing beyond beneficiation
611620 Karate instruction, camps or schools
713990 Kayaking, recreational
327420 Keene's cement manufacturing
321920 Kegs, wood, coopered, manufacturing
311119 Kelp meal and pellets, animal feed manufacturing
334515 Kelvin bridges (i.e., electrical measuring instruments) manufacturing
111998 Kenaf farming
112990 Kennels, breeding and raising stock for sale
711219 Kennels, dog racing
812910 Kennels, pet boarding
212391 Kernite mining and/or beneficiating
211111 Kerogen processing
324110 Kerosene manufacturing
333414 Kerosene space heaters manufacturing
311421 Ketchup manufacturing
325199 Ketone compounds, not specified elsewhere by process, manufacturing
332420 Kettles, heavy gauge metal, manufacturing
332510 Key blanks, metal, manufacturing
316993 Key cases (except metal) manufacturing
339911 Key cases, precious metal, manufacturing
333512 Key cutting machines, metal cutting type, manufacturing
811490 Key duplicating shops
332618 Key rings made from purchased wire
334119 Keyboards, computer peripheral equipment, manufacturing
339992 Keyboards, piano or organ, manufacturing
336322 Keyless entry systems, automotive, truck, and bus, manufacturing

337122	Knickknack shelves, wood, manufacturing
332211	Knife blades manufacturing
332211	Knife blanks manufacturing
335313	Knife switches, electric power switchgear-type, manufacturing
311812	Knishes (except frozen) made in commercial bakeries
311813	Knishes, frozen, manufacturing
315992	Knit gloves cut and sewn from purchased fabric (except apparel contractors)
315191	Knit gloves made in apparel knitting mills
315211	Knit gloves, men's and boys', cut and sew apparel contractors
315212	Knit gloves, women's, girls', and infants', cut and sew apparel contractors
313113	Knitting and crocheting thread manufacturing
313249	Knitting and finishing lace
313249	Knitting and finishing warp fabric
313241	Knitting and finishing weft fabric
313249	Knitting lace
333292	Knitting machinery manufacturing
313111	Knitting spun yarns (e.g., cotton, manmade fiber, silk, wool) made from purchased fiber
313249	Knitting warp fabric
313241	Knitting weft fabric
332211	Knives (e.g., hunting, pocket, table nonprecious, table precious plated) manufacturing
423710	Knives (except disposable plastics) merchant wholesalers
333515	Knives and bits for metalworking lathes, planers, and shapers manufacturing
332212	Knives and bits for woodworking lathes, planers, and shapers manufacturing
424130	Knives, disposable plastics, merchant wholesalers
335211	Knives, household-type electric carving, manufacturing
339112	Knives, surgical, manufacturing
339992	Knobs, organ, manufacturing
321999	Knobs, wood, manufacturing
333292	Knot tying machinery for textiles manufacturing
333513	Knurling machines, metalworking, manufacturing
322130	Kraft liner board manufacturing
322121	Kraft paper stock manufacturing
212325	Kyanite mining and/or beneficiating
339942	Label making equipment, handheld, manufacturing
333993	Labeling (i.e., packaging) machinery manufacturing
561910	Labeling services
323110	Labels, lithographic (offset) printing, on a job-order basis
424310	Labels, textile, merchant wholesalers
313221	Labels weaving
561320	Labor (except farm) contractors (i.e., personnel suppliers)
561320	Labor (except farm) pools
115115	Labor contractors, farm
813930	Labor federations
561330	Labor leasing services
926150	Labor management negotiations boards, government
541612	Labor relations consulting services
926110	Labor statistics agencies
813930	Labor unions (except apprenticeship programs)
	Laboratories (see specific type)
621512	Laboratories, dental X-ray
621511	Laboratories, medical (except radiological, X-ray)
621512	Laboratories, medical radiological or X-ray
334516	Laboratory analytical instruments (except optical) manufacturing
333314	Laboratory analytical optical instruments (e.g., microscopes) manufacturing
311119	Laboratory animal feed manufacturing

332999	Ladders, portable metal, manufacturing
332313	Ladle bails, fabricated metal plate work, manufacturing
332313	Ladles, fabricated metal plate work, manufacturing
312120	Lager brewing
237110	Lagoon, sewage treatment construction
483211	Lake freight transportation (except on Great Lakes system)
483113	Lake freight transportation, Great Lakes (including St. Lawrence Seaway)
483212	Lake passenger transportation (except on Great Lakes system)
483114	Lake passenger transportation, Great Lakes (including St. Lawrence Seaway)
325132	Lakes (i.e., organic pigments) manufacturing
311611	Lamb carcasses, half carcasses, primal and sub-primal cuts, produced in slaughtering plants
112410	Lamb feedlots (except stockyards for transportation)
311612	Lamb, primal and sub-primal cuts, made from purchased carcasses
327215	Laminated glass made from purchased glass
327211	Laminated glass made in glass making plants
326130	Laminated plastics plate, rod, and sheet, manufacturing
321213	Laminated structural wood members (except trusses) manufacturing
321213	Laminated veneer lumber (LVL) manufacturing
322225	Laminating foil for flexible packaging applications
332813	Laminating metals and metal formed products without fabricating

322222	Laminating purchased foil sheets for nonpackaging applications
322226	Laminating purchased paperboard
322222	Laminating purchased papers for nonpackaging applications
322221	Laminating purchased papers for packaging applications
313320	Laminating purchased textiles
335311	Lamp ballasts manufacturing
327112	Lamp bases, pottery, manufacturing
325182	Lamp black manufacturing
335110	Lamp bulb parts (except glass blanks), electric, manufacturing
335110	Lamp bulbs and tubes, electric (i.e., fluorescent, incandescent filament, vapor), manufacturing
335110	Lamp bulbs and tubes, health, infrared and ultraviolet radiation, manufacturing
332618	Lamp frames, wire, made from purchased wire
335931	Lamp holders manufacturing
332999	Lamp shade frames, metal, manufacturing
335121	Lamp shades (except glass, plastics), residential, manufacturing
327215	Lamp shades made from purchased glass
327212	Lamp shades made in glass making plants
326199	Lamp shades, plastics, manufacturing
442299	Lamp shops, electric
335931	Lamp sockets and receptacles (i.e., electric wiring devices) manufacturing
423220	Lamps (i.e., lighting fixtures) merchant wholesalers
335122	Lamps (i.e., lighting fixtures), commercial, industrial, and institutional, manufacturing
335121	Lamps (i.e., lighting fixtures), residential, electric, manufacturing

333512	Lathes, metalworking, manufacturing
333210	Lathes, woodworking-type, manufacturing
238310	Lathing contractors
321912	Lathmills, wood
316110	Latigo leather manufacturing
812332	Laundered mat and rug supply services
812332	Launderers, industrial
812310	Launderettes
812320	Laundries (except coin-operated, linen supply, uniform supply)
812310	Laundries, coin-operated or similar self-service
812331	Laundries, linen and uniform supply
812310	Laundromats
812320	Laundry and drycleaning agents
314911	Laundry bags made from purchased woven or knitted materials
812320	Laundry drop-off and pick-up sites
335224	Laundry equipment (e.g., dryers, washers), household-type, manufacturing
333312	Laundry extractors manufacturing
332439	Laundry hampers, light gauge metal, manufacturing
337125	Laundry hampers, rattan, reed, wicker or willow, manufacturing
812310	Laundry machine routes (i.e., concession operators), coin-operated or similar self-service
333312	Laundry machinery and equipment (except household-type) manufacturing
423620	Laundry machinery and equipment, household-type (e.g., dryers, washers), merchant wholesalers
423850	Laundry machinery, equipment, and supplies, commercial, merchant wholesalers
314999	Laundry nets made from purchased materials
333312	Laundry pressing machines (except household-type) manufacturing
812320	Laundry services (except coin-operated, linen supply, uniform supply)
812310	Laundry services, coin-operated or similar self-service
812332	Laundry services, industrial
812331	Laundry services, linen supply
325611	Laundry soap, chips, and powder manufacturing
424690	Laundry soap, chips, and powder, merchant wholesalers
332998	Laundry tubs, metal, manufacturing
326191	Laundry tubs, plastics, manufacturing
325199	Lauric acid esters and amines manufacturing
332998	Lavatories, metal, manufacturing
327111	Lavatories, vitreous china, manufacturing
922190	Law enforcement statistics centers, government
541110	Law firms
541110	Law offices
541110	Law practices
611310	Law schools
333112	Lawn and garden equipment manufacturing
811411	Lawn and garden equipment repair and maintenance services without retailing new lawn and garden equipment
713990	Lawn bowling clubs
561730	Lawn care services (e.g., fertilizing, mowing, seeding, spraying)
424910	Lawn care supplies (e.g., chemicals, fertilizers, pesticides) merchant wholesalers
332212	Lawn edgers, nonpowered, manufacturing
333112	Lawn edgers, powered, manufacturing
561730	Lawn fertilizing services

211111 Lease condensate production
213112 Lease tank cleaning and repairing on a contract basis
316999 Leashes, dog, manufacturing
****** Leasing—see type of property or article being leased
522220 Leasing in combination with sales financing
315292 Leather apparel (e.g., capes, coats, hats, jackets) (except apparel contractors) manufacturing
315211 Leather apparel (e.g., capes, coats, hats, jackets), men's and boys', cut and sew apparel contractors
315212 Leather apparel (e.g., capes, coats, hats, jackets), women's, girls', and infants', cut and sew apparel contractors
316999 Leather belting manufacturing
315292 Leather clothing (except apparel contractors) manufacturing
315212 Leather clothing manufacturing, women's, girls', and infants', cut and sew apparel contractors
315211 Leather clothing, men's and boys', cut and sew apparel contractors
448190 Leather coat stores
316110 Leather coloring, cutting, embossing, and japanning
316110 Leather converters
424990 Leather cut stock (except boot, shoe) merchant wholesalers
316999 Leather cut stock for shoe and boot manufacturing
424340 Leather cut stock for shoe and boot merchant wholesalers
316219 Leather footwear (except house slippers, men's, women's) manufacturing
316213 Leather footwear, men's (except athletic, slippers), manufacturing
316212 Leather footwear, slippers, manufacturing

316214 Leather footwear, women's (except athletic, slippers), manufacturing
812320 Leather garment cleaning services
315211 Leather gloves or mittens (except athletic), men's and boys', cut and sew apparel contractors
315212 Leather gloves or mittens (except athletic), women's, girls', and infants', cut and sew apparel contractors
315992 Leather gloves or mittens (except athletic, cut and sewn apparel contractors) manufacturing
339920 Leather gloves, athletic, manufacturing
424990 Leather goods (except belting, footwear, handbags, gloves, luggage) merchant wholesalers
811430 Leather goods repair shops without retailing new leather goods
448320 Leather goods stores
316993 Leather goods, small personal (e.g., coin purses, eyeglass cases, key cases), manufacturing
316992 Leather handbags and purses manufacturing
316212 Leather house slippers manufacturing
316991 Leather luggage manufacturing
316110 Leather tanning, currying, and finishing
316219 Leather upper athletic footwear manufacturing
316999 Leather welting manufacturing
333298 Leather working machinery manufacturing
313320 Leather, artificial, made from purchased fabric
322226 Leatherboard (i.e., paperboard based) made from purchased paperboard
322130 Leatherboard (i.e., paperboard based) made in paperboard mills

311225 Lecithin made from purchased oils
311223 Lecithin, cottonseed, made in crushing mills
311222 Lecithin, soybean, made in crushing mills
334413 LED (light emitting diode) manufacturing
111219 Leek farming, field, bedding plant and seed production
541110 Legal aid services
922130 Legal counsel offices, government
315119 Leggings knitting or knitting and finishing
315291 Leggings, infants', cut and sewn from purchased fabric (except apparel contractors)
316999 Leggings, welder's, leather, manufacturing
315212 Leggings, women's, girls', and infants', cut and sew apparel contractors
315239 Leggings, women's, misses' and girls', cut and sewn from purchased fabric (except apparel contractors)
315239 Leggings, women's, misses', and girls', cut and sewn from purchased fabric (except apparel contractors)
921140 Legislative and executive office combinations
921120 Legislative assemblies
921120 Legislative bodies (e.g., federal, local, and state)
921120 Legislative commissions
111320 Lemon groves
325998 Lemon oil manufacturing
519120 Lending libraries
423460 Lens blanks, ophthalmic, merchant wholesalers
327215 Lens blanks, optical and ophthalmic, made from purchased glass
327212 Lens blanks, optical and ophthalmic, made in glass making plants
326199 Lens blanks, plastics ophthalmic or optical, manufacturing

333314 Lens coating (except ophthalmic)
339115 Lens coating, ophthalmic
333314 Lens grinding (except ophthalmic)
339115 Lens grinding, ophthalmic (except in retail stores)
446130 Lens grinding, ophthalmic, in retail stores
333315 Lens hoods, camera, manufacturing
333314 Lens mounting (except ophthalmic)
339115 Lens mounts, ophthalmic, manufacturing
333314 Lens polishing (except ophthalmic)
339115 Lens polishing, ophthalmic
333314 Lenses (except ophthalmic) manufacturing
339115 Lenses, ophthalmic, manufacturing
111130 Lentil farming, dry, field and seed production
315191 Leotards made in apparel knitting mills
315212 Leotards, women's, girls', and infants', cut and sew apparel contractors
315239 Leotards, women's, misses', and girls', cut and sewn from purchased fabric (except apparel contractors)
212393 Lepidolite mining and/or beneficiating
622310 Leprosy hospitals
****** Lessors—see specific type of asset or property being rented or leased
531130 Lessors of miniwarehouses
531120 Lessors of nonresidential buildings (except miniwarehouses)
531110 Lessors of residential buildings and dwellings
531130 Lessors of self storage units
333313 Letter folding, stuffing, and sealing machinery manufacturing

333515 Letter pins (e.g., gauging, measuring) manufacturing
561410 Letter writing services
325910 Letterpress inks manufacturing
323122 Letterpress plate preparation services
333293 Letterpress printing presses manufacturing
339950 Letters for signs manufacturing
322231 Letters, die-cut, made from purchased cardboard
111219 Lettuce farming, field, bedding plant and seed production
237990 Levee construction
334513 Level and bulk measuring instruments, industrial process-type, manufacturing
334519 Level gauges, radiation-type, manufacturing
334519 Levels and tapes, surveying, manufacturing
332212 Levels, carpenter's, manufacturing
524126 Liability insurance carriers, direct
519120 Libraries (except motion picture stock footage, motion picture commercial distribution)
512199 Libraries, motion picture stock footage film
512199 Libraries, videotape, stock footage
236220 Library construction
561990 License issuing services (except government), motor vehicle
621399 Licensed practical nurses' (LPNs) offices (e.g., centers, clinics)
926130 Licensing and inspecting of utilities
926150 Licensing and permit issuance for business operations, government
926150 Licensing and permit issuance for professional occupations, government
926120 Licensing of transportation equipment, facilities, and services
311340 Licorice candy manufacturing

332431 Lids and ends, can, light gauge metal, manufacturing
332115 Lids, jar, metal, stamping
561611 Lie detection services
334519 Lie detectors manufacturing
611699 Life guard training
524210 Life insurance agencies
524113 Life insurance carriers, direct
339113 Life preservers manufacturing
326199 Life rafts, inflatable plastics, manufacturing
326299 Life rafts, inflatable rubberized fabric, manufacturing
524130 Life reinsurance carriers
541710 Life sciences research and development laboratories or services
423830 Lift trucks, industrial, merchant wholesalers
316999 Lifts, heel, leather, manufacturing
333298 Light bulb and tube (i.e., electric lamp) machinery manufacturing
335110 Light bulbs manufacturing
423610 Light bulbs merchant wholesalers
335110 Light bulbs, sealed beam automotive, manufacturing
334413 Light emitting diodes (LED) manufacturing
333315 Light meters, photographic, manufacturing
336510 Light rail cars and equipment manufacturing
237990 Light rail system construction
485119 Light rail systems (except mixed mode), commuter
334511 Light reconnaissance and surveillance systems and equipment manufacturing
334512 Light responsive appliance controls manufacturing
441110 Light utility truck dealers, new only or new and used
441120 Light utility truck dealers, used only
336112 Light utility trucks assembling on chassis of own manufacture

325998 Lighter fluids (e.g., charcoal, cigarette) manufacturing

483211 Lighterage (i.e., freight transportation except vessel supply services)

339999 Lighters, cigar and cigarette (except motor vehicle, precious metal), manufacturing

339911 Lighters, cigar and cigarette, clad with precious metal, manufacturing

424990 Lighters, cigar and cigarette, merchant wholesalers

488310 Lighthouse operation

335991 Lighting carbons manufacturing

423990 Lighting equipment, gas, merchant wholesalers

444190 Lighting fixture stores

335129 Lighting fixtures, airport (e.g., approach, ramp, runway, taxi), manufacturing

335122 Lighting fixtures, commercial electric, manufacturing

423610 Lighting fixtures, electric, merchant wholesalers

335122 Lighting fixtures, industrial electric, manufacturing

335122 Lighting fixtures, institutional electric, manufacturing

335129 Lighting fixtures, nonelectric (e.g., propane, kerosene, carbide), manufacturing

335121 Lighting fixtures, residential electric, manufacturing

561790 Lighting maintenance services (e.g., bulb and fuse replacement and cleaning)

238210 Lighting system installation

711510 Lighting technicians, theatrical, independent

335311 Lighting transformers manufacturing

335311 Lighting transformers, street and airport, manufacturing

335931 Lightning arrestors and coils manufacturing

238290 Lightning protection equipment (e.g., lightning rod) installation

335931 Lightning protection equipment manufacturing

238290 Lightning rod and conductor installation

325211 Lignin plastics manufacturing

213113 Lignite mining services (except site preparation and related construction contractor activities) on a contract basis

212111 Lignite surface mining and/or beneficiating

111130 Lima bean farming, dry, field and seed production

339113 Limbs, artificial, manufacturing

423320 Lime (except agricultural) merchant wholesalers

111320 Lime groves

325998 Lime oil manufacturing

327410 Lime production

212312 Lime rock, ground, mining and/or beneficiating

424910 Lime, agricultural, merchant wholesalers

212312 Limestone (except bituminous) crushed and broken stone mining and/or beneficiating

212312 Limestone beneficiating plants (e.g., grinding or pulverizing)

212311 Limestone mining or quarrying

212319 Limestone, bituminous, mining and/or beneficiating

325320 Lime-sulfur fungicides manufacturing

334512 Limit controls (e.g., air-conditioning, appliance, heating) manufacturing

511199 Limited editions art print publishers (except exclusive Internet publishing)

452990 Limited price variety stores

212210 Limonite mining and/or beneficiating

532111 Limousine rental without driver

485320 Limousine services (except shuttle services)

485320 Limousines for hire with driver (except taxis)

325320 Lindane pesticides manufacturing

334512 Line or limit control for electric heat manufacturing

561730 Line slash (i.e., rights of way) maintenance services

238910 Line slashing or cutting (except maintenance)

335311 Line voltage regulators (i.e., electric transformers) manufacturing

335999 Linear accelerators manufacturing

332991 Linear ball bearings manufacturing

334514 Linear counters manufacturing

325222 Linear esters fibers and filaments manufacturing

332991 Linear roller bearings manufacturing

442299 Linen stores

812331 Linen supply services

423220 Linens (e.g., bath, bed, table) merchant wholesalers

314129 Linens made from purchased materials

327123 Liner brick and plates, vitrified clay, manufacturing

332313 Liners, industrial, fabricated metal plate work, manufacturing

114111 Lingcod fishing

424330 Lingerie merchant wholesalers

448190 Lingerie stores

315212 Lingerie, women's, cut and sew apparel contractors

315231 Lingerie, women's, misses', and girls', cut and sewn from purchased fabric (except apparel contractors)

316110 Lining leather manufacturing

316999 Linings, boot and shoe, leather, manufacturing

314999 Linings, casket, manufacturing

315211 Linings, hat, men's, cut and sew apparel contractors

315999 Linings, hat, men's, cut and sewn from purchased fabric (except apparel contractors)

314999 Linings, luggage, manufacturing

332999 Linings, metal safe and vault, manufacturing

332994 Links, ammunition (i.e., 30 mm. or less, 1.18 inch or less), manufacturing

332995 Links, ammunition (i.e., more than 30 mm., more than 1.18 inch), manufacturing

325199 Linoleic acid esters and amines manufacturing

326192 Linoleum floor coverings manufacturing

238330 Linoleum, installation only

333293 Linotype machines manufacturing

311225 Linseed oil made from purchased oils

311223 Linseed oil, cake and meal, made in crushing mills

327390 Lintels, concrete, manufacturing

325412 Lip balms manufacturing

325620 Lipsticks manufacturing

424690 Liquefied gases (except LP) merchant wholesalers

424710 Liquefied petroleum gas (LPG) bulk stations and terminals

332420 Liquefied petroleum gas (LPG) cylinders manufacturing

454312 Liquefied petroleum gas (LPG) dealers, direct selling

221210 Liquefied petroleum gas (LPG) distribution through mains

324110 Liquefied petroleum gas (LPG) made in refineries

424720 Liquefied petroleum gas (LPG) merchant wholesalers (except bulk stations, terminals)

211112 Liquefied petroleum gases (LPG), natural

325120 Liquid air manufacturing

334513 Liquid analysis instruments, industrial process-type, manufacturing

311313 Liquid beet syrup manufacturing

334516 Liquid chromatographic instruments, laboratory-type, manufacturing

334513 Liquid concentration instruments, industrial process-type, manufacturing

334514 Liquid flow meters manufacturing

211112 Liquid hydrocarbons recovered from oil and gas field gases

334512 Liquid level controls, residential and commercial heating-type, manufacturing

334513 Liquid level instruments, industrial process-type, manufacturing

332420 Liquid oxygen tanks manufacturing

311313 Liquid sugar made from beet sugar

311312 Liquid sugar made from purchased raw cane sugar

311311 Liquid sugar made in sugarcane mill

211112 Liquids, natural gas (e.g., ethane, isobutane, natural gasoline, propane) recovered from oil and gas field gases

445310 Liquor stores, package

311320 Liquor, chocolate, made from cacao beans

311330 Liquor, chocolate, made from purchased chocolate

424820 Liquors merchant wholesalers

312130 Liquors, brandy, distilling and blending

424820 Liquors, distilled, merchant wholesalers

312140 Liquors, distilling and blending (except brandy)

339942 List finders and roledex address files manufacturing

531390 Listing services, real estate

711410 Literary agents

325131 Litharge manufacturing

335912 Lithium batteries, primary, manufacturing

325188 Lithium compounds, not specified elsewhere by process, manufacturing

212393 Lithium mineral mining and/or beneficiating

325910 Lithographic inks manufacturing

323122 Lithographic plate preparation services

323110 Lithographic printing (except books, manifold business forms, printing grey goods, quick printing)

333293 Lithographic printing presses manufacturing

325131 Lithopone manufacturing

334510 Lithotripters manufacturing

711310 Live arts center operators

424990 Live bait merchant wholesalers

711310 Live theater operators

332995 Livens projectors (i.e., ordnance) manufacturing

541690 Livestock breeding consulting services

115210 Livestock breeding services (except consulting)

424910 Livestock feeds merchant wholesalers

311119 Livestock feeds, supplements, concentrates and premixes, manufacturing

541940 Livestock inspecting and testing services, veterinary

115210 Livestock spraying

484220 Livestock trucking, local

484230 Livestock trucking, long-distance

541940 Livestock veterinary services

337124 Living room furniture (except upholstered), metal, manufacturing

337122 Living room furniture (except upholstered), wood, manufacturing

337121 Living room furniture, upholstered, manufacturing

112990 Llama production

334418 Loaded computer boards manufacturing

423430 Loaded computer boards merchant wholesalers

333120 Loaders, shovel, manufacturing

332993 Loading and assembling bombs

488490 Loading and unloading at truck terminals

488320 Loading and unloading services at ports and harbors

488210 Loading and unloading services at rail terminals

333131 Loading machines, underground mining, manufacturing

334418 Loading printed circuit boards

522310 Loan brokerages

522310 Loan brokers' or agents' offices (i.e., independent)

522291 Loan companies (i.e., consumer, personal, small, student)

522292 Loan correspondents (i.e., lending funds with real estate as collateral)

522390 Loan servicing

541820 Lobbying services

541820 Lobbyists' offices

114112 Lobster fishing

334210 Local area network (LAN) communications equipment (e.g., bridges, gateways, routers) manufacturing

541512 Local area network (LAN) computer systems integration design services

611420 Local area network (LAN) management training

485113 Local bus services (except mixed mode)

492210 Local letter and parcel delivery services (except as part of intercity carrier network, U.S. Postal Service)

492110 Local letter and parcel delivery services as part of intercity courier network

485112 Local passenger rail systems (except mixed mode)

813940 Local political organizations

517110 Local telephone carriers (except wireless)

485111 Local transit systems, mixed mode (e.g., bus, commuter rail, subway combinations)

561990 Locating underground utility lines prior to digging

237990 Lock and waterway construction

332722 Lock washers, metal, manufacturing

454390 Locker meat provisioners, direct selling

337215 Lockers (except refrigerated) manufacturing

423440 Lockers (except refrigerated) merchant wholesalers

812990 Lockers, coin-operated, rental

333415 Lockers, refrigerated, manufacturing

423740 Lockers, refrigerated, merchant wholesalers

332510 Locks (except coin-operated, time locks), metal, manufacturing

333311 Locks, coin-operated, manufacturing

423710 Locks, security, merchant wholesalers

423850 Locksmith equipment and supplies merchant wholesalers

561622 Locksmith services

561622 Locksmith services with or without sales of locking devices, safes, and security vaults

561622 Locksmith shops

488210 Locomotive and rail car repair (except factory conversion, factory overhaul, factory rebuilding)

336321 Locomotive and railroad car light fixtures manufacturing

333923 Locomotive cranes manufacturing

333618 Locomotive diesel engines manufacturing

336510 Locomotives manufacturing

423860 Locomotives merchant wholesalers

336510 Locomotives rebuilding

212221 Lode gold mining and/or beneficiating

321992 Log cabins, prefabricated wood, manufacturing

333120 Log debarking machinery, portable, manufacturing

333291 Log debarking machinery, stationary, manufacturing

113310 Log harvesting

484220 Log hauling, local

484230 Log hauling, long-distance

236117	Low income housing construction operative builders
236116	Low income housing, multifamily, construction general contractors
236115	Low income housing, single-family, construction general contractors
238160	Low slope roofing installation
238210	Low voltage electrical work
335121	Low voltage lighting equipment, residential, electric, manufacturing
236116	Low-rise apartment construction general contractors
236117	Low-rise apartment operative builders
311340	Lozenges, nonmedicated, candy, manufacturing
621399	LPNs' (licensed practical nurses) offices (e.g., centers, clinics)
484122	LTL (less-than-truckload) long-distance freight trucking
424710	Lubricating oils and greases bulk stations and terminals
324110	Lubricating oils and greases made in petroleum refineries
424720	Lubricating oils and greases merchant wholesalers (except bulk stations, terminals)
324191	Lubricating oils and greases, petroleum, made from refined petroleum
325998	Lubricating oils and greases, synthetic, manufacturing
811191	Lubrication shops, automotive
336510	Lubrication systems, locomotive (except pumps), manufacturing
332510	Luggage hardware, metal, manufacturing
314999	Luggage linings manufacturing
423990	Luggage merchant wholesalers
336399	Luggage racks, car top, automotive, truck, and bus, manufacturing
811430	Luggage repair shops without retailing new luggage
448320	Luggage stores
316991	Luggage, all materials, manufacturing
335931	Lugs and connectors, electrical, manufacturing
423610	Lugs and connectors, electrical, merchant wholesalers
423310	Lumber (e.g., dressed, finished, rough) merchant wholesalers
321113	Lumber (i.e., rough, dressed) made from logs or bolts
561990	Lumber grading services
444190	Lumber retailing yards
493190	Lumber storage terminals
321113	Lumber, hardwood dimension, made from logs or bolts
321912	Lumber, hardwood dimension, resawing purchased lumber
321999	Lumber, kiln drying
321213	Lumber, parallel strand, manufacturing
321113	Lumber, softwood dimension, made from logs or bolts
321912	Lumber, softwood dimension, resawing purchased lumber
335122	Luminous panel ceilings, electric, manufacturing
335311	Luminous tube transformers manufacturing
332439	Lunch boxes, light gauge metal, manufacturing
722330	Lunch wagons
311612	Luncheon meat (except poultry) made from purchased carcasses
311611	Luncheon meat (except poultry) produced in slaughtering plants
311615	Luncheon meat, poultry, manufacturing
532111	Luxury automobile rental
485320	Luxury automobiles for hire with driver (except taxis)
321213	LVL (laminated veneer lumber) manufacturing
325612	Lye, household-type, manufacturing
111335	Macadamia farming
424490	Macaroni merchant wholesalers
311823	Macaroni, dry, manufacturing
311991	Macaroni, fresh, manufacturing

311412 Macaroni, frozen, manufacturing

332212 Machetes manufacturing

332999 Machine bases, metal, manufacturing

332322 Machine guards, sheet metal (except stampings), manufacturing

332994 Machine gun belts (i.e., 30 mm. or less, 1.18 inch or less) manufacturing

332995 Machine gun belts (i.e., more than 30 mm., more than 1.18 inch) manufacturing

332994 Machine guns (i.e., 30 mm. or less, 1.18 inch or less) manufacturing

332995 Machine guns (i.e., more than 30 mm., more than 1.18 inch) manufacturing

332722 Machine keys, metal, manufacturing

332212 Machine knives (except metal cutting) manufacturing

333515 Machine knives, metal cutting, manufacturing

238290 Machine rigging

332710 Machine shops

333515 Machine tool attachments and accessories manufacturing

335311 Machine tool transformers manufacturing

423830 Machine tools and accessories merchant wholesalers

811310 Machine tools repair and maintenance services

333512 Machine tools, metal cutting, manufacturing

333513 Machine tools, metal forming, manufacturing

238290 Machinery and equipment, large-scale, installation

522220 Machinery finance leasing

238910 Machinery, construction (except cranes), rental with operator

423420 Machines, office, merchant wholesalers

332212 Machinists' precision measuring tools (except optical) manufacturing

423830 Machinists' precision measuring tools merchant wholesalers

334511 Machmeters manufacturing

114111 Mackerel fishing

315291 Mackinaws, infants', cut and sewn from purchased fabric (except apparel contractors)

315211 Mackinaws, men's and boys', cut and sew apparel contractors

315228 Mackinaws, men's and boys', cut and sewn from purchased fabric (except apparel contractors)

315212 Mackinaws, women's, girls', and infants', cut and sew apparel contractors

315239 Mackinaws, women's, misses', and girls', cut and sewn from purchased fabric (except apparel contractors)

541840 Magazine advertising representatives (i.e., independent of media owners)

511120 Magazine publishers (except exclusive Internet publishing)

511120 Magazine publishers and printing combined

516110 Magazine publishers, exclusively on Internet

337122 Magazine racks, wood, manufacturing

451212 Magazine stands (i.e., permanent)

323112 Magazines and periodicals flexographic printing without publishing

323111 Magazines and periodicals gravure printing without publishing

323110 Magazines and periodicals lithographic (offset) printing without publishing

323119 Magazines and periodicals printing (except flexographic, gravure, lithographic, quick, screen) without publishing

323113 Magazines and periodicals screen printing without publishing

424920   Magazines merchant wholesalers
711190   Magic shows
451120   Magic supply stores
711510   Magicians, independent
327125   Magnesia refractory cement manufacturing
325411   Magnesia, medicinal, uncompounded, manufacturing
212325   Magnesite mining and/or beneficiating
327992   Magnesite, crude (e.g., calcined, dead-burned, ground), manufacturing
331491   Magnesium and magnesium alloy bar, rod, shape, sheet, strip, and tubing made from purchased metals or scrap
325188   Magnesium carbonate manufacturing
331528   Magnesium castings (except die-castings), unfinished, manufacturing
325188   Magnesium chloride manufacturing
325188   Magnesium compounds, not specified elsewhere by process, manufacturing
331522   Magnesium die-castings, unfinished, manufacturing
331491   Magnesium foil made by rolling purchased metals or scrap
332999   Magnesium foil not made in rolling mills
331492   Magnesium recovering from scrap and/or alloying purchased metals
331419   Magnesium refining, primary
331491   Magnesium rolling, drawing, or extruding purchased metals or scrap
331422   Magnet wire, insulated, made from purchased copper in wire drawing plants
331319   Magnet wire, insulated, made in aluminum wire drawing plants

331491   Magnet wire, nonferrous metals (except aluminum, copper), made from purchased nonferrous metals (except aluminum, copper) in wire drawing plants
334613   Magnetic and optical media, blank, manufacturing
334514   Magnetic counters manufacturing
334513   Magnetic flow meters, industrial process-type, manufacturing
333513   Magnetic forming machines, metalworking, manufacturing
541360   Magnetic geophysical surveying services
334119   Magnetic ink recognition devices, computer peripheral equipment, manufacturing
334613   Magnetic recording media for tapes, cassettes, and disks, manufacturing
621512   Magnetic resonance imaging (MRI) centers
334510   Magnetic resonance imaging (MRI) medical diagnostic equipment manufacturing
334516   Magnetic resonance imaging (MRI) type apparatus (except medical diagnostic) manufacturing
334613   Magnetic tapes, cassettes and disks, blank, manufacturing
423690   Magnetic tapes, cassettes, and disks, blank, merchant wholesalers
334112   Magnetic/optical combination storage units for computers manufacturing
334519   Magnetometers manufacturing
334411   Magnetron tubes manufacturing
327113   Magnets, permanent, ceramic or ferrite, manufacturing
332999   Magnets, permanent, metallic, manufacturing
339115   Magnifiers, corrective vision-type, manufacturing
333314   Magnifying glasses (except corrective vision-type) manufacturing

333314 Magnifying instruments, optical, manufacturing
114111 Mahimahi fishing
561310 Maid registries
561720 Maid services (i.e., cleaning services)
238990 Mail box units, outdoor, multiple box-type, erection
337215 Mail carrier cases and tables, wood, manufacturing
332322 Mail chutes, sheet metal (except stampings), manufacturing
333313 Mail handling machinery, post office-type, manufacturing
561499 Mail presorting services
561431 Mailbox rental centers, private
561431 Mailbox rental services combined with one or more other office support services, private
332439 Mailboxes, light gauge metal, manufacturing
322214 Mailing cases and tubes, paper fiber (i.e., all-fiber, nonfiber ends of any material), made from purchased paperboard
532420 Mailing equipment rental or leasing
511140 Mailing list publishers (except exclusive Internet publishing)
423420 Mailing machines merchant wholesalers
454113 Mail-order houses
334111 Mainframe computers manufacturing
488190 Maintenance and repair services, aircraft (except factory conversion, factory overhaul, factory rebuilding)
561730 Maintenance of plants and shrubs in buildings
488210 Maintenance of rights-of-way and structures, railway
488119 Maintenance services, runway
488310 Maintenance services, waterfront terminal (except dredging)
711211 Major league baseball clubs
812112 Make-up (except permanent) salons

325620 Make-up (i.e., cosmetics) manufacturing
812199 Make-up salons, permanent
523110 Making markets for securities
337125 Malacca furniture (except upholstered), household-type, manufacturing
325320 Malathion insecticides manufacturing
325192 Maleic anhydride manufacturing
531120 Mall property operation (i.e., not operating contained businesses) rental or leasing
331511 Malleable iron foundries
332212 Mallets (e.g., rubber, wood) manufacturing
321999 Mallets, wood, manufacturing
325199 Malonic dinitrile manufacturing
524126 Malpractice insurance carriers, direct
311942 Malt extract and syrups manufacturing
424490 Malt extract merchant wholesalers
311213 Malt flour manufacturing
312120 Malt liquor brewing
311213 Malt manufacturing
424490 Malt merchant wholesalers
333294 Malt milling machinery manufacturing
311213 Malt sprouts manufacturing
311514 Malted milk manufacturing
311213 Malting (germinating and drying grains)
311221 Maltodextrins manufacturing
621512 Mammogram (i.e., breast imaging) centers
711410 Management agencies for artists, entertainers, and other public figures
611430 Management development training
561110 Management services (except complete operation of client's business)
115116 Management services, farm
711310 Managers of agricultural fairs with facilities
711320 Managers of agricultural fairs without facilities

711310	Managers of arts events with facilities
711320	Managers of arts events without facilities
711310	Managers of festivals with facilities
711320	Managers of festivals without facilities
711310	Managers of live performing arts productions (e.g., concerts) with facilities
711320	Managers of live performing arts productions (e.g., concerts) without facilities
711310	Managers of sports events with facilities
711320	Managers of sports events without facilities
531312	Managers' offices, commercial condominium
531312	Managers' offices, commercial real estate
531312	Managers' offices, nonresidential real estate
531311	Managers' offices, residential condominium
531311	Managers' offices, residential real estate
711410	Managers, authors'
711410	Managers, celebrities'
561920	Managers, convention
711410	Managers, entertainers'
711410	Managers, pubic figures'
711410	Managers, sports figures'
561920	Managers, trade fair or show
531312	Managing commercial condominiums
531312	Managing commercial real estate
531311	Managing cooperative apartments
523920	Managing investment funds
523920	Managing mutual funds
561110	Managing offices of dentists
561110	Managing offices of physicians and surgeons
561110	Managing offices of professionals (e.g., dentists, physicians, surgeons)
523920	Managing personal investment trusts
531311	Managing residential condominiums
531311	Managing residential real estate
523920	Managing trusts
111320	Mandarin groves
339992	Mandolins manufacturing
333515	Mandrels (i.e., a machine tool accessory) manufacturing
212299	Manganese concentrates beneficiating
325188	Manganese dioxide manufacturing
331112	Manganese metal ferroalloys manufacturing
212299	Manganese ores mining and/or beneficiating
212210	Manganiferous ores valued for iron content, mining and/or beneficiating
212299	Manganiferousares ores (not valued for iron content) mining and/or beneficiating
212299	Manganite mining and/or beneficiating
111339	Mango farming
325191	Mangrove extract manufacturing
331511	Manhole covers, cast iron, manufacturing
812113	Manicure and pedicure salons
611511	Manicure and pedicure schools
325620	Manicure preparations manufacturing
812113	Manicurist services
323116	Manifold business forms printing
336312	Manifolds (i.e., intake and exhaust), automotive and truck gasoline engine, manufacturing
332996	Manifolds, pipe, made from purchased metal pipe
322231	Manila folders, die-cut, made from purchased paper or paperboard
325221	Manmade cellulosic fibers manufacturing
313221	Manmade fabric, narrow woven, weaving

212393	Marcasite mining and/or beneficiating
325199	Margaric acid manufacturing
311221	Margarine and other corn oils made by wet milling corn
424490	Margarine merchant wholesalers
311225	Margarine-butter blend made from purchased fats and oils
311225	Margarines (including imitation) made from purchased fats and oils
713930	Marinas
335314	Marine and navy auxiliary controls, manufacturing
713930	Marine basins, operation of
488390	Marine cargo checkers and surveyors
488320	Marine cargo handling services
237990	Marine construction
928110	Marine Corps
541330	Marine engineering services
333618	Marine engines manufacturing
332510	Marine hardware, metal, manufacturing
332999	Marine horns, compressed air or steam, metal, manufacturing
524126	Marine insurance carriers, direct
712110	Marine museums
611519	Marine navigational schools
325510	Marine paints manufacturing
332410	Marine power boilers manufacturing
334220	Marine radio communications equipment manufacturing
524130	Marine reinsurance carriers
488330	Marine salvaging services
447190	Marine service stations
488510	Marine shipping agency
335911	Marine storage batteries manufacturing
423860	Marine supplies (except pleasure) merchant wholesalers
423910	Marine supplies, pleasure, merchant wholesalers
441222	Marine supply dealers
541990	Marine surveyor (i.e., ship appraiser) services
488330	Marine vessel traffic reporting services
339999	Marionettes (i.e., puppets) manufacturing
339942	Marker boards (i.e., whiteboards) manufacturing
523110	Market making for securities
541910	Marketing analysis services
541613	Marketing consulting services
541613	Marketing management consulting services
541910	Marketing research services
339943	Marking devices manufacturing
424120	Marking devices merchant wholesalers
333518	Marking machines, metal, manufacturing
212312	Marl crushed and broken stone mining and/or beneficiating
311421	Marmalade manufacturing
321999	Marquetry, wood, manufacturing
624190	Marriage counseling services (except by offices of mental health practitioners)
922120	Marshals' offices
311340	Marshmallow creme manufacturing
311340	Marshmallows manufacturing
611620	Martial arts instruction, camps, or schools
311340	Marzipan (i.e., candy) manufacturing
335999	Maser (i.e., microwave amplification by stimulated emission of radiation) amplifiers manufacturing
321999	Mashers, potato, wood, manufacturing
322222	Masking tape made from purchased paper
444190	Masonry (e.g., block, brick, stone) dealers
238140	Masonry contractors
238140	Masonry pointing, cleaning or caulking
332212	Mason's handtools manufacturing
423320	Mason's materials merchant wholesalers
334516	Mass spectrometers manufacturing

334516 Mass spectroscopy instrumentation manufacturing
335211 Massage machines, electric (except designed for beauty and barber shop use), manufacturing
812199 Massage parlors
611519 Massage therapist instruction
621399 Massage therapists' offices
512210 Master recording leasing and licensing
424690 Mastics (except construction) merchant wholesalers
321999 Masts, wood, manufacturing
812332 Mat and rug supply services
325998 Matches and match books manufacturing
424990 Matches and match books merchant wholesalers
238290 Materials handling equipment installation
811310 Materials handling equipment repair and maintenance services
423830 Materials handling machinery and equipment merchant wholesalers
532490 Materials handling machinery and equipment rental or leasing
541614 Materials management consulting services
562920 Materials recovery facilities (MRF)
236210 Materials recovery facility construction
923120 Maternity and child health program administration
315212 Maternity bras and corsets, women's, cut and sew apparel contractors
315231 Maternity bras and corsets, women's, misses', and girls', cut and sewn from purchased fabric (except apparel contractors)
622310 Maternity hospitals
448120 Maternity shops

541710 Mathematics research and development laboratories or services
332618 Mats and matting made from purchased wire
332212 Mattocks (i.e., handtools) manufacturing
326299 Mattress protectors, rubber, manufacturing
332612 Mattress springs and spring units, light gauge, made from purchased wire or strip
442110 Mattress stores (including waterbeds)
337910 Mattresses (i.e., box spring, innerspring, noninnerspring) manufacturing
337910 Mattresses made from felt, foam rubber, urethane and similar materials
423210 Mattresses merchant wholesalers
326199 Mattresses, air, plastics, manufacturing
326299 Mattresses, air, rubber, manufacturing
311812 Matzo baking made in commercial bakeries
332212 Mauls, metal, manufacturing
321999 Mauls, wood, manufacturing
236220 Mausoleum (i.e., building) construction
812220 Mausoleums
311941 Mayonnaise manufacturing
921110 Mayor's offices
321219 MDF (medium density fiberboard) manufacturing
621112 MDs' (medical doctors), mental health, offices (e.g., centers, clinics)
621111 MDs' (medical doctors, except mental health) offices (e.g., centers, clinics)
624210 Meal delivery programs
311119 Meal, alfalfa, manufacturing
311119 Meal, bone, prepared as feed for animals and fowls, manufacturing

311211   Meal, corn, for human consumption made in flour mills

423830   Measuring and testing equipment (except automotive) merchant wholesalers

333515   Measuring attachments (e.g., sine bars) for machine tool manufacturing

334515   Measuring equipment for electronic and electrical circuits and equipment manufacturing

811219   Measuring instrument repair and maintenance services

334515   Measuring instruments and meters, electric, manufacturing

334513   Measuring instruments, industrial process control-type, manufacturing

332212   Measuring tools, machinist's (except optical), manufacturing

334514   Measuring wheels manufacturing

311613   Meat and bone meal and tankage, produced in rendering plant

311612   Meat canning (except baby, pet food, poultry), made from purchased carcasses

311611   Meat canning (except poultry) produced in slaughtering plants

311422   Meat canning, baby food, manufacturing

311111   Meat canning, dog and cat, pet food, made from purchased carcasses

311615   Meat canning, poultry (except baby and pet food), manufacturing

311612   Meat extracts made from purchased carcasses

333294   Meat grinders, food-type, manufacturing

445210   Meat markets

311615   Meat products (e.g., hot dogs, luncheon meats, sausages) made from a combination of poultry and other meats

311612   Meat products canning (except baby, pet food, poultry) made from purchased carcasses

311111   Meat products, dog and cat, pet food, canning, made from purchased carcasses

311612   Meats (except poultry), cured or smoked, made from purchased carcasses

424470   Meats and meat products (except canned, packaged frozen) merchant wholesalers

311611   Meats fresh, chilled or frozen (except poultry and small game), produced in slaughtering plants

424490   Meats, canned, merchant wholesalers

424470   Meats, cured or smoked, merchant wholesalers

311611   Meats, cured or smoked, produced in slaughtering plants

311612   Meats, fresh or chilled (except poultry and small game), frozen, made from purchased carcasses

424470   Meats, fresh, merchant wholesalers

424470   Meats, frozen (except packaged), merchant wholesalers

424420   Meats, packaged frozen, merchant wholesalers

238220   Mechanical contractors

541330   Mechanical engineering services

238290   Mechanical equipment insulation

313311   Mechanical finishing of broadwoven fabrics

316110   Mechanical leather manufacturing

334513   Mechanical measuring instruments, industrial process-type, manufacturing

339942   Mechanical pencil refills manufacturing

339941   Mechanical pencils manufacturing

811310 Mechanical power transmission equipment repair and maintenance services

423840 Mechanical power transmission supplies (e.g., gears, pulleys, sprockets) merchant wholesalers

326291 Mechanical rubber goods (i.e., extruded, lathe-cut, molded) manufacturing

423840 Mechanical rubber goods merchant wholesalers

541380 Mechanical testing laboratories or services

611513 Mechanic's apprenticeship training

333924 Mechanic's creepers manufacturing

325611 Mechanic's hand soaps and pastes manufacturing

332212 Mechanic's handtools, nonpowered, manufacturing

611519 Mechanic's schools (except apprenticeship)

423120 Mechanic's tools merchant wholesalers

333311 Mechanisms for coin-operated machines manufacturing

334518 Mechanisms, clockwork operated device, manufacturing

541840 Media advertising representatives (i.e., independent of media owners)

541830 Media buying agencies

541830 Media buying services

541840 Media representatives (i.e., independent of media owners)

518210 Media streaming services

926150 Mediation and conciliation services, government

541990 Mediation product services (except by lawyer, attorney, paralegal offices, family and social services)

624190 Mediation, social service, family, agencies

811219 Medical and surgical equipment repair and maintenance services

541430 Medical art services

541430 Medical artists, independent

923130 Medical assistance programs administration, government

813920 Medical associations

531120 Medical building rental or leasing

334510 Medical cleaning equipment, ultrasonic, manufacturing

524298 Medical cost evaluation services

621112 Medical doctors' (MDs), mental health, offices (e.g. centers, clinics)

621111 Medical doctors' (MDs, except mental health) offices (e.g., centers, clinics)

423450 Medical dressings merchant wholesalers

532490 Medical equipment (except home health furniture and equipment) rental or leasing

446199 Medical equipment and supplies stores

423450 Medical equipment merchant wholesalers

423450 Medical furniture merchant wholesalers

327215 Medical glassware made from purchased glass

327212 Medical glassware made in glass making plants

423450 Medical glassware merchant wholesalers

541430 Medical illustration services

541430 Medical illustrators, independent

423450 Medical instruments merchant wholesalers

524114 Medical insurance carriers, direct

511120 Medical journal and periodical publishers (except exclusive Internet publishing)

511120 Medical journal and periodical publishers and printing combined

516110 Medical journal and periodical publishers, exclusively on Internet

621511	Medical laboratories (except radiological, X-ray)
621512	Medical laboratories, radiological or X-ray
541611	Medical office management consulting services or consultants
561110	Medical office management services
621511	Medical pathology laboratories
541922	Medical photography services
334517	Medical radiation therapy equipment manufacturing
621512	Medical radiological laboratories
524130	Medical reinsurance carriers
541710	Medical research and development laboratories or services
611310	Medical schools
315211	Medical service apparel, men's and boys', cut and sew apparel contractors
315225	Medical service apparel, men's and boys', cut and sewn from purchased fabric (except apparel contractors)
315212	Medical service apparel, women's, cut and sew apparel contractors
315239	Medical service apparel, women's, misses', and girls', cut and sewn from purchased fabric (except apparel contractors)
524114	Medical service plans without providing health care services
424210	Medical sundries, rubber, merchant wholesalers
423450	Medical supplies merchant wholesalers
611519	Medical technician schools
339112	Medical thermometers manufacturing
334510	Medical ultrasound equipment manufacturing
621512	Medical X-ray laboratories
923130	Medicare and Medicaid administration
325411	Medicinal chemicals, uncompounded, manufacturing
337110	Medicine cabinets (except freestanding), wood household-type, manufacturing
337124	Medicine cabinets, metal household-type, manufacturing
321219	Medium density fiberboard (MDF) manufacturing
212399	Meerschaum mining and/or beneficiating
531120	Meeting hall and room rental or leasing
325211	Melamine resins manufacturing
111219	Melon farming (e.g., cantaloupe, casaba, honeydew, watermelon), field, bedding plant and seed production
111419	Melon farming, grown under cover
313230	Melt blown nonwoven fabrics manufacturing
315291	Melton jackets, infants', cut and sewn from purchased fabric (except apparel contractors)
315211	Melton jackets, men's and boys', cut and sew apparel contractors
315228	Melton jackets, men's and boys', cut and sewn from purchased fabric (except apparel contractors)
315212	Melton jackets, women's, girls', and infants', cut and sew apparel contractors
315239	Melton jackets, women's, misses', and girls', cut and sewn from purchased fabric (except apparel contractors)
813410	Membership associations, civic or social
721110	Membership hotels
812220	Memorial gardens (i.e., burial places)
334418	Memory boards manufacturing
712130	Menageries
114111	Menhaden fishing
424320	Men's and boys' clothing merchant wholesalers

334519   Metal detectors manufacturing
339113   Metal fabric and mesh safety gloves manufacturing
332999   Metal foil containers (except bags) manufacturing
333513   Metal forming machine tools manufacturing
337121   Metal framed furniture, household-type, upholstered, manufacturing
238190   Metal furring contractors
339943   Metal hand stamps manufacturing
333994   Metal melting furnaces, industrial, manufacturing
213114   Metal mining support services (shaft sinking, tunneling, blasting) (except site preparation and related construction contractor activities)
336370   Metal motor vehicle body parts stamping
423520   Metal ores merchant wholesalers
334413   Metal oxide silicon (MOS) devices manufacturing
423510   Metal pipe merchant wholesalers
325612   Metal polishes (i.e., tarnish removers) manufacturing
331314   Metal powder and flake made from purchased aluminum
331423   Metal powder and flake made from purchased copper
331221   Metal powder and flake made from purchased iron or steel
331492   Metal powder and flake nonferrous (except aluminum, copper) made from purchased metal
236210   Metal processing plant construction
423510   Metal products (e.g., bars, ingots, plates, rods, shapes, sheets) merchant wholesalers
423930   Metal scrap and waste merchant wholesalers
238170   Metal siding installation

332116   Metal stampings (except automotive, cans, cooking, closures, crowns), unfinished, manufacturing
335991   Metal-graphite product manufacturing
423520   Metallic concentrates merchant wholesalers
325131   Metallic pigments, inorganic, manufacturing
325199   Metallic soap manufacturing
313320   Metallizing purchased textiles
541380   Metallurgical testing laboratories or services
423510   Metals sales offices
423510   Metals service centers
423510   Metals, ferrous and nonferrous, merchant wholesalers
423940   Metals, precious, merchant wholesalers
333512   Metalworking lathes manufacturing
423830   Metalworking machinery and equipment merchant wholesalers
532490   Metalworking machinery and equipment rental or leasing
334519   Meteorologic tracking systems manufacturing
811219   Meteorological instrument repair and maintenance services
334519   Meteorological instruments manufacturing
541990   Meteorological services
561990   Meter reading services, contract
334514   Metering devices (except electrical and industrial process control) manufacturing
335313   Metering panels, electric, manufacturing
334514   Meters (except electrical and industrial process control) manufacturing
423830   Meters (except electrical, parking) merchant wholesalers
334515   Meters, electrical (i.e., graphic recording, panelboard, pocket, portable), manufacturing

423610 Meters, electrical, merchant wholesalers
334513 Meters, industrial process control-type, manufacturing
334514 Meters, parking, manufacturing
423850 Meters, parking, merchant wholesalers
334515 Meters, power factor and phase angle, manufacturing
325320 Methoxychlor insecticides manufacturing
325191 Methyl acetone manufacturing
325211 Methyl acrylate resins manufacturing
325199 Methyl alcohol (i.e., methanol), synthetic, manufacturing
325191 Methyl alcohol (methanol), natural, manufacturing
325211 Methyl cellulose resins manufacturing
325199 Methyl chloride manufacturing
325211 Methyl methacrylate resins manufacturing
325199 Methyl perhydrofluorine manufacturing
325199 Methyl salicylate manufacturing
325132 Methyl violet toners manufacturing
325199 Methylamine manufacturing
325199 Methylene chloride manufacturing
311422 Mexican foods canning
311412 Mexican foods, frozen, manufacturing
212399 Mica mining and/or beneficiating
327992 Mica processing beyond beneficiation
327999 Mica products manufacturing
212319 Mica schist crushed and broken stone mining and/or beneficiating
212311 Mica schist mining or quarrying
311119 Micro and macro premixes, livestock, manufacturing
334516 Microbiology instruments manufacturing
325413 Microbiology, virology, and serology in-vitro diagnostic substances manufacturing

334111 Microcomputers manufacturing
334413 Microcontroller chip manufacturing
333315 Microfiche equipment (e.g., cameras, projectors, readers) manufacturing
518210 Microfiche recording and imaging services
333315 Microfilm equipment (e.g., cameras, projectors, readers) manufacturing
423420 Microfilm equipment and supplies merchant wholesalers
518210 Microfilm recording and imaging services
212299 Microlite mining and/or beneficiating
333295 Micro-lithography equipment, semiconductor, manufacturing
332212 Micrometers, machinist's precision tools, manufacturing
334310 Microphones manufacturing
334516 Microprobes (e.g., electron, ion, laser, X-ray) manufacturing
334413 Microprocessor chip manufacturing
333314 Microscopes (except electron, proton) manufacturing
334516 Microscopes, electron and proton, manufacturing
237990 Microtunneling contractors
334220 Microwave communications equipment manufacturing
334419 Microwave components manufacturing
811412 Microwave oven, household-type, repair and maintenance services, without retailing new microwave ovens
335221 Microwave ovens (including portable), household-type, manufacturing
333319 Microwave ovens, commercial-type, manufacturing
237130 Microwave relay tower construction
517310 Microwave telecommunication resellers
334515 Microwave test equipment manufacturing

326199   Microwaveware, plastics, manufacturing
315291   Middies, infants', cut and sewn from purchased fabric (except apparel contractors)
315212   Middies, women's, girls' and infants', cut and sew apparel contractors
315232   Middies, women's, misses', and girls', cut and sewn from purchased fabric (except apparel contractors)
611110   Middle schools
621399   Midwives' offices (e.g., centers, clinics)
721310   Migrant workers' camps
611310   Military academies, college level
611110   Military academies, elementary or secondary
928110   Military bases and camps
315211   Military dress uniforms, men's and boys', cut and sew apparel contractors
315222   Military dress uniforms, men's and boys', cut and sewn from purchased fabric (except apparel contractors)
315234   Military dress uniforms, tailored, women's, misses' and girls', cut and sewn from purchased fabric (except apparel contractors)
315212   Military dress uniforms, women's, cut and sew apparel contractors
332999   Military insignia, metal, manufacturing
314999   Military insignia, textile, manufacturing
712110   Military museums
928110   Military police
928110   Military reserve armories and bases
611310   Military service academies (college)
928110   Military training schools (except academies)
423860   Military vehicles (except trucks) merchant wholesalers

311511   Milk based drinks (except dietary) manufacturing
311514   Milk based drinks, dietary, manufacturing
322130   Milk carton board made in paperboard mills
322226   Milk carton board stock made from purchased paperboard
311511   Milk drink, chocolate, manufacturing
484220   Milk hauling, local
311511   Milk pasteurizing
311511   Milk processing (e.g., bottling, homogenizing, pasteurizing, vitaminizing) manufacturing
333294   Milk processing (except farm-type) machinery manufacturing
112120   Milk production, dairy cattle
311511   Milk substitutes manufacturing
115210   Milk testing for butterfat and milk solids
311511   Milk, acidophilus, manufacturing
424490   Milk, canned or dried, merchant wholesalers
311514   Milk, concentrated, condensed, dried, evaporated, and powdered, manufacturing
311511   Milk, fluid (except canned), manufacturing
424430   Milk, fluid (except canned), merchant wholesalers
311514   Milk, malted, manufacturing
311514   Milk, powdered, manufacturing
311514   Milk, ultra-high temperature, manufacturing
112120   Milking dairy cattle
112420   Milking dairy goat
112410   Milking dairy sheep
423820   Milking machinery and equipment merchant wholesalers
333111   Milking machines manufacturing
311514   Milkshake mixes manufacturing
314999   Mill menders, contract, woven fabrics
316999   Mill strapping for textile mills, leather, manufacturing

238310	Mineral wool insulation installation
327993	Mineral wool insulation materials manufacturing
327993	Mineral wool products (e.g., board, insulation, tile) manufacturing
423520	Minerals (except construction materials, petroleum) merchant wholesalers
335129	Miner's lamps manufacturing
332993	Mines, ammunition, manufacturing
713990	Miniature golf courses
337920	Miniblinds manufacturing
334111	Minicomputers manufacturing
331111	Mini-mills, steel
926150	Minimum wage program administration
******	Mining—see type
813910	Mining associations
333131	Mining cars manufacturing
423810	Mining cranes merchant wholesalers
541330	Mining engineering services
336510	Mining locomotives and parts manufacturing
423810	Mining machinery and equipment (except petroleum) merchant wholesalers
532412	Mining machinery and equipment rental or leasing
811310	Mining machinery and equipment repair and maintenance services
423830	Mining machinery and equipment, petroleum, merchant wholesalers
531190	Mining property leasing
336112	Minivans assembling on chassis of own manufacture
531130	Miniwarehouse rental or leasing
112930	Mink production
112511	Minnow production, farm raising
711211	Minor league baseball clubs
111998	Mint farming
238150	Mirror installation
423220	Mirrors (except automotive) merchant wholesalers

423120	Mirrors, automotive, merchant wholesalers
327215	Mirrors, framed (except automotive) or unframed, made from purchased glass
333314	Mirrors, optical, manufacturing
237990	Missile facility construction
332993	Missile warheads manufacturing
561611	Missing person tracing services
813110	Missions, religious organization
332212	Miter boxes manufacturing
315992	Mittens cut and sewn from purchased fabric (except apparel contractors)
315191	Mittens, knit, made in apparel knitting mills
315992	Mittens, leather (except apparel contractors), manufacturing
315211	Mittens, leather, men's and boys', cut and sew apparel contractors
315212	Mittens, leather, women's, girls', and infants', cut and sew apparel contractors
315211	Mittens, men's and boys', cut and sew apparel contractors
315212	Mittens, women's, girls', and infants', cut and sew apparel contractors
315992	Mittens, woven or knit, cut and sewn from purchased fabric (except apparel contractors)
315211	Mittens, woven or knit, men's and boys', cut and sew apparel contractors
315212	Mittens, woven or knit, women's, girls', and infants', cut and sew apparel contractors
311230	Mix grain breakfast manufacturing
311514	Mix, ice cream, manufacturing
312140	Mixed drinks, alcoholic, manufacturing
111940	Mixed hay farming
485111	Mixed mode transit systems (e.g., bus, commuter rail, subway combinations)
333120	Mixers, concrete, portable, manufacturing

424490 Mixes (e.g., cake, dessert, pie) merchant wholesalers

311211 Mixes, flour (e.g., biscuit, cake, doughnut, pancake) made in flour mills

311822 Mixes, flour (e.g., biscuit, cake, doughnut, pancake), made from purchased flour

325314 Mixing purchased fertilizer materials

531190 Mobile (manufactured) home parks

531190 Mobile (manufactured) home site rental or leasing

531110 Mobile (manufactured) home, on site, rental or leasing

621512 Mobile breast imaging centers

811192 Mobile car and truck washes

334220 Mobile communications equipment manufacturing

311119 Mobile feed mill

722330 Mobile food stands

453930 Mobile home dealers, manufactured

321991 Mobile home manufacturing

532120 Mobile home rental (except on site)

484220 Mobile home towing services, local

484230 Mobile home towing services, long-distance

712110 Mobile museums

624210 Mobile soup kitchens

333924 Mobile straddle carriers manufacturing

517212 Mobile telephone communication carriers

621512 Mobile X-ray facilities (medical)

316219 Moccasins manufacturing

325222 Modacrylic fibers and filaments manufacturing

313111 Modacrylic spun yarns made from purchased fiber

339932 Model kits manufacturing

423920 Model kits merchant wholesalers

339932 Model railroad manufacturing

561310 Model registries

561320 Model supply services

711410 Modeling agents

339942 Modeling clay manufacturing

611519 Modeling schools

711410 Models' agents or managers

339999 Models, anatomical, manufacturing

711510 Models, independent

339932 Models, toy and hobby (e.g., airplane, boat, ship), manufacturing

423690 Modems merchant wholesalers

334210 Modems, carrier equipment, manufacturing

711120 Modern dance companies

238390 Modular furniture system attachment and installation

337214 Modular furniture systems (except wood frame), office-type, manufacturing

337211 Modular furniture systems, wood frame office-type, manufacturing

236115 Modular house assembly on site by general contractors

236117 Modular housing, residential, assembled on site by operative builders

334518 Modules for clocks and watches manufacturing

112420 Mohair farming

313112 Mohair yarn twisting or winding of purchased yarn

424590 Mohair, raw, merchant wholesalers

334516 Moisture analyzers, laboratory-type, manufacturing

334513 Moisture meters, industrial process-type, manufacturing

311312 Molasses made from purchased raw cane sugar

311313 Molasses made from sugar beets

311311 Molasses made in sugarcane mill

424490 Molasses merchant wholesalers

311312 Molasses, blackstrap, made from purchased raw cane sugar

311311   Molasses, blackstrap, made in sugarcane mill

339991   Molded packings and seals manufacturing

322299   Molded pulp products (e.g., egg cartons, food containers, food trays) manufacturing

423310   Molding (e.g., sheet metal, wood) merchant wholesalers

332321   Molding and trim (except motor vehicle), metal, manufacturing

238350   Molding or trim, wood or plastic, installation

212322   Molding sand quarrying and/or beneficiating

336370   Moldings and trim, motor vehicle, stamping

321918   Moldings, clear and finger joint wood, manufacturing

321918   Moldings, wood and covered wood, manufacturing

333511   Molds (except steel ingot), industrial, manufacturing

331511   Molds for casting steel ingots manufacturing

333511   Molds for forming materials (e.g., glass, plastics, rubber) manufacturing

333511   Molds for metal casting (except steel ingot) manufacturing

333511   Molds for plastics and rubber working machinery manufacturing

331511   Molds, steel ingot, industrial, manufacturing

112512   Mollusk production, farm raising

212299   Molybdenite mining and/or beneficiating

331491   Molybdenum and molybdenum alloy bar, plate, pipe, rod, sheet, tubing, and wire made from purchased metals or scrap

212299   Molybdenum ores mining and/or beneficiating

331491   Molybdenum rolling, drawing, or extruding purchased metals or scrap

331112   Molybdenum silicon ferroalloys manufacturing

212299   Molybdite mining and/or beneficiating

813110   Monasteries (except schools)

212299   Monazite mining and/or beneficiating

521110   Monetary authorities, central bank

332999   Money chests, metal, manufacturing

525990   Money market mutual funds, closed-end

525910   Money market mutual funds, open-ended

522390   Money order issuance services

334119   Monitors, computer peripheral equipment, manufacturing

325120   Monochlorodifluoromethane manufacturing

334516   Monochrometers, laboratory-type, manufacturing

334413   Monolithic integrated circuits (solid-state) manufacturing

325199   Monomethylparaminophenol sulfate manufacturing

237990   Monorail construction

333923   Monorail systems (except passenger-type) manufacturing

485119   Monorail transit systems (except mixed mode), commuter

487110   Monorail, scenic and sightseeing, operation

325199   Monosodium glutamate manufacturing

611110   Montessori schools, elementary or secondary

236220   Monument (i.e., building) construction

453998   Monument (i.e., burial marker) dealers

423990   Monuments and grave markers merchant wholesalers

327991   Monuments and tombstone, cut stone (except finishing or lettering to order only), manufacturing

333319   Mop wringers manufacturing

441221   Moped dealers

423110   Moped merchant wholesalers

532292 Moped rental
336991 Mopeds and parts manufacturing
339994 Mops, floor and dust, manufacturing
325132 Mordant dyes manufacturing
325613 Mordants manufacturing
325411 Morphine and derivatives (i.e., basic chemicals) manufacturing
522190 Morris Plans (i.e., known as), depository
522298 Morris Plans (i.e., known as), nondepository
333120 Mortar mixers, portable, manufacturing
332993 Mortar shells manufacturing
327125 Mortar, nonclay refractory, manufacturing
332995 Mortars manufacturing
327124 Mortars, clay refractory, manufacturing
522292 Mortgage banking (i.e., nondepository mortgage lending)
522310 Mortgage brokerages
522310 Mortgage brokers' or agents' offices (i.e., independent)
522292 Mortgage companies
524126 Mortgage guaranty insurance carriers, direct
812210 Mortician services
333210 Mortisers, woodworking-type, manufacturing
812210 Mortuaries
334413 MOS (metal oxide silicon) devices manufacturing
327122 Mosaic tile, ceramic, manufacturing
238340 Mosaic work
813110 Mosques, religious
926130 Mosquito eradication districts
561710 Mosquito eradication services
113210 Moss gathering
531120 Motel building, not operating motel, rental or leasing
236220 Motel construction
561110 Motel management services (except complete operation of client's business)

721110 Motels
325320 Moth repellants manufacturing
423430 Mother boards merchant wholesalers
334290 Motion alarms (e.g., swimming pool, perimeter) manufacturing
334290 Motion detectors, security system, manufacturing
512110 Motion picture and video production
512110 Motion picture and video production and distribution
512191 Motion picture animation, post-production
512199 Motion picture booking agencies
333315 Motion picture cameras manufacturing
423410 Motion picture cameras, equipment, and supplies merchant wholesalers
541690 Motion picture consulting services
711510 Motion picture directors, independent
512120 Motion picture distribution exclusive of production
532490 Motion picture equipment rental or leasing
512131 Motion picture exhibition
512131 Motion picture exhibitors for airlines
512131 Motion picture exhibitors, itinerant
512120 Motion picture film distributors
512199 Motion picture film laboratories
512120 Motion picture film libraries
519120 Motion picture film libraries, archives
512199 Motion picture film libraries, stock footage
325992 Motion picture film manufacturing
512199 Motion picture film reproduction for theatrical distribution
512199 Motion picture laboratories
512191 Motion picture or video editing services

512191 Motion picture or video post-
        production services
512191 Motion picture or video titling
711510 Motion picture producers,
        independent
512110 Motion picture production
512110 Motion picture production and
        distribution
512191 Motion picture production
        special effects, post-
        production
333315 Motion picture projectors
        manufacturing
512110 Motion picture studios,
        producing motion pictures
512132 Motion picture theaters, drive-in
512131 Motion picture theaters, indoor
532220 Motion picture wardrobe and
        costume rental
711510 Motivational speakers,
        independent
441221 Motor bike dealers
926120 Motor carrier licensing and
        inspection offices
485210 Motor coach operation,
        interurban and rural
335314 Motor control accessories
        (including overload relays)
        manufacturing
335314 Motor control centers,
        manufacturing
335314 Motor controls, electric,
        manufacturing
423610 Motor controls, electric,
        merchant wholesalers
721110 Motor courts
484110 Motor freight carrier, general,
        local
484122 Motor freight carrier, general,
        long-distance, less-than-
        truckload (LTL)
484121 Motor freight carrier, general,
        long-distance, truckload (TL)
484210 Motor freight carrier, used
        household goods
335312 Motor generator sets (except
        automotive, turbine generator
        sets) manufacturing
333611 Motor generator sets, turbo
        generators, manufacturing

441210 Motor home dealers
423110 Motor home merchant
        wholesalers
532120 Motor home rental
336213 Motor homes, self-contained,
        assembling on purchased
        chassis
336120 Motor homes, self-contained,
        mounted on heavy truck
        chassis of own manufacture
336112 Motor homes, self-contained,
        mounted on light duty truck
        chassis of own manufacture
721110 Motor hotels without casinos
721110 Motor inns
721110 Motor lodges
324191 Motor oils, petroleum, made
        from refined petroleum
325998 Motor oils, synthetic,
        manufacturing
811310 Motor repair and maintenance
        services, commercial or
        industrial
441221 Motor scooters dealers
336991 Motor scooters manufacturing
335314 Motor starters, contractors, and
        controllers, industrial,
        manufacturing
561599 Motor travel clubs
333997 Motor truck scales
        manufacturing
236210 Motor vehicle assembly plant
        construction
326220 Motor vehicle belts, rubber or
        plastics, manufacturing
238290 Motor vehicle garage and
        service station mechanical
        equipment (e.g., gasoline
        pumps, hoists) installation
332510 Motor vehicle hardware, metal,
        manufacturing
326220 Motor vehicle hoses, rubber or
        plastics, manufacturing
334514 Motor vehicle instruments (e.g.,
        fuel level gauges, oil pressure,
        speedometers, tachometers,
        water temperature)
        manufacturing
423120 Motor vehicle instruments,
        electric, merchant wholesalers

621512 MRI (magnetic resonance imaging) centers
334510 MRI (magnetic resonance imaging) medical diagnostic equipment manufacturing
325520 Mucilage adhesives manufacturing
213112 Mud service for oil field drilling on a contract basis
238110 Mud-jacking contractors
811112 Muffler repair and replacement shops
336399 Mufflers and resonators, automotive, truck, and buses manufacturing
315191 Mufflers made in apparel knitting mills
423120 Mufflers, exhaust, merchant wholesalers
315211 Mufflers, men's and boys', cut and sew apparel contractors
315993 Mufflers, men's and boys', cut and sewn from purchased fabric (except apparel contractors)
315999 Mufflers, women's and girls', cut and sewn from purchased fabric (except apparel contractors)
315212 Mufflers, women's, girls', and infants', cut and sew apparel contractors
424910 Mulch merchant wholesalers
333112 Mulchers, lawn and garden-type, manufacturing
112920 Mule production
424590 Mules merchant wholesalers
114111 Mullet fishing
712110 Multidisciplinary museums
236116 Multifamily building construction general contractors
236117 Multifamily building operative builders
334515 Multimeters manufacturing
334210 Multiplex equipment, telephone, manufacturing
624190 Multiservice centers, neighborhood
212391 Muriate of potash, mining

325412 Muscle relaxant preparations manufacturing
212399 Muscovite mining and/or beneficiating
236220 Museum construction
712110 Museums
111411 Mushroom farming
111411 Mushroom spawn farming
311421 Mushrooms canning
519120 Music archives
711510 Music arrangers, independent
512230 Music book (i.e., bound sheet music) publishers
512230 Music book (i.e., bound sheet music) publishers and printing combined
323117 Music books printing or printing and binding without publishing
339999 Music boxes manufacturing
512230 Music copyright authorizing use
512230 Music copyright buying and licensing
711510 Music directors, independent
711310 Music festival managers with facilities
711320 Music festival managers without facilities
711310 Music festival organizers with facilities
711320 Music festival organizers without facilities
711310 Music festival promoters with facilities
711320 Music festival promoters without facilities
611610 Music instruction (e.g., guitar, piano)
515112 Music program distribution (except exclusively on Internet), radio
517510 Music program distribution, cable or satellite
512290 Music program distribution, pre-recorded
512230 Music publishers
339992 Music rolls, perforated, manufacturing
611610 Music schools (except academic)

451220   Music stores (e.g., cassette, compact disc, record, tape)
453310   Music stores (e.g., cassette, instrument, record, tape), used
451140   Music stores (i.e., instrument)
621340   Music therapists' offices (e.g., centers, clinics)
512110   Music video production
512110   Music video production and distribution
323112   Music, sheet, flexographic printing without publishing
323111   Music, sheet, gravure printing without publishing
323110   Music, sheet, lithographic (offset) printing without publishing
424990   Music, sheet, merchant wholesalers
323119   Music, sheet, printing (except flexographic, gravure, lithographic, quick, screen) without publishing
512230   Music, sheet, publishers and printing combined
323113   Music, sheet, screen printing without publishing
711130   Musical artists, independent
711130   Musical groups (except musical theater groups)
339992   Musical instrument accessories (e.g., mouthpieces, reeds, stands, traps) manufacturing
423990   Musical instrument accessories and supplies merchant wholesalers
316991   Musical instrument cases, all materials, manufacturing
532299   Musical instrument rental
811490   Musical instrument repair shops without retailing new musical instruments
451140   Musical instrument stores
339992   Musical instruments (except toy) manufacturing
423990   Musical instruments merchant wholesalers
339932   Musical instruments, toy, manufacturing

711130   Musical productions (except musical theater productions), live
512220   Musical recording, releasing, promoting, and distributing
423990   Musical recordings (e.g., compact discs, records, tapes) merchant wholesalers
711110   Musical theater companies or groups
711110   Musical theater productions, live
711130   Musicians, independent
111219   Muskmelon farming, field, bedding plant and seed production
114112   Mussel fishing
112512   Mussel production, farm raising
111120   Mustard seed farming, field and seed production
311941   Mustard, prepared, manufacturing
523120   Mutual fund agencies (i.e., brokerages)
523120   Mutual fund agents' (i.e., brokers') offices
523920   Mutual fund managing
525990   Mutual funds, closed-end
525910   Mutual funds, open-ended
522120   Mutual savings banks
621511   Mycology health laboratories
325191   Myrobalans extract manufacturing
333991   Nail guns, handheld power-driven, manufacturing
333513   Nail heading machines manufacturing
325620   Nail polish remover manufacturing
325620   Nail polishes manufacturing
812113   Nail salons
333991   Nailers and staplers, handheld power-driven, manufacturing
423510   Nails merchant wholesalers
331319   Nails, aluminum, made in wire drawing plants
332618   Nails, brads, and staples made from purchased wire
331222   Nails, iron or steel, made in wire drawing plants

331491 Nails, nonferrous metals (except aluminum, copper), made from purchased nonferrous metals (except aluminum, copper) in wire drawing plants

332999 Name plate blanks, metal, manufacturing

325998 Napalm manufacturing

325192 Naphtha made by distillation of coal tar

324110 Naphtha made in petroleum refineries

325192 Naphtha, solvent, made by distillation of coal tar

325192 Naphthalene made from refined petroleum or natural gas

325192 Naphthalenesulfonic acid manufacturing

325199 Naphthenic acid soaps manufacturing

325192 Naphthenic acids made from refined petroleum or natural gas

324110 Naphthenic acids made in petroleum refineries

325192 Naphthol, alpha and beta, manufacturing

325192 Naphtholsulfonic acids manufacturing

423220 Napkins (except paper) merchant wholesalers

314129 Napkins made from purchased fabrics

424130 Napkins, paper, merchant wholesalers

322291 Napkins, table, made from purchased paper

322121 Napkins, table, made in paper mills

313311 Napping broadwoven fabrics

333292 Napping machinery for textiles manufacturing

313312 Napping textile products and fabrics (except broadwoven fabrics)

313221 Narrow fabrics weaving

927110 National Aeronautics and Space Administration

522110 National commercial banks

522298 National Credit Union Administration (NCUA)

928110 National Guard

712190 National parks

926120 National Transportation Safety Board

311422 Nationality specialty foods canning

311412 Nationality specialty foods, frozen, manufacturing

212399 Native asphalt mining and/or beneficiating

327310 Natural (i.e., calcined earth) cement manufacturing

212399 Natural abrasives (e.g., emery, grindstones, hones, pumice) (except sand) mining and/or beneficiating

313113 Natural fiber (i.e., hemp, linen, ramie) thread manufacturing

313210 Natural fiber fabrics (i.e., jute, linen, hemp, ramie), broadwoven, weaving

313221 Natural fiber fabrics (i.e., jute, linen, hemp, ramie), narrow woven, weaving

313111 Natural fiber spun yarns (i.e., hemp, jute, ramie, flax) made from purchased fiber

221210 Natural gas brokers

221210 Natural gas distribution systems

333618 Natural gas engines manufacturing

211112 Natural gas liquids (e.g., ethane, isobutane, natural gasoline, propane) recovered from oil and gas field gases

486910 Natural gas liquids pipeline transportation

221210 Natural gas marketers

237120 Natural gas pipeline construction

486210 Natural gas pipeline transportation

238220 Natural gas piping installation

237120 Natural gas processing plant construction

211111 Natural gas production

315212	Needlework art contractors on women's, girls', and infants' apparel
315192	Negligees made in apparel knitting mills
315212	Negligees, women's, cut and sew apparel contractors
315231	Negligees, women's, misses', and girls', cut and sewn from purchased fabric (except apparel contractors)
813319	Neighborhood development advocacy organizations
325120	Neon manufacturing
339950	Neon signs manufacturing
325212	Neoprene manufacturing
212325	Nepheline syenite mining and/ or beneficiating
334516	Nephelometers (except meteorological) manufacturing
334519	Nephoscopes manufacturing
333292	Net and lace making machinery manufacturing
424310	Net goods merchant wholesalers
313210	Nets and nettings, more than 12 inches in width, weaving
313249	Netting made in warp knitting mills
313241	Netting made in weft knitting mills
313249	Netting made on a lace or net machine
326199	Netting, plastics, manufacturing
332618	Netting, woven, made from purchased wire
515111	Network broadcasting service, radio
515111	Network radio broadcasting
541512	Network systems integration design services, computer
515120	Network television broadcasting
515210	Networks, cable television
622310	Neurological hospitals
621111	Neurologists' offices (e.g., centers, clinics)
621111	Neuropathologists' offices (e.g., centers, clinics)
312140	Neutral spirit, beverages (except fruit), manufacturing
424820	Neutral spirits merchant wholesalers
334516	Neutron activation analysis instruments manufacturing
441110	New car dealers
541613	New product development consulting services
321918	Newel posts, wood, manufacturing
451212	News dealers
519110	News picture gathering and distributing services
519110	News reporting services
519110	News service syndicates
519110	News ticker services
511120	Newsletter publishers (except exclusive Internet publishing)
511120	Newsletter publishers and printing combined (except Internet)
516110	Newsletter publishers, exclusively on Internet
323112	Newsletters flexographic printing without publishing
323111	Newsletters gravure printing without publishing
323110	Newsletters lithographic (offset) printing without publishing
323119	Newsletters printing (except flexographic, gravure, lithographic, quick, screen) without publishing
323113	Newsletters screen printing without publishing
541840	Newspaper advertising representatives (i.e., independent of media owners)
424920	Newspaper agencies merchant wholesalers
511110	Newspaper branch offices
711510	Newspaper columnists, independent (freelance)
519110	Newspaper feature syndicates
333293	Newspaper inserting equipment manufacturing
511110	Newspaper publishers (except exclusive Internet publishing)
511110	Newspaper publishers and printing combined

315212 Nightshirts, women's, girls', and infants', cut and sew apparel contractors

315231 Nightshirts, women's, misses', and girls', cut and sewn from purchased fabric (except contractors)

315192 Nightwear made in apparel knitting mills

315291 Nightwear, infants', cut and sewn from purchased fabric (except apparel contractors)

315211 Nightwear, men's and boys', cut and sew apparel contractors

315221 Nightwear, men's and boys', cut and sewn from purchased fabric (except apparel contractors)

424320 Nightwear, men's and boys', merchant wholesalers

315212 Nightwear, women's, girls', and infants', cut and sew apparel contractors

315231 Nightwear, women's, misses', and girls', cut and sewn from purchased fabric (except apparel contractors)

331419 Niobium refining, primary

326299 Nipples and teething rings, rubber, manufacturing

332996 Nipples, metal, made from purchased pipe

325192 Nitrated hydrocarbon derivatives manufacturing

325311 Nitric acid manufacturing

325212 Nitrile rubber manufacturing

325212 Nitrile-butadiene rubber manufacturing

325212 Nitrile-chloroprene rubbers manufacturing

325192 Nitroaniline manufacturing

325192 Nitrobenzene manufacturing

325211 Nitrocellulose (i.e., pyroxylin) resins manufacturing

325920 Nitrocellulose explosive materials manufacturing

325221 Nitrocellulose fibers manufacturing

325120 Nitrogen manufacturing

325311 Nitrogenous fertilizer materials manufacturing

325314 Nitrogenous fertilizers made by mixing purchased materials

325920 Nitroglycerin explosive materials manufacturing

325192 Nitrophenol manufacturing

325192 Nitrosated hydrocarbon derivatives manufacturing

325132 Nitroso dyes manufacturing

325920 Nitrostarch explosive materials manufacturing

325199 Nitrous ether manufacturing

325120 Nitrous oxide manufacturing

325411 N-methylpiperazine manufacturing

924110 NOAA (National Oceanic and Atmospheric Administration)

339113 Noise protectors, personal, manufacturing

312120 Nonalcoholic beer brewing

312130 Nonalcoholic wines manufacturing

551112 Nonbank holding companies (except managing)

325222 Noncellulosic fibers and filaments manufacturing

325222 Noncellulosic filament yarn manufacturing

325222 Noncellulosic staple fibers and filaments manufacturing

111339 Noncitrus fruit farming

327125 Nonclay refractories (e.g., block, brick, mortar, tile) manufacturing

311514 Nondairy creamers, dry, manufacturing

311511 Nondairy creamers, liquid, manufacturing

541380 Non-destructive testing laboratories or services

425120 Nondurable goods agents and brokers, wholesale trade

425110 Nondurable goods business to business electronic markets, wholesale trade

325110 Nonene made from refined petroleum or liquid hydrocarbons

311514 Nonfat dry milk manufacturing

531120	Nonresidential building (except miniwarehouse) rental or leasing
481212	Nonscheduled air freight transportation
481211	Nonscheduled air passenger transportation
332214	Nonstick metal cooking utensils
337122	Nonupholstered, household-type, custom wood furniture, manufacturing
313230	Nonwoven fabric tapes manufacturing
313230	Nonwoven fabrics manufacturing
313230	Nonwoven felts manufacturing
311999	Noodle mixes made from purchased dry ingredients
311423	Noodle mixes made in dehydration plants
311823	Noodle mixes made in dry pasta plants
311823	Noodles, dry, manufacturing
311991	Noodles, fresh, manufacturing
311999	Noodles, fried, manufacturing
339113	Nose and ear plugs manufacturing
541199	Notary public services
541199	Notary publics' private practices
334111	Notebook computers manufacturing
322233	Notebooks (including mechanically bound by wire, or plastics) made from purchased paper
424120	Notebooks merchant wholesalers
332999	Novelties and specialties, nonprecious metal and precious plated, manufacturing
424990	Novelties merchant wholesalers
316999	Novelties, leather (e.g., cigarette lighter covers, key fobs), manufacturing
339999	Novelties, not specified elsewhere, manufacturing
339911	Novelties, precious metal (except precious plated), manufacturing
321999	Novelties, wood fiber, manufacturing
453220	Novelty shops
315211	Novelty stitching contractors on men's and boys' apparel
315212	Novelty stitching contractors on women's, girls', and infants' apparel
326199	Nozzles, aerosol spray, plastics, manufacturing
332919	Nozzles, fire fighting, manufacturing
332919	Nozzles, lawn hose, manufacturing
325212	N-type rubber manufacturing
332911	Nuclear application valves manufacturing
541690	Nuclear energy consulting services
926130	Nuclear energy inspection and regulation offices
325188	Nuclear fuel scrap reprocessing
325188	Nuclear fuels, inorganic, manufacturing
334519	Nuclear instrument modules manufacturing
334517	Nuclear irradiation equipment manufacturing
325412	Nuclear medicine (e.g., radioactive isotopes) preparations manufacturing
237130	Nuclear power plant construction
332410	Nuclear reactor steam supply systems manufacturing
332410	Nuclear reactors control rod drive mechanisms manufacturing
332410	Nuclear reactors manufacturing
332313	Nuclear shielding, fabricated metal plate work, manufacturing
332420	Nuclear waste casks, heavy gauge metal, manufacturing
237990	Nuclear waste disposal site construction
721214	Nudist camps with accommodation facilities
713990	Nudist camps without accommodations

621111   Obstetricians' offices (e.g., centers, clinics)
339992   Ocarinas manufacturing
926150   Occupational safety and health administration
926150   Occupational safety and health standards agencies
813920   Occupational therapists' associations
621340   Occupational therapists' offices (e.g., centers, clinics)
541710   Oceanographic research and development laboratories or services
212393   Ocher mining and/or beneficiating
325131   Ocher pigments manufacturing
339992   Octophones manufacturing
114112   Octopus fishing
621320   ODs' (doctors of optometry) offices (e.g., centers, clinics)
332995   Oerlikon guns manufacturing
721310   Off campus dormitories
624190   Offender self-help organizations
336999   Off-highway tracked vehicles (except construction, armored military) manufacturing
333120   Off-highway trucks manufacturing
561110   Office administration services
541512   Office automation computer systems integration design services
236220   Office building construction
531120   Office building rental or leasing
561720   Office cleaning services
423420   Office equipment merchant wholesalers
337214   Office furniture (except wood), padded, upholstered, or plain (except wood), manufacturing
423210   Office furniture merchant wholesalers
532420   Office furniture rental or leasing
442110   Office furniture stores
238390   Office furniture, modular system, installation
337211   Office furniture, padded, upholstered, or plain wood, manufacturing

561320   Office help supply services
811212   Office machine repair and maintenance services (except communication equipment)
532420   Office machinery and equipment rental or leasing
423420   Office machines merchant wholesalers
561110   Office management services
322121   Office paper (e.g., computer printer, photocopy, plain paper) made in paper mills
322233   Office paper (e.g., computer printer, photocopy, plain paper), cut sheet, made from purchased paper
424120   Office supplies (except furniture, machines) merchant wholesalers
322231   Office supplies, die-cut paper, made from purchased paper or paperboard
561320   Office supply pools
453210   Office supply stores
336999   Off-road all terrain vehicles (ATV's), wheeled or tracked, manufacturing
441221   Off-road all-terrain vehicles (ATV), wheeled or tracked, dealers
325910   Offset inks manufacturing
323122   Offset plate preparation services
323110   Offset printing (except books, manifold business forms, printing grey goods)
333293   Offset printing presses manufacturing
211111   Offshore crude petroleum production
211111   Offshore natural gas production
713290   Off-track betting parlors
334515   Ohmmeters manufacturing
324110   Oil (i.e., petroleum) refineries
325998   Oil additive preparations manufacturing
324110   Oil additives made in petroleum refineries
424690   Oil additives merchant wholesalers

424490	Oils, cooking and salad, merchant wholesalers
324110	Oils, fuel, manufacturing
424990	Oils, inedible, animal or vegetable, merchant wholesalers
324191	Oils, lubricating petroleum, made from refined petroleum
325998	Oils, lubricating, synthetic, manufacturing
324191	Oils, petroleum lubricating, re-refining used
325613	Oils, soluble (i.e., textile finishing assistants), manufacturing
325411	Oils, vegetable and animal, medicinal, uncompounded, manufacturing
325191	Oils, wood, made by distillation of wood
111191	Oilseed and grain combination farming, field and seed production
424990	Oilseed cake and meal merchant wholesalers
333294	Oilseed crushing and extracting machinery manufacturing
111120	Oilseed farming (except soybean), field and seed production
424590	Oilseeds merchant wholesalers
212399	Oilstones mining and/or beneficiating
333911	Oil-well and oil-field pumps manufacturing
111219	Okra farming, field, bedding plant and seed production
623312	Old age homes without nursing care
923130	Old age survivors and disability programs
623312	Old soldiers' homes without nursing care
325222	Olefin fibers and filaments manufacturing
325110	Olefins made from refined petroleum or liquid hydrocarbons
325199	Oleic acid (i.e., red oil) manufacturing

325199	Oleic acid esters manufacturing
325188	Oleum (i.e., fuming sulfuric acid) manufacturing
111339	Olive farming
311225	Olive oil made from purchased oils
311223	Olive oil made in crushing mills
311421	Olives brined
311423	Olives, dried, made in dehydration plant
212325	Olivine, non-gem, mining and/or beneficiating
334511	Omnibearing instrumentation manufacturing
621111	Oncologists' offices (e.g., centers, clinics)
812922	One-hour photofinishing services
111219	Onion farming, field, bedding plant and seed production
311421	Onions pickled
518111	On-line access service providers
212319	Onyx marble crushed and broken stone mining and/or beneficiating
212311	Onyx marble mining or quarrying
512132	Open air motion picture theaters
711110	Opera companies
315991	Opera hats cut and sewn from purchased fabric (except apparel contractors)
315211	Opera hats, men's and boys', cut and sew apparel contractors
315212	Opera hats, women's, girls', and infants', cut and sew apparel contractors
711130	Opera singers, independent
927110	Operating and launching government satellites
339111	Operating room tables manufacturing
511210	Operating systems software, computer, packaged
541614	Operations research consulting services

621991 Organ donor centers, body
424690 Organic chemicals merchant
wholesalers
325222 Organic fibers and filaments
(except cellulosic)
manufacturing
325132 Organic pigments, dyes, lakes,
and toners manufacturing
541612 Organization development
consulting services
928120 Organization for Economic
Coperation and Development
928120 Organization of American
States
326199 Organizers for closets, drawers,
and shelves, plastics,
manufacturing
711310 Organizers of agricultural fairs
with facilities
711320 Organizers of agricultural fairs
without facilities
711310 Organizers of arts events with
facilities
711320 Organizers of arts events
without facilities
711310 Organizers of festivals with
facilities
711320 Organizers of festivals without
facilities
711310 Organizers of live performing
arts productions (e.g.,
concerts) with facilities
711320 Organizers of live performing
arts productions (e.g.,
concerts) without facilities
711310 Organizers of sports events with
facilities
711320 Organizers of sports events
without facilities
325199 Organo-inorganic compound
manufacturing
325320 Organo-phosphate based
insecticides manufacturing
321219 Oriented strandboard (OSB)
manufacturing
327420 Ornamental and architectural
plaster work (e.g., columns,
mantels, molding)
manufacturing

112511 Ornamental fish production,
farm raising
423390 Ornamental ironwork merchant
wholesalers
238190 Ornamental metal work
installation
332323 Ornamental metalwork
manufacturing
111422 Ornamental plant growing
561730 Ornamental tree and shrub
services
321918 Ornamental woodwork (e.g.,
cornices, mantels)
manufacturing
339999 Ornaments, Christmas tree
(except electric, glass),
manufacturing
335129 Ornaments, Christmas tree,
electric, manufacturing
327212 Ornaments, Christmas tree,
glass, made in glass making
plants
327215 Ornaments, Christmas tree,
made from purchased glass
623990 Orphanages
325998 Orris oil manufacturing
325192 Orthodichlorobenzene
manufacturing
339116 Orthodontic appliance, custom
made in dental laboratories
339114 Orthodontic appliances
manufacturing
621210 Orthodontists' offices (e.g.,
centers, clinics)
339113 Orthopedic canes manufacturing
339113 Orthopedic device
manufacturing and sale in
retail environment
339113 Orthopedic devices
manufacturing
423450 Orthopedic equipment and
supplies merchant wholesalers
339113 Orthopedic extension shoes
manufacturing
339113 Orthopedic hosiery, elastic,
manufacturing
622310 Orthopedic hospitals
621111 Orthopedic physicians' offices
(e.g., centers, clinics)

327420 Orthopedic plaster, gypsum, manufacturing
316219 Orthopedic shoes (except extension shoes), children's, manufacturing
316213 Orthopedic shoes (except extension shoes), men's, manufacturing
316214 Orthopedic shoes (except extension shoes), women's, manufacturing
448210 Orthopedic shoes stores
621111 Orthopedic surgeons' offices (e.g., centers, clinics)
321219 OSB (oriented strandboard) manufacturing
334515 Oscillators (e.g., instrument type audiofrequency and radiofrequency) manufacturing
334515 Oscilloscopes manufacturing
212299 Osmium mining and/or beneficiating
334516 Osmometers manufacturing
325998 Ossein manufacturing
622110 Osteopathic hospitals
621111 Osteopathic physicians' (except mental health) offices (e.g., centers, clinics)
112390 Ostrich production
621111 Otolaryngologists' offices (e.g., centers, clinics)
334510 Otoscopes, electromedical, manufacturing
337121 Ottomans, upholstered, manufacturing
441222 Outboard motor dealers
811490 Outboard motor repair shops
333618 Outboard motors manufacturing
423910 Outboard motors merchant wholesalers
713990 Outdoor adventure operations (e.g., white water rafting) without accommodations
721214 Outdoor adventure retreats with accommodation facilities
541850 Outdoor display advertising services
423210 Outdoor furniture merchant wholesalers
237990 Outdoor recreation facility construction
451110 Outdoor sporting equipment stores
315191 Outerwear handknitted for the trade
424320 Outerwear, men's and boys', merchant wholesalers
424330 Outerwear, women's, children's, and infants', merchant wholesalers
335932 Outlet boxes, electrical wiring, manufacturing
335931 Outlets (i.e., receptacles), electrical, manufacturing
335931 Outlets, convenience, electrical, manufacturing
541850 Out-of-home media (i.e., display) advertising services
621420 Outpatient mental health centers and clinics (except hospitals)
621420 Outpatient treatment centers and clinics (except hospitals) for substance abuse (i.e., alcoholism, drug addiction)
621420 Outpatient treatment centers and clinics for alcoholism
621420 Outpatient treatment centers and clinics for drug addiction
541612 Outplacement consulting services
541990 Outplacement services
325612 Oven cleaners manufacturing
334512 Oven temperature controls, nonindustrial, manufacturing
811412 Oven, household-type, repair and maintenance services without retailing new ovens
236210 Oven, industrial plant, construction
423720 Ovens (except electric), household-type, merchant wholesalers
333294 Ovens, bakery, manufacturing
333319 Ovens, commercial-type, manufacturing
423440 Ovens, commercial-type, merchant wholesalers
423620 Ovens, electric household-type, merchant wholesalers

335221 Ovens, freestanding household-type, manufacturing

333994 Ovens, industrial process-type, manufacturing

423830 Ovens, industrial, merchant wholesalers

339111 Ovens, laboratory-type, manufacturing

335211 Ovens, portable household-type (except microwave and convection ovens), manufacturing

335221 Ovens, portable household-type convention and microwave, manufacturing

327215 Ovenware made from purchased glass

327212 Ovenware, glass, made in glass making plants

315211 Overall jackets, work, men's and boys', cut and sew apparel contractors

315225 Overall jackets, work, men's and boys', cut and sewn from purchased fabric (except apparel contractors)

315211 Overalls, work, men's and boys', cut and sew apparel contractors

315225 Overalls, work, men's and boys', cut and sewn from purchased fabric (except apparel contractors)

213113 Overburden removal for coal mining on a contract basis

213114 Overburden removal for metal mining on a contract basis

213115 Overburden removal for nonmetallic minerals mining (except fuels) on a contract basis

315211 Overcoats, men's and boys', cut and sew apparel contractors

315222 Overcoats, men's and boys', cut and sewn from purchased fabric (except apparel contractors)

315212 Overcoats, women's, girls', and infants', cut and sew apparel contractors

315234 Overcoats, women's, misses', and girls', cut and sewn from purchased fabric (except apparel contractors)

333922 Overhead conveyors manufacturing

238290 Overhead door, commercial- or industrial-type, installation

238350 Overhead door, residential-type, installation

333315 Overhead projectors (except computer peripheral) manufacturing

334119 Overhead projectors, computer peripheral-type, manufacturing

333923 Overhead traveling cranes manufacturing

237310 Overpass construction

316211 Overshoes, plastics or plastics soled fabric upper, manufacturing

316211 Overshoes, rubber, or rubber soled fabric, manufacturing

325199 Oxalates (e.g., ammonium oxalate, ethyl oxalate, sodium oxalate) manufacturing

325199 Oxalic acid manufacturing

532291 Oxygen equipment rental (i.e. home use)

325120 Oxygen manufacturing

339112 Oxygen tents manufacturing

114112 Oyster dredging

112512 Oyster production, farm raising

212399 Ozokerite mining and/or beneficiating

333319 Ozone machines for water purification manufacturing

621999 Pacemaker monitoring services

334510 Pacemakers manufacturing

326299 Pacifiers, rubber, manufacturing

713990 Pack trains (i.e., trail riding), recreational

445310 Package stores (i.e., liquor)

511210 Packaged computer software publishers

326112 Packaging film, plastics, single-web or multiweb, manufacturing

115114 Packaging fresh or farm-dried fruits and vegetables

424950 Paintbrushes merchant wholesalers

711510 Painters (i.e., artists), independent

424950 Painter's supplies (except artists', turpentine) merchant wholesalers

238320 Painting (except roof) contractors

238320 Painting and wallpapering

237310 Painting lines on highways, streets and bridges

332812 Painting metals and metal products for the trade

711510 Painting restorers, independent

237310 Painting traffic lanes or parking lots

238160 Painting, spraying, or coating, roof

325510 Paints (except artist's) manufacturing

424950 Paints (except artists') merchant wholesalers

339942 Paints, artist's, manufacturing

424990 Paints, artist's, merchant wholesalers

325510 Paints, emulsion (i.e., latex paint), manufacturing

325510 Paints, oil and alkyd vehicle, manufacturing

315192 Pajamas made in apparel knitting mills

315291 Pajamas, infants', cut and sewn from purchased fabric (except apparel contractors)

315211 Pajamas, men's and boys', cut and sew apparel contractors

315221 Pajamas, men's and boys', cut and sewn from purchased fabric (except apparel contractors)

315231 Pajamas, women's and girls', cut and sewn from purchased fabric (except apparel contractors)

315212 Pajamas, women's, girls', and infants', cut and sew apparel contractors

339942 Palettes, artist's, manufacturing

212299 Palladium mining and/or beneficiating

321920 Pallet containers, wood or wood and metal combination, manufacturing

333924 Pallet movers manufacturing

333924 Pallet or skid jacks manufacturing

332999 Pallet parts, metal, manufacturing

321920 Pallet parts, wood, manufacturing

532490 Pallet rental or leasing

423830 Pallets and skids merchant wholesalers

322211 Pallets, corrugated and solid fiber, made from purchased paper or paperboard

332999 Pallets, metal, manufacturing

321920 Pallets, wood or wood and metal combination, manufacturing

812990 Palm reading services

325199 Palmitic acid esters and amines manufacturing

311225 Palm-kernel oil made from purchased oils

311223 Palm-kernel oil, cake, and meal made in crushing mills

323121 Pamphlet binding without printing

511130 Pamphlet publishers (except exclusive Internet publishing)

511130 Pamphlet publishers and printing combined

516110 Pamphlet publishers, exclusively on Internet

424920 Pamphlets merchant wholesalers

323117 Pamphlets printing and binding without publishing

323117 Pamphlets printing without publishing

315991 Panama hats cut and sewn from purchased fabric (except apparel contractors)

315211 Panama hats, men's and boys', cut and sew apparel contractors

315291	Pants, infants', cut and sewn from purchased fabric (except apparel contractors)
315292	Pants, leather (except apparel contractors), manufacturing
315211	Pants, leather, men's and boys', cut and sew apparel contractors
315211	Pants, men's and boys', cut and sew apparel contractors
315191	Pants, outerwear, made in apparel knitting mills
315299	Pants, rubber and rubberized fabric, made in the same establishment as the basic material
315291	Pants, sweat, infant's, cut and sewn from purchased fabric (except apparel contractors)
315228	Pants, sweat, men's and boys', cut and sewn from purchased fabric (except apparel contractors)
315212	Pants, sweat, women's, girls', and infants', cut and sew apparel contractors
315239	Pants, sweat, women's, misses', and girls', cut and sewn from purchased fabric (except apparel contractors)
315211	Pants, unisex sweat, cut and sew apparel contractors
315228	Pants, unisex sweat, cut and sewn from purchased fabric (except apparel contractors)
315299	Pants, vulcanized rubber, manufacturing
315299	Pants, waterproof outerwear (except infants'), cut and sewn from purchased fabric (except apparel contractors)
315211	Pants, waterproof outerwear, men's and boys', cut and sew apparel contractors
315212	Pants, waterproof outerwear, women's, girls', and infants', cut and sew apparel contractors
315212	Pants, women's, girls', and infants', cut and sew apparel contractors
315239	Pants, women's, misses', and girls', cut and sewn from purchased fabric (except apparel contractors)
315211	Pants, work (except dungarees, jeans), men's and boys', cut and sew apparel contractors
315225	Pants, work (except dungarees, jeans), men's and boys', cut and sewn from purchased fabric (except apparel contractors)
315291	Pantsuits, infants', cut and sewn from purchased fabric (except apparel contractors)
315212	Pantsuits, women's, girls', and infants', cut and sew apparel contractors
315234	Pantsuits, women's, misses', and girls', cut and sewn from purchased fabric (except apparel contractors)
315212	Panty girdles cut and sew apparel contractors
315231	Panty girdles, women's, misses', and girls', cut and sewn from purchased fabric (except apparel contractors)
315111	Panty hose, women's and girls', knitting or knitting and finishing
111339	Papaya farming
327910	Paper (e.g., aluminum oxide, emery, garnet, silicon carbide), abrasive coated, made from purchased paper
424110	Paper (e.g., fine, printing, writing), bulk, merchant wholesalers
322121	Paper (except newsprint, uncoated groundwood) manufacturing
322121	Paper (except newsprint, uncoated groundwood) products made in paper mills

322121 Paper, asphalt, made in paper mills
423390 Paper, building, merchant wholesalers
339944 Paper, carbon, manufacturing
322211 Paper, corrugated, made from purchased paper or paperboard
523110 Paper, dealing of commercial (i.e., acting as principal in dealing securities to investors)
322122 Paper, newsprint and uncoated groundwood, manufacturing
424120 Paper, office (e.g., carbon, computer, copier, typewriter), merchant wholesalers
325992 Paper, photographic sensitized, manufacturing
423930 Paper, scrap, merchant wholesalers
339944 Paper, stencil, manufacturing
322130 Paperboard (e.g., can/drum stock, container board, corrugating medium, folding carton stock, linerboard, tube) manufacturing
424130 Paperboard and paperboard products (except office supplies) merchant wholesalers
333291 Paperboard box making machinery manufacturing
322130 Paperboard coating, laminating, or treating in paperboard mills
333291 Paperboard making machinery manufacturing
322130 Paperboard mills
322130 Paperboard products (e.g., containers) made in paperboard mills
322226 Paperboard, pasted, lined, laminated, or surface coated, made from purchased paperboard
238320 Paperhanging and removal contractors
238320 Paperhanging or removal contractors
327999 Papier-mache statuary and related art goods (e.g., urns, vases) manufacturing

713990 Para sailing, recreational
314999 Parachutes manufacturing
213112 Paraffin services, oil and gas field, on a contract basis
324110 Paraffin waxes made in petroleum refineries
325110 Paraffins made from refined petroleum or liquid hydrocarbons
541199 Paralegal services
321213 Parallel strand lumber manufacturing
621399 Paramedics' offices (e.g., centers, clinics)
325132 Pararosaniline dyes manufacturing
621511 Parasitology health laboratories
339999 Parasols manufacturing
325320 Parathion insecticides manufacturing
485991 Paratransit transportation services
561431 Parcel mailing services combined with one or more other office support services, private
561431 Parcel mailing services, private
333997 Parcel post scales manufacturing
316110 Parchment leather manufacturing
922150 Pardon boards and offices
624190 Parenting support services
813410 Parent-teachers' associations
325320 Paris green insecticides manufacturing
237990 Park and recreational open space improvement construction
922120 Park police
332812 Parkerizing metals and metal products for the trade
236220 Parking garage construction
812930 Parking garages, automobile
561790 Parking lot cleaning (e.g., power sweeping, washing) services
237310 Parking lot marking and line painting
238990 Parking lot paving and sealing

111339 Passion fruit farming
928120 Passport issuing services
541921 Passport photography services
311422 Pasta based products canning
333294 Pasta making machinery (i.e., food manufacturing-type) manufacturing
311999 Pasta mixes made from purchased dry ingredients
311823 Pasta, dry, manufacturing
311991 Pasta, fresh, manufacturing
331314 Paste made from purchased aluminum
331423 Paste made from purchased copper
331221 Paste made from purchased iron or steel
331111 Paste, iron or steel, made in iron and steel mills
331492 Paste, nonferrous metals (except aluminum, copper), made from purchased metal
325520 Pastes, adhesive, manufacturing
311421 Pastes, fruit and vegetable, canning
333294 Pasteurizing equipment, food, manufacturing
311511 Pasteurizing milk
311612 Pastrami made from purchased carcasses
311812 Pastries (e.g., Danish, French), fresh, made in commercial bakeries
311813 Pastries (e.g., Danish, French), frozen, manufacturing
311822 Pastries, uncooked, manufacturing
321999 Pastry boards, wood, manufacturing
541199 Patent agent services (i.e., patent filing and searching services)
541110 Patent attorneys' offices
541110 Patent attorneys' private practices
541990 Patent broker services (i.e., patent marketing services)
533110 Patent buying and licensing
533110 Patent leasing
316110 Patent leather manufacturing

325412 Patent medicine preparations manufacturing
621511 Pathological analysis laboratories
621111 Pathologists' (except oral, speech, voice) offices (e.g., centers, clinics)
621111 Pathologists', forensic, offices (e.g., centers, clinics)
621111 Pathologists', neuropathological, offices (e.g., centers, clinics)
621210 Pathologists', oral, offices (e.g., centers, clinics)
621340 Pathologists', speech or voice, offices (e.g., centers, clinics)
621111 Pathologists', surgical, offices (e.g., centers, clinics)
621511 Pathology laboratories, medical
334510 Patient monitoring equipment (e.g., intensive care, coronary care unit) manufacturing
423450 Patient monitoring equipment merchant wholesalers
327331 Patio block, concrete, manufacturing
238990 Patio construction
336611 Patrol boat building
561612 Patrol services, security
541990 Patrolling (i.e., visual inspection) of electric transmission or gas lines
511199 Pattern and plan (e.g., clothing patterns) publishers (except exclusive Internet publishing)
511199 Pattern and plan (e.g., clothing patterns) publishers and printing combined
516110 Pattern and plan (e.g., clothing patterns) publishers, exclusively on Internet
332997 Patterns (except shoe), industrial, manufacturing
423830 Patterns (except shoe), industrial, merchant wholesalers
323112 Patterns and plans (e.g., clothing patterns) flexographic printing without publishing

812113 Pedicure and manicure salons
812113 Pedicurist services
115210 Pedigree (i.e., livestock, pets, poultry) record services
334514 Pedometers manufacturing
813920 Peer review boards
212325 Pegmatite, feldspar, mining and/or beneficiating
316999 Pegs, leather shoe, manufacturing
332994 Pellet guns manufacturing
333131 Pellet mills machinery, mining-type, manufacturing
332992 Pellets, air rifle and pistol, manufacturing
316110 Pelts bleaching, currying, dyeing, scraping, and tanning
424590 Pelts, raw, merchant wholesalers
339112 Pelvimeters manufacturing
339941 Pen refills and cartridges manufacturing
339942 Pencil leads manufacturing
339942 Pencil sharpeners manufacturing
321999 Pencil slats, wood, manufacturing
339942 Pencils (except mechanical) manufacturing
424120 Pencils merchant wholesalers
339941 Pencils, mechanical, manufacturing
335122 Pendant lamps (except residential), electric, manufacturing
335121 Pendant lamps fixtures, residential electric, manufacturing
325613 Penetrants manufacturing
325998 Penetrating fluids, synthetic, manufacturing
325412 Penicillin preparations manufacturing
325411 Penicillin, uncompounded, manufacturing
922140 Penitentiaries
236220 Penitentiary construction
212113 Pennsylvania anthracite mining and/or beneficiating
339941 Pens manufacturing

424120 Pens, writing, merchant wholesalers
523920 Pension fund managing
524292 Pension fund, third party administrative services
525110 Pension funds
525110 Pension plans (e.g., employee benefit, retirement)
332313 Penstocks, fabricated metal plate, manufacturing
325192 Pentachlorophenol manufacturing
325199 Pentaerythritol manufacturing
325110 Pentanes made from refined petroleum or liquid hydrocarbons
325110 Pentenes made from refined petroleum or liquid hydrocarbons
325920 Pentolite explosive materials manufacturing
561330 PEO (professional employer organizations)
111219 Pepper (e.g., bell, chili, green, hot, red, sweet) farming
311942 Pepper (i.e., spice) manufacturing
325998 Peppermint oil manufacturing
313210 Percales weaving
114111 Perch fishing
325188 Perchloric acid manufacturing
325199 Perchloroethylene manufacturing
335211 Percolators, household-type electric, manufacturing
332992 Percussion caps (i.e., 30 mm. or less, 1.18 inch or less), ammunition, manufacturing
339992 Percussion musical instruments manufacturing
213112 Perforating oil and gas well casings on a contract basis
711510 Performers (i.e., entertainers), independent
711510 Performing artists, independent
711310 Performing arts center operators
611610 Performing arts schools (except academic)

333315 Photographic equipment (except lenses) manufacturing
423410 Photographic equipment and supplies merchant wholesalers
532210 Photographic equipment rental
811211 Photographic equipment repair shops without retailing new photographic equipment
423410 Photographic film merchant wholesalers
325992 Photographic film, cloth, paper, and plate, sensitized, manufacturing
333314 Photographic lenses manufacturing
812990 Photographic machine concession operators, coin-operated
443130 Photographic supply stores
326113 Photographic, micrographic, and X-ray plastics, sheet, and film (except sensitized), manufacturing
611610 Photography schools, art
611519 Photography schools, commercial
541922 Photography services, commercial
541921 Photography services, portrait (e.g., still, video)
541922 Photography studios, commercial
541921 Photography studios, portrait
327212 Photomask blanks, glass, made in glass making plants
325992 Photomasks manufacturing
334516 Photometers (except photographic exposure meters) manufacturing
334516 Photonexcitation analyzers manufacturing
325992 Photosensitized paper manufacturing
323122 Phototypesetting services
334413 Photovoltaic devices, solid-state, manufacturing
812990 Phrenology services
325199 Phthalate acid manufacturing
325211 Phthalic alkyd resins manufacturing

325192 Phthalic anhydride manufacturing
325211 Phthalic anhydride resins manufacturing
325132 Phthalocyanine pigments manufacturing
541614 Physical distribution consulting services
621340 Physical equestrian therapist offices (e.g., centers, clinics)
713940 Physical fitness centers
621999 Physical fitness evaluation services (except by offices of health practitioners)
713940 Physical fitness facilities
713940 Physical fitness studios
334519 Physical properties testing and inspection equipment manufacturing
622310 Physical rehabilitation hospitals
541710 Physical science research and development laboratories or services
621340 Physical therapists' offices (e.g., centers, clinics)
621340 Physical therapy offices (e.g., centers, clinics)
621340 Physical-integration practitioners' offices (e.g., centers, clinics)
621111 Physicians' (except mental health) offices (e.g., centers, clinics)
621399 Physicians' assistants' offices (e.g., centers, clinics)
621112 Physicians', mental health, offices (e.g., centers, clinics)
541690 Physics consulting services
541710 Physics research and development laboratories or services
621340 Physiotherapists' offices (e.g., centers, clinics)
339112 Physiotherapy equipment (except electrotherapeutic) manufacturing
325411 Physostigmine and derivatives (i.e., basic chemicals) manufacturing

332510 Piano hardware, metal, manufacturing

339992 Piano parts and materials (except piano hardware) manufacturing

532299 Piano rental

451140 Piano stores

339992 Piccolos and parts manufacturing

333292 Picker machinery for textiles manufacturing

333292 Picker sticks for looms manufacturing

311712 Picking crab meat

333516 Picklers and pickling machinery, metalworking, manufacturing

311421 Pickles manufacturing

311421 Pickling fruits and vegetables

332813 Pickling metals and metal products for the trade

332212 Picks (i.e., handtools) manufacturing

812320 Pickup and drop-off sites for drycleaners and laundries

336214 Pickup canopies, caps, or covers manufacturing

336112 Pick-up trucks, light duty, assembling on chassis of own manufacture

713990 Picnic grounds

326199 Picnic jugs, plastics (except foam), manufacturing

325920 Picric acid explosive materials manufacturing

334511 Pictorial situation instrumentation manufacturing

442299 Picture frame shops, custom

311822 Pie crust shells, uncooked, made from purchased flour

424310 Piece goods (except burlap, felt) merchant wholesalers

451130 Piece goods stores

424990 Piece goods, burlap and felt, merchant wholesalers

237990 Pier construction

531120 Piers and associated building rental or leasing

713110 Piers, amusement

424420 Pies (e.g., fruit, meat, poultry), frozen, merchant wholesalers

311812 Pies, fresh, made in commercial bakeries

311813 Pies, frozen, manufacturing

334419 Piezoelectric crystals manufacturing

334419 Piezoelectric devices manufacturing

112210 Pig farming

331111 Pig iron manufacturing

423510 Pig iron merchant wholesalers

325132 Pigment, scarlet lake, manufacturing

325132 Pigments (except animal black, bone black), organic, manufacturing

325131 Pigments (except bone black, carbon black, lamp black), inorganic, manufacturing

212393 Pigments, natural, mineral, mining and/or beneficiating

424950 Pigments, paint, merchant wholesalers

311612 Pig's feet, cooked and pickled, made from purchased carcasses

114111 Pilchard fishing

238910 Pile driving, building foundation

237990 Pile driving, marine

313249 Pile fabrics made in warp knitting mills

313241 Pile fabrics made in weft knitting mills

332313 Pile shells, fabricated metal plate, manufacturing

332322 Pile shells, sheet metal (except stampings), manufacturing

333120 Pile-driving equipment manufacturing

238910 Piling (i.e., bored, cast-in-place, drilled), building foundation, contractors

321114 Pilings, foundation and marine construction, treating

331111 Pilings, iron or steel plain sheet, made in iron and steel mills

321114 Pilings, round wood, cutting and treating

321114 Pilings, wood, treating
332991 Pillow blocks with ball or roller bearings manufacturing
812320 Pillow cleaning services
314129 Pillowcases, bed, made from purchased fabrics
314129 Pillows, bed, made from purchased materials
488490 Pilot car services (i.e., wide load warning services)
488330 Piloting services, water transportation
713120 Pinball arcades
713990 Pinball machine concession operators (i.e., supplying and servicing in others' facilities)
339999 Pinball machines, coin-operated, manufacturing
113210 Pine gum extracting
325191 Pine oil manufacturing
111339 Pineapple farming
325191 Pinene manufacturing
713990 Ping pong parlors
212325 Pinite mining and/or beneficiating
339993 Pins (except precious) manufacturing
339911 Pins and brooches, precious metal, manufacturing
712120 Pioneer villages
331210 Pipe (e.g., heavy riveted, lock joint, seamless, welded) made from purchased iron or steel
332996 Pipe and pipe fittings made from purchased metal pipe
331511 Pipe and pipe fittings, cast iron, manufacturing
333516 Pipe and tube rolling mill machinery, metalworking, manufacturing
332323 Pipe bannisters, metal, manufacturing
326299 Pipe bits and stems, tobacco, hard rubber, manufacturing
339999 Pipe cleaners manufacturing
332996 Pipe couplings made from purchased metal pipe
331511 Pipe couplings, cast iron, manufacturing
238290 Pipe covering

333512 Pipe cutting and threading machines, metalworking, manufacturing
332996 Pipe fabricating (i.e., bending, cutting, threading) made from purchased metal pipe
238220 Pipe fitting contractors
326122 Pipe fittings, rigid plastics, manufacturing
332323 Pipe guards, metal, manufacturing
332999 Pipe hangers and supports, metal, manufacturing
332996 Pipe headers made from purchased metal pipe
237120 Pipe lining (except thermal insulating) contractors
331316 Pipe made by extruding purchased aluminum
332323 Pipe railings, metal, manufacturing
325520 Pipe sealing compounds manufacturing
213112 Pipe testing services, oil and gas field, on a contract basis
424940 Pipe tobacco merchant wholesalers
312229 Pipe tobacco, prepared, manufacturing
331316 Pipe, aluminum, made in integrated secondary smelting and extruding mills
327332 Pipe, concrete, manufacturing
238290 Pipe, duct and boiler insulation
331421 Pipe, extruded and drawn, brass, bronze, and copper, made from purchased copper or in integrated secondary smelting and rolling, drawing or extruding plants
332313 Pipe, fabricated metal plate, manufacturing
331111 Pipe, iron or steel, made in iron and steel mills
423510 Pipe, metal, merchant wholesalers
331491 Pipe, nonferrous metals (except aluminum, copper), made from purchased metals or scrap

525120	Plans, health and welfare related employee benefit
522190	Plans, Morris (i.e., known as), depository
522298	Plans, Morris (i.e., known as), nondepository
525110	Plans, pension
561730	Plant and shrub maintenance in buildings
424990	Plant food merchant wholesalers
325311	Plant foods, mixed, made in plants producing nitrogenous fertilizer materials
325312	Plant foods, mixed, made in plants producing phosphatic fertilizer materials
325320	Plant growth regulants manufacturing
561730	Plant maintenance services
111422	Plant, ornamental, growing
111422	Plant, potted flower and foliage, growing
111339	Plantain farming
115112	Planting crops
423820	Planting machinery and equipment, farm-type, merchant wholesalers
333111	Planting machines, farm-type, manufacturing
333513	Plasma jet spray metal forming machines manufacturing
333512	Plasma process metal cutting machines (except welding equipment) manufacturing
333992	Plasma welding equipment manufacturing
621991	Plasmapheresis centers
325414	Plasmas manufacturing
424210	Plasmas, blood, merchant wholesalers
327420	Plaster and plasterboard, gypsum, manufacturing
423320	Plaster merchant wholesalers
327420	Plaster of paris manufacturing
327420	Plaster of paris products (e.g., columns, statuary, urns) manufacturing
327420	Plaster, gypsum, manufacturing
238310	Plastering (i.e., ornamental, plain) contractors
212325	Plastic fire clay mining and/or beneficiating
621111	Plastic surgeons' offices (e.g., centers, clinics)
325510	Plastic wood fillers manufacturing
325199	Plasticizers (i.e., basic synthetic chemicals) manufacturing
424610	Plasticizers merchant wholesalers
337125	Plastics (including fiberglass) furniture (except upholstered), household-type, manufacturing
326220	Plastics and rubber belts and hoses (without fittings) manufacturing
325211	Plastics and synthetic resins regenerating, precipitating, and coagulating
424130	Plastics bags merchant wholesalers
424610	Plastics basic shapes (e.g., film, rod, sheet, sheeting, tubing) merchant wholesalers
313320	Plastics coating of textiles and apparel
326113	Plastics film and unlaminated sheet (except packaging) manufacturing
424610	Plastics foam merchant wholesalers
423840	Plastics foam packing and packaging materials merchant wholesalers
424990	Plastics foam products (except disposable) merchant wholesalers
424130	Plastics foam products, disposable (except packaging, packing), merchant wholesalers
315299	Plastics gowns (except infants') cut and sewn from purchased fabric (except apparel contractors)
315291	Plastics gowns, infants', cut and sewn from purchased fabric (except apparel contractors)

315211 Plastics gowns, men's and boys', cut and sew apparel contractors

315212 Plastics gowns, women's, girls', and infants, cut and sew apparel contractors

423830 Plastics industries machinery, equipment, and supplies merchant wholesalers

337110 Plastics laminated over particleboard (e.g., fixture tops) manufacturing

424610 Plastics materials merchant wholesalers

315299 Plastics rainwear cut and sewn from purchased fabric (except apparel contractors)

315211 Plastics rainwear, men's and boys', cut and sewn apparel contractors

315212 Plastics rainwear, women's, girls', and infants', cut and sew apparel contractors

325991 Plastics resins compounding from recycled materials

424610 Plastics resins merchant wholesalers

325991 Plastics resins, custom compounding of purchased

423930 Plastics scrap merchant wholesalers

333220 Plastics working machinery manufacturing

325510 Plastisol coating compounds manufacturing

524126 Plate glass insurance carriers, direct

423390 Plate glass merchant wholesalers

333516 Plate rolling mill machinery, metalworking, manufacturing

332313 Plate work (e.g., bending, cutting, punching, shaping, welding), fabricated metal, manufacturing

331315 Plate, aluminum, made by continuous casting purchased aluminum

331315 Plate, aluminum, made by flat rolling purchased aluminum

331315 Plate, aluminum, made in integrated secondary smelting and continuous casting mills

331315 Plate, aluminum, made in integrated secondary smelting and flat rolling mills

331421 Plate, copper and copper alloy, made from purchased copper or in integrated secondary smelting and rolling, drawing or extruding plants

331111 Plate, iron or steel, made in iron and steel mills

326130 Plate, laminated plastics, manufacturing

331491 Plate, nonferrous metals (except aluminum, copper), made from purchased metals or scrap

332211 Plated metal cutlery manufacturing

423940 Plated metal cutlery or flatware merchant wholesalers

332211 Plated metal flatware manufacturing

332999 Plated ware (e.g., ecclesiastical ware, hollowware, toilet ware) manufacturing

335932 Plates (i.e., outlet or switch covers), face, manufacturing

322299 Plates, molded pulp, manufacturing

326140 Plates, polystyrene foam, manufacturing

332813 Plating metals and metal products for the trade

331491 Platinum and platinum alloy rolling, drawing, or extruding from purchased metals or scrap

331491 Platinum and platinum alloy sheet and tubing made from purchased metals or scrap

332999 Platinum foil and leaf not made in rolling mills

212299 Platinum mining and/or beneficiating

331492 Platinum recovering from scrap and/or alloying purchased metals

331419	Platinum refining, primary
237990	Play ground construction
423910	Playground equipment and supplies merchant wholesalers
238990	Playground equipment installation
423920	Playing cards merchant wholesalers
337124	Playpens, children's metal, manufacturing
337122	Playpens, children's wood, manufacturing
315291	Playsuits, infants', cut and sewn from purchased fabric (except apparel contractors)
315212	Playsuits, women's, girls', and infants', cut and sew apparel contractors
315239	Playsuits, women's, misses', and girls', cut and sewn from purchased fabric (except apparel contractors)
711510	Playwrights, independent
532292	Pleasure boat rental
336612	Pleasure boats manufacturing
423910	Pleasure boats merchant wholesalers
315211	Pleating contractors on men's and boys' apparel
315212	Pleating contractors on women's, girls', and infants' apparel
332212	Pliers, handtools, manufacturing
327331	Plinth blocks, precast terrazzo, manufacturing
334119	Plotters, computer, manufacturing
115112	Plowing
333120	Plows, construction (e.g., excavating, grading), manufacturing
423820	Plows, farm, merchant wholesalers
333111	Plows, farm-type, manufacturing
111422	Plug (i.e., floriculture products) growing
332911	Plug valves, industrial-type, manufacturing
213112	Plugging and abandoning wells on a contract basis
335931	Plugs, electric cord, manufacturing
332999	Plugs, magnetic metal drain, manufacturing
321999	Plugs, wood, manufacturing
111339	Plum farming
238220	Plumbers
611513	Plumbers' apprenticeship training
423720	Plumbers' brass goods merchant wholesalers
332212	plumbers' handtools, nonpowered, manufacturing
325520	plumbers' putty manufacturing
238220	Plumbing and heating contractors
332919	Plumbing and heating inline valves (e.g., check, cutoffs, stop) manufacturing
423720	Plumbing and heating valves merchant wholesalers
238220	Plumbing contractors
423720	Plumbing equipment merchant wholesalers
532490	Plumbing equipment rental or leasing
332913	Plumbing fittings and couplings (e.g., compression fittings, metal elbows, metal unions) manufacturing
332913	Plumbing fixture fittings and trim, all materials, manufacturing
238220	Plumbing fixture installation
326191	Plumbing fixtures (e.g., shower stalls, toilets, urinals), plastics or fiberglass, manufacturing
423720	Plumbing fixtures merchant wholesalers
332998	Plumbing fixtures, metal, manufacturing
327111	Plumbing fixtures, vitreous china, manufacturing
423720	Plumbing supplies merchant wholesalers
444190	Plumbing supply stores
423310	Plywood merchant wholesalers

922120 Police departments (except American Indian or Alaska Native)

315222 Police dress uniforms, men's, cut and sewn from purchased fabric (except apparel contractors)

315234 Police dress uniforms, women's, cut and sewn from purchased fabric (except apparel contractors)

453998 Police supply stores

611519 Police training schools

315211 Police uniforms, men's, cut and sew apparel contractors

315212 Police uniforms, women's, cut and sew apparel contractors

921150 Police, American Indian or Alaska Native tribal

311212 Polished rice manufacturing

333991 Polishers, handheld power-driven, manufacturing

325612 Polishes (e.g., automobile, furniture, metal, shoe) manufacturing

424690 Polishes (e.g., automobile, furniture, metal, shoe, stove) merchant wholesalers

333512 Polishing and buffing machines, metalworking, manufacturing

332813 Polishing metals and metal products for the trade

325612 Polishing preparations manufacturing

327910 Polishing wheels manufacturing

813940 Political action committees (PACs)

813940 Political campaign organizations

711510 Political cartoonists, independent

541820 Political consulting services

541910 Political opinion polling services

813940 Political organizations or clubs

813940 Political parties

115112 Pollinating

114111 Pollock fishing

423830 Pollution control equipment (except air) merchant wholesalers

423730 Pollution control equipment, air, merchant wholesalers

924110 Pollution control program administration

541380 Pollution testing (except automotive emissions testing) services

315191 Polo shirts made in apparel knitting mills

315211 Polo shirts, men's and boys', cut and sew apparel contractors

315223 Polo shirts, men's and boys', cut and sewn from purchased fabric (except apparel contractors)

315212 Polo shirts, women's, girls', and infants', cut and sew apparel contractors

315232 Polo shirts, women's, misses', and girls', cut and sewn from purchased fabric (except apparel contractors)

325211 Polyacrylonitrile resins manufacturing

325211 Polyamide resins manufacturing

325211 Polycarbonate resins manufacturing

325222 Polyester fibers and filaments manufacturing

313112 Polyester filament yarn throwing, twisting, texturizing, or winding of purchased yarn

326113 Polyester film and unlaminated sheet (except packaging) manufacturing

325211 Polyester resins manufacturing

313111 Polyester spun yarns made from purchased fiber

313113 Polyester thread manufacturing

326113 Polyethylene film and unlaminated sheet (except packaging) manufacturing

325211 Polyethylene resins manufacturing

325212 Polyethylene rubber manufacturing

325211 Polyethylene terephathalate (PET) resins manufacturing

325222 Polyethylene terephthalate (PET) fibers and filaments manufacturing
334519 Polygraph machines manufacturing
561611 Polygraph services
325211 Polyhexamethylenediamine adipamide resins manufacturing
325199 Polyhydric alcohol esters and amines manufacturing
325199 Polyhydric alcohols manufacturing
325211 Polyisobutylene resins manufacturing
325212 Polyisobutylene rubber manufacturing
325212 Polyisobutylene-isoprene rubber manufacturing
325211 Polymethacrylate resins manufacturing
325212 Polymethylene rubber manufacturing
325222 Polyolefin fibers and filaments manufacturing
313112 Polypropylene filament yarn throwing, twisting, texturizing, or winding of puchased yarn
326113 Polypropylene film and unlaminated sheet (except packaging) manufacturing
325211 Polypropylene resins manufacturing
313111 Polypropylene spun yarns made from purchased fiber
238310 Polystyrene board insulation installation
326140 Polystyrene foam packaging manufacturing
325211 Polystyrene resins manufacturing
325212 Polysulfide rubber manufacturing
325211 Polytetrafluoroethylene resins manufacturing
325510 Polyurethane coatings manufacturing
326150 Polyurethane foam products manufacturing

325211 Polyurethane resins manufacturing
325211 Polyvinyl alcohol resins manufacturing
325211 Polyvinyl chloride (PVC) resins manufacturing
325222 Polyvinyl ester fibers and filaments manufacturing
326113 Polyvinyl film and unlaminated sheet (except packaging) manufacturing
325211 Polyvinyl halide resins manufacturing
325211 Polyvinyl resins manufacturing
325222 Polyvinylidene chloride (i.e., saran) fibers and filaments manufacturing
111339 Pomegranate farming
315299 Ponchos and similar waterproof raincoats (except infants') cut and sewn from purchased fabric (except apparel contractors)
315291 Ponchos and similar waterproof raincoats, infants', cut and sewn from purchased fabric (except apparel contractors)
315211 Ponchos and similar waterproof raincoats, men's and boys', cut and sew apparel contractors
315212 Ponchos and similar waterproof raincoats, women's, girls', and infants', cut and sew apparel contractors
112920 Pony production
423910 Pool (billiards) supplies merchant wholesalers
423910 Pool (swimming) and equipment merchant wholesalers
713990 Pool halls
713990 Pool parlors
713990 Pool rooms
312111 Pop, soda, manufacturing
311919 Popcorn (except candy covered), popped, manufacturing
311999 Popcorn (except popped) manufacturing

311340 Popcorn balls manufacturing
111150 Popcorn farming, field and seed production
424450 Popcorn merchant wholesalers
335211 Popcorn poppers, household-type electric, manufacturing
311340 Popcorn, candy covered popped, manufacturing
313210 Poplins weaving
621391 Popopediatricians' offices (e.g., centers, clinics)
711130 Popular musical artists, independent
711130 Popular musical groups
532120 Popup camper rental
327113 Porcelain parts, electrical and electronic device, molded, manufacturing
327112 Porcelain, chemical, manufacturing
236118 Porch construction, residential-type
337122 Porch furniture (except upholstered), wood, manufacturing
337920 Porch shades. wood slat, manufacturing
337124 Porch swings, metal, manufacturing
321918 Porch work (e.g., columns, newels, rails, trellises), wood, manufacturing
114111 Porgy fishing
311422 Pork and beans canning
311611 Pork carcasses, half carcasses, and primal and sub-primal cuts produced in slaughtering plants
311919 Pork rinds manufacturing
311612 Pork, primal and sub-primal cuts, made from purchased carcasses
926120 Port authorities and districts, nonoperating
237990 Port facility construction
488310 Port facility operation
332311 Portable buildings, prefabricated metal, manufacturing
332998 Portable chemical toilets, metal, manufacturing

334111 Portable computers manufacturing
335211 Portable cooking appliances (except convection, microwave ovens), household-type electric, manufacturing
335211 Portable electric space heaters manufacturing
335211 Portable hair dryers, electric, manufacturing
335211 Portable humidifiers and dehumidifiers manufacturing
334290 Portable intrusion detection and signaling devices manufacturing
334310 Portable stereo systems manufacturing
334515 Portable test meters manufacturing
562991 Portable toilet pumping (i.e., cleaning) services
562991 Portable toilet renting and/or servicing
326191 Portable toilets, plastics, manufacturing
518112 Portals, web search
312120 Porter brewing
424810 Porter merchant wholesalers
812990 Porter services
523920 Portfolio fund managing
541921 Portrait photography services
541921 Portrait photography studios
621512 Positron emission tomography (PET) scanner centers
334511 Position indicators (e.g., for landing gear, stabilizers), airframe equipment, manufacturing
336312 Positive crankcase ventilation (PCV) valves, engine, manufacturing
334514 Positive displacement meters manufacturing
334510 Positron emission tomography (PET) scanners manufacturing
238130 Post frame contractors
332212 Post hole diggers, nonpowered, manufacturing
333120 Post hole diggers, powered, manufacturing

325181	Potassium hydroxide manufacturing
325188	Potassium hypochlorate manufacturing
325188	Potassium inorganic compounds, not specified elsewhere by process, manufacturing
325188	Potassium iodide manufacturing
325188	Potassium nitrate manufacturing
325199	Potassium organic compounds, not specified elsewhere by process, manufacturing
325188	Potassium permanganate manufacturing
325188	Potassium salts manufacturing
212391	Potassium salts, natural, mining and/or beneficiating
325188	Potassium sulfate manufacturing
424450	Potato chips and related snacks merchant wholesalers
311919	Potato chips manufacturing
115114	Potato curing
333111	Potato diggers, harvesters, and planters manufacturing
111211	Potato farming, field and seed potato production
311211	Potato flour manufacturing
332214	Potato mashers manufacturing
311999	Potato mixes made from purchased dry ingredients
311423	Potato products (e.g., flakes, granules) dehydrating
311221	Potato starches manufacturing
311919	Potato sticks manufacturing
311991	Potatoes, peeled or cut, manufacturing
334515	Potentiometric instruments (except industrial process-type) manufacturing
334513	Potentiometric instruments (except X-Y recorders), industrial process-type, manufacturing
237310	Pothole filling, highway, road, street or bridge
339999	Potpourri manufacturing
332420	Pots (e.g., annealing, melting, smelting), heavy gauge metal, manufacturing
332214	Pots and pans, fabricated metal, manufacturing
327124	Pots, glass-house, clay refractory, manufacturing
311612	Potted meats made from purchased carcasses
327112	Pottery made and sold on site
327112	Pottery products (except plumbing fixtures and porcelain electrical goods) manufacturing
325314	Potting soil manufacturing
311615	Poultry (e.g., canned, cooked, fresh, frozen) manufacturing
311615	Poultry (e.g., canned, cooked, fresh, frozen) processing
424440	Poultry and poultry products (except canned, packaged frozen) merchant wholesalers
333111	Poultry brooders, feeders, and waterers manufacturing
311615	Poultry canning (except baby, pet food)
115210	Poultry catching services
445210	Poultry dealers
423820	Poultry equipment merchant wholesalers
311119	Poultry feeds, supplements, and concentrates manufacturing
112340	Poultry hatcheries
332618	Poultry netting made from purchased wire
311615	Poultry slaughtering, dressing, and packing
424490	Poultry, canned, merchant wholesalers
424440	Poultry, live and dressed, merchant wholesalers
424420	Poultry, packaged frozen, merchant wholesalers
333991	Powder actuated handheld power tools manufacturing
332812	Powder coating metals and metal products for the trade
325510	Powder coatings manufacturing
331221	Powder made from purchased iron or steel
331314	Powder made from purchased aluminum

238910 Power, communication and pipe line right of way clearance (except maintenance)

333991 Power-driven handtools manufacturing

212399 Pozzolana mining and/or beneficiating

621399 Practical nurses' offices (e.g., centers, clinics), licensed

315299 Prayer shawls cut and sewn from purchased fabric (except apparel contractors)

315191 Prayer shawls made in apparel knitting mills

315211 Prayer shawls, men's and boys', cut and sew apparel contractors

315212 Prayer shawls, women's, girls', and infants', cut and sew apparel contractors

327331 Precast concrete block and brick manufacturing

238120 Precast concrete panel, slab, or form installation

327332 Precast concrete pipe manufacturing

327390 Precast concrete products (except brick, block, pipe) manufacturing

423940 Precious and semiprecious stones merchant wholesalers

423940 Precious and semiprecious stones merchant wholesalers

331491 Precious metal bar, rod, sheet, strip, and tubing made from purchased metals or scrap

423940 Precious metals merchant wholesalers

331492 Precious metals recovering from scrap and/or alloying purchased metals

331419 Precious metals refining, primary

212399 Precious stones mining and/or beneficiating

811219 Precision equipment calibration

332212 Precision tools, machinist's (except optical), manufacturing

332721 Precision turned product manufacturing

236117 Precut housing, residential, assembled on site by operative builders

236116 Precut multifamily housing assembled on site by general contractors

236115 Precut single-family housing assembly on site by general contractors

334514 Predetermined counters manufacturing

444190 Prefabricated building dealers

423390 Prefabricated buildings (except wood) merchant wholesalers

332311 Prefabricated buildings, metal, manufacturing

423310 Prefabricated buildings, wood, merchant wholesalers

236220 Prefabricated commercial building erection

321992 Prefabricated homes (except mobile homes), wood, manufacturing

332311 Prefabricated homes, metal, manufacturing

236210 Prefabricated industrial building (except warehouses) erection

236220 Prefabricated institutional building erection

238350 Prefabricated kitchen and bath cabinet, residential-type, installation

238350 Prefabricated sash and door installation

321992 Prefabricated wood buildings manufacturing

238130 Prefabricated wood frame component (e.g., trusses) installation

321211 Prefinished hardwood plywood manufacturing

321212 Prefinished softwood plywood manufacturing

621410 Pregnancy counseling centers

325413 Pregnancy test kits manufacturing

624410   Pre-kindergarten centers (except part of elementary school system)

334611   Prepackaged software, mass reproducing

424990   Pre-paid calling card distribution, merchant wholesalers

517310   Pre-paid calling cards, telecommunications resellers

213112   Preparation of oil and gas field drilling sites (except site preparation and related construction contractor activities) on a contract basis

212113   Preparation plants, anthracite

611110   Preparatory schools, elementary or secondary

311822   Prepared flour mixes made from purchased flour

311211   Prepared flour mixes made in flour mills

424490   Prepared foods (except frozen) merchant wholesalers

424420   Prepared foods, frozen (except dairy products), merchant wholesalers

424430   Prepared foods, frozen dairy, merchant wholesalers

311991   Prepared meals, perishable, packaged for individual resale

311941   Prepared sauces (except gravy, tomato based) manufacturing

488991   Preparing goods for transportation (i.e., crating, packing)

323122   Prepress printing services (e.g., color separation, imagesetting, photocomposition, typesetting)

541350   Prepurchase home inspection services

423990   Prerecorded audio and video tapes and discs merchant wholesalers

512220   Prerecorded audio tapes and compact discs integrated manufacture, release, and distribution

334612   Pre-recorded magnetic audio tapes and cassettes mass reproducing

454113   Prerecorded tape, compact disc, and record mail-order houses

624410   Preschool centers

424210   Prescription drugs merchant wholesalers

111421   Preseeded mat farming

311421   Preserves (e.g., imitation) canning

321114   Preserving purchased wood and wood products

313311   Preshrinking broadwoven fabrics

313312   Preshrinking textile products and fabrics (except broadwoven)

921110   President's office, United States

325611   Presoaks manufacturing

333513   Press brakes, metalworking, manufacturing

519190   Press clipping services

332111   Press forgings made from purchased iron or steel, unfinished

332112   Press forgings made from purchased nonferrous metals, unfinished

424130   Pressed and molded pulp goods (e.g., egg cartons, shipping supplies) merchant wholesalers

313230   Pressed felts manufacturing

321999   Pressed logs of sawdust and other wood particles, nonpetroleum binder, manufacturing

333513   Presses (e.g., bending, punching, shearing, stamping), metal forming, manufacturing

333294   Presses (i.e., food manufacturing-type) manufacturing

333210   Presses for making composite woods (e.g., hardboard, medium density fiberboard (MDF), particleboard, plywood) manufacturing

333111 Presses, farm-type, manufacturing
333999 Presses, metal baling, manufacturing
333293 Presses, printing (except textile), manufacturing
321999 Pressing blocks, wood, tailor's, manufacturing
336350 Pressure and clutch plate assemblies, automotive, truck, and bus, manufacturing
334519 Pressure and vacuum indicators, aircraft engine, manufacturing
332911 Pressure control valves (except fluid power), industrial-type, manufacturing
332912 Pressure control valves, fluid power, manufacturing
334512 Pressure controllers, air-conditioning system-type, manufacturing
332214 Pressure cookers, household-type, manufacturing
334513 Pressure gauges (e.g., dial, digital), industrial process-type, manufacturing
334513 Pressure instruments, industrial process-type, manufacturing
327332 Pressure pipe, reinforced concrete, manufacturing
322222 Pressure sensitive paper and tape (except medical) made from purchased materials
334519 Pressure transducers manufacturing
321113 Pressure treated lumber made from logs or bolts and treated
321114 Pressure treated lumber made from purchased lumber
561790 Pressure washing (e.g., buildings, decks, fences)
334512 Pressurestats manufacturing
238120 Prestressed concrete beam, slab or other component installation
327331 Prestressed concrete blocks or bricks manufacturing
327332 Prestressed concrete pipes manufacturing
327390 Prestressed concrete products (except blocks, bricks, pipes) manufacturing
722213 Pretzel shops, on premise baking and carryout service
424490 Pretzels (except frozen) merchant wholesalers
311919 Pretzels (except soft) manufacturing
424420 Pretzels, frozen, merchant wholesalers
311812 Pretzels, soft, manufacturing
335129 Prewired poles, brackets, and accessories for electric lighting, manufacturing
926150 Price control agencies
111339 Prickly pear farming
331312 Primary aluminum production and manufacturing aluminum alloys
331312 Primary aluminum production and manufacturing aluminum shapes (e.g., bar, ingot, rod, sheet)
335912 Primary batteries manufacturing
334513 Primary elements for process flow measurement (i.e., orifice plates) manufacturing
334512 Primary oil burner controls (e.g., cadmium cells, stack controls) manufacturing
334513 Primary process temperature sensors manufacturing
331312 Primary refining of aluminum
331411 Primary refining of copper
331419 Primary refining of nonferrous metals (except aluminum, copper)
611110 Primary schools
331312 Primary smelting of aluminum
331411 Primary smelting of copper
331419 Primary smelting of nonferrous metals (except aluminum, copper)
335312 Prime mover generator sets (except turbine generator sets) manufacturing
332993 Primers (i.e., more than 30 mm., more than 1.18 inch), ammunition, manufacturing

325510   Primers, paint, manufacturing
323115   Print shops, digital
323119   Print shops, engraving
323112   Print shops, flexographic
323111   Print shops, gravure
323119   Print shops, letterpress
323110   Print shops, lithographic (offset) (except grey goods, manifold business forms, printing books, quick printing)
323114   Print shops, quick
323113   Print shops, screen
334418   Printed circuit assemblies manufacturing
334418   Printed circuit boards loading
423690   Printed circuit boards merchant wholesalers
334412   Printed circuit boards, bare, manufacturing
334419   Printed circuit laminates manufacturing
334119   Printers, computer, manufacturing
423430   Printers, computer, merchant wholesalers
323117   Printing and binding books without publishing
323117   Printing books without publishing
313311   Printing broadwoven fabrics grey goods
561990   Printing brokers
313312   Printing fabric grey goods (except broadwoven)
325910   Printing inks manufacturing
423840   Printing inks merchant wholesalers
333292   Printing machinery for textiles manufacturing
323116   Printing manifold business forms
424120   Printing paper (except bulk) merchant wholesalers
424110   Printing paper, bulk, merchant wholesalers
236210   Printing plant construction
333293   Printing plate engraving machinery manufacturing
323122   Printing plate preparation services

333293   Printing plates, blank (except photosentive), manufacturing
323121   Printing postpress services (e.g., beveling, bronzing, folding, gluing, edging, foil stamping) to printed products (e.g., books, cards, paper)
323122   Printing prepress services (e.g., color separation, imagesetting, photocomposition, typesetting)
333293   Printing press rollers manufacturing
333293   Printing presses (except textile) manufacturing
313312   Printing textile products (except apparel)
811310   Printing trade machinery repair and maintenance services
423830   Printing trade machinery, equipment, and supplies merchant wholesalers
323115   Printing, digital (e.g., billboards, other large format graphical materials)
323115   Printing, digital (e.g., graphics, high resolution)
323119   Printing, engraving, on paper products
323112   Printing, flexographic (except books, grey goods, manifold business forms)
323111   Printing, gravure (except books, grey goods, manifold business forms)
323119   Printing, letterpress (except books, grey goods, manifold business forms)
323110   Printing, lithographic (except books, grey goods, manifold business forms, quick printing)
323110   Printing, photo-offset (except books, grey goods, manifold business forms, printing books)
323114   Printing, quick
323113   Printing, screen (except books, manifold business forms, grey goods)
333314   Prisms, optical, manufacturing

337127   Prison bed manufacturing
236220   Prison construction
922140   Prison farms
922140   Prisons
522190   Private banks (i.e., unincorporated)
334210   Private branch exchange (PBX) equipment manufacturing
611310   Private colleges (except community or junior college)
561611   Private detective services
238210   Private driveway or parking area lighting contractors
525920   Private estates (i.e., administering on behalf of beneficiaries)
814110   Private households employing domestic personnel
814110   Private households with employees
561611   Private investigation services (except credit)
561431   Private mail centers
561431   Private mailbox rental centers
624190   Private parole offices
624190   Private probation offices
611110   Private schools, elementary or secondary
561990   Private volunteer fire fighting
493190   Private warehousing and storage (except farm products, general merchandise, refrigerated)
493130   Private warehousing and storage, farm products (except refrigerated)
493110   Private warehousing and storage, general merchandise
493120   Private warehousing and storage, refrigerated
451110   Pro shops (e.g., golf, skiing, tennis)
922150   Probation offices
212391   Probertite mining and/or quarrying
334510   Probes, electric medical, manufacturing
339112   Probes, surgical, manufacturing
325411   Procaine and derivatives (i.e., basic chemicals) manufacturing

334513   Process control instruments, industrial, manufacturing
238220   Process piping installation
541199   Process server services
541199   Process serving services
311513   Processed cheeses manufacturing
424470   Processed meats (e.g., luncheon, sausage) merchant wholesalers
311612   Processed meats manufacturing
424440   Processed poultry (e.g., luncheon) merchant wholesalers
311615   Processed poultry manufacturing
522320   Processing financial transactions
314999   Processing of textile mill waste and recovering fibers
621111   Proctologists' offices (e.g., centers, clinics)
424910   Produce containers merchant wholesalers
445230   Produce markets
445230   Produce stands, permanent
454390   Produce stands, temporary
424480   Produce, fresh, merchant wholesalers
813910   Producers' associations
711510   Producers, independent
561910   Product sterilization and packaging services
541380   Product testing laboratories or services
524128   Product warranty insurance carriers, direct
334514   Production counters manufacturing
541614   Production planning and control consulting services
541614   Productivity improvement consulting services
813920   Professional associations
711219   Professional athletes, independent (i.e., participating in sports events)
711211   Professional baseball clubs
323121   Professional book binding without printing

511210	Programming language and compiler software publishers, packaged
541511	Programming services, custom computer
332993	Projectiles (except guided missile), jet propulsion, manufacturing
333315	Projection equipment (e.g., motion picture, slide), photographic, manufacturing
423410	Projection equipment (e.g., motion picture, slide), photographic, merchant wholesalers
333314	Projection lenses manufacturing
333315	Projection screens (i.e., motion picture, overhead, slide) manufacturing
334310	Projection television manufacturing
332995	Projectors (e.g., antisub, depth charge release, grenade, livens, rocket), ordnance, manufacturing
711310	Promoters of agricultural fairs with facilities
711320	Promoters of agricultural fairs without facilities
711310	Promoters of arts events with facilities
711320	Promoters of arts events without facilities
561920	Promoters of conventions with or without facilities
711310	Promoters of festivals with facilities
711320	Promoters of festivals without facilities
711310	Promoters of live performing arts productions (e.g., concerts) with facilities
711320	Promoters of live performing arts productions (e.g., concerts) without facilities
711310	Promoters of sports events with facilities
711320	Promoters of sports events without facilities

561920	Promoters of trade fairs or shows with or without facilities
561410	Proofreading services
111421	Propagation material farming
424710	Propane bulk stations and terminals
324110	Propane gases made in petroleum refineries
211112	Propane recovered from oil and gas field gases
333518	Propeller straightening presses manufacturing
334514	Propeller type meters with registers manufacturing
332999	Propellers, ship and boat, made from purchased metal
524126	Property and casualty insurance carriers, direct
524130	Property and casualty reinsurance carriers
524126	Property damage insurance carriers, direct
531312	Property managers' offices, commercial real estate
531312	Property managers' offices, nonresidential real estate
531311	Property managers' offices, residential real estate
531312	Property managing, commercial real estate
531312	Property managing, nonresidential real estate
531311	Property managing, residential real estate
813990	Property owners' associations
561612	Property protection services (except armored car, security systems)
921130	Property tax assessors' offices
326299	Prophylactics manufacturing
112910	Propolis production, bees
336415	Propulsion units and parts, guided missile and space vehicle, manufacturing
325199	Propylcarbinol manufacturing
324110	Propylene (i.e., propene) made in petroleum refineries
325199	Propylene glycol manufacturing

811213	Public address system repair and maintenance services
334310	Public address systems and equipment manufacturing
423690	Public address systems and equipment merchant wholesalers
423210	Public building furniture merchant wholesalers
922130	Public defenders' offices
711410	Public figures' agents or managers
923120	Public health program administration, nonoperating
541910	Public opinion polling services
541910	Public opinion research services
921190	Public property management services, government
922130	Public prosecutors' offices
541820	Public relations agencies
541820	Public relations consulting services
541820	Public relations services
813319	Public safety advocacy organizations
922190	Public safety bureaus and statistics centers, government
922190	Public safety statistics centers, government
926130	Public service (except transportation) commissions, nonoperating
813410	Public speaking improvement clubs
611699	Public speaking training
561492	Public stenography services
926120	Public transportation commissions, nonoperating
926130	Public utility (except transportation) commissions, nonoperating
813910	Public utility associations
551112	Public utility holding companies
236220	Public warehouse construction
493190	Public warehousing and storage (except farm products, general merchandise, refrigerated, self storage)
493110	Public warehousing and storage (except self storage), general merchandise
493130	Public warehousing and storage, farm products (except refrigerated)
493120	Public warehousing and storage, refrigerated
511130	Publishers (except exclusive Internet publishing), book
511140	Publishers (except exclusive Internet publishing), directory
511191	Publishers (except exclusive Internet publishing), greeting card
511120	Publishers (except exclusive Internet publishing), magazine
511130	Publishers (except exclusive Internet publishing), map
511120	Publishers (except exclusive Internet publishing), periodical
511199	Publishers (except exclusive Internet publishing), racing form
******	Publishers—see specific type
541840	Publishers' advertising representatives (i.e., independent of media owners)
******	Publishers and printing combined—see specific type of publisher
******	Publishers or publishing—see specific type
511130	Publishers, book, combined with printing
511191	Publishers, greeting card, combined with printing
516110	Publishers, Internet greeting card
516110	Publishers, Internet map
516110	Publishers, Internet racing form
511120	Publishers, magazine, combined with printing
512230	Publishers, music
511110	Publishers, newspaper (except exclusive Internet publishing)
511110	Publishers, newspaper, combined with printing
511210	Publishers, packaged computer software

333911	Pumps (except fluid power), general purpose, manufacturing
316214	Pumps (i.e., dress shoes) manufacturing
423830	Pumps and pumping equipment, industrial-type, merchant wholesalers
333911	Pumps for railroad equipment lubrication systems manufacturing
333996	Pumps, fluid power, manufacturing
333911	Pumps, industrial and commercial-type, general purpose, manufacturing
333913	Pumps, measuring and dispensing (e.g., gasoline), manufacturing
333911	Pumps, oil field or well, manufacturing
333911	Pumps, sump or water, residential-type, manufacturing
313230	Punched felts manufacturing
332212	Punches (except paper), nonpowered handtool, manufacturing
333514	Punches for use with machine tools manufacturing
333513	Punching machines, metalworking, manufacturing
711110	Puppet theaters
339999	Puppets manufacturing
921190	Purchasing and supply agencies, government
522298	Purchasing of accounts receivable
332323	Purlins, metal, manufacturing
316993	Purses (except precious metal), men's, manufacturing
316992	Purses (except precious metal), women's, manufacturing
339911	Purses, precious metal or clad with precious metal, manufacturing
333515	Pushers (i.e., a machine tool accessory) manufacturing
332212	Putty knives manufacturing
423920	Puzzles merchant wholesalers
326122	PVC pipe manufacturing
325320	Pyrethrin insecticides manufacturing
334519	Pyrheliometers manufacturing
212393	Pyrite concentrates mining and/or beneficiating
212393	Pyrite mining and/or beneficiating
325191	Pyroligneous acids manufacturing
212299	Pyrolusite mining and/or beneficiating
327112	Pyrometer tubes manufacturing
334513	Pyrometers, industrial process-type, manufacturing
327112	Pyrometric cones, earthenware, manufacturing
212399	Pyrophyllite mining and/or beneficiating
327992	Pyrophyllite processing beyond beneficiation
332994	Pyrotechnic pistols and projectors manufacturing
325998	Pyrotechnics (e.g., flares, flashlight bombs, signals) manufacturing
325211	Pyroxylin (i.e., nitrocellulose) resins manufacturing
212393	Pyrrhotite mining and/or beneficiating
112390	Quail production
611430	Quality assurance training
541990	Quantity surveyor services
327122	Quarry tiles, clay, manufacturing
333131	Quarrying machinery and equipment manufacturing
423810	Quarrying machinery and equipment merchant wholesalers
316999	Quarters (i.e., shoe cut stock), leather, manufacturing
212399	Quartz crystal, pure, mining and/or beneficiating
334419	Quartz crystals, electronic application, manufacturing
212319	Quartzite crushed and broken stone mining and/or beneficiating
212311	Quartzite dimension stone mining or quarrying

325191 Quebracho extracts manufacturing
112910 Queen bee production
325191 Quercitron extracts manufacturing
323114 Quick printing
327410 Quicklime (i.e., calcium oxide) manufacturing
811191 Quick-lube shops
212299 Quicksilver ores and metal mining and/or beneficiating
314999 Quilting of textiles
314129 Quilts made from purchased materials
111339 Quince farming
325411 Quinine and derivatives (i.e., basic chemicals) manufacturing
523999 Quotation services, securities
523999 Quotation services, stock
311119 Rabbit food manufacturing
112930 Rabbit production
311615 Rabbits processing (i.e., canned, cooked, fresh, frozen)
311615 Rabbits slaughtering and dressing
711219 Race car drivers
711219 Race car owners (i.e., racing cars)
336999 Race cars manufacturing
711219 Race dog owners (i.e., racing dogs)
711219 Racehorse owners (i.e., racing horses)
711219 Racehorse trainers
711219 Racehorse training
332991 Races, ball or roller bearings, manufacturing
511199 Racetrack program publishers (except Internet)
511199 Racetrack program publishers and printing combined
516110 Racetrack program publishers, exclusively on Internet
323112 Racetrack programs flexographic printing without publishing
323111 Racetrack programs gravure printing without publishing

323110 Racetrack programs lithographic (offset) printing without publishing
323119 Racetrack programs printing (except flexographic, gravure, lithographic, quick, screen) without publishing
323113 Racetrack programs screen printing without publishing
711212 Racetracks (e.g., automobile, dog, horse)
713990 Racetracks, slot car (i.e., amusement devices)
335932 Raceways manufacturing
713990 Raceways, gocart (i.e., amusement rides)
511199 Racing form publishers (except exclusive Internet publishing)
511199 Racing form publishers and printing combined
516110 Racing form publishers, exclusively on Internet
323112 Racing forms flexographic printing without publishing
323111 Racing forms gravure printing without publishing
323110 Racing forms lithographic (offset) printing without publishing
323119 Racing forms printing (except flexographic, gravure, lithographic, quick, screen) without publishing
323113 Racing forms screen printing without publishing
711219 Racing stables, horse
711219 Racing teams (e.g., automobile, motorcycle, snowmobile)
334417 Rack and panel connectors manufacturing
336330 Rack and pinion steering assemblies manufacturing
336399 Racks (e.g., bicycle, luggage, ski, tire), automotive, truck, and buses manufacturing
332313 Racks (e.g., trash), fabricated metal plate, manufacturing
332618 Racks, household-type, made from purchased wire
713940 Racquetball club facilities

811219	Radar and sonar equipment repair and maintenance services
334511	Radar detectors manufacturing
423690	Radar equipment merchant wholesalers
517910	Radar station operations
334511	Radar systems and equipment manufacturing
334515	Radar testing instruments, electric, manufacturing
334519	RADIAC (radioactivity detection, identification, and computation) equipment manufacturing
238220	Radiant floor heating equipment installation
334519	Radiation detection and monitoring instruments manufacturing
541380	Radiation dosimetry (i.e., radiation testing) laboratories or services
812332	Radiation protection garment supply services
339113	Radiation shielding aprons, gloves, and sheeting manufacturing
541380	Radiation testing laboratories or services
325998	Radiator additive preparations manufacturing
326220	Radiator and heater hoses, rubber or plastics, manufacturing
811118	Radiator repair shops, automotive
332322	Radiator shields and enclosures, sheet metal (except stampings), manufacturing
333414	Radiators (except motor vehicle, portable electric) manufacturing
336399	Radiators and cores manufacturing
423120	Radiators, motor vehicle, merchant wholesalers
335211	Radiators, portable electric, manufacturing

541840	Radio advertising representatives (i.e., independent of media owners)
236220	Radio and television broadcast studio construction
443112	Radio and television stores
332312	Radio and television tower sections, fabricated structural metal, manufacturing
488330	Radio beacon (i.e., ship navigation) services
515112	Radio broadcasting (except exclusively on Internet) stations (e.g., AM, FM, shortwave)
515111	Radio broadcasting network services
515111	Radio broadcasting networks
515111	Radio broadcasting syndicates
711510	Radio commentators, independent
541690	Radio consulting services
511120	Radio guide publishers (except exclusive Internet publishing)
511120	Radio guide publishers and printing combined
516110	Radio guide publishers, exclusively on Internet
323112	Radio guides flexographic printing without publishing
323111	Radio guides gravure printing without publishing
323110	Radio guides lithographic (offset) printing without publishing
323119	Radio guides printing (except flexographic, gravure, lithographic, quick, screen) without publishing
323113	Radio guides screen printing without publishing
334310	Radio headphones manufacturing
326199	Radio housings, plastics, manufacturing
334511	Radio magnetic instrumentation (RMI) manufacturing
517211	Radio paging services communication carriers

326299	Rafts, rubber inflatable, manufacturing
423930	Rags merchant wholesalers
335931	Rail bonds, propulsion and signal circuit electric, manufacturing
331111	Rail joints and fastenings made in iron and steel mills
336510	Rail laying and tamping equipment manufacturing
485112	Rail transportation (except mixed mode), commuter
332323	Railings, metal, manufacturing
321918	Railings, wood stair, manufacturing
926120	Railroad and warehouse commissions, nonoperating
333613	Railroad car journal bearings, plain, manufacturing
532411	Railroad car rental and leasing
336510	Railroad cars and car equipment manufacturing
423860	Railroad cars merchant wholesalers
336510	Railroad cars, self-propelled, manufacturing
237990	Railroad construction
331111	Railroad crossings, iron or steel, made in iron and steel mills
423860	Railroad equipment and supplies merchant wholesalers
336510	Railroad locomotives and parts (except diesel engines) manufacturing
339932	Railroad models, hobby and toy, manufacturing
923130	Railroad Retirement Board
531190	Railroad right of way leasing
336510	Railroad rolling stock manufacturing
336360	Railroad seating manufacturing
334290	Railroad signaling equipment manufacturing
238210	Railroad signalling equipment installation
488210	Railroad switching services
488210	Railroad terminals, independent operation
561599	Railroad ticket offices
321114	Railroad ties (i.e., bridge, cross, switch) treating
423990	Railroad ties, wood, merchant wholesalers
333997	Railroad track scales manufacturing
482111	Railroad transportation, line-haul
487110	Railroad transportation, scenic and sightseeing
482112	Railroad transportation, short-line or beltline
487110	Railroad, scenic and sightseeing, operation
482111	Railroads, line-haul
482112	Railroads, short-line or beltline
321999	Rails (except rough), wood fence, manufacturing
423510	Rails and accessories, metal, merchant wholesalers
331319	Rails made by rolling or drawing purchased aluminum
331111	Rails rerolled or renewed in iron and steel mills
331319	Rails, aluminum, made in integrated secondary smelting and drawing plants
331319	Rails, aluminum, made in integrated secondary smelting and rolling mills
331111	Rails, iron or steel, made in iron and steel mills
113310	Rails, rough wood, manufacturing
332312	Railway bridge sections, prefabricated metal, manufacturing
237990	Railway construction (e.g., interlocker, roadbed, signal, track)
335312	Railway motors and control equipment, electric, manufacturing
237990	Railway roadbed construction
236220	Railway station construction
485112	Railway systems (except mixed mode), commuter
488210	Railway terminals, independent operation

482111 Railway transportation, line-haul
487110 Railway transportation, scenic and sightseeing
482112 Railway transportation, short-line or beltline
334519 Rain gauges manufacturing
315211 Raincoats water resistant, men's and boys', cut and sew apparel contractors
313320 Raincoats waterproofing (i.e., oiling)
315299 Raincoats, rubber or rubberized fabric, manufacturing
315291 Raincoats, water resistant, infants', cut and sewn from purchased fabric (except apparel contractors)
315228 Raincoats, water resistant, nontailored, men's and boys', cut and sewn from purchased fabric (except apparel contractors)
315239 Raincoats, water resistant, nontailored, women's, misses', and girls', cut and sewn from purchased fabric (except apparel contractors)
315222 Raincoats, water resistant, tailored, men's and boys', cut and sewn from purchased fabric (except apparel contractors)
315234 Raincoats, water resistant, tailored, women's, misses', and girls', cut and sewn from purchased fabric (except apparel contractors)
315212 Raincoats, water resistant, women's, girls', and infants', cut and sew apparel contractors
315299 Raincoats, waterproof (except infants'), cut and sewn from purchased fabric (except apparel contractors)
315291 Raincoats, waterproof, infants', cut and sewn from purchased fabric (except apparel contractors)

315211 Raincoats, waterproof, men's and boys', cut and sew apparel contractors
315212 Raincoats, waterproof, women's, girls', and infants', cut and sew apparel contractors
315291 Raincoats, water-repellent, infants', cut and sewn from purchased fabric (except apparel contractors)
315211 Raincoats, water-repellent, men's and boys', cut and sew apparel contractors
315228 Raincoats, water-repellent, nontailored, men's and boys', cut and sewn from purchased fabric (except apparel contractors)
315239 Raincoats, water-repellent, nontailored, women's, misses', and girls', cut and sewn from purchased fabric (except apparel contractors)
315222 Raincoats, water-repellent, tailored, men's and boys', cut and sewn from purchased fabric (except apparel contractors)
315234 Raincoats, water-repellent, tailored, women's, misses', and girls', cut and sewn from purchased fabric (except apparel contractors)
315212 Raincoats, water-repellent, women's, girls', and infants', cut and sew apparel contractors
111332 Raisin farming
112990 Raising swans, peacocks, flamingos, or other adornment birds
311423 Raisins made in dehydration plants
333111 Rakes, hay, manufacturing
332212 Rakes, nonpowered handtool, manufacturing
313111 Ramie spun yarns made from purchased fiber

316999	Rands (i.e., shoe cut stock), leather, manufacturing
333315	Range finders, photographic, manufacturing
335211	Range hoods with integral lighting fixtures, household-type, manufacturing
335211	Range hoods, household-type, manufacturing
333319	Ranges, commercial-type, manufacturing
335221	Ranges, household-type cooking, manufacturing
624190	Rape crisis centers
311225	Rapeseed (i.e., canola) oil made from purchased oils
311223	Rapeseed (i.e., canola) oil made in crushing mills
111120	Rapeseed farming, field and seed production
336510	Rapid transit cars and equipment manufacturing
325188	Rare earth compounds, not specified elsewhere by process, manufacturing
212299	Rare earth metal concentrates beneficiating
212299	Rare earth metal ores mining and/or beneficiating
325188	Rare earth salts manufacturing
453310	Rare manuscript stores
111334	Raspberry farming
332212	Rasps, handheld, manufacturing
332212	Ratchets, nonpowered, manufacturing
524298	Rate making services, insurance
334511	Rate-of-climb instrumentation manufacturing
213112	Rathole and mousehole drilling at oil and gas fields on a contract basis
112390	Ratite production
337125	Rattan furniture, household-type, manufacturing
321999	Rattan ware (except furniture) manufacturing
112990	Rattlesnake production
311313	Raw beet sugar manufacturing
424590	Raw farm products (except field beans, grains) merchant wholesalers
316110	Rawhide manufacturing
114111	Ray fishing
325221	Rayon fibers and filaments manufacturing
313111	Rayon spun yarns made from purchased fiber
313113	Rayon thread manufacturing
313112	Rayon yarn throwing, twisting, texturizing, or winding purchased filament
331221	Razor blade strip steel made in cold rolling mills
332211	Razor blades manufacturing
424210	Razor blades merchant wholesalers
316999	Razor strops manufacturing
332211	Razors (except electric) manufacturing
424210	Razors (except electric) merchant wholesalers
335211	Razors, electric, manufacturing
423620	Razors, electric, merchant wholesalers
332313	Reactor containment vessels, fabricated metal plate, manufacturing
332410	Reactors, nuclear, manufacturing
333315	Readers, microfilm or microfiche, manufacturing
327320	Ready-mix concrete manufacturing and distributing
336211	Ready-mix concrete trucks assembling on purchased chassis
531190	Real estate (except building) rental or leasing
237210	Real estate (except cemeteries) subdividers
531210	Real estate agencies
531210	Real estate agents' offices
531320	Real estate appraisal services
531320	Real estate appraisers' offices
531390	Real estate asset management services (except property management)
813910	Real estate boards

711510	Record producers, independent
512210	Record production (except independent record producers) without duplication or distribution
512220	Record releasing, promoting, and distributing combined with mass duplication
451220	Record stores, new
453310	Record stores, used
423620	Recorders (e.g., tape, video), household-type, merchant wholesalers
334513	Recorders, industrial process control-type, manufacturing
334515	Recorders, oscillographic, manufacturing
512290	Recording books on tape or disc (except publishers)
512290	Recording seminars and conferences, audio
512240	Recording studios, sound, operating on a contract or fee basis
711510	Recording technicians, independent
541611	Records management consulting services
314999	Recovered fibers processing
331492	Recovering and refining of nonferrous metals (except aluminum, copper) from scrap
331492	Recovering silver from used photographic film or X-ray plates
237990	Recreation area, open space, construction
621340	Recreational (e.g., art, dance, music) therapists' offices (e.g., centers, clinics)
721214	Recreational camps with accommodation facilities (except campgrounds)
713990	Recreational camps without accommodations
713990	Recreational day camps (except instructional)
423910	Recreational equipment and supplies (except vehicles) merchant wholesalers

236220	Recreational facility building construction
532292	Recreational goods rental
924120	Recreational programs administration, government
713940	Recreational sports club facilities
713990	Recreational sports clubs (i.e., sports teams) not operating sports facilities
713990	Recreational sports teams and leagues
532120	Recreational trailer rental
441210	Recreational vehicle (RV) dealers
532120	Recreational vehicle (RV) rental or leasing
423110	Recreational vehicle merchant wholesalers
237990	Recreational vehicle park construction
721211	Recreational vehicle parks
441210	Recreational vehicle parts and accessories stores
335999	Rectifiers (except electronic component type, semiconductor) manufacturing
334419	Rectifiers, electronic component-type (except semiconductor), manufacturing
423690	Rectifiers, electronic, merchant wholesalers
334413	Rectifiers, semiconductor, manufacturing
333298	Rectifying equipment, chemical, manufacturing
562111	Recyclable material collection services
562111	Recyclable material hauling, local
484230	Recyclable material hauling, long-distance
423930	Recyclable materials (e.g., glass, metal, paper) merchant wholesalers
325612	Recycling drycleaning fluids
811212	Recycling inkjet cartridges

334512 Refrigeration controls, residential and commercial-type, manufacturing

423740 Refrigeration equipment and supplies, commercial-type, merchant wholesalers

811310 Refrigeration equipment repair and maintenance services, industrial and commercial-type

333415 Refrigeration equipment, industrial and commercial-type, manufacturing

238220 Refrigeration system (e.g., commercial, industrial, scientific) installation

334512 Refrigeration thermostats manufacturing

423740 Refrigeration units, motor vehicle, merchant wholesalers

333415 Refrigeration units, truck-type, manufacturing

334512 Refrigeration/air-conditioning defrost controls manufacturing

532210 Refrigerator rental

811412 Refrigerator, household-type, repair and maintenance services without retailing new refrigerators

335222 Refrigerator/freezer combinations, household-type, manufacturing

335222 Refrigerators (e.g., absorption, mechanical), household-type, manufacturing

423740 Refrigerators (e.g., reach-in, walk-in), commercial-type, merchant wholesalers

423620 Refrigerators, household-type, merchant wholesalers

624230 Refugee settlement services

562212 Refuse collecting and operating solid waste landfills

562111 Refuse collection services

562213 Refuse disposal combustors or incinerators

562212 Refuse disposal landfills

236210 Refuse disposal plant construction

562111 Refuse hauling, local

484230 Refuse hauling, long-distance

325221 Regenerated cellulosic fibers manufacturing

925120 Regional planning and development program administration

621399 Registered nurses' (RNs) offices (e.g., centers, clinics)

334514 Registers, linear tallying, manufacturing

332323 Registers, metal air, manufacturing

561310 Registries, employment ·

561310 Registries, teacher

335311 Regulating transformers, power system-type, manufacturing

926140 Regulation and inspection of agricultural products

926130 Regulation of utilities

335311 Regulators (i.e., electric transformers), feeder voltage, manufacturing

336322 Regulators, motor vehicle voltage for internal combustion engines manufacturing

335313 Regulators, power, manufacturing

423610 Regulators, voltage (except motor vehicle), merchant wholesalers

624190 Rehabilitation agencies for offenders

622310 Rehabilitation hospitals (except alcoholism, drug addiction)

622210 Rehabilitation hospitals, alcoholism and drug addiction

624310 Rehabilitation job counseling and training, vocational

922150 Rehabilitation services, correctional, government

332618 Reinforcing mesh, concrete, made from purchased wire

238120 Reinforcing rod, bar, mesh and cage installation

238120 Reinforcing steel contractors

524130 Reinsurance carriers

525930 REITs (real estate investment trusts)

213114	Removal of overburden for metal mining on a contract basis
213115	Removal of overburden for nonmetallic minerals mining (except fuels) on a contract basis
562920	Removal of recyclable materials from a waste stream
621492	Renal dialysis centers and clinics
311613	Rendering animals (carrion) for feed
311613	Rendering fats
311613	Rendering plants
424990	Rennets merchant wholesalers
926150	Rent control agencies
******	Rental—see type of article or property being rented
532310	Rent-all centers
532490	Renting coin-operated amusement devices (except concession operators)
531210	Renting real estate for others (i.e., agents, brokers)
541611	Reorganizational consulting services
522294	Repackaging loans for sale to others (i.e., private conduits)
******	Repair—see type of article being repaired
237310	Repair, highway, road, street, bridge or airport runway
323121	Repairing books
334210	Repeater and transceiver equipment, carrier line, manufacturing
711110	Repertory companies, theatrical
322231	Report covers made from purchased paper or paperboard
711510	Reporters, independent (freelance)
561491	Repossession services
512199	Reproduction of motion picture films for theatrical distribution
115210	Reproductive flushing services for animals
621410	Reproductive health services centers
561439	Reprographic services
712130	Reptile exhibits, live
324191	Re-refining used petroleum lubricating oils
321912	Resawing purchased lumber
621910	Rescue services, air
621910	Rescue services, medical
517410	Resellers, satellite telecommunication
517310	Resellers, telecommunication (except satellite)
325411	Reserpines (i.e., basic chemicals) manufacturing
561599	Reservation (e.g., airline, car rental, hotel, restaurant) services
522320	Reserve and iiquidity services (except central bank)
237110	Reservoir construction
721310	Residence clubs, organizational
531110	Residential building rental or leasing
561720	Residential cleaning services
721310	Residential clubs
236116	Residential construction, multifamily, general contractors
236115	Residential construction, single-family, general contractors
623220	Residential group homes for the emotionally disturbed
531110	Residential hotel rental or leasing
236117	Residential operative builders
531311	Residential property managing
531210	Residential real estate agencies
531210	Residential real estate agents' offices
531210	Residential real estate brokerages
531210	Residential real estate brokers' offices
531311	Residential real estate property managers' offices
531190	Residential trailer parks
211112	Residue gas production
326192	Resilient floor coverings (e.g., sheet, tile) manufacturing
238330	Resilient floor tile or sheet (e.g., linoleum, rubber, vinyl), installation only

525110	Retirement pension plans
332420	Retorts, heavy gauge metal, manufacturing
339112	Retractors, medical, manufacturing
326211	Retreading materials, tire, manufacturing
326212	Retreading tires
813110	Retreat houses, religious
115114	Retting flax
811420	Reupholstery shops, furniture
522292	Reverse mortgage lending
237990	Revetment construction
332994	Revolvers manufacturing
238290	Revolving door installation
811310	Rewinding armatures (except on an assembly line or factory basis)
213111	Reworking oil and gas wells on a contract basis
331419	Rhenium refining, primary
335931	Rheostats (i.e., dimmer switches), current carrying wiring device, manufacturing
334419	Rheostats, electronic, manufacturing
335314	Rheostats, industrial control, manufacturing
212299	Rhodium mining and/or beneficiating
212299	Rhodochrosite mining and/or beneficiating
111219	Rhubarb farming, field and seed production
111419	Rhubarb, grown under cover
339944	Ribbons (e.g., cash register, printer, typewriter), inked, manufacturing
314999	Ribbons made from purchased fabrics
313221	Ribbons made in narrow woven fabric mills
313230	Ribbons made in nonwoven fabric mills
339944	Ribbons, inked, manufacturing
424120	Ribbons, inked, merchant wholesalers
424310	Ribbons, textile, merchant wholesalers
111160	Rice (except wild rice) farming, field and seed production
311212	Rice bran, flour, and meals, manufacturing
311230	Rice breakfast foods manufacturing
311212	Rice cleaning and polishing
115114	Rice drying
311212	Rice flour manufacturing
311213	Rice malt manufacturing
311212	Rice meal manufacturing
311212	Rice milling
311999	Rice mixes (i.e., uncooked and packaged with other ingredients) made from purchased rice and dry ingredients
311423	Rice mixes (i.e., uncooked and packaged with other ingredients) made in dehydration plants
311212	Rice mixes (i.e., uncooked and packaged with other ingredients) made in rice mills
311221	Rice starches manufacturing
311212	Rice, brewer's, manufacturing
311212	Rice, brown, manufacturing
424490	Rice, polished, merchant wholesalers
424510	Rice, unpolished, merchant wholesalers
315211	Riding clothes, men's and boys', cut and sew apparel contractors
315228	Riding clothes, men's and boys', cut and sewn from purchased fabric (except apparel contractors)
315212	Riding clothes, women's and girls', cut and sew apparel contractors
315239	Riding clothes, women's, misses', and girls', cut and sewn from purchased fabric (except apparel contractors)
713990	Riding clubs, recreational
316999	Riding crops manufacturing
611620	Riding instruction academies or schools
713990	Riding stables

713990 Rifle clubs, recreational
332994 Rifles (except recoilless, toy) manufacturing
332994 Rifles, BB and pellet, manufacturing
332994 Rifles, pneumatic, manufacturing
332995 Rifles, recoilless, manufacturing
339932 Rifles, toy, manufacturing
333512 Rifling machines, metalworking, manufacturing
213112 Rig skidding, oil and gas field, on a contract basis
238290 Rigging large-scale equipment
238910 Right of way cutting (except maintenance)
336399 Rims, automotive, truck, and bus wheel, manufacturing
336311 Rings, piston, manufacturing
713940 Rinks, ice or roller skating
237990 Riprap installation
212319 Riprap (except granite, limestone) preparation plants
212319 Riprap (except limestone and granite) mining or quarrying
212313 Riprap, granite, mining or quarrying
212313 Riprap, granite, preparation plants
212312 Riprap, limestone, mining or quarrying
212312 Riprap, limestone, preparation plants
483211 River freight transportation
483212 River passenger transportation
713990 River rafting, recreational
713210 Riverboat casinos
333991 Riveting guns, handheld power-driven, manufacturing
333513 Riveting machines, metalworking, manufacturing
332722 Rivets, metal, manufacturing
621399 RNs' (registered nurses) offices (e.g., centers, clinics)
325320 Roach poisons manufacturing
711110 Road companies, theatrical
237310 Road construction
423810 Road construction and maintenance machinery merchant wholesalers

324199 Road oils made from refined petroleum
324110 Road oils made in petroleum refineries
311911 Roasted nuts and seeds manufacturing
112320 Roaster chicken production
335211 Roasters (i.e., cooking appliances), household-type electric, manufacturing
311920 Roasting coffee
333294 Roasting machinery manufacturing
315291 Robes, lounging, infants', cut and sewn from purchased fabric (except apparel contractors)
315192 Robes, lounging, made in apparel knitting mills
315211 Robes, lounging, men's and boys', cut and sew apparel contractors
315221 Robes, lounging, men's and boys', cut and sewn from purchased fabric (except apparel contractors)
315212 Robes, lounging, women's, girls', and infants', cut and sew apparel contractors
315231 Robes, lounging, women's, misses', and girls', cut and sewn from purchased fabric (except apparel contractors)
333120 Rock crushing machinery, portable, manufacturing
333131 Rock crushing machinery, stationary, manufacturing
333132 Rock drill bits, oil and gas field-type, manufacturing
333120 Rock drills, construction and surface mining-type, manufacturing
333131 Rock drills, underground mining-type, manufacturing
711130 Rock musical artists, independent
711130 Rock musical groups
237990 Rock removal, underwater
212393 Rock salt mining and/or beneficiating

336312   Rocker arms and parts, automotive and truck gasoline engine, manufacturing

337122   Rockers (except upholstered), wood, manufacturing

337121   Rockers, upholstered, manufacturing

332313   Rocket casings, fabricated metal work, manufacturing

336412   Rocket engines, aircraft, manufacturing

336415   Rocket engines, guided missile, manufacturing

332995   Rocket launchers manufacturing

336414   Rockets (guided missiles), space and military, complete, manufacturing

332993   Rockets, ammunition (except guided missiles, pyrotechnic), manufacturing

114111   Rockfish fishing

339932   Rocking horses manufacturing

331316   Rod made by extruding purchased aluminum

331319   Rod made by rolling purchased aluminum

333516   Rod rolling mill machinery, metalworking, manufacturing

331316   Rod, aluminum, made in integrated secondary smelting and extruding mills

331319   Rod, aluminum, made in integrated secondary smelting and rolling mills

331421   Rod, copper and copper alloy, made from purchased copper or in integrated secondary smelting and rolling, drawing or extruding plants

326130   Rod, laminated plastics, manufacturing

331491   Rod, nonferrous metals (except aluminum, copper), made from purchased metals or scrap

326121   Rod, nonrigid plastics, manufacturing

325320   Rodent poisons manufacturing

325320   Rodenticides manufacturing

711310   Rodeo managers with facilities

711320   Rodeo managers without facilities

711310   Rodeo organizers with facilities

711320   Rodeo organizers without facilities

711310   Rodeo promoters with facilities

711320   Rodeo promoters without facilities

339920   Rods and rod parts, fishing, manufacturing

326299   Rods, hard rubber, manufacturing

331111   Rods, iron or steel, made in iron and steel mills

423510   Rods, metal (except precious), merchant wholesalers

334519   Rods, surveyor's, manufacturing

238160   Roll roofing installation

332991   Roller bearings manufacturing

711211   Roller hockey clubs, professional or semiprofessional

316110   Roller leather manufacturing

339920   Roller skates manufacturing

713940   Roller skating rinks

333120   Rollers, road construction and maintenance machinery, manufacturing

321999   Rollers, wood, manufacturing

332321   Rolling doors for industrial buildings and warehouses, metal, manufacturing

333516   Rolling mill machinery and equipment, metalworking, manufacturing

333516   Rolling mill roll machines, metalworking, manufacturing

331511   Rolling mill rolls, iron, manufacturing

331513   Rolling mill rolls, steel, manufacturing

321999   Rolling pins, wood, manufacturing

336510   Rolling stock, railroad, rebuilding

311812   Rolls and buns (including frozen) made in commercial bakeries

321920 Round stave baskets (e.g., fruit, vegetable) manufacturing
321912 Rounds or rungs, furniture, hardwood, manufacturing
331111 Rounds, tube, steel, made in iron and steel mills
423990 Roundwood merchant wholesalers
213112 Roustabout mining services, on a contract basis
333991 Routers, handheld power-driven, manufacturing
333292 Roving machinery for textiles manufacturing
236115 Row house (i.e., single-family type) construction general contractors
236117 Row house construction operative builders
532292 Rowboat rental
336612 Rowboats manufacturing
713990 Rowing clubs, recreational
112910 Royal jelly production, bees
326220 Rubber and plastics belts and hoses (without fittings) manufacturing
326299 Rubber bands manufacturing
325520 Rubber cements manufacturing
212324 Rubber clay mining and/or beneficiating
238290 Rubber door installation
326192 Rubber floor coverings manufacturing
326291 Rubber goods, mechanical (i.e., extruded, lathe-cut, molded), manufacturing
423840 Rubber goods, mechanical (i.e., extruded, lathe-cut, molded), merchant wholesalers
424210 Rubber goods, medical, merchant wholesalers
325998 Rubber processing preparations (e.g., accelerators, stabilizers) manufacturing
423930 Rubber scrap and scrap tires merchant wholesalers
339943 Rubber stamps manufacturing
424120 Rubber stamps, merchant wholesalers
313221 Rubber thread and yarns, fabric covered, manufacturing
333220 Rubber working machinery manufacturing
424990 Rubber, crude, merchant wholesalers
325212 Rubber, synthetic, manufacturing
313320 Rubberizing purchased capes
313320 Rubberizing purchased cloaks
313320 Rubberizing purchased clothing
313320 Rubberizing purchased coats
313320 Rubberizing purchased textiles and apparel
212399 Rubbing stones mining and/or beneficiating
562111 Rubbish (i.e., nonhazardous solid waste) hauling, local
562111 Rubbish collection services
562213 Rubbish disposal combustors or incinerators
562212 Rubbish disposal landfills
484220 Rubbish hauling without collection or disposal, truck, local
484230 Rubbish hauling without collection or disposal, truck, long-distance
562119 Rubble hauling, local
562119 Rubble removal services
212399 Ruby mining and/or beneficiating
532299 Rug and carpet rental
561740 Rug cleaning plants
325612 Rug cleaning preparations manufacturing
561740 Rug cleaning services
442210 Rug stores
314110 Rugs and carpets made from textile materials
423220 Rugs merchant wholesalers
321999 Rulers and rules (except slide), wood, manufacturing
332212 Rulers, metal, manufacturing
326199 Rulers, plastics, manufacturing
334519 Rules, slide, manufacturing
624221 Runaway youth shelters
488119 Runway maintenance services
237310 Runway, airport, line painting (e.g., striping)

485210 Rural bus services
324191 Rust arresting petroleum compounds made from refined petroleum
325998 Rust preventive preparations manufacturing
325612 Rust removers manufacturing
238320 Rustproofing (except automotive)
332812 Rustproofing metals and metal products for the trade
811198 Rustproofing shops, automotive
111219 Rutabaga farming, field and seed production
212299 Ruthenium ore mining and/or beneficiating
212299 Rutile mining and/or beneficiating
721211 RV (recreational vehicle) parks
532120 RV (recreational vehicle) rental or leasing
441210 RV dealers
111199 Rye farming, field and seed production
311211 Rye flour manufacturing
311213 Rye malt manufacturing
111998 Ryegrass seed farming
114111 Sablefish fishing
325199 Saccharin manufacturing
325620 Sachet, scented, manufacturing
322224 Sacks, multiwall, made from purchased uncoated paper
424130 Sacks, paper, merchant wholesalers
713990 Saddle horse rental services, recreational
325612 Saddle soaps manufacturing
321999 Saddle trees, wood, manufacturing
316110 Saddlery leather manufacturing
424910 Saddlery merchant wholesalers
332999 Saddlery parts, metal, manufacturing
811430 Saddlery repair shops without retailing new saddlery
451110 Saddlery stores
316999 Saddles and parts, leather, manufacturing
332999 Safe deposit boxes and chests, metal, manufacturing

332999 Safe doors and linings, metal, manufacturing
332999 Safes, metal, manufacturing
423420 Safes, security, merchant wholesalers
332911 Safety (i.e., pop-off) valves, industrial-type, manufacturing
316999 Safety belts, leather, manufacturing
541690 Safety consulting services
325920 Safety fuses, blasting, manufacturing
327215 Safety glass (including motor vehicle) made from purchased glass
238990 Safety net system, erecting and dismantling at construction site
339993 Safety pins manufacturing
332211 Safety razor blades manufacturing
332211 Safety razors manufacturing
111120 Safflower farming, field and seed production
311225 Safflower oil made from purchased oils
311223 Safflower oil made in crushing mills
441222 Sail boat dealers
339920 Sailboards manufacturing
336612 Sailboat building, not done in shipyards
532292 Sailboat rental
713930 Sailing clubs with marinas
713990 Sailing clubs without marinas
336611 Sailing ships, commercial, manufacturing
314912 Sails made from purchased fabrics
325181 Sal soda (i.e., washing soda) manufacturing
311423 Salad dressing mixes, dry, made in a dehydration plant
311942 Salad dressing mixes, dry, manufacturing
311941 Salad dressings manufacturing
424490 Salad dressings merchant wholesalers
424490 Salad oils merchant wholesalers

311991	Salads, fresh or refrigerated, manufacturing
424120	Sales books merchant wholesalers
323116	Sales books, manifold, printing
522220	Sales financing
541613	Sales management consulting services
325199	Salicylic acid (except medicinal) manufacturing
325411	Salicylic acid, medicinal, uncompounded, manufacturing
212391	Salines (except common salt) mining and/or beneficiating
114111	Salmon fishing
236220	Salon construction
311421	Salsa canning
325998	Salt (except table) manufacturing
311942	Salt substitute manufacturing
213112	Salt water disposal systems, oil and gas field, on a contract basis
212393	Salt, common, mining and/or beneficiating
212393	Salt, rock, mining and/or beneficiating
311942	Salt, table, manufacturing
424490	Salt, table, merchant wholesalers
311612	Salted meats made from purchased carcasses
311821	Saltines manufacturing
424210	Salts, bath, merchant wholesalers
424690	Salts, industrial, merchant wholesalers
334516	Sample analysis instruments (except medical) manufacturing
316991	Sample cases, all materials, manufacturing
334519	Sample changers, nuclear radiation, manufacturing
541870	Sample direct distribution services
323121	Samples mounting
541910	Sampling services, statistical
423320	Sand (except industrial) merchant wholesalers
212321	Sand and gravel quarrying (i.e., construction grade) and/or beneficiating
213112	Sand blasting pipelines on lease, oil and gas field on a contract basis
331524	Sand castings, aluminum, unfinished, manufacturing
331525	Sand castings, copper and copper-base alloy, unfinished, manufacturing
331528	Sand castings, nonferrous metals (except aluminum, copper), unfinished, manufacturing
484220	Sand hauling, local
484230	Sand hauling, long-distance
333120	Sand mixers manufacturing
212322	Sand, blast, quarrying and/or beneficiating
212321	Sand, construction grade, quarrying and/or beneficiating
212322	Sand, industrial (e.g., engine, filtration, glass grinding), quarrying and/or beneficiating
423840	Sand, industrial, merchant wholesalers
316219	Sandals, children's (except rubber, plastics), manufacturing
316213	Sandals, men's footwear (except rubber, plastics), manufacturing
316211	Sandals, plastics or plastics soled fabric upper, manufacturing
316211	Sandals, rubber or rubber soled fabric upper, manufacturing
316214	Sandals, women's footwear (except rubber, plastics), manufacturing
332813	Sandblasting metals and metal products for the trade
238990	Sandblasting, building exterior
333991	Sanders, handheld power-driven, manufacturing
333319	Sanding machines, floor, manufacturing

333210 Sanding machines, woodworking-type, stationary, manufacturing
333291 Sandpaper making machines manufacturing
327910 Sandpaper manufacturing
212319 Sandstone crushed and broken stone mining
212311 Sandstone mining or quarrying
212399 Sandstone, bituminous, mining and/or beneficiating
722211 Sandwich shops, limited-service
311612 Sandwich spreads, meat, made from purchased carcasses
311941 Sandwich spreads, salad dressing based, manufacturing
335211 Sandwich toasters and grills, household-type electric, manufacturing
424490 Sandwiches merchant wholesalers
311991 Sandwiches, fresh (i.e., assembled and packaged for wholesale market), manufacturing
322212 Sanitary food container, folding, made from purchased paperboard
424130 Sanitary food containers (e.g., disposable plastics, paper, paperboard) merchant wholesalers
322215 Sanitary food containers (except folding) made from purchased paper or paperboard
562212 Sanitary landfills
322291 Sanitary napkins and tampons made from purchased paper or textile fiber
322121 Sanitary napkins and tampons made in paper mills
322121 Sanitary paper products (except newsprint, uncoated groundwood) made in paper mills
424130 Sanitary paper products merchant wholesalers
322121 Sanitary paper stock manufacturing

322291 Sanitary products made from purchased sanitary paper stock
322121 Sanitary products made in paper mills
237110 Sanitary sewer construction
332998 Sanitary ware (e.g., bathtubs, lavatories, sinks), metal, manufacturing
238220 Sanitary ware installation
423720 Sanitary ware, china or enameled iron, merchant wholesalers
541620 Sanitation consulting services
926130 Sanitation districts, nonoperating
924110 Sanitation engineering agencies, government
212399 Sapphire mining and/or beneficiating
325222 Saran (i.e., polyvinylidene chloride) fibers and filaments manufacturing
332612 Sash balance springs, light gauge, made from purchased wire or strip
332321 Sash, door and window, metal, manufacturing
321911 Sash, door and window, wood and covered wood, manufacturing
316991 Satchels, all materials, manufacturing
334220 Satellite antennas manufacturing
334220 Satellite communications equipment manufacturing
238290 Satellite dish, household-type, installation
517510 Satellite master antenna television service (SMATV)
515111 Satellite radio networks
237130 Satellite receiving station construction
517410 Satellite telecommunication carriers
517410 Satellite telecommunication resellers
517910 Satellite telemetry operations on a contract or fee basis
517510 Satellite television distribution systems

515210	Satellite television networks
517910	Satellite tracking stations on a contract or fee basis
325131	Satin white pigments manufacturing
335311	Saturable transformers manufacturing
324122	Saturated felts made from purchased paper
322121	Saturated felts made in paper mills
311423	Sauce mixes, dry, made in dehydration plants
311942	Sauce mixes, dry, manufacturing
311941	Sauces (except tomato based) manufacturing
311941	Sauces for meat (except tomato based) manufacturing
311941	Sauces for seafood (except tomato based) manufacturing
311941	Sauces for vegetable (except tomato based) manufacturing
311421	Sauces, tomato-based, canning
311421	Sauerkraut manufacturing
335211	Sauna heaters, electric, manufacturing
321992	Sauna rooms, prefabricated, wood, manufacturing
812199	Saunas
311612	Sausage and similar cased products made from purchased carcasses
424490	Sausage casings merchant wholesalers
311612	Sausage casings, collagen, made from purchased hides
311611	Sausage casings, natural, produced in slaughtering plant
326121	Sausage casings, plastics, manufacturing
522120	Savings and loan associations (S&L)
524113	Savings bank life insurance carriers, direct
522120	Savings banks
522120	Savings institutions
332213	Saw blades, all types, manufacturing
811411	Saw repair and maintenance (except sawmills) without retailing new saws
321113	Sawdust and shavings (i.e., sawmill byproducts) manufacturing
424990	Sawdust merchant wholesalers
321999	Sawdust, regrinding
321113	Sawed lumber made in sawmills
321912	Sawed lumber, resawing purchased lumber
333512	Sawing machines, metalworking, manufacturing
333210	Sawmill equipment manufacturing
532490	Sawmill machinery rental or leasing
423830	Sawmill machinery, equipment, and supplies merchant wholesalers
321113	Sawmills
333210	Saws, bench and table, power-driven, woodworking-type, manufacturing
332213	Saws, hand, nonpowered, manufacturing
333991	Saws, handheld power-driven, manufacturing
339112	Saws, surgical, manufacturing
339992	Saxophones and parts manufacturing
238990	Scaffold erecting and dismantling
423810	Scaffolding merchant wholesalers
532490	Scaffolding rental or leasing
332323	Scaffolds, metal, manufacturing
334519	Scalers, nuclear radiation, manufacturing
333997	Scales (except laboratory-type) manufacturing
339111	Scales and balances, laboratory-type, manufacturing
339111	Scales, laboratory, manufacturing
114112	Scallop fishing
812199	Scalp treating services
518210	Scanning services, optical

333210 Scarfing machines, woodworking-type, manufacturing
333516 Scarfing units, rolling mill machinery, metalworking, manufacturing
333120 Scarifiers, road, manufacturing
325132 Scarlet 2 R lake manufacturing
315191 Scarves made in apparel knitting mills
315211 Scarves, men's and boys', cut and sew apparel contractors
315993 Scarves, men's and boys', cut and sewn from purchased fabric (except apparel contractors)
315212 Scarves, women's, girls', and infants', cut and sew apparel contractors
315999 Scarves, women's, misses', and girls', cut and sewn from purchased fabric (except apparel contractors)
336350 Scattershield, engine, manufacturing
711510 Scenery designers, independent theatrical
532490 Scenery, theatrical, rental or leasing
487990 Scenic and sightseeing excursions, aerial
487110 Scenic and sightseeing excursions, land
487210 Scenic and sightseeing excursions, water
481112 Scheduled air freight carriers
481112 Scheduled air freight transportation
481111 Scheduled air passenger carriers
481111 Scheduled air passenger transportation
212299 Scheelite mining and/or beneficiating
313222 Schiffli machine embroideries manufacturing
333292 Schiffli machinery manufacturing
212319 Schist, mica, crushed and broken stone, mining and/or beneficiating
212311 Schist, mica, mining or quarrying
511120 Scholarly journal publishers (except exclusive Internet publishing)
511120 Scholarly journal publishers and printing combined
516110 Scholarly journal publishers, exclusively on Internet
323112 Scholarly journals flexographic printing without publishing
323111 Scholarly journals gravure printing without publishing
323110 Scholarly journals lithographic (offset) printing without publishing
323119 Scholarly journals printing (except flexographic, gravure, lithographic, quick, screen) without publishing
323113 Scholarly journals screen printing without publishing
813211 Scholarship trusts (i.e., grantmaking, charitable trust foundations)
511120 Scholastic magazine and periodical publishers (except exclusive Internet publishing)
511120 Scholastic magazine and periodical publishers and printing combined
516110 Scholastic magazine and periodical publishers, exclusively on Internet
323112 Scholastic magazines and periodicals flexographic printing without publishing
323111 Scholastic magazines and periodicals gravure printing without publishing
323110 Scholastic magazines and periodicals lithographic (offset) printing without publishing
323119 Scholastic magazines and periodicals printing (except flexographic, gravure, lithographic, quick, screen) without publishing

323113 Scholastic magazines and periodicals screen printing without publishing

611110 School boards, elementary and secondary

511130 School book publishers (except exclusive Internet publishing)

511130 School book publishers and printing combined

516110 School book publishers, exclusively on Internet

323117 School books printing and binding without publishing

323117 School books printing without publishing

236220 School building construction

611710 School bus attendant services

423110 School bus merchant wholesalers

532120 School bus rental or leasing

485410 School bus services

336211 School buses assembling on purchased chassis

611110 School districts, elementary or secondary

423490 School equipment and supplies (except books, furniture) merchant wholesalers

337127 School furniture manufacturing

423210 School furniture merchant wholesalers

541921 School photography (i.e., portrait photography) services

453210 School supply stores

511130 School textbook publishers (except exclusive Internet publishing)

511130 School textbook publishers and printing combined

516110 School textbook publishers, exclusively on Internet

323121 School textbooks binding without printing

448190 School uniform stores

611110 Schools for the handicapped, elementary or secondary

611110 Schools for the mentally retarded (except preschool, job training, vocational rehabilitation)

611110 Schools for the physically disabled, elementary or secondary

611512 Schools, aviation

611511 Schools, barber

611511 Schools, beauty

611410 Schools, business, not offering academic degrees

611310 Schools, correspondence, college level

611511 Schools, cosmetology

611610 Schools, drama (except academic)

611110 Schools, elementary

611210 Schools, junior college

611210 Schools, junior college vocational

611630 Schools, language

611310 Schools, medical

611610 Schools, music (except academic)

611310 Schools, professional (colleges or universities)

611110 Schools, secondary

611620 Schools, sports instruction

712110 Science and technology museums

339932 Science kits (e.g., chemistry sets, microscopes, natural science sets) manufacturing

327215 Scientific apparatus glassware made from purchased glass

813920 Scientific associations

327215 Scientific glassware made from purchased glass

327212 Scientific glassware, pressed or blown, made in glass making plants

423490 Scientific instruments merchant wholesalers

511120 Scientific journal and periodical publishers (except exclusive Internet publishing)

511120 Scientific journal and periodical publishers and printing combined

516110 Scientific journal and periodical publishers, exclusively on Internet

339920	Scuba diving equipment manufacturing
611620	Scuba instruction, camps, or schools
711510	Sculptors, independent
611610	Sculpture instruction
327420	Sculptures (e.g., gypsum, plaster of paris) manufacturing
327112	Sculptures, architectural, clay, manufacturing
332212	Scythes manufacturing
212399	Scythestones mining and/or beneficiating
114111	Sea bass fishing
114111	Sea herring fishing
713990	Sea kayaking, recreational
111998	Sea plant agriculture
114111	Sea trout fishing
114112	Sea urchin fishing
424460	Seafood (except canned, packaged frozen) merchant wholesalers
311711	Seafood and seafood products canning
311711	Seafood and seafood products curing
311712	Seafood dinners, frozen, manufacturing
445220	Seafood markets
311712	Seafood products, fresh prepared, manufacturing
311712	Seafood products, frozen, manufacturing
424490	Seafood, canned, merchant wholesalers
311712	Seafood, fresh prepared, manufacturing
311712	Seafood, frozen, manufacturing
424420	Seafoods, packaged frozen, merchant wholesalers
339943	Seal presses (e.g., notary), hand operated, manufacturing
424690	Sealants merchant wholesalers
335110	Sealed beam automotive light bulbs manufacturing
325520	Sealing compounds for pipe threads and joints manufacturing
423840	Seals merchant wholesalers
339991	Seals, grease or oil, manufacturing
333992	Seam welding equipment manufacturing
334511	Search and detection systems and instruments manufacturing
518112	Search portals, Internet
335129	Searchlights, electric and nonelectric, manufacturing
453220	Seasonal and holiday decoration stores
721110	Seasonal hotels without casinos
561730	Seasonal property maintenance services (i.e., snow plowing in winter, landscaping during other seasons)
311942	Seasoning salt manufacturing
336360	Seat belts, motor vehicle and aircraft, manufacturing
423120	Seat covers, automotive, merchant wholesalers
321999	Seat covers, rattan, manufacturing
326150	Seat cushions, foam plastics (except polystyrene), manufacturing
316999	Seatbelts, leather, manufacturing
336360	Seats for public conveyances, manufacturing
336360	Seats, railroad, manufacturing
321999	Seats, toilet, wood, manufacturing
237990	Seawall, wave protection, construction
488310	Seaway operation
111998	Seaweed farming
114119	Seaweed gathering
311711	Seaweed processing (e.g., dulse)
325199	Sebacic acid esters manufacturing
325199	Sebacic acid manufacturing
611630	Second language instruction
522294	Secondary market financing (i.e., buying, pooling, repackaging loans for sale to others)
331492	Secondary refining of nonferrous metals (except aluminum, copper)

331491 Selenium bar, rod, sheet, strip, and tubing made from purchased metals or scrap

325188 Selenium compounds, not specified elsewhere by process, manufacturing

325188 Selenium dioxide manufacturing

331492 Selenium recovering from scrap and/or alloying purchased metals

331419 Selenium refining, primary

611699 Self defense (except martial arts) instruction

624190 Self-help organizations (except for disabled persons, the elderly, persons diagnosed with mental retardation)

624120 Self-help organizations for disabled persons, the elderly, and persons diagnosed with mental retardation

624110 Self-help organizations, youth

525190 Self-insurance funds (except employee benefit funds)

811192 Self-service carwash

812310 Self-service drycleaners and laundries

531130 Self-storage unit rental or leasing

531130 Self-storage warehousing

531210 Selling real estate for others (i.e., agents, brokers)

115210 Semen collection

424590 Semen, bovine, merchant wholesalers

212111 Semianthracite surface mining and/or beneficiating

212112 Semianthracite underground mining or mining and beneficiating

212111 Semibituminous coal surface mining and/or beneficiating

212112 Semibituminous coal underground mining or mining and beneficiating

333295 Semiconductor assembly and packaging machinery manufacturing

335999 Semiconductor battery chargers manufacturing

334413 Semiconductor circuit networks (i.e., solid-state integrated circuits) manufacturing

334413 Semiconductor devices manufacturing

423690 Semiconductor devices merchant wholesalers

334413 Semiconductor dice and wafers manufacturing

335999 Semiconductor high-voltage power supplies manufacturing

333295 Semiconductor making machinery manufacturing

334413 Semiconductor memory chips manufacturing

334515 Semiconductor test equipment manufacturing

333618 Semidiesel engines manufacturing

423510 Semi-finished metal products merchant wholesalers

611110 Seminaries, below university grade

611310 Seminaries, theological, offering baccalaureate or graduate degrees

212399 Semiprecious stones mining and/or beneficiating

711211 Semiprofessional baseball clubs

711211 Semiprofessional football clubs

711211 Semiprofessional sports clubs

331511 Semisteel foundries

336212 Semi-trailer manufacturing

532120 Semi-trailer rental or leasing

311211 Semolina flour manufacturing

624120 Senior citizens activity centers

813311 Senior citizens advocacy organizations

813410 Senior citizens' associations, social

624120 Senior citizens centers

623312 Senior citizens' homes without nursing care

485991 Senior citizens transportation services

325992 Sensitized cloth or paper (e.g., blueprint, photographic) manufacturing

333315 Sensitometers, photographic, manufacturing

327332   Sewer pipe, concrete, manufacturing
221320   Sewer systems
424310   Sewing accessories merchant wholesalers
339999   Sewing and mending kits assembling
316993   Sewing cases (except metal) manufacturing
339911   Sewing cases, precious metal, manufacturing
315211   Sewing fabric owned by others for men's and boys' apparel
315212   Sewing fabric owned by others for women's, girls' and infants' apparel
337129   Sewing machine cabinets, wood, manufacturing
443111   Sewing machine stores, household-type
811412   Sewing machine, household-type, repair shops without retailing new sewing machines
333298   Sewing machines (including household-type) manufacturing
423620   Sewing machines, household-type, merchant wholesalers
423830   Sewing machines, industrial, merchant wholesalers
451130   Sewing supply stores
313113   Sewing threads manufacturing
334511   Sextants (except surveying) manufacturing
334519   Sextants, surveying, manufacturing
337920   Shade pulls, window, manufacturing
335121   Shades, lamp (except glass, plastics), residential-type, manufacturing
337920   Shades, window (except outdoor canvas awnings), manufacturing
213113   Shaft sinking for coal mines on a contract basis
213114   Shaft sinking for metal mines on a contract basis
238160   Shake and shingle, roof, installation

321113   Shakes (i.e., hand split shingles) manufacturing
212325   Shale (except oil shale) mining and/or beneficiating
327992   Shale, expanded, manufacturing
211111   Shale, oil, mining and/or beneficiating
111219   Shallot farming, field and seed production
325620   Shampoos and conditioners, hair, manufacturing
316999   Shanks, shoe, leather, manufacturing
333210   Shapers, woodworking-type, manufacturing
114111   Shark fishing
339994   Shaving brushes manufacturing
333512   Shaving machines, metalworking, manufacturing
325620   Shaving preparations (e.g., creams, gels, lotions, powders) manufacturing
424210   Shaving preparations merchant wholesalers
333513   Shearing machines, metal forming, manufacturing
316110   Shearling (i.e., prepared sheepskin) manufacturing
333991   Shears and nibblers, handheld power-driven, manufacturing
332211   Shears, nonelectric, household-type (e.g., kitchen, barber, tailor) manufacturing
332212   Shears, nonelectric, tool-type (e.g., garden, pruners, tinsnip), manufacturing
333111   Shears, powered, for use on animals, manufacturing
322121   Sheathing paper (except newsprint, uncoated groundwood) made in paper mills
324122   Sheathing, asphalt saturated, made from refined petroleum
238130   Sheathing, wood, installation
333613   Sheaves, mechanical power transmission, manufacturing
332311   Sheds, (e.g., garden, storage, utility) prefabricated metal, manufacturing

321992 Sheds, (e.g., garden, storage, utility) prefabricated wood, manufacturing
115210 Sheep dipping and shearing
112410 Sheep farming (e.g., meat, milk, wool production)
424520 Sheep merchant wholesalers
333111 Sheep shears, powered, manufacturing
326140 Sheet (i.e., board), polystyrene foam insulation, manufacturing
238220 Sheet metal duct work installation
333513 Sheet metal forming machines manufacturing
238160 Sheet metal roofing installation
423330 Sheet metal roofing materials merchant wholesalers
332322 Sheet metal work (except stampings) manufacturing
611513 Sheet metal workers' apprenticeship training
323112 Sheet music flexographic printing without publishing
323111 Sheet music gravure printing without publishing
323110 Sheet music lithographic (offset) printing without publishing
424990 Sheet music merchant wholesalers
323119 Sheet music printing (except flexographic, gravure, lithographic, qiuck, screen) without publishing
512230 Sheet music publishers
512230 Sheet music publishers and printing combined
323113 Sheet music screen printing without publishing
451140 Sheet music stores
331111 Sheet pilings, plain, iron or steel, made in iron and steel mills
331315 Sheet, aluminum, made by flat rolling purchased aluminum

331315 Sheet, aluminum, made in integrated secondary smelting and flat rolling mills
331421 Sheet, copper and copper alloy, made from purchased copper or in integrated secondary smelting and rolling, drawing or extruding plants
326130 Sheet, laminated plastics (except flexible packaging), manufacturing
326113 Sheet, plastics, unlaminated (except packaging), manufacturing
326299 Sheeting, rubber, manufacturing
314129 Sheets and pillowcases made from purchased fabrics
313210 Sheets and pillowcases made in broadwoven fabric mills
331111 Sheets, steel, made in iron and steel mills
311119 Shell crushing and grinding for animal feed
311119 Shell crushing for feed
332993 Shell loading and assembly plants
212399 Shell mining and/or beneficiating
339999 Shell novelties
331111 Shell slugs, steel, made in iron and steel mills
325510 Shellac manufacturing
424950 Shellac merchant wholesalers
311711 Shellfish and shellfish products canning
311711 Shellfish curing
114112 Shellfish fishing (e.g., clam, crab, oyster, shrimp)
112512 Shellfish hatcheries
311712 Shellfish products, fresh prepared, manufacturing
311712 Shellfish products, frozen, manufacturing
311712 Shellfish, fresh prepared, manufacturing
311712 Shellfish, frozen, manufacturing
332993 Shells, artillery, manufacturing
332992 Shells, small arms (i.e., 30 mm. or less, 1.18 inch or less), manufacturing

624310 Sheltered workshops (i.e., work experience centers)
624221 Shelters (except for victims of domestic or international disasters or conflicts), emergency
624230 Shelters for victims of domestic or international disasters or conflicts, emergency
624221 Shelters, battered women's
624221 Shelters, homeless
624221 Shelters, runaway youth
624221 Shelters, temporary (e.g., battered women's, homeless, runaway youth)
337215 Shelving (except wire) manufacturing
423440 Shelving, commercial, merchant wholesalers
238390 Shelving, metal, constructed on site
332618 Shelving, wire, made from purchased wire
238350 Shelving, wood, constructed on site
332812 Sherardizing of metals and metal products for the trade
311520 Sherbets manufacturing
922120 Sheriffs' offices (except court functions only)
922110 Sheriffs' offices, court functions only
332999 Shims, metal, manufacturing
321113 Shingle mills, wood
423330 Shingles (except wood) merchant wholesalers
324122 Shingles made from purchased asphaltic materials
423310 Shingles, wood, merchant wholesalers
321113 Shingles, wood, sawed or hand split, manufacturing
331525 Ship and boat propellers, cast brass, bronze and copper (except die-casting), unfinished, manufacturing
424990 Ship chandler merchant wholesalers

483113 Ship chartering with crew, coastal or Great Lakes freight transportation (including St. Lawrence Seaway)
483114 Ship chartering with crew, coastal or Great Lakes passenger transportation (including St. Lawrence Seaway)
483111 Ship chartering with crew, deep sea freight transportation to or from foreign ports
483112 Ship chartering with crew, deep sea passenger transportation to or from foreign ports
483211 Ship chartering with crew, freight transportation, inland waters (except on Great Lakes system)
483212 Ship chartering with crew, passenger transportation, inland waters (except on Great Lakes system)
333923 Ship cranes and derricks manufacturing
561310 Ship crew employment agencies
561310 Ship crew registries
423930 Ship dismantling (except at floating drydocks and shipyards) merchant wholesalers
488390 Ship dismantling at floating drydock
336611 Ship dismantling at shipyards
337127 Ship furniture manufacturing
488320 Ship hold cleaning services
238350 Ship joinery contractors
238320 Ship painting contractors
532411 Ship rental or leasing without operators
336611 Ship repair done in a shipyard
336611 Ship scaling services done at a shipyard
488390 Ship scaling services not done at a shipyard
332312 Ship sections, prefabricated metal, manufacturing
331422 Shipboard cable made from purchased copper in wire drawing plants

331319 Shipboard cable made in aluminum wire drawing plants

488510 Shipping agents (freight forwarding)

314911 Shipping bags made from purchased woven or knitted materials

332439 Shipping barrels, drums, kegs, and pails, light gauge metal, manufacturing

321920 Shipping cases and drums, wood, wirebound, manufacturing

321920 Shipping cases, wood, nailed or lock corner, manufacturing

813910 Shipping companies' associations

423840 Shipping containers (except disposable plastics, paper) merchant wholesalers

322211 Shipping containers made from purchased paperboard

322211 Shipping containers, corrugated, made from purchased paper or paperboard

321920 Shipping crates, wood, manufacturing

483113 Shipping freight to and from domestic ports (i.e., coastal, deep sea (including Puerto Rico), Great Lakes system (including St. Lawrence Seaway))

483111 Shipping freight to or from foreign ports, deep sea

483211 Shipping freight, inland waters (except on Great Lakes system)

326150 Shipping pads and shaped cushioning, foam plastics (except polystyrene), manufacturing

326140 Shipping pads and shaped cushioning, polystyrene foam, manufacturing

423840 Shipping pails, metal, merchant wholesalers

323112 Shipping registers flexographic printing without publishing

323111 Shipping registers gravure printing without publishing

323110 Shipping registers lithographic (offset) printing without publishing

323113 Shipping registers screen printing without publishing

424130 Shipping supplies, paper and disposable plastics, merchant wholesalers

336611 Ships (i.e., not suitable or intended for personal use) manufacturing

423860 Ships merchant wholesalers

517212 Ship-to-shore broadcasting communication carriers (except satellite)

336611 Shipyard (i.e., facility capable of building ships)

315223 Shirts, outerwear (except work shirts), men's and boys', cut and sewn from purchased fabric (except apparel contractors)

315225 Shirts, outerwear work, men's and boys', cut and sewn from purchased fabric (except apparel contractors)

315291 Shirts, outerwear, infants', cut and sewn from purchased fabric (except apparel contractors)

315191 Shirts, outerwear, made in apparel knitting mills

315211 Shirts, outerwear, men's and boys', cut and sew apparel contractors

315223 Shirts, outerwear, unisex (i.e., sized without regard to gender), cut and sewn from purchased fabric (except apparel contractors)

315212 Shirts, outerwear, women's, girls', and infants', cut and sew apparel contractors

315232 Shirts, outerwear, women's, misses', and girls', cut and sewn from purchased fabric (except apparel contractors)

315291 Shirts, underwear, infants', cut and sewn from purchased fabric (except apparel contractors)

315192 Shirts, underwear, made in apparel knitting mills

315211 Shirts, underwear, men's and boys', cut and sew apparel contractors

315221 Shirts, underwear, men's and boys', cut and sewn from purchased fabric (except apparel contractors)

315212 Shirts, underwear, women's, girls', and infants', cut and sew apparel contractors

315231 Shirts, underwear, women's, misses', and girls', cut and sewn from purchased fabric (except apparel contractors)

111411 Shitake mushroom farming

336330 Shock absorbers, automotive, truck, and bus, manufacturing

448210 Shoe (except bowling, golf, spiked) stores

326299 Shoe and boot parts (e.g., heels, soles, soling strips), rubber, manufacturing

322212 Shoe boxes, folding, made from purchased paperboard

322213 Shoe boxes, setup, made from purchased paperboard

541490 Shoe design services

321999 Shoe display forms, all materials, manufacturing

316991 Shoe kits (i.e., cases), all materials, manufacturing

333298 Shoe making and repairing machinery manufacturing

423830 Shoe manufacturing and repairing machinery merchant wholesalers

326199 Shoe parts (e.g., heels, soles), plastics, manufacturing

335211 Shoe polishers, household-type electric, manufacturing

325612 Shoe polishes and cleaners manufacturing

423850 Shoe repair materials merchant wholesalers

811430 Shoe repair shops without retailing new shoes

316999 Shoe soles, leather, manufacturing

448210 Shoe stores, orthopedic

451110 Shoe stores, specialty sports footwear (e.g., bowling, golf, spiked)

321999 Shoe stretchers manufacturing

321999 Shoe trees manufacturing

424340 Shoes merchant wholesalers

316219 Shoes, athletic (except rubber or plastics soled with fabric upper), manufacturing

316219 Shoes, ballet, manufacturing

316219 Shoes, children's and infant's (except house slippers, orthopedic extension, plastics, rubber), manufacturing

316219 Shoes, cleated or spiked, all materials, manufacturing

316213 Shoes, men's (except house slippers, athletic, rubber, orthopedic extension), manufacturing

339113 Shoes, orthopedic extension, manufacturing

316211 Shoes, plastics or plastics soled fabric upper (except cleated athletic), manufacturing

316211 Shoes, rubber or rubber soled fabric upper (except cleated athletic), manufacturing

316219 Shoes, theatrical, manufacturing

316214 Shoes, women's (except house slippers, athletic, orthopedic extension, plastic, rubber), manufacturing

316219 Shoes, wooden, manufacturing

812990 Shoeshine parlors

812990 Shoeshine services

321920 Shook, box, manufacturing

713990 Shooting clubs, recreational

713990 Shooting galleries

713990 Shooting ranges

423120 Shop equipment, service station, merchant wholesalers

424130 Shopping bags, paper and plastics, merchant wholesalers

531120 Shopping center (i.e., not operating contained businesses) rental or leasing

236220 Shopping center construction

236220 Shopping mall construction

812990 Shopping services, personal

****** Shops—see type

238990 Shoring, construction

111421 Short rotation woody tree growing (i.e., growing and harvesting cycle 10 years or less)

311223 Shortening (except soybean) made in crushing mills

311222 Shortening, soybean, made in crushing mills

311225 Shortening made from purchased fats and oils

424490 Shortening, vegetable, merchant wholesalers

482112 Short-line railroads

315291 Shorts, outerwear, infants', cut and sewn from purchased fabric (except apparel contractors)

315191 Shorts, outerwear, made in apparel knitting mills

315211 Shorts, outerwear, men's and boys', cut and sew apparel contractors

315228 Shorts, outerwear, men's and boys', cut and sewn from purchased fabric (except apparel contractors)

315212 Shorts, outerwear, women's, girls', and infants', cut and sew apparel contractors

315239 Shorts, outerwear, women's, misses', and girls', cut and sewn from purchased fabric (except apparel contractors)

315192 Shorts, underwear, made in apparel knitting mills

315211 Shorts, underwear, men's and boys', cut and sew apparel contractors

315221 Shorts, underwear, men's and boys', cut and sewn from purchased fabric (except apparel contractors)

522298 Short-term inventory credit lending

213112 Shot hole drilling, oil and gas field, on a contract basis

332811 Shot peening metal and metal products for the trade

332992 Shot, BB, manufacturing

332992 Shot, lead, manufacturing

332992 Shot, pellet, manufacturing

332992 Shot, steel, manufacturing

238110 Shotcrete contractors

332992 Shotgun shells manufacturing

332994 Shotguns manufacturing

333120 Shovel loaders manufacturing

332212 Shovels, handheld, manufacturing

333120 Shovels, power, manufacturing

337215 Showcases (except refrigerated) manufacturing

423440 Showcases (except refrigerated) merchant wholesalers

333415 Showcases, refrigerated, manufacturing

314129 Shower and bath curtains, all materials, made from purchased fabric or sheet goods

332913 Shower heads, plumbing, manufacturing

332998 Shower receptors, metal, manufacturing

332999 Shower rods, metal, manufacturing

316211 Shower sandals or slippers, rubber, manufacturing

332998 Shower stalls, metal, manufacturing

326191 Shower stalls, plastics or fiberglass, manufacturing

115210 Showing of cattle, hogs, sheep, goats, and poultry

333111 Shredders, farm-type, manufacturing

212399 Shredding peat mining and/or beneficiating

114112 Shrimp fishing

112512	Shrimp production, farm raising
813110	Shrines, religious
561910	Shrink wrapping services
313311	Shrinking broadwoven fabrics
313312	Shrinking textile products and fabrics (except broadwoven)
561730	Shrub services (e.g., bracing, planting, pruning, removal, spraying, surgery, trimming)
111421	Shrubbery farming
311712	Shucking and packing fresh shellfish
488490	Shunting of trailers in truck terminals
488210	Shunting trailers in rail terminals
334515	Shunts, instrument, manufacturing
238190	Shutter installation
332321	Shutters, door and window, metal, manufacturing
321918	Shutters, door and window, wood and covered wood, manufacturing
326199	Shutters, plastics, manufacturing
321918	Shutters, wood, manufacturing
485999	Shuttle services (except employee bus)
333292	Shuttles for textile weaving machinery manufacturing
446199	Sick room supply stores
332212	Sickles manufacturing
212210	Siderite mining and/or beneficiating
238990	Sidewalk construction, residential and commercial
237310	Sidewalk, public, construction
238170	Siding (e.g., vinyl, wood, aluminum) installation
423330	Siding (except wood) merchant wholesalers
238170	Siding contractors
444190	Siding dealers
324122	Siding made from purchased asphaltic materials
321113	Siding mills, wood
321113	Siding, dressed lumber, manufacturing
326199	Siding, plastics, manufacturing
332322	Siding, sheet metal (except stampings), manufacturing
423310	Siding, wood, merchant wholesalers
212393	Sienna mining and/or beneficiating
325131	Sienna pigment manufacturing
333294	Sieves and screening equipment (i.e., food manufacturing-type) manufacturing
333298	Sieves and screening equipment, chemical preparation-type, manufacturing
333999	Sieves and screening equipment, general purpose-type, manufacturing
333131	Sieves and screening equipment, mineral beneficiating, manufacturing
332618	Sieves, made from purchased wire, manufacturing
333294	Sifting machine (i.e., food manufacturing-type) manufacturing
333314	Sights, telescopic, manufacturing
487210	Sightseeing boat operation
487110	Sightseeing bus operation
487110	Sightseeing operation, human-drawn vehicle
238990	Sign (except on highways, streets, bridges and tunnels) erection
237310	Sign erection, highway, roads street or bridge
611630	Sign language instruction
611630	Sign language schools
541930	Sign language services
541890	Sign lettering and painting services
238990	Sign, building, erection
331422	Signal and control cable made from purchased copper in wire drawing plants
331319	Signal and control cable made in aluminum wire drawing plants
334515	Signal generators and averagers manufacturing

236115 Single-family attached housing construction general contractors
236115 Single-family detached housing construction general contractors
236115 Single-family homes built on land owned by others, general contractors of
236115 Single-family house construction by general contractors
236117 Single-family housing built on own land for sale (i.e., operative builders)
236117 Single-family housing construction operative builders
213113 Sinking shafts for coal mining on a contract basis
213114 Sinking shafts for metal mining on a contract basis
332998 Sinks, metal, manufacturing
326191 Sinks, plastics, manufacturing
327111 Sinks, vitreous china, manufacturing
212210 Sintered iron ore produced at the mine
212392 Sintered phosphate rock mining and/or beneficiating
334290 Sirens (e.g., air raid, industrial, marine, vehicle) manufacturing
541611 Site location consulting services
541620 Site remediation consulting services
562910 Site remediation services
541611 Site selection consulting services
812990 Sitting services, house
812910 Sitting services, pet
313311 Sizing of broadwoven fabrics
313312 Sizing of fabric (except broadwoven)
339920 Skateboards manufacturing
339920 Skates and parts, ice and roller, manufacturing
713990 Skeet shooting facilities
331111 Skelp, iron or steel, made in iron and steel mills
711510 Sketch artists, independent

321999 Skewers, wood, manufacturing
541320 Ski area design services
541320 Ski area planning services
532292 Ski equipment rental
713920 Ski lift and tow operators
721110 Ski lodges and resorts with accommodations
315191 Ski pants made in apparel knitting mills
315291 Ski pants, infants', cut and sewn from purchased fabric (except apparel contractors)
315211 Ski pants, men's and boys', cut and sew apparel contractors
315228 Ski pants, men's and boys', cut and sewn from purchased fabric (except apparel contractors)
315212 Ski pants, women's, girls', and infants', cut and sew apparel contractors
315239 Ski pants, women's, misses', and girls', cut and sewn from purchased fabric (except apparel contractors)
713920 Ski resorts without accommodations
315191 Ski suits made in apparel knitting mills
315291 Ski suits, infants', cut and sewn from purchased fabric (except apparel contractors)
315211 Ski suits, men's and boys', cut and sew apparel contractors
315228 Ski suits, men's and boys', cut and sewn from purchased fabric (except apparel contractors)
315212 Ski suits, women's, girls', and infants', cut and sew apparel contractors
315239 Ski suits, women's, misses', and girls', cut and sewn from purchased fabric (except apparel contractors)
237990 Ski tow construction
532490 Skid rental or leasing
213112 Skidding of rigs, oil and gas field, on a contract basis

333120	Slag mixers, portable, manufacturing
238140	Slate (i.e., masonry) contractors
212319	Slate crushed and broken stone mining and/or beneficiating
212311	Slate mining or quarrying
327991	Slate products manufacturing
238340	Slate, interior, installation
311611	Slaughtering, custom
311991	Slaw, cole, fresh, manufacturing
332212	Sledgehammers manufacturing
339932	Sleds, children's, manufacturing
621498	Sleep disorder centers and clinics, outpatient
337215	Sleeper mechanisms, convertible bed, manufacturing
314999	Sleeping bags manufacturing
316999	Sleeves, welder's, leather, manufacturing
333294	Slicing machinery (i.e., food manufacturing-type) manufacturing
339993	Slide fasteners (i.e., zippers) manufacturing
332618	Slings, lifting, made from purchased wire
212324	Slip clay mining and/or beneficiating
335312	Slip rings for motors and generators manufacturing
423220	Slipcovers merchant wholesalers
314129	Slipcovers, all materials, made from purchased materials
316212	Slipper socks made from purchased socks
315119	Slipper socks made in sock mills
424340	Slippers merchant wholesalers
316219	Slippers, ballet, manufacturing
316212	Slippers, house, manufacturing
315192	Slips made in apparel knitting mills
315212	Slips, women's and girls', cut and sew apparel contractors
315231	Slips, women's, misses', and girls', cut and sewn from purchased fabric (except apparel contractors)

522294	SLMA (Student Loan Marketing Association)
713990	Slot car racetracks (i.e., amusement devices)
713290	Slot machine concession operators (i.e., supplying and servicing in others' facilities)
713290	Slot machine parlors
339999	Slot machines manufacturing
333512	Slotting machines, metalworking, manufacturing
562212	Sludge disposal sites
333999	Sludge tables manufacturing
327331	Slumped brick manufacturing
486990	Slurry pipeline transportation
213112	Slush pits and cellars, excavation of, on a contract basis
541940	Small animal veterinary services
332992	Small arms ammunition (i.e., 30 mm. or less, 1.18 inch or less) manufacturing
926110	Small business development agencies
811411	Small engine repair and maintenance shops
311615	Small game, processing, fresh, frozen, canned or cooked
311615	Small game, slaughtering, dressing and packing
522291	Small loan companies (i.e., unsecured cash loans)
236210	Smelter construction
331492	Smelting and refining of nonferrous metals (except aluminum, copper), secondary
423830	Smelting machinery and equipment merchant wholesalers
331492	Smelting nonferrous metals (except aluminum, copper), secondary
331419	Smelting of nonferrous metals (except aluminum, copper), primary
333994	Smelting ovens manufacturing
332420	Smelting pots and retorts manufacturing
212231	Smithsonite mining and/or beneficiating

238210 Smoke detection system, installation only
334290 Smoke detectors manufacturing
423620 Smoke detectors, household-type, merchant wholesalers
332995 Smoke generators manufacturing
311612 Smoked meats made from purchased carcasses
424990 Smokers' supplies merchant wholesalers
453991 Smokers' supply stores
332313 Smokestacks, fabricated metal boiler plate, manufacturing
621999 Smoking cessation programs
312229 Smoking tobacco (e.g., cigarette, pipe) manufacturing
333311 Snack and confection vending machines manufacturing
722213 Snack bars (e.g., cookies, popcorn, pretzels), fixed location
722330 Snack stands, mobile
111219 Snap bean farming (i.e., bush and pole), field and seed production
335931 Snap switches (i.e., electric wiring devices) manufacturing
114111 Snapper fishing
488490 Snow clearing, highways and bridges, road transportation
321912 Snow fence lath manufacturing
321999 Snow fence, sections or rolls, manufacturing
333415 Snow making machinery manufacturing
238210 Snow melting cable, electric, installation
238220 Snow melting system (e.g., hot water, glycol) installation
111219 Snow pea farming, field and seed production
333120 Snow plow attachments (except lawn, garden-type) manufacturing
333112 Snow plow attachments, lawn and garden-type, manufacturing

561790 Snow plowing driveways and parking lots (i.e., not combined with any other service)
561730 Snow plowing services combined with landscaping services (i.e., seasonal property maintenance services)
423810 Snow plows merchant wholesalers
488490 Snow removal, highway
532292 Snow ski equipment rental
423810 Snowblowers (except household-type) merchant wholesalers
333112 Snowblowers and throwers, residential-type, manufacturing
423820 Snowblowers, household-type, merchant wholesalers
441229 Snowmobile dealers
423110 Snowmobile merchant wholesalers
711212 Snowmobile racetracks
711219 Snowmobile racing teams
336999 Snowmobiles and parts manufacturing
713990 Snowmobiling, recreational
339920 Snowshoes manufacturing
315191 Snowsuits made in apparel knitting mills
315291 Snowsuits, infants', cut and sewn from purchased fabric (except apparel contractors)
315211 Snowsuits, men's and boys', cut and sew apparel contractors
315228 Snowsuits, men's and boys', cut and sewn from purchased fabric (except apparel contractors)
315212 Snowsuits, women's, girls', and infants', cut and sew apparel contractors
315239 Snowsuits, women's, misses', and girls', cut and sewn from purchased fabric (except apparel contractors)
312229 Snuff manufacturing
424940 Snuff merchant wholesalers
327111 Soap dishes, vitreous china and earthenware, manufacturing

332999 Soap dispensers, metal, manufacturing
325611 Soaps (e.g., bar, chip, powder) manufacturing
212399 Soapstone mining and/or beneficiating
711211 Soccer clubs, professional or semiprofessional
713990 Soccer clubs, recreational
611620 Soccer instruction, camps, or schools
711211 Soccer teams, professional or semiprofessional
923130 Social assistance cost-sharing, government
813319 Social change advocacy organizations
813410 Social clubs
812990 Social escort services
813410 Social organizations, civic and fraternal
541720 Social science research and development services
923130 Social Security Administration (SSA), federal
813319 Social service advocacy organizations
624190 Social service agencies, family
624190 Social service centers, multipurpose
424120 Social stationery merchant wholesalers
813920 Social workers' associations
621330 Social workers' offices (e.g., centers, clinics)
541720 Sociological research and development services
541720 Sociology research and development services
332212 Sockets and socket sets manufacturing
335931 Sockets, electric, manufacturing
315119 Socks knitting or knitting and finishing
315119 Socks, men's and boy's, manufacturing
316212 Socks, slipper, made from purchased socks
315119 Socks, slipper, made in sock mills

111421 Sod farming
333111 Sod harvesting machines manufacturing
561730 Sod laying services
325181 Soda ash manufacturing
212391 Soda ash mining and/or beneficiating
212391 Soda ash, natural, mining and/or beneficiating
327213 Soda bottles, glass, manufacturing
312111 Soda carbonated, manufacturing
311821 Soda crackers manufacturing
333415 Soda fountain cooling and dispensing equipment manufacturing
423440 Soda fountain fixtures (except refrigerated) merchant wholesalers
311930 Soda fountain syrups manufacturing
312111 Soda pop manufacturing
325199 Sodium acetate manufacturing
325199 Sodium alginate manufacturing
325188 Sodium aluminate manufacturing
325188 Sodium aluminum sulfate manufacturing
325188 Sodium antimoniate manufacturing
325320 Sodium arsenite insecticides manufacturing
325188 Sodium arsenite (except insecticides) manufacturing
325199 Sodium benzoate manufacturing
325181 Sodium bicarbonate manufacturing
325188 Sodium bichromate and chromate manufacturing
325188 Sodium borate manufacturing
212391 Sodium borates, natural, mining and/or beneficiating
325188 Sodium borohydride manufacturing
325188 Sodium bromide manufacturing
325181 Sodium carbonate (i.e., soda ash) manufacturing
212391 Sodium carbonates, natural, mining and/or beneficiating
325188 Sodium chlorate manufacturing

325412　Sodium chloride pharmaceutical preparations manufacturing
212393　Sodium chloride, rock salt, mining and/or beneficiating
212391　Sodium compounds prepared at beneficiating plants
212391　Sodium compounds, natural (except common salt), mining and/or beneficiating
325188　Sodium cyanide manufacturing
325199　Sodium glutamate manufacturing
325188　Sodium hydrosulfite manufacturing
325181　Sodium hydroxide (i.e., caustic soda) manufacturing
325188　Sodium hypochlorite manufacturing
325188　Sodium inorganic compounds, not specified elsewhere by process, manufacturing
325188　Sodium molybdate manufacturing
325199　Sodium organic compounds, not specified elsewhere by process, manufacturing
325199　Sodium pentachlorophenate manufacturing
325188　Sodium perborate manufacturing
325188　Sodium peroxide manufacturing
325188　Sodium phosphate manufacturing
325188　Sodium polyphosphate manufacturing
325412　Sodium salicylate preparations manufacturing
325188　Sodium silicate (i.e., water glass) manufacturing
325188　Sodium silicofluoride manufacturing
325188　Sodium stannate manufacturing
325188　Sodium sulfate manufacturing
212391　Sodium sulfate, natural, mining and/or beneficiating
325199　Sodium sulfoxalate formaldehyde manufacturing
325188　Sodium tetraborate manufacturing

325188　Sodium thiosulfate manufacturing
325188　Sodium tungstate manufacturing
325188　Sodium uranate manufacturing
335110　Sodium vapor lamp bulbs manufacturing
337121　Sofa beds and chair beds, upholstered, manufacturing
337121　Sofas, convertible (except futons), manufacturing
337121　Sofas, upholstered, manufacturing
722213　Soft drink beverage bars, nonalcoholic, fixed location
332431　Soft drink cans manufacturing
311930　Soft drink concentrates (i.e., syrup) manufacturing
445299　Soft drink stores, bottled
333311　Soft drink vending machines manufacturing
312111　Soft drinks manufacturing
424490　Soft drinks merchant wholesalers
311812　Soft pretzels made in a commercial bakery
325613　Softeners, leather or textile, manufacturing
541511　Software analysis and design services, custom computer
611420　Software application training
511210　Software computer, packaged, publishers
541519　Software installation services, computer
541511　Software programming services, custom computer
511210　Software publishers
511210　Software publishers, packaged
443120　Software stores, computer
423430　Software, computer, packaged, merchant wholesalers
334611　Software, packaged, mass reproducing
321912　Softwood dimension lumber and stock, resawing purchased lumber
325191　Softwood distillates manufacturing
321212　Softwood plywood composites manufacturing

321212	Softwood veneer or plywood manufacturing
238910	Soil compacting
924120	Soil conservation services, government
331511	Soil pipe, cast iron, manufacturing
562910	Soil remediation services
238910	Soil test drilling
325998	Soil testing kits manufacturing
541380	Soil testing laboratories or services
334413	Solar cells manufacturing
423690	Solar cells merchant wholesalers
926130	Solar energy regulation
333414	Solar energy heating equipment manufacturing
238220	Solar heating equipment installation
423720	Solar heating panels and equipment merchant wholesalers
333414	Solar heating systems manufacturing
335122	Solar lighting fixtures (except residential), electric, manufacturing
335121	Solar lighting fixtures, residential, electric, manufacturing
237130	Solar power structure construction
238160	Solar reflecting coating, roof, application
423330	Solar reflective film merchant wholesalers
334519	Solarimeters manufacturing
331491	Solder wire, nonferrous metals (except aluminum, copper), made from purchased metals or scrap
333992	Soldering equipment (except hand held) manufacturing
332212	Soldering guns and irons, handheld (including electric), manufacturing
332212	Soldering iron tips and tiplets manufacturing
335931	Solderless connectors (electric wiring devices) manufacturing
316110	Sole leather manufacturing
335314	Solenoid switches, industrial, manufacturing
332911	Solenoid valves (except fluid power), industrial-type, manufacturing
332912	Solenoid valves, fluid power, manufacturing
334419	Solenoids for electronic applications manufacturing
316999	Soles, boot and shoe, leather, manufacturing
541110	Solicitors' offices, private
922130	Solicitors' offices, government
541110	Solicitors' private practices
325188	Solid fuel propellants, inorganic, not specified elsewhere by process, manufacturing
562213	Solid waste combustors or incinerators, nonhazardous
562212	Solid waste landfills combined with collection and/or local hauling of nonhazardous waste materials
562212	Solid waste landfills, nonhazardous
711130	Soloists, independent musical
325132	Solvent dyes manufacturing
324110	Solvents made in petroleum refineries
334511	Sonabuoys manufacturing
423690	Sonar equipment merchant wholesalers
334511	Sonar fish finders manufacturing
334511	Sonar systems and equipment manufacturing
512230	Song publishers
512230	Song publishers and printing combined
711510	Song writers, independent
325612	Soot removing chemicals manufacturing
325199	Sorbitol manufacturing
111199	Sorghum farming, field and seed production
311211	Sorghum flour manufacturing
111998	Sorghum sudan seed farming

325222   Spandex fiber, filaments, and yarn manufacturing
113210   Spanish moss gathering
212399   Spar, iceland, mining and/or beneficiating
327113   Spark plug insulators, porcelain, manufacturing
334515   Spark plug testing instruments, electric, manufacturing
336322   Spark plugs for internal combustion engines manufacturing
312130   Sparkling wines manufacturing
321999   Spars, wood, manufacturing
713940   Spas without accommodations, fitness
316999   Spats, leather, manufacturing
326299   Spatulas, rubber, manufacturing
337129   Speaker cabinets (i.e., housings), wood, manufacturing
813410   Speakers' clubs
334310   Speaker systems manufacturing
711410   Speakers' bureaus
711510   Speakers, independent
325998   Spearmint oil manufacturing
711510   Special effect technicians, independent
512191   Special effects for motion picture production, post-production
516110   Special interest portals (e.g., parents sharing information about child rearing, etc.), Internet
485991   Special needs passenger transportation services
336211   Special purpose highway vehicle (e.g., firefighting vehicles) assembling on purchased chassis
336211   Special purpose highway vehicle (e.g., firefighting vehicles) bodies manufacturing
336120   Special purpose highway vehicles (e.g., firefighting vehicles) assembling on heavy chassis of own manufacture

423830   Special purpose industrial machinery and equipment merchant wholesalers
525990   Special purpose financial vehicles
445299   Specialty food stores
316110   Specialty leathers manufacturing
515210   Specialty television (e.g., music, sports, news) cable networks
335311   Specialty transformers, electric, manufacturing
424210   Specialty-line pharmaceuticals merchant wholesalers
334516   Specific ion measuring instruments, laboratory-type, manufacturing
238390   Spectator seating installation
334516   Spectrofluorometers manufacturing
334516   Spectrographs manufacturing
334516   Spectrometers (e.g., electron diffraction, mass, NMR, Raman) manufacturing
334519   Spectrometers (e.g., liquid scintillation, nuclear) manufacturing
334516   Spectrophotometers (e.g., atomic absorption, atomic emission, flame, fluorescence, infrared, Raman, visible) manufacturing
334515   Spectrum analyzers manufacturing
236220   Speculative builders (i.e., building on own land, for sale), commercial and institutional building
236210   Speculative builders (i.e., building on own land, for sale), industrial building (except warehouses)
236117   Speculative builders (i.e., building on own land, for sale), multifamily housing
236117   Speculative builders (i.e., building on own land, for sale), residential
236117   Speculative builders (i.e., building on own land, for sale), single-family housing
339112   Speculums manufacturing

541930 Speech (i.e., language) interpretation services
621340 Speech clinicians' offices (e.g., centers, clinics)
621340 Speech defect clinics
621340 Speech pathologists' offices (e.g., centers, clinics)
621340 Speech therapists' offices (e.g., centers, clinics)
333612 Speed changers (i.e., power transmission equipment) manufacturing
611699 Speed reading instruction
333612 Speed reducers (i.e., power transmission equipment) manufacturing
441310 Speed shops
334511 Speed, pitch, and roll navigational instruments and systems manufacturing
711212 Speedways
621991 Sperm banks, human
113210 Sphagnum moss gathering
212231 Sphalerite mining and/or beneficiating
339112 Sphygmomanometers manufacturing
111998 Spice farming
111419 Spice farming, grown under cover
311942 Spice grinding and blending
311942 Spice mixtures manufacturing
445299 Spice stores
311942 Spices and spice mix manufacturing
424490 Spices merchant wholesalers
331112 Spiegeleisen ferroalloys manufacturing
332913 Spigots, plumbing fixture fitting, manufacturing
321999 Spigots, wood, manufacturing
331111 Spike rods made in iron and steel mills
332618 Spikes made from purchased wire
331222 Spikes, iron or steel, made in wire drawing plants
423510 Spikes, metal, merchant wholesalers

237990 Spillway, floodwater, construction
111219 Spinach farming, field, bedding plant and seed production
333292 Spindles for textile machinery manufacturing
313111 Spinning carpet and rug yarn from purchased fiber
333292 Spinning machinery for textiles manufacturing
333513 Spinning machines, metalworking, manufacturing
332116 Spinning unfinished metal products
313111 Spinning yarn from purchased fiber
332618 Spiral cloth made from purchased wire
312140 Spirits, distilled (except brandy), manufacturing
424820 Spirits, distilled, merchant wholesalers
333513 Spline rolling machines, metalworking, manufacturing
321920 Splint baskets for fruits and vegetables, manufacturing
339113 Splints manufacturing
316110 Splits, leather, manufacturing
212393 Spodumene mining and/or beneficiating
321999 Spokes, wood, manufacturing
114119 Sponge gathering
331111 Sponge iron
424990 Sponges merchant wholesalers
332999 Sponges, metal scouring, manufacturing
326199 Sponges, plastics, manufacturing
326299 Sponges, rubber, manufacturing
313311 Sponging broadwoven fabrics
313312 Sponging textile products and fabrics (except broadwoven)
313112 Spooling of yarn
313112 Spooling of yarns for the trade
321999 Spools (except for textile machinery), wood, manufacturing
333292 Spools for textile machinery manufacturing

332211	Spoons, table, nonprecious and precious plated metal, manufacturing
315222	Sport coats (except fur, leather), men's and boys', cut and sewn from purchased fabric (except apparel contractors)
315292	Sport coats, fur (except apparel contractors), manufacturing
315211	Sport coats, fur, men's and boys', cut and sew apparel contractors
315292	Sport coats, leather (including artificial and tailored) (except apparel contractors), manufacturing
315211	Sport coats, leather (including artificial and tailored), men's and boys', cut and sew apparel contractors
315211	Sport coats, men's and boys', cut and sew apparel contractors
315211	Sport shirts, men's and boys', cut and sew apparel contractors
315223	Sport shirts, men's and boys', cut and sewn from purchased fabric (except apparel contractors)
532112	Sport utility vehicle leasing
423110	Sport utility vehicle merchant wholesalers
532111	Sport utility vehicle rental
336112	Sport utility vehicles assembling on chassis of own manufacture
811490	Sporting equipment repair and maintenance without retailing new sports equipment
423910	Sporting firearms and ammunition merchant wholesalers
339920	Sporting goods (except ammunition, clothing, footwear, small arms) manufacturing
423910	Sporting goods and supplies merchant wholesalers
532292	Sporting goods rental
451110	Sporting goods stores
453310	Sporting goods stores, used
711510	Sports announcers, independent
711310	Sports arena operators
611620	Sports camps (e.g., baseball, basketball, football), instructional
315228	Sports clothing (except team uniforms), men's and boys', cut and sewn from purchased fabric (except apparel contractors)
315239	Sports clothing (except team uniforms), women's, misses', and girls', cut and sewn from purchased fabric (except apparel contractors)
315191	Sports clothing made in apparel knitting mills
315211	Sports clothing, men's and boys', cut and sew apparel contractors
315299	Sports clothing, team uniforms, cut and sewn from purchased fabric (except apparel contractors)
315212	Sports clothing, women's and girls', cut and sew apparel contractors
713940	Sports club facilities, physical fitness
713990	Sports clubs (i.e., sports teams) not operating sports facilities, recreational
711211	Sports clubs, professional or semiprofessional
423910	Sports equipment and supplies merchant wholesalers
532292	Sports equipment rental
711310	Sports event managers with facilities
711320	Sports event managers without facilities
711310	Sports event organizers with facilities
711320	Sports event organizers without facilities
711310	Sports event promoters with facilities

423820 Sprinklers, agricultural, merchant wholesalers
332919 Sprinklers, lawn, manufacturing
333613 Sprockets, power transmission equipment, manufacturing
113210 Spruce gum gathering
213111 Spudding in oil and gas wells on a contract basis
313230 Spunbonded fabrics manufacturing
332212 Squares, carpenters', metal, manufacturing
713940 Squash club facilities
339920 Squash equipment (except apparel) manufacturing
111219 Squash farming, field, bedding plant and seed production
114112 Squid fishing
332999 Stabilizing bars, cargo, metal, manufacturing
711219 Stables, horse racing
713990 Stables, riding
423830 Stackers, industrial, merchant wholesalers
333924 Stackers, industrial, truck-type, manufacturing
333924 Stackers, portable (except farm), manufacturing
236220 Stadium and arena construction
711310 Stadium operators
337127 Stadium seating manufacturing
531120 Stadium rental or leasing without promotion of events
561330 Staff leasing services
335129 Stage lighting equipment manufacturing
711510 Stage set (e.g., concert, motion picture, television) erecting and dismantling, independent
327211 Stained glass and stained glass products made in glass making plants
238150 Stained glass installation
327215 Stained glass products made from purchased glass
331513 Stainless steel castings (except investment), unfinished, manufacturing
331111 Stainless steel made in iron and steel mills

325510 Stains (except biological) manufacturing
424950 Stains merchant wholesalers
325132 Stains, biological, manufacturing
332323 Stair railings, metal, manufacturing
321918 Stair railings, wood, manufacturing
332323 Stair treads, metal, manufacturing
326299 Stair treads, rubber, manufacturing
332323 Staircases, metal, manufacturing
332323 Stairs, metal, manufacturing
238190 Stairway, metal, installation
238120 Stairway, precast concrete, installation
238350 Stairway, wood, installation
333921 Stairways, moving, manufacturing
321918 Stairwork (e.g., newel posts, railings, staircases, stairs), wood, manufacturing
321999 Stakes, surveyor's, wood, manufacturing
333111 Stalk choppers (i.e., shredders) manufacturing
332323 Stalls, metal, manufacturing
325998 Stamp pad ink manufacturing
339943 Stamp pads manufacturing
339943 Stamping devices, hand operated, manufacturing
333513 Stamping machines, metalworking, manufacturing
336370 Stamping metal motor vehicle body parts
336370 Stamping metal motor vehicle moldings and trims
332116 Stampings (except automotive, cans, cooking, closures, crowns), metal, unfinished, manufacturing
713210 Stand alone casinos (except slot machine parlors)
334515 Standards and calibration equipment for electrical measuring manufacturing
813920 Standards review committees, professional

926150 Standards, setting and management, agencies, government

334515 Standing wave ratio measuring equipment manufacturing

337215 Stands (except wire), merchandise display, manufacturing

711510 Standup comedians, independent

325188 Stannic and stannous chloride manufacturing

339942 Staple removers manufacturing

333991 Staplers and nailers, handheld power-driven, manufacturing

339942 Staplers manufacturing

332618 Staples made from purchased wire

423710 Staples merchant wholesalers

331222 Staples, iron or steel, made in wire drawing plants

325520 Starch glues manufacturing

311221 Starches (except laundry) manufacturing

325612 Starches, laundry, manufacturing

112310 Started pullet production

336322 Starter and starter parts for internal combustion engines manufacturing

522110 State commercial banks

522130 State credit unions

928120 State Department

923110 State education departments

561310 State operated employment job services offices

922120 State police

522120 State savings and loan associations

522120 State savings banks

921130 State tax commissions

334413 Static converters, integrated circuits, manufacturing

334512 Static pressure regulators manufacturing

332410 Stationary power boilers manufacturing

327112 Stationery articles, pottery, manufacturing

323112 Stationery, flexographic printing, on a job-order basis

323111 Stationery, gravure printing, on a job-order basis

323110 Stationery, lithographic (offset) printing, on a job-order basis

322233 Stationery made from purchased paper

323114 Stationery, quick printing, on a job-order basis

323113 Stationery, screen printing, on a job-order basis

453210 Stationery stores

424120 Stationery supplies merchant wholesalers

335312 Stators for motors manufacturing

327420 Statuary (e.g., gypsum, plaster of paris) manufacturing

424990 Statuary goods (except religious) merchant wholesalers

327112 Statuary, clay and ceramic, manufacturing

327991 Statuary, marble, manufacturing

327999 Statuary, vases, and urns, papier-mache, manufacturing

238990 Statue erection

212399 Staurolite mining and/or beneficiating

321920 Staves, barrel, sawed or split, manufacturing

316999 Stays, shoe, leather, manufacturing

722110 Steak houses, full service

722211 Steak houses, limited-service

812199 Steam baths

561790 Steam cleaning building exteriors

213112 Steam cleaning oil and gas wells on a contract basis

332410 Steam condensers manufacturing

333319 Steam cookers, commercial-type, manufacturing

335211 Steam cookers, household-type, manufacturing

611513 Steam fitters' apprenticeship training

238220 Steam fitting contractors

332919	Steam fittings, metal, manufacturing
221330	Steam heat distribution
333414	Steam heating equipment manufacturing
221330	Steam heating systems (i.e., suppliers of heat)
334512	Steam pressure controls, residential and commercial heating-type, manufacturing
221330	Steam production and distribution
333999	Steam separating machinery manufacturing
221330	Steam supply systems, including geothermal
333319	Steam tables manufacturing
487110	Steam train excursions
332911	Steam traps, industrial-type, manufacturing
333611	Steam turbine generator set units manufacturing
333611	Steam turbines manufacturing
532411	Steamship rental or leasing without operator
325199	Stearic acid esters manufacturing
325199	Stearic acid manufacturing
325199	Stearic acid salts manufacturing
311613	Stearin, animal, rendering
212399	Steatite mining and/or beneficiating
327113	Steatite porcelain insulators manufacturing
331111	Steel balls made in iron and steel mills
332431	Steel cans, light gauge metal, manufacturing
331513	Steel castings (except investment), unfinished, manufacturing
332111	Steel forgings made from purchased steel, unfinished
331513	Steel foundries (except investment)
238130	Steel framing contractors
331512	Steel investment castings, unfinished, manufacturing
331512	Steel investment foundries
332312	Steel joists manufacturing
331111	Steel manufacturing
423510	Steel merchant wholesalers
236210	Steel mill construction
331111	Steel mill products (e.g., bar, plate, rod, sheet, structural shapes) manufacturing
331111	Steel mills
332312	Steel railroad car racks manufacturing
238120	Steel reinforcing contractors
327910	Steel shot abrasives manufacturing
332999	Steel wool manufacturing
423510	Steel wool merchant wholesalers
331111	Steel, from pig iron, manufacturing
238160	Steep slope roofing installation
238990	Steeplejack work
311221	Steepwater concentrate manufacturing
336330	Steering boxes, manual and power assist, manufacturing
336330	Steering columns, automotive, truck, and bus, manufacturing
336330	Steering wheels, automotive, truck, and bus, manufacturing
327215	Stemware made from purchased glass
327212	Stemware, glass, made in glass making plants
325910	Stencil inks manufacturing
339944	Stencil paper manufacturing
339943	Stencils for painting and marking (e.g., cardboard, metal) manufacturing
561410	Stenographic services (except court or stenographic reporting)
333313	Stenography machinery manufacturing
561492	Stenography services, public
561492	Stenotype recording services
332999	Stepladders, metal, manufacturing
321999	Stepladders, wood, manufacturing
337129	Stereo cabinets (i.e., housings), wood, manufacturing
423620	Stereo equipment merchant wholesalers

212399	Stones, abrasive (e.g., emery, grindstones, hones, pumice), mining and/or beneficiating
423940	Stones, precious and semiprecious, merchant wholesalers
327999	Stones, synthetic, for gem stones and industrial use, manufacturing
327112	Stoneware (i.e., pottery products) manufacturing
212325	Stoneware clay mining and/or beneficiating
238140	Stonework (i.e., masonry) contractors
337124	Stools, metal household-type (except upholstered), manufacturing
337122	Stools, wood household-type (except upholstered), manufacturing
621999	Stop smoking clinics
332911	Stop valves, industrial-type, manufacturing
332913	Stopcock drains, plumbing, manufacturing
321999	Stoppers, cork, manufacturing
326299	Stoppers, rubber, manufacturing
423610	Storage batteries (except automotive) merchant wholesalers
335911	Storage batteries manufacturing
335312	Storage battery chargers (except internal combustion engine-type) manufacturing
423390	Storage bins merchant wholesalers
334112	Storage devices, computer, manufacturing
236220	Storage elevator construction
486210	Storage of natural gas
237120	Storage tank, natural gas or oil, tank farm or field construction
332420	Storage tanks, heavy gauge metal, manufacturing
423510	Storage tanks, metal, merchant wholesalers
236220	Store construction

541850	Store display advertising services
337215	Store display fixtures manufacturing
423440	Store equipment (except furniture) merchant wholesalers
423440	Store fixtures (except refrigerated) merchant wholesalers
238190	Store front, metal or metal frame, installation
423210	Store furniture merchant wholesalers
******	Stores—see type
562998	Storm basin cleanout services
332321	Storm doors and windows, metal, manufacturing
321911	Storm doors and windows, wood framed, manufacturing
237110	Storm sewer construction
711510	Storytellers, independent
312120	Stout brewing
332322	Stove boards, sheet metal (except stampings), manufacturing
327123	Stove lining, clay, manufacturing
332322	Stove pipes and flues, sheet metal (except stampings), manufacturing
811412	Stove, household-type, repair and maintenance services without retailing new stoves
335221	Stoves, ceramic disk element, household-type, manufacturing
333319	Stoves, commercial-type, manufacturing
423720	Stoves, cooking and heating (except electric), household-type, merchant wholesalers
335221	Stoves, household-type cooking, manufacturing
333924	Straddle carriers, mobile, manufacturing
332211	Straight razors manufacturing
332911	Straightway (i.e., Y-type) valves, industrial-type, manufacturing

333999 Strainers, pipeline, manufacturing

321219 Strandboard, oriented, manufacturing

332618 Stranded wire, uninsulated, made from purchased wire

316110 Strap leather manufacturing

332999 Strappings, metal, manufacturing

316999 Straps (except watch), leather, manufacturing

316993 Straps, watch (except metal), manufacturing

339911 Straps, watch, precious metal, manufacturing

541611 Strategic planning consulting services

213112 Stratigraphic drilling, oil and gas field exploration on a contract basis

321999 Straw baskets manufacturing

315991 Straw hats manufacturing

424910 Straw merchant wholesalers

111333 Strawberry farming

488490 Street cleaning service

237310 Street construction

335129 Street lighting fixtures (except traffic signals) manufacturing

516110 Street map and guide publishers, exclusively on Internet

511130 Street map guide publishers (except exclusive Internet publishing)

485119 Street railway systems (except mixed mode), commuter

423810 Street sweeping and cleaning equipment merchant wholesalers

454390 Street vendors (except food)

722330 Street vendors, food

238990 Street, interlocking brick (i.e., not mortared), installation

237990 Streetcar line construction

336510 Streetcars and car equipment, urban transit, manufacturing

713940 Strength development centers

336211 Stretch limousines assembling on purchased chassis

321999 Stretchers, curtain, wood, manufacturing

339113 Stretchers, medical, manufacturing

333513 Stretching machines, metalworking, manufacturing

111219 String bean farming, field and seed production

314991 Strings (except musical instrument) manufacturing

339992 Strings, musical instrument, manufacturing

212113 Strip mining, anthracite, on own account

212111 Strip mining, bituminous coal or lignite, on own account

212111 Strip mining, lignite, on own account

331421 Strip, copper and copper alloy, made from purchased copper or in integrated secondary smelting and rolling, drawing or extruding plants

331111 Strip, galvanized iron or steel, made in iron and steel mills

331111 Strip, iron or steel, made in iron and steel mills

331491 Strip, nonferrous metals (except aluminum, copper), made from purchased metals or scrap

211111 Stripper well production

213113 Stripping overburden services for coal mining on a contract basis

213114 Stripping overburden services for metal mining on a contract basis

213115 Stripping overburden services for nonmetallic minerals mining (except fuels) on a contract basis

334515 Stroboscopes manufacturing

335110 Strobotrons manufacturing

339932 Strollers, baby, manufacturing

212393 Strontianite mining and/or beneficiating

325188 Strontium carbonate manufacturing

325188 Strontium compounds, not specified elsewhere by process, manufacturing

212393 Strontium mineral mining and/or beneficiating

325188 Strontium nitrate manufacturing

423510 Structural assemblies, metal, merchant wholesalers

423390 Structural assemblies, prefabricated (except wood), merchant wholesalers

423310 Structural assemblies, prefabricated wood, merchant wholesalers

423320 Structural clay tile (except refractory) merchant wholesalers

327121 Structural clay tile manufacturing

321114 Structural lumber and timber, treating

321213 Structural members, glue laminated or pre-engineered wood, manufacturing

333516 Structural rolling mill machinery, metalworking, manufacturing

331319 Structural shapes made by rolling purchased aluminum

331319 Structural shapes, aluminum, made in integrated secondary smelting and rolling mills

331111 Structural shapes, iron or steel, made in iron and steel mills

238120 Structural steel contractors

332312 Structural steel, fabricated, manufacturing

339932 Structural toy sets manufacturing

321213 Structural wood members (except trusses), fabricated, manufacturing

336330 Struts, automotive, truck, and bus, manufacturing

325411 Strychnine and derivatives (i.e., basic chemicals) manufacturing

327999 Stucco and stucco products manufacturing

238140 Stucco contractors

321113 Stud mills

115210 Stud services

238130 Stud wall (e.g., wood, steel) installation

813410 Student clubs

611710 Student exchange programs

522291 Student loan companies

522294 Student Loan Marketing Association (SLMA)

813410 Students' associations

813410 Students' unions

334220 Studio equipment, radio and television broadcasting, manufacturing

541430 Studios, commercial art

321912 Studs, resawing purchased lumber

332322 Studs, sheet metal (except stampings), manufacturing

921120 Study commissions, legislative

339931 Stuffed toys (including animals) manufacturing

333294 Stuffer, sausage machinery, manufacturing

113310 Stump removing in the field

325212 S-type rubber manufacturing

325920 Styphnic acid explosive materials manufacturing

325110 Styrene made from refined petroleum or liquid hydrocarbons

324110 Styrene made in petroleum refineries

325211 Styrene resins manufacturing

325211 Styrene-acrylonitrile resins manufacturing

325212 Styrene-butadiene rubber containing less than 50 percent styrene manufacturing

325212 Styrene-chloroprene rubber manufacturing

325212 Styrene-isoprene rubber manufacturing

238310 Styrofoam insulation installation

212111 Subbituminous coal surface mining and/or beneficiating

212112 Subbituminous coal underground mining or mining and beneficiating

237210 Subdividers, real estate

237210 Subdividing real estate
332994 Submachine guns manufacturing
336611 Submarine building
333514 Subpresses, machine tool, manufacturing
334210 Subscriber loop equipment, telephone, manufacturing
515210 Subscription television networks
551114 Subsidiary management offices
623220 Substance abuse (i.e., alcoholism, drug addiction) halfway houses
623220 Substance abuse facilities, residential
813319 Substance abuse prevention advocacy organizations
621420 Substance abuse treatment centers and clinics (except hospitals), outpatient
237130 Substation and switching station, power transmission line, construction
335311 Substation transformers, electric power distribution, manufacturing
512191 Subtitling of motion picture film or video
485113 Suburban bus line services (except mixed mode)
485112 Suburban commuter rail systems (except mixed mode)
485111 Suburban transit systems, mixed mode (e.g., bus, commuter rail, subway combinations)
541850 Subway card display advertising services
336510 Subway cars manufacturing
423860 Subway cars merchant wholesalers
237990 Subway construction
485119 Subway systems (except mixed mode), commuter
339112 Suction therapy apparatus manufacturing
812320 Suede garment cleaning services
313311 Sueding broadwoven fabrics
313312 Sueding textile products and fabrics (except broadwoven)
111991 Sugar beet farming
115113 Sugar beets, machine harvesting

311221 Sugar made by wet milling corn
333294 Sugar refining machinery manufacturing
325998 Sugar substitutes (i.e., synthetic sweeteners blended with other ingredients) made from purchased synthetic sweeteners
325199 Sugar substitutes (i.e., synthetic sweeteners blended with other ingredients) made in synthetic sweetener establishments
311312 Sugar, cane, made from purchased raw cane sugar
311311 Sugar, clarified, granulated, and raw, made in sugarcane mill
311312 Sugar, confectionery, made from purchased raw cane sugar
311313 Sugar, confectionery, made from sugar beets
311311 Sugar, confectionery, made in sugarcane mill
311312 Sugar, granulated, made from purchased raw cane sugar
311313 Sugar, granulated, made from sugar beets
311311 Sugar, granulated, made in sugarcane mill
311312 Sugar, invert, made from purchased raw cane sugar
311313 Sugar, invert, made from sugar beets
311311 Sugar, invert, made in sugarcane mill
311313 Sugar, liquid, made from sugar beets
311311 Sugar, raw, made in sugarcane mill
424590 Sugar, raw, merchant wholesalers
311312 Sugar, refined, made from purchased raw cane sugar
424490 Sugar, refined, merchant wholesalers
111930 Sugarcane farming, field production
311311 Sugarcane mills
311311 Sugarcane refining
115113 Sugarcane, machine harvesting

624190	Suicide crisis centers
532220	Suit rental
315999	Suit trimmings cut and sewn from purchased fabric (except apparel contractors)
315211	Suit trimmings, men's and boys', cut and sew apparel contractors
332510	Suitcase hardware, metal, manufacturing
316991	Suitcases, all materials, manufacturing
315211	Suits (i.e., nontailored, tailored, work), men's and boys', cut and sew apparel contractors
315212	Suits (i.e., nontailored, tailored, work), women's, misses', girls', and infants', cut and sew apparel contractors
315191	Suits made in apparel knitting mills
339113	Suits, firefighting, manufacturing
315291	Suits, infants' (e.g., warm-up, jogging, snowsuits), cut and sewn from purchased fabric (except apparel contractors)
424320	Suits, men's and boys', merchant wholesalers
315239	Suits, nontailored (e.g., jogging, snowsuit, warm-up), women's, misses', and girls', cut and sewn from purchased fabric (except apparel contractors)
315228	Suits, nontailored (e.g., jogging, snow, ski, warm-up), men's and boys', cut and sewn from purchased fabric (except apparel contractors)
339113	Suits, space, manufacturing
315222	Suits, tailored, men's and boys', cut and sewn from purchased fabric (except apparel contractors)
315234	Suits, tailored, women's, misses', and girls', cut and sewn from purchased fabric (except apparel contractors)

325411	Sulfa drugs, uncompounded, manufacturing
212391	Sulfate, sodium, mining and/or beneficiating
325188	Sulfides and sulfites manufacturing
325188	Sulfocyanides manufacturing
325411	Sulfonamides, uncompounded, manufacturing
325188	Sulfur and sulfur compounds, not specified elsewhere by process, manufacturing
325188	Sulfur chloride manufacturing
325188	Sulfur dioxide manufacturing
325188	Sulfur hexafluoride gas manufacturing
325320	Sulfur insecticides manufacturing
212393	Sulfur mining and/or beneficiating
211112	Sulfur recovered from natural gas
325188	Sulfur recovering or refining (except from sour natural gas)
212393	Sulfur, native, mining and/or beneficiating
325188	Sulfuric acid manufacturing
424690	Sulfuric acid merchant wholesalers
325192	Sulphonated derivatives manufacturing
311423	Sulphured fruits and vegetables manufacturing
325191	Sumac extract manufacturing
721214	Summer camps (except day, instructional)
713990	Summer day camps (except instructional)
721110	Summer resort hotels without casinos
711110	Summer theaters
238220	Sump pump installation
333911	Sump pumps, residential-type, manufacturing
115114	Sun drying of dates, prunes, raisins, and olives
115114	Sun drying of fruits and vegetables
115114	Sun drying of tomatoes
812199	Sun tanning salons

111120 Sunflower farming, field and seed production
311223 Sunflower seed oil, cake and meal, made in crushing mills
446130 Sunglass stores
339115 Sunglasses and goggles manufacturing
423460 Sunglasses merchant wholesalers
336399 Sunroofs and parts, automotive, truck, and bus, manufacturing
236118 Sun-room additions, residential
325620 Sunscreen lotions and oils manufacturing
315291 Sunsuits, infants', cut and sewn from purchased fabric (except apparel contractors)
325620 Suntan lotions and oils manufacturing
331111 Superalloys, iron or steel, manufacturing
331492 Superalloys, nonferrous based, made from purchased metals or scrap
445110 Supermarkets
325312 Superphosphates manufacturing
452910 Superstores (i.e., food and general merchandise)
921190 Supply agencies, government
332913 Supply line assemblies, plumbing (i.e., flexible hose with fittings), manufacturing
624190 Support group services
339113 Supports, orthopedic (e.g., abdominal, ankle, arch, kneecap), manufacturing
325412 Suppositories manufacturing
524126 Surety insurance carriers, direct
325613 Surface active agents manufacturing
424690 Surface active agents merchant wholesalers
334516 Surface area analyzers manufacturing
334512 Surface burner controls, temperature, manufacturing
322226 Surface coating purchased paperboard

333120 Surface mining machinery (except drilling) manufacturing
333295 Surface mount machinery for making printed circuit boards manufacturing
237310 Surfacing, highway, road, street, bridge or airport runway
532292 Surfboard rental
339920 Surfboards manufacturing
335999 Surge suppressors manufacturing
621111 Surgeons' (except dental) offices (e.g., centers, clinics)
541940 Surgeons' offices, veterinary
621210 Surgeons', dental, offices (e.g., centers, clinics)
115112 Surgery on trees and vines
541940 Surgery services, veterinary
423450 Surgical appliances merchant wholesalers
339112 Surgical clamps manufacturing
339113 Surgical dressings manufacturing
339113 Surgical implants manufacturing
811219 Surgical instrument repair and maintenance services
423450 Surgical instruments and apparatus merchant wholesalers
339112 Surgical knife blades and handles manufacturing
621111 Surgical pathologists' offices (e.g., centers, clinics)
339112 Surgical stapling devices manufacturing
339113 Surgical supplies (except medical instruments) manufacturing
423450 Surgical supplies merchant wholesalers
334510 Surgical support systems (e.g., heart-lung machines) (except iron lungs) manufacturing
423450 Surgical towels merchant wholesalers
311711 Surimi canning
311712 Surimi, fresh and frozen, manufacturing

238210   Surveillance system, installation only

213112   Surveying (except seismographic) oil or gas wells on a contract basis

541370   Surveying and mapping services (except geophysical)

423490   Surveying equipment and supplies merchant wholesalers

811219   Surveying instrument repair and maintenance services

334519   Surveying instruments manufacturing

541360   Surveying services, geophysical

321999   Surveyor's stakes, wood, manufacturing

611699   Survival training instruction

238310   Suspended ceiling installation

315999   Suspenders cut and sewn from purchased fabric (except apparel contractors)

315211   Suspenders, men's and boys', cut and sew apparel contractors

315212   Suspenders, women's, girls', and infants', cut and sew apparel contractors

811118   Suspension repair shops, automotive

339113   Sutures, surgical, manufacturing

213112   Swabbing oil or gas wells on a contract basis

333513   Swaging machines, metalworking, manufacturing

487210   Swamp buggy operation

323121   Swatches and samples, mounting for the trade

332999   Swatters, fly, metal, manufacturing

315299   Sweat bands cut and sewn from purchased fabric (except apparel contractors)

315191   Sweat bands made in apparel knitting mills

315211   Sweat bands, men's and boys', cut and sew apparel contractors

315212   Sweat bands, women's, girls', and infants', cut and sew apparel contractors

315191   Sweat pants made in apparel knitting mills

315291   Sweat pants, infants', cut and sewn from purchased fabric (except apparel contractors)

315228   Sweat pants, men's, boys', and unisex (i.e., sized without regard to gender), cut and sewn from purchased fabric (except apparel contractors)

315211   Sweat pants, men's, boys', and unisex, cut and sew apparel contractors

315212   Sweat pants, women's, girls', and infants', cut and sew apparel contractors

315239   Sweat pants, women's, misses', and girls', cut and sewn from purchased fabric (except apparel contractors)

315191   Sweat suits made in apparel knitting mills

315291   Sweat suits, infants', cut and sewn from purchased fabric (except apparel contractors)

315211   Sweat suits, men's and boys', cut and sew apparel contractors

315228   Sweat suits, men's and boys', cut and sewn from purchased fabric (except apparel contractors)

315212   Sweat suits, women's, girls', and infants', cut and sew apparel contractors

315239   Sweat suits, women's, misses', and girls', cut and sewn from purchased fabric (except apparel contractors)

316110   Sweatband leather manufacturing

315191   Sweater jackets made in apparel knitting mills

315291   Sweater jackets, infants', cut and sewn from purchased fabric (except apparel contractors)

315211   Sweater jackets, men's and boys', cut and sew apparel contractors

333319	Swimming pool filter systems manufacturing
333414	Swimming pool heaters manufacturing
335129	Swimming pool lighting fixtures manufacturing
238990	Swimming pool screen enclosure construction
453998	Swimming pool supply stores
236220	Swimming pool, indoor, construction
238990	Swimming pool, outdoor, construction
713940	Swimming pools
423910	Swimming pools and equipment merchant wholesalers
339920	Swimming pools, above ground, manufacturing
326199	Swimming pools, fiberglass, manufacturing
315191	Swimsuits made in apparel knitting mills
315291	Swimsuits, infants', cut and sewn from purchased fabric (except apparel contractors)
315211	Swimsuits, men's and boys', cut and sew apparel contractors
315228	Swimsuits, men's and boys', cut and sewn from purchased fabric (except apparel contractors)
315212	Swimsuits, women's, girls', and infants', cut and sew apparel contractors
315239	Swimsuits, women's, misses', and girls', cut and sewn from purchased fabric (except apparel contractors)
448190	Swimwear stores
424320	Swimwear, men's and boys', merchant wholesalers
424330	Swimwear, women's, children's, and infants', merchant wholesalers
311119	Swine feed, complete, manufacturing
311119	Swine feed, supplements, concentrates, and premixes, manufacturing
424520	Swine merchant wholesalers
335932	Switch boxes, electrical wiring, manufacturing
335931	Switch cutouts manufacturing
335313	Switchboards and parts, power, manufacturing
423610	Switchboards, electrical distribution, merchant wholesalers
335931	Switches for electrical wiring (e.g., pressure, pushbutton, snap, tumbler) manufacturing
334419	Switches for electronic applications manufacturing
335313	Switches, electric power (except pushbotton, snap, solenoid, tumbler), manufacturing
423610	Switches, electrical, merchant wholesalers
423690	Switches, electronic, merchant wholesalers
335931	Switches, outlet box mounting-type, manufacturing
334512	Switches, pneumatic positioning remote, manufacturing
334512	Switches, thermostatic, manufacturing
335313	Switchgear and switchgear accessories manufacturing
335313	Switching equipment, power, manufacturing
334210	Switching equipment, telephone, manufacturing
488210	Switching services, railroad
114111	Swordfish fishing
332211	Swords, nonprecious and precious plated metal, manufacturing
212313	Syenite (except nepheline) crushed and broken stone mining and/or beneficiating
212311	Syenite (except nepheline) mining or quarrying
212325	Syenite, nepheline, mining and/or beneficiating
212221	Sylvanite mining and/or beneficiating
711130	Symphony orchestras
813110	Synagogues

337122	Tables, wood household-type, manufacturing
337211	Tables, wood, office-type, manufacturing
322233	Tablets (e.g., memo, note, writing) made from purchased paper
322121	Tablets (e.g., memo, note, writing) made in paper mills
332999	Tablets, metal, manufacturing
423220	Tableware (except disposable, plated, precious) merchant wholesalers
327215	Tableware made from purchased glass
327212	Tableware made in glass making plants
532299	Tableware rental
424130	Tableware, disposable, merchant wholesalers
423940	Tableware, precious and plated, merchant wholesalers
327112	Tableware, vitreous china, manufacturing
334515	Tachometer generators manufacturing
451110	Tack shops
321999	Tackle blocks, wood, manufacturing
451110	Tackle shops (i.e., fishing)
339920	Tackle, fishing (except line, nets, seines), manufacturing
423710	Tacks merchant wholesalers
331222	Tacks, iron or steel, made in wire drawing plants
332618	Tacks, metal, made from purchased wire
212210	Taconite concentrates or agglomerates beneficiating
212210	Taconite ores mining and/or beneficiating
334511	Taffrail logs manufacturing
213111	Tailing in oil and gas field wells on a contract basis
811490	Tailor shops, alterations only
315211	Tailored dress and sport coats, men's and boys', cut and sew apparel contractors
315222	Tailored dress and sport coats, men's and boys', cut and sewn from purchased fabric (except apparel contractors)
332211	Tailors' scissors, nonelectric, manufacturing
423850	Tailors' supplies merchant wholesalers
******	Tailors—see specific apparel manufacturing
722211	Take out eating places
212399	Talc mining and/or beneficiating
327992	Talc processing beyond beneficiation
325620	Talcum powders manufacturing
711410	Talent agencies
711410	Talent agents
541214	Talent payment services
325191	Tall oil (except skimmings) manufacturing
311611	Tallow produced in a slaughtering plant
311613	Tallow produced in rendering plant
334514	Tally counters manufacturing
334514	Tallying meters (except clocks, electricity meters, watches) manufacturing
333120	Tampers, powered, manufacturing
332995	Tampion guns manufacturing
111320	Tangelo groves
111320	Tangerine groves
332995	Tank artillery manufacturing
336211	Tank bodies for trucks manufacturing
562998	Tank cleaning and disposal services, commercial or industrial
562991	Tank cleaning services, septic
238990	Tank lining contractors
315291	Tank tops, infants', cut and sewn from purchased fabric (except apparel contractors)
315211	Tank tops, men's and boys', cut and sew apparel contractors
315191	Tank tops, outerwear, made in apparel knitting mills

1372   NORTH AMERICAN INDUSTRY CLASSIFICATION SYSTEM

423690	Tapes, blank, audio and video, merchant wholesalers
424120	Tapes, cellophane, merchant wholesalers
334613	Tapes, magnetic recording (i.e., audio, data, video), blank, manufacturing
339113	Tapes, medical adhesive, manufacturing
423450	Tapes, medical and surgical, merchant wholesalers
313230	Tapes, nonwoven fabric, manufacturing
423990	Tapes, prerecorded, audio or video, merchant wholesalers
334519	Tapes, surveyor's, manufacturing
424310	Tapes, textile, merchant wholesalers
313320	Tapes, varnished and coated (except magnetic), made from purchased fabric
238310	Taping and finishing drywall
311221	Tapioca manufacturing
333512	Tapping machines, metalworking, manufacturing
333515	Taps and dies (i.e., a machine tool accessory) manufacturing
335931	Taps, current, attachment plug and screw shell types, manufacturing
316999	Taps, shoe, leather, manufacturing
325211	Tar acid resins manufacturing
324121	Tar and asphalt paving mixtures made from purchased asphaltic materials
325191	Tar and tar oils made by distillation of wood
325192	Tar made by distillation of coal tar
324110	Tar made in petroleum refineries
324122	Tar paper made from purchased asphaltic materials and paper
324122	Tar paper, building and roofing, made from purchased paper
322121	Tar paper, building and roofing, made in paper mills

324122	Tar roofing cements and coatings made from purchased asphaltic materials
211111	Tar sands mining
336411	Target drones, aircraft, manufacturing
336413	Targets, trailer type, aircraft, manufacturing
541614	Tariff rate consulting services
541614	Tariff rate information services
111219	Taro farming, field and seed production
314912	Tarpaulins made from purchased fabrics
423330	Tarred felts merchant wholesalers
237310	Tarring roads
311941	Tartar sauce manufacturing
325199	Tartaric acid manufacturing
325199	Tartrates, not specified elsewhere by process, manufacturing
812199	Tattoo parlors
722410	Taverns (i.e., drinking places)
561440	Tax collection services on a contract or fee basis
541110	Tax law attorneys' offices
541110	Tax law attorneys' private practices
523910	Tax liens dealing (i.e., acting as a principal in dealing tax liens to investors)
541213	Tax return preparation services
921130	Taxation departments
541850	Taxicab card advertising services
485310	Taxicab dispatch services
485310	Taxicab fleet operators
423110	Taxicab merchant wholesalers
485310	Taxicab organizations
485310	Taxicab owner-operators
485310	Taxicab services
711510	Taxidermists, independent
423850	Taxidermy supplies merchant wholesalers
334514	Taximeters manufacturing
813319	Taxpayers' advocacy organizations
311920	Tea (except herbal) manufacturing

445299 Tea and coffee (i.e., packaged) stores

311920 Tea blending

111998 Tea farming

424490 Tea merchant wholesalers

311920 Tea, herbal, manufacturing

312111 Tea, iced, manufacturing

311920 Tea, instant, manufacturing

113210 Teaberries gathering

923110 Teacher certification bureaus

561310 Teacher registries

333319 Teaching machines (e.g., flight simulators) manufacturing

423490 Teaching machines (except computers), electronic, merchant wholesalers

332214 Teakettles and coffee pots, fabricated metal (except electric, glass), manufacturing

335211 Teakettles, electric, manufacturing

327212 Teakettles, glass and glass ceramic, made in glass making plants

315299 Team athletic uniforms cut and sewn from purchased fabric (except apparel contractors)

315211 Team athletic uniforms, men's and boys', cut and sew apparel contractors

315212 Team athletic uniforms, women's and girls', cut and sew apparel contractors

325199 Tear gas manufacturing

313311 Teaseling broadwoven fabrics

313312 Teaseling fabrics (except broadwoven)

325412 Technetium medicinal preparations manufacturing

327212 Technical glassware and glass products, pressed or blown, made in glass making plants

327215 Technical glassware made from purchased glass

511120 Technical magazine and periodical publishers (except exclusive Internet publishing)

511120 Technical magazine and periodical publishers and printing combined

516110 Technical magazine and periodical publishers, exclusively on Internet

323112 Technical magazines and periodicals flexographic printing without publishing

323111 Technical magazines and periodicals gravure printing without publishing

323110 Technical magazines and periodicals lithographic (offset) printing without publishing

323119 Technical magazines and periodicals printing (except flexographic, gravure, lithographic, quick, screen) without publishing

323113 Technical magazines and periodicals screen printing without publishing

511130 Technical manual and paperback book publishers (except exclusive Internet publishing)

511130 Technical manual and paperback book publishers and printing combined

323121 Technical manual paper (books) binding without printing

511130 Technical manual publishers (except exclusive Internet publishing)

516110 Technical manual publishers, exclusively on Internet

323117 Technical manuals and papers (books) printing and binding without publishing

323117 Technical manuals and papers (books) printing without publishing

711510 Technical writers, independent

315212 Teddies, women's, cut and sew apparel contractors

315231 Teddies, women's, misses', and girls', cut and sewn from purchased fabric (except apparel contractors)

624110 Teen outreach services

339114	Teeth (except customized) manufacturing
339116	Teeth, custom made in dental laboratories
423450	Teeth, dental, merchant wholesalers
517212	Telecommunications carriers, cellular telephone
517110	Telecommunications carriers, wired
238210	Telecommunications equipment and wiring (except transmission line) installation contractors
532490	Telecommunications equipment rental or leasing
541618	Telecommunications management consulting services
517110	Telecommunications networks, wired
517310	Telecommunications resellers
561499	Teleconferencing services
517110	Telegram services (except wireless)
812990	Telegram services, singing
423690	Telegraph equipment merchant wholesalers
561422	Telemarketing bureaus
561422	Telemarketing services on a contract or fee basis
334513	Telemetering instruments, industrial process-type, manufacturing
517910	Telemetry and tracking system operations on a contract or fee basis
334416	Telephone and telegraph transformers, electronic component-type, manufacturing
334210	Telephone answering machines manufacturing
423620	Telephone answering machines merchant wholesalers
561421	Telephone answering services
337215	Telephone booths manufacturing
5o1422	Telephone call centers

334210	Telephone carrier line equipment manufacturing
334210	Telephone carrier switching equipment manufacturing
517110	Telephone carriers, facilities-based (except wireless)
517410	Telephone communications carriers, satellite
517212	Telephone communications carriers, wireless (except satellite)
517310	Telephone communications resellers (except satellite)
624190	Telephone counseling services
323112	Telephone directories flexographic printing without publishing
323111	Telephone directories gravure printing without publishing
323110	Telephone directories lithographic (offset) printing without publishing
323119	Telephone directories printing (except flexographic, gravure, lithographic, quick, screen) without publishing
323113	Telephone directories screen printing without publishing
541870	Telephone directory distribution services, door-to-door
511140	Telephone directory publishers (except exclusive Internet publishing)
511140	Telephone directory publishers and printing combined
516110	Telephone directory publishers, exclusively on Internet
238210	Telephone equipment and building wiring installation
423690	Telephone equipment merchant wholesalers
811213	Telephone equipment repair and maintenance services without retailing new telephone equipment
517110	Telephone installation by telecommunications carriers, wired
238210	Telephone installation contractors

334512	Temperature controls, automatic, residential and commercial-types, manufacturing
334513	Temperature instruments, industrial process-type (except glass and bimetal thermometers), manufacturing
334512	Temperature sensors for motor windings manufacturing
327215	Tempered glass made from purchased glass
332811	Tempering metals and metal products for the trade
331111	Template, made in iron and steel mills, manufacturing
334519	Templates, drafting, manufacturing
339115	Temples and fronts (i.e., eyeglass frames), ophthalmic, manufacturing
813110	Temples, religious
561320	Temporary employment services
561320	Temporary help services
624221	Temporary housing for families of medical patients
624221	Temporary shelters (e.g., battered women's, homeless, runaway youth)
561320	Temporary staffing services
713950	Ten pin bowling alleys
713950	Ten pin bowling centers
813319	Tenants' advocacy associations
813990	Tenants' associations (except advocacy)
813319	Tenants' associations, advocacy
713940	Tennis club facilities
236220	Tennis court, indoor, construction
713940	Tennis courts
237990	Tennis courts, outdoor, construction
423910	Tennis equipment and supplies merchant wholesalers
339920	Tennis goods (e.g., balls, frames, rackets) manufacturing
611620	Tennis instruction, camps, or schools
711219	Tennis professionals, independent (i.e., participating in sports events)
315191	Tennis shirts made in apparel knitting mills
315291	Tennis shirts, infants', cut and sewn from purchased fabric (except apparel contractors)
315211	Tennis shirts, men's and boys', cut and sew apparel contractors
315223	Tennis shirts, men's and boys', cut and sewn from purchased fabric (except apparel contractors)
315212	Tennis shirts, women's, girls', and infants', cut and sew apparel contractors
315239	Tennis shirts, women's, misses', and girls', cut and sewn from purchased fabric (except apparel contractors)
315191	Tennis skirts made in apparel knitting mills
315212	Tennis skirts, women's and girls', cut and sew apparel contractors
315239	Tennis skirts, women's, misses', and girls', cut and sewn from purchased fabric (except apparel contractors)
334510	TENS (transcutaneous electrical nerve stimulator) manufacturing
334519	Tensile strength testing equipment manufacturing
321999	Tent poles, wood, manufacturing
336214	Tent trailers (hard top and soft top) manufacturing
532292	Tent, camping, rental
532299	Tent, party, rental
314912	Tents made from purchased fabrics
335931	Terminals and connectors for electrical devices manufacturing
334113	Terminals, computer, manufacturing
424710	Terminals, petroleum

561710 Termite control services
325320 Termite poisons manufacturing
331111 Terneplate made in iron and steel mills
423510 Terneplate merchant wholesalers
331111 Ternes, iron or steel, long or short, made in iron and steel mills
325199 Terpineol manufacturing
114119 Terrapin fishing
238340 Terrazzo and tile refinishing
238340 Terrazzo contractors
327390 Terrazzo products, precast (except brick, block and pipe), manufacturing
313210 Terry broadwoven fabrics weaving
325199 Tert-butylated bis (p-phenoxyphenyl) ether fluid manufacturing
238910 Test boring for construction
611710 Test development and evaluation services, educational
213114 Test drilling for metal mining on a contract basis
213115 Test drilling for nonmetallic minerals mining (except fuel) on a contract basis
334515 Test equipment for electronic and electrical circuits and equipment manufacturing
334515 Test sets, ignition harness, manufacturing
525920 Testamentary trusts
334519 Testers for checking hydraulic controls on aircraft manufacturing
423830 Testing and measuring equipment, electrical (except automotive), merchant wholesalers
334519 Testing equipment (e.g., abrasion, shearing strength, tensile strength, torsion) manufacturing
541380 Testing laboratories (except medical, veterinary)
621511 Testing laboratories, medical

541940 Testing laboratories, veterinary
541940 Testing services for veterinarians
488190 Testing services, aircraft
611710 Testing services, educational
333993 Testing, weighing, inspecting, packaging machinery manufacturing
325199 Tetrachloroethylene manufacturing
325411 Tetracycline, uncompounded, manufacturing
325199 Tetraethyl lead manufacturing
325920 Tetryl explosive materials manufacturing
323117 Textbooks printing and binding without publishing
323117 Textbooks printing without publishing
314911 Textile bags made from purchased woven or knitted materials
424990 Textile bags merchant wholesalers
313210 Textile broadwoven fabrics mills
561990 Textile cutting services
541490 Textile design services
325613 Textile finishing assistants manufacturing
333292 Textile finishing machinery (e.g., bleaching, dyeing, mercerizing, printing) manufacturing
314999 Textile fire hose made from purchased material
561910 Textile folding and packaging services
327212 Textile glass fibers made in glass making plants
327112 Textile guides, porcelain, manufacturing
316999 Textile leathers (e.g., apron picker leather, mill strapping) manufacturing
423830 Textile machinery and equipment merchant wholesalers
532490 Textile machinery rental or leasing

811310	Textile machinery repair and maintenance services
333292	Textile making machinery (except sewing machines) manufacturing
236210	Textile mill construction
313210	Textile mills, broadwoven fabrics
313221	Textile mills, narrow woven fabric
313221	Textile narrow woven fabric mills
325910	Textile printing inks manufacturing
333292	Textile printing machinery manufacturing
313210	Textile products (except apparel) made in broadwoven fabric mills
313249	Textile products (except apparel) made in lace mills
313221	Textile products (except apparel) made in narrow woven fabric mills
313249	Textile products (except apparel) made in warp knitting mills
313241	Textile products (except apparel) made in weft knitting mills
313312	Textile products finishing
325613	Textile scouring agents manufacturing
423930	Textile waste merchant wholesalers
313320	Textile waterproofing
424310	Textiles (except burlap, felt) merchant wholesalers
325221	Texturizing cellulosic yarn made in the same establishment
333292	Texturizing machinery for textiles manufacturing
325222	Texturizing noncellulosic yarn made in the same establishment
313112	Texturizing purchased yarn
212299	Thallium mining and/or beneficiating

711110	Theater companies (except dance)
711110	Theater companies (except dance), amateur
711120	Theater companies, dance
236220	Theater construction
423410	Theater equipment (except seats) merchant wholesalers
711310	Theater festival managers with facilities
711320	Theater festival managers without facilities
711310	Theater festival organizers with facilities
711320	Theater festival organizers without facilities
711310	Theater festival promoters with facilities
711320	Theater festival promoters without facilities
711310	Theater operators
611610	Theater schools
337127	Theater seating manufacturing
423210	Theater seats merchant wholesalers
531120	Theater, property operation, rental or leasing
711120	Theaters, dance
711110	Theaters, dinner
711110	Theaters, live theatrical production (except dance)
512131	Theaters, motion picture (except drive-in)
512132	Theaters, motion picture, drive-in
512131	Theaters, motion picture, indoor
711110	Theaters, musical
512132	Theaters, outdoor motion picture
711320	Theatrical booking agencies (except motion picture)
315299	Theatrical costumes cut and sewn from purchased fabric (except apparel contractors)
315211	Theatrical costumes, men's and boys', cut and sew apparel contractors
315212	Theatrical costumes, women's, girls', and infants', cut and sew apparel contractors

711120	Theatrical dance productions, live
561310	Theatrical employment agencies
532490	Theatrical equipment (except costumes) rental or leasing
711310	Theatrical production managers with facilities
711320	Theatrical production managers without facilities
711310	Theatrical production organizers with facilities
711320	Theatrical production organizers without facilities
711310	Theatrical production promoters with facilities
711320	Theatrical production promoters without facilities
711110	Theatrical repertory companies
711110	Theatrical road companies
339999	Theatrical scenery manufacturing
711110	Theatrical stock companies
711410	Theatrical talent agents
561599	Theatrical ticket offices
532220	Theatrical wardrobe and costume rental
334290	Theft prevention signaling devices (e.g., door entrance annunciation, holdup signaling devices, personal duress signaling devices), manufacturing
713110	Theme parks, amusement
325411	Theobromine and derivatives (i.e., basic chemicals) manufacturing
333314	Theodolites manufacturing
334519	Theodolites, surveying, manufacturing
611310	Theological seminaries offering baccalaureate or graduate degrees
334517	Therapeutic X-ray apparatus and tubes (e.g., medical, industrial, research) manufacturing
******	Therapists' offices—see type
423450	Therapy equipment merchant wholesalers
334516	Thermal analysis instruments, laboratory-type, manufacturing
334516	Thermal conductivity instruments and sensors manufacturing
334513	Thermal conductivity instruments, industrial process-type, manufacturing
326140	Thermal insulation, polystyrene foam, manufacturing
237130	Thermal power plant construction
541380	Thermal testing laboratories or services
334415	Thermistors manufacturing
334513	Thermistors, industrial process-type, manufacturing
334519	Thermocouples (except industrial process, aircraft type, glass vacuum) manufacturing
334512	Thermocouples, glass vacuum, manufacturing
334513	Thermocouples, industrial process-type, manufacturing
335999	Thermoelectric generators manufacturing
333993	Thermoform, blister, and skin packaging machinery manufacturing
333220	Thermoforming machinery for plastics manufacturing
334516	Thermogravimetric analyzers manufacturing
334519	Thermometer, liquid-in-glass and bimetal types (except medical), manufacturing
423450	Thermometers merchant wholesalers
334513	Thermometers, filled system industrial process-type, manufacturing
339112	Thermometers, medical, manufacturing
325211	Thermoplastic resins and plastics materials manufacturing
325211	Thermosetting plastics resins manufacturing

325212	Thermosetting vulcanizable elastomers manufacturing
332911	Thermostatic traps, industrial-type, manufacturing
334512	Thermostats (e.g., air-conditioning, appliance, comfort heating, refrigeration) manufacturing
336399	Thermostats, automotive, truck, and bus, manufacturing
334519	Thickness gauging instruments, ultrasonic, manufacturing
332999	Thimbles for wire rope manufacturing
334413	Thin film integrated circuits manufacturing
333295	Thin layer deposition equipment, semiconductor, manufacturing
115112	Thinning of crops, mechanical and chemical
325188	Thiocyanate manufacturing
325199	Thioglycolic acid manufacturing
325212	Thiol rubber manufacturing
212299	Thorite mining and/or beneficiating
212299	Thorium ores mining and/or beneficiating
711212	Thoroughbred racetracks
424310	Thread (except industrial) merchant wholesalers
333515	Thread cutting dies (i.e., a machine tool accessory) manufacturing
313312	Thread finishing
333292	Thread making machinery manufacturing
313113	Thread mills
333513	Thread rolling machines, metalworking, manufacturing
313113	Thread, all fibers, manufacturing
423840	Thread, industrial, merchant wholesalers
326299	Thread, rubber (except fabric covered), manufacturing
333512	Threading machines, metalworking, manufacturing
115113	Threshing service
453310	Thrift shops, used merchandise
333298	Through-hole machinery, printed circuit board loading, manufacturing
325221	Throwing cellulosic yarn made in the same establishment
325222	Throwing noncellulosic yarn made in the same establishment
313112	Throwing purchased yarn
334519	Thrust power indicators, aircraft engine, manufacturing
332991	Thrust roller bearings manufacturing
334413	Thyristors manufacturing
325412	Thyroid preparations manufacturing
325320	Tick powders or sprays manufacturing
561599	Ticket (e.g., airline, bus, cruise ship, sports, theatrical) offices
561599	Ticket (e.g., airline, bus, cruise ship, sports, theatrical) sales offices
561599	Ticket (e.g., amusement, sports, theatrical) agencies
561599	Ticket (e.g., amusement, sports, theatrical) sales agencies
561599	Ticket agencies, amusement
561599	Ticket agencies, sports
561599	Ticket agencies, theatrical
561599	Ticket offices for foreign cruise ship companies
331111	Tie plates, iron or steel, made in iron and steel mills
448150	Tie shops
331222	Tie wires made in wire drawing plants
315191	Ties made in apparel knitting mills
327390	Ties, concrete, railroad, manufacturing
315993	Ties, men's and boys' hand sewn (except apparel contractors), manufacturing
315211	Ties, men's and boys' hand sewn, cut and sew apparel contractors
321113	Ties, railroad, made from logs or bolts

325188   Tin compounds, not specified elsewhere by process, manufacturing

212299   Tin metal concentrates beneficiating

212299   Tin metal ores mining and/or beneficiating

325188   Tin oxide manufacturing

332431   Tin plate cans, light gauge metal, manufacturing

423510   Tin plate merchant wholesalers

331492   Tin recovering from scrap and/or alloying purchased metals

331419   Tin refining, primary

331491   Tin rolling, drawing, or extruding purchased metals or scrap

325188   Tin salts manufacturing

325412   Tincture of iodine preparations manufacturing

332999   Tinfoil not made in rolling mills

331111   Tin-free steel made in iron and steel mills

332212   Tinners' snips manufacturing

331111   Tinplate made in iron and steel mills

339999   Tinsel manufacturing

325998   Tint and dye preparations, household-type (except hair), manufacturing

325620   Tints, dyes, and rinses, hair, manufacturing

212111   Tipple operation, bituminous coal mining and/or beneficiating

236210   Tipple, mining, construction

316999   Tips, shoe, leather, manufacturing

423130   Tire and tube repair materials merchant wholesalers

332618   Tire chains made from purchased wire

314992   Tire cord and fabric, all materials, manufacturing

336360   Tire covers made from purchased fabric

441320   Tire dealers, automotive

325998   Tire inflators, aerosol, manufacturing

333220   Tire making machinery manufacturing

333319   Tire mounting machines, motor vehicle, manufacturing

333220   Tire recapping machinery manufacturing

423830   Tire recapping machinery merchant wholesalers

326211   Tire repair materials manufacturing

811198   Tire repair shops (except retreading), automotive

326212   Tire retreading, recapping or rebuilding

333220   Tire shredding machinery manufacturing

423130   Tire tubes, motor vehicle, merchant wholesalers

326211   Tires (e.g., pneumatic, semi-pneumatic, solid rubber) manufacturing

423130   Tires, new, motor vehicle, merchant wholesalers

326199   Tires, plastics, manufacturing

423930   Tires, scrap, merchant wholesalers

423130   Tires, used (except scrap), merchant wholesalers

111421   Tissue culture farming

322121   Tissue paper stock manufacturing

424130   Tissue paper, toilet and facial, merchant wholesalers

327113   Titania porcelain insulators manufacturing

212299   Titaniferous-magnetite ores, valued chiefly for titanium content, mining and/or beneficiating

331491   Titanium and titanium alloy bar, billet, rod, sheet, strip, and tubing made from purchased metals or scrap

325131   Titanium based pigments manufacturing

331528   Titanium castings (except die-castings), unfinished, manufacturing

212299   Titanium concentrates beneficiating

321999 Toilet seats, wood, manufacturing

325611 Toilet soaps manufacturing

424210 Toilet soaps merchant wholesalers

424130 Toilet tissue merchant wholesalers

332999 Toilet ware, precious plated metal, manufacturing

325620 Toilet water manufacturing

424210 Toiletries merchant wholesalers

334210 Toll switching equipment, telephone, manufacturing

325110 Toluene made from refined petroleum or liquid hydrocarbons

324110 Toluene made in petroleum refineries

325192 Toluidines manufacturing

111219 Tomato farming (except under cover), field, bedding plant and seed production

111419 Tomato farming, grown under cover

333111 Tomato harvesting machines manufacturing

325992 Toner cartridges manufacturing

424120 Toner cartridges merchant wholesalers

325992 Toner cartridges rebuilding

325132 Toners (except electrostatic, photographic) manufacturing

325992 Toners, electrostatic and photographic, manufacturing

339113 Tongue depressors manufacturing

316999 Tongues, boot and shoe, leather, manufacturing

339112 Tonometers, medical, manufacturing

332439 Tool boxes, light gauge metal, manufacturing

321920 Tool chests, wood, manufacturing

321999 Tool handles, wood, turned and shaped, manufacturing

541420 Tool industrial design services

337127 Tool stands, factory, manufacturing

331111 Tool steel made in iron and steel mills

444130 Tool stores, power and hand (except outdoor)

333515 Toolholders (i.e., a machine tool accessory) manufacturing

333515 Tools and accessories for machine tools manufacturing

423120 Tools and equipment, motor vehicle, merchant wholesalers

339114 Tools, dentists', manufacturing

423710 Tools, hand (except motor vehicle, machinists' precision tools), merchant wholesalers

332212 Tools, hand, metal blade (e.g., putty knives, scrapers, screwdrivers)

333991 Tools, handheld power-driven, manufacturing

332212 Tools, handheld, nonpowered (except kitchen-type), manufacturing

423830 Tools, machinists' precision, merchant wholesalers

332212 Tools, woodworking edge (e.g., augers, bits, countersinks), manufacturing

339994 Toothbrushes (except electric) manufacturing

424210 Toothbrushes (except electric) merchant wholesalers

335211 Toothbrushes, electric, manufacturing

423620 Toothbrushes, electric, merchant wholesalers

325611 Toothpastes, gels, and tooth powders manufacturing

321999 Toothpicks, wood, manufacturing

316999 Top lifts, boot and shoe, leather, manufacturing

212325 Topaz, non-gem, mining and/or beneficiating

315211 Topcoats, men's and boys', cut and sew apparel contractors

315222 Topcoats, men's and boys', cut and sewn from purchased fabric (except apparel contractors)

541370 Topographic mapping services

541370 Topographic surveying services
424490 Toppings (except fountain) merchant wholesalers
336399 Tops, convertible automotive, manufacturing
484220 Top-soil hauling, local
332995 Torpedo tubes manufacturing
332993 Torpedoes manufacturing
336350 Torque converters, automotive, truck, and bus, manufacturing
335312 Torque motors, electric, manufacturing
332611 Torsion bar, heavy gauge metal, manufacturing
334519 Torsion testing equipment manufacturing
311919 Tortilla chips manufacturing
311830 Tortillas manufacturing
334514 Totalizing fluid meters manufacturing
334514 Totalizing meters (except aircraft), consumption registering, manufacturing
339999 Toupees manufacturing
424990 Toupees merchant wholesalers
487110 Tour bus, scenic and sightseeing, operation
561520 Tour operators (i.e., arranging and assembling tours)
561591 Tourism bureaus
926110 Tourism development offices, government
713990 Tourist guide services
721199 Tourist homes
561591 Tourist information bureaus
721110 Tourist lodges
336413 Tow targets, aircraft, manufacturing
488410 Tow truck services
336211 Tow trucks (including tilt and load) assembling on purchased chassis
336611 Towboat building and repairing
532411 Towboat rental or leasing
812331 Towel (except shop, wiping) supply services
327111 Towel bar holders, vitreous china and earthenware, manufacturing

812332 Towel supply services, shop or wiping
325620 Towelettes, premoistened, manufacturing
313210 Towels and washcloths made in broadwoven fabric mills
313249 Towels and washcloths made in warp knitting mills
313241 Towels and washcloths made in weft knitting mills
423220 Towels and washcloths merchant wholesalers
314129 Towels or washcloths made from purchased fabrics
423840 Towels, industrial, merchant wholesalers
322291 Towels, paper, made from purchased paper
322121 Towels, paper, made in paper mills
423450 Towels, surgical, merchant wholesalers
237130 Tower, power distribution and communication, construction
336399 Towing bars and systems manufacturing
483211 Towing service, inland waters (except on Great Lakes system)
488410 Towing services, motor vehicle
236115 Town house (i.e., single-family type) construction by general contractors
236117 Town house construction operative builders
531110 Town house rental or leasing
541320 Town planners' offices
541320 Town planning services
562910 Toxic material abatement services
562910 Toxic material removal contractors
621511 Toxicology health laboratories
325414 Toxoids (e.g., diphtheria, tetanus) manufacturing
339932 Toy furniture and household-type equipment manufacturing
451120 Toy stores
339932 Toys (except dolls, stuffed toys) manufacturing

423920 Toys (including electronic) merchant wholesalers
339931 Toys, doll, manufacturing
339931 Toys, stuffed, manufacturing
333515 Tracer and tapering machine tool attachments manufacturing
332993 Tracer igniters, ammunition (i.e., more than 30 mm., more than 1.18 inch), manufacturing
339920 Track and field athletic equipment (except apparel, footwear) manufacturing
335121 Track lighting fixtures and equipment, residential, electric, manufacturing
484220 Tracked vehicle freight transportation, local
484230 Tracked vehicle freight transportation, long-distance
487110 Tracked vehicle sightseeing operation
339113 Traction apparatus manufacturing
811310 Tractor, farm or construction equipment repair and maintenance services
532490 Tractor, farm, rental or leasing
532490 Tractor, garden, rental or leasing
333120 Tractors and attachments, construction-type, manufacturing
333111 Tractors and attachments, farm-type, manufacturing
333112 Tractors and attachments, lawn and garden-type, manufacturing
333120 Tractors, crawler, manufacturing
423820 Tractors, farm and garden, merchant wholesalers
423110 Tractors, highway, merchant wholesalers
333924 Tractors, industrial, manufacturing
423830 Tractors, industrial, merchant wholesalers
811411 Tractors, lawn and garden repair and maintenance services without retailing new lawn and garden tractors

336120 Tractors, truck for highway use, assembled on chassis of own manufacture
813910 Trade associations
522293 Trade banks (i.e., international trade financing)
323121 Trade binding services
926110 Trade commissions, government
926110 Trade development program administration
561920 Trade fair managers
561920 Trade fair organizers
561920 Trade fair promoters
522293 Trade financing, international
511120 Trade journal publishers (except exclusive Internet publishing)
511120 Trade journal publishers and printing combined
516110 Trade journal publishers, exclusively on Internet
323112 Trade journals flexographic printing without publishing
323111 Trade journals gravure printing without publishing
323110 Trade journals lithographic (offset) printing without publishing
323119 Trade journals printing (except flexographic, gravure, lithographic, quick, screen) without publishing
323113 Trade journals screen printing without publishing
511120 Trade magazine and periodical publishers (except exclusive Internet publishing)
511120 Trade magazine and periodical publishers and printing combined
516110 Trade magazine and periodical publishers, exclusively on Internet
323112 Trade magazines and periodicals flexographic printing without publishing
323111 Trade magazines and periodicals gravure printing without publishing

323110 Trade magazines and periodicals lithographic (offset) printing without publishing

323119 Trade magazines and periodicals printing (except flexographic, gravure, lithographic, quick, screen) without publishing

323113 Trade magazines and periodicals screen printing without publishing

238390 Trade show exhibit installation and dismantling contractors

561920 Trade show managers

561920 Trade show organizers

561920 Trade show promoters

611513 Trade union apprenticeship training programs

813930 Trade unions (except apprenticeship programs)

813930 Trade unions, local

533110 Trademark licensing

523130 Trading companies, commodity contracts

452990 Trading posts, general merchandise

523110 Trading securities (i.e., acting as a principal in dealing securities to investors)

561990 Trading stamp promotion and sale to stores

561990 Trading stamp redemption services

334290 Traffic advisory and signalling systems manufacturing

922110 Traffic courts

541330 Traffic engineering consulting services

237310 Traffic lane painting

519110 Traffic reporting services

238210 Traffic signal installation

334290 Traffic signals manufacturing

237990 Trail construction

721214 Trail riding camps with accommodation facilities

713990 Trail riding, recreational

336399 Trailer hitches, motor vehicle, manufacturing

531190 Trailer park or court, residential

423120 Trailer parts, new, merchant wholesalers

532120 Trailer rental or leasing

336214 Trailers for transporting horses (except fifth-wheel-type) manufacturing

336214 Trailers, camping, manufacturing

336212 Trailers, fifth-wheel type, for transporting horses, manufacturing

423830 Trailers, industrial, merchant wholesalers

423110 Trailers, motor vehicle, merchant wholesalers

115210 Training horses (except racehorses)

315212 Training pants (i.e., underwear), infants', cut and sew apparel contractors

315291 Training pants (i.e., underwear), infants', cut and sewn from purchased fabric (except apparel contractors)

711219 Training race dogs

711219 Training racehorses

339932 Trains and equipment, toy, electric or mechanical, manufacturing

713990 Trampoline facilities, recreational

485119 Tramway systems (except mixed mode), commuter

487990 Tramway, aerial, scenic and sightseeing operation

332994 Tranquilizer guns, manufacturing

325412 Tranquilizer preparations manufacturing

336350 Transaxles, automotive, truck, and bus, manufacturing

334220 Transceivers (i.e., transmitter-receiver units) manufacturing

561410 Transcription services

334510 Transcutaneous electrical nerve stimulators (TENS) manufacturing

334419 Transducers (except pressure) manufacturing

334519 Transducers, pressure, manufacturing

484110 Transfer (trucking) services, general freight, local

523999 Transfer agencies, securities

237130 Transformer station and substation, electric power, construction

423610 Transformers (except electronic) merchant wholesalers

335311 Transformers, electric power, manufacturing

334416 Transformers, electronic component-types, manufacturing

423690 Transformers, electronic, merchant wholesalers

335311 Transformers, ignition, for use on domestic fuel burners, manufacturing

335311 Transformers, reactor, manufacturing

335311 Transformers, separate solid-state arc-welding, manufacturing

335912 Transistor radio batteries manufacturing

334413 Transistors manufacturing

423690 Transistors merchant wholesalers

541850 Transit advertising services

922120 Transit police

926120 Transit systems and authorities, nonoperating

485111 Transit systems, mixed mode (e.g., bus, commuter rail, subway combinations)

624229 Transitional housing agencies

327320 Transit-mixed concrete manufacturing

334519 Transits, surveying, manufacturing

541930 Translation services, language

237130 Transmission and distribution line construction

335311 Transmission and distribution voltage regulators manufacturing

316999 Transmission belting, leather, manufacturing

326220 Transmission belts, rubber, manufacturing

336399 Transmission coolers manufacturing

423610 Transmission equipment, electrical, merchant wholesalers

324191 Transmission fluids, petroleum, made from refined petroleum

325998 Transmission fluids, synthetic, manufacturing

221121 Transmission of electric power

486210 Transmission of natural gas via pipeline (i.e., processing plants to local distribution systems)

335932 Transmission pole and line hardware manufacturing

811113 Transmission repair shops, automotive

332312 Transmission tower sections, fabricated structural metal, manufacturing

336350 Transmissions and parts, automotive, truck, and bus, manufacturing

423690 Transmitters merchant wholesalers

334513 Transmitters, industrial process control-type, manufacturing

333111 Transplanters, farm-type, manufacturing

115112 Transplanting services

****** Transportation—see mode

481212 Transportation by spacecraft, freight

926120 Transportation departments, nonoperating

423860 Transportation equipment and supplies (except marine pleasure craft, motor vehicles) merchant wholesalers

336360 Transportation equipment seating manufacturing

541614 Transportation management consulting services

926120 Transportation regulatory agencies

926120 Transportation safety programs, government

311223	Tree nut oils (e.g., tung, walnut) made in crushing mill
561730	Tree pruning services
561730	Tree removal services
113210	Tree seed extracting
113210	Tree seed gathering
113210	Tree seed growing for reforestation
561730	Tree services (e.g., bracing, planting, pruning, removal, spraying, surgery, trimming)
333111	Tree shakers (e.g., citrus, nut, soft fruit) manufacturing
561730	Tree surgery services
561730	Tree trimming services
339999	Trees and plants, artificial, manufacturing
424930	Trees merchant wholesalers
321918	Trellises, wood, manufacturing
238910	Trenching (except underwater)
333120	Trenching machines manufacturing
237990	Trenching, underwater
237310	Trestle construction
321114	Trestle parts, wood, treating
325221	Triacetate fibers and yarns manufacturing
921150	Tribal chief's or chairman's office, American Indian or Alaska Native
921150	Tribal councils, American Indian or Alaska Native
921150	Tribal courts, American Indian or Alaska Native
325199	Trichloroethylene manufacturing
325199	Trichlorophenoxyacetic acid manufacturing
325199	Tricresyl phosphate manufacturing
339932	Tricycles (except metal) manufacturing
336991	Tricycles, metal, adult and children's, manufacturing
325199	Tridecyl alcohol manufacturing
238350	Trim and finish carpentry contractors
332321	Trim and molding (except motor vehicle), metal, manufacturing
332321	Trim, metal, manufacturing
321918	Trim, wood and covered wood, manufacturing
333112	Trimmers, hedge, electric, manufacturing
332212	Trimmers, hedge, nonelectric, manufacturing
333112	Trimmers, string, lawn and garden-type, manufacturing
315292	Trimmings, fur (except apparel contractors), manufacturing
315211	Trimmings, fur, men's and boys', cut and sew apparel contractors
315212	Trimmings, fur, women's, girls', and infants', cut and sew apparel contractors
316999	Trimmings, shoe, leather, manufacturing
325920	Trinitrotoluene (TNT) manufacturing
325199	Triphenyl phosphate manufacturing
333315	Tripods, camera and projector, manufacturing
212399	Tripoli mining and/or beneficiating
339112	Trocars manufacturing
485119	Trolley systems (except mixed mode), commuter
487110	Trolley, scenic and sightseeing, operation
339992	Trombones and parts manufacturing
212391	Trona mining and/or beneficiating
423940	Trophies merchant wholesalers
332999	Trophies, nonprecious and precious plated metal, manufacturing
339912	Trophies, precious metal, (except precious plated) manufacturing
453998	Trophy (including awards and plaques) shops
321999	Trophy bases, wood, manufacturing
424990	Tropical fish merchant wholesalers
112511	Tropical fish production, farm raising

561730 Tropical plant maintenance services
335129 Trouble lights manufacturing
332322 Troughs, elevator, sheet meta (except stampings), manufacturing
332313 Troughs, industrial, fabricated metal plate work, manufacturing
335211 Trouser pressers, household-type electric, manufacturing
315191 Trousers made in apparel knitting mills
315211 Trousers, men's and boys', cut and sew apparel contractors
315224 Trousers, men's and boys', cut and sewn from purchased fabric (except apparel contractors)
114111 Trout fishing
112511 Trout production, farm raising
332212 Trowels manufacturing
532120 Truck (except industrial) rental or leasing
811192 Truck and bus washes
336211 Truck bodies and cabs manufacturing
336211 Truck bodies assembling on purchased chassis
336214 Truck campers (i.e., slide-in campers) manufacturing
441310 Truck cap stores
611519 Truck driving schools
111219 Truck farming, field, bedding plant and seed production
522220 Truck finance leasing
423120 Truck parts, new, merchant wholesalers
811310 Truck refrigeration repair and maintenance services
811111 Truck repair shops, general
447190 Truck stops
236220 Truck terminal construction
532120 Truck tractor rental or leasing
336120 Truck tractors for highway use, assembling on chassis of own manufacture
336211 Truck tractors for highway use, assembling on purchased chassis

423110 Truck tractors, road, merchant wholesalers
811121 Truck trailer body shops
336212 Truck trailer manufacturing
423110 Truck trailer merchant wholesalers
811121 Truck trailer paint and body repair
488490 Truck weighing station operation
532490 Truck, industrial, rental or leasing
488490 Trucking terminals, independently operated
484210 Trucking used household, office, or institutional furniture and equipment
484110 Trucking, general freight, local
484122 Trucking, general freight, long-distance, less-than-truckload (LTL)
484121 Trucking, general freight, long-distance, truckload (TL)
484220 Trucking, specialized freight (except used goods), local
484230 Trucking, specialized freight (except used goods), long-distance
327320 Truck-mixed concrete manufacturing
336120 Trucks, heavy, assembling on chassis of own manufacture
333924 Trucks, industrial, manufacturing
423830 Trucks, industrial, merchant wholesalers
336112 Trucks, light duty, assembling on chassis of own manufacture
333120 Trucks, off-highway, manufacturing
423110 Trucks, road, merchant wholesalers
111419 Truffles farming, grown under cover
339992 Trumpets and parts manufacturing
316991 Trunks (i.e., luggage), all materials, manufacturing

332313	Truss plates, metal, manufacturing
321214	Trusses, glue laminated or pre-engineered wood, manufacturing
321214	Trusses, wood roof or floor, manufacturing
321214	Trusses, wood, glue laminated or metal connected, manufacturing
523991	Trust administration, personal investment
523991	Trust companies, nondepository
813211	Trusts, charitable, awarding grants
813211	Trusts, educational, awarding grants
525920	Trusts, estates, and agency accounts
813211	Trusts, religious, awarding grants
448190	T-shirt shops, custom printed
315291	T-shirts, outerwear, infants', cut and sewn from purchased fabric (except apparel contractors)
315191	T-shirts, outerwear, made in apparel knitting mills
315223	T-shirts, outerwear, men's and boys', cut and sewn from purchased fabric (except apparel contractors)
315211	T-shirts, outerwear, men's, boys' and unisex, cut and sew apparel contractors
315223	T-shirts, outerwear, unisex (i.e., sized without regard to gender), cut and sewn from purchased fabric (except apparel contractors)
315212	T-shirts, outerwear, women's, girls', and infants', cut and sew apparel contractors
315232	T-shirts, outerwear, women's, misses', and girls', cut and sewn from purchased fabric (except apparel contractors)
315291	T-shirts, underwear, infants', cut and sewn from purchased fabric (except apparel contractors)
315192	T-shirts, underwear, made in apparel knitting mills
315211	T-shirts, underwear, men's and boys', cut and sew apparel contractors
315221	T-shirts, underwear, men's and boys', cut and sewn from purchased fabric (except apparel contractors)
315231	T-shirts, underwear, women's, misses', and girls', cut and sewn from purchased fabric (except apparel contractors)
315212	T-shirts, underwear, women's, misses', girls', and infants', cut and sew apparel contractors
334519	T-squares (drafting) manufacturing
325612	Tub and tile cleaning preparations manufacturing
331210	Tube (e.g., heavy riveted, lock joint, seamless, welded) made from purchased iron or steel
332912	Tube and hose fittings, fluid power, manufacturing
331316	Tube blooms made by extruding purchased aluminum
331316	Tube blooms, aluminum, made in integrated secondary smelting and extruding mills
331316	Tube made by drawing or extruding purchased aluminum
333516	Tube rolling mill machinery, metalworking, manufacturing
331111	Tube rounds, iron or steel, made in iron and steel mills
331316	Tube, aluminum, made in integrated secondary smelting and drawing plants
331316	Tube, aluminum, made in integrated secondary smelting and extruding mills
331111	Tube, iron or steel, made in iron and steel mills
326121	Tube, nonrigid plastics, manufacturing
331315	Tube, welded, aluminum, made by flat rolling purchased aluminum

331315 Tube, welded, aluminum, made in integrated secondary smelting and flat rolling mills

325414 Tuberculin (i.e., tuberculo-protein derived) manufacturing

622310 Tuberculosis and other respiratory illness hospitals

332996 Tubes made from purchased metal pipe

334411 Tubes, cathode ray, manufacturing

334411 Tubes, electron, manufacturing

423690 Tubes, electronic (e.g., industrial, receiving, transmitting), merchant wholesalers

334411 Tubes, electronic, manufacturing

334411 Tubes, klystron, manufacturing

334517 Tubes, X-ray, manufacturing

331421 Tubing, copper and copper alloy, made from purchased copper or in integrated secondary smelting and rolling, drawing or extruding plants

332999 Tubing, flexible metal, manufacturing

331210 Tubing, mechanical and hypodermic sizes, cold-drawn stainless steel, made from purchased steel

423510 Tubing, metal, merchant wholesalers

331491 Tubing, nonferrous metals (except aluminum, copper), made from purchased metals or scrap

326299 Tubing, rubber (except extruded, molded, lathe-cut), manufacturing

331111 Tubing, seamless steel, made in iron and steel mills

331111 Tubing, wrought iron or steel, made in iron and steel mills

332998 Tubs, laundry and bath, metal, manufacturing

238140 Tuck pointing contractors

212312 Tufa, calcareous, crushed and broken stone, mining and/or beneficiating

212311 Tufa, calcareous, mining or quarrying

333292 Tufting machinery for textiles manufacturing

336611 Tugboat building

532411 Tugboat rental or leasing

488330 Tugboat services, harbor operation

326199 Tumblers, plastics, manufacturing

332813 Tumbling (i.e., cleaning and polishing) metal and metal products for the trade

114111 Tuna fishing

811118 Tune-up shops, automotive

325188 Tungstates (e.g., ammonium tungstate, sodium tungstate) manufacturing

331491 Tungsten bar, rod, sheet, strip, and tubing made by rolling, drawing, or extruding purchased metals or scrap

331492 Tungsten carbide powder made by metallurgical process

325188 Tungsten compounds, not specified elsewhere by process, manufacturing

212299 Tungsten concentrates beneficiating

212299 Tungsten ores mining and/or beneficiating

811490 Tuning and repair of musical instruments

339992 Tuning forks manufacturing

237990 Tunnel construction

238210 Tunnel lighting contractors

332313 Tunnel lining, fabricated metal plate work, manufacturing

213113 Tunneling services for coal mining on a contract basis

332313 Tunnels, wind, fabricated metal plate work, manufacturing

334513 Turbidity instruments, industrial process-type, manufacturing

334516 Turbidometers, laboratory-type, manufacturing

334513 Turbine flow meters, industrial process-type, manufacturing
333611 Turbine generator set units manufacturing
334514 Turbine meters, consumption registering, manufacturing
333611 Turbines (except aircraft) manufacturing
423830 Turbines (except transportation) merchant wholesalers
423860 Turbines, transportation, merchant wholesalers
561730 Turf (except artificial) installation services
238990 Turf, artificial, installation
424440 Turkey and turkey products (except canned and packaged frozen) merchant wholesalers
112330 Turkey egg production
311119 Turkey feeds, prepared, manufacturing
112340 Turkey hatcheries
112330 Turkey production
311615 Turkeys, processing, fresh, frozen, canned, or cooked
311615 Turkeys, slaughtering and dressing
812199 Turkish bathhouses
812199 Turkish baths
332722 Turnbuckles, metal, manufacturing
333512 Turning machines (i.e., lathes), metalworking, manufacturing
321912 Turnings, furniture, unfinished wood, manufacturing
111219 Turnip farming, field, bedding plant and seed production
325191 Turpentine made by distillation of pine gum or pine wood
424690 Turpentine merchant wholesalers
212399 Turquoise mining and/or beneficiating
333512 Turret lathes, metalworking, manufacturing
332995 Turrets, gun, manufacturing
114119 Turtle fishing
112519 Turtle production, farm raising
611691 Tutoring, academic
532220 Tuxedo rental

315222 Tuxedos cut and sewn from purchased fabric (except apparel contractors)
315211 Tuxedos, cut and sew apparel contractors
334310 TV (television) sets manufacturing
443112 TV (television) stores
532490 TV broadcasting and studio equipment rental or leasing
337124 TV stands and similar stands for consumer electronics, metal, manufacturing
337125 TV stands and similar stands for consumer electronics, plastics, manufacturing
337122 TV stands and similar stands for consumer electronics, wood, manufacturing
313210 Twills weaving
423840 Twine merchant wholesalers
314991 Twines manufacturing
423830 Twist drills merchant wholesalers
517211 Two-way paging communication carriers
323122 Typesetting (i.e., computer controlled, hand, machine)
333293 Typesetting machinery manufacturing
424120 Typewriter paper merchant wholesalers
811212 Typewriter repair and maintenance services
339944 Typewriter ribbons manufacturing
333313 Typewriters manufacturing
423420 Typewriters merchant wholesalers
561410 Typing services
212291 Tyuyamunite mining and/or beneficiating
922130 U. S. attorneys' offices
522320 U.S. Central Credit Union
311514 UHT (ultra high temperature) milk manufacturing
339992 Ukuleles and parts manufacturing
212391 Ulexite mining and/or beneficiating

315212   Underwear shorts, women's, girls', and infants', cut and sew apparel contractors

315231   Underwear shorts, women's, misses', and girls', cut and sewn from purchased fabric (except apparel contractors)

315291   Underwear, infants', cut and sewn from purchased fabric (except apparel contractors)

315211   Underwear, men's and boys', cut and sew apparel contractors

315221   Underwear, men's and boys', cut and sewn from purchased fabric (except apparel contractors)

424320   Underwear, men's and boys', merchant wholesalers

424330   Underwear, women's, children's, and infants', merchant wholesalers

315231   Underwear, women's, misses', and girls', cut and sewn from purchased fabric (except apparel contractors)

315212   Underwear, women's, misses', girls', and infants', cut and sew apparel contractors

523110   Underwriting securities

923130   Unemployment insurance program administration

812331   Uniform (except industrial) supply services

315991   Uniform hats and caps cut and sewn from purchased fabric (except apparel contractors)

315211   Uniform hats and caps, men's and boys', cut and sew apparel contractors

315212   Uniform hats and caps, women's, and girls', cut and sew apparel contractors

315232   Uniform shirts (except team athletic), women's, misses', and girls', cut and sewn from purchased fabric (except apparel contractors)

315223   Uniform shirts (except team athletic, work), men's and boys', cut and sewn from purchased fabric (except apparel contractors)

315211   Uniform shirts, men's and boys', cut and sew apparel contractors

315299   Uniform shirts, team athletic, cut and sewn from purchased fabric (except apparel contractors)

315212   Uniform shirts, women's and girls', cut and sew apparel contractors

315225   Uniform shirts, work, men's and boys', cut and sewn from purchased fabric (except apparel contractors)

448190   Uniform stores (except athletic)

451110   Uniform stores, athletic

812332   Uniform supply services, industrial

315299   Uniforms, band, cut and sewn from purchased fabric (except apparel contractors)

315211   Uniforms, band, men's and boys', cut and sew apparel contractors

315212   Uniforms, band, women's, girls', and infants', cut and sew apparel contractors

315211   Uniforms, dress (e.g., fire fighter, military, police), men's, cut and sew apparel contractors

315222   Uniforms, dress (e.g., fire fighter, military, police), men's, cut and sewn from purchased fabric (except apparel contractors)

315212   Uniforms, dress (e.g., military, police, fire fighter), women's, cut and sew apparel contractors

337121	Upholstered furniture, household-type, custom, manufacturing
337121	Upholstered furniture, household-type, on frames of any material, manufacturing
423850	Upholsterers' equipment and supplies (except fabrics) merchant wholesalers
314999	Upholstering filling (except nonwoven fabric) manufacturing
811420	Upholstery (except motor vehicle) repair services
561740	Upholstery cleaning on customers' premises
561740	Upholstery cleaning services
316110	Upholstery leather manufacturing
451130	Upholstery materials stores
811121	Upholstery shops, automotive
332612	Upholstery springs and spring units, light gauge, made from purchased wire or strip
316110	Upper leather manufacturing
316999	Uppers (i.e., shoe cut stock), leather, manufacturing
335999	UPS (uninterruptible power supplies) manufacturing
332111	Upset forgings made from purchased iron or steel, unfinished
332112	Upset forgings made from purchased nonferrous metals, unfinished
333513	Upsetters (i.e., forging machines) manufacturing
212291	Uraninite (pitchblende) mining and/or beneficiating
325188	Uranium compounds, not specified elsewhere by process, manufacturing
212291	Uranium ores mining and/or beneficiating
325188	Uranium oxide manufacturing
331419	Uranium refining, primary
325188	Uranium, enriched, manufacturing

212291	Uranium-radium-vanadium ore mine site development for own account
212291	Uranium-radium-vanadium ores mining and/or beneficiating
485113	Urban bus line services (except mixed mode)
485112	Urban commuter rail systems (except mixed mode)
541320	Urban planners' offices
925120	Urban planning commissions, government
541320	Urban planning services
485111	Urban transit systems, mixed mode (e.g., bus, commuter rail, subway combinations)
325311	Urea manufacturing
325211	Urea resins manufacturing
325211	Urea-formaldehyde resins manufacturing
238310	Urethane foam insulation application
326150	Urethane foam products manufacturing
325212	Urethane rubber manufacturing
621493	Urgent medical care centers and clinics (except hospitals), freestanding
332998	Urinals, metal, manufacturing
326191	Urinals, plastics, manufacturing
327111	Urinals, vitreous china, manufacturing
621511	Urinalysis laboratories
327420	Urns (e.g., gypsum, plaster of paris) manufacturing
335211	Urns, household-type electric, manufacturing
621111	Urologists' offices (e.g., centers, clinics)
441229	Used aircraft dealers
441310	Used automotive parts stores
441320	Used automotive tire dealers
453310	Used bicycle (except motorized) shops
441222	Used boat dealers
441120	Used car dealers
423110	Used car merchant wholesalers
484210	Used household and office goods moving

453930   Used manufactured (mobile) home dealers
453310   Used merchandise dealers (except motor vehicles and parts)
453310   Used merchandise stores
441221   Used motorcycle dealers
423140   Used parts, motor vehicle, merchant wholesalers
441210   Used recreational vehicle (RV) dealers
441320   Used tire dealers
423130   Used tires, motor vehicle, merchant wholesalers
441229   Used utility trailer dealers
541618   Utilities management consulting services
332311   Utility buildings, prefabricated metal, manufacturing
326199   Utility containers (e.g., baskets, bins, boxes, buckets, dishpans, pails), plastics (except foam), manufacturing
237130   Utility line (i.e., communication, electric power), construction
237110   Utility line (i.e., sewer, water), construction
511210   Utility software, computer, packaged
441229   Utility trailer dealers
423110   Utility trailer merchant wholesalers
532120   Utility trailer rental or leasing
336214   Utility trailers manufacturing
531190   Vacant lot rental or leasing
531190   Vacation and recreation land rental or leasing
721214   Vacation camps (except campgrounds, day instructional)
236115   Vacation home, single-family, construction by general contractors
236117   Vacation housing construction operative builders
115210   Vaccinating livestock (except by veterinarians)
541940   Vaccination services, veterinary

325414   Vaccines (i.e., bacterial, virus) manufacturing
424210   Vaccines merchant wholesalers
332439   Vacuum bottles and jugs, light gauge metal, manufacturing
336340   Vacuum brake booster, automotive, truck, and bus, manufacturing
326220   Vacuum cleaner belts, rubber or plastics, manufacturing
443111   Vacuum cleaner stores, household-type
335212   Vacuum cleaners (e.g., canister, handheld, upright) household-type electric, manufacturing
335212   Vacuum cleaners and sweepers, household-type electric, manufacturing
423620   Vacuum cleaners, household-type, merchant wholesalers
333319   Vacuum cleaners, industrial and commercial-type, manufacturing
238290   Vacuum cleaning system, built-in, installation
333912   Vacuum pumps (except laboratory) manufacturing
339111   Vacuum pumps, laboratory-type, manufacturing
335314   Vacuum relays manufacturing
332420   Vacuum tanks, heavy gauge metal, manufacturing
327215   Vacuum tube blanks, glass, made from purchased glass
327212   Vacuum tube blanks, glass, made in glass making plants
334411   Vacuum tubes manufacturing
488119   Vacuuming of airport runways
333112   Vacuums, yard, manufacturing
812930   Valet parking services
316991   Valises, all materials, manufacturing
325191   Valonia extract manufacturing
333512   Valve grinding machines, metalworking, manufacturing
423840   Valves (except hydraulic, plumbing, pneumatic) merchant wholesalers
332911   Valves for nuclear applications manufacturing

332911	Valves for water works and municipal water systems manufacturing
336311	Valves, engine, intake and exhaust, manufacturing
332912	Valves, hydraulic and pneumatic, fluid power, manufacturing
423830	Valves, hydraulic and pneumatic, merchant wholesalers
332911	Valves, industrial-type (e.g., check, gate, globe, relief, safety), manufacturing
332919	Valves, inline plumbing and heating (e.g., cutoffs, stop), manufacturing
423720	Valves, plumbing and heating, merchant wholesalers
316999	Vamps, leather, manufacturing
532120	Van (except passenger) rental or leasing without driver
532112	Van (passenger) leasing
532111	Van (passenger) rental
336213	Van and minivan conversions on purchased chassis
811121	Van conversion shops (except on assembly line or factory basis)
484210	Van lines, moving and storage services
212291	Vanadium ores mining and/or beneficiating
325199	Vanillin, synthetic, manufacturing
337110	Vanities (except freestanding), stock or custom wood, manufacturing
337122	Vanities, freestanding, wood, manufacturing
337124	Vanities, metal household-type, manufacturing
316993	Vanity cases, leather, manufacturing
337110	Vanity tops, wood or plastics laminated on wood, manufacturing
485999	Vanpool operation
488999	Vanpools, arrangement of

336112	Vans, commercial and passenger light duty, assembling on chassis of own manufacture
334512	Vapor heating controls manufacturing
335110	Vapor lamps, electric, manufacturing
333999	Vapor separating machinery manufacturing
335211	Vaporizers, household-type electric, manufacturing
334513	Variable control instruments, industrial process-type, manufacturing
311612	Variety meats, edible organs, made from purchased meats
311611	Variety meats, edible organs, made in slaughtering plants
452990	Variety stores
334415	Varistors manufacturing
325510	Varnishes manufacturing
424950	Varnishes merchant wholesalers
332812	Varnishing metals and metal products for the trade
313320	Varnishing purchased textiles and apparel
327420	Vases (e.g., gypsum, plaster of paris) manufacturing
327215	Vases, glass, made from purchased glass
327212	Vases, glass, made in glass making plants
327112	Vases, pottery (e.g., china, earthenware, stoneware), manufacturing
325132	Vat dyes, synthetic, manufacturing
332420	Vats, heavy gauge metal, manufacturing
332439	Vats, light gauge metal, manufacturing
711110	Vaudeville companies
332999	Vault doors and linings, metal, manufacturing
238290	Vault, safe and banking machine installation
332999	Vaults (except burial), metal, manufacturing

454210   Vending machine merchandisers, sale of products
532490   Vending machine rental
333311   Vending machines manufacturing
423440   Vending machines merchant wholesalers
333210   Veneer and plywood forming machinery manufacturing
321920   Veneer baskets, for fruits and vegetables, manufacturing
321211   Veneer mills, hardwood
321212   Veneer mills, softwood
321999   Veneer work, inlaid, manufacturing
811490   Venetian blind repair and maintenance shops without retailing new venetian blinds
321918   Venetian blind slats, wood, manufacturing
337920   Venetian blinds manufacturing
238390   Ventilated wire shelving (i.e., closet organizing-type) installation
238220   Ventilating contractors
423730   Ventilating equipment and supplies (except household-type fans) merchant wholesalers
333412   Ventilating fans, industrial and commercial-type, manufacturing
335211   Ventilating kitchen fans, household-type electric, manufacturing
335211   Ventilation and exhaust fans (except attic fans), household-type, manufacturing
561790   Ventilation duct cleaning services
561790   Ventilation duct cleaning services
332322   Ventilators, sheet metal (except stampings), manufacturing
523910   Venture capital companies
212319   Verde' antique crushed and broken stone mining and/or beneficiating

212311   Verde' antique mining or quarrying
212399   Vermiculite mining and/or beneficiating
327992   Vermiculite, exfoliated, manufacturing
325412   Vermifuge preparations manufacturing
325131   Vermilion pigments manufacturing
312130   Vermouth manufacturing
337920   Vertical blinds manufacturing
488390   Vessel supply services
332420   Vessels, heavy gauge metal, manufacturing
315299   Vestments, academic and clerical, cut and sewn from purchased fabric (except apparel contractors)
315211   Vestments, academic and clerical, men's and boys', cut and sew apparel contractors
315212   Vestments, academic and clerical, women's and girls', cut and sew apparel contractors
315292   Vests, leather, fur, or sheep-lined (except apparel contractors), manufacturing
315211   Vests, leather, fur, or sheep-lined, men's and boys', cut and sew apparel contractors
315212   Vests, leather, fur, or sheep-lined, women's, girls', and infants', cut and sew apparel contractors
315211   Vests, men's and boys', cut and sew apparel contractors
315228   Vests, nontailored, men's and boys', cut and sewn from purchased fabric (except apparel contractors)
315239   Vests, nontailored, women's, misses', and girls', cut and sewn from purchased fabric (except apparel contractors)
315222   Vests, tailored, men's and boys', cut and sewn from purchased fabric (except apparel contractors)

423690	Video tapes, blank, merchant wholesalers
423990	Video tapes, prerecorded, merchant wholesalers
541922	Video taping services for legal depositions
541921	Video taping services, special events (e.g., birthdays, weddings)
561499	Videoconferencing services
512199	Videotape libraries, stock footage
311941	Vinegar manufacturing
115112	Vineyard cultivation services
325199	Vinyl acetate (except resins) manufacturing
325211	Vinyl acetate resins manufacturing
326113	Vinyl and vinyl copolymer film and unlaminated sheet (except packaging) manufacturing
325211	Vinyl chloride resins manufacturing
313320	Vinyl coated fabrics manufacturing
325222	Vinyl fibers and filaments manufacturing
326192	Vinyl floor coverings manufacturing
238330	Vinyl flooring contractors
325211	Vinyl resins manufacturing
423330	Vinyl siding merchant wholesalers
238170	Vinyl siding, soffit and fascia, installation
316219	Vinyl upper athletic footwear manufacturing
325222	Vinylidene chloride fiber and filament manufacturing
325211	Vinylidene resins manufacturing
339992	Violas and parts manufacturing
339992	Violins and parts manufacturing
325413	Viral in-vitro diagnostic test substances manufacturing
325414	Virus vaccines manufacturing
325221	Viscose fibers, bands, strips, and yarn manufacturing
334519	Viscosimeters (except industrial process type) manufacturing
334513	Viscosimeters, industrial process-type, manufacturing
332212	Vises (except machine tool attachments) manufacturing
621610	Visiting nurse associations
561591	Visitors bureaus
325412	Vitamin preparations manufacturing
446191	Vitamin stores
424210	Vitamins merchant wholesalers
325411	Vitamins, uncompounded, manufacturing
711130	Vocalists, independent
611513	Vocational apprenticeship training
624310	Vocational habilitation job counseling
624310	Vocational habilitation job training facilities (except schools)
624310	Vocational rehabilitation agencies
624310	Vocational rehabilitation job counseling
624310	Vocational rehabilitation job training facilities (except schools)
624310	Vocational rehabilitation or habilitation services (e.g., job counseling, job training, work experience)
611610	Voice instruction
561421	Voice mailbox services
621340	Voice pathologists' offices (e.g., centers, clinics)
212399	Volcanic ash mining and/or beneficiating
212319	Volcanic rock crushed and broken stone mining and/or beneficiating
212311	Volcanic rock, mining or quarrying
335311	Voltage regulating transformers, electric power, manufacturing
423610	Voltage regulators (except motor vehicle) merchant wholesalers
336322	Voltage regulators for internal combustion engines manufacturing

236220　Warehouse, commercial and institutional, construction
236220　Warehouse, industrial, construction
332311　Warehouses, prefabricated metal, manufacturing
493190　Warehousing (except farm products, general merchandise, refrigerated)
493110　Warehousing (including foreign trade zones), general merchandise
493110　Warehousing and storage, general merchandise
813910　Warehousing associations
493130　Warehousing, farm products (except refrigerated)
493120　Warehousing, refrigerated
531130　Warehousing, self storage
334511　Warfare countermeasures equipment manufacturing
423730　Warm air heating equipment merchant wholesalers
238220　Warm air heating system installation
335211　Warming trays, electric, manufacturing
315191　Warmup suits made in apparel knitting mills
315291　Warmup suits, infants', cut and sewn from purchased fabric (except apparel contractors)
315211　Warmup suits, men's and boys', cut and sew apparel contractors
315228　Warmup suits, men's and boys', cut and sewn from purchased fabric (except apparel contractors)
315212　Warmup suits, women's, girls', and infants', cut and sew apparel contractors
315239　Warmup suits, women's, misses', and girls', cut and sewn from purchased fabric (except apparel contractors)
313249　Warp fabrics knitting
333292　Warping machinery manufacturing

524128　Warranty insurance carriers (e.g., appliance, automobile, homeowners, product), direct
315211　Washable service apparel (e.g., barbers', hospital, professional), men's and boys', cut and sew apparel contractors
315225　Washable service apparel (e.g., barbers', hospital, professional), men's and boys', cut and sewn from purchased fabric (except apparel contractors)
315212　Washable service apparel, women's and girls', cut and sew apparel contractors
315239　Washable service apparel, women's, misses', and girls', cut and sewn from purchased fabric (except apparel contractors)
321999　Washboards, wood and part wood, manufacturing
532210　Washer, clothes, rental
212113　Washeries, anthracite
212111　Washeries, bituminous coal or lignite
333131　Washers, aggregate and sand, stationary, manufacturing
332722　Washers, metal, manufacturing
236210　Washery, mining, construction
811412　Washing machine, household-type, repair and maintenance services without retailing new washing machine
335224　Washing machines, household-type, manufacturing
333312　Washing machines, laundry (except household-type), manufacturing
561720　Washroom sanitation services
562219　Waste (except sewage) treatment facilities, nonhazardous
562119　Waste (except solid and hazardous) collection services
562119　Waste (except solid and hazardous) hauling, local

335228	Water heaters (including nonelectric), household-type, manufacturing
423620	Water heaters, electric, merchant wholesalers
326220	Water hoses, rubber or plastics, manufacturing
213111	Water intake well drilling, oil and gas field on a contract basis
334519	Water leak detectors manufacturing
237110	Water main and line construction
238220	Water meter installation
713110	Water parks, amusement
238290	Water pipe insulating
331511	Water pipe, cast iron, manufacturing
335211	Water pulsating devices, household-type electric, manufacturing
237110	Water pumping or lift station construction
333319	Water purification equipment manufacturing
334513	Water quality monitoring and control systems manufacturing
325510	Water repellant coatings for wood, concrete and masonry manufacturing
315211	Water resistant apparel, men's and boys', cut and sew apparel contractors
315228	Water resistant jackets and windbreakers, nontailored, men's and boys', cut and sewn from purchased fabric (except apparel contractors)
315239	Water resistant jackets and windbreakers, not tailored, women's, misses' and girls', cut and sewn from purchased fabric (except apparel contractors)
315228	Water resistant outerwear (except overcoats), men's and boys', cut and sewn from purchased fabric (except apparel contractors)
315239	Water resistant outerwear (except overcoats), women's, misses', and girls', cut and sewn from purchased fabric (except apparel contractors)
315291	Water resistant outerwear infants', cut and sewn from purchased fabric (except apparel contractors)
315212	Water resistant outerwear, women's, girls', and infants', cut and sew apparel contractors
315222	Water resistant overcoats, men's and boys', cut and sewn from purchased fabric (except apparel contractors)
315234	Water resistant overcoats, women's, misses', and girls', cut and sewn from purchased fabric (except apparel contractors)
316211	Water shoes, plastics or plastics soled fabric upper, manufacturing
316211	Water shoes, rubber or rubber soled fabric upper, manufacturing
532292	Water ski rental
238220	Water softener installation
454390	Water softener service providers, direct selling
423720	Water softening and conditioning equipment merchant wholesalers
424690	Water softening compounds merchant wholesalers
333319	Water softening equipment manufacturing
237110	Water system storage tank and tower construction
445299	Water stores, bottled
221310	Water supply systems
238220	Water system balancing and testing contractors
332420	Water tanks, heavy gauge metal, manufacturing
483212	Water taxi services
332913	Water traps manufacturing
221310	Water treatment and distribution

334515	Watt-hour and time switch meters, combined, manufacturing
334515	Watt-hour meters, electric, manufacturing
325191	Wattle extract manufacturing
334515	Wattmeters manufacturing
713940	Wave pools
334515	Waveform measuring and/or analyzing equipment manufacturing
339999	Wax figures (i.e., mannequins) manufacturing
712110	Wax museums
325612	Wax removers manufacturing
322222	Waxed paper for nonpackaging applications made from purchased paper
322221	Waxed paper for packaging applications made from purchased paper
424130	Waxed paper merchant wholesalers
424690	Waxes (except petroleum) merchant wholesalers
324199	Waxes, petroleum, made from refined petroleum
324110	Waxes, petroleum, made in petroleum refineries
325612	Waxes, polishing (e.g., floor, furniture), manufacturing
313320	Waxing purchased textiles and apparel
115114	Waxing, fruits or vegetables
112210	Weaning pig operations
336992	Weapons, self-propelled, manufacturing
541990	Weather forecasting services
924120	Weather research program administration
321918	Weather strip, wood, manufacturing
238390	Weather stripping installation
423330	Weather stripping merchant wholesalers
334519	Weather tracking equipment manufacturing
333999	Weather vanes manufacturing

331422	Weatherproof wire or cable made from purchased copper in wire drawing plants
331319	Weatherproof wire or cable made in aluminum wire drawing plants
238390	Weatherproofing concrete
332321	Weatherstrip, metal, manufacturing
314999	Weatherstripping made from purchased textiles
313221	Weaving and finishing narrow fabrics
313210	Weaving and finishing of broadwoven fabrics (except rugs, tire fabric)
313210	Weaving broadwoven fabrics (except rugs, tire fabrics)
313210	Weaving broadwoven felts
313221	Weaving fabric less than 12 inches (30cm)
313210	Weaving fabrics more than 12 inches (30cm) in width
333292	Weaving machinery manufacturing
313221	Weaving narrow fabrics
314110	Weaving rugs, carpets, and mats
541511	WEB (i.e., Internet) page design services, custom
516110	Web broadcasting
516110	Web communities (except Web search portals)
518210	Web hosting
454111	Web retailers
518112	Web search portals
313221	Webbing weaving
321999	Webbing, cane, reed, and rattan, manufacturing
812990	Wedding chapels (except churches)
315212	Wedding dresses, women's, cut and sew apparel contractors
315233	Wedding dresses, women's, misses', and girls', cut and sewn from purchased fabric (except apparel contractors)
541921	Wedding photography services
812990	Wedding planning services
561730	Weed control and fertilizing services (except crop)

111140	Wheat farming, field and seed production
311211	Wheat flour manufacturing
311211	Wheat germ manufacturing
311213	Wheat malt manufacturing
334515	Wheatstone bridges (i.e., electrical measuring instruments) manufacturing
811118	Wheel alignment shops, automotive
532291	Wheel chair rental
334511	Wheel position indicators and transmitters, aircraft, manufacturing
332212	Wheel pullers, handtools, manufacturing
333924	Wheelbarrows manufacturing
339113	Wheelchairs manufacturing
423450	Wheelchairs merchant wholesalers
336399	Wheels (i.e., rims), automotive, truck, and bus, manufacturing
327910	Wheels, abrasive, manufacturing
331111	Wheels, car and locomotive, iron or steel, made in iron and steel mills
423120	Wheels, motor vehicle, new, merchant wholesalers
327910	Wheels, polishing and grinding, manufacturing
336330	Wheels, steering, automotive, truck, and bus, manufacturing
327910	Whetstones manufacturing
212399	Whetstones mining and/or beneficiating
311512	Whey butter manufacturing
311514	Whey, condensed, dried, evaporated, and powdered, manufacturing
311513	Whey, raw, liquid, manufacturing
311511	Whipped topping (except dry mix, frozen) manufacturing
311514	Whipped topping, dry mix, manufacturing
311412	Whipped topping, frozen, manufacturing
335211	Whippers, household-type electric, manufacturing
311511	Whipping cream manufacturing
316999	Whips, horse, manufacturing
316999	Whipstocks manufacturing
339113	Whirlpool baths (i.e., hydrotherapy equipment) manufacturing
423450	Whirlpool baths merchant wholesalers
493190	Whiskey warehousing
325131	White extender pigments (e.g., barytes, blanc fixe, whiting) manufacturing
331528	White metal castings (except die-castings), unfinished, manufacturing
713990	White water rafting, recreational
238320	Whitewashing contractors
212312	Whiting crushed and broken stone, mining and/or beneficiating
114111	Whiting fishing
325131	Whiting manufacturing
334519	Whole body counters, nuclear, manufacturing
******	Wholesale—see type of product
561520	Wholesale tour operators
813910	Wholesalers' associations
337125	Wicker furniture (except upholstered), household-type, manufacturing
313221	Wicks manufacturing
334210	Wide area network communications equipment (e.g., bridges, gateways, routers) manufacturing
448150	Wig and hairpiece stores
424990	Wigs merchant wholesalers
339999	Wigs, wiglets, toupees, hair pieces, manufacturing
712130	Wild animal parks
111199	Wild rice farming, field and seed production
721214	Wilderness camps
711510	Wildlife artists, independent
924120	Wildlife conservation agencies
813312	Wildlife preservation organizations
712190	Wildlife sanctuaries
212231	Willemite mining and/or beneficiating

336322	Windshield washer pumps, automotive, truck, and bus, manufacturing
336399	Windshield wiper blades and refills manufacturing
336322	Windshield wiper systems, automotive, truck, and bus, manufacturing
326199	Windshields, plastics, manufacturing
312130	Wine coolers manufacturing
424820	Wine coolers, alcoholic, merchant wholesalers
445310	Wine shops, packaged
312130	Wineries
312130	Wines manufacturing
424820	Wines merchant wholesalers
312130	Wines, cooking, manufacturing
325998	Wintergreen oil manufacturing
336399	Wipers, windshield, automotive, truck, and bus, manufacturing
313230	Wipes, nonwoven fabric, manufacturing
423840	Wiping cloths merchant wholesalers
423510	Wire (except insulated) merchant wholesalers
423510	Wire and cable (except electrical) merchant wholesalers
333298	Wire and cable insulating machinery manufacturing
331222	Wire cages, iron or steel, made in wire drawing plants
331222	Wire carts (e.g., grocery, household, industrial), iron or steel, made in wire drawing plants
331422	Wire cloth made from purchased copper in wire drawing plants
331319	Wire cloth made in aluminum wire drawing plants
331422	Wire cloth, copper, made in integrated secondary smelting and wire drawing plants
331222	Wire cloth, iron or steel, made in wire drawing plants
331491	Wire cloth, nonferrous metals (except aluminum, copper), made from purchased metals or scrap
423390	Wire fencing and fencing accessories merchant wholesalers
331222	Wire garment hangers, iron or steel, made in wire drawing plants
519110	Wire photo services
331111	Wire products, iron or steel, made in iron and steel mills
331222	Wire products, iron or steel, made in wire drawing plants
423510	Wire rope (except insulated) merchant wholesalers
333923	Wire rope hoists manufacturing
423510	Wire screening merchant wholesalers
331319	Wire screening, aluminum, made in integrated secondary smelting and drawing plants
331491	Wire screening, nonferrous metals (except aluminum, copper), made from purchased nonferrous metals (except aluminum, copper) in wire drawing plants
561422	Wire services (i.e., telemarketing services), floral
519110	Wire services, news
331319	Wire, armored, made in aluminum wire drawing plants
331319	Wire, bare, made in aluminum wire drawing plants
331422	Wire, copper (except mechanical) (e.g., armored, bare, insulated), made from purchased copper in wire drawing plants
331422	Wire, copper (except mechanical) (e.g., armored, bare, insulated), made in integrated secondary smelting and wire drawing plants
331221	Wire, flat, rolled strip, made in cold rolling mills
331319	Wire, insulated, made in aluminum wire drawing plants

321114	Wood products, creosoting purchased wood products
322110	Wood pulp manufacturing
424990	Wood pulp merchant wholesalers
423310	Wood shingles merchant wholesalers
321918	Wood shutters manufacturing
423310	Wood siding merchant wholesalers
238170	Wood siding, installation
333414	Wood stoves manufacturing
424690	Wood treating preparations merchant wholesalers
333210	Wood verneer laminating and gluing machines manufacturing
321911	Wood window frames and sash manufacturing
321999	Wood wool (excelsior) manufacturing
442299	Wood-burning stove stores
321999	Woodenware, kitchen and household, manufacturing
532490	Woodworking machinery and equipment rental or leasing
423830	Woodworking machinery merchant wholesalers
333210	Woodworking machines (except handheld) manufacturing
333292	Wool and worsted finishing machinery manufacturing
313210	Wool fabrics, broadwoven, weaving
313221	Wool fabrics, narrow woven, weaving
313111	Wool spun yarn made from purchased fiber
313312	Wool tops and noils manufacturing
424590	Wool tops and noils merchant wholesalers
314999	Wool waste processing
313112	Wool yarn, twisting or winding of purchased yarn
424590	Wool, raw, merchant wholesalers
311941	Worcestershire sauce manufacturing
333313	Word processing equipment, dedicated, manufacturing
561410	Word processing services
624229	Work (sweat) equity home construction organizations
337127	Work benches manufacturing
812332	Work clothing and uniform supply services, industrial
424320	Work clothing, men's and boys', merchant wholesalers
315211	Work coats and jackets, men's and boys', cut and sew apparel contractors
315225	Work coats and jackets, men's and boys', cut and sewn from purchased fabric (except apparel contractors)
624310	Work experience centers (i.e., sheltered workshops)
315191	Work gloves and mittens, knit, made in apparel knitting mills
315992	Work gloves, leather (except apparel contractors), manufacturing
315211	Work gloves, leather, men's and boys', cut and sew apparel contractors
315212	Work gloves, leather, women's and girls', cut and sew apparel contractors
315225	Work pants (except dungarees, jeans), men's and boys', cut and sewn from purchased fabric (except apparel contractors)
315211	Work pants, men's and boys', cut and sew apparel contractors
315211	Work shirts, men's and boys', cut and sew apparel contractors
315225	Work shirts, men's and boys', cut and sewn from purchased fabric (except apparel contractors)
316213	Work shoes, men's (except rubber or plastics protective footwear), manufacturing
721310	Workers' camps

325110 Xylene made from refined petroleum or liquid hydrocarbons
324110 Xylene made in petroleum refineries
339992 Xylophones and parts manufacturing
713930 Yacht basins
336612 Yacht building, not done in shipyards
713930 Yacht clubs with marinas
713990 Yacht clubs without marinas
532292 Yacht rental without crew
336611 Yachts built in shipyards
111219 Yam farming, field and seed production
424310 Yard goods, textile (except burlap, felt), merchant wholesalers
335121 Yard Lights, residential electric, manufacturing
332212 Yardsticks, metal, manufacturing
321999 Yardsticks, wood, manufacturing
313111 Yarn spinning mills
313111 Yarn spun from purchased fiber
333292 Yarn texturizing machines manufacturing
313112 Yarn throwing, twisting, and winding of purchased yarn
313111 Yarn, carpet and rug, spun from purchased fiber
325221 Yarn, cellulosic filament, manufacturing
325221 Yarn, cellulosic filament, manufacturing and texturizing
327212 Yarn, fiberglass, made in glass making plants
325222 Yarn, noncellulosic fiber and filament, manufacturing
325222 Yarn, noncellulosic fiber and filament, manufacturing and texturizing
424310 Yarns (except industrial), merchant wholesalers
424990 Yarns, industrial, merchant wholesalers

511199 Yearbook (e.g., high school, college, university) publishers (except exclusive Internet publishing)
511199 Yearbook (e.g., high school, college, university) publishers and printing combined
516110 Yearbook (e.g., high school, college, university) publishers, exclusively on Internet
323112 Yearbooks flexographic printing without publishing
323111 Yearbooks gravure printing without publishing
323110 Yearbooks lithographic (offset) printing without publishing
323119 Yearbooks printing (except flexographic, gravure, lithographic, quick, screen) without publishing
323113 Yearbooks screen printing without publishing
311999 Yeast manufacturing
424490 Yeast merchant wholesalers
611699 Yoga instruction, camps, or schools
311511 Yogurt (except frozen) manufacturing
424430 Yogurt merchant wholesalers
311514 Yogurt mix manufacturing
311520 Yogurt, frozen, manufacturing
111334 Youngberry farming
624110 Youth centers (except recreational only)
813410 Youth civic clubs
813410 Youth clubs (except recreational only)
813410 Youth farming organizations
624110 Youth guidance organizations
721199 Youth hostels
813410 Youth scouting organizations
624110 Youth self-help organizations
813410 Youth social clubs
713990 Youth sports leagues or teams
325222 Zein fibers and filaments manufacturing
325188 Zinc ammonium chloride manufacturing

Appendix C

2002 CHANGES to NAICS MATCHED to 1987 SIC

Table 3 - 2002 NAICS United States Matched to 1987 Standard Industrial Classification

2002 NAICS Code	2002 NAICS Description		1987 SIC Code	1987 SIC and Description
236	Construction of Buildings			
2361	Residential Building Construction			
23611	Residential Building Construction			
236115	New Single-Family Housing Construction (except Operative Builders)			
	Single-family housing general contractors	*	1521	General Contractors - Single-Family Houses (except remodeling contractors)
	Single-family housing construction management	*	8741	Management Services (single-family housing construction management)
236116	New Multifamily Housing Construction (except Operative Builders)			
	Multifamily housing general contractors	*	1522	General Contractors - Residential Buildings Other Than Single-Family (except remodeling contractors, hotel and motel construction contractors, and dormitory and barrack construction contractors)
	Multifamily housing construction management	*	8741	Management Services (multifamily housing construction management)
236117	New Housing Operative Builders	*	1531	Operative Builders (residential operative builders)
236118	Residential Remodelers			
	Single-family housing remodeling contractors	*	1521	General Contractors - Single-Family Houses (remodeling contractors)
	Multifamily housing remodeling contractors	*	1522	General Contractors - Residential Buildings Other Than Single-Family (remodeling contractors)
	Operative residential remodelers	*	1531	Operative Builders (residential operative remodelers)
	Construction management for residential remodeling projects	*	8741	Management Services (residential remodeling construction management)
2362	Nonresidential Building Construction			
23621	Industrial Building Construction			
	Operative builders of industrial buildings	*	1531	Operative Builders (Operative builders of industrial and manufacturing buildings except grain elevators, dry cleaning plants, and manufacturing and industrial warehouses)
	Industrial building general contractors	*	1541	General Contractors Industrial Buildings and Warehouses (except grain elevators; drycleaning plants; and manufacturing, public, and industrial warehouses)

NAICS	SIC Match
Industrial nonbuilding structures (except petrochemical plants and refineries)	* 1629 Heavy Construction, NEC (Industrial nonbuilding structures [except petrochemical plants and petroleum refineries])
Industrial building construction management	* 8741 Management Services (industrial building and nonbuilding structure construction management)
23622 Commercial and Institutional Building Construction	
Hotel, motel, dormitory and barrack general contractors	* 1522 General Contractors - Residential Buildings Other Than Single-Family (dormitory, barrack, hotel, and motel construction contractors)
Operative builders of commercial and institutional buildings	* 1531 Operative Builders (grain elevator, dry cleaning plant, and manufacturing and industrial warehouse operative builders)
Grain elevator; dry cleaning plant; and public, industrial, and public warehouse general contractors	* 1541 General Contractors - Industrial Buildings and Warehouses (general contractors of grain elevators; dry cleaning plants; and manufacturing, industrial, and public warehouses)
Nonresidential buildings, other than industrial buildings and warehouses general contractors	* 1542 General Contractors - Nonresidential Buildings, Other than Industrial Buildings and Warehouses
Indoor swimming pool construction	* 1799 Special Trade Contractors, NEC (indoor swimming pool construction contractors)
Commercial and institutional building construction management	* 8741 Management Services (Commercial and Institutional building construction management)
237 Heavy and Civil Engineering Construction	
2371 Utility System Construction	
23711 Water and Sewer Line and Related Structures Construction	
Water and sewer pipelines and related line construction	* 1623 Water, Sewer, Pipeline, and Communications and Power Line Construction (water and sewer pipelines and related construction)
Water and sewage treatment plants and related structures	* 1629 Heavy Construction NEC (irrigation systems, sewage treatment plants, and water treatment plants)
Water well drilling	* 1781 Water Well Drilling
Construction management for water and sewer lines and related structures	* 8741 Management Services (construction management of water, sewer, and related structure construction projects)
23712 Oil and Gas Pipeline and Related Structures Construction	
Construction of oil and gas field gathering lines on a contract basis	* 1389 Oil and Gas Field Services, NEC (construction of field gathering lines on a contract or fee basis)
Oil and gas pipelines, mains, pumping stations, and storage tanks	* 1623 Water, Sewer, Pipeline, and Communications and Power Line Construction (gas and oil pipelines, mains, and pumping stations)

Petrochemical plants and refineries

* 1629 Heavy Construction, NEC (petrochemical plants and refineries)

Oil and gas pipeline and related structure construction management

* 8741 Management Services (construction management of oil and gas pipelines and related structure construction projects)

23713 Power and Communication Line and Related Structures Construction

Power and communication line construction

* 1623 Water, Sewer, Pipeline, and Communications and Power Line Construction (power and communications transmission lines)

Transmission stations, distribution stations, and related structures

* 1629 Heavy Construction, NEC (power generation plants [except hydroelectric dams], transmission stations, and distribution stations)

Power and communication line and related structure construction management

* 8741 Management Services (construction management of power generation [except hydroelectric] facilities, and transmission and distribution station construction projects)

2372 Land Subdivision
23721 Land Subdivision

6552 Land Subdividers and Developers, Except Cemeteries

2373 Highway, Street, and Bridge Construction
23731 Highway, Street, and Bridge Construction

Highway and street construction

1611 Highway and Street Construction

Bridge and elevated highway construction

* 1622 Bridge, Tunnel, and Elevated Highway Construction (bridge and elevated highway construction)

Traffic lane painting

* 1721 Painting and Paper Hanging (traffic lane painting)

Highway, street, and bridge construction management

* 8741 Management Services (highway, street, and bridge construction management)

2379 Other Heavy and Civil Engineering Construction
23799 Other Heavy and Civil Engineering Construction

Tunnel construction

* 1622 Bridge, Tunnel, and Elevated Highway Construction (tunnel construction)

Transit, rail, port, dam, flood control, and other heavy and civil engineering construction

* 1629 Heavy Construction, NEC (except industrial nonbuilding structures, irrigation systems, sewage and water treatment plants, petrochemical plants and refineries, power generation plants [except hydroelectric dams] transmission and distribution stations, right-of-way clearing, line slashing, blasting, and trenching)

Anchored earth retention wall construction contractors

* 1799 Special Trade Contractors, NEC (anchored earth retention contractors)

Other heavy and civil engineering construction management
- * 8741 Management Services (construction management for other heavy and civil engineering construction)

238 Specialty Trade Contractors

2381 Foundation, Structure, and Building Exterior Contractors

23811 Poured Concrete Foundation and Structure Contractors
- * 1771 Concrete Work (except stucco work; and residential and commercial asphalt, brick, and paving)

23812 Structural Steel and Precast Concrete Contractors
- * 1791 Structural Steel Erection (except curtain wall installation, metal furring installation, and cooling tower installation)

23813 Framing Contractors
- * 1751 Carpentry Work (framing carpentry)

23814 Masonry Contractors
Masonry, stone setting, and other stone work
Stucco work
- * 1741 Masonry, Stone Setting, and Other Stone Work
- * 1771 Concrete Work (stucco work)

23815 Glass and Glazing Contractors
Glass and glazing work
Glass tinting work
- * 1793 Glass and Glazing Work
- * 1799 Special Trade Contractors, NEC (glass tinting work)

23816 Roofing Contractors
- * 1761 Roofing, Siding, and Sheet Metal Work (roofing contractors)

23817 Siding Contractors
- * 1761 Roofing, Siding, and Sheet Metal Work (siding contractors)

23819 Other Foundation, Structure, and Building Exterior Contractors
Curtain wall and metal furring installation
Forming and ornamental metal work contractors
- * 1791 Structural Steel Erection (curtain wall installation and metal furring installation)
- * 1799 Special Trade Contractors, NEC (forming contractors and ornamental metal work contractors)

2382 Building Equipment Contractors

23821 Electrical Contractors
Environmental control installation contractors
Electrical contractors
- * 1711 Plumbing, Heating, and Air-Conditioning (environmental control installation contractors)
- * 1731 Electrical Work (except burglar and fire alarm installation)

23822 Plumbing, Heating, and Air-Conditioning Contractors
Plumbing, heating, and air-conditioning contractors
Cooling tower installation contractors
- * 1711 Plumbing, Heating, and Air-Conditioning (except environmental controls installation; and septic tank, cesspool, and dry well construction)
- * 1791 Structural Steel Erection (cooling tower installation)

	NAICS	SIC
	Scrubber, dust collection, and other industrial ventilation equipment installation contractors	1796 Installation or Erection of Building Equipment, NEC (scrubber, dust collection, and other industrial ventilation installation)
	Boiler chipping, scaling, and cleaning	7699 Repair Shops and Related Services, NEC (boiler cleaning, chipping, and scaling)
23829	Other Building Equipment Contractors	
	Elevator, escalator, and other building equipment installation	1796 Installation or Erection of Building Equipment, NEC (except scrubber, dust collection, and other industrial ventilation installation)
	Installation of service station equipment, bowling alley equipment, church bells, clock towers, and similar equipment; and insulation of boilers, pipes, and ducts	1799 Special Trade Contractors, NEC (building equipment installation contractors for service station equipment; boiler, duct, and pipe insulation; lightning rod installation; bowling alley equipment installation; church bell installation; and clock tower installation)
	Household antenna installation	7622 Radio and Television Repair Shops (household antenna installation)
2383	Building Finishing Contractors	
23831	Drywall and Insulation Contractors	
	Plastering, drywall, acoustical, and insulation contractors	1742 Plastering, Drywall, Acoustical, and Insulation Work
	Fresco work	1743 Terrazzo, Tile, Marble, and Mosaic Work (fresco work)
23832	Paint and Wall Covering Contractors	
	Paint and wall covering contractors	1721 Painting and Paper Hanging (except traffic lane painting)
	Paint and wall covering removal contractors	1799 Special Trade Contractors, NEC (paint and wallpaper stripping and removing contractors)
23833	Flooring Contractors	1752 Floor Laying and Other Floor Work, NEC
23834	Tile and Terrazzo Contractors	1743 Terrazzo, Tile, Marble, and Mosaic Work (except fresco work)
23835	Finish Carpentry Contractors	1751 Carpentry Work (finish carpentry)
23839	Other Building Finishing Contractors	
	Sheet metal work (except roofing and siding)	1761 Roofing, Siding, and Sheet Metal Work (except roofing and siding work)
	Weather stripping and damp proofing, modular furniture installation, bathtub refinishing, window covering fixture installation, exhibit installation and removal, and spectator seating installation	1799 Special Trade Contractors, NEC (building finishing contractors for weather stripping and damp proofing, modular furniture installation, bathtub refinishing, window covering refinishing, trade show exhibit installation and dismantling, and spectator seating installation)

2389 Other Specialty Trade Contractors

23891 Site Preparation Contractors

Site preparation and related activities at metal ore mines
- * 1081 Metal Mining Services (site preparation and related construction activities on a contract basis)

Site preparation and related activities at coal mines
- * 1241 Coal Mining Services (site preparation and related construction activities on a contract basis)

Site preparation and related activities at oil and gas fields
- * 1389 Oil and Gas Field Services, NEC (site preparation and related construction activities on a contract basis)

Site preparation and related activities at nonmetallic mineral mines
- * 1481 Nonmetallic Minerals Services, Except Fuels (site preparation and related construction activities on a contract basis)

Right-of-way clearing, line slashing, blasting, and trenching
- * 1629 Heavy Construction, NEC (right-of-way clearing and line slashing, blasting, and trenching)

Septic tank, cesspool, and dry well contractors
- * 1711 Plumbing, Heating, and Air-Conditioning (septic tank, cesspool, and dry well construction contractors)

Excavation contractors
- 1794 Excavation Work

Wrecking and demolition contractors
- 1795 Wrecking and Demolition Work

Dewatering contractors, test boring for construction, and core drilling for construction
- * 1799 Special Trade Contractors, NEC (dewatering contractors, test drilling for construction, and core drilling for construction)

Rental of construction equipment (except cranes) with operator
- * 7353 Construction Equipment Rental and Leasing (rental of construction equipment [except cranes] with operator)

23899 All Other Specialty Trade Contractors

Residential and commercial concrete and asphalt paving
- * 1771 Concrete Work (residential and commercial asphalt, brick, and concrete paving)

Special trade contractors not specified elsewhere
- * 1799 Special Trade Contractors, NEC (except indoor swimming pool contractors, anchored earth retention contractors, glass tinting work, forming contractors, ornamental metal work contractors, service station equipment installation, pipe and duct insulation contractors, lightning rod installation contractors, bowling alley equipment installation, church bell installation, clock tower installation, paint and wall paper removal contractors, miscellaneous building finishing contractors, dewatering contractors, test drilling for construction, and core drilling for construction)

Crane rental with operator
- * 7353 Construction Equipment Rental and Leasing (crane rental with operator)

42 Wholesale Trade

423 Merchant Wholesalers, Durable Goods

NAICS		SIC	
4231	Motor Vehicle and Motor Vehicle Parts and Supplies Merchant Wholesalers		
42311	Automobile and Other Motor Vehicle Merchant Wholesalers	* 5012	Automobiles and Other Motor Vehicles (merchant wholesalers)
42312	Motor Vehicle Supplies and New Parts Merchant Wholesalers	* 5013	Motor Vehicle Supplies and New Parts (merchant wholesalers except selling via retail method)
42313	Tire and Tube Merchant Wholesalers	* 5014	Tires and Tubes (merchant wholesalers except selling via retail method)
42314	Motor Vehicle Parts (Used) Merchant Wholesalers	* 5015	Motor Vehicle Parts, Used (merchant wholesalers except selling via retail method)
4232	Furniture and Home Furnishing Merchant Wholesalers		
42321	Furniture Merchant Wholesalers	* 5021	Furniture (merchant wholesalers except selling via retail method)
42322	Home Furnishing Merchant Wholesalers	* 5023	Homefurnishings (merchant wholesalers except selling via retail method)
4233	Lumber and Other Construction Materials Merchant Wholesalers		
42331	Lumber, Plywood, Millwork, and Wood Panel Merchant Wholesalers		
	Lumber, plywood, millwork, and wood panels	* 5031	Lumber, Plywood, Millwork, and Wood Panels (merchant wholesalers except selling via retail method)
	Nonwood prefabricated buildings and structural assemblies	* 5039	Construction Materials, NEC (prefabricated buildings and structural assemblies, nonwood, merchant wholesalers)
42332	Brick, Stone, and Related Construction Material Merchant Wholesalers	* 5032	Brick, Stone, and Related Construction Materials (merchant wholesalers except selling via retail method)
42333	Roofing, Siding, and Insulation Material Merchant Wholesalers	* 5033	Roofing, Siding, and Insulation Materials (merchant wholesalers except selling via retail method)
42339	Other Construction Material Merchant Wholesalers	* 5039	Construction Materials, NEC (merchant wholesalers of construction materials, nec except selling via retail method)
4234	Professional and Commercial Equipment and Supplies Merchant Wholesalers		
42341	Photographic Equipment and Supplies Merchant Wholesalers	* 5043	Photographic Equipment and Supplies (merchant wholesalers)
42342	Office Equipment Merchant Wholesalers	* 5044	Office Equipment (merchant wholesalers except selling via retail method)

NAICS	NAICS Description		SIC	SIC Description
42343	Computer and Computer Peripheral Equipment and Software Merchant Wholesalers	*	5045	Computers and Computer Peripheral Equipment and Software (merchant wholesalers except selling via retail method)
42344	Other Commercial Equipment Merchant Wholesalers	*	5046	Commercial Equipment, NEC (merchant wholesalers)
42345	Medical, Dental, and Hospital Equipment and Supplies Merchant Wholesalers	*	5047	Medical, Dental, and Hospital Equipment and Supplies (merchant wholesalers except selling via retail method)
42346	Ophthalmic Goods Merchant Wholesalers	*	5048	Ophthalmic Goods (merchant wholesalers)
42349	Other Professional Equipment and Supplies Merchant Wholesalers	*	5049	Professional Equipment and Supplies, NEC (merchant wholesalers except selling via retail method)
4235	Metal and Mineral (except Petroleum) Merchant Wholesalers			
42351	Metals Service Centers and Other Metal Merchant Wholesalers	*	5051	Metals Service Centers and Offices (merchant wholesalers)
42352	Coal and Other Mineral and Ore Merchant Wholesalers	*	5052	Coal and Other Minerals and Ores (merchant wholesalers)
4236	Electrical and Electronic Goods Merchant Wholesalers			
42361	Electrical Apparatus and Equipment, Wiring Supplies, and Related Equipment Merchant Wholesalers	*	5063	Electrical Apparatus and Equipment, Wiring Supplies, and Construction Materials (merchant wholesalers except selling via retail method)
42362	Electrical and Electronic Appliance, Television, and Radio Set Merchant Wholesalers	*	5064	Electrical Appliances, Television and Radio Sets (merchant wholesalers except selling via retail method)
42369	Other Electronic Parts and Equipment Merchant Wholesalers	*	5065	Electronic Parts and Equipment, NEC (merchant wholesalers except selling via retail method)
4237	Hardware, and Plumbing and Heating Equipment and Supplies Merchant Wholesalers			
42371	Hardware Merchant Wholesalers	*	5072	Hardware (merchant wholesalers except selling via retail method)
42372	Plumbing and Heating Equipment and Supplies (Hydronics) Merchant Wholesalers	*	5074	Plumbing and Heating Equipment and Supplies (Hydronics) (merchant wholesalers except selling via retail method)
42373	Warm Air Heating and Air-Conditioning Equipment and Supplies Merchant Wholesalers	*	5075	Warm Air Heating and Air-Conditioning Equipment and Supplies (merchant wholesalers)

NAICS	Description		SIC	Description
42374	Refrigeration Equipment and Supplies Merchant Wholesalers	*	5078	Refrigeration Equipment and Supplies (merchant wholesalers)
4238	Machinery, Equipment, and Supplies Merchant Wholesalers			
42381	Construction and Mining (except Oil Well) Machinery and Equipment Merchant Wholesalers	*	5082	Construction and Mining (Except Petroleum) Machinery and Equipment (merchant wholesalers)
42382	Farm and Garden Machinery and Equipment Merchant Wholesalers	*	5083	Farm and Garden Machinery and Equipment (merchant wholesalers except lawn and garden equipment sold via retail method)
42383	Industrial Machinery and Equipment Merchant Wholesalers			
	Industrial machinery and equipment	*	5084	Industrial Machinery and Equipment (merchant wholesalers)
	Fluid power accessories	*	5085	Industrial Supplies (fluid power accessories merchant wholesalers)
42384	Industrial Supplies Merchant Wholesalers	*	5085	Industrial Supplies (merchant wholesalers - except selling via retail method and merchant wholesalers of fluid power accessories)
42385	Service Establishment Equipment and Supplies Merchant Wholesalers	*	5087	Service Establishment Equipment and Supplies (merchant wholesalers, except merchant wholesalers selling beauty and barbershop equipment and supplies via retail method)
42386	Transportation Equipment and Supplies (except Motor Vehicle) Merchant Wholesalers	*	5088	Transportation Equipment and Supplies, Except Motor Vehicles (merchant wholesalers)
4239	Miscellaneous Durable Goods Merchant Wholesalers			
42391	Sporting and Recreational Goods and Supplies Merchant Wholesalers			
	Sporting and recreational goods and supplies merchant wholesalers	*	5091	Sporting and Recreational Goods and Supplies (merchant wholesalers except selling via retail method)
	Men's and boy's athletic uniforms		5136	Men's and Boy's Clothing and Furnishing (athletic uniform merchant wholesalers except selling via retail method)
	Other athletic uniforms	*	5137	Women's, Children's, and Infant's Clothing and Accessories (other athletic uniform merchant wholesalers except selling via retail method)
42392	Toy and Hobby Goods and Supplies Merchant Wholesalers	*	5092	Toys and Hobby Goods and Supplies (merchant wholesalers except selling via retail method)

NAICS		SIC	
42393	Recyclable Material Merchant Wholesalers	5093	Scrap and Waste Materials (merchant wholesalers)
42394	Jewelry, Watch, Precious Stone, and Precious Metal Merchant Wholesalers	5094	Jewelry, Watches, Precious Stones, and Precious Metals (merchant wholesalers except selling via retail method)
42399	Other Miscellaneous Durable Goods Merchant Wholesalers	5099	Durable Goods, NEC (merchant wholesalers except selling via retail method)
	Durable goods, nec merchant wholesalers		
	Prerecorded video tape merchant wholesalers	7822	Motion Picture and Video Tape Distribution (merchant wholesalers)
424	Merchant Wholesalers, Nondurable Goods		
4241	Paper and Paper Product Merchant Wholesalers		
42411	Printing and Writing Paper Merchant Wholesalers	5111	Printing and Writing Paper (merchant wholesalers except selling via retail method)
42412	Stationary and Office Supplies Merchant Wholesalers	5112	Stationary and Office Supplies (merchant wholesalers except selling via retail method)
42413	Industrial and Personal Service Paper Merchant Wholesalers	5113	Industrial and Personal Service Paper (merchant wholesalers except selling via retail method)
4242	Drugs and Druggists' Sundries Merchant Wholesalers		
42421	Drugs and Druggists' Sundries Merchant Wholesalers	5122	Drugs, Drug Proprietaries, and Druggists' Sundries (merchant wholesalers except selling via retail method)
4243	Apparel, Piece Goods, and Notions Merchant Wholesalers		
42431	Piece Goods, Notions, and Other Dry Goods Merchant Wholesalers	5131	Piece Goods, Notions, and Other Dry Goods (merchant wholesalers- except selling via retail method and piece goods converters)
42432	Men's and Boys' Clothing and Furnishings Merchant Wholesalers	5136	Men's and Boys' Clothing and Furnishings (merchant wholesalers [except athletic uniforms and merchant wholesalers selling via retail method])
42433	Women's, Children's, and Infants' Clothing and Accessories Merchant Wholesalers	5137	Women's, Children's, and Infants' Clothing and Accessories (merchant wholesalers [except athletic uniforms and merchant wholesalers selling via retail method])
42434	Footwear Merchant Wholesalers	5139	Footwear (merchant wholesalers except selling via retail method)
	Footwear merchant wholesalers		

NAICS	SIC
Footwear cut stock merchant wholesalers	* 5199 Nondurable Goods, NEC (footwear cut stock merchant wholesalers)
4244 Grocery and Related Product Merchant Wholesalers	
42441 General Line Grocery Merchant Wholesalers	* 5141 Groceries, General Line (merchant wholesalers except selling via retail method)
42442 Packaged Frozen Food Merchant Wholesalers	* 5142 Packaged Frozen Foods (merchant wholesalers except selling via retail method)
42443 Dairy Product (except Dried or Canned) Merchant Wholesalers	* 5143 Dairy Products, Except Dried or Canned (merchant wholesalers except selling via retail method)
42444 Poultry and Poultry Product Merchant Wholesalers	* 5144 Poultry and Poultry Products (merchant wholesalers except selling via retail method)
42445 Confectionery Merchant Wholesalers	* 5145 Confectionery (merchant wholesalers except selling via retail method)
42446 Fish and Seafood Merchant Wholesalers	* 5146 Fish and Seafoods (merchant wholesalers except selling via retail method)
42447 Meat and Meat Product Merchant Wholesalers	* 5147 Meats and Meat Products (merchant wholesalers [except boxed beef manufacturers and merchant wholesalers selling via retail method])
42448 Fresh Fruit and Vegetable Merchant Wholesalers	* 5148 Fresh Fruits and Vegetables (merchant wholesalers except selling via retail method)
42449 Other Grocery and Related Products Merchant Wholesalers	* 5149 Groceries and Related Products, NEC (merchant wholesalers [except bottled water manufacturers and merchant wholesalers selling via retail method])
4245 Farm Product Raw Material Merchant Wholesalers	
42451 Grain and Field Bean Merchant Wholesalers	* 5153 Grain and Field Beans (merchant wholesalers except selling via retail method)
42452 Livestock Merchant Wholesalers	* 5154 Livestock (merchant wholesalers)
42459 Other Farm Product Raw Material Merchant Wholesalers	* 5159 Farm-Product Raw Materials, NEC (merchant wholesalers except selling via retail method)
4246 Chemical and Allied Products Merchant Wholesalers	

NAICS		SIC	
42461	Plastics Materials and Basic Forms and Shapes Merchant Wholesalers		
	Plastics materials and basic forms and shapes merchant wholesalers	* 5162	Plastics materials and Basic Forms and Shapes (merchant wholesalers except selling via retail method)
	Plastics foam merchant wholesalers	* 5199	Nondurable Goods, NEC (plastics foam merchant wholesalers)
42469	Other Chemical and Allied Products Merchant Wholesalers	* 5169	Chemicals and Allied Products, NEC (merchant wholesalers)
4247	Petroleum and Petroleum Products Merchant Wholesalers		
42471	Petroleum Bulk Stations and Terminals	* 5171	Petroleum Bulk Stations and Terminals (except petroleum sold via retail method)
42472	Petroleum and Petroleum Products Merchant Wholesalers (except Bulk Stations and Terminals)	* 5172	Petroleum and Petroleum Products Wholesalers, Except Bulk Stations and Terminals (merchant wholesalers)
4248	Beer, Wine, and Distilled Alcoholic Beverage Merchant Wholesalers		
42481	Beer and Ale Merchant Wholesalers	* 5181	Beer and Ale (merchant wholesalers except selling via retail method)
42482	Wine and Distilled Alcoholic Beverage Merchant Wholesalers	* 5182	Wine and Distilled Alcoholic Beverages (merchant wholesalers except selling via retail method)
4249	Miscellaneous Nondurable Goods Merchant Wholesalers		
42491	Farm Supplies Merchant Wholesalers	* 5191	Farm Supplies (merchant wholesalers except selling lawn and garden supplies via retail method)
42492	Book, Periodical, and Newspaper Merchant Wholesalers	* 5192	Books, Periodicals, and Newspapers (merchant wholesalers except selling via retail method)
42493	Flower, Nursery Stock, and Florists' Supplies Merchant Wholesalers	* 5193	Flowers, Nursery Stock, and Florists' Supplies (merchant wholesalers except selling via retail method)
42494	Tobacco and Tobacco Product Merchant Wholesalers	* 5194	Tobacco and Tobacco Products (merchant wholesalers except selling via retail method)
42495	Paint, Varnish, and Supplies Merchant Wholesalers	* 5195	Paints, Varnishes, and Supplies (merchant wholesalers)
42499	Other Miscellaneous Nondurable Goods Merchant Wholesalers	* 5199	Nondurable Goods, NEC (merchant wholesalers [except advertising specialties goods distributors, footwear cutstock, plastics foam, and merchant wholesalers selling nondurable goods, nec via retail method])

425 Wholesale Electronic Markets and Agents and Brokers
4251 Wholesale Electronic Markets and Agents and Brokers
42511 Business to Business Electronic Markets

- Motor vehicle business to business electronic markets
- Motor vehicle parts and supplies business to business electronic markets
- Tire and tube business to business electronic markets
- Used motor vehicle parts business to business electronic markets
- Furniture business to business electronic markets
- Homefurnishings business to business electronic markets
- Lumber, plywood, and panel business to business electronic markets
- Brick, stone, and related products business to business electronic markets
- Roofing, siding and insulation business to business electronic markets
- Construction materials, nec business to business electronic markets
- Photographic equipment and supplies business to business electronic markets
- Office equipment business to business electronic markets
- Computers and related equipment business to business electronic markets
- Commercial equipment, nec business to business electronic markets
- Medical, dental, and hospital equipment and supplies business to business electronic markets
- Ophthalmic goods business to business electronic markets
- Professional equipment and supplies business to business electronic markets
- Metals business to business electronic markets
- Coal and other mineral and ore business to business electronic markets
- Electrical apparatus and equipment and wiring supplies business to business electronic markets

- 5012 Automobiles and Other Motor Vehicles (business to business electronic markets)
- 5013 Motor Vehicle Supplies and New Parts (business to business electronic markets)
- 5014 Tires and Tubes (business to business electronic markets)
- 5015 Motor Vehicle Parts, Used (business to business electronic markets)
- 5021 Furniture (business to business electronic markets)
- 5023 Homefurnishings (business to business electronic markets)
- 5031 Lumber, Plywood, Millwork, and Wood Panels (business to business electronic markets)
- 5032 Brick, Stone, and Related Construction Materials (business to business electronic markets)
- 5033 Roofing, Siding, and Insulation Materials (business to business electronic markets)
- 5039 Construction Materials, NEC (business to business electronic markets)
- 5043 Photographic Equipment and Supplies (business to business electronic markets)
- 5044 Office Equipment (business to business electronic markets)
- 5045 Computers and Computer Peripheral Equipment and Software (business to business electronic markets)
- 5046 Commercial Equipment, NEC (business to business electronic markets)
- 5047 Medical, Dental, and Hospital Equipment and Supplies (business to business electronic markets)
- 5048 Ophthalmic Goods (business to business electronic markets)
- 5049 Professional Equipment and Supplies, NEC (business to business electronic markets)
- 5051 Metals Service Centers and Offices (business to business electronic markets)
- 5052 Coal and Other Minerals and Ores (business to business electronic markets)
- 5063 Electrical Apparatus and Equipment, Wiring Supplies, and Construction Materials (business to business electronic markets)

- 5064 Electrical Appliances, Television and Radio Sets (business to business electronic markets)
- 5065 Electronic Parts and Equipment, NEC (business to business electronic markets)
- 5072 Hardware (business to business electronic markets)
- 5074 Plumbing and Heating Equipment and Supplies (Hydronics) (business to business electronic markets)
- 5075 Warm Air Heating and Air-Conditioning Equipment and Supplies (business to business electronic markets)
- 5078 Refrigeration Equipment and Supplies (business to business electronic markets)
- 5082 Construction and Mining (Except Petroleum) Machinery and Equipment (business to business electronic markets)
- 5083 Farm and Garden Machinery and Equipment (business to business electronic markets)
- 5084 Industrial Machinery and Equipment (business to business electronic markets)
- 5085 Industrial Supplies (business to business electronic markets)
- 5087 Service Establishment Equipment and Supplies (business to business electronic markets)
- 5088 Transportation Equipment and Supplies, Except Motor Vehicles (business to business electronic markets)
- 5091 Sporting and Recreational Goods and Supplies (business to business electronic markets)
- 5092 Toys and Hobby Goods and Supplies (business to business electronic markets)
- 5093 Scrap and Waste Materials (business to business electronic markets)
- 5094 Jewelry, Watches, Precious Stones, and Precious Metals (business to business electronic markets)
- 5099 Durable Goods, NEC (business to business electronic markets)
- 5111 Printing and Writing Paper (business to business electronic markets)
- 5112 Stationary and Office Supplies (business to business electronic markets)
- 5113 Industrial and Personal Service Paper (business to business electronic markets)
- 5122 Drugs, Drug Proprietaries, and Druggists' Sundries (business to business electronic markets)
- 5131 Piece Goods, Notions, and Other Dry Goods (business to business electronic markets)

Electrical appliance business to business electronic markets

Electronic parts business to business electronic markets

Hardware business to business electronic markets

Plumbing and hot water heating equipment business to business electronic markets

Warm air heating and air-conditioning equipment business to business electronic markets

Refrigeration equipment and supplies business to business electronic markets

Construction and mining equipment business to business electronic markets

Farm and garden machinery business to business electronic markets

Industrial machinery and equipment business to business electronic markets

Industrial supplies business to business electronic markets

Service industry equipment and supplies business to business electronic markets

Transportation equipment and supplies, except motor vehicle, business to business electronic markets

Sporting goods business to business electronic markets

Toys and hobby supply business to business electronic markets

Scrap and waste material business to business electronic markets

Jewelry, watches, and related goods business to business electronic markets

Durable goods, nec business to business electronic markets

Printing and writing paper business to business electronic markets

Stationary and office supplies business to business electronic markets

Other paper business to business electronic markets

Drugs and related products business to business electronic markets

Dry goods business to business electronic markets

* 5136 Men's and Boy's Clothing and Furnishing (business to business electronic markets)
* 5137 Women's, Children's, and Infant's Clothing and Accessories (business to business electronic markets)
* 5139 Footwear (business to business electronic markets)
* 5141 Groceries, General Line (business to business electronic markets)
* 5142 Packaged Frozen Foods (business to business electronic markets)
* 5143 Dairy Products, Except Dried or Canned (business to business electronic markets)
* 5144 Poultry and Poultry Products (business to business electronic markets)
* 5145 Confectionery (business to business electronic markets)
* 5146 Fish and Seafoods (business to business electronic markets)
* 5147 Meats and Meat Products (business to business electronic markets)
* 5148 Fresh Fruits and Vegetables (business to business electronic markets)
* 5149 Groceries and Related Products, NEC (business to business electronic markets)
* 5153 Grain and Field Beans (business to business electronic markets)
* 5154 Livestock (business to business electronic markets)
* 5159 Farm-Product Raw Materials, NEC (business to business electronic markets)
* 5162 Plastics materials and Basic Forms and Shapes (business to business electronic markets)
* 5169 Chemicals and Allied Products, NEC (business to business electronic markets)
* 5172 Petroleum and Petroleum Products Wholesalers, Except Bulk Stations and Terminals (business to business electronic markets)
* 5181 Beer and Ale (business to business electronic markets)
* 5182 Wine and Distilled Alcoholic Beverages (business to business electronic markets)
* 5191 Farm Supplies (business to business electronic markets)
* 5192 Books, Periodicals, and Newspapers (business to business electronic markets)
* 5193 Flowers, Nursery Stock, and Florists' Supplies (business to business electronic markets)

Men's and boys' clothing business to business electronic markets

Women's and children's business to business electronic markets

Footwear business to business electronic markets
General line grocery business to business electronic markets

Frozen food business to business electronic markets

Dairy product business to business electronic markets

Poultry and poultry product business to business electronic markets

Confectionery business to business electronic markets
Fish and seafood business to business electronic markets

Meat and meat product business to business electronic markets

Fresh fruit and vegetable business to business electronic markets

Grocery and related product, nec business to business electronic markets

Grain and field bean business to business electronic markets

Livestock business to business electronic markets
Farm products, nec business to business electronic markets

Plastics business to business electronic markets

Chemicals business to business electronic markets

Petroleum and petroleum product business to business electronic markets

Beer and ale business to business electronic markets
Wine and distilled beverage business to business electronic markets

Farm supply business to business electronic markets
Book and other published material business to business electronic markets

Flower and nursery stock business to business electronic markets

		SIC	
Tobacco and tobacco product business to business electronic markets	*	5194	Tobacco and Tobacco Products (business to business electronic markets)
Paint and related product business to business electronic markets	*	5195	Paints, Varnishes, and Supplies (business to business electronic markets)
Nondurable goods, nec business to business electronic markets	*	5199	Nondurable Goods, NEC (business to business electronic markets)
42512 Wholesale Trade Agents and Brokers			
Motor vehicle wholesale trade agents and brokers	*	5012	Automobiles and Other Motor Vehicles (wholesale trade agents and brokers)
Motor vehicle parts and supplies wholesale trade agents and brokers	*	5013	Motor Vehicle Supplies and New Parts (wholesale trade agents and brokers)
Tire and tube wholesale trade agents and brokers	*	5014	Tires and Tubes (wholesale trade agents and brokers)
Used motor vehicle parts wholesale trade agents and brokers	*	5015	Motor Vehicle Parts, Used (wholesale trade agents and brokers)
Furniture wholesale trade agents and brokers	*	5021	Furniture (wholesale trade agents and brokers)
Homefurnishings wholesale trade agents and brokers	*	5023	Homefurnishings (wholesale trade agents and brokers)
Lumber, plywood, and panel wholesale trade agents and brokers	*	5031	Lumber, Plywood, Millwork, and Wood Panels (wholesale trade agents and brokers)
Brick, stone, and related products wholesale trade agents and brokers	*	5032	Brick, Stone, and Related Construction Materials (wholesale trade agents and brokers)
Roofing, siding and insulation wholesale trade agents and brokers	*	5033	Roofing, Siding, and Insulation Materials (wholesale trade agents and brokers)
Construction materials, nec wholesale trade agents and brokers	*	5039	Construction Materials, NEC (wholesale trade agents and brokers)
Photographic equipment and supplies wholesale trade agents and brokers	*	5043	Photographic Equipment and Supplies (wholesale trade agents and brokers)
Office equipment wholesale trade agents and brokers	*	5044	Office Equipment (wholesale trade agents and brokers)
Computers and related equipment wholesale trade agents and brokers	*	5045	Computers and Computer Peripheral Equipment and Software (wholesale trade agents and brokers)
Commercial equipment, nec wholesale trade agents and brokers	*	5046	Commercial Equipment, NEC (wholesale trade agents and brokers)
Medical, dental, and hospital equipment and supplies wholesale trade agents and brokers	*	5047	Medical, Dental, and Hospital Equipment and Supplies (wholesale trade agents and brokers)
Ophthalmic goods wholesale trade agents and brokers	*	5048	Ophthalmic Goods (wholesale trade agents and brokers)
Professional equipment and supplies wholesale trade agents and brokers	*	5049	Professional Equipment and Supplies, NEC (wholesale trade agents and brokers)
Metals wholesale trade agents and brokers	*	5051	Metals Service Centers and Offices (wholesale trade agents and brokers)
Coal and other mineral and ore wholesale trade agents and brokers	*	5052	Coal and Other Minerals and Ores (wholesale trade agents and brokers)

SIC		NAICS
5063 Electrical Apparatus and Equipment, Wiring Supplies, and Construction Materials (wholesale trade agents and brokers)	*	Electrical apparatus and equipment and wiring supplies wholesale trade agents and brokers
5064 Electrical Appliances, Television and Radio Sets (wholesale trade agents and brokers)	*	Electrical appliance wholesale trade agents and brokers
5065 Electronic Parts and Equipment, NEC (wholesale trade agents and brokers)	*	Electronic parts wholesale trade agents and brokers
5072 Hardware (wholesale trade agents and brokers)	*	Hardware wholesale trade agents and brokers
5074 Plumbing and Heating Equipment and Supplies (Hydronics) (wholesale trade agents and brokers)		Plumbing and hot water heating equipment wholesale trade agents and brokers
5075 Warm Air Heating and Air-Conditioning Equipment and Supplies (wholesale trade agents and brokers)	*	Warm air heating and air-conditioning equipment wholesale trade agents and brokers
5078 Refrigeration Equipment and Supplies (wholesale trade agents and brokers)	*	Refrigeration equipment and supplies wholesale trade agents and brokers
5082 Construction and Mining (Except Petroleum) Machinery and Equipment (wholesale trade agents and brokers)	*	Construction and mining equipment wholesale trade agents and brokers
5083 Farm and Garden Machinery and Equipment (wholesale trade agents and brokers)		Farm and garden machinery wholesale trade agents and brokers
5084 Industrial Machinery and Equipment (wholesale trade agents and brokers)	*	Industrial machinery and equipment wholesale trade agents and brokers
5085 Industrial Supplies (wholesale trade agents and brokers)	*	Industrial supplies wholesale trade agents and brokers
5087 Service Establishment Equipment and Supplies (wholesale trade agents and brokers)	*	Service industry equipment and supplies wholesale trade agents and brokers
5088 Transportation Equipment and Supplies, Except Motor Vehicles (wholesale trade agents and brokers)	*	Transportation equipment and supplies, except motor vehicle, wholesale trade agents and brokers
5091 Sporting and Recreational Goods and Supplies (wholesale trade agents and brokers)	*	Sporting goods wholesale trade agents and brokers
5092 Toys and Hobby Goods and Supplies (wholesale trade agents and brokers)	*	Toys and hobby supply wholesale trade agents and brokers
5093 Scrap and Waste Materials (wholesale trade agents and brokers)	*	Scrap and waste material wholesale trade agents and brokers
5094 Jewelry, Watches, Precious Stones, and Precious Metals (wholesale trade agents and brokers)	*	Jewelry, watches, and related goods wholesale trade agents and brokers
5099 Durable Goods, NEC (wholesale trade agents and brokers)	*	Durable goods, nec wholesale trade agents and brokers
5111 Printing and Writing Paper (wholesale trade agents and brokers)	*	Printing and writing paper wholesale trade agents and brokers
5112 Stationary and Office Supplies (wholesale trade agents and brokers)	*	Stationary and office supplies wholesale trade agents and brokers
5113 Industrial and Personal Service Paper (wholesale trade agents and brokers)	*	Other paper wholesale trade agents and brokers
5122 Drugs, Drug Proprietaries, and Druggists' Sundries (wholesale trade agents and brokers)	*	Drugs and related products wholesale trade agents and brokers

Code	Description	Matched description
5131	Piece Goods, Notions, and Other Dry Goods (wholesale trade agents and brokers)	Dry goods wholesale trade agents and brokers
* 5136	Men's and Boy's Clothing and Furnishing (wholesale trade agents and brokers)	Men's and boys' clothing wholesale trade agents and brokers
* 5137	Women's, Children's, and Infant's Clothing and Accessories (wholesale trade agents and brokers)	Women's and children's wholesale trade agents and brokers
* 5139	Footwear (wholesale trade agents and brokers)	Footwear wholesale trade agents and brokers
* 5141	Groceries, General Line (wholesale trade agents and brokers)	General line grocery wholesale trade agents and brokers
5142	Packaged Frozen Foods (wholesale trade agents and brokers)	Frozen food wholesale trade agents and brokers
* 5143	Dairy Products, Except Dried or Canned (wholesale trade agents and brokers)	Dairy product wholesale trade agents and brokers
* 5144	Poultry and Poultry Products (wholesale trade agents and brokers)	Poultry and poultry product wholesale trade agents and brokers
* 5145	Confectionery (wholesale trade agents and brokers)	Confectionery wholesale trade agents and brokers
* 5146	Fish and Seafoods (wholesale trade agents and brokers)	Fish and seafood wholesale trade agents and brokers
* 5147	Meats and Meat Products (wholesale trade agents and brokers)	Meat and meat product wholesale trade agents and brokers
* 5148	Fresh Fruits and Vegetables (wholesale trade agents and brokers)	Fresh fruit and vegetable wholesale trade agents and brokers
* 5149	Groceries and Related Products, NEC (wholesale trade agents and brokers)	Grocery and related product, nec wholesale trade agents and brokers
* 5153	Grain and Field Beans (wholesale trade agents and brokers)	Grain and field bean wholesale trade agents and brokers
* 5154	Livestock (wholesale trade agents and brokers)	Livestock wholesale trade agents and brokers
* 5159	Farm-Product Raw Materials, NEC (wholesale trade agents and brokers)	Farm products, nec wholesale trade agents and brokers
* 5162	Plastics materials and Basic Forms and Shapes (wholesale trade agents and brokers)	Plastics wholesale trade agents and brokers
* 5169	Chemicals and Allied Products, NEC (wholesale trade agents and brokers)	Chemicals wholesale trade agents and brokers
* 5172	Petroleum and Petroleum Products Wholesalers, Except Bulk Stations and Terminals (wholesale trade agents and brokers)	Petroleum and petroleum product wholesale trade agents and brokers
* 5181	Beer and Ale (wholesale trade agents and brokers)	Beer and ale wholesale trade agents and brokers
* 5182	Wine and Distilled Alcoholic Beverages (wholesale trade agents and brokers)	Wine and distilled beverage wholesale trade agents and brokers
* 5191	Farm Supplies (wholesale trade agents and brokers)	Farm supply wholesale trade agents and brokers
* 5192	Books, Periodicals, and Newspapers (wholesale trade agents and brokers)	Book and other published material wholesale trade agents and brokers
* 5193	Flowers, Nursery Stock, and Florists' Supplies (wholesale trade agents and brokers)	Flower and nursery stock wholesale trade agents and brokers

NAICS		SIC
	Tobacco and tobacco product wholesale trade agents and brokers	* 5194 Tobacco and Tobacco Products (wholesale trade agents and brokers)
	Paint and related product wholesale trade agents and brokers	* 5195 Paints, Varnishes, and Supplies (wholesale trade agents and brokers)
	Nondurable goods, nec wholesale trade agents and brokers	* 5199 Nondurable Goods, NEC (wholesale trade agents and brokers)
	Yacht brokers	* 7389 Business Services, NEC (yacht brokers)
4521	Department Stores	
4521	Department Stores	
452111	Department Stores (except Discount Department Stores)	* 5311 Department Stores (traditional department stores)
452112	Discount Department Stores	* 5311 Department Stores (discount department stores)
4541	Electronic Shopping and Mail-Order Houses	
45411	Electronic Shopping and Mail-Order Houses	
454111	Electronic Shopping	* 5961 Catalog and Mail-Order Houses (Internet shopping)
454112	Electronic Auctions	* 5961 Catalog and Mail-Order Houses (electronic retail auctions)
454113	Mail-Order Houses	* 5961 Catalog and Mail-Order Houses (except Internet shopping and electronic retail auctions)
51	Information	
511	Publishing Industries (except Internet)	
5111	Newspaper, Periodical, Book, and Directory Publishers	
51111	Newspaper Publishers	* 2711 Newspapers: Publishing or Publishing and Printing (except Internet newspaper publishing)
51112	Periodical Publishers	
	Periodical publishers (except Internet periodicals)	* 2721 Periodicals: Publishing or Publishing and Printing (except Internet periodical publishing)
	Shopping news publishing (except Internet)	* 2741 Miscellaneous Publishing (shopping news publishing except on-line shopping news)
51113	Book Publishers	
	Book publishers (except Internet)	* 2731 Books: Publishing or Publishing and Printing (except music books and Internet book publishing)
	Technical book and manual publishers (except Internet)	* 2741 Miscellaneous Publishing (technical books and manuals, except Internet publishing)
51114	Directory and Mailing List Publishers	

NAICS	Description		SIC	Description
51119	Directory and database publishers (except Internet)	•	2741	Miscellaneous Publishing (database and directory publishing, except Internet)
511191	Mailing list compilers	•	7331	Direct Mail Advertising Services (mailing list compilers)
	Other Publishers			
	Greeting Card Publishers	•	2771	Greeting Cards (publishing or publishing and printing greeting cards, except Internet greeting card publishing)
511199	All Other Publishers	•	2741	Miscellaneous Publishing (except database, directory, sheet music, shopping news, technical manuals, technical books, and Internet versions of these activities)
5112	Software Publishers			
51121	Software Publishers	•	7372	Prepackaged Software (software publishing)
512	Motion Picture and Sound Recording Industries			
5121	Motion Picture and Video Industries			
51211	Motion Picture and Video Production		7812	Motion Picture and Video Tape Production
51212	Motion Picture and Video Distribution			
	Motion picture and video distribution	•	7822	Motion Picture and Video Tape Distribution (except video tape and cassette wholesalers)
	Commercial distribution film libraries	•	7829	Services Allied to Motion Picture Distribution (commercial distribution film libraries)
51213	Motion Picture and Video Exhibition			
512131	Motion Picture Theaters (except Drive-Ins)	•	7832	Motion Picture Theaters, Except Drive-In
512132	Drive-In Motion Picture Theaters	•	7833	Drive-In Motion Picture Theaters
51219	Post Production Services and Other Motion Picture and Video Industries			
512191	Teleproduction and Other Postproduction Services	•	7819	Services Allied to Motion Picture Production (teleproduction and postproduction services)
512199	Other Motion Picture and Video Industries	•	7819	Services Allied to Motion Picture Production (except casting bureaus, wardrobe and equipment rental, talent payment services, teleproduction and postproduction services, reproduction of videos, film distributors, and other related motion picture production services)
5122	Sound Recording Industries			
51221	Record Production	•	8999	Services, NEC (record production)

NAICS			SIC	
51222	Integrated Record Production/Distribution	*	3652	Phonograph Records and Prerecorded Audio Tapes and Disks (integrated record companies, except duplication only)
51223	Music Publishers			
	Music book publishing	*	2731	Books: Publishing, or Publishing and Printing (music books)
	Sheet music publishing	*	2741	Miscellaneous Publishing (sheet music publishing)
	Music publishers	*	8999	Services, NEC (music publishing)
51224	Sound Recording Studios	*	7389	Business Services, NEC (recording studios)
51229	Other Sound Recording Industries			
	Audio taping services	*	7389	Business Services, NEC (audio taping services)
	Radio program producers	*	7922	Theatrical Producers (Except Motion Picture) and Miscellaneous Theatrical Services (producers of radio programs)
515	Broadcasting (except Internet)			
5151	Radio and Television Broadcasting			
51511	Radio Broadcasting			
515111	Radio Networks	*	4832	Radio Broadcasting Stations (radio networks)
515112	Radio Stations	*	4832	Radio Broadcasting Stations (radio stations)
51512	Television Broadcasting	*	4833	Television Broadcasting Stations
5152	Cable and Other Subscription Programming			
51521	Cable and Other Subscription Programming	*	4841	Cable and Other Pay Television Services (cable and other subscription programming)
516	Internet Publishing and Broadcasting			
5161	Internet Publishing and Broadcasting			
51611	Internet Publishing and Broadcasting			
	Internet newspaper publishers	*	2711	Newspapers: Publishing or Publishing and Printing (Internet newspaper publishing)
	Internet periodical publishers	*	2721	Periodicals: Publishing or Publishing and Printing (Internet newspaper publishing)
	Internet book publishers	*	2731	Books: Publishing or Publishing and Printing (Internet book publishing)
	Miscellaneous Internet publishing	*	2741	Miscellaneous Publishing (Internet publishing)
	Internet greeting card publishers	*	2771	Greeting Cards (Internet greeting card publishers)
	Internet broadcasting		8999	Services NEC (Internet broadcasting)

	NAICS		SIC
	517 Telecommunications		
	5171 Wired Telecommunications Carriers		
	51711 Wired Telecommunications Carriers		
	Wired telephone service	*	4813 Telephone Communications, Except Radiotelephone (except resellers)
	Other wired telecommunications services		4822 Telegraph and Other Message Communications
	5172 Wireless Telecommunications Carriers (except Satellite)		
	51721 Wireless Telecommunications Carriers (except Satellite)		
	517211 Paging	*	4812 Radiotelephone Communications (paging carriers)
	517212 Cellular and Other Wireless Telecommunications		
	Cellular carriers	*	4812 Radiotelephone Communications (cellular carriers)
	Other wireless telecommunications	*	4899 Radiotelephone Communications (ship-to-shore telecommunications)
	5173 Telecommunications Resellers		
	51731 Telecommunications Resellers		
	Wireless telecommunications resellers	*	4812 Radiotelephone Communications (cellular and paging resellers)
	Wired telecommunications resellers	*	4813 Telephone Communications, Except Radiotelephone (wired telecommunications resellers)
	5174 Satellite Telecommunications		
	51741 Satellite Telecommunications	*	4899 Communications Services, NEC (satellite telecommunications)
	5175 Cable and Other Program Distribution		
	51751 Cable and Other Program Distribution	*	4841 Cable and Other Pay Television Services (except cable and other subscription programming)
	5179 Other Telecommunications		
	51791 Other Telecommunications	*	4899 Communications Services, NEC (except radio dispatch, ship-to-shore, and satellite communications)
	518 Internet Service Providers, Web Search Portals, and Data Processing Services		
	5181 Internet Service Providers and Web Search Portals		
	51811 Internet Service Providers and Web Search Portals		
	518111 Internet Service Providers		7375 Information Retrieval Services
	518112 Web Search Portals	*	8999 Services, NEC (Internet web search portals)

5182 Data Processing, Hosting, and Related Services
51821 Data Processing, Hosting, and Related Services
Data processing and preparation services
  7374 Computer Processing and Data Preparation and Processing Services
Disk and diskette conversion and recertification
  * 7379 Computer Related Services, NEC (disk and diskette conversion and recertification)
Microfilm service
  * 7389 Business Services, NEC (microfilm services)

519 Other Information Services
5191 Other Information Services
51911 News Syndicates
  * 7383 News Syndicates (except independent news correspondents)

51912 Libraries and Archives
Film archives
  * 7829 Services Allied to Motion Picture Distribution (film archives)
Libraries
  8231 Libraries

51919 All Other Information Services
  * 7389 Business Services, NEC (stock photo agencies, press clipping services, and related information services)

Appendix D

1987 SIC MATCHED to 2002 CHANGES to NAICS

1987 SIC CODE	1987 SIC DESCRIPTION AND DESCRIPTION	2002 NAICS CODE	2002 NAICS AND DESCRIPTION
1081	Metal Mining Services (site preparation and related construction activities on a contract basis)	23891	Site preparation and related activities at metal ore mines(Site Preparation Contractors)
1241	Coal Mining Services (site preparation and related construction activities on a contract basis)	23891	Site preparation and related activities at coal mines(Site Preparation Contractors)
1389	Oil and Gas Field Services, NEC (construction of field gathering lines on a contract or fee basis)	23712	Construction of oil and gas field gathering lines on a contract basis(Oil and Gas Pipeline and Related Structures Construction)
1389	Oil and Gas Field Services, NEC (site preparation and related construction activities on a contract basis)	23891	Site preparation and related activities at oil and gas fields(Site Preparation Contractors)
1481	Nonmetallic Minerals Services, Except Fuels (site preparation and related construction activities on a contract basis)	23891	Site preparation and related activities at nonmetallic mineral mines(Site Preparation Contractors)
1521	General Contractors - Single-Family Houses (remodeling contractors)	236115	Single-family housing remodeling contractors(New Single-Family Housing Construction (except Operative Builders))
1521	General Contractors - Single-Family Houses (except remodeling contractors)	236118	Single-family housing general contractors(Residential Remodelers)
1522	General Contractors - Residential Buildings Other Than Single-Family (except remodeling contractors, hotel and motel construction contractors, and dormitory and barrack construction contractors)	236116	Multifamily housing general contractors(New Multifamily Housing Construction (except Operative Builders))
1522	General Contractors - Residential Buildings Other Than Single-Family (dormitory, barrack, hotel, and motel construction contractors)	23622	Hotel, motel, dormitory and barrack general contractors(Commercial and Institutional Building Construction)
1522	General Contractors - Residential Buildings Other Than Single-Family (remodeling contractors)	236118	Multifamily housing remodeling contractors(Residential Remodelers)
1531	Operative Builders (Operative builders of industrial and manufacturing buildings except grain elevators, dry cleaning plants, and manufacturing and industrial warehouses)	23621	Operative builders of industrial buildings(Industrial Building Construction)
1531	Operative Builders (residential operative builders)	236117	New Housing Operative Builders
1531	Operative Builders (residential operative remodelers)	236118	Operative residential remodelers(Residential Remodelers)
1531	Operative Builders (grain elevator, dry cleaning plant, and manufacturing and industrial warehouse operative builders)	23622	Operative builders of commercial and institutional buildings(Commercial and Institutional Building Construction)
1541	General Contractors Industrial Buildings and Warehouses (except grain elevators; drycleaning plants; and manufacturing, public, and industrial warehouses)	23621	Industrial building general contractors(Industrial Building Construction)
1541	General Contractors - Industrial Buildings and Warehouses (general contractors of grain elevators; dry cleaning plants; and manufacturing, industrial, and public warehouses)	23622	Grain elevator; dry cleaning plant; and public, industrial, and public warehouses general contractors(Commercial and Institutional Building Construction)

1987 SIC CODE	1987 SIC DESCRIPTION AND DESCRIPTION	2002 NAICS CODE	2002 NAICS AND DESCRIPTION
1542	General Contractors - Nonresidential Buildings, Other than Industrial Buildings and Warehouses	23622	Nonresidential buildings, other than industrial buildings and warehouses general contractors(Commercial and Institutional Building Construction)
1611	Highway and Street Construction	23731	Highway and street construction(Highway, Street, and Bridge Construction)
1622	Bridge, Tunnel, and Elevated Highway Construction (bridge and elevated highway construction)	23731	Bridge and elevated highway construction(Highway, Street, and Bridge Construction)
1622	Bridge, Tunnel, and Elevated Highway Construction (tunnel construction)	23799	Tunnel construction(Other Heavy and Civil Engineering Construction)
1623	Water, Sewer, Pipeline, and Communications and Power Line Construction (power and communications transmission lines)	23713	Power and communication line construction(Power and communication line and related structure construction)
1623	Water, Sewer, Pipeline, and Communications and Power Line Construction (water and sewer pipelines and related construction)	23711	Water and sewer pipelines and related line construction(Water and Sewer Line and Related Structures Construction)
1623	Water, Sewer, Pipeline, and Communications and Power Line Construction (gas and oil pipelines, mains, and pumping stations)	23712	Oil and gas pipelines, mains, pumping stations, and storage tanks(Oil and Gas Pipeline and Related Structures Construction)
1629	Heavy Construction, NEC (except industrial nonbuilding structures, irrigation systems, sewage and water treatment plants, petrochemical plants and refineries, power generation plants [except hydroelectric dams] transmission and distribution stations, righ	23799	Transit, rail, port, dam, flood control, and other heavy and civil engineering construction(Other Heavy and Civil Engineering Construction)
1629	Heavy Construction, NEC (power generation plants [except hydroelectric dams], transmission stations, and distribution stations)	23713	Transmission stations, distribution stations, and related structures(Power and communication line and related structure construction)
1629	Heavy Construction, NEC (petrochemical plants and refineries)	23712	Petrochemical plants and refineries(Oil and Gas Pipeline and Related Structures Construction)
1629	Heavy Construction, NEC (Industrial nonbuilding structures [except petrochemical plants and petroleum refineries])	23621	Industrial nonbuilding structures (except petrochemical plants and refineries(Industrial Building Construction) refineries)
1629	Heavy Construction, NEC (right-of-way clearing and line slashing, blasting, and trenching)	23891	Right-of-way clearing, line slashing, blasting, and trenching(Site Preparation Contractors)
1629	Heavy Construction NEC (irrigation systems, sewage treatment plants, and water treatment plants)	23711	Water and sewage treatment plants and related structures(Water and Sewer Line and Related Structures Construction)
1711	Plumbing, Heating, and Air-Conditioning (environmental control installation contractors)	23821	Environmental control installation contractors(Electrical Contractors)
1711	Plumbing, Heating, and Air-Conditioning (except environmental controls installation; and septic tank, cesspool, and dry well construction)	23822	Plumbing, heating, and air-conditioning contractors(Plumbing, Heating, and Air-Conditioning Contractors)
1711	Plumbing, Heating, and Air-Conditioning (septic tank, cesspool, and dry well construction contractors)	23891	Septic tank, cesspool, and dry well contractors(Site Preparation Contractors)

1987 SIC CODE	1987 SIC DESCRIPTION AND DESCRIPTION	2002 NAICS CODE	2002 NAICS AND DESCRIPTION
1721	Painting and Paper Hanging (traffic lane painting)	23731	Traffic lane painting(Highway, Street, and Bridge Construction)
1731	Electrical Work (except burglar and fire alarm installation)	23821	Electrical contractors(Electrical Contractors)
1741	Masonry, Stone Setting, and Other Stone Work	23814	Masonry, stone setting, and other stone work(Masonry Contractors)
1742	Plastering, Drywall, Acoustical, and Insulation Work	23831	Plastering, drywall, acoustical, and insulation contractors(Drywall and Insulation Contractors)
1743	Terrazzo, Tile, Marble, and Mosaic Work (fresco work)	23831	Fresco work(Drywall and Insulation Contractors)
1743	Terrazzo, Tile, Marble, and Mosaic Work (except fresco work)	23834	Tile and Terrazzo Contractors
1751	Carpentry Work (framing carpentry)	23813	Framing Contractors
1751	Carpentry Work (finish carpentry)	23835	Finish Carpentry Contractors
1752	Floor Laying and Other Floor Work, NEC	23833	Flooring Contractors
1761	Roofing, Siding, and Sheet Metal Work (roofing contractors)	23816	Roofing Contractors
1761	Roofing, Siding, and Sheet Metal Work (siding contractors)	23817	Siding Contractors
1761	Roofing, Siding, and Sheet Metal Work (except roofing and siding work)	23839	Sheet metal work (except roofing and siding)(Other Building Finishing Contractors)
1771	Concrete Work (stucco work)	23814	Stucco work(Masonry Contractors)
1771	Concrete Work (residential and commercial asphalt, brick, and concrete paving)	23899	Residential and commercial concrete and asphalt paving(All Other SpecialtyTrade Contraactors)
1771	Concrete Work (except stucco work; and residential and commercial asphalt, brick, and paving)	23811	Poured Concrete Foundation and Structure Contractors
1781	Water Well Drilling	23711	Water well drilling(Water and Sewer Line and Related Structures Construction)
1791	Structural Steel Erection (except curtain wall installation, metal furring installation, and cooling tower installation)	23812	Structural Steel and Precast Concrete Contractors
1791	Structural Steel Erection (curtain wall installation and metal furring installation)	23819	Curtain wall and metal furring installation(Other Foundation, Structure, and Building Exterior Contractors)
1791	Structural Steel Erection (cooling tower installation)	23822	Cooling tower installation contractors(Plumbing, Heating, and Air-Conditioning Contractors)
1793	Glass and Glazing Work	23815	Glass and glazing work(Glass and Glazing Contractors)
1794	Excavation Work	23891	Excavation contractors(Site Preparation Contractors)
1795	Wrecking and Demolition Work	23891	Wrecking and demolition contractors(Site Preparation Contractors)

1987 SIC CODE	1987 SIC DESCRIPTION AND DESCRIPTION	2002 NAICS CODE	2002 NAICS AND DESCRIPTION
1796	Installation or Erection of Building Equipment, NEC (except scrubber, dust collection, and other industrial ventilation installation)	23829	Elevator, escalator, and other building equipment installation(Other Building Equipment Contractors)
1796	Installation or Erection of Building Equipment, NEC (scrubber, dust collection, and other industrial ventilation installation)	23822	Scrubber, dust collection, and other industrial ventilation equipment(Plumbing, Heating, and Air-Conditioning Contractors) installation contractors
1799	Special Trade Contractors, NEC (forming contractors and ornamental metal work contractors)	23819	Forming and ornamental metal work contractors(Other Foundation, Structure, and Building Exterior Contractors)
1799	Special Trade Contractors, NEC (glass tinting work)	23815	Glass tinting work(Glass and Glazing Contractors)
1799	Special Trade Contractors, NEC (anchored earth retention contractors)	23799	Anchored earth retention wall construction contractors(Other Heavy and Civil Engineering Construction)
1799	Special-Trade Contractors, NEC (building finishing contractors for weather stripping and damp proofing, modular furniture installation, bathtub refinishing, window covering fixture installation, trade show exhibit installation and dismantling, and spectat	23839	Weather stripping and damp proofing, modular furniture installation, bathtub refinishing, window covering fixture installation, exhibit installation and removal, and spectator seating installation (Other Building Finishing Contractors)
1799	Special Trade Contractors, NEC (dewatering contractors, test drilling for construction, and core drilling for construction)	23891	Dewatering contractors, test boring for construction, and core drilling for construction(Site Preparation Contractors)
1799	Special Trade Contractors, NEC (except indoor swimming pool contractors, anchored earth retention contractors, glass tinting work, forming contractors, ornamental metal work contractors, service station equipment installation, pipe and duct insulation con	23899	Special trade contractors not specified elsewhere((All Other SpecialtyTrade Contraaactors))
1799	Special Trade Contractors, NEC (indoor swimming pool construction contractors)	23622	Indoor swimming pool construction(Commercial and Institutional Building Construction)
1799	Special Trade Contractors, NEC (paint and wallpaper stripping and removing contractors)	23832	Paint and wall covering removal contractors(Paint and wall covering contractors)
1799	Special Trade Contractors, NEC (building equipment installation contractors for service station equipment; boiler, duct, and pipe insulation; lightning rod installation; bowling alley equipment installation; church bell installation; and clock tower insta	23829	Installation of service station equipment, bowling alley equipment, church bells, clock towers, and similar equipment; and insulation of boilers, pipes, and ducts(Other Building Equipment Contractors)
2711	Newspapers: Publishing or Publishing and Printing (Internet newspaper publishing)	51611	Internet newspaper publishers(Internet Publishing and Broadcasting)
2711	Newspapers: Publishing or Publishing and Printing (except Internet newspaper publishing)	51111	Newspaper Publishers
2721	Periodicals: Publishing or Publishing and Printing (except Internet periodical publishing)	51112	Periodical publishers (except Internet periodicals)(Periodical Publishers)
2721	Periodicals: Publishing or Publishing and Printing (Internet newspaper publishing)	51611	Internet periodical publishers(Internet Publishing and Broadcasting)

1987 SIC CODE	1987 SIC DESCRIPTION AND DESCRIPTION	2002 NAICS CODE	2002 NAICS AND DESCRIPTION
2731	Books: Publishing or Publishing and Printing (Internet book publishing)	51611	Internet book publishers(Internet Publishing and Broadcasting)
2731	Books: Publishing or Publishing and Printing (except music books and Internet book publishing)	51113	Book publishers (except Internet)(Book Publishers)
2731	Books: Publishing, or Publishing and Printing (music books)	51223	Music book publishing(Music Publishers)
2741	Miscellaneous Publishing (Internet publishing)	51611	Miscellaneous Internet publishing(Internet Publishing and Broadcasting)
2741	Miscellaneous Publishing (sheet music publishing)	51223	Sheet music publishing(Music Publishers)
2741	Miscellaneous Publishing (except database, directory, sheet music, shopping news, technical manuals, technical books, and Internet versions of these activities)	511199	All Other Publishers
2741	Miscellaneous Publishing (shopping news publishing except on-line shopping news)	51112	Shopping news publishing (except Internet)(Periodical Publishers)
2741	Miscellaneous Publishing (technical books and manuals, except Internet publishing)	51113	Technical book and manual publishers (except Internet)(Book Publishers)
2741	Miscellaneous Publishing (database and directory publishing, except Internet)	51114	Directory and database publishers (except Internet)(Directory an d Mailing List Publishers)
2771	Greeting Cards (publishing or publishing and printing greeting cards, except Internet greeting card publishing)	511191	Greeting Card Publishers
2771	Greeting Cards (Internet greeting card publishers)	51611	Internet greeting card publishers(Internet Publishing and Broadcasting)
3652	Phonograph Records and Prerecorded Audio Tapes and Disks (integrated record companies, except duplication only)	51222	Integrated Record Production/Distribution
4812	Radiotelephone Communications (cellular and paging resellers)	51731	Wireless telecommunications resellers(Telecommunications Resellers)
4812	Radiotelephone Communications (paging carriers)	517211	Paging
4812	Radiotelephone Communications (cellular carriers)	517212	Cellular carriers(Cellular and Other Wireless Telecommunications)
4813	Telephone Communications, Except Radiotelephone (wired telecommunications resellers)	51731	Wired telecommunications resellers(Telecommunications Resellers)
4813	Telephone Communications, Except Radiotelephone (except resellers)	51711	Wired telephone service(Wired Telecommunications Carriers)
4822	Telegraph and Other Message Communications	51711	Other wired telecommunications services(Wired Telecommunications Carriers)
4832	Radio Broadcasting Stations (radio stations)	515112	Radio Stations
4832	Radio Broadcasting Stations (radio networks)	515111	Radio Networks

1987 SIC CODE	1987 SIC DESCRIPTION AND DESCRIPTION	2002 NAICS CODE	2002 NAICS AND DESCRIPTION
4833	Television Broadcasting Stations	51512	Television Broadcasting
4841	Cable and Other Pay Television Services (cable and other subscription programming)	51521	Cable and Other Subscription Programming
4841	Cable and Other Pay Television Services (except cable and other subscription programming)	51751	Cable and Other Program Distribution
4899	Communications Services, NEC (satellite telecommunications)	51741	Satellite Telecommunications
4899	Communications Services, NEC (except radio dispatch, ship-to-shore, and satellite communications)	51791	Other Telecommunications
4899	Radiotelephone Communications (ship-to-shore telecommunications)	517212	Other wireless telecommunications(Cellular and Other Wireless Telecommunications)
5012	Automobiles and Other Motor Vehicles (merchant wholesalers)	42311	Automobile and Other Motor Vehicle Merchant Wholesalers
5012	Automobiles and Other Motor Vehicles (business to business electronic markets)	42511	Motor vehicle business to business electronic markets(Business to Business Electronic Markets)
5012	Automobiles and Other Motor Vehicles (wholesale trade agents and brokers)	42512	Motor vehicle wholesale trade agents and brokers(Wholesale Trade Agents and Brokers)
5013	Motor Vehicle Supplies and New Parts (business to business electronic markets)	42511	Motor vehicle parts and supplies business to business electronic markets(Business to Business Electronic Markets)
5013	Motor Vehicle Supplies and New Parts (wholesale trade agents and brokers)	42512	Motor vehicle parts and supplies wholesale trade agents and brokers(Wholesale Trade Agents and Brokers)
5013	Motor Vehicle Supplies and New Parts (merchant wholesalers except selling via retail method)	42312	Motor Vehicle Supplies and New Parts Merchant Wholesalers
5014	Tires and Tubes (business to business electronic markets)	42511	Tire and tube business to business electronic markets(Business to Business Electronic Markets)
5014	Tires and Tubes (merchant wholesalers except selling via retail method)	42313	Tire and Tube Merchant Wholesalers
5014	Tires and Tubes (wholesale trade agents and brokers)	42512	Tire and tube wholesale trade agents and brokers(Wholesale Trade Agents and Brokers)
5015	Motor Vehicle Parts, Used (merchant wholesalers except selling via retail method)	42314	Motor Vehicle Parts (Used) Merchant Wholesalers
5015	Motor Vehicle Parts, Used (business to business electronic markets)	42511	Used motor vehicle parts business to business electronic markets(Business to Business Electronic Markets)
5015	Motor Vehicle Parts, Used (wholesale trade agents and brokers)	42512	Used motor vehicle parts wholesale trade agents and brokers(Wholesale Trade Agents and Brokers)
5021	Furniture (business to business electronic markets)	42511	Furniture business to business electronic markets(Business to Business Electronic Markets)
5021	Furniture (merchant wholesalers except selling via retail method)	42321	Furniture Merchant Wholesalers
5021	Furniture (wholesale trade agents and brokers)	42512	Furniture wholesale trade agents and brokers(Wholesale Trade Agents and Brokers)

1987 SIC CODE	1987 SIC DESCRIPTION AND DESCRIPTION	2002 NAICS CODE	2002 NAICS AND DESCRIPTION
5023	Homefurnishings (merchant wholesalers except selling via retail method)	42322	Home Furnishing Merchant Wholesalers
5023	Homefurnishings (wholesale trade agents and brokers)	42512	Homefurnishings wholesale trade agents and brokers(Wholesale Trade Agents and Brokers)
5023	Homefurnishings (business to business electronic markets)	42511	Homefurnishings business to business electronic markets(Business to Business Electronic Markets)
5031	Lumber, Plywood, Millwork, and Wood Panels (business to business electronic markets)	42511	Lumber, plywood, and panel business to business electronic markets(Business to Business Electronic Markets)
5031	Lumber, Plywood, Millwork, and Wood Panels (merchant wholesalers except selling via retail method)	42331	Lumber, plywood, millwork, and wood panels(Lumber, Plywood, Millwork, and Wood Panel Merchant Wholesalers)
5031	Lumber, Plywood, Millwork, and Wood Panels (wholesale trade agents and brokers)	42512	Lumber, plywood, and panel wholesale trade agents and brokers(Wholesale Trade Agents and Brokers)
5032	Brick, Stone, and Related Construction Materials (wholesale trade agents and brokers)	42512	Brick, stone, and related products wholesale trade agents and brokers(Wholesale Trade Agents and Brokers)
5032	Brick, Stone, and Related Construction Materials (merchant wholesalers except selling via retail method)	42332	Brick, Stone, and Related Construction Material Merchant Wholesalers
5032	Brick, Stone, and Related Construction Materials (business to business electronic markets)	42511	Brick, stone, and related products business to business electronic markets(Business to Business Electronic Markets)
5033	Roofing, Siding, and Insulation Materials (wholesale trade agents and brokers)	42512	Roofing, siding and insulation wholesale trade agents and brokers(Wholesale Trade Agents and Brokers)
5033	Roofing, Siding, and Insulation Materials (business to business electronic markets)	42511	Roofing, siding and insulation business to business electronic markets(Business to Business Electronic Markets)
5033	Roofing, Siding, and Insulation Materials (merchant wholesalers except selling via retail method)	42333	Roofing, Siding, and Insulation Material Merchant Wholesalers
5039	Construction Materials, NEC (prefabricated buildings and structural assemblies, nonwood, merchant wholesalers)	42331	Nonwood prefabricated buildings and structural assemblies(Lumber, Plywood, Millwork, and Wood Panel Merchant Wholesalers)
5039	Construction Materials, NEC (merchant wholesalers of construction materials, nec except selling via retail method)	42339	Other Construction Material Merchant Wholesalers
5039	Construction Materials, NEC (business to business electronic markets)	42511	Construction materials, nec business to business electronic markets(Business to Business Electronic Markets)
5039	Construction Materials, NEC (wholesale trade agents and brokers)	42512	Construction materials, nec wholesale trade agents and brokers(Wholesale Trade Agents and Brokers)
5043	Photographic Equipment and Supplies (wholesale trade agents and brokers)	42512	Photographic equipment and supplies wholesale trade agents and brokers(Wholesale Trade Agents and Brokers)

1987 SIC CODE	1987 SIC DESCRIPTION AND DESCRIPTION	2002 NAICS CODE	2002 NAICS AND DESCRIPTION
5043	Photographic Equipment and Supplies (business to business electronic markets)	42511	Photographic equipment and supplies business to business electronic markets(Business to Business Electronic Markets)
5043	Photographic Equipment and Supplies (merchant wholesalers)	42341	Photographic Equipment and Supplies Merchant Wholesalers
5044	Office Equipment (merchant wholesalers except selling via retail method)	42342	Office Equipment Merchant Wholesalers
5044	Office Equipment (wholesale trade agents and brokers)	42512	Office equipment wholesale trade agents and brokers(Wholesale Trade Agents and Brokers)
5044	Office Equipment (business to business electronic markets)	42511	Office equipment business to business electronic markets(Business to Business Electronic Markets)
5045	Computers and Computer Peripheral Equipment and Software (business to business electronic markets)	42511	Computers and related equipment business to business electronic markets(Business to Business Electronic Markets)
5045	Computers and Computer Peripheral Equipment and Software (wholesale trade agents and brokers)	42512	Computers and related equipment wholesale trade agents and brokers(Wholesale Trade Agents and Brokers)
5045	Computers and Computer Peripheral Equipment and Software (merchant wholesalers except selling via retail method)	42343	Computer and Computer Peripheral Equipment and Software Merchant Wholesalers
5046	Commercial Equipment, NEC (merchant wholesalers)	42344	Other Commercial Equipment Merchant Wholesalers
5046	Commercial Equipment, NEC (wholesale trade agents and brokers)	42512	Commercial equipment, nec wholesale trade agents and brokers(Wholesale Trade Agents and Brokers)
5046	Commercial Equipment, NEC (business to business electronic markets)	42511	Commercial equipment, nec business to business electronic markets(Business to Business Electronic Markets)
5047	Medical, Dental, and Hospital Equipment and Supplies (business to business electronic markets)	42511	Medical, dental, and hospital equipment and supplies business to business electronic markets(Business to Business Electronic Markets)
5047	Medical, Dental, and Hospital Equipment and Supplies (merchant wholesalers except selling via retail method)	42345	Medical, Dental, and Hospital Equipment and Supplies Merchant Wholesalers
5047	Medical, Dental, and Hospital Equipment and Supplies (wholesale trade agents and brokers)	42512	Medical, dental, and hospital equipment and supplies wholesale trade agents and brokers(Wholesale Trade Agents and Brokers)
5048	Ophthalmic Goods (business to business electronic markets)	42511	Ophthalmic goods business to business electronic markets(Business to Business Electronic Markets)
5048	Ophthalmic Goods (wholesale trade agents and brokers)	42512	Ophthalmic goods wholesale trade agents and brokers(Wholesale Trade Agents and Brokers)
5048	Ophthalmic Goods (merchant wholesalers)	42346	Ophthalmic Goods Merchant Wholesalers
5049	Professional Equipment and Supplies, NEC (business to business electronic markets)	42511	Professional equipment and supplies business to business electronic markets(Business to Business Electronic Markets)
5049	Professional Equipment and Supplies, NEC (merchant wholesalers except selling via retail method)	42349	Other Professional Equipment and Supplies Merchant Wholesalers

1987 SIC CODE	1987 SIC DESCRIPTION AND DESCRIPTION	2002 NAICS CODE	2002 NAICS AND DESCRIPTION
5049	Professional Equipment and Supplies, NEC (wholesale trade agents and brokers)	42512	Professional equipment and supplies wholesale trade agents and brokers(Wholesale Trade Agents and Brokers)
5051	Metals Service Centers and Offices (business to business electronic markets)	42511	Metals business to business electronic markets(Business to Business Electronic Markets)
5051	Metals Service Centers and Offices (merchant wholesalers)	42351	Metal Service Centers and Other Metal Merchant Wholesalers
5051	Metals Service Centers and Offices (wholesale trade agents and brokers)	42512	Metals wholesale trade agents and brokers(Wholesale Trade Agents and Brokers)
5052	Coal and Other Minerals and Ores (wholesale trade agents and brokers)	42512	Coal and other mineral and ore wholesale trade agents and brokers(Wholesale Trade Agents and Brokers)
5052	Coal and Other Minerals and Ores (business to business electronic markets)	42511	Coal and other mineral and ore business to business electronic markets(Business to Business Electronic Markets)
5052	Coal and Other Minerals and Ores (merchant wholesalers)	42352	Coal and Other Mineral and Ore Merchant Wholesalers
5063	Electrical Apparatus and Equipment, Wiring Supplies, and Construction Materials (business to business electronic markets)	42511	Electrical apparatus and equipment and wiring supplies business to business electronic markets(Business to Business Electronic Markets)
5063	Electrical Apparatus and Equipment, Wiring Supplies, and Construction Materials (merchant wholesalers except selling via retail method)	42361	Electrical Apparatus and Equipment, Wiring Supplies, and Related Equipment Merchant Wholesalers
5063	Electrical Apparatus and Equipment, Wiring Supplies, and Construction Materials (wholesale trade agents and brokers)	42512	Electrical apparatus and equipment and wiring supplies wholesale trade agents and brokers(Wholesale Trade Agents and Brokers)
5064	Electrical Appliances, Television and Radio Sets (business to business electronic markets)	42511	Electrical appliance business to business electronic markets(Business to Business Electronic Markets)
5064	Electrical Appliances, Television and Radio Sets (wholesale trade agents and brokers)	42512	Electrical appliance wholesale trade agents and brokers(Wholesale Trade Agents and Brokers)
5064	Electrical Appliances, Television and Radio Sets (merchant wholesalers except selling via retail method)	42362	Electrical and Electronic Appliance, Television, and Radio Set Merchant Wholesalers
5065	Electronic Parts and Equipment, NEC (business to business electronic markets)	42511	Electronic parts business to business electronic markets(Business to Business Electronic Markets)
5065	Electronic Parts and Equipment, NEC (wholesale trade agents and brokers)	42512	Electronic parts wholesale trade agents and brokers(Wholesale Trade Agents and Brokers)
5065	Electronic Parts and Equipment, NEC (merchant wholesalers except selling via retail method)	42369	Other Electronic Parts and Equipment Merchant Wholesalers
5072	Hardware (merchant wholesalers except selling via retail method)	42371	Hardware Merchant Wholesalers
5072	Hardware (business to business electronic markets)	42511	Hardware business to business electronic markets(Business to Business Electronic Markets)
5072	Hardware (wholesale trade agents and brokers)	42512	Hardware wholesale trade agents and brokers(Wholesale Trade Agents and Brokers)

1987 SIC CODE	1987 SIC DESCRIPTION AND DESCRIPTION	2002 NAICS CODE	2002 NAICS AND DESCRIPTION
5074	Plumbing and Heating Equipment and Supplies (Hydronics) (business to business electronic markets)	42511	Plumbing and hot water heating equipment business to business electronic markets(Business to Business Electronic Markets)
5074	Plumbing and Heating Equipment and Supplies (Hydronics) (merchant wholesalers except selling via retail method)	42372	Plumbing and Heating Equipment and Supplies (Hydronics) Merchant Wholesalers
5074	Plumbing and Heating Equipment and Supplies (Hydronics) (wholesale trade agents and brokers)	42512	Plumbing and hot water heating equipment wholesale trade agents and brokers(Wholesale Trade Agents and Brokers)
5075	Warm Air Heating and Air-Conditioning Equipment and Supplies (business to business electronic markets)	42511	Warm air heating and air-conditioning equipment business to business electronic markets(Business to Business Electronic Markets)
5075	Warm Air Heating and Air-Conditioning Equipment and Supplies (wholesale trade agents and brokers)	42512	Warm air heating and air-conditioning equipment wholesale trade agents and brokers(Wholesale Trade Agents and Brokers)
5075	Warm Air Heating and Air-Conditioning Equipment and Supplies (merchant wholesalers)	42373	Warm Air Heating and Air-Conditioning Equipment and Supplies Merchant Wholesalers
5078	Refrigeration Equipment and Supplies (wholesale trade agents and brokers)	42512	Refrigeration equipment and supplies wholesale trade agents and brokers(Wholesale Trade Agents and Brokers)
5078	Refrigeration Equipment and Supplies (business to business electronic markets)	42511	Refrigeration equipment and supplies business to business electronic markets(Business to Business Electronic Markets)
5078	Refrigeration Equipment and Supplies (merchant wholesalers)	42374	Refrigeration Equipment and Supplies Merchant Wholesalers
5082	Construction and Mining (Except Petroleum) Machinery and Equipment (merchant wholesalers)	42381	Construction and Mining (except Oil Well) Machinery and Equipment Merchant Wholesalers
5082	Construction and Mining (Except Petroleum) Machinery and Equipment (wholesale trade agents and brokers)	42512	Construction and mining equipment wholesale trade agents and brokers(Wholesale Trade Agents and Brokers)
5082	Construction and Mining (Except Petroleum) Machinery and Equipment (business to business electronic markets)	42511	Construction and mining equipment business to business electronic markets(Business to Business Electronic Markets)
5083	Farm and Garden Machinery and Equipment (business to business electronic markets)	42511	Farm and garden machinery business to business electronic markets(Business to Business Electronic Markets)
5083	Farm and Garden Machinery and Equipment (merchant wholesalers except lawn and garden equipment sold via retail method)	42382	Farm and Garden Machinery and Equipment Merchant Wholesalers
5083	Farm and Garden Machinery and Equipment (wholesale trade agents and brokers)	42512	Farm and garden machinery wholesale trade agents and brokers(Wholesale Trade Agents and Brokers)
5084	Industrial Machinery and Equipment (wholesale trade agents and brokers)	42512	Industrial machinery and equipment wholesale trade agents and brokers(Wholesale Trade Agents and Brokers)
5084	Industrial Machinery and Equipment (business to business electronic markets)	42511	Industrial machinery and equipment business to business electronic markets(Business to Business Electronic Markets)

1987 SIC CODE	1987 SIC DESCRIPTION AND DESCRIPTION	2002 NAICS CODE	2002 NAICS AND DESCRIPTION
5084	Industrial Machinery and Equipment (merchant wholesalers)	42383	Industrial machinery and equipment(Industrial Machinery and Equipment Merchant Wholesalers)
5085	Industrial Supplies (wholesale trade agents and brokers)	42512	Industrial supplies wholesale trade agents and brokers(Wholesale Trade Agents and Brokers)
5085	Industrial Supplies (fluid power accessories merchant wholesalers)	42383	Fluid power accessories(Industrial Machinery and Equipment Merchant Wholesalers)
5085	Industrial Supplies (merchant wholesalers - except selling via retail method and merchant wholesalers of fluid power accessories)	42384	Industrial Supplies Merchant Wholesalers
5085	Industrial Supplies (business to business electronic markets)	42511	Industrial supplies business to business electronic markets(Business to Business Electronic Markets)
5087	Service Establishment Equipment and Supplies (merchant wholesalers, except merchant wholesalers selling beauty and barbershop equipment and supplies via retail method)	42385	Service Establishment Equipment and Supplies Merchant Wholesalers
5087	Service Establishment Equipment and Supplies (wholesale trade agents and brokers)	42512	Service industry equipment and supplies wholesale trade agents and brokers(Wholesale Trade Agents and Brokers)
5087	Service Establishment Equipment and Supplies (business to business electronic markets)	42511	Service industry equipment and supplies business to business electronic markets(Business to Business Electronic Markets)
5088	Transportation Equipment and Supplies, Except Motor Vehicles (business to business electronic markets)	42511	Transportation equipment and supplies, except motor vehicle, business to business electronic markets(Business to Business Electronic Markets)
5088	Transportation Equipment and Supplies, Except Motor Vehicles (merchant wholesalers)	42386	Transportation Equipment and Supplies (except Motor Vehicle) Merchant Wholesalers
5088	Transportation Equipment and Supplies, Except Motor Vehicles (wholesale trade agents and brokers)	42512	Transportation equipment and supplies, except motor vehicle, wholesale trade agents and brokers(Wholesale Trade Agents and Brokers)
5091	Sporting and Recreational Goods and Supplies (merchant wholesalers except selling via retail method)	42391	Sporting and recreational goods and supplies merchant wholesalers(Sporting and Recreational Goods and Supplies Merchant Wholesalers)
5091	Sporting and Recreational Goods and Supplies (business to business electronic markets)	42511	Sporting goods business to business electronic markets(Business to Business Electronic Markets)
5091	Sporting and Recreational Goods and Supplies (wholesale trade agents and brokers)	42512	Sporting goods wholesale trade agents and brokers(Wholesale Trade Agents and Brokers)
5092	Toys and Hobby Goods and Supplies (merchant wholesalers except selling via retail method)	42392	Toy and Hobby Goods and Supplies Merchant Wholesalers
5092	Toys and Hobby Goods and Supplies (wholesale trade agents and brokers)	42512	Toys and hobby supply wholesale trade agents and brokers(Wholesale Trade Agents and Brokers)
5092	Toys and Hobby Goods and Supplies (business to business electronic markets)	42511	Toys and hobby supply business to business electronic markets(Business to Business Electronic Markets)
5093	Scrap and Waste Materials (merchant wholesalers)	42393	Recyclable Material Merchant Wholesalers
5093	Scrap and Waste Materials (wholesale trade agents and brokers)	42512	Scrap and waste material wholesale trade agents and brokers(Wholesale Trade Agents and Brokers)

1987 SIC CODE	1987 SIC DESCRIPTION AND DESCRIPTION	2002 NAICS CODE	2002 NAICS AND DESCRIPTION
5093	Scrap and Waste Materials (business to business electronic markets)	42511	Scrap and waste material business to business electronic markets(Business to Business Electronic Markets)
5094	Jewelry, Watches, Precious Stones, and Precious Metals (business to business electronic markets)	42511	Jewelry, watches, and related goods business to business electronic markets(Business to Business Electronic Markets)
5094	Jewelry, Watches, Precious Stones, and Precious Metals (merchant wholesalers except selling via retail method)	42394	Jewelry, Watch, Precious Stone, and Precious Metal Merchant Wholesalers
5094	Jewelry, Watches, Precious Stones, and Precious Metals (wholesale trade agents and brokers)	42512	Jewelry, watches, and related goods wholesale trade agents and brokers(Wholesale Trade Agents and Brokers)
5099	Durable Goods, NEC (business to business electronic markets)	42511	Durable goods, nec business to business electronic markets(Business to Business Electronic Markets)
5099	Durable Goods, NEC (wholesale trade agents and brokers)	42512	Durable goods, nec wholesale trade agents and brokers(Wholesale Trade Agents and Brokers)
5099	Durable Goods, NEC (merchant wholesalers except selling via retail method)	42399	Durable goods, nec merchant wholesalers(Other Miscellaneous Durable Goods Merchant Wholesalers)
5111	Printing and Writing Paper (business to business electronic markets)	42511	Printing and writing paper business to business electronic markets(Business to Business Electronic Markets)
5111	Printing and Writing Paper (wholesale trade agents and brokers)	42512	Printing and writing paper wholesale trade agents and brokers(Wholesale Trade Agents and Brokers)
5111	Printing and Writing Paper (merchant wholesalers except selling via retail method)	42411	Printing and Writing Paper Merchant Wholesalers
5112	Stationary and Office Supplies (merchant wholesalers except selling via retail method)	42412	Stationary and Office Supplies Merchant Wholesalers
5112	Stationary and Office Supplies (business to business electronic markets)	42511	Stationary and office supplies business to business electronic markets(Business to Business Electronic Markets)
5112	Stationary and Office Supplies (wholesale trade agents and brokers)	42512	Stationary and office supplies wholesale trade agents and brokers(Wholesale Trade Agents and Brokers)
5113	Industrial and Personal Service Paper (merchant wholesalers except selling via retail method)	42413	Industrial and Personal Service Paper Merchant Wholesalers
5113	Industrial and Personal Service Paper (wholesale trade agents and brokers)	42512	Other paper wholesale trade agents and brokers(Wholesale Trade Agents and Brokers)
5113	Industrial and Personal Service Paper (business to business electronic markets)	42511	Other paper business to business electronic markets(Business to Business Electronic Markets)
5122	Drugs, Drug Proprietaries, and Druggists' Sundries (wholesale trade agents and brokers)	42512	Drugs and related products wholesale trade agents and brokers(Wholesale Trade Agents and Brokers)
5122	Drugs, Drug Proprietaries, and Druggists' Sundries (business to business electronic markets)	42511	Drugs and related products business to business electronic markets(Business to Business Electronic Markets)

1987 SIC CODE	1987 SIC DESCRIPTION AND DESCRIPTION	2002 NAICS CODE	2002 NAICS AND DESCRIPTION
5122	Drugs, Drug Proprietaries, and Druggists' Sundries (merchant wholesalers except selling via retail method)	42421	Drugs and Druggists' Sundries Merchant Wholesalers
5131	Piece Goods, Notions, and Other Dry Goods (business to business electronic markets)	42511	Dry goods business to business electronic markets(Business to Business Electronic Markets)
5131	Piece Goods, Notions, and Other Dry Goods (merchant wholesalers- except selling via retail method and piece goods converters)	42431	Piece Goods, Notions, and Other Dry Goods Merchant Wholesalers
5131	Piece Goods, Notions, and Other Dry Goods (wholesale trade agents and brokers)	42512	Dry goods wholesale trade agents and brokers(Wholesale Trade Agents and Brokers)
5136	Men's and Boy's Clothing and Furnishing (wholesale trade agents and brokers)	42512	Men's and boys' clothing wholesale trade agents and brokers(Wholesale Trade Agents and Brokers)
5136	Men's and Boys' Clothing and Furnishings (merchant wholesalers [except athletic uniforms and merchant wholesalers selling via retail method])	42432	Men's and Boys' Clothing and Furnishings Merchant Wholesalers
5136	Men's and Boy's Clothing and Furnishing (athletic uniform merchant wholesalers except selling via retail method)	42391	Men's and boy's athletic uniforms(Sporting and Recreational Goods and Supplies Merchant Wholesalers)
5136	Men's and Boy's Clothing and Furnishing (business to business electronic markets)	42511	Men's and boys' clothing business to business electronic markets(Business to Business Electronic Markets)
5137	Women's, Children's, and Infant's Clothing and Accessories (other athletic uniform merchant wholesalers except selling via retail method)	42391	Other athletic uniforms(Sporting and Recreational Goods and Supplies Merchant Wholesalers)
5137	Women's, Children's, and Infant's Clothing and Accessories (business to business electronic markets)	42511	Women's and children's business to business electronic markets(Business to Business Electronic Markets)
5137	Women's, Children's, and Infants' Clothing and Accessories (merchant wholesalers [except athletic uniforms and merchant wholesalers selling via retail method])	42433	Women's, Children's, and Infants' Clothing and Accessories Merchant Wholesalers
5137	Women's, Children's, and Infant's Clothing and Accessories (wholesale trade agents and brokers)	42512	Women's and children's wholesale trade agents and brokers(Wholesale Trade Agents and Brokers)
5139	Footwear (wholesale trade agents and brokers)	42512	Footwear wholesale trade agents and brokers(Wholesale Trade Agents and Brokers)
5139	Footwear (merchant wholesalers except selling via retail method)	42434	Footwear merchant wholesalers(Footwear Merchant Wholesalers)
5139	Footwear (business to business electronic markets)	42511	Footwear business to business electronic markets(Business to Business Electronic Markets)
5141	Groceries, General Line (business to business electronic markets)	42511	General line grocery business to business electronic markets(Business to Business Electronic Markets)
5141	Groceries, General Line (merchant wholesalers except selling via retail method)	42441	General Line Grocery Merchant Wholesalers
5141	Groceries, General Line (wholesale trade agents and brokers)	42512	General line grocery wholesale trade agents and brokers(Wholesale Trade Agents and Brokers)

1987 SIC CODE	1987 SIC DESCRIPTION AND DESCRIPTION	2002 NAICS CODE	2002 NAICS AND DESCRIPTION
5142	Packaged Frozen Foods (merchant wholesalers except selling via retail method)	42442	Packaged Frozen Food Merchant Wholesalers
5142	Packaged Frozen Foods (wholesale trade agents and brokers)	42512	Frozen food wholesale trade agents and brokers(Wholesale Trade Agents and Brokers)
5142	Packaged Frozen Foods (business to business electronic markets)	42511	Frozen food business to business electronic markets(Business to Business Electronic Markets)
5143	Dairy Products, Except Dried or Canned (wholesale trade agents and brokers)	42512	Dairy product wholesale trade agents and brokers(Wholesale Trade Agents and Brokers)
5143	Dairy Products, Except Dried or Canned (merchant wholesalers except selling via retail method)	42443	Dairy Product (except Dried or Canned) Merchant Wholesalers
5143	Dairy Products, Except Dried or Canned (business to business electronic markets)	42511	Dairy product business to business electronic markets(Business to Business Electronic Markets)
5144	Poultry and Poultry Products (business to business electronic markets)	42511	Poultry and poultry product business to business electronic markets(Business to Business Electronic Markets)
5144	Poultry and Poultry Products (merchant wholesalers except selling via retail method)	42444	Poultry and Poultry Product Merchant Wholesalers
5144	Poultry and Poultry Products (wholesale trade agents and brokers)	42512	Poultry and poultry product wholesale trade agents and brokers(Wholesale Trade Agents and Brokers)
5145	Confectionery (business to business electronic markets)	42511	Confectionery business to business electronic markets(Business to Business Electronic Markets)
5145	Confectionery (wholesale trade agents and brokers)	42512	Confectionery wholesale trade agents and brokers(Wholesale Trade Agents and Brokers)
5145	Confectionery (merchant wholesalers except selling via retail method)	42445	Confectionery Merchant Wholesalers
5146	Fish and Seafoods (business to business electronic markets)	42511	Fish and seafood business to business electronic markets(Business to Business Electronic Markets)
5146	Fish and Seafoods (wholesale trade agents and brokers)	42512	Fish and seafood wholesale trade agents and brokers(Wholesale Trade Agents and Brokers)
5146	Fish and Seafoods (merchant wholesalers except selling via retail method)	42446	Fish and Seafood Merchant Wholesalers
5147	Meats and Meat Products (business to business electronic markets)	42511	Meat and meat product business to business electronic markets(Business to Business Electronic Markets)
5147	Meats and Meat Products (merchant wholesalers [except boxed beef manufacturers and merchant wholesalers selling via retail method])	42447	Meat and Meat Product Merchant Wholesalers
5147	Meats and Meat Products (wholesale trade agents and brokers)	42512	Meat and meat product wholesale trade agents and brokers(Wholesale Trade Agents and Brokers)
5148	Fresh Fruits and Vegetables (merchant wholesalers except selling via retail method)	42448	Fresh Fruit and Vegetable Merchant Wholesalers
5148	Fresh Fruits and Vegetables (business to business electronic markets)	42511	Fresh fruit and vegetable business to business electronic markets(Business to Business Electronic Markets)

1987 SIC CODE	1987 SIC DESCRIPTION AND DESCRIPTION	2002 NAICS CODE	2002 NAICS AND DESCRIPTION
5148	Fresh Fruits and Vegetables (wholesale trade agents and brokers)	42512	Fresh fruit and vegetable wholesale trade agents and brokers(Wholesale Trade Agents and Brokers)
5149	Groceries and Related Products, NEC (business to business electronic markets)	42511	Grocery and related product, nec business to business electronic markets(Business to Business Electronic Markets)
5149	Groceries and Related Products, NEC (merchant wholesalers [except bottled water manufacturers and merchant wholesalers selling via retail method)	42449	Other Grocery and Related Products Merchant Wholesalers
5149	Groceries and Related Products, NEC (wholesale trade agents and brokers)	42512	Grocery and related product, nec wholesale trade agents and brokers(Wholesale Trade Agents and Brokers)
5153	Grain and Field Beans (merchant wholesalers except selling via retail method)	42451	Grain and Field Bean Merchant Wholesalers
5153	Grain and Field Beans (business to business electronic markets)	42511	Grain and field bean business to business electronic markets(Business to Business Electronic Markets)
5153	Grain and Field Beans (wholesale trade agents and brokers)	42512	Grain and field bean wholesale trade agents and brokers(Wholesale Trade Agents and Brokers)
5154	Livestock (wholesale trade agents and brokers)	42512	Livestock wholesale trade agents and brokers(Wholesale Trade Agents and Brokers)
5154	Livestock (merchant wholesalers)	42452	Livestock Merchant Wholesalers
5154	Livestock (business to business electronic markets)	42511	Livestock business to business electronic markets(Business to Business Electronic Markets)
5159	Farm-Product Raw Materials, NEC (merchant wholesalers except selling via retail method)	42459	Other Farm Product Raw Material Merchant Wholesalers
5159	Farm-Product Raw Materials, NEC (wholesale trade agents and brokers)	42512	Farm products, nec wholesale trade agents and brokers(Wholesale Trade Agents and Brokers)
5159	Farm-Product Raw Materials, NEC (business to business electronic markets)	42511	Farm products, nec business to business electronic markets(Business to Business Electronic Markets)
5162	Plastics materials and Basic Forms and Shapes (business to business electronic markets)	42511	Plastics business to business electronic markets(Business to Business Electronic Markets)
5162	Plastics materials and Basic Forms and Shapes (merchant wholesalers except selling via retail method)	42461	Plastics materials and basic forms and shapes merchant wholesalers(Plastics Materials and Basic Forms and Shapes Merchant Wholesalers)
5162	Plastics materials and Basic Forms and Shapes (wholesale trade agents and brokers)	42512	Plastics wholesale trade agents and brokers(Wholesale Trade Agents and Brokers)
5169	Chemicals and Allied Products, NEC (merchant wholesalers)	42469	Other Chemical and Allied Products Merchant Wholesalers
5169	Chemicals and Allied Products, NEC (wholesale trade agents and brokers)	42512	Chemicals wholesale trade agents and brokers(Wholesale Trade Agents and Brokers)
5169	Chemicals and Allied Products, NEC (business to business electronic markets)	42511	Chemicals business to business electronic markets(Business to Business Electronic Markets)
5171	Petroleum Bulk Stations and Terminals (except petroleum sold via retail method)	42471	Petroleum Bulk Stations and Terminals

1987 SIC MATCHED TO 2002 CHANGES TO NAICS

1987 SIC CODE	1987 SIC DESCRIPTION AND DESCRIPTION	2002 NAICS CODE	2002 NAICS AND DESCRIPTION
5172	Petroleum and Petroleum Products Wholesalers, Except Bulk Stations and Terminals (business to business electronic markets)	42511	Petroleum and petroleum product business to business electronic markets(Business to Business Electronic Markets)
5172	Petroleum and Petroleum Products Wholesalers, Except Bulk Stations and Terminals (wholesale trade agents and brokers)	42512	Petroleum and petroleum product wholesale trade agents and brokers(Wholesale Trade Agents and Brokers)
5172	Petroleum and Petroleum Products Wholesalers, Except Bulk Stations and Terminals (merchant wholesalers)	42472	Petroleum and Petroleum Products Merchant Wholesalers (except Bulk Stations and Terminals)
5181	Beer and Ale (business to business electronic markets)	42511	Beer and ale business to business electronic markets(Business to Business Electronic MarketsBusiness to Business Electronic Markets
5181	Beer and Ale (wholesale trade agents and brokers)	42512	Beer and ale wholesale trade agents and brokers(Wholesale Trade Agents and Brokers)
5181	Beer and Ale (merchant wholesalers except selling via retail method)	42481	Beer and Ale Merchant Wholesalers
5182	Wine and Distilled Alcoholic Beverages (wholesale trade agents and brokers)	42512	Wine and distilled beverage wholesale trade agents and brokers(Wholesale Trade Agents and Brokers)
5182	Wine and Distilled Alcoholic Beverages (merchant wholesalers except selling via retail method)	42482	Wine and Distilled Alcoholic Beverage Merchant Wholesalers
5182	Wine and Distilled Alcoholic Beverages (business to business electronic markets)	42511	Wine and distilled beverage business to business electronic markets(Business to Business Electronic Markets)
5191	Farm Supplies (wholesale trade agents and brokers)	42512	Farm supply wholesale trade agents and brokers(Wholesale Trade Agents and Brokers)
5191	Farm Supplies (business to business electronic markets)	42511	Farm supply business to business electronic markets(Business to Business Electronic Markets)
5191	Farm Supplies (merchant wholesalers except selling lawn and garden supplies via retail method)	42491	Farm Supplies Merchant Wholesalers
5192	Books, Periodicals, and Newspapers (wholesale trade agents and brokers)	42512	Book and other published material wholesale trade agents and brokers(Wholesale Trade Agents and Brokers)
5192	Books, Periodicals, and Newspapers (merchant wholesalers except selling via retail method)	42492	Book, Periodical, and Newspaper Merchant Wholesalers
5192	Books, Periodicals, and Newspapers (business to business electronic markets)	42511	Book and other published material business to business electronic markets(Business to Business Electronic Markets)
5193	Flowers, Nursery Stock, and Florists' Supplies (merchant wholesalers except selling via retail method)	42493	Flower, Nursery Stock, and Florists' Supplies Merchant Wholesalers
5193	Flowers, Nursery Stock, and Florists' Supplies (wholesale trade agents and brokers)	42512	Flower and nursery stock wholesale trade agents and brokers(Wholesale Trade Agents and Brokers)
5193	Flowers, Nursery Stock, and Florists' Supplies (business to business electronic markets)	42511	Flower and nursery stock business to business electronic markets(Business to Business Electronic Markets)

1987 SIC CODE	1987 SIC DESCRIPTION AND DESCRIPTION	2002 NAICS CODE	2002 NAICS AND DESCRIPTION
5194	Tobacco and Tobacco Products (wholesale trade agents and brokers)	42512	Tobacco and tobacco product wholesale trade agents and brokers(Wholesale Trade Agents and Brokers)
5194	Tobacco and Tobacco Products (merchant wholesalers except selling via retail method)	42494	Tobacco and Tobacco Product Merchant Wholesalers
5194	Tobacco and Tobacco Products (business to business electronic markets)	42511	Tobacco and tobacco product business to business electronic markets(Business to Business Electronic Markets)
5195	Paints, Varnishes, and Supplies (wholesale trade agents and brokers)	42512	Paint and related product wholesale trade agents and brokers(Wholesale Trade Agents and Brokers)
5195	Paints, Varnishes, and Supplies (merchant wholesalers)	42495	Paint, Varnish, and Supplies Merchant Wholesalers
5195	Paints, Varnishes, and Supplies (business to business electronic markets)	42511	Paint and related product business to business electronic markets(Business to Business Electronic Markets)
5199	Nondurable Goods, NEC (merchant wholesalers [except advertising specialties goods distributors, footwear cutstock, plastics foam, and merchant wholesalers selling nondurable goods, nec via retail method)	42499	Other Miscellaneous Nondurable Goods Merchant Wholesalers
5199	Nondurable Goods, NEC (wholesale trade agents and brokers)	42512	Nondurable goods, nec wholesale trade agents and brokers(Wholesale Trade Agents and Brokers)
5199	Nondurable Goods, NEC (business to business electronic markets)	42511	Nondurable goods, nec business to business electronic markets(Business to Business Electronic Markets)
5199	Nondurable Goods, NEC (plastics foam merchant wholesalers)	42461	Plastics foam merchant wholesalers(Plastics Materials and Basic Forms and Shapes Merchant Wholesalers)
5199	Nondurable Goods, NEC (footwear cut stock merchant wholesalers)	42434	Footwear cut stock merchant wholesalers(Footwear Merchant Wholesalers)
5311	Department Stores (traditional department stores)	452111	Department Stores (except Discount Department Stores)
5311	Department Stores (discount department stores)	452112	Discount Department Stores
5961	Catalog and Mail-Order Houses (Internet shopping)	454111	Electronic Shopping
5961	Catalog and Mail-Order Houses (except Internet shopping and electronic retail auctions)	454113	Mail-Order Houses
5961	Catalog and Mail-Order Houses (electronic retail auctions)	454112	Electronic Auctions
6552	Land Subdividers and Developers, Except Cemeteries	23721	Land Subdivision
7331	Direct Mail Advertising Services (mailing list compilers)	51114	Mailing list compilers(Directory an d Mailing List Publishers)
7353	Construction Equipment Rental and Leasing (crane rental with operator)	23899	Crane rental with operator(All Other SpecialtyTrade Contraactors)

1987 SIC CODE	1987 SIC DESCRIPTION AND DESCRIPTION	2002 NAICS CODE	2002 NAICS AND DESCRIPTION
7353	Construction Equipment Rental and Leasing (rental of construction equipment [except cranes] with operator)	23891	Rental of construction equipment (except cranes) with operator(Site Preparation Contractors)
7372	Prepackaged Software (software publishing)	51121	Software Publishers
7374	Computer Processing and Data Preparation and Processing Services	51821	Data processing and preparation services(Data Processing, Hosting, and Related Services)
7375	Information Retrieval Services	518111	Internet Service Providers
7379	Computer Related Services, NEC (disk and diskette conversion and recertification)	51821	Disk and diskette conversion and recertification(Data Processing, Hosting, and Related Services)
7383	News Syndicates (except independent news correspondents)	51911	News Syndicates
7389	Business Services, NEC (audio taping services)	51229	Audio taping services(Other Sound Recording Industries)
7389	Business Services, NEC (yacht brokers)	42512	Yacht brokers(Wholesale Trade Agents and Brokers)
7389	Business Services, NEC (stock photo agencies, press clipping services, and related information services)	51919	All Other Information Services
7389	Business Services, NEC (microfilm services)	51821	Microfilm service(Data Processing, Hosting, and Related Services)
7389	Business Services, NEC (recording studios)	51224	Sound Recording Studios
7622	Radio and Television Repair Shops (household antenna installation)	23829	Household antenna installation(Other Building Equipment Contractors)
7699	Repair Shops and Related Services, NEC (boiler cleaning, chipping, and scaling)	23833	Boiler chipping, scaling, and cleaning(Plumbing, Heating, and Air-Conditioning Contractors)
7812	Motion Picture and Video Tape Production	51211	Motion Picture and Video Production
7819	Services Allied to Motion Picture Production (except casting bureaus, wardrobe and equipment rental, talent payment services, teleproduction and postproduction services, reproduction of videos, film distributors, and other related motion picture productio	512199	Other Motion Picture and Video Industries
7819	Services Allied to Motion Picture Production (teleproduction and postproduction services)	512191	Teleproduction and Other Postproduction Services
7822	Motion Picture and Video Tape Distribution (except video tape and cassette wholesalers)	51212	Motion picture and video distribution(Motion Picture and Video Distribution)
7822	Motion Picture and Video Tape Distribution (merchant wholesalers)	42399	Prerecorded video tape merchant wholesalers(Other Miscellaneous Durable Goods Merchant Wholesalers)
7829	Services Allied to Motion Picture Distribution (film archives)	51912	Film archives(Libraries and Archives)
7829	Services Allied to Motion Picture Distribution (commercial distribution film libraries)	51212	Commercial distribution film libraries(Motion Picture and Video Distribution)

1987 SIC CODE	1987 SIC DESCRIPTION AND DESCRIPTION	2002 NAICS CODE	2002 NAICS AND DESCRIPTION
7832	Motion Picture Theaters, Except Drive-In	512131	Motion Picture Theaters (except Drive-Ins)
7833	Drive-In Motion Picture Theaters	512132	Drive-In Motion Picture Theaters
7922	Theatrical Producers (Except Motion Picture) and Miscellaneous Theatrical Services (producers of radio programs)	51229	Radio program producers(Other Sound Recording Industries)
8231	Libraries	51912	Libraries(Libraries and Archives)
8741	Management Services (residential remodeling construction management)	236118	Construction management for residential remodeling projects-(Residential Remodelers)
8741	Management Services (single-family housing construction management)	236115	Single-family housing construction management(New Single-Family Housing Construction (except Operative Builders))
8741	Management Services (multifamily housing construction management)	236116	Multifamily housing construction management(New Multifamily Housing Construction (except Operative Builders))
8741	Management Services (industrial building and nonbuilding structure construction management)	23621	Industrial building construction management(Industrial Building Construction)
8741	Management Services (construction management of power generation [except hydroelectric] facilities, and transmission and distribution station construction projects)	23713	Power and communication line and related structure construction management(Power and communication line and related structure construction)
8741	Management Services (Commercial and Institutional building construction management)	23622	Commercial and institutional building construction management(Commercial and Institutional Building Construction)
8741	Management Services (construction management for other heavy and civil engineering construction)	23799	Other heavy and civil engineering construction management(Other Heavy and Civil Engineering Construction)
8741	Management Services (construction management of water, sewer, and related structure construction projects)	23711	Construction management for water and sewer lines and related structures(Water and Sewer Line and Related Structures Construction)
8741	Management Services (construction management of oil and gas pipelines and related structure construction projects)	23712	Oil and gas pipeline and related structure construction management(Oil and Gas Pipeline and Related Structures Construction)
8741	Management Services (highway, street, and bridge construction management)	23731	Highway, street, and bridge construction management(Highway, Street, and Bridge Construction)
8999	Services, NEC (Internet web search portals)	518112	Web Search Portals
8999	Services NEC (Internet broadcasting)	51611	Internet broadcasting(Internet Publishing and Broadcasting)
8999	Services, NEC (record production)	51221	Record Production
8999	Services, NEC (music publishing)	51223	Music publishers(Music Publishers)